Trust

Critical Studies in Economic Institutions

Series Editor: Geoffrey M. Hodgson
Research Professor, University of Hertfordshire Business School, UK

1. Competing Capitalisms: Institutions and Economies (Volumes I and II)
   Richard Whitley
2. Foundations of Social Capital
   Elinor Ostrom and T.K. Ahn
3. Trust
   Elias L. Khalil

Future titles will include:

Recent Developments in Institutional Economics
Geoffrey M. Hodgson

Knowledge, Learning and Routines
Nathalie Lazaric and Edward Lorenz

Networks
Gernot Grabher and Walter Powell

The State
Klaus Nielsen

Markets
Mitchel Y. Abolafia

Knowledge and Learning in the Firm
Bart Nooteboom

Wherever possible, the articles in these volumes have been reproduced as originally published using facsimile reproduction, inclusive of footnotes and pagination to facilitate ease of reference.

For a list of all Edward Elgar published titles visit our site on the World Wide Web at
http://www.e-elgar.co.uk

Trust

Edited by

Elias L. Khalil

Director
Behavioral Research Council,
American Institute for Economic Research, USA

CRITICAL STUDIES IN ECONOMIC INSTITUTIONS

An Elgar Reference Collection
Cheltenham, UK • Northampton, MA, USA

Published by
Edward Elgar Publishing Limited
Glensanda House
Montpellier Parade
Cheltenham
Glos GL50 1UA
UK

Edward Elgar Publishing, Inc.
136 West Street
Suite 202
Northampton
Massachusetts 01060
USA

A catalogue record for this book is available from the British Library.

Library of Congress Cataloguing in Publication Data

Trust / edited by Elias L. Khalil.
p. cm. — (Critical studies in economic institutions ; 3)
Includes bibliographical references and index.
1. Reciprocity. 2. Reliability. 3. Cooperation. I. Khalil, Elias L., 1957– II. Series.

HF1721.T745 2003
330'.01—dc21

2003043908

ISBN 1 84064 737 X

Printed and bound in Great Britain by MPG Books Ltd, Bodmin, Cornwall

Contents

Acknowledgements

The editor and publishers wish to thank the authors and the following publishers who have kindly given permission for the use of copyright material.

Academic Press, an imprint of Elsevier Science for article: Herbert Gintis (2000), 'Strong Reciprocity and Human Sociality', *Journal of Theoretical Biology*, **206**, 169–79.

American Association for the Advancement of Science for article: Robert Axelrod and Douglas Dion (1988), 'The Further Evolution of Cooperation', *Science*, **242** (4884), 9 December, 1385–90.

American Economic Association for articles and excerpt: Oliver E. Williamson (1983), 'Credible Commitments: Using Hostages to Support Exchange', *American Economic Review*, **73** (4), September, 519–40; Daniel Kahneman, Jack L. Knetsch and Richard Thaler (1986), 'Fairness as a Constraint on Profit Seeking: Entitlements in the Market', *American Economic Review*, **76** (4), September, 728–41; Robert H. Frank (1987), 'If *Homo Economicus* Could Choose His Own Utility Function, Would He Want One with a Conscience?', *American Economic Review*, **77** (4), September, 593–604; Alvin E. Roth, Vesna Prasnikar, Masahiro Okuno-Fujiwara and Shmuel Zamir (1991), 'Bargaining and Market Behavior in Jerusalem, Ljubljana, Pittsburgh, and Tokyo: An Experimental Study', *American Economic Review*, **81** (5), December, 1068–95; Richard H. Thaler with Robyn M. Dawes (1992), 'Cooperation', in *The Winner's Curse: Paradoxes and Anomalies of Economic Life*, Chapter 2, 6–20, references; Matthew Rabin (1993), 'Incorporating Fairness into Game Theory and Economics', *American Economic Review*, **83** (5), December, 1281–302; Ernst Fehr and Simon Gächter (2000), 'Fairness and Retaliation: The Economics of Reciprocity', *Journal of Economic Perspectives*, **14** (3), Summer, 159–81; Joseph Henrich, Robert Boyd, Samuel Bowles, Colin Camerer, Ernst Fehr, Herbert Gintis and Richard McElreath (2001), 'In Search of *Homo Economicus*: Behavioral Experiments in 15 Small-Scale Societies', *American Economic Review, Papers and Proceedings*, **91** (2), May, 73–8.

Blackwell Publishing Ltd for articles: Ulrich Witt (1986), 'Evolution and Stability of Cooperation without Enforceable Contracts', *Kyklos*, **39** (2), 245–66; Werner Güth, Hartmut Kliemt and Bezalel Peleg (2000), 'Co-evolution of Preferences and Information in Simple Games of Trust', *German Economic Review*, **1** (1), February, 83–110.

Cambridge University Press for article: Amitai Etzioni (1986), 'The Case for a Multiple-Utility Conception', *Economics and Philosophy*, **2** (2), October, 159–83.

Elsevier Science for articles: James Andreoni (1988), 'Why Free Ride? Strategies and Learning in Public Goods Experiments', *Journal of Public Economics*, **37** (3), December, 291–304; Werner Güth and Reinhard Tietz (1990), 'Ultimatum Bargaining Behavior: A Survey and Comparison of Experimental Results', *Journal of Economic Psychology*, **11** (4), December, 417–49; Elias L. Khalil (1999), 'Sentimental Fools: A Critique of Amartya Sen's Notion of Commitment', *Journal of Economic Behavior and Organization*, **40** (4), December, 373–86; Jörn P.W. Scharlemann, Catherine C. Eckel, Alex Kacelnik and Rick K. Wilson (2001), 'The Value of a Smile: Game Theory with a Human Face', *Journal of Economic Psychology*, **22**, 617–40.

Elsevier Science (USA) for articles: David M. Kreps, Paul Milgrom, John Roberts and Robert Wilson (1982), 'Rational Cooperation in the Finitely Repeated Prisoners' Dilemma', *Journal of Economic Theory*, **27** (2), August, 245–52; John Gale, Kenneth G. Binmore and Larry Samuelson (1995), 'Learning to Be Imperfect: The Ultimatum Game', *Games and Economic Behavior*, **8**, 56–90; Joyce Berg, John Dickhaut and Kevin McCabe (1995), 'Trust, Reciprocity, and Social History', *Games and Economic Behavior*, **10**, 122–42; David K. Levine (1998), 'Modeling Altruism and Spitefulness in Experiments', *Review of Economic Dynamics*, **1** (3), July, 593–622; Axel Ockenfels and Reinhard Selten (2000), 'An Experiment on the Hypothesis of Involuntary Truth-Signalling in Bargaining', *Games and Economic Behavior*, **33** (1), October, 90–116.

Diego Gambetta for excerpts: Keith Hart (1988), 'Kinship, Contract, and Trust: The Economic Organization of Migrants in an African City Slum', in Diego Gambetta (ed.), *Trust: Making and Breaking Cooperative Relations*, Chapter 11, 176–93; Edward H. Lorenz (1988), 'Neither Friends nor Strangers: Informal Networks of Subcontracting in French Industry', in Diego Gambetta (ed.), *Trust: Making and Breaking Cooperative Relations*, Chapter 12, 194–210.

Journal of Law and Economics, University of Chicago for article: Oliver E. Williamson (1993), 'Calculativeness, Trust, and Economic Organization', *Journal of Law and Economics*, **XXXVI** (1, Part 2), April, 453–86.

Kluwer Academic Publishers for articles: Jack Hirshleifer (1999), 'There are Many Evolutionary Pathways to Cooperation', *Journal of Bioeconomics*, **1** (1), 73–93; Andreas Ortmann, John Fitzgerald and Carl Boeing (2000), 'Trust, Reciprocity, and Social History: A Re-examination', *Experimental Economics*, **3** (1), June, 81–100.

Kluwer Academic Publishers B.V. for article: Bernd Lahno (2001), 'On the Emotional Character of Trust', *Ethical Theory and Moral Practice*, **4** (2), June, 171–89.

MIT Press for excerpt: Jack Hirshleifer (1987), 'On the Emotions as Guarantors of Threats and Promises', in John Depré (ed.), *The Latest on the Best: Essays on Evolution and Optimality*, Chapter 14, 307–26.

MIT Press Journals and the President and Fellows of Harvard College for articles: George A. Akerlof (1982), 'Labor Contracts as a Partial Gift Exchange', *Quarterly Journal of Economics*, **XCVII** (4), November, 543–69; Gordon Tullock (1985), 'Adam Smith and the Prisoners' Dilemma', *Quarterly Journal of Economics*, **100** (402), Supplement, 1073–81.

Bart Nooteboom for his own article: (1996), 'Trust, Opportunism and Governance: A Process and Control Model', *Organization Studies*, **17** (6), 985–1010.

Oxford University Press for article: Amartya K. Sen (1977), 'Rational Fools: A Critique of the Behavioral Foundations of Economic Theory', *Philosophy and Public Affairs*, **6** (4), 317–44.

Python (Monty) Pictures Ltd for excerpt from Merchant Banker sketch, originally published in *Monty Python's Flying Circus* included in article: Richard H. Thaler with Robyn M. Dawes (1992), 'Cooperation', in *The Winner's Curse: Paradoxes and Anomalies of Economic Life*, Chapter 2, 6–20, references.

University of Chicago Press for articles: Avner Greif, Paul Milgrom and Barry R. Weingast (1994), 'Coordination, Commitment, and Enforcement: The Case of the Merchant Guild', *Journal of Political Economy*, **102** (4), August, 745–76 ; Peter Kollock (1994), 'The Emergence of Exchange Structures: An Experimental Study of Uncertainty, Commitment, and Trust', *American Journal of Sociology*, **100** (2), September, 313–45.

University of Michigan Press for excerpt: Werner Güth and Menahem E. Yaari (1992), 'Explaining Reciprocal Behavior in Simple Strategic Games: An Evolutionary Approach', in Ulrich Witt (ed.), *Explaining Process and Change: Approaches to Evolutionary Economics*, Chapter 2, 23–34.

Every effort has been made to trace all the copyright holders but if any have been inadvertently overlooked the publishers will be pleased to make the necessary arrangement at the first opportunity.

In addition the publishers wish to thank the Marshall Library of Economics, Cambridge University, the Library of the University of Warwick and the Library of Indiana University at Bloomington, USA, for their assistance in obtaining these articles.

Introduction Why Does Trustworthiness Pay? Three Answers

Elias L. Khalil[1]

The Big Puzzle

The articles in this volume try to solve a puzzle facing standard evolutionary theory and standard rationality theory. Both engender, under some conditions, the same result: agents will choose the most advantageous, which can be the most opportunistic, strategy. If agents are irrational, according to neo-Darwinism,[2] the forces of evolutionary selection would delete them, before being able to leave offspring or copies behind, in favor of the rational ones. Of course, certain conditions have to be met, such as the existence of at least one rational agent that the selection process favors and that markets or niches are not insulated from competitive forces. The exemplar story is the single-shot prisoners' dilemma game, where noncooperation is the dominant strategy. If most agents are irrational and choose cooperation, they would be edited out in favor of the ones who choose defection. Once you accept either the rationality or evolutionary explanation, a big puzzle arises: Why then do trustworthy, nonopportunistic agents survive and even propagate their kind?

In the literature, there are basically three different answers to the big puzzle. Yet why is there a big puzzle in the first place? To be sure, trustworthiness is not a puzzle for functionalist analyses in traditional sociological and anthropological theories or their equivalent in biology, namely, group-selection evolutionary theory. For traditional sociological theory (e.g., Parsons, 1951), agents are socialized into behavioral roles through a complex web of approvals and sanctions. For traditional anthropological theory, agents are by nature norm following and, hence, tend to imitate the norms prevalent in their culture. The major problem with this approach is the phenomenon of free riding. Interestingly, this critique of functionalism, also informs greatly George Williams's (1966) critique of group-selection arguments in evolutionary biology. This should not mean that group-selection evolutionary theory *in toto* is doomed. Some recent effort to advance group-selection theory has been successful in circumventing the free-riding problem (e.g., Hayek, 1967; Cavalli-Sforza & Feldman, 1981; Boyd & Richerson, 1985; Wilson & Sober, 1989; Sober & Wilson, 1999; Richerson & Boyd, 2001). Nonetheless, the trend or intellectual fashion of the last quarter of the twentieth century has been, across the social sciences, to stay away from functionalist analyses and instead embrace rationality choice theory and neo-Darwinism. In this fashion, theoreticians do not have to deal with the free-riding problem.

However, the rationality and neo-Darwinian stories created their own puzzle. If it pays to free ride and act opportunistically, how do we explain that trustworthy, gullible agents have managed to survive and to propagate their kind in the population? The propagation of the opportunistic trait does not have to be through biological reproduction. It can be through imitation. Spectators, who see that trustworthy agents are losing money, learn quickly to behave like opportunists. Also, to act opportunistically there is no need to assume intelligence or intentionality on the part of agents. They only need to be programmed to want to live and their kind to survive. The neo-Darwinian story guarantees – under strict conditions[3] – that the least foolish of fools would survive while the rest would fail to propagate. If agents act in a trustworthy manner, and if there is at least one agent who is less gullible, the less gullible agent would amass greater profits and, hence, drive the trustworthy agents out of existence. Yet this did not happen. So, trustworthiness must have a payoff or a dividend. The question is, then, what is the payoff? There are three answers to the big puzzle, which inform the organization of the volume into three corresponding parts.

A World of Words: Trust, Altruism, Public Spiritedness, Faith, Confidence, Fidelity

Before reviewing the three answers, I need to specify what I mean by the word 'trust':

> Trust denotes the conviction that one (including the self) or anonymous others will act in a trustworthy way, i.e., carry out binding, fiduciary commitments towards specific individuals irrespective, but within limits, of *ex post* incentives.

This is similar to the definition provided by Harvey James (2002, p. 291): 'To say "A trusts B" means that A expects B will not exploit a vulnerability A has created for himself by taking the action.'

The agent may think that he is trustworthy, i.e., a future self will not betray the commitment promised by current self, or may think that others are trustworthy, i.e., current other selves will not take advantage of current self. In this manner, the problem of explaining why one acts in a trustworthy way is isomorphic to the problem of explaining why others act in a trustworthy manner. There is no need to distinguish, à la Russell Hardin (2001), trust from trustworthiness. The others can range from known partners and local politicians to anonymous bureaucrats and players that make up larger systems of government, finance, church, and so on. There must be a basis for trusting one's *ex post* intention or the *ex post* intention of anonymous others – a basis that resembles the capital stock that needs to be replenished through use.

The above definition of trust is intentionally broad. It does not necessarily require *ex post* and *ex ante* alignment or misalignment of incentives. This broad definition allows us to elucidate the three answers to the puzzle. However, this broad definition does not exclude one feature of trust, vulnerability. Even when it is in the best interest of an opponent to cooperate, there is always a chance that he might change his mind about what constitutes his best interest. So, although the proposed definition is broad, it still gives room to the idea that trust is always fraught with the possibility of abuse as Carol Heimer (2001) emphasizes.

There are other sentiments and motivations that need to be distinguished from trust. Human sentiments and motivations are complex if not messy. While it is very difficult to classify them, the classification is imperative for any attempt at theorizing. Part of the difficulty arises from the fact that one needs a theory in order to undertake the classification. To break through the impasse, I attempt here a classification by dissecting the nuances of the term 'trust' (see also Nooteboom, 2000, 2002, ch. 2; Heimer, 2001; Hardin, 2001). I propose to distinguish trust from altruism, public spiritedness, faith, confidence, and fidelity.

To start with altruism, many writers, with a few exceptions (e.g., Fehr & Gächter, Chapter 14 in this volume), conceive trust and altruism as belonging to the same category of 'non-self-interested' behavior (e.g., Sally, 2000). One reason behind this mode of conception is probably that some of the explanations of trust overlap with some of the explanations of altruism (Khalil, 2001, 2003b). However, to use common empiricism, when one acts with trustworthiness and leaves a tip in a far-away restaurant one cannot be acting out of altruism, i.e., out of care for the welfare of the waiter who is a stranger. Otherwise, he would have given the tip instead to a more needy person who might even be more familiar. Likewise, if the altruistic act to help a stranger to catch a taxi is a matter of trust, the stranger would have the right to demand it. Stated tersely, altruism expresses a voluntary action, while trust as defined here engenders a binding commitment in which the punishment of defectors is justified (Khalil, Chapter 28 in this volume). While the biological literature does not make a distinction between voluntary help and binding cooperative strategy, the difference is at least pertinent to human behavior at the intuitive level.

Another clarification, trust should be distinguished from public spiritedness which, in turn, differs from altruism or sympathy with people who need help. Trust informs action according to a promise to pay back, while public spiritedness is a voluntary undertaking to improve living conditions. However, public spiritedness differs from altruism that is also voluntary. Altruism involves depriving oneself of the resource for the benefit of others. Public spiritedness entails the desire to change institutions – which may entail changing laws or may be limited to changing the public perception of a problem. By changing institutions, the actor does not only give up a portion of his budget, but also convinces (compels?) others to act in a similar manner. Such public spiritedness stems from a desire to mold at least some institutions after what one thinks is the good way of life. Thus, public spiritedness falls better under the same motivation or aspiration that propels one to mold one's life (the entrepreneurship motive), the life of his offspring (the paternity motive), or the life of others (the philanthropy motive). Such a motive requires an expanded notion of rationality that takes into consideration not only given tastes, but also the desire of the ego to mold circumstances after its own image.

An additional clarification, the focus here on intention differs from another sense of the word 'trust' when used interchangeably with 'faith' in one's ability or competence (see Barber, 1983; Luhmann, 1988; Nooteboom, 2000; cf. Heimer, 2001). Trust as faith is about rhetoric and the power of belief as evident in statements such as 'I trust myself – I will pass the exam,' 'I will win the battle against smoking,' or 'I will prevail over my enemy.' Here the agent is concerned with one's ability. Likewise, one may trust a leader of an organization in the sense of faith, rather than in the sense of intention as usually discussed in the agency problem and public choice literature: Does the leader have the foresight, courage, and ability to lead the firm, tribe, or country? Also, when one states: 'I place my trust in God' (which is, incidentally, the literal meaning of the Arabic word 'islam'),[4] one is not stating: 'I do not think that God is opportunistic.' Rather, one is stating: 'Given my beliefs of God's omnipotence and love, I have the ability to face the challenges of life.'

If the distinction between faith and trust is granted, organizational arrangements such as the intra-firm contract are not simply about trust that informs commercial arrangements, such as the inter-firm contract. The intra-firm contract may involve faith, where the employee submits to the ability and authority of the firm (Masten in Williamson & Winter, 1993), besides the usual trust that characterizes also the commercial contract. While the faith/trust distinction is pivotal to the debate of the firm/market distinction, i.e., of whether the firm differs in a substantial way from market networks or alliances (Khalil, 1997c), it is outside the scope of this volume. The concern of this volume is not with trust as faith in ability, but rather with trust in intention, or simply 'trust,' that characterizes commercial contracts that informs both firms and networks.

Moreover, the term 'trust' is sometimes used interchangeably with the expression 'confidence.' I like to suggest reserving 'confidence' to denote another phenomenon, as when one utters: 'I trust that the weather will cooperate this weekend' or 'I trust that the car will keep going this winter.' Obviously, one is not doubting that an inanimate system (either natural such as the weather or artificial such as the car) may suffer from the agency problem and shirk – unless one has a particular religious belief about punishment. Also, one is not doubting that an inanimate system may suffer from weakness of will or lack of faith in its own ability to perform. The car's capacity or weather's dynamics is known according to a *given* risk distribution, while the agent's ability is unknown even according to risk distribution because it develops through the act of knowing it. It is outside the scope here to elaborate on doubt in the sense of confidence as opposed to doubt in the sense of faith (Khalil, 1997a,d). Neoclassical economists use the same category – either risk, uncertainty, or subjective uncertainty – to denote both kinds of doubt as if confidence and faith are identical. What matters here is that both kinds of doubt, confidence and faith, are different from the sense of trust as trust in intention, the focus of this volume.

A final clarification, trust in the sense of trusting the intention of contractual partners seems to differ, at first examination, from fidelity in the sense of bonding, intimacy, or solidarity – either with a mate, a god, a family, a community, a tribe, or a nation. In the sense of fidelity, a better word for denoting trust is probably 'love' as expressed in gift exchange. Trust as fidelity that is imperative to the cohesiveness of an entity such as the firm, tribe, or community informs greatly the sociological literature (e.g., Luhmann, 1979, 1988; Barber, 1983; Lewis & Weigert, 1985; Meeker, 1983; Eisenstadt & Roniger, 1984; Fox, 1974; Sztompka, 1999), the anthropological literature (e.g., Richerson & Boyd, 2001), and the organizational studies literature that is critical of the crudeness and reductionism of the transaction cost theory of the firm (e.g., Husted, 1989; Williamson & Winter, 1993; Noorderhaven, 1995; Hodgson, 1995; Mayer *et al.*, 1995; Kramer & Tyler, 1996, ch. 1; Tyler & Degoey, 1996; Nooteboom, Chapter 12 in this volume and 2000; Miller, 2001).

At least according to one interpretation of John Locke's social contract, namely the work of John Dunn (e.g., 1988), the sense of trust as fidelity – rather than verified commercial contracting – is how John Locke characterized the relationship of the citizens and their government. The sense of trust as communal solidarity is highlighted as imperative to political order, democracy, and governance by many contributors to the collection of Valerie Braithwaite and Margaret Levi (1998) such as Simon Blackburn, Valerie Braithwaite, Tom Tyler, Mark Peel, and John Braithwaite, as well as to the collection of Mark Warren (1999) such as Claus Offe, Jean Cohen, Jane Mansbridge, and Mark Warren. Yet we may not need to conceive communal solidarity or love as different from trust based on interest. It seems that one finds love, or at least one-sided love, where one finds mutual interest suitable. It seems that bonding is a by-product of interest (see Khalil, 1997e, 2000a). One expresses such a *by-product* by offering words of thanks or tangible gifts to people who are not opportunistic with regard to one's interest. While love may not characterize an exchange relation at the start, it arises from a contract that endures, where the partners do not take advantage of each other. So, the phenomenon of social bond or love should not call for another way to classify the theories of trust, if the social bond or love is a by-product or shadow of the underlying exchange relationship. This explains why I place some of the sociological and organizational studies literature that discusses long-term contracting in terms of bonding or solidarity alongside the transaction cost literature (e.g., Kollock, Chapter 9, in this volume; Nooteboom, Chapter 12, in this volume).

It seems that, in light of the above clarifications, the big puzzle can be explained in three ways that cut across the divides among disciplines.[5] The chapters selected for this volume are arranged into three parts that correspond to the three ways of solving the puzzle. The first answer is the idea that trust is a strategy in repeated games. The second answer is the notion that trust is a taste. The third answer is the thesis that trust is a trait favored by evolutionary selection forces.

As many contributors have noted, the three modes of explaining trust do not need to be exclusive alternatives. It might be the case that in some arenas, trust as strategy is the relevant one, while in other arenas, trust as taste seems to be more applicable. Further, trust as trait complements the trust as taste explanation by providing it with conditions of stability.

Trust as Strategy

Gordon Tullock (Chapter 1) employs the prisoners' dilemma game to argue that cooperative strategy would be the dominant one if the agents play under, to use Adam Smith's words, 'the discipline of continuous dealings.' Robert Axelrod and Douglas Dion (Chapter 2) extend Axelrod's model of repetitive prisoners' dilemma game to account for cooperation. Cooperation arises among egoists if each player knows that the other would retaliate in the next move if one fails to choose cooperation in the current move. William Hamilton, Robert Axelrod, and Reiko Tanese (1990) apply this Tit-for-Tat strategy to account for the origin of sex. Sexual reproduction can be modeled as cooperative strategy of egoistic organisms in order to vary the genetic stock and, hence, fend off against the invasion of parasites. To account for trust as strategy, the evolutionary mechanism is superfluous. One only needs the assumption of rational choice. In this regard, Jack Hirshleifer (Chapter 3; see also Hirshleifer, 2001) shows – in prisoners' dilemma, chicken, and tender trap games – that evolutionary selection, under certain conditions, traces optimal choice theory.

According to Hardin (2001, 2002), for one to be trustworthy, one's incentive must be aligned with one's obligated commitment. The fact that one may trust a loved one whose interest may not be aligned with obligated commitment does not contradict what Hardin calls the 'encapsulated-interest' view of trust. To have someone love you means that your interest is part of his or hers, and so he/she can be trusted because he/she is actually acting on an 'expanded' interest. Here Hardin is also providing a theory of altruism that is similar to Gary Becker's (1981; cf. Khalil, 2001).

The chapters so far discuss the basis upon which one may trust someone else. Yet how should the someone else act in order to gain the trust? Oliver Williamson (Chapter 4) discusses actions that corporations take, called 'hostage posting,' to exhibit credible commitment and, hence, worthy of the trust of others. Such credible commitments involve investment in buildings, advertisements, and other overhead costs to assure suppliers and customers that the corporation is not a fly-by-night operation.

Further, the chapters so far generally discuss cooperation in the context of *infinitely* repetitive games. However, if the repetitive games are finite, which is the usual case in everyday life, they should unravel through backward induction according to game theory – unless the payoffs and rules meet particular conditions as discussed by David Kreps *et al.* (Chapter 5).

In any case, you do not need repetitive game per se to explain trust as the dominant strategy. One can explain trust as strategy even in a single-shot game by introducing transaction cost and bounded rationality. It might be too costly for agents to switch the strategy on and off in the light of case-by-case calculations. One might adopt trust as a habit that minimizes the cost of calculation – similar to the habit of taking the stairs two floors up versus the elevator. If one decides habitually to take the stairs because it is faster, in many cases it might not be the case, but on average, the stairs are faster. The agent who acts habitually is ahead by economizing on his mental ability that is bounded. David Messick and Roderick Kramer (2001) rely on this explanation to discuss trust in single-shot interaction. They appeal to Herbert Simon's notion of 'satisficing' to explain the origin of the decision to trust or to be trustworthy – which they call shallow, rule-based psychology. It is shallow because agents, following some fine-tuned discriminatory judgment, decide that other agents follow the rules of trust, without reflecting on deep moral questions. Along this rationale, one acts with trustworthiness and leaves a tip in a far-from-home restaurant because it would be costly to calculate that he is now in a single-shot game and can cheat. John Gale *et al.* (Chapter 6) also provides a bounded-rationality account, but of the ultimatum game which is the focus of the next part on trust as taste.

Moving towards applications of the trust-as-strategy view, Edward Lorenz (Chapter 7) shows the importance of trust in an advanced capitalist economy like France. He argues that subcontracting among 'lock-in' firms in modern France is based on informal networks of trust, for which formal contracts cannot substitute. In contrast, Keith Hart (Chapter 8) thinks that less developed countries such as Ghana have the greatest needs for trust because their disintegrated, kinship-based organizations of traditional obligations have not been fully replaced by formal contracts. Jean Ensminger (2001) discusses how herd owners among the Orma of northeast Kenya developed 'fictive kinship' in order to minimize monitoring costs and solve the agency problem.

Starting with Kenneth Arrow's (1963) article on the economics of medical care and his article on exchange in general (Arrow, 1972), where information is imperfect, contributors to the growing literature on trust recognize that trust reduces transaction costs. Contributors to collections such as those of Diego Gambetta (1988), Roderick Kramer and Tom Tyler (1996), Valerie Braithwaite and Margaret Levi (1998), Karen Cook (2001), and Randolph Nesse (2001) generally concur that distrust increases transaction costs and, consequently, hinders division of labor and leads to economic stagnation, as in the case of political institutions in Southern Italy (Putnam, 1993; Gambetta, 1995; Galassi, 2000). They maintain that trust is a capital stock that underpins development and economic growth, the idea behind the categories 'social capital' or 'cultural institutions' stressed by James Coleman (1988), Mark Casson (1991), Robert

Putnam (1993, 1995; cf. Sobel, 2002), Francis Fukuyama (1996), Rafael La Porta *et al.* (1997), and Partha Dasgupta and Ismail Serageldin (1999). Stephen Knack and Philip Keefer (1997) find strong evidence linking social capital to economic performance in 29 market economies (see also Zak & Knack, 2001). Further, Edward Glaeser *et al.* (2000) provide experimental and survey-based methods to measure social capital.

However, social capital, like any other capital, is not costless. Agents have to spend resources to cultivate and replenish social capital. Such costs rise probably at an increasing rate with the size of the network. This may explain why enclaves of trust are easier to maintain at the scale of local neighborhood, ethnic clubs, church, and other small-scale networks. As some contributors have noted (e.g., Braithwaite & Levi, 1998), such small-scale networks bounded by trust usually harbor distrust to outsiders and the wider community – which may hinder development. Further, as Bart Nooteboom (2000) reminds us, there can be an over-investment in trust – as is probably the case with the once celebrated Japanese networks such as *kinyu keiretsu* (financial lineage) and *kigyo shudan* (enterprise group) (see Gerlach, 1987). An over-investment in trust may undermine innovation and may erect barriers to competition and free trade. Also, it goes without stating, the prisoners' dilemma insofar as it plagues criminal networks, mafia organizations, cartels, and old-boy's-network of corporate and political cliques is actually public delight.

Peter Kollock (Chapter 9) shows how long-term relations cemented with trust characterize the raw rubber market in Southeast Asia. Raw rubber belongs to the class of commodities that involves asymmetric information, namely, the lemon problem (see Sako, 1992). The seller knows the quality of the rubber, but the buyer would not know the quality until the passage of a few months after extraction. While Kollock discusses trust as social bond or solidarity, it can be fully accounted for as strategy in repetitive game – similar to Carol Heimer's (2001) account of the legal and reputational safeguards that buttress trustworthiness. The possibility of cheating, and the ability to enforce contracts also characterize merchant trading guilds that emerged in the late medieval period according to Avner Greif, Paul Milgrom, and Barry Weingast (Chapter 10). Robert Gibbons (2001) shows how repeated game theory can explain enforcement of law by the state as well as long-term contracting within and between firms.

In fact, with regard to long-term contracting, Oliver Williamson (Chapter 11) argues that the category 'trust' is redundant (see also Telser, 1980). Calculative self-interest would have taken care of vulnerability arising from opportunism that may arise in contracts between firms that involves asset specificity. For Williamson, the impetus behind economic organization is bounded rationality and opportunism. Bart Nooteboom (Chapter 12; see also Winter in Williamson & Winter, 1993; Noorderhaven, 1995; Hodgson, 1995) recognizes the opportunism problem and how governance devices are geared to minimize it. As an antidote to the transaction cost literature, however, Nooteboom argues that trust is not a redundant category. Similar to Kollock, Nooteboom maintains that trust adds ethical cement to an on-going, long-term relation (see also Hollis, 1998). Likewise, Bernd Lahno (Chapter 13) argues sharply that trust has an emotional component that is somewhat independent of rational deliberation. Lahno argues that the emotional component is necessary in order to cope with the risk associated with exchange relations that one needs.

Williamson seems more convincing, though. The explanation of trust as strategy makes the category of trust as an ethical or emotional cement ultimately redundant. Of course, one may add that trust as strategy has some by-product effects, similar to the sentiments associated with gift giving discussed above (Khalil, 1997e). These sentiments – such as love, appreciation, solidarity, loyalty, bonding, warmth – only add salt and pepper to the dish that is already cooked by egoistic agents whose eyes are fixed on the money. Salt and pepper might be important in accentuating the taste of the dish – as much as the gift is supposed to negate any crudeness or tackiness in hard-nosed contract negotiations. Yet salt and pepper, without the underlying ingredients, would be pointless and, in fact, repulsive. The ethical cement can go far, but ultimately is regulated by underlying mutual interest. So, the category 'trust' could be interchangeable with 'enlightened self-interest,' in repeated games, or with 'habit' and rule-based, ethical behavior in single-shot games characterized by bounded rationality. In this light, the trust-as-strategy explanation economizes on theory construction and, hence, following the Ockham's razor dictum, is a theoretical triumph.

However, as many thinkers – including some promoters of the trust-as-strategy explanation such as Hardin and Gibbons – have pointed out, trust is not a redundant category. It expresses something more than strategy. From casual empiricism, people do not usually want to end a relation 'on a bad note' – even when there would be no harm to reputation. Also, concerning bounded rationality, it costs one almost nothing to realize that he is in a far-from-home restaurant and to adjust strategy from cooperation to defection. In fact, such casual empiricism has been amplified and confirmed by an alternative literature that is inclined to explain trust as taste.

Trust as Taste

A body of experiments started to show that agents reciprocate *ex post*, i.e., repay kindness with kindness when there is no further gain in sight – contrary to what the trust-as-strategy view predicts. Ernst Fehr and Simon Gächter (Chapter 14) usefully call cooperative reciprocal tendencies 'positive reciprocity,' and the retaliatory tendencies 'negative reciprocity.' In this manner, cooperation and retaliation stem from the same tendency to respond to trust with cooperation, and to respond to deception with retaliation. They show that once subjects are allowed to punish defectors in public good games, they would do so even when it is a dominated strategy. Despite the fact that the dominant strategy is not to punish, agents on the whole punish defectors at their own personal expense whereas the benefit is public good.

The classic illustration of negative reciprocity is the ultimatum game (or the final round of a centipede experiment). Werner Güth *et al.* (1982) and Werner Güth & Reinhard Tietz (Chapter 15) show the tendency of agents to punish others for not cooperating according to some standard of fairness, even when such punishment is costly without engendering any benefit. Alvin Roth *et al.* (Chapter 16) confirm the results of the ultimatum game in many cities including Jerusalem, Ljubljana, Pittsburgh, and Tokyo. More recently, Joseph Henrich *et al.* (Chapter 17), conduct the same game in small-scale societies, arriving at similar results (see also Hoffman *et al.*, 1995, 1996).

The canonical illustration of positive reciprocity is the trust game. James Andreoni (Chapter 18) and Robyn Dawes and Richard Thaler (Chapter 19) conduct and review experiments where agents do not free ride in single-shot public-good decisions. They do not contribute zero as expected by the trust-as-strategy explanation. They contribute between 40 per cent and 60 per cent of what is socially optimal. Joyce Berg *et al.* (Chapter 20) and Andreas Ortmann *et al.* (Chapter 21) conduct experiments on the trust game (known also as the investment game), which confirms positive reciprocity. When agent 1 gives money to agent 2 in a single-shot game, agent 2 in most cases responds cooperatively despite the fact that agent 2 would make more money by defecting. In this situation, it benefits agent 1 greatly to 'mindread' the intentionality of agent 2, whether he is an opponent or a partner. The ability to identify cooperators or read the intentions of others, what is known in psychology as 'theory of mind,' has opened a new vista of research which Kevin McCabe coins 'neuroeconomics' (see Coricelli *et al.*, 2000; McCabe & Smith, 2000; McCabe *et al.*, 2000; Burnham *et al.*, 2000; Brosig, 2002).

What is the source of reciprocity – positive or negative? Daniel Kahneman *et al.* (Chapter 22) models retaliation as a taste for fairness that may reduce the payoff for the agent. George Akerlof (Chapter 23; see also Baron, 1988; Bishop, 1987) discusses the labor contract as partially a gift in the sense that loyalty is rewarded even when it pays to withhold the reward. Likewise, Mathew Rabin (Chapter 24) models trustworthiness as a taste that produces what he calls 'fairness equilibrium.' One is ready to pay the cost (in terms of not cheating cooperators, and punishing defectors) to satisfy the fairness taste by responding to the intention of the player (see Greenberg & Frisch, 1972). In David Levine's (Chapter 25) game-theoretic approach, agents respond to the kind of person, rather than to the intention of the person, to account for *ex post* reciprocity.

In contrast, Amitai Etzioni (Chapter 26) provides a multiple-self account for the taste of trustworthiness and commitment. He starts from a different background, namely, the Kantian imperative to act ethically. Etzioni distinguishes interests that generate 'pleasure utility' from ideal ends that engender 'moral "utility".' The two kinds of utility are supposedly incommensurable – a position also advocated by a number of economists (e.g., Sen, Chapter 27; Albert Hirschman, 1985). Etzioni rejects the neoclassical economic model that reduces moral 'utility' to pleasure utility. Similarly Valerie Braithwaite (1998) distinguishes between trust that is based on the knowledge of the motives of others and hence related to the trust-as-strategy view, and trust based on communal solidarity and connectedness to others, which is related to Etzioni 'moral "utility".' For Braithwaite, while both kinds of trust co-exist, they are based on different value systems that correspond to different institutional settings. Likewise, Philip Pettit (1998; see also Pettit, 1995) highlights trustworthiness as a virtue that cannot be reduced to economic calculation. According to Pettit's view of the republican theory of government, officials in government are kept trustworthy if the public is not cynical but rather upholds the virtue of trustworthiness. The virtue consists of the belief in exemplars of what it is to be honorable – even beyond whether officials are actually trustworthy. The belief sets in motion the incentive, what Pettit calls the 'trust-mechanism,' for officials to behave with honesty because they desire to be thought of as trustworthy.

Amartya Sen (Chapter 27) provides a direct critique of the neoclassical theory of optimization that treats moral commitments as ordinary tastes and part of the pecuniary, welfare function. For Sen, the treatment amounts to modeling agents as rational fools. Sen argues that moral commitments such as honesty and the pride one takes in achieving a task cannot be reduced to the standard sense of welfare. Elias Khalil (Chapter 28) argues that Sen and others who erect an iron wall between interest and commitment usually do not demarcate between two kinds of commitment. There is honesty or trust that involves '*binding* commitment.' This commitment differs from tenacity or perseverance to pursue a goal, such as a career as a singer, which entails a commitment also, but a *non-binding* one. One can always walk away from the commitment to be a singer, after failing so many times, without punishment or ostracism. However, one cannot walk away from debt without punishment or ostracism. The conception of the two kinds of commitment as essentially the same, especially in how they relate to interest or welfare, amounts to modeling agents as 'sentimental fools.'

While the different theories of trust as taste can account for trustworthiness in *ex post* settings when transaction cost is close to zero, there are two main problems with such theories. First, at first examination the solution seems a *deus ex machina*. It invokes tastes as the solution, instead of searching for an economic explanation in terms of prices and budgets (Stigler & Becker, 1977). However, at further examination, it might be the case that agents have always had a stable taste for trustworthiness, i.e., ready to incur costs to behave trustworthily or punish cheaters in single-shot encounters. In fact, the rise of experimental economics in the last two decades went a long way to measure tastes such as trustworthiness. There is one problem, though, with the view of trustworthiness as taste – even after treating it as a stable taste. Namely, if trustworthiness is a taste, why is there no 'open' market for dishonesty? Why is bribe-taking conducted in secret, even in single-shot games where there is no penalty? Why do some agents feel shameful for acting dishonestly? Also, why do the rest of them, who are not shameful, spend resources to explain away their acts, yet explain them mainly to themselves? The phenomena of shame and self-deception are mysterious in the temple of optimization where trustworthiness is treated as a taste (Khalil, 2002).

Second, the solution might be unstable. To have a taste for trust amounts to being gullible. Once others know that someone is gullible, that person would be the perfect partner in single-shot prisoners' dilemma games. While the agent might make the optimum consumption allocation, the agent who is inflicted with the taste for trust would be deleted from the population – given that the population includes others who have no taste for trustworthiness and that the selection process is efficient. However, this critique is weak as the third answer to the puzzle shows.

Trust as Trait

For Ulrich Witt (Chapter 29), trustworthiness need not be unstable. He argues that most cooperation is neither strategic nor expressive of taste. Rather, trustworthiness is expressive of a personality trait, that he calls 'social.' The prosocial trait is produced through indoctrination, preaching, and teaching – or what sociologists call 'socialization' – that manipulate the agent to act in roles that are beneficial to the collective. Such a functionalist account cannot address the free-riding problem as mentioned earlier. Nonetheless, Witt's account anticipates a whole literature that posits trustworthiness as a personality trait. One does not reap pleasure from having such a trait, just as one does not enjoy being tall. The trait is part of the budget function, a tool, and hence one rather enjoys, under certain conditions, the consequences of being trustworthy or being tall. So, similar to traditional sociological and psychological theories, one cannot help but act trustworthily if he possesses the prosocial trait. Witt here tries to solve a paradox: how could trustworthiness survive? For Witt, the prosocial trait survives only if there is a critical mass of such a trait in the population (see also Axelrod, 1986). Above the critical mass, the prosocial trait learns from experience to uphold what one was indoctrinated from childhood. Yet cooperation disappears if the frequency of the prosocial trait falls below the critical mass. In this sense, Witt provides the condition of stability for the unlikely character of trustworthiness.

Witt's theory is similar to Peyton Young's (1996) population dynamics account of social conventions, such as driving on the right-hand side of the road, as Nash equilibrium solutions. Werner Güth *et al.* (Chapter 30), also provide a population dynamics account to explain the trait of positive reciprocity. Under certain conditions, the trait succeeds through dynamic feedbacks. The success pushes the population composition to a unique rest point. Focusing on negative reciprocity, Werner Güth and Menahem Yaari (Chapter 31) provide an evolutionary game account. They show that mutants with the character to reciprocate harm have greater reproductive success than others. In the game where both players derive pleasure from revenge, the dominant strategy is to play fair. In the game where both players have distaste for revenge, the dominant strategy is to cheat. In the game where only one player has the taste for revenge, the dominant strategy for that player is to cheat the other, but not vice versa. The payoffs in the last two games in terms of reproductive success are less than when both players have the taste for revenge and, hence, the genetic make-up shifts towards agents with the taste for revenge. There is one weakness in this argument. The same framework could possibly account for the stability of the distaste for revenge as well. When revenge is costly, agents who are clever enough to exchange hostages to assure cooperation could reap greater payoffs than the agents who have the taste for revenge.

Herbert Gintis (Chapter 32) offers a model to account for the persistence of cooperation, what he calls 'strong reciprocity' as opposed to 'weak reciprocity' of the theories of trust as strategy. Gintis, through the mathematical machinery of group selection, establishes the conditions under which agents with 'strong reciprocity' can save their group from disintegration in the face of environmental challenges, securing in the meantime their trait. Robert Frank (Chapter 33) deals with the same problem: how can trustworthy agents survive? It is because others find it to their benefit to transact with such agents. Yet how can others distinguish agents equipped with the conscience trait from opportunists? There are signals, such as sweat and tone of voice, that opportunists cannot mimic without high cost. As long as the cost of signals of honesty is high enough, such as religious affiliation (Irons, 2001), or information about the trustworthy trait is low enough (Güth & Kliemt, 2000), agents who have conscience are chosen as partners and, hence, can propagate at least at the same rate as opportunistic agents.

As Jack Hirshleifer (Chapter 34; see also De Sousa, 1987) argues, the signals can be the outburst of emotions, where the other player in a conflict realizes that he/she had better choose cooperation in a single-shot game because the opponent is 'irrational;' i.e., the opponent would incur *ex post* cost in exacting revenge. Jörn P.W. Scharlemann *et al.* (Chapter 35) show that signals of trustworthiness, such as the smile, make players choose cooperative strategies that would be dominated in prisoners' dilemma game (see also Bacharach & Gambetta, 2001). Axel Ockenfels and Reinhard Selten (Chapter 36) also conduct experiments that show how trustworthiness is directly affected by involuntary signals.

In turn, Randolph Nesse (2001) offers a wide-ranging survey of the nuances of the neo-Darwinian evolutionary account of trustworthiness. He emphasizes that trustworthiness should be seen as a capacity rather than a prescribed behavior according to genetic determinism. Nesse distinguishes trustworthiness as 'subjective commitment,' i.e., involves caring and hence differs from the calculative notion of commitment as strategy. Oliver Goodenough (2001) argues that evolutionary theory must meet particular conditions in order to account for subjective commitment. He reviews the legal literature where subjective commitment is called 'fiduciary duty.' Fiduciary duty informs the modern corporation where ownership, represented in the board of trustees, is separated from control, represented by the chief executive officer of the corporation (Berle & Means, 1933).[6]

In short, the trust-as-trait model can explain trust in single shot games when transaction costs are low – without appealing to caring à la trust-as-taste explanation. Here, the cooperator trait prevails in the population because, if the trait exists beyond a critical threshold, it can persist. One does not need to care about the waiter at a restaurant in a far-away place in order to leave the tip. The tip is left behind because one simply possesses the prosocial trait. The agent just cannot not leave the tip. He/she does not want to go home with bad conscience. So, he/she does not need to be involved in repetitive games with the waiter, to suffer from bounded rationality, or to care about the welfare of the waiter in order to explain trust. We only need enough agents equipped with the moral gene to tip-off the propagation dynamics in their favor. However, is this neo-Darwinian, selection model convincing?[7]

There seem to be insurmountable weaknesses in the neo-Darwinian approach. First, the trust-as-trait approach cannot explain the *origin* of trustworthiness in the trust game or retaliation in the ultimatum game. At best, similar to all neo-Darwinian models, the trust-as-trait explanation can shed light on the *diffusion* of the trait. It takes as given that such a trait exists in the population – and exists in sufficient frequency. Neo-Darwinian theory proposes that the origin of the trait is accidental or subject to a stochastic dynamics that is oblivious to *ex post* benefit.

Second, if trust is a stable trait, why do we fail to find a one-to-one correspondence between trait and behavior? It is not unlikely to observe that agents who possess the trait for trust often act deceptively, and agents who possess the trait for deception often act trustworthily – even when incentives do not change. One may cheat on his taxes, but would never accept a bribe – even when costs and benefits are the same. One may also deceive a gullible customer, but never steal – even when the costs and benefits are the same. The variability of behavior of one agent, even when the incentives do not change, makes it doubtful that trustworthiness arises from some ingrained personality trait.

Third, if one accepts the neo-Darwinian story that the trait for trust arises randomly, why has nature so far failed to produce the dominance of 'natural cheaters,' driving honest agents to extinction – where it costs the socially pathological agents nothing to deceive and mimic the signals of honest agents? The socially pathological agents would inherit the neo-Darwinian Earth. The explanation of the existence of the trait for trust amounts to *deus ex machina*.

Then What – Trust as Identity?

What is the answer to the big puzzle? We cannot go back to functionalist analyses that invite the free-riding problem. We must adhere to the lesson that motivated the three answers reviewed above: Namely, any explanation must show that trust is sustainable; i.e., it pays to be trustworthy. However, any explanation must also meet the three following challenges – which help us avoid the pitfall of each of the three answers:

1. The explanation must explain trust in single-shot games without bounded rationality.

2. The explanation must explain trust in a systematic fashion; i.e. avoid invoking, in a *deus ex machina* fashion, trust as taste, which in turn raises the issue of stability.
3. The explanation must avoid neo-Darwinian selection stories, which actually explain the stability of trustworthiness, but not its origin.

I do not have an answer. However, I can propose a hypothesis to start from, which I can only mention here. Namely, people behave either as trustworthy or non-trustworthy – whatever it takes to preserve their identity under given circumstances (Khalil, 2003c). There is nothing inherent in their nature on how to behave. To elaborate, there is a little noticed fact about the prisoners' *story* (i.e., the actual story, not the game). Namely, the two criminals are friends. While the prisoners are playing a single-shot game, the prisoners' situation is underpinned by the particular institution of friendship. If the past does not matter, as we are led to believe by standard game theory, why would the prisoners' story be a dilemma? If the past is irrelevant, the prisoners' story would be indifferent from the institution-free 'Red Queen Paradox' (Khalil, 1997b).

What is salient about trustworthiness is that the past does matter. The agent, at least from casual empiricism, takes pride in acting according to trust, as if it is the smart choice. This is perplexing because if circumstances are different, the agent should rather take pride in being manipulative, nongullible, or, in short, street-smart. In some rough neighborhoods, trustworthiness borders on stupidity. What seems to matter is that the person chooses optimally what he thinks of as his identity. Yet once chosen, the agent is committed, but of course *within limits*, to the choice: he acts trustworthily in order to self-verify his optimally chosen identity – if the choice was trustworthiness (see Swann, 1983; Burke & Stets, 1999; Stets & Burke, 2000). This resembles the choice of one's favorite church, ideology, football team, or profession. The choice seems to be nonflexible, at least in the short-term, even when transactions costs are zero. It might be nonflexible because it becomes part of one's identity.

So, *identity* might be the proper metaphor for trust. What distinguishes trust-as-identity metaphor from trust-as-trait metaphor? To model trust as identity, there is no need for an evolutionary mechanism. Identity arises from the nature of cognitive activity as the agent tries to make sense of the world around him. It is what defines the agent as an actor per se.

The idea that identity, such as street-smartness, is chosen optimally would sound unconventional to social scientists trained to think of identity as an exogenous category or as fixed as one's gender, ethnicity, or shape of body. However, some of the categories that are considered to be fixed can be changed. Even when they are fixed, such as hair color, the agent still has the choice of whether to make them an important part of his/her identity. If one has great difficulty in exercising or in disciplining the appetite, one may not want to choose shape of body as part of identity, and instead opt for ethnicity or quickness of mind as more important components of identity. This should not deny the roles of past consumptions (habits) and social influences (peer pressure) in the choice of one's identity. Yet such cultural and social factors do not mean that one does not make choices. One can model such factors as part of the constraint function if the agent has no choice over past mistakes or social networks (see Becker, 1996).

However, the demand for identity may not be the result of optimal calculations as the neoclassical theory may suggest. Identity goods may not be ordinary products. If rationality involves intentionality, and not only passive optimization (Khalil, 1997a), identity goods, such as trustworthiness or street-smartness, would have peculiar characteristics. To stipulate that agents act with intentionality means that agents conceive resources, such as their skill in relation to the goods and capital they possess, in innovative ways. The conception depends greatly on their beliefs of their ability and the challenges they face. Given that one is uncertain about one's ability, one needs to hang onto a belief about one's prowess. The agent usually resists adjusting his identity to circumstances, even when transaction costs are zero. The agent's particular belief would be shaken and, hence, one might be unable to undertake action. Even if one finds it more suitable to adopt another identity in a different circumstance, one would lose the orientation that is necessary for action. If one's identity is street-smartness, it should not be subject to evaluation with each circumstance. In order to assess each circumstance the belief in one's ability has to be stable. Such a belief is a meta-choice that cannot be assessed simultaneously with the assessment of each particular action.

From the standard neoclassical point of view, identity is superfluous and should be treated as sunk cost. It is not needed in the formation of belief because belief is supposedly forward looking, based on information about expected resources. However, this assumes that resources, including one's ability, are given data, only subject to some stochastic noise. Recent developments in neuroscience (Damasio, 1994, 2000) show this not to be the case. Humans act with intentionality, which makes them articulate information in different ways, according to one's needs or ends. John Dewey (1972 [1896]) over a hundred years ago criticized the view of resources or stimuli as given data. For behaviorism, the stimulus precedes the response. For Dewey, the agent acting intentionally defines the stimulus as stimulus. Later, John Dewey and Arthur Bentley (1973 [1949]) as well as Maurice Merleau-Ponty (1994 [1945]) offered a theory of cognition where the mind is seen as part of the body and, hence, cognition is embodied with the biological needs of the organism (Khalil, 2003a). They argued that even when one studies the environment, one is not a mirror reflecting innocently what is out there. One rather sees in light of one's goals, which makes the agent at least partially see things in one particular form or gestalt rather than another. Such an ecological view of perception (see Rogers, 1998) presents resources and the organism as united, part of the same transactional field. Resources cannot be defined independently of the acting organism; and the acting organism cannot be defined independently of the resources.

The embodied cognitive approach, where cognition is seen as an extension of the body, shows that trust as identity is endemic to the nature of action. Action expresses the unity of the subject (actor) with the object (resources). Agents with slippery or ever-flexible identity cannot act in the world; they would be dysfunctional and ever uncertain of their self. Yet agents with excessive stickiness or stubbornness may not survive a competitive environment. While the embodied cognitive approach explains the origin of the demand for identity, the evolutionary story has a role to play. It may explain why excessively stubborn agents, insensitive to overwhelming incentives, are few and far between.

The suggested embodied cognitive approach seems to meet the three challenges mentioned above. Concerning the first challenge, the trust-as-identity view shows that trust can be exhibited in single-shot games without invoking bounded rationality. Regarding the second challenge, the trust-as-identity view avoids the main pitfall of the trust-as-taste approach: why is the taste for trust stable? In relation to the third challenge, the trust-as-identity view does not need the neo-Darwinian story of selection to establish the conditions of stability and, hence, avoids its central weakness: what is the origin of trust as a trait?

Notes

1. Behavioral Research Council, a division of American Institute for Economic Research, and Department of Economics, Vassar College. Email: elk@aier.org. The Introduction benefited from the comments of Herbert Gintis, Margaret Levi, Laszlo Zsolnai, Simon Gächter, Oliver Goodenough, Geoffrey Hodgson, and especially Jack Hirshleifer and Paul Saka. However, none of them should be held responsible for any remaining mistakes.
2. The core of neo-Darwinian theory is the negation of the idea that purposefulness of the organism or agent plays a role in the development of new traits that can be passed on to progeny (Ghiselin, 1969). Neo-Darwinism consists basically of two principles. First, traits arise randomly in the sense that there is no relation between the generation of traits and their *ex post* benefit. Second, selection forces (which can be the market, the environment, or natural predators) are sufficiently effective or efficient to discern the differences among the range of traits. In this fashion, agents with the most adapted traits are allowed to propagate faster than the rest. The rest of agents, if they fail to imitate, they would be edited out of the population.
3. One of these conditions is that all agents have the same skill or productivity. Otherwise, we could have foolish agents with high productivity surviving, while rational agents with low productivity failing (Khalil, 2000b).
4. 'Islam' comes from the same family of Arabic nouns such as 'salaam' ('shalom' in Hebrew) for peace, and 'saalem' ('shalem' in Hebrew) for wholeness: to be complete, full, and sound. This may suggest that faith in one's ability, which can be mediated through faith in God, approximates reaching the state of wholeness as an individual and, hence, peace in the sense of freedom from anxiety.
5. There are different ways to classify the literature, depending on one's question. In the proposed classification, I do not observe a difference between human and non-human animal behavior. Both agents are assumed to behave rationally and subject to evolutionary selection pressures. In many classifications, rational behavior is restricted to humans, and when it is attributed to non-human agents, such as in game theoretic discussions (e.g., Trivers, 1971; Maynard Smith, 1982; Dugatkin, 1998), the term of acting strategically or selfishly is used as a short-cut, as if evolutionary selection has chosen the agent that is programmed to act in a selfish manner.
6. Interestingly, however, the modern usage of the term 'trust' in the sense of anti-trust law has a different origin in American legal history. In the nineteenth century, US corporation statutes did not permit one corporation to own the stock of another corporation. If a corporation wanted to combine separate corporations under consolidated ownership structure (as Rockefeller did with Standard Oil), the corporation needed to use another form. The familiar 'trust' in which property was entrusted to the care of trustees to hold for the benefit of a third party, such as a child, was picked up and adapted to this business need. 'Anti-trust' and 'trust-busting' were so named because they originally aimed at attacking this method of combination. Around the beginning of the twentieth century, the prohibition on using corporations as holding companies was dropped in many states, and so the corporate form replaced the cumbersome, but available, trust format. While currently the trust form is hardly used for business combination, the expression 'anti-trust' stuck. (I owe this clarification to Oliver Goodenough.)
7. There is no need for the other two answers to appeal to neo-Darwinism. In fact, when biologists use the trust-as-strategy model as the case with reciprocity games (Trivers, 1971) or the trust-as-taste model as the case with the inclusive fitness hypothesis (Hamilton, 1964), the biologists do not need neo-Darwinian theory. The two explanations are rather about rational decision making.

References

Arrow, Kenneth. 'Uncertainty and the Welfare Economics of Medical Care.' *American Economic Review*, December 1963, 53:5, 941–73.

Arrow, Kenneth. 'Gifts and Exchanges.' *Philosophy & Public Affairs*, 1972, 1, 343–62.

Axelrod, Robert. 'An Evolutionary Approach to Norms.' *American Political Science Review*, 1986, 80, 1095–111.

Bacharach, Michael and Diego Gambetta. 'Trust in Signs.' In Karen S. Cook (ed.), *Trust in Society*, Volume II in the Russell Sage Foundation Series on Trust. New York: Russell Sage Foundation, 2001, ch. 5, 148–84.

Barber, Bernard. *The Logic and Limits of Trust*. New Brunswick, NJ: Rutgers University Press, 1983.

Baron, James N. 'The Employment Relation as a Social Relation.' *Journal of the Japanese and International Economies*, December 1988, 2, 492–525.

Becker, Gary S. 'Altruism in the Family and Selfishness in the Market Place.' *Economica*, February 1981, 48, 1–15.

Becker, Gary S. *Accounting for Tastes*. Cambridge, MA: Harvard University Press, 1996.

Berle, Adolf A., Jr. and Gardiner C. Means. *The Modern Corporation and Private Property*. New York: Macmillan, 1933.

Bishop, John. 'The Recognition and Reward of Employee Performance.' *Journal of Labor Economics*, October 1987, 5, S36–56.

Boyd, Robert and Peter J. Richerson. *Culture and the Evolutionary Process*. Chicago: University of Chicago Press, 1985.

Braithwaite, Valerie. 'Communal and Exchange Trust Norms: Their Value Base and Relevance to Institutional Trust.' In Valerie Braithwaite and Margaret Levi (eds), *Trust and Governance*, Volume I in the Russell Sage Foundation Series on Trust. New York: Russell Sage Foundation, 1998, ch. 3, 46–74.

Braithwaite, Valerie and Margaret Levi (eds). *Trust and Governance*, Volume I in the Russell Sage Foundation Series on Trust. New York: Russell Sage Foundation, 1998.

Brosig, Jeannette. 'Identifying Cooperative Behavior: Some Experimental Results in a Prisoner's Dilemma Game.' *Journal of Economic Behavior & Organization*, March 2002, 47:3, 275–90.

Burke, Peter J. and Jan E. Stets. 'Trust and Commitment through Self-Verification.' *Social Psychology Quarterly*, 1999, 62, 347–60.

Burnham, Terence, Kevin McCabe, and Vernon L. Smith. 'Friend-or-Foe Intentionality Priming in an Extensive Form Trust Game.' *Journal of Economic Behavior & Organization*, September 2000, 43:1, 57–73.

Casson, Mark C. *The Economics of Business Culture*. Oxford: Clarendon Press, 1991.

Cavalli-Sforza, Luigi L. and Marcus W. Feldman. *Cultural Transmission and Evolution*. Princeton: Princeton University Press, 1981.

Coleman, James S. 'Social Capital in the Creation of Human Capital.' *American Journal of Sociology*, 1988, 94, S95–120.

Cook, Karen S. (ed.). *Trust in Society*, Volume II in the Russell Sage Foundation Series on Trust. New York: Russell Sage Foundation, 2001.

Coricelli, Georgio, Kevin McCabe, and Vernon Smith. 'Theory-of-Mind Mechanism in Personal Exchange.' In Giyoo Hatano, Naoyuki Okada, Hirotaka Tanabe (eds), *Affective Minds*. Amsterdam: Elsevier, 2000, 249–59.

Damasio, Antonio R. *Descartes' Error: Emotion, Reason, and the Human Brain*. New York: G.P. Putnam's Sons, 1994.

Damasio, Antonio R. *The Feeling of What Happens: Body and Emotion in the Making of Consciousness*. New York: Harcourt Brace, 2000.

Dasgupta, Partha and Ismail Serageldin (eds). *Social Capital: A Multifaceted Perspective*. Washington, DC: The World Bank, 1999.

De Sousa, Ronald. *The Rationality of Emotions*. Cambridge, MA: MIT Press, 1987.

Dewey, John. 'The Reflex Arc Concept in Psychology.' In *The Early Works, 1882–1898, 5: 1895–1898*. Carbondale and Edwardsville: Southern Illinois University Press, and London and Amsterdam: Feffer & Simons, 1972, 96–109. (Originally published in *Psychological Review*, July 1896, 3, 357–70.)

Dewy, John and Arthur F. Bentley. *Knowing and the Known*. In Rollo Handy and E.C. Harwood (eds), *Useful Procedures of Inquiry*. Great Barrington, MA: Behavioral Research Council, [1949] 1973.

Dugatkin, Lee Alan. 'Game Theory and Cooperation.' In Lee Alan Dugatkin and Hudson Kern Reeve (eds), *Game Theory and Animal Behavior*. Oxford: Oxford University Press, 1998, 38–63.

Dunn, John. 'Trust and Political Agency.' In Diego Gambetta (ed.), *Trust: Making and Breaking Cooperative Relations*. Oxford: Basil Blackwell, 1988, ch. 5, 73–93.

Eisenstadt, S.N. and Louis Roniger. *Patrons, Clients and Friends: Interpersonal Relations and the Structure of Trust in Society*. Cambridge: Cambridge University Press, 1984.

Ensminger, Jean. 'Reputations, Trust, and the Principal Agent Problem.' In Karen S. Cook (ed.), *Trust in Society*, Volume II in the Russell Sage Foundation Series on Trust. New York: Russell Sage Foundation, 2001, ch. 6, 185–201.

Fox, Alan. *Beyond Contract: Work, Power and Trust Relations*. London: Faber, 1974.

Fukuyama, Francis. *Trust: The Social Virtues and the Creation of Prosperity*. New York: Free Press, 1996.

Galassi, Francesco L. 'A Measure of Culture: Trust and Defection in Southern Italy.' In Mark Casson and Andrew Godley (eds), *Cultural Factors in Economic Growth*, Springer, 2000, ch. 3, 69–110.

Gambetta, Diego (ed.). *Trust: Making and Breaking Cooperative Relations*. Oxford: Basil Blackwell, 1988.

Gambetta, Diego. 'Fragments of an Economic Theory of the Mafia.' In Nikos Passas (ed.), *Organized Crime*. Aldershot: Dartmouth, 1995, ch. 9, 171–90.

Gerlach, Michael. 'Business Alliances and the Strategy of the Japanese Firm.' *California Management Review*, Fall 1987, 30:1, 126–42

Ghiselin, Michael T. *The Triumph of the Darwinian Method*. Berkeley: University of California Press, 1969.

Gibbons, Robert. 'Trust in Social Structures: Hobbes and Coase Meet Repeated Games.' In Karen S. Cook (ed.), *Trust in Society*, Volume II in the Russell Sage Foundation Series on Trust. New York: Russell Sage Foundation, 2001, ch. 11, 332–53.

Glaeser, Edward L., David I. Laibson, José A. Scheinkman, Christine L. Soutter. 'Measuring Trust.' *Quarterly Journal of Economics*, August 2000, 115:3, 811–46.

Goodenough, Oliver R. 'Law and the Biology of Commitment.' In Randolph M. Nesse (ed.), *Evolution and the Capacity for Commitment*, Volume III in the Russell Sage Foundation Series on Trust. New York: Russell Sage Foundation, 2001, ch. 12, 262–91.

Greenberg, Martin and David Frisch. 'Effect of Intentionality on Willingness to Reciprocate a Favor.' *Journal of Experimental Social Psychology*, March 1972, 8, 99–111.

Güth, Werner, Rolf Schmittberger, and Bernd Schwarze. 'An Experimental Analysis of Ultimatum Bargaining.' *Journal of Economic Behavior and Organization*, December 1982, 3:4, 367–88.

Güth, Werner and Hartmut Kliemt. 'Evolutionarily Stable Co-Operative Commitments.' *Theory and Decision*, 2000, 49, 197–221.

Hamilton, William D. 'The Genetical Evolution of Social Behavior, I, II.' *Journal of Theoretical Biology*, 1964, 7, 1–16, 17–52.

Hamilton, William D., Robert Axelrod, and Reiko Tanese, 'Sexual Reproduction as an Adaptation to Resist Parasites (A Review).' *Proceedings of the National Academy of Sciences*, May 1990, 87, 3566–73.

Hardin, Russell. 'Conceptions and Explanations of Trust.' In Karen S. Cook (ed.), *Trust in Society*, Volume II in the Russell Sage Foundation Series on Trust. New York: Russell Sage Foundation, 2001, ch. 1, 3–39.

Hardin, Russell. *Trust and Trustworthiness*. New York: Russell Sage Foundation, 2002.

Hayek, Friedrich A. 'Notes on the Evolution of Systems of Rules of Conduct: (The Interplay between Rules of Individual Conduct and the Social Order of Actions).' In *Studies in Philosophy, Politics and Economics*. Chicago: University of Chicago Press, 1967, 66–81.

Heimer, Carol. 'Solving the Problem of Trust.' In Karen S. Cook (ed.), *Trust in Society*, Volume II in the Russell Sage Foundation Series on Trust. New York: Russell Sage Foundation, 2001, ch. 2, 40–88.

Hirschman, Albert O. 'Against Parsimony: Three Ways of Complicating Some Categories of Economics Discourse.' *Economics and Philosophy*, April 1985, (1) ch. 1, 7–21.

Hirshleifer, Jack. 'Game-Theoretic Interpretations of Commitment,' In Randolph M. Nesse (ed.), *Evolution and the Capacity for Commitment*, Volume III in the Russell Sage Foundation Series on Trust. New York: Russell Sage Foundation, 2001, ch. 4, 77–93.

Hodgson, Geoffrey M. 'Corporate Culture and Evolving Competences: An "Old" Institutionalist Perspective on the Nature of the Firm.' In John Groenewegen (ed.), *Transaction Cost Economics and Beyond*. Dordrecht, Netherlands: Kluwer Academic Publishers, 1995, ch. 13, pp. 249–70.
Hoffman, Elizabeth, Kevin McCabe, and Vernon Smith. 'Ultimatum and Dictator Games.' *Journal of Economic Perspectives*, Fall 1995, 9:4, 236–39.
Hoffman, Elizabeth, Kevin McCabe, and Vernon Smith. 'Social Distance and Other-Regarding Behavior in Dictator Games.' *American Economic Review*, June 1996, 86:3, 653–60.
Hollis, Martin. *Trust within Reason*. Cambridge: Cambridge University Press, 1998.
Husted, Bryan W. 'Trust in Business Relations: Directions for Empirical Research.' *Business & Professional Ethics Journal*, Summer 1989, 8:2, 23–40.
Irons, William. 'Religion as a Hard-to-Fake Sign of Commitment.' In Randolph M. Nesse (ed.), *Evolution and the Capacity for Commitment*, Volume III in the Russell Sage Foundation Series on Trust. New York: Russell Sage Foundation, 2001, ch. 13, 292–309.
James, Harvey S., Jr. 'The Trust Paradox: A Survey of Economic Inquiries into the Nature of Trust and Trustworthiness.' *Journal of Economic Behavior & Organization*, March 2002, 47:3, 291–307.
Khalil, Elias L. 'Buridan's Ass, Uncertainty, Risk, and Self-Competition: A Theory of Entrepreneurship.' *Kyklos*, 1997a, 50:2, 147–63.
Khalil, Elias L. 'The Red Queen Paradox: A Proper Name for a Popular Game.' *Journal of Institutional and Theoretical Economics*, June 1997b, 153:2, 411–15.
Khalil, Elias L. 'Is the Firm an Individual?' *Cambridge Journal of Economics*, July 1997c, 21:4, 519–44.
Khalil, Elias L. 'Chaos Theory versus Heisenberg's Uncertainty: Risk, Uncertainty and Economic Theory.' *American Economist*, Fall 1997d, 41:2, 27–40.
Khalil, Elias L. 'Etzioni *versus* Becker: Do Moral Sentiments Differ from Ordinary Tastes?' *De Economist*, December 1997e, 145:4, 491–520.
Khalil, Elias L. 'Symbolic Products: Prestige, Pride and Identity Goods.' *Theory and Decision*, August 2000a, 49:1, 53–77.
Khalil, Elias L. 'Survival of the Most Foolish of Fools: The Limits of Evolutionary Selection Theory.' *Journal of Bioeconomics*, 2000b, 2:3, 203–20.
Khalil, Elias L. 'Adam Smith and Three Theories of Altruism.' *Recherches Économiques de Louvain – Louvain Economic Review*, 2001, 67:4, 421–35.
Khalil, Elias L. 'The Economist Liar Paradox.' Working paper, 2002.
Khalil, Elias L. 'A Transactional View of Entrepreneurship: A Deweyan Approach.' *Journal of Economic Methodology*, June 2003a, 10:2.
Khalil, Elias L. 'What is Altruism?' *Journal of Economic Psychology*, 2003b.
Khalil, Elias L. 'Why does Irrationality Pay? Three Answers: An Introduction.' In Elias L. Khalil (ed.), *The New Behavioral Economics*. A volume of 'The International Library of Critical Writings in Economics,' series editor: Mark Blaug. Cheltenham and Northampton, MA: Edward Elgar, 2004.
Knack, Stephen and Philip Keefer. 'Does Social Capital Have an Economic Payoff? A Cross-Country Investigation.' *Quarterly Journal of Economics*, 1997, 112, 1251–88.
Kramer, Roderick M. and Tom R. Tyler (eds). *Trust in Organizations: Frontiers of Theory and Research*. Thousand Oaks, CA: Sage, 1996.
La Porta, Rafael, Florencio Lopez-de-Silanes, Andrei Shleifer, and Robert W. Vishny. 'Trust in Large Organizations.' *American Economic Review, Papers and Proceedings*, May 1997, 87:2, 333–38.
Lewis, David J. and Andrew J. Weigert, 'Social Atomism, Holism, and Trust.' *The Sociological Quarterly*, Winter 1985, 26:4, 455–71.
Luhmann, Niklas. *Trust and Power*, two works, trans. by Gianfranco Poggi. Chichester: John Wiley & Sons, 1979.
Luhmann, Niklas. 'Familiarity, Confidence, Trust: Problems and Alternatives.' In Diego Gambetta (ed.), *Trust: Making and Breaking Cooperative Relations*. Oxford: Basil Blackwell, 1988, ch. 6, 94–107.
Masten, Scott E. 'A Legal Basis for the Firm.' In Oliver E. Williamson and Sidney G. Winter (eds), *The Nature of the Firm: Origins, Evolution, and Development*. Oxford: Oxford University Press, 1993, 196–212.
Mayer, Roger C., James H. Davis, and F. David Schoorman. 'An Integrative Model of Organizational Trust.' *Academy of Management Review*, 1995, 20:3, 709–34.

Maynard Smith, John. *Evolution and the Theory of Games*. Cambridge: Cambridge University Press, 1982.

McCabe, Kevin A. and Vernon L. Smith. 'A Comparison of Naïve and Sophisticated Subject Behavior with Game Theoretic Predictions.' *Proceedings of the National Academy of Sciences*, March 28, 2000, 97:7, 3777–81.

McCabe, Kevin A., Vernon L. Smith, and Michael LePore. 'Intentionality Detection and "Mindreading": Why Does Game Form Matter?' *Proceedings of the National Academy of Sciences*, April 11, 2000, 97:8, 4404–09.

Meeker, Barbara F. 'Cooperative Orientation, Trust, and Reciprocity.' *Human Relations*, 1983, 37:3, 225–43.

Merleau-Ponty, Maurice. *Phenomenology of Perception*, translated from the French by Colin Smith. London: Routledge, [1945] 1994.

Messick, David M. and Roderick M. Kramer. 'Trust as a Form of Shallow Morality.' In Karen S. Cook (ed.), *Trust in Society*, Volume II in the Russell Sage Foundation Series on Trust. New York: Russell Sage Foundation, 2001, ch. 3, 89–117.

Miller, Gary. 'Why is Trust Necessary in Organizations? The Moral Hazard of Profit Maximization.' In Karen S. Cook (ed.), *Trust in Society*, Volume II in the Russell Sage Foundation Series on Trust. New York: Russell Sage Foundation, 2001, ch. 10, 307–31.

Nesse, Randolph M. 'Natural Selection and the Capacity for Subjective Commitment.' In Randolph M. Nesse (ed.), *Evolution and the Capacity for Commitment*, Volume III in the Russell Sage Foundation Series on Trust. New York: Russell Sage Foundation, 2001, ch. 1, 1–44.

Nesse, Randolph M. (ed.). *Evolution and the Capacity for Commitment*, Volume III in the Russell Sage Foundation Series on Trust. New York: Russell Sage Foundation, 2001.

Noorderhaven, Niels G. 'Opportunism and Trust in Transaction Cost Economics.' In John Groenewegen (ed.), *Transaction Cost Economics and Beyond*. Dordrecht, Netherlands: Kluwer Academic Publishers, 1995, ch. 6, 105–28.

Noorderhaven, Niels G. 'Trust as a Governance Device.' In Mark Casson and Andrew Godley (eds), *Cultural Factors in Economic Growth*, Springer, 2000, ch. 2, 44–68.

Noorderhaven, Niels G. *Trust: Forms, Foundations, Functions, Failures, and Figures*. Cheltenham and Northampton, MA: Edward Elgar, 2002.

Parsons, Talcott. *The Social System*. Glencoe, IL: The Free Press, 1951.

Pettit, Philip. 'The Cunning of Trust', *Philosophy and Public Affairs*, 1995, 24:3, 202–25.

Pettit, Philip. 'Republican Theory and Political Trust.' In Valerie Braithwaite and Margaret Levi (eds), *Trust and Governance*, Volume I in the Russell Sage Foundation Series on Trust. New York: Russell Sage Foundation, 1998, ch. 12, 295–314.

Putnam, Robert. *Making Democracy Work: Civic Traditions in Modern Italy*. Princeton: Princeton University Press, 1993.

Putnam, Robert. 'Bowling Alone: America's Declining Social Capital.' *Journal of Democracy*, 1995, 6:1, 65–78.

Richerson, Peter J. and Robert Boyd. 'The Evolution of Subjective Commitment to Groups: A Tribal Instincts Hypothesis.' In Randolph M. Nesse (ed.), *Evolution and the Capacity for Commitment*, Volume III in the Russell Sage Foundation Series on Trust. New York: Russell Sage Foundation, 2001, ch. 9, 186–220.

Rogers, W. Kim. 'On the Mode of Being of Living Beings and Their Environment: Preliminary Ideas for an Ecological Approach in Philosophy.' *Analecta Husserliana*, 1998, 52, 531–47.

Sako, Mari. *Prices, Quality and Trust: Inter-firm Relations in Britain and Japan*. Cambridge: Cambridge University Press, 1992.

Sally, David. 'A General Theory of Sympathy, Mind-Reading, and Social Interaction, with an Application to the Prisoner's Dilemma.' *Social Science Information*, December 2000, 39:4, 567–634.

Sobel, Joel. 'Can We Trust Social Capital?' *Journal of Economic Literature*, March 2002, 40:1, 139–54.

Sober, Elliott and David Sloan Wilson. *Unto Others: The Evolution and Psychology of Unselfish Behavior*. Cambridge, MA: Harvard University Press, 1999.

Stets, Jan E. and Peter J. Burke. 'Identity Theory and Social Identity Theory.' *Social Psychology Quarterly*, 2000, 63, 224–37.

Stigler, George J. and Gary S. Becker. '*De Gustibus Non Est Disputandum.*' *American Economic Review*, March 1977, 67:1, 76–90.
Swann, William B. Jr. 'Self-Verification: Bringing Reality into Harmony with the Self.' In Jerry Suls (ed.), *Psychological Perspectives on the Self.* Hillsdale, NJ: Lawrence Erlbaum, 1983, 33–66.
Sztompka, Piotr. *Trust: A Sociological Theory*. Cambridge: Cambridge University Press, 1999.
Telser, Lester G. 'A Theory of Self-Enforcing Agreements.' *Journal of Business*, 1980, 53, 27–44.
Trivers, Robert L. 'The Evolution of Reciprocal Altruism.' *Quarterly Review of Biology*, 1971, 46, 35–57.
Tyler, Tom R. and Peter Degoey. 'Trust in Organizational Authorities: The Influence of Motive Attributions on Willingness to Accept Decisions.' In Roderick M. Kramer and Tom R. Tyler (eds), *Trust in Organizations: Frontiers of Theory and Research*. Thousand Oaks, CA: Sage, 1996, 331–56.
Warren, Mark E. (ed.). *Democracy and Trust*. Cambridge: Cambridge University Press, 1999.
Williamson, Oliver E. and Sidney G. Winter (eds). *The Nature of the Firm: Origins, Evolution, and Development*, Oxford, Oxford University Press, 1993.
Williams, George C. *Adaptation and Natural Selection: A Critique of Some Current Evolutionary Thought*. Princeton, NJ: Princeton University Press, 1966.
Wilson, David Sloan and Elliott Sober. 'Reviving the Superorganism.' *Journal of Theoretical Biology*, 1989, 136, 337–56.
Winter, Sidney G. 'On Coase, Competence, and the Corporation.' In Oliver E. Williamson and Sidney G. Winter (eds), *The Nature of the Firm: Origins, Evolution, and Development*, Oxford: Oxford University Press, 1993, 179–95.
Young, H. Peyton. 'The Economics of Convention.' *Journal of Economic Perspectives*, Spring 1996, 10:2, 105–22.
Zak P.J. and S. Knack. 'Trust and Growth.' *Economic Journal*, April 2001, 111:470, 295–321.

Part I
Trust as Strategy

[1]

ADAM SMITH AND THE PRISONERS' DILEMMA

GORDON TULLOCK

In ordinary life we engage in many transactions with other people in which there is potential profit for both parties from some kind of cheating. Normally, we do not see much of this cheating. I have no doubt that the merchant will put in the package the merchandise which I buy, or which I ordered, even though if he put in something else cheaper it is quite dubious that I would be able to win a lawsuit. On my part, if I decide I did not like the product and returned it with the remark that it was defective, having first damaged it so that it is indeed defective, I could get a gain. Neither I nor the merchant worries particularly about this kind of behavior, although the merchant worries more than I do for reasons that will become plain below. If we worried about it, we would both take precautions, with the result that socially we would be worse off by the cost of these precautions. We have here what appears to be a prisoners' dilemma matrix, but the two parties are behaving cooperatively.

What Adam Smith called "the discipline of continuous dealings" takes care of the matter. The point of this article is to work out Adam Smith's insight in the terminology of a modern game theory. We shall see that Smith was right, and there are some cases, indeed practically very important cases, where what appears to be a prisoners' dilemma in fact leads to cooperative behavior.

Consider the prisoners' dilemma game shown in Figure I. It is orthodox that if *A* and *B* are playing a single turn of this particular game, they will end up in the lower right-hand corner with a net loss of one dollar each. If we go from a single game to a long series of games played by the same players, however, there is no agreed-upon solution.[1] Experimental evidence seems to indicate that the players play a mixed strategy with some cooperative plays and some noncooperative plays, and the mixture can be modified by changing the payoffs.[2] All of these situations are simplifications of the real world, and it is a point of this article to suggest that if we make the game more like many real world

1. The author of this article is one of the people who has attempted to solve the problem. See Overcast and Tullock [1971].
2. *The Journal of Conflict Resolution* has run an immense number of articles with varying payoffs.

The Quarterly Journal of Economics, Vol. 100, Supplement, 1985

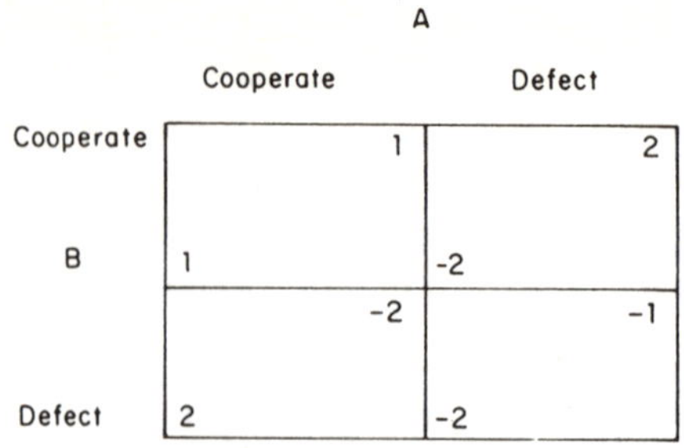

FIGURE I

games, then there will be a very high tendency for play to concentrate in the upper left-hand corner.

If we compare a prisoners' dilemma game and an ordinary competitive market, there is an immediate, obvious difference. The partners in the prisoners' dilemma game are pre-selected and cannot change. The partners in the competitive market select their opposite numbers.[3]

To illustrate, let us follow the physicists and perform a thought experiment. Suppose that we have a large room and along one wall a series of isolation booths. There are about 30 experimental subjects in the room. They are free to communicate with each other in any way they want, and if they wish to make side payments, they are also free to do that, but it does not seem likely that they will. It is, however, possible for any two of them who wish to play the game shown in Figure I. They simply go into two adjacent isolation booths and make their strategy choices on a game matrix on a computer terminal. They are immediately paid the amount that they win or charged the amount that they lose. They are free, of course, to communicate the outcome of the game to anyone else they wish, and they are free to play more games if they wish or to change partners. All that is required is that the people who play the games do so in voluntarily chosen pairs.

I take it that all of my readers will agree that under these

3. Robert Rosenthal and Henry J. Landau have looked into the situation in which prisoners' dilemma games are played by pairs of people who are changed randomly but who know the reputation for the previous players. This mathematically fascinating situation turns out to have a reasonably well specified equilibrium. See Rosenthal [1979] and Rosenthal and Landau [1979].

circumstances all plays would be in the upper left-hand corner except possibly by mistake or possibly in the "end game" if the time at which the experiment was to be ended was announced in advance. In the real world, of course, the game or, to be more precise, the series of games never ends, although individual players are removed by death, etc. If some individual player did for some reason, possibly mental pathology, make a mistake and play a noncooperative strategy, he would find it very difficult to get people to play with him in the future. Almost certainly, he would have to offer some side-payments until he had established something in the way of a reputation.

We can complicate the game yet further by, for example, assuming that the experimenters charge a small fee for playing the game. This fee could be high enough so that the two parties only made a modest profit if they played the cooperative strategy, but the person who double-crosses his cooperative partner would do quite well—for example, a 50 cent fee or even a 75 cent fee.

This is one type of ownership price; another type would be to assume that some of the people in our room are landlords and some peasants. The landlords each own the right to one pair of isolation booths and the games played there. The peasants own only themselves. Assuming that the peasants are numerous, we would presumably reach an equilibrium solution in which the peasants received only the value of their services. If the peasants were less numerous than the landlords, there would be nothing to prevent landlords from playing with each other, so the peasants' bargaining situation would not be perfect, but nevertheless, they should be able to do well.

Games are not necessarily two-party. Figure II represents the payoff to one player in a five-sided prisoner dilemma game. He has the choices represented by the columns of either cooperating or defecting, and the rows show the payoff to him, granted that the other four players cooperated or defected in the numbers shown. It will be seen that the defect column always dominates the cooperating column, but if we repeat our experiment, i.e., permit people voluntarily to make up little groups of five in which each individual is free to enter or leave as he wishes and permit public communication so that the reputation of the individual is well-known, all of them would play the cooperative strategy, and the payoff to each would be nine in each game played. Anyone who chose to defect in any given game would, in essence, put

		Cooperate	Defect
4 Cooperate		9	10
3 Cooperate	1 Defect	7	8
2 Cooperate	2 Defect	5	6
1 Cooperate	3 Defect	3	4
0 Cooperate	4 Defect	1	2

FIGURE II

himself in a situation where it would be extremely difficult for him to get partners for any future game.[4]

In all of these cases, the prisoners' dilemma vanishes because the individual players have a strong desire to establish credibility so that they can play in future games. The basic reason is simply that people voluntarily choose their own partners. As far as I know, this aspect of the prisoners' dilemma has never been discussed before. It has pretty clearly, however, been in at least the subconscious mind of almost everybody who has written in this field. All of the previous articles that I have seen are situations in which the individual does not have a choice of partners. Either he is stuck with his colleague, like the two prisoners in the initial story, or the state of nature is such that he cannot change partners. Consider, for example, an industry in which there are five firms. They get together and form a cartel. Any individual member of this cartel has a motive to cheat, and it is not possible for the other partners to exclude him from the cartel because that, in essence, would give him the best of all possible worlds. He would be under no obligation whatsoever to restrict production, and the other four companies would be attempting to raise prices. The only threat that the other four companies have against a possible cheater is that they shall all stop cooperating, and that threat has limitations which are known to all economists. Simi-

4. He could perhaps get back into the game by elaborate promises of good behavior and side-payments, but certainly a second defection would finish that.

larly, in international relations problems, countries cannot chose their neighbors.

Although this is true of existing games, in the real world something can be done to make credibility valuable. The two prisoners in *The Prisoners' Dilemma* could have originally formed their partnership in crime because each had a well-established reputation for keeping his mouth shut. Each could think that talking under these circumstances would reduce his prospects for future profitable criminal activity jointly with any partner, not just with this particular partner and, hence, remain silent. With the flexibility of modern economic production, the possibility of companies chosing industries to enter in terms of the cooperativeness of other members is real, and establishing a reputation of being a good cartel partner might be quite valuable to a company that produced products in a number of different lines. Only in those particular industries where all members had a reputation for keeping their cartel agreements would any cartel agreements be entered into. As far as I know, this is not a conscious part of the strategy of any American conglomerate, but it is at least possible.

There are, of course, other techniques for establishing credibility. The businessman who regularly goes to church and regularly makes contributions to all kinds of worthy causes may be attempting to convince people that he is a safe partner. It is after all true that in a very large number of economic dealings it is possible for either, and in most cases both, parties to cheat. We do not usually tie our transactions so tightly in legal strings that there is not some room for uncooperative behavior on the part of either or both parties. Parties presumably refrain from this because of Adam Smith's discipline of continuous dealings or, in my more modern terminology, because they want to be partners in further prisoners' dilemma games.

Novelists and other critics have frequently made fun of the conformists' attitude that we frequently see in American business communities. As a matter of fact, conformism is found in all sorts of communities, including those of letters and social critics, although they, of course, conform to a different set of standards. This conformism is, in a way, an effort to convince people that you are the standard individual; i.e., the individual who, in the prisoners' dilemma situation, will not choose the noncooperative play. Similarly, if you have considerable hostages, you are, for example, a member of a fairly tight social group, and you and your family would be severely injured if you were, in essence, removed from the social group for bad behavior; you are more trustworthy.

The same rule applies to politicians, and for that matter to a somewhat limited extent in international dealings. Dishonesty is, of course, so common in international dealings that it would take a long time for anyone to produce a reputation for honesty (see Beilsenson [1969]). A reputation for being "sound" is a valuable asset, and we should expect people to make every effort to get it. In many cases these efforts seem to an outsider prosaic, dull, or even foolish, but there is every reason to believe that most of us would, in fact, prefer to enter into deals with the prosaic, conventional businessman with a well-established business, than with a long-haired radical poet if there was something we could lose if the person we were dealing with decided to take advantage of us.[5]

We can see here also why I can be much more trusting in dealing with a merchant than he can in dealing with me. His reputation spreads over far more people, and it is harder for him to change partners readily. Blacksburg is a small town, but I am about to move to Washington. In Washington I presumably could spend a long time regularly returning products because I decided I did not want them, damaging them and claiming that they were damaged when I received them, without running out of new merchants to deal with. Merchants knowing this do take rather more precautions than the customer needs to. They are particularly concerned, of course, about the creditworthiness of their customers.

Of course, the game does not have to be symmetric. I referred earlier to the fact that I do not worry very much about stores cheating me, but they may worry about my credit card. The explanation here is simple: they are heavily dependent on their reputation, but probably they do not know me. It is, of course, true that credit card companies do their best to make holders of bogus or stolen credit cards known, i.e., to create a negative reputation for them, and checking that list is probably the only thing the store will do. Still, the situation is, with respect to reputation,

5. Of course, the radical, long-haired poet might simply behave erratically without any calculation.

asymmetrical in the sense that the store has to do research to find out the reputation of its customers.

It is likely that almost all interactions between human beings can be drawn as prisoners' dilemmas because it is possible for one party, or all parties, to make a one-time gain by cheating. In practice, almost no one even thinks of this opportunity in a competitive market in which he intends to remain for a while because the cost of getting a reputation for cheating is too high. In essence, the two-strategy prisoners' dilemmas' matrix is extended by a third strategy—refuse to play with some specified person as shown in Figure III. Under these circumstances, the cooperative solution is usually an optimum.

There is another application of this analysis. If an individual has lost reputation, there is little or no reason why he should play cooperative strategies in the future. If anyone agrees to play with him, which is not terribly likely, it would take a large number of plays before his reputation for reliability was as good as that of the person who had not already blotted his copy book even if he played cooperatively each time. Under the circumstances, he should attempt to con people into games, and when he gets them in, the decision to play noncooperatively may well be perfectly rational.

All of this would provide one more explanation for the tendency of people who once slipped to continue on that course of action. Thus, the habitual criminal or the "shady" businessman who continues to be "shady" are both responding rationally to their situation. Once they have a bad reputation, the cost of building up a reputation for reliability is extremely high.

There are many other examples. When individuals can freely

	Cooperate	Defect	Don't Play
Cooperate	1 / 1	2 / -2	0 / 0
Defect	-2 / 2	-1 / -1	0 / 0
Don't Play	0 / 0	0 / 0	0 / 0

FIGURE III

change the jurisdiction in which they live, then governmental "cheating" has only short-run payoffs. Note that there usually are at least some barriers to changing one's residence, and the height of these barriers in a way provides a threshold. With respect to a small suburban town, outside a major city, this threshold is apt to be very low, indeed. For a major nation, on the other hand, it can be quite large.

It is notable that this kind of threshold can be increased. The United States has elaborate and not very effective procedures along its border that are supposed to prevent outsiders from coming in. The Soviet Union has much more elaborate, and much more effective barriers around its border, the purpose of which is to prevent its own citizens from going out. The direction of the American barriers indicates that the American polity must be rather attractive by world standards. The need to have such extremely high barriers around the Soviet Union indicates that its internal practices are much more objectionable to the average Russian than the practices of most countries.

Hirschman, in a famous book, *Exit Voice and Loyalty* [1970], argued that if people for one reason or another do not want to change their bargaining partners, the railroads they use, etc., then they will exert pressure to improve the quality of the services they receive. This may indeed be so, but if it is, we are dealing there with a quite different phenomenon. It is certainly true that the individual who can readily change from the railroad in Nigeria, with which Hirschman [1970] starts, to trucks is better off then he would be if he were compelled to use the railroads. Perhaps, of course, Hirschman is correct that railway service would be markedly better if this alternative did not exist.

But this is more an exercise in general political philosophy than a discussion of the market. It is, indeed, true that the freedom to change what government you serve under will make it easier for you to better your lot. It is also true that this privilege will mean that governments, regardless of their formal structure, will find it necessary to pay considerable attention to the wishes of their citizenry. Individuals in a democracy must consider to at least some extent when they vote, not only the effect of that vote on themselves but its effect on their neighbors who might conceivably decide to move to the next suburb, thus lowering real estate values in this suburb if they are sufficiently offended.

But the main theme of this discussion has been that the prisoners' dilemma, strictly speaking, occurs only in a rather narrow area. Where there are a number of potential players available, the dilemma is proportionately weakened. Indeed, here we have what amounts to a mapping of the usual economic distinction between monopoly on the one side and competition on the other. If there is only one person with whom I can play the game, both he and I very likely will decide not to cooperate. As the number of people playing increases, the prospect that either he or I can get another partner, if we find our current partner objectionable, exerts steadily increasing pressure to always play cooperatively. In the limit, as in the limit of perfect competition, behavior is always mutually advantageous with the individual not taking a course of action which with respect to a particular play of the game seems desirable.

It is not only numbers here, it is also improved information. Brokers are specialists in this kind of thing. I have just finished selling a house in Blacksburg and buying an apartment in Washington. Brokers who assisted me were, among other things, very knowledgeable not only on what was in the market and the legal precautions necessary to see to it that I was not cheated, but also on the reputation of various parties. Additional precautions were sometimes suggested. Brokers themselves, of course, live and die with a reputation for efficiency and fairness.

All of this, however, was known to Adam Smith and has probably been known to successful merchants from time immemorial. Where the market is broad and there are many alternatives, you had better cooperate. If you choose the noncooperative solution, you may find you have no one to noncooperate with.

GEORGE MASON UNIVERSITY

REFERENCES

Beilenson, Laurence W., *The Treaty Trap* (Washington, D.C.: Public Affairs Press, 1969).

Hirschman, Albert O., *Exit Voice and Loyalty* (Cambridge, MA: Harvard University Press, 1970).

Overcast, H. Edwin, and Gordon Tullock, "A Differential Approach to the Repeated Prisoner's Dilemma," *Theory and Decision,* I (1971), 350–58.

Rosenthal, R. W., "Sequences of Games with Varying Opponents," *Econometrica,* IIIL (1979).

Rosenthal, R. W., and Henry J. Landau, "A Game-Theoretic Analysis of Bargaining with Reputations," *Journal of Mathematical Psychology,* XX (1979), 233–55.

[2]

The Further Evolution of Cooperation

ROBERT AXELROD AND DOUGLAS DION

Axelrod's model of the evolution of cooperation was based on the iterated Prisoner's Dilemma. Empirical work following this approach has helped establish the prevalence of cooperation based on reciprocity. Theoretical work has led to a deeper understanding of the role of other factors in the evolution of cooperation: the number of players, the range of possible choices, variation in the payoff structure, noise, the shadow of the future, population dynamics, and population structure.

COOPERATION IS A TOPIC OF CONTINUING INTEREST FOR the social and biological sciences. A theory of cooperation based upon reciprocity (*1–3*) has engendered a wide literature concerning the evolution of cooperation. In this article, we survey this literature in order to determine what new insights have been gained.

Although we shall concentrate on theoretical work, it is important to note that scholars have been active in pursuing empirical applications of the theory. Huth (*4*) found that military conflict during the last century was most successfully deterred when a challenge was met with reciprocity. Cooperation based on reciprocity has been supported for vampire bats (*5, 6*), vervet monkeys (*7*), and sessile invertebrates (*8*). Experimental simulations of defection have been presented to stickleback fish (*9*) and tree swallows (*10*); the findings are consistent with reciprocity. On the other hand, Nol (*11*) rejected reciprocity as an explanation of cooperation between the sexes in chick-rearing by the American oyster catcher, arguing that data on foraging trips and energy use support a theory based on the efficient allocation of energy by the birds. Other investigators have pointed to the difficulties in determining whether observed cooperation is due to a tit-for-tat-like process (*12*). Despite these difficulties, cooperation based upon reciprocity has received substantial empirical support.

In addition, advice has been offered for problems of breach of contracts (*13*), child custody (*14*), superpower negotiations (*15*), and international trade (*16, 17*).

We begin our analysis of recent theoretical work on the evolution of cooperation by reviewing Axelrod's original formulation and theoretical results (*2*). Is there any reason for an individual to cooperate when noncooperative behavior is rewarded? This question underlies the problem of cooperation in the Prisoner's Dilemma. In the Prisoner's Dilemma, each player has two choices: cooperate or defect (Fig. 1). The choice may or may not be made rationally. In either case, if the game is only played once, then each player gets a higher payoff from defecting than from cooperating, regardless of what the other player does. However, if both players defect, they both do worse than had both cooperated.

If the game is played repeatedly (the iterated Prisoner's Dilemma, or IPD), there is greater room for cooperation. To see which strategies would be effective in exploiting this opportunity for cooperation, game theorists were invited to submit programs for a round-robin IPD computer tournament having the following properties:

1) The interactions were between pairs of players.

2) Each player had two available choices on each move: cooperate or defect. Choices were made simultaneously.

3) The payoffs (Fig. 1) were fixed before play and announced to all players.

4) At each move in the game, each player had access to the history of the game up to that move—in short, there was no noise in the transmission of strategy choices between players.

Rankings of the strategies were determined by the number of points achieved overall. The winner of the first tournament was TIT FOR TAT (TFT), a program that uses cooperation on the first move of the game and then plays whatever the other player chose on the previous move. Results of this tournament were publicized and a second tournament received 62 entries. Unlike the first tournament, in which the number of iterations was known beforehand, the second tournament had the following additional characteristic.

5) There was a fixed probability (called the "shadow of the future") of the game ending on the next move.

The winner of this second tournament was again TFT. TFT's success was due to its being nice (not the first to defect), provokable (responding to the other player's defection with a defection), forgiving (punishing and then cooperating after a defection), and clear (easy for other players to understand) (*2*).

But success in the computer tournaments did not prove that TFT would perform well as an evolutionary strategy. After all, TFT's success might have been due to its performance with other strategies that would not themselves survive for very long. To check this possibility, an ecological simulation was conducted. The initial population consisted of the entries to the second round of the computer tournament with the following characteristic:

6) The population dynamics of the ecological simulation were determined by setting the change in frequency of each strategy in

Player A \ Player B	C Cooperation	D Defection
C Cooperation	R=3 Reward for mutual cooperation	S=0 Sucker's payoff
D Defection	T=5 Temptation to defect	P=1 Punishment for mutual defection

Fig. 1. The Prisoner's Dilemma game. The payoff to player A is shown with illustrative numerical values. The game is defined by $T > R > P > S$ and $R > (S + T)/2$.

R. Axelrod is a professor of political science and public policy at the Institute of Public Policy Studies, University of Michigan, Ann Arbor, MI 48109. D. Dion is a graduate student in the Department of Political Science, University of Michigan.

any given round to be proportional to its relative success in the previous round.

In this ecological simulation, TFT quickly became the most common strategy.

Once cooperation based upon reciprocity is established, no player can do any better than to cooperate as well, provided the chance for future interaction, w, is high enough. For example, if everyone is using TFT then no one mutant can do better if $w \geq \max [T - R)/(R - S), (T - R)/(T - P)]$ (2, pp. 207–208). In game theory terms, this means that everyone using TFT is a Nash equilibrium when the shadow of the future is sufficiently high (*18*).

Getting cooperation started required something more because a single cooperative player can never do better than the population average of a group of noncooperating players. So the implications of clustering of strategies were explored by supposing the following condition holds (at least initially).

7) Populations are structured in the sense that strategies have more-than-random interaction with strategies of their own type.

Axelrod (*2*, pp. 63–69) showed that even a small cluster of players who used cooperation based upon reciprocity could establish themselves in a population of noncooperative players, and even take over such a population. Moreover, once established, the reciprocating cooperative players would be immune from re-invasion by a similar cluster of noncooperating players. Thus, the evolution of cooperation contains a ratchet.

In the remainder of this article, we review the work that has been done on altering or relaxing each of the seven assumptions listed above.

Interactions

In the original formulation, the interactions are between pairs of players (*2*, p. 30). For certain applications, however, interactions involve more than two players. Consequently, the corresponding game is the n-player PD (NPD), in which players make a choice (cooperate or defect) which they play with all other players.

Theorists have shown that increasing the number of individuals in the NPD makes cooperation more difficult (*19–22*). Taylor (*19*), in a nonevolutionary framework, proved that for cooperation to be part of an equilibrium in an NPD when some players are playing ALL D (the strategy which defects on each move), it is necessary that either the shadow of the future is long or the number of cooperators is large. In an evolutionary setting, Joshi (*20*) has found that if individuals play a "hard" TFT (meaning that they will cooperate until one player defects), and the number of individuals playing a hard TFT passes a certain threshold, then hard TFT can dominate a population of ALL D players. But this threshold rises as the number of individuals in the society increases.

The effectiveness of TFT in the NPD, however, depends upon the type of NPD that is being played. Pettit (*23*) has distinguished "free-riding" from "foul-dealing" NPDs. In a free-riding NPD, a lone defection places the remainder of the population worse off than total cooperation but still better off than complete defection. In a foul-dealing NPD, the defection of one individual places some subset of the population in a position worse than universal defection. Pettit argues that only in the foul-dealing iterated NPD is the retaliation implied by TFT rational, since in the free-ridng iterated NPD each player would rather cooperate with the remainder of the population than lose the benefits of cooperation by punishing the lone defector.

Pettit's distinction raises two questions. First, is it true that the coalition behavior Pettit suggests would actually be effective in a variegated environment? An answer is provided by Fader and Hauser (*24*) who ran a computer tournament involving a three-firm oligopoly game. They found that effective strategies tended to take advantage of the opportunity for cooperating with other players, including cooperating with the remaining player if the third player defects (charged the competitive price). Winners in the Fader and Hauser tournament also tended to be magnanimous, offering potential partners a coalition price that was slightly above the optimal coalition price (in this way, they avoided being misperceived as competitive). This work is paralleled in the study of alliances among primates (*25*). Alliances potentially can form when a pair of organisms is engaged in a game with each other as well as a game against a common enemy. Aoki (*26*) has formally demonstrated that if the gains to altruism (both in terms of direct benefits and inclusive fitness) exceed the coats to altruism, then a genetic trait for forming reciprocal alliances will increase in the population.

The second question: if there is an incentive not to punish defectors, can some change in the game structure reintroduce the incentive to retaliate? Axelrod's (*27*) analysis of the metanorms game suggests there is. In the metanorms game, individuals still have the option to punish a defector. However, individuals also have the opportunity to punish others who have failed to punish defectors. An evolutionary simulation of the metanorms game shows that the population quickly becomes vengeful in their punishment of defections and not so bold in the attempting of defections. This suggests the establishment of a norm of cooperation. This analysis of the evolution of norms may give us a solution to the difficulty posed by Pettit. Although individual punishment of defection may not be individually optimal in the free-riding iterated NPD, in the context of a metanorm it may be optimal for individuals to punish defectors.

Choices

One limitation of the IPD is the assumption of two possible choices (cooperate and defect) chosen simultaneously by the two players. In many applications there is an option to leave the game (exit) or to force others to leave the game (ostracism). One might suppose that when exit was possible, the cooperators would leave first to avoid exploitation by the defectors. But in an experiment allowing human subjects to exit from a nine-player PD, this did not happen (*28*). The reason was the cooperators' greater concern for the welfare of the group that led them to cooperate in the first place. Hirshleifer and Rasmusen (*29*) have used the presence of ostracism to derive the stability of cooperation in the finitely repeated PD in all but the last round. The cooperation-inducing effects of ostracism have been empirically supported in a case study by Barner-Barry (*30*), who found that ostracism of a school-yard bully led to the bully's eventual attempts at cooperation. The assumption of simultaneous choice has been relaxed by Kondo (*31*), who has shown that the stable equilibria of the nonsimultaneous move game are either ALL D or a form of conditional cooperation.

Payoffs

How robust are the original solutions to changes in the payoff matrix? Lipman (*32*) has generalized the Nash equilibrium results to iterated Chicken, a game that models crisis bargaining. Dacey and Pendegraft (*33*) ran a computer tournament in which programs played both the IPD and Chicken. They found that TFT does well in the provokable worlds of the simulation, but that PERMANENT RETALIATION (cooperate until the other player defects and then defect for the remainder of the game) excelled in the Chicken games.

In the IPD, the shadow of the future and reciprocity help support cooperation. This is a special case of the folk theorem, a theorem that applies to all iterated games. The folk theorem states that any individually rational outcome (34) of any one-shot game can be supported as a Nash equilibrium of the infinitely repeated game, assuming the future is important enough (35). In the strategies constructed in the proof of this (and similar theorems) conditional cooperation is used as the basis for deterring defecton. Such theorems also show the variety of outcomes (besides mutual cooperation) that can be supported in equilibrium in the IPD.

Noise

Faulty transmission of strategy choices (noise) severely undercuts the effectiveness of reciprocating strategies. Molander (36) has shown that in the presence of any amount of noise, two TFT players will in the long run average the payoffs of two interacting RANDOM players, each of whom cooperates and defects with equal probability. In fact, a risk-averse player would prefer a strategy of any weighted average reciprocator (reciprocates based upon a longer history of the game than TFT) to TFT, as Bendor (37) has shown.

If few environments were characterized by noise, then TFT's vulnerability would not be very important, but this is not the case. Various species lack the capacity for individual recognition, which implies that they will be unable to determine the history of interaction with any given individual. Species with individual recognition may still only imperfectly recognize others. Noise can even be a serious problem between people or between nations (15, 38) and can occur in any game in which monitoring of the other player is difficult.

Two tournaments have been conducted to see how TFT would do in a noisy variegated environment. The first is reported in Axelrod (2, p. 183), who noted that rerunning the first round of the computer tournament with a 1 percent probability of misperceiving the other player's choice still found TFT to be the best decision rule. The second tournament, by Donninger (39), used a 10 percent chance of misperception. In this tournament, TFT finished sixth out of 21. In variegated populations, then, TFT may still perform fairly well, even with noise.

How can TFT be modified to more easily cope with environments of noise? The solutions depend on the type of noise. One type of noise can be labeled "misimplementation." In this case, the player making the mistake knows that a mistake has been made and that the other player cannot distinguish the mistake from an intentional cooperation or defection. A variety of authors have suggested some unconditional cooperation (increasing the probability of playing C after misimplementing a prior C choice) on the part of the individual making the error as a response to small probabilities of misimplementation (40).

A second type of noise is misperception, where a player actually does make one choice but the other player believes that a different choice was made. In the case of misperception, if there is no information that the players can use to distinguish an intentional from an unintentional defection (or cooperative move), then there is no (game-theoretic) difference between the noiseless IPD and the IPD with misperception.

A variant of misperception is "noisy channels," where neither player knows that an error has been committed but they both know that such errors have some probability of occurring. In environments with sufficiently small amounts of this type of noise, risk-averse, self-interested players will both converge on the same level of generosity (defined as the probability that one's strategy plays C after the other player has played D) (36). Mueller (41) finds that the best strategy to maintain already established cooperation is a more or less restrained version of TFT, with the amount of restraint depending on the necessary safety margin against an eventual reinvasion of noncooperators.

Finally, another sort of noise, in which players observe each other's choices but a stochastic variable affects the payoffs, has been considered for the case of a "favor granting" game by Calvert (42). In equilibrium each player grants all favors asked to the other player. Intuitively, each player takes into account the stochastic element of the game, and therefore is not provoked when low payoffs are realized. If strategy choices are unobservable then cooperative outcomes may still be obtained, even in the NPD, by the use of trigger strategies (22, 43). A trigger strategy specifies defection for t moves whenever the player's payoff falls below a certain level. Such strategies are restrained in their retaliation, and explain temporary failures of cooperation as elements of Nash equilibrium behavior.

We have dealt so far with responses that players can make to noise within the context of the IPD, but it is important to note that changing the structure of the game can give players additional ways of dealing with noise. Players can choose strategies which are less ambiguous, as Dixit (16) has suggested for U.S. trade policy. There can be an explicit convention about what constitutes defection and cooperation (44). And players can unilaterally take steps that minimize the probability of error. For example, vampire bats tend to have very poor individual recognition. However, grooming behavior, with its attendant close contact, may provide the clues needed for a system of reciprocal food sharing to overcome the effects of noise from inadequate individual recognition (6).

The lessons of the literature on noise in the IPD suggest that for sufficiently small amounts of noise, unilateral generosity is the best response. However, for larger amounts of noise, there is a trade-off: unnecessary conflict can be avoided by generosity, but generosity invites exploitation.

The Shadow of the Future

The original paradigm assumed an indefinite ending to the game, with the probability of the game ending with the current move equal to w. This probability is called the shadow of the future and is equivalent to a discount rate. As mentioned earlier, if $w \geq \max[(T - R)/(R - S), (T - R)/(T - P)]$, there exists a Nash equilibrium in which all players use TFT. In this section, we shall see how various changes in the paradigm affect the way in which the shadow of the future supports cooperation.

If cooperation depends on a long enough shadow of the future, then it should not be surprising that variation in w can affect observed patterns of cooperation. In research on the implications of a nonconstant discount parameter, behavior-dependent contexts of play and finite repetition have been studied.

In work on behavior-dependent contexts of play, it is assumed that choices affect the probability of future interaction. Eshel and Weinshall (45) consider an iterated game with a stochastic payoff matrix. In some moves of this game, the players are in a PD, while in other moves cooperation is the dominant choice. If the probability of surviving the current move depends on the cumulative payoffs, an egoist may cooperate on the PD iterations of the game to guarantee the presence of a partner for reaping the benefits of mutual assistance in other iterations. In work reviewed below, Feldman and Thomas (46) investigate the case where the probability of future interactions depends on the choices of the players.

In work on finite repetition, the possibility of cooperation in the finitely repeated prisoner's dilemma, or FRPD, has been analyzed. Luce and Raiffa (47) proved by backward induction that cooperation was not rational in the FRPD (cooperation does not pay in the last round, and hence cannot pay in the next to last round, and so forth). In recognition of this problem, the second computer tournament used a probabilistic treatment of the possibility that the two players will meet again (*2*, p. 42).

Efforts to establish conditions for cooperation in the FRPD fall into three categories. The first employs the theory of automata to study players with limited computational ability. These theoretical results have been mixed, with cooperation being obtained in some models (*48*) but not in others (*49*). A second approach uses various combinations of player beliefs about payoffs and strategies. In one model, each player attaches a certain probability to the proposition that the other player will use TFT even if it is irrational to do so (*50*). A final approach uses learning theory to account for the tendency of college students engaged in a series of FRPDs to start defecting more and more moves before the end of the game (*51*). The results of these three lines of inquiry are particularly relevant because the rationality and information of people as well as animals is incomplete.

In a similar attempt at realism, finite population versions of the Nash equilibrium result have been presented (*21, 52, 53*). Aoki (*53*) has noted that if the size of the group numbers several tens, as is the case with primate groups or many human societies, then the infinite population theorem provides a good approximation to the finite population case. Pollock (*54*), however, notes that if the population consists of a single dyad, then for any discount rate TFT is not stable in the presence of an ALL D mutant. This point emphasizes the value to a TFT player of the presence of other reciprocating players.

The theoretical work on the importance of the shadow of the future has received empirical support from social and biological scientists. Moore (*55*) has found that the continued interactions among individuals in the Lebanese banking community laid the groundwork for the stability of that sector despite the great instability of Lebanese affairs. In a more rarefied setting, Murnighan and Roth (*56*) found that the probability of repeated play had a significant impact on the number of cooperative choices made in an IPD by undergraduates. In avian studies, Davies and Houston (*57*) suggest that the failure of two male dunnocks to practice cooperative polyandry reflects the low chance of their surviving the season and meeting again.

Population Dynamics

Readers familiar with the literature on game-theoretic models of evolution will note the difference between an evolutionarily stable strategy (ESS) (*58*) and a strategy that is in Nash equilibrium with itself. Let $V(X|Y)$ be the payoff to an X player when playing with a Y player. A strategy X is said to be an ESS if for all Y either (i) $V(X|X) > V(Y|X)$, or (ii) $V(X|X) = V(Y|X)$ and $V(X|Y) > V(Y|Y)$. By contrast, the Nash condition is that a strategy is stable if there is no Y such that $V(Y|X) > V(X|X)$. All strategies that are ESS are stable in the Nash sense but the converse need not hold.

The implications of this distinction can be best understood in terms of stability versus neutral stability. A strategy that is evolutionarily stable can completely overcome invasion by mutants. This is stability. A strategy that is stable in the Nash sense may be only neutrally stable for a unilateral deviation from the equilibrium (*59*). This allows mutants to drift into the population.

As it turns out, if one allows invasion by multiple mutants, there is no single strategy that is evolutionarily stable (ESS) in the IPD. This fact was discovered, apparently independently, by Pudaite (*60*) and Boyd and Lorberbaum (*61*). Pudaite showed that if there is some chance for future interaction, then for each strategy X there is always some set of strategies Z such that X is not an ESS against Z. Boyd and Lorberbaum showed that no pure strategy whose behavior is determined solely by the history of the game is an ESS if the future is important enough (that is, if $w > \min[(T - R)/(T - P), (P - S)/(R - S)]$).

These negative results place new value on the intensive analysis of sets of strategies, because it is only by understanding the set of possible competitors that we can understand the particular evolutionary path of cooperation. Two procedures seem particularly well adapted for such analysis.

The first procedure applies the mathematics of dynamical systems to the interactions of sets of representative strategies in order to determine the full characteristics of possible dynamics. We already noted the work of Feldman and Thomas (*46*) in which behavior-dependent discount parameters were used. One of their results points to, not only the existence, but also the local stability of a full polymorphic equilibrium (composed of TFT, ALL D, and a strategy that defects on all but the first move) given certain conditions on the discount rates. This result is of particular importance in determining whether observed genotypic variation is merely transitory or in fact stable. Other population dynamic treatments are presented in Blad (*62*), Cave (*21*), and Pudaite (*60*).

A limitation of these dynamic treatments, as well as the ecological tournament, is their inability to develop new strategies. One method of overcoming this limitation is to use a genetic approach to develop new strategies for playing the IPD. A good method of implementing this on a computer is Holland's genetic algorithm (*63*). A strategy can be represented as a "chromosome" describing what to do in each different context that the strategy can distinguish. The genetic algorithm simulates the evolutionary process by mutating the chromosomes and by allowing sexual reproduction to recombine features from two different strategies. It then subjects the resulting offspring to competition with other programs in the population. Axelrod (*64*) used the genetic algorithm and a chromosome of 70 genes to study the evolution of strategies in a fixed environment composed of eight representative strategies from his second computer tournament. From a random start, strategies similar to TFT often evolved within a few dozen generations. Strategies sometimes evolved that outperformed TFT in this environment. These well-adapted strategies were not nice: they defected initially to discriminate between the representatives they were facing so that they could exploit those that were exploitable and cooperate with the others.

These two methods of overcoming the limitations of an ecological simulation approach are complementary. The differential equations approach allows a relatively complete analysis of the interactions among a small set of selected strategies or strategy types. The genetic algorithm approach provides a way of exploring a potentially huge strategy space, making possible the discovery of new strategies not previously specified.

Population Structure

As noted earlier, the initiation of cooperation in a population of noncooperators was possible if the cooperative strategies invaded in clusters (*2*, p. 63–68). Can cooperation evolve without the presence of population structure?

The theoretical results on ESS supply one answer. Because no strategy is ESS if the future is important enough, cooperation may be started without population structure if the "correct" combination of strategies is present (*60, 61*). This also undoes the "ratchet effect" discovered by Axelrod. Boyd and Lorberbaum (*61*) suggest the following example. Suppose that a population consists of TFT, SUSPICIOUS TFT (or STFT, exactly like TFT but defects on the initial move) and TIT FOR TWO TATS (or TF2T, which defects only if the other player defected on the two preceding moves). STFT and TF2T will end up cooperating after the first move, STFT and TFT will each continue cooperating while the other defects (and vice versa), and TFT and TF2T will cooperate on every move. In such a situation, TF2T will be able to invade both TFT and STFT, even without clustering. This example would not be so startling (since a cooperative strategy is merely invading another cooperative strategy), except that TF2T is easily invaded by a strategy which initially defects and then alternates cooperation and defection (*65*).

Other attempts at minimizing the need for clustering in order to initiate cooperation have relied on certain informational requirements. Examples are positive assortative mating and meeting (*66*). Intuitively, cooperative strategies "pick" fellow cooperators and shun noncooperators, an outcome that is quite similar to ostracism.

Informational requirements may not be necessary, however, if the payoffs reflect certain behavioral characteristics of the game. For instance, Peck and Feldman (*67*) prove that cooperation can get started in a population of defectors if the payoffs to cooperative acts depend on the frequency with which those acts are performed. And Feldman and Thomas (*46*) have found that in the case where the probability of another interaction depends on the choices of the players, TFT can increase when rare, although this does not guarantee that TFT will increase to fixation. In particular, in a population of mostly ALL D, where w is the probability that a player continues to interact after choosing cooperation and u is the probability that a player continued to interact after defection, a rare TFT trait can increase if $S(1 - u) > P(1 - w)$.

Work on initial viability of cooperative strategies has mixed implications for the evolution of cooperation. On the plus side, initial viability of cooperation may not require the assumption of population structure. On the minus side, however, such theoretical results imply that cooperative strategies need not be stable against invading ensembles of strategies.

Conclusion

Research has shown that many of Axelrod's findings (*2*) can be generalized to settings that are quite different from the original two-player iterated Prisoner's Dilemma game. Our review has identified the following extensions. Increasing the number of players who simultaneously interact tends to make cooperation more difficult. The results on the importance of reciprocity and the shadow of the future apply not only to the iterated Prisoner's Dilemma, but also to Chicken and more generally to any game in which individually rational choices lead to suboptimal decisions. Altering the set of strategies to include nonsimultaneous play and options for exit and ostracism does not disturb Axelrod's conclusions. Several solutions to the problem of noise and misperception have been suggested; the prescriptions entail increased generosity for small amounts of noise. However, for larger amounts of noise, increased generosity may invite exploitation. The empirical relevance of the shadow of the future in inducing cooperation has been demonstrated, and theoretical researchers have been pushing beyond the IPD formulation to derive cooperation for the finitely repeated Prisoner's Dilemma. The sophistication of evolutionary models of cooperation has been advanced by the introduction of full population dynamics and by the use of the genetic algorithm for the discovery of entirely new strategies. Work in theoretical biology has demonstrated that no strategy is evolutionarily stable in the iterated Prisoner's Dilemma if the shadow of the future is long enough and multiple mutants occur. This also implies that it is possible for cooperation to begin without a structured population.

Further exploration of the evolution of cooperation can profit from the greater specification of the pattern of interactions and the process by which those interactions themselves evolve. Research along such lines will not only help unite theoretical and empirical work even further than has so far been possible, but may also deepen our understanding of the initiation, maintenance, and further evolution of cooperation.

REFERENCES AND NOTES

1. R. Axelrod, *J. Conflict Resolut.* **24**, 389 (1980); *ibid.*, p. 379; *Am. Polit. Sci. Rev.* **75**, 306 (1981).
2. ———, *The Evolution of Cooperation* (Basic Books, New York, 1984).
3. ——— and W. Hamilton, *Science* **211**, 1390 (1981).
4. P. Huth, *Extended Deterrence and the Prevention of War* (Yale Univ. Press, New Haven, CT, in press).
5. G. Wilkinson, *Nature* **308**, 181 (1984).
6. ———, *Behav. Ecol. Sociobiol.* **17**, 111 (1985).
7. R. M. Seyfarth and D. L. Cheney, *Nature* **308**, 541 (1984).
8. L. W. Buss, *Science* **213**, 1012 (1981).
9. M. Milinski, *Nature* **325**, 433 (1987).
10. M. P. Lombardo, *Science* **227**, 1363 (1985).
11. E. Nol, *Behavior* **95**, 232 (1985).
12. H. R. Pulliam, G. H. Pyke, T. Caraco, *J. Theor. Biol.* **95**, 89 (1982); R. L. Mumme and A. De Queiroz, *Behavior* **95**, 290 (1985).
13. S. B. Katz, *Southern Calif. Law Rev.* **60**, 509 (1987).
14. A. Schepard, *Texas Law Rev.* **64**, 687 (1985).
15. S. Brown, *Negotiation J.* **2**, 371 (1986).
16. A. Dixit, in *U.S. Trade Policies in a Changing World*, R. M. Stern, Ed. (MIT Press, Cambridge, MA, 1987), p. 245.
17. J. L. Goldstein and S. D. Krasner, *Am. Econ. Rev.* **74**, 282 (1984).
18. Axelrod (*2*) termed a strategy that is in Nash equilibrium with itself is called a collectively stable strategy.
19. M. Taylor, *Anarchy and Cooperation* (Wiley, New York, 1976).
20. N. V. Joshi, *J. Genet.* **66**, 69 (1987).
21. J. A. K. Cave "A formal analysis of the evolution of cooperation" (Rand Paper Series P-7031, Santa Monica, CA, 1984).
22. J. Bendor and D. Mookherjee, *Am. Polit. Sci. Rev.* **81**, 129 (1987).
23. P. Pettit, *J. Philos.* **83**, 361 (1986).
24. P. Fader and J. R. Hauser, *J. Conflict Resolut.* **32**, 553 (1988).
25. A. H. Harcourt, in *Comparative Socioecology of Mammals and Humans*, V. Standen and R. A. Foley, Eds. (Blackwell, Oxford, in press).
26. K. Aoki, in *Population Genetics and Molecular Evolution*, T. Ohta and K. Aoki, Eds. (Springer-Verlag, Berlin, 1985), p. 429.
27. R. Axelrod, *Am. Polit. Sci. Rev.* **80**, 1095 (1986).
28. J. M. Orbell, P. Schwartz-Shea, R. T. Simmons, *ibid.* **78**, 147 (1984).
29. D. Hirshleifer and E. Rasmusen, *Cooperation in a Repeated Prisoners' Dilemma with Ostracism* (Graduate School of Management, UCLA, 1988).
30. C. Barner-Barry, *Ethol. Sociobiol.* **7**, 281 (1986).
31. T. Kondo, *Int. Relat. Stud.* **5**, 3 (1986).
32. B. J. Lipman, *Public Choice* **51**, 315 (1986).
33. R. Dacey and N. Pendegraft, *Int. Interactions*, in press.
34. An outcome is individually rational if it provides each player with at least that payoff below which the player cannot be forced by the other players.
35. For a review of work since 1976, see D. Fudenberg and E. Maskin, *Econometrica* **54**, 533 (1986).
36. P. Molander, *J. Conflict Resolut.* **29**, 611 (1985).
37. J. Bendor, *Am. J. Polit. Sci.* **31**, 531 (1987).
38. J. Gowa, *Int. Org.* **40**, 167 (1986); R. Axelrod and R. Keohane, *World Polit.* **38**, 226 (1985).
39. C. Donninger, in *Paradoxical Effects of Social Behavior*, A. Diekmann and P. Mitter, Eds. (Physica-Verlag, Heidelberg, 1986), p. 123.
40. R. Sugden, *The Economics of Rights, Co-operation and Welfare* (Basil Blackwell, New York, 1986); P. S. Segerstrom, *J. Econ. Theor.*, in press.
41. U. Mueller, *J. Conflict Resolut.* **31**, 692 (1987).
42. R. Calvert, *Reciprocity Among Self-Interested Actors: Asymmetry, Uncertainty and Bargaining* (Carnegie-Mellon University and Washington University, Pittsburgh, 1985).
43. E. J. Green and R. H. Porter, *Econometrica* **52**, 87 (1984).
44. R. Keohane, *After Hegemony* (Princeton Univ. Press, Princeton, 1984).
45. I. Eshel and D. Weinshall, *Theor. Popul. Biol.*, in press.
46. M. W. Feldman and E. R. C. Thomas, *J. Theor. Biol.* **128**, 297 (1987).
47. R. D. Luce and H. Raiffa, *Games and Decisions* (Wiley, New York, 1957).
48. A. Neyman, *Econ. Lett.* **19**, 227 (1985); N. Megiddo and A. Wigderson, "On play by means of computing machines" (IBM Research Report RJ 4984, Computer Science, Yorktown Heights, NY, 1986).
49. A. Rubinstein, *J. Econ. Theor.* **39**, 83 (1986).
50. D. M. Kreps, P. Milgrom, J. Roberts, R. Wilson, *ibid.* **27**, 245 (1982).
51. R. Selten and R. Stoecker, *J. Econ. Behav. Organ.* **7**, 47 (1986).
52. I. McLean, *Public Choice* (Basil Blackwell, New York, 1987).
53. K. Aoki, *Proc. Natl. Acad. Sci. U.S.A.* **80**, 4065 (1983).
54. G. Pollock, *Am. J. Phys. Anthropol.*, in press.
55. C. H. Moore, *Am. Polit. Sci. Rev.* **81**, 201 (1987).
56. J. K. Murninghan and A. Roth, *J. Conflict Resolut.* **27**, 279 (1983).
57. N. B. Davies and A. I. Houston, *J. Anim. Ecol.* **55**, 139 (1986).
58. J. Maynard Smith and G. R. Price, *Nature* **246**, 15 (1973).
59. W. G. S. Hines, *Theor. Popul. Biol.* **31**, 195 (1987).
60. P. Pudaite, *On the Initial Viability of Cooperation* (Merriam Laboratory for Analytic

Political Research, University of Illinois, Urbana–Champaign, 1985).
61. R. Boyd and J. P. Lorberbaum, *Nature* **327**, 58 (1987).
62. M. C. Blad, *Int. J. Game Theory* **15**, 83 (1986).
63. J. Holland, *Adaptation in Natural and Artificial Systems* (Univ. of Michigan Press, Ann Arbor, 1975).
64. R. Axelrod, in *Genetic Algorithms and Simulated Annealing*, L. Davis, Ed. (Pitman, London, 1987), p. 32.
65. R. M. May, *Nature* **327**, 15 (1987).
66. L. L. Cavalli-Sforza and M. W. Feldman, *Proc. Natl. Acad. Sci. U.S.A.* **80**, 2017 (1983); I. Eshel and L. L. Cavalli-Sforza, *ibid.* **79**, 1331 (1982).
67. J. R. Peck and M. W. Feldman, *Am. Nat.* **127**, 209 (1986).
68. We thank the anonymous reviewers for helpful suggestions. Supported by the MacArthur Foundation through a grant to the University of Michigan and by the NSF grant SES-8808459.

[3]

Journal of Bioeconomics 1: 73–93, 1999

There are Many Evolutionary Pathways to Cooperation

JACK HIRSHLEIFER
Department of Economics, University of California, Los Angeles, Los Angeles, CA 90095-1477, USA (jhirshle@ucla.edu)

Synopsis: Current sociobiological discussions attribute the evolution of cooperation to only two main influences: kinship and reciprocity. As a baseline, the paper analyzes the extent of incidental cooperation achieved in three important 2 × 2 payoff environments (Prisoners' Dilemma, Chicken, and Tender Trap) and the two simplest 'rules of the game' or protocols of play (single-round simultaneous-move and single-round sequential move). Kinship promotes cooperation beyond these base levels by modifying payoffs of selfish versus unselfish behaviors. Reciprocity may also promote cooperation, but its expression requires protocols that widen available strategy sets (in comparison with the basic strategies in the underlying 2 × 2 payoff matrices). Once payoff modifications and/or more elaborate protocols are allowed, many other pathways to cooperation are opened up. Among them are punishment options, complementary strategy mixes, recognition effects, coordination using external clues, and group selection.

Key words: evolution of cooperation, payoff environments, protocols of play

Introduction

A key question for all the social sciences is why cooperation occurs in some contexts but not in others. Cooperation poses an especially pressing challenge for sociobiology, founded as it is upon the central principle of the selfish gene—that the elements of our genetic heritage have been selected solely for strictly self-interested reproductive survival. The issue is, how can unselfish genes outcompete selfish ones? Or put another way, how can selfish genes translate into unselfish organisms?[1]

A somewhat impoverished view of this profoundly complex problem has become current in the sociobiological literature. To wit, that genetically driven cooperation stems, almost entirely, from only two sources: kinship and reciprocity (see, e.g., Ridley (1996)).[2] Although most sociobiological expositors limit their attention to this very narrow list of influences [Tooby & Cosmides (1988) is a praiseworthy exception], social scientists in other disciplines recognize a far wider range of bases for prosocial behaviors.[3] My intention here is to indicate the richness of the factors influencing the evolution of cooperation among living beings. First, I provide an interpretation of how evolutionary selection leads to subtly different kinds and degrees of cooperation in a variety of different payoff environments and under differing protocols or 'rules of the game'. In doing so I will compare evolutionary selection with self-interested rational choice as an alternative process that also might conduce to mutually helpful behavior.[4] Next I review the extent to which kinship and reciprocity may contribute to the evolution of cooperation. Finally, without attempting an overview of all possible pathways, I shall describe just a few of the many routes to cooperation that need not involve kinship or reciprocity.

1. Cooperation and helping in alternative social contexts

On the level of unilateral action, the kind of behavior that needs to be explained is best described by the psychologically neutral word helping. A pattern of mutual helping among two or more parties constitutes cooperation. (An unfortunate rhetorical tradition in the sociobiological literature confounds helping, an action, with altruism, which properly speaking refers to motivation. A person can have altruistic motives without engaging in helpful acts, owing perhaps to their high cost or insufficient effectiveness. Conversely, aid might be conferred for any number of reasons apart from friendly feeling.) Of course a great deal of the helping that occurs, whether unilateral or reciprocal, turns out to be merely incidental to self-interested behavior. The analytic difficulty arises only in connection with assistance to others that is actually costly to the donor. It might seem that costly helping necessarily requires altruistic motivation. But, as will be seen, this is not always the case.

The matrices in Table 1 are numerical instances[5] of social contexts in which greater or lesser degrees of cooperation might be achieved. Two familiar payoff patterns appear, Prisoners' Dilemma (PD) and Chicken (CH), together with one other called Tender Trap (TT).[6] Letting a_{ij} and b_{ij} be the Row and Column players' payoff elements in the cell located at the ith row and jth column, these matrices display a pattern of symmetry such that $a_{ij} = b_{ji}$. Thus the Row and Column roles can be transposed.

The three matrices illustrate characteristic social problems. Prisoners' Dilemma hardly needs explanation: it represents situations where the players could choose helpful behaviors to their mutual advantage, yet, in terms of unilateral decisions, each is motivated to defect. In the Chicken environment the parties can cooperate by coordinating on different actions,

Table 1. Three payoff environments (numerical illustrations).

	C_1	C_2
Prisoners' Dilemma (PD)		
R_1	3, 3	0, 5
R_2	5, 0	1, 1
Chicken (CH)		
R_1	3, 3	1, 5
R_2	5, 1	0, 0
Tender Trap (TT)		
R_1	5, 5	0, 1
R_2	1, 0	3, 3

a kind of complementary division of labor, but the payoff from doing so is asymmetrical. In the hope of getting the better of the bargain each side is tempted to behave aggressively, yet to some extent is deterred by the severe penalties suffered when both sides are too assertive. In Tender Trap, cooperation requires adopting the same action. Here interests are pretty much in harmony, yet unilateral decisions in ignorance of one another's choices may not achieve the needed coordination.[7]

Figure 1 illustrates the associated opportunity sets. In each diagram the four labeled nodes correspond to the cells of the associated payoff matrix, that is, to the pure-strategy outcomes. The convex hull bounding the nodes indicates the expanded set of outcomes attainable when mixed strategies are also considered.

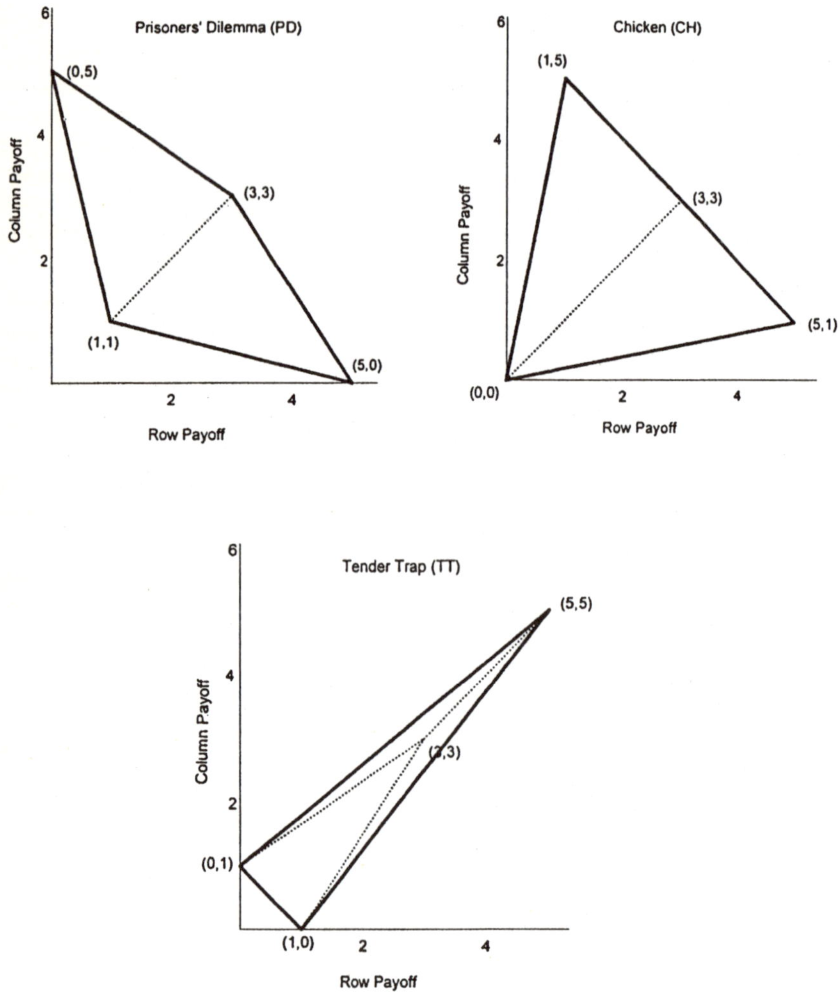

Figure 1. Three payoff environments.

Full cooperation can be regarded as attaining one or more of the Pareto-efficient outcomes, shown diagrammatically by the northeast boundary of the convex hull. There will always be a unique symmetrical 'most cooperative' outcome, for example, the (5, 5) payoff point in the TT diagram.

As for helping, in Prisoners' Dilemma Row's first strategy R_1 is always 'more helpful' to his opponent than R_2—since, whatever her strategy might be, Column does better when Row chooses R_1 rather than R_2—and similarly Column's C_1 is 'more helpful' to the Row player than C_2. This nice separation holds also for Chicken, but not for Tender Trap. In TT when Column is playing her first strategy C_1, Row's R_1 is 'more helpful' than R_2—but when Column is playing C_2 the reverse is true. The matrices of Table 1 have been set up so as to make the move-pair $[R_1, C_1]$ be the symmetrical 'most cooperative' choices in each case.

So, even avoiding the unfortunate term 'altruism', the psychologically neutral concepts of helping and cooperation remain somewhat soft around the edges. Still, the meanings are clear enough in many important contexts, and in others they retain at least suggestive validity. I will therefore continue to use these terms, indeed one could hardly do without them, but keeping the possible ambiguities in mind.

2. Optimization versus selection: one-round simultaneous-move protocol

Can evolutionary selection simulate, replace, or surpass self-interested rational optimization in leading to cooperative outcomes? Despite their limited mental powers, 'lower' animals often display impressive patterns of teamwork. And perhaps the cooperation observed among humans may stem more from evolutionary selection for instinctive behaviors than from calculated rational choices. I will be emphasizing that the relative efficacy of rationality and selection varies depending upon the environmental context (the pattern of payoffs) and also upon the operative 'rules of the game' (the protocol).

Starting with the evolutionary mechanism, think of populations of self-interested players randomly encountering one another in alternative payoff environments represented by some one of the PD, CH, and TT matrices in Table 1. And suppose that, in each one-on-one meeting, the protocol of interaction dictates single-round simultaneous-move choices by the Row and Column players. (Other possible protocols will be considered later on.) The basic principle of evolutionary selection is that more successful strategies multiply, while less successful ones suffer reduced representation within the population. An evolutionary equilibrium (EE) is achieved when, for a given strategy or combination of strategies (the 'incumbents'), no other strategies (the 'mutants') can successfully invade.[8]

For each matrix of Table 1, let α be the average payoff over all the individuals following the first strategy and β be the corresponding average payoff for the second strategy. Also, let p be the fraction of the population following the first strategy. The first strategy will tend to proliferate within the population when $\alpha - \beta > 0$, where:[9]

$$\begin{aligned} \alpha &\equiv pa_{11} + (1-p)a_{12} \\ \beta &\equiv pa_{21} + (1-p)a_{22} \end{aligned} \qquad (1)$$

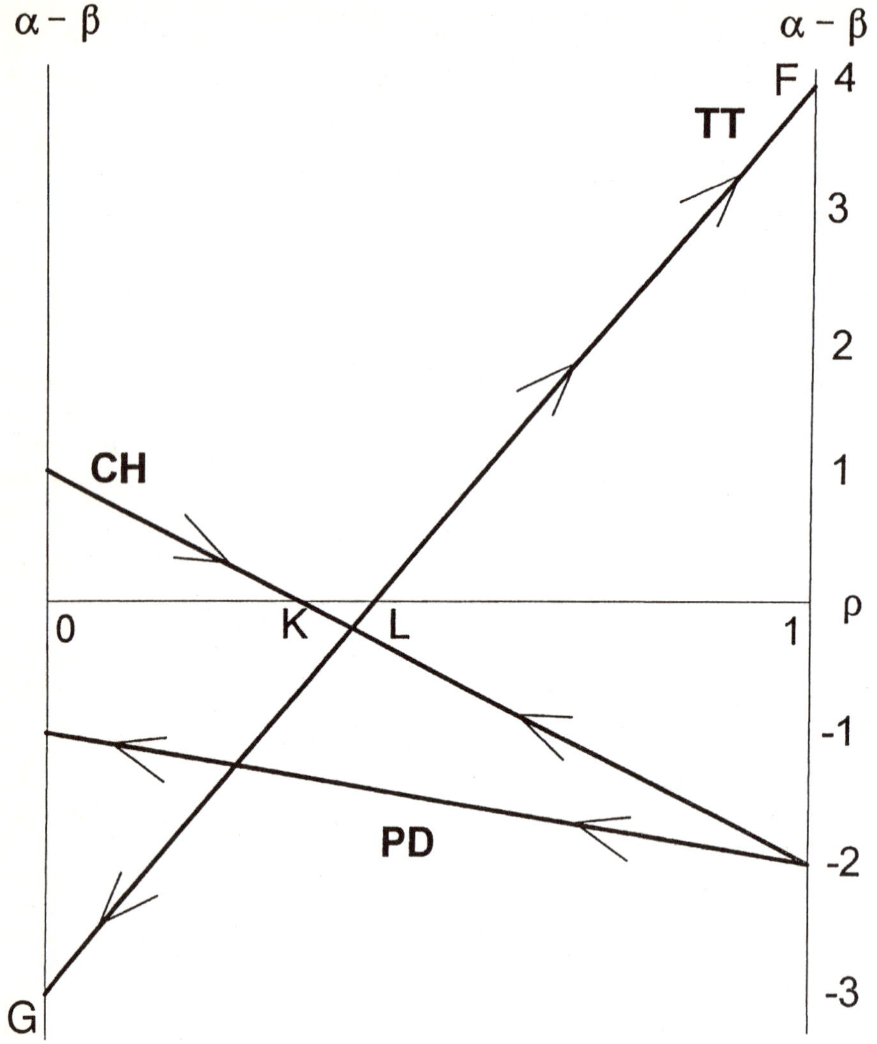

Figure 2. Progress toward cooperation in three evolutionary environments.

For the numerical matrices of Table 1, the associated courses of evolutionary development are pictured in figure 2. The arrows indicate the direction of movement from any momentarily given level of p. The evolutionary equilibria pictured in figure 2 are summarized in the first columns of Table 2.

In Prisoners' Dilemma $\alpha - \beta$ is always negative, hence (as indicated by the arrows) the population inevitably progresses toward an EE at $p = 0$—the familiar PD 'trap'—regardless of the starting point. In each interaction the players end up at the move-pair [R_2, C_2], so

Table 2. Rationality versus selection in three payoff environments (simultaneous-move protocol).

	Evolutionary equilibrium (EE)		Nash equilibrium (NE)	
	Proportion cooperating (p^*)	Payoffs	Strategy-pair	Payoffs
PD	0	1	[R2, C2]	(1, 1)
CH	1/3	5/3	(i) [R2, C1]	(5, 1)
			(ii) [R1, C2]	(1, 5)
			(iii) mixed-strategy ($\pi = 1/3$)	(5/3, 5/3)
TT	(i) 1	5	(i) [R1, C1]	(5, 5)
	(ii) 0	3	(ii) [R2, C2]	(3, 3)
			(iii) mixed-strategy ($\pi = 3/7$)	(15/7, 15/7)

the mean payoff is 1. Thus, under the assumed protocol, the evolutionary equilibrium for PD excludes both cooperation and helping.

For Chicken the 'more cooperative' (first) strategy has higher mean payoff when it is relatively rare (when p is low) while the reverse occurs when it is numerically more common (when p is high). Consequently, as the arrows indicate, regardless of the starting point the progression will be toward an interior evolutionary equilibrium at point K where the two strategies are equally profitable: $\alpha - \beta = 0$. At this EE a fraction p^* of the population will be using the first strategy and the remainder the second strategy. Numerically here, $p^* = 1/3$. The average payoff to each strategy, and therefore for the population as a whole, is 5/3.[10]

Finally, Tender Trap is the evolutionary reverse of Chicken: now either strategy becomes the more profitable when it is sufficiently popular. The crossover point L occurs numerically at $p = 3/7$. So, as the arrows indicate, there are two possible corner EE's. Depending upon whether the starting point is to the right or the left of L in figure 2, the evolutionary outcome will be the 'more cooperative' [R_1, C_1] strategy combination at point F with payoffs of 5 for each player or the 'less cooperative' combination [R_2, C_2] at point G with payoffs of 3. (Note that the mixed population represented by point L is not an EE.)

To interpret these results in terms of achieved cooperation, it seems reasonable to choose as point of comparison the symmetrical most Pareto-inferior outcome within the opportunity set defined by the convex hull. Measured against this base point, the progress toward cooperation achieved by the evolutionary process under the assumed protocol can be summarized:

For Prisoners' Dilemma—no progress at all:
  At the EE the proportion making the more cooperative (first row or first column) move is $p = 0$.

For Chicken—an intermediate degree of progress:
  In evolutionary equilibrium the fraction choosing the more cooperative strategy is $p^* = 1/3$. The average payoff to each strategy of 5/3 is short of the symmetrical 'fully cooperative' payoff of 3 but a considerable improvement over the symmetrical 'most Pareto-inferior' payoff of 0.

For Tender Trap—either full or partial cooperation:

If the initial situation is to the right of the cross-over point in figure 2, in equilibrium everyone uses the first strategy with payoffs of 5 to each; otherwise, at the EE everyone uses the second strategy with payoffs of 3. In comparison, the 'most Pareto-inferior' symmetrical payoffs are 0.5 to each—midway along the line connecting the (1, 0) and (0, 1) points in figure 1.

Thus, depending upon the payoff environment, greater or lesser degrees of cooperation can come about simply by evolutionary selection.

A comparison of these results with what would be achieved under the alternative 'rationality mechanism' is provided in Table 2, taking the game theorists' Nash equilibrium (NE) as the standard of rational play.[11] In Prisoners' Dilemma the unique NE is at the 'trap' move-pair [R_2, C_2], which of course matches the EE at $p^* = 0$. So, in terms of achieved cooperation, the results are equally unsatisfactory under either mechanism.

For Chicken there are three NE's. The two solutions in pure strategies—[R_1, C_2] and [R_2, C_1]—are Pareto-efficient but asymmetrical. Of main interest to us is the symmetrical but Pareto-inefficient mixed-strategy NE. For the numerical payoffs of the CH matrix, this mixed strategy has each player choosing the more cooperative move with probability $\pi = 1/3$—numerically the same as the proportion of the population who cooperative ($p^* = 1/3$) in the corresponding EE solution. (In fact, for Chicken it is true generally that $p^* = \pi$.)[12] And so once again the two mechanisms arrive at essentially equivalent levels of cooperation, in this case intermediate between full cooperation and none.

For Tender Trap the two symmetrical NE's in pure strategies evidently match up with the corresponding EE's in Table 2. But whereas the 'evolutionary mixture' corresponding to point L in figure 2 was not an EE, the corresponding symmetrical mixed strategy is an NE with $\pi = 3/7$, the level of efficiency being lower than at either of the two pure-strategy solutions. It appears that here again the evolutionary process seems to do at least as well as the kind of rationality associated with the Nash equilibrium concept in game theory.

So, under the single-round simultaneous-move protocol, the two mechanisms—rational optimization and evolutionary selection—do about equally well in the PD and CH payoff contexts, while selection has perhaps an edge in the TT environment.

3. Kinship effects

As has just been seen, a substantial amount of cooperation may—the Prisoners' Dilemma apart—emerge simply as a consequence of incidental helping. The next question is the degree to which kinship and/or reciprocity effects can induce even higher levels of mutual aid. Kinship will be examined in this section, and reciprocity in the next. Since we are concerned here with the possible evolutionary emergence of additional helping, for any given payoff environment it is natural to take the evolutionary equilibrium EE of the previous section as base point. That leaves some residual ambiguity in the Chicken and Tender Trap environments, where the EEs may be mixed or non-unique. So let us start with Prisoners' Dilemma, where (at least for the simultaneous-move protocol) the EE is not only unique but represents a zero level of helping.

Table 3. Effect of kinship in prisoners' dilemma.

	C_1	C_2
Original PD matrix		
R_1	3, 3	0, 5
R_2	5, 0	1, 1
Adjusted for relatedness ($r = 1/2$)		
R_1	4.5, 4.5	2.5, 5
R_2	5, 2.5	1.5, 1.5

One of the key concepts of sociobiology is inclusive fitness (Hamilton 1964). As usually expressed, the evolutionary payoff of any trait or behavior should be evaluated not in terms of its contribution to the organism's own reproductive survival alone. Instead, the contribution to the reproductive survival of relatives should also be counted, weighted by the degree of relatedness (50% for full siblings, 25% for half-sibs, etc.). So any fitness advantage conferred on a sibling would be added, with weight of 50%, to the direct own-fitness gain associated with that gene. (It is important to appreciate, since there has been some confusion on this score, that this adjustment is not valid for the purpose of showing or predicting how an organism would or should count benefits conferred on relatives in any and all contexts. It is only valid for determining the stability of an evolutionary equilibrium EE involving such benefits.)[13]

In Table 3 the first matrix repeats the PD matrix of Table 1. The new matrix in Table 3 illustrates the kinship adjustment for interaction between siblings. In the upper-left cell the old (3, 3) payoffs have become (4.5, 4.5), with the other cells adjusted accordingly. Inspection of the new matrix reveals the crucial point: it is no longer a Prisoners' Dilemma! In fact, it is in the form of the Chicken (CH) matrix of Table 1. As was pictured in figure 2, for the Chicken environment there is evolutionary convergence toward an interior solution, in which part (but not all) of the population now adopts the more cooperative strategy. For the numerical example here, at equilibrium 77.8% of the population will be doing so. Thus, we have seen how kinship may bring about some partial escape from the PD trap.

More generally, it has been shown (Bergstrom and Stark 1993, Bergstrom 1995) that, starting from the non-cooperative 'trap' PD solution, allowing for sibling relatedness opens up four possible classes of solutions: (1) a monomorphic cooperative EE (upper-left cell of the matrix); (2) a monomorphic non-helping equilibrium (lower-right cell); (3) EE's at either of the above, depending upon the initial starting-point; and (4) no monomorphic EE at all (so that the population converges to an interior equilibrium in which the more and the less cooperative strategies both survive in the population). Which type of EE comes about depends upon the specific numerical parameters assumed for the PD matrix. The numbers employed in Table 3 are associated with an equilibrium of type (4) above. Had we started with somewhat different numbers in the source PD, any of the other three classes of solutions might have been obtained.

That interacting with one's kin tends to improve the prospects for achieving a cooperative outcome is of course not very surprising. But the analysis here does tend to indicate the

Table 4. Prisoners' dilemma in cost-benefit form.

	C_1	C_2
General cost-benefit PD matrix		
R_1	$b-c,\ b-c$	$-c,\ b$
R_2	$b,\ -c$	0, 0
Numerical illustration ($b=3,\ c=1$)		
R_1	2, 2	−1, 3
R_2	3, −1	0, 0

various provisos and limitations under which this kinship effect operates in Prisoners' Dilemma environments. (Somewhat parallel results would apply also in Chicken and Tender Trap environments, but will not be covered here.)

The remainder of this section is devoted to the special class of Prisoners' Dilemma matrices illustrated in Table 4. Matrix 1 is a generic payoff table in 'cost-benefit form', where b stands for benefit and c for cost. As in all PD matrices, the lower-right cell (adoption of the less cooperative strategies on each side) is the Nash equilibrium NE and evolutionary equilibrium EE as well. The cost-benefit form sets these payoffs at (0, 0). If Row were to shift unilaterally to his more cooperative strategy, he would incur cost c while conferring benefit b upon Column. So the payoffs in the upper-right cell are $(-c, b)$. The diagonally opposite cell is defined correspondingly. Finally, if both sides cooperate, the payoffs in the upper-left cell become $(b-c, b-c)$. Matrix 2 is a specific numerical instance where $b = 3$ and $c = 1$.[14]

PD matrices in cost-benefit form permit a more intuitive answer to the question of when a 'gene for helping' H would win out in evolutionary competition against the 'gene for not-helping' NH. Let W_H and W_{NH} represent the 'fitnesses' of the two genes, and define two new parameters: N is the population size, and m is the 'discrimination factor' (that is, the proportion of helping acts received by fellow-helpers). Then, for the condition $W_H > W_{NH}$ to be met, it must be that:[15]

$$-c + \frac{bmNp}{Np} > \frac{b(1-m)Np}{N(1-p)} \tag{2}$$

On the left-hand side, $-c$ is the fitness loss or cost to the helper (assuming one helping act per unit of time). In the second term on the left, the numerator $bmNp$ represents the aggregate benefit of helping acts per time-period that are directed at fellow-helpers, while the denominator Np is the number of helpers in the population. The ratio of the two then shows the average per-helper benefit of helping acts, in fitness units per time-period. The right-hand side similarly shows the average per-non-helper benefit of having helpers in the population. Simplifying, inequality (3) reduces to:

$$\frac{c}{b} < \frac{m-p}{1-p} \tag{3}$$

As a corollary, for costly helping to evolve, at least the condition $m > p$ must be met: fellow-helpers must receive helping acts in bigger proportion than their representation in the population. Kin selection is a way of achieving this. For siblings, and assuming that H is a new mutation in the parent, initially p is effectively zero in the population. If so, the probability that one's sibling also bears the H gene is one-half. As p goes to unity, m must also approach unity, in accordance with the algebraic relation:

$$m = \frac{1+p}{2} \tag{4}$$

Making this substitution in (4) leads directly to:

$$\frac{c}{b} < \frac{1}{2} \tag{5}$$

This is Hamilton's Rule (Hamilton 1964) for siblings. Generalizing for any level of relatedness r:

$$\frac{c}{b} < r \tag{6}$$

Thus, if the c/b ratio is less than the degree of relatedness, the NH gene will eventually be swamped by organisms carrying the H gene.

It will be of interest to bring in one other important factor: competition. The cost and benefit parameters c and b (and the payoff patterns from which they were derived) have so far been taken as constants independent of population size. But any fitness gain due to mutual helping would presumably lead to population growth, implying increased pressure upon resources. The consequent intensification of rivalry could then be expected to affect the cost-benefit calculations. The influence of competition can be explored using a generalized helping/hurting rule (following West-Eberhard 1975):

$$\sum_{\text{losers}(i)} r_{i\text{D}} c_i < \sum_{\text{gainers}(j)} r_{j\text{D}} b_j \tag{7}$$

That is, a donor D will be motivated to take any action on the margin for which the relatedness-weighted sum of benefits exceeds the corresponding sum of costs, where i is an index running over all the losers whereas j is an index running over all the gainers. (The donor will count himself, with a relatedness of unity, on whichever side of the inequality is appropriate.)

Turning now to the constraints upon the costs and benefits dictated by pressure on resources, as an extreme absolute competition could be defined by the condition (Hirshleifer 1978):

$$\sum_i c_i = \sum_j b_j \tag{8}$$

That is, the individuals are playing a constant-sum game.

In two-party absolute competition the ratio c_i/b_j is necessarily unity, so in such an environment we would not expect to observe costly helping even toward close kin. In fact, extreme sibling hostility has been known to evolve—for example, in bird species for whom within-nest competition is severe—and possible human analogs come to mind. Rewriting the generalized helping/hurting rule (7), where $\bar{r}$ is the average relatedness of members of the population to the donor:

$$\sum_i c_i(r_{i\mathrm{D}} - \bar{r}) < \sum_j b_j(r_{j\mathrm{D}} - \bar{r}) \tag{9}$$

So, under absolute competition, it is not simple relatedness but relatedness greater or less than the average in the population that serves as the factor weighting costs and benefits. Paraphrasing Hamilton (1970): 'Anyone is your enemy who is less closely related to you than the average in the population'. In sum, relatedness does certainly tend to promote cooperation. But as competition intensifies, the effect weakens and it may actually become selectively advantageous to injure not only strangers but even one's kin.

4. Reciprocity and other sequential strategies

The discussion so far has analyzed three important payoff patterns, each representing a possible environment in which one-on-one interactions might take place, but under only a single protocol: single-round simultaneous-move play. Under that protocol there was no way for reciprocative behavior to express itself. In this section I will consider two (among an indefinitely large number of) alternative 'rules of the game' that allow reciprocity to play a role.[16] The first to be considered is the simplest possible sequential arrangement: a single round, but now the players move in turn. Then the later-mover can adapt his choice in response to the opponent's earlier move in the same round. The other protocol to be examined involves simultaneous moves in any given round, but allows for an indefinitely large number of rounds. In that case a player's subsequent-round choices could be conditioned upon what the opponent has done in prior rounds.[17]

Single-round sequential protocol

The change from single-round simultaneous play to single-round sequential play opens up a surprising range of strategy choices. The earlier-mover still has only two options: (1) the 'more helpful' R_1 or (2) the 'less helpful' R_2. (It will be assumed that the Row player has the earlier move.) The later-mover has four reactive options:

(i) Respond to R_1 with C_1 and to R_2 with C_1 (always follow with the more helpful C_1)
(ii) Respond to R_1 with C_1 and to R_2 with C_2 (echo the opponent's earlier move)
(iii) Respond to R_1 with C_2 and to R_2 with C_1 (reverse the opponent's earlier move)
(iv) Respond to R_1 with C_2 and to R_2 with C_2 (always follow with the less helpful C_2)

Since any individual might either be the earlier-mover or later-mover, there are in all eight possible sequential strategies.

In this context, reciprocity is represented by the strategy 1(ii): pick the 'more helpful' R_1 on the earlier move, and the echoing option ii on the later move.[18] Interacting with one another, reciprocative players would always end up at the move-pair [R_1, C_1] achieving

Table 5. Rationality versus selection in three payoff environments (sequential-move protocol).

	Evolutionary equilibrium (EE)		Subgame-perfect equilibrium (SGPE)	
	Is reciprocity strategy 1(ii) a possible EE?	Payoffs	Strategy (see text) (earlier-move, later-move)	Payoffs
PD	No	—	2(iv)	(1, 1)
CH	No	—	2(iii)	(3, 3)[a]
TT	Yes[b]	5	1(ii)	(5, 5)

[a]Average of (5, 1) and (1, 5). (Earlier-mover has advantage, but each player has a 50% chance of being the earlier-mover.)
[b]As part of 'drifting equilibrium' with 1(i).

payoffs (3, 3) in PD and CH and payoff (5, 5) in TT. I will be asking here, for the different payoff environments, whether reciprocative behavior is consistent with equilibrium under either the rationality or the evolutionary mechanisms.

The 'rational' game theory solution concept for this sequential protocol is subgame-perfect equilibrium (SGPE). The essential idea is that the player with the earlier move will choose his most profitable option, on the assumption that the reactive later-mover will similarly be choosing whatever is most profitable for herself when her turn comes up. Table 5 indicates that, for Prisoners' Dilemma, the SGPE is 2(iv)—in short, never cooperate. Thus the adopted move-pair remains [R_2, C_2] with payoff 1 to each player. (Reciprocity behavior is an available strategy, but it is not consistent with self-interested rational play). Despite the changed protocol, under the rationality mechanism the PD trap still grips as tightly as ever.

For Chicken the SGPE solution is 2(iii): as earlier-mover choose the less helpful option, and as later-mover always reverse the opponent's prior choice. In any single run of the game the result is asymmetrical, the earlier-mover having the advantage. But recall that each player is equally likely to be the earlier-mover or later-mover. Then, taking the average of the asymmetrical (5, 1) and (1, 5) payoffs, the mean return is 3—exactly the same as at the reciprocative outcome. This equivalence is however an accidental result of the specific payoff numbers used in the CH matrix of Table 1. If the payoffs in the upper-left cell were changed from (3, 3) to say (2, 2), the game would still be Chicken but the parties would now both do better under self-interested rationality than by following the reciprocity strategy! The opposite would hold if, say, the upper-left payoffs were changed to (4, 4). Finally, for Tender Trap, the SGPE is 1(ii). Here, under the assumed sequential protocol, reciprocity behavior coincides with rational self-interest, and leads to the unique 'most cooperative' outcome with payoff 5.

Now let us turn to the evolutionary process. Having to deal with eight different pure strategies is more than a little troublesome. In addition to a number of more complicated possibilities, the evolutionary equilibrium EE in pure strategies could involve only one strategy surviving, or two, or any number up to the full eight.[19] To keep the problem within bounds, I ask only whether the reciprocity strategy 1(ii) can ever be a single-strategy evolutionary equilibrium.

In the Prisoners' Dilemma environment, 1(ii) cannot be a single-strategy EE. In a population with 1(ii) as sole 'incumbent', every possible 'mutant' strategy involving C_2 or R_2—that is, any strategy for which the less cooperative option is chosen on the earlier move or on the later move or both—will strictly defeat 1(ii) in one-on-one play and thus successfully invade. True, the reciprocative players will be making $[R_1, C_1]$ moves with one another and achieving handsome (3, 3) payoffs. But against these incumbents a mutant choosing the less cooperative R_2 on the earlier move will be earning the higher of the payoff-pair (5, 0), and similarly an entrant choosing the less cooperative C_2 on the later move will receive the higher of (0, 5).

The analysis of Chicken is very similar. If 1(ii) is the incumbent, once again the reciprocative players receive (3, 3) when they interact with one another. But a less cooperative mutant would now earn the higher of (5, 1) on the earlier move and/or the higher of (1, 5) on the later move. For Tender Trap the situation is somewhat trickier. As incumbent, the reciprocative strategy 1(ii) cannot be strictly defeated by any other. However, the Always-Cooperate (AC) strategy 1(i) ties 1(ii) in any one-on-one interaction between them—since both lead to the move-pair $[R_1, C_1]$ with payoffs (5, 5). So we can expect a kind of meta-stable 'drifting equilibrium' for some range of combinations of 1(i) and 1(ii).

Summarizing, in both the Prisoners' Dilemma and Chicken environments under the single-round sequential protocol, reciprocative behavior does not in general succeed in maintaining itself either as the rational subgame-perfect equilibrium or as an evolutionary equilibrium. However, in Tender Trap the reciprocative strategy is indeed the sole SGPE, and it is an element in a 'drifting' EE in combination with the Always-Cooperate strategy 1(i).

Multiple-round simultaneous-move protocol

A variety of other 'rules of the game' provide ways for reciprocity behavior to be expressed. Let us suppose here that the players choose simultaneously in any given round, but the interaction is repeated over an indefinite number of rounds. Then a less cooperative move in a prior round could conceivably be penalized by the opponent's refusal to play cooperatively in one or more subsequent rounds. Under the famous Tit-for-Tat (TFT) strategy popularized in the well-known work of Axelrod (1984), initially the player would choose the more helpful option (first row or column in the matrices of Table 1), thereafter echoing the opponent's behavior in the previous round. Unhelpful behavior would be punished, but in a proportionate eye-for-an-eye way that leaves open the possibility of later reversion to more cooperative play. In two tournaments conducted by Axelrod using the Prisoners' Dilemma payoffs of Table 1, TFT scored higher than any other of the strategies considered. It has come to be widely believed that TFT is, in a very sweeping sense, the 'best' strategy to follow and constitutes the key to the emergence of cooperation.[20]

A systematic investigation of these issues is out of the question here. Instead, I shall limit myself to a few points bearing specifically upon TFT as one possible reciprocative strategy:

1. Not all social interactions correspond to evolutionary competition. So even if TIT FOR TAT were a universal evolutionary equilibrium, that would not warrant using the TFT strategy in non-evolutionary contexts such as labor-management relations or international policy.[21]
2. For evolutionary processes quite generally, it is unreasonable to expect a 'corner solution' in which only a single strategy such as TFT survives. In almost all real-world

contexts a coexisting mix of strategies—more cooperative ones together with less cooperative ones—is observed.[22] (This point will be discussed further under the heading of 'complementary strategy mixes' in the next section.)

3. TFT has been discussed almost exclusively in the context of the multiple-round simultaneous-move Prisoners' Dilemma. Even if it were successful under those conditions, that success would not necessarily remain valid for other environments and protocols.
4. But in fact, as has just been seen, although there are a huge number of EE's in the multiple-round simultaneous-move Prisoners' Dilemma, an all-TFT population is not one of them! In parallel with the corresponding result for the single-round sequential-move PD, Tit for Tat as incumbent can never do better than tie with (and thus be subject to invasion by) the Always-Cooperate strategy.

The upshot, then, is that reciprocity, like kinship, can indeed promote cooperation in a number of important specific contexts. But it is no panacea.

5. Other pathways

So far the analysis has examined two influences—kinship and reciprocity—that, in certain circumstances, lead to cooperation. These are the forces emphasized in sociobiological summaries and textbook discussions. Yet appearing here and there in the vast literatures of sociobiology, economics, and other social sciences are indications of a great many other possible pathways to cooperation. Kinship promotes cooperation by modifying the payoffs of helpful actions. (Discounted by the degree of relatedness, benefits to others are counted as equivalent to benefits to self.) And reciprocative behavior requires consideration of a number of alternative protocols of play, with a consequent need to deal with extended strategy sets in comparison with the elemental Row and Column strategies of Table 1. However, once adjustments of payoffs, protocols, and/or strategy sets are permitted, many other possible routes to cooperation are opened up. A very few of these additional routes are briefly covered in this section.

Punishment opportunities

Reciprocative strategies such as Tit-for-Tat penalize an opponent's failure to cooperate by reactive non-cooperation. But this is a mild penalty. In some circumstances it may be possible to impose stronger penalties, as exemplified by what has been termed Punisher strategies (Hirshleifer & Martinez Coll 1988). Punisher players gain at the expense of non-cooperators, just as the latter 'make a living' by exploiting cooperators. In the realm of Nature, for example, super-predator species prey upon lower-level predators. In human terms, bounty-hunters specialize in capturing criminals.

When Punisher strategies are available in the PD environment, the typical evolutionary outcome is a mixed population in which the more cooperative, less cooperative, and Punisher strategies are all represented—rather like the continuing survival of ranchers, rustlers, and bounty-hunters in the Old West.[23] Thus, introducing Punisher is a way of modeling the fact that what we observe in the real world is almost never the total victory of any single strategy but rather a co-existing set of differentiated strategies.[24]

Complementary strategy mixes

Extending this idea for the Prisoners' Dilemma payoff environment and multiple-round simultaneous-move protocol, Lomborg (1996) generated simulations taking account of all the strategies that can 'remember' and thus react to the opponent's three prior moves. (There are 32,768 such strategies!) Over the evolutionary generations meta-stable (but never fully stable) equilibria[25] emerge. These typically involve a considerable number of mutually supportive strategies, commonly falling into two types labeled 'nucleus' and 'shield'. The nucleus strategies are highly cooperative ones, reacting very little or not at all to opponents' unhelpful moves but scoring well in encounters with other members of the incumbent strategy set. The shield strategies, in contrast, provide protection by reacting adversely to uncooperative deviants.

Despite chaotic periods that show up when an existing meta-equilibrium collapses, the system as a whole spends most of its time at or near the meta-equilibria. Furthermore, these equilibria yield very high average payoffs (high levels of cooperation). In fact, the mean evolutionary payoffs were generally higher than what an all-TFT population would achieve![26]

Recognition and prompt response

While ordinarily it is assumed that a TFT player can react to the opponent's prior move in the very next round of play, that is only one of many possibilities. If response delay were greater, the TFT strategy would not do so well. Conversely, however, Tit-for-Tat would do even better than in the standard formulation if a TFT player could recognize and respond to the opponent's choice earlier, perhaps even in the very same round. This last could occur if, for example, the situation dictated that the opponent's action, hostile or friendly, had to be overt rather than covert. In the arms race preceding World War I, it was impossible for open societies like Britain or Germany to hide the numbers of battleships under construction. So a hostile move by either nation (deciding to build more battleships) could not gain much lead time over the opponent's response. Alternatively, by paying a 'cost of scrutiny' (Frank 1988, pp. 59–63) it might be possible to identify a covertly hostile action in good time—an instance of trading off payoff numbers to gain promptness of response.

Allowing perfect recognition and timely response makes Tit-for-Tat an available strategy even when the protocol is single-round simultaneous-move.[27] Martinez Coll & Hirshleifer (1991) analyzed the Prisoners' Dilemma and Chicken environments under this protocol, with three strategies in contention: TFT, Always-Cooperate (AC), and Never-Cooperate (NC). In such a simple context it was possible to find all the evolutionary equilibria. For PD a 'drifting' EE was found involving TFT and AC, provided the proportion of the latter was not too large. In the Chicken environment there was a similar drifting equilibrium, but also a separate non-drifting EE in which the population ended up with a specific division between AC and NC. (Note the similarity of the latter equilibrium to the EE for Chicken in figure 2.)

Once again, these extended strategy sets allowed the continuing survival of more and less cooperative players in a variety of contexts.

Control

In some circumstances a person might be in a position to 'commit' to a particular strategy, or alternatively to foreclose his ever employing certain other strategies. (As in 'burning your bridges behind you'.) Commitment or foreclosure can affect the rational equilibrium. If you burn your bridges behind you the enemy knows you can no longer retreat, which might affect his calculation whether or not to attack. However, neither commitment nor foreclosure on the part of an individual can affect the evolutionary equilibrium, since your self-denied strategies still remain available to other players present in the population. Conceivably, however, a player might have the ability to dictate or control the *opponent's* possible actions. Control might be effected by physical means like imprisonment, or psychological means like hypnotism or indoctrination.[28] The controlling party would ordinarily incur some cost, yet the trade-off might prove advantageous.

As one example, for Prisoners' Dilemma using the single-round simultaneous-play protocol 'with recognition' (as described just above), Heckathorn (1996) found that the reciprocative Tit for Tat strategy was driven to extinction by a control strategy termed 'hypocritical cooperation'. Under that strategy the player does not cooperate voluntarily, but is willing to incur a cost to force the opponent into a cooperative move. So in a world where such control is not too costly, a great deal of cooperation might emerge, even if unwilling.

Coordination by external clues

The three payoff contexts of Table 1 displayed different types of obstacles hampering mutually advantageous coordination of strategies. Sometimes, however, external clues may provide the basis for harmonizing the players' moves. Starting from the underlying Chicken environment under the single-round simultaneous-move protocol, Maynard Smith (1978) described a strategy termed Bourgeois. The idea is that, in competing for use of a resource, one animal typically arrives earlier and the other later. Using this external clue, the Bourgeois strategy is: As earlier-comer, play aggressively, as later-comer, play submissively. In terms of the CH matrix of Table 1, the moves would be $[R_2, C_1]$ with payoffs (4, 2) the earlier-comer having the advantage. But on average each animal can expect to be in either situation half the time, so the mean payoff would be 3—higher than 5/3 payoff shown in Table 2 for the symmetrical EE when only the simpler more cooperative and less cooperative strategies are available.

Group selection

Although currently highly controversial among biologists, group selection as a possible force favoring cooperation has a long intellectual history. Darwin suggested that the habit of cooperation, even where disadvantageous to the individual, might be evolutionarily viable owing to its impact upon the differential survival of groups (Darwin 1871 n.d. 498). But, at least if we think in terms of environments like the Prisoners' Dilemma matrix of Table 1, group selection for cooperative behavior runs against the fact that individual selection favors selfish actions. And in fact the current standard view among sociobiologists is that individual selection for selfishness must dominate (Williams 1966). The key argument has been that individuals within a population have shorter 'turnover times' (are differentially selected faster) than populations as a whole. So the internal within-group trend toward selfishness will proceed more rapidly than any collective between-group gain from the displacement of less unselfish populations.

But recall that kin selection, whose power no sociobiologist questions, operates essentially by concentrating helping acts upon fellow-carriers of the helping gene. Much the same would hold even for unrelated individuals living in groups characterized by preferential interaction with one another—possibly due simply to propinquity. Group selection is also favored by frequent exterminations of entire clans and tribes, a condition that very likely characterized primal mankind (Alexander 1979, chapter 4). In recent years biological opinion has been swinging back toward assigning a substantial evolutionary role to group selection (Wilson and Sober 1994).

The discussion in this section could do no more than suggest the huge number of pathways to cooperation opened up once we allow for wider ranges of payoff patterns and protocols, and consequently enlarged strategy sets. Sociobiologists have not overlooked these other pathways; indeed, most of the examples in this section derive from the sociobiological literature. What I have tried to critique is the tendency in textbooks and other summary discussions to recognize only kinship and reciprocity as systematic factors tending to produce cooperative evolutionary outcomes.

6. Concluding thoughts

Cooperation takes many forms and emerges through many channels and pathways. Game-theoretic analyses in the sociobiological literature have concentrated excessively upon just one or a very few payoff environments (notably Prisoners' Dilemma) and similarly only one or a very few of the enormous range of possible protocols of play ('rules of the game'). It is probably owing to this excessive narrowness of viewpoint that usually only kinship and reciprocity have been recognized as systematic influences favoring the rise of cooperation.

As a baseline, this paper first assessed three important payoff environments (Prisoners' Dilemma, Chicken, and Tender Trap) illustrating different types of obstacles hampering the evolution of mutual helping, and using only the two simplest possible protocols (single-round simultaneous-move and single-round sequential move). In these contexts, by and large, comparable levels of cooperation were achieved by the different mechanisms of evolutionary selection and rational self-interested choice. The degree to which kinship and/or reciprocity improved upon these results varied with the specifics of the payoff environment and protocol assumed.

Allowing for kinship and reciprocity already involves a certain widening of horizons in comparison with the baseline conditions. Kinship and reciprocity effects modify the payoffs of cooperative versus uncooperative behaviors and/or require consideration of more complex protocols, the latter implying an extension of the sets of strategies assumed available. Once such alterations of payoffs and protocols are permitted, however, a vast number of other routes to cooperation are opened up. The final main section of the paper summarized a number of these other pathways: punishment opportunities, complementary strategy mixes, recognition effects, techniques of control, coordination with the help of external clues, and group selection.

A few other points relate to limitations of the present analysis. First, not all competition is evolutionary competition. The relations among nations and social classes certainly change over time, but are not usually best modeled as involving large populations of entities subject to evolutionary influences such as inheritance, mutation, multiplication, and selection. Second, the analysis here dealt almost exclusively with symmetrical solutions. But a degree of cooperation is often achieved in asymmetrical ways, for example by systems of dominance and deference that keep internal power struggles within bounds.

As a coda to the main discussion, I will offer a further comment on a secondary theme of the paper: the relative efficacy of evolutionary selection versus rational optimization as mechanisms of competition and cooperation. Section 2 above suggested there was little to choose between them; if anything, selection had the edge over rationality. But, I now want to argue, the very simple protocols of play postulated in Section 2 led to an under-estimate of what interacting rational choices can actually achieve in the way of cooperation. In the single-round sequential-move Prisoners' Dilemma, for example, the Subgame-perfect equilibrium associated with rational play offers no escape from the PD 'trap' outcome (Table 5). However, rational players can (and are observed to) do much better under quite reasonable though somewhat more complex protocols, in particular one that might be termed the Standard Negotiation Protocol (SNP).[29]

The SNP, while single-round, allows for an indefinite number of negotiation cycles before moves are finalized and payoffs are made. In each cycle players tentatively choose either the more cooperative move (first row or column of the PD matrix in Table 1) or the less cooperative move (second row or column). After these tentative choices are revealed at the end of a cycle, either or both players may stand pat or switch. Since any player can always switch away from the exploitative outcome in which he/she would have received zero payoff, there is no reason not to try the cooperative move. The only stable equilibrium involves the mutually advantageous (3, 3) payoffs. So rational players can, given this quite realistic protocol, escape the PD trap after all. More generally, rational players can frequently treat the rules of the game as endogenous, and hence should be able to hit upon a protocol leading to mutually advantageous outcomes. Economists will of course recognize this as a version of the famous 'Coase theorem'.

Acknowledgements

For helpful comments I especially thank David Hirshleifer, Theodore C. Bergstrom, Michael Ghiselin, and two anonymous referees of this Journal.

Notes

1. Classic treatments include Dawkins (1976) and Trivers (1985). A valuable recent discussion is Ridley (1996).

2. A third force, parental manipulation, has also received some attention. Parents, aiming at their own evolutionary advantage, may manipulate offspring to act unselfishly toward one another (Alexander 1974, West Eberhard 1975, Trivers 1985, chapter 7). Parental manipulation is however only a very special kind of kinship effect.
3. One attempt to connect these up with sociobiological considerations is Hirshleifer (1982).
4. It might be thought that, since the realms of evolutionary selection and rational choice do not ordinarily overlap, no actual choice can be exercised between them. Still, in certain contexts—for example, software design—researchers have at times employed a kind of artificial evolutionary selection as an alternative to explicit optimization.
5. The specific numbers in the Prisoners' Dilemma matrix are those used in the famous tournaments conducted by Robert Axelrod (Axelrod 1984, p. 8). The numbers in the other two matrices have been designed to correspond.
6. Tender Trap (Hirshleifer 1982, p. 14) somewhat resembles other payoff patterns known as the Assurance Game and Stag Hunt.
7. Many more payoff environments exist than the very few considered here. Even counting only the matrices with four distinct levels of payoff to each player—i.e., excluding ties—there are 78 essentially distinct 2×2 patterns (Rapoport & Guyer 1966). Allowing for ties increases the number substantially, and the range of possibilities becomes mind-boggling when more strategy options are allowed (e.g., 3×3 matrices). And of course all this is within the context of two-party games; with three or more players the number of possible situation increases almost unimaginably. ('Parental manipulation', as described in an earlier footnote, is an example of an interaction involving at least three parties: one parent and two offspring.)

   Within the set of two-person 2×2 matrices, the symmetry restriction reduces the number of possibilities. On this basis, and ruling out certain other patterns as well, Heckathorn (1996) boils down the number of patterns to just five—essentially our three, plus two others that could not be covered here. (In contrast, when it comes to explicit game-theoretic modeling, with a few important exceptions the sociobiological literature deals only with the Prisoners' Dilemma environment.)
8. What is here termed evolutionary equilibrium is often referred to by biologists as an Evolutionarily Stable Strategy or ESS (Maynard Smith 1982), where the strategy can be pure or mixed. (Unless indicated to the contrary, only pure strategies will be dealt with in this paper.) The EE terminology is preferable, since only in special cases does the equilibrium take the form of a single strategy engaged in by all members of the population.
9. The symmetry assumption permits us to employ only the a_{ij} parameters in these equations, omitting Column's b_{ij} payoff elements.
10. If mixed strategies were also considered, there would also be a monomorphic ESS in the form of the mixture involving the more cooperative strategy with probability 1/3 and the other with probability 2/3.
11. At a Nash equilibrium, each player's choice is a 'best response' to the opponent's strategy. I pass over some subtle intellectual issues about the nature of rationality and how it relates to the Nash equilibrium concept. One approach to the NE, in fact, justifies it not so much as the 'eductive' outcome of rational play but rather as the 'evolutive' consequence of a trial-and-error process (Binmore 1992).
12. In Chicken, at the cross-over proportion p^* the two strategies have equal payoffs. And it is a feature of all mixed-strategy Nash equilibria that each element of a player's mixture yields the same payoff—else he would shift out of the mixture to whichever element thereof had highest payoff.
13. Consider a sexual haploid. (Sexual diploids have two genes at each locus, one inherited from the father and one from the mother. A sexual haploid has only one gene at each locus, equally likely to have been inherited from father or mother. Thinking in terms of the latter avoids complications associated with dominant versus recessive genes.) Starting with a hypothetical non-helping EE, imagine a mutation in the form of a new help-your-sibling gene. In the interaction between two offspring of a mutant organism, if one sibling bears the new gene, there is a 50% chance that the other does so as well. Hence, from the point of view of the gene, any benefit conferred on the recipient sibling would be counted, to the extent of 50%, in calculating the fitness of the mutant helping gene in comparison with the incumbent non-helping gene at that locus. (If the helping gene were not initially rare, there would be a more than 50% chance that the second sibling carries it, having possibly inherited it from the other parent. But it is only the 'rare gene' case that is relevant in determining when the mutant helping gene can invade a previous non-helping EE.) I thank T. C. Bergstrom for clarifying my thinking on this score.

14. It is important to note that PD matrices cannot always be put into cost-benefit form, because the costs and benefits of helping may depend on what the recipient is doing as well. In the PD matrix of Table 1, for example, the cost to Row of moving from lower-right to upper-right is not the same as the cost to him of moving from lower-left to upper-left. (I thank an anonymous referee of this journal for this point.)
15. This discussion, applying once again to sexual haploids, is adapted from a development in Hirshleifer (1978) based upon Charnov (1977).
16. Comparative studies of different protocols are quite rare in the game-theoretic literature. One important exception is Brams (1993).
17. Reciprocity brings to mind the institutions of contract and market exchange. These forms of interaction involve a variety of possible negotiation protocols too complex to be examined here. In addition, owing to the need for enforcement, contract and market exchange typically constitute games with three or more players and so are beyond the scope of the present paper. (Some further comments on negotiation and exchange will be offered below.)
18. This form of reciprocity corresponds to the 'Tit for Tat' strategy that has received a great deal of attention in the sociobiological literature (see below).
19. Up to eight distinct single-strategy EE's might coexist, as many as $8 \times 7/2 = 28$ EEs involving mixtures of two strategies, etc.
20. For a critique of these claims see Martinez Coll and Hirshleifer (1991). Some qualifying statements also appear in Axelrod (1984), pp. 176–177.
21. Contra occasional suggestions in Axelrod (1984), for example, p. 190.
22. See, e.g., Dugatkin (1990). For the PD environment and the multiple-round simultaneous-move protocol, Boyd and Lorberbaum (1987) have shown that no single strategy can ever be an EE.
23. The relation among ranchers, rustlers, and bounty-hunters is somewhat like the children's game of Rock-Paper-Scissors. When ranchers preponderate, it is most profitable to be a rustler. When rustlers are very numerous, it's advantageous to be a bounty-hunter. And when almost everyone is a bounty-hunter, it pays best to be a rancher.
24. On the other hand, for unfavorable values of the parameters an interior solution involving all three strategies might not be viable. If bounty-hunting were too ineffective ever to be profitable, the EE might consist of ranchers and rustlers only.
25. Meta-stable equilibria are strategy combinations that persist more or less unchanged over a considerable number of generations, but eventually succumb to the invasion of 'mutants' who find a basis for entry.
26. This was possible because the simulations allowed for 'noise', that is, for the possibility that a TFT player misperceives and therefore responds incorrectly to the opponent's prior move. Absent noise, in a hypothetical all-TFT world everyone would score 3 per move, and it is not possible to do better. But the all-TFT payoffs decline considerably with even modest levels of noise.
27. Recall that we have heretofore allowed TFT to play a role only in the single-round sequential-play or the multiple-round simultaneous-play protocols.
28. Parental manipulation, discussed in an earlier endnote, is an example of such control.
29. This discussion is an adaptation of a development in Brams (1993).

References cited

Alexander, Richard D. 1974. The evolution of social behavior. Annual Review of Ecology and Systematics 5:325–383.

Alexander, Richard D. 1979. Darwinism and human affairs. University of Washington Press, Seattle.

Axelrod, Robert. 1984. The evolution of cooperation. Basic Books, New York.

Bergstrom, Theodore C. 1995. On the evolution of altruistic ethical rules for siblings. American Economic Review 85:58–81.

Bergstrom, Theodore C. & Oded Stark. 1993. How altruism can prevail in an evolutionary environment. American Economic Review, Papers and Proceedings 83:149–155.

Binmore, Ken. 1992. Fun and games. D.C. Heath and Co., Lexington.

Boyd, Robert & Jeffrey P. Lorberbaum. 1987. No pure strategy is evolutionarily stable in the repeated Prisoner's Dilemma game. Nature 274:58–59.

Brams, Steven J. 1993. Theory of moves. American Scientist 81:562–570.

Charnov, Eric L. 1977. An elementary treatment of the genetical theory of kin-selection. Journal of Theoretical Biology 66:541–550.

Darwin, Charles. 1871. The descent of man, and selection in relation to sex. John Murray, London. [Modern Library re-issue of second 1874 edition.]

Dawkins, Richard. 1976. The selfish gene. Oxford University Press, Oxford.

Dugatkin, Lee Alan. 1990. N-person games and the evolution of co-operation: a model based on predator inspection in fish. Journal of Theoretical Biology 142:123–135.

Frank, Robert H. 1988. Passions within reason: the strategic role of the emotions. W.W. Norton, New York.

Hamilton, William D. 1964. The genetical evolution of social behaviour, I. Journal of Theoretical Biology 7:1–16.

Hamilton, William D. 1970. Selfish and spiteful behaviour in an evolutionary model. Nature 228:1218–1220.

Heckathorn, Douglas D. 1996. The dynamics of collective action. American Sociological Review 61:250–277.

Hirshleifer, Jack. 1978. Natural economy versus political economy. Journal of Social and Biological Structures 1:319–337.

Hirshleifer, Jack. 1982. Evolutionary models in economics and law: cooperation versus conflict strategies. Research in Law and Economics 4:1–60.

Hirshleifer, Jack & Juan Carlos Martinez Coll. 1988. What strategies can support the evolutionary emergence of cooperation? Journal of Conflict Resolution 32:367–398.

Lomborg, Bjorn. 1996. Nucleus and shield: the evolution of social structure in the iterated Prisoner's Dilemma. American Sociological Review 61:278–307.

Martinez Coll, Juan Carlos & Jack Hirshleifer. 1991. The limits of reciprocity. Rationality and Society 3:35–64.

Maynard Smith, John. 1978. The evolution of behavior. Scientific American 239:176–192.

Maynard Smith, John. 1982. Evolution and the theory of games. Cambridge University Press, Cambridge.

Rapoport, Anatol & Melvin Guyer. 1966. A taxonomy of 2 × 2 games. General Systems 11:203–214.

Ridley, Matt. 1996. The origins of virtue. Penguin Books, New York.

Tooby, John & Leda Cosmides. 1985. Friendship and the banker's paradox: other pathways to the evolution of adaptations for altruism. Proceedings of the British Academy 88:119–143.

Trivers, Robert. 1985. Social evolution. Benjamin/Cummings Publishing Co., Menlo Park.

West Eberhard, Mary Jane. 1975. The evolution of social behavior by kin selection. Quarterly Review of Biology 50:1–32.

Williams, George C. 1966. Adaptation and natural selection: a critique of some current evolutionary thought. Princeton University Press, Princeton.

Wilson, David Sloan & Elliot Sober. 1994. Reintroducing group selection to the human behavioral sciences. The Behavioral and Brain Sciences 17:585–608.

[4]

Credible Commitments: Using Hostages to Support Exchange

By OLIVER E. WILLIAMSON*

Credible commitments and credible threats share the following common attribute: both appear mainly in conjunction with irreversible, specialized investments. But whereas credible commitments are undertaken in support of alliances and to promote exchange, credible threats appear in the context of conflict and rivalry.[1] The former involve reciprocal acts designed to safeguard a relationship, while the latter are unilateral efforts to preempt an advantage. Efforts to support exchange generally operate in the service of efficiency; preemptive investments, by contrast, are commonly antisocial. Both are plainly important to politics and economics, but the study of credible commitments is arguably the more fundamental of the two.

Interest in credible threats is much more widespread and the credible threat literature is more fully developed,[2] however, than is the interest and economic literature dealing with credible commitments. This disparity is consistent with the treatment accorded to each in Thomas Schelling's classic essay (1956) on bargaining, where the main emphasis is placed on tactics by which one party can realize an advantage in relation to a rival by credibly "tieing ones hands." But Schelling also, albeit briefly, addresses the matter of promise. He observes in this connection that "Bargaining may have to concern itself with an 'incentive' system as well as the division of gains" (p. 300) and adds in a footnote that the exchange of hostages served incentive purposes in an earlier age (p. 300, fn. 17).

That the study of credible commitments has been relatively neglected is explained by the assumption, common to both law and economics, that the legal system enforces promises in a knowledgeable, sophisticated, and low-cost way. Albeit instructive, this convenient assumption is commonly contradicted by the facts—on which account additional or alternative modes of governance have arisen. Bilateral efforts to create and offer hostages are an interesting and, as it turns out, economically important illustration. Absent a recognition and appreciation for the merits of "private ordering," the suggestion that hostages are used to support contemporary exchange is apt to be dismissed as fanciful. I submit, however, that not only are the economic equivalents of hostages widely used to effect credible commitments, but failure to recognize the economic pur-

*Department of Economics, Yale University, New Haven, CT 06520. This paper has benefited from the comments of participants in the Sloan Foundation Workshops in Transaction Cost Economics at the University of Pennsylvania and the University of Minnesota, and from seminar presentations at Oxford University, Williams College, and Yale University. Comments by Dennis Carlton, Frank Easterbrook, Benjamin Klein, Scott Masten, Michael Riordan, David Sappington, Richard Stewart, and Lester Telser, and from the referees of this journal are gratefully acknowledged. Research support from the National Science Foundation is gratefully acknowledged.

[1]It should be noted that I use the terms threat and commitment differently than do Curtis Eaton and Richard Lipsey (1981). They distinguish between empty and credible threats and use the term commitment to refer to the latter. I submit that the language of rivalry is well serviced by reference to threats; and I suggest that the term commitment be reserved to describe exchange. Thus both credible and noncredible threats would be distinguished in assessing rivalry. Similarly, credible and noncredible commitments are distinguished in evaluating exchange. Alliances complicate matters in that these are organized in relation to another party. This could be wholly beneficial, but it need not be. Thus suppliers could form an alliance in relation to buyers, with possible antisocial results. Credible commitments which simultaneously support exchange and promote alliances thus sometimes pose tradeoffs.

[2]Recent applications within economics involve investments in specific capital undertaken for the purpose of impeding new entry (Avinash Dixit, 1979; 1982; Eaton and Lipsey, 1981; Richard Schmalensee, 1981). For a discussion of reputation effects and quasi credibility in the economics literature, see David Kreps and Robert Wilson (1982), Paul Milgrom and John Roberts (1982), and myself (1982b).

poses served by hostages has been responsible for repeated policy error.

The private ordering approach to the study of contract is sketched in Section I. A simple model for assessing the efficiency ramifications of alternative contracts, one of which involves hostages, is developed in Section II. The model demonstrates that the investments made by suppliers are influenced by the incentives experienced by buyers. Incentive complications that reach beyond the model are discussed in Section III. Applications of the argument to unilateral and to bilateral exchange are set out in Sections IV and V. Some evidence bearing on petroleum exchanges and public policy attitudes that relate thereto are examined in Section VI.

I. Private Ordering

A. *Contracting Traditions*

Most studies of exchange assume that efficacious rules of law regarding contract disputes are in place and that these are applied by the courts in an informed, sophisticated, and low-cost way. These assumptions are convenient, in that lawyers and economists are relieved of the need to examine the variety of ways by which individual parties to exchange "contract out of or away from" the governance structures of the state by devising private orderings. A division of effort thus arises whereby economists are preoccupied with the economic benefits that accrue to specialization and exchange, while legal specialists focus on the technicalities of contract law.[3]

The "legal centralism" tradition reflects this orientation. It maintains that "disputes require 'access' to a forum external to the original social setting of the dispute...[and that] remedies will be provided as prescribed in some body of authoritative learning and dispensed by experts who operate under the auspices of the state" (Marc Galanter, 1981, p. 1). The facts, however, disclose otherwise. Most disputes, including many of those which, under current rules, could be brought to a court, are resolved by avoidance, self-help, and the like (Galanter, p. 2).

The unreality of the assumptions of legal centralism can be defended by reference to the fruitfulness of the pure exchange model. This is not disputed here. My concern with this tradition is that the law and economics of private ordering have been pushed into the background as a consequence. This is unfortunate, since "In many instances the participants can devise more satisfactory solutions to their disputes than can professionals constrained to apply general rules on the basis of limited knowledge of the dispute" (Galanter, p. 4).[4]

Four distinct, albeit related, literatures within economics[5] have developed over the past decade in which private ordering is expressly or implicitly featured: the incentive compatibility literature (Leonid Hurwicz, 1972); the literature on the economics of internal organization (Ronald Coase, 1937; Kenneth Arrow, 1963, 1974; myself, 1971, 1975, 1979; Benjamin Klein et al., 1978; David Teece, 1982; Eugene Fama and Michael Jensen, 1983); the financial economics literature dealing with bonding (Joseph Stiglitz, 1974; Jensen and William Meckling, 1976; Sanford Grossman and Oliver Hart, 1982); and the study of self-enforcing agreements (Lester Telser, 1981; Klein and Keith Leffler, 1981). The first two of these have been reviewed elsewhere (Hurwicz, 1973; myself, 1981, 1982b). The third takes issue

[3]Lawyers do not have a monopoly on refining contractual rules. For recent contributions by economists, see Peter Diamond and Eric Maskin (1979) and Steven Shavell (1980). Such an economic approach to contract focuses on the technicalities of legal rules. The approach taken here holds that even refined rules of law are costly to implement, whence private ordering is widely employed.

[4]Galanter elaborates as follows: "The variability of preferences and of situations, compared to the small number of things that can be taken into account by formal rules..., and the loss of meaning in transforming the dispute into professional categories suggest limits on the desirability of conforming outcomes to authoritative rules" (1981, p. 4).

[5]There is also a long legal tradition in which contract as legal rule is disputed. Karl Llewellyn's views regarding "contract as framework" (1931) are especially important. Recent significant contributions include Stewart Macaulay (1963) and Ian Macneil (1974). For a discussion, see my 1979 article.

with the Modigliani-Miller theorem that the firm's production plan is independent of its financial structure.[6] The fourth deals with contracting in intermediate product markets and expressly relies on private ordering.

Telser characterizes a self-enforcing agreement as one which, if "one party violates the terms the only recourse of the other is to terminate the agreement" (p. 27). Contrary to legal centralism, the courts and other third parties are assumed away. Klein and Leffler are explicit on this: "we assume throughout... that contracts are not enforceable by the government or any third party" (p. 616). Commercial contract law in late nineteenth-century Taiwan evidently approximated this condition (Rosser Brockman, 1980). Stewart Macaulay's remarks about the informality of contract in business are likewise in this spirit: "Often businessmen do not feel they have 'a contract'—rather they have 'an order.' They speak of 'cancelling the order' rather than 'breaching our contract'" (1963, p. 61).

To be sure, pure private ordering is extreme. As Robert Mnookin and Lewis Kornhauser state, private ordering invariably operates in "the shadow of the law" (1979).[7] It suffices for my purposes to argue that the incentives of private parties to devise bilateral contractual safeguards is a function of the efficacy of court adjudication, and that this varies with the attributes of transactions. Specifically the courts experience serious disabilities with respect to the transactions of the kinds herein described.

B. *Some Attributes of this Article*

This article examines self-enforcing agreements in transaction cost terms. Contracting agents are thus assumed to be subject to bounded rationality and, where circumstances permit, are given to opportunism.[8]

Although hostages can have both *ex ante* (screening) and *ex post* (bonding) effects, the *ex post* contract execution consequences are of principal interest here.[9] This is also the focus of the self-enforcing agreement literature. Additionally, like both Telser and Klein-Leffler, the intertemporal contracts of concern here feature both uncertainty and transaction-specific capital. But in other respects there are important differences.

Thus, whereas Telser deals with "a sequence of transactions over time such that the ending date is unknown and uncertain" (p. 30), because any finite sequence of transactions using his model will unravel (p. 29), the transactions that I consider can be (indeed, normally are) finite. Furthermore, the role of transaction specific capital is more explicit and fully developed in this article than in Telser's.

The self-enforcing contracts studied by Klein and Leffler are likewise of indefinite rather than finite duration. The hostage model is further distinguishable from Klein-Leffler in that 1) they deal with quality un-

[6]Grossman and Hart make the interesting distinction between a bonding and a signaling equilibrium: in the former, agents communicate "their endogenous intentions, while the latter involves agents communicating their exogenous characteristics" (p. 110). Put differently, bonding has reference to the incentives of agents at the contract execution stage (an *ex post* condition), whereas signaling involves inferring the directly unobservable *ex ante* attributes of agents, which are fully prespecified. Thus whereas Stephen Ross (1977) uses the debt-equity ratio to signal objective (exogenous) differences in the quality of management, Grossman and Hart use debt to *precommit* managers to a course of action whereby closer *ex post* adherence to profit maximization is induced. Specifically, debt becomes an instrument by which managers place themselves at hazard, in recognition of which the financial market places a higher value on the firm (Grossman and Hart, p. 130). Since managers are assumed to benefit from this higher market valuation (Grossman and Hart, p. 109), they self-consciously accept the hazards of bankruptcy which debt financing poses.

[7]Galanter suggests that a better way to characterize the study of contract is "law in the shadow of indigenous ordering" (p. 23). There is a good deal to be said for this. The main point is that a place for law is properly provided in any comprehensive study of contract.

[8]Whereas previously I have emphasized firm versus market governance, here I focus strictly on market-mediated exchange. The governance issue of interest thus involves choice among alternative contracts.

[9]*Ex ante* screening attributes are briefly examined in an earlier version of this paper (1982a, pp. 6–9). The assessment of a screening equilibrium is complex, however, and is not central to the main argument. See Michael Rothschild and Stiglitz (1976) and John Riley (1979a, b) for a discussion of screening equilibrium issues.

certainty in final goods markets, whereas I assume that quality is known and focus on stochastic demand in intermediate product markets;[10] 2) their "fundamental theoretical result" involves the assurance of quality through the sacrifice of "minimum-cost production techniques" (pp. 618, 628–29), while the hostage model involves no such sacrifice (indeed, the use of hostages to support exchange encourages investment in specific asset technologies which have *lower* expected costs);[11] and 3) suppliers in their model are confronted neither with expropriation nor adaptation hazards, while these are both of concern to me. More generally, the hostage model and imagery have application to a quite different set of contractual circumstances than the analysis of quality assurance contemplates.

II. The Hostage Model

The simple hostage model serves to illuminate both unilateral and bilateral exchange, permits the concept of specific capital to be extended beyond earlier uses, and clarifies how costs should be described in assessing exchange. While it is primitive and suggestive, rather than refined and definitive, it serves as a paradigmatic wedge by which the importance of private ordering is exposed and is easily made the vehicle for further analysis.

A. *Technologies and Costs*

The assessment of alternative contracts will be facilitated by assuming that the product in question can be produced by either of two technologies. One is a general purpose technology; the second is a special purpose technology. The special purpose technology requires greater investment in transaction specific durable assets and, as described below, is more efficient for servicing steady-state demands.

Costs that are highly specific to a transaction have two attributes: they are incurred in advance of the contemplated exchange; and their value in alternative uses, or by alternative users, is greatly reduced.[12] As Klein and Leffler put it, the irreversible, nonsalvageable part of an advance commitment is sunk (p. 619). It is common to think of this as applying to physical plant or accounting costs that are reported as fixed, but this is not the critical distinction. Thus investments in labor (transaction specific human capital) can be highly specific. And many costs that for accounting purposes are reported to be fixed are in fact nonspecific, hence can be recovered (salvaged) by redeployment. Durable but mobile assets such as general purpose trucks or airplanes are illustrations.

The two technologies in question will thus be described in value realization terms. The value that can be realized by redeploying variable and fixed costs will be given by v. The nonsalvageable value of advance commitments will be denoted by k. The two technologies can thus be described as T_1: the general purpose technology, all advance commitments of which are salvageable, the redeployable unit operating costs of which are v_1; and T_2: the special purpose technol-

[10] My discussion of franchising in Section IV.C parallels Klein-Leffler and assumes that quality uncertainty is responsible for a demand externality. The hostage model developed in Section II does not apply directly to this case, but the spirit carries over in three respects: 1) franchisees, like buyers, are given a choice among alternative contracts; 2) the decision to expose specific assets is deliberately taken because this has superior incentive effects; and 3) the sunk cost technology is *more* efficient, which vitiates the inefficiency tradeoff that is central to the Klein-Leffler paper.

[11] Contrary to the argument advanced by Klein and Leffler, total costs need not increase in a quality assurance model because investments are shifted from a reversible (fixed cost) to an irreversible (sunk cost) technology. Thus instead of a general purpose building of nondescript design, the producer could construct a building with a distinctive "signature." The durable investments could be the same, but the alternative value that can be realized from the second building might be much lower. The long-term commitments that are signaled by this second design relieve customers of quality shading hazards, which is the central issue with which Klein and Leffler are concerned.

[12] Klein et al. use the term "appropriable quasi rent" to describe this condition. Use vs. user distinctions are relevant in this connection: "The quasi-rent value of the asset is the excess of its value over its salvage value, that is, its value in its next best *use* to another renter. The potentially appropriable specialized portion of the quasi-rent is the portion, if any, in excess of its value to the second highest-valuing *user*" (p. 298).

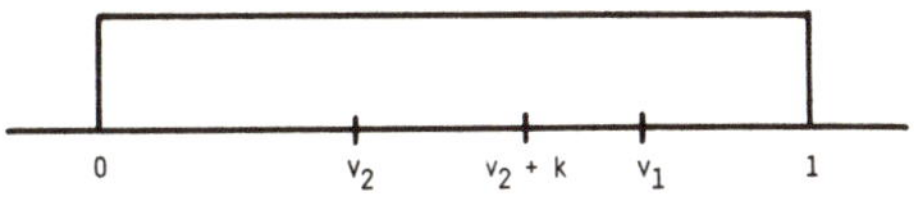

FIGURE 1

ogy, the nonsalvageable value of advance commitments of which are k and the redeployable unit operating costs of which are v_2.

B. *Contracting*

There are two periods. Orders are placed in the first, and production if any occurs in the second. Buyers can either take delivery or refuse it. Demand is stochastic. The gross value to buyers is assumed to be uniformly distributed over the interval [0, 1], and the quantity demanded at every price will be assumed to be constant, which it will be convenient to set equal to unity. Sunk costs, if any, are incurred in the first period. Inasmuch as sunk costs are incurred for certain while the decision to incur redeployable costs is contingent on the buyer's decision to confirm or cancel an order, a choice between technologies is interesting only if $k + v_2 < v_1$. The demand and cost relations are set out in Figure 1.

1. *Net Benefits*

The criterion by which decisions to take or refuse delivery will be evaluated is that of joint profit maximization. Feasibility and/or bureaucratic disabilities aside, vertical integration assuredly accomplishes the joint profit-maximization result. Thus the reference condition for evaluating contracts will be an integrated firm with two divisions, a producing division and a marketing division. The producing division has access to the same two technologies described above, one of which involves specific assets, the other of which does not. Whichever technology is employed, product is transferred between divisions at marginal cost.

That $k + v_2 < v_1$ does not establish that the special purpose technology (T_2) is the more efficient. Whether it is or not depends on a net benefit calculation. The expected net benefits of using the general purpose technology (T_1) are given by the product of the probability that the integrated firm will decide to produce and the average net benefits that are realized when product is supplied. The integrated firm will decide to produce only if the realized demand price exceeds marginal costs, whence the probability of production under T_1 is $1 - v_1$. The mean net benefits during production periods are $(1 - v_1)/2$, whence the expected net benefits for technology T_1 are

$$(1) \quad b_1 = (1 - v_1)(1 - v_1)/2 = (1 - v_1)^2/2.$$

The expected net benefits for the specific asset technology (T_2) are found similarly. Again, the integrated firm will produce whenever realized demand price exceeds marginal costs. Expected net receipts, however, must be reduced by the amount of the earlier investment in specific assets, k, in computing expected net benefits. Thus we have

$$(2) \quad b_2 = (1 - v_2)(1 - v_2)/2 - k = (1 - v_2)^2/2 - k,$$

where the first term is the expected excess of revenue over out-of-pocket costs.

The specific asset technology will be selected only if $b_2 > b_1$, which requires that

$$(3) \quad k < (1 - v_2)^2/2 - (1 - v_1)^2/2.$$

2. *Autonomous Contracting*

Assume that the inequality in (3) holds and consider the case of autonomous contracting between a buyer, who services final demand, and a producer, who manufactures the product. Assume that demand and production technologies are as described above. Efficient contracting relations are those that replicate the vertical integration result,[13]

[13] Here and throughout the remainder of this article I assume that exchange is governed by contract rather than by vertical integration. Vertical integration is thus used merely as a reference condition. That manufacturers do not integrate forward or distributors integrate backward can be explained on a number of

namely, 1) select the specific asset technology, and 2) produce and sell product whenever realized demand price exceeds v_2. Assume that both parties are risk neutral and that the production side of the industry is competitively organized. Whatever contracting relation is described, producers will be willing to supply if a break-even condition (expressed in expected value terms) can be projected.[14]

Recall that orders are placed in the first period. Specific assets, if any, are committed in the first period in anticipation of second-period supply. Whether second-period production actually occurs, however, is contingent on demand realizations. Buyers have the option of confirming or cancelling orders in the second period. Consider three contracting alternatives:

I. The buyer purchases specific assets and assigns them to whichever seller submits the lowest bid, p;

II. The producer makes the specific asset investment himself and receives a payment of $\bar{p}$ in the second period if the buyer confirms the order but nothing otherwise; and

III. The producer makes the specific asset investment himself and receives $\hat{p}$ from the buyer if the buyer confirms the order, is paid $\alpha h, 0 \leqslant \alpha \leqslant 1$, if the order is cancelled while the buyer pays $\hat{p}$ upon taking delivery and experiences a reduction in wealth of h if second-period delivery is cancelled.

The third scenario can be thought of as one where the buyer posts a hostage that he values in amount h, which hostage is delivered to the producer, who values it in amount αh if the order is cancelled.

The producer will break even under contracting relation I if he is compensated in amount v_2, which is his out of pocket cost, for each unit demanded. The low bidder will thus offer to supply product for $p = v_2$. Since the buyer's net benefits are maximized if he invests in the specific assets, and since product is transferred on marginal cost terms, this contract replicates the vertical integration relation. Contracts of type I are feasible, however, only if the specialized assets are mobile and the specificity is attributable to physical features (for example, specialized dies). Market procurement can then service the needs of the parties without posing hold-up problems by concentrating the ownership of the specific assets on the buyer (who then assigns them to the low bidder). Inasmuch as the buyer can reclaim the dies and, without cost, solicit new bids should contractual difficulties develop, type I contracts yield an efficient result.[15]

Attention hereafter will be focused on contracts II and III, the assumption being that asset specificity is of the human or dedicated asset kinds (see Part C, below). The autonomous buyer will confirm an order under contract II whenever realized demand price exceeds $\bar{p}$ but not otherwise. The producer will thus break even if $(1-\bar{p})\bar{p} - [(1-\bar{p})v_2 + k] = 0$, whence

$$\bar{p} = v_2 + k/(1-\bar{p}). \tag{4}$$

Product will thus be exchanged at a price that exceeds marginal cost under this contracting scenario.[16] Plainly if $\bar{p} \geqslant v_1$, the

grounds—one of which is that there are economies of scope at both stages, but that very different product mixes are needed to realize these scope economies at each stage.

[14]There is no problem in principle in allowing suppliers to extract positive profits as a condition of supply. The salient features of the hostage model are all preserved if, instead of an expected break-even condition, the supplier was assumed to realize expected profits of $\bar{\pi} > 0$ on each contract. Although final demands will be choked off as a consequence, the main features of the contractual argument survive.

[15]This ignores the possibility that suppliers will abuse the dies if ownership resides with the buyer.

[16]Conceivably $\bar{p}$ will exceed v_1, in which event the buyer who is contemplating contract II will prefer instead to purchase from sellers who use the general purpose technology. The comparison in the text implicitly assumes that $\bar{p} < v_1$. Also note that a standby technology that can be costlessly switched into and out of the product in question could effectively truncate demand at v_1. This would be true if potential middlemen could place orders to take product at v_1 from general purpose manufacturers, which orders could be costlessly cancelled (and general purpose assets redeployed) if demands fell below this value. I will arbitrarily assume that this is not feasible. The problem could, however, be reformulated by describing demand as uniformly distributed over the interval 0 to v_1, with v_1 having measure $1 - v_1$.

buyer is better off to scuttle contract II and purchase instead from producers who utilize the (inferior) variable cost technology T_1 (and will break even by supplying product on demand for a price of v_1).

The buyer will confirm an order under contract III whenever the realized demand price exceeds $\hat{p} - h$. Let $\hat{p} - h$ be denoted by m. The seller will then break even when $(1-m)\hat{p} + m\alpha h - [(1-m)v_2 + k] = 0$, whence

$$(5) \qquad \hat{p} = v_2 + (k - m\alpha h)/(1-m).$$

The case where $h = k$ and $\alpha = 1$ is one where the buyer gives up wealth in amount of the investment in specific assets in cancellation states and this is delivered to the producer who values it in amount k. Under these circumstances, (5) becomes

$$(5') \qquad \hat{p} = v_2 + k.$$

Since the buyer places an order whenever demand exceeds $m = \hat{p} - h$, this yields the result that $m = v_2$, whence orders will be placed whenever demand exceeds v_2, which is the efficient (marginal cost) supply criterion.

The buyer's net benefits under contracting scheme III are

$$(6) \quad b_3 = (1-m)\left[\left(m + \frac{1-m}{2}\right) - \hat{p}\right] - mh,$$

where $(1-m)$ is the probability of placing an order, $m + (1-m)/2$ is the expected demand price for all orders that are placed, $\hat{p}$ is the payment in demand confirmation states to the producer, and h is the wealth sacrifice in cancellation states (which occur with probability m). Under the assumptions that $h = k$ and $\alpha = 1$, this reduces to

$$(6') \qquad b_3 = (1-v_2)^2/2 - k,$$

which is identical to the net benefit calculation for technology T_2 under the vertical integration reference condition (see equation (2)).

Accordingly, contracting scheme III accompanied by the stipulations that $h = k$ and $\alpha = 1$ replicates the efficient investment and supply conditions of vertical integration. Problems arise, however, if $h < k$ or $\alpha < 1$. The disadvantage, moreover, accrues entirely to the buyer—since the seller, by assumption, breaks even whatever contracting relation obtains. Thus although *after* the contract has been made, the buyer would prefer to offer a lesser-valued hostage and cares not whether the hostage is valued by the producer, at the time of the contract he will wish to assure the producer that a hostage of k for which the producer realizes full value ($\alpha = 1$) will be transferred in nonexchange states. Failure to make this commitment will result in an increase in the contract price. Thus, whereas producers who are concerned only with *ex ante* screening can tolerate values of α less than one—see the discussion of ugly princesses in Section III.A, below—this is not the case at all when *ex post* opportunism is the concern. If the producer is not indifferent, as between two princesses, each of whom is valued identically by the buyer, the producer's preferences now need to be taken into account.[17]

To summarize, therefore, it can be observed that contract I mimics vertical integration, but only under special asset specificity conditions; contract II is inferior; and contract III yields the vertical integration result if $h = k$ and $\alpha = 1$. Furthermore, note that an important feature of contract III is that the buyer takes delivery in all demand states for which realized demand exceeds $m = \hat{p} - h$. Since the supplier is always paid $\hat{p}$ upon execution, the buyer sometimes takes delivery when his realized receipts (upon resale of the product) are less than $\hat{p}$. This does not, however, signal inefficiency, since orders are never confirmed when realized demand price falls below marginal cost (v_2). Indeed, it is precisely because of the hostage feature that efficiency is realized and contract III is superior to contract II.

[17]Placing an upper bound of unity on α precludes the possibility that the supplier values the hostages more than does the buyer. Potential gains from trade would exist for all hostages for which α exceeds unity. A case for negatively valued hostages could be made in the context of ugly princesses (see Section III, Part A).

C. *Dedicated Assets*

Three types of asset specificity have been recognized in earlier discussions: site specificity—as where successive stations are located in a cheek-by-jowl relation to each other so as to economize on inventory and transportation expenses;[18] physical asset specificity—such as specialized dies that are required to produce a component; and human asset specificity that arises in a learning-by-doing fashion. A fourth type, previously unremarked but nevertheless important for some transactions, needs to be added: dedicated assets. Such assets represent a discrete investment in plant. Although these assets add to the firm's generalized (as contrasted with special purpose) production capability, the investment would not be undertaken but for the prospect of selling a significant amount of product to a specific customer. As with other types of asset specificity, dedicated assets lose value if employed in alternative uses (or by or to service alternative users). Dedicated assets thus are those that are put in place contingent upon particular supply agreements and, should such contracts be prematurely terminated, would result in significant excess capacity.

III. Engaging the Supplier

Suppliers are passive instruments in this model. They are indifferent among contracts, since their expected profits are the same (zero) whichever choice the buyer makes. What drives the argument is that buyers can secure better terms only by relieving producers of demand cancellation penalties. Buyers cannot have their cake (product supplied by the efficient technology at a price of $\hat{p}$) and eat it too (cancel without cost).

Inasmuch as optimality is realized if $h=k$ and $\alpha=1$, the ideal hostage would appear to be an offer of generalized purchasing power: money. A security bond in amount $h=k$ would serve this purpose. That the argument does not terminate here is because such an arrangement does not assuredly engage the interests and cooperation of the supplier. Three reasons can be adduced for this condition: contrived cancellation, uncertain valuation, and incomplete contracting. All are a consequence of joining bounded rationality with opportunism.

A. *Supplier Opportunism*

1. *Contrived Cancellation*

The issue of contrived cancellation has been addressed by Kenneth Clarkson, Roger Miller, and Timothy Muris in their discussion of refusal of the courts to enforce stipulated damage clauses where breach has been deliberately induced (1978, pp. 366–72). Induced breach could arise where a party intentionally withholds relevant information, yet complies with the letter of the contract. Or it might involve perfunctory fulfillment of obligations where more resourceful cooperation is needed (Clarkson et al., pp. 371–72). In either case, induced breach is costly to detect and/or prove (Clarkson et al., p. 371).

This explanation for selective enforcement of liquidated damage clauses has troubled other legal scholars (Richard Posner, 1979, p. 290), but a more satisfactory explanation has yet to be advanced. At the very least, the Clarkson et al. treatment reflects a sensitivity to the subtleties of opportunism—on which account private ordering is more complicated than the bare bones hostage model would suggest. Among other things, the expropriation hazard to which they refer may explain the use of ugly princesses.

Thus suppose that demand uncertainties are negligible, whence order cancellation hazards can be disregarded. Suppose further, however, that buyers differ in credit risk respects, and that producers would, if they could, refuse sales to poor risks. Assuming that the difference between good and poor risks is sufficiently great that a separating equilibrium is feasible,[19] producers could demand hostages (or, put differently, good risks could offer hostages) as a way by which to

[18] Common ownership is the preponderant response to site specificity. Close proximity is desired because of inventory or related processing cost (for example, thermal economy) savings. Once sited, the assets in question are highly immobile—which is to say that the setup and/or relocation costs are great.

[19] See fn. 9.

screen. Given, moreover, that the only use to which hostages are put is as a screen, a value of $\alpha = 0$ would accomplish this purpose without exposing the buyer to an expropriation hazard (based, say, on a legal technicality). Specifically, a king who is known to cherish two daughters equally and is asked, for screening purposes, to post a hostage is better advised to offer the ugly one.

2. *Uncertain Valuation*

The model assumes that the value of the specific investment (k) is well specified. This need not be the case. Indeed, it may be difficult for buyers to ascertain whether the investments made in response to first-period orders are of the amount or of the kind that producers claim. This is not a serious problem if the production side of the market is competitively organized and fly-by-night concerns can be disregarded. Where, however, this cannot be presumed, the possibility that buyers will be expropriated arises. Producers may feign delivery competence (claim to have invested in specific assets in amount k but only committed $k' < k$) and expropriate bonds for which $h = k$ by contriving breach or invoking a technicality.

This hazard is especially great if the producer, who retains possession of the assets for which specificity is claimed, can preserve asset values by integrating forward into the buyer's market upon taking possession of the hostage. Even though the producer is poorly suited to perform successor stage functions, the possession of specialized stage I assets effectively reduces the costs that would otherwise attend de novo stage II entry.

To be sure, the buyer who offers a hostage and recognizes a risk of contrived expropriation will adjust the original terms to reflect this. Specifically, contracts supported by hostages for which expropriation risks are believed to be great will command less than those where these same hazards are believed to be lower. But this is to concede that, absent additional safeguards, neither the transfer of product on marginal cost terms nor the efficient level and kind of investment will assuredly attend contracts of type III. Deeper governance issues than those contemplated by the simple model are evidently posed.

3. *Incomplete Contracts/Haggling*

For the reasons and in the ways described elsewhere (see my 1975 study, pp. 20–36; 91–94), complex contracts are invariably incomplete and many are maladaptive. The reasons are two: many contingencies are unforeseen (and even unforeseeable); and the adaptations to those contingencies that have been recognized and for which adjustments have been agreed to are often mistaken—possibly because the parties acquire deeper knowledge of production and demand during contract execution than they possessed at the outset (Richard Nelson and Sidney Winter, 1982, pp. 96–136). Instrumental gap filling, thus, is an important part of contract execution. Whether this is done easily and effectively, or if instead reaching successive agreements on adaptations and their implementation is costly, makes a huge difference in evaluating the efficacy of contracts.

Thus even if contrived breach hazards could be disregarded, producers who are entirely open and candid about contract execution may nevertheless be in a position to haggle—thereby to expropriate sellers—because contracts are incomplete or maladaptive. Specialized governance structures that have the purpose and effect of promoting harmonious adaptations and preserving the continuity of exchange relations arise in response to this condition. Knowledgeable third parties and reciprocal exposure of specialized assets are two possibilities.

B. *Protective Governance Structures*

1. *Arbitration*

Institutions that have the capacity to evaluate disputes in a more knowledgeable way than the courts may arise in this way. The parties, for example, may agree to submit disputes over contract execution to arbitrators who have specialized knowledge of the industry. Lon Fuller's remarks concerning procedural differences between arbitration and litigation are instructive:

> ...there are open to the arbitrator... quick methods of education not open to the courts. An arbitrator will frequently interrupt the examination of witnesses with a request that the parties

> educate him to the point where he can understand the testimony being received. The education can proceed informally, with frequent interruptions by the arbitrator, and by informed persons on either side, when a point needs clarification. Sometimes there will be arguments across the table, occasionally even within each of the separate camps. The end result will usually be a clarification that will enable everyone to proceed more intelligently with the case. [1963, pp. 11–12]

Many agreements which, were it not for arbitration, would be regarded as excessively hazardous can, in this way, be reached and implemented.[20]

2. *Reciprocal Exposure*

An alternative way by which to protect contracts against expropriation is to expand the contractual relation. One way of accomplishing this is for buyer and seller to devise a *mutual reliance relation*. Thus suppose that the buyer does not post a hostage as such, but himself invests in specific capital that has value only in conjunction with servicing final demands for the product in question. Assume that these are valued in amount k''. The buyer then has the incentive to take delivery as long as realized demand exceeds $\hat{p} - k''$. If $k'' = k$, this yields the marginal cost supply result,[21] and the producer will be satisfied with the buyer's incentives. Or suppose that producer and buyer engage in reciprocal trade. Specifically, suppose that the producer contracts to procure product from the buyer, the supply of which requires the buyer to invest in specific assets in amount k'''. Each party to this reciprocal trade will experience appropriate incentives if 1) $k''' = k$, 2) demand variation in the two markets is perfectly correlated, and 3) each party has the option to cancel an order if a cancellation notice is received from his opposite.[22] As discussed in Section V, bilateral trades (reciprocity; swaps) can sometimes be made to approximate these conditions.

IV. Unilateral Trading

The argument that buyers can affect the terms and manner of supply by offering (or refusing to offer) hostages has ramifications for Robinson-Patman price discrimination and to an understanding of franchising and two-part pricing.

A. *Robinson-Patman*

The Robinson-Patman Act has been interpreted as an effort "to deprive a large buyer of [discounts] except to the extent that a lower price could be justified by reason of a seller's diminished costs due to *quantity* manufacture, delivery, or sale, or by reason of the seller's good faith effort to meet a competitor's equally low price."[23] Plainly, that $\hat{p}$ is less than $\bar{p}$ in the hostage model has neither quantity nor meeting competition origins. Neither is it contrary to the public interest. Indeed, it would be inefficient and unwarranted for a producer to charge the same price to two customers who order an identical amount of product, but only one of which offers a hostage, if 1) investments in specialized assets are required to support the transactions in question, or 2) if, because of a refusal to make a credible commitment, transactions of the second kind are produced

[20] Labor unions can help to assure integrity in contractual relations where workers are asked to accept assignments that involve considerable investments in human capital. Not only can the union intercede on behalf of the worker(s) where an expropriation effort is suspected, but it provides an institutional memory whereby reputation effects can be communicated to successor generations of workers. For both of these reasons, the firm is deterred from attempting expropriation. Setting aside the possibility that unions will attempt to negotiate monopoly wages, perceptive firms will prefer and actively assist in the creation of unions if these serve to attenuate expropriation risks—since otherwise workers may refuse to make (or will need to be bribed to make) mutually beneficial investments in human capital.

[21] The buyer must, of course recover his full costs if he is to place specialized marketing assets at hazard. This will obtain if final demand is uniformly distributed over the interval k'' to $1 + k''$ and derived demand is as described earlier.

[22] This last condition protects each against a prisoner's dilemma result.

[23] *FTC v. Morton Salt Co.*, 334 U.S. 37 (1948); emphasis added.

with a general purpose (but high cost) technology.

The missing ingredients, plainly, are the differential commitment to buy (as reflected by the willingness to offer hostages) and the differential incentives to breach once hostages have been posted. The confusion is explained by the propensity to employ conventional (steady state) microtheory to the neglect of transaction cost aspects. Rectifying this involves examination of the microanalytics of transactions, with special reference to asset specificity and the hazards thereby posed, and evaluating alternative contracts with respect to a *common reference condition*—prospective break even being a useful standard. Once this is done, a different understanding of many nonstandard or unfamiliar contracting practices, many of which are held to be presumptively unlawful, frequently emerges.[24]

B. *Franchising*

Klein and Leffler argue that franchisees may be required to make investments in transaction specific capital as a way by which to safeguard the franchise system against quality shading. As Klein puts it, franchisers can better

> ...assure quality by requiring franchisee investments in specific...assets that upon termination imply a capital loss penalty larger than can be obtained by the franchisee if he cheats. For example, the franchiser may require franchisees to rent from them short term (rather than own) the land upon which their outlet is located. This lease arrangement creates a situation where termination can require the franchisee to move and thereby impose a capital loss on him up to the amount of his initial non-salvageable investment. Hence a form of collateral to deter franchisee cheating is created.
>
> [1980, p. 359]

The arrangement is tantamount to the creation of hostages to restore integrity to an exchange.

This logic notwithstanding, the use of hostages to deter franchisees from exploiting demand externalities is often regarded as an imposed (top down) solution. Franchisees are "powerless"; they accept hostage terms because no others are available. Such power arguments are often based on *ex post* reasoning. That the use of hostages to support exchange can be and often is an efficient systems solution, hence is independent of who originates the proposal, can be seen from the following revised sequence.[25]

Suppose that an entrepreneur develops a distinctive, patentable idea that he sells outright to a variety of independent suppliers, each of which is geographically dispersed and is assigned an exclusive territory. Each supplier expects to sell only to the population located within its territory, but all find to their surprise (and initially to their delight) that sales are also made to a mobile population. Purchases by the mobile population are based not on the reputation of individual franchisees but on customers' perceptions of the reputation of the system. A demand externality arises in this way.

Thus, if sales were made only to the local population, each supplier would fully appropriate the benefits of its promotional and quality enhancement efforts. Population mobility upsets this; since the costs savings that result from local quality debasement accrue to the local operator while the adverse demand effects are diffused throughout the system, suppliers now have an incentive to free ride off of the reputation of the system. Having sold the exclusive territory rights outright, the entrepreneur who originated the program is indifferent to these unanticipated demand developments. It thus remains for the collection of independent franchisees to devise a correction themselves—lest the value of the system deteriorate to their individual and collective disadvantage.

[24] Note that the argument applies only to $\hat{p}$ vs. $\bar{p}$ comparisons in trades where specific assets are involved. The efficiency properties of customer price differentials that do have these origins are not reached by the argument in this paper.

[25] That this is a useful way to pose the franchise issue evolved out of discussions that I had with Jeffrey Goldberg. For a more complete development, see Goldberg's dissertation, 1982.

The franchisees, under this revised scenario, thus create an agent to police quality or otherwise devise penalties that deter quality deterioration. One possibility is to return to the entrepreneur and hire him to provide these services. Serving now as the agent of the franchisees, the entrepreneur may undertake a program of quality checks (certain purchasing restraints are introduced, whereby franchisees are required to buy only from qualified suppliers; periodic inspections are performed). The incentive to exploit demand externalities may further be discouraged by requiring each franchisee to post a hostage and by making franchises terminable.[26]

This indirect scenario serves to demonstrate that it is the *system* that benefits from the control of externalities. But this merely confirms that the normal scenario in which the franchiser controls the contractual terms is not an arbitrary exercise of power. Indeed, if franchisees recognize that the demand externality exists from the outset, if the franchiser refuses to make provision for the externality in the original contract, and if it is very costly to reform the franchise system once initial contracts are set, franchisees will bid less for the right to a territory than they otherwise would. It should not therefore be concluded that perceptive franchisers, who recognize the demand externality in advance and make provision for it, are imposing objectionable *ex ante* terms on unwilling franchisees. They are merely taking steps to realize the full value of the franchise. Here as elsewhere, contracts need to be examined in their entirety.

C. *Two-Part Pricing*

Victor Goldberg and John Erickson (1982) describe an interesting two-part pricing scheme that they observed in the sale of coke. The producer both sold coke to the calciner, and owned and leased the land upon which the plant of the calciner was built. Inasmuch as the coke was sold for "about one-quarter the current market price of equivalent quality coke" (p. 25), Goldberg and Erickson conjecture that "the rental rate was above the fair market rate and that the contract was designed to ensure that [the calciner] would continue to perform" (p. 25). Assuming that marginal costs are much less than average, such an arrangement can be interpreted as one by which the parties are attempting to strike efficient pricing terms that approximate those of the hostage model.

The pricing of utility services, whereby *ex ante* installation fees are paid by subscribers, also have interesting two-part pricing attributes.[27] The risk that sellers will expropriate buyers upon receipt of advance payment can be mitigated by creating a specialized third party, which for convenience may be referred to as a regulatory commission (Goldberg, 1976). Utilization of utility services can then be priced so as to more nearly approximate marginal cost.

More generally, Goldberg and Erickson conjecture that nonlinear pricing schemes are much more widespread than is commonly believed. They further point out that such arrangements are often very subtle and will require detailed knowledge of contracts to investigate (pp. 56–57).

V. Bilateral Applications

As indicated, the offer of hostages poses a hazard of expropriation. One way to deter this is to expand the contracting relationship from one of unilateral to bilateral exchange. Credible commitments are signaled without exposing assets to expropriation hazards. Reciprocal trades, especially those that involve product exchanges (swaps), sometimes come about in this way.

A. *Reciprocity, General*

Reciprocity transforms a unilateral supply relation—whereby A sells X to B—into a bilateral one, whereby A agrees to buy Y

[26]Termination is a credible threat only if the franchisee who cheats on the system bears a capital loss. This is the basic Klein and Leffler message. It would not do, therefore, if the terminated franchisee were permitted to sell the franchise to a highest bidder unless the investment in specific capital took the form of the franchisee's specialized knowledge of the system, and the terminated franchisee were thereafter prohibited from participating in owner, adviser, or employee status.

[27]This possibility was suggested to me by Alvin Klevorick.

from *B* as a condition for making the sale of *X* and both parties understand that the transaction will be continued only if reciprocity is observed. Although reciprocal selling is widely held to be anticompetitive (George Stocking and Willard Mueller, 1957; Harlan Blake, 1973), others regard it more favorably. George Stigler offers the following affirmative rationale for reciprocity:

> The case for reciprocity arises when prices cannot be freely varied to meet supply and demand conditions. Suppose that a firm is dealing with a colluding industry which is fixing prices. A firm in this collusive industry would be willing to sell at less than the cartel price if it can escape detection. Its price can be reduced in effect by buying from the customer-seller at an inflated price. Here reciprocity restores flexibility of prices. [1969, p. 39]

Inasmuch as, however, many industries do not satisfy the prerequisites for oligopolistic price collusion (Posner; myself, 1975, ch. 12) and as reciprocity is sometimes observed among these, reciprocity presumably has other origins as well. Tie breaking is one of these. A second is that reciprocity can have advantageous governance structure benefits. These two can be distinguished by the type of product being sold.

The tie-breaker explanation applies where firm *B*, which is buying specialized product from *A*, asks that *A* buy standardized product from *B* on the condition that *B* meets market terms. Other things being equal, procurement agents at *A* are apt to accede. F. M. Scherer notes that "Most of the 163 corporation executives responding to a 1963 survey stated that their firms' purchases were awarded on the basis of reciprocity only when the price, quality, and delivery conditions were equal" (1980, p. 344).

The more interesting case is where reciprocity involves the sale of specialized product to *B* conditioned on the procurement of specialized product from *B*. The argument here is that reciprocity can serve to equalize the exposure of the parties, thereby reducing the incentive of the buyer to defect from the exchange—leaving the supplier to redeploy specialized assets at greatly reduced alternative value. Absent a hostage (or other assurance that the buyer will not defect), the sale by *A* of specialized product to *B* may never materialize. The buyer's commitment to the exchange is more assuredly signaled by his willingness to accept reciprocal exposure of specialized assets. Defection hazards are thereby mitigated.

Lest the argument be uncritically considered to be a defense for reciprocal trading quite generally, note that it applies only where specialized assets are placed at hazard by *both* parties. Where only one or neither invests in specialized assets, the practice of reciprocity plainly has other origins.[28]

B. *Exchanges*

Although reciprocal trading among nonrivals may occasionally be justified, the exchange of product among nominal rivals is surely more puzzling and troublesome. Firms that are presumed to be in head-to-head competition ought to be selling product against one another rather than to one another. What explains the reverse?

Several distinctions are useful in considering exchanges. First, trade among rivals—short term or long term, unilateral or bilateral—is feasible only if product is fungible. This is not true for many differentiated goods and services, whence the issue of trade among rivals never arises for these. Second, short-term supply agreements are usefully distinguished from long term. The former may be explained as an "occasional exception," whereby one rival will sell product to another on a short-term, gap-filling basis so as to provide temporary relief against unanticipated product shortfalls (occasioned by either demand or supply changes). Recognizing that the shoe may be on the other foot next time, otherwise rivalrous firms may assist one another for stop-gap purposes. Public policy can presumably recognize merit in such trades and, so long as they lack a pat-

[28]Possible trading objections are discussed by Scherer (pp. 344–45). Another objection is that reciprocity becomes a bureaucratic habit that salesmen and purchasing agents find convenient and that outsiders are thereby disadvantaged in attempting to secure sales. See my 1975 study, pp. 163–64.

tern, hence do not give rise to a "web of interdependence," will regard these as unobjectionable. Long-term trading among rivals is, however, much less consistent with the notion of effective head-to-head rivalry. At the very least, such arrangements warrant scrutiny.

Whether there are efficiency incentives for rivals to supply product to one another on a long-term basis turns initially on prospective realization of production cost savings. The realization of production cost savings through long-term trade between rivals requires that economies of scale be large in relation to the size of geographic markets and, if they are, that firm-specific reputation effects extend across geographic market boundaries. The former is obvious since, absent economies of scale, every firm would presumably supply everywhere to its own long-term needs. Where, however, scale economies are significant, each market will support only a limited number of plants of minimum efficient size.

But fungibility and scale economies do not establish that gains from trade will be realized from such sales. This will obtain only if the value of (identical) product sold by rivals exceeds that sold by the local supplier. The issue here is whether valued reputation effects will go unrealized if rivals are unable to secure local product on favorable terms. Firms that possess valued reputations that extend beyond their local market to include distant markets are thus the ones for which long-term supply by rivals will be attractive.[29]

Even supposing that fungibility, scale economy, and reputation effect conditions are satisfied, this merely establishes that *unilateral* long-term trade among rivals can yield economies. A justification for *bilateral* (exchange) agreements is not reached by these arguments. Indeed, the usual defense for exchanges—that inefficient cross-hauling will occur if every firm is required to supply everywhere to its own needs—conveniently suppresses the obvious alternative, which is not zero trade, but rather unilateral long-term trade. Failure to address these matters directly and demonstrate wherein exchanges enjoy comparative institutional advantages over more standard and familiar forms of unilateral trade presumably explains the suspect or hostile attitude with which exchanges are typically regarded. The argument that emerges from this paper is that bilateral exchanges offer prospective advantages over unilateral trade *if* the resulting exposure of transaction specific assets effects a credible commitment without simultaneously posing expropriation hazards.

The type of specific asset that is placed at hazard by unilateral long-term trade, but which a reciprocal long-term exchange agreement serves to protect, is that of a dedicated asset. Recall that dedicated assets were described as discrete additions to generalized capacity that would not be put in place but for the prospect of selling a large amount of product to a particular customer. Premature termination of the contract by the buyer would leave the supplier with a large excess of capacity that could be disposed of only at distress prices. Requiring buyers to post a bond would mitigate this hazard, but only by posing another: the supplier may contrive to expropriate the bond. More generally, the interests of the supplier in adapting efficiently to new circumstances are not fully engaged. Reciprocal trading supported by separate but concurrent investments in specific assets provides a mutual safeguard against this second class of hazards. The hostages that are thereby created have the interesting property, moreover, that they are *never exchanged*. Instead, each party retains possession of its dedicated assets should the contract be prematurely terminated.

The usual argument that exchanges are justified because they avoid costly cross-hauling does not get to these issues and, by itself, is not an adequate justification for widespread use of exchanges. Were it only that transportation cost savings were realized, unilateral trading would suffice. Indeed, petroleum firms should be expected to create a central exchange in which supplies and demands were brought into correspondence by an auctioneer. Firms would end up selling to each other only by accident in

[29]Reputation effect valuations may be illusory or real. Those that are real take the form of customer convenience (billing, contracting) or assured knowledge of product characteristics.

these circumstances. Where dedicated assets are exposed, however, *the identity of the parties clearly matters*. Trades of this kind will not go through an auction market but will be carefully negotiated between the parties. Reciprocity in these circumstances is thus a device by which the continuity of a specific trading relation is promoted with risk attenuation effects.

VI. Petroleum Exchanges

"The task of linking concepts with observations demands a great deal of detailed knowledge of the realities of economic life" (Tjalling Koopmans, 1957, p. 145). The phenomenon of petroleum exchanges has puzzled economists for a long time. It routinely comes up in antitrust cases and investigations. The 1973 case brought by the United States Federal Trade Commission against the major petroleum firms maintained the view that exchanges were instrumental in maintaining a web of interdependencies among these firms, thereby helping to effect an oligopolistic outcome in an industry that was relatively unconcentrated on normal market structure criteria.[30] The more recent study on *The State of Competition in the Canadian Petroleum Industry* likewise regards exchanges as objectionable.[31] The Canadian Study, moreover, produces documents—contracts, internal company memoranda, letters, and the like—as well as deposition testimony to support its views that exchanges are devices for extending and perfecting monopoly among the leading petroleum firms. Such evidence on the details and purposes of contracting is usually confidential and hence unavailable. But detailed knowledge is clearly germane—and sometimes essential—to a microanalytic assessment of the transaction cost features of contract.

A. *The Evidence from the Canadian Study*

Volume V of the Canadian Study deals with the refining sector. Arguments are advanced and supporting evidence is developed that interfirm supply arrangements permit the major refiners to perfect oligopolistic restrictions in the following four respects:[32] 1) valuable knowledge about investment and marketing plans of rivals are disclosed by such agreements (p. 56); 2) leading firms are able to control lesser firms by exercising discretionary power through the terms of exchange (pp. 49–50); 3) competition is impaired by conditioning supply on the payment of an "entry fee" (pp. 53–54); and 4) exchange agreements impose limits on growth and supplementary supply (pp. 51–52).

The first two of these fail to pass scrutiny of the most rudimentary comparative institutional kind. Thus assuming that trade between rivals is efficient and that unilateral supply agreements (if not exchange) will be permitted, the objectionable information disclosures attributed to exchanges would presumably continue—since investment and marketing plans will be unavoidably disclosed in the process. Accordingly, evaluated in comparative institutional terms, the information disclosure objection is properly regarded as an objection to long term trade of any kind. Exchanges are not uniquely culpable.

The suggestion that exchanges are anticompetitive because they permit firms to realize bargaining advantages is similarly misplaced. The correct view is that firms should always be expected to realize such bargaining advantages as their positions lawfully permit. Absent a showing that exchanges are different from unilateral trades in bargaining respects, this objection is properly disregarded also.

[30] *FTC v. Exxon et al.*, Docket No. 8934 (1963).

[31] Robert J. Bertrand, Q. C., Director of Investigation and Research, Combines Investigation Act, coordinated the eight-volume study, *The State of Competition in the Canadian Petroleum Industry* (Quebec, 1981). All references in this paper are to Vol. V, *The Refining Sector*. This study will hereinafter be referred to as the Canadian Study.

[32] The Canadian Study contends that "a close examination of the interest of the [major refiners] and their actions shows that refining arrangements were meant to restrict competition. The collection of information, the intent to control lesser firms, the imposition of an 'entry fee,' the use of restrictions on downstream growth are not characteristics that would be expected normally from a competitive market" (Vol. V, p. 76).

The entry fee and marketing restraint objections are more substantial, however, and warrant elaboration.

1. *Entry Fees*

The entry fee objection to exchanges is that this has foreclosure consequences. That such fees are required as a precondition for trade, or at least the sale of product at favorable prices, is set out in the Canadian Study as follows:

> Evidence of an understanding that a fee relating to investment was required for acceptance into the industry can be found in the following quotation from Gulf: "We do believe that the oil industry generally, although grudgingly, will allow a participant who has paid his ante, to play the game; the ante in this game being the capital for refining, distributing and selling products" (Document #71248, undated, Gulf). The significance of the quotation lies equally in the notion that an "entry fee" was required and in the notion that the industry set the rules of the "game." The meaning of the "entry fee" as well as the rules of the "game" as understood by the industry can be found in the actual dealings between companies where the explicit mention of an "entry fee" arises. These cases demonstrate the rules that were being applied—the rules to which Gulf was referring. Companies which had not paid an "entry fee", that is, companies which had not made a sufficient investment in refining capacity or in marketing distribution facilities would *either not be supplied or would be penalized in the terms of the supply agreement*.
> [pp. 53–54, emphasis added]

2. *Marketing Restraints*

The Canadian Study notes that exchanges were made conditional on growth and territorial restraints and regards both as objectionable. The Imperial-Shell exchange agreement, under which Imperial supplied product to Shell in the Maritimes and received product in Montreal, is cited in both connections.

> The agreement between Imperial and Shell, originally signed in 1963, was renegotiated in 1967. In July 1972, Imperial did this because Shell had been growing too rapidly in the Maritimes. In 1971/72, Imperial had expressed its dissatisfaction with the agreement because of Shell's marketing policies. Shell noted:
> "There [sic] [Imperial's] present attitude is that we have built a market with their facilities, we are aggressive and threatening them all the time, and they are not going to help and in fact get as tough as possible with us" (Document #23633, updated, Shell). [Vol. 5, p. 51]

Imperial renewed the agreement with Shell only after imposing a price penalty if expansion were to exceed "normal growth rates" and furthermore stipulated that "Shell would not generally be allowed to obtain product from third party sources" to service the Maritimes (p. 52).

Gulf Oil likewise took the position that rivals receiving product under exchange agreements should be restrained to normal growth: "Processing agreements (and exchange agreements) should be entered into only after considering the overall economics of the Corporation and should be geared to providing competitors with volumes required for the normal growth only."[33] It furthermore sought and secured assurances that product supplied by Gulf would be used only by the recipient and would not be diverted to other regions or made available to other parties (p. 59).

B. *Interpretations*

These practices are subject to several interpretations. One is that the entry fees and marketing restraints are both anticompetitive. A second is that efficiency purposes are arguably served, especially by the former. A third is that there are mixed effects.

[33] The Canadian Study (p. 59) identifies the source as Document #73814, January 1972, Gulf.

1. *The Inhospitality Tradition*

The two polar contracting traditions for evaluating nonstandard or unfamiliar contracting practices are the common law tradition, and the antitrust or inhospitality tradition. Donald Turner makes reference to both of them in expressing his views about vertical market restrictions: "I approach territorial and customer restrictions not hospitably in the common law tradition, but inhospitably in the tradition of antitrust law."[34] Thus whereas contractual irregularities are presumed to serve affirmative economic purposes under the common law tradition, a deep suspicion of anticompetitive purposes is maintained by the antitrust (or inhospitality) tradition.

The inhospitality tradition is supported by the widespread view that economic organization is technologically determined. Economies of scale and technological nonseparabilities explain the organization of economic activity within firms. All other activity is appropriately organized by market exchanges. Legitimate market transactions will be mediated entirely by price; restrictive contractual relations signal anticompetitive intent.

The authors of the Canadian Study are evidently persuaded of the merits of this tradition. Long-term trade among rivals of any kind is suspect. And exchanges, which represent an irregular if not unnatural contracting form, are especially objectionable. Not only do exchanges facilitate information disclosure and permit bargaining strength, but they are used punitively against nonintegrated independents who, because they have not paid an entry fee, are denied product on parity terms. Furthermore, the marketing restraints that are associated with exchanges are patently offensive.

2. *An Efficiency Assessment*

Unlike the inhospitality tradition, the transaction cost approach is in the common law tradition. A comparative institutional orientation (Coase, 1964) is maintained. "Defects" are thus objectionable only where superior feasible alternatives can be described. Inasmuch as the information disclosure and bargaining concerns raised by the authors of the Canadian Study continue under unilateral trading, these are set aside and attention is focused on other matters.

(a) Entry Fees. The entry fee issue is a matter of special interest to this paper. Long-term exchange agreements permit firms to secure product in geographic markets where own-production is not feasible because economies of scale are large in relation to their own needs. The amount of product in question may nevertheless be substantial. Firms with whom exchange agreements are reached will thus construct and maintain larger plants than they otherwise would. Specific investments in dedicated assets are made as a consequence of such agreements.

Were it that supply agreements were of a unilateral kind and the buyer was unable or unwilling to offer a hostage, contracts of type II would presumably be negotiated—whence the trading price would be $\bar{p} = v_2 + k/(1-\bar{p})$. If, instead, the contract is extended to include bilateral rather than unilateral trade, the contract is converted to one of type III. Although exchange agreements stipulate the physical flows of product, the effective price is $\hat{p} = v_2 + k$, which is less than $\bar{p}$. Moreover, the parties have the incentive to exchange product so long as realized demand price in both regions exceeds v_2,[35] which is the marginal cost supply criterion. Assuming that demands in the two regions are highly correlated, the parties will normally reach common decisions on the desirability of trade.[36]

[34] The quotation is attributed to Turner by Stanley Robinson, 1968, N.Y. State Bar Association, Antitrust Symposium, p. 29.

[35] This assumes common costs, which condition will normally be approximated in exchanges of product between firms within a single country where factor prices are very similar.

[36] The possibility that the contract will drift out of alignment nevertheless needs to be recognized. Should one of the firms in an exchange agreement operate much closer to its capacity limits than the other, the latter party would incur much higher costs of termination than would the former. Recognition of this may explain

(b) Marketing Restraints. The supply and growth restraints discussed by the Canadian Study can be looked at in three ways. First, these can be viewed as a means by which to protect the exchange agreement against unilateral defection. Second, such restraints may serve strategic market division purposes. Third, restraints may serve to regularize markets. These are not mutually exclusive.

Only the first of these purposes is consonant with an efficiency interpretation. The argument here is that marketing restraints help to preserve symmetrical incentives. Such symmetry could be upset if one of the firms were to receive product in its deficit region from third parties. Such a firm might then be in a position to play one supplier off against the other. Or symmetry could be placed under strain if one party were to receive product from the other such that it began to grow "in excess of normal"—in which event it might be prepared to construct its own plant and scuttle the exchange agreement. Marketing restraints which help to forestall such outcomes encourage parties to participate in exchanges that might otherwise be unacceptable.

3. *A Mixed View*

Monopoly explanations are commonly advanced when economists, lawyers, or other interested observers come across contractual practices that they do not understand. Inasmuch as "we are very ignorant [in this field], the number of ununderstandable practices tends to be very large, and the reliance on a monopoly explanation frequent" (Coase, 1972, p. 67). A rebuttable presumption that nonstandard contracting practices are serving affirmative economic purposes, rather than monopoly purpose, would arguably serve antitrust law and economics better than the inhospitality presumption which, until recently, has prevailed.[37]

The presumption that exchanges have efficiency purposes could be challenged on any or all of three grounds. First, it might be argued that exchanges are merely a clever device by which to deny product to nonintegrated rivals. Refusals to sell to nonintegrated firms on $\bar{p}$ terms would support this contention. (It is plainly unrealistic, however, for buyers that have not made credible commitments to expect to receive product at $\hat{p}$.) Second, the market in question could be shown to have troublesome structural properties. The issue here is whether the requisite preconditions for market power—mainly high concentration coupled with high barriers to entry[38]—are satisfied. A third would be that the preconditions for efficiency are not satisfied. Factors favorable to the efficiency interpretation are the following: the exchange should be of a long-term kind; the amount of product exchanged should represent a significant fraction of plant capacity; and economies of plant scale should be large in relation to the amount of product traded. Exchanges for a small quantity of product where economies of scale are insubstantial are much more problematic.

To be sure, exchanges might simultaneously service efficiency and anticompeti-

why "during the renegotiation of a reciprocal purchase/sale agreement covering Montreal and the Maritimes," Shell noted that Imperial advised them that "they were not satisfied with the extent of Shell's investment in the Maritimes" (p. 54). In addition to the investment in refining in Montreal, which Shell interpreted as an investment "by exchange" in the Maritimes, Imperial wanted Shell to make direct investment in a Maritime distribution network (p. 54). Shell observed in this connection that although it had made no significant investment of its own in the Maritimes, "we have invested in Montreal and by exchange invested in the Maritimes so we have paid an entrance fee, although we have not paid for distribution network." The Canadian Study (p. 54) identifies the source as Document #23633, updated, Shell.

[37]To be sure, this is an oversimplification. Antitrust, has been loath to declare contractual constraints to be per se illegal. It came perilously close to taking this step in *U.S. v. Arnold Schwinn & Co.*, 388 U.S. 365 (1967), however. The prevailing enforcement view toward contractual restraints in the 1960's is accurately characterized as inhospitable.

[38]There is growing agreement that the structural preconditions that must be satisfied before claims of strategic anticompetitive behavior are seriously entertained are very high concentration coupled with barriers to entry (my 1977 article, pp. 292–93; P. L. Joskow and A. K. Klevorick, 1979, pp. 225–31; Janusz Ordover and Robert Willig, 1981, pp. 307–08).

tive purposes. Here as elsewhere, where tradeoffs are posed, they need to be evaluated.

VII. Concluding Remarks

The study of contract in both law and economics has mainly emphasized legal rules and technicalities. Such an orientation is supported by the implicit assumption that the courts "work well." Whether they work well or poorly, however, requires a comparative institutional assessment. There is growing awareness that the (comparative) limitations of the courts are more severe than the legal cêntralism tradition admits.

The severity of these limitations is not uniform but varies with the circumstances. A discriminating approach to the study of contract will necessarily make provision for this. Specifically, if different transactions have different governance needs, these will be expressly recognized. Accordingly, the study of contract is appropriately extended from legal rules to include an assessment of alternative governance structures, of which the courts are only one. Of special interest in this connection is the use of bilateral governance structures (private ordering) to implement nonstandard contracts where the adaptation and continuity needs of the parties are especially great.

This paper is an effort to deepen the understanding of private ordering. The central points are these:

1) Hostages: Contrary to the prevailing view that hostages are a quaint concept with little or no practical importance to contemporary contracting, the use of hostages to support exchange is widespread and economically important. But hostage creation is only part of the story. Expropriation hazards and prospective maladaptation conditions also need to be considered. Complex governance structures, of which reciprocal trading is one, arise in response to such conditions.

2) Asset Specificity: The organization of economic activity is massively influenced by the degree to which the transactions under examination are supported by assets that are specific to the parties. This paper 1) reaffirms the basic proposition that governance structures need to be matched to the underlying attributes of transactions in a discriminating way if the efficiency purposes of economic organization are to be realized, 2) extends the scope of asset specificity to include dedicated assets, and 3) establishes that, as between two buyers, one of whom posts a hostage in support of specific asset investments by suppliers while the other does not, suppliers will offer better terms to the former, *ceteris paribus*.

3) Microanalytics: The relevant unit of analysis for studying exchange relations of the kinds discussed in this article is the transaction. Assessing transactions and assigning them to governance structures in a discriminating (mainly transaction cost economizing) way requires much more microanalytic knowledge of economic activity and organization than is customary within economics. Empirical work will necessarily reflect this.[39] Price and quantity of course remain relevant, but the contractual devices by which prices are made to track costs, the manner in which adaptations are effected, and the safeguards that are provided are not only germane but are sometimes decisive.

4) Contracting in its Entirety: Not every transaction poses defection hazards, and it may not be possible to safeguard all that do. Where the potential hazards that beset contracts are evident to the parties from the outset, however, studies of contracts and of contracting institutions arguably start "at the beginning." This has ramifications for assessing the importance of the prisoners' dilemma and for understanding the administration of justice.

(a) Prisoners' Dilemma: The benefits of cooperation notwithstanding, the achievement of cooperation is widely thought to be frustrated by the relentless logic of the prisoners' dilemma. To be sure, it has always been evident that defection can be deterred if payoffs are appropriately altered. But this stratagem is held to be infeasible or is other-

[39]Examples of microanalytic studies of contract include myself (1976), Thomas Palay (1981), Goldberg and Erickson (1982), and Scott Masten (1982).

wise dismissed—on which account the dilemma persists or appeal is made to "exogenous norms of cooperative behavior [that are] adhered to by the actors" (Albert Hirschman, 1982, p. 1470). I submit that the feasibility of crafting superior *ex ante* incentive structures warrants more attention. A leading reason for its neglect is because the study of the institutions of contract has occupied such a low place on the research agenda. Subtle incentive features that are incorporated in nonstandard contracting practices have gone undetected as a consequence of this nonchalance—on which account the practical significance of the prisoners' dilemma to the study of exchange has been vastly exaggerated.

(b) Justice: The notion that hostages are demanded as a condition for supplying product on favorable terms has the appearance of an arbitrary exercise of power: the stronger party "demands" a hostage from the weaker, who accedes it because it has no other choice. In fact, a comparative institutional assessment of contractual alternatives discloses that efficiency purposes are often served by hostages and that it is in the mutual interest of the parties to achieve this result. Not only can producers be induced to invest in the most efficient technology, but buyers can be induced to take delivery whenever demand realizations exceed marginal cost. More generally, contracts need to be examined *in their entirety*, with special attention to their governance features. Principles of justice or competition that look at the relation between the parties at the execution stage without examining the *ex ante* bargaining relation are at best incomplete and are frequently mistaken.[40] Parties to a contract should not expect to have their cake (low price) and eat it too (no hostage).

[40] Robert Nozick's views on justice are apposite: "whether a distribution is just depends upon how it came about. In contrast, *current-time-slice* principles of justice hold that the justice of a distribution is determined by how things are distributed (who has what)" (1975, p. 153). What he refers to as the current-time-slice approach to justice neglects *ex ante* bargaining and evaluates justice in terms of outcomes alone. Upon realization that justice is administered in this way, initial bargains will be struck on different terms than they would if the parties were given assurance that the complete contract would be subject to review in evaluating the merits of a contracting relation. Two difficult issues nevertheless remain if the comprehensive bargain orientation to justice is adopted: the initial distribution of resources; and the competence of the parties to evaluate complex contracts. The relative importance of these varies with the circumstances.

REFERENCES

Arrow, Kenneth J., "Control in Large Organization," *Management Science*, September 1963, *10*, 397–408.

______, *Limits of Organization*, New York: W. W. Norton, 1974.

Blake, Harlan M., "Conglomerate Mergers and the Antitrust Laws," *Columbia Law Review*, March 1973, *73*, 555–92.

Brockman, Rosser H., "Commercial Contract Law in Late Nineteenth Century Taiwan," in Jerome Alan Cohen et al., eds., *Essays on China's Legal Tradition*, Princeton: Princeton University Press, 1980, 76–136.

Clarkson, Kenneth W., Miller, Roger L. and Muris, Timothy J., "Liquidated Damages v. Penalties," *Wisconsin Law Review*, 1978, 351–90.

Coase, Ronald H., "The Nature of the Firm," *Economica*, November 1937, *4*, 386–405; reprinted in George J. Stigler and Kenneth E. Boulding, eds., *Readings in Price Theory*, Homewood: Richard D. Irwin, 1952.

______, "The Regulated Industries: Discussion," *American Economic Review Proceedings*, May 1964, *54*, 194–97.

______, "Industrial Organization: A Proposal for Research," in Victor R. Fuchs, ed., *Policy Issues and Research Opportunities in Industrial Organization*, Vol. 3, New York: National Bureau of Economic Research, 1972, 59–73.

Diamond, Peter A. and Maskin, Eric, "An Equilibrium Analysis of Search and Breach of Contract," *Bell Journal of Economics*, Spring 1979, *10*, 282–316.

Dixit, Avinash, "A Model of Duopoly Suggesting a Theory of Entry Barriers," *Bell Journal of Economics*, Spring 1979, *10*, 20–32.

______, "Recent Developments in Oligopoly Theory," *American Economic Review Proceedings*, May 1982, *72*, 12–17.

Eaton, B. Curtis and Lipsey, Richard G., "Capital, Commitment, and Entry Equilibrium," *Bell Journal of Economics*, Autumn 1981, *12*, 593–604.

Fama, Eugene F. and Jensen, Michael C., "Separation of Ownership and Control," *Journal of Law and Economics*, June 1983, *26*.

Fuller, Lon L., "Collective Bargaining and the Arbitrator," *Wisconsin Law Review*, January 1963, 3–46.

Galanter, Marc, "Justice in Many Rooms: Courts, Private Ordering, and Indigenous Law," *Journal of Legal Pluralism*, No. 19, 1981, 1–47.

Goldberg, Jeffrey, "A Theoretical and Econometric Analysis of Franchising," draft, doctoral dissertation, University of Pennsylvania, 1982.

Goldberg, Victor P., "Regulation and Administered Contracts," *Bell Journal of Economics*, Autumn 1976, *7*, 426–48.

______ **and Erickson, John E.**, "Long-Term Contracts for Petroleum Coke," Department of Economics Working Paper Series No. 206, University of California-Davis, September 1982.

Grossman, Sanford J. and Hart, Oliver D., "Corporate Financial Structure and Managerial Incentives," in John J. McCall, ed., *The Economics of Information*, Chicago: University of Chicago Press, 1982, 107–40.

Hirschman, Albert, "Rival Interpretations of Market Society: Civilizing, Destructive, or Feeble?," *Journal of Economic Literature*, December 1982, *20*, 1463–84.

Hurwicz, Leonid, "On Informationally Decentralized Systems," in C. B. McGuire and R. Radner, eds., *Decision and Organization*, Amsterdam: North-Holland 1972, 297–336.

______, "The Design of Mechanisms for Resource Allocation," *American Economic Review Proceedings*, May 1973, *63*, 1–30.

Jensen, Michael and Meckling, William, "Theory of the Firm: Managerial Behavior, Agency Costs, and Capital Structure," *Journal of Financial Economics*, October 1976, *3*, 305–60.

Joskow, P. L. and Klevorick, A. K., "A Framework for Analyzing Predatory Pricing Policy," *Yale Law Journal*, December 1979, *89*, 213–70.

Klein, Benjamin, "Transaction Cost Determinants of 'Unfair' Contractual Relations," *American Economic Review Proceedings*, May 1980, *70*, 356–62.

______, **Crawford, R. A. and Alchian, A. A.**, "Vertical Integration, Appropriable Rents, and the Competitive Contracting Process," *Journal of Law and Economics*, October 1978, *21*, 297–326.

______ **and Leffler, K. B.**, "The Role of Market Forces in Assuring Contractual Performance," *Journal of Political Economy*, August 1981, *89*, 615–41.

Koopmans, Tjalling C., *Three Essays on the State of Economic Science*, New York: McGraw-Hill, 1957.

Kreps, David M. and Wilson, Robert, "Reputation and Imperfect Information," *Journal of Economic Theory*, August 1982, *27*, 253–79.

Llewellyn, Karl N., "What Price Contract?—An Essay in Perspective," *Yale Law Journal*, May 1931, *40*, 704–51.

Macaulay, Stewart, "Non-Contractual Relations in Business," *American Sociological Review*, February 1963, *28*, 55–70.

Macneil, Ian R., "The Many Futures of Contract," *University of California Law Review*, May 1974, *67*, 691–816.

Masten, Scott, "Transaction Costs, Institutional Choice, and the Theory of the Firm," unpublished doctoral dissertation, University of Pennsylvania, 1982.

Milgrom, Paul and John Roberts, "Predation, Reputation, and Entry Deterrence," *Journal of Economic Theory*, August 1982, *27*, 280–312.

Mnookin, Robert H. and Kornhauser, Lewis, "Bargaining in the Shadow of the Law: The Case of Divorce," *Yale Law Journal*, March 1979, *88*, 950–97.

Nelson, Richard R. and Winter, Sidney G., *An Evolutionary Theory of Economic Change*, Cambridge: Harvard University Press, 1982.

Nozick, Robert, *Anarchy, State, and Utopia*, New York: Basic Books, 1975.

Ordover, Janusz A. and Willig, Robert D., "An Economic Definition of Predatory Product Innovation," in S. Salop, ed., *Strategic Views of Predation*, Washington: Federal Trade Commission, 1981, 301–96.

Palay, Thomas, "The Governance of Rail-Freight Contracts: A Comparative Institutional Approach," unpublished doctoral dissertation, University of Pennsylvania, 1981.

Posner, Richard A., "Some Uses and Abuses of Economics in Law," *University of Chicago Law Review*, Winter 1979, *46*, 281–306.

Riley, John G., (1979a) "Informational Equilibrium," *Econometrica*, March 1979, *47*, 331–53.

______, (1979b) "Noncooperative Equilibrium and Market Signaling," *American Economic Review Proceedings*, May 1979, *69*, 303–07.

Ross, Stephen, "The Determination of Financial Structure: The Incentive Signaling Approach," *Bell Journal of Economics*, Spring 1977, *8*, 23–40.

Rothschild, Michael and Stiglitz, Joseph, "Equilibrium in Competitive Insurance Markets," *Quarterly Journal of Economics*, November 1976, *80*, 30–49.

Schelling, Thomas C., "An Essay on Bargaining," *American Economic Review*, June 1956, *46*, 281–306.

Scherer, F. M., *Industrial Market Structure and Economic Performance*, Chicago: Rand McNally, 1980.

Schmalensee, Richard, "Economies of Scale and Barriers to Entry," *Journal of Political Economy*, December 1981, *89*, 1228–38.

Shavell, Steven, "Damage Measures for Breach of Contract," *Bell Journal of Economics*, Autumn 1980, *11*, 446–90.

Stigler, George J., in *President's Task Force on Productivity and Competition*, reprinted in CCH *Trade Regulation Reporter*, No. 419, June 24, 1969.

Stiglitz, Joseph, "Incentives and Risk Sharing in Sharecropping," *Review of Economic Studies*, June 1974, *41*, 219–57.

Stocking, George W. and Mueller, Willard F., "Business Reciprocity and the Size of Firms," *Journal of Business*, April 1957, *30*, 73–95.

Teece, David J., "Economics of Scope and the Scope of the Enterprise," *Journal of Economic Behavior and Organization*, September 1980, *1*, 223–45.

______, "A Transaction Cost Theory of the Multinational Enterprise," unpublished manuscript, 1982.

Telser, L. G., "A Theory of Self-Enforcing Agreements," *Journal of Business*, February 1981, *53*, 27–44.

Wachter, Michael L. and Williamson, Oliver E., "Obligational Markets and the Mechanics of Inflation," *Bell Journal of Economics*, Autumn 1978, *9*, 549–71.

Williamson, Oliver E., "The Vertical Integration of Production: Market Failure Considerations," *American Economic Review Proceedings*, May 1971, *61*, 112–23.

______, *Markets and Hierarchies: Analysis and Antitrust Implications*, New York: Free Press, 1975.

______, "Franchise Bidding for Natural Monopolies—in General and with Respect to CATV," *Bell Journal of Economics*, Spring 1976, *7*, 73–104.

______, "Predatory Pricing: A Strategic and Welfare Analysis," *Yale Law Journal*, December 1977, *87*, 284–340.

______, "Transaction-Cost Economics: The Governance of Contractual Relations," *Journal of Law and Economics*, October 1979, *22*, 233–61.

______, "The Modern Corporation: Origins, Evolution, Attributes," *Journal of Economic Literature*, December 1981, *19*, 1537–68.

______, (1982a) "Mitigating Contractual Hazards: Using Hostages to Support Exchange," Discussion Paper No. 126, Center for the Study of Organizational Innovation, University of Pennsylvania, April 1982.

______, (1982b) "Antitrust Enforcement: Where It has Been; Where It is Going," in John Craven, ed., *Industrial Organization, Antitrust, and Public Policy*, Boston: Kluwer-Nijhoff Publishing, 1982, 41–68.

[5]

JOURNAL OF ECONOMIC THEORY 27, 245–252 (1982)

Rational Cooperation in the Finitely Repeated Prisoners' Dilemma

DAVID M. KREPS

Graduate School of Business, Stanford University, Stanford, California 94305

PAUL MILGROM

Graduate School of Management, Northwestern University, Evanston, Illinois 60201

JOHN ROBERTS AND ROBERT WILSON

Graduate School of Business, Stanford University, Stanford, California 94305

Received July 8, 1981

A common observation in experiments involving finite repetition of the prisoners' dilemma is that players do not always play the single-period dominant strategies ("finking"), but instead achieve some measure of cooperation. Yet finking at each stage is the only Nash equilibrium in the finitely repeated game. We show here how incomplete information about one or both players' options, motivation or behavior can explain the observed cooperation. Specifically, we provide a bound on the number of rounds at which Fink may be played, when one player may possibly be committed to a "Tit-for-Tat" strategy. *Journal of Economic Literature* Classification Numbers: 026, 213.

The purpose of this note is to demonstrate how reputation effects due to informational asymmetries can generate cooperative behavior in finitely repeated versions of the classic prisoners' dilemma. The methods employed are those developed in our work on the chain-store paradox (Kreps and Wilson [2], Milgrom and Roberts [4]). We refer the reader to those papers for motivation, formal definitions, and interpretation.

The basic game that we consider consists of N repetitions of the following two person, bimatrix, stage game:

	COL	
ROW	Fink	Cooperate
Fink	0, 0	a, b
Cooperate	b, a	1, 1

0022-0531/82/040245–08$02.00/0

We require $a > 1$, $b < 0$, and $a + b < 2$.[1] At each stage, each of the two players, ROW and COL, recalls his previous actions and is informed about those of his opponent. The players move simultaneously at each stage. Payoffs in the overall game are the (undiscounted) sums of the stage payoffs.

This game has a unique Nash equilibrium path, which involves each player choosing to fink at every stage. The logic is similar to Selten's backwards induction in the chain-store game (although the argument there shows the uniqueness of the perfect equilibrium). In the final stage (which we call stage 1), finking strongly dominates cooperating, and so must ensue. Then, in the penultimate stage, finking does better than cooperating in terms of the current stage, while the choice at this stage cannot affect the outcome in stage 1. Thus finking will again be adopted by both players. And so on, for any finite N.[2] This outcome is clearly and dramatically inefficient.

This uniqueness result is disturbing in light of experiments with this game, of which there have been a very large number. (See Axelrod [1] and Smale [5] for references.) A common pattern in these experiments is that, at least for some time, both players cooperate and, in the process, end up with payoffs that are strictly greater than they would obtain under equilibrium play. The issue then is whether this puzzle can be resolved in the context of rational, self-interested behavior. The approach we adopt is to admit a "small amount" of the "right kind" of incomplete information.

In fact, we are able to show that certain kinds of informational asymmetries *must* yield a significant measure of cooperation in equilibrium, and that other plausible asymmetries may produce cooperation as well. Throughout, the equilibrium concept is that of sequential equilibrium (Kreps and Wilson [3]). Sequential equilibrium in a game of incomplete information requires that the action taken by any player at any point in the game tree must be part of an optimal strategy from that point forward, given his beliefs about the evolution of the game to this point (which must, to the extent possible, be consistent with Bayesian updating on the hypothesis that the equilibrium strategies have been used to date) and given that future play will be governed by the equilibrium strategies. The various models we use parallel those in [2, 4]. Each involves some element of uncertainty in the mind of (at least) one player about the other, and they can all be viewed in terms of a lack of common knowledge (between ROW and COL) that both

[1] If $a + b > 2$, then the strategy of both cooperating at each stage is Pareto-dominated by alternating between fink–cooperate and cooperate–fink. Much of our analysis can be adapted to handle this case.

[2] Note the sharp contrast with the infinitely repeated case, where any average payoff vector in the intersection of the positive orthant and the convex hull of the four possible stage payoff vectors can be achieved through a perfect equilibrium. Note also that in the finitely repeated case, Nash equilibrium behavior *off* the equilibrium path may involve some cooperation. But finking is required *everywhere* in any perfect equilibrium.

are rational players playing precisely the game specified above. The possibilities for more detailed analysis of this model and its application in economic, political, and military contexts appear to be very rich. Various combinations of the authors hope to report on such work in the future.

Model 1: *ROW Might Play Tit-for-Tat*

The first approach we consider supposes that, when the game begins, one of the players (say COL) is not absolutely certain that the other (ROW) will play "rationally" according to the payoffs specified above. Specifically, COL assigns probability $1-\delta$ to the possibility of a "rational" opponent, and he allows a (very small) chance, δ, that ROW has available only the Tit-for-Tat strategy.[3] The Tit-for-Tat strategy requires the player using it to begin by cooperating and then to cooperate at stage $n+1$ if and only if his opponent cooperated at the preceding stage, n. It is worth noting that this strikingly simple and quite natural strategy emerged as the winner in Axelrod's prisoners' dilemma tournament [1].

To present a sequential equilibrium in full detail for this game is difficult. There is no question that such equilibria exist: See Kreps and Wilson [3, Prop. 1]. But the "end play" of such equilibria are very complex. So we shall be content here to prove that in any sequential equilibrium, the number of stages where one player or the other finks is bounded above by a constant depending on δ but independent of N. Further, if we restrict attention to sequential equilibria that are not Pareto-dominated by any other sequential equilibria, then there is cooperation in all but the last "few" stages.

We prove these statements in a number of steps. The statement of each step except the last should be prefaced: In every sequential equilibrium...

Step 1. ...if it becomes common knowledge[4] before some stage that ROW is rational, then both ROW and COL fink at this and every succeeding stage, and their payoffs from the remainder of the game are zero.

The proof is by induction on the number of stages remaining. It is apparent if there is only one stage remaining. Suppose that it is true if there

[3] An alternative way to model this is to assume that ROW has available *all* the strategies above, but that with probability δ, ROW's payoffs are not as above but rather make playing Tit-for-Tat strongly dominant. The results given below can be proved for this alternative model, although the simple "common knowledge" arguments that we use are no longer available, and slightly more complex arguments are required. An advantage of this alternative model is that it eases interpretation of the probability assessed by COL that ROW is the Tit-for-Tat player as ROW's "reputation."

[4] It is common knowledge that ROW is rational if both players know this, both know that both know this, *ad infinitum*. More formally, an event E is common knowledge between two individuals at a state $\omega \in \Omega$ if there is some A in the finest common coarsening (meet) of their information partitions with $\omega \in A \subseteq E$. The crucial role of common knowledge will be illustrated shortly.

are $n-1$ or fewer stages to go. Then with n stages remaining, the rational ROW must foresee that his present choice of action cannot influence the future course of the game, since it will remain common knowledge that he is rational when stage $n-1$ arrives. Therefore he will maximize his immediate payoff, which means finking. Similarly, COL anticipates that no matter what he does at this stage, finking will occur at all later stages. In this round, finking is strictly better, so COL finks as well. Since both sides fink, their payoffs are each zero, and the induction is complete.

Step 2. ...if COL finks at stage $n+1$, then ROW finks at stage n with probability one.

If ROW did cooperate in these circumstances, it would become common knowledge that he was rational. (The "Tit-for-Tat" ROW does not have this action available.) Thus cooperation nets zero in the continuation game. But finking can do no worse than zero in the continuation game and it is strictly dominant in the stage game. Thus finking does strictly better overall. This means that ROW must fink with probability one.

Step 3. ...starting from any point in the game tree (i), where COL assesses probability q that ROW is the Tit-for-Tat player, (ii), where there are n stages to go, and (iii), where COL *cooperated* on the previous stage, the expected payoff to COL for the remainder of the game is at least $qn+b$.

To show this, consider the strategy for COL of cooperating until the next time that ROW finks, and then finking ever after. Against the Tit-for-Tat player, this yields a payoff of n. Against the rational ROW, it yields no worse than b. Thus it yields an expected payoff that is at least $qn+(1-q)\,b \geqslant qn+b$, and any equilibrium strategy must do at least as well.

Step 4. ...starting from any point in the game tree (i), where COL assesses probability q that ROW is the Tit-for-Tat player, (ii), where there are n stages to go, and (iii), where COL *finked* on the previous stage, the expected payoff to COL for the remainder of the game is at least $q(n-1)+2b$.

Because ROW is sure to fink (see step 2), COL knows that his assessment in the subsequent stage will again be q. So by cooperating at this stage, COL gets b immediately and at least $q(n-1)+b$ in the continuation game. His overall expected payoff can be no worse than the sum of these, or $q(n-1)+2b$.

Step 5. ...starting at a point in the game tree (i), where COL assesses probability q that ROW is the Tit-for-Tat player, and (ii), where there are n stages to go, the expected payoff to the rational ROW player is no less than $q(n-1)+3b-a$.

Note first that COL will do no worse if the rational ROW plays Tit-for-Tat than if the rational ROW plays his equilibrium strategy. This is easily verified inductively, using steps (1) and (2). Thus the bounds obtained in steps (3) and (4) apply equally well if the rational ROW were to play Tit-for-Tat. And by playing Tit-for-Tat, the rational ROW nets within $b - a$ of whatever COL gets, path by path. This gives us the bound on ROW's payoff stated above.

Step 6. ...if COL assesses probability q that ROW is the Tit-for-Tat player, and if there are more than $(2a - 4b + 2q)/q$ stages left to go, then ROW plays the Tit-for-Tat strategy with probability one. Thus along the equilibrium path, until the first stage less than $(2a - 4b + 2\delta)/\delta$, COL infers nothing from the observed behavior of ROW, and COL's assessment that ROW is the Tit-for-Tat player remains at δ.

In light of Step 2, all that is needed here is to show that ROW cooperates if COL has just cooperated in these circumstances. (The second part of the statement follows trivially from the first.) If ROW were to fink, it would become common knowledge that ROW is rational. Thus the total payoff from finking cannot exceed a—ROW gets at most a immediately (if COL cooperates) and then zero in the continuation game (by Step 1)). By cooperating, ROW will do no worse than b in this round (if COL finks) and, by Step 5, $q(n-2) + 3b - a$ in the continuation game, where n is the number of stages remaining. If n exceeds $(2a - 4b + 2q)/q$, then cooperating is strictly better.

Step 7. ...the total number of stages where one side or the other finks is bounded above by

$$\frac{2a - 4b + 2\delta}{\delta} \cdot \left[1 + \frac{2}{\min\{2 - a - b, 1\}}\right].$$

As seen in Step 6, ROW plays Tit-for-Tat until stage $(2a - 4b + 2\delta)/\delta$. If COL cooperates until ROW finks and then finks thereafter, his payoff must be at least $N - (2a - 4b + 2\delta)/\delta$. If COL finks before this date, then in that stage he gets a. If he then returns m stages later to cooperating, he gets b in the stage where he cooperates and zero in between. Thus he gives up $1 + m - a - b$ in this circumstance. A string of finks costs him $1 + (1 - (a + b))/m$ per round in comparison to cooperating. Thus, each time COL finks it costs him at least $\min\{2 - a - b, 1\}$. If he finks k times prior to stage $(2a - 4b + 2\delta)/\delta$, his payoff cannot exceed $N - k \cdot \min\{2 - a - b, 1\}$. These two bounds on COL's payoffs yield $k \leqslant (2a - 4b + 2\delta)/(\delta \cdot \min\{2 - a - b, 1\})$. Each such act of finking by COL provokes a Tit-for-Tat response from ROW in the next round, so there are at most $2k$ rounds before stage $(2a - 4b + 2\delta)/\delta$ when finking occurs. Thus the maximum number of rounds with finking is that given above.

Step 8. In any sequential equilibrium that is not Pareto-dominated by some other sequential equilibrium, there is no finking along the equilibrium path when more than $1 + (2a - 4b + 2\delta)/\delta$ stages remain.

For any equilibrium where there is finking before this date, a Pareto-superior equilibrium consists of not having that finking, and then continuing to play the game as if it had occurred.

Note that these bounds are not tight: If $\delta = 1$ they yield $n = 10$ in Step 8 for $a = 1.5$ and $b = -1$, yet in this circumstance one should see finking only in the last period. The looseness of these bounds suggests the need for further work.

The Tit-for-Tat theme can also be developed so as to further emphasize the role of lack of common knowledge. This development is in the spirit of Milgrom and Roberts [4, Appendix B].

Suppose that there are three states of the world. In state 1, ROW is the Tit-for-Tat player; in stages 2 and 3 he is rational. ROW learns whether he is Tit-for-Tat or not—his information partition (at the outset) is $\{1\}$, $\{2, 3\}$. COL, on the other hand, is given the information partition $\{1, 2\}$, $\{3\}$: In state 3 he knows whether ROW is the Tit-for-Tat player; in state 2 he does not. Suppose that state 3 prevails with very high probability. Then with very high probability, Row is not Tit-for-Tat, and COL *knows* that ROW is not Tit-for-Tat. But ROW is not sure that COL knows this, and one can show that the qualitative results proved for model 1 hold here. ROW will play Tit-for-Tat until near the end of the game, hoping that COL will be "deceived." And COL will pretend to be "deceived" even if he is not, as this improves his lot as well.

Or consider a four state case. In state 1 ROW is the Tit-for-Tat player—in states 2, 3 and 4 he is not. ROW is endowed with the information partition $\{1\}$, $\{2, 3\}$, $\{4\}$; COL with $\{1, 2\}$, $\{3, 4\}$. State 4 prevails with probability close to one. Then with probability close to one, ROW is not Tit-for-Tat, COL knows that this is so, ROW knows that COL knows this, but COL is not sure that ROW knows that COL knows. Once more the qualitative results for the original model hold up—ROW tries to "deceive" COL, knowing full well that COL will not be deceived but will act as if he is, and COL will do this in the hope that ROW may be unaware that is COL is not being deceived. One could go on like this forever: The general structure is that ROW's information partition should involve sets $\{1\}$, $\{2, 3\}$,..., $\{2m, 2m + 1\}$,... and COL's should involve $\{1, 2\}$, $\{3, 4\}$,..., $\{2m + 1, 2m + 2\}$,... (with termination eventually). The point is simply that so long as it is not common knowledge that ROW is not Tit-for-Tat, cooperation until near the end of the game will be rational.

Model 2: *Two-Sided Uncertainty about the Stage Payoffs*

In Model 1, COL entertains a hypothesis about ROW's behavior that cannot be generated if ROW is rational and has some stage game payoffs that he sums to arrive at his overall payoff. That is, COL's hypothesis, in terms of ROW's "true" utility function, necessarily involves payoffs for ROW that cut across stages. We might then wonder: Can long-run cooperation be attained if the only alternative hypotheses that are allowed (besides the hypothesis that the player is rational with the given stage payoffs) involve changes in the stage game payoffs? (This approach is used in [2].) The answer is a qualified yes.

Suppose that *each* player originally assesses a small probability that his opponent "enjoys" cooperation when it is met by cooperation. Given our zero-one normalization, we model this by assuming that COL assigns a small probability $\delta > 0$ that $a < 1$ for ROW, and ROW entertains a similar hypothesis about COL. We can then produce a sequential equilibrium wherein each side cooperates until the last few stages of the game, although again the end-game play is rather complex. In this equilibrium, if either side ever fails to cooperate, then the other side takes this as a sure sign that the defector has stage game payoffs with $a > 1$, and the noncooperative equilibrium ensues. As the details of this equilibrium are quite complex, we refrain from giving them here. Note, however, that if we move directly to a continuous-time formulation of this game, as in Kreps and Wilson [2, Sect. 4], then one equilibrium has cooperation throughout.

There are two qualifications to be made. First, two-sided uncertainty is required. If ROW, say, is uncertain about COL's stage payoffs, but it is common knowledge that $a > 1$ for ROW, then the only sequential equilibrium has finking throughout. (This is true for any "incomplete information" about one player's stage payoffs.) The second qualification, and certainly the more important, is that this game admits sequential equilibria in which long-run cooperation does not ensue, unlike the game with a Tit-for-Tat possibility. This is true even if we make a "plausibility" restriction on beliefs off the equilibrium path in the spirit of Section 3 of Kreps and Wilson [2]. Cooperation here requires a "boot-strapping" operation: Even if each side is *certain* that the other has $a < 1$, cooperation ensues only if each side hypothesizes that the other side will cooperate. (This is a fancy way of saying: If both sides have payoffs with $a < 1$, then there are two Nash equilibria in the stage game.) One might justify the cooperative equilibrium on "efficiency" grounds, but one cannot guarantee that cooperation will prevail in every sequential equilibrium.

Acknowledgments

Financial support from the following grants is gratefully acknowledged: National Science Foundation Grants SOC 79-07542 and SES 80-01932 to Northwestern University and SES 80-06407 and SES 81-08226 to Stanford University, and Office of Naval Research Grant N00014-79-C-0685 to Stanford University. We are grateful to William Stanford for pointing out an error in an earlier version of this paper.

References

1. R. Axelrod, The emergence of cooperation among egoists, *Amer. Pol. Sci. Rev.* **75** (1981), 306–318.
2. D. Kreps and R. Wilson, Reputation and imperfect information, *J. Econ. Theory* **27** (1982), 253–279.
3. D. Kreps and R. Wilson, Sequential equilibrium, *Econometrica*, in press.
4. P. Milgrom and J. Roberts, Predation, reputation and entry deterrence, *J. Econ. Theory* **27** (1982), 280–312.
5. S. Smale, The prisoner's dilemma and dynamical systems associated to non-cooperative games, *Econometrica* **48** (1980), 1617–1634.

[6]

GAMES AND ECONOMIC BEHAVIOR **8**, 56–90 (1995)

Learning To Be Imperfect: The Ultimatum Game*

JOHN GALE

Department of Economics, University of Wisconsin, 1180 Observatory Drive, Madison, Wisconsin 53706

KENNETH G. BINMORE

Department of Economics, University College London, Gower Street, London WC1E 6BT England

AND

LARRY SAMUELSON

Department of Economics, University of Wisconsin, 1180 Observatory Drive, Madison, Wisconsin 53706

Received August 22, 1994

This paper studies interactive learning processes that are subject to constant perturbations or "noise." We argue that payoffs in the Ultimatum Game are such that responders are more apt to be "noisy" than are proposers and show that as a result the learning process readily leads to outcomes that are Nash equilibria but not subgame-perfect. We conclude that game theorists should not restrict attention to the subgame-perfect equilibrium when predicting laboratory behavior in the Ultimatum Game. *Journal of Economic Literature* Classification Numbers: C70, C72. © 1995 Academic Press, Inc.

* Financial support from National Science Foundation Grant SES-9122176 and the Deutsche Forschungsgemeinschaft, Sonderforschungsbereich 303 at the University of Bonn, is gratefully acknowledged. We thank Drew Fudenberg and Joseph Harrington for helpful discussions, and thank two referees and an associate editor for helpful comments. We are grateful to the Department of Economics at the University of Bonn and the Institute for Advanced Studies at the Hebrew University of Jerusalem, where part of this work was done, for their hospitality. The authors first encountered the possibility of using the replicator dynamics to obtain unusual results in the Ultimatum Game in a manuscript of James Andreoni and John Miller. This paper was prepared for the Nobel Symposium at Björkborn, Sweden, 18–20 June 1993.

0899-8256/95 $6.00

1. The Ultimatum Game

Consider two players with a dollar to divide. The rules of the *Ultimatum Game* specify that player I begins by making an offer of $x \in [0, 1]$ to player II, who then accepts or refuses. If player II accepts, player I gets $1 - x$ and player II gets x. If player II refuses, both get nothing. Traditional game theory predicts that the play of this game will result in the unique subgame-perfect equilibrium in which player II plans to accept whatever she is offered and player I offers player II nothing.[1]

In the first of many experiments on this and related games by numerous authors, Güth *et al.* (1982) found that the modal offer was $\frac{1}{2}$ and that player I had roughly half a chance of being rejected if he offered about $\frac{1}{3}$ of the sum of money available. Binmore *et al.* (1989) reported qualitatively similar results in their replication of the Ultimatum Game experiment. There have been many related studies in the interim, surveyed by Bolton and Zwick (1993), Güth and Tietz (1990), Roth (1994), and Thaler (1988).

Critics of traditional game theory have quoted these results (along with the early results on the finitely repeated Prisoners' Dilemma and games involving the private provision of public goods) as demonstrating that the optimizing paradigm on which game theory is based is fundamentally mistaken. Instead, so the story goes, people simply honor whatever social norm is appropriate to the situation. Frank (1988) is particularly eloquent on this subject. In bargaining games, for example, it is popular to assert that people "just play fair."

Many game theorists have responded by dismissing laboratory results as irrelevant to actual behavior. We agree that the results of poorly designed experiments are irrelevant. Binmore (1992, p. 51) stresses that an experimentalist or game theorist should be cautious about making predictions unless the following criteria are satisfied:[2]

- The game is reasonably simple;
- The incentives are adequate;
- Sufficient opportunity for trial-and-error learning is provided.

[1] If offers must be made in whole numbers of cents, other subgame-perfect equilibria also exist, but player II never gets more than one cent in any of these.

[2] As experimental techniques in economics have become increasingly sophisticated, the importance of these factors has come to the fore. As advocated by Smith (1991), it is now commonplace to offer experimental subjects large incentives instead of the negligible amounts considered appropriate by many psychologists. At the same time, the introduction of computer technology has made it possible to use interactive demonstrations to teach subjects the rules of the game quickly and efficiently and to give the subjects the experience of large numbers of repetitions of the game. A survey to Ledyard (1992) of recent experiments concerning the private provision of public goods is revealing. In experiment after experiment, subjects are reported to approach the game-theoretic equilibrium as the incentives increase and the subjects' experience with the game becomes extensive.

On the other hand, game theorists cannot ignore experiments that persistently refute their predictions when all three criteria are satisfied. In the case of the Ultimatum Game, the relevant experiments have been replicated too often for doubts about the data to persist. A theory predicting that real people will use the subgame-perfect equilibrium in the Ultimatum Game is therefore open to question.

At first glance, the case for subgame-perfection in the Ultimatum Game seems ironclad. This is a two-player game of perfect information in which each player moves only once.[3] Player I need only believe that player II will not play a weakly dominated strategy to arrive at the subgame-perfect offer. But the deletion of weakly dominated strategies is an *eductive* principle (cf. Binmore (1987, 1988)), whereas we believe that the principles to which one must appeal when predicting actual behavior, in the laboratory or elsewhere, are almost always *evolutive* in character. That is to say, the outcomes we observe are not the product of careful reasoning but of trial-and-error learning.

This paper demonstrates that interactive learning processes readily lead to outcomes in the Ultimatum Game that are Nash equilibria but not subgame-perfect.[4] We argue that game theorists were therefore wrong to put all their eggs in the subgame-perfect basket when predicting laboratory behavior in the Ultimatum Game. A case exists for predicting that interactive learning will result in the selection of one of the other Nash equilibria of the game.

Section 2 begins by showing that if the initial conditions are not too close to the subgame-perfect equilibrium, then the replicator dynamics can converge to Nash equilibria in the Ultimatum Game that are not subgame-perfect. Given the relation between trembles and subgame-perfect equilibria (Selten (1975)), such a result is of interest only if it is robust in the presence of relevant perturbations. We therefore introduce noise into the replicator dynamics. When this noise is small in absolute terms but relatively larger in the population of responders, we find that asymptotic attractors survive which are Nash equilbria but not subgame-perfect. But why do we expect responders to be noisier than proposers? Our reason is to be found in the structure of the Ultimatum Game. When noise levels are allowed to depend on the potential cost of making an error, the system

[3] In particular, the criticism that subgame-perfection calls for players to regard their opponents as perfectly rational after having received evidence to the contrary (cf. Binmore (1987/1988) has no force in the Ultimatum Game.

[4] This finding is not without precedent. Binmore (1990), Samuelson (1988, 1993, 1994), and Samuelson and Zhang (1992) give simple examples showing that the deletion of weakly dominated strategies is at best a dubious activity in an evolutionary context.

can endogenously produce a situation with more noise in the responding population.

Section 3 explains how we think these calculations should be interpreted in the light of the experimental data. In the process, we comment on a complementary learning-based analysis of the Ultimatum Game due to Roth and Erev (1993). We also explain why we expect to see initial conditions in laboratory experiments that lead the dynamics to equilibria that are not subgame-perfect. In particular, we suggest that initial play reflects decision rules that have evolved in real-life bargaining situations that are superficially similar to the Ultimatum Game. These bargaining games generally feature more symmetric allocations of bargaining power than the Ultimatum Game, yielding initial play in Ultimatum Game experiments that need not be close to the subgame-perfect equilibrium.

Section 4 discusses how we think (out-of-equilibrium) behavior can persist in which people "leave money on the table." This section also comments on the use of "fairness" explanations for the outcomes of Ultimatum Game experiments.

The results of Section 2 are established by numerically computing trajectories for the replicator dynamics. In order to provide some insight into the forces that drive these results, Section 5 studies a variant of Selten's (1978) Chain-Store Game, which we reinterpret as a two-offer simplification of the Ultimatum Game. In this simpler setting, an analytic study of the evolutionary dynamics is possible. The same analysis also provides a possible resolution of the well-known chain-store paradox that does not require incomplete information assumptions and applies even when only one potential entrant exists.

We employ the replicator dynamics throughout. Why are such biologically motivated dynamics relevant? First, Section 6 presents an aspiration-level model of learning that leads to the replicator dynamics. Börgers and Sarin (1993), Binmore and Samuelson (1993), Cabrales (1993), and Schlag (1994) similarly present learning models that lead to the replicator dynamics, suggesting that the replicator dynamics are of more than merely biological interest. Second, the analysis of Section 5 isolates the smoothness properties of the learning model that drive our results, revealing that qualitatively similar results will hold in a wide variety of learning models (including variants of Roth and Erev's (1993) model).

2. Numerical Calculations

This section studies a version of the Ultimatum Game. The players must split a "pie" of size 40. The set of offers available to the proposer is $I = \{1, 2, \ldots, 40\}$.[5] (Note that an offer i is the amount that player I proposes that player II should get rather than the amount player I demands for himself.) An action for player II is a choice from the set $\{Y, N\}$. Her strategies are therefore functions f: $\{1, 2, \ldots, 40\} \rightarrow \{Y, N\}$. However, we assume that player II is restricted to functions of the form $f(i) = Y$ $(i \geq j)$ and $f(i) = N$ $(i < j)$ for some $j \in \{1, 2, \ldots, 40\}$. We can then identify player II's strategy with the minimum acceptable offer j and the set of pure-strategy pairs can be identified with $I \times I$. The forty pure-strategy Nash equilibria are (i, i) $(i = 1, 2, \ldots, 40)$. Since $i = 0$ is excluded, the unique subgame-perfect equilibrium is (1, 1).

For an evolutionary analysis, we assume that player I is drawn from an infinite population of proposers and that player II is drawn from an infinite population of responders. The fraction of proposers who make offer i at time t is denoted by $x_i(t)$. The fitness $\pi_i(t)$ of a proposer using offer i at time t is taken to be the expected payoff to a player I who makes offer i when his opponent is drawn at random from the population of responders at time t. Average fitness in the population of proposers at time t is $\overline{\pi}_I(t) = x_1(t)\pi_1(t) + \cdots + x_{40}\pi_{40}(t)$. The standard replicator equation for the evolution of $x_i(t)$ is given by

$$\dot{x}_i = x_i(\pi_i - \overline{\pi}_I) \qquad i \in \{1, 2, \ldots, 40\}. \tag{1}$$

Similarly, we let $y_j(t)$ be the fraction of responders playing strategy j at time t, with $\pi_j(t)$ being the fitness of a responder using strategy j and $\overline{\pi}_{II}(t)$ be the average fitness of responders, so that

$$\dot{y}_j = y_j(\pi_j - \overline{\pi}_{II}) \qquad j \in \{1, 2, \ldots, 40\}. \tag{2}$$

The evolution of the whole system is determined by the 80 equations given by (1) and (2).

In the terminology of Hofbauer and Sigmund (1988), every Nash equilibrium is a rest point of the replicator dynamics.[6] It is easy to show that many of these Nash equilibria are local attractors. In addition, the calculation reported in cell (0, 0) of Table I shows that, with uniform initial conditions,[7]

[5] In what seemed crucial cases, we also computed solutions for games with $I = \{1, 2, \ldots, 100\}$ without significantly altering the results.

[6] A *rest point* r is a fixed point of the dynamics. A *local attractor* l has the property that, for each neighborhood V with $l \in V$, there is another neighborhood U with $l \in U \subseteq V$ such that any trajectory that begins in U remains in V. An *asymptotic attractor* a is a local attractor with the property that all trajectories which begin in a small enough neighborhood of a converge to a.

[7] That is, each population begins with each strategy being played by $\frac{1}{40}$ of the agents in that population.

the system converges to an equilibrium in which player II receives a little more than 20% of the pie. We therefore have immediate occasion to cast doubt on the subgame-perfect prediction in an evolutive context.

However, it may appear that Nash equilibria which fail to be subgame-perfect equilibria are attractors only because the long-run operation of the replicator dynamics allows some strategies to approach extinction, and hence artificially excludes the evolutionary pressure against weakly dominated strategies that would otherwise eliminate them. We therefore turn our attention to models in which small fractions of all possible strategies are continually injected into the population—including those that test the "rationality" of responders who refuse positive offers. Only if the survival of Nash equilibria that are not subgame-perfect is robust in the presence of such noise can we realistically argue against the subgame-perfect prediction.

It is natural to see the noisy model as an evolutionary gloss on Selten's (1975) trembling-hand story, which he used to justify subgame-perfect equilibria in games like the Ultimatum Game. However, caution is necessary before pressing the analogy too far. Samuelson and Zhang (1992) show that adding noise to the replicator and other evolutionary dynamics does not necessarily lead to the elimination of weakly dominated strategies. The question of whether only subgame-perfect equilibria can survive in a noisy evolutionary environment therefore remains open.

Noise in an interactive learning system may arise in many ways and cause perturbations of various types. We therefore think it important to be clear on the source of the noise to be studied.[8] This in turn requires that we take a little more care than is usual in modeling the agents.

We envisage an agent as a stimulus–response mechanism with two modes of operation: a playing mode and a learning mode. Its playing mode operates when it is called upon to choose a strategy in one of a large number of games that it repeatedly plays against different opponents. Its behavior in each game is triggered by a stimulus that is determined by the manner in which the game is framed. (By a "game-frame," we mean more than the game itself. We include also the context in which the game is encountered and the manner in which its rules are described.[9]) When it receives such a stimulus s it responds by playing a strategy $D(s)$. If the learning mode were absent, an agent could therefore be identified with a fixed decision rule D that maps a set of stimuli into a set of strategies.

[8] We depart from that part of the refinement literature which follows Kohlberg and Mertens (1986) in demanding robustness in the face of all conceivable perturbations. There is no reason to suppose that a system will necessarily be adapted to types of noise that it has experienced only rarely if at all.

[9] For example, it may be relevant whether the interacting agents are a monopoly seller and a buyer, or whether they are the joint winners of a lottery.

However, sometimes an agent will enter its learning mode between games to adjust its current decision rule. When learning, it takes a stimulus s and some information f about the relative success of strategies in the game labeled by s to modify the value of $D(s)$. The learning rule L that it uses for this purpose is assumed to be fixed. We restrict our attention to learning rules that lead to the replicator dynamics largely because this dynamic has been widely discussed in the literature on evolutionary game theory and hence will be familiar (but see Section 6).

Noise may perturb an agent in its decision mode or in its learning mode. Here and in Section 6, we simplify by considering only the second possibility. We then simplify further by assuming that the only source of error lies in the possibility that an agent may mistakenly learn to play a strategy that is adapted to the wrong game.[10] We do not explicitly model the situations that may be confused with the Ultimatum Game. In the case of a misguided proposer, we simply assume that he makes each offer i in the Ultimatum Game with probability θ_i. If the fraction of proposers at time t who misread the game is always δ_I, and the usual arguments leading to the replicator equation apply to the fraction $1 - \delta_I$ of the proposing population who do not misread the game, then we are led to the "noisy replicator equation"

$$\dot{x}_i = (1 - \delta_I)x_i(\pi_i - \overline{\pi}_I) + \delta_I(\theta_i - x_i) \tag{3}$$

for the evolution of the fraction $x_i(t)$ of agents in the proposing population who play strategy i. The corresponding equation for the population of responders is

$$\dot{y}_j = (1 - \delta_{II})y_j(\pi_j - \overline{\pi}_{II}) + \delta_{II}(\psi_j - y_j), \tag{4}$$

where δ_{II} is the fraction of the responding population who misread the game and ψ_j describes the choices of such agents.

Section 6 derives (1)–(2) and (3)–(4) from an explicit choice model in which agents sometimes misread their strategic situation. Other choice models can lead to different versions of the dynamics. For example, if a proportion $\delta_I\tau$ of the agents die (or leave the game, or choose to experiment with new strategies) in each time period of length τ, to be replaced by

[10] Although the English language forces us into speaking of players' misreading the game or learning to play better, it should be emphasized that our agents do not monitor what is going on except insofar as this is modeled by the learning rule with which they are endowed. The fact that they have a learning rule at all makes them more flexible than the stimulus–response machines that are often considered, since their decision rules for playing games evolve over time, but the learning rule that governs how decision rules evolve is fixed.

TABLE I

FIXED NOISE CALCULATIONS

		δ_{II}				
		0.1	0.01	0.001	0.0001	0
	0.1	7	2	1	1	1
	0.01	9	7	3	1	1
δ_I	0.001	9	9	7	3	1
	0.0001	9	9	9	7	1
	0	9	9	9	9	9

novices who play each strategy i with probability θ_i, then we are led to the equation $\dot{x}_i = x_i(\pi_i - \bar{\pi}_I) + \delta_I(\theta_i - x_i)$. This corresponds to noise in agents' playing mode rather than their learning mode. Our theoretical analysis in Section 5 includes this case as well as (3) by examining dynamics of the form $\dot{x}_i = \Delta_I x_i(\pi_i - \bar{\pi}_I) + \delta_I(\theta_i - x_i)$. Alternatively, Binmore *et al.* (1993) examine a choice model that gives rise to the dynamics $\dot{x}_i = x_i(\pi_i - \bar{\pi}_I)/\bar{\pi}_I$. Van Damme (1987) and others work with a discrete version of this dynamic. We have reported numerical calculations using this discrete dynamic in Binmore and Samuelson (1994), and we indicate how the results differ from those reported here as we proceed.

What determines θ_i and ψ_j? These presumably reflect rules of thumb or behavior learned in other games, and as a result we have little to say about their precise form. For most of our calculations, we will assume that these represent a uniform distribution over strategies. We discuss how the specification of θ_i and ψ_j affects the results at the end of this section.

Table I reports calculations for various values of δ_I and δ_{II}.[11] The rows in Table I correspond to different values of δ_I. The columns correspond to different values of δ_{II}. In each case, the system was initialized with each of the 40 possible strategies being played by $\frac{1}{40}$ of each population. The mistake probabilities were also taken to be uniform, so that $\theta_i = \psi_j = \frac{1}{40}$.

The entries in Table I are the model offers made by player I after the system has converged to a point where the proportion of each population playing each strategy is unchanging in its first 15 decimal places. In each case, the frequency with which the model offer is played at this point is 1.00 to at least two decimal places. The equilibrium behavior of responders

[11] The difference equation $x_i(t + \tau) - x_i(t) = \tau[(1 - \delta_I)x_i(\pi_i - \bar{\pi}) + \delta_I(\theta_i - x_i)]$ is used to approximate Eq. (3) where we set $\tau = 0.01$. The robustness of the approximation was tested by repeating a sample of the calculations with much smaller values of τ.

is much more diffuse, but is very highly concentrated on strategies less than or equal to the modal offer. Hence, offers are rejected with only a very tiny probability. For example, in the cases when the model equilibrium offer made by player I is 9, a significant fraction of responders would accept each of the offers between 1 and 9 in equilibrium (with virtually no responders insisting on more than 9)—but the fraction of responders who will refuse anything lower than 9 is high enough to make it unprofitable for proposers to reduce their offer.

Table I shows that, if the noise level among responders is sufficiently small relative to that of proposers, then the subgame-perfect equilibrium appears. However, if the noise level in the responding population fails to be small enough compared with the noise level in the proposing population, then outcomes appear that are far from the subgame-perfect equilibrium. If responders are noisy enough compared with proposers, then player II gets a little more than 20% of the pie.[12]

Section 5 provides an analytic explanation of these results for a simple special case, but the intuition is straightforward. It is, for example, weakly dominated for player II to refuse an offer of 10%. There will therefore always be some evolutionary pressure against this strategy because, in a noisy population, the set of proposers who make such low offers is continually renewed. However, if this fraction of the proposing population becomes sufficiently small, the pressure against refusals of 10% will be negligible compared with the drift engendered by the noise in the responding population. Hence, if responders are noisy enough relative to proposers, then sufficiently many responders can reject offers of 10% that it is not a best response for proposers to offer less and we can reach outcomes that are not subgame-perfect.

Why should we anticipate that there will be more noise in the population of responders than in the population of proposers? Recall that we envision the noise arising as a result of an agent misreading the game when learning and hence acquiring an inappropriate behavior. The context is that of a boundedly rational agent without sufficient computational power to devote full attention to all of the many games that compete for its attention. However, the frequency with which learning errors are made is unlikely to be independent of the potential costs. Instead, we expect the likelihood of a learning error to depend on how much it currently matters in payoff

[12] For the dynamic $x_i(t + 1) = x_i(t) + x_i(t)(\pi_i - \bar{\pi})/\bar{\pi}$, Binmore and Samuelson (1994) find results that are much the same as reported in this paper, though in (1994) we find that player I's noise level need only be at least as high as player II's in order to give subgame-perfection. The outcome for cases in which player II's noise level is higher is again 9. This difference arises because, near the subgame-perfect equilibrium, the divisor π becomes especially small for responders. This accentuates the learning portion of the noisy replicator dynamic, causing the responding population to seem less noisy.

terms what strategy is played in the game.[13] In more familiar terms, the assumption will be that the players are more diligent in identifying games correctly when their potential gains and losses are large, and more prone to misread games when their potential gains or losses are small.[14]

In the Ultimatum Game, the result of making such an assumption is that responders will tend to be noisier when proposers are making low offers, because the responders will then have less at stake. In particular, such endogenously determined noise will lead responders to be noisier than proposers if the system should get close to the subgame-perfect equilibrium.

To explore this question further, we performed calculations in which the noise levels were endogenized along the lines discussed above. We took

$$\delta_k(t) = \frac{\alpha\beta}{\alpha + \lambda_k(t)} \qquad k = \mathrm{I}, \mathrm{II}, \tag{5}$$

where α and β are constant and $\lambda_k(t)$ is the difference between the maximum and minimum of the expected payoffs attached to player k's strategies, given the current distribution of strategies in the opposing population. When this difference is zero, as is nearly the case for responders at the subgame-perfect equilibrium, the noise level takes its highest value of β. If the difference could increase all the way to infinity, $\delta_k(t)$ would decrease to zero.[15]

[13] This formulation is consistent with the spirit of Myerson's (1991) proper equilibrium, which refines the idea of a trembling-hand equilibrium by making more costly mistakes less likely.

[14] Such an assumption adds more complexity to the stimulus–response mechanism used to model an agent. The mechanism must now incorporate a device that responds to changes in its environment by diverting computational capacity between monitoring and other tasks according to the estimated rewards from the different activities. Like the learning rule, this device is assumed to be fixed.

[15] The difference between the maximum and minimum payoff is an arbitrary measure of the payoffs that are at stake in a game. Calculations using alternative measures, such as the variance of the payoffs to player k's strategies, with each strategy taken to be equally likely in the variance calculation, produced analogous results (Binmore and Samuelson (1994)). A more realistic measure would perhaps use a sample of past payoffs rather than employing all current payoffs. On the other hand, we suspect that people are indeed often able to make educated guesses about their compatriots' current payoffs without necessarily being at all well informed about the strategies that secure the payoffs. Academic economists, for example, are often able to estimate their colleagues' salaries quite closely. Extreme payoffs are especially likely to attract comment.

TABLE II

CALCULATIONS WITH ENDOGENOUS NOISE

α	β	Offer	$\delta_I(\infty)$	$\delta_{II}(\infty)$
10	1	9	0.26	0.52
10	0.1	9	0.024	0.053
10	0.01	9	0.0024	0.0053
10	0.001	9	0.00024	0.00053
1	1	9	0.032	0.1
1	0.1	9	0.0031	0.01
1	0.01	9	0.00031	0.001
1	0.001	9	0.000031	0.0001
0.1	1	9	0.0032	0.011
0.1	0.1	9	0.00032	0.0011
0.1	0.01	9	0.000032	0.00011
0.1	0.001	9	0.0000032	0.000011
0.01	1	9	0.00032	0.0011
0.01	0.1	9	0.000032	0.00011
0.01	0.01	9	0.0000032	0.000011
0.01	0.001	9	0.00000032	0.0000011

Table II summarizes calculations with endogenized noise for various values of the two constants α and β listed in the first and second columns. The third column shows the modal offer made in equilibrium. The frequency with which the modal offer made in equilibrium is again 1.00 to at least two decimal places, and responders' strategies range between the modal offer and zero, with virtually no rejections. The fifth and sixth columns show the noise levels in the two populations after equilibrium is achieved.

Endogenizing the noise leads to an equilibrium in which the responder population is noisier than the proposer population. It is therefore not surprising that the equilibrium outcome is not subgame-perfect. In fact, the equilibrium offer is again close to 20%.

How robust are these results? First, consider the question of initial conditions. The calculations reported in Tables I and II are based on a uniform initial distribution of offers over $I \times I$. We also performed $1600 = 40 \times 40$ other calculations to explore the dependence of the results on the initial conditions. Table III shows the modal equilibrium offers for some of these initial conditions for the case of endogenous noise with $\alpha = 1$ and $\beta = 0.1$. The entry in row i and column j is the modal equilibrium offer when the system is started with all proposers playing i and all responders playing j. The frequency of the modal equilibrium offer remains 1.00 to at least two decimal places.

Space precludes showing the whole table. The table extends downward

TABLE III

CALCULATIONS WITH VARYING INITIAL CONDITIONS

	1	2	3	4	5	6	7	8	9	10	11	12	13	14	...
1	1	2	3	4	5	6	7	8	9	10	10	10	10	10	...
2	1	2	3	4	5	6	7	8	9	10	10	10	10	10	...
3	1	2	3	4	5	6	7	8	9	10	10	10	10	10	...
4	1	2	3	4	5	6	7	8	9	10	10	10	10	10	...
5	1	2	3	4	5	6	7	8	9	10	10	10	10	10	...
6	1	2	3	4	5	6	7	8	9	10	10	10	10	10	...
7	1	2	3	4	5	6	7	8	9	10	10	10	10	10	...
8	1	2	3	4	5	6	7	8	9	10	10	10	10	10	...
9	1	2	3	4	5	6	7	8	9	10	10	10	10	10	...
10	1	2	3	4	5	6	7	8	9	10	10	10	10	10	...
11	1	2	3	4	5	6	7	8	9	10	10	10	10	10	...
12	1	2	3	4	5	6	7	8	9	10	10	10	10	10	...
13	1	2	3	4	5	6	7	8	9	10	10	10	10	10	...
14	1	2	3	4	5	6	7	8	9	10	10	10	10	10	...
15	1	2	3	4	5	6	7	8	9	10	10	10	10	10	...
16	1	2	3	4	5	6	7	8	9	10	10	10	10	10	...
17	1	2	3	4	5	6	7	8	9	10	10	10	10	10	...
18	1	2	3	4	5	6	7	8	9	10	10	10	10	10	...
19	1	2	3	4	5	6	7	8	9	10	10	10	10	10	...
20	1	2	3	4	5	6	7	8	9	10	10	10	10	10	...
21	1	2	3	4	5	6	7	8	9	10	10	10	10	10	...
22	1	2	3	4	5	6	7	8	9	10	10	10	10	10	...
23	1	2	3	4	5	6	7	8	9	10	10	10	10	10	...
24	1	2	3	4	5	6	7	8	9	10	10	10	10	10	...
25	1	2	3	4	5	6	7	8	9	10	10	10	10	10	...
⋮	⋮	⋮	⋮	⋮	⋮	⋮	⋮	⋮	⋮	⋮	⋮	⋮	⋮	⋮	

just as one would anticipate on the basis of its existing pattern. For cases in which proposers initially play at least 10, it extends to the right as one would expect (except that the cells (38, 37), (38, 38), (39, 37), (39, 38), (39, 39), (40, 37), (40, 38), (40, 39), and (40, 40) yield outcomes of 9 rather than 10). For cases in which the initial offer is less than 10, we find the outcome to be 10 as long as the initial response is not too high (generally, up to 25, though higher for lower initial proposals). Higher initial responses yield lower final outcomes. We found the outcomes of initial conditions in which the proposer offers at least 10 to be robust to the values of α and β.[16] The outcomes for cases in which proposers initially offered less

[16] Using the specification of the basic dynamic as $x_i(t+1) = x_i(t) + x_i(t)(\pi_i - \bar{\pi})/\bar{\pi}$ and taking $\lambda_k(t)$ to be the variance of the payoffs accruing to each of agent k's strategies (rather than the difference between the maximum and minimum payoff) gives similar results, though the 10's are replaced by 9's.

than 10 were somewhat more sensitive, though the outcome was always at least as large as the minimum of the initial offer and initial proposal.[17]

The most striking feature of Table III is the robustness of a modal equilibrium offer above 20%. This offer appears for a large collection of initial conditions, including all those in which the initial proposal and response are at least 20%. The next section explains why we believe these are most likely to be the relevant initial conditions.

How do our results depend upon the specification of noise, i.e., on θ_i and ψ_j? By changing these specifications, we can obtain different results. The distribution of noise among the responders is especially important. If we alter ψ_j to put relatively more weight on offers and responses near zero, equilibrium outcomes can be achieved in which the responder gets less that 20% of the pie. Causing more weight to be put on somewhat higher offers gives outcomes in which the responders get more than 20% of the pie.

It is interesting to note, however, that changing the values of θ_i and ψ_j that are attached to relatively high offers has virtually no effect on the outcome. For example, we changed the mistake probabilities so that θ_{20} and ψ_{20}, the probabilities of the "fair" offer and response, took various values up to 0.95 (with the remaining values of θ_i and ψ_j remaining equal to one another). We might view this as a case in which the rule of thumb to which most noisy players resort when not paying attention to the game is to split the pie evenly, with a minority of such players adopting completely random rules of thumb that attach equal probability to all strategies. This change had almost no impact on the results of the calculations.

Probability attached to the "fair" response of 20 has little effect because this offer lies above the range of potential modal equilibrium offers (given that the remaining noise is uniformly distributed). As a result, the response earns a low payoff and the learning dynamics ensure that little probability accumulates on this response. The important considerations involve the distribution of noise over those responses that are lower than potential modal equilibrium offers. These responses earn almost identical payoffs and noise plays a major role in determining the equilibrium proportions of responders choosing each of these strategies. The key here is whether the noise in the responder population can amass a sufficient proportion of responders on a strategy y to make it unprofitable for proposers to make offers $x < y$ and hence sustain an outcome in which the modal offer is y. This depends upon the relative noise level of the two populations

[17] Whenever proposers initially make smaller offers than responders will accept, the dynamics begin with a race between proposers and responders, with each adjusting to match the other's strategy. The outcome of this race can be sensitive to parameters of the model when all responders initially get very low payoffs, as is the case for low proposer offers.

and on the specification of the noise. With uniform noise and sufficiently noisy responders, offers less than or equal to 10 can be sustained (cf. Table III) but higher offers cannot. If the responder's noise concentrates more of its probability near (away from) zero, then lower (higher) modal offers will result (provided in the latter case that the increased weight is not directed to offers such as 20 that are too high to be possible equilibrium modal offers).

It is clear that we cannot place too much significance on the particular value of the equilibrium offer of a little more than 20% that repeatedly emerges in the calculations, and we are anxious that our results not be remembered for this number. Different specifications of the model can give different numbers. The important feature of the results is that the equilibrium offer is frequently far from subgame-perfect, even when the noise levels are made very small indeed. This result requires primarily that the responding population be relatively more noisy than the proposing population. But this is the configuration of noise levels that appears if players tend to be less noisy when making decisions that are more important.

3. Relevance to Experimental Data?

How do we think the calculations of the previous section might be relevant to the experimental data? We think it useful to distinguish four time spans:[18]

1. In the *short run*, one should anticipate that behavior is driven primarily by norms that are triggered by the framing of the problem. The framing may well elicit norms that are ill-adapted to the laboratory situation. If these norms have been strongly reinforced outside the laboratory, they may be hard to shift. We suspect that the "irrational" behavior studied by the school of Kahneman and Tversky (1987) often falls into this category.

2. In the *medium run*, subjects begin to learn—as emphasized by Andreoni and Miller (1993), Crawford (1991, 1992), Miller and Andreoni (1991), Roth and Erev (1993), and numerous other authors.

3. In the *long run*, this interactive learning process may converge on an equilibrium of the game.

4. In the *ultralong run*, there may be jumps between equilibria when

[18] Our general views on the evolution of social norms inside and outside laboratories have been reported elsewhere (Binmore and Samuelson (1994)).

random shocks jolt the system from one basin of attraction to another—as emphasized by Young (1993), Kandori *et al.* (1993), and Samuelson (1994).

In the ultralong run, we expect an evolutionary process to select the subgame-perfect equilibrium. However, our guess is that the ultralong run is *too* long a run to be relevant to the available experimental data. We also do not think that the replicator dynamics provide a useful model of the ultralong run.[19]

But, as we have argued, the replicator dynamics do have a role to play as long-run approximations to certain simple learning rules. We therefore believe that the asymptotic properties of the replicator dynamics may be relevant to the long-run outcome of interactive learning in the laboratory. If so, then it is significant that our calculations of the long-run behavior of noisy replicator dynamics in the Ultimatum Game should generate equilibria that are far from subgame-perfect.

We believe that our calculations are relevant to the short run as well as the long run. As Section 6 explains, we think it possible to regard our dynamics as a crude but instructive model of social evolution (as well as of interactive learning in the laboratory).

More importantly, the social norm (or norms) triggered in the short term by laboratory experiments on the Ultimatum Game have presumably evolved to guide behavior in real-life bargaining situations that are superficially similar to the Ultimatum Game in some respects. We must therefore examine long-run behavior in these external situations for the origin of the norms that guide short-run behavior in laboratory experiments on the Ultimatum Game.

The real-life bargaining situations that have shaped the norms which subjects bring to the laboratory will be complicated by informational, reputational and other effects that are controlled away in the laboratory. The pure Ultimatum Game represents an extremal case in the class of real-life bargaining situations, because all the power is on the side of the proposer. If a social norm adapted to the pure Ultimatum Game leads to the proposer offering about 20% to the responder, we should therefore anticipate that bargaining norms adapted to a wider class of bargaining games will assign *more* than 20% to the responder. If this guess is correct,

[19] In Section 6, an implicit appeal is made to the law of large numbers when studying the long run, so that the underlying stoachastic learning is smoothed into a deterministic process. Binmore and Samuelson (1993) argue that one must refrain from such appeals when studying the ultralong run, and work directly with the stochastic system instead. If one were to work directly with the stochastic system in the current paper, results would emerge concerning the expected waiting time until reaching the subgame-perfect equilibrium in the ultralong run. The noisier the responding population relative to the proposing population, the longer the system lingers near long-run equilibria that are not subgame-perfect—and hence the longer and less relevant the ultralong run.

TABLE IV

MEDIUM RUN EQUIVALENT OF TABLE I

		δ_{II}				
		0.1	0.01	0.001	0.0001	0
	0.1	9 (13)	7 (74)	7 (69)	7 (69)	7 (69)
	0.01	9 (15)	9 (12)	9 (12)	9 (12)	9 (12)
δ_I	0.001	9 (15)	9 (12)	9 (12)	9 (12)	9 (12)
	0.0001	9 (15)	9 (12)	9 (12)	9 (12)	9 (12)
	0	9 (15)	9 (12)	9 (12)	9 (12)	9 (12)

we should therefore envisage the initial conditions for learning in the laboratory as allocating more than 20% to the responder and hence as lying in the basin of attraction of the 20% equilibrium offer of Table III.

What do our calculations tell us about the medium run? Table IV is a medium-run version of Table I. It differs from Table I in that the modal offer is reported on the first occasion at which no change in consecutive iterations was detected in the first five decimal places of the fractions of proposers making each offer. (Table I does the same, but with fifteen decimal places.) The number in parentheses following each modal offer is a measure of how much learning was necessary before a temporary stability in the first five decimal places was achieved.[20] In Table I, the frequency with which modal offers were used was 1.00 to at least two decimal places. The frequency with which the modal offers were used at the time reported in Table IV is at least .98.[21]

Table IV shows that the system *always* (with uniform initial conditions and perturbations) goes quite quickly to a modal offer of about 20%. But Table I shows this to be a medium-run result. In the long run, the system sometimes moves away to the subgame-perfect equilibrium. Only when $\delta_I < \delta_{II}$ is the medium-run behavior a useful guide to the long-run behavior of the system.

These results complement those of Roth and Erev (1993), who report Ultimatum-Game simulations that spend extended periods of time, in the

[20] The measure is the number of iterations of the discrete dynamic described in note 11 multiplied by the step size. In the model of Section 6, τ of the population has an opportunity to change strategies in each iteration of the discrete equation. Our measure therefore provides a crude approximation to the aggregate number of times that members of the entire population have assessed their strategies. The measure is intended to serve as a correlate for the number of rounds of an experiment required to reach temporary stability.

[21] If we ask for stability in only the first three decimal places, the first line of this table would read 9 (7) 9 (6) 9 (6) 9 (6), with the modal offer being played with frequency at least 0.85 in each case.

medium run, near equilibria that are Nash but not subgame-perfect. Roth and Erev suggest explaining the experimental data on the Ultimatum Game as a set of medium-run observations of a learning process.

We agree that much experimental data consists of a series of snapshots of medium-run phenomena. This is especially true of Ultimatum Game experiments, where both dispersion in proposals as well as rejected offers often persist into the later rounds of the experiments, both of which can only be medium-run phenomena in our model. However, we do not think it follows that theories of long-run behavior can be neglected. As our analysis of Section 5 suggests, long-run predictions of theoretical models of interactive learning will often depend only on *qualitative* features of the models. By contrast, medium-run predictions must be expected to depend upon the fine details of the interactive learning process. We therefore think that current theoretical techniques are more likely to be successful when applied to long-run rather than medium-run phenomena. Rather than seeking to explain experimental data in which medium-run behavior has been elicited, we therefore think there is a strong case for designing experiments with a view to eliciting long-run behavior.[22] The contribution of this paper is to argue that, in such experiments, there is no compelling reason why predictions should favor subgame-perfect equilibria over other Nash equilibria.

4. Leaving Money on the Table

The previous sections argue that attention needs to be paid to Nash equilibria in the Ultimatum Game that are not subgame-perfect. Such equilibria require that the responder be prepared to refuse low positive offers. If offered a choice between something and nothing, such a responder would therefore sometimes choose nothing. Such behavior is outlawed in conventional economic modeling. Perhaps for this reason, a common response to our argument is an incredulous "Why would anyone leave money on the table?"

That positive offers should be refused in the short term is easy to understand. Short-term behavior in the Ultimatum Game is likely to be governed by social norms that are triggered by the framing of the laboratory experiment. Rather than being adapted to the pure Ultimatum Game, such social norms will presumably have evolved for use in everyday cousins of the Ultimatum Game. In everyday life, we rarely play pure

[22] Binmore *et al.* (1992), for example, obtain very close convergence to equilibrium in less than 40 repetitions in a complicated bargaining game by offering high incentives and helping the subjects with sophisticated computer graphics.

take-it-or-leave-it games. In particular, real-life games are seldom played under conditions of total anonymity. A refusal of something positive may therefore serve to maintain a reputation for toughness. Even when we do play anonymously, outside options are often available. For example, in the take-it-or-leave-it auction used by stores to sell their goods, a refusal of something positive may simply indicate a willingness to search elsewhere for a better deal. Norms that call for refusals in commonly occurring "take-it-or-leave-it" situations therefore make good evolutionary sense. Given that such norms exist, it is unsurprising if they are sometimes inappropriately triggered in laboratory experiments. Short-run refusals of positive offers in the pure Ultimatum Game therefore create no problem for orthodox game theory.

However, we argue that Nash equilibria that are not subgame-perfect should be taken seriously even in the long run. Notice first that such equilibria actually require very few offers to be rejected, because proposers learn not to make such offers. Nevertheless, responders must stand ready to reject some positive offers.

On this subject, it is useful to observe that people clearly *do* sometimes leave money on the table. Frank (1988), for example, reminds us about tipping behavior in restaurants that are never to be visited again. After the waiter makes your change, you can either pocket the entire amount or leave the customary percentage on the table. Nearly everyone chooses the latter option—including economists!

A kibitzer may ask *why* we leave money on the table. Most people are satisfied with the explanation that leaving a tip is a custom that it would be uncomfortable to violate. If pressed, they might attribute the discomfort to the unfairness involved in disappointing the server's expectations.

Such considerations have led a number of authors to downplay strategic explanations of experimental behavior in favor of various theories of "fair play". Sophisticated versions of this approach sometimes build a taste for "fairness" into the utility functions attributed to the subjects. Ochs and Roth (1989) discuss such a utility function in explaining the medium-run results of an alternating offers bargaining experiment. Bolton (1991) explicitly constructs such a utility function for this purpose.

We agree that subjects find their emotions engaged in bargaining situations. They also frequently explain their bargaining behavior in the laboratory in terms of "fairness." But an approach that takes these facts at their face value is in danger of explaining too much and too little. Fairness theories explain too much because, by choosing one's fairness notion with sufficient care, one can justify a very wide range of outcomes. At the same time, such theories explain too little because they provide no insight into the origin of the fairness norms to which appeal is made.

We believe that a more fruitful approach is to ask how the custom of leaving money on the table can survive. Our answer is quite simple. The amounts involved and the frequency with which the situation arises are too small to provide sufficient evolutionary pressure to eliminate the phenomenon in a noisy environment. What then of the folk explanation in terms of the discomfort felt at violating a fairness norm?

In responding to such questions, it is important to appreciate that the evolutionary approach we advocate reverses the standard *explicans* and *explicandum* of the folk explanation and of economic theory. Our players are not members of the species *Homo economicus*. They do not optimize relative to fixed preferences. They simply have decision rules for playing games. When a player switches from a less profitable to a more profitable strategy, he does not do so because he thinks that the switch is optimal—he is just acting as a stimulus–response mechanism.

This model of *Homo sapiens* raises the question of how it *feels* for one's actions to be programmed as a result of past experience. Here the *post hoc, ergo propter hoc* fallacy awaits the unwary. It is easy to say that I preferred to take this foolish action rather than that wise action *because* I got angry. But we feel angry because adrenalin and other chemicals have been released into our bloodstream by a process which is only very partially under our conscious control. Angry feelings are a conditioned reflex to certain learned stimuli. Such conditioned reflexes survive because the behaviors they induce have evolutionary advantages. Rather than seeking to explain a particular behavior in terms of the angry feelings that accompany it, we therefore do better to explain the angry feelings in terms of the evolutionary advantages of the behavior. In brief, being angry or fearful or amorous is how it feels to be a stimulus–response mechanism.

Of course, none of us like to admit that much of our behavior is little more than a set of conditioned reflexes. We prefer to offer more flattering rationalizations of the behavior. For example, the stimulus of receiving an offer of only 10% in the Ultimatum Game may be sufficiently irritating that we turn the offer down. If asked *why* we refused, we may then rationalize our behavior by arguing that irritation is an entirely appropriate response to an "unfair" offer of 10%. Indeed, such an explanation may become institutionalized and so reinforce the behavior that it "explains." But we see no more reason to believe that "fairness norms" are fixed and immutable than that economic agents always maximize money. We believe that players usually find their way to a long-run equilibrium of trial-and-error learning without having any clear understanding of the strategic realities of the game they are playing. They simply learn that certain stimulus–response behaviors are effective. After the game, they may rationalize their behavior in various ways. In bargaining experiments, they often say that the long-run equilibrium to which they found their way is "fair." But, from an evolutionary perspective, how they explain

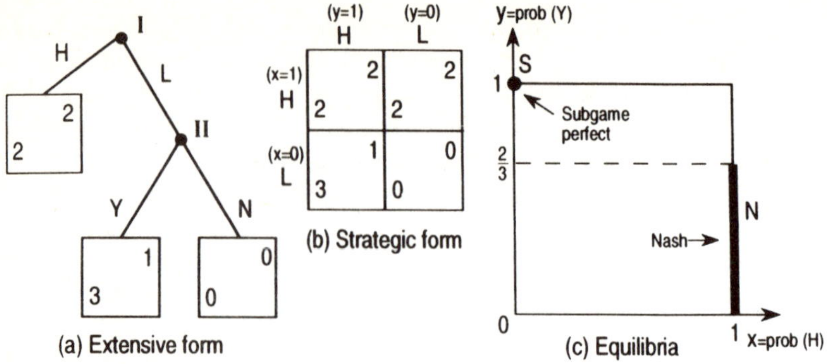

FIG. 1. Ultimatum Minigame.

their own behavior to themselves and others is an epiphenomenon. If they had found their way to another equilibrium, they would be offering some other explanation.[23] Economists who fit utility functions to observed behavior would similarly find themselves proposing a different utility function.

In summary, we believe that attention should be focused on the evolution of *behavior*. If a type of behavior that prompts people to leave money on the table survives, it will be because there is insufficient evolutionary pressure to remove it. Fairness explanations may be offered as rationalizations of the behavior. Such stories may even be incorporated into the workings of the stimulus–response mechanism. But the details of how the mechanism actually works or how we explain its workings to ourselves are secondary. The primary consideration is why some behavior patterns survive in a population while others will necessarily perish. Only after this question has been answered is it worthwhile to ask why some of the stories we tell ourselves are washed away by the evolutionary tide while others remain high and dry.

5. An Ultimatum Minigame

To identify the forces that drive our computational results, this section provides an analytical study of the simplified version of the Ultimatum Game shown in Fig. 1. In this Ultimatum Minigame, player I can make

[23] One can observe the fairness norms evolving in the laboratory. In Binmore *et al.* (1992), the median long-run equilibrium claim in a laboratory implementation of the Nash Demand Game turns out to be a very good predictor of the median claim said to be "fair" in a computerized postexperimental debriefing, even though subjects are randomly chosen for an initial conditioning that directs their subsequent play to different long-run equilibrium claims.

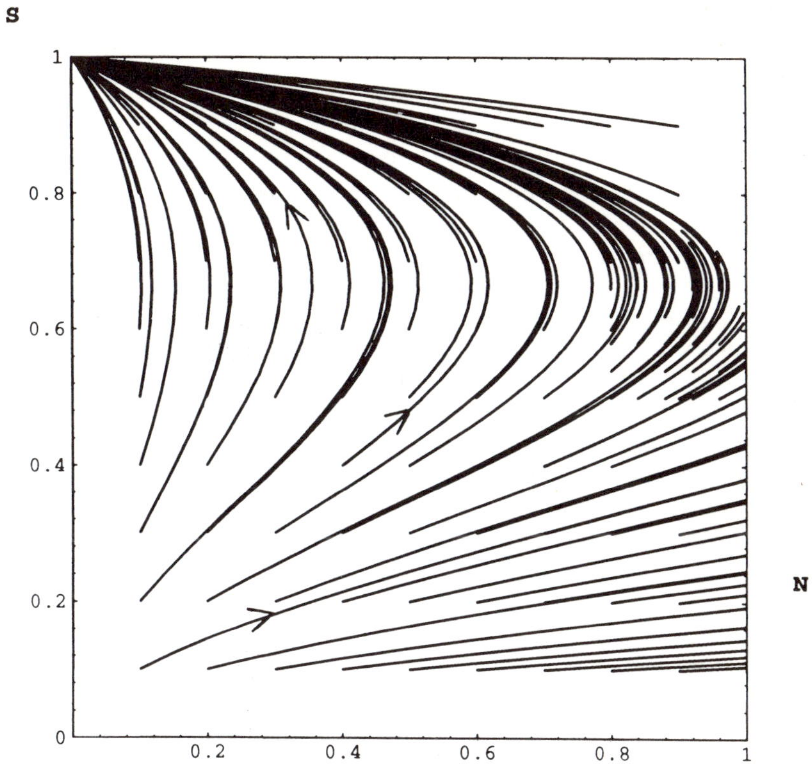

FIG. 2. Phase diagram, no noise.

a high offer (H) or a low offer (L). If he makes a high offer, it is assumed that player II accepts. If he makes a low offer, player II may accept (Y) or refuse (N).

The Ultimatum Minigame has the same structure as Selten's (1978) Chain-Store Game. Although we do not press the point, our conclusions in this section therefore provide a possible resolution of the chain-store paradox that applies even in the case when there is just one potential entrant.

Figure 1(c) shows the pairs (x, y) that represent equilibria in the Ultimatum Minigame, where x and y are the probabilities with which H and Y are played. There is a unique subgame-perfect equilibrium S at (0, 1) in Fig. 1(c), and a component N of Nash equilibria occupying the closed line segment joining $(1, \frac{2}{3})$ and (1, 0).

Figure 2 shows the trajectories of the standard replicator dynamics in the Ultimatum Minigame:

$$\dot{x} = x(1 - x)(2 - 3y) \tag{6}$$

$$\dot{y} = y(1 - y)(1 - x). \tag{7}$$

We summarize the key properties of these trajectories in Proposition 1 (cf. note 6):

PROPOSITION 1. *The subgame-perfect equilibrium S is the unique asymptotic attractor of the unperturbed replicator dynamics. With the exception of* $(1, \frac{2}{3})$, *the Nash equilibria in the set N are local attractors.*

The fact that interior points of N are local attractors does not seem to us an adequate reason for regarding them as alternatives to the subgame-perfect equilibrium S. To draw this conclusion, we feel it necessary that the result should survive in the presence of noise that continually replaces strategies that the replicator dynamics drives to extinction. We accordingly require strategies to be at least local attractors in slightly perturbed versions of the dynamics where extinction is not a possibility. We accordingly study the perturbed replicator dynamics, defined by

$$\dot{x} = \Delta_I x(1 - x)(2 - 3y) + \delta_I(\tfrac{1}{2} - x) \tag{8}$$

$$\dot{y} = \Delta_{II} y(1 - y)(1 - x) + \delta_{II}(\tfrac{1}{2} - y). \tag{9}$$

In the case when $\Delta_k = 1 - \delta_k$ $(k = \text{I, II})$, these equations are analogues to (3)–(4) of Section 3.

Figures 3 and 4 show the trajectories for the perturbed replicator dynamics. None of the points in N is a local attractor in Fig. 3, where responders and proposers are equally noisy; but there exists an asymptotic attractor in Fig. 4, where responders are noisier than proposers.

More formally, we are interested in what happens when the noise in (8)–(9) is small, so that $(\delta_I, \delta_{II}, \Delta_I, \Delta_{II})$ is close to $(0, 0, 1, 1)$. We fix $\phi = \delta_{II}\Delta_I/\delta_I\Delta_{II}$ and consider the limit as $(\delta_I, \delta_{II}, \Delta_I, \Delta_{II}) \to (0, 0, 1, 1)$ in two cases:

Case 1: $0 < \phi < 3 + 2\sqrt{2}$.

Case 2: $3 + 2\sqrt{2} < \phi$.

Since $3 + 2\sqrt{2} \sim 5.8$, responders are appreciably noisier than proposers in the second case.

LEMMA 1. *Let R be the set of rest points of the system* (8)–(9) *for values of* $(\delta_I, \delta_{II}, \Delta_I, \Delta_{II})$ *near* $(0, 0, 1, 1)$.

In Case 1, the set R has at most one limit point, which is the subgame-perfect equilibrium $S = (0, 1)$.

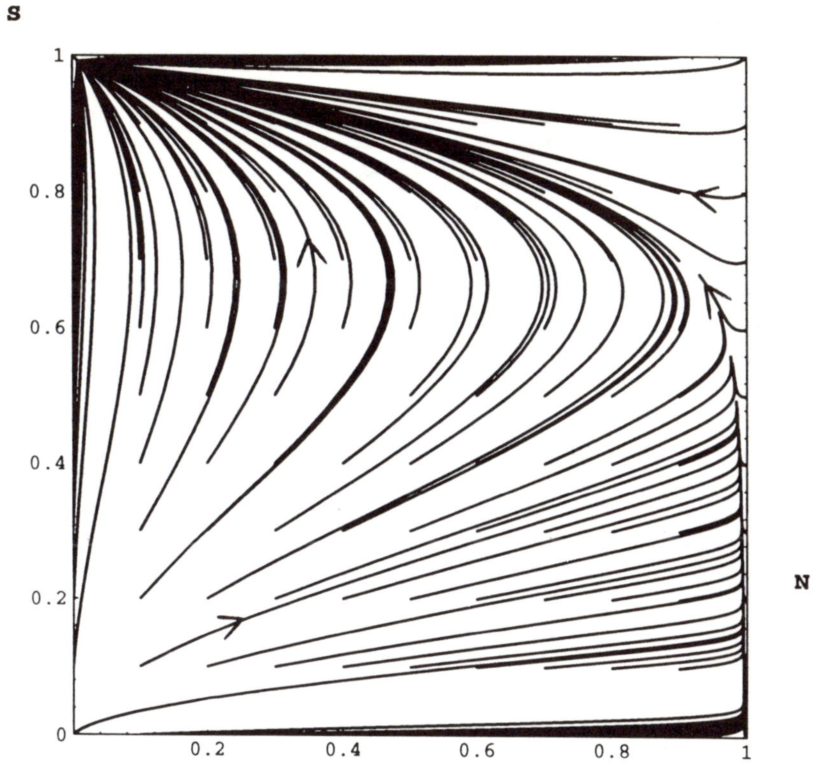

FIG. 3. Phase diagram, comparable noise ($\delta_{\mathrm{I}} = \delta_{\mathrm{II}} = 0.01$).

In Case 2, the set R has at most three limit points $S = (0, 1), (1, \underline{y})$ *and* $(1, \bar{y})$. *The points* $(1, \underline{y})$ *and* $(1, \bar{y})$ *lie in the set N of Nash equilibria.*

Proof. Writing $\dot{x} = \dot{y} = 0$ and $(\delta_{\mathrm{I}}, \delta_{\mathrm{II}}, \Delta_{\mathrm{I}}, \Delta_{\mathrm{II}}) = (0, 0, 1, 1)$ in (8)–(9) yields (0, 0), (0, 1) and $(1, y)$ as candidates for the limit points of R. The first point is a source for the unperturbed dynamics, and is easily excluded as a limit point of R. We now consider the possible values of y. To this end, write $\dot{x} = \dot{y} = 0$ in (8)–(9) and then set $x = 1$. We then obtain the equation

$$\phi = \frac{y(1 - y)}{(2 - 3y)(2y - 1)}.$$

This equation, illustrated in Fig. 6, has two solutions, $\underline{y}$ and $\bar{y}$, satisfying $\frac{1}{2} < \underline{y} < 2 - \sqrt{2} < \bar{y} < \frac{2}{3}$ when $\phi > 3 + 2\sqrt{2}$. When $\phi < 3 + \sqrt{2}$, the equation has no solutions y satisfying $0 \leq y \leq 1$. ■

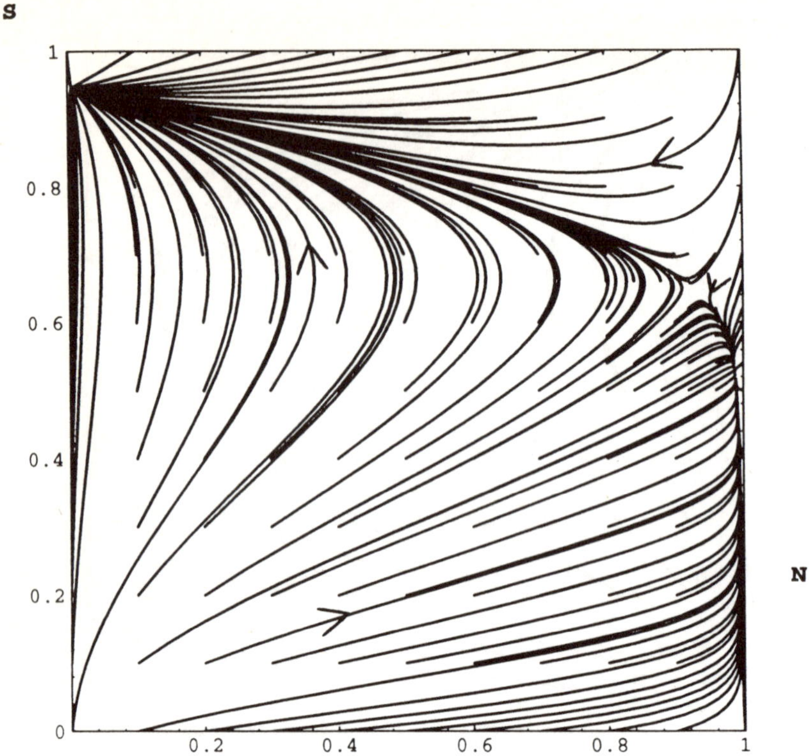

FIG. 4. Phase diagram, more noise in population II ($\delta_I = 0.01$, $\delta_{II} = 0.1$).

PROPOSITION 2. *Let* $A(\delta_I, \delta_{II}, \Delta_I, \Delta_{II})$ *be the set of asymptotic attractors of the system* (8)–(9) *given values* $(\delta_I, \delta_{II}, \Delta_I, \Delta_{II})$.

In Case 1, the set A has a unique limit point as $(\delta_I, \delta_{II}, \Delta_I, \Delta_{II}) \to (0, 0, 1, 1)$, *which is the subgame-perfect equilibrium* $S = (0, 1)$.

In Case 2, the set A has two limit points as $(\delta_I, \delta_{II}, \Delta_I, \Delta_{II}) \to (0, 0, 1, 1)$, *which are* $S = (0, 1)$ *and* $(1, \underline{y})$. *(The point* $(1, \bar{y})$ *is a limit of saddles.)*

The first case gives rise to the phase diagram in Fig. 3; the second case to the phase diagram in Fig. 4.

Proof. The proof of the first statement is straightforward, and we consider only the second. The right side of (8)–(9) defines a function F: $\mathbb{R}^2 \to \mathbb{R}^2$ for which

$$DF(x, y) = \begin{pmatrix} \Delta_I(2 - 3y)(1 - 2x) - \delta_I & -3\Delta_I x(1 - x) \\ -\Delta_{II} y(1 - y) & \Delta_{II}(1 - 2y)(1 - x) - \delta_{II} \end{pmatrix}.$$

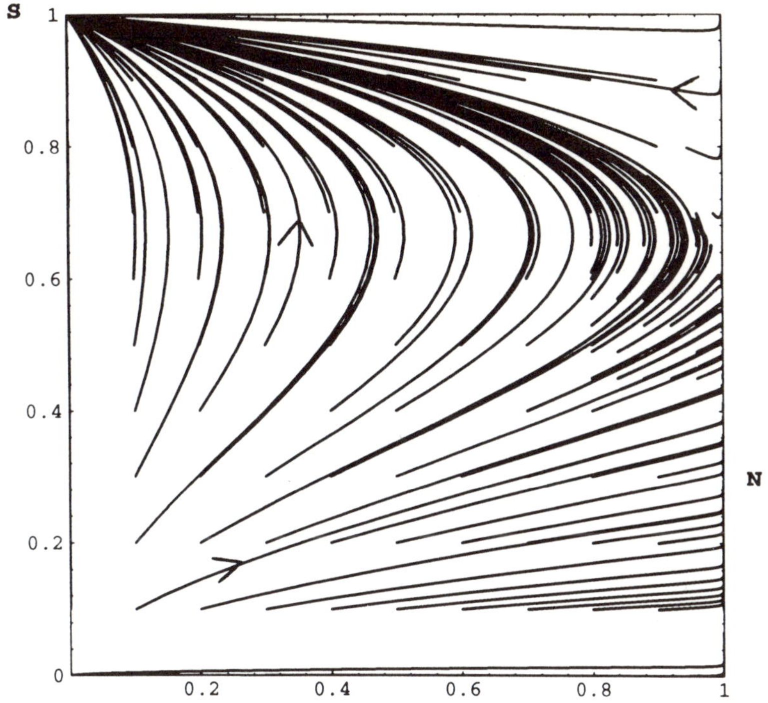

FIG. 5. Phase diagram, endogenous noise ($\alpha = \beta = 0.01$).

The trace of this matrix is negative when $\frac{1}{2} < y < \frac{2}{3}$ and $x > \frac{1}{2}$. We therefore consider the limiting value of its determinant.

Multiply the second column of det $DF(x, y)$ by $2y - 1$ and then make the substitution $\delta_{II}(2y - 1) = 2\Delta_{II}y(1 - y)(1 - x)$, which holds at a rest point by virtue of (8)–(9). Factor out the term $\Delta_I\Delta_{II}(1 - x)$ and write $\delta_I = 0$ and $x = 1$ in what remains. We then have to sign the determinant

$$\begin{vmatrix} 2 - 3y & 3(2y - 1) \\ y(1 - y) & 2y^2 - 2y + 1 \end{vmatrix} = y^2 - 4y + 2.$$

The roots of the quadratic equation $y^2 - 4y + 2 = 0$ are $2 - \sqrt{2}$ and $2 + \sqrt{2}$. It follows that the determinant is positive when $y = \underline{y} \leq 2 - \sqrt{2}$ and negative when $y = \overline{y} < \frac{2}{3} < 2 + \sqrt{2}$. Thus $\underline{y}$ is an asymptotic attractor and $\overline{y}$ is not. ∎

We next briefly consider the effect of endogenizing the noise in (8)–(9) by writing $\Delta_I = c_I(1 - \delta_I(t))$ and $\Delta_{II} = c_{II}(1 - \delta_{II}(t))$, where c_I and c_{II} are

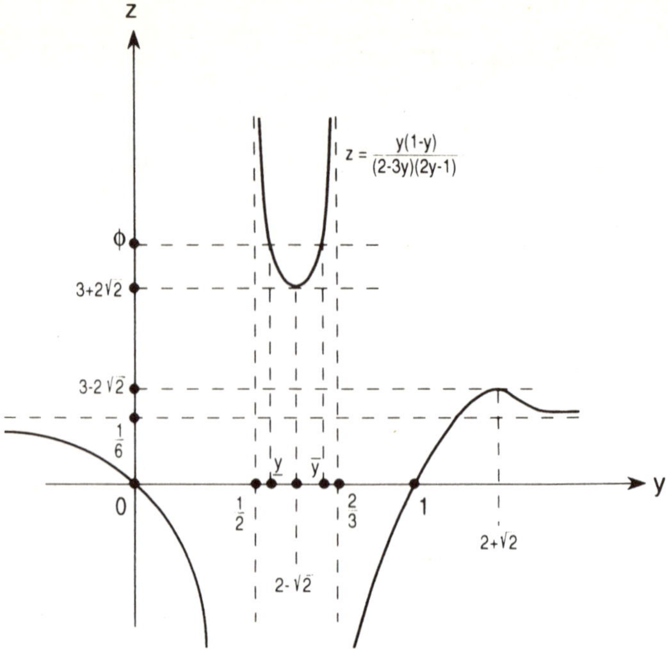

FIG. 6. Determining $\underline{y}$ and $\bar{y}$.

constants and $\delta_{I}(t)$ and $\delta_{II}(t)$ are given by (5). We study the rest points of this system as β approaches zero, for small values of α. Figure 5 shows the trajectories for this case.[24] We have:

PROPOSITION 3. *Let A be the set of asymptotic attractors for* (8)–(9) *with endogenous noise when* $\beta > 0$ *is small. For sufficiently small* α, *A has two limit points* $S = (0, 1)$ *and* $(1, \underline{y})$ *as* $\beta \to 0$. As $\alpha \to 0$, *these limit points converger to* $(0, 1)$ *and* $(1, \frac{1}{2})$.

Proof. The first statement follows from an argument analogous to that of the previous proposition, along with the observation that, as $x \to 1$, the difference between the minimum and maximum of player II's payoffs approaches zero, so that $\delta_{II}(t)/\delta_{I}(t)$ gets very large for sufficiently small α. As $\alpha \to 0$, the limiting ratio of $\delta_{II}(t)/\delta_{I}(t)$ approaches infinity, in which case we see from Fig. 6 that the limiting values of $\underline{y}$ and $\bar{y}$ approach $\frac{1}{2}$ and $\frac{2}{3}$ respectively. ■

We can identify the forces behind these results. When nearly all proposers are playing H, the pressure for a responder to play Y is weak.

[24] An asymptotic attractor exists, though it is difficult to see, at approximately (1, 0.505).

Adding noise to the strategies of the proposer pushes the population of proposers away from H, and increases the pressure for responders to move towards Y. This pushes the system toward the subgame-perfect equilibrium. However, the responders are also noisy. In the absence of other forces, this noise creates a drift that would eventually result in the responding population being split equally between agents who play Y and agents who play N. But the best reply for a proposer against such a mix in the responding population is to play H. If the drift in the responding population is sufficiently strong, it overpowers the countervailing tendency towards the subgame-perfect equilibrium. As a result, the responding population remains close enough to a half–half mix of Y and N that the best reply for proposers continues to be H. The subgame-perfect equilibrium then fails to be selected.

The same intuition can be expressed in a more quantitative form. The dynamic system give by (6)–(7) can be represented as a vector field on the state space $[0, 1]^2$, associating with each point (x, y) a vector

$$(x(1 - x)(2 - 3y), y(1 - y)(1 - x)) \tag{10}$$

indicating the direction and strength of moment at (x, y). Along the component N illustrated in Fig. 1c, these vectors are all zero vectors. The perturbed system (8)–(9) is the sum of the vector field given by (10) and a vector field of perturbations given by

$$\begin{aligned}((\Delta_I - 1)x(1 - x)(2 - 3y) + \delta_I(\tfrac{1}{2} - x),\\ (\Delta_{II} - 1)y(1 - y)(1 - x) + \delta_{II}(\tfrac{1}{2} - y)).\end{aligned} \tag{11}$$

Because the vector (10) is zero on N, the behavior of (8)–(9) on N is driven by the perturbations given in (11). The key question here is whether we can find a subset $\overline{N} \subset N$ such that the perturbations on $\overline{N}$ point into the basin of attraction of $\overline{N}$ in the *unperturbed* dynamics given by (10). If such an $\overline{N}$ exists, then the perturbations have the effect of continually pushing points near $\overline{N}$ back into the basin of attraction of $\overline{N}$. The dynamics (8)–(9) will then have an asymptotic attractor that is close to $\overline{N}$ and which converges to $\overline{N}$ as noise levels become small.

What does this have to do with relative noise levels? Let $\overline{N} = [0, \underline{y} + \varepsilon]$ for some small $\varepsilon > 0$. Notice that this set includes the half-half mixture between Y and N, and recall that responder perturbations are pushing responders toward the half–half mixture of Y and N. At the same time, proposer perturbations are pushing proposers towards the strategy L, which in turn creates pressure for responders to switch to Y. The larger the ratio δ_{II} to δ_{I}, the stronger the net perturbation pushing responders toward the half–half mixture, and the more likely the resulting perturbations to point into the basin of attraction of $\overline{N}$. Notice that only relative noise levels matter in determining the *direction* of the perturbation vectors, which (combined with the fact that (10) is zero on N) explains why the argument holds for arbitrarily small absolute noise levels.

Two implications of this argument are immediate. First, if the payoff 3 is replaced by 5 in the Ultimatum Minigame, then the best response to a half–half mixture of Y and N is L, so that the preturbed dynamics can never point into the basin of attraction of a subset of N. The dynamics then lead to the subgame-perfect equilibrium regardless of relative noise levels. Second, even after replacing 3 by 5, we could induce the perturbations to point into the basin of attraction of a subset of N if we altered the specification of the responders' behavior (when noisy) to put a large probability on N rather than a probability of $\frac{1}{2}$ on N. We see here the sensitivity of the results to the specification of noisy behavior.

Second, this argument also provides an idea as to how sensitive our results are to the specification of the unperturbed learning dynamic, which we have taken to be the replicator dynamic. The precise form of this dynamic is not particularly important, as long as the points in N are rest points and the set N has a basin of attraction into which perturbations can point. This excludes pure best-reply dynamics, in which even an arbitrarily small payoff difference between Y and N causes all responders to immediately switch to Y. However, virtually any system in which growth rates of strategy proportions are smooth, increasing functions of expected payoff differences (with growth rates being zero when all strategies have the same expected payoff) has the desired property.[25] The existence of an asymptotic attractor close to the component of equilibria that are not subgame perfect therefore holds for a wide class of dynamic processes, although the precise location of this attractor will be sensitive to the specification of the process.

These results address long-run behavior. What about the medium run? Figures 3 and 4 reveal medium-run behavior matching that reported in Table IV for the full Ultimatum Game. The trajectories in Fig. 3 reach the subgame-perfect equilibrium S in the long run, but in the medium run they can first approach the set N of Nash equilibria that are not subgame perfect. In Fig. 4 (where $\delta_{I} < \delta_{II}$), some trajectories again approach N in the medium run, but in these case these trajectories never leave the vicinity of N.

These results allow us to return to the question of fairness. Experimental results in bargaining games are now seldom explained *purely* in terms of

[25] Samuelson (1988) describes such systems as "cardinal" (as opposed to "ordinal").

fairness norms. Prasnikar and Roth (1992) and Roth *et al.* (1991), for example, suggest that some experimental results are best described in terms of a trade-off between strategic and fairness factors. Their most striking example contrasts the Ultimatum Game with the Best Shot Game. The latter is a public-goods-provision game that, like the Ultimatum Game, features a unique subgame-perfect equilibrium in which the first mover's payoff is much higher than the second mover's.

Prasnikar and Roth find experimental outcomes for the Ultimatum Game that are not close to subgame perfection. On the other hand, their Best Shot outcomes are consistent with a subgame-perfect explanation. They suggest that fairness considerations are able to wrestle outcomes away from subgame-perfection in the Ultimatum Game, but are overwhelmed by strategic considerations in the Best Shot game. In adopting this interpretation, they note that the Best Shot Game has only one pure-strategy Nash equilibrium that is not subgame perfect. The payoff pair resulting from this Nash equilibrium is (0.4, 3.7). The payoff pair at the rival subgame-perfect equilibrium is (3.7, 0.4). Prasnikar and Roth argue that there is then very little scope for learning to reinforce movements of behavior away from the subgame-perfect equilibrium, and hence very little scope for fairness considerations to gain a foothold. This contrasts with the Ultimatum Game, where the presence of Nash equilibria that are close to the unique subgame-perfect outcome provides opportunity for movements away from subgame perfection (perhaps induced by fairness considerations) to be reinforced.

Our methodology offers a potential explanation of such results that, in keeping with our discussion in Section 4, does not require treating "fairness" as a primitive concept. To make this point, we contrast the Best Shot Minigame of Figure 7 with the Ultimatum Minigame of Figure 1. In the Best Shot Minigame, player I has the option of making a high (H) or low (L) contribution to the public good. If player I makes a high contribution, the player II is assumed to make a low contribution. If player I makes a low contribution, then player II has the choice of a high or low contribution. The payoffs are such that there is no gain to both players making a high contribution and each player is better off if the other player makes the high contribution.

As Fig. 7 indicates, the Best Shot Minigame has the same qualitative features as the Ultimatum Game, with a subgame-perfect equilibrium S of (L, H) and a component N of Nash equilibria in which player I plays H. However, the strategic incentives associated with these equilibria differ, with this difference making it very much more likely that our model will select a Nash equilibrium that is not subgame-perfect in the Ultimatum Minigame than in the Best Shot Minigame. In particular, notice that N is much smaller than the corresponding Ultimatum Game component. Nash

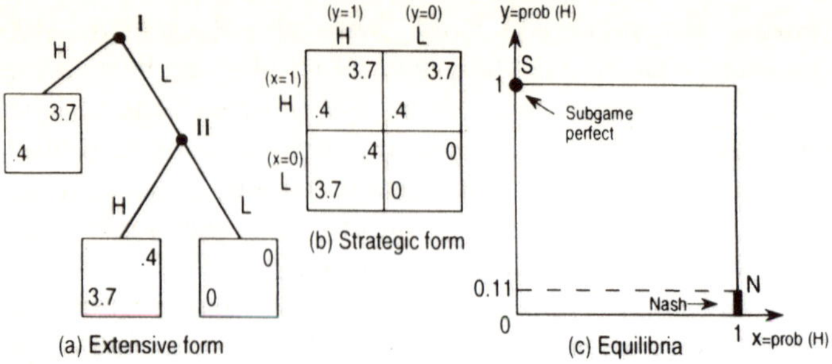

FIG. 7. Best Shot Minigame.

equilibria that are not subgame perfect in the Best Shot Game require that player II uses *H* with a probability no higher than approximately 0.11. As a result, the basin of attraction of this component relative to the unperturbed replicator dynamics is small. Moreover, if perturbations are introduced in which *H* and *L* receive the same probability from players who misread the game, then the perturbed dynamics cannot point into the basin of attraction of *N*. In contrast to the Ultimatum Minigame, no local attractor can therefore be found close to *N* and the subgame-perfect equilibrium is necessarily selected in the Best Shot Minigame.[26]

6. The Relevance of Replicator Dynamics

Why do we think the replicator dynamics, with their origins in biology, are relevant? Börgers and Sarin (1993) have shown that the replicator dynamics can serve as an approximation to simple learning models related to that used by Roth and Erev (1993). In this section we present a simple model of social evolution that also leads to the replicator dynamic. Our purpose is not to argue that the replicator dynamics represent "the" right model, but only to argue that dynamics of their general type are worthy of our attention.[27]

We interpret our model as one of social evolution because it relies on the ability of players to observe others' strategies; information that is generally not available in the laboratory. The reinforcement learning model of Börgers and Sarin (1993) is perhaps better suited as a model of learning

[26] A local attractor could be created close to *N*, but this requires perturbations that are very heavily weighted toward *L*.

[27] See Binmore and Samuelson (1993) and Cabrales (1993) for similar arguments. See Bendor *et al.* (1991) for another aspiration learning model.

in experiments. As explained in Section 3, both types of learning seem relevant to explaining experimental data.

Divide time into discrete periods of length τ. In every period, each agent retains his current strategy with probability $1 - \tau$. With probability τ, the agent compares his payoff with an aspiration level Λ, which is random and uniformly distributed on $[l, L]$. If the agent receives a payoff exceeding Λ, then the agent does not switch strategies. If the agent's payoff falls short of Λ, then the agent randomly chooses a new strategy. The probability that a given strategy is chosen is taken to be the proportion of the population playing that strategy. For example, it may be that the agent chooses a new strategy by randomly selecting another member of the population and imitating his strategy.

Why is Λ random? Our preferred interpretation here is that the aspiration level is actually fixed while the payoffs in the game are random,[28] though we find it analytically convenient to work with the equivalent formulation of a random aspiration level. This is consistent with the view we used to motivate our noisy dynamics, namely that players are constantly involved in a multitude of different games and may misperceive the precise nature of the game.

Let $p_i(t)$ be the probability that the aspiration level Λ exceeds the payoff from a proposer's strategy i in period t. We assume that exactly $p_i(t)$ of the proposers playing strategy i at time t are dealt an aspiration level in excess of their payoffs, and that these proposers switch to new strategies in exactly the same proportions as these strategies are used in the population of proposers. Then,

$$x_i(t + \tau) = x_i(t)(1 - \tau p_i(t)) + \sum_{j \in S} \tau p_j(t) x_j(t) x_i(t). \tag{12}$$

Note that $p_i(t) = (L - \pi_i(t))/(L - l)$, where $\pi_i(t)$ is the payoff to strategy i in period t. Hence,

$$\frac{x_i(t + \tau) - x_i(t)}{\tau} = x_i(t)\frac{\pi_i(t) - \overline{\pi}_{\mathrm{I}}(t)}{L - l},$$

where $\overline{\pi}_{\mathrm{I}}(t)$ is the average payoff over all proposers' strategies. Taking the limit as $\tau \to 0$ leads to a continuous-time version of the dynamic:

$$\dot{x}_i = x_i \frac{\pi_i - \overline{\pi}_{\mathrm{I}}}{L - l}. \tag{13}$$

[28] We then implicitly assume that the dispersion of the payoff distribution around its mean does not vary over strategies or players. More realistic assumptions would lead to more complex dynamics.

A similar equation can be derived for responders. The replicator dynamic given by (1)–(2) is the special case in which time has been rescaled so as to eliminate the constant $L - l$.[29]

Now suppose that each proposer ignores the learning process with probability δ_{I} in each period. Given that the learning process is ignored, with probability τ such an agent abandons his strategy regardless of aspiration level considerations and randomly chooses a new strategy, giving strategy i probability θ_i.

The dynamic given by (12) now becomes:[30]

$$x_i(t+\tau) = (1-\delta_{\mathrm{I}})\{x_i(t)(1-\tau p_i(t)) + \sum_{j \in S} \tau p_j(t) x_j(t) x_i(t)\} + \delta_{\mathrm{I}}[x_i(t) + \tau(\theta_i(t) - x_i(t))].$$

But $p_i(t) = (L - \pi_i(t))/(L - l)$. As $\tau \to 0$, we obtain that

$$\dot{x}_i = (1-\delta_{\mathrm{I}}) x_i(t) \frac{\pi_i(t) - \bar{\pi}_{\mathrm{I}}(t)}{L - l} + \delta_{\mathrm{I}}(\theta_i - x_i(t)). \tag{14}$$

The noisy replicator dynamic given by (3)–(4) is the special case in which $L - l = 1$ for both populations.

We have assumed that the two populations are governed by identical learning rules. There are two obvious ways in which they may not be. First, the populations may be characterized by different values of $L - l$. This is equivalent to saying that the unperturbed dynamics presented in (1)–(2) may proceed at different speeds of the two populations.[31] Consider the Ultimatum Minigame. The faster is the relative rate at which population I learns, the larger is the basin of attraction of the component of Nash equilibria N that are not subgame perfect. This makes it more likely that the perturbations on this component will point into its basin of attraction, and hence more likely that the dynamics do not lead to the subgame-perfect equilibria.

Alternatively, the rates of learning in the perturbed dynamics (3)–(4) may be different. This would correspond to a situation in which learn draws come at different rates for the two populations.[32] It is easy to show

[29] See Taylor and Jonker (1978) and Hofbauer and Sigmund (1988). This rescaling depends on an assumption that the distribution of the aspiration level is the same for the two players.

[30] Samuelson and Zhang (1992) examine an analogous dynamic, with the random choices interpreted as errors in passing strategies (or genes) from one generation to the next.

[31] One might, for example, make the speed of learning endogenous by linking it to the payoff magnitudes involved, just as we have done with noise levels.

[32] Again, these rates might be linked to payoff differences.

that changing the rate at which learning proceeds is equivalent to rescaling payoffs (i.e., multiplying by a constant) and noise levels.[33] As the relative rate at which learning procees for population II increases, we are again more likely to observe outcomes that are not subgame-perfect.

7. CONCLUSION

To the question of whether the subgame-perfect equilibrium should be regarded as the one and only game-theoretic prediction for the Ultimatum Game, we hope that we have provided a convincing and firmly negative answer. But what distinguishes our model from other theories of equilibrium selection in the long run, notably fairness theories? Neither our theory nor fairness theories are open to straightforward refutation, since both leave an apologist with ample room for maneuver in explaining the data. In particular, our theory requires tailoring the initial conditions and the noise that perturbes the dynamics to the experimental environment. We hope that our models will not have to be altered radically in moving between environments, as seems to be necessary with fairness models. However, the final word on these questions will have to await further research on a variety of other games. We hope to report such results soon.

References

Andreoni, J., and Miller, J. H. (1993). "Auctions with aritificial adaptive agents," mimeo, University of Wisconsin, Madison, WI; Carnegie Mellon University, Pittsburgh, PA.

Bendor, J., Mookherjee, D., and Ray, D. (1991). "Aspiration-based adaptive learning in two person repeated games," mimeo, Indian Statistical Institute, 1991.

Binmore, K. (1987/1988). "Modeling Rational Players: I and II," *Economics and Philosophy*, **3,** 179–214; **4,** 9–55.

Binmore, K. (1990). *Essays on the Foundations of Game Theory*, Cambridge, MA: Basil Blackwell.

Binmore, K., (1992). *Fun and Games*. Lexington, MA: Heath.

Binmore, K., and Samuelson, L. (1993). "Muddling through: Noisy equilibrium selection," mimeo, University College London; University of Wisconsin.

Binmore, K., and Samuelson, L. (1994). "An Economist's Perspective on the Evolution of Norms," *J. Institutional Theoretical Economics* **150,** 45–63.

Binmore, K., Samuelson, L., and Vaughan, R. (1993). "Musical chairs: Modelling noisy evolution," mimeo, University College London; University of Wisconsin.

[33] For example, increasing the rate at which time proceeds by replacing $\dot{x}$ with $k\dot{x}$ for $k < 1$ is equivalent to multiplying all payoffs by $1/k > 1$ and multiplying the noise level by $1/k$ (or multiplying the parameters α and β by $1/k$ in our endogenous noise cases).

BINMORE, K., SHAKED, A., AND SUTTON, J. (1989). "An Outside Option Experiment," *Quart. J. Econ.* **104,** 753–770.

BINMORE, K., SWIERZBINSKI, J., HSU, S., AND PROULX, C. (1992). "Focal points and Bargaining," Discussion Paper, University of Michigan.

BOLTON, G. E. (1991). "A Comparative Model of Bargaining: Theory and Evidence," *Amer. Econ. Rev.* **81,** 1096–1136.

BOLTON, G. E., AND ZWICK, R. (1993). "Anonymity versus punishment in ultimatum bargaining," mimeo, Pennsylvania State University.

BÖRGERS, T., AND SARIN, R. (1993). "Learning through reinforcement and replicator dynamics," technical report, University College London.

CABRALES, A. (1993). "Stochastic replicator dynamics," mimeo, University of California, San Diego.

CRAWFORD, V. P. (1991). "An 'Evolutionary' Interpretation of Van Huyck, Battalio, and Beil's Experimental Results on Coordination," *Games Econ. Behav.* **3,** 25–59.

CRAWFORD, V. P. (1992). "Adaptive dynamics in coordination games," Department of Economics Working Paper 92-02R, University of California, San Diego.

FRANK, R. (1988). *Passions within Reason*. New York: Norton.

GUTH, W., SCHMITTBERGER, R., AND SCHWARZE, B. (1982). "An Experimental Analysis of Ultimatum Bargaining," *J. Econ. Behav. Organ.* **3,** 367–388.

GÜTH, W., AND TIETZ, R. (1990). "Ultimatum Bargaining Behavior: A Survey and Comparison of Experimental Results," *J. Econ. Psychol.* **11,** 417–449.

HOFBAUER, J., AND SIGMUND, K. (1988). *The Theory of Evolution and Dynamical Systems*. Cambridge: Cambridge Univ.

KAHNEMAN, D. AND TVERSKY, A. (1988). "Rational Choice and the Framing of Decisions," in *Decision Making*. Cambridge: Cambridge Univ.

KANDORI, M., MAILATH, G. J., AND ROB, R. (1993). "Learning, Mutation, and Long Run Equilibria in Games," *Econometrica* **61,** 29–56.

KOHLBERG, E., AND MERTENS, J.-F. (1986). "On the Strategic Stability of Equilibria," *Econometrica* **54,** 1003–1038.

LEDYARD, J. (1992). "Public goods: A survey of experimental research," working paper, California Institute of Technology.

MILLER, J. H., AND ANDREONI, J. (1991). "Can Evolutionary Dynamics Explain Free Riding in Experiments?" *Econ. Lett.* **36,** 9–15.

MYERSON, R. B. (1991). *Game Theory: Analysis of Conflict*. Cambridge, MA: Harvard University Press.

OCHS, J., AND ROTH, A. E. (1989). "An Experimental Study of Sequential Bargaining," *Amer. Econ. Rev.* **79,** 355–384.

PRASNIKAR, V., AND ROTH, A. E. (1992). "Considerations of Fairness and Strategy: Experimental Data from Sequential Games," *Quart. J. Econ.* **106,** 865–888.

ROTH, A. E. (1994). "Bargaining Experiments," in *Handbook of Experimental Economics* (J. Kagel and A. E. Roth, Eds). Princeton, NJ: Princeton University Press, forthcoming.

ROTH, A. E., AND EREV, I. (1993). "Learning in Extensive-Form Games: Experimental Data and Simple Dynamic Models in the Intermediate Term," mimeo, University of Pittsburgh; The Technion.

ROTH, A. E., PRASNIKAR, V., OKUNO-FUJIWARA, M., AND ZAMIR, S. (1991). "Bargaining and Market Power in Jerusalem, Ljubljana, Pittsburgh, and Tokyo: An Experimental Study," *Amer. Econ. Rev.* **81,** 1068–1095.

SAMUELSON, L. (1988). "Evolutionary Foundations of Solution Concepts for Finite, Two-Player, Normal-Form Games," in *Theoretical Aspects of Reasoning about Knowledge* (M. Y. Vardi, Ed.). San Mateo, CA: Morgan Kaufmann.

SAMUELSON, L. (1993). "Does Evolution Eliminate Domianted Strategies?" *Frontiers of Game Theory* (K. Binmore, A. Kirman, and P. Tani, Eds). Cambridge, MA: MIT Press.

SAMUELSON, L., (1994). "Stochastic Stability in Games with Alternative Best Replies," *J. Econ. Theory* **64,** 35–65.

SAMUELSON, L., AND ZHANG, J. (1992). "Evolutionary Stability in Asymmetric Games," *J. Econ. Theory* **57,** 363–391.

SCHLAG, K. H. (1994). "Why imitate, and if so, how?" mimeo, University of Bonn.

SELTEN, R. (1975). "Reexamination of the Perfectness Concept for Equilibrium Points in Extensive-Form Games," *Int. J. Game Theory* **4,** 25–55.

SELTEN, R. (1978). "The Chain-Store Paradox," *Theory Dec.* **9,** 127–159.

SMITH, V. (1976). "Experimental Economics: Induced Value Theory," *Amer. Econ. Rev.* **66,** 274–279.

TAYLOR, P. D., AND JONKER, L. B. (1978). "Evolutionarily Stable Strategies and Game Dynamics," *Math. Biosci.* **40,** 145–156.

THALER, R. H. (1988). "Anomalies: The Ultimatum Game," *J. Econ. Perspect.* **2,** 185–206.

VAN DAMME, E. (1987). *Stability and Perfection of Nash Equilibria*. Berlin: Springer-Verlag.

YOUNG, P. (1993). "The Evolution of Conventions," *Econometrica* **61,** 57–84.

[7]

Neither Friends nor Strangers: Informal Networks of Subcontracting in French Industry

Edward H. Lorenz

Economists as a rule have attached little importance to the role of such social ties as trust and friendliness in market exchange. As Albert Hirschman (1982) has observed, this can be explained by the fact that the ideal market upon which claims of allocative efficiency rest involves large numbers of price-taking anonymous buyers and sellers supplied with perfect information. With such markets there is no room for bargaining, negotiation, or mutual adjustment, and the operators that contract together need not enter into a recurrent or continuing relationship.

This paper considers a case which does not conform to the economist's competitive ideal, that of continuing and recurrent relations between French firms and their subcontractors.[1] These are relations involving mutual dependency, where each firm's actions influence the other. The situation by its very nature calls for cooperation, and it is reasonable to ask whether trust plays a role in this process.

In order to motivate the discussion, I will first describe the context in which I decided to focus on the theme of trust and subcontracting. In 1985 I began a study of the introduction of new technology in small and medium French engineering firms.[2] This was prompted by a number of intriguing bits of evidence. From 1975 firms in this category had improved their performance relative to large firms in terms of profitability and rates of growth of output and employment. Further, in terms of the

[1] I would like to thank Diego Gambetta, Frank Wilkinson, Willy Brown, and Christina Ocampo for their interest in and suggestions for improving this paper. I also benefited from the comments of the participants in the trust seminar.

[2] The small and medium category (*petites et moyennes entreprises* or PME) refers to enterprises employing between 20 and 499 employees.

latter two criteria, the smaller firms in this category (between 10 and 100 employees) had outperformed the larger (Delattre 1982). Secondary sources also showed that small and medium firms had been some of the most dynamic investors in advanced computer-based technology, primarily NC and CNC machine tools (Cavestro 1984).

This picture of comparatively rapid growth and technological sophistication contradicted established views of the role of small firms in the French economy. In particular, it was inconsistent with the dualist model which predicted technological backwardness in accordance with the confinement of small firms to unstable portions of the product market. In order to come to some understanding of these unorthodox shifts in relative performance, I decided to investigate the process of mechanization in a selected number of mechanical engineering firms in the Lyons conurbation.

Preliminary visits to firms with 200 to 500 employees revealed that most had substantially reduced their employment levels since 1980. The value of their sales, however, had in most cases increased after a dip in 1982–83. This could be explained in part by improvements in their productivity, but also by a substantial increase in their use of subcontracting for intermediate component production.

To some extent, of course, the firms had used subcontracting before; few were of sufficient scale in their operations to warrant investing in plant for such specialized tasks as gear grinding or heat treatment. And they all made use of subcontracting to meet temporary capacity constraints.[3] What I was observing, however, was different. It was a shift to subcontracting on a permanent basis for such standard operations as turning, milling, and drilling. It allowed the firms to avoid making investments in up-to-date machine tools and was frequently the occasion for a reduction in capacity, with some existing plant being sold off. While the general type of operation subcontracted was not specialised or specific to the particular firm in question, the design and specifications of the components were. Thus it was not a case of substituting in-house production for standardized components available in the market: rather, components were being machined (turned, milled, etc.) by subcontractors according to firm-specific plans produced in the design offices of the client firm.

What appeared to be taking place, then, was a process of industrial disintegration similar to the well-documented Italian *decentramento*

[3] This form of subcontracting is encouraged by the rigid restrictions French legislation places on laying off workers. During the 1970s these restrictions spawned a proliferation of temporary help agencies whose employees do not benefit from the same protective legislation. Another common arrangement is the use of so-called *intérimaires*, permanent employees of one firm with an excess supply who are loaned on a temporary basis to a firm facing a capacity constraint.

(Piore and Sabel 1984; Sabel and Zeitlin 1985). The small-firm sector was benefiting from large firms hiving off some of the activities formerly undertaken in-house. When I questioned management about these policies, they generally attributed the decision to increase subcontracting to the 1981–82 depression in engineering together with the tremendous improvements in productivity then being made possible through the introduction of the CNC machine tools. Most argued that given the slow-growing and uncertain markets in which their firms operated, it would be impossible to amortize investments in CNC equipment. They were not in a position to continuously operate the equipment for the 12 to 16 hours a day required to achieve a satisfactory return on the investment. Smaller specialists, on the other hand, were in a position to do this, in part because they aggregated demands from multiple clients, and in part because of their greater internal flexibility in terms of shift work and overtime. In short, subcontractors could do it more cheaply.

Cost considerations, then, dictated the initial switch from in-house production to reliance on the market. Further discussion showed, however, that these evolving market relations were a far cry from those of the standard textbook, where 'faceless buyers and sellers meet for an instant to exchange standardized goods.' By 1984–85 the firms had begun to use a suggestive word to describe their relationship to these new subcontractors: partnership (*partenariat*). In the course of conversations in which I myself participated, other equally emotive terms evoked the nature of interfirm relations: the importance of loyalty (*fidélité*); the existence of a moral contract (*contrat moral*); and the need for mutual trust (*confiance mutuelle*). This language suggests a certain anxiety inherent in subcontracting, and the need for something like trust if the relationship was to work smoothly. Such considerations led me to structure my interviews around the following set of questions:

1 What risks does subcontracting pose, and what safeguards do firms make use of to minimize these risks?
2 What are the mutual obligations implicit in the relation of partnership?
3 What is the role of reputation in ensuring that contractual obligations are met?
4 How does a firm decide if it can trust another, and can this trust be intentionally created?

The remainder of the paper will be concerned with these issues, both at the analytical and the empirical level. I begin with some general remarks on the meaning of trust.

I

From my introductory comments it is no doubt evident that my notion of trust has something to do with relations of mutual dependency. I will now give a more precise definition of trusting behaviour in social relations.[4] This will clarify at least some of the semantic difficulties involved in employing a word with such varied usage. I will then turn to a discussion of the theoretical literature on vertical integration and subcontracting which shaped my empirical investigation. In the process, the relevance of the general definition of trust to subcontracting relations in particular will be made clear.

Trusting behaviour consists in action that (1) increases one's vulnerability to another whose behaviour is not under one's control, and (2) takes place in a situation where the penalty suffered if the trust is abused would lead one to regret the action. In economic terms this implies that the action would not be taken in the absence of trust because the expected net benefit is lower than if some alternative is chosen. In short, there is no best strategy independent of trust.

It is perhaps worth while to elaborate further on the implications of this definition. Firstly, trust presupposes decision-making in a situation of risk, where the risk is attributable to the strategic behaviour of others or to the possibility that they will behave opportunistically. By opportunistic behaviour I have in mind not only such blatant forms as stealing and lying, but also more subtle techniques such as withholding information in an effort to confuse. As Dasgupta (this volume) has noted, the possibility of such behaviour is a necessary condition for the question of trust to arise. If all people are invariably honest, doing their best to fulfil their commitments, then there is no problem of trust as I have defined it.

Secondly, the action and hence the risks are avoidable: one does not have to engage in trade with another firm (although this implies forgoing the potential benefits of trade). Being able to avoid the relation is fundamental. If you could not, you might say something like: 'I have no choice but to trust this person, institution, etc.' Clearly, there being no choice, we need not invoke trust to explain our behaviour. Of course, as Luhmann (this volume) points out, whether or not a relation is seen to be avoidable is often highly subjective, and presumably varies in accordance with the structure of institutions and political power.

Thirdly, it is useful to distinguish between risk associated with the behaviour of others and the risk of what economists call uncertain or exogenous events, such as acts of Nature or unpredictable changes in

[4] In common with Luhmann (this volume), I draw on the psychological literature, particularly Deutsch (1973).

consumer demand and prices. Trust in this context is unrelated to our concerns of possible opportunism and the violation of commitment.

II

Hirschman (1982) suggests that recent approaches in economics can address the role of social ties such as trust in market exchange. These approaches are concerned to explain the existence of continuing relations between economic actors by placing stress on such factors as transaction cost, limited information and imperfect maximization.

I would like to suggest that the transaction cost literature (associated notably with Williamson 1975; 1985) can tell us something about the role of trust in the economy. As the term 'transaction cost' suggests, this literature is concerned with the organizational implications of the costs of making a transaction. This includes not only the cost of reaching an agreement satisfactory to both sides, but also that of adapting the agreement to unanticipated contingencies and of enforcing its terms. Enforcement refers not only to potential litigation, but also to the use of private safeguards to prevent violation, a point I discuss in some detail in the empirical section below. The relation of transaction costs to the economy parallels that of friction to a physical system: it is often ignored in formal models but is none the less of great practical significance.

How does this relate to our concern? Trust enters into the argument because the presence of these costs is directly linked to the possibility that economic actors will be have opportunistically. This is obvious enough in the case of contract enforcement, but perhaps less so in those of negotiation and adaptation. Surely these latter costs are attributable to the time and expense of drafting a comprehensive agreement that attempts to account for all possible contingencies. But Williamson (1985) has made the point that in the absence of opportunistic behaviour there would be no need to attempt such costly planning: it would suffice for the two parties to agree always to adapt output to unanticipated contingencies in a jointly optimal way and always to share profits according to some general rule established in advance. Sequential adaptations would not pose risks if one could trust the other to behave honestly.

The tenor of my argument is probably becoming clear. If transaction costs are thought of as friction in the economy, then trust can be seen as an extremely effective lubricant. To quote Arrow (1974: 23): 'It saves a lot of trouble to have a fair degree of reliance in other people's word.'

I should emphasize that my use of the legalistic term 'contract' does not imply a comprehensive written agreement. In the subcontracting cases in question, agreements are never written. The only written document is the order form. Certainly there is no effort to engage in comprehensive planning. The initial agreement is a reference point, the gaps in planning being intentional, and it is understood that adaptations will have to be made if the relation is to continue. This incompleteness of contracts is one of the reasons (though not the only one) why, to my knowledge, there is no use of the courts to resolve disputes. It requires both subcontractor and client to engage in an ongoing process of discussion in order to resolve misunderstandings and ambiguities and arrive at acceptable terms. The court system is simply not designed to provide these services is an efficient manner.

Given the possibility of opportunistic behaviour, trust is an essential ingredient in intermediate product subcontracting in so far as the two firms are locked into the relation. By lock-in effects I mean not only that the mutual benefits will be achieved only if trade takes place, but that the identity of the partners counts. Switching partners involves a loss for both sides. As Klein, Crawford, and Alchian (1978) have argued, firms become locked into a relation when investments in specific assets have been made. This results in a bilateral monopoly. Specific assets are those whose value is less if switched to alternative transactions and consequently whose value is not fully salvageable if the relation breaks down. This situation would arise, for instance, if a subcontractor invested in machinery dedicated to the production of a specific component for a particular client and if the subsequent use of the machinery to service other clients' needs then entailed a costly retooling process.

An example may help to illustrate my point. Suppose a subcontractor invests in specialized fixtures and tooling to grind gears specific to a particular product. The amortized fixed cost of the tooling is £1000 per day and the daily operating costs are £200. Any contract price above £1200 per day for the subcontractor's services will allow a positive return on the investment. Suppose further, because the tooling and fixtures can only be adapted to other requirements at considerable cost, that the salvage value of the equipment if sold is £500 (daily rental equivalent). Consequently, if the contract is prematurely terminated the subcontractor faces a daily equivalent loss of £500. On the other hand, the client faces a potential loss associated with having to pay more for the components to be produced elsewhere with general purpose – and hence less efficient – equipment. He may also face costs due to the disruption of production while a replacement subcontractor is being found. The situation clearly calls for discussion and understanding, since without cooperation either side can block trade, thereby incurring mutual losses.

There is a large game-theoretic literature on such bilateral monopolies, concerned to find 'solutions' in terms of a determinant price for the supplier's services and hence for a division of joint profits (Rapoport

1970; Shubik 1959). The outcome is indeterminate in the sense that individual profit-maximizing decisions by the supplier and the buyer lead to an impasse. This is partly resolved in some models by explicitly taking into account the relative bargaining power of the two actors, represented by the magnitude of the loss each faces if the other carries out the threat to block trade.

My concern here is less with the terms of the original bargain than with the possibility of *ex post* opportunism: either reneging on the agreement or using the occasion of unanticipated contingencies to try to shift the distribution of joint profits in one's favour.[5] Returning to our example, suppose the subcontractor and the client agree on a contract price of £1200, allowing the subcontractor to break even on the proposed investment. Once the investment is made, however, the subcontractor's vulnerability is increased. The client is in a position to appropriate the subcontractor, demanding a new contract price slightly greater than £700 (the £500 salvage value if the assets are sold off and the £200 daily operating costs). He may justify this in the name of unexpected financial difficulties, which the subcontractor is generally not in a position to verify. Conversely, the subcontractor, realizing that the client faces stiff penalties for late delivery of the product to the final customer, may opportunistically use his bargaining power to push up the contract price, similarly claiming unforeseen costs. Verification may again be both difficult and expensive.

The main point is that even a situation of *ex ante* competitive supply, with a large number of subcontractors tendering bids for the contract, can be transformed into one of bilateral monopoly due to investment in specific assets. Once this occurs there is scope for opportunistic behaviour. If assets are general and products standardized, on the other hand, there is not. In this case the identity of the partners is not important, since if problems develop each can go his own way and fully redeploy his assets in other transactions without loss of value.[6]

[5] This is not to preclude the possibility of opportunism at the negotiation stage. Less trust implies that each side will take more costly measures to ensure that the other is truthfully disclosing their costs and revenues.

[6] This precludes the special hazard of fly-by-night firms. Suppose a subcontractor agrees to invest in a quality-improving asset (say a high-precision inspection device) for the purpose of a particular client's order. They agree on a price per component that allows the subcontractor a certain percentage return on the investment. The subcontractor, who has no intention of maintaining the relation, dishonestly avoids the investment, delivers a product below the specified quality, and receives the agreed price. The problem is discovered only when the component is assembled in the final product, whereupon the client responds by terminating the relation. The subcontractor gains from cheating and faces no loss associated with having invested in a specific asset that is not fully salvageable. The argument rests, of course, on asymmetric information, the subcontractor knowing more about the quality of the component than the client. In the empirical section below I discuss the safeguards whereby firms seek to protect themselves from such hazards.

The implication of this discussion is that the problem of trust in economic exchange is raised by the potential for opportunism inherent in investment in specific assets. Arguably, the contracting parties would avoid this problem if they could reach self-enforcing agreements. An agreement is defined as self-enforcing if the threat to terminate transactions (with a subsequent loss of business) if one party is caught cheating is sufficient to deter opportunism and ensure that contractual obligations are met. If such threats were sufficient, this would appear to resolve the problem of trust since each side would then be certain of the (rational) behaviour of the other.

The necessary conditions for self-enforcing agreements to be feasible have been enumerated in an interesting article by Telser (1980). His conclusions conform to the familiar results for infinitely repeated games which are discussed in this volume by Dasgupta.[7] Firstly, the sequence of transactions must be open-ended. There must always be a positive probability of continuing the sequence or else the relation will unravel. Secondly, for each player the discount rate has to be low enough for the one-off gains from cheating to be less in value than the expected net benefits that will be lost as a consequence of termination. Thirdly, the common knowledge assumption must hold. The players must share the knowledge that they share this ranking of the respective gains to be had from either violating or upholding the agreement.

There are two reasons why I believe this argument does not circumvent the need for trust. First of all it confuses information and trust. Clearly it is not enough for two firms to come together and share information on their costs and revenues. They also must trust each other's word. In other words, for common knowledge to play its assigned role in self-enforcing agreements there must exist a prior bond of trust between the contracting parties. Secondly, it does not adequately address the probability that unexpected developments in an unforeseeable future will trigger opportunistic responses. Trust will be essential to reassure those contemplating a long-term relation that adaptations to such future contingencies will be made in a jointly optimal way. The problem of trust in this context could only be avoided by making one of the following highly implausible assumptions about the nature of economic agents or the economic environment respectively. One could assume perfect rationality on the part of the actors: unlimited and costless ability to collect and process information. This would allow them to fully anticipate all relevant future eventualities. Alternatively one could simply assume what economists call a static world: a world without uncertainty due to exogenous events.

[7] See also Klein and Leffler (1982) for the case of quality assurance in final product markets.

In fact, with either of these admittedly unrealistic assumptions, it can be argued that the need for self-enforcing agreements would be eliminated due to the efficiency of third-party assistance in dispute resolution. If there were no limits to rationality, the two firms could costlessly negotiate a comprehensive agreement accounting for all possible circumstances. As Meade (1971) suggested, the world would be reduced once and for all to a giant higgle-haggle. Any subsequent efforts to alter the terms of the agreement could easily be rejected by the courts or by a third party as necessarily an effort to shift the distribution of joint gains to the favour of one side.[8] Much the same conclusion follows if we assume a world without uncertainty. In such a world, lacking in unanticipated contingencies, it would likewise be easy to negotiate a comprehensive agreement which the legal system could efficiently enforce.

In conclusion, then, once firms are locked into a relation, trust is essential. The need for trust can be circumscribed through the efforts of the parties to engage in comprehensive contracting. But the limits to our rationality in a world where surprise is inevitable ensure that such efforts will be imperfect at best. Trust cannot be disposed of entirely. The implications of this for economic exchange are threefold:

1 The right sort of investments may not be made, since actors do not trust each other to refrain from abusing their bargaining power to renege on contract terms or to use a shift in circumstances to shift the division of profits in their favour.
2 A considerable amount of expense may go into fashioning safeguards designed to minimize the risks of being a victim of opportunistic behaviour. These expenses could be avoided if there were mutual trust.
3 More subtly, those in a bilateral monopoly may hesitate to demand legitimate adaptations to changed conditions, fearing such demands may cause conflict owing to a suspicion that they are in fact illegitimate, and intended only to change the agreed distribution of profits.

III

The theoretical discussion implies that given plausible assumptions about the economic world, trust has an important role to play in facilitating efficient contractual relations. Is this borne out in practice? I now turn to

[8] This of course assumes that the courts are trustworthy. I make this assumption in the empirical section which follows, and I think it is a reasonable one. The French firms I interviewed never suggested that a concern over honesty prevented them from using the courts.

an interpretation of the empirical results, addressing in turn each of the questions raised in the introductory section. These results are based on interviews conducted with the managerial personnel of ten client firms, all located in the Lyons conurbation.[9] The firms include the following subsectors of mechanical engineering: machine tools, textile machinery, packaging machinery, mining equipment, and industrial filters. They are not mass producers: their products are large, complex, customized, and expensive. As production is to order they find it difficult to predict their requirements with any accuracy beyond a horizon of six months to a year.

The size of the firms varies between 100 and 400 employees. In most cases, as noted, employment levels have declined since 1980, owing in part to improvements in productivity and in part to increased use of subcontracting. Even those firms with expanding sales are not taking on additional labour. With one exception the firms experienced a decline in sales between 1980 and 1982 and subsequently have recovered to varying degrees. The size of the subcontracting firms they use, with few exceptions, is between 3 or 4 employees and 60. The average is between 10 and 20.

The first point to be made is that there is extensive use of safeguards by client firms to minimize the possibility of being the victim of opportunistic behaviour and hence the need to rely on trust. There is an Italian saying which captures much of the sentiment: 'It is good to trust but it is better not to trust.' First, client firms prefer to solicit tenders from a minimum of three subcontractors in order to preclude an opportunistic distortion of production costs. They also prefer to split an order between a minimum of two subcontractors so that if difficulties develop with one it is possible to switch to the other. This practice may, of course, entail a loss of potential scale economies depending on batch size.

Once firms are locked into a relation owing to investment in specific assets, such policies no longer apply. It is then impossible to refer to the market to ensure competitive pricing. In the case of physical assets (machine tools etc.) it is extremely rare for subcontractors to invest in machinery specific to a particular client's requirements. I only came across one significant example. The problem potentially arises in the case of tooling, that is specialized dies and moulds for forging and casting, and specialized fixtures and cutting tools for component machining. But

[9] The firms were initially visited in 1985. Five were revisited approximately one year later. In each case the production manager responsible for the firm's overall subcontracting policy was interviewed and in most cases so too was the buying agent. While these interviews constitute the principal source of information for this study, I also visited five subcontractors who work for three of the client firms. In each case I spoke to the owner or managing director. These interviews were less systematic than those conducted with the clients. The aim was simply to check for major discrepancies between the two sides' characterization of the subcontracting relationship.

risks are easily avoided: these physical assets are mobile and the client purchases them and retains control. If problems develop with one subcontractor the tooling is recovered and transferred to another. The rule is that subcontractors invest only in general purpose equipment. It is unclear whether this entails significant losses, however, since the more specific the machinery the less the sacrifice in scale economies from retaining production in-house. More suggestive of loss is the fact that when production of a particular type of component is carried out both in-house and externally (which does occur), the in-house machinery tends to be more specific.

Specific investment can take other forms, for example in training and skills. In the case of component machining this is relatively unimportant. As one production manager observed, 'nobody has a monopoly position in turning or milling.' There is a degree of skill specificity in the case of assembly work, and the general policy is that employees of the subcontracting firm undergo a period of on-the-job training in the assembly shops of the client firm before undertaking subcontracting on their own premises. In short, the costs of training in specific skills are borne by the client. The hazards implicit in such an arrangement no doubt help explain why so little assembly work is contracted out.

Assembly subcontracting poses a further hazard of the fly-by-night kind through private information on quality. In the case of individual component production, quality can be readily controlled. The client firm is as technically knowledgeable as the subcontractor. As a rule individual components are inspected on delivery and payment is made only after ascertaining that they meet the stipulated standards. In the case of subassemblies or entire machine assemblies, however, it is impossible to check the individual components, and problems due to poor workmanship may appear some time after the machine has been sold to the final customer. According to the client firms, it is primarily this problem of quality assurance which discourages them from resorting to assembly subcontracting on a regular basis.

Quality can pose a serious problem when components are delivered at the last moment, thus holding up completion of the machine and its delivery to the customer. This is costly since firms face severe penalties for late delivery on contracts which can sometimes amount to over £1 million. The risk of late delivery, accompanied by poor quality or not, is apparently the most difficult to safeguard against. Bear in mind that we are not talking about standardized components. The market cannot supply an instantaneous replacement; nor can the component easily be produced in-house.

In such cases, how is the firm to interpret a request from the subcontractor for an extension on delivery? Is it a legitimate request due to an unanticipated machine breakdown or some other unfortunate difficulty? Or is it opportunistic, the work having been taken on in the full knowledge that the capacity to complete the order on time was lacking? Given the difficulties of verification, repeated problems of delivery lead to the latter conclusion, with the subcontractor being dropped. When client firms say a subcontractor is trustworthy they invariably have in mind the question of prompt delivery as well as quality and price.[10]

Even when a subcontractor takes the precaution of investing solely in general purpose equipment it is possible to be locked into a relation. This occurs when a generalized capacity expansion is made only because of the prospect of selling a large amount of a particular product to a particular client. If the contract is then prematurely terminated the subcontractor is left with a large overhang of excess capacity that can only be sold off at distress prices. This clearly was recognized as a problem by the subcontractors interviewed, though they had varying degrees of success in coping with it. One quite successful subcontractor, for example, stated that occasionally it found it necessary to refuse orders from established customers so as to avoid the risks of a high degree of dependency. Others, who had grown up in close association with individual firms, had over 50 per cent of their sales directed to a single client. In such cases the loss of that client could prove crippling.

One of the most interesting results of the study is that not only do subcontractors seek to diversify their clients in order to reduce the risks of dependency, but so too do client firms. The accepted rule among the engineering employers of Lyons is that orders should be limited to between 10 and 15 per cent of a subcontractor's sales. The maximum figure is set to avoid the possibility of one's own market difficulties having a crippling effect on the subcontractor. Any figure less than 10 per cent, however, would imply too insignificant a position in the subcontractor's order book to warrant the desired consideration.

Effectively, then, clients put themselves in the position of the subcontractor in determining the optimal level of orders, much as game theorists have argued they should. From the subcontractor's perspective a reliable client is one who maintains a level of work. If a client firm wants a subcontractor to take its interests into account on recurrent contracts regarding quality and delivery, it is simply not acceptable to pull the work back in-house (assuming this were possible) whenever the firm faces a fall in final demand. Quantity adaptations also pose a trust

[10] Another potential hazard is that the subcontractor, recognizing his enhanced bargaining power at such times, will demand an increase in the contract price, claiming perhaps exceptional breakdown costs. In the short run the client may have no choice but to accede to the demand. A number of firms described such instances. There do not appear to be any effective safeguards. The only response is to seek an alternative supplier while completing the contract and subsequently break off the relation.

problem. How is a subcontractor to interpret a decline in the level of work from a particular client? Is the client facing legitimate difficulties, or is it opportunistically pulling work back in-house having first encouraged a capacity expansion? In the case of dedicated capacity expansions of a general purpose nature, quantity adaptations can be quite as contentious as price adaptations.

The 10 to 15 per cent figure seems to represent an optimum. It allows the client a degree of flexibility without undermining the viability of the subcontractor, and at the same time ensures the client is considered sufficiently important to make a continuing relation of interest.

This brings us to my second point, the meaning of the term 'partnership' or the expectations implicit in the moral contract. Partnership clearly implies something more than what is stated on the order form. It is not merely a question of not buying more than you know you can pay for. It seems rather to involve the following: in exchange for improved performance by the subcontractor on quality and delivery, the client firm will make every effort to guarantee a level of work; furthermore, any adaptations to price, quantity, and delivery are to be made in a non-opportunistic way by both sides, with full disclosure of the relevant information. In particular, this implies that the subcontractor will not be unconditionally dropped if a differential in terms of price or quality emerges with respect to competitors. Rather, clients stated that they operate a system of advance warnings; a reasonable period is allowed to their partner to match the competition. It also implies that clients will not pull back work in-house each time product demand falls. A number of firms observed explicit sharing rules to resolve problems associated with uncontrollable fluctuations in demand. A typical procedure was to guarantee that a constant fraction of work would be produced both in-house and by subcontractors regardless of the absolute level of output.

To sum up, partnership entails a long-term commitment and reflects a condition of mutual dependency where both client and subcontractor are in a position to influence the other by their behaviour. Partnership is a set of normative rules, determining what behaviour is permissible and what constitutes a violation of trust. The rules are designed to facilitate exchange in a situation otherwise open to exploitation.

The third point under consideration is the role of reputation in assuring compliance with the terms of the 'moral contract'. To put this question in another way: do firms rely on reputation alone in determining whether to trust each other? The evidence suggests that reputation is important but no substitute for experience. My information pertains primarily to the client's perception of the subcontractor and I would not want to exclude entirely the likelihood of asymmetry here. The client firms are comparatively visible, being prominent members of the Lyons engineering community and in most cases larger than the subcontractors. My interviews suggested that they are acutely aware of their reputation for reliability. When asked how they signalled their trustworthiness to potential subcontractors, they invariably referred to this.

But let us consider the conditions necessary for reputation effects to deter defection, here defined as violating the implicit terms of the partnership relation:

1 Common knowledge: all defections have to be made public. This does not simply mean a public announcement. It has to be possible to distinguish between real and bogus claims, to know who really was the offending party. This is frequently impossible.
2 The defector has to pay the full penalty: the firm cannot simply change its management team and ask for and receive forgiveness from the community.[11]

These are stringent conditions. In general, it is clear that client firms do not rely solely on reputation to determine the trustworthiness of a subcontractor, in the sense of his willingness to uphold the terms of the moral contract. To know whether a subcontractor is trustworthy (and this is my fourth point) they rely additionally on their own experience. One manager said a minimum of a year and a number of contracts was required, though he claimed that after three months he had an intuitive sense of how things would turn out based on personal contact with his opposite number. Another firm gave the figure of two to three years. During this period they operated a conscious testing process. Initially short-term contracts were given, it being understood that renewal would depend on performance. Once satisfied, a one-year contract was offered in which for a fixed price they guaranteed a level of work. At this point, according to the manager, the two firms were partners.

Time and experience were critical elements in deciding whether or not to trust. This suggests, much along the lines of Good's argument (this volume), an incremental notion of trust, of trust being built up in successive stages. It should be stressed, however, that it is not simply a question of registering performance on successive contracts and assigning a probability of trustworthiness on that basis. Invariably interviewees stressed the need for personal contact, and a number of firms stated that geographical proximity was desirable because it facilitated this. Thus one manager observed: 'It is important to visit and to talk, to know each other. This is partnership. If we know each other it is easier to resolve problems and to

[11] One client firm, close to bankruptcy in 1980 and now supported by the state, was actively trying to improve its reputation for reliability. Management spoke as if the world began in 1983. The success of the publicity campaign was not entirely clear, but there was no evidence that this firm experienced greater problems with subcontracting than others in the region.

adjust. So the closer we are to each other the easier it is. The Rhône-Alpes has an advantage owing to the availability of subcontractors.

How are we to interpret this stress on the importance of personal relations? Is this evidence that friendship or caring is involved in efficient economics? Are we to conclude that trust between firms depends on bonds of friendship between the respective employers or managers? From the structure of this paper you can probably foresee that my answer is negative. It would be difficult to explain how trust could be present as often as it is in subcontracting if it were to depend on sentiments of friendship. If this were true, we would have to adopt in the economic sphere Hawthorn's (this volume) conclusion in the political: that any attempt to produce trust which was not in fact an attempt to produce something else, something self-reinforcing, must fail. It seems implausible to entertain feelings of friendship for someone when it is realized that he or she is acting in a friendly way solely for the purpose of facilitating an economic transaction.

I interpret the stress on personal contact in a different way and as primarily to do with a pervasive problem in continuing economic relations: the need to adapt to contingency. Personal contact facilitates this by allowing for an easier exchange of information. You learn about the other person's idiosyncracies and together you forge a special language which permits more sensitive interpretation. In short, you develop what might be called an understanding.

This is what I take the French managers to mean when they say they know each other and are partners. Perhaps this relation can best be conceived as an intermediate level between friends and stranger, for which capitalist societies have developed a distinctive tolerance. Of course, nothing I say precludes the possibility that those involved in recurrent economic relations may develop deeper personal bonds and that this may also become a reason for trusting. But the evidence of French subcontracting shows that such bonds are not a necessary precondition for trust. If this interpretation is correct, then there is nothing to prevent firms (if they consider it worth while) making a concerted effort to inspire confidence. Certain types of behaviour, certain types of personal contact involving the exchange of information and the giving of mutual assurances, plus a considerable time for the consistency of one's behaviour to be observed and tested: an effective combination of these things will surely enhance a reputation for trustworthiness.

IV

Economists generally assume that the narrow pursuit of interest results in efficient economic exchange. The aim of this paper has been to dispute this assumption.

The theoretical section addressed two issues: to determine the conditions under which the need for trust develops in relations of economic exchange, and to show that business interests cannot negate that need because human rationality is limited and the environment is uncertain. Trust is crucial when contracting parties invest in specific assets, locking them into a relation. Limited rationality means that efforts to protect ourselves from opportunism through comprehensive contracting will inevitably be deficient. Rational comprehensive contracting is impossible. Trust is expedient.

The empirical investigation of machinery producers and their subcontractors in Lyons illustrates these themes. Firstly, it indicates that promoting trust is costly. In addition to the time it takes to establish a personal rapport between client and subcontractor, it involves a set of policies referred to as partnership. Client firms offer substantial guarantees on the level of orders and prices in exchange for improved performance on quality and delivery. Secondly, it demonstrates that while trust is costly, lack of trust is more costly still. Without the long-term commitment of partnership, the client's use of subcontractors is dictated by the changing demands of his market. This makes the subcontractor's orders volatile. Volatility inhibits quality-improving investment in up-to-date technology. It discourages flexibility in recontracting terms. Competitive success increasingly depends on cooperation as requirements for quality have escalated internationally and markets have become more uncertain. Clients should be called upon to recognize their dependence on subcontractors in this respect. Thirdly, it is apparent that where possible clients and subcontractors limit the dependence that creates the need for trust in the first place. Subcontractors avoid investing in capital equipment or skills specific to the client's needs. For similar reasons, clients avoid subcontracting final assembly operations. These are general rules with few exceptions: the exceptions that occur do so within trust.

Finally, the broader implication of this research is that trust can be created intentionally. This is not to preclude multiple mechanisms. Trust between firms in Lyons may have resulted in part from the shared values of community members. Yet it is clear that trust was more than a by-product of actions directed towards other ends. This was amply demonstrated in the practice of partnership, which sacrifices short-term gains for the long-term benefits of mutual cooperation.

REFERENCES

Arrow, K. 1974: *The Limits of Organization*. New York: Norton.
Cavestro, W. 1984: L'automation dans les industries de biens d'équipement. II.

Collection des Études. Paris: Centre d'Études et de Recherches sur les Qualifications.

Delattre, M. 1982: Les PME face aux grandes entreprises. *Economie et statistique* 148, 3–19.

Deutsch, M. 1973: *The Resolution of Conflict: constructive and destructive processes*. New Haven: Yale University Press.

Hirschman, A. O. 1982: Rival interpretations of market society: civilizing, destructive, or feeble? *Journal of Economic Literature* 20, 1463–84.

Klein, B. and Leffler, K. B. 1981: The role of market forces in assuring contractual performance. *Journal of Political Economy* 89, 615–41.

Klein, B., Crawford, R. A., and Alchian, A. A. 1978: Vertical integration, appropriable rents, and the competitive contracting process. *Journal of Law and Economics* 21, 297–326.

Meade, J. E. 1971: *The Controlled Economy*. London: George Allen and Unwin.

Piore, S. and Sabel, C. 1984: *The Second Industrial Divide*. New York: Basic Books.

Rapoport, A. 1970: *Two-Person Game Theory*. Ann Arbor: University of Michigan Press.

Sabel, C. and Zeitlin, J. 1985: Historical alternatives to mass production: politics, markets and technology in nineteenth-century industrialization. *Past and Present* 108, 133–76.

Shubik, M. 1959: *Strategy and Market Structure*. New York: Wiley.

Telser, L. 1980: A theory of self-enforcing agreements. *Journal of Business* 53, 27–44.

Williamson, O. E. 1975: *Market and Hierarchies: analysis and antitrust implications*. New York: Free Press.

Williamson, O. E. 1985: *The Economic Institutions of Capitalism*. New York: Free Press.

[8]

Kinship, Contract, and Trust: The Economic Organization of Migrants in an African City Slum

Keith Hart

PROBLEM

This paper[1] is based on fieldwork done 20 years ago in the slums of Accra, Ghana's capital city.[2] For two and a half years I lived among migrants from north-east Ghana called Frafras who included the Tallensi, the object of a classic study by Meyer Fortes (1945; 1949; see Hart 1978). At home these were a traditionally stateless people, huddled together in densely packed egalitarian settlements, millet farmers and raisers of livestock. In 1960 only 1 in 16 was Muslim or Christian; fewer adults had even a modicum of schooling. Their political organization and religion were based on descent ties, neighbourhood (manifested as an earth cult), ritual specialization of clans, and marriage exchange. The largest corporate units (patrilineages) were linked to the constant flux of self-reproducing domestic groups by a common ideology of kinship and the practice of ancestor worship. Age and genealogical seniority conferred office and stewardship of collective assets, principally cattle for bridewealth, on an informal gerontocracy. But individual mobility and small-scale accumulation were widespread; and the frequency of raiding between quite close neighbours lent considerable uncertainty to the social life of these fighting hill tribesmen.

[1] I am grateful for their comments on earlier drafts of this paper to Ray Abrahams, Eduardo da Fonseca, Tanya Luhrmann, Alan Macfarlane, Anthony Pagden, Johnny Parry, and especially to Diego Gambetta and Geoff Hawthorn.

[2] The fieldwork took place in 1965–68 and is embodied in a Cambridge PhD thesis (Hart 1969). There are many reasons why I balked at publishing the enthnography in subsequent years, most of them to do with my criminal associations.

By the 1960s the Frafras were dispersed throughout Ghana as unskilled labourers, petty traders, soldiers and, in popular repute, thieves. They circulated between town and countryside, being usually linked to an extended family network based on their home village. When I first went there maybe 10,000 Frafras (out of a total of a quarter million) were living in Accra, many of them in a sprawling slum called Nima. This was a migrant shanty town, the chief red light district of the city's lower classes, and a criminal 'badlands' only sporadically policed from the outside. I lived with a Frafra 'fence' (receiver) and before long became involved in a series of criminal and semi-legitimate enterprises which formed the backbone of my fieldwork. Having intended to study political and associational life, I found the focus of my research gravitating towards the self-made economic activities which sustained Nima's inhabitants. Many Frafras had poorly paid wage jobs, many had none. Virtually all of them derived income from what I later (Hart 1973) came to call the 'informal economy': a sphere of self-employment, casual labour, petty accumulation, and illegal transfers defined at its apex by the corruption of public life. I concentrated on the few successful Frafra entrepreneurs to be found in Accra and scattered elsewhere throughout Ghana (about 70 cases in all);[3] but I also tried to capture the style of economic life for the mass of transients and longer-term residents who made up the migrant community, one of scores of ethnic groups retaining a distinctive identity in Nima's melting-pot.

I was captivated by what seemed a paradox: on the one hand the banality of a barely differentiated Dickensian mob, of water carriers, bread sellers, shit shovellers, taxi drivers, pickpockets, and prostitutes; on the other the communal spirit of hill tribesmen whose fathers were earth priests and who expected to end their days as custodians of ancestral shrines. I was impressed by the energy and ingenuity of their efforts to enrich themselves and by the inevitability of long run failure for all but a handful. It seemed as if the economy was being made, unmade and remade from day to day. The central task for everyone was to find a reasonably durable basis for livelihood and even for accumulation, a stable core in the chaos of everyday life. That was why even a poorly paid job was valued: it was an island of regularity and predictability in a sea of ephemeral opportunities. I now think of this as the search for economic *form*, the search for the invariant in the variable, for rules and regularity in a world constituted by flux, emergence, informality.

The Frafra migrants were doubly hampered in this task. Firstly, they lacked effective legal sanctions; the state's presence in the slum was intermittent and punitive (occasional police raids). They knew well

[3] Details of the entrepreneurs' sample may be found in Hart (1969). Another paper (Hart 1975) discusses a number of issues germane to the present enquiry.

enough about the contractual ethos of bourgeois civil society, but it was not evident how such an ethos could be translated into the social conditions typical of Nima. They were in many ways pre-adapted to the statelessness of the slum, less suited perhaps than migrants from the savannah's Islamic civilization to the emergent mercantile society which was growing up in the interstices of state rule. Secondly, even as many aspects of their traditional mores were reinforced by slum conditions, it was not easy to transfer their customary rural institutions to the city. At home kinship is structured by lineage organization, lending the full authority of ancestors to fathers, husbands, and senior brothers. Away from home the migrants abjured any simulation of this religion of descent. Genealogical differences of generation were collapsed into a single conceptual brotherhood; ancestor worship could not be practised since the structure of home groups necessary to make up a sacrificial congregation could never be replicated. The sheer unequal power of parenthood writ large was mainly absent in the slums, where ethnic solidarity found expression in beer talk and kinship was a domestic relationship of uncertain moral provenance.

To summarize, Frafra migrants were faced with the need to build economic relations from scratch in a world lacking both orderly state regulation and the segmentary political structure of their customary society. I shall argue that they had three basic models for such relationships, none of them unproblematic. One, *kinship*, is an extrapolation from statuses typical of traditional ideology and practice; its antithesis is the legally sanctioned *contract* of the modern state and civil society. There remains the zone of free-floating social relationships formed by choice in the expectation of mutuality. The most neutral term for this zone is *association*, but its strongest form of expression is *friendship*, the negotiated order of free individuals joined by affection and shared experience rather than by legal sanction or the ties of blood. It is in this third area of social life that trust plays so prominent a role, relatively unmediated by the formal obligations of kinship and contract.

The remainder of the paper is divided into three sections. Only in the last of these ('Argument') will I return to explicit consideration of the issues raised here. The main problem I address is the basis of durable economic relations in an environment that is marginal to both traditional and modern society. The section on ethnography is primarily concerned with indicating, by way of examples, the tenor of commercial life and petty enterprise in Accra's slums. It is not structured explicitly to highlight specific points about trust. This description is contextual to the later analysis of the significance of trust in migrants' attempts to build viable patterns of enterprise. The third section of the paper ('Definition') prepares the ground for such an analysis by exploring the semantics of trust and cognate terms.

ETHNOGRAPHY

My main concern is with the difficulties Frafras faced in trying to establish enterprises; but firstly we should consider the more diffuse issue of commodity exchange, the ordinary business of buying and selling. Most sellers in Nima are women, although the upper echelons of trade in Accra are dominated by men, often European or Lebanese men. There is a general lack of liquidity, that is the women's customers generally run out of cash before each montly pay period is half over. Indeed budgeting is extremely rare, especially for single men. Expenditures are normally erratic, even when individuals succeed in stabilizing some part of their income by earning wages. In this situation continuous commerce would be impossible without a high level of credit. Credit is thus the most prominent feature of buyer–seller relations; and you do not bargain if each side has a long-term arrangement to protect. This is particularly true of the purchase of daily comestibles, less so of occasional deals involving consumer durables like items of furniture. The higgling or sliding price mechanism that Westerners imagine is endemic to foreign bazaars is absent from large sections of Nima's market.

Prices normally vary by volume for a fixed price. Thus a woman will buy her goods from a wholesaler, often on a daily basis, take out a third of the total quantity to give away as sweeteners to preferred customers, and divide the rest into equal piles sufficient to give her a profit if sold for a standard sum. The customers always buy, say, a shilling of yams; what they get for it varies. The interdependence of both parties is based on the fact that sellers are subject to unpredictable shortages and gluts of supply and must have a steady clientele, while the buyers of course need to eat when they have no cash. Since bargaining depends on the ability of each party to walk away from the deal, this pervasive structure of credit and clientelistic particularism restricts the scope for such behaviour. It is not accidental that game theorists talk about used cars and 'lemons'. The rational negotiation of risk is less appropriate when most purchases go on the slate.

The problem of default was omnipresent. The women were usually illiterate and relied on fantastic memories to keep a register of customers' debts. If challenged they could always list each purchase over several weeks, persuading the client by sheer power of mental arithmetic. This reliance on memory placed an upper limit – perhaps eight to ten – on the number of debtors each trader could support. Capital shortage was another restrictive consideration, of course. As partial defence against default, traders of a given commodity would stick together where possible and share information on their clients' trustworthiness. They could also ostracize persistent offenders and avoid being played off against each other. Interest rates in Nima were high, 25 to 50 per cent per month, and outstanding debts at the end of the month would often be increased by such an amount. The high price of money reflected not just the obvious risk of default, but rather its extreme scarcity and the inefficiency of commercial institutions.

I noticed that something like chains of debt were commonplace. Each migrant made and received loans (including traders' credit). If a man came into a windfall – a stolen wallet or a back-dated pay rise – he was as likely to lend the money as to pay off existing debts. This meant that when he was being dunned by a creditor, he could pass on the pressure to one of his debtors. There is an analogy with traditional bridewealth transactions where in-laws typically chase an infinitely regressive chain of debt in order to retrieve an outstanding cow. Another metaphor for this process, besides that of a chain, might be the ripples caused by a stone dropped into a pool. Beer drinking (a traditional millet beer from the north) is the main activity of Frafra men at weekends. I calculated that women beer brewers generally sold a volume valued at five to six times their initial production costs. But they gave away a third, and most of the rest was sold on credit; so that they often had difficulty finding the cash to start off another three-day brewing cycle. Every now and then a major millet trader would arrive to collect on credit sales to the brewers. These impressive ladies would sit in the courtyard of their principal customer, for all to see. The brewers would put the squeeze on their clients, the clients would turn to their debtors, and so on.

The sanctions available to traders when dealing with defaulters were weak. One woman was reduced to entering a client's room at 4 a.m. to steal his only pair of trousers, which she then waved triumphantly in the courtyard while shouting out his crimes: 'You think Alhassan is a big man because he walks around in trousers and white shirt, but he won't pay a poor woman for the bread and cola he eats!' Public humiliation of this sort is a poor substitute for legal sanctions. But, as we know, small debt settlement is hard to secure anywhere. Although Nima was beyond the law and a violent place to live in, traders rarely if ever resorted to force in settlement of debts incurred by legitimate commerce. Usury and criminal enterprise were often a different matter, but even in the area of casual sex, pimps were rare and most women relied on informal moral sanctions to extract money from their lovers, so that prostitution as we know it was not common. That is to say that what Durkheim ([1893] 1933) called the 'non-contractual element of the contract', the non-rational conditions for rational negotiation, assumed a dominant role in shaping commercial life in Nima. Markets were normally far from competitive, and price-setting mechanisms were governed by relatively long-term considerations of credit that helped to stabilize turnover and to regulate the erratic fluctuations which buffeted parties on both sides.

Frafra migrants were well aware that much of this commercial activity depended on the establishment of trust between free agents whose scope for default was palpable. The protagonist in the following example laid great stress on the importance of a personal style capable of winning and sustaining the friendship and trust of strangers. His conversation often turned to episodes such as the time when, as a house servant, he refused to steal from his white employer, with beneficial long-term results. He had once been a part-time photographer, and his account of that period of his life epitomizes the precarious, highly individuated casual enterprises which many Frafra migrants sought to combine with wage employment.

Atia had been hawking a camera around with intermittent success: the problem was that it was 35 mm and his customers were often unwilling to wait until the film was used up. His breakthrough came when he went to a girls' secondary school with 600 pupils and persuaded the principal to allow him to take the girls' photographs at weekends. Many others had tried and failed; but, as he put it, his sweet approach worked. He spent over £10 on chickens, eggs, and gifts of money before she agreed and gave him exclusive photographic rights in the school.

Trade was brisk: every weekend he got through two or three films 'cutting' the girls. Whenever they saw him, they all wanted photos to send to their boyfriends and families. Some asked to be taken in the nude: 'I was trusted by all of them; they knew that I was there for the money, that's all. If one asked me to stay and do something, another will call for photo before.' He used to try to get an advance where possible, usually half. Those who gave him an advance were asked to write their names in a book, although he was himself illiterate. This was to stop any false claims; but in general he worked on a degree of mutual trust. If no advance had been paid and he made two copies which were refused, he couldn't force them to pay. If he had tried force, he said, maybe they would have ganged up against him and stopped buying his pictures altogether. So he relied on goodwill. Some girls would pay for a bad photo and later tear it up. If he heard of this, he would do them a new set free. Sometimes he 'fell down' when he spoiled the whole negative and had to refund all the advances. Atia claims his average profit was 50 per cent. Good photos fetched more or less what he asked for. If a customer was pleased, she might not ask for change from a banknote. By buying wholesale from one man and using another individual for enlarging, Atia could often get his production costs reduced. So the profit from two films over one weekend, although highly variable, could be substantial, more than a week's wages for steward work.

Later he had to give up photography after joining the army; he was put on a charge for spending too many weekends out of barracks. Despite the doubling of army pay after the 1966 coup and the benefits of being a regularly paid soldier, Atia was chronically indebted and looked back on his work as a weekend photographer with some nostalgia, as a time when he was free. Be that as it may, Atia's enterprise was short-lived and unstable. He depended on the patronage of a headmistress and on his ability to step through a minefield of adolescent girls. Having failed to place his enterprise on a more durable basis, he fell back on a securely paid job. His willingness to invent the conditions of his participation in the market economy, rather than accept passively whatever its formal institutions had to offer, was typical of Frafra migrants. A few of them were more successful.

In the space of two and a half years, I built up case records on 71 Frafra entrepreneurs living in southern cities and their homeland (including both villages and the main town of Bolgatanga). One in five had assets worth more than £10,000 in the mid 1960s; half had accumulated £2,000 or more. These were substantial sums by Frafra standards, but only three were rich on a national scale. Men outnumbered women four to one. They usually maintained a diverse portfolio of investments; few were committed to managing a single enterprise. They were part-time petty capitalists: in the south, a third were still employed for wages and a further half had been employed fairly recently. The most common medium for investment was housing for rent (three-quarters of the sample); next in priority (each being an interest of half the sample) were trade – wholesale, retail, and commodity speculation; bars – beer and gin, food (most of the women were traders or caterers); machinery and plant producing services – flour mills, water supplies; and crime, including money lending at usurious interest rates. A third of the sample owned one or more commercial vehicles; transport was the riskiest but most lucrative form of investment. In addition, some Frafras were contractors in the construction industry.

Many of these activities belong to the sphere of circulation – rent, interest, trading profit, theft – which make few labour demands. But half of the entrepreneurs employed five or more workers and 80 per cent at least two. For most of them the key problem of accumulation was that of organizing a labour force in such a way as to secure routine transfer of surplus value to the owner of an enterprise. Trust enters into this issue, but it was much more prominent in the sphere of circulation, where economic organization is shaped by credit and debt and the partnership of equals rather than by productive hierarchy. I will return to this question in the concluding section. Half the sample neither spoke nor wrote any English (Ghana's official language) and only one in six was literate. Yet, as a group, they were remarkable for having made a break with traditional religion; whereas more than nine out of ten Frafra migrants were pagans, 21 per cent of the entrepreneurs were Muslim and 18 per cent were Christian or some agnostic mixture, a total of almost 40 per cent in the Ghana sample. This figure rose to near 50 per cent in urban areas and 60 per cent in the southern cities of Accra and Kumasi.

As an example of enterprise involving the hierarchical organization of labour, I will briefly describe transport operations. The richest Frafra entrepreneurs all owned commercial vehicles, but the risks of failure were very high; the abandoned hulks which litter Ghana's roadsides offer silent testimony to the idea that transport is an entrepreneur's graveyard. In their home town of Bolgatanga, several Frafras ran long-distance trucking firms, mostly using 7 ton lorries. In the south, it was more common for individuals to operate small vehicles on a part-time basis: taxis, intercity estate wagons ('Peugeot') and minibuses ('Benz').

If you buy a car or lorry, there are three things you can do with it: drive it yourself, hire a driver, or sell to a driver on a hire purchase basis ('work and pay'). No one who spends his days behind a wheel is in a position to accumulate. Most naïve operators opt for hiring a driver for fixed wages, since the prospective profit is greater. This is why they usually fail: a wage employee has no incentive to maintain the vehicle or to be honest with the takings. One alternative is to make a driver pay the owner a fixed sum daily; but again, he has no stake in the vehicle and there is nothing to stop him making common cause with a crooked fitter to supply inflated repair bills or to certify that the vehicle was legitimately off the road for several days owing to breakdown. The most secure method is to sell the vehicle to the driver on an instalment plan and make him responsible for maintenance, a method pioneered in Ghana by Lebanese traders. Some owners would run the risk of hiring a driver for the first trouble-free year of a new vehicle and then sell it second-hand on the work-and-pay basis.

One Tallensi entrepreneur, after several false starts, evolved his own method of running a transport enterprise. He would buy driving licences for young men from his home area and let them serve an apprenticeship on someone else's taxi until he was convinced they were a good risk. When he had enough cash in hand to buy a vehicle for £2000–£3000, he would pick out one from his pool in reserve (many of whom lived in his household of some 80 persons). He would then write up a contract, adding £1000 to the sale price, selling it to the driver at £10 a day, with a clause giving him the right to seize the bus if the driver missed three successive days' payments. The driver is responsible for maintenance, but if he is in difficulties the entrepreneur pays for the repairs and adds the cost to the total to be repaid. In the interest of quick turnover, he is anxious that the vehicle should not lie idle for long. Most drivers take one to one and a half years to buy their bus or taxi. This case is remarkable for being largely independent of the Muslim-controlled lorry-park system in Ghana. It is also worth noting that kinship, self-reinforcing agreements, and legally binding contracts played a more important part in his enterprise than friendship and trust. He was not a trusting man – in contrast to Atia, the unsuccessful photographer – and this was reflected in his preference for hire purchase agreements over direct employment for wages.

On the face of it, another alternative to wage employment is family labour. Many small enterprises – a bar, a flour mill, a market stall – are well suited to family labour. But in practice it often turned out differently. Many of the catering and retail entrepreneurs were single women; and few of the men had conjugal relations which allowed them to enter into partnership with their wives, since the traditional role pattern is typically both patriarchal and segregated. Few had children old enough to be much help, and most of those were busy acquiring the qualifications for a career of literate employment. The fact that descent organization did not travel to the south meant that kinship ties were much more fluid and the authority of household heads was frequently weak. Here the contrast is with Asian minority communities whose tight cohesion provides patriarchs with external support to domestic hierarchy. Frafra migrants were mostly an undifferentiated brotherhood of mobile single men, linked to a few prominent married men by ties of patronage and pseudo-kinship or descent. Such a community did not lend support to domestic hierarchy. Consequently, family labour was problematic. One significant exception consisted of a group of Christian entrepreneurs for whom marriage meant an egalitarian partnership with a wife conceived of as friend.

Employment of workers involves supervision, delegation, and control on a scale which many enterprises in the sphere of circulation largely avoided. Usury, speculation, landlordism, and theft are usually intermittent activities, lacking the routinized preoccupations of most productive enterprises. Here the main problems concern extraction of rents or debts from clients, establishing cooperative relations with partners, and negotiating obstacles imposed by public authorities. In a place like Nima, even more than in Ghana generally, legal sanction for contracts is weak or non-existent, so that most activities are outside the law, whether or not they self-consciously infringe it. Rates of return are nominally very high, interest rates of 25 to 50 per cent per month being normal as against the legal maximum of 30 per cent per annum and current bank lending rates of under 10 per cent per annum. On the other hand, default may be as high as four loans out of five, an expression both of the general lack of trust and of the value attached to trustworthy relationships. Recalcitrant tenants are hard to budge; and market fluctuations trap all but the most expert speculators. Rational calculation of profit under these circumstances is virtually impossible, leading to an atmosphere of windfall and catastrophe which is not conducive to sustained accumulation.

My field notes are full of unexpected deductions from profits that had been calculated on paper. My landlord and I once speculated in the grain market by buying 50 bags of maize in anticipation of a substantial price rise before the next harvest. Not only did many hidden expenses arise (a bag shortage, the market porters' union, pesticide for the insects), but the USA flooded the market with a donation of surplus maize. This left us scrambling to sell on credit as our only chance of making a small profit; and it took us a lot of effort to get our money back.

This raises the question of what takes the place of law as the major source of sanctions in economic relations. From where do the forms of economic life draw their effectiveness? Clearly force was far from centralized; but systematic use of violence to enforce payment was relatively rare in Nima, as I have already indicated. Criminals used force in their relations with each other and with the police but not normally on the local public, from whom they expected and received a considerable measure of communal support. Reputation, name, honour, the macho complex offered much more scope for creditors and rentiers hoping to shame their clients into payment. Of course, successful entrepreneurs did use forms of contractual agreement; for example, a client might agree to sign a document for a loan of £150, when he had in fact received only £100, thereby evading the law on usurious interest rates. Pawnbrokers acquired real assets and thereby reduced risks. Above all, economic life depended on the discovery of complementary or shared interests which might make commercial agreements self-reinforcing in the short and medium term.

Nevertheless, a significant part of all this wheeler-dealing hinged on friendship, on the trust generated by shared experience, mutual knowledge and the affection that comes from having entered a relationship freely, by choice rather than status obligation. Whenever my landlord introduced me to one of his 'good friends', I knew that he was almost certainly a crook, probably from another ethnic group, a member of a criminal fraternity stretching back decades with a common background of gambling dens, police raids, gaols, diamond smuggling, drug rings, and all the rest. These were the men he turned to when he needed to trust someone, not his family or his fellow tribesmen. Elsewhere in Nima these friendship networks were solidified into more corporate brotherhoods by religious organization, especially by Islamic control of the cattle trade and long-distance transport. And in West Africa, but not for the Frafras, such informal organization was often provided by secret societies. Meyer

Fortes (1969) argued that kinship carries an 'axiom of amity' and perhaps it does; but another Tallensi proverb says *maalong gaat soog* 'familiarity is better than kinship' (literally 'making sweet', the experience of being treated well). In the fourth section the contrast between kinship and friendship lies at the core of an attempt to assess the significance of trust in Frafra economic relations.

DEFINITION

I study dictionaries. Our words contain a sort of archaeological stratigraphy representing great historical shifts in society *and* the continuing evolution of meaning and usage. Words do not stand still, and any attempt to fix them will fail. Some words change fast (compare Jane Austen's 'economist', an efficient housekeeper, with today's academic fraternity); others less so. Perhaps *trust* belongs to this latter category.

The Germanic stratum of English stresses the active voice of *ich*; it is personal and transitive. Latin-based constructions yield agency to abstractions, camouflage the speaker's voice in passive or intransitive verbs. Beyond this ancient distinction, modern society has exposed us to mass anonymous phenomena like markets and states which have removed from sight the intermediate pattern of human interdependence that give rise to the words we now use. In particular, modern English usage frequently collapses the distinction between persons and things, so that trust can refer equally to a person, an idea, or an object. Nothing stands between the individual subject and a depersonalized, abstract world; and our words reflect this fact. But in origin they referred to another world explicitly founded on concrete human relationships, on activities and passions: love, persuasion, coercion.

The discovery of such a world depends heavily on the achievements of British social anthropology. By investigating societies without states in Africa and Oceania, my predecessors revealed patterns of social organization and human interdependence that we had forgotten and could not recreate in our philosophical speculations. Hence the power of *African Political Systems* (1940) and of monographs on the Nuer and Tallensi. Unfortunately the lessons Fortes and Evans-Pritchard taught are easily lost. We need this knowledge if we are to escape the tyranny of modern conceptions of the world. For this reason, I wish to distinguish carefully between trust in persons and more abstract understandings, so that we can contrast what we are with what we are not.

The set of synonyms to which *trust* belongs is unusually confusing.[4] Faith, trust, and confidence all express belief. *Belief* is originally

[4] The principal sources for the etymological argument are the appendix on Indo-European roots in the *American Heritage Dictionary* (Morris 1969: 1505–50) and Buck's

something held dear (compare with *love*). To believe is to accept something as *true*. To *believe in* is to have *faith*, *trust*, or *confidence* in someone or something. Faith and confidence both come from Latin *fides*, which is the nearest thing to the Germanic *trust*. Since the Middle Ages, faith has replaced belief as the strongest word for trust placed in a person or thing. To cut through the detail, I wish to propose a continuum of words connoting *belief* based on the degree to which they rest on evidence of the senses. Faith requires no evidence; trust is an expectation based on inconclusive evidence, is tolerant of uncertainty or risk; confidence is a strong conviction based on substantial evidence or logical deduction. These are all subjective attitudes.

The notion of *reliance* expresses complete confidence, a presumptively objective state where belief is no longer necessary. To rely on something is to be tied to it, bound (compare with *religion*), as to an objective condition of existence. When there is no choice, *reliance* become *dependence*. Belief, by contrast, connotes freedom of the subject to make commitments in the absence of full knowledge. Belief is a feeling that a person or thing will not fail in performance. Feeling varies inversely with evidence or proof. Thus *faith* is an emotionally charged, unquestioning acceptance. *Trust* implies depth and assurance of such feeling, with inconclusive evidence or proof. *Confidence* involves less intensity of feeling, being based often on good evidence for being sure. *Trust* thus stands in the middle of a continuum of words for belief mixing extremes of blind faith and open-eyed confidence. Its etymology shows trust to be *true* like a *tree*, firm, steadfast, and loyal; not impervious to the evidence of the senses, but founded on a willingness to endure risk and uncertainty.

I wish to suggest that *Trust* has been historically associated with the notion of friend. Modern usage restricts the number of our friends to a narrow circle of intimates, narrower by far than those whom we might occasionally be inclined to trust. But among the Frafras of my study – and perhaps for medieval Englishmen – trust was closely bound up with an idiom of classificatory friendship which had a relatively broad range of application. One definition of *friend* (*American Heritage Dictionary*) is 'a person whom one knows, likes, and trusts'. This is superior to the *Oxford English Dictionary*'s retention of Johnson's definition: 'one joined to another in mutual benevolence and intimacy'. A *friend* is someone to whom one is not bound, and hence etymologically speaking *free*, based on choice not status obligation. A friend is not a kinsman. Friend is free and analogous to *wife* in some Germanic dialects (Frigg, Friya – wife of Odin), someone chosen. If friendship no longer means to

Dictionary of Selected Synonyms in the Principal Indo-European Languages (1949). Much of this work is highly speculative, even poetic.

us what it used to, neither does trust, when we can place trust in persons and things with no semantic discontinuity.

Social relations have generally evolved from a concrete, interpersonal basis to the abstract mass anonymities of political economy, an evolution obscured by a modern usage which tends to objectify persons as abstractions, much as pre-industrial cultures personify objects. Social theorists perennially ask how qualities of trust, fairness, and cooperation which belong naturally to intimate social worlds might be projected on to the modern stage of markets and states. Neoclassical economists, however, by basing their most general propositions on a formal rational calculus of individual decision-making, have tended to obscure the sociological distinction on which this paper hinges.

I agree with the emphasis placed by both Partha Dasgupta and Niklas Luhmann (in this volume) on the importance of personal agency in defining trust. Thus Dasgupta identifies trust as an expectation about another *person*'s actions which influences our own actions before we have full knowledge of the outcome; and Luhmann exposes to full view the distinction between personal and impersonal social organization. Clearly trust is the predication of one's own actions on actions of others which bear an identifiable risk of turning out unfavourably. The problem is to control extrapolation from a theory of rational choice to the larger frameworks of modern mass society.

To some extent, the institutions of industrial society justify a theoretical stance in which the personal–impersonal distinction remains blurred. But a study such as this one, of life on the margins of the modern state, requires that the difference between levels of social experience be kept in sharp focus. A similar problem arose when anthropologists turned to the analysis of kinship in stateless societies. Here the largest political groups, such as clans, are often represented as being *like* families. Yet Fortes (for example 1958) showed that the political and domestic levels were often contradictory and should be kept analytically separate. An anthropological approach to the problem of trust would insist on no less a degree of analytical discrimination. To summarize, I situate the notion in a set of belief concepts bounded at the extremes by faith and confidence, where the variable significance of evidence or proof is matched by a compensating level of affectivity. As such, trust is located in the no man's land between status and contract, the poles of primitive and modern society in evolutionary theory (Maine 1861).

ARGUMENT

The specific sociological analysis goes something like this. The Frafra migrants face the problem of establishing economic forms, durable relations of partnership and hierarchy, in the city slum. Three basic models for how to go about this present themselves. The most obvious and apparently profitable of these is the contractual ethos of the civil society they think they have joined, that is individualism, rationality, market, impersonal law – the bourgeois package of city life. Here economic relations are in principle entered into freely and by choice, but the contract imposes binding obligations sanctioned by state law. There are several reasons why this does not generally work. State law does not apply except in the form of occasional punishment. Markets are erratic and the substantive conditions of rational calculation are largely absent. The Frafras have not been socialized to make and keep contracts of this sort (they are, for instance, rarely on time), and the impersonal disciplines involved have to be invented from scratch. They lack education. They have no grounds for *confidence* in outcomes established by contract.

Looking for some alternative form of guarantee, the migrants turn to the antithesis of modern civilization, their own customary moral institutions founded on the identities of kinship, descent, and family, reinforced as they are by a common language and religion, by the certain obligations of birth and community. This option too is fallible. The institutions do not travel *en bloc* to Accra, and some of the important public sanctions of domestic hierarchy are missing: lineages, ancestor worship, the security of their homeland. The migrant community is an egalitarian brotherhood of floating young men anchored in the patronage of a few resident big men. It is not closed or powerful enough to shore up the authority and reliability of kinsmen. In any case kinship is a poor foundation for the reckoning of two-sided economic relations, especially unequal relations, since its central postulate is identity, sameness, a collective self defined by opposition to the generalized other. The idea of shared but separate interests cannot be expressed through a kinship idiom. Not surprisingly, Frafra migrants lose *faith* in their traditions as a viable framework for urban economic life.

Almost *faute de mieux*, denied the opportunity to rely on the poles of primitive and modern society, they fall back on the sphere of social life that people, perhaps friends, make out of their free-floating association. This, as Mauss (1967) argued most cogently, is the true locus of society, where self and other meet in some reciprocal understanding, where interests and risk are negotiated within relations formed by shared experience (even secrets), by love, knowledge, choice. Friends are free, and they remain free or they are no longer friends. Society in this sense is always personal, active, concrete: perhaps inevitably charismatic or magical, straddling as it does the abstract tyrannies of nature and reason, of totality and isolation.

Does friendship work for the Frafras? In a way it has to work, although rarely without the reinforcement of some other social interest. The case of money lending illustrates the point. Loans in Nima are never made to strangers. Landlords lend to tenants, patrons to clients. The borrower often invokes friendship as a way of soliciting a loan; the pretension of familiarity is the normal rhetoric of economic life in a place like Accra. Kinsmen make poor borrowers since they equate their interests with those of the lender. Again, small traders sell to strangers for cash. Once their customers become more familiar, they grant them special privileges (extras and, more important, credit), engendering trust by means of the gift and making a kind of friendship between buyer and seller, even when it was not a precondition for their association. Regular clients with substantial debts are few, and the traders must pick them carefully: in this respect they are as selective as we are with our personal friendships. But this does not prevent Frafras and others like them from invoking friendship quite casually in their economic relations, a sort of inflation of the social currency that members of our civil society would be likely to resist.

Most migrants fail to transcend the mores of fighting hill tribesmen in the social chaos of the slum. But some of them do. They are aided in this process if they make a break with traditional religion, for both negative and positive reasons. They need some social and cultural distance from the axioms of a society where personal freedom is hedged in by kinship obligations on all sides. World religions also confer membership of new associations which lend organization and sanctions to negotiated social relations. Similar claims could be made for secret societies and criminal fraternities. In Accra, Islamic brotherhoods controlled much of the intermediate level of business between the state-made corporate zone and its amorphous hinterland. They did so in informal ways which have been documented brilliantly by Cohen (1969) for the Hausa trading diaspora. Christians, at least the few Frafra Christians, did not join organizations relevant to their enterprise, such as Masons, Rotary, Lions etc. But they were encouraged to elevate their wives to the position of friend, partner, and equal, just as Anthony Pagden tells us (in this volume) Neapolitan social theorists (and, for that matter, a long list of more familiar thinkers) argued we all should, if we are to break down the wearing inertia of familism and segmentary politics which finds expression in the macho complex of public rivalry and private partiarchy. And the idea of two working as one, the ancient but often abused notion of wife as friend, is surely a recurrent theme in the history of enterprise.

Some Frafra migrants learnt to *trust* those whom they chose as friends, especially if they could draw on associations or on conjugal partnership. Impersonal pieces of paper were largely worthless. But personal relationships are created over time; so that exchange relations in Nima were above all a *learning* process. People found out by trial and error what worked for them; and the failure rate was very high. Accordingly, the problems of managing information and developing effective social tactics severely restricted ease of entry into the sort of market that most economists would characterize as competitive. The contrasting case studies presented in the second section make it clear that no easy correlation can be drawn between entrepreneurial success and an ability to make friends or engender trust. Indeed the highly successful transport entrepreneur relied on kinship and contract, while the hustler made more of the need for trust.

Frafras relied on trust as a last resort, for good reasons. Trust is essential to dealing, as is known by the diamond traders and by the game theorists, with their suckers, free-riders, and lemons. But the routines of productive organization are not easily managed by an ethos of personal freedom. Kinship and contract each offer a durable model for hierarchy and control: parental and legal sanctions respectively. This is why traditional rural society has room only in the margins for achieved relations of friendship and why trust accumulates in the interstices of mass societies organized by markets and states. Trust is central to social life when neither traditional certainties nor modern probabilities hold – in weak states or relatively lawless zones of public life, and in the transition to capitalism, especially in the mercantile sphere of circulation where credit is so important – but not as a basis for industrial production and division of labour. In other words trust is the negotiation of risk occasioned by the freedom of others, whom we know personally, to act against our interests in the relative absence of constraints imposed by kinship identity or legal contract. Domination and interest offer a more pervasive and durable basis for society than friendship and trust.

The list of triadic word sets shown in table 11.1 captures some of this argument. Like all words, these are ideal types: they either make for good communication and rational insight or they do not. Real people and societies do not conform to these types: empirical life is always a mixture, and our interest is in the varying emphasis of different arrangements. The most important observation is that, whereas many languages have words which identify some of the conceptual oppositions in the table, such as kinship and friendship, confidence and trust, it is normal for cultural categories and social organizations to be formed out of hybrid constructs. This was pointed out by Pitt-Rivers (1973) in his excellent paper 'The kith and the kin', written for Fortes's Festschrift.

Starting from the premiss that Fortes's link between kinship and the 'axiom of amity' was odd in view of the conceptual opposition most cultures make between kinship and friendship, Pitt-Rivers went on to

TABLE 11.1 *Elements of a triadic model of social organization*

KINSHIP	ASSOCIATION	CIVIL SOCIETY
Status	Relation	Contract
Family	Personal	Impersonal
Community	Network	Individual
Nation/descent	Social life/alliance	Market/state
Nature	Love/friendship	Mind
Self	Self/other	Other
Same	Like/analogous	Different
Custom	Experience	Law
Habit/conviction	Sentiment	Calculation
Traditional	Charismatic	Rational
Religion	Magic	Science
Language	Poetry	Logic
Closed	Secret	Open
Obligatory	Free	Free/obligatory
Certainty	Risk	Probability
Long term	Medium term	Short term
No evidence	Some evidence	Strong evidence
High feeling	Intermediate	Low feeling
FAITH	TRUST	CONFIDENCE

argue that, in the Mediterranean region at least, the key social relations are a fusion of the two polar types, both obligatory and free, a sort of pseudo-familism of the kinsman-friend: patron, godfather, brother-in-law, indeed affinal relations in general. Something similar can be discerned in religious brotherhoods and in the sworn secrecy of associates who take on the symbolic attributes of blood and common substance in their rituals. We can go further. A familiar critique of utilitarianism is that the contract rests on a non-contractual element which is both prior and irreducible to its logic. Hence capitalist firms are organized not just by a state-made legal sanction for exploitation, but by having recourse to the ideology of paternalism and mutual trust. Real social organization depends on creative combinations of the types, and successful mixtures will vary according to their situational effectiveness. It is the intellectuals who suppose that modern society could ever be founded on rational choice alone or that the simple-minded identities of primitive kinship-based societies have no room for person or the individual, as in practice all societies must.

My most general point has been made several times in this paper. Our modern English usage, inured as it is to the abstractions of mass society, makes no systematic discrimination between persons and things. But, if we rely on the language and ideology of our times alone, we will fail to understand a social evolution which crucially entails a shift in emphasis from personal to impersonal relations as a function of society's greater size and complexity. The value of the Frafra case study is that it forces us to conceptualize social life on the margins of the industrial world; and to concede that 'trust' may occupy a rather different place in the spectrum of social organization there than it does in the imagination of economists.

REFERENCES

Buck, C. S. 1949: *A Dictionary of Selected Synonyms in The Principal Indo-European Languages*. Chicago: University of Chicago Press.

Cohen, A. 1969: *Custom and Politics in Urban Africa*. London: Routledge and Kegan Paul.

Durkheim, E. [1893] 1933: *The Division of Labour in Society*. Glencoe, Ill.: Free Press.

Fortes, M. 1945: *The Dynamics of Clanship among the Tallensi*. London: Oxford University Press.

Fortes, M. 1949: *The Web of Kinship among the Tallensi*. London: Oxford University Press.

Fortes, M. 1958: Introduction. In J. Goody (ed.), *The Development Cycle in Domestic Groups*, Cambridge: Cambridge University Press, 1–14.

Fortes, M. 1969: *Kinship and the Social Order*. London: Routledge and Kegan Paul.

Fortes, M. and Evans-Pritchard, E. (eds) 1940: *African Political Systems*. London: Oxford University Press.

Hart, J. K. 1969: Entrepreneurs and migrants: a study of modernization among the Frafras of Ghana. Cambridge University, PhD thesis.

Hart, J. K. 1973: Informal income opportunities and urban employment in Ghana. *Journal of Modern African Studies* 11, 61–89.

Hart, J. K. 1975: Swindler or public benefactor? The entrepreneur in his community. In J. Goody (ed.), *Changing Social Structure in Ghana*, London: International African Institute, 1–35.

Hart, J. K. 1978: The economic basis of Tallensi social history in the early twentieth century. In G. Dalton (ed.), *Research in Economic Anthropology*, vol. 1, Greenwich, Conn.: JAI Press, 185–216.

Maine, H. S. 1861: *Ancient Law*. London: Murray.

Mauss, M. 1967: *The Gift*. New York: Norton.

Morris, W. (ed.) 1969: *The American Heritage Dictionary of the English Language* (first college edition). Boston: Houghton Mifflin.

Pitt-Rivers, J. 1973: The kith and the kin. In J. Goody (ed.), *The Character of Kinship*, Cambridge: Cambridge University Press, 89–105.

[9]

The Emergence of Exchange Structures: An Experimental Study of Uncertainty, Commitment, and Trust[1]

Peter Kollock
University of California, Los Angeles

An experiment is used to investigate the effects of uncertainty on patterns of exchange. The role of reputation as an important factor related to the formation of stable exchange relations is examined. In addition, some of the consequences of different patterns of exchange—in particular, how different exchange conditions lead to different levels of trust among trading partners—are investigated. The results of the experiment indicate significant differences in the level of commitment, concern for one's own and others' reputation, and the level of trust that emerge when uncertainty (in the form of information asymmetries) is varied.

INTRODUCTION

The emergence of social structure has been a chronically underexamined topic across all areas in sociology (Coleman 1986). In particular, the feature of social structure that is examined here—the emergence of stable exchange relationships—has received very little empirical attention. The purpose of this study is to begin to explore this issue experimentally, examining the effects of a crucial variable—uncertainty—on the patterns of exchange that emerge. A further goal is to examine the role of reputation as an important factor related to the formation of stable exchange relations and to examine some of the consequences of different patterns

[1] Earlier versions of this article were presented at the annual meeting of the American Sociological Association, Pittsburgh, 1992, and at the Fourth Annual International Conference of the Society for the Advancement of Socio-Economics, Irvine, California, 1992. I wish to thank Gerrie Lemus, Elisabeth Schmutzer, and Martin Monto for their help in the design and implementation of this project. I also thank Phillip Bonacich, James Carrier, Harold Kelley, Toshio Yamagishi, Ronald Obvious, and the *AJS* reviewers for comments on earlier drafts. Correspondence may be directed to Peter Kollock, Department of Sociology, University of California, Los Angeles, California 90024-1551. E-mail: kollock@soc.sscnet.ucla.edu.

0002-9602/95/10002-0001$01.50

of exchange—in particular, how different exchange conditions lead to different levels of trust among trading partners.

This project brings together elements from two research traditions: social exchange theory and work on social dilemmas.[2] While the majority of research to date in these traditions has examined the effects of preexisting social structures on exchange and cooperation, this experiment is directed toward studying the *emergence* of different kinds of exchange structures. In addition, this project examines exchange situations in which deceit and opportunism are possible (in contrast to most work in social exchange theory) and where actors can move into and out of different exchange relations (in contrast to most work on social dilemmas).

A particularly evocative example of the kind of situation I wish to investigate is given in the work of Siamwalla (1978) and Popkin (1981) on the structure of commodity exchange in Thailand. Two contrasting cases are highlighted. The first is the market for rubber. Rubber is an interesting commodity in that at the time of sale it is impossible to determine its quality. It is not until months later, after extensive processing, that the buyer can determine whether the grower took the extra time and expense to insure a high-quality crop. Within this situation the buyers are not motivated to pay a high price for goods of unknown quality and the growers are not motivated to produce high quality goods as there is no simple, objective way of displaying the care they took. The participants are faced with a type of Prisoner's Dilemma that is the result of asymmetric information. Further, there are no regulatory agencies to monitor and sanction the actions of each exchange partner.

It is a difficult situation and one possible conclusion is that the buyers and sellers could not escape their fate, that is, cooperation would not emerge and the market would "fail" in that only low-quality goods would be bought and sold despite the fact that everyone could earn more buying and selling high-quality goods. And yet the growers and buyers of rubber have escaped this fate. Not because they decided to trust each other blindly or because they managed to create an institution to monitor and sanction themselves, but because they abandoned the anonymous exchange of the market for personal, long-term exchange relationships between particular buyers and sellers. Within this framework it is possible for the growers to establish reputations for fairness and trustworthiness.

[2] I use the term *social dilemmas* to refer to the broad range of work that has been done in a number of disciplines on situations in which individually rational behavior leads to collectively irrational outcomes. This includes work on the Prisoner's Dilemma, the problem of collective action, public goods and the free-rider problem, etc. For reviews see Messick and Brewer (1983), Orbell and Dawes (1981).

In contrast, if the uncertainty regarding the good is low, the need for commitment and the concern over reputation will be lower. An example is the market for rice (Siamwalla 1978; Popkin 1981). Unlike rubber, the quality of rice can be ascertained directly and at essentially no cost by rubbing a few grains together between blocks of wood. In this situation, exchange more closely resembles the neoclassical model of the market: "Since quality is easy to assess instantaneously, rice markets are generally auction markets: immediate, relatively impersonal transactions. Or what Adam Smith thought all capitalism was like—information easily and readily ascertainable, easy switching of buyers, little reason for loyalty to any marketer or to any buyer. The grower's reputation matters relatively little since direct quality assessments are so easy to perform" (Popkin 1981, pp. 72–73).

This pair of examples captures the key points of this article. In essence, the goal was to create experimental analogs of the rubber and rice markets in order to examine the effects of uncertainty on the emergence of commitment and trust, as well as the importance of reputation in these settings.[3]

Commitment in Exchange Relations

Social exchange theory has a long and fruitful history of examining the *effects* of different exchange structures (networks of various shapes) on patterns of interaction, but very little research has investigated the emergence of these networks. Within a given network structure, researchers have sometimes had something to say about which pairs of actors are likely to trade (e.g., Bienenstock and Bonacich 1993; Cook, Emerson, Gillmore, and Yamagishi 1983; Markovsky, Willer, and Patton 1988). Of particular importance is an early experiment by Cook and Emerson (1978), who developed a measure of commitment as part of a study on power use in two four-person networks. I use the term *commitment* in the same sense they do to refer to *behavioral* patterns of exchange—that is, who trades with whom and to what extent. Because their focus was on power, they did not study patterns of commitment per se but rather the mediating effects of commitment on power use. One of the very few studies that has experimentally examined commitment is Lawler and Yoon (1993). This research focused on dyads, with each member of the dyad having a single, less attractive (i.e., less profitable) alternative. Their results indicated that the distribution of power, and whether a

[3] Note that the rubber and rice markets are used here simply as examples. The point of the present study is to experimentally examine the emergence of commitment, not to create a detailed simulation of commodity markets in Thailand.

bargaining situation is zero sum or is not zero sum, can indirectly affect the frequency of trading between two exchange partners.[4]

However, in each of these studies the researchers created particular network structures within which subjects interacted. The question addressed here—What pattern of committed exchange relations emerges in a situation where anyone might interact with anyone else?—has received almost no empirical attention.[5]

A second limitation in current work within social exchange theory is the neglect of deceit and opportunism in exchange relations. That is, in the typical exchange experiment actors bargain over the price of their goods or how to divide a set number of points, but there is never the possibility of lying about the value of what one has, receiving a good without paying the agreed price, or backing out of a contract after it has been agreed upon. In other words, the typical social exchange experiment guarantees the terms of the exchange. In one sense this is an understandable feature of an experimental paradigm if one wishes to study, for example, the dynamics of power in a controlled way, but in another sense it sidesteps much that is crucial in actual interaction (concerns of uncertainty, risk, and being taken advantage of) and thus much that may be central in explaining why social structure in the form of networks of commitment exists.

If actors are not required to trade "in good faith," the interaction can have the structure of a social dilemma in that (like the rubber market) individuals gain by being deceitful, but all are hurt if all choose this course of action. Work on social dilemmas thus treats as its central concern the kind of deceit and uncertainty (caused by the tension between individual and collective rationality) that is usually ignored in exchange theory. The emergence of social structure, however, has also been taken for granted in much of the literature on social dilemmas.

In some of the best known work on the emergence of cooperation in

[4] While Lawler and Yoon (1993) studied frequency of exchange, as I do, they use the term *commitment* to refer to an *affective* bond. Again, I am using the term here to refer to *behavioral* patterns of exchange. *Commitment* has also been used to refer to phenomena such as moral obligations or feelings of attachment. For further discussions of these other forms of commitment, see Becker (1960), Johnson (1991), Kanter (1972), Kelley (1983), Leik and Leik (1977), Levinger (1979), Rosenblatt (1977), Rubin and Brown (1973), and Rusbult and Buunk (1993).

[5] One study that does address these issues is Podolny (1990). Unfortunately, the experiment in this study is seriously limited, as the author himself acknowledges. Experimental economists (e.g., Fehr, Kirchsteiger, and Riedl 1993; Lynch et al. 1984; Plott 1986) do often examine situations where there are no restrictions on who might exchange with whom, but they are interested in very different issues and so have focused on questions of efficiency, price estimation, etc., rather than studying the emergence of stable exchange relations.

the face of social dilemmas (e.g., Axelrod 1984; Hardin 1982; Taylor 1987), the structural property that is doing most of the work in these analyses—the fact that transactions occur repeatedly with the same actors—is fixed by assumption. Said another way, these scholars provide no mechanism to explain commitment to an exchange partner or group: commitment is fixed and unvarying across actors and time. Each actor is forced to interact with every other actor and is unable to choose partners or to leave unsatisfactory exchange relations. This is troubling because according to these theorists conditional cooperation occurs only because of iterated transactions with identifiable others; yet there is no explanation of how a longitudinal exchange relation is established or maintained or what pattern those networks of relations might take.

Recent work has begun to relax some of these stringent assumptions. Studying the emergence of committed exchange requires that actors be able to move into and out of relationships, and Schuessler (1989) as well as Orbell and Dawes (1991) have conducted computer simulations of groups of actors playing an iterated Prisoner's Dilemma game. In this work, actors had the option of exiting, that is, leaving their current partner for a new one, after each round. Because these researchers wished to study whether cooperation could emerge under very harsh conditions, in both cases the models assumed that actors could not recognize each other. Thus, issues such as commitment and reputation were irrelevant.

Research on social dilemmas in which actors can recognize each other as well as exit from the relationship includes computer simulations by Vanberg and Congleton (1992) and Yamagishi, Hayashi, and Jin (1992), and experimental work by Marwell and Schmitt (1975), Orbell, Schwartz-Shea, and Simmons (1984), and Yamagishi (1992). In each case, however, the focus was on the level of cooperation; the emergence of committed exchange relationships was not studied.

Uncertainty and Trust

As I discussed above, an important limitation in current work in social exchange theory is the absence of deceit or opportunism in experimental designs. Yet situations in which we can be taken advantage of are pervasive in every realm of our lives. The motivations of those we interact with can be inferred but never known directly and the quality of goods and services we are offered is often unknown or known only approximately. In the language of game theory, we are often faced with *information asymmetries:* you and I have different bundles of information. This lack of information about the motivations of others and the quality of what is exchanged can open one up to serious risks and lead to unfortunate outcomes.[6]

A classic example of this sort of situation is the market for "lemons" (i.e., used cars of poor quality) analyzed by Akerlof (1970). The problem faced by the buyer of a used car is that he or she often cannot know the true quality of a car until after the car has been purchased and driven for a time. The car seller often does have a good idea of the car's quality, but there is no simple means of conveying this information in a believable way. The buyer realizes that the seller is motivated to describe the car as reliable regardless of the true nature of the car and that the seller stands to make an especially large profit if a "lemon" can be sold as a reliable car. According to Akerlof's analysis, because of this risk a buyer will be unwilling to purchase a used car at a high price. If the seller cannot get a high price the seller will be motivated to sell only lemons. The pessimistic conclusion is that in the absence of other factors only low-quality cars will be bought and sold at a low price. Both buyers and sellers are hurt by this outcome, and so the situation has the structure of a social dilemma in that individually rational behavior leads to a collectively irrational outcome.[7]

Faced with a situation in which one can be taken advantage of, a natural response is to restrict one's transactions to those who have shown themselves to be trustworthy (i.e., becoming committed to particular exchange partners). This is not a possibility in Akerlof's original analysis because he assumes the purchase of a used car between a particular buyer and seller is a one-time transaction. In contrast, the market for rubber involves the same problem of information asymmetries but in a situation in which buyers and sellers might encounter each other from one season

[6] There are other sources of uncertainty, but in this article I restrict my attention to uncertainty that is the result of information asymmetries. To define the term more precisely, "In a game of asymmetric information, the information sets of players differ in ways relevant to their behavior. . . . The essence of asymmetric information is that some player has useful *private information*" (Rasmusen 1989, p. 53; emphasis in original). This same situation is sometimes referred to as a game of *incomplete* information (Dasgupta 1988; Kreps 1990). Because this latter term is used inconsistently in the literature I will not use it here. For a detailed analysis that distinguishes perfect, certain, symmetric, and complete information from each other, see Rasmusen (1989, pp. 51–54). Note that he uses these terms in a particular, restricted sense—his usage does not always coincide with common usage, and while I borrow his definition of asymmetries, I do not use such terms as "uncertainty" in the same restricted sense he does. For a discussion of the sources of information asymmetries, see Kollock and O'Brien (1992).

[7] There are a variety of institutional arrangements that can help alleviate this kind of risk. Examples include enforceable warranties and contracts (e.g., Heimer 1985) or regulatory agencies (e.g., Zucker 1986). These solutions have their own set of limitations and risks (cf. Coleman 1990; Shapiro 1987).

to the next. The possibility of repeated exchanges means commitment can be used as a response to the risks that derive from information asymmetries.

As sellers and buyers repeatedly trade with each other it will be possible for trust to develop. As I use the term here, an action demonstrates *trust* if it "increase[s] one's vulnerability . . . to another whose behavior is not under one's control. [It refers to] the conscious regulation of one's dependence on another" (Zand 1972, p. 230; cf. Deutsch 1962).[8] Thus, the development of high levels of trust requires more than just ongoing interaction. Some level of risk must also be present so that there is a *test* of trust (Dasgupta 1988). As Kelley and Thibaut (1978, p. 237) observe in a discussion of the development of exchange relations: "If the [situation] is extremely correspondent [i.e., what is good for one actor is good for the other], there is . . . no basis for the development of trust, for there is nothing to risk, hence no test of willingness to take risks: cooperative overtures will be attributed to the structure of the situation rather than to dispositional . . . properties of the participants. Therefore it is in the middle regions of the continuum of outcome correspondence, in which elements of both conflict and cooperation are present as temptations, that attributions of trust have their origins." The implication is that trust is likely to be higher among actors who manage to establish successful exchange relations in situations such as the rubber market (where information asymmetries introduce significant risks), as opposed to actors in situations similar to the rice market (where more information is available and the risks are significantly lower). Of course, risk creates a breeding ground not only for trust but for exploitation as well. It may be then that in looking at the trust actors have for each other in a risky exchange situation one will find extremes of both trust and distrust. This will be one of the issues explored in the experiment.

Granovetter (1985) has also argued that ongoing experience within a network of exchange relationships is likely to be a key source of trust. Indeed, his claim is that this may be the most important source: "The widespread preference for transacting with individuals of known reputation implies that few are actually content to rely on either generalized morality *or* institutional arrangements to guard against trouble. . . . [Instead] social relations, rather than institutionalized arrangements or generalized morality, are mainly responsible for the production of trust in economic life" (pp. 490–91; emphasis in original).

His comment also raises the issue of reputation. A *reputation,* as defined by Robert Wilson (1985, pp. 27–28), is a "characteristic or attribute

For further elaboration on the concept of trust, see Coleman (1990), Dasgupta (1988), Gambetta (1988), and Yamagishi and Yamagishi (1993).

ascribed to one person . . . by another (e.g., '*A* has a reputation for courtesy'). Operationally, this is usually represented as a prediction about likely future behavior (e.g., '*A* is likely to be courteous'). It is, however, primarily an empirical statement (e.g., '*A* has been observed in the past to be courteous'). Its predictive power depends on the supposition that past behavior is indicative of future behavior." If actors encounter each other repeatedly in a risky situation, reputation is likely to be an important concern, both in terms of establishing a particular reputation for oneself as well as making some judgment about the reputation of one's potential exchange partners.

In recent years there has been a great deal of theoretical work in game theory and microeconomics on the important effects of reputations in situations with information asymmetries (Kreps and Wilson 1982; Kreps et al. 1982; Milgrom and Roberts 1982; Shapiro 1982; Wilson 1985).[9] This research has argued that "differences in the information available to participants make their strategies acutely sensitive to their beliefs and expectations" (Wilson 1985, p. 59), and hence actors will be concerned about both their own and their partners' reputation. A further conclusion is that this concern will vary depending upon the amount of risk in the exchange, with situations characterized by a high degree of uncertainty (such as the rubber market) leading to a greater concern for reputation.

There have also been theoretical discussions of the importance of reputation in the literature on social dilemmas (e.g., Axelrod 1984) as well as in the rational choice tradition within sociology (e.g., Coleman 1990; Raub and Weesie 1990). Curiously, the concept of reputation has been all but absent in social exchange theory.[10] Exchange theory has focused on the flow of tangible resources through an exchange network, but the work that has been done on reputation suggests that the flow and management of information will likely be as important a determinant of exchange processes and structures.[11]

In sum, this discussion suggests that variations in the initial structural constraints that affect the availability of information should have predictable effects on the strategies of exchange that actors adopt in their trans-

[9] For general overviews of the topic, see Kreps (1990) and Rasmusen (1989).

[10] An important exception is the work by Bacharach and Lawler (1981) on bargaining.

[11] From a sociological point of view, considering reputation and its effects also brings a dramaturgical element into the study of exchange. To date the possible relevance of research on dramaturgy to work on social exchange has hardly been explored. A more complete analysis of exchange should bring in *both* the structural conditions of exchange and dramaturgical activity to examine the conditions under which such factors as reputation become important. For an extended discussion of the issues of commitment, reputation, and the relevance of dramaturgy to social exchange theory, see Kollock and O'Brien (1992).

actions and therefore on the structure of the exchange networks that emerge. Specifically, if the uncertainty regarding a good that is exchanged is high, actors will enter into committed exchange relations with those partners who have shown themselves to be trustworthy. In this setting commitment will be high, actors will be very concerned about reputations, and trust is likely to be high (at least among committed exchange partners). It will be a system of exchange marked by a network of personalized, long-term exchange relations. In contrast, the example of the market for rice implies that when uncertainty is low, commitment will be low, actors will not be as concerned about reputations, and the level of trust between exchange partners will be lower. These are the hypotheses that will be explored in the experiment. Thus, at least in a limited way both sides of the micro-macro relationship are brought in: I investigate how the initial structural conditions of exchange affect interaction which in turn reproduces or reforms the exchange structure.

METHOD

Design

I created two experimental conditions. The single factor varied (between subjects) was the information subjects had about the quality of goods they were trading. In the first condition the quality of the goods being sold was public knowledge. In the second condition buyers discovered the quality of the goods they had purchased only after the sale was made. It is important to note that the unit of analysis is the group as a whole. This is necessary both because the key dependent variable of interest (the degree of commitment in the exchange system) is a property of the group as a whole and because actors within a given group are of course interdependent, making statistical tests at the individual level inappropriate.

Subjects

The experiment was run during the spring of 1991. Subjects were recruited from undergraduate social science courses at the University of California, Los Angeles, during the winter of 1990–91 and at the beginning of spring. Recruitment was based solely on the opportunity to earn money, and prospective subjects were told they could earn from $10 to $30 (depending on their performance in the experiment) for two hours of their time. A total of 80 subjects participated in groups of eight.[12] The

[12] Because the group is the unit of analysis, although 80 subjects participated in the experiment, for the purpose of tests of statistical significance, $N = 10$.

subjects ranged from 18 to 33 years of age, with a mean age of 21.5 years.

Procedure

Subjects were scheduled in groups of eight. Four subjects were randomly assigned the role of seller and four were assigned the role of buyer. The experiment took place in a room with a divider so that sellers could not see buyers and vice versa. At the front of the room, in view of all of the subjects, was a large erasable board on which were recorded the subjects' offers to buy and sell. Subjects made offers and accepted them by writing messages on small individual boards; talking was prohibited. Thus buyers and sellers could neither see nor hear each other and were identified only on the basis of a letter each had been assigned. They were also explicitly told that they would not see each other after the experiment was over.

Subjects read a set of instructions and went through a training period before the experiment began. In both experimental conditions, buyers and sellers traded goods of different qualities in order to earn points (which were converted to money at the end of the experiment). In the uncertain-quality condition (as in the rubber market) buyers did not discover the quality of what they had purchased until after the sale, and the quality was disclosed only to that particular buyer, not to the group as a whole. In the certain-quality condition (as in the rice market) the quality of the goods being sold was public knowledge.

In the uncertain-quality condition, the instructions read by the subjects were as follows:

> *For sellers.*—During each trading period you will have an opportunity to sell *one* shipment of "goods" to one of the buyers. The shipment you sell can vary in terms of its quality. There are three levels of quality (low, regular, super) and the higher the quality the more it will cost you to produce a shipment (a low costs 20 points, a regular costs 60 points, and a super costs 100 points). You will be asked at the beginning of each trading period what quality of goods you wish to produce. The higher the quality, the more the shipment is worth to a buyer. However, *at the time you sell the shipment the buyer will not know the quality.* After the purchase the buyer will be told the quality of the shipment he or she just bought from you.
>
> *For buyers.*—During each trading period you will have an opportunity to buy *one* shipment of "goods" from one of the sellers. The value of a shipment to you depends on its quality. There are three levels of quality (low, regular, super) and the higher the quality, the higher its value to you (this value is known as the "redemption value"). A low is worth 40 points, a regular is worth 120 points, and a super is worth 200 points. *At the time*

you buy the shipment you will not know the quality but after the purchase you will be told the quality of the shipment you bought.

In the certain-quality condition, the instructions informed the subjects that the quality of goods being sold would be public knowledge. The value of the goods for buyers and sellers was designed to create a situation that had two key characteristics. First, the higher the quality, the greater the cost to produce, but the higher the value to buyers; second, the higher the quality, the more profit there was to split up. Subjects were aware of these two features, which were emphasized during the training period. Subjects did not know, however, the exact value of the goods for the people with whom they were trading. That is, buyers did not know exactly how much it cost sellers to produce a good and sellers did not know the exact redemption value of a given quality of goods for buyers.

While actual quality was unknown in the uncertain-quality condition, sellers were allowed to advertise if they wished; that is, they could claim the shipment they were trying to sell was of a particular grade. It was emphasized (and buyers quickly discovered this) that sellers were under no obligation to advertise truthfully.

Each trading period lasted a maximum of five minutes, during which buyers and sellers could make as many offers and counteroffers as they wished (though they could complete only one trade during a given period). These offers and counteroffers were listed on the large board at the front of the room and so could be seen by all subjects.[13] There were two types of offers that could be made: *public* offers, which could be accepted by anyone, or *private* offers, which were directed toward a particular person and could be accepted only by that person. This feature allowed subjects to enter into restricted trading relations if they so desired.

Buyers and sellers were free to accept or not to accept an offer at any time. Once an offer was accepted it became binding. In the uncertain-quality condition the buyer was then privately informed of the quality of the good he or she had just purchased (of course, this information was already known to the buyer in the certain-quality condition). Once the sale was made, the relevant information was recorded on a data sheet, and the subjects calculated their profits for the round. In order to eliminate endgame effects, the number of trading periods was varied and subjects did not know which period would be their last. All groups traded for at least 20 rounds.

[13] Buyers and sellers could make any offer they desired, subject only to the constraint that they needed to make a profit in order to earn money. Subjects were restricted to making one trade per round in order to be consistent with the important body of work on negatively connected exchange networks (Cook and Emerson 1978; Cook et al. 1983; Markovsky et al. 1988), which imposes the same restriction.

After the experiment, subjects were given a questionnaire that contained (1) items designed to serve as manipulation tests, (2) questions regarding demographic characteristics, (3) items designed to measure how concerned they were about their own and their partners' reputation and how likely they were to switch partners, and (4) ratings of others in the group on a variety of dimensions.

The Measurement of Commitment

The key dependent variable of interest is commitment. The variable will be defined and measured at the behavioral level; that is, the question will be, Who traded with whom and to what extent? Even when the variable is defined strictly in behavioral terms, there are a number of complexities that emerge in designing a measure of commitment.

One possibility for assessing commitment would be to compare the number of trades two actors engaged in to the total number of trades. That is, if A and B trade seven times out of 15 possible trades, one could compute a commitment measure that is simply the ratio of trades completed to total trades possible (a score of .467 in this case). Such "pair-based" measures, however, are local measures that examine only one relationship at a time. This can lead to counterintuitive results in which actors might be given the same commitment score despite very different patterns of exchange.[14]

The alternative would be a measure that took into account the entire set of possible exchange relationships each actor faced. Such a measure (which can be termed "network-based" rather than "pair-based") was developed by Cook and Emerson (1978). For each actor, this measure compares the number of trades made with different partners. That is, it contrasts each possible exchange relationship with every other possible exchange relationship in which an actor might take part.

A revised version of their measure will be used here. Specifically, for an exchange system in which each actor has four potential trading part-

[14] For example, in a situation in which an actor has three possible exchange partners and completed 15 trades, consider two possible distribution of trades:

Case 1 Actor A completes seven trades with B, seven trades with C, and one trade with D;

Case 2 Actor A completes seven trades with B, four trades with C, and four trades with D.

Using a pair-based measure, the commitment score for the exchange relation between A and B would be identical in both case 1 and case 2, as will the average level of commitment across partners. Yet A's overall pattern of trade in case 1 (where A is equally committed to both B and C) is very different than case 2 (where B is clearly the partner A is most committed to).

ners, the level of commitment for actor I with potential partners J, K, L, and M, after t trading periods will be defined as

$$(C_i)_t = [(T_{ij} - T_{ik})^2 + (T_{ij} - T_{il})^2 + (T_{ij} - T_{im})^2 + (T_{ik} - T_{il})^2 + (T_{ik} - T_{im})^2 + (T_{il} - T_{im})^2]/[3(t^2)], \tag{1}$$

where T_{ij} signifies the number of trades I completed with J. The commitment measure has a maximum value of 1.0 when an actor has completed a trade every round and always with the same partner, and a minimum value of 0.0 when trades are evenly distributed among all possible trading partners. As Cook and Emerson (1978, p. 735) point out, while each person in the group "can have a different commitment score, the [eight] scores are obviously interdependent. To the extent that any person becomes committed, others, losing 'choice' in partner selection, become structurally committed of necessity."

As the term is used here, commitment also implies that an actor will resist at least some levels of temptation (e.g., a better price from another potential partner). The implication is that once a committed exchange relationship forms, actors will not abandon the relationship the moment a slightly better alternative presents itself. To tap into this possibility, on the postexperimental questionnaire subjects were asked to report how often they kept trading with a buyer/seller even when they could get a better price from someone else.[15]

Other Measures

On the postexperiment questionnaire, subjects were also asked a variety of questions designed to serve as manipulation tests, including how realistic they felt the study was, how clear the instructions were, how strongly motivated they were to earn as much as possible, and how much they enjoyed the experiment.

In addition to the question concerning commitment, subjects were asked how concerned they were about both their own and their partners' reputation for being fair in their trades.[16]

[15] Subjects responded on a seven-point scale, ranging from *never* (1) to *always* (7). A direct behavioral measure of such actions would be preferable. However, recording the kind of fine moment-to-moment detail necessary to make such calculations (every offer and counteroffer and the sequence in which they were made) was simply not possible given that data was being recorded with paper and pencil. A future set of studies currently being planned will be run through a computer network, which will allow the recording of every offer and counteroffer throughout the length of the experiment.

[16] The questions read, "How strongly were you concerned about your reputation for being a fair seller [buyer]?" and "How strongly were you concerned about the buyers' [sellers'] reputations for being fair in their trades?" As with all questionnaire items, subjects responded on a seven-point scale.

Finally, the postexperiment questionnaire allowed subjects to evaluate each person the subject might have traded with (i.e., the four buyers if a seller was answering the questionnaire, and the four sellers if the subject had been a buyer) on 12 bipolar scales. Of particular importance is the scale which asked subjects to rate how untrustworthy/trustworthy each of their potential trading partners was.[17]

Hypotheses

Note that the sellers and buyers in the uncertain-quality condition are not exposed to the same level of risk. The seller does face some risk (producing a costly, high-quality good and then not being able to get a high price for it), but the risks for the buyer are much greater. The seller makes a trade with full information about the quality of the good and the price being paid. In contrast, the buyer must trade blindly, knowing the price but learning the quality only after the exchange is consummated. The experiment was designed with this structure for two reasons: first, this structure models a great many empirical situations; and second, for some variables this allows one to make hypotheses not simply about differences between the two conditions (certain vs. uncertain quality), but also about differences between the role subjects played in the experiment (seller vs. buyer).

Seven hypotheses will be investigated. Based on the discussion above, the key prediction is the effect of uncertainty on commitment:

HYPOTHESIS 1.—*Commitment will be greater in the uncertain-quality condition.*

Related to this prediction is the hypothesis concerning subjects' response to tempting offers by other exchange partners:

HYPOTHESIS 2.—*Subjects will be more likely to report staying with an exchange partner even when they could get a better price from someone else in the uncertain-quality condition.*

The second variable of interest is trust. As discussed above, developing high levels of trust requires that there be some test of trust, that is, risk. Assuming buyers and sellers establish successful exchange relations in both conditions, the prediction is

HYPOTHESIS 3.—*Subjects will rate their partners as significantly more trustworthy in the uncertain-quality condition.*

[17] Subjects were asked to indicate their overall impression of each potential trading partner on the following scales: intelligent/unintelligent, honest/dishonest, reliable/unreliable, likable/unlikable, irrational/rational, untrustworthy/trustworthy, kind/unkind, incompetent/competent, fair/unfair, unfriendly/friendly, rigid/flexible, and aggressive/unaggressive.

Exchange Structures

The uncertain-quality condition could produce extremes of both trust (for one's favored trading partner) and distrust (for other partners, who perhaps tried to take advantage of the subject). This possibility will be investigated by examining not just the overall level of trust within the group, but the average trustworthiness rating for one's most trusted and least trusted trading partner as well. Because of the asymmetric risk in the uncertain-quality condition, I also expect that the trustworthiness ratings made by buyers will be more "extreme" than those made by sellers. Specifically

HYPOTHESIS 4.—*Within the uncertain-quality condition, the trustworthiness rating of one's* most *trusted partner will be higher for buyers than sellers, and the trustworthiness rating for one's* least *trusted partner will be lower for buyers than sellers.*

The reason for this prediction is that, since buyers face much greater risk in their trading, they will have particularly strong evidence about the trustworthiness or untrustworthiness of their partners. One should also expect to find a relationship between commitment and trust in that there should be higher trust among partners who frequently trade with each other. Hence

HYPOTHESIS 5.—*The trustworthiness rating for one's most frequent exchange partner will be greater than the rating for one's least frequent exchange partner.*[18]

A positive relationship between commitment and trust should definitely be found in the uncertain-quality condition. I also expect to find this relationship in the certain-quality condition despite the absence of significant risk. Previous research (Homans 1961; Lawler and Yoon 1993; Molm 1991) has suggested that frequent exchange is sufficient in itself to produce positive evaluations of one's partner. However, while commitment and trust are likely to be related in both conditions, the average level of trust should be higher in the uncertain-quality condition.[19]

The final variable of interest is concern for reputation, and it is expected that greater risk leads to greater concern for reputation. Hence

HYPOTHESIS 6.—*Subjects will be significantly more concerned about*

[18] Note that in order to test this prediction it is necessary to examine the exchange patterns of particular dyads rather than the group as a whole. Thus for this hypothesis, and only for this hypothesis, a pair-based measure of commitment was used. This measure consists of the ratio of trades completed with a particular partner to total trades possible.

[19] I do not make an assumption about the direction of causality between commitment and trust, simply that the two will be positively related. Trust and commitment are likely to mutually reinforce each other over time. Tracking the fine details of how the two develop (which would require an experimental design that measured trust repeatedly over time) would be an interesting possibility for a future study.

both their own and their partners' reputation in the uncertain-quality condition.

Here, as with trust, I expect a difference between buyers and sellers in the uncertain-quality situation, and for a similar reason. Because buyers face a much greater risk—being exploited by a seller—the prediction is that buyers will be particularly concerned about the reputation of sellers and sellers will be especially concerned about their own reputation. Hence

HYPOTHESIS 7.—*Within the uncertain-quality condition, the concern for* one's partners' *reputation will be higher for buyers than sellers, and the concern for one's* own *reputation will be higher for sellers than buyers.*

RESULTS

Analysis of the postexperimental questionnaire provides evidence that the subjects were highly motivated to earn as much as possible (mean = 6.01, SD = 0.38; seven-point scale), rated the instructions they received as very clear (mean = 6.28, SD = 0.38), found the study realistic (mean = 4.89, SD = 0.30), and greatly enjoyed participating in the experiment (mean = 6.16, SD = 0.41). Only one of these scores differed significantly between the two experimental conditions (the question concerning the motivation to earn as much as possible; this result is discussed below).

The results will be grouped according to the dependent variables, beginning with the measures of commitment, then reporting on the level of trust in the groups, variables relevant to concerns about reputation, and finally a section on other findings that were not explicitly predicted. Because the group is the unit of analysis, all variables consist of group averages.

Commitment

Figure 1 displays the average level of commitment across time for both experimental conditions. The trading rounds were grouped into five blocks of four rounds each. The effect of uncertainty on commitment was significant and in the direction hypothesized: commitment was significantly greater in the uncertain-quality condition ($F_{1,8} = 5.46$; $P < .05$), supporting hypothesis 1.

There were no significant differences across blocks of trading rounds ($F_{4,32} = 0.72$; $P = .581$), nor was the interaction of uncertainty × blocks significant ($F_{4,32} = 0.73$; $P = .577$).[20]

[20] Because the commitment measure takes into account the entire group, it is impossible to test for differences between sellers and buyers (the mean score for one subgroup will always equal the mean of the other subgroup). Despite the limitations of a pair-based measure of commitment (i.e., a simple ratio of completed trades to possible trades), statistical tests were run using this measure because it allows comparisons

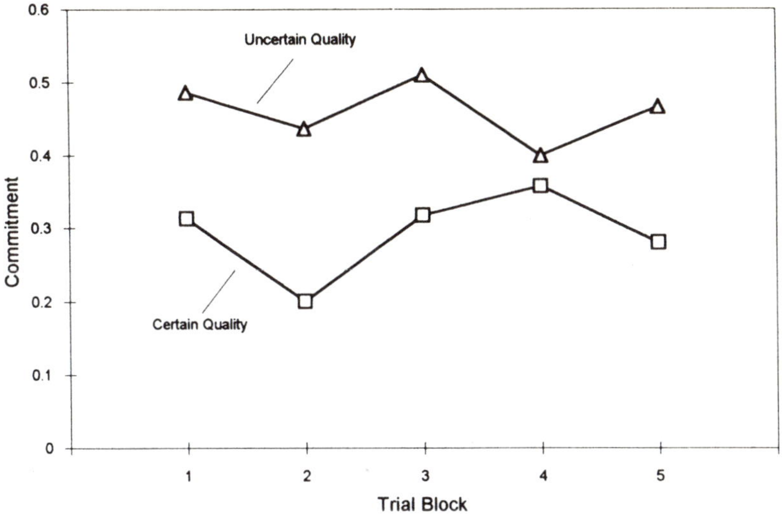

FIG. 1.—Average level of commitment

Consistent with the hypothesis 2, subjects in the uncertain-quality condition were significantly more likely to report that they sometimes kept trading with a particular partner even when they could get a better price from someone else. (Mean = 2.68, 3.98 for the certain- and uncertain-quality conditions, respectively; $P < .05$. Means are based on a seven-point scale with a higher score indicating a greater tendency to remain with one's partner.)

Trust

The average trust rating for all potential partners was significantly higher in the uncertain-quality condition, supporting hypothesis 3. (Mean = 4.08, 4.62 for the certain- and uncertain-quality conditions, respectively; $P < .01$.)

Because this overall average could be masking extremes of both trust and distrust, the average trustworthiness ratings of subjects' most and least trusted partner were examined separately. Figure 2 displays the trustworthiness rating of subjects' *most* trusted partner for sellers and buyers in both experimental conditions.

There is a very strong main effect for the influence of uncertainty,

between sellers and buyers. There were no significant or near-significant differences in commitment between sellers and buyers in either experimental condition.

FIG. 2.—Trustworthiness rating for *most* trusted partner

indicating that the level of trustworthiness for one's most trusted partner is significantly higher in the uncertain-quality condition ($F_{1,8}$ = 41.26; $P < .001$). There was also a significant effect for the role subjects occupied (seller vs. buyer), with buyers on average rating their most trusted partner higher than sellers ($F_{1,8}$ = 9.26; $P < .05$; role is treated as a repeated measure). However, this effect is largely the result of the difference between sellers and buyers in the uncertain-quality condition; sellers and buyers do not differ significantly in the certain-quality condition. This results in a significant interaction effect between uncertainty (certain vs. uncertain quality) and role (seller vs. buyer; $F_{1,8}$ = 5.60; $P < .05$). Note that subjects in the uncertain condition rated their most trusted partner higher than did subjects in the certain-quality condition and that the buyers in the uncertain condition rated their most trusted partner exceptionally high (mean = 6.80 on a seven-point scale).

Figure 3 displays the trustworthiness rating of subjects' *least* trusted partner. The main effect for uncertainty was not significant (P = .918), but the effect for role was significant ($F_{1,8}$ = 13.68; $P < .01$). Once again, this effect is due to the difference between sellers and buyers in the uncertain-quality conditions, a difference that results in a significant interaction effect ($F_{1,8}$ = 11.36; $P < .01$). In this case sellers in the uncertain-quality condition rated their least trustworthy partner higher than other experimental subjects, whereas buyers in the uncertain-quality condition rated their least trusted partner lower than other subjects.

Looking at both figures 2 and 3, one can see that buyers in the uncertain condition rated their most trusted partner higher than sellers in the uncertain condition and they rated their least trusted partner lower than

FIG. 3.—Trustworthiness rating for *least* trusted partner

sellers, all of which supports hypothesis 4. Note also that in the certain-quality condition there is essentially no difference between buyers and sellers in their ratings of their partners' trustworthiness.

One should also expect to find a relationship between trust and commitment. Figure 4 displays the trustworthiness rating of subjects' most and least frequent trading partner for the two experimental conditions.

As predicted by hypothesis 5, the difference between the trustworthiness rating of subjects' least and most frequent exchange partner is sig-

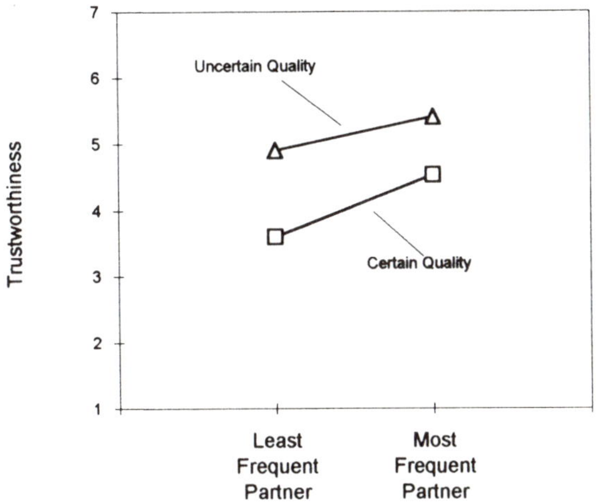

FIG. 4.—Trustworthiness rating of most and least frequent exchange partner

nificant in both conditions, with subjects rating their most frequent partner as more trustworthy ($F_{1,8}$ = 10.35; $P < .05$). The effect for uncertainty is also significant, indicating that subjects in the uncertain-quality condition on average rated their trading partners as more trustworthy ($F_{1,8}$ = 20.24; $P < .01$). The interaction effect was not significant (P = .365).

Concern for Reputation

The remaining hypotheses deal with subjects' concern for their own and their partners' reputation. Figure 5 displays subjects' concern for their *own* reputation for being fair in their trades. There is a significant effect for uncertainty, with subjects in the uncertain-quality condition being more concerned on average about their own reputation ($F_{1,8}$ = 20.17; $P < .01$). The effect for role was not significant (P = .693), but the interaction effect between uncertainty and role was nearly significant ($F_{1,8}$ = 4.76; P = .061).

Figure 6 displays how concerned subjects were about their potential *partners'* reputation. Again, there is a significant uncertainty effect ($F_{1,8}$ = 6.07; $P < .05$). Subjects in the uncertain-quality condition on average were more concerned about their partners' reputation. There is a nearly significant role effect ($F_{1,8}$ = 3.68; P = .091). As was true with the trust variables, this effect is the result of the difference between sellers and buyers in the uncertain-quality condition, which results in a significant interaction effect ($F_{1,8}$ = 6.66; $P < .05$).

In each case subjects in the uncertain-quality condition were on aver-

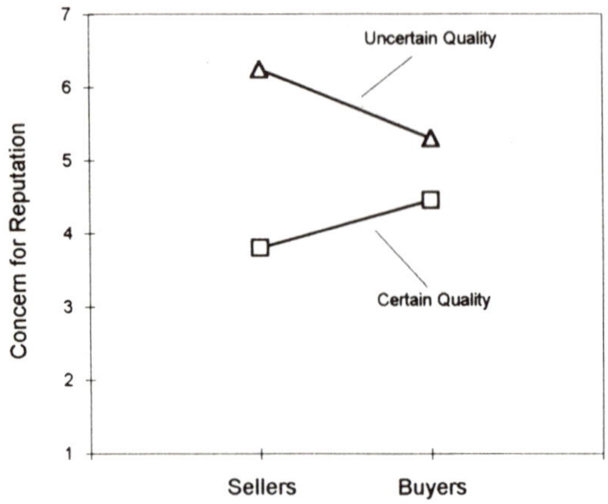

FIG. 5.—Concern for *own* reputation for being fair

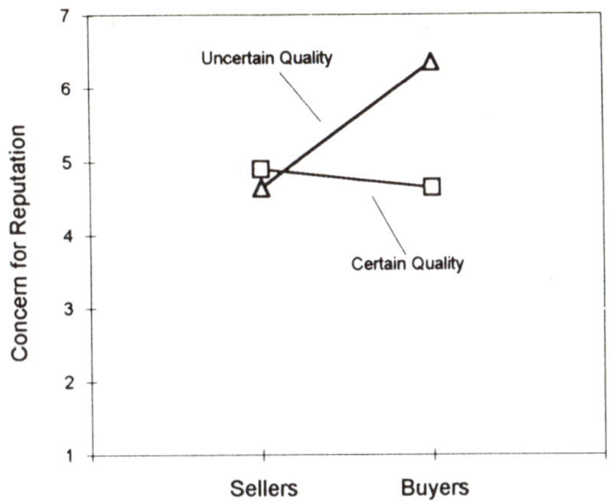

FIG. 6.—Concern for *partners'* reputation for being fair

age significantly more concerned about both their own and their potential partners' reputation, confirming hypothesis 6. In addition, within the uncertain-quality condition, sellers were more concerned about their own reputation and buyers were more concerned about their partners' reputation. In other words, subjects in the uncertain condition were especially concerned about sellers' reputation. This finding confirms hypothesis 7.

Other Findings

The average quality of goods exchanged in each experimental condition is shown in figure 7. Again, the trading periods are aggregated into five blocks of four trading periods each.

There is a significant rise in the average quality of goods traded for both experimental conditions ($F_{4,32} = 5.33$; $P < .01$). Although the overall quality of goods traded in the certain-quality condition is a little higher than in the uncertain-quality condition, the difference was not significant ($F_{1,8} = 2.14$; $P = .182$). The interaction between uncertainty and trial blocks was also not significant ($F_{4,32} = 0.80$; $P = .533$). Note that the average level of quality is quite high in both conditions.

Four other findings were significant or nearly significant. First, in a question that asked how motivated subjects were to be fair when they made trades, the average level of motivation for being fair was significantly higher in the uncertain-quality condition (mean = 4.18, 5.58 on a seven-point scale for the certain- and uncertain-quality conditions, respectively; $P < .01$). Second, although subjects in both conditions reported they were highly motivated to earn as much as possible, subjects

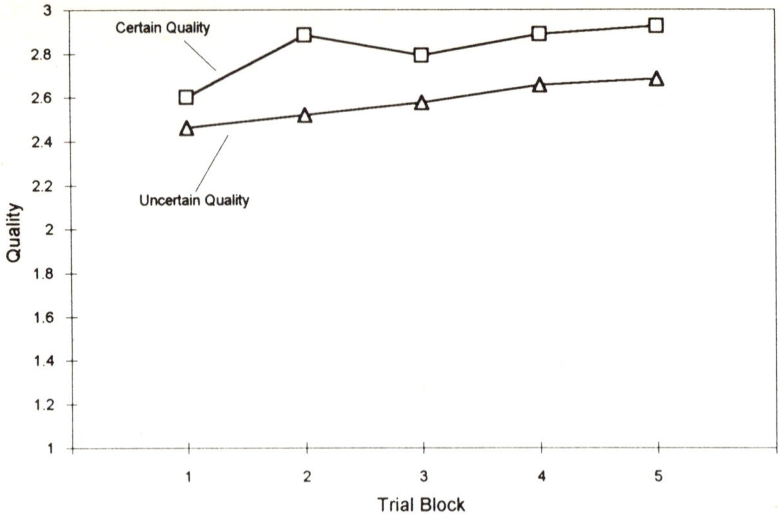

FIG. 7.—Average level of quality (3 = super, 2 = regular, 1 = low)

in the *certain* quality condition had significantly higher scores on this measure—that is, they were more motivated to earn as much as possible (mean = 6.28, 5.75 for the certain- and uncertain-quality conditions, respectively; $P < .05$). Third, an unanticipated finding was that when subjects were asked their impression of how rational their potential trading partners were, the overall rationality rating was significantly higher in the uncertain-quality condition (mean = 4.29, 4.81 for the certain- and uncertain-quality conditions, respectively; $P < .01$). Finally, it seems that subjects in the uncertain-quality condition attributed more "extreme" personality characteristics (whether in the positive or negative direction) to their trading partners than did subjects in the certain-quality condition. By "extreme" I mean the extent to which ratings on the bipolar personality scales departed from the midpoint. A measure was constructed that summed the absolute value of each rating minus four points (the midpoint). The average departure from the midpoint was greater for the uncertain-quality condition (mean = 1.103, 1.455 for the certain- and uncertain-quality conditions, respectively; $P = .056$).

DISCUSSION

All the hypotheses were supported by the results. Commitment, the reported tendency to remain with a partner despite a better offer, the average level of trust, and concern for one's own and others' reputation were all significantly higher in the uncertain-quality condition.

Although commitment, as operationalized by the Cook and Emerson measure, was significantly higher in the uncertain-quality condition, observations of subjects' trading behavior suggest a more complex definition of commitment may be needed. In some cases, sellers were observed advertising truthfully when trading with some buyers and trying to exploit others. For example, in one case a seller established a trading relationship with one favored buyer within which the seller always advertised truthfully and sold the goods at a reasonable price. When interacting with other buyers however, the seller tried to pass on low-quality goods as high-quality goods. When trying to sell a "lemon," the seller was very careful to shut out the favored buyer by making only private offers and only to the other three buyers. In that way the favored buyer could not inadvertently buy the shipment thinking it was a high-quality good (which would damage the relationship the seller had carefully nurtured).[21]

This example demonstrates the kind of sophisticated strategic behavior that some subjects engaged in. It also illustrates a different way of thinking about commitment. Intuitively, it seems reasonable to say that this seller was committed to the favored buyer. Yet simply looking at the number of trades the seller made and with whom would not uncover the kind of commitment expressed here. While the Cook and Emerson measure clearly taps into an important behavioral pattern, future work would likely benefit from using a more complex operational definition of commitment.

It is also important to note that the difference in commitment between the two experimental conditions was relative rather than absolute—commitment was definitely present in the certain quality condition. This suggests that commitment will be present to some degree in any exchange system. Indeed, Baker (1984) has shown that even in exchange situations that have been designed to eliminate quality uncertainty and transaction costs as much as possible, such as the Chicago Options Exchange, commitment between particular buyers and sellers emerges.

Trust was significantly higher on average in the uncertain-quality condition, though this general result ignores interesting interaction effects. As I discussed above, sellers and buyers both face risks in the uncertain condition, but buyers face much greater risks—they are always in danger of being exploited by sellers because of their lack of knowledge about the quality of the good being sold. This means that sellers face a particularly severe test of their trustworthiness, and so it is not surprising to see that, in the uncertain-quality condition, buyers' most trusted partners were

[21] These observations were confirmed in a discussion this seller had with the experimenter after the experiment had been completed.

ranked exceptionally high in trustworthiness and their least trusted partners were ranked exceptionally low (figs. 2 and 3). Buyers' ratings of their least trusted partner was the one case in which the level of trust was lower in the uncertain condition. It is noteworthy that there were no differences between sellers and buyers in the certain-quality condition. This is understandable given that sellers and buyers are in equivalent situations in that each has full information about quality and price.

The other finding regarding trust was the relationship between commitment and trust (fig. 4), and as expected the results demonstrate that subjects rank their most frequent exchange partner as more trustworthy than their least frequent partner. This relationship held in both conditions, although the level of trustworthiness was once again significantly higher in the uncertain-quality condition. The fact that the relationship between trading frequency and trust also existed in the certain-quality case is interesting. It seems that ongoing interaction, even in the absence of significant uncertainty, can lead to an increase in trust. Note however that the level of trust for subjects' *most* frequent partner in the certain-quality condition was still lower than the trust rating for subjects' *least* frequent partner in the uncertain condition.

Concern about reputation was also significantly higher in the uncertain-quality condition. Once again, this general finding ignores a variety of interesting interaction effects that can be seen once sellers and buyers are examined individually. In the uncertain-quality condition sellers had the opportunity to exploit buyers, and so it is understandable that buyers in this condition were especially concerned about sellers' reputation for being fair and sellers were especially concerned about their own reputation for being fair (figs. 5, 6). This concern about fairness in the uncertain-quality condition is also reflected in the finding that subjects in this condition were more likely to report that they were motivated to be fair in their trades with others.

The finding that subjects' impressions of each other's rationality was higher in the uncertain-quality condition was unexpected, and I am not certain how to interpret the result. One tentatively offered possibility is that the greater challenge of completing successful trades under conditions of uncertainty required sophisticated strategies and decision making, and so when subjects looked back on the actions of their trading partners they were inclined to rate them as quite rational. As for the finding that subjects in the uncertain-quality condition attributed more "extreme" personality characteristics to their trading partners, a possible interpretation is that trading under conditions of risk leads to subjectively more secure assessments of others' characteristics. Whatever the case, it is interesting that different structural conditions of exchange can lead to significantly different attributional patterns about individuals' underlying dispositions and capacities.

Observations of subjects' trading behavior in the uncertain-quality condition also revealed interesting details about their approach and reactions to risky exchange. Subjects seemed to follow a number of different strategies in trying to make successful trades. In the uncertain-quality condition there were some buyers who started off selling high-quality goods from the beginning and never tried to take advantage of buyers. Although no communication was permitted between subjects and the quality of the good was disclosed only to the buyer, because subjects had an opportunity to trade with each other over a number of rounds, those sellers who were reliable sources of high-quality goods were quickly discovered, and buyers often bid each other up in price for the opportunity of trading with the trusted seller. Indeed, the prices buyers were willing to pay for goods from a particular seller and the rush by some buyers to complete a trade with particular sellers seemed to be sources of information for other buyers—if other buyers were eager to trade with seller X, then perhaps they should be too. In this way sellers who established a reputation for selling high-quality goods could demand a premium for their goods because of the identity they had established for themselves.

Other sellers in the uncertain-quality condition tried to get away with all they could, sometimes stringing a buyer along with a few good trades and then exploiting them by passing on a low-quality good that they advertised as a high-quality good. Still other sellers, as was illustrated in the commitment example above, were always fair with some buyers (to the extent that they advertised truthfully) while not hesitating to exploit other buyers.

Also noteworthy was the exceptional involvement of subjects in the experiment and a moral element that seemed to color the experience. Those buyers in the uncertain-quality condition who were betrayed by a seller (having been sold low-quality goods that were advertised as high-quality goods) appeared very disturbed and often wrote notes in the margins of their data sheets such as "Never trade with C again!" Conversely, when successful exchange relations were established under conditions of risk, subjects reacted very positively. In two groups in the uncertain-quality condition, a pair of subjects formed exclusive trading relations (all trades were completed with only one partner) that were also highly successful (only high-quality goods were traded). The outcome was very interesting: although subjects were told they would not meet each other afterward and would not be able to identify each other, in these two cases the trading partners sought each other out, asking subjects as they left the experiment what position they held. When they found each other they greeted one another as old friends even though they had not known each other prior to the experiment (and of course knew each other during the experiment simply by an identifying letter, their only source of information about the other being their trading behavior). They congratulated each other, praised each other, exchanged "high-fives," and in one case even made plans to meet for lunch the next day. It is also noteworthy that exclusive exchange relations never developed in the certain-quality condition.

Risk, Regulation, and Trust

It is possible to think about the *certain*-quality condition as an exchange system in which a third party (the experimenter) served as a regulatory agency to insure the terms of the transaction. Indeed, it was an ideal regulatory system in that it operated perfectly (no seller could misrepresent the quality of his or her goods, and no one could back out of a contract once it had been made) and at no cost to the participants.

The quality of goods traded in the certain condition was a little higher than the goods traded in the uncertain condition, which suggests the advantage of a formal regulatory system. Yet this difference was not significant and, given that there was a significant increase in quality over time in both conditions, it may be that even this small difference would disappear. Further, the results indicated that there may be some drawbacks to a system that relies on an outside party to provide guarantees even when the monitoring system works perfectly. The average level of interpersonal trust was significantly lower in the certain-quality condition compared to the uncertain-quality condition. To the extent this finding is robust, one implication is that in some situations an external, formal regulatory system might work against the emergence of trust within a group or result in the atrophy of already existing trust. This possibility has been discussed by a number of theorists. At the most general level, Taylor (1987, p. 168) has argued that "the more the state intervenes . . . the more 'necessary' (on this view) it becomes, because positive altruism and voluntary cooperative behavior *atrophy* in the presence of the state and *grow* in its absence. Thus, again, the state exacerbates the conditions which are supposed to make it necessary. We might say that the state is like an addictive drug: the more of it we have, the more we 'need' it and the more we come to 'depend' on it" (emphasis in original).

Hirschman (1984, p. 93) makes a similar point, stating that trust and other "moral resources" are "resources whose supply may well increase rather than decrease through use; these resources do not remain intact if they stay unused; like the ability to speak a foreign language or to play the piano, these moral resources are likely to become depleted and to atrophy if *not* used" (emphasis in original).

An interesting empirical example that is consistent with these views comes from research by Light, Kwuon, and Zhong (1990). Their research contrasts the effects of rotating credit associations with bureaucratized financial institutions as a source of capital in a Korean-American community. Rotating credit associations are informal lending circles that often involve a significant risk (the possibility that one of the participants will default). They argue that these informal exchange systems can actually encourage trust and solidarity within the community: "Like ethnic business generally, [Korean rotating credit associations] encourage the ethnic solidarity they require. In short, social trust reciprocally shapes credit institutions and is shaped by them, being helped to persist where credit institutions require a high level of social solidarity in the user population, and damaged where general social (not economic) life undermines the requisite solidarity. This result supports the claim that bureaucratized financial institutions accelerated the atomization of the population rather than having, as previously thought, served the otherwise intractable needs of already atomized people" (Light et al. 1990, p. 48).[22]

While the links between these larger issues of social order and the experiment are speculative, the results do indicate that the presence of uncertainty in the form of information asymmetries can promote high levels of interpersonal trust.[23] It is conceivable that the higher levels of trust that emerged in this condition could serve as a form of "social capital" (Coleman 1988), making possible various actions that might otherwise not be successful (e.g., contributing toward the provision of some public good or managing a commons). Messick et al. (1983), for example, have demonstrated empirically that individuals who rated their exchange partners as trustworthy were more likely to cooperate in an *N*-person social dilemma (by reducing their own "harvest" in a commons type of collective dilemma).

This would be a very interesting route to solving group-level dilemmas because it would not require a formal control system. Undoubtedly, for-

[22] And as Taylor (1987, p. 177) notes, "It has often been argued that the choice of the scope and form of social institutions (such as the state) must be based on 'pessimistic' assumptions, so that they will be 'robust' against the worst possible conditions . . . in which they might be required to operate. . . . But if the institutions themselves affect preferences . . . then this approach is inappropriate and may be dangerously misleading."

[23] This is not to say that uncertainty *guarantees* high levels of trust. I discuss this issue below.

mal controls will often be needed, but there is an argument to be made against the inevitable *necessity* of formal controls as a solution to *N*-person social dilemmas. It is possible that endogenous solutions to *dyadic* dilemmas based on such features as commitment and reputation (as demonstrated in this experiment) could create the trust and solidarity necessary to solve *collective* dilemmas. An empirical test of these ideas is currently being designed.

Stable versus Optimal Outcomes

While the emergence of commitment, trust, and successful trading relations are possible results of an exchange system resembling the uncertain-quality condition, in no way are they inevitable results. I do not assume that the effects of commitment and reputation will always solve such problems as trading under conditions of uncertainty. That is, I wish to avoid a functionalist or "adaptionist" (Gould and Lewontin 1984) argument that would assume exchange systems inevitably converge on one optimal outcome.

That more than one stable outcome is possible is suggested by the pretrials that were run for this experiment. In the first pretrials, sellers in the uncertain-quality condition were not allowed to advertise. Under this condition two different groups reached different stable outcomes: for one group the transactions resembled the ones reported here (high-quality goods being exchanged), while in the other group the market "failed" in that after a short length of time only low-quality goods were being sold at low prices (and so resulting in low profits for everyone). It seemed that the first few trades subjects made had a great effect on subsequent transactions. In the group where the first few moves were trusting (producing high-quality goods, and offering a high price in buying goods), these actions seemed to encourage a trend toward high prices and high quality, but in the group where the first few moves were exploitative (trying to get a high price for low-quality goods), low-quality goods were soon the only ones available in the group.[24]

One possible interpretation is that although sellers were not required to be truthful in their advertising, it still served to communicate information that had a beneficial impact on trading. To put it differently, restricting the flow of information seemed to increase the sensitivity to initial conditions (i.e., the first few trades subjects made). Again, these are not established results, merely impressions from the pretrials, but the implications are certainly important enough to warrant future research,

[24] Compare Gamson, Fireman, and Rytina (1982) on the effects of early disagreement in a group on the group's subsequent capacity for collective action.

and they do make the point that an outcome of high quality and high profits is not inevitable.[25]

Thus, the kind of model of exchange and the emergence of social structure I have in mind is a contingent, "multiple equilibrium" one. In contrast, "in less contingent arguments—including most neoclassical economic work, many versions of Marxism or population ecology, and functionalism of all varieties—outcomes are predicted without the necessity of looking closely at the historical background of particular settings, the preexisting economic institutions, or the social structure and collective action of individuals" (Granovetter 1990, p. 106). While unique predictions might not be possible, "such multiple equilibrium models, even if underdetermined, are far from the historicist argument that every case is unique and anything is possible" (Granovetter 1990, p. 107). The challenge then is to specify the crucial parameters and the outcomes that will follow.

If uncertainty is too high, the risks too large, or perhaps the temptations of exploitation too great, high trust and successful exchange relations may not emerge. On the other hand, the quote from Kelley and Thibaut (1978, p. 237) in the introduction makes the point that if there is no risk in an exchange situation, exploitation will not occur, but neither will high levels of trust develop. Thus, one way of thinking about this experiment is as an investigation into the *structural* origins of trust in a system of exchange, rather than treating trust as an individual personality variable (e.g., Messick et al. 1983; Yamagishi 1986). It seems that it is in the broad middle range of risk and uncertainty that both the emergence of trust and the possibility of endogenous solutions to the problem of risky trade emerge. Here we see such possibilities as commitment and reputation as social solutions to uncertainty in exchange relations.

CONCLUSIONS

The results clearly indicate that it is possible to study experimentally the emergence of different exchange structures as well as the consequences

[25] Looking at another possible factor, it is interesting to note that reputations did not seem to provide a solution to a lemons market in a study conducted by Lynch et al. (1984). They believe it is likely that because only two extreme grades of quality were possible (lows and supers), the decision to offer high-quality goods was a very risky one—there was no way to temper one's risk by, for example, offering goods of intermediate quality until trust was established. In addition to the above discussion on advertising and the flow of information, this suggests another situation in which reputation and commitment might not solve the problem of information asymmetries: an exchange system in which the risks to cooperating initially (by offering to buy at a high price or produce a high-quality good) are extreme.

of different patterns of exchange. While this study obviously does not capture all the important processes involved in the emergence of structure and commitment (which might require following groups for weeks or months), it is equally important to note that for at least some important features, this experiment produced stable results and significant differences after 20 periods of exchange.

There are a number of important directions for future research. Using a behavioral measure of trust, perhaps in connection with the provision of a public good, would allow one to test some of the ideas discussed above in the section on risk and regulation. Another variation would be to allow the buyers and sellers to talk among themselves (i.e., buyers with buyers, and sellers with sellers). Presumably this would accelerate the development of reputation and might also lead to organized sanctioning of untrustworthy actors. Increasing the flow of information further by allowing face-to-face interaction of all the subjects would be another interesting variation. Research on social dilemmas (e.g., Messick and Brewer 1983; Orbell and Dawes 1981) and in experimental economics (e.g., Radner and Schotter 1989) has demonstrated that face-to-face communication can promote cooperation and increase bargaining efficiency. The general theme would be to study the effects of variations in the communication network *and* the exchange network (which can vary independently of each other) on the processes and emergent structures of exchange. Other possible modifications to this design include allowing more than one exchange per round or varying the number of buyers and sellers so that the two groups would not be evenly matched. Finally, commitment and trust are not the only important variables in exchange relations, and my future work will examine the effects of sociological variables on price and profit dynamics in risky trading situations.

In sum, this research demonstrates that uncertainty can have significant effects on the emergence of exchange structures, the level of interpersonal trust in a group, and the concern actors have for their own and their partners' reputation. The lessons for social exchange theory include recognizing the important effects of deceit and opportunism on exchange, the need to investigate the emergence of social structure as well as its effects, and the relevance of reputation (and other factors related to the signaling and collection of information) to exchange processes.

REFERENCES

Akerlof, George A. 1970. "The Market for 'Lemons': Quality Uncertainty and the Market Mechanism." *Quarterly Journal of Economics* 84:488–500.

Axelrod, Robert. 1984. *The Evolution of Cooperation*. New York: Basic.

Exchange Structures

Bacharach, Samuel B., and Edward J. Lawler. 1981. *Bargaining: Power, Tactics, and Outcomes*. San Francisco: Jossey-Bass.

Baker, Wayne. 1984. "Floor Trading and Crowd Dynamics." Pp. 107–28 in *Social Dynamics of Financial Markets,* edited by Patricia Adler and Peter Adler. Greenwich, Conn.: JAI Press.

Becker, H. S. 1960. "Notes on the Concept of Commitment." *American Journal of Sociology* 66:32–40.

Bienenstock, Elisa, and Phillip Bonacich. 1993. "Game Theory Models for Exchange Networks: Experimental Results." *Sociological Perspectives* 36 (2): 117–35.

Coleman, James S. 1986. "Social Theory, Social Research, and a Theory of Action." *American Journal of Sociology* 91:1309–35.

———. 1988. "Social Capital in the Creation of Human Capital." *American Journal of Sociology* 94 (suppl.): S95–S120.

———. 1990. *Foundations of Social Theory*. Cambridge, Mass.: Harvard University Press.

Cook, Karen S., and Richard M. Emerson. 1978. "Power, Equity and Commitment in Exchange Networks." *American Sociological Review* 43:721–39.

Cook, Karen S., Richard M. Emerson, Mary R. Gillmore, and Toshio Yamagishi. 1983. "The Distribution of Power in Exchange Networks: Theory and Experimental Results." *American Journal of Sociology* 89:275–305.

Dasgupta, Partha. 1988. "Trust as a Commodity." Pp. 49–72 in *Trust: Making and Breaking Cooperative Relations,* edited by Diego Gambetta. New York: Basil Blackwell.

Deutsch, Morton. 1962. "Cooperation and Trust: Some Theoretical Notes." Pp. 275–319 in *Nebraska Symposium on Motivation,* edited by M. Jones. Lincoln: University of Nebraska Press.

Fehr, Ernst, Georg Kirchsteiger, and Arno Riedl. 1993. "Does Fairness Prevent Market Clearing? An Experimental Investigation." *Quarterly Journal of Economics* 108 (2): 437–59.

Gambetta, Diego. 1988. "Can We Trust Trust?" Pp. 213–37 in *Trust: Making and Breaking Cooperative Relations,* edited by Diego Gambetta. New York: Basil Blackwell.

Gamson, William A., Bruce Fireman, and Steven Rytina. 1982. *Encounters with Unjust Authority*. Chicago: Dorsey Press.

Gould, Stephen Jay, and Richard C. Lewontin. 1984. "The Spandrels of San Marco and the Panglossian Paradigm: A Critique of the Adaptionist Programme." Pp. 252–70 in *Conceptual Issues in Evolutionary Biology,* edited by Elliot Sober. Cambridge, Mass.: MIT Press.

Granovetter, Mark. 1985. "Economic Action and Social Structure: The Problem of Embeddedness." *American Journal of Sociology* 91:481–510.

———. 1990. "The Old and the New Economic Sociology: A History and an Agenda." Pp. 89–112 in *Beyond the Marketplace: Rethinking Economy and Society,* edited by Roger Friedland and A. F. Robertson. New York: Aldine de Gruyter.

Hardin, Russel. 1982. *Collective Action*. Baltimore: Johns Hopkins University Press.

Heimer, Carol A. 1985. *Reactive Risk and Rational Action: Managing Moral Hazard in Insurance Contracts*. Berkeley and Los Angeles: University of California Press.

Hirschman, Albert O. 1984. "Against Parsimony: Three Easy Ways of Complicating Some Categories of Economic Discourse." *American Economic Review* 74 (2): 89–96.

Homans, George C. 1961. *Social Behavior: Its Elementary Forms*. New York: Harcourt Brace & World.

Johnson,. Michael. 1991. "Commitment to Personal Relationships." Pp. 117–43 in *Advances in Personal Relationships,* vol. 3. Edited by W. Jones and D. Perlman. London: Jessica Kingsley.

Kanter, R. M. 1972. *Commitment and Community: Communes and Utopias in Sociological Perspective*. Cambridge, Mass.: Harvard University Press.

Kelley, Harold H. 1983. "Love and Commitment." Pp. 265–314 in *Close Relationships,* by H. H. Kelley, E. S. Berscheid, A. Christensen, J. Harvey, T. L. Huston, G. Levinger, E. McClintock, L. A. Peplau, and D. R. Peterson. New York: Freeman.

Kelley, Harold H., and John W. Thibaut. 1978. *Interpersonal Relations: A Theory of Interdependence*. New York: Wiley.

Kollock, Peter, and Jodi O'Brien. 1992. "The Social Construction of Exchange." Pp. 89–112 in *Advances in Group Processes,* vol. 9. Edited by E. J. Lawler, B. Markovsky, C. Ridgeway, and H. A. Walker. Greenwich, Conn.: JAI Press.

Kreps, David M. 1990. *A Course in Microeconomic Theory*. Princeton, N.J.: Princeton University Press.

Kreps, David M., Paul Milgrom, John Roberts, and Robert Wilson. 1982. "Rational Cooperation in the Finitely Repeated Prisoners' Dilemma." *Journal of Economic Theory* 27:245–52.

Kreps, David M., and Robert Wilson. 1982. "Reputation and Imperfect Information." *Journal of Economic Theory* 27:253–79.

Lawler, Edward, and Jeongkoo Yoon. 1993. "Power and the Emergence of Commitment Behavior in Negotiated Exchange." *American Journal of Sociology* 58 (4): 465–81.

Leik, R. K., and S. A. Leik. 1977. "Transition to Interpersonal Commitment." Pp. 123–45 in *Behavioral Therapy in Sociology,* edited by R. L. Hamblin and J. H. Kunkel. New Brunswick, N.J.: Transaction.

Levinger, George. 1979. "A Social Exchange View on the Dissolution of Pair Relationships." Pp. 169–93 in *Social Exchange in Developing Relationships,* edited by R. Burgess and T. Huston. New York: Academic Press.

Light, Ivan, Im Jung Kwuon, and Deng Zhong. 1990. "Korean Rotating Credit Associations in Los Angeles." *Amerasia* 16 (1): 35–54.

Lynch, Michael, Ross M. Miller, Charles R. Plott, and Russel Porter. 1984. "Product Quality, Information Efficiency, and Regulations in Experimental Markets." Social Science Working Paper no. 528, California Institute of Technology.

Markovsky, Barry, David Willer, and Travis Patton. 1988. "Power Relations in Exchange Networks." *American Sociological Review* 53:220–36.

Marwell, Gerald, and David R. Schmitt. 1975. *Cooperation: An Experimental Analysis*. New York: Academic Press.

Messick, David M., and Marilynn B. Brewer. 1983. "Solving Social Dilemmas." Pp. 11–44 in *Review of Personality and Social Psychology,* vol. 4. Edited by L. Wheeler and P. Shaver. Beverly Hills, Calif.: Sage.

Messick, David M., H. Wilke, M. B. Brewer, R. M. Kramer, P. E. Zemke, and L. Lui. 1983. "Individual Adaptations and Structural Change as Solutions to Social Dilemmas." *Journal of Personality and Social Psychology* 44:294–309.

Milgrom, Paul, and John Roberts. 1982. "Predation, Reputation, and Entry Deterrence." *Journal of Economic Theory* 27:280–312.

Molm, Linda. 1991. "Affect and Social Exchange: Satisfaction in Power-Dependence Relations." *American Sociological Review* 56:475–93.

Orbell, John, and Robyn M. Dawes. 1981. "Social Dilemmas." Pp. 37–65 in *Progress in Applied Social Psychology,* vol. 1. Edited by G. Stephenson and J. Davis. New York: Wiley.

———. 1991. "A 'Cognitive Miser' Theory of Cooperators' Advantage." *American Political Science Review* 85 (2): 515–28.

Orbell, John, Peregine Schwartz-Shea, and Randy Simmons. 1984. "Do Cooperators Exit More Readily Than Defectors?" *American Political Science Review* 78: 147–62.

Plott, Charles R. 1986. "Rational Choice in Experimental Markets." *Journal of Business* 59, no. 4, pt. 2: S301–S327.

Podolny, Joel. 1990. "On the Formation of Exchange Relations in Political Systems." *Rationality and Society* 2 (3): 359–78.

Popkin, S. 1981. "Public Choice and Rural Development—Free Riders, Lemons, and Institutional Design." Pp. 43–80 in *Public Choice and Rural Development,* edited by C. Russel and N. Nicholson. Washington, D.C.: Resources for the Future.

Radner, Roy, and Andrew Schotter. 1989. "The Sealed-Bid Mechanism: An Experimental Study." *Journal of Economic Theory* 48:179–220.

Rasmusen, Eric. 1989. *Games and Information: An Introduction to Game Theory.* New York: Basil Blackwell.

Raub, Werner, and Jeroen Weesie. 1990. "Reputation and Efficiency in Social Interactions: An Example of Network Effects." *American Journal of Sociology* 96 (3): 626–54.

Rosenblatt, Paul C. 1977. "Needed Research on Commitment in Marriage." Pp. 73–86 in *Close Relationship: Perspectives on the Meaning of Intimacy,* edited by George Levinger and Harold L. Raush. Amherst: University of Massachusetts Press.

Rubin, J. A., and Bert R. Brown. 1973. "Becoming Committed." Pp. 157–81 in *Liking and Loving,* edited by Z. Rubin. New York: Holt.

Rusbult, Caryl E., and Bram P. Buunk. 1993. "Commitment Processes in Close Relationships: An Interdependence Analysis." *Journal of Social and Personal Relationships* 10:175–204.

Schuessler, Rudolf. 1989. "Exit Threats and Cooperation under Anonymity." *Journal of Conflict Resolution* 33 (4): 728–49.

Shapiro, Carl. 1982. "Consumer Information, Product Quality and Seller Reputation." *Bell Journal of Economics* 13:20–35.

Shapiro, Susan P. 1987. "The Social Control of Impersonal Trust." *American Journal of Sociology* 93:623–58.

Siamwalla, Ammar. 1978. "Farmers and Middlemen: Aspects of Agricultural Marketing in Thailand." *Economic Bulletin for Asia and the Pacific* (June): 38–50.

Taylor, Michael. 1987. *The Possibility of Cooperation.* Cambridge: Cambridge University Press.

Vanberg, Viktor J., and Roger D. Congleton. 1992. "Rationality, Morality, and Exit." *American Political Science Review* 86 (2): 418–31.

Wilson, Robert. 1985. "Reputations in Games and Markets." Pp. 27–62 in *Game-Theoretic Models of Bargaining,* edited by Alvin Roth. Cambridge: Cambridge University Press.

Yamagishi, Toshio. 1986. "The Provision of a Sanctioning System as a Public Good." *Journal of Personality and Social Psychology* 51 (1): 110–16.

———. 1992. "Prisoner's Dilemma Networks: Simulations and Experimental Work." Paper presented at the annual meeting of the American Sociological Association, Pittsburgh.

Yamagishi, Toshio, Nahoko Hayashi, and Nobuhito Jin. 1992. "Prisoner's Dilemma Networks: Selection Strategy versus Action Strategy." Paper presented at the Fifth International Conference on Social Dilemmas, Bielfeld, Germany.

Yamagishi, Toshio, and Midori Yamagishi. 1993. "Trust and Commitment as Alternative Responses to Social Uncertainty." Paper presented at the Social Network Conference, Whistler, British Columbia.

Zand, D. E. 1972. "Trust and Managerial Problem Solving." *Administrative Science Quarterly* 17:229–39.

Zucker, Lynne G. 1986. "Production of Trust: Institutional Sources of Economic Structure, 1840–1920." Pp. 53–111 in *Research in Organizational Behavior,* edited by B. Staw and L. Cummings. Greenwich, Conn.: JAI Press.

[10]

Coordination, Commitment, and Enforcement: The Case of the Merchant Guild

Avner Greif, Paul Milgrom, and
Barry R. Weingast

Stanford University

We interpret historical evidence in light of a repeated-game model to conclude that *merchant guilds* emerged during the late medieval period to allow rulers of trade centers to commit to the security of alien merchants. The merchant guild developed the theoretically required attributes, secured merchants' property rights, and evolved in response to crises to extend the range of its effectiveness, contributing to the expansion of trade during the late medieval period. We elaborate on the relations between our theory and the monopoly theory of merchant guilds and contrast it with repeated-game theories that provide no role for formal organization.

One of the central questions about the institutional foundations of markets concerns the power of the state. The simplest economic view of the state as an institution that enforces contracts and property rights and provides public goods poses a dilemma: A state with suffi-

This paper was originally prepared for the conference on Economic Policy in Political Equilibrium, June 14–16, 1990. We thank Yoram Barzel, Douglass C. North, Jean-Laurent Rosenthal, Nathan Sussman, and an anonymous referee for helpful comments; Esther-Mirjam Sent and Joshua Gans for editorial assistance; and the National Science Foundation for financial support. The participants at the conference on Markets and Organizations organized by the Center for Economic Research at Tilburg and seminar participants at the University of California at Berkeley, Boston University, Indiana University, the University of Illinois at Urbana-Champaign, Harvard University, the Hebrew University, Stanford University, and Tel-Aviv University contributed helpful comments.

[*Journal of Political Economy*, 1994, vol. 102, no. 4]

cient coercive power to do these things also has the power to withhold protection or confiscate private wealth, undermining the foundations of the market economy. In the particular case of medieval cities, these threats were sometimes realized, discouraging trade by foreign merchants to the mutual disadvantage of the ruler and the merchants. It is our thesis that merchant guilds emerged with the encouragement of the rulers of trading centers to be a countervailing power, enhancing the ruler's ability to commit and laying an important institutional foundation for the growing trade of that period.

European economic growth between the tenth and the fourteenth centuries was facilitated by the "Commercial Revolution of the Middle Ages"—the reemergence of Mediterranean and European long-distance trade after an extended period of decline (e.g., Lopez 1976). For this commercial expansion to be possible, institutions had to be created to mitigate the many kinds of contractual problems associated with long-distance trade. Assessing the significance of these institutions requires a subtle analysis. Indeed, the effectiveness of institutions for punishing contract violations is sometimes best judged like that of peacetime armies: by how little they must be used. Thus, when one reads the historical record to determine whether a major role of merchant institutions was to ensure contract compliance, the number of instances of enforcement is not a useful indicator. Instead, one must ask, What were the things that threatened, and on occasion thwarted, efficient trading? Can the powers and organizational details of merchant institutions be explained as responses to those threats? Did failures of enforcement trigger major changes in these institutions?

A comprehensive analysis of a contract enforcement institution must consider why the institution was needed, what sanctions were to be used to deter undesirable behavior, who was to apply the sanctions, how the sanctioners learned or decided what sanctions to apply, why they did not shirk from their duty, and why the offender did not flee to avoid the sanction. Some analyses meeting these criteria have been developed. One is Greif's (1989, 1993*a*) analysis of the contractual relations between merchants and their overseas agents in eleventh-century Mediterranean trade. To reap the benefit of employing overseas agents, an institution was required to enable the agents to commit to act on behalf of the merchants. One group of merchants known as the "Maghribi traders" managed their agency relations by forming a coalition whose members ostracized and retaliated against agents who violated their commercial code. Interrelated contractual arrangements motivated merchants to participate in the collective retaliation against agents who had cheated, and close community ties assured that each member had the necessary information to participate in sanctions when necessary.[1] Similarly, Milgrom, North, and Weingast (1990) have argued that the use of merchant courts in the Champagne fairs during the twelfth and the thirteenth centuries can be analyzed as an institution that created proper incentives for gathering information, honoring agreements, reporting disputes, and adhering to the judgments of the merchant courts. Moreover, by centralizing certain record-keeping functions and effectively permitting only merchants in good standing to remain at the fairs, this institution also achieved significant economies in transaction costs relative to other feasible enforcement institutions.

The cited papers provide consistent analyses of institutions used to overcome contractual problems among individual merchants active in long-distance trade. Individual merchants, however, were not the only important parties: the rulers of the trading centers at which the merchants met and brought their goods were an important independent force. Trading centers needed to be organized in ways that secured the person and property of the visiting merchants. Before a trading center became established, its ruler might be inclined to pledge that alien traders would be secure and that their rights would be respected. Once trade was established, however, the medieval ruler faced the temptation to renege on that pledge, failing to provide the promised protection or abusing the merchants' property rights by using his coercive power. In the age prior to the emergence of the nation-state, alien merchants could expect little military or political aid from their countrymen. Without something tangible to secure the ruler's pledge, alien merchants were not likely to frequent that trading center—an outcome that could be costly for both the ruler and the merchants. That rulers recognized the importance of this problem is well reflected in the words of the English king, Edward I, who noticed in 1283 that because alien merchants' property rights were not properly protected, "many merchants are put off from coming to this land with their merchandise to the detriment of merchants and of the whole kingdom" (*English Historical Documents*, 3:420).[2]

On the basis of the theory of repeated games, one might conjecture that since trade relationships between a specific merchant and ruler consist of a potentially long sequence of trading visits, the rulers' commitment problem could be overcome by either a *bilateral reputa-*

[1] For an analysis of the institution that governed agency relations in twelfth-century Genoa, see Greif (1993*b*). For game-theoretical and comparative historical analysis of the evolution and functioning of various trading institutions among the twelfth-century Genoese and the eleventh-century Maghribi traders from the Muslim world, see Greif (1994).

[2] The recognition that unprotected alien merchants would not come to England is also expressed in the *Carta Mercatoria* of 1303 (*English Historical Documents*, 3:515).

tion mechanism, in which a merchant whose rights were abused ceased trading, or a *multilateral reputation mechanism,* in which the cheated merchant and his close associates ceased trading. Yet the historical records indicate that, by and large, the ruler-merchant relations were governed by neither bilateral nor informal multilateral arrangements. On the contrary, ruler-merchant relations were governed by administrative bodies rooted outside the territory of the ruler, which held certain regulatory powers over their member merchants in their own territory and supervised the operation of these merchants in foreign lands. What roles could these administrative bodies theoretically play in overcoming the ruler's commitment problem? What roles did they play in fact?

To investigate these questions, we utilize historical records to develop a series of game-theoretic models corresponding to different institutional arrangements. The theoretical analyses indicate that although some trade is possible even without supporting organizations, sustaining the efficient level of trade is more demanding. Without administrative bodies capable of coordinating and sometimes compelling merchants' responses to a ruler's transgressions, trade could not expand to its efficient level. The corresponding historical analysis then suggests that during the late medieval commercial revolution, a specific institution—the *merchant guild*—developed the necessary attributes to enforce agreements with rulers, thus overcoming the commitment problem and enabling trade expansion. Merchant guilds exhibited a range of administrative forms from subdivision of a city administration to an intercity organization. Yet these forms all shared the common function of ensuring the coordination and internal enforcement required to surmount the commitment problem by permitting effective collective action. We emphasize two points at the outset. First, our argument concerns merchant guilds and not craft guilds.[3] Second, we define merchant guilds according to their function rather than their "official," late medieval name. Hence, as we discuss below, our theory applies to a wider range of medieval merchant organizations than those labeled as merchant guilds.

The evaluation of merchant guilds as supporting efficient trade is complementary to the view more common among economic historians that merchant guilds emerged to reduce negotiation costs, to administer trade and taxation, to extract privileges from foreign cities, and to shift rent in their own city (see, e.g., Gross 1890; Thrupp 1965; North and Thomas 1973). While the existence of merchant

[3] Economists have long associated the latter with the monopolization of a given craft within a specific town. For a recent economic analysis of craft guilds, see Hickson and Thompson (1991). See also Gustafsson (1987).

guilds could affect the distribution of rents besides enhancing the security of agreements, the unadorned theory of merchant guilds as cartels presents a puzzle: If the purpose of the guilds was to create monopoly power for the merchants and to increase their bargaining power with the rulers, why did *powerful* rulers during the late medieval period cooperate with alien merchants to establish guilds in the first place? What offsetting advantages did the rulers enjoy? The puzzle is resolved if the guild's power enabled trade to expand to the benefit of the merchants and rulers alike.[4]

While this paper emphasizes the function of the merchant guild in facilitating trade between political units during the late medieval period, it also sheds light on the changing nature of guilds over time and the complex nature of guilds at any point in time. Although certain features of the merchant guild enabled it to advance trade during the late medieval period, these same features were, in some cases, utilized during the premodern period to restrict trade. Furthermore, even during the late medieval period, some merchant guilds had quasi-monopoly rights in their own territories. These rights were part of the relations between rulers and local merchants. Since our paper concentrates on the relations between ruler and *alien* merchants, such rights are not considered here. It is interesting to note, however, that our theory suggests that a merchant guild's monopoly rights in its home locality may have been instrumental in advancing trade between different localities. This type of monopoly rights generated a stream of rents that depended on the support of other members and so served as a bond, allowing members to commit themselves to collective action in response to a ruler's transgressions.[5]

The paper proceeds as follows. Section I reports the relevant history. It describes the serious problems trading centers and merchants faced in providing security for merchants and their goods, demonstrates that the guild structure had the features required to resolve the problem, and recounts milestones in the evolution of the guild among German traders and the related expansion of trade. Section II formalizes the analysis. Its game-theoretic model allows us to explore the incentives of traders and cities and explain why a guild organization could sometimes successfully support an efficient level

[4] De Roover (1965) asserts that the guild's role "was, of course, to provide collective protection in foreign lands, to secure trade privileges, if possible, and to watch over the strict observance of those already in effect" (p. 111). While his intuition carried him a long way, it did not explain how the guilds could provide protection and assure observance of rights by local rulers in foreign lands in which the ruler had a preponderance of military force.

[5] This is not to argue, however, that this function was necessarily the main reason for these local monopoly rights.

of trading activity when a simple reputation mechanism could not. Section III concludes the paper by considering the subsequent history—the transformation and decline of the merchant guild associated with the rise of the state—and suggests other applications of the theoretical framework.

I. The Commitment Problem and the Role of Merchant Guilds

Institutions and Commitment

Long-distance trade in late medieval Europe was based on the exchange of goods brought from different parts of the world to central cities or fairs located in geographically or politically favorable places. Yet the presence of gains from trade and locations suitable to conduct exchange does not imply that exchange could occur without an institutional environment in which the merchants and their property were secure. The concern that rulers felt to provide security, reflected in the words of Edward I quoted above, should be understood against the background of events such as the following one that occurred in Boston, England, in, or shortly before, 1241. A Flemish merchant accused an English trader of not repaying a commercial loan. This resulted in

> an uproar on all sides and the English merchants assembled to attack the Flemings, who retired to their lodging in the churchyard. . . . The English threw down the pailings, broke the doors and windows and dragged out Peter Balg [the lender] and five others, whom they foully beat and wounded and then set in the stocks. All the other Flemings they beat, ill-treated and robbed, and pierced their cloths with swords and knives. . . . Their silver cups were carried off as they sat at table, their purses cut and the money in them stolen, [and] their chests broken open and money and goods, to an unknown extent, taken away. [Curia Regis, 121, m. 6; published by Salzman (1928)]

Such disorders were not peculiar to England but mark the history of long-distance medieval trade. For example, the commercial relations between Byzantine and Italian city-states were often hindered by insecurity during the twelfth century. The Genoese quarter in Constantinople was attacked by the Pisans in 1162. At least one merchant was killed, and the other Genoese merchants had to escape to their ship leaving all their valuables behind them. In 1171 the Venetians attacked and destroyed the same Genoese quarter. About 10 years later a mob destroyed all the Italian quarters in Constantinople during the "Latin massacre" of 1182 (Day [1988]; for additional examples, see also De Roover [1965, p. 61]; Lane [1973, p. 34]; Kedar [1976, p. 26 ff.]).

In light of the theory of repeated games, one might conjecture that a ruler's commitment problem could be solved by a *bilateral reputation mechanism* in which individual merchants whose person and property were not protected by a local ruler would refuse to return with their goods in the future. The ruler, while perhaps reaping short-run gains from ignoring a merchant's rights, stood to lose the future stream of rents from the cheated merchant's trade.[6] As we demonstrate formally in Section II, this intuition is misleading. At the level of trade that maximizes the total net value of trade—that is, at the *efficient volume of trade*—a bilateral reputation mechanism cannot resolve the commitment problem. In our formal theory, the reason is that, at the efficient volume of trade, the value of the stream of future rents collected by the ruler from an individual marginal merchant is almost zero and is therefore smaller than the value of the goods that can be seized or the cost of the services that can be withheld. The same conclusion would hold even at lesser volumes of trade if the frequency of visits by an individual trader were low. As long as ruler-merchant relations are governed only by a bilateral reputation mechanism, our theory holds that trading volume cannot expand to its efficient level.

The preceding discussion and the formal model below allow only one kind of sanction for cheated merchants: the withdrawal of trade. Military action might seem another important alternative. In the late medieval period, however, defensive technology was superior to offensive technology, and the costs and risks of offensive military action at distant ports limit its credibility as a sanction for trade violations.[7]

A possible means to increase the punishment is a multilateral response by all the merchants to transgressions against any subgroup of merchants. Indeed, the history of the relations between trade centers and alien merchants presents several examples of multilateral retaliations against rulers who had reneged on their contractual obli-

[6] Clearly, there was a limit to the security a ruler could provide the merchants. Accordingly, we have detailed above instances in which rights were abused in major cities or trade centers in which the relevant ruler had a relatively high level of ability to secure rights.

[7] Parker (1988, p. 7) comments that "After the proliferation of stone-built castles in western Europe, which began in the eleventh century . . . in the military balance between defence and offense, the former had clearly become predominant." This situation changed only during the so-called Military Revolution of the fifteenth century.

gations. For example, circa 1050 the Muslim ruler of Sicily imposed a 10 percent tariff (instead of the 5 percent tariff specified in the Islamic law) on goods imported to Sicily by Jewish traders. The traders responded by imposing an embargo and sending their goods to the rival trade center, Tunisia. The embargo was effective, and after a year the Sicilian ruler relented and removed the tariff (David Kaufmann Collection, Hungarian Academy of Science, Budapest, document no. 22, pt. a, lines 29–31; pt. b, lines 3–5; Gil [1983, pp. 97–106]; Taylor-Schechter Collection, University Library, Cambridge, document no. 10 J 12, folio 26, p. a, lines 18–20; Michael [1965, 2:85]).

The examples above suggest that a *multilateral reputation mechanism* might be able to surmount the commitment problem without the aid of any formal organization. In each case, merchants imposed a collective punishment on the city that included participation by merchants who had not been directly injured. Several of the cited offenses were offenses *against an entire group of merchants*. In medieval trade, however, a city could also discriminate among merchants, abusing or not protecting them selectively. For example, a city could confiscate the belongings of some traders or withhold legal protection from them without directly harming other alien merchants. Indeed, the Sicilian rulers increased the tariff only to Jewish traders; and during two attacks on the Genoese quarter in Constantinople, other Italian merchants were not harmed. This suggests two interconnected reasons why, without a supporting organization, a multilateral reputation mechanism may be insufficient to surmount the commitment problem at the efficient level of trade. The first involves contract ambiguities and asymmetric information, whereas the second reflects the distinct incentives among different traders generated by a multilateral response.

Long-distance premodern trade took place in a highly complex and uncertain environment. Unanticipated events and multiple interpretations of existing agreements were always possible under these circumstances, implying that the definition of a "contract violation" was often ambiguous. Information asymmetry, slow communication, and different interpretations of facts among merchants imply that without an organization that coordinates responses, it was not likely that all the merchants would respond to the abuse of any group of merchants. As demonstrated formally in Section II, if the fraction of merchants who detect and react to an abuse against any group of merchants is only proportionate to the number abused, then a multilateral reputation mechanism is ineffective at the efficient volume of trade. It is ineffective for the same reason that a bilateral reputation mechanism is ineffective: a threat by a group of marginal traders to withdraw their trade is barely significant once trade has expanded to its efficient level.

To permit an efficient expansion of trade in the medieval environment, there was a need for an organization that would supplement the operation of a multilateral reputation mechanism by *coordinating* the responses of a large fraction of the merchants. Only when a coordinating organization exists can the multilateral reputation mechanism potentially overcome the commitment problem. In our formal model, when a coordinating organization exists there is a Markov perfect equilibrium at which traders come to the city (at the efficient level of trade) as long as a boycott has never been announced; none of them comes to trade if a boycott has been announced. The ruler respects merchants' rights as long as a boycott has never been announced but abuses their rights otherwise. Thus, when a coordinating institution exists, trade may plausibly expand to its efficient level.

Although the behavior described forms a perfect equilibrium, the theory in this form remains unconvincing. According to the equilibrium strategies, when a coordinating institution organizes an embargo, merchants are deterred from disregarding it because they expect the ruler to abuse violators' trading rights. But are these expectations reasonable? Why would a city not *encourage* embargo breakers rather than punish them? As verified in Section II, this encouragement is potentially credible. During an effective embargo, the volume of trade shrinks and the value of the marginal trader increases; it is then possible for bilateral reputation mechanisms to become effective. That is, there may exist mutually profitable terms between the city and the traders that the city will credibly respect. This possibility limits the potential severity of an embargo and, correspondingly, potentially hinders the ability of any coordinating organization to support efficient trade. To support the efficient level of trade, a multilateral reputation mechanism may need to be supplemented by an organization with the ability both to *coordinate* embargo decisions and to *enforce* them by applying sanctions on its own members.

Evidence of the Role of Formal Organizations

The discussion so far has focused on two issues: a demonstration that guaranteeing the security of alien merchants and their goods was problematic in medieval Europe and that both historical evidence and theoretical reasoning suggest that a simple reputation mechanism could not completely resolve the problem. In this subsection, we identify more direct evidence that merchants and rulers recognized the need to provide believable assurances of security for traders and their goods, that they negotiated trading arrangements that often included a role for formal organizations, that these organizations served an important coordination and enforcement role, and that trade expanded in cities that negotiated these agreements. Notice that this pattern of facts is inconsistent with at least the simplest cartel theories of guilds, which predict that guilds would form only after trade relations were already established and would limit entry and price competition, leading to the trading of *smaller* quantities.

That medieval rulers and merchants recognized the need to secure alien merchants' property rights before trade expansion could occur is borne out repeatedly in the historical record. Christians traders, for example, did not dare to trade in the Muslim world unless they received appropriate securities. Similarly, throughout Europe itself, merchants did not trade in locations in which they did not have security agreements. The Italians began traveling to other European cities and to the Champagne fairs, and the Germans began traveling to Flanders, England, and the Slavic East only after negotiating appropriate safety agreements (see, e.g., De Roover 1948, p. 13; De Roover 1965; Dollinger 1970).

Safety agreements allowing the merchants some measure of internal organization appear crucial to trade expansion. The Genoese trade with North Africa provides an instructive illustration. Prior to 1160, the Genoese trade with North Africa never exceeded 500 lire. In 1161, the Genoese legate, Otobonus d'Albericis, and the local ruler of North Africa, Abd alMumin, signed a 15-year agreement securing the property rights of the Genoese. Genoese trade more than doubled to 1,057 lire and remained at this higher level in later years. Moreover, the agreement focused on security issues. Though it specified a 2 percent reduction in the 10 percent custom, it was hardly concerned with the distribution of gains from trade. Given that the expected gains from goods that reached North Africa were, on average, more than 26 percent during this period, it is highly unlikely that the custom reduction accounts for the expansion of trade that followed (Krueger 1932, pp. 81–82; Krueger 1933, pp. 379–80).

Merchants from other trading cities had similar experiences. For example, the Catalan merchants' trade expanded "within only a few months" after they received, in 1286, privileges and the right to have a consul in Sicily (Abulafia 1985, pp. 226–27). The trade of the German merchants in Bruges expanded after they received privileges and the right to have a *Kontor* (establishment or office) (Dollinger 1970, p. 41). The Italians' trade with Flanders flourished only after they were allowed to establish local organizations, called *nations* (De Roover 1948, p. 13).

There also exists indirect evidence that the parties recognized the importance of an *institutionalized commitment* to security rather than mere promises. Muslim rulers provided European traders with *aman,* a religious obligation to secure the merchants' rights. Some cities in England went so far as to elect an alien merchant as mayor. Yet it seems that a specific institution—the *merchant guild*—was the most common successful institution. The core of a merchant guild was an administrative body that supervised the overseas operation of merchant residents of a specific territorial area and held certain regulatory powers within that territorial area. In England, for example, the merchants of a town were granted the right to establish a society of merchants that retained specific commercial privileges in the internal and external trade of the town and usually had representation in the trade centers in which its members traded. On the European continent, many towns were controlled by the mercantile elite who organized a merchant guild to advance their interests. In some Italian and German towns the merchant guilds were virtually identical with the town's government itself, and in some Italian cities the merchants' operations were supervised by the city (Gross 1890; Rashdall 1936, pp. 150–53; Rorig 1967).[8]

Guilds provided merchants with the leadership and the information transmission mechanisms required for coordinated action. In the examples we have studied, it was the guild that decided when to impose a trade embargo and when to cancel it.[9] The trade center usually provided the guild with the right to obtain information about disputes between its members and that center's authorities or between its members and other traders. The guild's regulations facilitated the collection and transmission of information among its members.[10]

Though the term "merchant guild" was not used in Italy, the Italian cities served the same functions on behalf of their resident merchants. The city's role in coordinating embargo decisions is well reflected in the relationships between Genoa and Tabriz, a vital city on the trade route to the Persian Gulf and the Far East. In 1340 Tabriz's ruler confiscated the goods of many Genoese traders. Genoa responded by declaring a *devetum* (a commercial embargo) against Tabriz. In 1344, however, Tabriz's ruler sent ambassadors to Genoa promising an indemnity for everything that had been taken from the Genoese and

[8] For a general discussion of the concept of corporation in medieval English law, see Pollock and Maitland (1968, 1:486 ff.).

[9] An exception is the case of the Maghribi traders. That case, however, seems to reflect the situation in the Muslim world rather than in Europe (see Greif 1994).

[10] Guild members were required to travel together, to live and store their goods throughout their stay in quarters that belonged to the guild, to examine the quality of each other's goods, and to witness each other's sales (see, e.g., Moore 1985, p. 63 ff.). As De Roover (1948, p. 20) noted, the "main purpose of the consular organization [of the Italians in Bruges] was . . . to facilitate the exchange of information."

favorable treatment in the future. As a consequence, the *devetum* was removed and the Genoese traders flocked to Persia. However, the ruler of Tabriz did not keep his promise to protect their rights, and the Genoese traders were robbed and many of them were killed. The material damage reached 200,000 lire, an immense sum. When the ruler later invited the Venetians and Genoese to trade, he "could not give them the guarantees they required. . . . [Hence] the Italian merchants, eager as they were to recover their prosperous trade in Persia and to reopen the routes to India and China, felt it was unsafe to trust a mere promise" (Lopez 1943, pp. 181–84). As discussed below, however, it was the Genoese traders as a whole who could not trust a "mere promise"; an individual Genoese trader might still be able to trust the ruler of Tabriz while the *devetum* was in force.

An incident that occurred during the Genoese embargo of Tabriz confirms the historical importance of enforcement within the merchant group and confirms that merchant guilds assumed this enforcement role. In 1343, during the *devetum* against Tabriz, a Genoese merchant named Tommaso Gentile was on his way from Hormuz to China. Somewhere in the Pamir plateau he became sick and had to entrust his goods with his companions and head back to Genoa the shortest way. That way, however, passed through Tabriz. When knowledge concerning his journey through Tabriz reached Genoa, Tommaso's father had to justify this transgression with the "Eight Wisemen of Navigation and the Major [Black] Sea," that is, the superior colonial board of Genoa. These officers accepted the thesis of an act of God and acquitted Tommaso from every penalty, inasmuch as he had gone through Tabriz without merchandise (Lopez 1943, pp. 181–83).

The merchant guild's strategy of conditioning future trade on adequate past protection, the use of ostracism to achieve security (rather than privileges or low prices), and the relationship between acquiring information, coordination, and the ability to boycott are reflected again in the agreement made in 1261 between the Flemish merchants from Ghent, Ypres, Douai, Cambray, and Dixmude who purchased English wool. "For the good of the trade," they decided that "if it should happen that any cleric or any other merchant anywhere in England who deals with sales of wool deals falsely with any merchant in this alliance . . . , by giving false weight or false dressing of the wool or a false product, . . . and if they do not wish to make amends, we have decided that no present or future member of this alliance will be so bold as to trade with them" (Moore 1985, p. 301). To make this threat of boycott functional, they "decided that there will be in each of these cities one man to view and judge the grievances, and to persuade the wrongdoers to make amends" (p. 301).

The credibility and force of a coordinating organization's threat to embargo depended crucially on the ruler's ability to undermine an embargo by offering special terms to embargo violators. In theory, the marginal gains from additional trade rise during an embargo. Both this theoretical observation and the observation that guilds needed to take special measures to prevent shipments to the embargoed city are confirmed by the historical evidence. For example, in 1284, a German trading ship was attacked and pillaged by the Norwegians. The German towns responded by imposing an embargo on Norway. The export of grain, flour, vegetables, and beer was prohibited. According to the chronicler Detmar, "there broke out a famine so great that [the Norwegians] were forced to make atonement" (Dollinger 1970, p. 49). The temptation for an individual merchant to smuggle food to Norway in this situation is clear. To sustain the embargo, the German towns had to post ships in the Danish Straits.[11] The fact that the success of a trade embargo depended crucially on obtaining the support of virtually all the merchants involved was also clear to the cities on which an embargo was inflicted. When, in 1358, the German towns imposed an embargo on Bruges, the city attempted to defeat the embargo by offering merchants from Cologne extensive trade privileges (pp. 65–66).

Placing ships in a strait and imposing fines are specific ways to overcome the distinct incentives problem. The evidence, however, suggests that the credibility of the threat to carry out an embargo was, in many cases, sustained by a different means. Credibility was established by endowing guilds with the ability to impose commercial sanctions on their member merchants. In England and other regions in Europe a local guild usually had exclusive trade privileges in its own town, typically including monopoly rights over retail trade within the town, exclusive exemption from tolls, and so forth, as well as the right to exclude, under certain circumstances, members from the guild (Gross 1890, pp. 19–20, 38 ff., 65; De Roover 1948, pp. 18–19).[12] These guilds, therefore, were able to provide their members with streams of rents in their hometowns. Receiving these rents, how-

[11] See also Dollinger's description of the embargo on Novgorod (p. 48). Anyone who broke the embargo was to suffer the death penalty and the confiscation of his goods.

[12] Exclusive commercial rights for the guild should not be confused with monopoly rights. Entry into the guild was permitted during the period under consideration. The German *Kontore* were established by the merchants who actually traveled abroad to trade. In England, e.g., even individuals who did not live in a specific town could join its merchant guild, and each member had to pay an entry fee (see, e.g., Gross 1890; Dollinger 1970). Note that by creating barriers and consequent rents, such a system also motivates each merchant to adhere to the guild rules, including honoring guild-sponsored embargoes. As shown below, this in turn permits a higher volume of trade than would be possible without the entry restrictions.

ever, could have been made conditional on following the recommendations, rules, and directives of the guild. Hence these rents could serve to tie a member to the guild by making change of residence costly and to ensure solidarity among the guild's members.[13]

The Flemish regulations of 1240 illustrate the role of the stream of rents in providing the appropriate incentives: A merchant who ignored the ban imposed by the guild on another town was expelled, losing his rent stream: "If any man of Ypres or Daouai shall go against those decisions [made by the guild] . . . for the common good, regarding fines or anything else, that man shall be excluded from selling, lodging, eating, or depositing his wool or cloth in ships with the rest of the merchants. . . . And if anyone violates this ostracism, he shall be fined 5s" (Moore 1985, p. 298).

Evolution of Guild Organizations

Perhaps the best example of the guild's contribution to fostering the growth of trade is the evolution and operation of the institution that governed the relations among the German merchants, their towns, and the foreign towns with which they traded. To achieve the coordination and enforcement that was required for the reputation mechanism to operate effectively, a means was needed to influence the behavior of merchants from *different* towns. This fact led to the rise of an interesting form of guild—the German Hansa.[14] Several extensive studies have mined the abundant historical records of the Hansa and enable us to examine its evolution in light of our theoretical analysis.

Our analysis of the evolution of the guild in northern Europe emphasizes episodes in which conflict occurred and trade was affected. In purely theoretical terms, conflict can be explained as an equilibrium phenomenon when information about the behavior of the parties is imperfect,[15] as it surely was in the periods we are studying. Moreover, in the episodes we study, conflict was followed by institutional change, and it seems implausible to model them as equilibrium outcomes. Instead, we shall regard the episodes themselves as disequilibrium outcomes and the resulting changes as adaptations to chang-

[13] This is not to claim that this was the chief role of these rents. Our analysis examines the role of the merchant guild in the expansion of trade between political units and not within political units.

[14] Clearly, we do not claim that the efficiency attributes of the Hansa that we discuss below were sufficient for its emergence. For a general discussion of the relationships between social and political institutions, gains from trade, and the emergence of institutions that facilitate trade, see Greif (1992, in press).

[15] For the imperfect monitoring approach, see the pioneering work by Green and Porter (1984). For refinements of this approach, see Abreu, Pearce, and Stacchetti (1986) and Abreu, Milgrom, and Pearce (1991).

ing circumstances or as improvements based on accumulated experience.

Specifically, we focus on the development of the German Hansa. For historical reasons, membership in the basic organizational unit that coordinated the activities of German merchants abroad—the *Kontor*—was not conditional on residency in one particular town. Any German merchant who arrived in a non-German city could join the local *Kontor.* A *Kontor* had the same function as the guild in coordinating the responses of the German merchants in disputes with the town; however, it lacked the ability to punish merchants in the towns in which they resided, weakening its ability to enforce sanctions against its members. If our theory is correct, the difference between the German *Kontore* and other guilds should have made the *Kontore* less effective and should have led to changes in or the dissolution of that form of merchant organization. The history of the contractual relations among the city of Bruges, the local *Kontor,* and the German towns provides a clear illustration of the evolution of merchant organization.

In 1252, a *Kontor* of German merchants obtained extensive trading privileges from Bruges, and a permanent settlement followed (Weiner 1932, p. 218). The *Kontor* was led by six aldermen elected by the German merchants present in the town. Two of the aldermen were from Rhenish towns, two from Westphalian-Wendish towns, and two from Prussian-Baltic towns, reflecting the range of origins of the participating German merchants (De Roover 1965, p. 114; Dollinger 1970, p. 86). The trading privileges given to the alien merchants in Bruges were continually abused, and eventually riots broke out, endangering both people and property. The situation is described in a document dated 1280 reporting that "it is unfortunately only too well known that merchants travelling in Flanders have been the objects of all kinds of maltreatment in the town of Bruges and have not been able to protect themselves from this" (Urkundenbuch der Stadt Lubeck, vol. 1, no. 156, p. 371; translated by Dollinger [1970, p. 383]). Along with most of the other alien traders who operated in Bruges, the German merchants retaliated in 1280 by transferring their trade to Aardenburg. After 2 years of negotiation, a new agreement was reached and the *Kontor* returned to Bruges.

Seemingly successful, the embargo failed to guarantee the property rights of the German merchants, since Bruges simply ignored its agreement with them (Dollinger 1970, pp. 48–51). It should be noted, however, that Bruges did respect the rights of other alien merchants who frequented the city. Our analysis points to the reason for that discrimination. The embargo was not imposed by the German merchants alone but by all alien merchants in Bruges, including the important and well-organized Italian and Spanish *nations*. While the lesson for Bruges from that episode was to respect the rights of those well-organized groups, it became clear to the city that the German merchant organizations were different. The *Kontor* proved incapable of enforcing its decisions on its members. Because the *Kontor* encompassed only the German merchants actually present in Bruges—rather than all the potential German traders who might want to trade during a boycott—its threat of sanctions was not credible. For a time, German merchants had to accept inferior treatment.

Another embargo, from 1307 to 1309, was thus required to force Bruges to respect its contractual agreements with the Germans, and in this embargo, only they participated. What had changed between 1280 and 1307 was the ability of the German traders from different towns to coordinate their responses and enforce their embargo. A milestone occurred in 1284 when the Wendish German towns imposed an embargo on Norway. Merchants from the city of Bremen refused to cooperate in the embargo, and the other German towns excluded Bremen's merchants from all German *Kontore*. The German towns had achieved the coordination needed to expel one of their members. The importance of the achievement is indicated by the fact that the act of expelling a city came to be referred to by a special word, *Verhansung* (Weiner 1932, p. 219; Dollinger 1970, p. 49).

After 1307, the ability of the German merchants to commit themselves to coordinate their actions and to enforce their decisions on individual merchants and towns was rather advanced, thus guaranteeing Bruges's adherence to its contractual obligations. Bruges respected the charters agreed on in 1307 and 1309, and consequently Flanders's trade flourished and expanded for the next 50 years (Dollinger 1970, p. 51). As our theoretical analysis indicates, once the ability of the German *Kontor* to coordinate and enforce its decisions on its members was well developed, the contract enforcement problem could be resolved and trade expanded.

It was not until the middle of the century, when the cost of providing security around Bruges rose drastically, that a new level of cooperation among the German towns was required to force Bruges to provide the security required to support efficient trade. The Hansa relations with Bruges deteriorated around 1350, mainly because Bruges was not ready to compensate the Germans for their damages in Flanders from the war between England and France. The Hansa responded by strengthening its internal organization. In 1356 the German Hansa held its first *diet*. It was decided that the *Kontor* of Bruges should be operated according to the decisions of the diet. Apparently recognizing the need for coordination among towns, the *Kontor* accepted this decision. The prominent historian of the Hansa,

Dollinger, has emphasized the importance of this change: "In law, and not only in fact, the towns, acting through the general diet were establishing their authority over their merchants in foreign ports" (Dollinger 1970, p. 63).

A Hanseatic embargo of Bruges followed in 1358. It was announced that any disobedience, whether by a town or an individual, was to be punished by perpetual exclusion from the Hansa. Bruges attempted to defeat the embargo by offering trade privileges to individual cities, including both non-Hanseatic ones such as Kampen and a Hanseatic one, Cologne. Our theory suggests that by offering these privileges it hoped to undermine the effectiveness of the new leadership. While the non-Hanseatic cities accepted Bruges's terms, Cologne refused to cooperate. The embargo proved a success, and in 1360, Bruges came to terms with the Hansa. This time, reflecting the parties' more complete understanding of the range of circumstances in which the city would have to provide services, the privileges were written "in much detail as to prevent any one-sided interpretations" (Dollinger 1970, p. 66).[16]

The institution of the German Hansa was now crystallized. It was a nexus of contracts among merchants, their towns, and foreign cities that advanced exchange. The Hansa's leadership served to coordinate and enforce cooperation between German merchants and towns—a cooperation that served the interests of all sides. The trade of northern Europe prospered for generations under the supremacy of the Hansa. Although the trade embargo of 1360 was not the last, later trade disputes seemed to center around distributive issues such as the provision of trade privileges. Commitment for security was no longer an issue.

It is illuminating to contrast the development of the Hansa among German towns with the rather different organization among the Italian merchants. The solid internal political and commercial organization of the Italian cities and their prominence in trade enabled them to overcome the coordination and internal enforcement problems. Collective action among the merchants from Italian cities was ensured. And, because none of the cities was a "marginal player" in the ports in which they traded, coordination among the cities was unnecessary.[17] In contrast, the German *Kontor* was a local organization in a trading center that lacked the ability to enforce its decisions on its members, who came from various German towns. As noted,

[16] For further details of this embargo, see Weiner (1932, p. 220) and Dollinger (1970, pp. 63–66).

[17] For the relative size of Italian and German cities, see Bairoch, Batou, and Chèvre (1988). Some intercity cooperation was also practiced among the Italians when smaller cities "affiliated" themselves with larger ones. See the discussion below.

the German towns were small, and before the establishment of the Hansa, most were relatively insignificant in large trading centers such as Bruges.

The historical analysis presented in this section supports our hypothesis that the medieval merchant guild was an institution that overcame the ruler's commitment problem and facilitated trade expansion. Although the merchant guilds exhibited a range of administrative forms—from subdivision of a city administration (such as that of the Italian city-states) to the intercity organization (of the Hansa)—their functions were the same: to ensure the coordination and internal enforcement required to surmount the commitment problem by permitting effective collective action. The actions taken by rulers and traders, their strategies as reflected in their regulations, and the expansion of trade that followed the establishment of guilds all confirm the importance of this role of the guild organization.

II. The Formal Model

The theoretical modeling is kept intentionally simple and is directed to analyzing the potential of various plausible mechanisms for overcoming the ruler's commitment problem. Each of the mechanisms we consider might feasibly permit commitment by the ruler at some levels of trade; we focus on the growing need for more sophisticated mechanisms as the level of trade rises and approaches the efficient level.

We model the basic environment in which trade took place as having two kinds of players: a city and individual merchants. The merchants, identical and large in number, are identified with the points on the interval $[0, \bar{x}]$. The city—a potential trading center—has the following trading technology: If the number of traders passing through the city in a single period is x, the gross value of trade in that period is $f(x)$. In addition, we suppose that there is a cost of $c > 0$ per unit of value traded incurred by the city for the services it provides and a cost $\kappa > 0$ per unit of value incurred by each trader, so that the net value of trade is $f(x)(1 - c - \kappa)$. We assume that trade is profitable, that is, $c + \kappa < 1$. We also assume that f is nonnegative and differentiable, that $f(0) = 0$, and that f achieves a maximum at some unique value $x^* > 0$, which we call the *efficient volume of trade*. In our model, the city funds its services and earns additional revenues by charging a toll or tax of $\tau \geq c$ per unit of value passing through its ports, so that its total tax revenues are $\tau f(x)$. If it provides the services contracted for, then its net revenue for the period is $f(x)(\tau - c)$. If the city breaches its contract by failing to provide services to a fraction ϵ of the traders, it saves costs of $\epsilon c f(x)$, so its payoff for the trading period is $f(x)[\tau - c(1 - \epsilon)]$.[18] Traders who are not cheated each earn profits—net of costs, tolls, and taxes—of $(1 - \tau - \kappa)f(x)/x$. Traders who are cheated pay taxes and incur costs κ but receive no revenues; they each earn $-(\tau + \kappa)f(x)/x$.

All of this is repeated period after period, and the players' payoffs from the whole repeated game are the discounted sum of the periodic payoffs using discount factor δ. Thus the city's payoff when the trading volume is x_t in period t is given by

$$\sum_{t=0}^{\infty} \delta^t f(x_t)[\tau - c(1 - \epsilon_t)], \qquad (1)$$

and the payoffs of the individual traders are determined similarly as the discounted sum of their periodic payoffs.

The specification of the model captures the idea that merchants are substitutes as far as the ruler is concerned and each of them is relatively "small." The historical observation that rulers could discriminate between traders is captured through the specification of the ruler's strategy. We abstract away from the issue of competition among alternative trade centers since an essence of medieval trade was that it was based on exchange of goods brought by traders from several regions to a specific trading place. Thus, by and large, the threat of a group of traders from a specific region to permanently switch to an alternative potential trade center, without the cooperation of traders from other regions, was not credible.

The historical records also indicate, as discussed above, that merchants were most likely to trade abroad when they perceived their rights to be secure. The specification of the merchants' payoffs is based on this observation. The specification of the ruler's payoff reflects the fact that a ruler could gain from abusing rights or from allowing his subjects to do so. While the model equates the gains from abusing rights with the protection costs saved, one can alternatively think of gains from abuse as reflecting gains from the ruler's confiscation of merchants' goods. This specification of the ruler's and the merchants' payoffs also allows us to distinguish between issues of distribution and efficiency. We treat the tax rate as given and hence abstract away from examining the process through which the gains from trade are allocated. Any losses to the merchants above the agreed-on rate of taxation, however, are defined to be an abuse. Analytically, this specification implies that any first-best arrangement is characterized by the level of trade x^* in every period and no cheating

[18] Note that this formulation captures the gains to the ruler from either abusing rights directly or neglecting to provide merchants with costly protection.

by the city. Different first-best utility allocations are achieved by setting different tax rates τ. Technically, this conclusion reflects our assumption that some value is being lost when the ruler fails to provide protection, which reflects events such as those that took place in Boston, as described earlier: Failure to provide protection led to a destruction of goods and loss of value. Whatever the merchants were willing to pay the ruler—namely all issues of transfer—is modeled here as part of the tax.

Game 1: Informationally Isolated Traders: Bilateral Reputation Mechanism

Our first model represents the situation of traders who travel alone or in small groups with no social or economic organization, so that they remain unaware of how the city has treated other merchants. Although this model is surely too extreme to be fully descriptive, it highlights the difficulties faced by individual traders negotiating with the city on their own.

In this game, a trader must decide whether to bring his goods to the city in each period, knowing only the history of his own decisions and his own past treatment by the city. A strategy for the trader is a sequence of functions mapping the trader's personal history into decisions about whether to offer his goods for trade in that period. Similarly, the city must decide whom to cheat under various conditions. A strategy for the city is a sequence of functions identifying a (measurable) subset of the current traders for the city to cheat as a function of who shows up to trade currently and the full past history of the game.

Readers familiar with either the economics of reputations or the theory of repeated games will recognize that the repetition of the interactions between the city and the individual traders creates the possibility for reputations to be created that enforce good behavior by the city. The idea is that a trader who is once cheated might refuse to return to the city in future periods, leading to a loss of profits for the city. The effectiveness of this threat depends on both the frequency of trade and the periodic value of the individual merchant's trade to the city. If the frequency of trade is sufficiently high and the volume sufficiently low, so that the value of the repeat business of any individual trader to the city is high, the simple reputation mechanism can be effective for providing incentives to the city to protect individual rights. In our model, however, when the volume of trade rises to the efficient level, the value of repeat business to the city falls to zero, so the usual conclusions of the Folk theorem of repeated games do not apply.

PROPOSITION 1. No Nash equilibrium of game 1 can support honest trade ($\epsilon_t \equiv 0$) at the efficient level ($x_t \equiv x^*$), regardless of the levels of c, τ, κ, or δ.

Proof. Suppose that there was such an equilibrium, and consider the payoff to the city if it deviates from the equilibrium strategy and cheats a fraction ϵ of the first-period traders. In the initial period, its payoff is $f(x^*)[\tau - c(1 - \epsilon)]$. In subsequent periods, the informational assumptions of the model imply that the play of at most ϵ traders is affected. Consequently, at least $1 - \epsilon$ traders come to the city in each future period, and the city's payoff from treating them honestly is, in present value terms, at least $\gamma(\tau - c)f(x(1 - \epsilon))$, where, for convenience, we define $\gamma = \delta/(1 - \delta)$. So the city's total payoff from cheating a fraction ϵ of the traders in the first period and adhering to the purported equilibrium thereafter is at least

$$f(x)[\tau - c(1 - \epsilon)] + \gamma(\tau - c)f(x(1 - \epsilon)), \qquad (2)$$

and this expression coincides exactly with the actual payoff when $\epsilon = 0$, that is, when the city adheres to the purported equilibrium. The derivative of expression (2) with respect to ϵ at $\epsilon = 0$ and $x = x^*$ is

$$cf(x^*) - \gamma(\tau - c)x^*f'(x^*) = cf(x^*) > 0, \qquad (3)$$

because $f'(x^*) = 0$. This establishes that the city has a profitable deviation; that is, the specified behavior is not consistent with Nash equilibrium. Q.E.D.

No mechanism based only on sanctions by those who are cheated can support honest trading at the efficient level, x^*, because when trading is conducted at that level, the marginal trader has zero net value to the city. By cheating a few marginal traders, the city loses nothing in terms of future profits but saves a positive expense in the present period. To support the efficient level of trading, some kind of collective action among merchants is needed.[19]

We have stated the proposition in terms of a Nash equilibrium because it is a negative result and we want to emphasize that, even with the most inclusive of noncooperative equilibrium concepts, there is no way to support the efficient volume of trade. For our later

[19] This result is not an artifact of our specification of costs. For example, if we had specified that the costs borne by the city include some fixed costs per trader (possibly in addition to the proportional costs), the city would have an even stronger incentive to reduce the number of traders, because it bears only a fraction τ of the resulting loss of value but saves all the service costs. Making costs proportional to value minimizes the distortion in the city's incentives but still leaves it tempted to seek short-term gains by cutting services at the expense of individual traders when only the bilateral reputation mechanism is at work.

positive results, we shall utilize stronger, more convincing equilibrium concepts.

Game 2: Informationally Isolated Small Groups of Traders: An Uncoordinated Multilateral Reputation Mechanism

While information in medieval times was slow to diffuse by modern standards, it was nevertheless available. In particular, if a specific merchant was ever abused, even in the absence of any organization for information diffusion, some of his peers were likely to learn of it. For example, the traders cheated in Bruges might become known to some others from the same hometown or to their traveling companions. Can this process of limited, uncoordinated information diffusion enable the ruler to commit himself at the efficient level of trade?

To examine this issue, suppose that an incident in which the city cheats a group of traders always becomes known to a larger group of traders. Formally, whenever a set T of traders is cheated, there is a set of traders $\hat{T} \supset T$, each of whom learns of the event. We assume that there is some constant K ($1 \leq K < \infty$) such that if the number of traders cheated is $\mu(T)$, then the number of those who learn about the event, $\mu(\hat{T})$, is no more than $K\mu(T)$: If few traders are cheated, then proportionately few discover that the event has occurred. In game 2, traders make their decisions to bring goods on the basis of what they know of their own past behavior and the city's, including whatever they may know about how the city has cheated others. Potentially, an incident of cheating may then lead to a withdrawal of trade by a group that is many times larger than the group that was cheated. Even if this potentiality could be realized, however, it would not be sufficient to support an efficient volume of trade.

PROPOSITION 2. No Nash equilibrium of game 2 can support honest trade ($\epsilon_t \equiv 0$) at the efficient level ($x_t \equiv x^*$), regardless of the levels of c, τ, κ, or δ.

The proof is essentially the same as for proposition 1, except that the bound on the number who decline to trade in the future is multiplied by K. In particular, (3) is replaced by $cf(x^*) - \gamma K(\tau - c)x^*f'(x^*) = cf(x^*) > 0$.

Violations against a few merchants that are noticed by proportionately few cannot be deterred by a threat of retaliation by just those with firsthand knowledge.

The real situation faced by the traders is considerably more complicated than what we have modeled in games 1 and 2. One important missing element concerns informal and word-of-mouth communication. Although we allowed that some traders were informed when the city cheated another trader, we also assumed that traders knew nothing about who else was currently trading. This assumption was a device to rule out endogenous communication among the traders in the game, by which one trader may infer that another was cheated because someone did not show up to trade. In theory, this kind of communication can be significant (Kandori 1992). No doubt, both word of mouth and some inferences of this kind could take place, but we have built our formal model to disallow them on the assumption that they were of minor importance for enforcing contract compliance. To the extent that informal communications and indirect inferences could provide effective information, the need for organized communication and coordination is reduced.

Game 3: Guild with Coordinating Ability

We have now seen that it is impossible for the city and the traders to sustain an efficient level of trade based only on sanctions applied by small groups. Given the historical evidence of the existence of organizations that governed the relationships between the traders and the city, it is natural to examine whether these relationships could contribute to trade expansion.

There is a serious issue of how the guild ought to be modeled. In our view, a crucial characteristic that separates formal institutions such as guilds from informal codes of behavior is the creation of specialized roles such as those of the guild's aldermen. Determining how the guild selects its aldermen, what private interests those merchants may have, and how the guild manages the principal-agent problem of controlling the aldermen is a serious and complex issue that merits close analysis. Nonetheless, including such a model here would only obscure the main point of this paper. So we set these issues aside for future research and model the guild here as a mere automaton. By assigning different information and behavioral rules to the guild, we can evaluate its contribution to trade expansion.

In this subsection, we examine the role of the guild as an *organization* for communication and coordination. In our formal model, if the city cheats a set of traders, T, then the guild is assumed to discover the event and announce a boycott with probability $\alpha(T) \geq \mu(T)$. This specification entails that the more merchants were abused, the more likely the guild is to conclude that some abuse has occurred. On the other hand, it does not imply that the guild has information superior to that available to the merchants under the uncoordinated reputation mechanism examined in game 2.

In this game, the guild makes boycott announcements mechanically and without any means of enforcement. Traders learn the guild's announcement in each period, but they are not forced to heed it. It simply becomes part of the information that is available to them and to the city. Otherwise, the game is the same as game 1. Despite the guild's lack of enforcement ability, the mere change in information alters the set of equilibria.

PROPOSITION 3. Suppose that $\tau + \kappa \leq 1$ and

$$c \leq \gamma(\tau - c). \tag{4}$$

Then the following strategies form a Markov perfect equilibrium of game 3:[20] The city does not cheat unless a boycott is announced by the guild leader; after a boycott is announced, it cheats any trader who offers to trade. Traders offer to trade in a given period if and only if no boycott has been announced.

The proposition is formally proved by direct verification. The condition (4) is just the condition that what the city stands to gain by cheating a trader, which is proportional to $cf(x^*)$, be less than the average future profits from each trader, which are $\gamma(\tau - c)f(x^*)$. With group enforcement, it is *average* trading profits rather than marginal profits that determine the city's incentives. It is that fact that accounts for the continued effectiveness of group sanctions even at the efficient level of trade.

As remarked earlier, the equilibrium strategies contain a counterintuitive element: that the city cheats any trader who offers to trade during a boycott. It is the traders' unanimous expectations that the city will behave that way that cause them all to honor the boycott. But why should the city not welcome traders during the boycott rather than cheat them? Since we are looking at a Markov perfect equilibrium, the city can be expected to cheat embargo-breaking traders only if it is actually in the city's interest to do so once the embargo has been announced. Given the specified strategies, if y traders violate the boycott and offer their goods, the city expects a payoff of $(\tau - c)f(y)$ in the current period and zero in future periods, if it acts honestly. If it cheats, it expects $\tau f(y)$ in the current period and zero in the future, so cheating is, indeed, optimal.

Although the strategies described in proposition 3 do constitute an equilibrium, the expectations and behavior that they entail seem implausible. The equilibrium requires, for example, that no matter how desperate the city may be for renewed trade relationships once

[20] This is a Nash equilibrium of the game with the properties that (1) the player's strategies at any date depend only on whether a boycott has been announced and (2) each player's strategy at each date maximizes his payoff from that date onward, given the equilibrium strategies of the other players.

a boycott has been announced, the city must nevertheless cheat anyone who ventures to trade with it. In addition, the traders must expect that behavior. By the equilibrium logic, the city does this because it expects the boycott to take full hold in the next round anyway, so it anticipates that any cooperation it may offer would be fruitless.

This equilibrium behavior does not match the historical facts very well, and it is of doubtful import even as theory, because it supposes that the city and potential embargo breakers play the equilibrium with the lowest possible value for themselves. Similar criticisms have been leveled at the equilibria of other repeated-game models, notably by Pearce (1987), Bernheim and Ray (1989), Farrell and Maskin (1989), and Abreu and Pearce (1991). None of the alternative solution concepts that these authors suggest applies directly to our model, but all suggest that it is more reasonable to suppose that some cooperation may be achieved between traders and the city even after a boycott is announced. As an example, we emphasize the possibility that mutually profitable *bilateral* agreements between the city and individual traders may be reached even during a boycott. It will be apparent from the logic of the arguments that any other kind of cooperation would lead to qualitatively similar conclusions.

Let us therefore suppose that if some traders agree to trade with the city despite the embargo, they cannot rely on the threat of a group boycott to enforce their own claims against the city. What, then, can enforce honest behavior by the city during the boycott? We consider that it is the threat by a cheated trader to withdraw his own future trade. Proposition 1 established that the efficient level of trade x^* could not be supported by such an equilibrium, but it leaves open the possibility that some inefficiently low level of trade can be supported. We are therefore led to ask, What is the highest level of exchange, x', that can be supported in this way?

PROPOSITION 4. Assume that f is concave. Consider the strategies in which the city cooperates in each period with just those traders that it has never before cheated and each trader offers to trade in each period if and only if he has not been cheated before. These strategies constitute a subgame perfect equilibrium of game 1 when the volume of traders is x and the taxes are τ if and only if, for all $y \leq x$,

$$0 \geq cf(y) - \gamma(\tau - c)yf'(y). \tag{5}$$

A sufficient condition is that (i) $0 \geq cf(x) - \gamma(\tau - c)xf'(x)$ and (ii) the elasticity $e(x) = [d \ln f(x)]/[d \ln(x)]$ be a decreasing function of x.

Proof. It is obvious that the traders' strategies are best replies from any point in the history of the game to the strategy of the city, so we need consider only the optimality of the city's strategy.

Beginning with x current traders, consider the subgame achieved after $x - y$ traders depart, when there are $y \le x$ traders remaining. By cheating a fraction ϵ of the y current traders, the city's payoff will be $g(\epsilon; y) = [\tau - (1 - \epsilon)c]f(y) + \gamma f(y(1 - \epsilon))(\tau - c)$. A necessary condition for the optimality of $\epsilon = 0$ is $\partial g(\epsilon; y)/\partial\epsilon \le 0$ at $\epsilon = 0$. An easy calculation verifies that this is just the same as condition (5), so the latter condition is necessary for all y.

By the optimality principle of dynamic programming, it is sufficient to show that there is no subgame in which the city would do strictly better by setting $\epsilon > 0$ in the initial period and then adhering to its equilibrium strategy thereafter, given the strategies of the others. If f is concave, then, for all y, $g(\epsilon; y)$ is concave in ϵ, so a sufficient condition is that, for all y, $\partial g(\epsilon; y)/\partial\epsilon \le 0$ at $\epsilon = 0$, which is again equivalent to (5), proving sufficiency.

The elasticity can be rewritten as $e(x) = xf'(x)/f(x)$. The condition (5) is that $e(y) \ge c/[\gamma(\tau - c)]$ for all $y \le x$, which follows from $e(x) \ge c/[\gamma(\tau - c)]$ and the hypothesis that $e(\cdot)$ is decreasing. Q.E.D.

Let x' be the largest solution of (5). The equilibrium described by proposition 4 suggests an interesting interpretation of the levels of trade x' observed during boycotts and explains why some merchants continued to trade but others did not. According to the theory, additional traders, beyond the number x', would be cheated by the city and would be unable to exact retribution for their losses. Alternatively, if we think of the level of trade $x < x^*$ during the boycott as being determined by factors outside the model (such as existing alliances or other interests), then condition (5) implies that the minimum tax rate necessary to deter cheating is less the lower x is. This confirms the intuition that an embargo breaker may be able to negotiate an unusually attractive deal, both because the value of trade per trader $(f(x)/x)$ is higher when x is small and because the minimum tax rate τ necessary to prevent cheating is lower for small x.

Proposition 4 implies that in the absence of a strong guild—one that can enforce the boycott on its members—the guild cannot credibly threaten to reduce the city's income to less than $f(x')$. This threat may or may not be sufficient to support honest trade, depending on the parameters γ, τ, and c. That is, a boycott with leaks may or may not be enough to deter the city from violating its agreement. If this kind of boycott is not enough, then there may be mutual gains to be had by strengthening the guild and enabling it to make a more powerful threat. In particular, a guild with ability to enforce its boycott decision on all the merchants may be able to assure trade expansion.

The force of any potential boycott depends not only on $f(x')$ and $f(x^*)$ but also on the net rate of profit, $\tau - c$, earned by the city. Incentives for honest behavior by the city are stronger when the taxes and tolls are high, because the city then has more to lose from a boycott. A strong guild can make it feasible to offer lower taxes and tolls while still promoting honest behavior by the city, which, in a richer model, could lead to additional advantages in terms of an increased value of trade.

Game 4: The Guild with Coordination and Enforcement Abilities

The final variant is a game in which the guild has the ability to enforce compliance from the individual traders. We offer no formal analysis of this case. It is obvious that the only role of enforcement by the guild against member merchants in our formal model is to prevent trade during boycotts. Accordingly, the results are the same as in proposition 3, but now the traders participate in the boycott because they are required to do so rather than because they expect participation to serve their individual interests.

III. Discussion

All models in economics are stylized to highlight particular points, and ours are no exception. Our game models treat all merchants as small and perfect substitutes for one another; they abstract from the costs of running a guild and the problems of enforcing good behavior on the part of guild leaders; they omit the issues of competition among different trading centers and do not delve into how organized merchants actually enforce sanctions against their own members. Although the models' narrow focus highlights the need for cohesiveness among merchants and gives what we think is a convincing account of many details of the historical record, the omitted features are also important for understanding the history of merchant guilds. Merchant guilds were primarily an urban rather than rural phenomenon. That may be accounted for by the costs of organizing merchants over large geographic areas. Guild membership also extended gradually. In Germany, large cities took the lead in forming intercity guilds. This pattern, too, seems to reflect the costs and other barriers to forming large organizations, and the potential for success for small guilds is surely an important part of the dynamics of guild development.

Although our models treat merchants as homogeneous in their commercial affairs with the city, their geographic diversity was the very basis for the trade. There were exports of timber and Senegalese gold from North Africa; silk, spices, drugs, flax, and wine from the Middle East and Byzantium; luxury furs, cheese, butter, fish, and iron from Scandinavia and Russia; grains from Germany; wine from France and Spain; textiles from Flanders; wool, copper, dried fish, and goat- and sheepskins from England; and so on.

When groups of merchants are close substitutes for one another, competition among them can undermine the joint action needed to enforce rights obtained from rulers of trading centers. The patterns of guild membership along product lines that the theory implies are nearly identical to the patterns implied by a theory of the merchant guild as an instrument of monopoly, so it is important to emphasize how the other predictions of the theories differ.

Our theory predicts that rulers will *encourage* the establishment of merchant guilds with specific rights and an effective organization. Such encouragement would not be expected if the sole purpose of guilds was to shift some of the fixed gains from trade from rulers to merchants unless the encouragement itself reflects the merchants' ability to coerce the rulers to shift rent in merchants' favor. The evidence reveals that, even when merchants could not coerce rulers by the threat of embargo and even when the privileges provided to the merchants did not entail any shift in the rent, rulers did grant merchants various rights,[21] including the rights to organize, to hold courts and assemblies, to elect their own consuls, and to participate on juries when merchants were being tried. Our theory predicts that establishment of these guild rights would lead to trade *expansion,* but a cartel theory of guilds would suggest that guilds would form to reduce trade in goods in order to drive up relative prices. The evidence cited earlier supports the conclusion that, at least during the late medieval period, guilds led to trade expansion. While it is likely that the merchant guilds sought to advance the merchants' interests in many ways, including negotiating for rights to control prices, these rent-seeking activities cannot account for the patterns we have identified.

Of special interest for our theory are the richness and complexity of the guild system. The guild functioned as a nexus of contracts, weaving separate agreements with the individual merchants and the cities in which its members traded into a system whose parts were mutually supporting. Exclusive (but not necessarily monopolistic!) trading arrangements with the city allowed the guild to organize merchants, and other rights helped it to keep informed about disputes and to help the city enforce good behavior by merchants. The guild's

[21] In addition to the evidence mentioned above, see Carus-Wilson (1967, p. xviii) and *English Historical Documents,* 3:515–16. The role of the guild in securing rights rather than in achieving privileges in Bruges is suggested by the city policy to provide all *nations* with the same rights (see De Roover 1948, p. 15).

contracts with the merchants were fundamental to allow it to enforce its agreements with the city and with other merchants, including those from towns that tried to smuggle goods past its embargoes. The Hansa, effectively involving intercity contracts, further strengthened the merchants' hands in enforcement.

As centuries passed and trade gave impetus to political integration, larger political units emerged, taking on themselves the functions that the merchant guild previously had performed. The political, commercial, and military relations among rulers enabled each to commit to the safety of the alien merchants frequenting his realm. Illustrative are such acts as those of the English kings, who made agreements and enforced embargoes to provide the English Merchants of the Staple and the Merchant Adventurers with security in their dealings with the Hanseatic league. As the state system evolved, the need for the merchant guilds to secure merchants' rights declined.[22]

Merchant guilds, however, did not necessarily disappear, and some guilds became fiscal instruments that hindered trade expansion in the emerging states. Other guilds consolidated their political power and, after securing their members' rights, turned to limit the rights of their competitors. For example, the German Hansa of the late medieval period was a new political entity aimed at preserving the property rights of German merchants. Although its establishment enabled northern European trade to flourish, once organized, the Hansa's concern was not efficiency but profitability. In its constant efforts to preserve trade rights and supremacy, the Hansa crushed the advance of other traders' groups without consideration of their comparative efficiencies. Thus a merchant guild that had facilitated trade in the late medieval period was transformed into a monopolistic organization that hindered trade expansion during the premodern period.[23]

Up to this point, we have focused exclusively on the role of the merchant guild in a particular time and place, but we believe that the principles that applied then help to explain the emergence of other organizations in other places and times. Our analysis explains why a powerful party might find it advantageous to help weaker powers organize themselves into entities that can exert countervailing power, in order to allow itself to commit to certain mutually beneficial arrangements. For example, prior to the Revolution, the French kings developed an elaborate system to help secure their borrowing and

[22] For the relations between the Hansa and England during this later period, see Colvin (1971) and Postan (1973).

[23] See the discussion above regarding the Hansa embargoes during the late fourteenth century. Regarding the English traders, see Dollinger (1970) and Lloyd (1991). For a general discussion, see Greif (in press).

thereby enhance their ability to borrow (see Bien 1987; Root 1989; Hoffman 1994). The ingredients of this system—using the officer corps both to aggregate loans and to help borrowers coordinate and relying on the *parlements* to authorize the legality of royal edicts—suggest an attempt by the kings to create organizations capable of collective action to enforce the king's fiscal promises. Similarly, part of Britain's financial and military success following the Glorious Revolution in 1688 involved creating the Bank of England. This organization seems to have had the necessary attributes identified by our theory, for instance, the ability to announce the initiation of a credit boycott and to punish lenders who attempted to lend to the government.[24] The theoretical ideas introduced in this paper provide a promising new framework for analyzing these events and institutions.

References

Abreu, Dilip; Milgrom, Paul; and Pearce, David. "Information and Timing in Repeated Partnerships." *Econometrica* 59 (November 1991): 1713–33.

Abreu, Dilip, and Pearce, David. "A Perspective on Renegotiation in Repeated Games." In *Game Equilibrium Models,* vol. 2, *Methods, Morals and Markets,* edited by Reinhard Selten. New York: Springer-Verlag, 1991.

Abreu, Dilip; Pearce, David; and Stacchetti, Ennio. "Optimal Cartel Equilibria with Imperfect Monitoring." *J. Econ. Theory* 39 (June 1986): 251–69.

Abulafia, David. "Catalan Merchants and the Western Mediterranean, 1236–1300: Studies in the Notarial Acts of Barcelona and Sicily." *Viator* 16 (1985): 209–42.

Bairoch, Paul; Batou, Jean; and Chèvre, Pierre, eds. *The Population of European Cities from 800 to 1850: Data Bank and Short Summary of Results.* Geneva: Droz (for Center Internat. Econ. Hist.), 1988.

Bernheim, B. Douglas, and Ray, Debraj. "Collective Dynamic Consistency in Repeated Games." *Games and Econ. Behavior* 1 (December 1989): 295–326.

Bien, David D. "Offices, Corps, and a System of State Credit: The Uses of Privilege under the Ancien Regime." In *The French Revolution and the Creation of Modern Political Culture,* vol. 1, *The Political Culture of the Old Regime,* edited by Keith M. Baker. Oxford: Pergamon, 1987.

Carus-Wilson, Eleanora M. *Medieval Merchant Venturers: Collected Studies.* 2d ed. London: Butler and Tanner, 1967.

Colvin, Ian D. *The Germans in England, 1066–1598.* 1915. Reprint. London: Kennikat, 1971.

Day, Gerald W. *Genoa's Response to Byzantium, 1155–1204: Commercial Expansion and Factionalism in a Medieval City.* Urbana: Univ. Illinois Press, 1988.

De Roover, Raymond. *Money, Banking and Credit in Mediaeval Bruges: Italian Merchant-Bankers, Lombards and Money-Changers.* Cambridge, Mass.: Mediaeval Acad. America, 1948.

———. "The Organization of Trade." In *Cambridge Economic History of Europe,* vol. 3, *Economic Policies in the Middle Ages,* edited by M. Michael Postan, E. E. Rich, and Edward Miller. Cambridge: Cambridge Univ. Press, 1965.

[24] This argument is developed at length in Weingast (1992).

Dollinger, Philippe. *The German Hansa.* Stanford, Calif.: Stanford Univ. Press, 1970.

English Historical Documents. Vol. 3, *1189–1327.* Edited by Harry Rothwell. London: Eyre and Spottiswoode, 1975.

Farrell, Joseph, and Maskin, Eric. "Renegotiation in Repeated Games." *Games and Econ. Behavior* 1 (December 1989): 327–60.

Gil, Moshe. "The Jews in Sicily under the Muslim Rule in the Light of the *Geniza* Documents." Manuscript. Tel Aviv: Tel Aviv Univ., 1983. Also in Italian in *Italia Judaaica.* Rome: Inst. Poligrafico e Zecca dello Stato.

Green, Edward J., and Porter, Robert H. "Noncooperative Collusion under Imperfect Price Information." *Econometrica* 52 (January 1984): 87–100.

Greif, Avner. "Reputation and Coalitions in Medieval Trade: Evidence on the Maghribi Traders." *J. Econ. Hist.* 49 (December 1989): 857–82.

———. "Institutions and International Trade: Lessons from the Commercial Revolution." *A.E.R. Papers and Proc.* 82 (May 1992): 128–33.

———. "Contract Enforceability and Economic Institutions in Early Trade: The Maghribi Traders' Coalition." *A.E.R.* 83 (June 1993): 525–48. (*a*)

———. "On the Nature and Evolution of Political and Economic Institutions: Commitment, Reputation, and Self-Enforcing Institutions in Late Medieval Genoa." Manuscript. Stanford, Calif.: Stanford Univ., Dept. Econ., 1993. (*b*)

———. "Cultural Beliefs and the Organization of Society: A Historical and Theoretical Reflection on Collectivist and Individualist Societies." *J.P.E.* 102 (October 1994), in press.

———. "Trading Institutions and the Commercial Revolution in Medieval Europe." In *Proceedings of the Tenth World Congress of the International Economic Association,* edited by Michael Kaser. London: Macmillan, in press.

Gross, Charles. *The Gild Merchant: A Contribution to British Municipal History.* Oxford: Clarendon, 1890.

Gustafsson, Bo. "The Rise and Economic Behavior of Medieval Craft Guilds: An Economic-Theoretical Interpretation." *Scandinavian Econ. Hist. Rev.* 35, no. 1 (1987): 1–40.

Hickson, Charles R., and Thompson, Earl A. "A New Theory of Guilds and European Economic Development." *Explorations Econ. Hist.* 28 (April 1991): 127–68.

Hoffman, Philip. "Taxes, Fiscal Crises, and Representative Institutions: The Case of Early Modern France." In *Fiscal Crises and the Growth of Representative Institutions,* edited by Philip Hoffman and Kathryn Norberg. Stanford, Calif.: Stanford Univ. Press, 1994.

Kandori, Michihiro. "Social Norms and Community Enforcement." *Rev. Econ. Studies* 59 (January 1992): 63–80.

Kedar, Benjamin Z. *Merchants in Crisis: Genoese and Venetian Men of Affairs and the Fourteenth-Century Depression.* New Haven, Conn.: Yale Univ. Press, 1976.

Krueger, Hilmar C. "The Commercial Relations between Genoa and Northwest Africa in the Twelfth Century." Ph.D. dissertation, Univ. Wisconsin—Madison, 1932.

———. "Genoese Trade with Northwest Africa in the Twelfth Century." *Speculum* 8 (July 1933): 377–95.

Lane, Frederic C. *Venice: A Maritime Republic.* Baltimore: Johns Hopkins Univ. Press, 1973.

Lloyd, Terrence H. *England and the German Hanse, 1157–1611: A Study of*

Their Trade and Commercial Diplomacy. Cambridge: Cambridge Univ. Press, 1991.

Lopez, Robert Sabatino. "European Merchants in the Medieval Indies: The Evidence of Commercial Documents." *J. Econ. Hist.* 3 (November 1943): 164–84.

———. *The Commercial Revolution of the Middle Ages, 950–1350.* New York: Cambridge Univ. Press, 1976.

Michael, M. "The Archives of Naharay ben Nissim, Businessman and Public Figure in Eleventh Century Egypt." Ph.D. dissertation, Hebrew Univ., 1965.

Milgrom, Paul R.; North, Douglass C.; and Weingast, Barry R. "The Role of Institutions in the Revival of Trade: The Medieval Law Merchant, Private Judges, and the Champagne Fairs." *Econ. and Politics* 2 (March 1990): 1–23.

Moore, Ellen Wedemeyer. *The Fairs of Medieval England.* Toronto: Pontifical Inst. Mediaeval Study, 1985.

North, Douglass C., and Thomas, Robert Paul. *The Rise of the Western World: A New Economic History*. Cambridge: Cambridge Univ. Press, 1973.

Parker, Geoffrey. *The Military Revolution: Military Innovation and the Rise of the West, 1500–1800.* Cambridge: Cambridge Univ. Press, 1988.

Pearce, David. "Renegotiation-Proof Equilibria: Collective Rationality and Intertemporal Cooperation." Manuscript. New Haven, Conn.: Yale Univ., Dept. Econ., 1987.

Pollock, Frederick, and Maitland, Frederic William. *The History of English Law before the Time of Edward I.* 2 vols. 2d ed. Cambridge: Cambridge Univ. Press, 1968.

Postan, M. Michael. "The Trade of Medieval Europe: The North." In *Cambridge Economic History of Europe*, vol. 2, *Trade and Industry in the Middle Ages*, edited by M. Michael Postan and Edward Miller. Cambridge: Cambridge Univ. Press, 1965.

———. "The Economic and Political Relations of England and the Hanse from 1400 to 1475." In *Medieval Trade and Finance.* Cambridge: Cambridge Univ. Press, 1973.

Rashdall, Hastings. *The Universities of Europe in the Middle Ages.* Vol. 1, *Salerno, Bologna, Paris.* Edited by F. M. Powicke and A. B. Emden. Oxford: Oxford Univ. Press, 1936.

Root, Hilton L. "Tying the King's Hands: Credible Commitments and Royal Fiscal Policy during the Old Regime." *Rationality and Society* 1 (October 1989): 240–58.

Rorig, Fritz. *The Medieval Town.* Berkeley: Univ. California Press, 1967.

Salzman, L. F. "A Riot at Boston Fair." *Hist. Teachers' Miscellany* 6 (1928): 2–3.

Thrupp, Sylvia L. "The Gilds." In *Cambridge Economic History of Europe*, vol. 3, *Economic Organization and Policies in the Middle Ages*, edited by M. Michael Postan, E. E. Rich, and Edward Miller. Cambridge: Cambridge Univ. Press, 1965.

Weiner, A. "The Hansa." In *The Cambridge Medieval History*, vol. 7, *Decline of Empire and Papacy*, edited by J. R. Tanner, C. W. Previté-Orton, and Z. N. Brooke. Cambridge: Cambridge Univ. Press, 1932.

Weingast, Barry R. "Institutional Foundations of the 'Sinews of Power': British Financial and Military Success Following the Glorious Revolution." Manuscript. Stanford, Calif.: Stanford Univ., Hoover Inst., 1992.

[11]

CALCULATIVENESS, TRUST, AND ECONOMIC ORGANIZATION*

OLIVER E. WILLIAMSON
University of California, Berkeley

My main purpose in this article is to explicate what Diego Gambetta has referred to as "the elusive notion of trust."[1] As the literature on trust reveals, and as developed here, "trust" is a term with many meanings. The relentless application of calculative economic reasoning is the principal device that I employ to define and delimit the elusive notion of trust.

The calculative approach to economic organization is sketched in Section I. The concept of "calculative trust," which enjoys widespread and growing acceptance but with which I take exception, is examined in Section II. Societal trust, which works through the institutional environment and takes a series of hyphenated forms, is briefly treated in Section III. Nearly noncalculative uses of trust of a personal kind are developed in Section IV. Concluding remarks follow in Section V.

I. Calculativeness

As compared with the other social sciences, the economic approach to economic organization is decidedly more calculative. That is widely regarded as both the distinctive strength and the Achilles' heel of economics. A failure to appreciate the limits of calculativeness purportedly gives rise to excesses, as a consequence of which economists are prone to make mistaken assessments of many economic phenomena.

* Presented at the John M. Olin Centennial Conference in Law and Economics at the University of Chicago Law School, April 7–9, 1992. The author is Transamerica Professor of Business, Economics, and Law, University of California, Berkeley. This article has benefitted from comments from the participants at the Institutional Analysis Workshop at the University of California, Berkeley, and at the Research Conference on Industrial Organization in Toulouse. The helpful comments of James March, Claude Menard, and Vai-Lam Mui are also acknowledged, as are those of my two discussants, Richard Craswell and Lars Stole, and the conference participants at Chicago.

[1] Diego Gambetta, Can We Trust Trust? in Trust: Making and Breaking Cooperative Relations, at ix (Diego Gambetta ed. 1988).

[*Journal of Law & Economics*, vol. XXXVI (April 1993)]

I do not disagree, but I contend that the excesses to which calculativeness is sometimes given are usually remediable. I furthermore contend that the analytical reach of the calculative approach to economic organization is *extended rather than diminished by admitting to these limitations*. Once the excesses to which calculativeness is given are displayed and understood, the distortions can be anticipated and can thereafter be folded in at the design stage. A (more farsighted) calculative response to the (myopic) excesses of calculativeness thereby obtains. Provided that bounds on rationality are respected, calculativeness opens the door to a deeper understanding of economic organization.

A. *Economics and the Contiguous Disciplines*[2]

Applications of economic analysis and economic reasoning to the contiguous social sciences—principally law, political science, and sociology—have increased considerably in the past thirty years. To be sure, John R. Commons deserves credit for his early recognition that "law and economics" was a combined enterprise.[3] The institutional economics program with which he was involved enjoyed only limited success,[4] however, and the first concerted applications of economics to the law were mainly concentrated on antitrust.[5] That quickly changed after 1960 with the publication of Ronald Coase's "Social Cost" article[6] and Guido Calabresi's related work on torts.[7] Economics has since made its way into virtually every field of legal scholarship.[8]

The joinder of economics and political science has also undergone a

[2] The heading is borrowed from Ronald Coases's article on this subject, Economics and Contiguous Disciplines, 7 J. Legal Stud. 201 (1978).

[3] See John R. Commons, Legal Foundations of Capitalism (1924); and John R. Commons, Law and Economics, 34 Yale L. J. 371 (1925).

[4] The most significant contribution to law and economics stemming from the Commons's tradition is his book Legal Foundations of Capitalism, *supra* note 3. Albeit important, older-style institutional economics became embroiled in methodological controversy and failed to develop a research agenda to rival orthodoxy (see George Stigler's remarks appearing in Edmund W. Kitch, The Fire of Truth: A Remembrance of Law and Economics at Chicago, 1932–1970, 26 J. Law & Econ. 163, 170 (1983)). Some concluded, too harshly I think, that the work of American institutionalists "led to nothing . . . [since] without a theory, they had nothing to pass on" (Ronald H. Coase, The New Institutional Economics, 140 J. Inst. & Theor. Econ. 229, 230 (1984)).

[5] Richard A. Posner, The Chicago School of Antitrust Analysis, 127 U. Pa. L. Rev. 925 (1979).

[6] Ronald H. Coase, The Problem of Social Cost, 3 J. Law & Econ. 1 (1960).

[7] Guido Calabresi, Some Thoughts on Risk Distribution and the Law of Torts, 70 Yale L. J. 499 (1961).

[8] Richard A. Posner, Economic Analysis of Law (1977).

significant transformation. Kenneth Arrow's work on social choice,[9] Anthony Downs's treatment of an economic theory of democracy,[10] Mancur Olson's logic of collection action,[11] and James Buchanan and Gordon Tullock's work on constitutions[12] were all implicated in this transformation. As recent conference volumes in the *Journal of Law, Economics, and Organization* make clear,[13] the use of economic reasoning to examine politics and political institutions has become widespread and, for some issues, even essential.

Economics and sociology bear a more distant relation to each other,[14] although this too has been changing, especially as the "rational choice" approach to sociology[15] has been taking shape. A wide gulf between them nevertheless needed to be bridged. Thus, Paul Samuelson distinguished economics and sociology in terms of their rationality orientations, with rationality being the domain of economics and nonrationality being relegated to sociology.[16] James Duesenberry subsequently quipped that economics was preoccupied with how individuals made choices, whereas sociology maintained that individuals did not have any choices to make.[17] Both George Homans[18] and Herbert Simon[19] protested that sociology had a stake in rationality analysis and could not accept this division of labor, but such a division persisted.

What, it might be asked, is behind the successes of economics in moving into law, political science, and sociology? Coase observes that what binds a group of scholars together is "one or more of the following:

[9] Kenneth J. Arrow, Social Choice and Individual Values (1951).

[10] Anthony Downs, An Economic Theory of Democracy (1957).

[11] Mancur Olson, The Logic of Collective Action (1965).

[12] James Buchanan & Gordon Tullock, The Calculus of Consent (1964).

[13] The 1990 conference volume is entitled "The Organization of Political Institutions," while the 1992 conference volume deals with "The Economics and Politics of Administrative Law and Procedures."

[14] Much of the distance between economics and sociology appears to be attributable to the need for sociology, as a new discipline, to define itself in such a way as to avoid confrontation with economics, from which it had been spun off. See Richard Swedberg, Economic Sociology: Past and Present, 35 Current Soc. 1 (1987).

[15] See James Coleman, Foundations of Social Theory (1990); Siegwart Lindenberg, Homo Socio-oeconomicus: The Emergence of a General Model of Man in the Social Sciences, 146 J. Inst. & Theor. Econ. 727 (1990); and Michael Hecter, Principles of Group Solidarity (1987).

[16] Paul Samuelson, Foundations of Economic Analysis (1947).

[17] James Duesenberry, An Economic Analysis of Fertility: Comment, in Demographic and Economic Change in Developed Countries 233 (1960).

[18] George Homans, Social Behavior as Exchange, 62 Am. J. Sociol. 597 (1958).

[19] Herbert Simon, Rationality as Product and Process of Thought, 68 Am. Econ. Rev. 1 (1978).

common techniques of analysis, a common theory or approach to a subject, or a common subject matter."[20] Although, in the short run, the use of certain techniques or a distinctive approach may provide the means by which economists are able to move successfully into another field,[21] Coase argues that the subject matter is decisive in the long run: "What economists study is the working of the social institutions which bind together the economic system: firms, markets for goods and services, labor markets, capital markets, the banking system, international trade, and so on. It is the common interest in these social institutions which distinguishes the economics profession."[22] He subsequently remarks, however, that it is because economists "study the economic system as a unified whole, . . . [that they] are more likely to uncover the basic interrelationships within a social system than is someone less accustomed to looking at the working of a system as a whole. . . . [Also, the] study of economics makes it difficult to ignore factors which are clearly important and which play a part in all social systems [such as relative prices]."[23]

These last remarks seem to me to be more an endorsement of the economic approach than of the economic subject matter. Be that as it may, the economic approach, rather than the subject matter, is what I emphasize here. Calculativeness is the general condition that I associate with the economic approach and with the progressive extension of economics into the related social sciences. (I view it as the strategy that Gary Becker[24] has applied so widely and effectively.)[25] Note in this con-

[20] Coase, *supra* note 2, at 204.

[21] *Id.*

[22] *Id.* at 206–7.

[23] *Id.* at 209–10.

[24] Gary Becker. The Economic Approach to Human Behavior (1976).

[25] Note that there are real differences between the incomplete contracting approach out of which transaction cost economics works, in which bounded rationality is featured, and the optimality setup out of which Becker works. Herbert Simon, however, takes exception with both. Becker is scored for excesses of hyperrationality (Simon, *supra* note 19, at 2), while I am scored for using an incomplete contracting setup for which empirical support is purportedly lacking (Herbert Simon, Organization and Markets, 5 J. Econ. Persp. 25, 26–27 (1991)). Becker is his own best agent. As for myself, I would observe that empirical work in transaction cost economics is much greater than Simon indicates (see Oliver E. Williamson, The Economic Institutions of Capitalism (1985), ch. 5; Paul Joskow, Asset Specificity and the Structure of Vertical Relationships: Empirical Evidence, 4 J. L. Econ. & Org. 95 (1988); Paul Joskow, The Role of Transaction Cost Economics in Antitrust and Public Utility Regulatory Policies, 7 J. L. Econ. & Org. 53 (1991); and Howard Shelanski, Empirical Research in Transaction Cost Economics: A Survey and Assessment (unpublished manuscript, Univ. California, Berkeley 1991)) and is growing exponentially. Joskow concludes that the empirical research in transaction cost economics "is in much better shape than much of the empirical work in industrial organization generally" (The Role of Transac-

nection that calculative economic reasoning can take several forms—of which price theory, property rights theory, agency theory, and transaction cost economics are all variants.[26]

B. Transaction Cost Economics

Institutional Economics. Institutional economics works at two levels of analysis. The macro variant, which is especially associated with the work of Douglass North,[27] deals with the institutional environment. The micro variant deals with the institutions of governance. Lance Davis and North[28] distinguish between these two as follows (emphasis in original):

> The *institutional environment* is the set of fundamental political, social and legal ground rules that establishes the basis for production, exchange and distribution. Rules governing elections, property rights, and the right of contract are examples. . . .
>
> An *institutional arrangement* is an arrangement between economic units that governs the ways in which these units can cooperate and/or compete. It . . . [can] provide a structure within which its members can cooperate . . . or [it can] provide a mechanism that can effect a change in laws or property rights.

The way that I propose to join these two is to treat the institutional environment in which a transaction (or a related set of transactions) is embedded as a set of shift parameters, changes in which elicit shifts in the comparative costs of governance.[29] These issues are developed further in Section III below. My main purpose here is to examine the rudiments of governance.

---

tion Cost Economics, *supra*, at 81)—to which, however, he quickly adds that more and better theoretical and empirical work is needed: "[T]here is no rest for the weary" (*id.* at 82). I concur.

[26] Note in this connection is that the massive expansion of economic reasoning out of antitrust law into the law more generally had transaction cost economics origins (Coase, *supra* note 6). Many of the initial applications of economic reasoning to economic organization also rely, directly and indirectly, on transaction cost arguments (Arrow, *supra* note 9; Kenneth J. Arrow, The Organization of Economic Activity: Issues Pertinent to the Choice of Market versus Nonmarket Allocation, in 1 U.S. Joint Economic Committee, 91st Cong., 1st Sess., The Analysis and Evaluation of Public Expenditure: The PPB System 59 (1969); Oliver E. Williamson, Markets and Hierarchies: Analysis and Antitrust Implications (1975); Armen Alchian & Harold Demsetz, Production, Information Costs, and Economic Organization, 62 Am. Econ. Rev. 777 (1972); and Michael Jensen & William Meckling, Theory of the Firm, 3 J. Fin. Econ. 305 (1976)).

[27] Douglass North, Institutions, 5 J. Econ. Persp. 97 (1991).

[28] Lance E. Davis & Douglass C. North, Institutional Change and American Economic Growth 6–7 (1971).

[29] Oliver E. Williamson, Comparative Economic Organization: The Analysis of Discrete Structural Alternatives, 36 Admin. Sci. Q. 269 (1991).

Governance. Although hyperrationality has been responsible for some of the truly deep insights of economics, there is a need, at some stage, to describe "man as he is, acting within the constraints imposed by real institutions."[30] What are the key attributes of economic actors?

Opportunism and bounded rationality are the key behavioral assumptions on which transaction cost economics relies.[31] Bounded rationality is a cognitive assumption, according to which economic agents are "*intendedly* rational, but only *limitedly* so."[32] An immediate ramification of bounded rationality is that impossibly complex forms of economic organization (such as complete contingent-claims contracting)[33] are infeasible. Standing alone, that is a negative result. But there is more to it than that. If mind is a scarce resource,[34] then economizing on bounded rationality is warranted. This expands, rather than reduces, the range of issues to which the economic approach can be applied. Among other things, the "conscious, deliberate, purposeful" use of organization as a means by which to economize on bounded rationality is made endogenous.[35]

Opportunism is a self-interest-seeking assumption. By contrast with simple self-interest seeking, according to which economic agents will continuously consult their own preferences but will candidly disclose all pertinent information on inquiry and will reliably discharge all covenants, opportunistic agents are given to self-interest seeking with guile. Whether economic agents will tell the truth, the whole truth, and nothing but the truth and will reliably self-enforce covenants to behave "responsibly" are therefore problematic. Accordingly, "contract as promise" is fraught with hazards. Although that too is a negative result, again there is a positive research agenda.

[30] Coase, *supra* note 4, at 231.

[31] The aspect of bounded rationality that is most frequently emphasized is that of limited cognitive competence, on which account irrationality or satisficing are often thought to be implied. Intended (but limited) rationality, however, is a broader concept. Not only are intendedly rational agents attempting effectively to cope, whence irrationality (except, perhaps, for certain pathological cases) is not implied, but satisficing is merely one manifestation of coping. The satisficing approach, which appeals to psychology and works out of an aspiration level mechanics, has not found wide application within economics (Robert Aumann, What Is Game Theory Trying to Accomplish? in Frontiers of Economics 35 (Kenneth Arrow & Seppo Honkapohja eds. 1985)). Also see Kenneth Arrow, Reflections on the Essays, in Arrow and the Foundations of the Theory of Economic Policy 734 (George Feiwel ed. 1987).

[32] Herbert Simon, Administrative Behavior, at xxiv (2d ed. 1957).

[33] Roy Radner, Competitive Equilibrium under Uncertainty, 36 Econometrica 31 (1968).

[34] Simon, *supra* note 19, at 12.

[35] Chester Barnard, The Functions of the Executive 4 (15th printing 1962) (1st printing 1938).

The lessons of opportunism can be construed broadly or narrowly. The myopic construction is associated with Machiavelli, who advised his prince that he both could and should breach contracts with impunity.[36] By contrast, transaction cost economics advises that, once alerted to the *systematic hazards* of opportunism, the wise (farsighted) prince will both give and receive credible commitments. That more deeply calculative response permits superior deals to be made than could otherwise be supported.[37] Machiavellian grabbing is not implied if economic agents have a more farsighted understanding of the economic relation of which they are a part than myopic Machiavellianism ascribes to them.

Note, moreover, that the idea of credible commitments is a thoroughly hardheaded one. Contracts that have no need for added support (the "ideal" contracts of both law and economics)[38] will not be provided with them. More generally, contracts will be provided with added supports only in the degree to which these are cost-effective. Calculativeness is thus pervasive.

Taken together, the lessons of bounded rationality and opportunism lead to the following combined result: organize transactions so as to economize on bounded rationality while simultaneously safeguarding them against the hazards of opportunism. Not only do credible commitments arise when incomplete contracts are examined in their entirety, but complaints over obsessive calculativeness, truncated calculativeness, and anticalculativeness are mitigated as well.

C. Purported Excesses of Calculativeness

Obsessive Calculativeness. A calculative approach to economic organization can and sometimes does result in obsessive demands for control. One of the prescient lessons of sociology is that demands for control can

[36] Niccolò Machiavelli, The Prince 92–93 (1952).

[37] See Oliver E. Williamson, Credible Commitments: Using Hostages to Support Exchange, 73 Am. Econ. Rev. 519 (1983). The remarks of Richard Dawkins about conscious foresight, expressed in the context of selfish genes, are pertinent (Richard Dawkins, The Selfish Gene 215 (1976)):

> One unique feature of man . . . [is] his capacity for conscious foresight. Selfish genes . . . have no foresight.
>
> [Thus] even if we look on the dark side and assume that individual man is fundamentally selfish, our conscious foresight . . . could save us from the worst selfish excesses of the blind replicators. We have at least the mental equipment to foster our long-term selfish interests rather than merely our short-term selfish interests. We can see the long-term benefits of participating . . . , and we can sit down to discuss ways of making . . . [agreements] work.

[38] Ian Macneil, The Many Futures of Contract, 47 S. Cal. L. Rev. 691 (1974), at 738.

have both intended and unintended effects and that unintended effects often have dysfunctional consequences.[39]

One possible response to this finding is to argue that the economic approach is flawed because of its preoccupation with intended effects to the neglect of unintended effects. But that assumes that the economic approach is unable or unwilling to take into account all relevant regularities whatsoever. If the deeper lesson is to design control systems with reference to all consequences—both those that are intended and those that were (originally) unanticipated—and if economics can implement this deeper lesson, then the claim that the economic approach is mindlessly given to obsessive calculativeness is overdrawn. The correct view is that a naive application of calculativeness can be and sometimes is given to excesses but that this is often remediable. On being informed about added consequences, these will be factored into the design exercise from the outset. (A calculative response to the excesses of calculativeness thereby obtains.)

Truncated Calculativeness. Many models of economic organization work out of truncated logic, according to which economic actors are assumed to be myopic. Aspects of the Keynesian macro model work out of a myopic logic. The same is true of the cobweb cycle,[40] barriers to entry arguments,[41] and the resource dependency approach to economic organization.[42]

Transaction cost economics responds to all of these conditions identically: although complex contracts are unavoidably incomplete, a farsighted approach to contract is often feasible. Many of the problems associated with truncated contracting are relieved in the process.

The differences between the resource dependency and credible commitment approaches to economic organization are illustrative. The resource dependency approach is concerned with power disparities that arise when contractual dependency comes as an unwanted surprise. That occurs frequently if myopic agents are unable to project and make provision for the Fundamental Transformation—according to which a large-numbers bidding situation at the outset is (sometimes) transformed into a small-numbers supply relation during contract execution and at the

[39] See Robert Merton, The Unanticipated Consequences of Purposive Social Action, 1 Am. Sociol. Rev. 894 (1936); James G. March & Herbert Simon, Organizations (1958).

[40] Ronald H. Coase & Ronald Fowler, Bacon Production and the Pig Cycle in Great Britain, 2 Economica 142 (1935).

[41] George Stigler, The Organization of Industry (1968).

[42] See Jeffrey Pfeffer & Gerald Salancik, The External Control of Organizations (1978); and Jeffrey Pfeffer, Power in Organizations (1981).

contract renewal interval.[43] If this transformation is unforeseen, then one of the parties may find itself at a power disadvantage in relation to the other after the initial contract has been agreed to.

Transaction cost economics employs an efficiency perspective and treats dependency as a (broadly) foreseeable condition. In the degree, therefore, to which asset specificity (which is responsible for bilateral dependency) yields benefits (added revenues and/or production cost savings) that are not more than offset by the added governance costs, added asset specificity is deliberately incurred. Accordingly, farsighted parties purposefully create bilateral dependency and support it with contractual safeguards, but only in the degree to which the associated investments are cost-effective. Because price, asset specificity, and contractual safeguards are all determined simultaneously, calculativeness is the solution to what would otherwise be a problem (unwanted resource dependency).

Anticalculativeness: Voice. Yet another view is that the calculative approach to economic organization emphasizes exit (the traditional economic means by which to express dissatisfaction) to the neglect of voice (which is associated with politics and is purportedly less calculative).[44] Transaction cost economics is sometimes held to be especially reprehensible.[45]

My response is twofold. First, if voice in the absence of an exit option is relatively ineffective, which evidently it is,[46] then voice really does have a calculative aspect. Second, voice works through mechanisms, and those mechanisms are often carefully designed.

Karl Llewellyn's view of contract as framework,[47] as against contract as legal rules, is pertinent (emphasis added): "[The] major importance of legal contract is to provide a framework for well-nigh every type of group organization and for well-nigh every type of passing or permanent relation between individuals and groups . . . a *framework highly adjustable,* a framework which almost never accurately indicates real working relations, but which affords a rough indication around which such relations vary, an occasional guide in cases of doubt, and a norm of *ultimate appeal* when the relations cease in fact to work."

[43] Williamson, *supra* note 25, at 61–63.

[44] Albert O. Hirschman, Exit, Voice and Loyalty (1970).

[45] See Mark Granovetter, Economic Action and Social Structure: The Problem of Embeddedness, 91 Am. J. Sociol. 481 (1985); and Mark Granovetter, The Sociological and Economic Approaches to Labor Market Analysis, in Industries, Firms, and Jobs (George Farkas & Paula England eds. 1988).

[46] Hirschman, *supra* note 44.

[47] Karl N. Llewellyn, What Price Contract? An Essay in Perspective, 40 Yale L. J. 704, 736–37 (1931).

Plainly, Llewellyn provides for voice: parties to a (bilaterally dependent) contract will try to work things out when confronted by unanticipated disturbances. Within a broad range, the contract serves as framework. Llewellyn nevertheless observes that the contract serves also as a norm of ultimate appeal if the parties are unable to reconcile their differences. An exit option is thereby preserved, but court ordering of the contract serves to delimit threat positions. Bargaining through voice is thus greatly influenced by knowledge that the terms of exit are defined by the contract.

But there is more to it than that. The voice mechanics are often defined by the terms of the contract. Consider the provisions in the thirty-two-year coal supply agreement[48] between the Nevada Power Company and the Northwest Trading Company:

> In the event an inequitable condition occurs which adversely affects one Party, it shall be the joint and equal responsibility of both Parties to act promptly and in good faith to determine the action required to cure or adjust for the inequity and effectively to implement such action. Upon written claim of inequity served by one Party upon the other, the Parties shall act jointly to reach an agreement concerning the claimed inequity within sixty (60) days of the date of such written claim. An adjusted base coal price that differs from market price by more than ten percent (10%) shall constitute a hardship. The Party claiming inequity shall include in its claim such information and data as may be reasonably necessary to substantiate the claim and shall freely and without delay furnish such other information and data as the other Party reasonably may deem relevant and necessary. If the Parties cannot reach agreement within sixty (60) days the matter shall be submitted to arbitration.

Plainly, the procedures through which voice is expected to work are laid out in advance. Again, therefore, calculativeness is implicated in the design of ex post governance (voice).

As previously remarked, moreover, transaction cost economics maintains that ex post governance is aligned with the needs of transactions in a discriminating way. Some, but not all, transactions are provided with voice mechanisms. Specifically, classical transactions in which each party can go its own way without cost to the other will not be supported with voice.

The upshot is that calculativeness, albeit of a much richer and more varied kind than the orthodox exit-without-voice approach contemplates, applies throughout. The importance of voice is not in the least discredited. Instead, voice is encompassed within the extended calculative perspective.

[48] Reproduced from Williamson, *supra* note 25, at 164–65.

II. Calculative Trust[49]

My purpose in this and the next two sections is to examine the aforementioned "elusive notion of trust."[50] That will be facilitated by examining a series of examples in which the terms trust and risk are used interchangeably—which has come to be standard practice in the social science literature—after which the simple contractual schema out of which transaction cost economics works is sketched. As set out there, transaction cost economics refers to contractual safeguards, or their absence, rather than trust, or its absence. I argue that it is redundant at best and can be misleading to use the term "trust" to describe commercial exchange for which cost-effective safeguards have been devised in support of more efficient exchange. Calculative trust is a contradiction in terms.

A. *Trust as Risk*

"Trust" is a good word. So is "risk." Social scientists have begun to describe situations of trust as "a subclass of those involving risk. They are situations in which the risk one takes depends on the performance of another actor."[51] According to this formulation, trust is warranted when the expected gain from placing oneself at risk to another is positive, but not otherwise. Indeed, the decision to accept such a risk is taken to imply trust.[52]

This theme is repeated throughout the influential seminar series organized by Gambetta and published under the title *Trust: Making and Breaking Cooperative Relations*. That volume closes with the following unifying observation:[53] "[T]here is a degree of convergence in the definition of trust which can be summarized as follows: trust . . . is a particular level of the subjective probability with which an agent assesses that another agent or group of agents will perform a particular action. . . . When we say we trust someone or that someone is trustworthy, we implicitly mean that the probability that he will perform an action that is beneficial or at least not detrimental to us is high enough for us to consider engaging in some form of cooperation with him." Jeffrey Bradach and Robert Eccles expressly embrace this view in their recent treatment of "Price,

49 There is an enormous literature on trust. Some of that will be apparent from the discussion. For a more expansive survey, see Craig Thomas, Public Trust in Organizations and Institutions: A Sociological Perspective (1991).

50 Gambetta, *supra* note 1, at ix.

51 Coleman, *supra* note 15, at 91.

52 *Id.* at 105.

53 Gambetta, *supra* note 1, at 217.

Authority, and Trust'' in the *Annual Review of Sociology*.[54] As discussed below, David Kreps[55] and Partha Dasgupta[56] employ similar notions in their game theoretic treatments of trust. The upshot is that trust is purportedly made more transparent and operational by treating calculated trust as a subset of calculated risk.

James Coleman's chapter on ''Relations of Trust'' develops the rational choice approach to trust through three examples.[57] The first involves a Norwegian shipowner who is urgently seeking a £200,000 loan, thereby to release a ship of his that had undergone repairs in Amsterdam. The second involves the arrival of a farmer to a new area and the unexpected breakdown of his equipment. The third is that of an immigrant high school girl who lacked companionship in her new surroundings.

Confronted by the unwillingness of the Amsterdam shipyard to release his ship, the Norwegian shipowner telephoned his merchant banker, Hambros, in the City of London to arrange a loan. Within three minutes, the Hambros banker had arranged for an Amsterdam bank to deliver the money, whereupon the shipowner was told that his ship would be released. Coleman summarizes this case as follows:[58]

> This case clearly involves trust. The manager of the Norwegian department at Hambros placed trust in the Norwegian shipowner who telephoned him—trust to the extent of £200,000 of Hambros's money. There was no contract signed, no paper involved in the transaction, nothing more substantial than the shipowner's intention to repay the money and the Hambros man's belief in both the shipowner's honesty and his ability to repay. Similarly, the bank in Amsterdam trusted Hambros to the extent of £200,000, again merely on the basis of a verbal request over the telephone. It committed £200,000 of its money on the assumption that Hambros would, on Monday morning, repay the sum.

The farmer example involves the breakdown of a hay baler and the prospect that the crop would be ruined by rain. This was avoided by a neighbor's offer to use his baler and to help bale the hay without charge. When the farmer who had received the assistance asked what was needed in return, he was told ''all he wants is the gasoline it took to bale the hay.'' Coleman interprets this as the ''placement of trust by the second

[54] Jeffrey Bradach & Robert Eccles, Price, Authority, and Trust, 15 Am. Rev. Sociol. 97 (1989).

[55] David M. Kreps, Corporate Culture and Economic Theory, in Perspectives on Positive Political Economy (James Alt & Kenneth Shepsle eds. 1990).

[56] Partha Dasgupta, Trust as a Commodity, in Gambetta ed., *supra* note 1, at 49.

[57] Coleman, *supra* note 15.

[58] *Id*. at 92.

farmer in the first—trust that in a situation of need or time of trouble, when he might call on the first farmer, that farmer would provide help, as he had in this case."[59]

The third example begins with the assent by a high school girl to be walked home by a boy. She further assented, at his request, to take a shortcut through the woods. He then made a sexual advance, which she resisted. She was thereupon roughed up and sexually assaulted. Coleman interprets this as "a special case of a special circumstance involving trust" in which weaker women place themselves at hazard where "[s]ometimes, as in this episode, that trust is misplaced."[60]

Another example that is widely believed to reflect trust is that of diamond dealers in New York City. Yoram Ben-Porath describes the relationship as one in which major deals are "sealed by a handshake."[61] Such deals would not be possible were it not for the prevalence of trust within the Jewish community. Interestingly, those conditions of trust are said to be undergoing a change. An elderly Israeli diamond dealer has described the changes as follows: "[W]hen I first entered the business, the conception was that truth and trust were simply the way to do business, and nobody decent would consider doing it differently. Although many transactions are still consummated on the basis of trust and truthfulness, this is done because these qualities are viewed as good for business, a way to make a profit."[62]

James Henlin's account of the decisions by cab drivers to pick up a fare or not is used by Craig Thomas[63] to illustrate "characteristic-based trust": "Since cabbies do not know anything specific about the prospective passenger based through past experiences with that person, they must make their decision to stop based on what they can infer from the setting, the physical appearance of the person, and the manner in which the person presents himself. Henlin . . . argues that trust consists of an actor offering a definition of herself, and an audience choosing either to interact with (trust) or not to interact with (distrust)."

Recent game theoretic treatments of economic organization routinely refer to trust, usually in the context of parties engaged in sequential, repeated games. David Kreps's description of the game is typical. The

[59] *Id.* at 93.

[60] *Id.* at 94.

[61] Yoram Ben-Porath, The F-Connection: Families, Friends, and Firms and the Organization of Exchange, 6 Population & Dev. Rev. 1 (1980).

[62] Quoted in Lisa Bernstein, The Choice between Public and Private Law (Discussion Paper No. 70, Harvard Law School, Program in Law and Economics, 1990), at 38.

[63] Thomas, *supra* note 49, at 22.

basic setup is a one-sided version of the Prisoner's Dilemma game in which there is a sequence of two moves on every play of the game. First, Party X decides whether to put himself at hazard ("trust Y") or not ("do not trust Y"). If Party X accepts the hazard, then Party Y decides whether to take advantage of X ("abuse X's trust") or not ("honor X's trust"). The payoffs are such that the joint gain is maximized by the trust/honor outcome. But since Y's immediate gains are maximized if he abuses X's trust, the no-trust/no-play result will obtain if presented as a one-shot game.

Kreps thereupon converts the relation to a repeated game in which there is a high probability that each round will be followed by another. This changes the analysis "dramatically."[64] Say, for example, X tells Y, "I will begin by trusting you, hoping that you will honor that trust. Indeed, I will continue to trust you as long as you do not abuse that trust. But if ever you abuse that trust, I will never again trust you." If Y hears and believes that statement, and if the game is played repeatedly (with high probability), then the honor-trust arrangement is self-enforcing.[65] The commercial context notwithstanding, trust and honor are evidently what this game is all about.

Probably the most expansive treatment of trust in a gaming context is Partha Dasgupta's chapter on "Trust as a Commodity." He begins with the claim that "[t]rust is central to all transactions and yet economists rarely discuss the notion."[66] He elaborates as follows:[67] "For trust to be developed between individuals they must have repeated encounters, and they must have some memory of previous experiences. Moreover, for honesty to have potency as a concept there must be some *cost* involved in honest behavior. And finally, trust is linked with reputation, and reputation has to be acquired." Dasgupta further remarks that "[i]f the incentives are 'right,' even a trustworthy person can be relied upon to be untrustworthy."[68]

B. The Simple Contractual Schema

Risk entails exposure to probabilistic outcomes. If a gamble has two outcomes, good and bad, the utility valuation of each is G and B, respectively, and if the probability of a good outcome is q, then the expected utility of the gamble can be expressed as $V = qG + (1 - q)B$.

[64] Kreps, *supra* note 55, at 102.

[65] *Id.* at 103.

[66] Dasgupta, *supra* note 56, at 49.

[67] *Id.* at 59.

[68] *Id.* at 54.

Actions can sometimes be taken to mitigate bad outcomes and/or enhance good outcomes. I will define competent calculativeness as a situation in which the affected parties (1) are aware of the range of possible outcomes and their associated probabilities, (2) take cost-effective actions to mitigate hazards and enhance benefits, (3) proceed with the transaction only if expected net gains can be projected, and, (4) if X can complete the transaction with any of several Ys, the transaction is assigned to that Y for which the largest net gain can be projected.[69]

Parties to such transactions understand a great deal about the contractual relation of which they are a part and manage it in a calculative way.[70] The simple contractual schema to which transaction cost economics makes repeated reference describes exchange as a triple (p, k, s), where p refers to the price at which the trade takes place, k refers to the hazards that are associated with the exchange, and s denotes the safeguards within which the exchange is embedded. The argument is that price, hazards, and safeguards are determined simultaneously.

The schematic and the values that each element in the vector take on are shown in Figure 1. As shown, Node A involves no hazards. The good or service in question is completely generic. Goods or services are exchanged now for prices paid now. This is the classical market exchange that Ian Macneil has described as "sharp in by clear agreement; sharp out by clear performance."[71]

It will facilitate comparisons to assume that suppliers are competitively organized and are risk neutral. The prices at which product will be supplied therefore reflect an expected break-even condition. The break-even price that is associated with Node A is p. There being no hazards, $k = 0$. And since safeguards are unneeded,[72] $s = 0$.

Node B is more interesting. The contractual hazard here is $\bar{k}$. If the buyer is unable or unwilling to provide a safeguard, then $s = 0$. The corresponding break-even price is $\bar{p}$.

[69] This may appear to be indistinguishable from maximizing—at least if due allowance is made for (1) the incompleteness of contracting, (2) the crude quality of information, and (3) discrete choices. For a discussion of satisficing versus maximizing, see Oliver Williamson, Transaction Cost Economics and Organization Theory, 2 Indus. & Corp. Change 165 (1993).

[70] Pervasive calculativeness notwithstanding, the rhetoric of exchange often employs the language of promises, trust, favors, and cooperativeness. That is understandable, in that the artful use of language can produce deals that would be scuttled by abrasive calculativeness. If, however, the basic deal is shaped by objective factors, then calculativeness (credibility, hazards, safeguards, net benefits) is where the crucial action resides.

[71] Macneil, *supra* note 38, at 738.

[72] Another way of putting it is that (transition problems aside) each party can go its own way without cost to the other. Competition provides a safeguard.

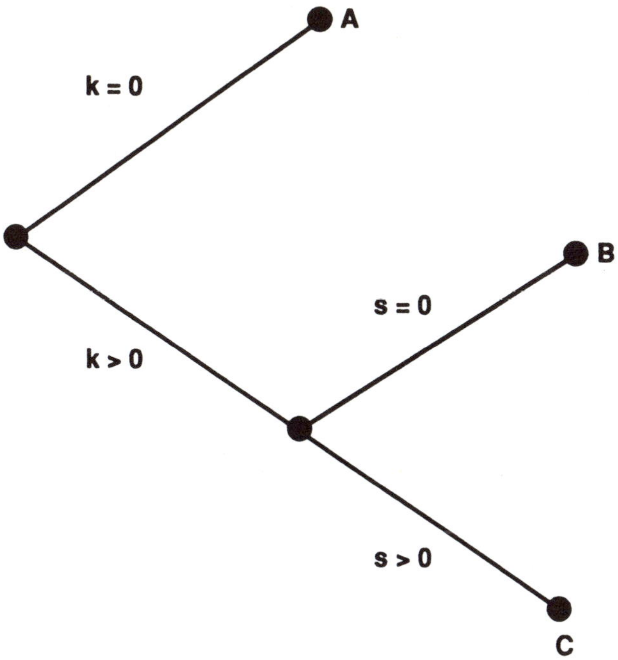

	p	k	s
Node A	p_1	0	0
Node B	$\bar{p}$	$\bar{k}$	0
Node C	$\hat{p}$	$\bar{k}$	$\hat{s}$

FIGURE 1.—Simple contractual schema

Node C poses the same contractual hazard, namely, $\bar{k}$. In this case, however, a safeguard in amount $\hat{s}$ is provided. The break-even price that is projected under these conditions is $\hat{p}$. It is elementary[73] that $\hat{p} < \bar{p}$.

In the language of Section II*A* above, Node A poses no risk, hence trust is unneeded. Nodes B and C, by contrast, do pose a risk. In the

[73] For a more systematic development, see Williamson, *supra* note 37. For related empirical work, see Scott Masten & Keith Crocker, Efficient Adaptation in Long-Term Contracts: Take or Pay Provisions for Natural Gas, 75 Am. Econ. Rev. 1085 (1985), and the surveys reported by Paul Joskow, *supra* note 25.

language of trust, Node B is the low-trust and Node C is the high-trust outcome.

Note that Bradach and Eccles contend that "mutual dependence [i.e., $k > 0$] between exchange partners . . . [promotes] trust, [which] contrasts sharply with the argument central to transaction cost economics that . . . dependence . . . fosters opportunistic behavior."[74] What transaction cost economics says, however, is that because opportunistic agents will not self-enforce open-ended promises to behave responsibly, efficient exchange will be realized only if dependencies are supported by credible commitments. Wherein is trust implicated if parties to an exchange are farsighted and reflect the relevant hazards in the terms of the exchange? (A better price ($\hat{p} < \bar{p}$) will be offered if the hazards ($k > 0$) are mitigated by cost-effective contractual safeguards ($s > 0$).) Indeed, I maintain that trust is irrelevant to commercial exchange and that reference to trust in this connection promotes confusion.

Note further that while credible commitments deter breach and support more efficient exchange, breach is not wholly precluded. On the contrary, if it is inefficient to supply under some state realizations, then an optimal contract will project breach for those states. Whereas *efficient breach* of commercial contract is easy to reconcile with a calculative approach to contract, the notion that trust can be efficiently breached experiences considerable strain. Much of the contract law literature would be clarified if trust were consistently used in a delimited way.

C. Applications

If calculative relations are best described in calculative terms, then diffuse terms, of which trust is one, that have mixed meanings should be avoided when possible. As discussed below, all of the above examples save one can be interpreted in terms of efficiency and credibility. (The exception is the assaulted girl, but that, I contend, is not properly described as a condition of trust either.) Were my arguments to prevail, the word "trust" would hereafter be used much more cautiously—at least among social scientists, if not more generally.

The Norwegian Shipowner. The Norwegian shipowner required a loan. Let q_1, q_2, and q_3 be the probabilities of a good outcome (timely loan repayment and profitable future business) that are projected by the shipyard, the Amsterdam bank, and the London merchant banker (Hambros), respectively. Let G_1, G_2, and G_3 be the corresponding gains and B_1, B_2, and B_3 be the corresponding losses that each associates with

[74] Bradach & Eccles, *supra* note 54, at 111.

dealing with the Norwegian shipowner directly. The expected net gains are then given by $V_i = q_iG_i + (1 - q_i)B_i$. As I interpret Coleman, the reason why the Hambros deal went through, while the other two did not, is because $V_3 > 0$ (the merchant banker trusts) and $V_1 < 0$, $V_2 < 0$ (the shipyard and Amsterdam bank distrust). But that is not necessary. As a matter of good business practice, the Hambros deal should go through if $V_3 > 0$ and $V_3 > V_1$ and V_2.

On my interpretation, (1) all parties were calculative, (2) the loan was made by the party that projected the largest expected net gain, and (3) no trust is implied. That the merchant banker was best suited to bear the risk is, I conjecture, because it had the most knowledge of the shipowner and the best prospect of future business. Indeed, the Amsterdam shipbuilder may have the policy of never releasing ships without payment. That is not because he always projects a net negative outcome. Instead, his policy is one of efficient decision making in the context of the *system* of which shipbuilding is a part.[75] Shipbuilders know shipbuilding but have much less experience with and knowledge of clients' financial conditions, have less assurance of repeat business, and have less competence to pursue their claims for unpaid debts in court. Since the merchant banker is more well-suited in all of these respects, the shipbuilder adopts a policy whereby production is specialized to one party and financial risk is specialized to another.

Even assuming, arguendo, that the merchant banker in London was better suited than the Amsterdam bank or the shipbuilder to bear the risk, might not trust come in through knowledge possessed by the London banker of the personal integrity of the Norwegian shipowner? That is, in addition to the objective features mentioned above, might idiosyncratic knowledge of personal integrity also favor running the transaction through London? Is trust then implicated after all?

I would argue that the London banker's deep knowledge of the personal integrity of the Norwegian shipowner merely permitted him to improve his estimate of integrity. That the London banker has a better estimate, in this sense, does not imply that he has a more favorable estimate of the Norwegian shipowner's integrity. (Indeed, the London banker may refuse the loan because he knows the Norwegian shipowner to be a crook.) More generally, if N shipowners approach Hambros with

[75] The main systems argument is in the text. But there is another possibility. Shipbuilders (or, more generally, businessmen—as opposed to bankers) are optimistic fellows, on which account they project subjective probabilities for good outcomes that exceed the objective conditions. Refusing to release ships may be a good policy for bringing such excesses of optimism under control. An important but little remarked purpose of having "firm but arbitrary" policies is to protect parties against idiosyncratic appeals.

the same request and only $M < N$ are approved, what are we to infer? I submit that calculativeness is determinative throughout and that invoking trust merely muddies the (clear) waters of calculativeness.

The Hay Baler. The hay baler case is one where issues of informal organization are posed. If accidents occur with stochastic regularity and if there is a great deal of indeterminacy in setting the price for emergency aid, then there are advantages to embedding these transactions in an institutional form in which quick responsiveness on nonexploitative terms will obtain. An informal, reciprocal aid mechanism is one possible institutional response.

Cheating is nevertheless a hazard. Sanctions are needed lest opportunistic farmers abuse informal supports. Thus, although almost all requests for emergency aid elicit quick and favorable responses, failures to reciprocate are not forgotten or forgiven and, if they persist, will elicit moral suasion and, eventually, sanctions—such as ostracism and refusals of assistance. The efficacy of informal organization thus turns on calculative supports. If almost-automatic and unpriced assistance is the most efficient response, provided that the practice in question is supported by sanctions and is ultimately made contingent on reciprocity, then calculativeness obtains and appeal to trust adds nothing.

The proviso that "the practice in question is supported by sanctions" is, however, crucial. In regions where informal organization delivers very weak sanctions, deferred payment schemes that rely on a reciprocal sense of responsibility will be less viable. Less "spontaneous" cooperation will therefore be observed and/or immediate payment will be expected (demanded) on providing emergency assistance.

Diamond Dealers. The appearance of trust among diamond dealers is deceptive. As Mark Granovetter observes, these transactions are "embedded in a close-knit community of diamond merchants who monitor one another's behavior closely."[76] Lisa Bernstein[77] elaborates:

> What is unique about the diamond industry is not the importance of trust and reputation in commercial transactions, but rather the extent to which the industry is able to use reputation/social bonds at a cost low enough to be able to create a system of private law which enables most transactions to be consummated and most contracts enforced completely outside of the legal system. . . . This is accomplished in two main ways: (1) through the use of reputation bonds; (2) through a private arbitration system whose damage awards are not bounded by expectancy damages, and whose judgments are enforced by both reputation bonds and social pressure.

[76] Granovetter, Economic Action and Social Structure, *supra* note 45, at 492.

[77] Bernstein, *supra* note 62, at 35–36.

Put differently, Node C "trust relations" do not obtain because the diamond industry had the good luck to be organized by an ethnic community in which trust is pervasive. On the contrary, the Jewish ethnic community that organized this market succeeded because it was able to provide cost-effective sanctions more efficiently than rivals. Until recently, moreover, the efficacy of those sanctions[78] depended on restrictive entry: In the past, Jews formed a cohesive geographically concentrated social group in the countries in which they lived. Jewish law provided detailed substantive rules of commercial behavior, and the Jewish community provided an array of extralegal dispute resolution institutions. Non-Jews to whom the sanctions for rule violation were weak—hence, would follow the rules only if that suited their convenience—could not be admitted without jeopardy to the Node C condition.[79]

The organization of this industry has nevertheless been changing in response to new information and monitoring technologies. (Conceivably, the efficacy of ethnic sanctions may be weakening, too.) Despite resistance by "older dealers accustomed to dealing primarily with friends and long standing business acquaintances,"[80] new governance structures[81] are making headway: "Among the proposals currently being considered by

[78] *Id.* at 41.

[79] The question of endgames sometimes arises. If Jews do not defect on the last play, does that imply that trust is operative after all? I would respond negatively if retired Jews remain in their community (in which event they would be subject to sanctions) or have active religious consciences. The contrast between a retiring Jew who remains within the community and the illicit deal related by Dostoyevsky in *The Brothers Karamozov* is instructive. Russell Hardin (Trusting Persons, Trusting Institutions, in Strategy and Choice 185 (Richard J. Zeckhauser ed. 1991)) retells that event as follows:

> [A] lieutenant colonel . . . managed substantial sums of money on behalf of the army. Immediately after each periodic audit of his books, he took the available funds to the merchant Trifonov, who soon returned them with interest and a gift. In effect, both the lieutenant colonel and Trifonov benefited from funds that would otherwise have lain idle, producing no benefit for anyone. Because it was highly irregular, theirs was a secret exchange that depended wholly on personal trust not backed by the law of contracts. When the day came that the lieutenant colonel was to be abruptly replaced in his command, he asked Trifonov to return the last sum, 4,500 rubles, entrusted to him.
>
> Trifonov replied, "I've never received any money from you, and couldn't possibly have received any."

Although Hardin describes the relation between the lieutenant colonel and Trifonov as "personal trust," I submit that Trifonov did view (and the lieutenant colonel should have viewed) the relation calculatively—as a self-enforcing contract to which no legal or social sanctions apply (Lester Telser, A Theory of Self-enforcing Agreements, 53 J. Bus. 27 (1981)).

[80] Bernstein, *supra* note 62, at 42.

[81] *Id.* at 43.

the World Federation of Diamond Bourses are: setting up an international computer database with reports of arbitration judgments from all member bourses in an attempt to foster international uniformity in trade customs, and a rule requiring that every bourse be equipped with a fax machine for rapid transmission of credit worthiness information. Also under consideration, although staunchly opposed by many dealers, is the creation of an international computer database describing goods available for sale worldwide."

The change is akin to a new technology, where the need for learning-by-doing is reduced by the appearance of a standardized machine. In the diamonds case, a new information technology makes it possible to support greater dealer diversity. To be sure, ethnic identity within markets may still have value. But ethnic disparity between markets is now easier to support. To describe the earlier arrangement as a high-trust condition and the emerging arrangement as a low-trust condition confuses rather than illuminates. Both reflect calculativeness.

Put differently, it is a mistake to suppose that commercial trust has supplanted real trust. Rather, the basis for commercial trust has become more transparently calculative as new communication technologies have made inroads into this small trading community by making it possible to track commercial reputation effects in larger trading networks. As a consequence, the diamond market has become larger and more faceless.[82]

Cab Drivers. Cab drivers need to decide whether to pick up a fare or not. Although the probability assessment out of which they work is highly subjective (it reflects risk attitudes, knowledge of particular circumstances, and prior own—and indirect—experience), this is an altogether calculative exercise. There is no obvious value added by describing a decision to accept a risk (pick up a fare) as one of trust.

Game Theory. The "dramatic" change in the games described by Kreps comes about on moving from a one-shot game (where refusal to play was the rational choice) to a game that is repeated with high probability. Given the behavioral rules stipulated by Kreps, reputation effects relentlessly track those who breach contracts. Trading hazards are thus mitigated by embedding trades in networks in which reputation effects are known to work well.

Again, that can be interpreted as a Node C outcome. The parties have examined alternative trading scenarios and have opted for one in which the immediate gains of breach are deterred by the prospective loss of

[82] Ethnic groups that greatly prefer continued trading within an identifiable membership, but whose costs are great in comparison with the new alternative, may need to accept lower compensation to be competitively viable, ceteris paribus.

future business. To be sure, some markets are better able to support reputation effects than others. Reputation effects can and sometimes do break down[83] and are not therefore a trading panacea. Calculative assessments of the efficacy of reputation effects are, however, properly included within the efficient contracting exercise. Reference to trust adds nothing.

Kreps might agree, but he could argue that this misconstrues his enterprise. What Kreps is really concerned with is the evolution of trading relationships—these being the product of learning, social conditioning, corporate culture, and the like. His use of the word "trust" is merely incidental. The intertemporal mechanisms are the key.

I am not only sympathetic with this line of argument, but I would call attention to the fact that the static schema in Figure 1 oversimplifies, in that it takes these types of intertemporal effects as given. I submit, however, that Kreps's use of the term "trust," especially as stated in the behavioral rules that he employs, obscures rather than illuminates these mechanisms. More microanalytic attention to the *processes* through which trading relationships evolve[84] is indeed a rewarding research enterprise.

The Assaulted Girl. Consider finally the case of the assaulted girl and suppose that the matter is put to her in the abstract: should she take shortcuts through the woods with ostensibly friendly boys of slight acquaintance? I submit that the girl in question would assign a nontrivial probability to a bad outcome $(1 - q)$, and a large negative value to B. Even for large values of G, the expected net gain from such walks would commonly be negative. Posed therefore as an abstract policy decision, the rational choice result is this: do not walk in the woods with strangers.

People, however, often cross bridges when they come to them rather than develop an abstract policy in advance. Still, why did she make the "wrong" decision when faced with the particulars?

One possibility is that she did not have the time to work out the calculus. Another possibility is that she had the time but got rattled. Still another possibility is that there is a dynamics to the situation which complicated matters. She cannot simply say no but needs a reason, otherwise her negative response to a "friendly" invitation will appear to be antiso-

[83] See Kreps, *supra* note 55; Bernard Williams, Formal Structure and Social Reality, in Gambetta ed., *supra* note 1, at 14; Oliver E. Williamson, Economic Institutions: Spontaneous and Intentional Governance, 7 J. L. Econ. & Org. 159 (1991).

[84] See Kenneth J. Arrow, Uncertainty and the Welfare Economics of Medical Care, 53 Am. Econ. Rev. 941 (1963); Kreps, *supra* note 55 (and see Section III*F* below); and John Orbell & Robyn Dawes, A "Cognitive Miser" Theory of Cooperators' Advantage, 85 Am. Polit. Sci. Rev. 515 (1991).

cial. Lacking a previously prepared response such as "I am sorry but I cannot walk in the woods because my hay fever is bothering me," and not wanting to appear unfriendly, she takes a chance.

This last involves a two-stage net benefit calculus. The first stage is as described earlier and, if the expected net gain comes out positive, the person assents and events thereafter unfold. If, however, the first stage comes out net negative, then the issue of tactful refusal must be faced. If a tactful refusal quickly presents itself, then the first stage calculus rules. But if a tactful refusal cannot be devised, then a choice between two net negatives needs to be made. Is a blunt refusal, which gives offense and/or results in a reputation for unfriendliness, more or less negative than the projected net loss from accepting the invitation (taking the risk)? Expressed in this way, the assaulted girl was caught up in a coercive situation. She was confronted with a contingency for which she was not prepared, and the social forces coerced her into taking a risky choice.

Situations that are mainly explained by bounded rationality—the risk was taken because the girl did not get the calculus right or because she was not clever enough to devise a contrived but polite refusal on the spot—are not illuminated by appealing to trust.[85]

III. Hyphenated Trust

Opportunism and bounded rationality are the key behavioral assumptions on which transaction cost economics relies. That parsimonious description is suitable for some purposes. But if man, after all, is a "social animal," then socialization and social approvals and sanctions are also pertinent. How can these be accommodated?

My response is suggested, if not evident, from my discussions of embeddedness and the institutional environment above. The Norwegian shipowner was part of a network, the farmer and diamond dealers are part of a community, and the assaulted high school girl is presented with a coercive situation. More generally, the argument is that trading hazards vary not only with the attributes of transaction but also with the trading environment of which they are a part.

[85] To be sure, individuals trapped in coercive situations are attempting to cope. Is it really useful, however, to interpret a bad outcome from a coercive event as a bad draw? It is more instructive, I submit, to regard coercive events as a special class of problems that "invite" people to make risky choices from which they should be shielded (for example, by protecting them against exposure to coercive situations—possibly through training, possibly through draconian penalties against those who contrive coercion). Becker's recent treatment of addiction affords a somewhat different perspective—see Gary Becker, Habits, Addictions, and Traditions (unpublished manuscript, Univ. Chicago 1991).

Although the environment is mainly taken as exogenous, calculativeness is not suspended but remains operative. That is because the need for transaction-specific safeguards (governance) varies systematically with the institutional environment within which transactions are located. Changes in the condition of the environment are therefore factored in—by adjusting transaction-specific governance in cost-effective ways. In effect, institutional environments that provide general purpose safeguards relieve the need for added transaction-specific supports. Accordingly, transactions that are viable in an institutional environment that provides strong safeguards may be nonviable in institutional environments that are weak—because it is not cost-effective for the parties to craft transaction-specific governance in the latter circumstances.

One should not, however, conclude that stronger environmental safeguards are always better than weaker. Not only can added environmental sanctions be pushed to dysfunctional extremes in purely commercial terms, but the environment can be oppressive more generally. My purpose here is merely to describe some of the contextual features with respect to which transaction-specific governance is crafted, rather than to prescribe an optimal institutional environment. Embeddedness attributes of six kinds are distinguished: societal culture, politics, regulation, professionalization, networks, and corporate culture.[86] Each can be thought of as institutional trust of a hyphenated kind: "societal-trust," "political-trust," and so forth.

A. *Societal Culture*

Culture applies to very large groups, sometimes an entire society, and involves very low levels of intentionality. The degree of trading trust in Japan, for example, is said to be much higher than in Great Britain.[87] By contrast, the villages in southern Italy described by Edward Banfield[88] are characterized by very low trading trust outside of the family.

The main import of culture, for purposes of economic organization, is that it serves as a check on opportunism. Social conditioning into a culture that condones lying and hypocrisy limits the efficacy of contract in three respects. First, social sanctions against strategic behavior (such as contrived breach) are weak. Second, court enforcement is problematic—

[86] For more expansive discussions of the institutional environment, see Lynne Zucker, Production of Trust: Institutional Sources of Economic Structure, 1849–1920, 6 Res. Org. Behav. 53 (1986); Susan Shapiro, The Social Control of Impersonal Trust, 93 Am. J. Sociol. 623 (1987); and Thomas, *supra* note 49.

[87] Ronald Dore, Goodwill and the Spirit of Market Capitalism, 39 Brit. J. Soc. 459 (1983).

[88] E. C. Banfield, The Moral Basis of a Backward Society (1958).

since bribery is widespread. Third, individuals feel slight remorse when they behave in opportunistic ways. Given the added hazards, transactions will tend to be of a more generic (Node A, spot market) kind in societies where cultural checks on opportunism are weak, ceteris paribus.

B. Politics

Legislative and judicial autonomy serve credibility purposes. As Harold Berman observes, credibility will be enhanced if a monarch who has made the law "may not make it arbitrarily, and until he has remade it—lawfully—he is bound by it."[89] Self-denying ordinances and, even more, inertia that have been crafted into the political process have commitment benefits.[90]

That this had not fully registered on Eastern Europe and the Soviet Union is suggested by the following remarks of Mikhail Gorbachev (advising U.S. firms to invest quickly in the Soviet Union rather than wait): "Those [companies] who are with us now have good prospects of participating in our great country . . . [whereas those who wait] will remain observers for years to come—*we will see to it*."[91] That the leadership of the Soviet Union "will see to it" that early and late movers will be rewarded and punished, respectively, reflects conventional carrot-and-stick incentive reasoning. What it misses is that ready access to administrative discretion is the source of contractual hazard. The paradox is that fewer degrees of freedom (rules) can have advantages over more (discretion) because added credible commitments can obtain in this way. Effective economic reform thus requires that political reneging options be foreclosed if investor confidence is to be realized.

C. Regulation

As Victor Goldberg[92] and Lynne Zucker[93] have explained, regulation can serve to infuse trading confidence into otherwise problematic trading relations. The creation and administration of a regulatory agency are both very intentional acts—although that is not to say that regulation does not have a (spontaneous) life of its own.[94] Provided that the regulation in

[89] Harold Berman, Law and Revolution (1983).

[90] Douglass North & Barry Weingast, Constitutions and Commitment: The Evolution of Institutions Governing Public Choice in 17th Century England, 49 J. Econ. Hist. 803 (1989).

[91] Quoted from the International Herald Tribune, June 5, 1990, at 5; emphasis added.

[92] Victor Goldberg, Toward an Expanded Economic Theory of Contract, 10 J. Econ. Issues 45 (1976).

[93] Zucker, *supra* note 86.

[94] Marver Bernstein, Regulating Business by Independent Commission (1955).

question is "appropriate," both parties to the transaction—the regulated firm and its customers—will be prepared to make investments in specialized assets on better terms than they would in the absence of such regulation.

D. *Professionalization*

The obligation to fulfill the definition of a role is especially important for professionals—physicians, lawyers, teachers, and so on. Although these roles generally arise in a spontaneous (evolutionary) manner, they are thereafter supported by entry limitations (such as licensing), specific ethical codes, added fiduciary obligations,[95] and professional sanctions. Such support features are highly intentional. They can have the effect of infusing trading confidence into transactions that are characterized by costly information asymmetries, although sometimes the (intentionality) purposes served are strategic.[96]

E. *Networks*

The diamond dealers described above are an example of a trading network. So are the network forms of organization that have recently appeared in northern Italy.[97] Other ethnic trading groups also qualify.[98] Although many of these networks have spontaneous origins, the maintenance of these networks depends on the perfection of intentional trading rules, the enforcement of sanctions, and the like. Credibility turns on whether these reputation effects work well or poorly.

F. *Corporate Culture*

The above-described features of the institutional environment are population-level effects, mainly of a spontaneous kind. Corporate culture displays both spontaneous and intentional features and works mainly within particular organizations. Informal organization[99] is one example; the use of focal points[100] is another.

[95] Fiduciary obligations arise in the context of information asymmetries where the less informed party is exposed to serious losses by failures of "due care."

[96] Arrow, *supra* note 84.

[97] S. Mariotti & G. Cainara, The Evolution of Transaction Governance in the Textile-Clothing Industry, 7 J. Econ. Behav. & Org. 351 (1986).

[98] Janet T. Landa, A Theory of the Ethnically Homogeneous Middleman Group: An Institutional Alternative to Contract Law, 10 J. Legal Stud. 349 (1981).

[99] Barnard, *supra* note 35.

[100] Kreps, *supra* note 55.

Barnard argued that formal and informal organization always and everywhere coexist[101] and that informal organization contributes to the viability of formal organization in three significant respects: "One of the indispensable functions of informal organizations in formal organizations . . . [is] that of communication. . . . Another function is that of maintaining the cohesiveness in formal organizations through regulating the willingness to serve and the stability of objective authority. A third function is the maintenance of the feeling of personal integrity, of self-respect, and independent choice."[102] That has turned out to be a productive formulation. Economic activity will be better organized where there is an appreciation for and intentional use of informal organization.

Internal effects spill over, moreover, onto external trade if firms take on distinctive trading reputations by reason of the corporate culture through which they come to be known and evaluated.[103] Whether added corporate culture is warranted, however, varies with the circumstance: "In general, it will be crucially important to align culture with the sorts of contingencies that are likely to arise."[104] Accordingly, calculativeness characterizes even such apparently "soft" notions as corporate culture, of which Japanese economic organization is an example.[105]

IV. Nearly Noncalculative Trust

Just as it is mind-boggling to contemplate hyperrationality of a comprehensive contracting kind, so is it mind-boggling to contemplate the absence of calculativeness. That is not to say that calculativeness cannot be suppressed or to deny that some actions or individuals are more spontaneous than others. Indeed, I shall argue that it is sometimes desirable to suppress calculativeness. If, however, the decision to suppress calculativeness is itself purposive and calculative, then the true absence of calculativeness is rare if not nonexistent.[106]

Unable to foreclose some shred of calculativeness in the personal trust relations described here, I describe personal trust as nearly noncalculative. The argument proceeds in two stages. Discrete structural analysis,

[101] Barnard, *supra* note 35, at 20.

[102] *Id.* at 122.

[103] Kreps, *supra* note 55.

[104] *Id.* at 128.

[105] Oliver E. Williamson, Strategizing, Economizing, and Economic Organization, 12 Strategic Mgt. J. 75 (1991).

[106] Conceivably, some situations are so complicated that we decide to throw darts or examine entrails. But we are attempting to cope nonetheless. My discussion assumes that noncontingently selfless behavior of a Good Samaritan kind is the exception.

with special reference to the economics of atmosphere, is discussed first. Personal trust is then examined.

A. *Discrete Structural Analysis*

A colleague noted that the economics of atmosphere plays a larger role in *Markets and Hierarchies*[107] than in *The Economic Institutions of Capitalism*[108] and asked about the de-emphasis. I replied that I thought atmosphere at least as important to an understanding of economic organization in 1985 as I had in 1975. Not having made more headway, however, I had little to add.

One of the lessons of the economics of atmosphere is that calculativeness can be taken to dysfunctional extremes. That can show up within governance structures as well as between them. The employment relation is one such context.

Suppose that a job can be split into a series of separable functions. Suppose further that differential metering at the margin is attempted with reference to each. What are the consequences?

If functional separability does not imply attitudinal separability, then piecemeal calculativeness can easily be dysfunctional. The risk is that pushing metering at the margin everywhere to the limit will have spillover effects from easy-to-meter onto hard-to-meter activities. If cooperative attitudes are impaired, then transactions that can be metered only with difficulty, but for which consummate cooperation is important, will be discharged in a more perfunctory manner. The neglect of such interaction effects is encouraged by piecemeal calculativeness, which is to say by an insensitivity to atmosphere.

A related issue is the matter of externalities. The question may be put as follows: ought all externalities to be metered that, taken separately, can be metered with net gains? Presumably, this turns partly on whether secondary effects obtain when an externality is accorded legitimacy. All kinds of grievances may be "felt," and demands for compensation made accordingly, if what had hitherto been considered to be harmless by-products of normal social intercourse are suddenly declared to be compensable injuries. The transformation of relationships that will ensue can easily lead to a lower level of felt satisfaction among the parties than prevailed previously—at least transitionally and possibly permanently.

Part of the explanation is that filing claims for petty injuries influences attitudes toward other transactions. My insistence on compensation for

[107] Williamson, *supra* note 26.

[108] Williamson, *supra* note 25.

A leads you to file claims for *B*, *C*, and *D*, which induces me to seek compensation for *E* and *F*, and so on. Although an efficiency gain might be realized were it possible to isolate transaction *A*, the overall impact can easily be negative. Realizing this to be the case, some individuals would be prepared to overlook such injuries. But everyone is not similarly constituted. Society is rearranged to the advantage of those who demand more exacting correspondences between rewards and deeds if metering at the margin is everywhere attempted. Were the issue of compensation to be taken up as a constitutional matter, rather than on a case-by-case basis, a greater tolerance for spillover would commonly obtain.[109]

Also pertinent is that individuals keep informal social accounts and find the exchange of reciprocal favors among parties with whom uncompensated spillovers exist to be satisfying.[110] Transforming these casual social accounts into exact and legal obligations may well be destructive of atmosphere and lead to a net loss of satisfaction between the parties. Put differently, pervasive pecuniary relations impair the quality of "contracting"—even if the metering of the transactions in question were costless.[111]

The argument that emerges from the above is not that metering ought to be prohibited but that the calculative approach to organization that is associated with economics can be taken to extremes. An awareness of attitudinal spillovers and nonpecuniary satisfactions serves to check such excesses of calculativeness. Consider now a more extreme possibility: there are some transactions for which the optimal level of *conscious* metering is zero.[112]

The idea here is that conscious monitoring, even of a low-grade kind, introduces unwanted calculativeness that is contrary to the spirit of certain very special relations and poses intertemporal threats to their viability. Not only can intendedly noncalculative relations can be upset by Type I error, according to which a true relation is incorrectly classified as false, but calculativeness may be subject to (involuntary) positive feed-

[109] Thomas Schelling, Micromotives and Macrobehavior (1978).

[110] A. W. Goulder, Industrial Bureaucracy (1954).

[111] The buying of "rounds" in English pubs is an example. Would a costless meter lead to a superior result? Suppose that everyone privately disclosed a willingness to pay and that successive bids were solicited until a break-even result was projected. Suppose that the results of the final solicitation are either kept secret or posted, depending on preferences, and that rounds are thereafter delivered to the table on request. Monthly bills are sent out in accordance with the break-even condition. How is camaraderie effected?

[112] Unconscious or subconscious metering is another problem. Observations that are not consciously processed may be processed by the subconscious nonetheless, and their ramifications may insistently intrude on consciousness.

back. Intendedly noncalculative relations that are continuously subject to being reclassified as calculative are, in effect, calculative.

Issues akin to those examined by Robert Nozick in his discussion of "Love's Bond" are implicated.[113] Nozick contends that the idea of "trading up" is inimical to a loving relationship: "The intention in love is to form a *we* and to identify with it as an extended self, to identify one's fortunes in large part with its fortunes. A willingness to trade up, to destroy the *we* you largely identify with, would then be a willingness to destroy yourself in the form of your own extended self" (emphasis in original).[114] If entertaining the possibility of trading up devalues the relation, a discrete structural shift that disallows trading up, which is a variety of calculativeness, is needed.

B. Personal Trust

John Dunn's recent treatment of "Trust and Political Agency"[115] raises many of the pertinent issues. Thus, Dunn distinguishes between trust as a "human passion" and trust as a "modality of human action," where the latter is "a more or less consciously chosen policy for handling the freedom of other human agents or agencies."[116] He subsequently remarks that "trust as a passion is the confident expectation of benign intentions by another agent," but as a "modality of action, . . . trust is ineluctably strategic."[117] He also contends that "the twin of trust is betrayal"[118] and avers that "human beings need, as far as they can, to economize on trust in persons and confide instead in well-designed political, social, and economic institutions."[119]

Trust as a passion versus trust as a modality corresponds in my treatment to personal trust and calculative trust, respectfully. Moreover, Dunn's characterization of calculative trust as strategic, whereas personal trust is not, is exactly right. But whereas Dunn contends that the twin of trust is betrayal, I would reserve betrayal for personal trust and would use breach of contract to describe calculative relations. As hitherto remarked, breach of contract is sometimes efficient, even in a commercial contract that is supported by perfect safeguards.[120] By contrast, betrayal of a personal trust can never be efficient. Betrayal is demoralizing.

[113] Robert Nozick, An Examined Life (1988), ch. 8, Love's Bond.

[114] *Id.* at 78.

[115] John Dunn, Trust and Political Agency, in Gambetta ed., *supra* note 1, at 73.

[116] *Id.* at 73.

[117] *Id.* at 74.

[118] *Id.* at 81.

[119] *Id.* at 85.

[120] Williamson, *supra* note 37.

Also, although I subscribe to the notion of economizing on trust, I would put the issue somewhat differently. Trust, I submit, should be concentrated on those personal relations in which it really matters, which will be facilitated by the use of "political, social, and economic institutions" to govern calculative relations.[121]

If calculativeness is inimical to personal trust, in that a deep and abiding trust relation cannot be created in the face of calculativeness, and if preexisting personal trust is devalued by calculativeness, then the question is how to segregate and preserve relations of personal trust.[122] I will take it that X reposes personal trust in Y if X (1) consciously refuses to monitor Y, (2) is predisposed to ascribe good intentions to Y when things go wrong, and (3) treats Y in a discrete structural way. Conditions 1 and 3 limit calculativeness. Under condition 2, "bad outcomes" are given a favorable construction: they are interpreted by X as stochastic events, or as complexity (Y didn't fully understand the situation), or as peccadillos (Y was inebriated).

To be sure, there are limits. An event where Y unambiguously violates the trust that X reposes in him threatens the relationship. Also (and here is where calculativeness creeps back in), a succession of minor violations may jeopardize the condition of trust. What further distinguishes personal trust, however, is that X insists that Y "reform" rather than merely "do better." That is because experience rating with continuous updating of the trustworthiness of Y places X in a calculative relation to Y. That degrades the relationship. Rather than do that, X elevates the relationship by placing it on all-or-none terms. Should Y refuse to make a discrete structural break with his past, then X will no longer trust him.[123] If instead Y agrees to reform, then trust will be renewed.

Personal trust is therefore characterized by (1) the absence of monitor-

[121] Dennis Robertson's remark is pertinent: "[I]f we economists mind our own business, and do that business well, we can, I believe, contribute mightily to the economizing, that is to the full but thrifty utilization, of that scarce resource Love—which *we* know, just as well as anybody else, to be the most precious thing in the world" (Dennis Robertson, What Does the Economist Economize? in Economic Commentaries 154 (1976)).

[122] There is nonetheless a sense in which incomplete contracts are continuously calculative, and that is in relation to reputation effects. If one party cannot make significant commercial moves without notice of the other—even moves that have no direct bearing on the immediate contract but involve different contracts with different trading partners—then continuous Bayesian updating may "ineluctably" obtain. In that event, reputation effects are pervasive (Kreps, *supra* note 55).

[123] That does not mean that X will no longer have anything to do with Y. If, however, the relation continues, X will thereafter treat Y in a calculative way.

Note in this connection that any shred of calculativeness does not imply that the relation is calculative. Rather, calculativeness needs to cross some (rather low) threshold before the relation is classified as calculative. The line is drawn—that is, a discrete structural break occurs—where X asks Y to reform.

ing, (2) favorable or forgiving predilections, and (3) discreteness. Such relations are clearly very special. Although some individuals may have the natural instincts to behave noncalculatively, others will need to figure it out—to look ahead and recognize that calculativeness will devalue the relation, which is a farsighted view of contract. It does not, moreover, suffice merely to figure it out, in that some of those who do may be unable to shed calculativeness—because calculativeness (or fear) is so deeply etched by their experience.[124] Be that as it may, trust, if it obtains at all, is reserved for very special relations between family, friends, and lovers. Such trust is also the stuff of which tragedy is made. It goes to the essence of the human condition.[125]

V. Concluding Remarks

A. *Linguistic and Conceptual Tools*

A case can be made, and I will assume here, that a science of organization is in progress.[126] The development of "specialized vocabularies" and "new languages" commonly attend such a project.[127]

The development of a science of administration,[128] which was Simon's objective in *Administrative Behavior,*[129] posed exactly those needs. Given the deep insights afforded by Chester Barnard's path-breaking book *The Functions of the Executive,*[130] how could that project be advanced? Simon observed in this connection that "we do not yet have, in this field, adequate linguistic and conceptual tools for realistically and significantly describing even a simple administrative organization—describing it, that is, in a way that will provide the basis for scientific analysis of the effectiveness of its structure and operation."[131] The need, as he saw it, was to

124 Joseph Raz makes a related argument: some people "fail to see that personal relations cannot be valued in terms of commodities" (Joseph Raz, The Morality of Freedom 353 (1986)).

125 See Nozick, *supra* note 113. Note that to repose trust in someone does not imply confidence in their judgment. Rather, as Dunn (*supra* note 115) has put it, to trust is to ascribe benign intent. Selective delegation is consistent with trust if the judgment of the trusted delegatee is believed to be better in some contexts than in others.

126 See Oliver E. Williamson, Chester Barnard and the Incipient Science of Organization, in Orgainzation Theory (Oliver Williamson ed. 1990); as well as Williamson, *supra* note 29; and the special issue on The New Science of Organization, 7 J. L. Econ. & Org. 1 (1991).

127 Thomas S. Kuhn, The Structure of Scientific Revolutions 203–4 (1970).

128 A science of organization deals with markets, hybrids, hierarchies, bureaucracies, and the like, whereas the science of administration is preoccupied with internal organization.

129 Simon, *supra* note 32, at 44, 248–53.

130 Barnard, *supra* note 35.

131 Simon, *supra* note 32, at xlv.

"be able to describe, in words, exactly how an administrative organization looks and how it works. . . . I have attempted to construct a vocabulary which will permit such a description."[132]

B. Calculativeness

The way in which human actors are described and the processes through which contracting is perceived to work are both crucial to the development of a science of organization. Human actors are described here as boundedly rational and opportunistic, while the contracting process entails "incomplete contracting in its entirety."[133] This last views the governance of contractual relations broadly, including an examination of the systems context within which contracts are embedded. A very calculative orientation to commercial contracting is the result.

Such a farsighted approach to contract (in which credible commitments, or the lack thereof, play a key role) collides with sociological views on power and trust. As James March has observed, power is a diffuse and disappointing concept.[134] I contend that the same is true of trust. The recent tendency for sociologists and economists alike to use the terms "trust" and "risk" interchangeably is, on the arguments advanced here, ill-advised.

Not only is "calculated trust" a contradiction in terms, but user-friendly terms, of which "trust" is one, have an additional cost. The world of commerce is reorganized in favor of the cynics, as against the innocents, when social scientists employ user-friendly language that is not descriptively accurate—since only the innocents are taken in. Commercial contracting will be better served if parties are cognizant of the embeddedness conditions of which they are a part and recognize, mitigate, and price out contractual hazards in a discriminating way.[135]

C. Categories of Trust

Without purporting to be exhaustive, trust differences of three types are distinguished: calculative trust, personal trust, and institutional (or hyphenated) trust. For the reasons given above, calculative relations should be described in calculative terms, to which the language of risk is

[132] *Id.*

[133] This phrase is my own.

[134] James G. March, Decisions and Organizations 6 (1988).

[135] This is not to deny the excesses of calculativeness that sociologists (for example, Merton, *supra* note 39) and contract law specialists (for example, Stewart Macauley, Noncontractual Relations in Business, 28 Am. Soc. Rev. 55 (1963)) have forcefully called to our attention. Transaction cost economics takes a farsighted view of contract in which "feasible" calculativeness is featured.

exactly suited. The practice of using "trust" and "risk" interchangeably should therefore be discontinued.

Personal trust is made nearly noncalculative by switching out of a regime in which the marginal calculus applies into one of a discrete structural kind. That often requires added effort and is warranted only for very special personal relations that would be seriously degraded if a calculative orientation were "permitted." Commercial relations do not qualify.[136]

Institutional trust refers to the social and organizational context within which contracts are embedded. In the degree to which the relevant institutional features are exogenous, institutional trust has the appearance of being noncalculative. In fact, however, transactions are always organized (governed) with reference to the institutional context (environment) of which they are a part. Calculativeness thus always reappears.[137]

Should these arguments prevail, trust will hereafter be reserved for noncalculative personal relations (and, possibly, in a hyphenated form, to describe differences in the institutional environment). Although this is a long article to reach such a modest result, the literature on trust is truly enormous, and the confusions associated with calculativeness are growing. The incipient science of organization needs common concepts and language as the productive dialogue between law, economics, and organization takes shape. The irony is that the limits on calculativeness are realized by examining user-friendly terms—of which "trust" is one—in a thoroughly calculative way.

[136] I subscribe to the proposition that "[t]he core idea of trust is that it is not based on an expectation of its justification. When trust is justified by expectations of positive reciprocal consequences, it is simply another version of economic exchange" (James March & Johan Olsen, Rediscovering Institutions 27 (1989)).

[137] Also, the parties to a transaction sometimes influence the context, the capture (Bernstein, *supra* note 94) or precapture (George Stigler, The Theory of Economic Regulation, 2 Bell J. Econ. 3 (1971)) of regulation being examples.

Trust, Opportunism and Governance: A Process and Control Model

Bart Nooteboom

Bart Nooteboom
School of Management and Organization, University of Groningen, The Netherlands

Abstract

In this paper a process and control model is developed for the analysis and design of inter-firm relations, in which both opportunism and trust play a role. Its aim is to develop a tool for the analysis, diagnosis and design of inter-firm partnerships. It takes into account the value of the partner, relative to alternatives, and the risk of the relation. Risk depends on the incentives that the partner may have towards opportunism, his opportunities for opportunism and his 'propensity' towards opportunism. The latter is related to trust. A partner's incentives towards opportunism depend on the uniqueness of the value that he offers, on one's own switching costs and on the partner's dependence on the relation. The underlying theory employs both transaction cost economics and social exchange theory. On the basis of the model, values and risks can be balanced in different ways: there are adversarial strategies that jeopardize value, and cooperative strategies that build value. The model can be used to explore viable sequences of strategies of governance, depending on different conditions. As an illustration, it is used for an analysis of ways to initiate a relation.

Descriptors: transaction cost economics, governance, trust, inter-firm alliances, inter-firm partnerships.

Introduction

The purpose of the present paper is to set up a process and control model for the analysis of the process of development of inter-firm relations, and the design of their control ('governance'), in which allowance is made for both opportunism and trust. This aligns with the conclusion by Smith Ring and Van de Ven (1994: 113) that:

> 'As the uncertainty, complexity, and duration of economic transactions within and between firms increase, it becomes increasingly important for scholars and managers to understand developmental processes of how equity, trust, conflict-resolution and procedures and internal governance structures emerge, evolve, and dissolve over time.'

As Joag (1995: 406) noted concerning vertical relations between suppliers and users:

Organization Studies
1996, 17/6
985–1010

01708406-99606
0017–0041 $3.00

'Even though marketing aims at understanding, explaining, predicting and influencing exchanges in human society (Bagozzi 1975; Dwyer et al. 1987), most research has been concentrated only on steps leading to choice . . . that end in the selection of suppliers (Webster and Wind 1972), thus leaving all processes beyond unmentioned.'

Taking such views into account, we focus on the process of development and governance after an exchange relation has been started. Transaction costs comprise costs of search and evaluation, costs of setting up governance prior to transactions and costs of control and redesign of the relation. Here, we focus on the third kind.

The question arises of how the present study fits in the growing literature on institutions, and in particular how it relates to transaction cost economics (TCE). TCE, as developed by Williamson (1975, 1985), has been called 'new institutionalist' economics, but shortcomings have been identified from a 'neo-institutionalist' perspective, which harks back to the older American institutionalists like Veblen, Commons and Mitchell (see, e.g. Johanson and Mattson 1987; Dietrich 1993; Foss 1993; Hodgson 1993; Nooteboom 1992, 1993b; Pitelis 1993, 1994). We position the present paper in terms of the differences between these schools of thought.

The 'new-institutionalism' of TCE maintains important parts of the core of neo-classical economics, while 'neo-institutionalist' economics includes perspectives from sociology. Some of the characteristic differences between the two schools are summarized in Table 1. Emboldened material in the table indicates the perspective of the present paper, and shows that it goes beyond traditional perspectives of mainstream economics, into the neo-institutionalist branch.

We aim to develop a model for studying the process of developing institutional arrangements between firms, which takes into account the possibility of trust next to the possibility of opportunism, allowing for the possibility that the relations between the firms may get locked into

Table 1
New and Neo-institutionalist Economics

Neo-institutionalism	New Institutionalism
Emphasis on explanation of the institutional environment (norms, habits)	**Emphasis on institutional arrangements** (governance between and within firms)
Homo socialis; methodological interactionism	*Homo economicus*; methodological individualism
Trust may build up	Opportunism prevails; trust is an irrelevant category
Emphasis on process	Emphasis on outcomes
There is path dependency, which may yield inefficient outcomes	Evolutionary pressures guarantee convergence on efficient outcomes
Preference formation and learning are inherent to the process	Preferences and knowledge are given

Cf. Nooteboom (1992), Groenewegen and Vromen (1995).

efficient or inefficient paths. It should yield a tool to explore balances and imbalances of dependence between parties, mixes of trust and opportunism, and of formal and informal forms of governance. It should also serve to identify instruments for governance, and to select them in relation to events that might trigger action. The ultimate objective, beyond the present paper, is to employ the model as a basis for simulation studies of the evolution of relations, and for applications of game theory in the analysis of governance. For the use of game theory in an attempt to reconstruct different generic forms of supplier–user relations ('Western, Japanese and a third way'), see Nooteboom (1994).

In contrast with TCE, we accept the relevance of sociological categories such as trust, power, social cohesion and social exchange, but we also acknowledge possible inclinations towards opportunism, and we preserve notions concerning governance from TCE.

In game-theoretic terms, this paper does not take the perspective of cooperative games, in the usual sense employed in the literature, that agreements are assumed to be binding from the start. The challenge is to show *how* agreements can be made binding; how cooperation can be achieved in spite of opportunities and possible inclinations towards opportunism. So, we are oriented towards cooperation as something to be explained rather than assumed (cf. Hargreaves et al. 1995: 38).

The basic analysis, in the present paper, is applicable to relations in general, including both horizontal relations between competitors and vertical relations of subcontracting, or even entirely different relations, such as marriages, but subcontracting forms the main intended area of application.

Trust and Opportunism

Transactions are to be seen as being embedded in relations that develop in time, while these relations in turn are socially embedded in their environment (Granovetter 1985). It is a peculiar thing in TCE that, on the one hand, passage of time is crucial, but on the other, relevant parameters are seen as timeless. According to TCE, a crucial condition for dependence is that time is required, with repeated transactions, to recoup transaction-specific investments, and allowance is made for the emergence of unpredictable contingencies that preclude closed contracts. On the other hand, TCE implicitly assumes the continuation of *ex ante* inability to judge propensities towards opportunism, unchanged supply and demand conditions (in which no novel and perhaps more attractive customers or suppliers appear on the scene), productive competencies and abilities to monitor partner's actions. But surely, ongoing interaction will modify those parameters? It is reasonable to say that prior to transaction one is uncertain about the partner's potential opportunism, and hence should take opportunism into account. Once one takes time into account, in ongoing transactions, it is unreasonable to ignore the formation of perceptions about propensities towards opportunism, and the possibility of building trust.

In spite of Williamson's acknowledgement of 'atmosphere' as a relevant factor in transactions, he neglects issues of trust and power. The view of the present paper is that these issues are important, and that a dynamic treatment of ongoing relations allows for the building of trust. To study this, we need contributions from sociology and anthropology on trust and social exchange (Homans 1961; Blau 1964; Luhmann 1979, 1988; Granovetter 1982, 1985; Gambetta 1988a).

The view that transactions are embedded in relations that develop in time has been advocated for a number of years in marketing and purchasing by the International Marketing and Purchasing Group (IMP; Hakansson 1982, 1987; Hagg and Johanson 1983; Easton 1989) and others (Jarillo 1988; Semlinger 1991; Lamming 1993). Exchange leads to mutual adaptation, which entails investment in a relation. As a result of this, bonding between the actors develops, trust is generated and a lasting relation emerges (Johanson and Mattson 1987, Easton 1989). A comparable attempt towards a process approach was recently published by Smith Ring and Van de Ven (1994).

However, if the IMP view can be taken to imply a rejection of the TCE view as a whole, it runs the risk of throwing away the baby with the bathwater. Doubtless, in present conditions of turbulence, firms require interactions in networks. Trust forms an important dimension in such relations, and, as pointed out by Hirschmann (1984), trust may increase with its usage. However, there are risks as well: trust is not unbounded, it cannot be taken for granted and it may break down. As Dasgupta (1988: 54) put it: 'If the incentives are right a trustworthy (untrustworthy) person may be relied upon to be untrustworthy (trustworthy)'. 'Golden opportunities' of defection are tempting, even to the trustworthy.

TCE has contributed greatly by specifying rigorously what the nature and extent of risk in transactions is: *to the extent that* agents are inclined towards opportunism, and if bounded rationality makes it impossible to foresee it and to foreclose its undesirable consequences, then one runs the risk of loss of investment to the extent that investments are relation specific, or of 'hold-up' situations as a consequence of that risk. Next, TCE has supplied indications of how to construct schemes for 'governing' transactions in such a way that risks are reduced: in bilateral private ordering, the use of different guarantees to compensate for one-sided, transaction-specific investments (symmetrical specific investments, cross-ownership of specific assets, hostages, guaranteed price, volume or period of purchase), and countermeasures to guard against invalid use and expropriation of such guarantees. In infrequent transactions: trilateral governance, with some third party acting as an arbitrator. These concepts are of theoretical and practical use, and it is unwise to ignore them.

Transaction on the basis of trust, with its implicit, pre-existing and unspecified conditions for cooperation, economizes on the specification and monitoring of contracts and material incentives for cooperation. This makes it not only cheaper (and to the taste of many, also more agreeable), but also makes for greater flexibility. With detailed formal contracts it is more difficult (slow and costly) to modify terms for changed conditions. Apart from its own worth, trust pays, but it also carries a risk of betrayal. One cannot simply buy into trust. If it is not already in place prior to transaction, trust has to be built up. It is as much the result of cooperation as a condition for it. All one can do is to select conditions that are conducive to the emergence of trust, such as placing not too much focus on mistrustful means of governance.

It is a long-standing argument in economics that optimal behaviour prevails among firms, not because agents are calculatively competent, but because the pressures of selection in markets extinguish sub-optimal behaviour, either because it loses its resources for survival to agents with more optimal conduct, or because it turns around to emulate more optimal conduct. It is, in fact, questionable whether this mechanism is indeed always so rigorous as to allow only the 'single exit' (Latsis 1980) of optimal behaviour. There may be slack due to lack of competition, due to mono- or oligopoly and lack of contestability of markets, or due to product differentiation. But that is not an issue we will discuss here.

The argument also appears in transaction cost economics (TCE). Williamson (1975, 1985) argued that among alternative governance structures (market, 'hierarchy', forms 'between market and hierarchy') one will survive which is optimal, i.e. minimizes the sum of production, transaction and organization costs, in a given technological and institutional environment. The argument was carried further by Hill (1990). He argued that since trust economizes on the cost of governance, the selection pressures of markets will lead to the prevalence of trust, so that 'in the long run' we can forget about opportunism.

However, the argument is flawed in the same way as, more often, arguments for group selection are flawed: it neglects the tension between collective and individual interest. While it is clearly in the interest of a group as a whole for everyone to be trustworthy and trusting, since that would greatly reduce transaction costs for all, individuals may be tempted to defect and be opportunistic while pretending to be trustworthy. The extent of this temptation increases as more people are trustworthy, and it further depends on the efficiency and reliability by which such defection can be detected and communicated, and the ensuing risk of a loss of reputation that is detrimental to future partnerships.

Nooteboom (1995) developed a model to analyse the issue. It is concluded that even if loss of reputation becomes infinitely costly, there still arises some non-zero equilibrium value of the percentage of opportunistic agents. If we allow only for self-interest, opportunism will not disappear, and Williamson remains correct on this, if not on other points: there is always a chance that a transaction partner may be opportunistic. Nevertheless, it helps considerably if, next to self-interest, there are other sources of cooperation in the institutional environment in which firms are embedded. Norms and values of conduct may mitigate inclinations towards opportunism; they may cause people to forego opportunities for opportunism, at least within reasonable bounds (short of 'golden opportunities' that are too tempting to resist). Here, Hill's (1990) argument carries conviction: societies with such institutional mitigation of opportunism have a competitive advantage over societies that do not, and they may thereby have a better chance of surviving in world markets.

We conclude that both trust and opportunism are likely to arise in transaction relations. Neither should be ignored, and we should find a way of systematically exploring their joint occurrence. Therefore, in spite of the differences between economics and sociology, we should seek to integrate them.

Dimensions of Trust

The concept of trust is subtle, diffuse and elusive. One feels some sympathy for the economist's inclination to evade the issue, but we cannot afford to do that. Here, I try to employ the concept with all the subtleties found for it in the literature (Gambetta 1988a).

Since our focus is on relations between organizations, the question arises as to what the relation is between the conduct of individuals and the conduct of firms: the 'micro–micro' problem. As argued by Smith Ring and Van de Ven (1994), these two sets of conduct are related by roles to which individuals are assigned in organizations. Conduct '*qua persona*' is restricted and guided by organizational roles and alignment between the two can be a problem. If cooperation is founded on trust based on personal bonding, problems may arise concerning the exigencies of organizational role. Personal loyalty may deviate from organizational interest, and may even lead to corruption or embezzlement. Too strong personal ties may need to be prevented by turnover of personnel across roles. Conversely, personnel change may lead to a breakdown of relations based on personal trust. Such considerations should be part of governance.

Trust may concern a partner's *ability* to perform according to agreements (competence trust), or his *intentions* to do so (goodwill trust). Here, we focus on the latter type of trust. Of course, risks due to failures of competence are important in subcontracting relations, but they do not form the focus here. The focus is on the relations between goodwill trust and cooperation. Whenever we use the term 'trust', this denotes goodwill trust.

According to Williams (1988), cooperation requires willingness to accept dependence, which requires assurance that other, non-dependent (or less dependent) parties will not defect in the cooperation. According to Dasgupta (1988), trust is associated with expectations regarding the other's choice of actions that have a bearing on one's own choice of action. Such expectations may have a strong or a weak basis, ranging from assurance from objective facts and logical reason, through belief which is less firmly based on experience and argument, to unsubstantiated faith. Gambetta (1988b: 217) summarized different views on trust as the subjective probability that one assigns to action by another agent (or group of agents) which affects one's own action. Luhmann (1988) emphasized that in trust there is an element of choice. If there is no choice, and one simply has to surrender to the powers that be, the belief that no harm will occur is a matter of confidence, not trust. Trust entails an action that one has a choice to conduct, and that one may later regret. One may or may not trust a potential business partner, and accept or refuse him as a partner. If it goes wrong, one attributes blame also to oneself for engaging in the relation. One has confidence or not in the law, or the political system, or God, without a choice as to whether or not to participate in them. If one is treated unjustly, the blame is on the system; not one's own choice.

Williams (1988) distinguished between macro and micro, and between egotistic and non-egotistic sources of cooperation. Micro sources depend on the specific relation at hand, while macro sources apply more generally. This yields four sources of cooperation, as indicated in Table 2.

Table 2
Sources of Cooperation

	Macro	Micro
Egotistic	Coercion or fear of sanctions from authority (God, law)	Material advantage or 'interest'
Non-egotistic	Ethics: values/norms of proper conduct	Bonds of friendship, kinship or empathy

Williams argued that none of these sources suffices by itself, and that in cooperation some mix will always be operative, while no universally best mix, regardless of specific conditions, can be specified. As set out by Gambetta (1988b), the Mafia employs all four sources, in ways that mutually reinforce each other. Cooperation is forced by violent means, is materially rewarded, is enhanced by bonds of friendship and pseudo family relationships (Mafia 'families', brotherhood, godfathers, etc.) and an ethic of non-betrayal ('*omerta*').

If trust is associated with a subjective probability that a partner will not misuse one's dependence, without further qualifications, then anything that contributes to such subjective probability would belong to trust. However, trust is generally not associated with motives of self-interest; at least not self-interest in a restricted material, economic sense.

We trust someone if he is likely to cooperate, even if he is not coerced to do so and has no direct material interest in doing so. Thus, trust is associated with the non-egotistic sources of cooperation; with loyalty to a partner due to ethics or bonds of friendship or kinship rather than coercion or material self-interest. The Mafia needs to employ coercion and the lure of material interest because trust will not suffice as a basis for cooperation. Conversely, material self-interest and coercion are seldom sufficient as a basis for cooperation; one needs trust to the extent that one cannot fully control the partner's conduct by threat and reward (cf. Deutsch 1962, quoted in Zand 1972).

One can object that the narrower concept of trust, when based on ties of ethics or kinship, is not really beyond self-interest, because they constitute social coercion rather than choice. In friendship or, more weakly, in relations of empathy or familiarity, trust in the sense of non-obligational and non-material sources of cooperation appears to be most 'thick'. But even there, one can argue that it is based on self-interest, in the form of the 'emotional utility' derived from it. One could argue, therefore, as economists do, that in the last analysis, motivation on the basis of norms, bonding, social exchange, kinship, friendship or whatever, is also egotistic. In fact, anything that anyone does can be interpreted as 'revealed preference'. One objection to this view is that it has made itself unfalsifiable, but there are two other objections.

The first objection is taken from social exchange theory (Blau 1964). In addition to an economic dimension (extrinsic utility), exchange often has a social dimension (intrinsic utility). Economists tend to think of value in exchange as something that exists independently from the transaction. As formulated by Murakami and Rohlen (1992: 70); 'The value of the relationship itself is typically ignored and the impersonality of the transaction is assumed'. In intrinsic utility, the exchange process itself matters, in addition to the economic surplus and its division that the exchange yields. People may *prefer* to transact on the basis of trust and its concomitants of ethics, kinship, friendship or empathy. Social exchange relies more on unspecified, implicit obligations, which depend on shared systems of meaning, belief and ethics. The idea that exchange includes non-contractual elements, of course, goes back (at least) to Durkheim (1893). The economist will answer that there are apparently two dimensions of utility (extrinsic and intrinsic), and if one prefers to transact with party *X* in spite of higher extrinsic returns from a transaction with party *Y*, apparently intrinsic utility dominates extrinsic utility, but self-interest as a driver of conduct remains in the seat. Be that as it may, the point is that economists tend to neglect intrinsic utility and its implication that it does matter who the transaction partner is. What matters is that personality and social embeddedness enter as dimensions of transactions.

The second, more general, objection is that there is often tension between private material interest (monetary gain) and interest in ethical norms, social cohesion, kinship, friendship and the like. There is a real issue of sacrificing one for the sake of the other. This goes beyond material interest in the form of maintaining reputation as a basis for future material benefit. One should include in one's investigation how these conflicts are resolved, and how one dimension may mitigate the effect of the other. How opportunism may be mitigated by trust, and how loyalty may be broken by some 'golden opportunity' to defect.

Trustworthiness varies between agents. It is to some extent personal, in bonds of kinship and friendship, but also to some extent impersonal, when a person observes a given ethic or set of behavioural routines. When the agent is a firm, its trustworthiness is associated with ethics and behavioural routines, which are part of an organization's culture. Again, firm and individual are connected by organizational roles, and again, the alignment between a person *qua persona* and his organizational role may not be perfect. That depends, among other things, on the care in role allocation and discipline in role observance that the firm exercises. Variability of trustworthiness, and hence of its opposite propensity towards opportunism, underlines the need to extend TCE with considerations of trust. If not, everyone is equally opportunistic; then, in the selection of a partner and in governing a relation with him, one should try to establish his particular propensity towards opportunism (cf. Noorderhaven 1995).

Social exchange, by its nature, is restricted to insiders: people with whom one shares the basis for trust. Trust requires familiarity and mutual understanding, and hence depends on time and context.

Definition of Trust

On the basis of the above, we adopt the following conceptualization:

X is willing to engage in cooperation with *Y* (i.e. enter upon cooperation or continue it), even if it makes *X* dependent, if *X* has a more or less well-grounded belief, in the form of a subjective probability, that *Y* will cooperate in the sense of not mis-using such dependence. This belief may be based on (perceived) available **opportunities** for misuse on the part of *Y*, *Y*'s **incentives** towards misuse and *Y*'s **propensity** to employ the opportunities. Propensity to use opportunities for defection is related to trust, which has its basis in ethics, kinship, friendship or empathy.

My **definition of (goodwill) trust** would now be as follows:

X trusts *Y* to the extent that X chooses to cooperate with *Y* on the basis of a subjective probability that *Y* will choose not to employ opportunities for defection that *X* considers damaging, even if it is in the interest of *Y* to do so. The trustworthiness of *Y* depends on *Y*'s true propensity to employ those opportunities. (1)

Note that (1) indicates that:

- *X* and *Y* have a choice: to engage upon cooperation, at the risk of dependence (*X*), and to forego opportunities to misuse such dependence (*Y*). This distinguishes trust from confidence.

– there are two mutually dependent types of choice: a choice of whether to enter upon a relation of cooperation and to continue with it, and a choice of whether or not to misuse dependence of one's partner in the relation (called 'defection')
– the second type of choice (defection) is based on a combination of opportunities for defection, interest in defection and propensity not to employ opportunities for defection
– trust relates to the last factor: the partner's choice not to defect in spite of both a motive and an opportunity to do so
– trust is related to a propensity, not a certainty: it may not be resistant to golden opportunities.

Defection is closely related to the concept of opportunism, as employed in TCE: 'interest seeking with guile', and to make the connection with TCE we will equate the two. Thus, we will speak of 'opportunities for opportunism', and the 'propensity' to employ them. We may define power as opportunities to act against someone's interest in a way that he cannot control. Then power is close to opportunities for opportunism. Trust is then associated with the voluntary submission to power, on the belief that it will not be exercised.

In the case of an organization, the subjective probability associated with trust depends on an assessment of: the ethical stance and routines that form part of the culture of the firm, the 'tightness' with which individuals are tied to it in their organizational roles, relevant characteristics of the individual one is dealing with (his personal ethics, bonding) and the net effect on his propensity towards opportunism.

Now, is reputation a basis for trust, or is it part of interest? It can be either or both. In economics, the rationale for reputation is that it is built upon investments in the form of opportunities for opportunism foregone. To behave opportunistically is to surrender the investment, if opportunism is both detected and communicated at large, and this yields a rational basis for people to rely on reputation, at least to some extent (reputation may be surrendered when a 'golden opportunity' presents itself). A complication is that reputation may be based on the rational calculation of its benefit, as indicated, but may also be based on genuine trustworthiness in the sense of a non-egotistic propensity to forego opportunities for opportunism (on the basis of ethics, kinship, friendship, empathy). While both may be sensitive to temptation, trustworthiness is more robust than calculation. It is less sensitive to the condition of detectability and communicability of a breach, and is less likely to unravel when the end of a relation is in sight. The difference may not be easy to establish: that may require some minimum degree of experience and familiarity with a partner, or joint membership of a social community with sufficiently strong norms and values of cooperation.

In our study there are two fundamental questions:

A. On the basis of what motives will agents enter upon and maintain a relation?

B. How will agents act and react within that relation? They may be jockeying for advantage, short of breaking up the relation. This question can be broken down into two questions:
   B1. How do agents behave in a relation, i.e. in a setting with given parameters of the relation? For example: when will they act opportunistically?
   B2. How do they behave in trying to change the relation, i.e. change the parameters of the relation? For example: how can they balance risk and value?

The answer to question A seems simple: people engage upon a relation because it yields value, which may have many (extrinsic and intrinsic) dimensions. In this paper we focus on question B. We consider question B1 in the next section, and question B2 in the one after that.

Model of Conduct

Relations of cooperation are incurred from an expectation of value. Thus, the value to *X* of a partner *Y* (*VYX*) is a key variable. Here, it is specified as value relative to the next best alternative, which becomes negative when a more attractive partner presents himself. This allows for the event of a more attractive alternative partner emerging on the scene, and the analysis of its consequences for the relation.

This concept of the value of a partner in relative terms (excess value with respect to the next best alternative) is not present, at least not explicitly, in TCE. TCE, as developed by Williamson, assumes that for contracting out, there is a specialized supplier who offers value in terms of an ability to produce more efficiently, because he produces in larger volumes for more than one user. The search for a focal user, and the evaluation of such a partner's worth, is not part of the analysis (in contrast with Coase, who does pay attention to transaction costs in the form of search). One could perhaps argue that, implicitly, such an evaluation is nevertheless present in Williamsonian TCE, in the possibility of new contingencies ('external uncertainty'), that may arise which a partner might exploit opportunistically. However that may be, we need to make it explicit, for two reasons. First, to deal with the risk that a relation will become destabilized due to the emergence of a novel, more attractive alternative for one of the partners. Second, to allow for investments for the increase of value, on either or both sides of the relation. Both are part of the project of making TCE dynamic, by looking at the evolution of relations in the light of changing conditions, learning, etc.

Value may include many dimensions, such as: efficiency, developmental capability, flexibility, adherence to specifications, network position, value as a source of learning, international presence, continuity. It has been suggested by a reviewer that there is redundancy here: that value *of the partner to you* and *your switching costs* can be collapsed into a single variable from the beginning. However, analytically, it is useful to maintain the distinction. First of all, switching costs are related to specific investments that *cause* value. Second, they primarily contribute to one's *own value to the partner*, rather than his value for you. Value also includes competence trust: an assessment of the partner's capability to perform and to achieve goals of quality, service, delivery time, knowledge transfer, payment, etc.

Value is assessed not only in the present, but also on the basis of potential for the future. This is taken to imply some assessment of the probability that the relation will proceed in the future. As is well known from repeated games (Axelrod 1984), this is crucial: a rational decision to defect opportunistically is then based on a trade-off between advantage now and possible loss of value from an ongoing relation in the future. In particular, opportunism affects perceived probabilities of an ongoing relation. Renunciation of opportunities for opportunism will enhance trust. This may contribute directly to value by increasing intrinsic value, and indirectly by increasing perceived probabilities of an ongoing relation.

The other side of the coin is risk, due to dependence, and as a result of that: the size of damage that the partner may do, and the probability that he will do it:

$$LOX = SLX \times PRLX \tag{2}$$

where: LOX = possible loss for X; SLX = size of the loss for X; PLX = probability of loss for X.

The damage may consist of several things:

- Loss of extrinsic value, in the economic surplus from the exchange (due to neglect or accident). This may include disasters, with a cost that exceeds (one's share in) the value of the surplus.
- Redistribution of the economic surplus (due to opportunism).
- Damage due to a break of the relation (which may be non-intentional, e.g. when the partner goes bankrupt).
- Loss due to spill-over of proprietary information.
- Loss of intrinsic value.

Spill-over of sensitive information to competitors, via the partner, is a risk to the extent that knowledge is transferred, but while the relation lasts, the partner has an interest in preventing it. The risk is particularly high if the relation is broken opportunistically; on purpose rather than by accident. In fact, sensitive information may be treated as a 'hostage'.

The loss for X due to a break of the relation equals switching costs (SWX) plus the relative value of the partner Y (VYX). The cost of breakage determines dependence on cooperation in the sense of the 'captiveness' of X ($CAPX$): damage due to the redistribution of surplus cannot systematically exceed the damage due to a break of the relation, because if it did, X would be likely to break the relation. Disasters, however, could exceed that limit. Like the accidental damage of breakage, they are associated with competence trust rather than goodwill trust.

Switching costs (*SWX*) include the costs associated with specific investments that are typical of TCE: e.g. specific investments that one has oneself incurred; guarantees given to cover the risk of specific investments by the partner; the value to *X* of hostages supplied, etc.

If we look only at goodwill trust and ignore disasters, risk depends wholly on the possibility of opportunism. In formula:

$$SLX < CAPX = SWX + VYX \quad (3)$$

The probability of damage to (*PLX*) then equals the probability of opportunism by *Y*, and depends on:

- incentives towards opportunism by *Y* (*IOY*)
- opportunities for opportunism by *Y* (*OOY*)
- propensity towards opportunism by *Y* (inverse of trustworthiness — *POY*). (4)

Here, we recognize the sources of cooperation from Table 2.

Each of the above form a necessary condition for opportunistic acts, which is expressed by the following multiplicative specification:

$$PLX = IOY \times OOY \times POY \quad (5)$$

where: *IOY*, *OOY* and *POY* are normalized to take values between 0 and 1 — $OOY = 0$ for a closed contract and =1 for the absence of any formal constraints on action; *POY* is the probability that *Y* will utilize opportunities for opportunism.

There is similarity here to the notion in TCE that there are transaction costs only if there are specific assets *and* there is bounded rationality *and* there is opportunism. As we shall argue, specific assets yield switching costs and hence captivity and hence an incentive to opportunism; bounded rationality precludes closed contracts with perfect monitoring and thereby opens opportunities for opportunism; the possibility of opportunistic conduct is here reconstructed as 'propensity towards opportunism'.

Incentives towards opportunism (*IOY*) belong to the dimension of interest as a source of cooperation (Table 2), and are associated with what in TCE is called 'private ordering' or 'relational contracting'. It depends on the captiveness of *X* (*CAPX*), and hence on the value of *Y* to *X* and on switching costs. The first depends on the degree to which *Y* has adapted to the specific demands of *X*, which is likely to yield specific assets (but not necessarily — flexible production technology allows for specific products with non-specific assets, see Nooteboom 1993c), and the latter on how the risks of specific investments are distributed, for example, by cross-ownership or guarantees, exchange of hostages, etc. The incentive for *Y* also depends on pressures from competition or owners/shareholders on *Y* to utilize opportunities for short-term profit or saving.

> An earlier prototype of the model was discussed with representatives from several industries. One was the automobile industry, at a time of declining sales (1993), which yielded great competitive pressure, and consequently high pressure on suppliers. Here, our ideas concerning the role of trust met with scepsis bordering on ridicule: trust was something they could not afford to build on. Other representatives were from the firm that has a monopoly in the exploration and production of natural gas. They balked at our discussion of potential opportunism: they had easy, amicable, generous relations with their suppliers. Unlike the automobile industry, they could easily afford to.

Y's incentives towards opportunism also depend on the extent to which *Y* perceives himself to be dependent on *X*: if *Y* is more dependent on *X* than vice versa, it is in *Y*'s interest to be careful about opportunism. *Y* should also take into account the effect that opportunistic action may have on the intrinsic value of the relation and on perceived probabilities of an ongoing relation, and hence future value and particularly if he takes into account the possible retaliation by *X*, which may yield a downward spiral of mutual retaliation. *Y* should take into account the risk of breakdown of the relation, yielding complete loss of the relative value of his partner, switching costs, loss of hostages, spill-over to competitors.

Note that this part of our model (*IOY*) incorporates what is studied in game-theoretic studies of the *outcomes* of interaction, except that here we set up a framework for reproducing the *process* of strategic interaction. The literature (Axelrod 1984) demonstrates that there is an infinite number of equilibria in the repeated prisoner dilemma game. Rather than taking any of these for granted, we want to reproduce the emergence of sequences of choices and their effects on further choices.

Opportunities for opportunism (*OOY*) belong to the source of coercion (Table 2), by contractual, legally enforceable restrictions on *Y*'s conduct, or what in TCE is called 'legal ordering'. As recognized in TCE, they also depend on the occurrence of unforeseen contingencies ('external uncertainty'), which arise to the extent that the environment is volatile (shifts in technologies or markets, for example). They also depend on *X*'s ability to monitor *Y*'s actions ('asymmetric information'), and on *Y*'s competence to utilize the opportunities. In connection with this, they are also related to firm size: due to a greater spread of activities over more products and wider markets, larger firms have more diversified partnerships and thereby are better able to spread risk and cross-subsidize activities (Nooteboom 1993a).

Propensity towards opportunism belongs to the category of trust: norms/values, ethics, customs and bonds of kinship or friendship. Trust tends to grow as the relation proceeds successfully, because bonds of empathy may get stronger, or because habituation occurs. The setting up of a

Figure 1 Determinants of Risk of Opportunism for X

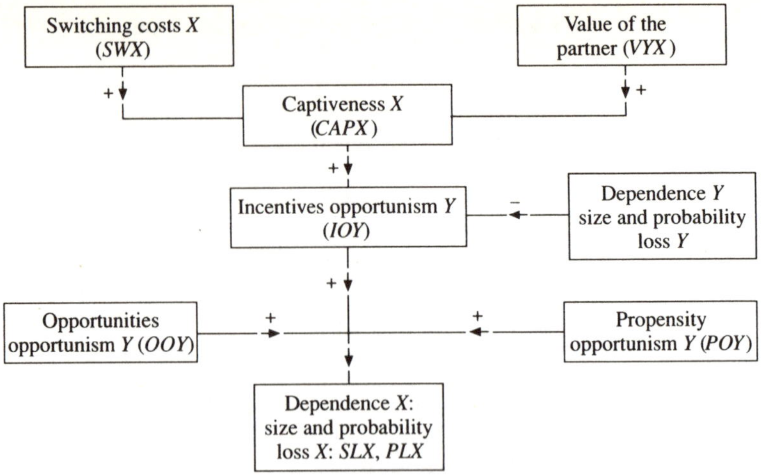

common cognitive base (getting to know who is who in each other's organizations, mutual understanding, development of procedures and routines) can be seen as mutual specific investments.

The results so far are illustrated in Figure 1. Note that through the basic variables in Figure 1, opportunism may be triggered or lessened by external events (not created by the partners), such as (the list is not exhaustive):

- emergence of a new potential partner for *X*, lessening the relative value of *Y* (*VYX*), and possibly reducing switching costs for *X* (*SWX*), thereby reducing the captiveness of *X*
- some unexpected situation presents a novel opportunity for *Y* to exercise opportunism (*OOY*)
- the information *X* has for monitoring changes, perhaps due to a change of technology (*OOY*)
- a change of law or regulation affects opportunities for opportunism (*OOY*)
- appearance of a novel competitor puts pressure on *Y* to utilize opportunities for opportunism (*IOY*)
- *Y* is taken over by a more or a less aggressive firm or the contacts of *X* at *Y* are replaced (*POY*).

Note also that the arrows from *IOY*, *OOY* and *POY* intersect, rather than going directly to the outcome of opportunistic conduct. This is designed to reflect the possibility of interaction effects. A large value of *X*'s captivity (*CAPX*) determines the gain that *Y* may take from opportunism ['golden opportunity', see (3)], and this may affect his incentive to grasp the opportunity (*IOY*). The incentive interacts with propensity towards opportunism (*POY*), in that it may exceed the boundaries of *Y*'s trustworthiness. If *X* seeks to restrict *Y*'s opportunities by detailed legal contracts and close monitoring (*OOY* ↓), this may antagonize trust and *Y*'s propensity to opportunism may increase (*POY* ↑). Restrictions on *Y*'s conduct signal to *Y* that *X* has no trust, which may suggest to *Y* that *X* himself is not trustworthy, so that *Y* is more inclined to take countermeasures of limiting *X*'s actions. Thus, we may arrive at a cycle of mutual limitation and breakdown of trust.

This scheme has been tested in empirical research (Berger et al. 1995; Nooteboom et al. 1995), and has been used for preliminary attempts to diagnose buyer–supplier relations in practice. The empirical research was aimed at testing the model on the basis of surveys. Psychometric techniques were used for measuring variables, and these were fed into econometric models to test hypotheses derived from Figure 1. The first study (Berger et al. 1995) involved a survey of 80 suppliers to a producer of state-of-the-art photocopying machines. The second (Nooteboom et al. 1995) involved 10 customer relations each for 10 suppliers of sub-assemblies to end-producers of electrical/electronic apparatus. Examples of the exploratory use of the model in practice will be discussed in the text. Below is an illustration.

> Analysis of the relation between a supplier of hard/software (*Y*) to a consortium of firms that develop worldwide telecom services (*X*) showed that the buyer was extremely dependent on the supplier: it was their single supplier (in our model: causing high *VYX*), and switching costs (*SWX*) were extremely high, thus yielding high captivity (*CAPX*). On the other hand, the supplier had multiple customers, suggesting a modest relative value of the buyer (*VXY*), faced limited switching costs (*SWY*), thus yielding low captivity (*CAPY*). This suggested a danger of one-sided dependence of the buyer, in terms of the size of the possible loss (*SLX*). The buyer recognised this, and was contemplating a switch to dual suppliership, in spite of the enormous duplication of costs involved. On the basis of the model, we found that, nevertheless, dependence was balanced in that the buyer supplied such a unique opportunity for the supplier to penetrate fast-growing world markets in telecom that the supplier would have absolutely no interest in exploiting the one-sided dependence of the buyer (low incentive *IOY*) and, furthermore, was large enough not to run the risk of default. As a result, the extent and size of possible loss to the buyer (*SLX*) was compensated by a low probability (*PLX*). The buyer decided not to go for dual sourcing, for the time being.

Model of Governance

So far, we have considered the implications of given parameter values in the relation. Now we turn to the possibilities of control by modifying the parameters. Figure 1 applies to both sides of a relation, as illustrated in Figure 2. For governance (control), we must add a control loop, whereby partners can redesign the relationship to lessen dependence. This yields actions which constitute events that are internal to the relation, and may call forth reactions by the other side, and so on, perhaps until some equilibrium arises, possibly in the nature of a Nash equilibrium. In Figure 2, single lines indicate effects of parameters; double

Figure 2
Interaction between *X* and *Y*

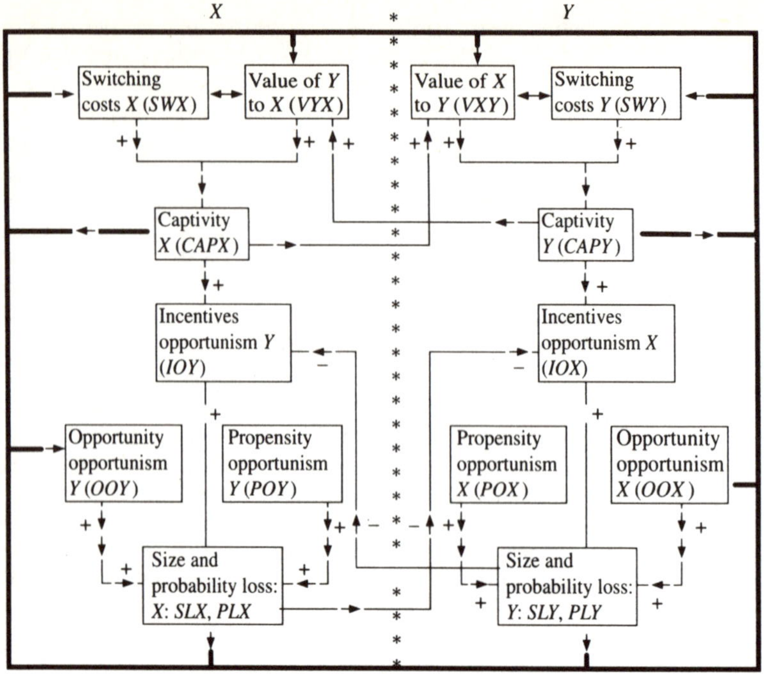

lines in the control loop indicate governance by change of parameters. Note that we include the (negative) effect of one's own perceived dependence on one's incentives towards opportunism. Trust-related variables, such as ethics, habituation and bonding determine the propensity towards opportunism. We again take an illustration from practice.

> In a relation between a supplier of specialty chemicals (*Y*) to a producer of semi-conductors (*X*), there appeared to be extreme captiveness of the buyer (single supply, yielding high *VYX*, and high investments dedicated to receiving the specific products and services from the supplier, yielding high *SWX*). The supplier, on the other hand, had many alternative customers (ostensibly yielding modest *VXY*)and limited switching costs (*SWY*), due to limited specific investments. On further inspection, *VXY* turned out to be higher, since the buyer was yielding the supplier access and prestige in a vital growth market. This might yield balance of dependence, but it seemed to be wearing off: the supplier seemed to have learned most of what there was to learn, and was already cashing in on the prestige. Meanwhile, the dependence of the buyer was only increasing, with an ostensible increase of both size and probability of loss (*SLX*, *PLX*). On the other hand, the relation was characterized by extreme openness. In our analysis we conducted interviews at both sides, with a proposal for holding answers to certain potentially sensitive questions secret from the other side, but this offer was rejected by both sides. We were encouraged

to present our analysis, including opportunities for opportunism, etc., without holding anything back, in a meeting with representatives from both sides. Both sides acknowledged that our analysis was valid, and they would certainly use that kind of thinking in other relations, but in this particular relation there was no need, because 'both sides fully trusted each other'. The relation had developed over a protracted period of time, with great mutual benefit, and strong bonding and social exchange had developed. Thus, there seemed to be a very low propensity towards opportunism on both sides (low *POY* and *POX*), which also appeared to reduce the probability of loss for the buyer. Yet, we felt more confident when we heard that the next stage in the development of the relation involved a much higher level of specific investments (notably high location specificity) on the part of the supplier (yielding higher *SWY*).

Figure 2 shows that if one is concerned about risk, there are two basic options for redesign of the relation:

Modify the causative parameters of risk for X *in Figure 2*:
VYX = value of the partner. Lessen dependence by decreasing the value of the partner, by developing alternatives (remember that value is relative to the next best alternative).
SWX = one's switching costs. This can be changed by reducing the specificity of investments, or of the underlying technology; demanding more guarantees; redistributing their ownership; changing guarantees given to the partner; adding or retracting hostages, etc.
OOY = the partner's opportunities for opportunism. This can be changed by changing contractual terms or one's capacity for monitoring, or by trying to stabilize the environment that generates unforeseen contingencies.
IOY = the partner's incentives towards opportunism. This can be reduced above all by increasing his perceived dependence. We return to this later.
POY = the partner's propensity towards opportunism. This is the most difficult to change directly: it is dependent on the growth of trust in time, which one can try to affect by building friendship or empathy, and trying to develop further joint ethics, procedures or routines.

One can also modify the parameters in the scheme that structures risk for one's partner *Y*, in the mirror image of Figure 2. There, *SLY* indicates the size of the loss for *Y* due to opportunism by *X*, and *PLY* its probability.

Modify the causative parameters affecting partner Y*'s risk*:
VXY = one's value to the partner. This can be increased, by investing in one's capabilities, or by eliminating alternatives for the partner (remember that one's value is relative to *Y*'s alternative partners).
SWY = the partner's switching costs. These can be changed analogously to the change of one's own switching costs, discussed before.
OOX = one's opportunities for opportunism. These can be changed by changing contractual terms, affecting the partner's capability of monitoring (e.g. closing oneself off from scrutiny), or creating a more turbulent environment, in which novel opportunities may arise.
IOX = one's own incentives towards opportunism. This can be changed especially by changing one's dependence.

POX = one's propensity towards opportunism. Relevant here is the propensity as perceived by the partner. This may be affected by signalling: either to exaggerate or to hide true propensity. One may also redistribute roles of personnel, e.g. by replacing trusted long-term contacts by new ones, replacing technical personnel by legal formalists, etc.

Note that apparently perverse acts of governance may be rational for the sake of committing oneself and thereby facilitating participation by the partner. For example, one may bind oneself with an increase of switching costs (*SWX*), thereby increasing one's dependence, aligning it better, for example, with high dependence of the partner, due perhaps to high specific investments. This may be done by participating in their ownership, or by giving hostages.

This yields an interpretation of the previous illustration. The chemical supplier was willing to increase his specific investments at the plant of the buyer, both for further improvement of mutual value, but also to redress an imbalance of dependence that was in his favour, but might jeopardize the buyer's confidence.

Another noteworthy strategy is the following. If one's captivity becomes negative ($CAPX < 0$), perhaps because one has found a more attractive alternative partner (with an excess of value greater than switching costs), a plausible action would be to try and get out of the relation at the lowest possible cost. However, there is the alternative of investing in one's partner (increasing *VYX*) to such an extent that one no longer wants to get out.

When analysing actions and their triggers, we should consider the possibility of imperfect perception. The most crucial problem of limited perception pertains to the partner's propensity towards opportunism (*POY*). This seems so basic to the issue that it cannot be ignored. One will form an opinion on the partner' propensity on the basis of:

- true propensity, to the extent that one can infer such propensity directly, on the basis of experience or reputation;
- actual opportunistic behaviour.

For modelling purposes, one might envisage a Bayesian procedure, whereby prior estimates of propensity towards opportunism are adapted as a function of events. If no opportunism is perceived, the subjective probability of the partner's taking advantage of opportunities for opportunism may decline; when opportunism is perceived, it will increase.

A further complication arises when something happens to the detriment of *X*, but *Y* claims that it is due to some mishap beyond his control. Is this true or is *Y* trying to mask opportunism?

Parameters concerning value (*VYX*, *VXY*), switching costs (*SWX*, *SWY*), opportunities for opportunism (*OOY*, *OOX*) and incentives for opportunism (*IOY*, *IOX*) may more reasonably be assumed to be observable, with some qualifications:

- Note that *OOY*/*OOX* include the possibly limited capacities of monitoring. In assuming that *OOY*/*OOX* are known, we also assume that partners are aware of each other's limitations in monitoring.

– The assessment of value includes expectations about a prolonged relationship, which depend on imperfectly perceived propensities of the partner. Furthermore, since the values of partners are relative, they presume knowledge about alternative partners and their value, which presupposes an ongoing collection of information on such alternatives. It is possible that this is, in fact, neglected.

A striking illustration of this latter point is offered by Joag (1995).

> 'A firm that made the transition from customary multiple, price-oriented sourcing to single sourcing aimed at cooperation in development, on the basis of long term contracts, failed to monitor the performance of the single sources relative to outside producers, and thereby made it too easy for them to relax and concentrate on other more demanding and competitive customer relations. After seven years the firm found out by coincidence that its suppliers had seriously lagged behind potential competitors.'

Generic Strategies

We have generated quite a rich structure of interaction. To maintain grasp of complexity we now reduce the multitude of possible actions of governance to a small set of 'generic strategies', in Table 3.

Note that there are adversarial and cooperative means of increasing a partner's captivity (*CAPY* ↑). Cooperative: increase one's value relative to the partner (*VXY* ↑) by investing in further adaptation to the partner, and thereby incurring specific investments; invite hostages in the form of information about the partner's technology in order to improve cooperation in development of his products or processes (*SWY* ↑). Adversarial: increase one's relative value (*VXY* ↑) by blocking *Y*'s access to alternative partners; demand 'improductive hostages', without adding value for *Y* (*SWY* ↑).

We now have an instrument for exploring time paths of relations: sequences of actions that affect the parameters of the relation in response to outside events or internal events in the form of actions of the partner that influence the parameters of the relation. We could do that by simulation, on the basis of assumed perceptions, behavioural routines (responses to different types of perceived phenomena, in terms of attempts to change the parameters of the relation) and their possible adaptation. We could also employ game theory, using backward induction to see what (sub-game perfect) equilibria may appear.

Many situations can be set up for analysis, but for the purpose of illustration we will discuss only one particularly interesting situation: the beginning of a relation. At the beginning of a relation, a key problem, as indicated also in TCE, is that, *ex ante*, it is difficult to judge propensity towards opportunism. Then, as argued in TCE, one should take the

Table 3
Typology of Strategy (for *X*)

	Fastening	Loosening
Adversarial	Constrain partner ($CAPY\uparrow$, $OOY\downarrow$) Block alternatives Unproductive hostages Restrict actions Close monitoring → *binding*	Reduce own constraints ($SWX\downarrow$, $OOX\uparrow$) reduce values ($VYX\downarrow$, $VXY\downarrow$) decrease own bonding ($POX\uparrow$) → *breaking up*
Cooperative	Increase values ($VYX\uparrow$, $VXY\uparrow$) Increase bonding ($POX\downarrow$, $POY\downarrow$) Increase own constraints ($SWX\uparrow$, $ROX\downarrow$) Productive hostages ($SWX\uparrow$, $SWY\uparrow$) → *making attractive*	reduce switching costs ($SWX\downarrow$, $SWY\downarrow$) decrease bonding partner ($POY\uparrow$) → *setting free*

A cooperative strategy is also: *submission*; i.e. accept an aggressive strategy (binding, breaking up) of the partner, e.g. by accepting constraints ($OOX\downarrow$, $SWX\uparrow$).

possibility of opportunism into account. According to Table 3, fastening can occur by 'binding' or by 'making attractive'. Which, though, is preferable in view of the partner's likely reactions? How do choices of strategy affect the development of trust under different conditions of external events, availability of information, etc.? Should one begin with formal, contractual measures until trust has been built up to relax them, or vice versa: build trust first and formalize later? How should one set the ball rolling? Many readers will have more or less informal experience in this case. We have not yet constructed a systematic empirical case that may serve as an illustration, but our theoretical analysis is given below.

Suppose that *X* chooses binding. If this takes the form of tying *Y* down in a formal detailed contract ($OOY\downarrow$), the danger is that this may antagonize any inclination towards trust that *Y* may have, or may create the impression that, in his expectation of opportunism, *X* himself is inclined towards it. The first may increase *Y*'s propensity towards opportunism ($POY\uparrow$), and the second may cause *Y* to retaliate with restrictive measures ($OOX\downarrow$). There is a danger of a vicious cycle of distrust and mutual restrictions. Game theory also teaches us that it is unwise to demand that the precise date of terminating the relation be set in advance, as part of formal, legal ordering, because then, cooperation may unravel before it can properly start. Jockeying for the best exit condition rather than exploring novel potentialities then determines the relation. Private ordering is also cheaper, and allows for greater flexibility. Thus, this approach is ill-advised if *X* wants to develop the relation. Other adversarial measures of binding, such as blocking the partner's access to alternatives or demanding improductive hostages, likewise invites retaliation and a closing rather than opening of the relation. *Y* would be unwise to react by using the alternative strategy of 'making attractive', since that would make him extremely vulnerable, given *X*'s adversarial orientation, and *Y* would be virtually forced to retaliate with the same actions of binding.

Alternatively, *X* could choose 'making attractive'. He could invest in his value to the partner by engaging in modest initial specific investments (*VXY* ↑). This would contribute to fastening: the partner becomes more captive (*CAPY* ↑). This argument is also present in TCE. *X* may also offer productive hostages in the form of information about his technology, for the purpose of helping *Y* to develop his competence. A particularly interesting form of doing this is to invite specialists from *Y* to develop his competence. A particularly interesting form of doing this is to invite specialists from *Y* for a stay at *X*'s facilities. This simultaneously yields improvement of *Y*'s monitoring of *X* (*OOX* ↓). Conversely, *X* may supply specialists for a stay at *Y*, which increases *X*'s monitoring of *Y* (*OOY* ↓). The possible conflict between people '*qua persona*' and their organizational roles presents a complication here. People stationed at *Y* may establish personal bonds beyond the interest of *X*. Their value for monitoring, for example, may become void.

Y would be very unwise not to respond in the same fashion if he is interested in developing the relation. He would thereby forego the opportunity of a virtuous circle of mutual investment and the development of trust that promises to increase extrinsic, as well as intrinsic, value. If he reacted with binding, then so would *X*, with the negative results discussed above.

Note that the exchange of hostages in the form of information about one's technology carries the risk of spill-over (that is what makes it a hostage). Some guarantees are then required that the partner will be careful to control accidental spill-overs.

In view of uncertainty about propensities to opportunism, this build-up

Figure 3 Starting a Relation (*VYX* > 0; *VXY* > 0)

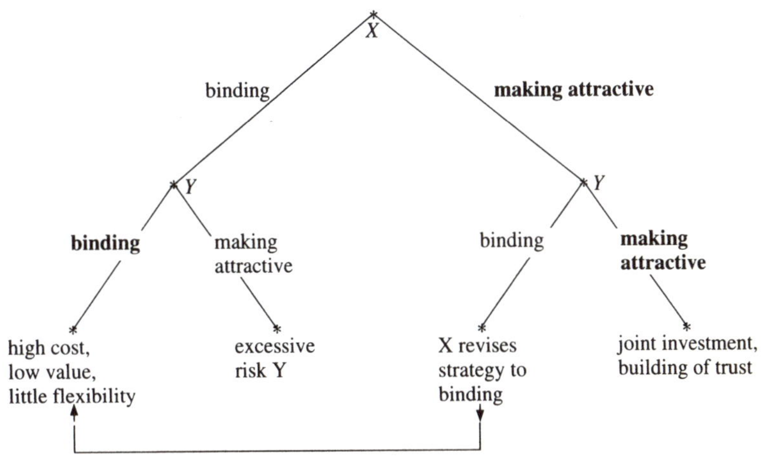

of the relation under private rather than legal ordering should proceed cautiously, and step by step. In the process, if parties refrain from opportunism, trust may grow, on the basis of bonding and habituation, and perhaps the development of a joint ethic. This game is illustrated in Figure 3, where italicized material indicates preferred strategies, forming a unique sub-game perfect equilibrium.

In a similar fashion, we could analyse the perhaps more difficult issue of ending a relation, but this would require too much space. The analysis has been conducted, and applied, by way of experiment, to ways of divorce.

Further Studies

The use of the model can be taken further, and the model can be developed in more detail. Both are under way. To give an example: a particularly interesting avenue of study is to see what the effects are of increased turbulence of technology and markets. If conditions are turbulent, in the sense that there is much entry and exit of firms, relative value is subject to shifts that may destabilize a relation. We have already indicated the cost of adjustment, the inflexibility of formal contracts and the greater relative attraction of trust, when changes in demands upon the relation are to be expected. On the other hand, if trust is based on close personal bonds, this can yield a conflict with organizational roles and tasks, particularly when the relation needs to be stopped, and replacement of personnel may be required. When technology progresses to become more flexible, and enables differentiated production at low costs of switching between products, the level of specificity of investments declines, resulting in lower switching costs and less need to control the hold-up risk. The first may destabilize a relation, and the latter may stabilize it.

Some issues can best be studied with the help of game theory, in a loose or formal way, and others by means of simulating the development of the relation. In comparison to simulation, game theory is useful for its analytical parsimony, but it leaves questions of how, and by what paths, Nash equilibria may be reached. In repeated interaction, parameters are likely to shift along the way, such as the build-up of trust and shifting goals, and analysis by repeated games may be either unrealistic (not taking into account such shifts) or no longer soluble analytically (cf. Gilbert 1989). For the evolution of relations, it might be better to resort to simulation, particularly if we want to investigate the robustness of a strategy under different conditions, events and parameter shifts. The problem with simulation is often that it generates too much complexity in terms of numbers of potential parameter constellations. Perhaps the two methods can be combined, with game theory to provide benchmarks to give some order and direction to simulation to test how Nash equilibria may be achieved. For practical purposes of the diagnosis and design of relations, complexity should be reduced by setting parameters to values that represent the case at hand. Whether this works will be further explored using case studies of firms.

References

Axelrod, R.
1984 *The evolution of cooperation.* New York: Basic Books.

Bagozzi, R. P.
1975 'Marketing as exchange'. *Journal of Marketing* 39: 32–39.

Berger, J., N. G. Nooderhaven, and B. Nooteboom
1995 'The determinants of supplier dependence: An empirical study' in *On economic institutions: Theory and applications.* J. Groenewegen, C. Pitelis, and S. E. Sjöstrand (eds.), 195–212. Aldershot: Edward Elgar.

Blau, P. M.
1964 *Exchange and power in social life.* New York: Wiley.

Dasgupta, P.
1988 'Trust as a commodity' in *Trust: Making and breaking of cooperative relations.* D. Gambetta (ed.), 49–72. Oxford: Blackwell.

Deutsch, M.
1962 'Cooperation and trust: Some theoretical notes' in *Nebraska symposium on motivation.* M. R. Jones (ed.), 275–319. Lincoln, Nebraska: University of Nebraska Press.

Dietrich, M.
1993 *Transaction cost economics and beyond: Towards a new economics of the firm.* London: Routledge.

Durkheim, E.
1893 (1933) *The division of labour in society.* Glencoe, IL: Free Press.

Dwyer, F. R., P. Schurr, and S. Oh
1987 'Developing buyer–seller relationships'. *Journal of Marketing* 51: 11–27.

Easton, G.
1989 *Industrial networks — A review.* 5th IMP conference: 161–182.

Foss, N. J.
1993 'Theories of the firm: Contractual and competence perspectives'. *Journal of Evolutionary Economics* 3/2: 127–144.

Gambetta, D., *editor*
1988a *Trust: Making and breaking of cooperative relations.* Oxford: Blackwell.

Gambetta, D.
1988b 'Can we trust trust?' in *Trust: making and breaking of cooperative relations.* D. Gambetta (ed.), 213–237. Oxford: Blackwell.

Gilbert, R. J.
1989 'Mobility barriers and the value of incumbency' in *Handbook of industrial organization.* R. Schmalensee and R. D. Willig (eds.), 475–531. Amsterdam: North Holland.

Granovetter, M.
1982 'The strength of weak ties' in *Social structure and network analysis.* P. Marsden and N. Lin (eds.), 105–130. Beverly Hills, CA: Sage.

Granovetter, M.
1985 'Economic action and social structure: the problem of embeddedness' *American Journal of Sociology* 91: 481–510.

Groenewegen, J., and J. Vromen
1995 'Theories of the firm revisited: New and neo-institutional perspectives'. Paper presented at the symposium on 'Evolutionary Economics and Path Dependency', 20–21 May, Uppsala University.

Hagg, I., and J. Johanson
1983 *Firms in networks.* Stockholm: Business and Social Research Institute.

Hakansson, H., *editor*
1982 *International marketing and purchasing of industrial goods, an interaction approach.* Chichester: Wiley.

Hakansson, H., *editor*
1987 *Industrial technological development — A network approach.* London: Croom Helm.

Hargreaves Heap, S. P., and Y. Varoufakis
1995 *Game theory: A critical introduction.* London: Routledge.

Hill, C. W. L.
1990 'Cooperation, opportunism and the invisible hand: Implications for transaction cost theory'. *Academy of Management Review* 15/3: 500–513.

Hirschman, A. O.
1984 'Against parsimony: Three easy ways of complicating some categories of economic discourse'. *American Economic Review* 74: 88–96.

Hodgson, G. M., *editor*
1993 *The economics of institutions.* Aldershot: Edward Elgar.

Homans, G.
1961 *Social behavior: Its elementary forms.* New York: Harcourt.

Jarillo, J. C.
1988 'On strategic networks'. *Strategic Management Journal* 9: 31–41.

Joag, S. G.
1995 'Supplier partnerships: The dream and the reality' in *Looking to the 21st century in purchasing and supply chain management.* R. A. Kemp and R. C. Lamming (eds.), 455–475. Proceedings of the first worldwide research symposium on purchasing and supply chain management, Tempe, Arizona, 23–25 March.

Johanson, J., and L. G. Mattson
1987 'Interorganisational relations in industrial systems — A network approach compared with the transaction cost approach'. *International Studies of Management and Organization* 17/1.

Lamming, R.
1993 *Beyond partnership.* New York: Prentice-Hall.

Latsis, S. J., *editor*
1980 *Method and appraisal in economics.* Cambridge: Cambridge University Press.

Luhmann, N.
1979 *Trust and power.* Chichester: Wiley.

Luhmann, N.
1988 'Familiarity, confidence, trust: Problems and alternatives' in *Trust: Making and breaking of cooperative relations.* D. Gambetta (ed.), 94–107. Oxford: Blackwell.

Murakami, Y., and T. P. Rohlen
1992 'Social-exchange aspects of the Japanese political economy: Culture, efficiency and change' in *The political economy of Japan,* Vol. 3, *Cultural and social dynamics.* S. Kumon and H. Rosorsky (eds.), 63–105. Stanford, CA: Stanford University Press.

Noorderhaven, N. G.
1995 'Trust and transactions: Towards transaction cost analysis with a differential behavioral assumption'. *Tijdschrift voor Economie en Management* 15: 5–18.

Nooteboom, B.
1992 'Towards a dynamic theory of transactions'. *Journal of Evolutionary Economics* 2: 281–299.

Nooteboom, B.
1993a 'Firm size effects on transaction costs'. *Small Business Economics* 5: 283–295.

Nooteboom, B.
1993b 'Transactions and networks: Do they connect?' in *Dynamics of the firm: Strategies of pricing and organisation.* J. Groenewegen (ed.), 9–26. Aldershot: Edward Elgar.

Nooteboom, B.
1993c 'An analysis of specificity in transaction cost economics'. *Organization Studies* 14/3: 443–451.

Nooteboom, B.
1994 'Cost, quality and learning based governance of transactions: Western, Japanese and a third way'. Paper EMOT conference (European Science Foundation), Como, October.

Nooteboom, B.
1995 'Will opportunism go away?' Research Report, SOM Research School, Groningen University, The Netherlands.

Nooteboom, B., J. Berger, and N. G. Noorderhaven
1995 'Sources, measurement and effect of trust in the governance of buyer–supplier relations'. Paper for the EMOT workshop (European Science Foundation), Geneva, 1–3 December.

Pitelis, C.
1993 *Transaction costs, markets and hierarchies*. Oxford: Basil Blackwell.

Pitelis, C.
1994 'On the nature of the firm' in *Market evolution: Competition and cooperation across markets and over time*. A. van Witteloostuijn (ed.), 11–37. Dordrecht: Kluwer Academic Publishers.

Semlinger, K.
1991 'New developments in subcontracting: Mixing market and hierarchy' in *Towards a new Europe? Structural change in the European economy*. A. Amin and M. Dietrich (eds.), 96–115. Aldershot: Edward Elgar.

Smith Ring, P., and A. H. Van de Ven
1994 'Developmental processes of cooperative interorganizational relationships'. *Academy of Management Review* 19/1: 90–118.

Webster, F. E., and Y. Wind
1972 *Organizational buyer behavior*. Englewood Cliffs, NJ: Prentice-Hall.

Williams, B.
1988 'Formal structures and social reality' in *Trust: Making and breaking of cooperative relations*. D. Gambetta (ed.), 3–13. Oxford: Blackwell.

Williamson, O. E.
1975 *Markets and hierarchies: Analysis and antitrust implications*. New York: Free Press.

Williamson, O. E.
1985 *The economic institutions of capitalism: Firms, markets, relational contracting*. New York: Free Press.

Zand, D. E.
1972 'Trust and managerial problem solving'. *Administrative Science Quarterly* 17/2: 229–239.

[13]

BERND LAHNO

ON THE EMOTIONAL CHARACTER OF TRUST

ABSTRACT. Trustful interaction serves the interests of those involved. Thus, one could reason that trust itself may be analyzed as part of rational, goal-oriented action. In contrast, common sense tells us that trust is an emotion and is, therefore, independent of rational deliberation to some extent. I will argue that we are right in "trusting" our common sense. My argument is conceptual in nature, referring to the common distinction between trust and pure reliance. An emotional attitude may be understood as some general pattern in the way the world or some part of the world is perceived by an individual. Trust may be characterized by such a pattern. I shall focus on two central features of a trusting attitude. First, trust involves a participant attitude (Strawson) toward the person being trusted. Second, a situation of trust is perceived by a trusting person as one in which shared values or norms motivate both his own actions as well as those of the person being trusted. As an emotional attitude, trust is, to some extent, independent of objective information. It determines what a trusting person will believe and how various outcomes are evaluated. Hence, trust is quite different from rational belief and the problem with trust is not adequately met in minimizing risk by supplying extensive information or some mechanism of sanctioning. Trust is an attitude that enables us to cope with risk in a certain way. If we want to promote trustful interaction, we must form our institutions in ways that allow individuals to experience their interest and values as shared and, thus, to develop a trusting attitude.

KEY WORDS: cooperation, emotion, faith, rational choice, trust

Introduction

Risk is generally held to be a central characteristic of trustful interaction. In a trust situation, one person allows another to exercise a certain amount of control over matters that are of some importance to him. A trusting person is vulnerable. She is open to harm caused by the actions of the person being trusted; and, in trusting she intentionally accepts being vulnerable in this way. To illustrate, let us think of a mother who asks her neighbor to babysit her daughter. If her neighbor accepts, but does not properly care for the child, the little girl could be seriously injured. In this case the mother would suffer some harm from the neighbor's actions, harm she could have prevented by not trusting her neighbor and taking care of her daughter herself.

Why should anyone voluntarily make herself vulnerable to the actions of another person? There is one easy answer to this question: In trusting another person, one does not merely risk being harmed, one usually also

Ethical Theory and Moral Practice **4**: 171–189, 2001.

has good prospects of some particular benefit. Trusting behavior usually generates new options and it often opens the door to certain opportunities. Thus, the mother who trusts her neighbor with the care of her child would benefit by possibly being able to go back to work or, at least, having a bit of time for herself.

When trust is not misguided, it promotes the interests of individuals. It is advantageous to both those, who are being trusted (which might seem questionable in some cases) as well as, and even more so, to those who are doing the trusting. Moreover, it seems impossible to live a satisfying life entirely without trust. In daily life everybody is in many respects necessarily dependent on the performance of others. It is often possible to exercise some influence on exactly who gains what amount of control over which things or events in our lives, but it is impossible to be independent of all others. As we do not have the power to control other people's actions completely, we must necessarily trust. In addition, given the complexity of life today, in many ways, we are subject to the decisions of mere acquaintances or even complete strangers. Traditional bonds or personal relationships cannot (maybe not anymore) suffice as a general foundation of trustful interaction.

Thus, trust serves our interests. It is not far from this insight to the claim that trust is merely one aspect of interest-driven and goal-oriented behavior (Coleman, 1990). According to what could possibly be the most consequent and which certainly is the most influential form of such a theory, trust is nothing but a rational belief about the character or the probable behavior of another person (see, e.g., Dasgupta, 1988; Gambetta, 1988; Hardin, 1991). Based on the information available to him the trustor believes that the trustee will behave in a way, which is favorable for him. This, according to this theory, is the essence of trust. We trust if and only if we have a belief like this.

From a common sense point of view, such a concept of trust is met with consternation. This theory, so it is said, does not take into account that trust is a specific source of cooperative expectations. It gives the impression that trust is essentially only a question of rationally calculated risk. Yet, one may protest that calculating behavior in fact contradicts real trust (see also Williamson, 1993). Genuine trust is an emotion and emotions are, in general, not subject to direct rational control.

I believe that, despite the general advantages of an analysis of trust from a Rational Choice point of view,[1] there is some truth in this popular view,

[1]But see Hollis, 1998, for an analysis of the limited explanatory force of a concept of trust based solely on instrumental rationality.

which should be taken into account when carefully analyzing the social phenomenon of trust. Trust does in fact possess emotional character in some important respects. It is an emotional attitude. Now, before I delve into the justification of this claim in more detail, it is necessary to clarify how the term "emotional attitude" is used in this context.

1. Faith

John Wisdom's (1944–45) famous parable of the invisible gardener is an illuminating example of an emotional attitude:

> Two people return to their long neglected garden and find among the weeds a few of the old plants surprisingly vigorous. One says to the other 'It must be that a gardener has been coming and doing something about the plants.'

The second person is skeptical. They ask the neighbors but nobody has ever seen a gardener in the garden. Still, the fist person sticks to his opinion and presumes that the unknown gardener must have done his work in a way not noticeable to the neighbors. He points to the harmony and the beauty of some of the spots in the garden. How could this come about if it was not purposely created by some conscious, planning mind? He concludes that since no gardener has ever been seen in the garden and possibly never will, the gardener must be invisible to mortal eyes.

The two painstakingly investigate the garden. Some of the things they see seem to confirm the first person's assumption but others seem to oppose it. They gather all available information that could possibly be relevant to resolving the dispute. In the end, both share the same factual knowledge of the general condition of the garden, the same knowledge of the laws of nature that govern the vegetation of a garden and the same knowledge of all possible ways to intervene in structuring the garden. They even agree on what further changes are likely to be seen in the future. Still, the first person insists that an invisible gardener is secretly intervening, while the second asserts that there is simply no such gardener.

Although the two have the very same information at their disposal, they are holding different beliefs. Obviously, no sensory experience – except them actually seeing the mysterious gardener – could settle their dispute. Yet, these two people do not just differ in their attitude towards a proposition that is relatively independent of the world of experience, they perceive the garden through different eyes. While the first sees the expression of some planning intellect in the garden, the second chalks it all up to coincidences of natural order. When looking at the garden the one is filled with admiration, the other with wonder. The one concentrates on the hidden beauty of the garden, while the other simply finds occasional natural harmony amongst the dirt and disorder.

The way the garden is perceived is obviously not determined by rational considerations. Experience and rationality simply do not suffice for drawing a clear and unambiguous picture. There is something about the picture each of the observers has which is direct and spontaneous. The picture is not completely independent of their beliefs, but it is certainly not inferred. It is simply given in this way and no other.

The aim of Wisdom's parable is to illustrate the difference between a person who has faith in God and someone who is a skeptic or atheist. The crux of the parable is that the religious believer does not generally differ from other people in his knowledge of empirical facts of the world or in his expectations of the world. He rather merely takes a different stance toward the world. Although this may have no immediate impact on his cognitive beliefs regarding the empirical world, it is obviously not irrelevant. It is easy to imagine that the two protagonists of the parable will be differently motivated when beginning the restoration of the garden. Thus, their different attitudes toward the garden will most likely result in different actions. Moreover, the well-being of the individuals is probably tied to their attitude. One may expect that the first person, impressed by what she perceives as harmony, will set out to work in the garden feeling optimistic and happy. This is exactly what religious people usually – and possibly correctly – maintain: a person with faith in God will enjoy a richer and happier life on earth regardless of what her expectations of the afterlife may be. However, it would, of course, be completely misguided to infer that this is her reason for believing in God.

2. Emotion and Perception

What is an emotion? This question has a long tradition in philosophy (see, e.g., Calhoun and Solomon, 1984). Emotions have been defined as specific inner experiences or feelings, as the perception of certain physiological disturbances, as patterns of behavioral dispositions, or as a certain kind of belief. Each of these definitions emphasizes one particular aspect of emotional reactions in humans, but it would seem that none meets the demand of actually giving a comprehensive and suitable account of the concept. I also have no such account to offer, but I shall still try to clarify what I mean by characterizing trust as an emotional attitude in this discussion[2].

[2]My argument owes a lot to the theory of emotion as developed by Ronald de Sousa (1987) and to Calhoun (1985).

In Aristotle's Rhetoric, he defines emotions in the following way:

> The emotions are all those feelings that so change men as to affect their judgements, and that are also attcmpted by pain or pleasure. (Rhetoric 1378a).

Although Aristotle links emotions to the basic feelings of pain and pleasure, he does not define them as certain mental events of a specific quality. The crux of the matter for him is rather that emotions serve a particular function in organizing conscious life: They lead us to perceive and judge the world in a specific way.

It is debatable whether Aristotle generally understood emotions in this way (see, e.g., Elster, 1999, 54f.). Nevertheless, the basic idea formulated here seems to be of the utmost importance for an adequate understanding of emotional phenomena. Emotions are characterized by how they guide our thoughts.

There is a popular aphorism in Germany, which illustrates this point: Lovers see the world through rose-colored glasses. A person who is in love tends to see everything around him in a positive light and often just does not take notice of anything negative. Almost everything reminds him of his beloved and seems to obtain a new meaning in the light of his beloved's well-being and their shared happiness. All this may, of course, vary from person to person and according to the particular circumstances of the relationship. Still, there is some basic general pattern in the way the world is represented in the thoughts of a person in love. This basic pattern characterizes the emotion of love and other emotions may be characterized in similar ways. That some mental state may be understood as part of the realization of such a pattern shows its emotional character.

Emotions are like glasses, through which we perceive the world. Three aspects of how emotions shape our thoughts may be differentiated in the following way:

1. Emotions determine how we perceive the world in a direct manner. They do so by giving us a certain perspective on the world. They guide our attention by making some things appear more salient than others.
2. Emotions determine how we think and what judgments we make on matters of fact. That is not to say that an emotion necessarily annuls reason. Instead, it directs reason by stimulating certain associations and suggesting certain patterns of interpretation.
3. Emotions guide our evaluation of some aspects of the world and motivate our actions.

This last normative aspect of an emotion is frequently emphasized (see, e.g., Solomon, 1993). However, it is not true that emotions are just a special form of normative judgment. First of all, if one were to accept this narrow view, it would mean the first two aspects involved with emotions would have to be disregarded and, thus, their complex character would be ignored. Moreover, a judgment is usually understood as a particular act of reason, whereby a person takes on an attitude of assent or dissent toward some proposition. In contrast, emotions do not require the mediation of reason. They are more immediate in this respect. A person in love experiences the presence of his be-loved as pleasant; there is no reasoning involved. If the person in love does not merely feel, but judge that his be-loved is pleasant, this is simply a consequence of the fact that being in love he can only perceive of his be-loved in this favorable way.

At this point a decisive difference between emotion and belief becomes clear. Beliefs are much more closely linked to the operations of reason than emotions are. Our beliefs have some influence on how we perceive the world, too. Thus, how large an object appears to some observer usually depends on what he knows about the distance to the object. But in contrast to emotions, beliefs generally are the result of rational reflection, they are the starting point and basis of further reflection and they cannot be maintained when acknowledged as wrong. By comparison, if a person has doubts about whether the world is, in fact, such as he experiences it through his emotions, the experience itself will not be changed by that doubt alone. To bring about a change, one has to alter one's perspective. One may try to achieve such a change in perspective because of some rational insight, but a change in perspective cannot come from insight alone.

Furthermore, a belief is tied to a specific content while the intentional character of emotions is much more difficult to grasp. An emotion is not characterized by a specific content but rather by the way the world is represented in thought and by the way the contents of thought are associated with each other.

All this does not mean that emotions are completely independent of beliefs or reason. Anything we perceive is already structured by concepts. Our beliefs color our picture of the world and, conversely, what we believe about the world is influenced, to a large extent, by our perceptions. But the connection between the two is best understood as causal. Emotions are relatively independent of beliefs in that they do not immediately come with our beliefs. Because they determine the contents of our thoughts, which are the bases for all our reasoning, and because they invoke particular thought patterns, they take precedence over thought. Since emotions affect our insights and, conversely, since no insight has a direct and necessary impact on our emotions, they in fact evade rational control to some extent.

Thus, when trust is referred to as an emotional attitude, the following is meant: Trust is necessarily tied to a particular perception of the world or some part of the world. It may be characterized by certain patterns in the way the world is represented in thought and the way certain contents of thought are associated with each other. There is a causal relationship between trust and belief. Yet, because trust somehow determines how we think, it cannot be understood as the immediate result of rational consideration.

3. Trust in Personal Relationships

Faith as analyzed by John Wisdom evidently is an emotional attitude in this sense. But faith is not the same as trust. Still, it does come from the Latin word "fidere". Webster's Dictionary defines faith as "complete trust" or "belief and trust in and loyalty to God". So, faith may be understood as a special and particularly strong form of trust. The emotional character of faith is exceptionally clear, but other forms of trust exhibit the same emotional elements.

Suppose a good friend is suspected of having committed a serious crime; he is, for instance, said to have embezzled a considerable sum of money. All circumstantial evidence is against your friend. You do not have any special knowledge about the case yourself. You know, just as well as everyone else, that the evidence is against your friend. Your friend claims he is innocent. You know, just as all others do, that your friend denies the embezzlement. But you trust him. Why?

First of all, you know your friend better than anyone else. Thus, you might have some exclusive information that does not seem to be in accord with the accusation. As far as this is concerned the difference between your trust and the commonly held suspicion may be put down to a cognitive difference. Suppose, however, that the evidence against your friend is overwhelming. What would you do? In this case you would ask yourself how the evidence might have truly come about. You would try to overcome the obvious incompatibility of your personal beliefs about your friend's character and the incriminating evidence presented. You might, for instance, consider how the evidence could be explained without incriminating your friend. You would not simply evaluate the given information and come to an objective judgement; instead, your special relationship to your friend would induce you to see him and his situation in a certain favorable light and call the information into question.

Now, your trust can not be understood as the result of a cognitive learning process or pure rational refection. It is not simply a matter of analyzing the given information to get to some factual expectation on what will happen or has happened. It rather amounts to evaluating information in a certain way and asking certain questions. Moreover, the trust of a friend encompasses patterns of normative evaluation that will motivate the trusting friend in a certain way (compare Govier, 1993, 1997).[3] The trusting person perceives the friend and that part of the world that is related to the friend and his actions in a certain light. This is the core of his trust. It is an emotional attitude as defined above.

In contrast to the case of faith in God the trusting friend differs from others in his beliefs about empirical facts. Still, his trust is, to some extent, independent of the given information. In determining what information is relevant and in suggesting particular questions and patterns of interpretation, his trust rather determines what he believes.

Again, one may want to object that trust in a friend is a special kind of trust. Personal relationships are, by definition, emotional in character, so it is hardly surprising that the specific form of trust, which is essential to this form of human relationship, is itself characterized as emotional.

4. Trust and Reliance

In my opinion, genuine trust is basically an emotional attitude or at least essentially contains such an attitude in any social relationship. My argument for this claim is conceptual in nature. If certain features, which make up an emotional attitude, are not present, we do not in general speak of trust, or we will use the word trust under such circumstances in a very wide and vague sense only. My argument aims at the differentiation of trust and pure reliance.

Imagine the mother again, who trusts her neighbor to take care for her daughter in her own home. Now compare her situation with that of a burglar, who has observed the situation and who now grasps the opportunity to rob the neighbor's home undisturbed. Both the mother and the burglar

[3]I am indebted to an anonymous referee for drawing my attention to the later work of Professor Govier. The relevant passages may be found in chapter 1. There, Professor Govier also gives an account of faith based on Wisdom's parable, which is similar to my argument in section 1.

expect the neighbor to look after the child carefully. Both consider this favorable in the light of their own interests. The mother does so because she cares for her daughter's well-being and the burglar is looking forward to being undisturbed in his disreputable job. Both are led by their expectation to make themselves vulnerable to the actions of the neighbor. Yet, while the mother's is an ordinary case of trust, we would definitely hesitate to ascribe trust to the burglar. Admittedly, the burglar is relying on the neighbor to stay away, but there seems to be more to genuine trust than just simple reliance. What does this "more" consist of?

For Annette Baier the difference between simple reliance and genuine trust is that, with trust, a person relies on the partner being motivated in a specific way. In a most influential article she characterizes trust as the 'accepted vulnerability to another's possible but not expected ill will (or lack of good will) toward one' (Baier, 1986, p. 235).

This intuitively plausible definition rules out the burglar scenario as a case of trust. The burglar does not believe in the good will of the neighbor toward himself, and, even if he did, he would not expect her to leave him undisturbed for this reason.

Baier wants her characterization of trust to be understood as a 'first approximation'. In fact, the criterion given seems to be too restrictive. In particular, it might rule out the case of the mother as a case of trust, too. Imagine that the mother has a strained relationship with her neighbor. The neighbor does not like her and the mother knows this very well. Now, she can still believe that the neighbor likes her daughter and that these two get along quite well. In this case, we might still attribute trust to the mother although she does not count on the neighbor's good will toward herself personally. Her favorable expectations are based on the neighbor's affection for the daughter. *This* good will is the object of her trust.

Annette Baier is obviously right in stating that trust, in contrast to simple reliance, is associated with ascribing a certain motivation to the trustee. Yet, her 'first approximation' of the concept of trust imposes too hard restrictions on what exactly this motivation may be. Our example suggests the following distinction: The motive a trustor attributes to his partner in trusting is such that the trustor himself acknowledges it as a justified and valuable motive. Interest in the trustor's wellbeing is one such motive, but it is not the only one. In contrast to Baier's criterion, this wider criterion also applies to all those obvious cases of trust where no mutual affection is present but where norms are involved, for instance, if a promise has been given.

Yet, our criterion is possibly too wide now. The burglar can also base his confidence on the belief that the neighbor will look after the girl carefully. He might even have some interest in the well-being of the girl himself and, thus, endorse the neighbor's presumed motive. We would, nevertheless, still hesitate to attribute trust to him. The point here is that the ascribed and favored motive does not play any essential role for the burglar in pursuing his aims in the given situation. In contrast to the mother, the burglar is not at all motivated by the girl's welfare, he is only looking to promote his own interests. So, it does not only matter what kind of motivation is attributed to the partner. How the trustor perceives his partner's motives and interests as connected to his own motives is also important.

It is noteworthy that it does not really matter what the actual properties of the situation are nor what the actual motivation of the trustee is. Everything depends on how the situation and the partner are perceived by the trustor. Trust is connected to a certain point of view. He who trusts another makes himself vulnerable because he perceives his partner as being connected to himself by shared aims or values. For the trustor, the situation is one that calls for the realization of such aims or for observing shared norms as part of a cooperative enterprise. For the burglar, the welfare of the girl is, at best, a pleasant side effect, but his guiding interest is opposed to the aims of the neighbor.

This explication of the concept of trust also explains the normative character of those expectations that usually come with trust. If a person trusts someone because of a promise given, she does not only believe that the other will in fact keep his promise, she is also convinced that her partner is obliged to do so, that he knows that this is so and that this is one of the main reasons for keeping his promise. The situation of the mother's case is similar. Based on her knowledge about the relationship between her neighbor and her daughter, she can be fairly certain that the neighbor will take care of the girl. The mother's knowledge is sufficient for her to rely on her neighbor and the burglar's reliance could be justified in the same way. However, the mother's trust goes beyond reliance. She has the firm conviction that the relationship between her neighbor and her daughter implies an obligation to care and that her neighbor is well aware of this. Therefore, if her trust is disappointed, she will not only be dismayed because of the possible consequences, but, what is more, she will hold her neighbor responsible. This follows simply from the fact that the mother perceives the situation as defined by shared values that allow for demands.

The burglar can be annoyed, too, if the neighbor does not follow her duties and he is caught as a result of this. Still, his annoyance is not really elicited by the violation of the duty to care for the girl but rather by the accidental consequences of that violation. He may be annoyed, but he has no reason to be angry *with the neighbor*.

5. Trust and Person

These last remarks show that trust not only implies a certain view of a situation but that it principally includes a special attitude toward the person trusted. The conceptual differentiation, introduced by Peter Strawson (1974) between two general attitudes that one may take toward other persons may be helpful at this point (compare also Holton, 1994).

In a participant attitude, a person regards herself and another person as being involved in interaction. The acts of the other person are seen as part of a larger context in which the person herself plays a role. Thus, the other is looked at from a perspective within the interaction. A participant attitude toward another person is characterized by the disposition to have certain feelings or emotions that are directed toward that person. Strawson calls these emotions 'reactive attitudes', some examples being anger, revenge or gratitude. What makes these emotions special is that a person can only have them if she is immediately engaged in interaction with the person or people they are directed at. These emotions are, in fact, part of the interaction and cannot be separated from it. To have these emotions is to take part in the interaction.

By contrast, an objective attitude toward another person implies a certain distance. It is the attitude of an uninvolved and detached observer. Although the actions of the other person might provoke some reaction, these reactions will not be directed toward that person. The other person's actions are not seen as part of any genuine interaction but as one link of a more extensive independent chain of cause and effect. Social scientists and psychologists typically take up an objective attitude when analyzing or trying to manipulate the behavior of other human beings. The individual is seen as an external object that is driven by the laws of nature and as the object of indifferent observation or manipulation.

Such an attitude is obviously incompatible with trust. If we perceive another person as someone who shares goals and values with us, we are involved and we cannot but do this from an inner perspective directed toward understanding and not toward causal explanation. Thus, trust presupposes that the trustor takes up a participant attitude toward the trustee.

For Strawson, a participant attitude is completely determined by the disposition to have reactive emotions. The normative character of trustful expectations implies that trust involves such a disposition. Yet, there is something that goes beyond the simple and possibly merely accidental disposition for certain feelings.

He who emotionally reacts to the actions of another person and directs his emotions to the person acting is assuming (or, at least, acts as if he assumes) that the other person is the author of his actions. Thus, we have here a deeper reason for trust necessarily involving a participant attitude: One can only believe that another individual may act for the sake of some common goal or shared value if she is perceived as a person with personal goals, a personal standard of value and the capability of choosing her actions accordingly.

Kant taught us that the concept "person" is necessarily tied to the concept "autonomy". A person does not only have personal aims and values to guide her actions, a person has the faculty of setting goals for herself and choosing values. Because we see our fellow human beings as persons, we judge their actions not only by how effectively they pursue their goals but by the very goals they set for themselves. Another person is someone who is fully responsible for her actions and can, therefore, be held responsible. In this sense, to trust someone presupposes treating her as a person.

We have another reason here for the fact that we cannot attribute trust to the burglar relying on the neighbor's taking care of the girl. He knows very well that the neighbor is a person who makes her decisions to fit in with her personal goals. He simply exploits this fact for his own interests. Still, the burglar sees the neighbor from the position of an uninvolved observer and from that position the acts of the neighbor do not differ in character from any other event governed by the laws of nature. To him the neighbor is simply like a mechanism, whose performance is to be observed in order to realize the burglar's very own goals effectively. This is why one would not speak of trust in this case. The burglar does not really interact with the neighbor. He uses her as a means to his private ends and disregards her as a person.

6. Trust Determines the Context of Action

John Wisdom described faith in God as an attitude that gives a believer a certain impression of the world. Now, I have argued that genuine interpersonal trust in general is ascribed only to those persons who perceive the person they rely on as connected to themselves by shared values or common goals. The context of interaction with the trustee is viewed from this perspective and the impression of the world is characteristically formed thus.

Faith was found to be relatively independent of the available empirical information. Since the impression of the world mediated by faith cannot be understood as an immediate result of rational reflection and since faith, in contrast, determines to some extent our thoughts, faith has been characterized as an emotional attitude.

Something similar is true of interpersonal trust in general. Although the mother and the burglar may have the very same information regarding the empirical facts, they, nevertheless, view the situation and the neighbor's expected actions through different eyes. This difference does not only concern immediate perception. As I have argued, a trusting person will think about the situation in a way characteristic only to trusting persons and will evaluate the possible outcomes of the situation in a certain manner. If this is correct, trust has an immediate impact on the beliefs and preferences of a trusting person. It follows that trust may not be understood as an element of instrumental rationality in a decision situation, which is defined by pre-set beliefs and goals. There are no such pre-set goals and beliefs on the side of the trustor. His beliefs and evaluations are first formed by his trust.

Wisdom claims that, although the faithful person does not differ from the skeptic in his expectations regarding empirical facts, faith does have some cognitive value. In his faith, the believer may perceive something which is hidden from the skeptic or atheist and which is, nonetheless, part of the objective independent world. Wisdom relates this to the situation of a person who discovers a certain harmony in a piece of art, a harmony which is characteristic of the art object and not just some subjective feature of the person's faculty of perception.

John Wisdom's argument is questionable in many respects (see Flew and Macintyre, 1955). Yet, when carried over to the problem of interpersonal trust, the thesis may gain some plausibility. For, in social interaction, the impression the individual has generally has some influence on his expected decision. The trustor's beliefs and preferences as affected by his perception of the situation are themselves part of the situation. They are not just an inner reaction to an independent outside world. They rather manifest themselves in the situation through the behavior expected.

In some cases, the impact of trust on the structure of a social context may go beyond forming the incentives of the trustor. It is a well-known phenomenon, often noted and discussed by philosophers (Horsburgh, 1960; Hartmann, 1962; Pettit, 1995), that trust may create trustworthiness. This phenomenon has some particular relevance in education.

It is a fairly common experience to people concerned with the education of young persons that they feel unable to trust one of their pupils in some certain respect. Thus, a teacher may know that one of his students is extremely impulsive in ordinary circumstances and that it is, therefore, fairly risky to entrust him with tasks, which require a sense of responsibility. Still, on some occasion this teacher may, nevertheless, give his student a task of exactly this kind. He is, thus, signaling firm confidence that the student will do his duty when the situation calls for it. And, the teacher ostensibly confirms this impression. In fact, this sort of behavior is reinforced by the advice of prominent educationalists (see, for example, Bollnow, 1959, 143ff.; Makarenko, 1974, 208ff.).

Although the teacher does not really trust in the strength of the pupil's character, he takes a considerable risk regarding the action of his pupil. But, why should anybody do such a thing? The answer lies in the expected impact of a signal of trust on the student's attitude and behavior. The teacher may count on the pupil being additionally motivated by the signal of trust to do what is right. Not only will there be some prospect that the student will act in desired ways in spite of the fact that he has not yet morally matured. The essential educational point of the measure is that by such exercise, by and by, exactly those virtues and human faculties will be developed which – in the eyes of the teacher – are still absent.

There is some fundamental form of trust involved here, namely trust in the responsiveness and malleability of the pupil, trust in his good core and his capability to develop his person favorably if assisted in suitable ways. This sort of trust is at the heart of any genuine educational enterprise. It requires a positive sympathetic attitude toward the pupil as an evolving person. Still, as far as the actual present person and the signal of trust given to him by the teacher is concerned, one may feel that trust is somehow feigned. This may be true even if the teacher does in fact expect the pupil to act in desired ways as a result of his educational measure.

The picture of trust that I have drawn endorses this impression. The teacher is lacking the attitude necessary for the sort of trust he is signaling. He simply does not see the student as a person who has already internalized the essential normative demands necessary for deliberately doing the job in a responsible fashion. He actually does not believe that the student has the sense of responsibility needed and it is precisely because of this that he aims to arouse just such a sense of responsibility in him. There is even a manipulative element in his behavior. In counting on the effects of his behavior while concealing his actual motivation, he treats the student like an external object that can readily be manipulated. In this regard he is pursuing his (private) educational aims and does not participate in a cooperative project with the actual person in front of him (although one might say that he is cooperating with the person to evolve).

The manipulative element in the teacher's behavior becomes salient when one takes into consideration that the success of the operation essentially depends on how successful he is in concealing his real beliefs and motivation. If the student finds out that his teacher does not in fact believe in his sense of responsibility, he will most probably turn away disappointed and will not behave as expected and/or hoped for. Two things become clear from this.

Firstly, the effect in the student's behavior is obviously not caused by the mere expectations of the teacher, but by the specific source of those expectations, namely by the trust signaled. The student may still quite reasonably assume that the teacher expected his educational measure to be successful. It is the student's insight that the teacher's expectations were not really based on the trust he signaled, not his discovery that the teacher did not truly expect him to do his duty, that induces the student to reject the role of responsibility the teacher had hoped for.

The example shows, secondly, that trust obviously has intrinsic value. We appreciate someone trusting us and we are displeased if trust is withdrawn. The theory of learning may provide a simple explanation for this fact. Since we experience cooperative enterprises as beneficial and pleasant, we appreciate the social relationships they are based on and we carry our appreciation over onto the kind of attitude that seems to be the essence of those relationships. But this undoubtedly plausible and, in many cases, applicable explanation is not very convincing in the case at hand. The student will most likely lack those positive experiences. The concept of trust, which I have developed here, throws a new light on the case. Trust requires that we treat each other as persons. The experience of being acknowledged as a person by others is of extreme importance for the development of personal identity and self-esteem and, thus, is naturally an object of high regard.

7. Conclusion

To conclude: I have argued that common sense is right in maintaining that trust has emotional character. In some specifiable sense, trust is an emotional attitude. In particular, trust is beyond the direct control of reason and cannot be understood as the result of rational calculation.

My argument has rested upon a conceptual analysis and in particular on the commonly made distinction between trust and pure reliance. One may object here that such an analysis inevitably results in a very narrow concept of trust. Although we make this conceptual differentiation we also use the concept of trust in a much wider sense in everyday life. Sometimes we even use the term "trust" as a synonym for "reliance". Now, one could argue that this is particularly true for those cases that deal with cooperation between people who are basically strangers. Of course, these are precisely the cases of major interest under the given social conditions. They constitute the problem of cooperation and, thus, the social problem of trust. So, one could argue that, although genuine trust is in some sense rightly characterized as an emotional attitude, genuine trust, in this strict sense, is not truly the problem.

Several studies of the problem of trust indicate that this is not true. In organization science, for instance, scholars have devoted some effort to the problem of trust in the last few years. A considerable number of the studies concur in one respect: The perception of shared values plays a decisive role for cooperation in organizations based on trust (see, for example, Sitkin and Roth, 1993; Morgan and Hunt, 1994; Mayer, Davies and Schoorman, 1995; Tyler and Degoey, 1995).

Even in some studies in experimental gaming, where great pains have traditionally been taken to secure anonymity, a connection between trusting cooperation and emotional attitude has been observed. Thus, the classic studies by Deutsch (1958) and Solomon (1960) have proven that there is a direct connection between trust and what they term a "cooperative attitude". [More recently Peter Kollock (1994) made a remarkable experience, when two of his subjects succeeded in breaking his careful arrangements for anonymity. These two turned out to be very successful partners in the experiment. Although they never saw each other directly prior to or during the experiment, they met as friends, exchanged high fives and went out for dinner together.]

Even if we grant that trust, as an emotional attitude, is not merely some marginal problem of thick personal relationships, one might still object that this is irrelevant from a practical point of view. Although people may have emotions when they trust someone, these emotions may not have an essential impact on what is, in fact, going on. Interest and cognitive beliefs might suffice to explain cooperative behavior, whether based on an emotional attitude called trust or not. The example of the teacher who signals trust for educational purposes shows that this is not true. The emotional attitude does have important consequences for behavior. Of course, this is, again, a special case, one whose general social relevance could still be doubted. Nevertheless, I believe experience tells us that emotional attitudes do play a major role in social interaction in general. And again, results in organizational science indicate that this is especially true in the case of trust. The perception of shared values has proven to be a reliable indicator of organizational efficiency.

If trust were only an aspect in the rational pursuit of interests, then the problem of trust would predominantly be one of minimizing risk. From a Rational Choice point of view, there are basically two ways to cope with risk in cooperative interaction. Firstly, one can try to affect the incentives of the interacting individuals directly, for instance, by supplying suitable mechanisms of sanctioning. Trusting behavior is more probable if trustworthiness is rewarded and/or if breaches of trust are made costly and if the interacting individuals are well aware of this. One may, secondly, engage in forming social institutions that guarantee that the decisive information for a cooperative decision is easily available. This allows for qualified, rationally justifiable trust. And, at the same time, it produces indirect incentives for trustworthy behavior by increasing the value of a good reputation and decreasing its price.

Without doubt, these are important measures. Still, it seems to me that, in regard to trust, they miss a substantial point. They only help reduce objective uncertainty and this is precisely why they can only be effective to a limited extent under the conditions of the modern world (Shapiro, 1987). But trust is a mechanism that allows people to cope with uncertainty.

As I have argued, there is a substantial presupposition for trust to be effective. There must be some measure of shared values or shared goals in any context if trustful interaction is to be expected. Yet, this does not mean that we should cultivate all our traditional values or that we should even try to unite the individuals under one common and all embracing ideology. Nothing has been said here that would support conservatism. The simple examples, which I have offered, show that very little is needed to make that minimal common spirit possible which is necessary for trustful interaction. In any society, most people agree on at least some of their values and many people will have some common interests. In order to promote opportunities to pursue interests in mutual cooperation based on trust, we must design our institutions such that we may experience that we have common interests and such that some sense of "connectedness" in pursuing individual aims may be developed.

References

Aristotle, "Rhetoric", in Jonathan Barnes (ed.) *The Complete Works of Aristotle*, Vol. 2. Princeton, N.J.: Princeton University Press, 1984, pp. 2152–2269.

Baier, Annette, Trust and Antitrust, *Ethics* 96 (1986), pp. 231–260.

Bollnow, Otto Friedrich, *Existenzphilosophie und Pädagogik*. Stuttgart: W. Kohlhammer, 1959.

Coleman, James S., *Foundations of Social Theory*, Cambridge, MA/London: The Belknap Press of Harvard University Press, 1990.

Calhoun, Cheshire, Cognitive Emotions?, in C. Calhoun and R.C. Solomon (eds) *What is an Emotion? Classical Readings in Philosophical Psychology*. New York/Oxford: Oxford University Press, 1984, pp. 327–342.

Calhoun, Cheshire and Solomon, Robert C., (eds), *What is an Emotion? Classical Readings in Philosophical Psychology*. New York/Oxford: Oxford University Press, 1984.

Dasgupta, Partha, Trust as a Commodity, in D. Gambetta (ed.), *Trust: Making and Breaking Cooperative Relations*. Oxford/New York: Basil Blackwell, 1988, pp. 49–72.

Dennet, Daniel C., Intentional Systems, *Journal of Philosophy* 8 (1987), pp. 87–106.

de Sousa, Ronald, *The Rationality of Emotion*, Cambridge, MA/London: MIT Press, 1987.

Deutsch, Morton, Trust and Suspicion, *Journal of Conflict Resolution*, 4 (1958), pp. 265–279.

Elster, Jon, *Alchemies of The Mind. Rationality and the Emotions*. New York/Cambridge: Cambridge University Press, 1999.

Flew, Antony and Macintyre, A., *New Essays in Philosophical Theology*. London, 1955.

Gambetta, Diego, Can We Trust Trust, in D. Gambetta (ed.), *Trust: Making and Breaking Cooperative Relations*. Oxford/New York: Basil Blackwell, 1988, pp. 213–238.

Govier, Trudy, An Epistemology of Trust, *International Journal of Moral and Social Studies*, 8(2) (1993), pp. 155–174.

Govier, Trudy, *Social Trust and Human Communities*. Montreal/Kingston/London/Buffalo: McGill-Queen's University Press, 1997.

Hardin, Russell, Trusting Persons, Trusting Institutions, in R. Zeckhauser (ed.), *Strategy and Choice*. Cambridge, MA: The MIT Press, 1991, pp. 183–209.

Hartmann, Nicolai, *Ethik*. Berlin: Walter de Gruyter, 1962.

Hollis, Martin, *Trust within Reason*. Cambridge, UK/New York: Cambridge University Press, 1998.

Holton, Richard, Deciding to Trust, Coming to Believe, *Australian Journal of Philosophy*, 72(1) (1994), pp. 63–76.

Horsburgh, H.J.N., The Ethics of Trust, *Philosophical Quarterly* 10, (1960), pp. 343–354.

Kollock, Peter, The Emergence of Exchange Structures: An Experimental Study of Uncertainty, Commitment and Trust", *The American Journal of Sociology*, 100(2) (1994), pp. 313–345.

Makarenko, A.S., *Der Weg ins Leben*. Berlin/Weimar: Aufbau-Verlag, 1974.

Mayer, Roger C., Davis, James H. and Schoorman, F. David, An Integrative Model of Organizional Trust, *Academy of Management Review*, 20(3) (1995), pp. 709–734.

Morgan, Robert M. and Hunt, Shelby D., The Commitment-Trust Theory of Relationship Marketing, *Journal of Marketing*, 58 (1994), 20–38.

Pettit, Philip, The Cunning of Trust, *Philosophy and Public Affairs*, 24(3) (1995), pp. 202–225.

Shapiro, Susan P., The Social Control of Impersonal Trust, *American Journal of Sociology* 93 (1987), pp. 623–658.

Sitkin, Sim B. and Roth, Nancy L., Explaining the Limited Effectiveness of Legalistic, Remedies' for Trust/Distrust, *Organization Science*, 4(3) (1993), pp. 367–392.

Solomon, Leonard, The Influence of Some Types of Power Relationships and Game Strategies upon the Development of Interpersonal Trust, *Journal of Abnormal and Social Psychology*, 61(2) (1960), pp. 223–230.

Solomon, Robert, *The Passions. Emotions and The Meaning of Life*. Indianapolis: Hackett Publishing Company, 1993.

Strawson, Peter F., *Freedom and Resentment*. London: Methuen, 1974.

Tyler, Tom R. and Degoey, Peter, Trust in Organizational Authorities: The Influence of Motive Attributions on Willingness to Accept Decisions, in R.M. Kramer and T.R. Tyler (eds), *Trust in Organizations. Frontiers of Theory and Research*. Thousand Oaks/London/New Delhi: SAGE, 1996.

Williamson, Oliver E., Calculativeness, Trust, and Economic Organization, *Journal of Law and Economics* 36(1) (1993), pp. 453–486.

Wisdom, John, Gods, *Proceedings of the Aristotelian Society* 45 (1944-45), pp. 185–206.

Heinrich-Heine Universität Düsseldorf
Sozialwissenschaftliches Institut, Soziologie I
Universitätsstrasse 1
D-40224 Düsseldorf
Germany
E-mail: lahno@phil-fak.uni-duesseldorf.de; B. Lahno@t-online.de

Part II
Trust as Taste

[14]

Journal of Economic Perspectives—Volume 14, Number 3—Summer 2000—Pages 159–181

Fairness and Retaliation: The Economics of Reciprocity

Ernst Fehr and Simon Gächter

A long-standing tradition in economics views human beings as exclusively self-interested. In most economic accounts of individual behavior and aggregate social phenomena, the "vast forces of greed" (Arrow, 1980) are put at the center of the explanation. In economic models human actors are typically portrayed as "self-interest seeking with guile (which) includes . . . more blatant forms, such as lying, stealing, and cheating . . . (but) more often involves subtle forms of deceit" (Williamson, 1985).

However, as we will document below, many people deviate from purely self-interested behavior in a reciprocal manner. Reciprocity means that in response to friendly actions, people are frequently much nicer and much more cooperative than predicted by the self-interest model; conversely, in response to hostile actions they are frequently much more nasty and even brutal. The *Edda*, a 13th century collection of Norse epic verses, gives a succinct description of reciprocity: "A man ought to be a friend to his friend and repay gift with gift. People should meet smiles with smiles and lies with treachery." There is considerable evidence that a substantial fraction of people behave according to this dictum: People repay gifts and take revenge even in interactions with complete strangers and even if it is costly for them and *yields neither present nor future material rewards*. Our notion of reciprocity is thus very different from kind or hostile responses in repeated interactions that are solely motivated by future material gains.

■ *Ernst Fehr is Professor of Economics and a Core Member of the MacArthur Foundation Network on Economic Environments and the Evolution of Individual Preferences and Social Norms, while Simon Gächter is Assistant Professor of Economics, both at the University of Zurich, Institute for Empirical Economic Research, Zurich, Switzerland. Their web page is ⟨http://www.unizh.ch/iew/grp/fehr/index.html⟩. Their e-mail addresses are ⟨efehr@iew.unizh.ch⟩ and ⟨gaechter@iew.unizh.ch⟩, respectively.*

We term the cooperative reciprocal tendencies "positive reciprocity" while the retaliatory aspects are called "negative reciprocity." In this paper, we first offer a brief overview of the evidence for reciprocal actions in relatively abstract one-shot games. Then, we show that reciprocity has powerful implications for many important economic domains. George Stigler (1981) wrote that when "self-interest and ethical values with wide verbal allegiance are in conflict, much of the time, most of the time in fact, self-interest-theory . . . will win." Our evidence indicates that Stigler's position is often not valid. When the world is made up of self-interested types and reciprocal types, interacting with each other, the reciprocal types dominate the aggregate outcome in certain circumstances, while the self-interested types will dominate the aggregate outcome in other circumstances. We will provide evidence that there are important conditions in which the self-interest theory is unambiguously refuted. For example, in competitive markets with incomplete contracts, the reciprocal types dominate the aggregate results. Similarly, when people face strong material incentives to free ride, the self-interest model predicts no cooperation at all. However, if there are individual opportunities to punish others, then the reciprocal types vigorously punish free riders even when the punishment is costly for the punisher. As a consequence of the punishing behavior of the reciprocal types, a very high level of cooperation can in fact be achieved. Indeed, the power to enhance collective actions and to enforce social norms is probably one of the most important consequences of reciprocity.

This line of thought brings out another important implication of the presence of reciprocal types: Details of the institutional environment, like the presence of incomplete contracts or of costly individual punishment opportunities, determine whether the reciprocal or the selfish types are pivotal. Institutional features like this may thus have a tremendous impact on patterns of aggregate behavior that are neglected by the self-interest model. As a consequence, economic predictions regarding the impact of different institutions will be questionable if they do not take into account the presence of reciprocal types. Moreover, it turns out that the existence of reciprocal types may actually give rise to a world of incomplete contracts, so that reciprocity helps to generate those conditions under which it can flourish.

Positive and Negative Reciprocity: Some Evidence

Reciprocity is fundamentally different from "cooperative" or "retaliatory" behavior in repeated interactions. These behaviors arise because actors expect future material benefits from their actions; in the case of reciprocity, the actor is *responding* to friendly or hostile actions even if no material gains can be expected. Reciprocity is also fundamentally different from altruism. Altruism is a form of *unconditional* kindness; that is, altruism given does not emerge as a response to altruism received. Again, reciprocity is an in-kind response to beneficial or harmful acts.

Examples of retaliatory behavior abound. Many wars and gang crimes fit well into this category. A vivid example is provided by the recent events in Kosovo when many Albanian refugees took bloody revenge after the victory of NATO over Serbian forces. Other examples are given by the rise in employees' theft rates after firms have cut employees' wages (Giacalone and Greenberg, 1997) or by the social ostracism exercised by coworkers against strikebreakers during and after industrial disputes.

Likewise, positive reciprocity is deeply embedded in many social interactions. Psychological studies show, for example, that smiling waitresses get tipped much more than less friendly ones (Tidd and Lochard, 1978). Calls for contributions to charities are often accompanied by small gifts. Apparently, charities believe that this raises the propensity to donate. Uninvited favors, in general, are likely to create feelings of indebtedness obliging many people to repay the psychological debt. A particularly powerful example of this is the use of free samples as a sales technique (Cialdini, 1993). In supermarkets, customers are frequently given small amounts of a certain product for free. For many people it seems to be very difficult to accept samples from a smiling attendant without actually buying anything. Some people even buy the product although they do not like it very much. The normative power of reciprocity is also likely to have an important impact on social policy issues (Bowles and Gintis, 1998b). Social policies are much less likely to be endorsed by public opinion when they reward people independent of whether and how much they contribute to society.

Since in real world interactions, it is very difficult to rule out with certainty that an actor derives a future material benefit from a reciprocal response, we provide in the following discussion evidence on reciprocity from controlled laboratory experiments. In these experiments, real subjects interact anonymously and face real, and sometimes rather high, material costs of reciprocal actions, in a context where it can be precluded that reciprocal responses will lead to future material rewards.

Perhaps the most vivid game to demonstrate negatively reciprocal behavior is the ultimatum bargaining experiment. In this game, two subjects have to agree on the division of a fixed sum of money. Person A, the Proposer, can make exactly one proposal of how to divide the amount. Person B, the Responder, can accept or reject the proposed division. In the case of rejection, both receive nothing; in the case of acceptance, the proposal is implemented. A robust result in this experiment, across hundreds of trials, is that Proposers who offer the Responder less than 30 percent of the available sum are rejected with a very high probability (for example, see Güth, Schmittberger and Schwarze, 1982; Camerer and Thaler, 1995; Roth, 1995, and the references therein). Apparently, Responders do not behave in a self-interest maximizing manner. In general, the motive indicated for the rejection of positive, yet "low," offers is that subjects view them as unfair.

Negative reciprocity in an ultimatum game has been observed in many countries, including Indonesia, Israel, Japan, many European countries, Russia and the United States (for example, see Roth, Prasnikar, Okuno-Fujiwara and Zamir,

1991).[1] Moreover, rather high monetary stakes do not change or have only a minor impact on these experimental results. In the study of Cameron (1999), the amount to be divided represented the income of three months for the subjects. Other studies with relatively high stakes have involved college students dividing amounts of $100 or more (Hoffman, McCabe and Smith, 1995; Henrich, forthcoming; Slonim and Roth, 1998).

Positive reciprocity has been documented in many trust or gift exchange games (for example, Fehr, Kirchsteiger and Riedl, 1993; Berg, Dickhaut and McCabe, 1995; McCabe, Rassenti and Smith, 1996). In a trust game, for example, a Proposer receives an amount of money x from the experimenter, and then can send between zero and x to the Responder. The experimenter then triples the amount sent, which we term y, so that the Responder has $3y$. The Responder is then free to return anything between zero and $3y$ to the Proposer. It turns out that many Proposers send money and that many Responders give back some money. Moreover, there is frequently a positive correlation between y and the amount sent back at the individual as well as at the aggregate level. Again, positive reciprocity does not appear to diminish even if the monetary stake size is rather high; for example, Fehr and Tougareva (1995) found strong positive reciprocity in experiments conducted in Moscow, where their subjects earned on average the monetary income of ten weeks in an experiment that lasted for two hours.

The fraction of subjects who show a concern for fairness and behave reciprocally in one-shot situations is relatively high. Many studies have carried out detailed analyses of individual decisions and found that the fraction of subjects exhibiting reciprocal choices is between 40 and 66 percent (Gächter and Falk, 1999; Berg, Dickhaut and McCabe, 1995; Fehr and Falk, 1999; Abbink, Irlenbusch and Renner, forthcoming). However, these same studies also find that between 20 and 30 percent of the subjects do not reciprocate and behave completely selfishly. Thus, a nontrivial minority of subjects exhibits selfish behavior. Burnham (1998) found that male behavior in the ultimatum game is systematically linked to testosterone levels. Males who reject unfair offers have higher testosterone levels than males who accept unfair offers. This is interesting because testosterone levels are thought to be important mediators of male willingness to engage in aggressive behavior.

There is now little disagreement among experimental researchers about the facts indicating reciprocal *behavior.* There also seems to be an emerging consensus that the propensity to punish harmful behavior is stronger than the propensity to reward friendly behavior (Offerman, 1999; Charness and Rabin, 2000). There is, however, disagreement regarding the main sources of reciprocal behavior. Some believe that the desire to maintain equity is most important (Bolton and Ockenfels, forthcoming). Others emphasize that the desire to punish hostile *intentions* and to reward kind *intentions* is also important (Rabin, 1993; Blount, 1995; Dufwenberg and Kirchsteiger, 1999; Falk and Fischbacher, 1999). A third possibility

[1] The only exception is the study of Henrich (forthcoming) among the Machiguenga in the Peruvian Amazon. Machiguengas exhibit very low rejection rates.

is that people do not respond to the intention but to the type of person they face (Levine, 1998). A fourth group of researchers, in contrast, views the reciprocal actions in laboratory experiments as a form of boundedly rational behavior (Gale, Binmore and Samuelson, 1995; Roth and Erev, 1995). However, differences in interpretation notwithstanding, many researchers now agree that reciprocity is a rather stable behavioral response by a nonnegligible fraction of the people that can be reliably elicited under appropriate circumstances.[2]

In our view, this stability and reliability renders reciprocity important for economics and raises exciting questions: How do reciprocal types change the nature of collective action problems that permeate people's interactions in firms, public bureaucracies, markets and the political sphere? To what extent can reciprocal people constrain the opportunistic tendencies of selfish people? Which institutions render the reciprocal types decisive in shaping aggregate social phenomena and when are the selfish types pivotal? How does the presence of reciprocal types change organizational outcomes, contractual and institutional choices, and the interactions in competitive markets? How do explicit economic incentives affect the propensity for voluntary cooperation among the reciprocal people? Do explicit incentives crowd out or enhance voluntary cooperation? In the rest of this paper, we offer answers to these questions.

Public Goods

Many societies face the problem of how to provide public goods. For a group of self-interested agents, of course, public goods present the difficulty that since all agents will want to be free riders on the efforts of others, no agent will contribute willingly to the public good.

To take a specific example of this situation, consider the basic structure of a public good experiment run by Fehr and Gächter (forthcoming). In this experiment, there are four group members who are each given 20 tokens. All four subjects decide simultaneously how many tokens to keep for themselves and how many tokens to invest in a common public good project. For each token that is privately kept by a subject, that subject earns exactly one token. For each token a subject invests into the project *each* of the four subjects, whether they have invested in the public good or not, earns .4 tokens. Thus, the private return for investing one additional token into the public good is .4 tokens while the social return is 1.6 tokens. Since the cost of investing one token is exactly one token while the private return is only .4 tokens, it is always in the material self-interest of a subject to keep all tokens. Yet, if all group members keep all tokens privately, each subject earns only 20 tokens, while if all invest their total endowment in the public good, each

[2] The stability of reciprocal behavior suggests that it has deep evolutionary roots. For evolutionary explanations see Güth and Yaari (1992); Bowles and Gintis (1999); Sethi and Somananthan (2000); and Gintis (forthcoming).

subject earns 32 tokens. Thus, in this simple example, the highest level of social welfare would be achieved if everyone contributed all of their assets to the public good, but it is in the self-interest of each individual to free ride, regardless of what others contribute, and to contribute nothing.[3]

To what extent can reciprocity provide the basis for agents deciding to make at least some contribution to the public good? Positive reciprocity implies that subjects are willing to contribute something to the public good if others are also willing to contribute, because a contribution to the public good represents a kind action, which induces reciprocally motivated people to contribute, too (Sugden, 1984; Keser and van Winden, forthcoming). However, to sustain contributing to the public good as a stable behavioral regularity, a sufficiently high proportion of the agents in the game have to be reciprocally motivated. Since we know that a nonnegligible minority of subjects is motivated by pure self-interest, not reciprocity, it is unlikely that a positive level of contributions to the public good can be sustained as an equilibrium.

Up to this point, negative reciprocity has not played a role, because in the game as described there are no opportunities for *direct* retaliation in response to observed free riding. However, negative reciprocity can play the role that if subjects expect that others free ride, and if they interpret that as a hostile act, then they can "punish" others by free riding, too. The result is likely to be that self-interested types choose to free ride because they are self-interested, and reciprocal types free ride because they observe others free riding. Although the motivation to free ride is different for the reciprocal type, in the end the behavior of the selfish and the reciprocal type is indistinguishable. This public good game provides, therefore, an example where selfish types can induce reciprocal types to make "selfish" choices.[4]

However, the impact of negative reciprocity changes radically if subjects are given the opportunity to observe the contributions of others, and to punish those who do not contribute. Suppose, for example, that each subject in a group has the opportunity to *reduce* the income of each other subject in the group. Suppose further, that a reduction of the income of one other group member by x tokens costs the punisher $(1/3)x$ tokens. It is important that punishment be costly to the agent who imposes it. After all, if punishing is costly for the punisher, selfish subjects will never punish. Hence, if all subjects were purely self-interested, contribution decisions would be unaffected by the punishment opportunity. However, negatively reciprocal subjects, who are willing to pay a price to act reciprocally, will use the costly punishment opportunity to punish free riders. This, in turn, will induce self-interested subjects to contribute to avoid the punishment. The public good game with *direct* punishment opportunities provides, therefore, an example where the reciprocal types can induce the selfish types to make "cooperative"

[3] For a survey on public goods experiments, see Ledyard (1995).

[4] Fehr and Schmidt (1999, Proposition 4) provide a formal proof of these arguments. They show that even a small minority of purely selfish subjects can induce the reciprocal subjects to behave "selfishly" in this game.

choices. Fehr and Schmidt (1999, Proposition 5) show theoretically that even a *minority* of reciprocal subjects is capable of inducing a *majority* of selfish subjects to cooperate in these circumstances.

Fehr and Gächter (forthcoming) have conducted a variety of public good experiments with and without punishment opportunities, using the basic structure of the four-person, 20-token public good game just described.[5] The experiment was conducted in two versions: a Perfect Stranger version and a Partner version. In an experimental session of the Perfect Stranger version, 24 subjects formed six groups with four members in each group. The public good games were repeated for six periods and in each period completely new groups were formed so that nobody met another group member more than once. The Perfect Stranger version ensures that the actions in a particular period have no rewards in future periods. In contrast, in the Partner version the *same* four members played ten times.[6] In this version there are possible strategic spillovers across periods so that present actions can have future returns. However, as in the Perfect Stranger version, all subjects knew the total number of periods in advance.

Figure 1 shows how much a subject is punished for a given negative deviation from the average contribution of other members in the group. The punishment is measured by the average percentage reduction in the incomes of the punished subject. It turns out that the negative deviation from others' average contributions to the public good is a strong determinant of punishment. The more a subject free rides *relative* to the others the more it gets punished. Moreover, this pattern is almost the same in the two versions of the game: Free riders are punished irrespective of whether there are future rewards for the punisher. Questionnaire evidence that elicits subjects' motives and emotions indicates that the deviation from the norm of cooperation causes resentment and the impulse to punish.[7]

The heavy punishment of free riders, in turn, has a large disciplining effect on subjects' cooperation behavior, as indicated in Figure 2. This figure compares the time paths of the average contributions in the two versions of the public good game. The first observation is that in the absence of a punishment opportunity, average cooperation converges to very low levels in the later periods. For instance, in period six of the Perfect Stranger version, 79 percent of the subjects free ride completely and the rest contributes little. This high defection rate stands in sharp contrast to the contribution behavior in the games with a punishment opportunity: When subjects are perfect strangers they can at least stabilize contributions at

[5] For an exciting experiment with punishment opportunities in a common pool resource context, see Ostrom, Walker and Gardner (1992).

[6] In the Partner and the Perfect Stranger version, experiments with and without the punishment opportunity were conducted and all interactions were completely anonymous. In the presence of the punishment opportunity, subjects could punish in each period after they observed others' contributions in this period.

[7] On the role of emotions in similar contexts, see also the experimental study by Bosman and van Winden (1999).

Figure 1
Mean Income Reduction for a Given Negative Deviation from the Mean Contribution of Other Group Members

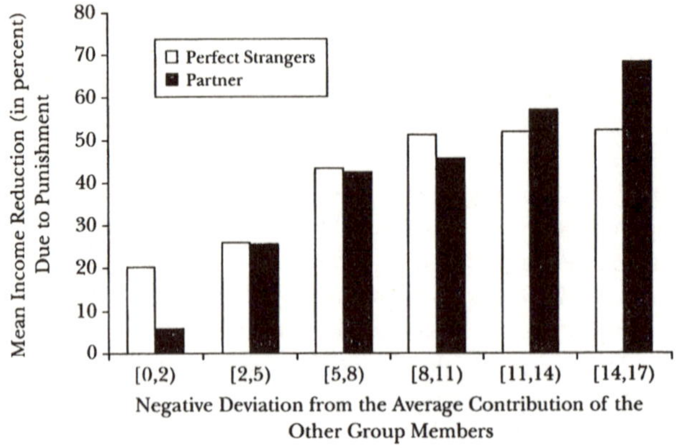

Source: Fehr and Gächter (forthcoming).

relatively high levels. In the Partner version they almost converge to the maximum level of contributions. It is particularly remarkable that in the *final* period of the Partner version subjects still contribute 90 percent of the endowment (of 20 tokens), indicating the disciplining force of the punishment opportunity.

From Public Goods to Social Norms

The problem of public goods may seem a rather limited economic application, and it may seem farfetched to link the experiment here to government spending on basic research and development or national defense. While we believe that such links can be made, we readily concede that the most important applications of this line of thought are not found in government budget decisions. Instead, we believe that the analytical structure of the public good problem is a good approximation to the question of how social norms are established and maintained.

At this point, it is useful to define a social norm more precisely. It is: 1) a behavioral regularity; that is 2) based on a socially shared belief of how one ought to behave; which triggers 3) the enforcement of the prescribed behavior by informal social sanctions. Thus, a social norm can be thought of as a sort of behavioral public good, in which everybody should make a positive contribution—that is, follow the social norm—and also where individuals must be willing to enforce the social norm with informal social sanctions, even at some immediate cost to themselves.

Casual evidence and daily experience suggests that social norms are pervasive in social and economic life. The large majority of interactions in people's lives take

Figure 2
Evolution of Average Contributions with and without the Punishment Option in the Partner and the Perfect Stranger Condition

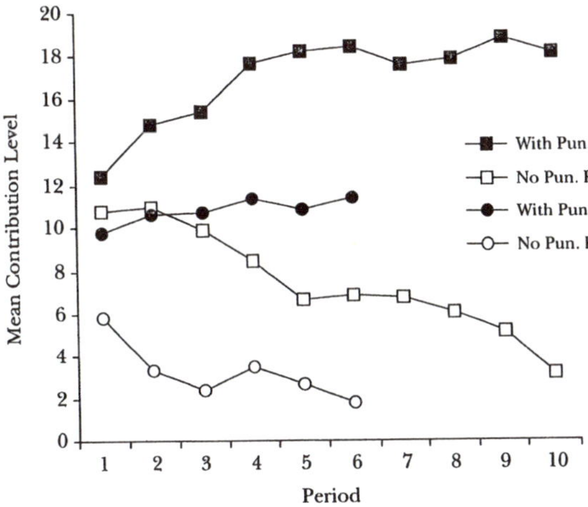

Source: Fehr and Gächter (forthcoming).

place in the family, in residential neighborhoods, in formal or informal clubs and at people's workplaces. Typically, these interactions are not regulated by explicit contracts but by informal social norms.

For example, it has been observed in many studies that social norms influence work morale and behavior against "rate busters" (Roethlisberger and Dickson, 1947). Social sanctions by peer members are probably a very important determinant of effort behavior in work relations. It has often been observed that consumption and savings decisions are to a large degree affected by social norms that determine what others regard as "appropriate" consumption. Norm-governed attitudes, social interactions and conformism among peers, relatives, and in neighborhoods may have important consequences for human capital decisions, for the decision to take part in elections, and for criminal activities. Social norms also often regulate the use of common pool resources (Ostrom, 1998) and the ways landowners settle disputes (Ellickson, 1994). There is a huge literature that argues that in collective action problems and in the provision of public goods, social norms play a decisive role (Elster, 1989; Ostrom, 1998). There is also reason to believe that social norms are relevant for the amount of tax evasion and the abuse of welfare payments, and for attitudes towards the welfare state in general. Social norms also constitute perhaps one of the most important elements of what recently has been termed "social capital"—the informal cooperative infrastructure of our societies. Finally, there are powerful arguments that social norms also have a decisive impact on the functioning of markets. Solow (1990), for instance, has argued that they can lead to involuntary unemployment. The above examples also indicate that social norms are not necessarily beneficial for society. Depending on the specific context of the norm, norms may deter or encourage socially beneficial behavior.

In our view, there can be little doubt that human behavior is shaped by social norms. They constitute constraints on individual behavior beyond the legal, information and budget constraints usually considered by economists. In view of the fact that most social relations in neighborhoods, families and work places are not governed by explicit agreements but by social norms, the role of reciprocity as a norm enforcement device is perhaps its most important function.

Reciprocity as a Contract Enforcement Device

Real-world contracts are often highly incomplete, which gives rise to strong incentives to shirk (Williamson, 1985). Economic historians like North (1990) have argued that differences in societies' contract enforcement capabilities are probably a major reason for differences in economic growth and human welfare.

The employment relationship, in particular, is characterized by incomplete contracts. Labor contracts often take the form of a fixed wage contract without explicit performance incentives and in which workers have a considerable degree of discretion over effort levels. In such a situation, a worker's general job attitude, loyalty (Simon, 1991), or what Williamson (1985) called "consummate cooperation," which is "an affirmative job attitude whereby gaps are filled, initiative is taken, and judgment is exercised in an instrumental way," becomes important. Under a complete labor contract, of course, a generally cooperative job attitude would be superfluous, because all relevant actions would be unambiguously described and enforceable. But how can any explicit contract unambiguously describe, assess, and enforce terms like "initiative," "good judgment" and "potentially arising gaps"?

The requirement of a generally cooperative job attitude renders reciprocal motivations potentially very important in the labor process. If a substantial fraction of the work force is motivated by reciprocity considerations, employers can affect the degree of "cooperativeness" of workers by varying the generosity of the compensation package—even without offering explicit performance incentives.

The conjecture that reciprocity plays a role in the choice of effort has been investigated in several tightly controlled laboratory experiments. For example, in Fehr, Gächter and Kirchsteiger (1997), experimental employers could offer a wage contract that stipulated a binding wage w and a desired effort level $\hat{e}$. If an experimental worker accepted this offer, the worker was free to choose the actual effort level e between a minimum and a maximum level. The employer always had to pay the offered wage irrespective of the actual effort level. In this experiment effort is represented by a number e between 1 and 10. Higher numbers represent higher effort levels and, hence, a higher profit π for the employer and higher effort costs $c(e)$ for the worker. The effort cost for $e = 1$ was zero. The profit π from the employment of a worker was given by $\pi = 10e - w$ and the monetary payoff for the experimental worker was $u = w - c(e)$. In each experimental session there were eight workers and six employers, who could employ at most one worker. All participants knew the excess supply of workers. It ensured that a worker's reservation wage, if the worker is purely selfish, was zero so that employers could, in principle, enforce very low wages. The crucial point in this experiment is that selfish workers have no incentives to provide effort above the minimum level $e = 1$. The question, therefore, is to what extent experimental employers do appeal to workers' reciprocity by offering generous compensation packages and to what extent workers honor generous offers.

It turns out that many employers indeed make quite generous offers. On average, the offered contracts stipulate a desired effort of $\hat{e} = 7$ and the offered wage implied that the worker receives 44 percent of the total surplus $u + \pi$. Interestingly, many workers honor this generosity somewhat but not fully. The actual average effort is given by $e = 4.4$, which was substantially above the selfish choice of $e = 1$. However, only in 14 percent of all cases workers abide by the terms of the contract, while in 83 percent of all cases they shirk. Still, in 74 percent of all instances of shirking they do *not* shirk fully. Thus, although shirking is still quite prevalent in this situation the evidence suggests that in response to generous job offers, people are on average willing to put forward extra effort above what is implied by purely pecuniary considerations.

A large interview study conducted by Bewley (1995, 1999) provides field evidence supporting this view. The managers who were interviewed stress "that workers have so many opportunities to take advantage of employers that it is not wise to depend on coercion and financial incentives alone as motivators. . . . Employers believe that other motivators are necessary, which are best thought of as having to do with generosity" (Bewley, 1995, p. 252).

In the situation described above, only workers can react reciprocally while employers cannot. Employers can only try to elicit reciprocal effort choices from the workers. Yet, what happens if employers can also respond reciprocally by rewarding or punishing workers after they observe actual effort choices? This question is examined as well in Fehr, Gächter and Kirchsteiger (1997). In this experiment everything is kept identical to the previous experiment, except that employers could now reward or punish the workers after the effort decision is revealed. For every token spent on rewards they could raise the worker's monetary income by 2.5 tokens (reflecting the possible higher marginal utility of income for workers in reality). Likewise, for every token spent on punishment, they could reduce the worker's income by 2.5 tokens. Since rewarding and punishing is costly, a selfish employer will never reward or punish. Hence, the reward and punishment opportunity is irrelevant according to the self-interest model.

If workers shirked in the experiments, however, employers punished in 68 percent of these cases. If there was overprovision, employers rewarded in 70 percent of these cases. If workers exactly met the desired effort, employers still rewarded in 41 percent of the cases. As a consequence, workers chose much higher effort levels when employers have a reward/punishment opportunity. Indeed, although in these experiments the average *desired* effort level is slightly higher than in the previous experiment, the shirking rate declined from 83 percent to 26 percent. In

38 percent of the cases, workers even provided a higher effort than requested. An important consequence of this increase in average effort was that the aggregate monetary payoff increased by 40 percent—even if one takes the payoff reductions that result from actual punishments into account.

This evidence strongly suggests that reciprocity substantially contributes to the enforcement of contracts. The power of reciprocity derives from the fact that it provides incentives for the potential cheaters to behave cooperatively or at least to limit their degree of noncooperation. In the above experiments, for example, even purely selfish employers have an incentive to make a generous job offer, if they expect sufficiently many workers to behave in a reciprocal manner. Similarly, even purely selfish workers have an incentive to provide a high effort in case of a reward/punishment opportunity, if they expect that sufficiently many employers respond reciprocally to their effort choices.

Work Motivation and Performance Incentives

The previous experiments focus on fairness and reciprocity as a means to enforce contracts. In reality, material incentives are, of course, also used to mitigate the enforcement problem. The question, therefore, arises, how explicit material incentives to abide by the terms of the contract interact with motivations of fairness and reciprocity. One possibility is that reciprocity gives rise to extra effort on top of what is enforced by material incentives alone. However, it is also possible that explicit incentives may cause a hostile atmosphere of threat and distrust, which reduces any reciprocity-based extra effort. Bewley (1995, p. 252), for example, reports that many managers stress that explicit "punishment should be rarely used as a way to obtain co-operation" because of the negative effects on work atmosphere.

In a new series of experiments, Fehr and Gächter (2000) examine this possibility. They implement a control treatment that is identical to the previous contract enforcement experiment *without* reward and punishment opportunities. Remember that in this treatment there are no material incentives. In addition, they also implement a treatment with explicit performance incentives. This treatment keeps everything constant relative to the control treatment, except that employers now have the possibility to stipulate a fine, to be paid by the worker to the employer in case of verified shirking. The probability of verification is .33 and the fine is restricted to an interval between zero and a maximal fine. The maximal fine is fixed at a level such that a selfish risk-neutral worker will choose an effort level of 4 when faced with this fine.[8]

The line with the black dots in Figure 3 shows workers' effort behavior in the control treatment. It depicts the average effort on the vertical axis as a function of

[8] To prevent hostility from being introduced merely by the use of value-laden terms we avoided terms like "fine," "performance," and so on. Instead we used a rather neutral language like, for example, "price deduction."

Figure 3
Actual Effort-Rent Relation in the Absence and Presence of Explicit Performance Incentives

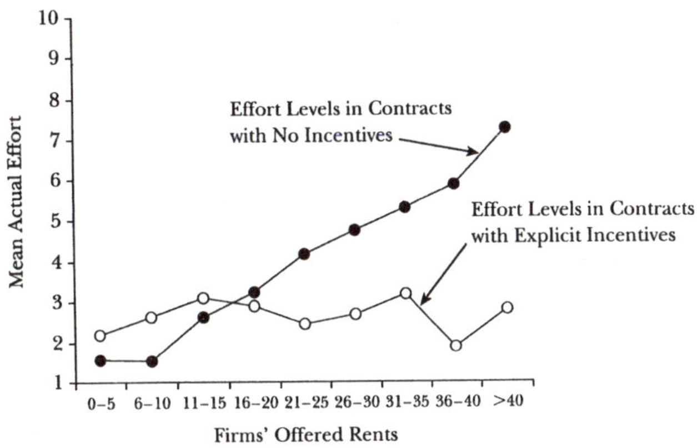

Source: Fehr and Gächter (forthcoming).

the rent offered to the workers. The offered rent is implied by the original contract offer; it is defined as the wage minus the cost of providing the desired effort level. Due to the presence of many reciprocal workers, the average effort level is strongly increasing in the offered rent and rises far above the selfish level of $e = 1$. The line with the white dots in Figure 3 shows the relationship of rent to effort in the presence of the explicit performance incentive. Except at the low rent levels, the average effort is *lower* in the presence of the explicit incentives!

This result suggests that reciprocity-based effort elicitation and explicit performance incentives may indeed be in conflict with each other. In particular, explicit incentives may "crowd out" reciprocal effort choices. In the experiments of Fehr and Gächter (2000), the average effort taken over all trades and, hence, the aggregate monetary surplus, is lower in the incentive treatment than in the control treatment. However, employers' profits are higher because in the incentive treatment they rely much less on the "carrot" of generous wage offers. Instead, they threaten the maximal fine in most cases. For the employers, the savings in wage costs more than offset the reductions in revenues that are caused by the lower effort in the incentive treatment. However, while the wage savings merely represent a transfer from the workers to the firms, the reduction in effort levels reduces the aggregate surplus. This shows that, in the presence of reciprocal types, efficiency questions and questions of distribution are inseparable. Since the perceived fairness of the distribution of the gains from trade affects the effort behavior of the reciprocal types, different distributions are associated with different levels of the aggregate gains. Thus, lump-sum transfers between trading parties have allocative consequences.

Our "crowding out" result may seem counterintuitive, since it is almost axiomatic to some economists that material incentives should produce a better outcome. However, this position neglects the existence of reciprocity-based voluntary cooperation. Similar problems with explicit incentives are obtained in the experiments of Gneezy and Rustichini (forthcoming) and Bohnet, Frey and Huck (1999)—explicit material incentives may have counterproductive effects. These results, of course, do not provide a general case against the use of explicit incentives.[9] In some cases, there is evidence that explicit incentives can leave voluntary cooperation intact (for example, Güth, Klose, Königstein and Schwalbach, 1998). In particular, notice that the incentive devices discussed here involved punishments and it may well be that reward-based explicit incentives do not destroy reciprocal inclinations, or may even strengthen them. However, the results do indicate that in the presence of reciprocity-based voluntary cooperation, the task of providing explicit incentives is considerably more complicated than envisaged by standard principal-agent theory.

Wage Rigidity, Rent-Sharing and Competition

In a seminal paper, Akerlof (1982) argued that labor markets are characterized by considerations of "gift exchange," by which he meant that employers offer a gift of pay which is more than labor's opportunity cost and employees offer a gift of more than minimal effort. This exchange may explain why employers are reluctant to cut wages in a recession, as found by many researchers (see Bewley, 1999, and the references therein). The reason is that wage cuts may decrease productivity. In addition, the gift exchange notion implies that, ceteris paribus, more profitable firms pay on average higher wages. Higher profitability is likely to be associated with a higher marginal product of effort. Therefore, the return of a given effort increase is higher and employers have an incentive to pay higher wages.

The fact that the presence of reciprocal types in the labor market gives rise to downward wage rigidity has been demonstrated in a number of experiments. In the following we draw on Fehr and Falk (1999), because they confirmed the existence of downward wage rigidity in a version of the most competitive environment—the competitive double auction. In this environment, both experimental firms and workers can make wage bids. A large body of research has shown the striking competitive properties of experimental double auctions. In hundreds of such experiments, prices and quantities quickly converged to the competitive equilibrium predicted by standard self-interest theory (Holt, 1995, presents a survey of important results). Therefore, showing that reciprocity causes wage rigidity in a double auction provides a strong piece of evidence in favor of the importance of reciprocity in markets.

[9] There exists a large psychological literature on the crowding out of intrinsic motivation by explicit rewards (Deci and Ryan, 1985). For applications of intrinsic motivation theory to economics, see Frey (1997). There are, however, considerable differences between the literature discussed above and the psychological studies on crowding out (Fehr and Gächter, 2000).

Fehr and Falk (1999) carried out a series of double auction experiments set in the context of a labor market. Both experimental firms and experimental workers could make wage bids. If a bid was accepted, a labor contract was concluded. There were eight firms and twelve workers and each firm could employ at most one worker. A worker who concluded a contract had costs of 20. Therefore, due to the excess supply of labor, the competitive wage level was 20. Within this broader context, Fehr and Falk (1999) considered two treatment conditions: one condition in which the labor contract was complete because the experimenter enforced a given effort level; and one where the labor contract was incomplete because employees could choose an effort level between a minimum and maximum after the wage contract was concluded, and the employers could neither stipulate nor enforce an effort level above the minimum level.[10]

The time path of the average wage in a typical double auction with incomplete contracts is shown in Figure 4a. Figure 4b shows average wages in a typical double auction with complete contracts. In addition, both figures show workers' wage bids. Clearly, wage levels are radically different in the two conditions. In the market with complete contracts, employers take full advantage of the low wage offers made by the workers and, as a consequence, wages are close to the competitive level in this market. In contrast, in the market with incomplete contracts employers are very reluctant to accept workers' underbidding of prevailing wages. From period 4 onwards, wages move even further away from the competitive level—despite fierce competition among workers for scarce jobs. The data analysis in Fehr and Falk (1999) shows that employers' high wage policy in the market with incomplete contracts was quite rational, because in this way they could sustain higher effort levels and increase profits relative to a low wage policy.

The big difference in the impact of reciprocity on wage formation in markets with complete and incomplete contracts illustrates again the importance of institutional details. In the incomplete contracts condition, a reciprocal worker can punish the firm by choosing a low effort level after the labor contract has been concluded. Since firms anticipate this possibility, they have a reason to pay generous wages. In contrast, in the complete contracts condition, the only method for a worker to punish a firm who offers a low wage is to reject such an offer. However, due to the presence of a certain proportion of purely self-interested workers, the reciprocal worker knows that others will accept low wage offers. Thus, reciprocal workers have, in fact, no possibility to punish firms—which induces them to accept low wage offers, too. Since firms anticipate or notice this willingness to accept low offers, they have no reason to offer generous wages. Thus, the ability to punish is

[10] One double auction lasted for ten periods and a period lasted for three minutes. In each period the same stationary situation was implemented; that is, there were twelve workers, eight firms, and each worker's reservation wage was 20. In a given period, employers and workers could make as many wage bids as they liked, as long as they had not yet concluded a contract. In the condition with incomplete contracts, workers had to choose an effort between a minimum and a maximum level after they had concluded a contract.

Figure 4a
Workers' Offers and Mean Contract Wages in the Double Auction Market with Incomplete Contracts

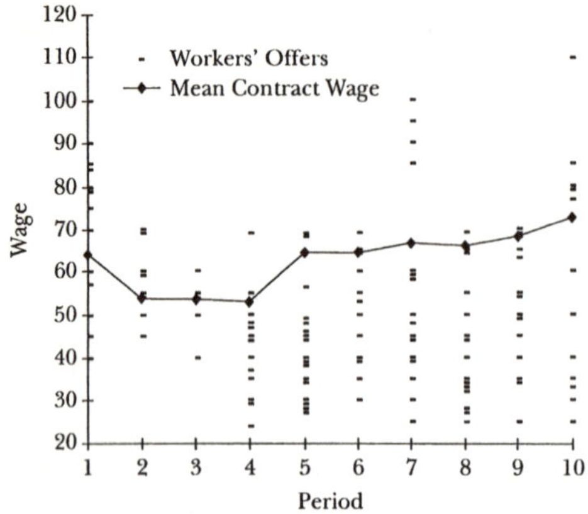

Figure 4b
Workers' Offers and Mean Contract Wages in the Double Auction Market with Complete Contracts

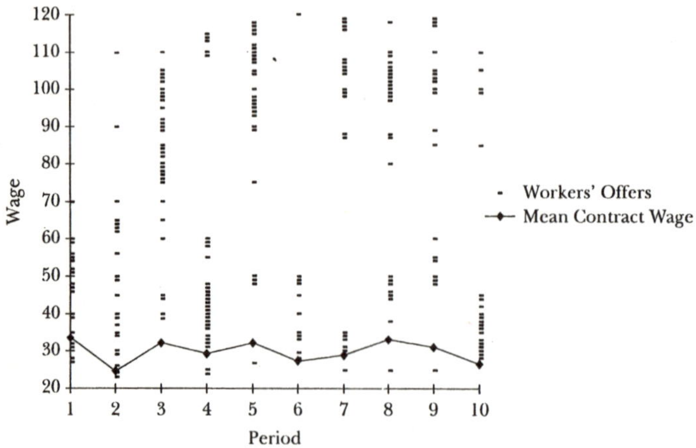

Source: Fehr and Falk (1999).

an institutional detail that means that reciprocity will have a very different impact on wage formation in the two conditions. Fehr and Schmidt (1999) provide a rigorous derivation of this argument.

A variety of studies have found that one major reason why managers are reluctant to cut wages in a recession is the fear that wage cuts may inhibit work performance. Among others, Bewley (1999) reports that managers are afraid that pay cuts "express hostility to the work force" and will be "interpreted as an insult."

A comparison of wage levels in Figure 4a and 4b shows that workers earn rents in the market with incomplete contracts. The existence of rents is also indicated by the many wage bids below the prevailing wage level in Figure 4a. This raises two questions: 1) Does reciprocity also cause a reduction in employment if employers can hire more than one worker? 2) Do the rents vary systematically with firms' profitability? In a recent paper, Falk and Fehr (2000) addressed the first question. They show that firms indeed reduce employment in response to workers' reciprocity. The second question is examined in Fehr, Gächter and Kirchsteiger (1996) who conducted competitive market experiments in which experimental firms differed according to their profit opportunities. They found a clear positive correlation between firms' profit opportunities and the rents paid to workers.

This result is compatible with empirical evidence on rent-sharing in real companies. For example, Blanchflower, Oswald and Sanfey (1996) show that there is a positive relation between long-run wages and the profitability of nonunionized companies or nonunionized industries, respectively. Also, Krueger and Summers (1987), for instance, have shown that estimated industry wage differentials are positively correlated in a cross section with industry profitability. Such findings are not consistent with competitive theories of the labor market, because in those theories, firms should pay no more than the opportunity cost of wages, and there is no reason that the profit opportunities of a certain firm should affect those market-determined opportunity costs. However, this finding is predicted by rent-sharing theories of the labor market based on the presence of reciprocal agents in the market.

The combination of the findings of laboratory studies on rent-sharing and the field evidence on rent-sharing suggests that rent-sharing theories have explanatory power. The laboratory results have the advantage that they unambiguously show the existence of profit-related job rents, due to their ability to control fully for other factors like unobservable heterogeneity in working conditions or skill levels. Such factors can create havoc in interpreting the results of real world studies of wage differentials (for example, Gibbons and Katz, 1992). In addition, the laboratory approach allows for the isolation of the gift-exchange mechanism as a cause for noncompensating wage differentials. The disadvantage of the laboratory data is that further assumptions are necessary to render the results relevant for real labor markets. This comparison illustrates that field and laboratory studies should be viewed as complementary methods of economic exploration.

Foundations of Incomplete Contracts

Standard principal-agent models predict that contracts should be made contingent on all verifiable measures that are informative with regard to the agent's effort. But in reality, we often observe highly incomplete contracts. For example, as noted earlier, wages are often paid without explicit performance incentives. To this point, the discussion has focused on demonstrating that reciprocity has powerful economic effects in situations where contracts are incomplete.

This section seeks to explore the underlying causes for the prevalence of incomplete contracts in the first place. One common explanation for the absence of explicit incentives is that when employees are expected to carry out multiple tasks or when the measures of effort and performance are distorted in some way, providing powerful incentives will induce agents to focus too much on what is being measured and not enough on the other dimensions and tasks of the job (Holmström and Milgrom, 1991). This line of explanation certainly has some truth in it. However, our aim here is to show that the presence of reciprocal types is an independent source of the absence of explicit incentives.

To study the impact of reciprocity on contractual choices, Fehr, Klein and Schmidt (2000) conducted an experiment in which principals had the choice between an explicit contract and an implicit, less complete, contract. In a typical session of this experiment, there are 12 principals and 12 agents who play for ten periods. In each of the ten periods, an employer faces a different principal, which ensures that all matches are one-shot. A period consists of three stages. At stage one of a period, the principal has to decide whether to offer the agent an implicit or an explicit contract. The implicit contract specifies a fixed wage and a desired effort level (where effort choices can range from one to ten). In addition, the principal can promise a bonus that may be paid after actual effort has been observed. In the implicit contract, there is no contractual obligation to pay the announced bonus, nor is the agent obliged to choose the desired effort level. The principal is, however, committed to pay the wage. An explicit contract also specifies a binding fixed wage and a desired effort level between one and ten. Here, however, the principal can impose a fine on the agent that has to be paid to the principal in case of verifiable shirking. Except for one detail, the explicit contract is identical to the performance contract discussed above in the context of "crowding out" of reciprocity. The difference concerns the fact that the choice of the explicit contract involves fixed verification cost. This reflects the fact that the verification of effort is, in general, costly. Note that the implicit contract does not require third-party verification of effort. It is only necessary that effort is observable by the principal.[11] The explicit contract is more complete than the implicit contract, because in the explicit contract the employer conditions the fine on the actual effort level in a

[11] Employers are, in general, not free to cut a worker's wage for shirking but they have little legal problem when they refuse to pay a promised bonus.

credible manner, while in the implicit contract, no such credible commitments are possible.

At stage two, the agent observes which contract has been offered and decides whether to accept or reject the offer. If the agent rejects the offer, the game ends and both parties get a payoff of zero. If the agent accepts, the next step is for the agent to choose an actual level of effort between one and ten.

At stage three, the principal observes the actual effort level. If the principal has offered an implicit contract, the next decision is whether to award the bonus payment to the agent. If the principal offered an explicit contract and if the agent's effort falls short of the agreed effort, a random draw decides with probability of one-third whether shirking is verifiable, in which case the agent has to pay the fine.

If all players have purely selfish preferences, the analysis of this game is straightforward. A selfish principal would never pay a bonus. Anticipating this, there is no incentive for the agent to spend more than the minimum effort. If the principal chooses the explicit contract, the principal should go for the maximum punishment because this is the best deterrence for potential shirkers. The parameters of the experiment are chosen such that a risk-neutral and selfish agent maximizes expected utility by choosing an effort level of four if faced with the maximum fine. Since the enforceable effort level is four under the explicit contract while it is only one under an implicit contract, the self-interest model predicts that principals prefer the explicit contract.

The experimental evidence is completely at odds with these predictions. In total, the implicit contract was chosen in 88 percent of the cases. In view of the relative profitability of the different contracts, the popularity of the implicit contract is not surprising. Those principals who chose the explicit contract made an average loss of nine tokens per contract, while those who chose the implicit contract made an average profit of 26 tokens per contract. Since the fixed verification cost in the explicit contract was ten tokens, the explicit contract would have been much less profitable even in the absence of these costs. For both contracts, the average income of the agents was roughly 18 tokens. Implicit contracts were more profitable because—contrary to the standard prediction—they induced much higher effort levels. The effort level in the implicit contract was 5.2 on average (on a scale of one to ten), while the effort level in the explicit contract was 2.1 on average.

How did implicit contracts induce effort levels so much higher than expected? A major reason is that in the presence of reciprocal principals, the promised bonus does not merely represent cheap talk, because reciprocal principals can—and actually do—condition the bonus payment on the effort level. The average data clearly reflect this impact of the reciprocal types because the actual average bonus rises steeply with the actual effort level. The principals' capability to commit to paying a conditional bonus is based on their reciprocal inclinations. Conditional bonus payments, in turn, provide a strong pecuniary incentive for the agents to perform as desired by the principals. Why did explicit contracts induce effort levels lower than expected? A likely reason is that these contracts crowd out positive reciprocity, and perhaps even induce negative reciprocity, as shown in the section on work motivation above.

One also might conjecture that the preference for implicit contracts in this particular experiment is caused by the fact that the explicit contract involves a punishment while the implicit contract involves a reward. However, further experiments in Fehr, Klein and Schmidt (2000) cast doubt on this explanation. If the above-described implicit contract competes with a piece rate contract, the vast majority of principals still prefer the implicit contract.

The endogenous formation of incomplete contracts through reciprocal choices shows that reciprocity may not only cause substantial changes in the functioning of given economic institutions but that it also may have a powerful impact on the selection and formation of institutions. To provide a further example: The present theory of property rights predicts that joint ownership will in general severely inhibit relation-specific investments, so that it emerges only under very restrictive conditions (Hart, 1995). This may no longer be true in the presence of reciprocal actors who are willing to cooperate if they expect the trading partner to cooperate as well, and who are willing to punish even at a cost to themselves.

Concluding Remarks

The assumption that economic agents make their decisions based on pure self-interest has served economists well in many areas. In situations where contracts are reasonably complete, the underlying assumption of self-interest should continue to be especially important. However, the self-interest model has also failed to give satisfactory explanations for a wide variety of questions of interest to economists, including questions about labor market interactions, public goods, and social norms. We believe that for important questions in these areas, progress will not come from additional tweaking of a pure self-interest model, but rather from recognizing that a sizeable proportion of economic actors act on considerations of reciprocity.

In view of the powerful implications of reciprocity, it is also important to know why a sizeable fraction of the people have reciprocal inclinations. Which factors in the evolution of the human species have contributed to this? Which social and economic conditions produce the propensity to reciprocate? There are now several evolutionary models (see footnote 3) that provide answers to this question. At the empirical level, however, little is known.

■ *This paper is part of the MacArthur Foundation Network on Economic Environments and the Evolution of Individual Preferences and Social Norms. Some research reported in this paper has also been funded by the EU-TMR research network ENDEAR (FMRX-CT98-0238). We are grateful for helpful comments by Alan Krueger, Timothy Taylor and J. Bradford De Long, as well as by Ken Binmore, Iris Bohnet, Terence Burnham, Colin Camerer, Gary Charness, Jim Cox, Vince Crawford, Armin Falk, Urs Fischbacher, Diego Gambetta, Robert Gibbons,*

Herbert Gintis, Felix Oberholzer, Larry Samuelson, Rajiv Sethi, Herbert Simon, Vernon Smith and Frans van Winden. We regret that—in view of the very large number of comments we received—we could not do justice to all of them.

References

Abbink, Klaus, Bernd Irlenbusch and Elke Renner. 2000. "The Moonlighting Game. An Experimental Study on Reciprocity and Retribution." *Journal of Economic Behavior and Organization.* 42:2, pp. 265-77.

Akerlof, George. 1982. "Labor Contracts as Partial Gift Exchange." *Quarterly Journal of Economics.* 97, pp. 543-69.

Arrow, Kenneth. 1980. "Discrimination in the Labour Market," in J.E. King, ed. *Readings in Labour Economics.* Oxford: Oxford University Press.

Berg, Joyce, John Dickhaut and Kevin McCabe. 1995. "Trust, Reciprocity and Social History." *Games and Economic Behavior.* 10, pp. 122-42.

Bewley, Truman. 1995. "A Depressed Labor Market as Explained by Participants." *American Economic Review, Papers and Proceedings.* 85, pp. 250-54.

Bewley, Truman. 2000. *Why Wages Don't Fall During a Recession.* Cambridge: Harvard University Press.

Blanchflower, David, Andrew Oswald and Peter Sanfey. 1996. "Wages, Profits, and Rent-Sharing." *Quarterly Journal of Economics.* 111:2, pp. 227-52.

Blount, Sally. 1995. "When Social Outcomes aren't Fair: The Effect of Causal Attributions on Preferences." *Organizational Behavior and Human Decision Processes.* 63, pp. 131-44.

Bohnet, Iris, Bruno Frey and Steffen Huck. 1999. "More Order with Less Law: On Contract Enforcement, Trust, and Crowding," mimeo, Harvard University.

Bolton, Gary and Axel Ockenfels. Forthcoming. "ERC - A Theory of Equity, Reciprocity, and Competition." *American Economic Review.*

Bosman, Ronald and Frans van Winden. 1999. "The Behavioral Impact of Emotions in a Power-to-Take Game: An Experimental Study," CREED/Tinbergen Institute working paper, Amsterdam.

Bowles, Samuel and Herbert Gintis. 1998. "Is Equality Passé?" *Boston Review.* December/January, 23:6.

Bowles, Samuel and Herbert Gintis. 1999. "The Evolution of Strong Reciprocity," mimeo, University of Massachusetts.

Burnham, Terence. 1999. "Testosterone and Negotiations," mimeo, John F. Kennedy School of Government, Harvard University.

Camerer, Colin and Richard Thaler. 1995. "Anomalies: Ultimatums, Dictators and Manners." *Journal of Economic Perspectives.* 9:2, pp. 209-19.

Cameron, Lisa. 1999. "Raising the Stakes in the Ultimatum Game: Experimental Evidence from Indonesia." *Economic Inquiry.* 37:1, pp. 47-59.

Charness, Gary and Matthew Rabin. 2000. "Social Preferences: Some Simple Tests and a New Model," mimeo, University of Berkeley.

Cialdini, Robert. 1993. *Influence–The Psychology of Persuasion.* New York: Quill William Morrow.

Deci, Edward and Richard Ryan. 1985. *Intrinsic Motivation and Self-Determination in Human Behavior.* New York and London: Plenum Press.

Dufwenberg, Martin and Georg Kirchsteiger. 1998. "A Theory of Sequential Reciprocity," mimeo, CentER Tilburg.

Ellickson, Robert. 1994. *Order without Law—How Neighbors Settle Disputes.* Cambridge, Massachusetts: Harvard University Press.

Elster, Jon. 1989. *The Cement of Society—A Study of Social Order.* Cambridge: Cambridge University Press.

Falk, Armin and Ernst Fehr. 2000. "Fair Wages and Unemployment," mimeo, University of Zürich.

Falk, Armin and Urs Fischbacher. 1999. "A Theory of Reciprocity," Working paper No. 6, Institute for Empirical Research in Economics, University of Zurich.

Fehr, Ernst and Armin Falk. 1999. "Wage Rigidity in a Competitive Incomplete Contract Market." *Journal of Political Economy.* 107, pp. 106-34.

Fehr, Ernst and Simon Gächter. Forthcoming. "Cooperation and Punishment in Public Goods Experiments." *American Economic Review.*

Fehr, Ernst and Simon Gächter. 2000. "Do Incentive Contracts Crowd-Out Voluntary Cooperation?" Working paper No 34, Institute for Empirical Research in Economics, University of Zurich.

Fehr, Ernst and Klaus Schmidt. 1999. "A Theory of Fairness, Competition, and Cooperation." *Quarterly Journal of Economics.* 114, pp. 817-68.

Fehr, Ernst and Elena Tougareva. 1995. "Do High Stakes Remove Reciprocal Fairness—Evidence from Russia," discussion paper, University of Zurich.

Fehr, Ernst, Simon Gächter and Georg Kirchsteiger. 1996. "Reciprocal Fairness and Noncompensating Wage Differentials." *Journal of Institutional and Theoretical Economics.* 152:4, pp. 608-40.

Fehr, Ernst, Simon Gächter and Georg Kirchsteiger. 1997. "Reciprocity as a Contract Enforcement Device." *Econometrica.* 65:4, pp. 833-60.

Fehr, Ernst, Georg Kirchsteiger and Arno Riedl. 1993. "Does Fairness Prevent Market Clearing? An Experimental Investigation." *Quarterly Journal of Economics.* 108:2, pp. 437-60.

Fehr, Ernst, Alexander Klein and Klaus Schmidt. 2000. "Endogenous Incomplete Contracts," mimeo, University of Munich.

Frey, Bruno. 1997. *Not Just For the Money—An Economic Theory of Personal Motivation.* Cheltenham: Edward Elgar Publishing.

Gächter, Simon and Armin Falk. 1999. "Reputation or Reciprocity?" Working paper No. 19, Institute for Empirical Research in Economics, University of Zurich.

Gale, John, Ken Binmore and Larry Samuelson. 1995. "Learning to Be Imperfect: The Ultimatum Game." *Games and Economic Behavior.* 8, pp. 56-90.

Giacalone, Robert and Jerald Greenberg. 1997. *Antisocial Behavior in Organizations.* Thousand Oaks: Sage Publications.

Gibbons, Robert and Lawrence Katz. 1992. "Does Unmeasured Ability Explain Inter-Industry Wage Differentials?" *Review of Economic Studies.* 59, p. 515-35.

Gintis, Herbert. Forthcoming. "Strong Reciprocity and Human Sociality." *Journal of Theoretical Biology.*

Gneezy, Uri and Aldo Rustichini. Forthcoming. "A Fine is a Price." *Journal of Legal Studies.*

Güth, Werner and Menachem Yaari. 1992. "Explaining Reciprocal Behavior in Simple Strategic Games: An Evolutionary Approach," in Ulrich Witt, ed. *Explaining Process and Change: Approaches to Evolutionary Economics.* Ann Arbor: University of Michigan Press.

Güth, Werner, Rolf Schmittberger and Bernd Schwarze. 1982. "An Experimental Analysis of Ultimatum Bargaining." *Journal of Economic Behavior and Organization.* 3:3, pp. 367-88.

Güth, Werner, Wolfgang Klose, Manfred Königstein and Joachim Schwalbach. 1998. "An Experimental Study of a Dynamic Principal-Agent Relationship." *Managerial and Decision Economics.* 19, pp. 327-41.

Hart, Oliver. 1995. *Firms, Contracts, and Financial Structure.* Oxford: Clarendon Press.

Henrich, Joe. Forthcoming. "Does Culture Matter in Economic Behavior? Ultimatum Game Bargaining among the Machiguenga of the Peruvian Amazon. *American Economic Review.*

Hoffman, Elizabeth, Kevin McCabe and Vernon Smith. 1996. "On Expectations and Monetary Stakes in Ultimatum Games." *International Journal of Game Theory.* 25, pp. 289-301.

Holmström, Bengt and Paul Milgrom. 1991. "Multi-Task Principal-Agent Analyses: Incentive Contracts, Asset Ownership and Job-Design." *Journal of Law, Economics and Organization.* 7, pp. 24-52.

Holt, Charles. 1995. "Industrial Organization: A Survey of Laboratory Research," in Alvin Roth and John Kagel, eds. *Handbook of Experimental Economics.* Princeton: Princeton University Press.

Keser, Claudia and Frans van Winden. Forthcoming. "Conditional Cooperation and Voluntary Contributions to Public Goods." *Scandinavian Journal of Economics.*

Krueger, Alan and Lawrence Summers. 1987. "Reflections on the Inter-Industry Wage Structure," in Kevin Lang and Jonathan Leonhard, eds. *Unemployment and the Structure of Labor Markets.* New York: Basil Blackwell.

Ledyard, John. 1995. "Public Goods: A Survey of Experimental Research," in Alvin Roth and John Kagel, eds. *Handbook of Experimental Economics.* Princeton: Princeton University Press.

Levine, David. 1998. "Modeling Altruism and Spitefulness in Experiments." *Review of Economic Dynamics.* 1, pp. 593-622.

Lindbeck, Assar, Sten Nyberg and Jörgen Weibull. 1999. "Social Norms and Economic Incentives in the Welfare State." *Quarterly Journal of Economics.* 116:1, pp. 1-35.

McCabe, Kevin, Stephen Rassenti and Vernon Smith. 1996. "Game Theory and Reciprocity in Some Extensive Form Experimental Games." *Proceedings National Academy of Science.* 93, pp. 13,421-13,428.

North, Douglass. 1990. *Institutions, Institutional Change and Economic Performance.* Cambridge: Cambridge University Press.

Offerman, Theo. 1999. "Hurting Hurts More than Helping Helps: The Role of the Self-Serving Bias," mimeo, CREED, University of Amsterdam.

Ostrom, Elinor, James Walker and Roy Gardner. 1992. "Covenants with and without a Sword: Self-Governance is Possible." *American Political Science Review.* 86, pp. 404-17.

Ostrom, Elinor. 1998. "A Behavioral Approach to the Rational Choice Theory of Collective Action." *American Political Science Review.* 92, pp. 1-22.

Rabin, Matthew. 1993. "Incorporating Fairness into Game Theory and Economics." *American Economic Review.* 83:5, pp. 1,281-1,302.

Roethlisberger, F. J. and W. J. Dickson. 1947. *Management and the Worker: An Account of a Research Program Conducted by the Western Electric Company, Hawthorne Works, Chicago.* Cambridge, MA: Harvard University Press.

Roth, Alvin. 1995. "Bargaining Experiments," in Alvin Roth and John Kagel, eds. *Handbook of Experimental Economics.* Princeton: Princeton University Press.

Roth, Alvin and Ido Erev. 1995. "Learning in Extensive-Form Games: Experimental Data and Simple Dynamic Models in the Intermediate Term." *Games and Economic Behavior.* 8, pp. 164-212.

Roth, Alvin, Vesna Prasnikar, Masahiro Okuno-Fujiwara and Shmuel Zamir. 1991. "Bargaining and Market Behavior in Jerusalem, Ljubljana, Pittsburgh, and Tokyo: An Experimental Study." *American Economic Review.* 81, pp. 1,068-1,095.

Sethi, Rajiv and E. Somanathan. 2000. "Preference Evolution and Reciprocity," mimeo, Columbia University.

Simon, Herbert. 1991. "Organizations and Markets." *Journal of Economic Perspectives.* Spring, 5:2, pp. 25-44.

Slonim, Robert and Alvin Roth. 1998. "Financial Incentives and Learning in Ultimatum and Market Games: An Experiment in the Slovak Republic." *Econometrica.* 66, pp. 569-96.

Solow, Robert. 1990. *The Labor Market as a Social Institution.* Oxford: Basil Blackwell.

Stigler, George. 1981. "Economics or Ethics?" In S. McMurrin, ed. *Tanner Lectures on Human Values.* Cambridge: Cambridge University Press.

Sugden, Robert. 1984. "Reciprocity: The Supply of Public Goods through Voluntary Contributions." *Economic Journal.* 84, pp. 772-87.

Tidd, K.L and J.S. Lochard. 1978. "Monetary Significance of the Affiliative Smile: A Case for Reciprocal Altruism." *Bull. Psychonom. Soc.* 11, pp. 344-46.

Williamson, Oliver. 1985. *The Economic Institutions of Capitalism.* New York: Free Press.

[15]

Journal of Economic Psychology 11 (1990) 417–449
North-Holland

ULTIMATUM BARGAINING BEHAVIOR
A survey and comparison of experimental results *

Werner GÜTH and Reinhard TIETZ

Johann Wolfgang Goethe-Universität, Frankfurt/Main, FRG

Received March 26, 1989; accepted March 21, 1990

In an ultimatum bargaining game players 1 and 2 can distribute a positive amount of money in the following way: first, player 1 determines his demand which player 2 can then either accept or induce conflict, i.e. player 2 faces the ultimatum either to accept player 1's proposal or to have no agreement at all. Experimentally observed ultimatum bargaining decisions with amounts ranging from 0.50 to 100 German marks are statistically analysed. The demands of player 1 are compared with the acceptance behavior of player 2 with the help of consistency tests in which a subject has to decide in the position of both players. Finally, we consider ultimatum bargaining games with more than just one round where, except for the final round, nonacceptance does not cause conflict but another round of ultimatum bargaining for a smaller cake.

1. Introduction

In many bargaining situations it seems possible to terminate bargaining by imposing an ultimatum. Even if this possibility would not be used frequently, this still would have to be explained. Therefore one needs a theory of ultimatum bargaining behavior.

Bargaining games with the possibility to terminate bargaining by imposing an ultimatum are also interesting from a game-theoretic perspective. Since the solution of such games can be rather extreme, the game-theoretic solution is socially rather unacceptable. Therefore ultimatum bargaining is important for testing the predictive power of the game-theoretic solution. Richard H. Thaler (1988) even includes ultimatum bargaining in his list of 'Anomalies' and relates it to other

* The authors gratefully acknowledge the helpful comments by an anonymous referee.

Requests for reprints should be sent to W. Güth, Fachbereich Wirtschaftswissenschaften, J.W. Goethe Universität, Postfach 111932, 6000 Frankfurt/Main 11, FRG.

social decision problems.

In all the studies which we consider, only two players, 1 and 2, negotiate how to distribute a given positive amount c of money. Thus, if one player wants to impose an ultimatum on the other, he only has to determine his own demand. The other player can then only either accept the residual amount or choose conflict which implies 0 payoffs for both players. In section 2 we consider one-round ultimatum bargaining games or subgames. Our statistical analysis of experimentally observed decision data compares and analyses all available results of one-round ultimatum bargaining games.

A disadvantage of these experiments is that we only know player 2's reaction to player 1's specific demand but not how he would have reacted to other demands by player 1. This can be avoided if, before knowing player 1's actual demand d_1, player 2 is asked for any possible demand d_1 whether he will accept it or not. In this way one observes not only player 2's acceptance decision but a complete acceptance strategy of player 2. In section 3 we compare the results of Güth et al. (1982) and Kahneman et al. (1986a,b) who both, although in slightly different ways, have tried to observe the complete acceptance strategy of player 2. Since player 2 determines his strategy independently from player 1's demand d_1, the same subject could assume the position of player 1 and the position of player 2. Güth et al. and Kahneman et al. both have exploited this possibility to compare how a given subject's demand d_1 as player 1 is related to his acceptance behavior as player 2.

Binmore et al. (1984,1985) performed experiments with two rounds of ultimatum bargaining: in the first round player 1 first determines his demand d_1 which 2 can then either accept or not, as before. But if 2 does not accept player 1's proposal this does not necessarily imply conflict. Instead there follows another round of ultimatum bargaining for a 'smaller cake' c' where now player 2 can first determine his demand $d_2(0 \leq d_2 \leq c')$ which player 1 can then either accept or choose conflict. Their conclusions have inspired further experiments with more than one round of bargaining. In section 4 we compare the results of Binmore et al. with those of Güth and Tietz (1986), Neelin et al. (1988) as well as with the comparable decision data of Ochs and Roth (1989). The final remarks summarize the results and indicate lines of future research.

2. Strategic power versus distributive justice

The game-theoretic solution of one-round ultimatum bargaining games is rather obvious. If $d_1 < c$, player 2 should obviously accept player 1's proposal. Thus player 1 can ask for nearly all of c and leave only a crumb of the 'cake' c for player 2. Let $\epsilon(>0)$ be the smallest positive unit of money. If player 2 would not accept the demand $d_1 = c$ by player 1 the optimal demand of player 1 would be $d_1^* = c - \epsilon$ (otherwise $d_1 = c$ can also be an equilibrium demand). Since this demand will be accepted by player 2, the solution payoffs are $c - \epsilon$ for player 1 and ϵ for player 2, i.e. player 1 receives nearly the whole amount c. Due to this extremely 'unfair' distribution of rewards one-round ultimatum bargaining games are one of the most critical paradigms for testing the predictive power of the game-theoretic solution. Since ultimatum bargaining games are extensive games with perfect information (all information sets are singletons), the appropriate solution concept for such games is that of a subgame perfect equilibrium point (see Selten 1975).

In a simple reward allocation experiment (see, for instance, Mikula 1973; and Kahneman et al. 1986a,b) a subject has to allocate the total reward $c(>0)$ among two individuals who both contributed to obtain the total reward c. Viewed as a game the solution of such an allocation problem is clearly that the allocator takes all of c for himself, thereby leaving nothing for his partner. This similarity of the game-theoretic allocation explains why the two decision problems, ultimatum bargaining games and reward allocation problems, are often seen as closely related (see Thaler 1988; and Forsythe et al. 1988). The essential differences between the two decision problems are, of course, that the allocator in reward allocation does not have to fear a rejection by his partner and that reward allocation problems are neither presented as strategic games nor usually perceived as situations where egoistic motivations should dominate. The reward allocation experiments of Hoffman and Spitzer (1982,1985) are more complicated since the total reward depends on the allocation result and since players can agree on side payments.

In the study of Güth et al. (1982) the amount c varied from 4 to 10 German marks. Furthermore, all subjects played successively two games with different partners in order to observe whether experience affects ultimatum bargaining behavior. In table 1 the 'low rewards' data of

Table 1
The plays of ultimatum games.

Experiment	1st game			2nd game			3rd game		
	c	d_1	$\delta_2(d_1)$	c	d_1	$\delta_2(d_1)$	c	d_1	$\delta_2(d_1)$
Low rewards	4.00	2.00	1	4.00	3.00	0			
	4.00	4.00	0	4.00	3.00	0			
	4.00	4.00	1	4.00	3.00	1			
	5.00	2.50	1	5.00	3.00	1			
	5.00	3.00	1	5.00	4.00	0			
	5.00	3.50	1	5.00	4.99	0			
	6.00	3.00	1	6.00	3.00	1			
	6.00	4.00	1	6.00	3.80	1			
	6.00	4.80	0	6.00	5.00	0			
	7.00	3.50	1	7.00	4.00	0			
	7.00	5.00	1	7.00	4.00	1			
	7.00	5.85	1	7.00	5.00	1			
	8.00	4.00	1	8.00	5.00	1			
	8.00	4.35	1	8.00	6.50	1			
	8.00	5.00	1	8.00	7.00	1			
	9.00	5.00	1	9.00	4.50	1			
	9.00	5.55	1	9.00	4.50	1			
	9.00	8.00	1	9.00	6.00	1			
	10.00	5.00	1	10.00	6.00	1			
	10.00	5.00	1	10.00	7.00	1			
	10.00	6.00	1	10.00	7.50	1			
Auction winners	15.00	8.00	1	15.00	10.00	1	15.00	7.50	1
	15.00	8.00	1	15.00	10.00	1	15.00	9.00	1
	15.00	8.50	0	15.00	10.00	1	15.00	9.50	1
	15.00	9.00	1	15.00	11.00	0	15.00	10.00	1
	55.00	28.00	1	55.00	30.00	1	55.00	20.00	1
	55.00	35.00	1	55.00	35.00	1	55.00	36.00	1
	55.00	40.00	1	55.00	37.00	1	55.00	41.25	1
	55.00	45.00	1	55.00	50.00	0	55.00	45.00	1
	100.00	55.00	1	100.00	60.00	1	100.00	60.00	1
	100.00	55.00	1	100.00	65.00	1	100.00	70.00	1
	100.00	60.00	1	100.00	67.00	1	100.00	78.00	1
	100.00	61.00	1	100.00	70.00	1	100.00	81.00	0

continued overleaf

Second round subgames									
Güth and Tietz	0.50	0.50	0	3.50	2.00	0			
	3.50	3.50	0	4.50	2.50	1			
	4.50	2.50	0	4.50	2.50	1			
	4.50	3.50	0	4.50	3.00	1			
	13.50	8.00	1	31.50	15.75	1			
	13.50	8.50	1	31.50	20.00	1			
	13.50	9.50	0	31.50	21.50	0			
	31.50	22.50	1						
	31.50	27.50	0						
Neelin et al.	$1.25	$0.25	0						
	$1.25	$0.50	1						
	$1.25	$0.60	1						
	$1.25	$0.62	1						
	$1.25	$1.00	0						
	$1.25	$1.20	0						
	$1.25	$1.20	0						
	$1.25	$1.24	0						
	$1.25	$1.25	0						
	Games 1–3			Games 4–6			Games 7–10		
Ochs and Roth [a]	12.0	6.00	1	12.00	6.00	1	12.00	7.80	1
	12.00	10.80	0	12.00	9.60	0	12.00	8.40	0
	12.00	11.88	0	12.00	11.88	0	12.00	8.40	0
	18.00	9.00	1	18.00	9.54	1	12.00	10.00	0
	18.00	9.36	1	18.00	9.90	1	18.00	9.00	1
	18.00	9.90	1	18.00	10.80	1	18.00	9.90	0
	18.00	9.90	1	18.00	13.50	0	18.00	9.90	0
	18.00	13.50	1				18.00	10.80	0
	18.00	14.40	0				18.00	13.50	0
Third round subgames [a]	5.00	4.00	0	11.00	5.50	1	5.00	2.50	1
	11.00	5.50	0	11.00	6.49	0	11.00	5.50	1
				11.00	9.35	0	11.00	6.60	1

[a] Normal amounts in $; note that subjects were paid only in one of ten games. (When comparing the various data sets of table 1 we therefore have to multiply these amounts by $\frac{2}{10}$ based on an exchange rate $1 for DM2.)

games with c ranging from 4 to 10 German marks were observed by Güth et al. (1982: tables 4 and 5). Due to random pairing the (sorted) results listed in table 1 usually are decision data of different subjects. We first indicate whether it was the 1st or 2nd game. For each game we give the amount c and the play, consisting of players 1's demand d_1 and player 2's acceptance decision $\delta_2(d_1)$. Here $\delta_2(d_1) = 1$ means that 2 accepts proposal d_1 whereas $\delta_2(d_1) = 0$ means that 2 chooses conflict.

The 'auction winners' (data) in table 1 are the plays observed by Güth and Tietz (1985, 1986) who auctioned the position of ultimatum bargainers before letting the auction winners play the ultimatum bargaining game. In their experiments subjects were first informed about the rules of second highest bid-price auctions and that it is a dominant strategy to bid the true value in such auctions. In a second highest price auction (see Vickrey 1961) the object is sold to the highest bid(der) at the price of the second highest bid. After these instructions all subjects participated in normal, 4-person, second highest bid-price auctions so that the authors could assess the proportion of subjects who accepted that bidding the true value is optimal. The share of inessential deviations from bidding truthfully (less than 5% of the true value) was 85%.

Once subjects were familiar with bidding in second highest bid-price auctions they were told that they were then going to bid for strategic positions. They were informed how to play ultimatum bargaining games with amounts c of 15, 55, and 100 German marks and then asked to bid either for the position of player 1 or for the one of player 2, i.e., we conducted an independent auction for both ultimatum bargaining positions and every single game. Afterwards the auction winners were determined and privately informed about the price (the next highest bid for the same position) which they had to pay for their strategic position. Then, knowing their own price but not the one of their opponent, the two auction winners played the ultimatum bargaining game. Denote by x_i player i's win in the ultimatum bargaining game and by p_i the price which i has to pay for his position i in the ultimatum bargaining game. The final win of the subject who became player i is $x_i - p_i$. These final payoffs were paid immediately after the game. As can be seen from table 1 three games were played successively. It should be noted that the decision data in the 1st, 2nd, and 3rd game for the amounts $c = 15$, 55, and 100 German marks usually came

Table 2
Average results of table 1.

Experiment	Repetition: 1st game				2nd game				3rd game				All games			
	c	d_1	$\underline{d}_1$	δ_2	c	d_1	$\underline{d}_1$	δ_2	c	d_1	$\underline{d}_1$	δ_2	c	d_1	$\underline{d}_1$	δ_2
Low rewards	7 (2) $N = 21$	4.43 (1.32)	0.65 (0.162)	0.905 (0.294)	7 (2) $N = 21$	4.75 (1.42)	0.691 (0.13)	0.714 (0.452)					7 (2) $N = 42$	4.59 (1.38)	0.67 (0.148)	0.81 (0.393)
Auction winners	56.67 (34.7) $N = 12$	34.38 (20.6)	0.603 (0.086)	0.917 (0.276)	56.67 (34.7) $N = 12$	37.92 (23.1)	0.676 (0.083)	0.833 (0.373)	56.67 (34.7) $N = 12$	38.94 (26.9)	0.656 (0.127)	0.917 (0.276)	56.67 (34.7) $N = 36$	37.08 (23.8)	0.645 (0.105)	0.889 (0.314)
Second round subgames																
Güth and Tietz	12.94 (10.9) $N = 9$	9.56 (8.81)	0.761 (0.156)	0.333 (0.471)	15.93 (13.5) $N = 7$	9.61 (8.36)	0.595 (0.062)	0.714 (0.452)					14.25 (12.21) $N = 16$	9.58 (8.62)	0.688 (0.149)	0.5 (0.5)
Neelin et al.	2.5 (0) $N = 9$	1.75 (0.722)	0.699 (0.289)	0.333 (0.471)									2.5 (0) $N = 9$	1.75 (0.722)	0.699 (0.289)	0.333 (0.471)
	Games 1–3				Games 4–6				Games 7–10							
Ochs and Roth	3.2 (0.566) $N = 9$	2.11 (0.475)	0.673 (0.179)	0.667 (0.471)	3.09 (0.594) $N = 7$	2.04 (0.432)	0.674 (0.166)	0.571 (0.495)	3.07 (0.596) $N = 9$	1.97 (0.328)	0.656 (0.117)	0.222 (0.416)	3.12 (0.588) $N = 25$	2.04 (0.419)	0.667 (0.156)	0.48 (0.5)
Third round subgames	Games 1–3				Games 4–6				Games 7–10							
Ochs and Roth	1.6 (0.6) $N = 2$	0.95 (0.15)	0.65 (0.15)	0 (0)	2.2 (0) $N = 3$	1.42 (0.326)	0.647 (0.148)	0.333 (0.471)	1.8 (0.566) $N = 3$	0.973 (0.347)	0.533 (0.047)	1 (0)	1.9 (0.52) $N = 8$	1.14 (0.374)	0.605 (0.133)	0.5 (0.5)
All experiments	16.1 (25.7) $N = 62$	10.1 (15.5)	0.667 (0.183)	0.677 (0.467)	19.33 (27.8) $N = 50$	12.81 (18.5)	0.669 (0.124)	0.7 (0.458)	29.71 (36.5) $N = 24$	20.3 (26.6)	0.641 (0.123)	0.667 (0.471)	19.69 (29.0) $N = 136$	12.92 (19.3)	0.663 (0.154)	0.684 (0.464)

Note: Standard deviations are given in parentheses.

from different groups of subjects since the strategic positions of each game were auctioned independently.

The next data set of table 1, named '2nd round subgames' (data), are the plays which were observed in the second round of two-round ultimatum bargaining games where no agreement has been reached in the first round. The first subset of decision data in the 1st and 2nd games gives the corresponding results of Güth and Tietz (1988a), and the second subset with observations only for the 1st game contains the results of Neelin et al. (1988). The data of Ochs and Roth (1989) are listed by aggregating the first three games, games 4 to 6, and games 7 to 10, respectively. The '3rd round subgames' are the corresponding data of Ochs and Roth (1989). We only included results of last-round subgames with equal discount factors for both players. The corresponding results of Binmore et al. (1984, 1985) were not available.

In table 2 we give the mean reward amount c, the mean demand d_1, the mean relative demand $\underline{d}_1$ ($\underline{d}_1 = d_1/c$), and the mean acceptance decision δ_2 individually for the different sets of experimentally observed data shown in table 1 as well as for their aggregates. It should be mentioned that all ultimatum bargaining games presented in tables 1 and 2 are strategically equivalent although they are embedded in different scenarios. When playing the ultimatum game the costs of strategic positions as well as the loss of efficiency implied by not reaching an agreement for the bigger pie in the first rounds are both sunk costs which do not have any impact on the optimal decision behavior.

If $N > 10$, the mean relative demanded shares $\underline{d}_1$ ranging from 0.6 to 0.69 do not vary dramatically. Nevertheless, table 2 reveals how strongly strategically irrelevant aspects can influence ultimatum bargaining decisions. This is most clearly demonstrated by the mean acceptance decision δ_2 varying from 0.22 in the 3rd games of the 2nd round subgames of the shrinking cake experiments to 0.92 in the auction winners experiments. Auctioning strategic positions seems to induce the most consistent kind of behavior.

Game theory predicts $\underline{d}_1$ to be nearly 1 and $\delta_2 = 1$ for $d_1 < c$ since $d_1 = c$ and $d_1^* = c - \epsilon$ are the only equilibrium demands. Contrary to this, $\underline{d}_1$ was consistently and significantly smaller than 1. Furthermore, the sometimes extremely low acceptance rates δ_2 in table 2 indicate that players 2 are often enough willing to sacrifice quite a monetary amount in order to punish player 1 for making an 'unfair' proposal (see

Güth (1988) who relates such a behavior to equity theory). A previous loss of efficiency by failing to reach an agreement on the bigger cake seems to increase this willingness to punish dramatically. Of course, in most last-round subgames of table 2 the mean amount c to be distributed has been rather low. The only exceptions are the second round subgames of Güth and Tietz (1988a) with $c = 12.94$ and $c = 15.93$ German marks as a result of the games with an almost unshrinking cake.

An attempt to explain the relative demand behavior of player 1 globally by a linear regression function of the amount c and the experience parameter 'game' fails. Dummy variables for the different experiments also do not influence demand behavior significantly.

For the 'auction winners' experiments it has been shown that the demand behavior was positively influenced by the bids in the auction (cf. Güth and Tietz 1985,1986). More globally, $\underline{b}_1$, i.e. the bid b_1 of player 1 divided by c, has a distinct influence on $\underline{d}_1$:

$$\begin{array}{llll} \underline{d}_1 = & 0.372 + & 0.422\,\underline{b}_1, & R^2 = 0.400,\ N = 36 \\ \sigma & (0.059) & (0.088) & \\ t & 5.42 & 4.80 & \\ \alpha & < 0.001 & 0.001. & \end{array} \tag{1}$$

R^2 is the coefficient of determination and N the number of observations. σ denotes the standard deviation of the regression coefficients, t the corresponding t-statistic, and α the significance level.

For the last-round subgames let c_p denote the cake size of the second last round. The relation c/c_p is called the cake-shrinking parameter of the previous round. We have tried to explain the relative demand behavior $\underline{d}_1$ by the cake-shrinking parameter c/c_p, by the cake size c, the experience parameter 'game', the previous sacrifices (i.e. the amounts given up by turning down the previous offer), and the experimental dummies reflecting the various experimental procedures. None of the variables has a statistically significant influence.

Since δ_2 assumes only values of 0 and 1, the assumptions of the classical linear regression model with regresssand δ_2 are not fulfilled. The optimal separation function for acceptance decisions (see Hartung and Elpelt (1986: 140 f.) as well as Güth and Tietz (1988b) for details), which maximizes the number of correctly explained acceptance decisions, is given by

$$\delta_2(\underline{s}_2) = \begin{cases} 0 & \text{for } \underline{d}_1 \geq \underline{s}_2 \\ 1 & \text{otherwise,} \end{cases} \tag{2a}$$

with

$$\underline{s}_2 = 0.737 + 0.00262c. \tag{2b}$$

According to $\underline{s}_2$ player 2 is willing to accept a lower share if the cake is bigger. Function (2) explains 83% of the 136 observed acceptance decisions. Similar results can be obtained if the cake size parameter c is substituted by dummy variables for different experiments. The mean of the 93 accepted relative demands $\underline{d}_1^a$ is with 0.61 significantly smaller than the mean of the 43 rejected relative demands $\underline{d}_1^r$ (Mann-Whitney U test, $\alpha < 0.00001$).

Kravitz and Gunto (1988) as well as Güth et al. (1990) try to explore psychological reasons for ultimatum bargaining behavior. In the experiment of Kravitz and Gunto subjects do not play the ultimatum bargaining game properly. As player 2, subjects are confronted with predetermined demands (robot strategies) by player 1 where in two of three conditions the greedy proposal is supplemented by a nasty (the 'power comment') or a justifying (the 'need comment') remark. Subjects were paid a fixed amount unrelated to the offer and their reaction to it. Especially, in the case of the power comment subjects should have recognized that they were not faced with a real opponent. Before the experiment subjects were asked which demand they would choose as player 1, which proposal they considered as fair, and what they required as player 2 to accept. In a post-experimental questionnaire they were furthermore asked to rate the personality of their 'opponent' and the procedure of ultimatum bargaining on discrete bipolar scales.

Subjects in the Güth et al. (1990) experiment first answered the personality questionnaire 16PA, developed by Brandstätter (1988). In addition to some personal characteristics like sex, age, education, subjects were required to rate their personality on 33 discrete bipolar scales. We do not give a detailed description of this personality questionnaire as it is not related to ultimatum bargaining. The main reason for using it is an explorative attempt to explain ultimatum bargaining behavior by general psychological characteristics. To reduce the number of dimensions Güth et al. (1990) apply factor analysis and then use these factors to explain experimentally observed ultimatum bargaining decisions by these subjects. Psychological variables were useful in explaining the bidding and bargaining decisions but usually for different variables different factors were relevant.

For their ultimatum bargaining experiment Güth et al. (1990) uses the auctioning procedure of Güth and Tietz (1985, 1986) in a 2-factorial design: each of the amounts $c =$ DM18, DM32, and DM54 is played once in the usual way and once with an additional transfer payment to player 2 which equals the cake size c and which is paid independently of what happens in bargaining. Thus player 2 is sure to receive c in addition to what he earns in ultimatum bargaining. As a consequence, the game-theoretic solution gives both players nearly the same amount ($c - \epsilon$ and $c + \epsilon$, respectively) so that the game-theoretic solution is supported by the distribution standard of equal monetary rewards (see Homans 1961; and Güth 1988). Unfortunately, the hypothesis that player 1 will demand significantly more in case of the transfer payment had to be rejected.

Prasknikar and Roth (1989) compare ultimatum bargaining behavior with the experimental results for sequential best shot games (Harrison and Hirshleifer 1989). In a sequential best shot game player 1 first determines his contribution and then, knowing 1's decision, player 2 chooses how much he contributes. For both players the level of the public good is determined purely by the maximal individual contribution. The unique subgame perfect equilibrium point (Selten 1975) prescribes a 0 contribution by player 1, i.e. only player 2 has to bear the burden of providing the public good. In the experiment of Harrison and Hirshleifer (1989) the equilibrium payoff of player 1 and 2 was \$3.70 and \$0.42, respectively. Nevertheless their experimental results strongly support the game-theoretic prediction.

Since in the Harrison and Hirshleifer experiment a subject knew only his own payoff function, these best shot games can be viewed as games with incomplete information whereas ultimatum bargaining, as defined above, relies on complete information (i.e., all payoff functions are common knowledge). Prasknikar and Roth (1989) experimentally compare best shot games with and without complete information with ultimatum bargaining games. They confirm the conclusions by Harrison and Hirshleifer for best shot games with complete information. For best shot games with incomplete information the behavior is different from equilibrium behavior although it is moving in the direction of the equilibrium decisions. Most importantly, for both variants of best shot games the observed means are much closer to equilibrium behavior than for the ultimatum bargaining.

To explain the puzzling difference in the predictive power of game theory for best shot games and ultimatum bargaining Prasknikar and Roth (1989) explore the experimentally observed reaction behavior to non-equilibrium opening moves. Whereas in best shot games the game-theoretic opening move yields the highest payoff expectation, the best opening move in ultimatum bargaining is to leave a significant amount (about 40% of the cake) for player 2.

Equal positive contributions in best shot games are obviously inefficient since one of the two contributions is completely useless. If sharing the burden of providing the public good is impossible, fairness considerations cannot be applied. Furthermore, the very obvious aspect of efficiency requires extreme payoff distributions. The results of Hoffman and Spitzer (1982, 1985) demonstrate that the desire for efficiency can be a strong motivation. In ultimatum bargaining, efficiency does not have any impact on the payoff distribution since it only excludes conflict. Best shot games are therefore more complex than ultimatum bargaining games and more comparable to the 'complicated games' of Güth et al. (1982) which allow for efficient and inefficient payoff distributions.

3. Consistency of demand and acceptance behavior

In games without chance moves a (pure) strategy vector uniquely determines a play but many different strategy vectors might imply the same play. In the specific context of ultimatum bargaining games a play consists of players 1's proposal d_1 and 2's reaction $\delta_2(d_1)$ to this specific proposal by player 1. Whereas the choice of d_1 corresponds to choosing a strategy for player 1, the same is not true for player 2. A pure strategy of player 2 is a function $\delta_2(\cdot)$ which assigns to all possible demands d_1 by player 1 a decision $\delta_2(d_1) = 1$ or $\delta_2(d_1) = 0$. Thus the plays listed in table 1 give only a point information about the general decision behavior $\delta_2(\cdot)$.

An obvious way to observe the strategy $\delta_2(\cdot)$ instead of only a reaction $\delta_2(d_1)$ to one specific demand d_1 is to ask player 2 how he would react to all possible demands d_1 before being confronted with the specific decision d_1 of player 1, and to determine the result of ultimatum bargaining by the demand d_1 of player 1 as well as by the hypothetical decision behavior $\delta_2(\cdot)$ of player 2, i.e., if $\delta_2(d_1) = 1$, player 1's proposal is accepted whereas for $\delta_2(d_1) = 0$ conflict results. In the consistency test of Güth et al. (1982) every subject first had to determine his demand d_1 as player 1 and then this minimal acceptance payoff m_2 as player 2, presuming that the subject will only accept proposals d_1 with $c - d_1 \geq m_2$. Subjects were informed in advance that both their decisions d_1 and m_2 matter since every subject is engaged in two ultimatum bargaining games, once as player 1 and once as player 2.

Because of the experimental procedure Güth et al. (1982) were able to identify both decisions d_1 and m_2 of a given subject. There were 6 cases with $d_1 + m_2 > c$, 15 with $d_1 + m_2 = c$, and 17 with $d_1 + m_2 < c$. Apparently, subjects with $d_1 + m_2 > c$ consider themselves as exceptionally tough whereas subjects with $d_1 + m_2 < c$ would accept more ambitious demands d_1 than their own one. Subjects with $d_1 + m_2 = c$ seem to rely on a point solution, i.e., they consider one and only one agreement as acceptable. For instance, 7 of the 15 subjects with $d_1 + m_2 = c$ proposed the equal split of c. We will not investigate the individual decisions in further detail since we want to compare the results of Güth et al. (1982) with those of Kahneman et al. (1986a and b), who provide only aggregated data.

Kahneman et al. (1986) use ultimatum bargaining games to demonstrate the discrepancy between the 'assumptions of economics' like, for instance, profit maximization for firms and the actually observable decision behavior. In their 'Study 1: Resisting Unfairness', they tried to investigate how a subject as player 2 would react to 'unfair' payoff proposals by player 1. Their subjects also assumed both the position of player 1 and the one of player 2. First a subject had to decide as player 2 for any possible allocation of $c = \$10$ ranging from $d_1 = \$0.50$ to $d_1 = \$9.50$ in steps of $c = \$0.50$ whether he would accept it or not. Afterwards he had to allocate c as player 1 by choosing his demand d_1 out of $\{\$0.50, \ldots, \$9.50\}$.

The experiment was conducted in a psychology and a commerce class where psychology students were matched with psychology stu-

Table 3
Mean offered share, proportion of equal splits, mean minimal demanded share, proportion of demanded shares > 0.15 of Kahneman et al. (1986: table 1) and Güth et al. (1982: table 7) as well as the corresponding results from table 1 whenever they are defined.

	Subject group			Consis-tency test		From table 1			All games
	Psych/ Psych	Psych/ Com	Com/ Psych			1st game	2nd game	3rd game	
Mean share offered to player 2	0.476	0.447	0.421	0.419	Low rewards	0.35	0.31	–	0.33
					Auction winners	0.40	0.32	0.34	0.35
					Last round sg.	0.29	0.36	0.38	0.33
					Mean	0.33	0.33	0.36	0.34
Proportion of equal splits					Low rewards	33%	14%	–	24%
	81%	78%	63%	43%	Auction winners	–	–	8%	3%
					Last round sg.	14%	18%	25%	17%
					Mean	18%	12%	13%	15%
Mean minimal demanded share by player 2	0.259	0.224	0.200	0.363		–	–	–	–
Proportion of minimal demanded shares > 0.015	58%	59%	51%	78%		–	–	–	–
					Low rewards	21	21	–	42
					Auction winners	12	12	12	36
					Last round sg.	29	17	12	58
Number of subjects	43	37	35	37	Total	62	50	24	136

dents (the 'Psych/Psych' column of table 3), psychology students as player 1 were facing commerce students being player 2 (the 'Psych/Com' column of table 3), and vice versa (the 'Com/Psych' column of table 3). The aggregate data given by Kahneman et al. (1986b: table 1) are the mean share $(c - d_1)/c$ offered to player 2, the proportion of equal splits $d_1 = c/2$, the mean minimal demanded share m_2/c, the proportion of minimal demands m_2 with $m_2 \geq 0.15c$, and the number of subjects. In table 3 we give these results in the first three columns mentioned above. The fourth column of table 3 contains the corresponding values for the consistency test of Güth et al. (1982: table 7). Whenever they are defined we also list the corresponding results of table 1 individually for the 1st, 2nd, and 3rd game as well as for all three games together. For the sake of completeness we specify the corresponding values separately for low-rewards, auction-winners, and last-round subgame experiments as well as for the whole set of data contained in table 1.

Table 3 reveals some surprising differences in the results. We focus our attention on the proportion of equal splits proposed by player 1. A similar analysis could be performed for the proportion of minimal demanded shares > 0.15 but the results of consistency tests could not be compared with those of normal ultimatum bargaining games.

There is no significant difference in the proportion of equal splits of the Psych/Psych and the Psych/Com group ($\alpha = 0.37$), but the average share of both these groups is significantly greater than the corresponding value of the Com/Psych group ($\alpha < 0.05$). Thus, psychology students tend to propose equal splits more often than students of business administration. However, the Com/Psych group has a significantly greater proportion of equal splits than the one observed in the consistency test of Güth et al. ($\alpha < 0.05$). We suppose that this is mainly due to the way of performing experiments (e.g. only a random sample of subjects was paid in the Kahneman et al. experiment).

But even the proportion of equal splits (43%) observed by Güth et al. (1982) is much higher ($\alpha < 0.001$) than the one in normal ultimatum bargaining games (15% in average). Thus, consistency tests seem to induce subjects to consider and to perceive the situation in quite a different way. Analysing the situation both from the viewpoint of player 1 and 2 apparently reduces the incentive to exploit the strategic advantage of player 1. Altogether this shows that subjects hardly ever apply game-theoretic reasoning to determine their behavior but that the extent of paying attention to strategic aspects can be strongly affected by the experimental environment whenever the monetary incentives are rather low.

Bolle (1988) uses consistency tests to explore whether high reward experiments can be substituted by low cost experiments with high potential rewards but a rather low reward expectation. The paper is mainly an attempt to justify experiments where not all subjects are paid according to their success but only a random sample. Bolle performed four different experiments: in the D2 experiment 12 pairs of subjects played for an amount $c =$ DM2; in the P20 experiment with $c =$ DM20 the monetary reward expectation was the same since only 1 of 10 pairs of subjects was actually paid. A similar distinction holds for the D20 and P200 experiment with a deterministic or probabilistic monetary reward expectation of DM20 per pair.

The proportion of equal splits with 62.5%, 50%, 41.7%, and 55% for the D2, P20, D20, and P200 experiment was always higher than the one of the consistency test by Güth et al. which already exceeded considerably the corresponding quota of 15% for usual ultimatum bargaining games. On the other hand, the proportion of minimal demanded shares (> 0.15) by player 2 with 79.2%, 80%, 66.7%, and 80% was always higher than the corresponding data of Kahneman et al. (1986b). One could say that Bolle's observations reveal a demand behavior of player 1 similar to Kahneman et al. and an acceptance behavior of player 2 corresponding to the results of Güth et al.

4. How to bargain for a shrinking cake?

The speciality of the bargaining situations analysed above is that there is just one round of ultimatum bargaining, i.e., one player proposes an agreement which the other can accept or not and then the game is over. The other extreme is the case of infinitely many rounds of ultimatum bargaining where in each round one player suggests an agreement which the other can accept or reject and where in the latter case a new round of ultimatum bargaining follows.

A model of the latter type has been rigorously analysed by Rubinstein (1982) who assumes that the two players take turns in being the proposer. Thus in all odd rounds $t = 1, 3, 5, \ldots$ player 1 would be proposing whereas in all even rounds $t = 2, 4, 6, \ldots$ this would be done by player 2. If no agreement is reached in finite time, both players receive nothing. In case an agreement to distribute c is reached in round t, player $i = 1, 2$ receives $x_i \rho_i^{t-1}$. Here x_i is the amount allocated to i and ρ_i with $0 < \rho_i < 1$ is player i's discount factor.

Thus the two players can only allocate the full amount c if they reach an agreement immediately, i.e. in round $t = 1$. Otherwise the 'cake', the amount which can be distributed, will shrink with each round not yielding an agreement.

Rubinstein (1982) has shown that the game-theoretic solution implies an immediate agreement according to which player 1 receives the share $(1 - \rho_2)/(1 - \rho_1\rho_2)$ of the amount c whereas 2's share is $\rho_2(1 - \rho_1)/(1 - \rho_1\rho_2)$. Thus the more patient player 1 is the more successful he will be. Furthermore, the special case $\rho = \rho_1 = \rho_2$ with $0 < \rho < 1$ illustrates that it is usually better to be first in proposing an agreement. For $\rho = \rho_1 = \rho_2$ the share of both player 1 and 2 is $1/(1 + \rho)$ and $\rho/(1 + \rho)$, respectively. Thus player 1's share approaches 1 for $\rho \to 0$ whereas for $\rho \to 1$ the solution agreement approaches the equal split of c.

The experiment of Binmore et al. (1984, 1985) deviates from the previous ultimatum bargaining experiments in the direction of the game model analysed by Rubinstein (1982). Instead of just one round Binmore et al. assume that there are two rounds of ultimatum bargaining. In the first round player 1 proposes d_1 with $0 \leq d_1 \leq c$ which 2 can accept or reject. If 2 rejects d_1 the second round follows where now player 2 can propose how to allocate the smaller cake c' with $0 < c' < c$ by choosing his demand d_2 with $0 \leq d_2 \leq c'$. In case that 1 rejects d_2 the game is over and both players receive nothing. Otherwise the payoff result is determined by the accepted proposal, i.e., players 1 and 2 receive d_1 and $c - d_1$, respectively, in case of an agreement in the first round and $c' - d_2$ and d_2 if an agreement is reached in the second round.

If the second round is reached, player 1 should accept any proposal d_2 satisfying $d_2 < c'$. Assuming that 1 will not accept the proposal $d_2 = c'$ leaving nothing for him player 2's optimal demand d_2 is therefore $d_2^* = c' - \epsilon$ where again ϵ denotes the smallest money unit. Anticipating this result for the second round, player 2, in turn, will accept any proposal d_1 with $c - d_1 > c' - \epsilon$ which shows that player 1 can demand $d_1^* = c - c'$ without having to fear a rejection by player 2.

Table 4
Relative opening demands $\underline{d}_1$ by player 1 in two-round ultimatum bargaining for a shrinking cake.

Interval for relative demands	Binmore et al. exp.			Güth and Tietz exp.					
	1st game	2nd game	both games	1st game		2nd game		Both games	
$c'/c =$	0.25	0.25	0.25	0.1	0.9	0.1	0.9	0.1	0.9
$\underline{d}_1 \leq 0.05$	–	–	–	–	–	–	–	–	–
$0.05 < \underline{d}_1 \leq 0.15$	–	–	–	–	– *	–	– *	–	– *
$0.15 < \underline{d}_1 \leq 0.25$	–	–	–	–	–	–	–	–	–
$0.25 < \underline{d}_1 \leq 0.35$	3	2	5	–	–	–	–	–	–
$0.35 < \underline{d}_1 \leq 0.45$	12	3	15	–	–	–	3	–	3
$0.45 < \underline{d}_1 \leq 0.55$	30	14	44	1	4	2	5	3	9
$0.55 < \underline{d}_1 \leq 0.65$	13	8	21	–	2	2	2	2	4
$0.65 < \underline{d}_1 \leq 0.75$	16 *	50 *	66 *	3	2	3	1	6	3
$0.75 < \underline{d}_1 \leq 0.85$	6	3	9	5	2	2	–	7	2
$0.85 < \underline{d}_1 \leq 0.95$	2	1	3	2 *	–	1 *	–	3 *	–
$0.95 < \underline{d}_1$	–	–	–	–	–	–	–	–	–
N	82	81	163	11	10	10	11	21	21

continued overleaf

Table 4 (continued)

Interval for relative demands	Neelin et al. exp.	Ochs and Roth exp.							
		Games 1–3		Games 4–6		Games 7–10		All games	
$c'/c =$	0.25	0.4	0.6	0.4	0.6	0.4	0.6	0.4	0.6
$d_1 \leq 0.05$	–	–	–	–	–	–	–	–	–
$0.05 < \underline{d}_1 \leq 0.15$	–	–	–	–	–	–	–	–	–
$0.15 < \underline{d}_1 \leq 0.25$	–	–	–	–	–	–	–	–	–
$0.25 < \underline{d}_1 \leq 0.35$	–	–	–	–	–	–	–	–	–
$0.35 < \underline{d}_1 \leq 0.45$	–	–	– *	–	– *	–	– *	–	– *
$0.45 < \underline{d}_1 \leq 0.55$	2	11	18	8	20	9	26	28	64
$0.55 < \underline{d}_1 \leq 0.65$	1	18 *	6	19 *	4	30 *	6	67 *	16
$0.65 < \underline{d}_1 \leq 0.75$	33 *	1	–	3	–	1	–	5	–
$0.75 < \underline{d}_1 \leq 0.85$	4	–	–	–	–	–	–	–	–
$0.85 < \underline{d}_1 \leq 0.95$	–	–	–	–	–	–	–	–	–
$0.95 < \underline{d}_1$	–	–	–	–	–	–	–	–	–
N	40	30	24	30	24	40	32	100	80

Thus the game-theoretic solution predicts an immediate agreement determined by player 1's demand $d_1^* = c - c'$.

In the experiment of Binmore et al. (1984, 1985) the initial cake was $c = 100$ pence and the smaller cake $c' = 25$ pence. Thus the solution payoffs of player 1 and 2 are 75 pence and 25 pence, respectively. Compared to the one-round ultimatum bargaining games, described and analysed in sections 2 and 3, the relation of equilibrium payoffs $c'/(c - c') = 1/3$ between player 2 and 1 in the Binmore et al. experiment is rather moderate. In the one-round ultimatum bargaining games the relation of equilibrium payoffs $\epsilon/(c - \epsilon)$ between players 2 and 1 is nearly zero.

Table 4 contains the experimental results of Binmore et al. (1985: fig. 1). The level of aggregation in table 4 is determined by Binmore et al. who do not list individual decision data. Whereas the main tendency (30 out of 82 observations) in the 1st game is to propose an equal split, the strong tendency (50 out of 81 observations) in the 2nd game is to play like a game theorist (Binmore et al. 1985: 1179). For Binmore et al. the equal division of c is an obvious and acceptable compromise for an unexperienced subject. However, once a subject is fully aware of the game structure, considerations of strategic power should dominate.

The study of Binmore et al. has inspired further experiments with at least two rounds of ultimatum bargaining. Güth and Tietz (1985, 1986) have explored more extreme equilibrium payoff relations $c'/(c - c')$ for the different initial cake sizes $c = 15$, 35, and 55 German marks by using $c' = 0.1c$ and $c' = 0.9c$. In table 4 we have listed their results in the same way as those of Binmore et al. individually for the two values of the 'cake shrinking' parameter $c'/c = 0.1$ and $c'/c = 0.9$. The game-theoretic relative demand $\underline{d}_1^* = 0.9$ for $c'/c = 0.1$ and $\underline{d}_1^* = 0.1$ for $c'/c = 0.9$ was rarely observed. For $c'/c = 0.1$ only 2 out of 11 observations in the 1st game and 1 out of 10 in the 2nd game lie in the corresponding range $0.85 \leq \underline{d}_1 \leq 0.95$; for $c'/c = 0.9$ no observed value $\underline{d}_1$ coincides with the game-theoretic solution $\underline{d}_1^*$. Thus the conclusion of Binmore et al. that more experienced subjects confirm with the game-theoretic prediction is limited to rather moderate equilibrium payoff relations. As in one-round ultimatum bargaining games the game-theoretic solution looses nearly all its predictive power if it induces payoff results which are socially unacceptable.

Neelin et al. (1988) keep the equilibrium payoff relation 1/3 between player 2 and player 1 of Binmore et al. (1984, 1985) but vary the possible length of bargaining plays. The 'framing' of this experiment has been criticised by Binmore et al. (1988) (see Forsythe et al. (1988: table 1) for some differences in the experimental design of ultimatum bargaining experiments). With two possible rounds of ultimatum bargaining the initial cake $c = \$5$ shrinks to \$1.25, with three rounds it shrinks first to \$2.50 and then to \$1.25, whereas for five possible rounds the initial cake $c = \$5$ shrinks to \$1.70, then to \$0.58, then to \$0.20, and finally to \$0.07. Backward induction shows that in all cases the optimal opening demand is $d_1^* = \$3.75$, i.e. the equilibrium payoff relation (between players 2 and 1) is 1/3 regardless of whether bargaining can extend over two, three of five rounds.

For two rounds of ultimatum bargaining Neelin et al. confirm in a surprisingly clear way the major tendency in the 2nd game of the Binmore et al. experiment. It can be seen from table 4 that 33 out of 40 observations lie in the corresponding range $0.65 < \underline{d}_1 \leq 0.75$. Since all subjects participated in a trial session with four possible rounds of ultimatum bargaining, the subjects in the Neelin et al. experiment can be regarded as experienced.

But with more than two possible rounds of ultimatum bargaining the game-theoretic solution is a rather poor prediction. The general tendency observed by Neelin et al. (1988) is that the initial demands d_1 leave just the second round cake for player 2, i.e. d_1 is equal to c minus the second round cake. The means of the observed relative demands are 0.73, 0.53, and 0.66 for 2-round, 3-round, and 5-round ultimatum games, respectively (computed from Neelin et al. 1988: appendix 2). Only for two possible rounds of ultimatum bargaining such a behavior confirms the game-theoretic prediction $d_1^* = \$3.75$.

In a second experiment Neelin et al. (1988) allowed for more experience by letting subjects play the 5-round game four times, once for practice and three times for an initial cake of size \$15. Neither experience nor the increase of rewards changed the major conclusions described above.

The general observation by Neelin et al. that player 1 leaves the second round cake for player 2 in ultimatum bargaining games with at least two possible rounds seems to suggest the following limited rationality approach to ultimatum bargaining (see Güth and Tietz (1988) for another attempt): instead of backward induction underlying the game-theoretic solution concept of 'subgame perfect equilibrium points' (Selten 1975) subjects use a rather crude form of forward induction according to which player 1 rightly concludes that he can demand all of the difference between the initial amount c and the second round cake. However, he avoids a more detailed analysis of further strategic interaction by assuming that player 2 completely controls the situation once the second round of ultimatum bargaining is reached.

Unfortunately, the results of Güth and Tietz (1988a) show that subjects entertain such considerations only in very special situations, e.g. in situations where the equilibrium payoff relation is rather moderate. Neither the mean demanded share $\underline{d}_1 = 0.72$ for $c'/c = 0.1$ nor the one of $\underline{d}_1 = 0.57$ for $c'/c = 0.9$ confirm the hypothesis that player 1 leaves the second-round cake c' for player 2. Neelin et al. themselves have already expected that their hypothesis will not be confirmed in extreme situations where the equilibrium payoff relation is socially unacceptable.

But do the experimental results of Güth and Tietz (1988a) really reject the hypothesis that subjects rely on the limited rationality approach: 'Leave the second round cake for player 2'. In our view, the impressing results of Neelin et al. (1988) indicate that subjects first calculate the difference between the initial and the second round cake in order to derive an aspiration level. If the implied payoff distribution is either socially acceptable or such that player 2 will not dare to reject it, then this amount is really demanded. But if the cost of rejecting an unfair proposal is rather low for player 2, player 1 obviously gives up this initial aspiration level and applies other considerations to determine his demand. In this sense the empirical results of the shrinking cake experiments seem to provide a promising starting point for a limited rationality approach: subjects first apply a rather simple procedure like the 'leave the 2nd round cake for player 2' considerations. The recommendation of this procedure then has to pass an acceptability test. Only in case this test fails a more complicated procedure for analysing the situation is used, etc. We think that viewing decision making as a process of subsequent decision filters corresponding to an increasing degree of sophistication is probably the most fruitful way to derive a concept of limited rationality. It has been suggested by an anonymous referee that one should debrief subjects in order to test whether this corresponds to the intellectual process actually employed by the subjects.

Since our main intention is to compare the different experimental results of ultimatum bargaining behavior, we do not list and analyse the decision data which Neelin et al. observed for more than two possible rounds. In table 4 one can therefore find only the results for two possible rounds of ultimatum bargaining listed in the same way as the results of Binmore et al. (1984, 1985) and Güth and Tietz (1988a). Since the game was not repeated we cannot account for experience effects. Before playing the two-round games, subjects in the Neelin et al. experiment participated in a trial run with four possible rounds. From the instructions (see Neelin et al. 1988: appendix 1) we induce that the two-round games were the first decision problem that subjects had to face after their trial run.

The very systematic study of Ochs and Roth (1989) is based on a 4 by 2 factorial experimental design. All four constellations with approximate discount factors (0.4; 0.4), (0.4; 0.6), (0.6; 0.4), and (0.6; 0.6) for players 1 and 2 have been explored with two and three rounds of ultimatum bargaining. In table 4 we only included the results of games with two rounds of proposals and equal discount factors, since in games with unequal discount factors players 1 and 2 cannot divide a constant amount in later rounds in the same way as in the 'complicated' games of Güth et al. (1982). The results of Ochs and Roth are listed in the same way as the other results contained in table 4 where experience is reflected by summarizing the results of games 1–3, 4–6, and 7–10, respectively.

There is a weak tendency in the game-theoretic direction in the sense that most observations for the discount factor 0.4 lie in the interval for the game-theoretic relative opening demand $\underline{d}_1^* = 0.6$, and that the interval $0.45 < \underline{d}_1 \leq 0.55$ contains most observations if, due to the discount factor 0.6, the relative opening demand $\underline{d}_1^*$ is equal to 0.4. This influence of the discount factor or cake-shrinking parameter is highly significant ($\alpha < 0.001$). But similarly to the results of Güth and Tietz (1988a) for $c'/c = 0.9$ players 1 rarely go below the equal share of c with their demand d_1 if game-theoretic reasoning tells them to do so (the whole range $\underline{d}_1 \leq 0.45$ contains no observation in spite of $\underline{d}_1^* = 0.4$ for the discount factor 0.6).

Since payoffs were actually paid in only one of ten successive games, subjects in the experiment of Ochs and Roth faced a rather low probability that their decision will actually matter. Since experience did not have any significant influence, one might have preferred fewer repetitions with more significant payoffs. It is an interesting observation that the discount factor of player 1 influences the behavior in two-round bargaining games although the game-theoretic solution does not depend at all on this parameter. Ochs and Roth try to explain their observations by modifying the 'utility function'. Unlike our implicit assumption when determining the game-theoretic solution that players are solely motivated by monetary rewards they incorporate distributional concerns directly into the utility functions.

We strictly reject the idea to include results of analysing a social decision problem into the utility functions of the interacting agents. Utility functions are an instrument of describing individual characteristics needed to define a social decision problem. Furthermore, all our experiences from ultimatum bargaining experiments indicate that subjects do not 'maximize' but are guided by sometimes conflicting behavioral norms (see, for instance, the discussion of Güth (1988)). The utility approach necessarily neglects the dynamic nature of the intellectual process which subjects apply to derive their decision behavior as, for instance, indicated in our discussion of the Neelin et al. results.

Ultimatum bargaining with alternating offers and no announced upper bound for the number of rounds has been experimentally investigated by Weg et al. (1990). Of course, it will always be common knowledge that bargaining has to end after finitely many rounds. Actually, bargaining was not allowed to last for more than 20 periods. As Ochs and Roth, the authors used equal and unequal discount factors by providing tables showing the cumulative discounts up to 44 periods. The major conclusions are that the subgame perfect equilibrium point, i.e. the game-theoretic solution, is rejected and that norms of equality and equity seem to be more consistent with the experimentally observed decision data.

We now would like to compare the various data sets contained in table 4. '* ' indicates the interval containing the game-theoretic relative opening demand $\underline{d}_1^* = d_1^*/c$ by player 1. Whereas for Binmore et al. and Neelin et al. the * interval is one of the focal points, this is never true for the true for the Güth and Tietz results. As already indicated above, the corresponding results of Ochs and Roth depend crucially on the cake-shrinking parameter: If c'/c is 0.4, then the * interval is the main focal point. But if the cake-shrinking parameter is 0.6, the game-theoretic predicition has lost all its predictive power. In these cases the interval containing the equal split $\underline{d}_1 = 0.5$ becomes the main focal point. But even here still 16 of 80 players 1 (i.e. 20%) ask for more than half of the original cake. The distributions observed by Binmore et

Table 5

Average results of the first rounds of two-round ultimatum bargaining for a shrinking cake analogous to table 4.

	Binmore et al. exp.			Güth and Tietz exp.					
	1st game	2nd game	Both games	1st game		2nd game		Both games	
$c'/c=$	0.25	0.25	0.10.25	0.9	0.1	0.9	0.1	0.9	
c	3.50	3.50	3.50	18.64	18.00	18.00	18.64	18.33	18.33
	(0)	(0)	(0)	(13.00)	(11.9)	(11.9)	(13.0)	(12.5)	(12.5)
d_1	1.98	2.24	2.11	14.55	10.96	12.55	9.72	13.60	10.31
	(0.476)	(0.392)	(0.459)	(10.6)	(6.88)	(9.11)	(7.61)	(9.94)	(7.3)
$\underline{d}_1$	0.565	0.641	0.602	0.76	0.631	0.674	0.515	0.719	0.570
	(0.136)	(0.112)	(0.131)	(0.111)	(0.103)	(0.113)	(0.091)	(0.120)	(0.113)
$\delta_2(\underline{d}_1)$	–	–	–	0.727	0.3	0.9	0.455	0.81	0.381
	–	–	–	(0.445)	(0.458)	(0.3)	(0.498)	(0.393)	(0.486)
N	82	81	163	11	10	10	11	21	21

	Neelin et al. exp.	Ochs and Roth exp.							
		Games 1–3		Games 4–6		Games 7–10		All games	
$c'/c=$	0.25	0.4	0.6	0.4	0.6	0.4	0.6	0.4	0.6
c	10.00	6.00	6.00	6.00	6.00	6.00	6.00	6.00	6.00
	(0)	(0)	(0)	(0)	(0)	(0)	(0)	(0)	(0)
d_1	7.25	3.45	3.21	3.55	3.14	3.54	3.13	3.52	3.16
	(0.605)	(0.292)	(0.206)	(0.305)	(0.194)	(0.273)	(0.198)	(0.292)	(0.202)
$\underline{d}_1$	0.725	0.575	0.535	0.591	0.523	0.591	0.522	0.586	0.526
	(0.061)	(0.049)	(0.034)	(0.051)	(0.032)	(0.046)	(0.033)	(0.049)	(0.034)
$\delta_2(\underline{d}_1)$	0.775	0.9	0.75	0.9	0.833	0.9	0.844	0.9	0.813
	(0.418)	(0.3)	(0.433)	(0.3)	(0.373)	(0.3)	(0.363)	(0.3)	(0.39)
N	40	30		30	24	40	32	100	80

al. reveal most clearly double peakedness where the two focal points correspond to the equal split $\underline{d}_1 = 0.5$ and the game-theoretic relative opening demand $\underline{d}_1^* = 0.75$. Whereas for rather unexperienced players the main focal point of these two is the equal split interval, the opposite is true for more experienced subjects.

Table 5 contains more illustrative average results of table 4 as the average size c of the original cake, the average (relative) opening demand $d_1(\underline{d}_1)$, the average acceptance rate $\delta_2(d_1)$ of the opening demand d_1, and the number N of observations. All amounts have been expressed in German marks by evaluating 1 English pound ($\mathscr{L}$) by DM3.50 and 1 American dollar ($) by DM2. The amounts of Ochs and Roth have been divided by 10 to take account of the fact that subjects were paid in only one of 10 games. The values d_1 and $\underline{d}_1$ of Binmore et al. have been computed by setting $\underline{d}_1$ equal to the midpoint of the concerning interval in table 4. A '–' indicates that the corresponding observations were not available to us.

Güth and Tietz are the only ones who have varied monetary incentives. Furthermore, they have used the strongest average monetary motivation. Compared to the studies of Neelin et al. and Ochs and Roth there is a surprising variance in the average acceptance rates observed by Güth and Tietz. Whereas these range from 0.75 to 0.9 for Neelin et al. and Ochs and Roth, the corresponding interval for Güth and Tietz is from 0.3 to 0.9. Here one should, of course, keep in mind that Güth and Tietz have considerably fewer observations ($N = 10$ or 11 as compared to $N \geq 24$). But in our view the decisive reason for the extreme differences in the average acceptance rates is the fact that Güth and Tietz have imposed extreme cake-shrinking parameters c'/c. More specifically, the extremely low average acceptance rates have been caused by the almost unshrinking cake $c'/c = 0.9$.

The average relative opening demands $\underline{d}_1$ are consistently greater than 0.5 even in the cases with $c'/c > 0.5$ where $\underline{d}_1^* < 0.5$. Thus players 1 do not seem to trust game-theoretic reasoning when it yields them less than half of the initial cake. There is no significant effect of experience in the average data of Ochs and Roth. The observations of Güth and Tietz reveal a slight influence of experience in the sense that the mean demanded shares $\underline{d}_1$ decrease and that average acceptance rates $\delta_2(d_1)$ increase with more experience. Compared to this Binmore et al. have observed a significant increase of $\underline{d}_1$ with experience so that there is a puzzling difference in the effects of experience observed in the two experiments. It should be mentioned that, due to the games with $c'/c = 0.9$, Güth and Tietz observed quite a number of conflicts or nonefficient agreements and that all subjects could notice this (all players 1 were seated in one room and all players 2 in a neighboring room and games were played simultaneously). This common experience of conflicts or inefficient agreements could have induced subjects to be less demanding in the subsequent repetition. In the Binmore et al. experiment subjects had to rely purely on individual experiences.

A linear regression of the acceptance behavior of player 2 with the cake-shrinking parameter c'/c and the relative demand $\underline{d}_1$ of player 1 as regressors for the 262 first rounds of two-round games (withouth the data of Binmore et al. 1985) yields the following optimal separation function:

$$\delta_2(\underline{s}_2) = \begin{cases} 0 & \text{for } \underline{d}_1 > \underline{s}_2 \\ 1 & \text{otherwise,} \end{cases} \tag{3a}$$

with

$$\underline{s}_2 = 0.867 - 0.449\, c'/c. \tag{3b}$$

Other variables as the cake size c and the experience parameter 'game' have no significant influence. Function (3) explains 86.6% of the 262 acceptance decisions by player 2. The cake-shrinking parameter has significant impact on acceptance behavior. Observe that game theory predicts $\underline{s}_2 = 1 - c'/c$ and that the equal split solution implies $\underline{s}_2 = 0.5$. According to function (3) players 2 seem to determine their behavior by balancing the incentives to comply with both extreme principles. More specifically, the value $\underline{s}_2$ is always higher than the relative demand $\underline{s}_2 = 0.75 - 0.5c'/c$ implied by giving equal weights for both principles. The latter phenomenon could be justified by the hypothesis that players 2 want to allow for small deviations from a certain distribution norm, e.g. the one implied by equal weights for the game-theoretic and the fifty-fifty solution.

In the following we want to analyse the average demand behavior $\underline{d}_1$ over all 425 observations by some regressions. Postulating significance levels of $\alpha < 0.0001$ for the regression coefficients we obtain the following result:

$$\underline{d}_1 = 0.679 - 0.210\ c'/c, \quad R^2 = 0.126,\ N = 425. \tag{4}$$

The coefficient of determination can be improved by including the cake size c as regressor:

$$\underline{d}_1 = 0.659 - 0.242\ c'/c + 0.00488\ c, \quad R^2 = 0.189,\ N = 425. \tag{5}$$

Thus a bigger cake leads to higher relative demands. The highly significant influence of c (the partial correlation coefficient is 0.270) illustrates how important it is to vary the cake size c when exploring ultimatum bargaining behavior.

A further increase of R^2 to 0.266 is achieved if one substitutes c by the (0, 1) dummy variables for the experiments of Binmore et al. and of Ochs and Roth:

$$\underline{d}_1 = 0.769 - 0.225\ c'/c - 0.109\ \text{Binmore} - 0.0997\ \text{Ochs},$$

$$R^2 = 0.266,\ N = 425. \tag{6}$$

A corresponding dummy variable for the experiments of Neelin et al. has no significant influence. Compared to the results of Güth and Tietz and Neelin et al. the observations of Binmore et al. and Ochs and Roth indicate demands which ask for about 10% less of the cake. This can be revealed by separate regressions yielding similar coefficients for the cake-shrinking parameter c'/c.

An analysis of variance shows a sufficiently significant ($\alpha < 0.02$) interaction effect between the experience parameter game and c'/c. Separate regressions for the three experience conditions lead to

$$\underline{d}_1 = 0.656 - \underset{(\alpha < 0.005)}{0.137\ c'/c}, \quad R^2 = 0.039,\ N = 197,\ \text{for game} = 1, \tag{7a}$$

$$\underline{d}_1 = 0.698 - 0.246\ c'/c, \quad R^2 = 0.227,\ N = 156,\ \text{for game} = 2, \tag{7b}$$

$$\underline{d}_1 = 0.729 - 0.346\ c'/c, \quad R^2 = 0.420,\ N = 72,\ \text{for game} = 3. \tag{7c}$$

Eqs. (7) indicate a monotonic shift towards the compromise solution $\underline{d}_1 = 0.75 - 0.5c'/c$ implied by giving equal weights to the game-theoretic and the fifty-fifty solution. The asymptotic F-test (Amemiya 1985) for unequal variances shows with $F^2_{419} = 6.68$ that the structural change is highly significant ($\alpha < 0.002$). The increase of R^2 is accompanied by a reduction of the standard error from 0.125 to 0.092 to 0.041 underlining the importance of experiments in which subjects can learn successful behavior by experience. A theory of limited rational behavior, which can be classified as rational in the sense of goal-oriented behavior, should not be based only on experiments without repetitions. That experience influences the coefficient of c'/c is also demonstrated by a global regression which uses the product of c'/c and game (game = 1, 2, 3) as regressor instead of c'/c. Analogously to (6) we obtain

$$\underline{d}_1 = 0.665 + 0.0743 \text{ game} - 0.147 \text{ game} * c'/c - 0.118 \text{ Binmore}$$

$$- 0.112 \text{ Ochs}, \quad R^2 = 0.294, \; N = 425. \tag{8}$$

Better explanations can be obtained by separate investigations of accepted and refused demands. The gap $\Delta = |c'/c - 0.5|$ measures how the game-theoretic prediction deviates from the equal split solution and indicates the cognitive pressure due to these two competing behavioral norms. Using the gap Δ as an additional regressor yields the following result for the accepted relative demands $\underline{d}_1^a$:

$$\underline{d}_1^a = 0.728 - 0.140 \text{ game} * c'/c - 0.291 \text{ game} * \Delta + 0.0981 \text{ game}$$

$$- 0.176 \text{ Ochs}, \quad R^2 = 0.653, \; N = 211. \tag{9}$$

For the rejected relative demands $\underline{d}_1^r$ the regressor 'game $*\ \Delta$' is not significant. Eliminating this regressor yields

$$\underline{d}_1^r = 0.724 - 0.185 \text{ game} * c'/c + 0.097 \text{ game} - 0.133 \text{ Ochs},$$

$$R^2 = 0.724, \; N = 51. \tag{10}$$

The variable 'game $*\ \Delta$' indicates learning behavior in situations where Δ is large, i.e., when the two behavioral norms $\underline{d}_1^* = 1 - c'/c$ and $\underline{d}_1 = 0.5$ predict very different outcomes. From eqs. (9) and (10) one might therefore conclude that acceptance results from learning to make reasonable offers when Δ is large. In general, the mean accepted relative demand is significantly smaller with 0.586 than the mean rejected relative demand of 0.655 ($\alpha < 0.0001$).

5. Final remarks

Güth et al. (1982) examined experimentally ultimatum bargaining behavior in order to develop bargaining theory by first looking at the most basic bargaining situations and then trying to proceed with more complicated situations. Unfortunately, although ultimatum bargaining seems to be the most primitive form of negotiations, a satisfying descriptive theory of ultimatum bargaining is not yet available. As indicated by the results of sections 2 and 3 ultimatum bargaining behavior depends crucially on the experimental environment, i.e. on how the ultimatum bargaining game is embedded. Since a similar dependency on environmental aspects will be true for most (bargaining) experiments, we will not discuss this here in more detail.

One reason why ultimatum bargaining became a widely known experimental paradigm is that experimentally observed ultimatum bargaining behavior clearly contradicts the most obvious rationality requirements of game theory and also of economic theory. For somebody who always thougth that human decision making will be characterized at most by limited rationality, this controversy must be somewhat surprising. Apparently this debate is far from being settled.

Experimentally observed ultimatum bargaining behavior reveals how considerations of distributive justice seriously destroy the prospects of exploiting strategic power. Our analysis has indicated which factors influence demand and acceptance behavior in ultimatum bargaining experiments.

It could be shown that the cake-shrinking parameter had a distinct negative influence on $\underline{d}_1$ and δ_2 in first rounds. Its influence on the acceptance behavior in last-round subgames is still open. The strong effects of the dummy variables for the experimental procedure underline their importance. To explore the influence of experimental procedures one might consider to replicate previous experiments of other authors as closely as possible. This might, for instance, indicate whether the way of recruiting, advising, and introducing subjects is responsible for the differing results.

The empirical results for ultimatum bargaining behavior will help to explain decisions in other and probably more complicated situations of strategic interaction. What we have learned is that people are willing to sacrifice considerable monetary amounts in order to punish someone who has been too greedy and that they do so even if it will not be of any help for them in the future. As a consequence the usual backward induction procedure underlying the concept of subgame perfect equilibria is no reliable *behavioral* concept. Actual decision behavior is obviously a result of both forward and backward induction. This is clearly illustrated by the impressing results of Neelin et al. (1988) which indicate some crude form of forward induction.

In our view, this has important implications for the interpretation of many game-theoretic results as, for instance, the Folk Theorems of game theory (see Aumann 1981; Fudenberg and Maskin, 1986; and also the critical discussion of Güth et al. 1988). On the one hand, Folk Theorems apply the concept of subgame perfect equilibria, i.e. backward induction rationality. On the other hand, Folk Theorems allow to vary the decision behavior in strategically equivalent subgames in a forward induction manner as most clearly illustrated by tit for tat or grim strategies. What the empirical evidence of ultimatum bargaining experiments demonstrates is that people are really willing to punish as supposed by tit for tat or grim strategies. There is apparently a rather sound behavioral basis for establishing Folk Theorem-like behavioral conjectures. This explains the frequent use and wide acceptance of Folk Theorem-like arguments although Folk Theorems as normative statements are rather questionable (see Güth et al. 1988).

The study of Neelin et al. (1988) is interesting since it illustrates how backward induction fails to be used when extending the possible length of bargaining plays from two to more bargaining rounds. One should try to find out whether this result is still valid when the stakes are higher and/or when subjects can lose money as, for instance, in the experiments where positions were auctioned. Of course, one should also vary the equilibrium payoff distribution in order to see how the breakdown of backward induction is influenced by the payoff distribution which it determines.

There are plans to further explore ultimatum bargaining behavior which, as far as we know, go back to the basic situation of just one bargaining round. Eric van Damme has suggested to investigate situations where player 1 can allocate $c - d_1$ among several players and where he, furthermore, can select who of the other players determines whether his proposal is accepted or not. More specifically, player 1 can choose any payoff vector $x = (x_1, \ldots, x_n)$ with $x_i \geq 0$ for $i = 1, \ldots, n$ and $x_1 + \ldots + x_n = c$, where n (≥ 3) is the number of players, as well as the responder $r \in \{2, \ldots, n\}$. The main hypotheses concern how variations in the responder r's information about x influence the decision behavior of 1 and r. The responder, for instance, might know the whole vector x, or x_r only, the amount allocated to him, or x_1 and x_r.

Other attempts concern ultimatum bargaining experiments in which player 2 is only incompletely informed about the cake size c. Again there are various possibilities to define the rules of such games, especially the a priori beliefs of player 2 about the cake size c.

References

Amemiya, T., 1985. Advanced econometrics, Oxford: Basil Blackwell.

Aumann, R.J., 1981. 'Survey of repeated games'. In: Essays in game theory and mathematical economics in honor of Oskar Morgenstern. Mannheim/Wien/Zürich: Bibliographisches Institut. pp. 11–42.

Binmore, K.G., A. Shaked and J. Sutton, 1984. Fairness of gamesmenship in bargaining? – An experimental study. Unpublished working paper, The London School of Economics and Political Science, London.

Binmore, K.G., A. Shaked and J. Sutton, 1985. Testing noncooperative bargaining theory: A preliminary study. American Economic Review 75, 1178–1180.

Binmore, K.G., A. Shaked and J. Sutton, 1988. A further test of noncooperative bargaining theory: Reply. American Economic Review 78, 837–839.

Bolle, F., 1988. Are there high reward experiments without high expenditure for the experimenter? Discussion paper, Universität Hamburg, Sozialökonomisches Seminar.

Brandstätter, H., 1988. Sechzehn Persönlichkeits-Adjektivskalen (16PA) als Forschungsinstrument anstelle des 16PF. Zeitschrift für experimentelle und angewandte Psychologie 35, 370–391.

Forsythe, R., J.L. Horowitz, N.E. Savin and M. Sefton, 1988. Replicability, fairness and pay in experiments with simple bargaining games. Working paper 88-30, University of Iowa, IA.

Fudenberg, D. and E. Maskin, 1986. The fold theorem in repeated games with discounting and with incomplete information. Econometrica 54, 533–554.

Güth, W., 1988. 'On the behavioral approach to distributive justice – A theoretical and experimental investigation'. In: S. Maital (ed.), Applied behavioral economics, Vol. II. Brighton: Wheatsheaf Book Ltd. pp. 703–717.

Güth, W. and R. Tietz, 1985. 'Strategic power versus distributive justice. An experimental analysis of ultimatum bargaining'. In: H. Brandstätter and E. Kirchler (eds.), Economic psychology. Proceedings of the 10th IAREP Annual Colloquium. Linz: Rudolf Trauner Verlag. pp. 129–137.

Güth, W. and R. Tietz, 1986. 'Auctioning ultimatum bargaining positions. How to decide if rational decisions are unacceptable?' In: R.W. Scholz (ed.), Current issues in West German decision research. Frankfurt: Verlag Peter Lang. pp. 173–185.

Güth, W. and R. Tietz, 1988a. 'Ultimatum bargaining for a shrinking cake - An experimental analysis'. In: R. Tietz, W. Albers and R. Selten (eds.), Bounded rational behavior in experimental games and markets. Lecture notes in economics and mathematical systems, Vol. 314. Berlin: Springer. pp. 111-128.

Güth, W. and R. Tietz, 1988b. Ultimatum bargaining behavior - A survey. ZiF-Group on Game Theory in the Behavioral Science, ZiF-working paper, University of Bielefeld, No. 21, and Frankfurter Arbeiten zur Experimentellen Wirtschaftsforschung, discussion paper No. A 26.

Güth, W., W. Leininger and G. Stephan, 1988. 'On supergames and folk theorems, A conceptual discussion'. In: R. Selten (ed.), Game equilibrium models, Vol. II: Methods, morals, and markets. Berlin: Springer.

Güth, W., P. Ockenfels and R. Tietz, 1990. Distributive justice versus bargaining power - Some experimental results. Discussion paper, Frankfurt/Main.

Güth, W., R. Schmittberger and B. Schwarze, 1982. An experimental study of ultimatum bargaining. Journal of Economic Behavior and Organizations 3, 367-388.

Harrison, G.W. and J. Hirshleifer, 1989. An experimental evaluation of weakest link-best shot models of public goods. Journal of Political Economy 97, 201-255.

Hartung, J. and B. Elpelt, 1986. Multivariate statistik (2nd ed.). München: Oldenburg Verlag.

Hoffman, E. and M.L. Spitzer, 1982. The coase theorem: Some experimental tests. Journal of Law and Economics 25, 73-98.

Hoffman, E. and M.L. Spitzer, 1985. Entitlements, rights and fairness: An Experimental examination of subjects' concepts of distributive justice. Journal of Legal Studies 14, 259-297.

Homans, G.C., 1961. Social behavior: Its elementary forms. London: Routledge and Kegan Paul.

Kahneman, D., J.L. Knetsch and R.H. Thaler, 1986a. Fairness as a constraint on profit-seeking: Entitlements in the market. American Economic Review 76, 728-741.

Kahneman, D., J.L. Knetsch and R.H. Thaler, 1986b. Fairness and the assumptions of economics. Journal of Business 59, 285-300.

Kravitz, D.A. and S. Gunto, 1988. Decisions and perceptions of recipients in ultimatum bargaining games. Manuscript, Department of Psychology, Bowling Green State University, Bowling Green, OH.

Mikula, G., 1973. Gewinnaufteilungsverhalten in Dyaden bei variierten Leistungsverhältnis. Zeitschrift für Sozialpsychologie 3, 126-133.

Neelin, J., H. Sonnenschein and M. Spiegel, 1988. A further test of noncooperative bargaining theory: Comment. American Economic Review 78, 824-836.

Ochs, J. and A.E. Roth, 1989. An experimental study of sequential bargaining. The American Economic Review 79, 355-384.

Prasknikar, V. and A.E. Roth, 1989. Fairness and considerations of strategy in bargaining: Some experimental data. University of Pittsburgh.

Rubinstein, A., 1982. Perfect equilibrium in a bargaining model. Econometrica 50, 97-109.

Selten, R., 1975. Reexamination of the perfectness concept for equilibrium points in extensive games. International Journal of Game Theory 4, 25-55.

Thaler, R.H., 1988. Anomalies: The ultimatum game. The Journal of Economic Perspective 2(4), 195-206.

Vickrey, W., 1961. Counterspeculation, auctions and competitive sealed tenders. Journal of Finance 16, 8-37.

Weg, E., A. Rapoport and D.S. Felsenthal, 1990. Two-person bargaining behavior in fixed discounting factors games with infinite horizon. Games and Economic Behavior 2, 76-95.

[16]

Bargaining and Market Behavior in Jerusalem, Ljubljana, Pittsburgh, and Tokyo: An Experimental Study

By ALVIN E. ROTH, VESNA PRASNIKAR, MASAHIRO OKUNO-FUJIWARA, AND SHMUEL ZAMIR*

In an experiment comparing related two-person bargaining and multiperson market environments in Israel, Japan, the United States, and Yugoslavia, market outcomes converged to equilibrium everywhere, and there were no payoff-relevant differences among countries. However, bargaining outcomes were everywhere different from the equilibrium predictions (both in observed agreements and in the substantial frequency of observed disagreements), and substantial differences were observed among countries. Because of the way the experiment was designed, the fact that the market behavior is the same in all countries supports the hypothesis that the differences in bargaining behavior among countries are not due to differences in languages, currencies, or experiments but may tentatively be attributed to cultural differences. (*JEL* C78, C90, C92)

This paper reports an experiment in which data were collected for a simple one-period bargaining situation (an ultimatum game) and a simple one-period market in four countries: Israel, Japan, the United States, and Yugoslavia. The experiment had three substantive goals: (i) to compare behavior in related bargaining and market environments; (ii) to compare behavior in very different subject pools in order to assess the effect that subject-pool differences may have and to assess how this effect may differ in the bargaining and market environments; and (iii) to use such differences as may be found between subject pools to test and refine hypotheses about the out-of-equilibrium behavior that has frequently been observed in bargaining games of the kind examined here.

In addition, a major methodological goal of the present investigation was to give us the opportunity to learn from experience how to deal with the formidable problems of experimental design that come to the fore in constructing a multinational experiment, particularly if one of the goals of the experiment is to investigate possible *cultural* differences. These problems include how to control for potential experimental artifacts arising from the different languages in which instructions are given, the different currencies in which subjects are paid, and the different experimenters who conduct the trials in each country. To the extent that these factors can be controlled, different behavior in the different subject pools can cautiously be used as the basis for preliminary conjectures about cultural differences that might account for the different observed behavior.

The two-player bargaining environment we look at is an ultimatum game: one bargainer makes a proposal of how to divide a certain sum of money with another bargainer, who has the opportunity to accept or reject the proposed division. If the second bargainer accepts, each bargainer earns the amount proposed for him by the first bar-

*Roth: Department of Economics, University of Pittsburgh, Pittsburgh, PA 15260; Prasnikar: University of Pittsburgh and University of Ljubljana; Okuno-Fujiwara: University of Tokyo; Zamir: Hebrew University of Jerusalem and University of Pittsburgh.

This work has been partially supported by grants from the National Science Foundation, the Russell Sage Foundation, and the Alfred P. Sloan Foundation. We also thank Roy Navon in Israel, Janez Prasnikar and Lado Rupnik in Yugoslavia, and Koji Ishibashi and Noriyuki Yanagawa in Japan for assistance at critical junctures, and we thank J. Kadane for statistical advice.

gainer, and if the second bargainer rejects, then each bargainer earns zero. To allow us to observe the effects of experience, subjects in the bargaining part of the experiment each participate in ten bargaining sessions against different opponents. Although different pairs of bargainers interact simultaneously, each bargainer learns only the result of his own negotiation.

The multiplayer market environment we examine has a similar structure: multiple buyers (nine, in most sessions) each submit an offer to a single seller to buy an indivisible object worth the same amount to each buyer (and nothing to the seller). The seller has the opportunity to accept or reject the highest price offered. If the seller accepts, then the seller earns the highest price offered, the buyer who made the highest offer (or, in case of ties, a buyer selected by lottery from among those who made the highest offer) receives the difference between the object's value and the price he offered, and all other buyers receive zero. If the seller rejects, then all players receive zero. Each player learns whether a transaction took place and at what price. To allow us to observe the effects of experience, subjects in the market part of the experiment each participate in ten markets, with a changing population of buyers.

In both the market and bargaining environment, the prediction of the unique subgame-perfect equilibrium (under the auxiliary assumption that subjects seek to maximize their monetary payoffs) is that one player will receive all the wealth (or almost all, if payoffs are discrete). To see why this is so, suppose for specificity that the total value of a transaction is $10 and that offers can be made in units no smaller than $0.05. In the bargaining game, the assumption of subgame perfectness means that the second bargainer will accept any positive offer, rather than reject it and earn zero. Therefore, at equilibrium, no first bargainer will offer the second more than $0.05, since even that amount will surely be accepted. Thus, there are two subgame-perfect equilibria: in one of them, the first bargainer offers the second $0.05, keeping $9.95 for himself, and the second bargainer accepts (but would have rejected a proposal in which the first bargainer kept everything for himself). In the second equilibrium, the first bargainer offers zero to the second, keeping everything for himself, and the second bargainer (nevertheless) accepts. These two equilibria become one as the smallest unit of transaction goes to zero, and even with the $0.05 unit, both equilibria give virtually all the gains from trade to the first bargainer.

The computation of pure-strategy perfect equilibria is almost equally simple in the case of the market game. Here again, the assumption of subgame perfectness means that the seller never rejects the maximum bid when it is positive. Because any buyer who does not submit the maximum bid earns zero with certainty, there cannot be any equilibria at which the high bidder makes a positive profit (by bidding $9.95 or less) and some other bidder submits a lower bid, since a low bidder could do better by raising his bid to the high bid, which would then give him a positive expected payoff. If the high bid is no greater than $9.95, all bids must be equal. However, if all bids are equal, they cannot be less than $9.95, since if they were, then a bidder who raised his bid by $0.05 would increase his expected payoff because he would win with certainty instead of with probability $\frac{1}{9}$. Thus, the only perfect equilibrium at which the maximum bid is not $10.00 has all bids equal to $9.95, so that the seller earns virtually all of the profit. There are also equilibria at which the maximum bid is $10.00. In fact, *any* distribution of bids in which two or more buyers bid $10.00 is an equilibrium, since in this case no buyer can earn a positive payoff (even) by changing his bid. Thus, there are many equilibria, but only two equilibrium prices, $10.00 and $9.95, so the seller gets (virtually) all the wealth. The situation is the same when we consider perfect equilibria in mixed strategies.[1]

[1]Consider an equilibrium in which at least one buyer has a positive expected payoff (i.e., in which there is a positive probability that the high bid will be less than $10.00). Then, at equilibrium every buyer must have a positive expected payoff (since a bid of $9.95 with

Various experimenters (see Werner Guth and Reinhard Tietz [1990] and Roth [1992] for surveys) have previously noted that observed payoffs in ultimatum bargaining are much less extreme, with the second bargainer reliably receiving significantly more than zero when agreement is reached. In contrast, preliminary evidence from the pilot markets used to assess the viability of the present experiment, which were included in an experiment reported in Prasnikar and Roth (1991),[2] suggested that, after subjects had acquired a little experience with the market, prices would conform very closely to the perfect-equilibrium prediction that the single seller in each market would receive all the gains from trade. Thus, there was reason to believe that, despite their similar equilibria, these two economic environments would yield very different behavior.

The principal patterns of behavior observed in the data from the four countries in which this experiment was run are as follows.

1) Regarding the observed market behavior: (a) In every country, the observed market outcomes converge quickly to the perfect equilibrium, and do not deviate from equilibrium once it has been achieved. (In no country was the highest offered price ever rejected in any round, and so the observed outcomes were always Pareto-efficient.) (b) Hence, there are no payoff-relevant differences observed in market behavior between countries.
2) Regarding the observed bargaining behavior: (a) In every country, the observed bargaining outcomes are significantly different from the perfect-equilibrium predictions. (Further, in every country, there was a substantial frequency of rejected offers, resulting in Pareto-inefficient outcomes.) (b) However there are substantial differences observed between countries, such as a pronounced shift in the distribution of offers that the first bargainer makes to the second. (The highest offers are made in the United States and Yugoslavia, and the lowest offers are made in Israel, with Japan in the middle. Except for the United States and Yugoslavia, all between-country differences are statistically significant, and between-country differences are bigger than within-country differences among different experimental sessions.) (c) Within every country, the probability that an offer will be rejected is inversely related to the size of the offer (i.e., low offers are rejected more frequently than high offers). However, this pattern does not hold between countries: higher disagreement rates are *not* observed in countries where lower offers are observed. Further, the probability that a given offer is rejected is *lower* in countries where lower offers are observed. (This will allow us to distinguish between

---

certainty will have a positive expected payoff in this case). Let x be the smallest bid that some buyer makes with positive probability. At equilibrium the bid of x must have a positive expected payoff, so the event that all buyers bid x must have positive probability (since only in this event can a buyer who bids x be the winning bidder). Suppose a buyer changes his mixed strategy by reducing to zero the probability that he bids x and increasing the probability that he bids $x+0.5$. Then, in the event that all other buyers bid x, he will win with certainty instead of with probability $\frac{1}{9}$, so this increases his expected payoff, provided his expected payoff is positive when he wins with a bid of $x+0.05$ (i.e., provided x is less than \$9.95). Therefore, in the only equilibrium in which buyers have positive expected payoff, all buyers bid \$9.95 with certainty (and have expected payoff \$0.05/9). As already noted, any strategies are in equilibrium so long as two or more bidders bid \$10.00 with certainty, so even in mixed strategies there are only two equilibrium prices.

Note that, in addition to having extreme perfect-equilibrium distributions, both games have a continuum of other (imperfect) Nash equilibria. Any offer x in the bargaining game can occur at an (imperfect) equilibrium if the second bargainer's strategy is to reject all offers but x, and the same is true in the market game.

Finally, recall that the auxiliary assumption under which all these calculations are made, namely, that subjects are seeking simply to maximize income, has been shown to be questionable in environments such as this (see Jack Ochs and Roth, 1989). We will return to this point when we discuss the results of this experiment.

[2]See also J. Keith Murnighan and Roth (1980) for an earlier study of this kind of market, conducted under different conditions.

alternative hypotheses about the role that perceptions of fairness may play in this behavior and how it may vary across cultures.)

3) Regarding other comparisons: (a) Differences between countries evolved differently in the market and bargaining environments: as subjects gained experience, the between-country differences in market outcomes became smaller (and ultimately vanished), while the differences among bargaining outcomes in different countries grew larger as subjects gained experience. (b) Because of the way our experiment is designed, the pattern of bargaining results and the fact that the observed market behavior is essentially the same in all countries supports the hypothesis that the differences observed in bargaining behavior are not due to differences in languages, currencies, or experimenters but result from other causes.

Most of the conclusions we draw about the susceptibility of these two economic environments to subject-pool differences and the nature of those differences, do not depend on interpreting the causes of observed differences between countries as being cultural in origin. However, many aspects of the design of this experiment were concerned with controlling for the effects of extraneous variables in an experiment conducted in different countries. These and other aspects of the design are described in detail next.

I. Experimental Design

A. *Controlling for Between-Country Variables*

We first discuss several features of the experimental design which specifically address problems arising from the multinational character of this experiment, namely, the problems of controlling for the effects of different experimenters, different languages, and different currencies. (So far as we are aware, the design issues concerning languages and currencies have not previously been considered in the manner we propose here.) After discussing these elements of the design, we will return to those features of the design that are particular to the bargaining and market environments that are the focus of this experiment.

Our discussion of those aspects of the experimental design motivated by the multinational character of the experiment will be organized as a statement of a particular problem, followed by the element of the design that addresses this problem.

Problem 1: Experimenter Effects.—Since the experiment involves several experimenters in different locations, between-country differences might arise because of uncontrolled procedural differences or because of uncontrolled personal differences among the experimenters.

Design Solution.—After the procedures were initially designed, each of the experimenters came to Pittsburgh, where they ran (at least) a bargaining session and a market session. The Pittsburgh data were therefore gathered by all of the experimenters before they returned to their home countries to gather the data there.[3] In this way, we were able to coordinate the detailed operational procedures among the different experimenters. Also, the Pittsburgh data can be used to detect any pure experimenter effect in the between-country comparisons (i.e., any effect due to personal characteristics of the experimenters), since if these effects exist they will show up not only in the comparisons between countries, but in comparisons of the Pittsburgh sessions conducted by the different experimenters.

Problem 2: Language Effects.—Because the instructions for the experiment are presented in English, Hebrew, Japanese, and Slovenian, systematic differences between countries might be observed because of

[3]The Yugoslav data were gathered by Prasnikar, who ran the first Pittsburgh sessions with Roth observing. The remaining Pittsburgh data were gathered by Zamir (the Israeli experimenter) and Okuno-Fujiwara (the Japanese experimenter) with Roth and Prasnikar observing.

the way the instructions are translated. (For example, the English words "bargaining," "negotiating," and "haggling" are all approximate synonyms but have different connotations which might elicit differences in behavior.)[4]

Design Solutions.—We addressed the problem of language effects both through the way in which the translations were made and, more formally, through the way the instructions for the bargaining and market environments were related. (The instructions in all four languages are available from the first author upon request.)

1) Translations: The experimenter responsible for each translation is a national of the country in question who is both linguistically and culturally fluent in American English (all three non-American experimenters had lived for extended periods in the United States). Efforts were made to phrase the English instructions in terms that could be faithfully translated into each of the languages. Aside from avoiding terms with heavy or ambiguous connotations either in English or in translation, this also led to phrasing in less abstract terms than are sometimes used in single-culture experiments. (For example, subjects in bargaining experiments are sometimes instructed that they will be in the position of "player 1" or "player 2," but this turns out to be difficult to translate into Slovenian without sounding frivolous.)
2) Control for translation differences: The instructions for the bargaining and market environments were written in parallel, using the same vocabulary. (For example, in both environments, those subjects who made proposals were referred to as "buyers," while those who made acceptances or rejections were termed "sellers.") If a translation difference is responsible for an observed behavior difference between countries, it should show up in both the market and bargaining data. In particular, the pattern of results that would allow us to be most confident that a between-country difference in bargaining behavior, for example, was not due to translation differences would be if there were no between-country difference observed in the market behavior and if the market and bargaining behavior were also different from each other in each country. That is, suppose we observe a pattern of results of the following sort, in which the data differ between two countries for one of the environments (in this case, the bargaining environment), but not the other:

$$\begin{array}{ccc} \text{market/country 1} & \neq & \text{bargaining/country 1} \\ = & & \neq \\ \text{market/country 2} & \neq & \text{bargaining/country 2} \end{array}$$

If the market data (like the bargaining data) also showed differences between the two countries, or if the market and bargaining data were the same in one of the countries, then we could not be sure that the between-country difference in the bargaining data was not due to some property of the translation. However, if the pattern of results is as above, then we can at least put an upper bound on the effect of the translation: it is not large enough to cause the markets to yield different results in the different countries or to cause the bargaining to yield the same results as the market in one of the countries. This would thus support the hypothesis that the translation is not the cause of the observed difference in the bargaining.[5]

[4]This problem could not have been avoided by presenting the identical instructions in English to English-speaking subjects in each of the countries. Aside from the selection effects of choosing only English-speakers, there is no way to control the different connotations that various English terms and phrases might have to nonnative English-speakers in different countries.

[5]A priori, either environment might have served as a control for the other, but the strong convergence to equilibrium observed in the preliminary trials of the market in the United States made us anticipate that greater between-country differences would be observed in the bargaining. Another common approach for controlling for translation differences in survey research is "back translation," in which a second translator trans-

Problem 3: Currency Effects.—Because the subjects were paid in dinars, dollars, shekels, and yen, systematic differences between countries might be observed because of the different incentives that the potential payments give to subjects or because of the different numerical scale on which payments are made. (That is, subjects in experiments often tend to choose round numbers [see e.g., Wulf Albers and Gisela Albers, 1983], and these may depend on the units involved, so that subjects proposing prices in dollars might choose different numbers than those dealing in thousands of yen, or hundreds of thousands of dinars.)[6]

Design Solutions.—(a) To assess the extent to which between-country differences might be due to differences in purchasing power, the Pittsburgh data establish a baseline by including sessions in which the potential payoff ranged from $10 to $30. In each country, the size of the payoffs was then chosen to give a purchasing power on the high side of $10. If observed differences between countries fall outside the range of differences due to payoffs observed in Pittsburgh, they are likely to be due to other factors. (b) To control for differences in units, proposed prices in all countries were made in terms of 1,000 tokens, with increments being made in units of five tokens.

We hasten to note that there remain uncontrolled differences between subject pools that might not be regarded as "cultural." For example, in Israel and Yugoslavia, a much higher percentage of our sample of subjects are army veterans than in the United States or Japan. Therefore, any conclusions about the *causes* of between-country differences have to be circumspect.

B. *Other Aspects of the Experimental Design and Procedures*

In order that experimental sessions could be easily arranged in multiple locations, a "one-classroom" set of procedures was adopted for each of the two experimental environments. Parallel procedures were used in both environments, so that any observed differences between environments would be attributable to differences in the economic environment, such as the number of buyers or the information available to buyers and sellers.

Subjects who participated in a bargaining session were randomly divided into buyers and sellers and then separated into two rows on opposite sides of the room. After the instructions were read aloud, subjects played a practice round (to verify that everyone understood how to make and respond to proposals) and then ten rounds, changing partners after each round. Buyers made a price proposal by filling out a message form, on which they were identified only by a coded identification number. These message forms were then sorted and distributed to the sellers. The sellers' responses were returned to the buyers in the same way, so that in any round no buyer knew with which seller he was matched and vice versa, and each bargainer learned only the result of his own negotiation. At the conclusion of the session, one round was chosen at random, and subjects were paid their earnings for that round.[7]

Subjects who participated in a market session were also divided into buyers and sellers but were not separated by category, since there were only two sellers. In each round, the buyers were divided into two markets, A and B. The market in which a buyer was participating in a given round was

lates the instructions back into the original language, so that the two versions can be compared for substantive differences. For our purposes in the present experiment, we felt that this would not be adequate, because the issue was to control for subtle connotations. For a recent market experiment that uses back translation, see Steven Kachelmeier and Mohamed Shehata (1990).

[6]Since the Yugoslav data were collected, a devaluation has reduced currency units by a factor of 10,000.

[7]In all countries except Yugoslavia, where university authorities deemed it inappropriate, subjects were also paid a fixed amount for showing up on time ($5 in the United States, 10 IS in Israel, and 1,000 yen in Japan, with an additional 500 yen in travel expenses for University of Tokyo students who traveled to Keio University).

indicated on his message form for that round, but no subject knew which (other) buyers were in each market in each round. (The motivations for this arrangement were to prevent the ten rounds from becoming a repeated game among a constant group of buyers and to parallel the bargaining sessions, in which bargaining partners changed each round.) After buyers' proposed prices for a given round were collected, the highest proposed price in each market was posted on the blackboard, together with the identification number of the buyer who had proposed it (or who had been selected at random from among the high proposers). The seller in each market then accepted or rejected this offer. This decision was also posted on the blackboard, and the round ended.

In order that no subject in a market session should know which of the others were sellers and which were buyers, subjects were instructed to fill out forms at each opportunity (so that there would be no point at which only sellers or only buyers were writing). When buyers were recording their proposed prices, sellers were asked to estimate what the high price would be in their market, and while sellers were recording their acceptance or rejection, buyers were asked to estimate the likelihood that the posted high price would be accepted. In order that the procedures in the bargaining sessions would parallel those in the market sessions, buyers and sellers in the bargaining sessions also filled out these additional forms. However, only the offers and acceptances/rejections influenced each subject's payoff from the experiment, and therefore these are the primary data which will be the focus of the analysis.

In each country, a pilot session was conducted with experienced bargainers, recruited from subjects who had completed a bargaining session. All other bargaining and market sessions used subjects who had not previously participated in any other part of this or related experiments. Each session lasted ten rounds, which was announced at the beginning of the session and just prior to the last (tenth) round.

The tenth-round data will therefore be of particular interest, for two reasons. First, it represents the round at which these subjects had acquired the most experience with the game and with the reactions of the other subjects. Second, because the tenth round was the last, the experimental environment gave subjects no incentives extending beyond the play of that round. (In earlier rounds, even though subjects are not engaged in a repeated game with the same players, they may have some incentive to make proposals that will help them gather information about the likely reactions that different prices will elicit, in order to use this information in subsequent rounds.) However, the data from earlier rounds will also be of interest, in order to permit us to investigate the different dynamics by which behavior evolves in the market and bargaining environments in the various subject pools examined.

C. *Session Parameters*

The basic data in each of the four countries come from three bargaining sessions and two market sessions. In the United States, the value of the object being negotiated or bid for in the bargaining and market sessions was \$10, in Yugoslavia it was 400,000 dinars, in Japan 2,000 yen, and in Israel 20 shekels.[8] In the United States, an additional session of each of the market and bargaining environments was conducted with a \$30 value, to establish a baseline on the effect of changing the amount of the monetary payoffs.

Recall that all proposed prices were translated into units of 1,000 tokens, with

[8]The Yugoslav data were collected from 14 through 28 December 1989, a period during which there was substantial inflation, and the figure of 400,000 dinars was reached on the basis of a comparison of student wages and a price-index calculation at the beginning of that period. In Israel and Japan, the figures were set on the basis of comparisons of student wages and published figures of purchasing-power parity. In each case, the aim was to choose a figure that would yield a purchasing power slightly on the high side of \$10 in the United States.

the requirement that prices be stated in increments of 5. Thus, in both the market and bargaining environments, there are two perfect-equilibrium prices, differing by 5 tokens. These prices are 995 and 1,000 in the market, and 0 and 5 in the bargaining.[9] The difference of 5 tokens between the two equilibrium prices is negligible in terms of the payoff to any subject in any of the countries.

Subjects were recruited from the student populations of the University of Pittsburgh, the University of Ljubljana, the Hebrew University, and Keio University and the University of Tokyo. In Pittsburgh, subjects were drawn from undergraduate economics classes and M.B.A. business classes; in Israel, they were drawn from undergraduate first- and second-year economics classes (except for the 16 May 1990 bargaining session, which had a mixture of economics, business and psychology students); in Ljubljana, they were drawn from economics students (the 14 December 1989 bargaining session consisted entirely of first-year students, the other sessions consisted of second-, third-, and fourth-year students mixed together); and in Tokyo, they were drawn from third- and fourth-year economics students at the two universities (mixed together in each session).

In each session, we tried to have 20 subjects, so that there would be nine buyers in each of the two markets operating in each round of each market session and so that in the bargaining sessions each buyer would interact exactly once with each seller. On those occasions when fewer than 20 subjects reported for a session (in one market session and two bargaining sessions in the United States and in one bargaining session in Japan), the session proceeded with fewer subjects. In the market session, this meant that there were fewer buyers in each market, but in the bargaining session it meant that some buyers and sellers would interact twice in the course of the ten-round session. To prevent such a session from taking on some of the character of repeated play, buyers and sellers were therefore each assigned two coded identification numbers, so that they could not know when they were matched with someone for a second time.

II. Results

A. *Market Behavior*

Perhaps the single most striking result of this experiment was the remarkably consistent convergence to equilibrium observed in the markets. Recall that two markets, A and B, operated simultaneously in each of the ten rounds of each session. In no nonpractice round[10] was the maximum proposed price ever rejected, and in every session the transaction price in both markets rose to the equilibrium price of either 995 or 1,000. In one session (Israel, 4 April 1990), this double convergence was achieved as early as round 3, and in no session did it occur later than round 7. Furthermore, in no session did the transaction price in either market fall below 995 in any subsequent round.

Since the transaction price in each market is the maximum price offered, the convergence to equilibrium could conceivably be the consequence of one aggressive bidder in each market. However, this is not the case: the markets exhibit a high concentration of bids at or near the equilibrium bids. For example, there is no market session in which fewer than a third of the buyers proposed prices of 995 or 1,000 in round 10 (and in most sessions the percentage is far higher). In every country, over half of the

[9]The decision to use a market with many buyers (i.e., proposers) and a single seller, rather than one with one buyer and many sellers (which would have had equilibrium prices of 0 and 5), was made so as to gather more data on price proposals from each market and in the anticipation that competition might act more forcefully on the active (proposer) side of the market. Prasnikar and Roth (1991) compared bargaining and market games of the kind studied in this paper with an additional two-person game in which the perfect equilibrium gave almost all the wealth to the proposer and in which equilibrium was observed experimentally. The relationships among all three kinds of games will be discussed in Section III.

[10]And only once in a practice round.

TABLE 1—THE FIRST TWO HIGHEST PRICES p OFFERED IN EACH OF THE MARKETS AND THE BASIC DESCRIPTIVE STATISTICS

A. *Pittsburgh*:

		29 June 1989, Prasnikar ($N = 9$)			22 February 1990, Zamir ($N = 7$)			14 March 1990, Okuno-Fujiwara, $30 ($N = 9$)		
Period	Market	Highest price p	Second-highest price p	Mean (SD)	Highest price p	Second-highest price p	Mean (SD)	Highest price p	Second-highest price p	Mean (SD)
1	A	800	775	575	800	700	586	900	885	772
		(1)	(1)	(198)	(1)	(2)	(165)	(1)	(1)	(152)
	B	900	800	581	805	800	629	850	805	664
		(3)	(1)	(338)	(1)	(1)	(153)	(1)	(1)	(151)
2	A	935	900	665	900	825	758	965	950	721
		(1)	(2)	(299)	(1)	(1)	(119)	(1)	(1)	(205)
	B	900	855	676	1,000	900	635	930	880	684
		(1)	(1)	(269)	(1)	(1)	(262)	(1)	(1)	(252)
3	A	950	900	711	950	900	678	985	970	708
		(1)	(2)	(237)	(1)	(1)	(258)	(1)	(1)	(273)
	B	985	925	827	1,000	950	778	970	950	753
		(1)	(1)	(148)	(1)	(1)	(213)	(1)	(1)	(171)
4	A	995	990	864	955	935	613	960	930	748
		(1)	(1)	(177)	(1)	(1)	(326)	(1)	(1)	(218)
	B	990	940	674	995	925	737	985	980	782
		(1)	(1)	(335)	(1)	(1)	(272)	(1)	(2)	(307)
5	A	995	990	909	975	900	721	975	965	824
		(1)	(2)	(075)	(1)	(1)	(176)	(1)	(3)	(203)
	B	1,000	990	641	1,000	995	925	995	990	799
		(2)	(1)	(403)	(1)	(1)	(146)	(1)	(1)	(193)
6	A	1,000	950	581	995	990	822	990	970	879
		(1)	(1)	(376)	(1)	(1)	(216)	(2)	(1)	(161)
	B	995	980	868	925	750	539	995	970	782
		(4)	(1)	(325)	(1)	(1)	(298)	(1)	(1)	(199)
7	A	995	955	744	995	980	631	1,000	995	858
		(1)	(1)	(327)	(1)	(1)	(382)	(1)	(2)	(151)
	B	995	990	834	995	955	700	1,000	995	848
		(4)	(1)	(325)	(1)	(1)	(298)	(1)	(2)	(189)
8	A	995	990	758	995	990	796	995	960	811
		(3)	(1)	(377)	(1)	(1)	(221)	(2)	(1)	(191)
	B	1,000	995	809	995	990	669	995	975	789
		(1)	(3)	(330)	(1)	(1)	(319)	(1)	(1)	(176)
9	A	1,000	995	853	995	990	501	995	990	804
		(1)	(4)	(324)	(1)	(1)	(373)	(1)	(1)	(196)
	B	995	990	531	995	990	775	995	985	906
		(1)	(1)	(426)	(3)	(1)	(367)	(4)	(1)	(163)
10	A	1,000	995	621	995	990	534	1,000	995	807
		(1)	(3)	(457)	(2)	(1)	(458)	(1)	(1)	(216)
	B	1,000	995	741	1,000	995	699	1,000	995	916
		(1)	(2)	(342)	(1)	(2)	(390)	(2)	(3)	(170)

ctd. overleaf

buyers proposed a price of 995 or 1,000 at least once (18 out of 32 buyers in the $10 sessions in the United States; 31 out of 36 buyers in Yugoslavia; 29 out of 36 buyers in Japan; and 19 out of 36 buyers in Israel).

The market data are summarized in Table 1. For example, looking at Table 1A one sees that in the market conducted in Pittsburgh on 29 June 1989, with a transaction value of $10, there were nine buyers in each market (so there were 20 subjects, two of whom were sellers). In round 1, the high bid in market A was 800, and only one bidder in that market proposed that price, while the second-highest price was 775, also proposed by only one buyer. In the same round, the

TABLE 1—(CONTINUED)

B. *Ljubljana*:

		14 December 1989, Prasnikar ($N = 9$)			28 December 1989, Prasnikar ($N = 9$)		
Period	Market	Highest price p	Second-highest price p	Mean (SD)	Highest price p	Second-highest price p	Mean (SD)
1	A	875	840	730	920	890	795
		(2)	(1)	(113)	(1)	(2)	(97)
	B	825	820	664	870	835	736
		(1)	(1)	(158)	(1)	(1)	(89)
2	A	885	875	767	950	940	835
		(1)	(1)	(90)	(1)	(1)	(105)
	B	950	880	845	960	955	835
		(1)	(1)	(52)	(1)	(1)	(147)
3	A	965	930	893	985	980	836
		(1)	(1)	(62)	(1)	(2)	(186)
	B	975	955	787	990	975	894
		(1)	(1)	(211)	(1)	(1)	(152)
4	A	1,000	975	803	1,000	995	858
		(1)	(1)	(307)	(2)	(2)	(201)
	B	985	980	836	995	990	903
		(1)	(1)	(153)	(1)	(2)	(141)
5	A	995	975	858	1,000	995	959
		(1)	(1)	(154)	(1)	(3)	(67)
	B	1,000	995	833	1,000	995	874
		(1)	(1)	(316)	(3)	(2)	(196)
6	A	995	990	839	1,000	995	856
		(3)	(1)	(319)	(1)	(2)	(192)
	B	995	985	783	1,000	995	974
		(1)	(1)	(330)	(2)	(5)	(65)
7	A	995	990	846	1,000	995	947
		(2)	(3)	(327)	(2)	(4)	(131)
	B	995	990	928	995	990	943
		(1)	(5)	(162)	(4)	(2)	(96)
8	A	995	990	933	1,000	995	989
		(2)	(3)	(163)	(1)	(4)	(10)
	B	995	990	852	1,000	995	995
		(3)	(2)	(329)	(2)	(5)	(4)
9	A	995	990	791	1,000	995	994
		(1)	(4)	(340)	(1)	(5)	(3)
	B	995	990	988	995	990	991
		(3)	(4)	(8)	(6)	(2)	(7)
10	A	995	975	827	995	975	993
		(6)	(1)	(350)	(8)	(1)	(7)
	B	1,000	995	941	1,000	995	993
		(1)	(7)	(165)	(1)	(5)	(6)

highest price proposed in market B was 900, and this price was proposed by three different buyers. (Notice that, when proposing their prices, the buyers have no way of knowing which other buyers are in the market with them: a different sorting of buyers could easily have made 900 the transaction price in both markets, or 775 the transaction price in market A.) By round 5, however, both markets have a transaction price of 995 or 1,000, and the transaction price never drops below 995 in either market in any subsequent round. By round 10, the modal proposed price is 995, with 7 out of 18 buyers proposing prices of 995 or 1,000.

Notice that the pattern is very similar both in the other $10 Pittsburgh market (Table 1A, 22 February 1990), in which 5

TABLE 1—(CONTINUED)

C. *Tokyo*:

		17 May 1990, Okuno-Fujiwara ($N = 9$)			18 May 1990, Okuno-Fujiwara ($N = 9$)		
Period	Market	Highest price p	Second-highest price p	Mean (SD)	Highest price p	Second-highest price p	Mean (SD)
1	A	900	850	764	875	855	778
		(1)	(2)	(132)	(1)	(1)	(77)
	B	990	950	735	910	850	784
		(1)	(1)	(180)	(1)	(1)	(71)
2	A	955	925	750	925	920	783
		(1)	(1)	(295)	(1)	(1)	(267)
	B	995	990	803	950	930	812
		(1)	(2)	(234)	(1)	(1)	(133)
3	A	980	975	849	965	950	802
		(1)	(1)	(134)	(1)	(2)	(286)
	B	965	950	694	950	910	812
		(1)	(2)	(392)	(1)	(1)	(175)
4	A	975	955	933	975	970	895
		(2)	(1)	(44)	(1)	(1)	(122)
	B	995	985	968	975	960	886
		(1)	(2)	(19)	(1)	(2)	(135)
5	A	995	985	970	1,000	990	976
		(1)	(2)	(17)	(1)	(1)	(15)
	B	995	985	928	980	975	919
		(1)	(1)	(79)	(2)	(2)	(121)
6	A	995	985	963	990	975	901
		(2)	(2)	(45)	(3)	(1)	(127)
	B	995	990	961	995	990	968
		(2)	(2)	(69)	(3)	(2)	(47)
7	A	995	990	858	1,000	995	898
		(1)	(2)	(215)	(1)	(2)	(191)
	B	995	990	976	995	990	982
		(3)	(2)	(31)	(2)	(5)	(24)
8	A	1,000	995	988	995	970	934
		(1)	(4)	(15)	(6)	(1)	(161)
	B	1,000	995	909	1,000	995	984
		(1)	(3)	(175)	(2)	(4)	(32)
9	A	995	950	906	1,000	995	967
		(6)	(1)	(175)	(1)	(5)	(80)
	B	995	990	967	1,000	995	919
		(6)	(2)	(81)	(1)	(4)	(161)
10	A	995	990	958	1,000	995	961
		(7)	(1)	(110)	(1)	(4)	(44)
	B	995	950	979	1,000	995	880
		(7)	(1)	(33)	(2)	(3)	(328)

out of 14 buyers propose 995 or 1,000 in round 10, and in the Pittsburgh market in which the value of a transaction was $30 (Table 1A, 14 March 1990), in which 7 out of 18 buyers propose the equilibrium price. Therefore, the change in the scale of the payoffs makes no important difference, as might be expected in a market in which no buyer is making more than pennies in any of the final rounds.[11]

[11]The pattern was very similar in the pilot market session reported and analyzed in Prasnikar and Roth (1991).

TABLE 1—(CONTINUED)

D. *Jerusalem*:

Period	Market	4 April 1990, 1st session, Zamir ($N = 9$) Highest price p	Second-highest price p	Mean (SD)	4 April 1990, 2nd session, Zamir ($N = 9$) Highest price p	Second-highest price p	Mean (SD)
1	A	900	850	806	900	850	733
		(3)	(2)	(126)	(2)	(1)	(148)
	B	900	850	728	975	960	854
		(1)	(2)	(215)	(1)	(1)	(145)
2	A	950	930	872	1,000	990	877
		(1)	(1)	(66)	(1)	(1)	(102)
	B	995	950	862	985	975	913
		(1)	(1)	(89)	(1)	(1)	(81)
3	A	950	900	794	995	990	942
		(2)	(3)	(267)	(1)	(2)	(65)
	B	950	925	783	995	990	899
		(1)	(1)	(178)	(1)	(3)	(159)
4	A	965	950	846	1,000	995	924
		(1)	(2)	(145)	(1)	(2)	(80)
	B	960	955	875	995	990	891
		(2)	(1)	(131)	(2)	(2)	(195)
5	A	960	955	931	1,000	995	877
		(2)	(2)	(39)	(1)	(2)	(164)
	B	980	970	874	995	990	986
		(2)	(2)	(189)	(5)	(1)	(16)
6	A	1,000	990	959	1,000	995	937
		(1)	(2)	(37)	(1)	(4)	(84)
	B	1,000	980	919	995	975	945
		(1)	(1)	(74)	(4)	(1)	(67)
7	A	995	990	806	1,000	995	920
		(1)	(1)	(317)	(2)	(2)	(161)
	B	995	990	911	995	985	802
		(1)	(1)	(157)	(4)	(1)	(310)
8	A	995	990	978	1,000	995	843
		(3)	(2)	(20)	(2)	(2)	(305)
	B	995	980	869	1,000	995	926
		(1)	(1)	(185)	(1)	(5)	(197)
9	A	1,000	995	968	1,000	995	835
		(2)	(1)	(64)	(1)	(5)	(337)
	B	995	990	810	995	985	847
		(1)	(2)	(342)	(3)	(1)	(212)
10	A	995	990	820	1,000	995	769
		(2)	(2)	(329)	(1)	(2)	(339)
	B	1,000	995	964	1,000	995	903
		(1)	(3)	(41)	(1)	(5)	(149)

Notes: The numbers in parentheses under the prices are the numbers of buyers who offered that price. N represents the number of buyers in each market (i.e., in each round there are two sellers and $2N$ buyers, half in market A and half in market B.

Similarly, parts B–D of Table 1 show that by the tenth round the two Yugoslav markets both have 14 out of 18 buyers proposing 995 or 1,000, the two Japanese markets have 14 out of 18 and 10 out of 18 buyers proposing 995 or 1,000, and the two Israeli markets have 6 out of 18 and 9 out of 18 buyers proposing 995 or 1,000.

Figure 1 shows the distributions and cumulative distributions of proposed prices for rounds 1 and 10 for the two U.S. markets in which the transaction value was $10 and for

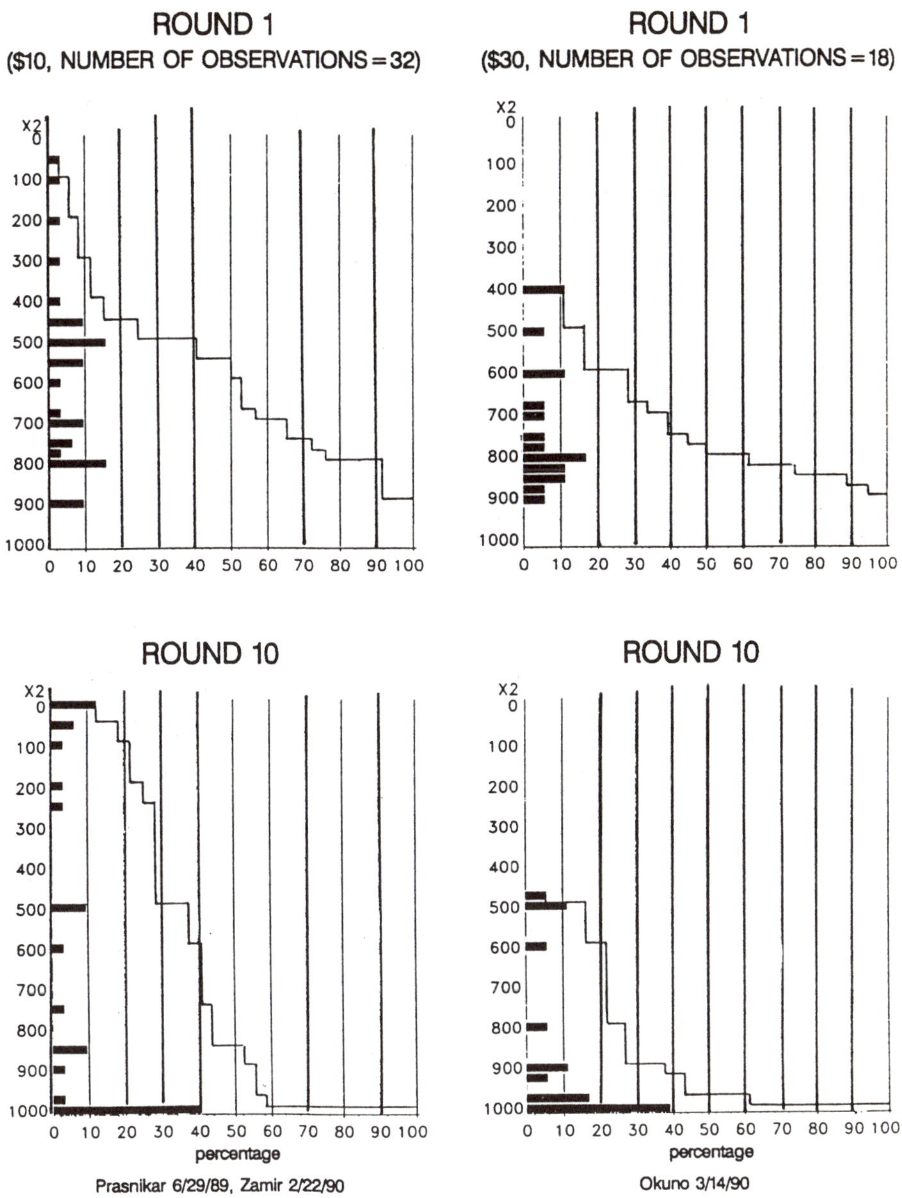

FIGURE 1. DISTRIBUTION OF MARKET OFFERS IN THE UNITED STATES

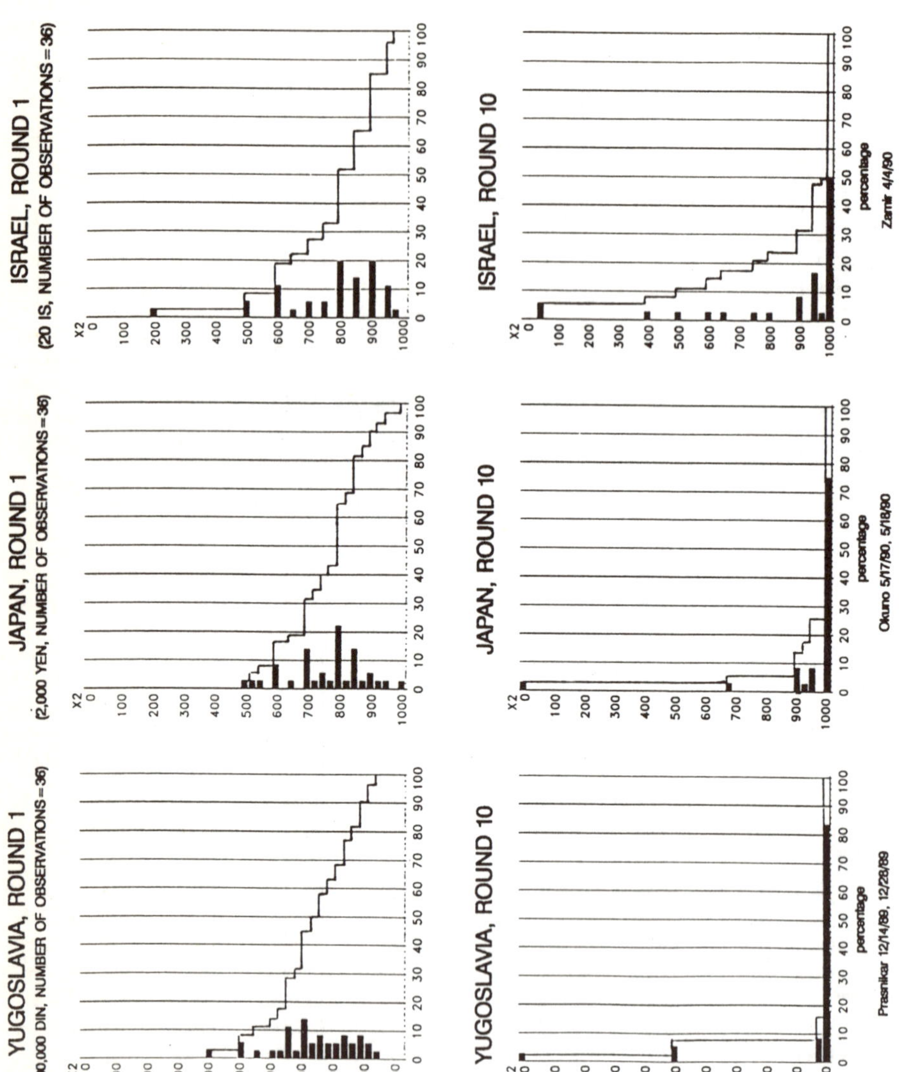

FIGURE 2. DISTRIBUTIONS OF MARKET OFFERS IN YUGOSLAVIA, JAPAN, AND ISRAEL

the one in which it was $30. (The histogram bars group price intervals of 25. Since price proposals are in increments of five tokens, this means that an interior bar on the graph, such as 500, contains the proposals from 490 through 510, while an endpoint, such as 1,000, contains the proposals of 990, 995, and 1,000.) Figure 2 contains the distributions and cumulative distributions of proposed prices for rounds 1 and 10 in Yugoslavia, Japan, and Israel. The pattern of how proposed prices changed over time is the same for all countries (and for $10 and $30 transaction values in the United States). In round 1, no more than 14 percent of the proposals are higher than 910 in any country, and except for a single offer in Japan, there are no proposals in the 990–1,000 range. However, in round 10, at least 39 percent of the proposals are from 990 to 1,000 in every country (and the concentration of proposals in this highest range goes up to over 80 percent). Thus, the shift in proposed prices from the first to tenth rounds in each country is clear.

While there are some detectable differences between the distributions in different countries,[12] we attach little significance to them for two reasons. First, none of these differences influences the payoffs to any agent: in the final rounds of the market sessions, any buyer who proposes a price of less than 900, say, has every reason to expect (correctly) that his earnings will be zero for that round. For this reason, economic theory makes no prediction about what the distribution of low offers will look like. Indeed, recall that, at any equilibrium in which two or more buyers propose a price of 1,000, no further prediction can be made about the price proposals of any other buyers, since these neither influence any payoff nor move the market out of equilibrium.

What Figures 1 and 2 and Table 1 make clear is that, while there is some variation in transaction prices in round 1, this has disappeared by round 10, when all transactions in all markets in all countries are at equilibrium prices.

B. *Bargaining Behavior*

The contrast between the bargaining data and the market data is striking: in the bargaining sessions, equilibrium price proposals (of 0 or 5) make up less than 1 percent of the data from any country. In all countries the price proposals made by bargainers are much nearer the middle of the range, and in all countries low offers are rejected at a substantially higher rate than higher offers.

However, despite the gross similarity of the bargaining data from all countries, especially when compared to the market data, there are notable differences between the distributions of bargaining proposals in different countries. The most obvious of these is seen in the different modal proposals (aggregated over all rounds of bargaining). In the United States (for bargaining both over $10 and $30) and in Yugoslavia the modal proposal is 500, while in Japan and Israel the modal proposal is 400.

To test formally whether these differences are reliable, we must disaggregate the data by rounds. The reason is that data from different rounds of the same bargaining session are not independent, since the same bargainers are involved (even though they are not paired in the same way). However, the proposals made in a given round by bargainers in different experimental sessions are independent, and so we can look at all the data for each country, round by round.

Before describing the formal tests, we first consider these distributions graphically. Figure 3 presents the round-1 and round-10 distributions and cumulative distributions for the $10 and $30 bargaining sessions in the United States, and Figure 4 presents the round-1 and round-10 distributions and cumulative distributions of offers in Yugoslavia, Japan, and Israel. In addition, the figures show the proportion of offers in each interval that were accepted (the black

[12] The Mann-Whitney U test reveals significant differences in most comparisons of the distributions, but all of the distributions are very highly concentrated in the highest prices.

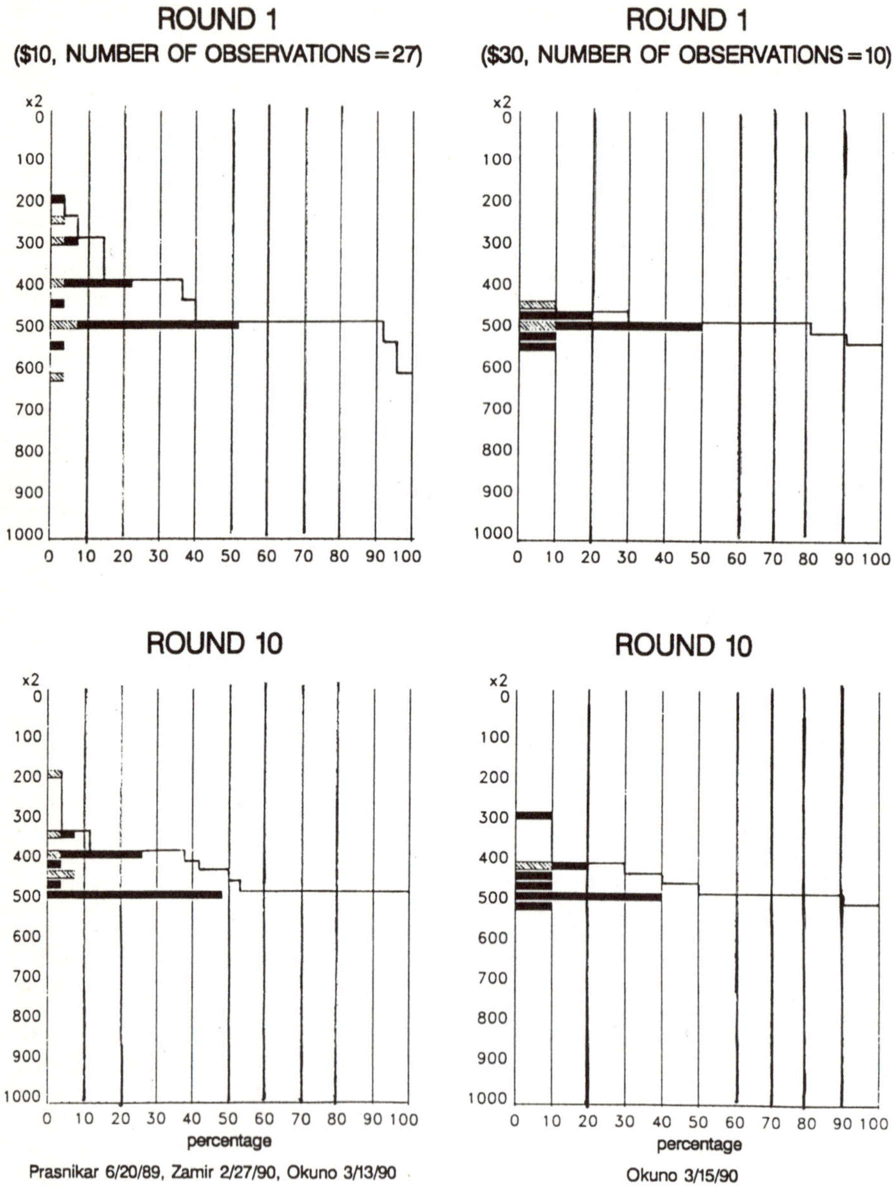

FIGURE 3. DISTRIBUTION OF BARGAINING OFFERS IN THE UNITED STATES (SOLID BARS = ACCEPTED OFFERS; STRIPED BARS = REJECTED OFFERS)

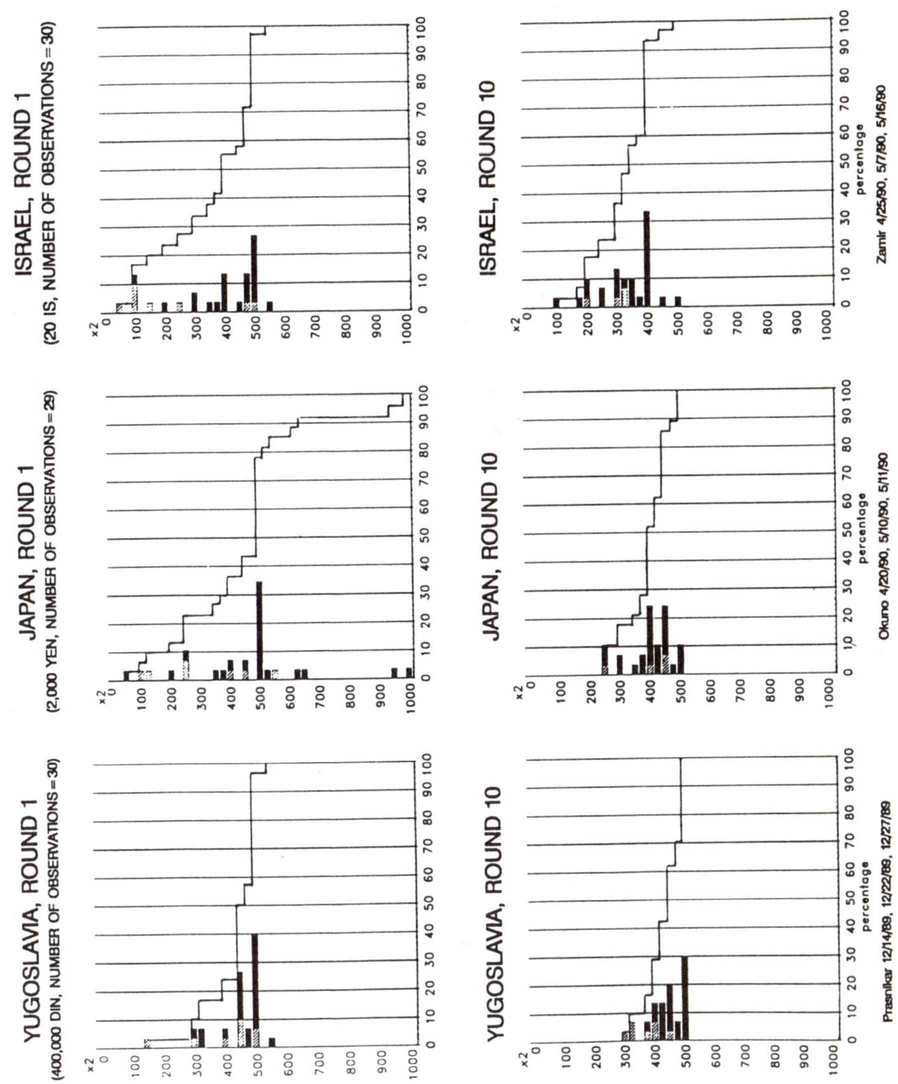

FIGURE 4. DISTRIBUTIONS OF BARGAINING OFFERS IN YUGOSLAVIA, JAPAN, AND ISRAEL (SOLID BARS = ACCEPTED OFFERS; STRIPED BARS = REJECTED OFFERS)

region) and rejected (the lighter, striped region).

In choosing the appropriate statistical test to compare the distributions between countries, we had to take into account the following features of these empirical distributions:

1) The distributions are highly asymmetric, with few observations higher than the mode. The distributions are clearly not normal and in fact fail the Kolmogorov-Smirnov test for normality.[13]
2) The sample sizes we are dealing with are relatively small. In each session involving 20 bargainers, there are 100 offers made by the 10 buyers in 10 rounds. However, because of the dependence between offers made by the same buyer in different rounds, we compare data round by round, which means that we base our tests on samples of size 10 when comparing two sessions and on samples of size 30 when we compare two countries with three sessions in each.

Guided by these considerations we used the nonparametric Mann-Whitney U test based on ranks (see e.g., Sidney Siegel, 1956). The idea of the test is as follows. Assume we are comparing two samples from variables X (offers in population 1) and Y (offers in population 2). Line up all the observations of both variables, from smallest to largest. The U statistic is then the number of times an X observation precedes a Y observation (with some adjustment for ties). If U is very small, this should be an indication that the distribution of X is "higher" than the distribution of Y. The distribution of U is known when X and Y have the same distribution, and therefore we can test the null hypothesis that X and Y have the same distribution against the alternative hypothesis that the two distributions are different.

The U statistics also provide an estimate of the magnitude of the difference between the two groups. A measure for this difference is $P(X>Y)$; that is, the probability that a random observation from X will be higher than a random observation from Y. If X and Y have the same distribution, then clearly $P(X>Y)=P(Y>X)$, and the higher the distribution of X compared to that of Y, the higher will be $P(X>Y)$ minus $P(Y>X)$. With the U statistics and a routine counting of the number of ties in the two samples of offers, we estimated $P(X>Y)$, $P(Y>X)$, and $P(X=Y)$. These estimates have the following probabilistic interpretation: assume that we draw two random offers x and y from the given samples of offers in group 1 and 2, respectively; our estimates are then the probabilities $P(x>y)$, $P(y>x)$, and $P(x=y)$, respectively.

Table 2 presents the results of the comparisons of the round-10 bargaining propos-

TABLE 2—MANN-WHITNEY TEST BETWEEN COUNTRIES: POOLED ROUND-10 BARGAINING

	Country		
Country	United States	Yugoslavia	Japan
Yugoslavia	0.35 0.45 (0.51)		
Japan	0.26 0.62 (0.02)*	0.29 0.59 (0.04)*	
Israel	0.10 0.79 (0.00)*	0.11 0.81 (0.00)*	0.21 0.69 (0.00)*

Notes: In each cell, the first number is the probability that an offer from the row country exceeds an offer from the column country. The second number is the probability that an offer from the column country exceeds an offer from the row country. The third number (in parentheses) is the significance level for the two-sided test of the null hypothesis that the offers are drawn from identical distributions (i.e., the probability that a difference as extreme as the observed difference would arise from two identical distributions). Cells in which this probability is less than 0.05 are marked with an asterisk.

[13]In each of the four countries, the pooled sample of all offers failed the Kolmogorov-Smirnov test at the 0.01 significance level. The same test by round in each country rejects the normal-distribution hypothesis in 27 out of 40 cases (the exceptions are eight rounds in Israel and five in Japan, and even there the maximum significance level was less than 0.4).

TABLE 3—MANN-WHITNEY *U* TEST, BY SESSION: NUMBER OF DIFFERENCES AT SIGNIFICANCE LEVEL 0.05 FOR ROUND-10 BARGAINING

	Country			
Country	United States	Yugoslavia	Japan	Israel
United States	0/6			
Yugoslavia	3/12	2/3		
Japan	5/12	3/9	0/3	
Israel	11/12	6/9	6/9	0/3

Notes: Each diagonal cell indicates how many significant differences were found when the round-10 bargaining data were compared for each pair of sessions in that country. Each off-diagonal cell indicates how many significant differences were found when the round-10 data from each session in the row country were compared with the round-10 data from each session in the column country. Since there are four sessions in the United States (one for each experimenter plus a $30 session) and three in each of the other countries, there are six pairwise comparisons within the United States and three within each other country, and there are 12 pairwise comparisons between the United States and each other country and nine pairwise comparisons between each other pair of countries.

als in all countries. The observed distributions are significantly different between every pair of countries except the United States and Yugoslavia.

This raises the question of whether these differences can be accounted for by currency or experimenter effects. As discussed earlier, tests for this possibility were built into the experimental design by having the three $10 bargaining sessions in Pittsburgh run by the three different experimenters and by having a fourth, $30, Pittsburgh bargaining session. If the distributions of offers are responding to changes in the value of a transaction, this should show up as a difference between the $30 bargaining session and the other sessions, while if there is an effect due to one of the experimenters, this should show up in comparisons involving the Pittsburgh session run by that experimenter. Contrary to either of these hypotheses, the first cell of Table 3 reports that there are no significant differences among the six pairwise comparisons of these four sessions.

When we compare the data for a given round from different sessions in this way, we are of course looking at smaller samples than when we pooled the data for a given round from all sessions in each country, as in Table 2. Therefore, one issue we need to consider is whether the lack of significant differences in the Pittsburgh sessions, in contrast to the significant differences between countries, might be due to the small sample sizes. Table 3 addresses this by reporting the results of pairwise comparisons between the unpooled round-10 bargaining data from all sessions in all countries. Note first that, except in Yugoslavia where one of the sessions was significantly different from the other two, there are no significant differences between sessions from the same country. The one Yugoslav session that differs from the others also differs from three of the U.S. sessions. Otherwise, the between-country differences by sessions mirror the between-country differences pooled across sessions.

So far we have concentrated on the round-10 data. Looking back at the comparison of rounds 1 and 10 given in Figures 3 and 4, we see that the differences between countries appear to increase from round 1 to round 10: the modal offer in round 1 is 500 in every country, whereas by round 10 the modal offer has shifted to 400 in Israel and Japan (which has a second mode of 450), while in the United States and Yugoslavia the round-10 mode remains at 500. Table 4 confirms this impression and shows that the differences between the distribu-

TABLE 4—PROBABILITY MEASURE Δp OF DIFFERENCE BETWEEN COUNTRIES' BARGAINING, BY ROUNDS

Round	US–YU	US–JA	US–IS	YU–JA	YU–IS	JA–IS
1	0.099	0.051	0.365	−0.038	0.271	0.264
2	0.042	0.330	0.446	0.313	0.429	0.076
3	−0.217	−0.022	0.221	0.139	0.438	0.192
4	−0.153	−0.031	0.178	0.122	0.329	0.207
5	0.132	0.169	0.505	0.015	0.422	0.364
6	0.332	0.301	0.575	−0.014	0.364	0.364
7	0.091	0.243	0.530	0.160	0.486	0.368
8	0.133	0.321	0.604	0.218	0.527	0.331
9	−0.054	0.161	0.496	0.259	0.590	0.377
10	0.099	0.360	0.695	0.302	0.703	0.479

Notes: US = United States, YU = Yugoslavia, JA = Japan, and IS = Israel.

tions of proposals by bargainers in different countries, as measured by $\Delta p = P\{x > y\} - P\{y > x\}$, tend to *increase* as the bargainers gain more experience. Although this increase is not monotonic, the difference in the last round is greater than the difference in the first round in every comparison, except between the United States and Yugoslavia, where it is constant (which is consistent with our general finding of no significant differences between those two countries' data).

This is confirmed by a simple regression model $\Delta p = \beta_0 + \beta n + \varepsilon$ which gives an estimate of β that is positive in all six comparisons. In the test of the hypothesis $\beta = 0$ against $\beta > 0$, the three comparisons involving Israel are significant at conventional levels (0.001 in two cases and 0.01 in one), and the comparisons of Japan with the United States and Yugoslavia have significance levels of 0.055 and 0.095, respectively. For the United States and Yugoslavia, β is not significantly different from zero ($P = 0.26$). (All tests passed the Kolmogorov-Smirnov test for the normality of the residuals.)

Another perspective on the differences between bargaining behavior in different countries comes from looking not at proposed prices, but at acceptances and rejections. We first look at overall disagreement rates in each country (i.e., the percentage of all offers that are rejected, without conditioning on the offer). Table 5 presents these

TABLE 5—REJECTION FREQUENCIES IN BARGAINING, BY ROUND AND COUNTRY

	United States		Yugoslavia		Japan		Israel	
Round	Frequency	Percentage	Frequency	Percentage	Frequency	Percentage	Frequency	Percentage
1	6	22	8	27	7	24	8	27
2	7	26	6	20	11	38	6	20
3	10	37	7	23	10	34	8	27
4	12	44	9	30	10	34	8	27
5	12	44	10	33	9	31	7	23
6	7	26	10	33	10	34	8	27
7	7	26	11	37	4	14	9	30
8	3	11	10	33	9	31	6	20
9	7	26	9	30	8	28	3	10
10	5	19	7	23	4	14	4	13
Total:	76	28	87	29	67	22	83	28

figures for rounds 1–10. The clear pattern within each country, that higher offers are accepted more frequently than lower offers (see Fig. 5),[14] is not mirrored at all when we compare countries where offers are high (the United States and Yugoslavia) with those where they are low (Japan and Israel). Over all rounds, the disagreement rates, which are 28 percent, 29 percent, 22 percent, and 28 percent, respectively, are certainly not rising. At round 10, the disagreement rates of 19 percent, 23 percent, 14 percent, and 13 percent are actually *lower* for the two low-offer countries. (However, we can only speculate whether the relationship among these last-round rates is robust, since the disagreement rates fluctuate so widely between rounds.)

A more detailed comparison of acceptances and rejections between countries can be made by considering how often the proposal of a given price is accepted. These comparisons are slightly complicated by the facts that the number of proposals of a given price is different in different countries and that observed rates of acceptance fluctuate widely for offers that were observed only rarely.[15] However, the underlying pattern is clear, as is demonstrated by Figure 5. The curves for each country represent the percentage of acceptances for each price that was proposed at least 10 times (over all rounds). Each cell of Figure 5 compares the resulting curves for a pair of countries, and these comparisons mirror those concerning the distribution of proposals. In each case, the country with the lower distribution of offered prices has a higher rate of acceptance for each proposed price. Thus, we see that the acceptance rate in Israel for each offer is higher than the corresponding rates in the United States, Yugoslavia, and Japan, while the acceptance rates in Japan are higher than those in the United States and Yugoslavia. Only in the comparison of the United States and Yugoslavia do we have two acceptance-rate curves such that the one that begins consistently lower ends consistently higher.

Given that different offers are accepted with different probabilities, it is natural to ask, for each country, what is the expected payoff to a buyer from making a particular offer. Since the behavior of the bargainers changes from round to round, this is something of a moving target. Nonetheless, Figure 6 presents the curves based on the pooled data from all rounds in each country for all offers that were made at least ten times. Thus, for example, if a buyer proposes a price of 300, he will earn 700 if it is accepted and 0 if it is rejected. In the United States, the price 300 was proposed 15 times and accepted four times (26.7 percent), so on average the proposal earned $(700 \times 0.267) = 186.9$, which can be read from the graph for the United States in Figure 6. It is instructive to compare these graphs to the modal offers observed in round 10 in each country (in Figs. 3 and 4). The modal offer in the final round in both the United States and Yugoslavia is 500, which is also the proposed price that maximizes a buyer's average earnings in these countries. The modal offer in the final round in Israel is 400; here too, this is the price that maximizes a buyer's average earnings. Finally, in Japan there are two modal offers in round 10, 400 and 450, and the latter maximizes a buyer's average earnings. Thus, by round 10, the buyers seem to be adapting to the experience of the prior rounds in a manner roughly consistent with simple income-maximization. (The same cannot be said of the sellers, who continue to reject low positive offers.) Of course, since we have observed that subjects are changing their behavior as they gain experience, the round-10 offers may not meet with the same average responses as in the earlier rounds, and to the extent that this is the case, there is reason

[14]The increasing acceptance rate of higher offers within each country is not completely monotonic, and in fact a small "kink" is visible in each country's acceptance-rate curve, which may possibly indicate a small bias related to whether offers are made in round numbers of tokens.

[15]For example, if a particular price is proposed only once, the percentage of acceptances will be either 100 percent or 0 percent.

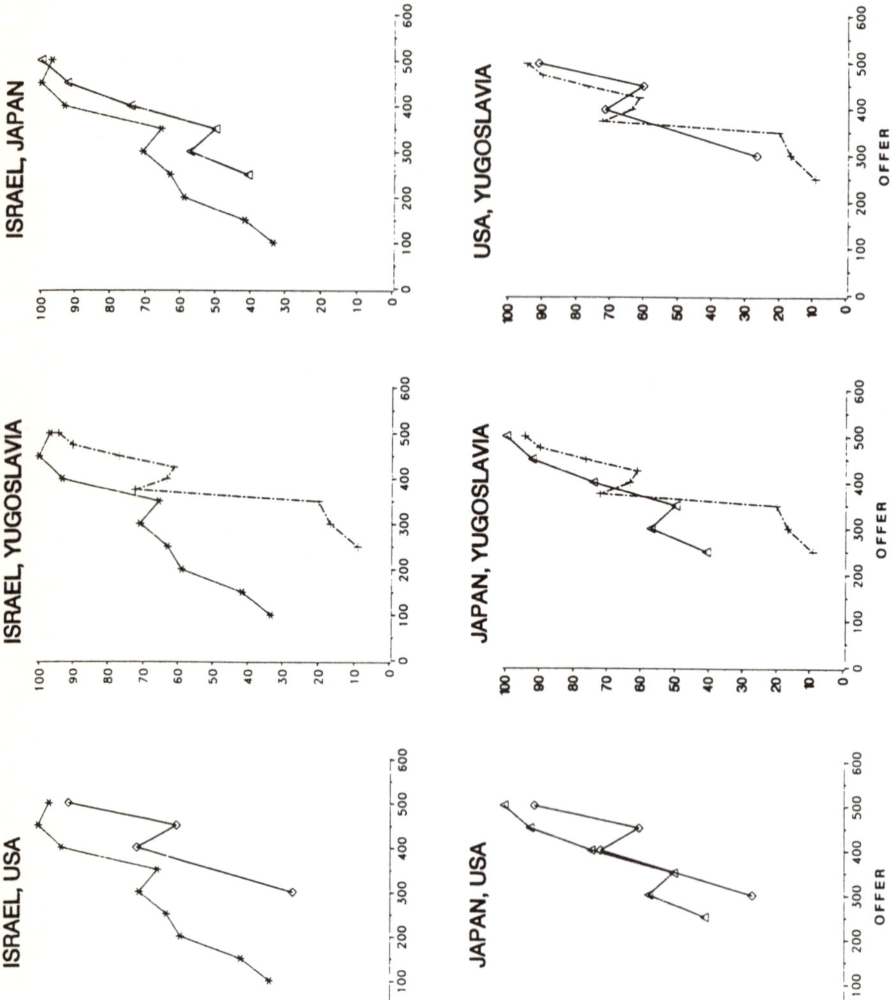

FIGURE 5. PAIRWISE COMPARISONS OF ACCEPTANCE RATES IN BARGAINING SESSIONS (POOLED DATA OF 10 ROUNDS; * = ISRAEL, ◇ = UNITED STATES, + = YUGOSLAVIA, △ = JAPAN)

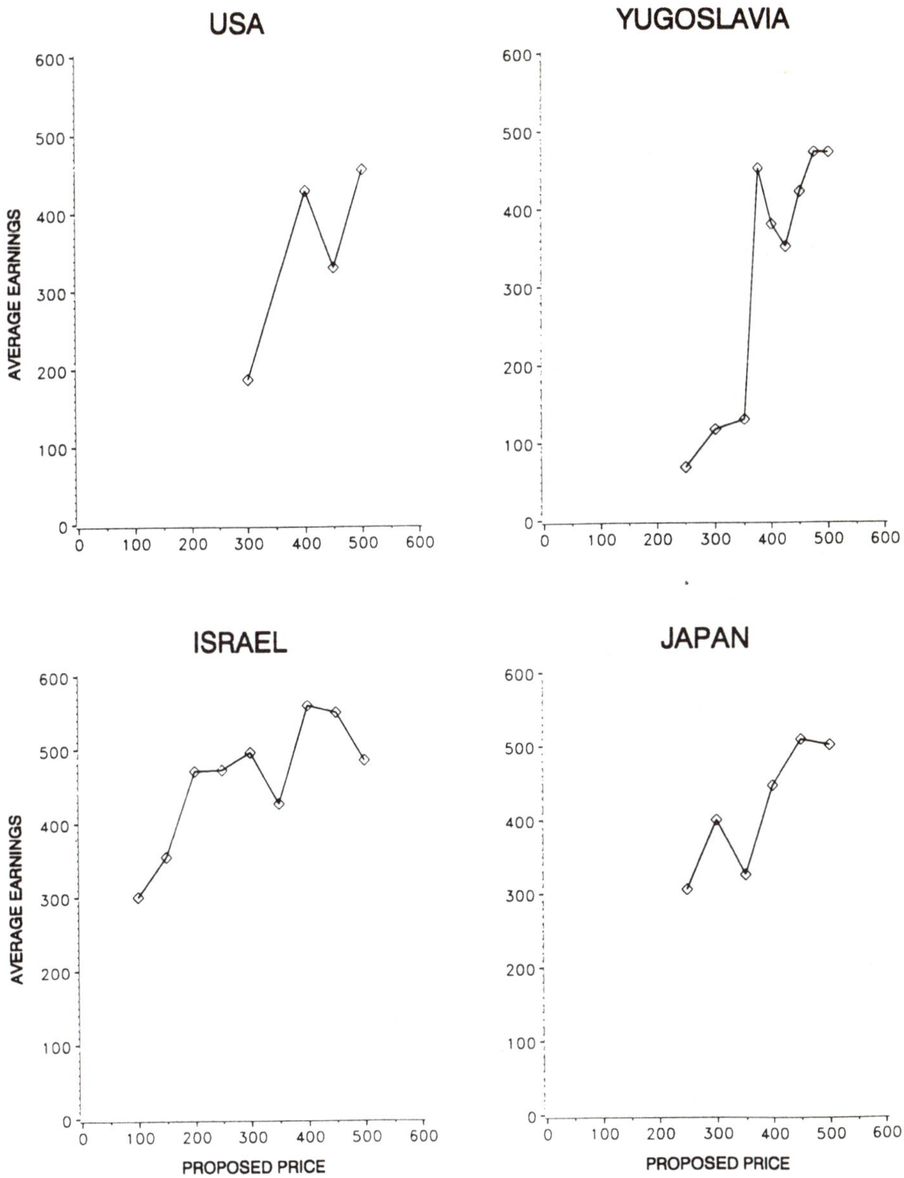

FIGURE 6. BUYERS' EARNINGS IN BARGAINING SESSIONS, BY PROPOSED PRICES (POOLED DATA OF 10 ROUNDS)

to believe that the process has not yet converged by round 10.[16]

III. Discussion

Both the market and bargaining environments chosen for this experiment have extreme perfect-equilibrium predictions, in which one player receives all the benefit from the transaction. Nevertheless, the market sessions exhibited a vigorous convergence to equilibrium that was robust to subject-pool differences and transaction values.[17]

In contrast to the market sessions, the bargaining sessions did not show any tendency toward the equilibrium prediction in any of the subject pools. Furthermore, there were clear differences in the outcomes of bargaining in different subject pools. These differences cannot be attributed simply to variations among inexperienced subjects, since they grew larger from round 1 to round 10, as the bargainers gained experience with the game and with each other.

The out-of-equilibrium behavior in the bargaining game is consistent with the behavior that has been uniformly observed by experimenters who have looked at ultimatum-bargaining games of this kind, starting with the paper by Guth et al. (1982). Prominent in the discussion of this phenomenon has been the idea that bargainers' conceptions of fairness might be an important explanatory variable, particularly insofar as such conceptions might explain the propensity of bargainers in the position of the second mover to reject positive offers (see Guth and Tietz [1990], Prasnikar and Roth [1991], and Roth [1992] for discussions of this literature). The relationship observed in this experiment between offers and acceptance rates in different subject pools can help distinguish between alternative hypotheses about how ideas about the fairness (or "reasonableness") of different proposals might account for these subject-pool differences.

One hypothesis is that the different subject pools share a common idea about what constitutes a fair or reasonable proposal (an obvious candidate is the fifty-fifty proposal of 500) and that the difference among subject pools is in something like their aggressiveness or "toughness." In this view, buyers in more aggressive subject pools would be more inclined to take advantage of their first-mover position to try to obtain more for themselves than might be considered fair. That is, such a buyer would recognize that a fifty-fifty split is "fair," but would seek to take more. However, if aggressiveness is a property of the subject pool, the sellers would share it and would presumably be less inclined to accept unfair offers than

[16] In an ideal world, we would at this point compare the experienced-bargainer sessions we conducted in each country. Instead, we have a cautionary tale about the difficulty of maintaining common procedures (and consequently experimental control) in an experiment conducted in four countries. Despite our efforts to remain in almost constant contact by electronic mail when the experimental sessions were in progress, in this aspect of the experiment our coordination failed. In Yugoslavia, the experienced subjects had all taken part in the same previous bargaining session (which turns out to have been the one Yugoslav bargaining session whose results were different from the other two), while in the other three countries, experienced bargainers were recruited from all three prior sessions. Furthermore, in Yugoslavia and the United States, the final experienced bargaining encounters occurred in the 20th round, while in Israel and Japan the sessions ended after the 10th round (with a subsequent experienced session in Japan lasting for 20 rounds). These procedural inconsistencies, together with the fact that we have many fewer experienced sessions than inexperienced sessions, make the comparisons of these groups less reliable than we would like. Consequently, we will simply note that the pooled data from all rounds of the experienced bargaining in each country are consistent with the between-country differences we have reported above. The experienced data also suggest that the evolution of behavior noted above from round 1 through round 10 may continue to evolve. However, a further exploration of these issues must await more data.

[17] The strength of the forces pushing buyers to propose prices that gave them zero profit can perhaps be better appreciated by noting that buyers in the market sessions appeared to find the experience quite frustrating. It was not uncommon, when subjects were being individually paid at the end of each session, for someone to ask why all the other buyers had behaved so foolishly. (When asked about his own bidding behavior, such a buyer would typically respond that the actions of the others had forced him to bid high as well.)

less aggressive sellers in other subject pools. Under this hypothesis, high rates of disagreement would be associated with subject pools in which offers are low. This is not what we observe.[18]

Instead, the subject pools where offers are low (Japan and Israel) do not exhibit any higher rates of disagreement than the high-offer subject pools. This suggests that what varies between subject pools is not a property like aggressiveness or toughness, but rather the perception of what constitutes a reasonable offer under the circumstances. That is, suppose that in all subject pools it seems reasonable for the first mover to ask for more than half the profit from the transaction and that what varies between subject pools is how much more seems reasonable. To the extent that offers tend toward what is commonly regarded as reasonable, and assuming that offers regarded as reasonable are accepted, there would be no reason to expect disagreement rates to vary between subject pools, even when offers do. Our data thus lend some support to the hypothesis that the subject-pool differences observed in this experiment are related to different expectations about what constitutes an acceptable offer, rather than different propensities to trespass on a shared notion of what constitutes such an offer.

This brings us to the question of whether such differences can be attributed to *cultural* differences between subject pools, where for an operational definition of "cultural" we mean differences that cannot be attributed to variables other than the nation in which the data were gathered. As we have already indicated, there are uncontrolled differences in subject pools (such as differences in military service) that must make any such attribution speculative. However, the experiment was designed to control for those variables that seemed to us to be potentially most troublesome, namely, currency, experimenter, and language effects. To the extent that the experimental controls were adequate, the results indicate that the subject-pool differences cannot be attributed to any of these variables.[19] Consequently, we offer the conjecture that the observed subject-pool differences are cultural in character. Such a conjecture must stand or fall on the repeatability and robustness of these results and on the extent to which similar differences among these countries can be observed in related economic environments. In this connection, and in view of the difficulty of controlling for between-country variables, laboratory experimentation seems to us to offer the possibility of focusing on some kinds of cultural differences in behavior that cannot be studied in any other way.[20]

Finally, we consider what implications the results of this experiment have for the ongoing assessment of the extent to which dif-

[18]Another way to make more or less the same point about the "toughness hypothesis" is to note that we are sometimes asked in which country the bargainers proved to be the toughest. Our data suggest that this is not a well-posed question, in the sense that the "toughest" buyers are found in the same place as the least tough sellers.

[19]Recall, however, that the control for translation differences built into our design provides only an upper bound on how great an effect might be due to linguistic factors. In particular, if the differences observed in bargaining behavior are due to translation differences, they must be due to differences too small to have had an effect on the market behavior. Given the robust convergence to equilibrium observed in the market, one might conjecture that it would take large translation differences indeed to affect market behavior, and in this case there is a possibility that the observed bargaining differences might nevertheless be due to differences in the translations, rather than to subject-pool differences. While such a possibility is not entirely ruled out by the data, we are skeptical that the bargaining differences are primarily linguistic in origin.

[20]At the same time, to the extent that experiments control for extraneous variables by eliminating much of the natural context in which negotiations may take place, there are aspects of cultural differences in bargaining behavior that cannot be studied in the laboratory. For example, differences such as how and when negotiations begin and end or how disagreement is expressed may involve important cultural differences that can only be observed in the natural context of negotiations; and of course, critical features of a negotiating environment, such as the legal framework in which negotiations take place, are important between-country variables that influence the outcome of bargaining in natural contexts but are deliberately excluded here.

ferent game-theoretic predictions may be descriptive of observed behavior. Diverse opinions on this subject have been expressed in the experimental literature.

Our evidence lends little support to the view that perfect-equilibrium predictions are not at all descriptive of observable behavior or to the view that they are only descriptive when they are not extreme.[21] Equilibrium prices are clearly reached in the markets we study, even though the equilibrium is so extreme that the buyers who find themselves proposing these prices earn nothing or next to nothing.

At the same time, the failure of observed behavior in the bargaining games even to approach the equilibrium prediction (and in particular the readiness of sellers in that game to earn zero by rejecting offers that would give them positive earnings) raises questions about the auxiliary assumption under which the equilibrium predictions were made, namely, that the players are attempting to maximize their earnings.[22] However, if players are not attempting to maximize their earnings, then why do the equilibrium predictions made under that assumption for the market games do so well? Preliminary discussions with various investigators in this area suggest at least two possible explanations. One is that the observed bargaining behavior is dominated by concerns about fairness which are context-dependent and do not arise in the market environment. Another is that whatever nonmonetary concerns enter bargainers' preferences do so in both environments, but the competitive pressure toward equilibrium in the market overwhelms any such factors in players' preferences.[23]

Whether or not nonmonetary factors play a role in either or both environments, the results of this experiment lend strong support to the hypothesis that the different outcomes observed in these two environments result from different behavior *away* from the equilibrium. This helps explain the relation between the equilibrium predictions and the observed bargaining and market behavior. To see why this is so, we need to compare these two games once again, both from the point of view of the equilibrium predictions and the observed behavior.

From the point of view of the equilibrium predictions, the two games are similar in that both predictions give one player 0, but they are dissimilar in that it is the buyer in the market game who is predicted to get 0, while the buyer in the bargaining game is predicted to get 1,000. This dissimilarity largely disappears when we look at observed behavior. In the market sessions, a buyer who proposes the equilibrium price certainly will earn 0; but a buyer who proposes the equilibrium price in the bargaining will earn 0 with very high probability, because

[21] See, for example, Matthew Spiegel et al. (1990), who review evidence from sequential bargaining games from a variety of subject pools, for a recent suggestion that the degree of inequality in the equilibrium payoff division may be the decisive element in determining its descriptive ability.

[22] See Ochs and Roth (1989) for a discussion of the consistency of this kind of disadvantageous rejection among a number of bargaining experiments; see Gary Bolton (1991) for a model in which a player's utility depends both on absolute and relative earnings and for a carefully conducted series of experimental tests of that model.

[23] These competitive pressures need not be due to simple income-maximization. For example, consider a hypothetical buyer whose preference for equality is such that his first-choice outcome would be to have all buyers submit identical bids of \$5 (or \$1) and who bids accordingly in the first two rounds. When he sees how high the actual transaction price is, he becomes annoyed with the other buyers, and (with the same motivation that would have caused him to express his displeasure by rejecting too small an offer if he were a seller in the ultimatum game) he decides to become the high bidder in round 3 in order to deprive other buyers of the benefits of what he sees as their unreasonable behavior. The point in considering such a hypothetical buyer is to observe that in the market game his nonmonetary preferences cause him to behave in a manner indistinguishable from an income-maximizer, while in the ultimatum game his preferences lead away from the equilibrium predicted for income-maximizers. The difference lies not in the preferences, or in the "social norms" elicited by the game which these preferences may reflect, but in how such preferences interact in the different games and in the outcome that emerges. (The above example is from Prasnikar and Roth [1991].)

low offers were accepted only with low probability (Figs. 5, 6). Despite the similarity of actual payoffs at the equilibrium offer, the payoffs away from the equilibrium proposals are quite different. In the market sessions, a buyer who consistently proposes a price of 500, say, will earn 0 in every round; but a buyer who consistently proposes a price of 500 in the bargaining sessions will with high probability reach an agreement in every round and will receive \$5 (or \$15, 10 shekels, 1,000 yen, or 200,000 dinars, depending on which session he is in). Thus, buyers in both environments earn little or nothing when they make equilibrium proposals, but in the markets we observed, buyers also earned nothing when they made nonequilibrium proposals, whereas buyers in the bargaining sessions could maximize their earnings by moving substantially away from the equilibrium proposal (see Fig. 6).

This conclusion is similar to that reached in Prasnikar and Roth (1991), on the basis of comparisons between some of the U.S. bargaining data considered here with another two-player game in which the first player was (also) a proposer and the second an accepter/rejecter.[24] In that game, as in the bargaining game, the equilibrium prediction gave almost nothing to the second player, but unlike the bargaining game, first players who deviated from equilibrium were not rewarded. After players gained experience with this game, the observed behavior converged to equilibrium.

In all these games, the behavior of the first mover is well accounted for by applying standard game-theoretic analysis, together with the (usual) assumption that first movers are income-maximizers, to the empirically observed behavior of the second mover. However, in the bargaining game, the behavior of the second movers (i.e., the sellers who refuse positive offers) cannot be accounted for by a standard game-theoretic model built on the usual auxiliary assumption of income-maximization. Therefore, Figure 6 suggests that the buyers in the bargaining games adapt to the "nonstandard" behavior of the sellers in a "standard" game-theoretic way. Thus, these data suggest to us that, while the problem of developing descriptively powerful theory for games of this sort does not call for anything like the wholesale abandonment of the apparatus of game theory, neither is it likely that game-theoretic analysis unaided by empirical observation will lead to reliable models of behavior.

[24]Glenn Harrison and Jack Hirshleifer (1989) earlier studied the same game as a model of public-goods provision and called it the "best-shot" game. The rules are that player 1 proposes the amount of public good he will provide and then player 2 does, with the amount provided being the *maximum* provided by either player. However, each player must pay for the full amount that he agreed to provide. Consequently, both players have an incentive to free-ride, and at perfect equilibrium the first player does so.

REFERENCES

Albers, Wulf and Albers, Gisela, "On the Prominence Structure of the Decimal System," in R. W. Scholz, ed., *Decision Making under Uncertainty*, Amsterdam: Elsevier, 1983, pp. 271–87.

Bolton, Gary, "A Comparative Model of Bargaining: Theory and Evidence," *American Economic Review*, December 1991, *81*, 1096–1136.

Guth, Werner, Schmittberger, R. and Schwarz, B., "An Experimental Analysis of Ultimatum Bargaining," *Journal of Economic Behavior and Organization*, December 1982, *3*, 367–88.

______ **and Tietz, Reinhard,** "Ultimatum Bargaining Behavior: A Survey and Comparison of Experimental Results," *Journal of Economic Psychology*, September 1990, *11*, 417–49.

Harrison, Glenn W. and Hirshleifer, J., "An Experimental Evaluation of Weakest Link/Best Shot Models of Public Goods," *Journal of Political Economy*, February 1989, *97*, 201–25.

Kachelmeier, Steven J. and Shehata, Mohamed, "Culture and Competition: A Laboratory Market Comparison Between the People's Republic of China, the United States, and Canada," mimeo, University of Texas at Austin, 1990.

Murnighan, J. Keith and Roth, Alvin E., "The Effect of Group Size and Communication Availability on Coalition Bargaining in a Veto Game," *Journal of Personality and Social Psychology*, January 1980, *39*, 92–103.

Ochs, Jack and Roth, Alvin E., "An Experimental Study of Sequential Bargaining," *American Economic Review*, June 1989, *79*, 355–84.

Prasnikar, Vesna and Roth, Alvin E., "Considerations of Fairness and Strategy: Experimental Data from Sequential Games," *Quarterly Journal of Economics*, 1991, forthcoming.

Roth, Alvin E., "Bargaining Experiments," in J. Kagel and A. E. Roth, eds., *Handbook of Experimental Economics*, Princeton: Princeton University Press, 1992, forthcoming.

Siegel, Sidney, *Nonparametric Statistics for the Behavioral Sciences*, New York: McGraw-Hill, 1956.

Spiegel, Matthew, Currie, Janet, Sonnenschein, Hugo and Sen, Arunava, "First-Mover Advantage and the Division of Surplus in Two-Person, Alternating-Offer Games: Results from Bargaining Experiments," mimeo, Columbia University, 1990.

[17]

In Search of Homo Economicus: Behavioral Experiments in 15 Small-Scale Societies

By JOSEPH HENRICH, ROBERT BOYD, SAMUEL BOWLES, COLIN CAMERER, ERNST FEHR, HERBERT GINTIS, AND RICHARD MCELREATH*

Recent investigations have uncovered large, consistent deviations from the predictions of the textbook representation of *Homo economicus* (Alvin E. Roth et al., 1991; Ernst Fehr and Simon Gächter, 2000; Colin Camerer, 2001). One problem appears to lie in economists' canonical assumption that individuals are entirely self-interested: in addition to their own material payoffs, many experimental subjects appear to care about fairness and reciprocity, are willing to change the distribution of material outcomes at personal cost, and are willing to reward those who act in a cooperative manner while punishing those who do not even when these actions are costly to the individual. These deviations from what we will term the canonical model have important consequences for a wide range of economic phenomena, including the optimal design of institutions and contracts, the allocation of property rights, the conditions for successful collective action, the analysis of incomplete contracts, and the persistence of noncompetitive wage premia.

Fundamental questions remain unanswered. Are the deviations from the canonical model evidence of universal patterns of behavior, or do the individual's economic and social environments shape behavior? If the latter, which economic and social conditions are involved? Is reciprocal behavior better explained statistically by individuals' attributes such as their sex, age, or relative wealth, or by the attributes of the group to which the individuals belong? Are there cultures that approximate the canonical account of self-regarding behavior?

Existing research cannot answer such questions because virtually all subjects have been university students, and while there are cultural differences among student populations throughout the world, these differences are small compared to the range of all social and cultural environments. To address the above questions, we and our collaborators undertook a large cross-cultural study of behavior in ultimatum, public good, and dictator games. Twelve experienced field researchers, working in 12 countries on five continents, recruited subjects from 15 small-scale societies exhibiting a wide variety of economic and cultural conditions. Our sample consists of three foraging societies, six that practice slash-and-burn horticulture, four nomadic herding groups, and three sedentary, small-scale agriculturalist societies. Our results are described in detail, with extensive ethnographic accounts of the cultures we studied and citations to the relevant literature, in Henrich et al. (2001); an extended overview paper is available online.[1]

We can summarize our results as follows. First, the canonical model is not supported in any society studied. Second, there is considerably more behavioral variability across groups than had been found in previous cross-cultural research, and the canonical model fails in a wider variety of ways than in previous experiments. Third, group-level differences in economic organization and the degree of market

* Henrich: School of Business Administration, University of Michigan, Ann Arbor, MI 48109; Boyd and McElreath: Department of Anthropology, University of California at Los Angeles, Los Angeles, CA 90095; Bowles: Department of Economics, University of Massachusetts, Amherst, MA 01003, and Santa Fe Institute; Camerer: Department of Economics, California Institute of Technology, Pasadena, CA 91125; Fehr: Institute for Empirical Research in Economics, University of Zürich, Blümlisalpstrasse 10, CH-8006, Zurich, Switzerland; Gintis: University of Massachusetts, Amherst, MA 01003. The research described in this paper was funded by the MacArthur Foundation's Research Group on the Nature and Origin of Norms and Preferences, directed by Robert Boyd and Herbert Gintis. The field experiments were carried out by Henrich, McElreath, Michael Alvard, Abigail Barr, Jean Ensminger, Francisco Gil-White, Michael Gurven, Kim Hill, Frank Marlowe, John Patton, Natalie Smith, and David Tracer.

[1] URL: ⟨www.santafe.edu⟩

integration explain a substantial portion of the behavioral variation across societies: the higher the degree of market integration and the higher the payoffs to cooperation, the greater the level of cooperation in experimental games. Fourth, individual-level economic and demographic variables do not explain behavior either within or across groups. Fifth, behavior in the experiments is generally consistent with economic patterns of everyday life in these societies.

I. The Evidence

Because the ultimatum game (UG) has been conducted throughout the world with student populations and has generated robust violations of the canonical model, we conducted this game in all of our 17 societies. The "proposer" in this game is provisionally assigned an amount equivalent to a day or two's wages in the society and asked to propose an offer to a second person, the "respondent." The respondent may then either accept the offer, in which case the two players receive the proposed amounts, or reject it, in which case the two receive nothing. If both players conform to the canonical model and if this is common knowledge, it is easy to see that the proposer will know that the respondent will accept any positive offer and so will offer the smallest possible amount, which will be accepted.

In most of our field experiments subjects played anonymously, not knowing the identity of the person or persons with whom they were paired. The stakes of most games were denominated in money (though in some cases tobacco or other goods were used). In all cases, we tested prospective participants for their comprehension of the experiment and eliminated any who appeared not to grasp the game.

The systematic deviations from the canonical model in our sample of simple societies can be inferred from Table 1, which lists all groups where UG's were conducted. Contrary to the prediction of the standard model, even the groups with the smallest offers have mean offers greater than 25 percent of stake size. Illustrating our second result (the large variation in mean offers across societies), others, including the Torguud and the Mapuche, offered between 30 percent and 40 percent, while still others, including the Achuar and the Sangu, offered between 40 percent and 50 percent. Finally, the Aché and the Lamelara had mean offers greater than 50 percent.

These group differences are strikingly large compared to previous cross-cultural work comparing ultimatum-game behavior among university students (Roth et al., 1991). While mean offers in industrial societies are typically close to 44 percent, the mean offers in our sample range from 26 percent to 58 percent. Similarly, while modal offers are consistently 50 percent

TABLE 1—THE ULTIMATUM GAME IN SMALL-SCALE SOCIETIES

Group	Country	Mean offer[a]	Modes[b]	Rejection rate[c]	Low-offer rejection rate[d]
Machiguenga	Peru	0.26	0.15/0.25 (72)	0.048 (1/21)	0.10 (1/10)
Hadza (big camp)	Tanzania	0.40	0.50 (28)	0.19 (5/26)	0.80 (4/5)
Hadza (small camp)	Tanzania	0.27 (38)	0.20 (8/29)	0.28 (5/16)	0.31
Tsimané	Bolivia	0.37	0.5/0.3/0.25 (65)	0.00 (0/70)	0.00 (0/5)
Quichua	Ecuador	0.27	0.25 (47)	0.15 (2/13)	0.50 (1/2)
Torguud	Mongolia	0.35	0.25 (30)	0.05 (1/20)	0.00 (0/1)
Khazax	Mongolia	0.36	0.25		
Mapuche	Chile	0.34	0.50/0.33 (46)	0.067 (2/30)	0.2 (2/10)
Au	PNG	0.43	0.3 (33)	0.27 (8/30)	1.00 (1/1)
Gnau	PNG	0.38	0.4 (32)	0.4 (10/25)	0.50 (3/6)
Sangu farmers	Tanzania	0.41	0.50 (35)	0.25 (5/20)	1.00 (1/1)
Sangu herders	Tanzania	0.42	0.50 (40)	0.05 (1/20)	1.00 (1/1)
Unresettled villagers	Zimbabwe	0.41	0.50 (56)	0.1 (3/31)	0.33 (2/5)
Resettled villagers	Zimbabwe	0.45	0.50 (70)	0.07 (12/86)	0.57 (4/7)
Achuar	Ecuador	0.42	0.50 (36)	0.00 (0/16)	0.00 (0/1)
Orma	Kenya	0.44	0.50 (54)	0.04 (2/56)	0.00 (0/0)
Aché	Paraguay	0.51	0.50/0.40 (75)	0.00 (0/51)	0.00 (0/8)
Lamelara[e]	Indonesia	0.58	0.50 (63)	0.00 (3/8)	0.00 (4/20)

Note: PNG = Papua New Guinea.

[a] This column shows the mean offer (as a proportion) in the ultimatum game for each society.

[b] This column shows the modal offer(s), with the percentage of subjects who make modal offers (in parentheses).

[c] The rejection rate (as a proportion), with the actual numbers given in parentheses.

[d] The rejection rate for offers of 20 percent or less, with the actual numbers given in parentheses.

[e] Includes experimenter-generated low offers.

in industrialized societies, our sample modes vary from 15 percent to 50 percent.

As shown in the last two columns of Table 1, rejections are also much more variable than previously observed. While in industrial societies offers below 20 percent are rejected with probability 0.40 to 0.60, rejections of low offers are extremely rare among some groups. In other groups, however, we observe substantial rejections rates, including frequent rejections of offers above 50 percent. Among the Achuar, Aché and Tsimané, we observe zero rejections after 16, 51, and 70 proposer offers, respectively. Moreover, while the Aché and Achuar made fairly equitable offers, nearly 50 percent of Tsimané offers were at or below 30 percent, yet all were accepted. Similarly, Machiguenga responders rejected only one offer, despite the fact that over 75 percent of their offers were below 30 percent. At the other end of the rejection scale, Hadza responders rejected 24 percent of all proposer offers and 43 percent of offers at 20 percent and below. Unlike the Hadza, who preferentially rejected low offers, the Au and Gnau of Papua New Guinea rejected both unfair and hyper-fair (greater than 50 percent) offers with nearly equal frequency.

In experiments with university subjects, offers are generally consistent with income-maximization, given the distribution of rejections. In our sample, however, in the majority of groups the modal behavior of the proposers is not consistent with expected income-maximization. In the Tsimané and Aché cases, for instance, there are no rejections of offers below 20 percent, although there were several low offers. The rejection rate for all other offers is also zero. Yet the modal offer in both groups is 50 percent, and the average offers are 37 percent and 51 percent, respectively. Where possible, we used the relationship between the size of the offer and the fraction of rejections to estimate income-maximizing offers for the group in question. In one group, the Hadza proposers approximated the income-maximizing offer quite closely, thus confirming the canonical model; but Hadza responders frequently rejected substantial positive offers, thus violating the canonical model. In all other groups, average offers exceeded the income-maximizing offer, in most cases by a substantial amount.

Data from public-goods games played in seven of these societies also show much greater variation than previously found, and again they exhibit novel deviations from the predictions of the canonical model. Public-goods games ask subjects to contribute to a common pool that will be expanded by the experimenter and then redistributed to all subjects. The canonical prediction is that everyone will free-ride, contributing nothing. Typical distributions of public-goods game contributions with students have a U-shape, with the mode at contributing nothing, a secondary mode at full cooperation, and mean contribution between 40 percent and 60 percent. By contrast, for instance, the Machiguenga have a mode at contributing nothing, with not a single subject cooperating fully, yielding a mean contribution of 22 percent. Also, the Aché and Tsimané both exhibit inverted distributions, with few or no contributions at full free-riding or full cooperation.

In three dictator games played in three of these societies, groups also deviate both from typical behavior in industrialized societies and the canonical predictions. The dictator game allows the proposer simply to assign some fraction of the stake to a passive second party who receives that amount. Among university students, the distribution of "offers" in the dictator game typically has a mode at zero and a secondary mode at 50/50, while the canonical model predicts that people will give zero. Contrasting with both, the Orma have a mode at 50 percent and a secondary mode at 20 percent. Hadza dictators show a mode at 10 percent. Offers of 0 percent and 50 percent are also popular. Among the Tsimané, there were no zero offers; the mean was 32 percent, and the mode was 25 percent.

II. What Explains Group-Level Differences?

The large variations across the different cultural groups suggest that preferences or expectations are affected by group-specific conditions, such as social institutions or cultural fairness norms. The large variance in institutions and norms in our sample allowed us to address this question systematically. Because of space limits we here concentrate on the behavior of proposers in the UG. We rank-ordered the societies along two dimensions:

(i) *Payoffs to cooperation (PC).*—How important and how large is a group's payoff from cooperation in economic production?
(ii) *Market integration (MI).*—How much do people rely on market exchange in their daily lives?

On the first dimension, payoffs to cooperation, the Machiguenga and Tsimané rank the lowest; they are almost entirely economically independent at the family level and engage rarely in productive activities involving more than members of a family. By contrast, the Lamelara whale-hunters go to sea in large canoes manned by a dozen or more individuals. The rationale for PC as a predictor of UG offers is that with little cooperative production there will be little necessity to share returns, while those whose livelihood depends on large-scale cooperation like the Lamelara must develop ways of sharing the joint surplus. Thus we might expect that a higher level of PC will increase sharing behavior in the UG. The rationale for market integration as an explanatory variable is that the more frequently people experience market transactions, the more they will also experience abstract sharing principles concerning behaviors toward strangers of which the UG is an example.

We sought to explain group mean UG offers on the basis of these two dimensions of economic structure. In a regression, both PC and MI were highly significant, their (positive) normalized regression coefficients were large in magnitude (about 0.3), and the two measures jointly explained 68 percent of the variance. The impact of PC and MI remains large and robust in an equation predicting individual offers, including individual measures such as sex, age, relative wealth, village population size, stake size, and experimenter experience with the group. Surprisingly, none of these individual level measures was significantly related to offers.

A plausible interpretation of our subjects' behaviors is that, when faced with a novel situation (the experiment), they looked for analogues in their daily experience, asking "What familiar situation is this game like?" and then acted in a way appropriate for the analogous situation. For instance, the hyper-fair UG offers (greater than 50 percent) and the frequent rejections of these offers among the Au and Gnau reflect the culture of gift-giving found in these societies. Among these groups, like many in New Guinea, accepting gifts, even unsolicited ones, commits one to reciprocate at some future time to be determined by the giver. Receipt of large gifts also establishes one in a subordinate position. Consequently, excessively large gifts, especially unsolicited ones, will frequently be refused because of the anxiety about the unspecific strings attached. Similarly the low offers and high rejection rates of the Hadza appear to reflect their reluctant process of sharing (termed "tolerated theft" by a leading ethnographer of the Hadza). While the Hadza extensively share meat, many hunters look for opportunities to avoid sharing and share only because they fear the social consequences of not sharing, in the form of informal social sanctions, gossip, and ostracism. This behavior is apparently transferred to the experimental setting.

Unlike the Hadza, the Aché did not reject low offers, and despite this the vast majority of the Aché (94 percent) made offers above 40 percent of the stake size. This coincides neatly with ethnographic descriptions indicating widespread meat-sharing and cooperation in community projects despite the absence of a fear of punishment in Aché society. Aché hunters, returning home, quietly leave their kill at the edge of camp, often claiming that the hunt was fruitless; their catch is later discovered and collected by others and then meticulously shared among all in the camp. We think it likely that the stake in the game seemed to some of the Aché subjects as analogous to their catch.

The Machiguenga show the lowest cooperation rates in public-good games, reflecting ethnographic descriptions of Machiguenga life, which report little cooperation, exchange, or sharing beyond the family unit. By contrast, Orma experimental subjects quickly dubbed the public-goods experiment a *harambee* game, referring to the widespread institution of village-level voluntary contributions for public-goods projects such as schools or roads. Not surprisingly, they contributed generously (58 percent of the stake), somewhat higher than most U.S. subjects contribute in similar experiments.

III. Discussion

Our data indicate that the degree of cooperation, sharing, and punishment exhibited by experimental subjects closely corresponds to templates for these behaviors in the subjects' daily lives, and that the substantial variability in experimental behaviors across groups is an expression of the large between-group differences in the structures of social interaction and modes of livelihood. How do we interpret these results?

Some of the variability among groups may be due to variations in implementation. We doubt that this explains the markedly differing behaviors across groups, however, since the experiments were run from identical protocols across groups and were thus as similar in procedures and stake size as we could achieve. Where we could test for experimenter effects we found none. It is possible also that our subjects presumed that their actions would somehow become public. In a good many of our cases, however, subsequent conversations with participants convinced us that this was not the case. Finally, it could be that participants thought they were in a repeated interaction, even though the games we used were clearly one-shot. We do not find this interpretation compelling, however, since there is extensive evidence from experiments in advanced economies that subjects understand the game very well, and those who reject a positive offer in the ultimatum game, when interviewed by the experimenter, typically do not say that they made an error, but rather affirm having goals besides maximizing a monetary payoff.

Why are many subjects willing to share resources and undertake costly reciprocal actions in anonymous one-shot interactions? Bowles et al. (2001) will provide a more extensive response than can be offered here. We suspect that a proximate reason for these behaviors is that situations cue emotional responses which induce the behaviors we have measured. For example, many ultimatum-game responders from advanced societies, when facing a low offer, experience an emotional impulse to hurt the proposer for being unfair, just as the subject might in a real-life bargaining situation. Similarly, the New Guinea responders who rejected hyper-fair offers in the UG may have experienced the same anxiety that emerges when somebody gives them an unsolicited gift in everyday life.

What are the ultimate determinants of our emotions and situation-specific cues? Here long-run evolutionary processes governing the distribution of genes and cultural practices could well have resulted in a substantial fraction of each population being predisposed in certain situations to forgo material payoffs in order to share with others, or to punish unfair actions, as our experimental subjects did. A number of recent contributions have shown that, under conditions that appear to approximate the social and physical environments of early human populations, prosocial behavior can proliferate in a population in which it is initially rare (Bowles et al., 2001).

IV. Conclusion

While our results do not imply that economists should abandon the rational-actor framework, they do suggest two major revisions. First, the canonical model of the self-interested material payoff-maximizing actor is systematically violated. In all societies studied, UG offers are strictly positive and often substantially in excess of the expected income-maximizing offer, as are contributions in the public-goods game, while rejections of positive offers in some societies occur at a considerable rate. Second, preferences over economic choices are not exogenous as the canonical model would have it, but rather are shaped by the economic and social interactions of everyday life. This result implies that judgments in welfare economics that assume exogenous preferences are questionable, as are predictions of the effects of changing economic policies and institutions that fail to take account of behavioral change. Finally, the connection between experimental behavior and the structure of everyday economic life should provide an important clue in revising the canonical model of individual choice behavior.

REFERENCES

Bowles, Samuel; Boyd, Richard; Fehr, Ernst and Gintis, Herbert, eds. *The foundations of social reciprocity*. Unpublished manuscript, University of Massachusetts, 2001.

Camerer, Colin F. *Behavioral economics*. Princeton, NJ: Princeton University Press, 2001 (forthcoming).

Fehr, Ernst and Gächter, Simon. "Fairness and Retaliation: The Economics of Reciprocity." *Journal of Economic Perspectives*, Summer 2000, *14*(3), pp. 159–81.

Henrich, Joseph; Boyd, Robert; Bowles, Samuel; Camerer, Colin; Fehr, Ernst; Gintis, Herbert and McElreath, Richard. "Cooperation, Reciprocity and Punishment in Fifteen Small-Scale Societies." Working paper, Santa Fe Institute, 2001.

Roth, Alvin E.; Prasnikar, Vesna; Okuno-Fujiwara, Masahiro and Zamir, Shmuel. "Bargaining and Market Behavior in Jerusalem, Ljubljana, Pittsburgh, and Tokyo: An Experimental Study." *American Economic Review*, December 1991, *81*(5), pp. 1068–95.

[18]

Journal of Public Economics 37 (1988) 291–304. North-Holland

WHY FREE RIDE?

Strategies and Learning in Public Goods Experiments

James ANDREONI*

The University of Wisconsin–Madison, Madison, WI 53706, USA

Received May 1987, revised version received August 1988

Laboratory experiments on free riding have produced mixed results. Free riding is seldom observed with single-shot games; however, it is often approximated in finitely repeated games. There are two prevailing hypotheses for why this is so: strategies and learning. This paper discusses these hypotheses and presents an experiment that examines both.

1. Introduction

The free riding hypothesis has been the subject of laboratory experiments for more than a decade. While the extent of free riding has often varied across experiments, three observations are consistently replicated. First, there is no significant evidence of free riding in single-shot games. Marwell and Ames (1981), for instance, found that subjects generally provide the public good at levels halfway between the Pareto efficient level and the free riding level. Second, when subjects play a repeated game, provision of the public good 'decays' toward the free riding level with each repetition. This decay phenomenon is observed when subjects know the length of the game for sure [Isaac, Walker and Thomas (1984), Isaac and Walker (1988)], and also when they do not [Isaac, McCue and Plott (1985), Kim and Walker (1984)]. Third, free riding is often approximated after subjects play several trials, although exact free riding is seldom realized.

These observations appear to provide mixed support for free riding. It seems clear that the free riding incentives are important – subjects consistently attain outcomes that are closer to the free riding levels than the Pareto efficient levels. On the other hand, the exact predictions of the model are seldom confirmed. The phenomenon of decay is particularly pronounced.

*Thanks to Theodore Bergstrom, Robyn Dawes, Mark Isaac, Gerald Marwell, Michael McKee, Thomas Palfrey, Hal Varian, James M. Walker and some referees for helpful comments. I am especially grateful for the advice and assistance of John H. Miller.

0047-2727/88/$3.50

Repetition appears to be necessary for subjects to approach free riding behavior.

Naturally, researchers have looked for explanations of these results. The two hypotheses that are most often proposed are strategies and learning. The learning hypothesis holds that a single shot of the game is not sufficient to allow subjects to learn the incentives. Repeated play allows such learning, and hence learning could explain decay. However, this test of learning is confounded by the fact that repetition allows subjects to signal future moves to each other. This is the basis for the strategies hypothesis. In a repeated game it may be rational for subjects to develop multiperiod strategies that allow for some cooperative behavior, even after the free riding incentives are learned. If this is the case, then these strategies may be responsible for decay.

This paper discusses a laboratory experiment designed to examine the strategies and learning hypotheses directiy. Section 2 describes the hypotheses in detail, and indicates how they are tested. The results of the experiment are given in section 3, with a discussion in section 4. The evidence from the experiment suggests, first, that a hypothesis of rational strategic play cannot be supported, and second, that learning may play little or no role in explaining the phenomenon of decay. Moreover, the data are consistent with other predictions based on theories of non-standard behavior, such as altruism, social norms, or bounded rationality.[1] The evidence suggests greater consideration of such non-standard behavior in both theoretical and experimental research.

2. Strategies and learning

2.1. Theory and evidence

The experiment reported in this paper is typical of most public goods experiments. It consists of a simple public goods game that is iterated 10 times. Every iteration operates as follows. Five subjects form a group. Each subject in the group is given a budget of 50 'tokens'. The tokens can be redeemed for cash only when they are 'invested' in either a private good (called an 'Individual Exchange') or a public good (called a 'Group Exchange'). A token in the private good earns one cent for the person who invests it. However, earnings from the public good depend on what the group as a whole invents. Each token in the public good earns one half cent for the person investing it, as well as one half cent for each other member of the group. Subjects always move simultaneously, and cannot communicate at any point in the experiment. Subjects are only told the total amount of the public good for their own group. Specific contributions of other individuals,

[1]For examples of such theories see Margolis (1982), Sugden (1984), Frank (1985), Palfrey and Rosenthal (1987), and Andreoni (1987).

and outcomes of other groups, are not known. For ease of reference, the precise details of the experiment are summarized in the appendix.[2]

With the payoffs just described, the equilibrium and efficiency conditions are easily calculated. Investing a token in the public good has a private return of one half cent, while it has a social return of 2.5 cents. Hence, it is Pareto efficient for all subjects to invest all tokens in the public good. On the other hand, since the private return from the private good exceeds the private return from the public good, the rational Nash equilibrium behavior in the single-shot game is to invest zero in the public good, i.e. to free ride. Moreover, the free riding equilibrium is unique. In fact, it is simple to verify that zero investment in the public good is a dominant strategy for each player.

The single-shot equilibrium is easily extended to a finitely repeated game. In the finitely repeated game, each round is an exact replication of the single-shot game. Subjects accumulate earnings each round, but they are not allowed to carry over earnings to succeeding rounds. As shown by Friedman (1986), there is again a unique equilibrium for this game: zero investment in the public good in every round. For both the single-shot and the finitely repeated game the same Nash prediction holds: subjects should invest zero in the public good. This will be called the *free riding* hypothesis.[3]

As already noted, free riding is seldom observed, but instead provision decays with repeated play. The learning hypothesis attempts to explain this by noting that subjects may not immediately understand the incentives of the game, but need repetition to help them learn. Once they recognize the dominant strategy, they will adopt free riding behavior. Since some learn more quickly than others, we should observe, on average, decay toward zero provision. With enough repetition, all subjects will eventually choose their optimal Nash investment. I will call this the *learning* hypothesis.

The second conjecture to explain decay is that rational subjects are playing strategically. This hypothesis is derived from the Kreps et al. (1982) discussion of the Prisoners' Dilemma under incomplete information. The free riding equilibrium rests on an assumption that all subjects believe that all other subjects will be behaving rationally. However, this information may be incomplete. In particular, subject Y may believe that his partners will possibly behave irrationally (perhaps because they have not yet learned the incentives). Then if Y free rides he will educate his partners. As a result, any initial cooperation will unravel to the (less lucrative) free riding equilibrium. Moreover, if Y believes that his partners think *he* does not understand free riding, then by free riding he would reveal himself to be rational. Again, any cooperation would unravel to free riding. Hence, even if all subjects

[2]The instructions provided to the subjects are available from the author on request.

[3]Some have termed this *strong* free riding or *pure* free riding. I will simply call it free riding, since distinctions between strong and weak free riding are not useful here.

understand free riding, they may choose a strategy of investing some in the public good to conceal the fact that they are rational. However, in the known end-period free riding is always optimal. In anticipation of the end-period (using backward induction), subjects are likely to start 'bailing-out.' Hence, it may be an incomplete information Nash equilibrium strategy to cooperate early in the game, but free ride late in the game. Stated differently, decay may be a rational strategy. This will be called the *strategies* hypothesis.[4]

Previous work sheds some light on strategies and learning. For instance, Isaac and Walker (1988, henceforth IW) found conditions under which more than 80 percent of the subjects chose the dominant strategy in the tenth and final round of a game. This suggests that subjects do learn to free ride. IW then repeated their experiment with experienced subjects, i.e. subjects who had participated in a public goods experiment in the past. However, they again observed high levels of provision early and decay with repetition. This suggests that learning alone is not responsible for decay, and provides some support for strategies. The next subsection describes a method of testing both hypotheses directly.

2.2. *Testing strategies and learning*

The experiment reported in this paper is intended to separate learning from strategic play. The design is *subtractive*: subjects participate in a repeated-play environment, but are denied the opportunity to play strategically. Without strategic play, we can isolate the learning hypothesis. Furthermore, by comparing this group to one that *can* play strategically, we can attribute the difference, if any, to strategic play.

Strategies were subtracted by putting subjects in one of two conditions. In the first condition, 20 subjects were randomly assigned (by a computer) to one of 4 groups (containing 5 subjects each). Subjects were told that they would play the game exactly 10 times, but that after each repetition the composition of their group would change in an unpredictable way. In particular, after each decision round, the computer randomly reassigned subjects. Subjects knew they would be reassigned, but were never told which 4 of the remaining 19 subjects were in their group at any time. Thus, no subject could expect to gain by playing strategically.[5] This can be called a

[4]Note that these rational strategies do not include the possibility of punishing strategies like *tit-for-tat*. This is because the game is finite. However, the equilibrium is driven by the *belief* that some subjects might actually adhere to such strategies.

[5]There is, of course, the chance that a subject's actions could eventually feed back to him. However, such feedback will come in a very unpredictable fashion. Moreover, the influence will be mitigated by the actions of all of the other players and their histories. Feedback, therefore, should not figure in the predictions. As will be seen, this is verified by the results.

'repeated single-shot' game. Since subjects in this condition only meet by chance, they will be called *Strangers*.

At the same time as the Strangers were playing, 15 different subjects assembled in an adjacent room. These subjects provided a control group. They played a standard finitely repeated game, again in groups of 5. In each repetition of the game, subjects played with the *same* group of 5 subjects. They knew the composition of their group was fixed, but they did not know which 4 of the remaining 14 subjects composed their group. To contrast with Strangers, call this group the *Partners*. Notice, Partners *can* play strategically. Aside from these two controls on group composition, both Partners and Strangers faced exactly the same game.[6]

The Partners and Strangers conditions test strategies and learning in the following way. Consider strategies first. Suppose a subject is initially investing some positive amount in the public good, but learns in round t that free riding is the single-shot dominant strategy. If she is a Partner – playing strategically – she may continue to contribute to the public good. On the other hand, if she is a Stranger, she has no incentive to continue cooperation – every game for a Stranger is, after all, an end-game. Therefore, under the strategies hypothesis, we expect that giving by Partners will be greater than giving by Strangers, especially early in the game (before the Partners begin to 'bail out'). In the tenth round, however, both Partners and Strangers are playing an end-game, hence both are predicted to free ride.

To isolate the learning hypothesis, the experiment included a 'restart'. The basic experiment just described was performed twice (using a total of 70 subjects). In the second experiment, subjects in both the Partners and the Strangers conditions were unexpectedly told, after their tenth round of play, that they would restart a new set of 10 rounds. Partners would stay in the same group, while Strangers would continue to be randomly reassigned.[7] However, play was suspended after only three additional rounds.[8] If learning is primarily responsible for decay, then both Partners and Strangers should be unaffected by the restart. If either is affected, then this would imply that learning alone cannot explain decay.

Finally, the restart may provide insights into theories of non-standard behavior. Suppose Partners are following a rule-of-thumb for participating in repeated social dilemmas. Then even if they are fully informed and understand free riding, they may deliberately give on the first round. Hence,

[6]The experimental design originally called for 40 subjects – 20 in each condition. However, only 35 subjects agreed to participate, despite attempts to over-book. Hence, 20 were randomly assigned to be Strangers, and 15 to be Partners. This does not affect the result.

[7]In particular, subjects were told that they had finished ahead of schedule, so there was just enough time remaining to complete another set. This was done to make the promise that they would not be restarted a second time appear credible.

[8]Had the budget for subjects been bigger, this would have been unnecessary. Such deceptive practices are, under less restrictive circumstances, not recommended.

Table 1
Average investment in public good per subject.[a]

	Round										
	1	2	3	4	5	6	7	8	9	10	All
Partners	24.1	22.9	21.5	18.8	18.4	16.8	12.8	11.2	13.7	5.8	16.6
Strangers	25.4	26.6	24.3	22.2	23.1	21.9	17.8	19.7	14.0	12.2	20.7
Difference	−1.3	−3.7	−2.8	−3.4	−4.7	−5.1	−5.0	−8.5	−0.3	−6.4	−4.1

[a] $n_P = 30$; $n_S = 40$.

Partners may return to the same point on the restart. For Strangers, on the other hand, the restart represents nothing new. Even if they are playing by a rule-of-thumb, they will be applying a single-shot rule. Hence, Strangers should be unaffected by the restart – even if they are not free riding.

3. Experimental results

The results of the experiment are summarized as a series of six observations. The first three deal primarily with the strategies hypothesis, while the last three deal primarily with the learning hypothesis.

3.1. The strategies hypothesis

Observation 1. Giving by Partners is less than giving by Strangers, in all 10 rounds. Moreover, the difference tends to grow as the last round approaches.

Table 1 reports the average giving per subject in the first 10 rounds. The table includes data on all subjects. Recall that the strategies hypothesis predicts that giving by Partners will be *greater* in all 10 rounds, with the gap *narrowing* as the game progresses. As can be seen, this is exactly the opposite of what occurred, hence is evidence against strategies.

To test whether the difference between Partners and Strangers is significant, assume that the gifts of Partners and Strangers represent random draws from identical probability distributions. A rejection of this hypothesis would indicate that the two populations are significantly different. The test has a chi-squared distribution with one degree of freedom.[9] For the data in table 1, $\chi^2 = 11.3$, which is significant beyond the 0.01 level. Hence, the behavior of Partners and Strangers differs significantly, but in the direction opposite of what the strategies hypothesis predicts.

[9] Pool the data on Partners and Strangers over all 10 rounds. Find the median of the combined sample. If Partners and Strangers are drawn from the same distribution, we should expect half of the observations on Partners, and half on Strangers, to be above the median. If they differ significantly on this respect, we can reject the hypothesis. A discussion of this test can be found in Hogg and Craig (1978, pp. 320–322).

Table 2
Percent of subjects free riding.[a]

	Round										
	1	2	3	4	5	6	7	8	9	10	All
Partners	16.6	13.3	20.0	23.3	33.3	30.0	40.0	40.0	40.0	70.0	34.3
Strangers	15.0	12.5	15.0	15.0	15.0	17.5	22.5	25.0	30.0	42.5	20.5
Difference	1.6	0.8	5.0	8.3	18.3	12.5	17.5	15.0	10.0	27.5	13.8

[a]$n_P = 30$; $n_S = 40$.

Observation 2. The percent of Partners choosing to free ride is greater than the percent of Strangers, in all 10 rounds. The difference is greatest in round 10.

Looking to table 2, it can be seen that Partners free ride more than Strangers in each round, with the overall difference of 34 percent for Partners and 20 percent for Strangers. Again, the difference is the reverse of prediction of the strategies hypothesis, and can be shown to be statistically significant. This is based on a binomial distribution (calling free riding a success and giving a failure). The test for comparing the means of two samples from a binomial distribution has a t-distribution.[10] For proportions in the 'All' column $t = 4.06$, which is significant beyond the 0.01 level.

This difference in free riding is especially strong in round 10. However, recall that in round 10 each group is playing an end-game and each has the same degree of experience. The prediction is identical for both, yet Strangers free ride much less often. Again, this contradicts the strategies hypothesis.

Observation 3. Giving by Partners is least in round 10, but is still above the free riding levels.

Looking again at tables 1 and 2, 70 percent of Partners are free riders in the last round, and average giving is 5.8 tokens (11.6 percent of the Pareto efficient amount). However, only two of the six partners groups reach the free riding equilibrium in round 10. Nine of 30 Partners contribute to the public good, investing an average of 19.4 tokens each (38.8 percent of their tokens). Of that nine, five had been free riders at some point prior to round 10. Hence, many Partners – including those who have shown an understanding of free riding – continue to give even when free riding is a dominant strategy.[11] Again, this opposes the strategies hypothesis.

[10]Let p_1 be the proportion of Partners free riding, and n_1 be the number of observations on Partners. Define p_2 and n_2 similarly for Strangers. Then

$$t = \frac{p_1 - p_2}{\sqrt{p_1(1-p_1)/n_1 + p_2(1-p_2)/n_2}}.$$

[11]Future experiments may want to test whether this end-period effect can be enhanced by using subjects with lots of experience. I thank Mark Isaac and James Walker for this suggestion.

Observations 1, 2 and 3 now provide direct evidence on the strategies hypothesis. When we compare subjects who can play strategically with those who cannot, we expect to observe that strategic play will produce relatively more cooperative outcomes. As was shown, this was not the case. Subjects who simply met like strangers were more cooperative – and significantly so.

3.2. The learning hypothesis

The next three observations focus on the learning hypothesis as an explanation of decay in repeated-play experiments.

Observation 4. Giving by Strangers is greater than giving by Partners in the last round.

As already noted, round 10 is an end-game for both Partners and Strangers. The incentives are thus equivalent for both, and, moreover, they have had the same opportunity for learning. Nevertheless, Strangers give significantly more, and free ride significantly less. Since the situations are exactly the same for both Partners and Strangers, the only way that this observation can be ascribed to learning is if we accept that Partners learn *faster* than Strangers. Most people would, I suspect, be unwilling to accept that such a difference in learning could be so profound. Hence, this observation seems to suggest that learning alone is not responsible for decay.

Observation 5. Strangers appear to be only temporarily affected by the restart.

Observation 6. Partners return to high levels of giving in the restart. Their choices in period 11 largely mirror their choices in round 1. The restart also seems to have a lasting effect.

Table 3 summarizes the average giving in the restart. Average giving by Strangers is 9.9 in round 10, increases to 14.5 in round 11, but is down to 5.3 by round 13. Thus, any effect of the restart appears to be mostly corrected by round 12, and totally eliminated by round 13. This suggests that the Strangers treatment did successfully subtract the strategic play – the restart was treated largely as continuation of the repeated single-shot game.

On the other hand, average giving by Partners in round 11 was only 0.2 below giving in round 1. Of those 15 Partners who restarted, 5 increased their donations, 4 reduced them, and 6 made exactly the same donation as they did in round 1. Furthermore, giving did not fall off rapidly (as it did with the Strangers), but nearly tracked the round 1–3 levels of giving.

Recall that the learning hypothesis predicts that both Partners and Strangers should be unaffected by the restart. This is borne out by Strangers,

Table 3
Average investment in the public good per subject, for subjects who restarted.[a]

	Round												
	1	2	3	4	5	6	7	8	9	10	11	12	13
Partners	19.9	21.3	19.7	18.3	17.5	11.9	10.0	7.0	13.7	5.3	19.7	19.5	16.6
Strangers	22.2	22.9	20.1	21.2	23.0	22.4	15.2	18.8	13.0	9.9	14.5	11.8	5.3
Difference	−2.3	−1.6	−0.4	−2.9	−5.5	−10.5	−5.2	−11.8	0.7	−4.6	5.2	7.7	11.3

[a] $n_P = 15$; $n_S = 20$.

who verify that they are (largely) treating each round as single-shot game. Partners, on the other hand, are strongly affected. In fact, they appear to return to their original round 1 choices. Note that Observation 6 is consistent with the prediction based on non-standard behavior, i.e. that round 1 decisions are part of a reasoned (if non-rational) rule for social dilemmas. This suggests that there may actually be very little learning about free riding, and that subjects mostly understand the incentives from the start – given the opportunity to repeat their moves, they by and large do. Hence, learning, like strategies, is unlikely to provide an explanation of decay.

3.3. Summary

The strategies hypothesis predicts that rational strategic play is responsible for excessive giving in repeated games. However, as Observations 1, 2 and 3 show, subjects who cannot play strategically actually provide more of the public good than subjects who can. This is a contradiction of the strategies hypothesis. Likewise, Observations 5 and 6 indicate that subjects continue to give to the public good, even after revealing an understanding of the free riding incentives. In addition, Observation 4 notes that in round 10 – when all subjects are playing a true end-game, and all have had the same opportunity to learn – Strangers give significantly more to the public good than Partners. It seems unlikely that learning alone can explain this difference. In summary, both the strategies and learning hypotheses are contradicted in the experiment.

4. Discussion and conclusion

This paper contends that neither strategies nor learning can be supported as explanations of decay in public goods experiments. It is natural to ask, therefore, if these hypotheses focus on the right kind of learning. For instance, it is possible that subjects have learned the single-shot dominant strategy, but have not learned the backward induction necessary to understand the equilibrium. Hence, experimenters may turn to a more general learning hypothesis that incorporates learning about both single-shot and repeated-play incentives. This point may also generalize the rational strategies hypothesis. In particular, revealing an understanding of the single-shot equilibria (free riding on round 10) does not necessarily reveal an understanding of the repeated-game structure. This introduces another form of asymmetric information. Therefore, rational players may choose to give on round 11, even after free riding on round 10.

One way to address both of these generalizations of strategies and learning is to use subjects with lots of experience. However, appealing to results from the Prisoners' Dilemma literature, it seems unlikely that even this will change the conclusions. Selten and Stoecker (1986), for instance, examined a finitely repeated Prisoners' Dilemma game where subjects played a series of supergames (of 10 periods), although with a different partner in each restart. The results revealed a restart effect similar to that observed for Partners above and, moreover, the effect did not disappear – even after 25 supergames.

These results suggest that we may need to turn to theories of non-standard behavior. This will require that we look beyond the characteristics of the equilibrium, and examine how subjects make their decisions. For instance, the difference between Partners and Strangers may be due to different decision-making processes, where each process is suitable for the game being played. One example is that subjects may get non-monetary pleasure from cooperative outcomes [Kreps et al. (1982), Stark (1985), and Palfrey and Rosenthal (1987)]. After every round, subjects may be updating prior beliefs on the likelihood of cooperation. One would expect that, for any given outcome, Partners would adjust their priors more rapidly than Strangers. Since Partners and Strangers started period 1 in almost exactly the same place, this could be consistent with what was observed.

Another alternative is that giving is consistent with social norms about participation in social dilemmas. Social norms tend to be enforced by punishing the deviants. Decay may simply represent the groups' struggles to establish a norm. When the game is restarted, it would be natural for Partners to try to establish a norm at the highest level of cooperation achieved in the previous 10 rounds – round 1 giving. Strangers, who have less enforcement power, are likely to ignore the restart.

Further explanation might also be found in what has been called Regret Theory in the economics of uncertainty [Loomis and Sugden (1982)]. For instance, if a subject discovers that she did better than expected, she is 'elated' and will likely choose the same action again. However, if she did worse than expected, she has 'regret'. She is likely to choose more cautiously next time – and probably reduce her donation. The dynamic of this game could result in decay. For example, if the elated subjects repeat their moves, but the regretful subjects cut their gifts in half, then the formerly elated subjects will end up doing worse than expected but the formerly regretful subjects will do better than expected. Hence, giving will ratchet downward after every round. Certainly there are many more possibilities.

In conclusion, the results of this paper fail to confirm that subjects adhere to our standard notions of free riding behavior. This does not suggest foreclosing attempts to confirm rational free riding behavior; however, it does suggest a broader set of alternatives. The study of free riding may benefit from experiments that allow the decision processes of agents to reveal themselves in natural and predictable ways. Focusing on testable alternatives may help us better understand both when and why free riding occurs.

Appendix: Experimental design and procedures

A.1. The single-shot game

Group size. Each group contained five individuals.

Payoff function. Each subject had a budget of 50 tokens. Tokens invested in the Private Exchange earned 1 cent for sure. Tokens invested in the Group Exchange earned 0.5 cent for each subject in the group, regardless of which subject invested it. Earnings in each round were set aside and could not be reinvested in later rounds.

Information. The payoff schedule, group size, total amount of tokens in the group, and the features of the repetition (below) were all common knowledge. After each decision round subjects were told only the total investment in group exchange and their own payoff. They did not know the identities of the other players in their group, the specific contributions of individual group members, or the outcomes of other groups in the experiment. Subjects were instructed not to converse at any time during the experiment.

Subjects. Subjects were recruited from undergraduate Introductory Economics courses at the University of Michigan.

A.2. Finitely repeated play

Repetition. The single-shot game was repeated 10 times for all subjects.

Partners. Fifteen subjects were randomly divided into 3 groups of 5 subjects. These subjects played a finitely repeated game with the other members of their group.

Strangers. Twenty subjects were randomly divided into 4 groups of 5 subjects. After each decision round the computer randomly reassigned the subjects to 4 new groups. Hence, these subjects played a repeated single-shot game.

Replication. Thirty-five subjects were required for each run of the experiment: 15 Partners and 20 Strangers. The basic experiment was run twice, using a total of 70 subjects.

Restart. After the tenth round of the second run, subjects were unexpectedly told that they would restart another set of 10 rounds. The rules of the restart would be identical to the first repeated game. In particular, Partners would be matched with the same group members, and Strangers would continue to be randomly reassigned. After 3 more rounds, however, play was stopped.

A.3. Procedures

Subjects were randomly assigned to either Partners or Strangers conditions. Each subject was given written instructions, which included a schedule of the returns from the group exchange. In addition, the instructions were read aloud to the subjects. Subjects were given a stack of 10 Investment Decision Forms, one for each round, and were asked to record their decisions on the Investment Decision Form for round 1. The forms were then collected by the experimenter and each subject's Subject Number and decision were typed into a computer. The computer calculated the payoff to each subject, and printed an Earnings Report form for every subject. The Earnings Report listed the subject's choice, total group provision of the public good, and the subject's payoff. All information about payoffs, therefore, was strictly private. This was repeated for 10 rounds. For the Strangers, the computer also randomized the groups in each round. For the restart, the subjects were given a new batch of 10 Investment Decision Forms. They were told that they had finished ahead of schedule, so that there was just enough time to play again. This was done to make the promise that the game would not restart a second time appear credible. The standard 10-period experiment was completed in about 50 minutes (including administering instructions). At the end of the experiment, subjects were paid in cash.

A.4. Instructions

The instructions given to both Partners and Strangers were identical, except for one paragraph. The paragraph was under the heading 'Your Group'. Partners received the following paragraph:

> You have been preassigned to a group of 5 participants. The composition of participants in your group will **never** change. During all 10 decision rounds you will be a member of the **same group** of 5 participants.

Strangers received the following paragraph:

> The composition of your group will be changing every decision round. After each decision round you will be **reassigned** to a **new group** of 5 participants. None of the 5 group members will ever have been members of the same group in the past. The chance that any other participant will ever be in a group with you more than one time is very small.

References

Andreoni, James, 1987, Private charity, public goods, and the crowding out hypothesis, University of Wisconsin, Social Systems Research Institute, Working paper 8706.

Frank, Robert H., 1985, The demand for unobservable and other nonpositional goods, American Economic Review 75, 101–116.

Friedman, James W., 1986, Game theory with applications to economics (Oxford University Press, New York).

Hogg, Robert V. and Allen T. Craig, 1978, Introduction to mathematical statistics, 4th ed (Macmillan, New York).

Isaac, R. Mark and James M. Walker, 1988, Group size effects in public goods provision: The voluntary contributions mechanism, Quarterly Journal of Economics 53, 179–200.

Isaac, R. Mark, Kenneth F. McCue and Charles R. Plott, 1985, Public goods provision in an experimental environment, Journal of Public Economics 26, 51–74.

Isaac, R. Mark, James M. Walker and Susan H. Thomas, 1984, Divergent evidence on free riding: An experimental examination of possible explanations, Public Choice 43, 113–149.

Kim, Oliver and Mark Walker, 1984, The free rider problem: Experimental evidence, Public Choice 43, 3–24.

Kreps, David M., Paul Milgrom, John Roberts and Robert Wilson, 1982, Rational cooperation in finitely repeated Prisoners' Dilemma, Journal of Economic Theory 27, 245–252.

Loomis, Graham and Robert Sugden, 1982, Regret theory: An alternative theory of rational choice under uncertainty, Economic Journal 92, 805–824.

Margolis, Howard, 1982, Selfishness, altruism and rationality (Cambridge University Press).

Marwell, Gerald and Ruth E. Ames, 1981, Economists free ride, does anyone else?, Journal of Public Economics 15, 295–310.

Palfrey, Thomas R. and Howard Rosenthal, 1987, Private incentives in social dilemmas, Working paper (Carnegie–Mellon University).

Selten, Reinhard and Rolf Stoecker, 1986, End behavior in sequences of finite Prisoner's Dilemma supergames: A learning theory approach, Journal of Economic Behavior and Organization 7, 47–70.

Stark, Oded, 1985, On private charity and altruism, Public Choice 46, 325–332.

Sugden, Robert, 1984, Reciprocity: The supply of public goods through voluntary contributions, Economic Journal 94, 772–787.

[19]
Cooperation

A Monty Python sketch[1] keeps coming back to you. The two characters are a banker (played by John Cleese) and a Mr. Ford (played by Terry Jones), who is collecting money for charity with a tin cup.

BANKER: How do you do. I'm a merchant banker.

FORD: How do you do Mr. . . .

BANKER: Er . . . I forgot my name for a moment but I *am* a merchant banker.

FORD: Oh. I wondered whether you'd like to contribute to the orphan's home. (*He rattles the tin.*)

BANKER: Well I don't want to show my hand too early, but actually here at Slater Nazi we are quite keen to get into orphans, you know, developing market and all that . . . what sort of sum did have in mind?

FORD: Well . . . er . . . you're a rich man.

BANKER: Yes, I am. Yes, very, very, very, very, very, very, very, very, very, very, very rich.

FORD: So er, how about a pound?

BANKER: A pound. Yes, I see. Now this loan would be secured by the . . .

FORD: It's not a *loan,* sir.

BANKER: What?

FORD: It's not a loan.

BANKER: Ah.

With Robyn M. Dawes.

[1]This sketch is reproduced with permission from *The Complete Monty Python's Flying Circus: All the Words, Vol.2* (New York: Pantheon Books, 1989), pp. 92–94. Copyright Python Productions 1989.

Cooperation 7

FORD: You get one of these, sir. (*He gives him a flag.*)

BANKER: It's a bit small for a share certificate isn't it? Look, I think I'd better run this over to our legal department. If you could possibly pop back on Friday.

FORD: Well, do you have to do that, couldn't you just give me the pound?

BANKER: Yes, but you see I don't know what it is *for.*

FORD: It's for the orphans.

BANKER: Yes?

FORD: It's a gift.

BANKER: A what?

FORD: A gift?

BANKER: Oh a *gift!*

FORD: Yes.

BANKER: A tax dodge.

FORD: No, no, no, no.

BANKER: No? Well, I'm awfully sorry I don't understand. Can you explain exactly what you want?

FORD: Well, I want you to give me a pound, and then I go away and give it to the orphans.

BANKER: Yes?

FORD: Well, that's it.

BANKER: No, no, no, I don't follow this at all, I mean, I don't want to seem stupid but it looks to me as though I'm a pound down on the whole deal.

FORD: Well, yes you are.

BANKER: I am! Well, what is my incentive to give you the pound?

FORD: Well, the incentive is—to make the orphans happy.

BANKER: (*genuinely puzzled*) Happy? . . . Are you quite sure you've got this right?

FORD: Yes, lots of people give me money.

BANKER: What, just like that?

FORD: Yes.

BANKER: Must be sick. I don't suppose you could give me a list of their names and addresses could you?

FORD: No, I just go up to them in the street and ask.

BANKER: Good lord! That's the most exciting new idea I've heard in years! It's so simple it's brilliant! Well, if that idea of yours isn't worth a pound I'd like to know what is. (*He takes the tin from Ford.*)

FORD: Oh, thank you sir.

BANKER: The only trouble is, you gave me the idea before I'd given you the pound. And that's not good business.

FORD: It isn't?

BANKER: No, I'm afraid it isn't. So, um, off you go. (*He pulls a lever opening a trap door under Ford's feet and Ford falls through with a yelp.*)
Nice to do business with you.

Much economic analysis—and virtually all game theory—starts with the assumption that people are both rational and selfish. An example is the analysis of the famous prisoner's dilemma (Rapoport and Chammah, 1965). A prisoner's dilemma game has the following structure. Two players must each select a strategy simultaneously and secretly. In the traditional story, the two players are prisoners who have jointly committed some crime and are being held separately. If each stays quiet (cooperates) they both are convicted of a minor charge and receive a one-year sentence. If just one confesses and agrees to testify against the other (defects), he goes free while the other receives a ten-year sentence. If both confess, they both receive a five-year sentence. The game is interesting because confessing is a dominating strategy—it pays to confess no matter what the other person does. If one player confesses and the other doesn't, he goes free rather than spend five years in jail. If, on the other hand, the other player also confesses, then confessing means a five-year sentence instead of ten. The assumptions of rationality and self-interest yield the prediction that people playing a game with this structure will defect. People are assumed to be clever enough to figure out that defection is the dominant strategy, and are assumed to care nothing for outcomes to other players; they will, moreover, have no qualms about their failure to do ''the right thing.''

A similar analysis applies to what economists call *public goods.*

Cooperation 9

A public good is one which has the following two properties: (1) once it is provided to one person, it is costless to provide to everyone else; (2) it is difficult to prevent someone who doesn't pay for the good from using it. The traditional example of a public good is national defense. Even if you pay no taxes, you are still protected by the Armed Forces. Another example is public radio and television. Even if you do not contribute, you can listen and watch. Again, economic theory predicts that when confronted with public goods, people will "free ride." That is, even if they enjoy listening to public radio, they will not make a contribution because there is no (selfish) reason to do so. (For a modern treatment of the theory of public goods, see Bergstrom, Blume, and Varian, 1986.)

The predictions derived from this assumption of rational selfishness are, however, violated in many familiar contexts. Public television in fact successfully raises enough money from viewers to continue to broadcast. The United Way and other charities receive contributions from many if not most citizens. Even when dining at a restaurant away from home in a place never likely to be visited again, most patrons tip the server. And people vote in presidential elections where the chance that a single vote will alter the outcome is vanishingly small. As summarized by Jack Hirshleifer (1985, p. 55), "the analytically uncomfortable (though humanly gratifying) fact remains: from the most primitive to the most advanced societies, a higher degree of cooperation takes place than can be explained as a merely pragmatic strategy for egoistic man." But why?

In this chapter and the next one, the evidence from laboratory experiments is examined to see what has been learned about when and why humans cooperate. This chapter considers the particularly important case of cooperation versus free riding in the context of public good provision.

SINGLE-TRIAL PUBLIC GOODS EXPERIMENTS

To investigate why people cooperate, it is necessary to examine behavior in both single-play and multiple-play environments. Does cooperation evolve, for instance, only as individuals repeatedly interacting with each other find it in their interests to cooperate? A typical public goods experiment uses the following procedures. A group of subjects (often, college students) is brought to the laboratory. Groups vary in size, but experiments usually have between four and ten subjects. Each subject is given a sum of money, for example, $5. The money can either be kept and taken home, or some or all of the money can be invested in a public good, often called a *group exchange.* Money invested in the group exchange for the n participants is multiplied by some factor k, where k is greater than one but less than n. The money invested, with its returns, is distributed equally among all group members. Thus, while the entire group's monetary resources are increased by each contribution (because k is greater than one), each individual's share of one such contribution is less than the amount she or he invests (because k is less than n). To take a concrete example, suppose k=2 and n=4. Then if everyone contributes all $5 to the public good, each ends up with $10. This is the unique Pareto efficient allocation: no other solution can make everyone better off. On the other hand, any one individual is always better off contributing nothing, because in exchange for a player's $5 contribution, that player receives only $2.50, while the rest of the payoff ($7.50) goes to the other players. In this game, the rational, selfish strategy is to contribute nothing and hope that the other players decide to invest their money in the group exchange. If one player contributes nothing while all the others contribute $5, then that player will end up with $12.50, while the other players end up with $7.50. These conditions constitute what is sometimes called a ''social dilemma.''

What does economic theory predict will happen in such a game? One prediction, called the *strong free rider hypothesis,* is that everyone will choose the dominant strategy, that is, nothing will be contributed to the public good. This is surely the outcome predicted by the selfish rational model. A less extreme prediction, called the *weak free rider hypothesis,* is that some people will free ride while others will not, yielding a suboptimal level of the public good, though not necessarily zero. The weak free rider hypothesis obviously does not yield very precise predictions.

The results of single play (''one shot'') public goods experiments lend little support to the strong free rider hypothesis. While not everyone contributes, there is a substantial number of contributors, and the public good is typically provided at 40–60 percent of the optimal quantity. That is, on average, the subjects contribute 40–60 percent of their stake to the public good. In a study by Marwell and Ames (1981), these results held in many conditions: for subjects playing the game for the first time, or after a previous experience; for subjects who believed they were playing in groups of 4 or 80; and for subjects playing for a range of monetary stakes, though in the experiments with the highest stakes, contribution rates were somewhat lower. Indeed, Marwell and Ames found only one notable exception to this 40–60 percent contribution rate. When the subjects were a group of University of Wisconsin economics graduate students, the contribution rate fell to 20 percent, leading them to title their article "Economists Free Ride: Does Anyone Else?"[2] (Interestingly, economists told about the experiments predicted on the average a rate of about 20 percent—but for all participants, not just their students.)

MULTIPLE TRIAL EXPERIMENTS

A natural question to ask about the surprisingly high level of cooperation observed by Marwell and Ames is what would happen if the same players repeated the game several times. This question has been investigated by Kim and Walker (1984), Isaac, Walker, and Thomas (1984), and Isaac, McCue, and Plott (1985). The experimental design in these papers is similar to that of Marwell and Ames, except that there are usually ten repetitions of the game. Two major conclusions emerge from these papers. First, on the initial trial, cooperation is observed at rates similar to those obtained by Marwell and Ames. For example, across nine different experiments with varying designs, Isaac, McCue, and Plott obtained a 53 percent contribution rate to the public good. Second, within a few repetitions, cooperation declines sharply. After five trials, the contributions to the public good were only 16 percent of the optimum. The experiments by Isaac, Walker, and Thomas also obtained a decline in the contribution rate over time, though the decline was not as abrupt.[3]

Why does the contribution rate decline with repetition? One

[2]This result has never been replicated, and so should be treated as preliminary. We wonder, however, whether economists *are* different. Do economists as a group donate less to charity than other similar groups? Are they less likely to leave tips in out-of-town restaurants?

[3]For experiments with a high return to contributing to the public good, the initial contribution rate was 52 percent which fell to 32 percent on trial 10. In versions with low returns to contributing, the initial rate was 40 percent and the final rate was 8 percent.

reasonable conjecture is that subjects learn something during the experiment that induces them to adopt the dominant strategy of free riding. Perhaps the subjects did not understand the game in the first trial and only learned that free riding was dominant over time. This possibility, however, appears unlikely in light of other experimental evidence. For example, the usual cooperation rates of roughly 50% are observed on trial 1 even for *experienced* subjects, that is, subjects who have participated in other multiple trial public goods experiments (e.g., Isaac and Walker, forthcoming). Also, Andreoni (1987a) has investigated the learning hypothesis directly using the simple procedure of restarting the experiment. Subjects were told they would play a ten-period public goods game. When the ten periods were completed, the subjects were told they would play again for another ten rounds with the same other players. In the first ten trials Andreoni replicated the decaying contribution rate found by previous investigators, but upon restarting the game contributions went back up to virtually the same contribution rates observed on the initial trial in the first game (44 percent on trial 1 of the second game versus 48 percent in the first). Such results seem to rule out any explanation of cooperation based on subjects' misunderstanding the task.[4]

RECIPROCAL ALTRUISM

One currently popular explanation of why we observe so much cooperation in and outside of the laboratory invokes reciprocal altruism as the mechanism. This explanation, most explicitly developed by Axelrod (1984), is based on the observation that people tend to reciprocate—kindness with kindness, cooperation with cooperation, hostility with hostility, and defection with defection. Thus, being a free rider may actually be a less fruitful strategy when the chooser takes account of the probable future response of others to his or her cooperation or defection. A cooperative act itself—or a reputation for being a cooperative person—may with high probability be reciprocated with cooperation, to the ultimate benefit of the cooperator.

The most systematic strategy based on the principle of reciprocal altruism is a TIT-FOR-TAT one first suggested by Anatol Rapoport, in which a player begins by cooperating and then chooses

[4]A similar conclusion is reached by Goetze and Orbell (forthcoming).

the same response the other player has made on the previous trial. The real strength of this explanation lies in demonstrating, both analytically and by computer tournaments of interacting players (programs) in iterated social dilemmas, that any person or small group of people practicing such reciprocal altruism will have a statistical tendency to receive higher payoffs ''in the long run'' than those who don't practice it. In fact, TIT-FOR-TAT ''won'' two computer tournaments Axelrod conducted in which game theorists proposed various strategies that were compared to each other in pairwise encounters with repeated plays. Because evolution is concerned with such long-run probabilistic phenomena, it can be inferred that reciprocating people have greater ''inclusive fitness'' than do non-reciprocating ones. Hence, to the degree to which such a tendency has some genetic basis, it should evolve as an adaptation to the social world.

An implication of reciprocal altruism is that individuals will be uncooperative in dilemma situations when there is no possibility of future reciprocity from others, as in situations of anonymity or interacting with people on a ''one-shot'' basis. Yet we observe 50 percent cooperation rates even in single-trial experiments, so reciprocal altruism cannot be used directly to explain the experimental results described so far. Also, of course, it is very difficult to play TIT-FOR-TAT, or any other strategy based on reciprocal altruism, when more than two people are involved in the repeated dilemma situation. If some members of a group cooperate on trial t while others defect, what should a player attempting to implement a TIT-FOR-TAT type strategy choose on the subsequent trial?

A related hypothesis that appears consistent with the decaying contribution rates observed in the multiple-trial experiments is suggested by the theoretical work of Kreps, Milgrom, Roberts, and Wilson (1982). They investigate the optimal strategy in a repeated prisoner's dilemma game with a finite number of trials. If both players are rational then the dominant strategy for both is to defect on every trial. While TIT-FOR-TAT has been shown to be effective in infinitely repeated prisoner's dilemma games (or equivalently, games with a constant small probability of ending after any given trial), games with a known end point are different. In any finite game both players know that they should defect on the last trial, so there is no point in cooperating on the penultimate trial, and by backward induction, it is never in one's best interest to cooperate. What Kreps et al. show is that if you are playing against an opponent who you think may be irrational (i.e., might play TIT-FOR-TAT even in a game with finite trials), then it may be rational to cooperate early in the game (to induce your irrational opponent to cooperate too). Since the public goods games have a similar structure, it could be argued that players are behaving rationally in the Kreps et al. sense. Once again, however, the data rule out this explanation. Cooperation never falls to zero, even in one-trial games or in the last period of multi-trial games when it can never be selfishly rational to cooperate.

Additional evidence against the reciprocity hypothesis comes from another experiment designed by Andreoni (1988). One group of 15 subjects played repeated trials in groups of five as described above. Another group of 20 subjects played the same game in groups of five, but the composition of the group varied on each trial. Moreover, the subjects did not know which four of the other 19 subjects would constitute their group in any given round of the game. In this condition, there can be no strategic advantage to cooperation, since the players in the next round will be, in essence, strangers. If cooperation in early rounds of these experiments is observed, strategic cooperation can be ruled out. Indeed, Andreoni found that cooperation was actually a bit higher in the stranger condition than in a comparable condition where the groups remained intact. (This effect was statistically significant, though slight.)

One conclusion which emerges from these experiments is that people have a tendency to cooperate until experience shows that those with whom they're interacting are taking advantage of them. This *norm of cooperation* will resemble reciprocal altruism in infinite repeated games; but, the behavior, as we have seen, is also observed in cases when reciprocal altruism would be inappropriate. One explanation for this type of behavior is offered by Robert Frank (1987). Frank argues that people who adopt a norm of cooperation will do well by eliciting cooperation from others, and attracting interaction with other cooperators. The key to Frank's argument is that one cannot successfully fake being cooperative for an extended period of time—just as one cannot be successful getting people to believe too many lies.[5] Furthermore, be-

[5] As the late Senator Sam Ervin said: "The problem with lying is that you have to have a perfect memory for what you said." None of us do. It's easier to remember what actually happened, although that is not easy either.

cause cooperators are, by assumption, able to identify one another, they are able to interact selectively and exclude defectors.

ALTRUISM

There are other explanations of why people cooperate both in the lab and in the real world. One is that people are motivated by "taking pleasure in others' pleasure." Termed *pure altruism* by Andreoni (1987b), this motive has been eloquently stated by Adam Smith, in *The Theory of Moral Sentiments* (1759; 1976): "how selfish soever man may be supposed to be, there are evidently some principles in his nature, which interest him in the fate of others, and render their happiness necessary to him, though he derive nothing from it, except the pleasure of seeing it." While the pleasure involved in seeing it may be considered "selfish" (following the sophomoric argument that altruism is by definition impossible, because people do what they "want" to do), the passage captures the idea that people are motivated by positive payoffs for others as well as for themselves. Consequently, they may be motivated to produce such results through a cooperative act. One problem with postulating such pure altruism as a reason for contributing to public goods is that such contributions cannot be explained purely in terms of their effects. If they could, for example, then governmental contributions to the same goal should "crowd out" private contributions on a dollar-for-dollar basis, since the results are identical no matter where the funding comes from. Such crowding out does not appear to be nearly complete. In fact, econometric studies indicate that an increase in governmental contribution to such activities is associated with a decrease in private contribution of only 5–28 percent (Abrams and Schmitz, 1978, 1984; Clotfelter, 1985).

Another type of altruism that has been postulated to explain cooperation is that involved in the act of cooperating itself, as opposed to its results. "Doing the right (good, honorable, . . .) thing" is clearly a motive for many people. Sometimes termed *impure altruism*, it generally is described as satisfaction of conscience, or of noninstrumental ethical mandates.

The roles of pure and impure altruism, and other causes for cooperation (or the lack thereof) have been investigated over the last decade by the team of Robyn Dawes, John Orbell, and Alphons van de Kragt. In one set of experiments (Dawes et al., 1986), they examined the motives for free riding. The game used for these experiments had the following rules. Seven strangers were given $5 each. If enough people contributed their stake to the public good (either three or five depending on the experiment), then every person in the group would receive a $10 bonus whether or not they contributed. Thus, if enough subjects contribute, each contributor would leave with $10 and each non-contributor would leave with $15. If too few contributed then non-contributors would keep their $5 while contributors would leave with nothing. Subjects were not permitted to talk to one another (though this was modified in subsequent experiments). In this context two reasons for not contributing can be identified. First, subjects may be afraid that they will contribute but not enough others will, so their contribution will be futile. This motive for defecting was termed ''fear.'' Second, subjects may hope that enough others will contribute and hope to receive $15 instead of $10. This motive was called ''greed.'' The relative importance of fear and greed was examined by manipulating the rules of the game. In the ''no greed'' condition, payoffs were changed so that all subjects would receive $10 if the number of contributors was sufficient (rather than $10 for contributors and $15 for free riders). In the ''no fear'' condition contributors were given a ''money back guarantee'': if a subject contributed and not enough others did, the subject would receive the money back. (However, in this condition if the public good was provided, contributors would receive only $10 while free riders would get $15.) The results suggested that greed was more important than fear in causing free riding. In the standard game contribution rates averaged 51 percent. In the no fear (money back) game contributions rose to 58 percent, but in the no greed game contributions were 87 percent.[6]

Another possible interpretation is that the no greed condition can produce a stable equilibrium, while the no fear cannot. If subjects in the no greed condition believe that the mechanism of

[6] Notice that contributing could be selfishly rational if a subject thought that the probability his or her contribution would be critical (that is, exactly M-1 others will contribute) was greater than one-half. However, subjects who contributed did not generally believe that their contribution was necessary. Virtually no contributors believed they were critical to obtaining the public good with a probability greater than .5. In fact, pooling across all conditions, 67 percent of the contributors believed so many others would contribute that their own contributions would be redundant.

truncating payoffs works to motivate others to contribute, their motive will be enhanced as well, because the only negative result of contributing occurs if enough others *don't* contribute. In contrast, subjects in the no fear condition who conclude that the conditions will encourage others to contribute will be tempted to free ride themselves, leading to the conclusion that others will be tempted as well, leading to the conclusion that they should themselves contribute, etc.—an infinite loop.

One of the most powerful methods for inducing cooperation in these games is to permit the subjects to talk to one another. Twelve groups were run with the same payoffs described earlier, but under conditions in which discussions were allowed. The effect of this discussion was remarkable (van de Kragt et al., 1983). Every group used the discussion period to specify a group of people who were designated to cooperate. The most common means of making the distributional decision was by lottery, though volunteering was also observed. One group attempted interpersonal utility comparisons to determine relative ''need.'' Whatever methods the groups used, they worked. All 12 groups provided the public good, and in three of the groups more than the required number of subjects contributed. These results are consistent with the earlier ones. Subjects designated as contributors cannot greedily expect more from free riding, because their contributions are (believed to be) crucial for their obtaining the bonus (and were in all but three groups). Moreover, belief that others in the designated set of contributors will be motivated to contribute by the designated contributor mechanism will enhance—rather than diminish—each designated contributor's motive to contribute.

One possible explanation for the value of discussion is that it ''triggers'' ethical concerns that yield a utility for doing the ''right'' thing (i.e., impure altruism). Elster (1986), for example, has argued that group discussions in such situations yield arguments for group-regarding behavior (it is hard to argue for selfishness), and that such arguments have an effect not only on the listener but on the person making them as well. To test this hypothesis, a new set of experiments was conducted (van de Kragt et al., 1986). In this set of experiments all seven subjects were given $6 each. They could either keep the money or contribute it to the public good in which case it would be worth $12 to the other six members of the group. In this case, keeping the $6 is a dominant strategy, because the person who does so receives both that $6 and $2 from each of the other six group members who gave away the money.

Subjects first met in groups of 14 in a waiting room in which they were not allowed to talk, and were then divided into the two groups on a clearly random basis. Half of these sub-groups were allowed to talk about the decision, half not. The experimenters told half of the groups that the $12 given away would go to the other six people in their own group, while the other half of the groups were told that the money would go to six people in the other group. There are thus four conditions—discussion or no discussion crossed with money goes to own group or other group. If discussion simply makes individuals' egoistic payoffs clear, then it should not increase cooperation rates in any of these conditions since free riding is dominant. If, however, discussion increases utility for the act of cooperation per se, then discussion should be equally effective whether the money given away goes to members of their own group or to the other group—consisting, after all, of very similar people who were indistinguishable prior to the random drawing (usually college students or poorer members of the community).

The results were clear. In the absence of discussion, only about 30 percent of the subjects gave away the money, and those who did so indicated that their motive was to "do the right thing," irrespective of the financial payoffs.[7] Discussion raises the cooperation rate to 70 percent, but only when the subjects believe the money is going to members of their own groups: otherwise, it is usually less than 30 percent. Indeed, in such groups it was common to hear comments that the "best" possible outcome would be for all group members to keep their money while those in the other group gave it away (again, people from whom the subjects have been randomly separated about ten minutes earlier).

Thus, group identity appears to be a crucial factor in eschewing the dominating strategy. That result is compatible with previous

[7] In a similar—but simulated—"one shot" experiment, Hofsteadter (1983) discovered a roughly identical cooperation rate among his eminent friends. Most defect, but some cooperate, and for reasons of impure altruism. As one cooperator, Professor Daniel C. Dennett of Tufts, put it: "I would rather be the person who bought the Brooklyn Bridge than the person who sold it. Similarly, I feel better spending $3 gained by cooperation than $10 gained by defection." (Hofsteadter terms that a "wrong reason" for cooperating in a dilemma situation; yet it is the one often given by the subjects who cooperate without discussion in the experiments described above, and similar ones.)

social-psychological research on the "minimal group" paradigm (e.g. Tajfel and Turner, 1979; and the papers contained in Turner and Giles, 1981), which has repeatedly demonstrated that allocative decisions can be sharply altered by manipulations substantially weaker than ten minutes of discussion. For example, a "common fate" group identity—where groups received differing levels of payoffs depending on a coin toss—led subjects to attempt to "compensate" for non-cooperators in their own group by increasing cooperation rates, while simultaneously decreasing cooperation when the non-cooperators were believed to be in the other group, even when the identities of the people involved were unknown (Kramer and Brewer, 1986).

In the groups in which discussion was permitted it was very common for people to make promises to contribute. In a second series of experiments, Orbell, Dawes, and van de Kragt (forthcoming) investigated whether these promises were important in generating cooperation. Perhaps people feel bound by their promises—or believe they will receive a "satisfactory" payoff if they give away the money when others promise to do so because others will be bound by such promises. The main result was that promise making was related to cooperation only when every member of the group promised to cooperate. In such groups with universal promising, the rate of cooperation was substantially higher than in other groups. In groups in which promising was not universal there was no relationship between each subject's choice to cooperate or defect and: (1) whether or not a subject made a promise to cooperate, and (2) the number of other people who promised to cooperate. Consequently, the number of promises made in the entire group and the group cooperation rate were unrelated. These data are consistent with the importance of group identity if (as seems reasonable) universal promising creates—or reflects—group identity.

COMMENTARY

In the rural areas around Ithaca it is common for farmers to put some fresh produce on a table by the road. There is a cash box on the table, and customers are expected to put money in the box in return for the vegetables they take. The box has just a small slit, so money can only be put in, not taken out. Also, the box is attached to the table, so no one can (easily) make off with the money. We think that the farmers who use this system have just about the right model of human nature. They feel that enough people will volunteer to pay for the fresh corn to make it worthwhile to put it out there. The farmers also know that if it were easy enough to take the money, someone would do so.

In contrast to these farmers, economists either avoid judgments of human nature, or make assumptions that appear excessively harsh. It is certainly true that there is a "free rider problem." Not all people can be expected to contribute voluntarily to a good cause, and any voluntary system is likely to produce too little of the public good (or too much of the public bad in the case of externalities). On the other hand, the strong free rider prediction is clearly wrong—not everyone free rides all of the time.

There is a big territory between universal free riding and universal contributing at the optimal rate. To understand the problems presented by public goods and other dilemmas it is important to begin to explore some issues that are normally ignored in economics. For example, what factors determine the rate of cooperation? It is encouraging to note that cooperation is positively related to the investment return on the public good. The more the group has to gain through cooperation, the more cooperation is observed—the supply of cooperation is upward sloping. The results involving the role of discussion and the establishment of group identity are, however, more difficult to incorporate into traditional economic analyses. (One economist attempting to do so proposed that group discussion simply confuses subjects to the point that they no longer understand it is in their best interests to be defectors.)

More generally, the role of selfish rationality in economic models needs careful scrutiny. Amartya Sen (1977) has described people who are always selfishly rational as "rational fools," because mutual choices based only on egoistic payoffs consistently lead to suboptimal outcomes for all involved. Perhaps we need to give more attention to "sensible cooperators."

References

Abrams, Burtran A., and Mark A. Schmitz (1978). "The Crowding Out Effect of Government Transfers on Private Charitable Contributions." *Public Choice*, 33, 29–39.

Abrams, Burtran A., and Mark A. Schmitz (1984). The Crowding Out Effect of Government Transfers on Private Charitable Contributions: Cross Sectional Evidence." *National Tax Journal*, 37, 563–68.

Andreoni, James (1988). "Why Free Ride? Strategies and Learning in Public Goods Experiments." *Journal of Public Economics*, 37, 291–304.

Axelrod, Robert (1984). *The Evolution of Cooperation*. New York: Basic Books.

Bergstrom, Theodore, Lawrence E. Blume, and Hal Varian (1986). "On the Private Provision of Public Goods." *Journal of Public Economics*, 29, 25–49.

Clotfelter, Charles T. (1985). *Federal Tax Policy and Charitable Giving*. Chicago: The University of Chicago Press.

Elster, Jon (1986). "The Market and the Forum: Three Varieties of Political Theory." In Jon Elster and Aanund Hylland, eds., *Foundations of Social Choice Theory: Studies in Rationality and Social Change*. Cambridge, U.K.: Cambridge University Press, 103–132.

Frank, Robert (1987), "If *Homo Economicus* Could Choose His Own Utility Function, Would He Want One with a Conscience?" *American Economic Review*, 77, September, 593–605.

Goetze, David, and John M. Orbell (forthcoming). "Understanding and Cooperation." *Public Choice*.

Hirshleifer, Jack (1985). "The Expanding Domain of Economics." *American Economic Review*, 75, 6, December, 53–70.

Hofsteadter, Douglas (1983). "Metamagical Themas." *Scientific American*, 248, 14–28.

Isaac, R. Mark, Kenneth F. McCue, and Charles Plott (1985). "Public Goods Provision in an Experimental Environment." *Journal of Public Economics*, 26, 51–74.

Isaak, R. Mark, and James M. Walker (forthcoming). "Group Size Effects in Public Goods Provision: The Voluntary Contributions Mechanism." *Quarterly Journal of Economics*.

Isaak, R. Mark, James M. Walker, and Susan H. Thomas (1984). "Divergent Evidence on Free Riding: An Experimental Examination of Possible Explanations." *Public Choice*, 43, 113–49.

Kim, Oliver, and Mark Walker (1984). "The Free Rider Problem: Experimental Evidence." *Public Choice*, 43, 3–24.

Kramer, R. M., and Marilyn Brewer (1986). "Social Group Identity and the Emergence of Cooperation in Resource Conservation Dilemmas." In H. Wilke, D. Messick, and C. Rutte, eds, *Psychology of Decision and Conflict* Vol. 3, *Experimental Social Dilemmas*. Frankfurt am Main: Verlag Peter Lang, 205–30.

Kreps, David, Paul Milgrom, John Roberts, and Robert Wilson (1982). "Rational Cooperation in Finitely Repeated Prisoner's Dilemmas." *Journal of Economic Theory*, 27, 245–52.

Marwell, Gerald, and Ruth Ames (1981). "Economists Free Ride, Does Anyone Else?" *Journal of Public Economics*, 15, 295–310.

Orbell, John M., Robyn M. Dawes, and Alphons J. C. van de Kragt (forthcoming). "Explaining Discussion Induced Cooperation." *Journal of Personality and Social Psychology.*

Rapoport, Anatol, and A. M. Chammah (1965). *Prisoner's Dilemma.* Ann Arbor: University of Michigan Press.

Sen, Amartya K. (1977). "Rational Fools: A Critique of the Behavioral Foundations of Economics Theory." *Journal of Philosophy and Public Affairs*, 6, 317–44.

Smith, Adam (1976). *The Theory of Moral Sentiments.* Oxford: Clarendon Press. (Originally published in 1759).

Tajfel, Henri, and John C. Turner (1979). "An Integrative Theory of Intergroup Conflict." In W. Austin and S. Worchel, eds., *The Social Psychology of Intergroup Relations.* Monterey, Calif.: Brooks/Cole, 33–47.

Turner, John C., and Howard Giles (1981). *Intergroup Behavior.* Chicago: University of Chicago Press.

Van de Kragt, Alphons J. C., John M. Orbell, and Robyn M. Dawes (1983). "The Minimal Contributing Set as a Solution to Public Goods Problems." *American Political Science Review*, 77, 112–22.

Van de Kragt, Alphons J. C., John M. Orbell, and Robyn M. Dawes, with Sandford L. Braver and L. A. Wilson, II (1986). "Doing Well and Doing Good as Ways of Resolving Social Dilemmas." In H. Wilke, D. Messick, and C. Rutte, eds., *Psychology of Decision and Conflict*, Vol. 3, *Experimental Social Dilemmas.* Frankfurt am Main: Verlag Peter Lang, 177–203.

[20]

GAMES AND ECONOMIC BEHAVIOR **10**, 122–142 (1995)

Trust, Reciprocity, and Social History*

JOYCE BERG

University of Iowa, Iowa City, Iowa 52442

AND

JOHN DICKHAUT AND KEVIN MCCABE

Department of Accounting, University of Minnesota, 645 Management and Economics, 271 19th Avenue South, Minneapolis, Minnesota 55455-0413

Received September 15, 1994

We designed an experiment to study trust and reciprocity in an investment setting. This design controls for alternative explanations of behavior including repeat game reputation effects, contractual precommitments, and punishment threats. Observed decisions suggest that reciprocity exists as a basic element of human behavior and that this is accounted for in the trust extended to an anonymous counterpart. A second treatment, social history, identifies conditions which strengthen the relationship between trust and reciprocity. © 1995 Academic Press, Inc.

1. INTRODUCTION

A fundamental assumption in economics is that individuals act in their own self interest. To enable explanation and prediction this assumption is often combined with other assumptions: (1) the objects of interest are restricted to personal consumption; (2) more consumption is preferred to less; and (3) only current consumption possibilities and plans for future consumption can influence current behavior. In individual choice settings, behavior that deviates from self interest is viewed as irrational. However,

* The authors thank Richard Thaler for extensive conversations concerning the design of this experiment. John Carter, Werner Guth, Tom Palfrey, Reinhard Selten, the participants of the Second Amsterdam Workshop on Experimental Economics (AWEE '93), and two anonymous referees have provided valuable insights into our study.

0899-8256/95 $12.00

in group settings there exist situations where self-interested behavior makes everyone worse off. This paradox has led to the consideration of modes of behavior that are not so restrictive. In this paper we consider the role of trust in a two-person exchange.

In his lectures on the limits of organizations, Arrow (1974) notes that in the face of transaction costs trust is ubiquitous to almost every economic transaction. This observation raises important questions about economic behavior. Is trust a primitive in economic models of behavior? What factors increase (or decrease) the likelihood of trust in economic transactions? We provide answers to these questions in a specific experimental setting, the investment game. By guaranteeing complete anonymity and by having subjects play the investment game only once, we eliminate mechanisms which could sustain investment without trust; these mechanisms include reputations from repeat interactions, contractual precommitments, and potential punishment threats. We then show that positive investments still occur, suggesting that trust is an economic primitive.

The investment game is played as follows. Subjects in room A decide how much of their $10 show-up fee to send to an anonymous counterpart in room B. Subjects were informed that each dollar sent would triple by the time it reached room B. Subjects in room B then decide how much of the tripled money to keep and how much to send back to their respective counterparts. The unique Nash equilibrium prediction for this game, with perfect information, is to send zero money.[1] This prediction is rejected in our first (no history) treatment where 30 of 32 room A subjects sent money ($5.16 on average). How can we explain this behavior?

From a rational choice perspective, subjects who sent money must have believed their expected return would be positive; but given the noncooperative prediction, why would they believe this? One approach is to derive trust as an equilibrium of a repeated game or as reputation building in a

[1] The investment game is similar to the trust game in Kreps (1990), the centipede game in Rosenthal (1982), and the peasant–dictator game studied by Van Huyck, *et al.* (1993). The trust game has the same basic two-stage structure as the investment game, that is, passing money to the other player is risky but leads to an expanded pie, some of which may be returned. The centipede game may go on for many stages, but any two consecutive stages involve the same basic structure. While the trust game and the centipede game have two choices at each stage, the investment game has a larger choice space allowing for different degrees of trust and reciprocity. All of these games have the same noncooperative prediction that play should end immediately even though strict Pareto improvements to payoffs can be found in later stages. McKelvey and Palfrey (1992) study repeated, one-shot, plays of four- and six-stage centipede games where subjects are paired with a different counterpart at the end of each game. Subjects in centipede games must cooperate to reach later stages. McKelvey and Palfrey find that a game of incomplete information based on a reputation for altruism, i.e., always willing to continue to later stages, explains their data. The investment game proposed in this paper provides a "boundary" design for the centipede game.

sequence of games; see for example Kreps (1990). Kreps notes that equilibria where trust emerges are but a small subset of the possible equilibria that may occur. While the theory of repeated games is useful for explaining how trust relationships become stable or unstable, it is not useful in discovering whether trust will exist absent repeat interactions, reputations, contracts, and punishment options.

A second approach is to derive trust as an evolutionarily stable strategy. Arrow (1974) refers to trust as an "important lubricant of a social system." While the emergence of trust is not formalized, he does categorize trust as a positive externality and suggests that evolutionary models may be able to explain the emergence of trust. The evolutionary approach is currently being studied in economics by Hirshleifer (1977), Guth and Kliment (1993), Guth *et al.* (1993), and Selten (1989) and in psychology by Cosmides and Tooby (1992). Evolutionary models predict the emergence of trust because it maximizes genetic fitness even though myopic self interest suggests cheating. From this perspective, trust can be viewed as a behavioral primitive that guides behavior in new situations; however, it may in some circumstances become extinct or it may be superseded by an individual's capacity to engage in self-interested decisionmaking.

Our "no history" results suggest that reciprocity does occur. We conjectured that the decision to reciprocate may depend on a counterpart's interpretation of room A behavior. If the counterpart interprets the decision to send money as an attempt to use trust to improve the outcome for both parties, then the counterpart is more likely to reciprocate. This lead to the consideration of factors that encourage the trust interpretation. One such factor is social history. There are many instances within organizations where public information reflects an organization's social history. Since social history provides common information about the use of trust within an organization, such a history may reinforce individuals' predispositions toward trust. This observation led to a second (social history) treatment. The following changes were made to the no history treatment: (1) subjects were recruited who had not participated in the previous sessions and (2) these subjects were given a summary of the no history results as part of their instructions.

2. Hypotheses and Procedures

The investment game is played as follows. In stage one, the subjects in rooms A and B are each given \$10 as a show-up fee. While subjects in room B pocket their show-up fees, subjects in room A must decide how much of their \$10 to send to an anonymous counterpart in room B. We denote this amount by M_a. The amount sent is then tripled, resulting in a total return of $3M_a$. In stage two, a counterpart in room B is given the tripled money. The counterpart must decide how much money to return, which is denoted $k_b(3M_a)$. The room A subject chooses the strategy M_a in {0, 1, 2, ..., 10}, while the counterpart in room B chooses the strategy

$$k_b\colon \{0, 3, ..., 30\} \rightarrow \{0, 1, ..., 30\},$$

which satisfies $0 \leq k_b(3M_a) \leq 3M_a$.

These strategies result in the payoffs

$$P_a(M_a, k_b) = \$10 - M_a + k_b(3M_a),$$

and

$$P_b(M_a, k_b) = 3M_a - k_b(3M_a).$$

A subject's initial wealth is denoted W_i. If subjects have strictly increasing indirect utility function for wealth, given by $V_i(W_i + P_i(M_a, k_b))$ for i = a, b, and each subject, i, maximizes $V_i(\cdot)$, then subjects in room B have a dominant strategy to keep all the money, that is, $k_b(3M_a) = 0$ for all M_a. If room A subjects infer their counterpart's dominant strategy, then they should send nothing, i.e., $M_a = 0$.

Evidence from other experiments suggests that subjects do consider their counterparts move in two-stage sequential games.[2] One hypothesis for the investment game is that subjects will make decisions consistent with the subgame perfect prediction,

$$N_0\colon M_a = 0 \qquad \text{for all a.}$$

If for some reason a positive amount is sent, i.e., $M_a > 0$, then we can test for the dominant strategy property by room B subjects.

$$N_1\colon \text{If } M_a > 0, \text{ then } k_b(3M_a) = 0, \qquad \text{for all b.}$$

The investment game provides a role for the use of trust in achieving a joint improvement to the subgame perfect outcome. For purposes of this

[2] See for example the two- versus three-stage bargaining results in Neelin *et al.* (1988) and Harrison and McCabe (1993) and the mouselab studies of bargaining by Camerer, *et al.* (1991). See also the baseline results for extensive form play by McCabe, *et al.* (1994). The conclusion from this research is that subjects do look at least one stage ahead. This observation is sufficient for assuming that subjects in room A did consider their counterpart's dominant strategy in the two-stage investment game.

paper, our definition of trust is similar to Coleman's (1990, Chap. 5). In Coleman's terminology a room A subject is known as the "trustor"; sending $M_a > 0$ is said to "place a trust" in the trustee. The trustee is said to "keep the trust," i.e., reciprocate, when $k_b(3M_a) > M_a$. Trust can be defined in terms of the following two actions: first, the trustor gives a trustee the right to make a decision; and, second, the trustee makes a decision which affects both trustor and trustee. Subjects have used trust to facilitate exchange, if the following conditions are met. (1) Placing trust in the trustee puts the trustor at risk; (2) relative to the set of possible actions, the trustee's decision benefits the trustor at a cost to the trustee; and (3) both trustor and trustee are made better off from the transaction compared to the outcome which would have occurred if the trustor had not entrusted the trustee.[3]

The conditions for trust can be satisfied in the investment game as follows: (1) Sending money in stage one is risky since the counterpart may or may not reciprocate; (2) in stage two, the counterpart has to give up money to make the room A subject better off; and (3) since the money triples both parties can be made better off relative to the subgame perfect outcome. The existence of trust and reciprocity in these experiments support the following alternative hypotheses,

$$A_0\colon M_a > 0 \qquad \text{for some a,}$$

and

$$A_1\colon k_b(3M_a) > M_a.$$

From a learning or evolutionary games standpoint, a strategy will become extinct if its relative payoff is poor. Since the simple strategy of not investing results in zero profit, trust cannot emerge as a norm unless it satisfies the positive profits hypothesis that, for at least some amounts M_a, the average net return is positive; i.e., if there are N room B subjects each receiving the total amount $3M_a$, then

A_2: There exist amounts M_a such that

$$\sum_b \frac{k_b(3M_a)}{N} > M_a.$$

[3] Williamson (1993) uses the same basic definition of trust in his review of the trust literature, but he distinguishes between calculative trust and personal trust. Calculative trust occurs when the trustor decides whether or not to entrust the trustee on the basis of an expected utility calculation. Personal trust is based on more of a noncalculative "feeling" that entrusting the trustee is the correct decision. In summary, trust is understood as a reliance on the reciprocity of others where a return is made for something done or given. Different forms of trust emerge depending on the basis of the reliance.

An important feature of the investment game is that different amounts M_a can be sent from room A. It seems plausible that the amount sent may have an impact on reciprocity. At one extreme, sending \$1 may signal a very weak belief in reciprocity; at the other extreme, sending \$10 may signal a strong belief in reciprocity. From an evolutionary perspective, someone with a predisposition to reciprocate may be more willing to reciprocate when they believe their counterpart shares a common regard for trust. Rabin (1993) makes such an assumption by incorporating a "kindness" function into subjects' utility in such a way as to capture the following behavior: as one's counterpart increases his or her "kindness," the utility maximizing response is to be kinder in return. These observations suggest the following hypothesis.

A_3: M_a and $k_b(M_a)$ are positively correlated.

A. *The Double Blind Procedure*

Stage two of the investment game is a dictator game[4], except that now subjects in room B, acting as dictators, have been entrusted with the money by a counterpart in room A. Dictator games without this element of trust have been studied extensively by experimentalists in order to understand bargaining behavior. Forsythe *et al.* (1994; henceforth FHSS) ran a \$10 dictator game where the amount given by the subject dictators is higher than the self-interested prediction of zero. The FHSS results were replicated by Hoffman *et al.* (1994; henceforth HMSS), who further find that self-interested behavior is significantly increased by using a procedure (double-blind) which guarantees complete anonymity with respect to other subjects and the experimenter.

In implementing the investment game, we incorporated the double-blind procedures used by HMSS. Our choice was motivated by the desire to control for the possibility of repeat game effects and thus protect any observed results from being attributed to reputation, collusion, or the threat of punishment. Such phenomena become impossible when no one, including the experimenter, is able to map individual decisions back to the identity of the decision maker. Yet it must be possible for the experimenter to gather data.

[4] In a dictator game player one, called the dictator, is given a sum of money, often \$10. The dictator must then decide how much if any to send player two. A theory which assumes self-interested, non-satiated behavior predicts that the dictator will keep all the money.

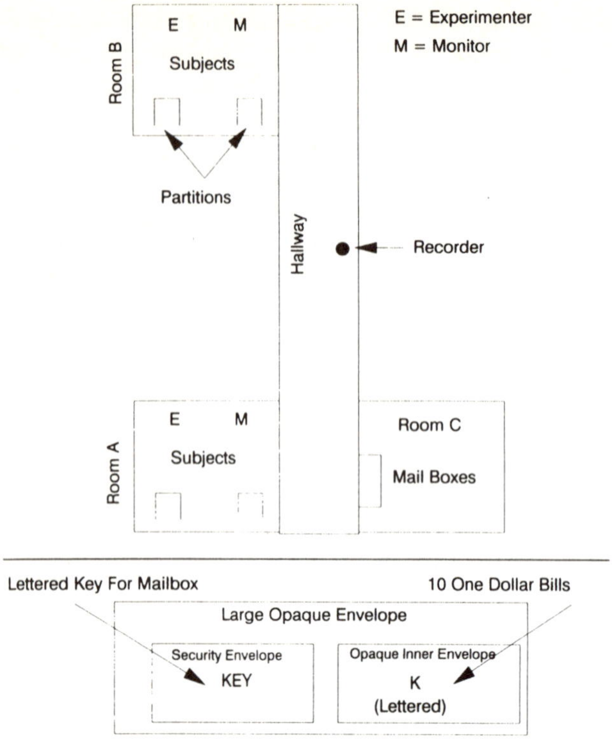

FIG. 1. Diagram of trust experiment.

Figure 1 shows the physical implementation of the investment game. This hand-run implementation involves passing envelopes among three rooms. Rooms A and B contain subjects, while room C contains a bank of 14 mailboxes. The experiment begins by having an experimenter (E) in each room read aloud the instructions that appear in appendix A. Once the instructions are finished, subjects in room A are called one at a time by the monitor (M). Once called, a subject receives a large unmarked opaque envelope which contains: (1) an inner envelope with a lettered mailbox key, (2) a smaller lettered opaque envelope which will contain the money to be invested, and (3) the subject's show-up fee of 10 one-dollar bills. The letter on the smaller envelope corresponds to the letter on the key, thus enabling subjects in room A to receive the return from their own investment decision.

Upon receiving the envelope a subject then proceeds to the back of the room, to a privacy preserving partition, and decides (1) how many dollars to send, i.e., put in the smaller opaque envelope which is then put back into the larger opaque envelope, and (2) how many dollars to keep along with the lettered mailbox key. Upon completing the task, the subject drops the large opaque envelope into a return box and returns to his or her seat. Once all decisions in room A are made, the monitor from room A takes the envelopes to the recorder (R) in the hallway. At this time the amounts sent are recorded by subject letter and the amount invested is tripled and returned to the lettered envelope, which is placed back into the unmarked envelope.

When the recording is finished, the monitor from room A returns to room A and the monitor from room B is called to get the envelopes. In room B subjects are called up one at a time and given one of the large unmarked opaque envelopes. Subjects then go to the back of the room where they privately open the outer and inner envelopes and learn how many dollars are in the inner envelope. The subject then decides the amount he or she wants to pay back, by putting that amount of money back in the inner envelope, and keeps the remaining dollars. The inner envelope is then returned to the unmarked outer envelope and is placed in the return box. At this point the subject in room B exits the experiment.

Once all decisions in room B are made, the monitor from room B takes the envelopes back to the recorder in the hallway. At this time the money paid back to subjects in room A is recorded by the letter on the inner envelope. Once recording is done, the inner envelopes are then placed in their corresponding mailboxes in room C. At this point the monitor from room B and the recorder both return to room B.

The monitor from room A then calls one subject at a time to go to room C and privately open his or her mailbox. The subject then pockets the money in the inner envelope, returns the key to a drop box, and exits the experiment. At no time does anyone else learn what key or mailbox was used. This procedure continues until all subjects in room A are finished.

B. *Subjects*

Subjects were recruited from the undergraduate student population at the University of Minnesota. All subjects were recruited by phone and had previously participated in at least one unrelated paid laboratory experiment. Subjects received $10 for showing up and $3 if they were bumped due to overbooking. Subjects were told to report directly to either room A or room B. Once an equal number of subjects were in each room, monitors were chosen from each room by having subjects draw without replacement

TABLE I
EXPERIMENTAL SESSIONS

Treatment	Date	Number of pairs
No history	7/13/93	10
	7/19/93	10
	7/23/93	12
Social history	7/27/93	10
	7/31/93	9
	8/03/93	9

a chip from a cup until the chip marked M appeared. Experiments lasted from 60 to 90 min. Table I summarizes our sessions.

3. No History Results

Our no history treatment consisted of 32 pairs of subjects run over 3 days. Figure 2 graphs the resulting data from these sessions. The data are presented in descending order using the amount sent from room A,

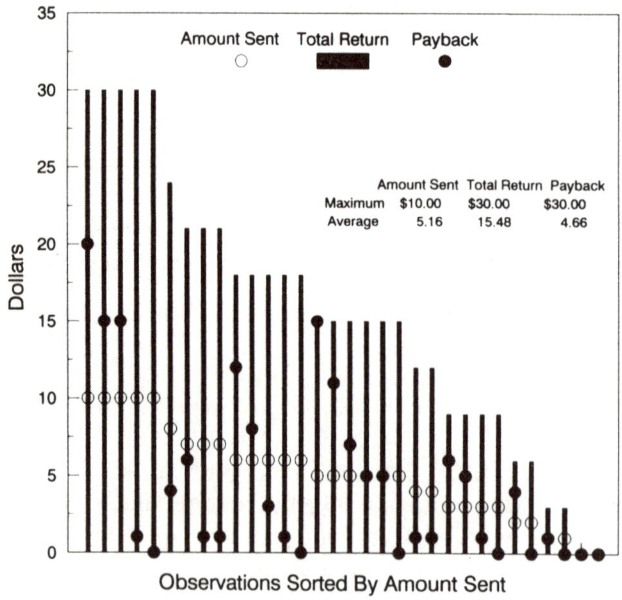

FIG. 2. Trust experiment results showing amount sent (○), total return (■), and payback (●). No history was provided to the subjects.

shown as an open circle, as the primary key. For example, 5 of 32 subjects in room A sent their entire show up fee of $10. Gray bars indicate the amount received by the counterpart in room B. The data are further sorted in descending order using the payback, the amount sent back to room A (shown as a black circle), as the secondary key. On average, $5.16 is sent by room A, resulting in an average payback of $4.66 by room B.

A. *Room A Decisions*

We make the following observations about room A decisions. (1) Only 2 of 32 subjects sent zero. (2) The amounts sent are highly variable, ranging from $1 to $10. These observations provide very little support for Hypothesis N_0. Furthermore, we cannot reject the null hypothesis that our sample of room A decisions was drawn from a uniform distribution over the amounts {0, 1, 2, . . . , 10}. Consider the following approximate randomization test; see Edington (1987). Randomly assign the (N = 32) decisions to the possible amounts sent, $m = 0, 1, 2, \ldots, 10$, under the assumption that each amount is equally likely. The resulting sample can be denoted s_i and the frequency of each amount, m, can be denoted f_m. We then measure the variation in the sample, s_i as

$$v(s_n) = \sum_{m=0}^{11} \left(f_m - \frac{N}{11}\right)^2.$$

Given our actual sample denoted d, we can now ask what is the probability, p, that $v(s_i)$ is greater than or equal to $v(d)$. We then draw 100,000 random samples to calculate p to be 0.29.

B. *Room B Decisions*

We make the following observations about room B decisions (1) Of the 28 room B subjects who were sent $M_a >$ \$1, 12 returned \$0 or \$1 to their counterparts. This behavior is supportive of hypothesis N_1. (2) However, 11 of the same 28 subjects returned more than their counterpart sent, resulting in positive net returns. This behavior is supportive of hypothesis A_1. (3) Investments of $5 had an average payback of $7.17, while investments of $10.00 had an average payback of $10.20. This observation provides some support for hypothesis A_2.

To examine hypothesis A_3 we calculate Spearman's rank correlation coefficient, r_s, between the paired room A and room B decisions. Since absolute amounts sent and amounts returned will bias our correlation statistic upwards, i.e., low amounts sent preclude some high returns, we compare amount sent to percentage returned. An $r_s = 0.01$ suggests no correlation between amounts sent and payback decisions.

4. Social History Results

The decisions to send money and reciprocate, in the no history treatment, raises the possibility that subjects decisions in the investment game are influenced by social norms.[5] Coleman (1990) defines a norm on a specific action to be a socially defined right by others to control an individual's action. Such control can be achieved through the use of sanctions or rewards. In Coleman's terminology there is a prescriptive norm to reinforce the room B decision to keep a trust, i.e., reciprocate. In light of this norm it is rational for individuals in room A to place a trust, i.e., send money.

In cases where outside sanctions or rewards are not available, norms may still exist if sanctions or rewards have been internalized by the decision maker. Coleman argues that norms are more likely to be internalized when an individual clearly identifies with a particular group. The process of having an individual identify with a group is termed socialization. In the no history experiment subjects were all University of Minnesota undergraduates. From this viewpoint, social history provides common information about the use of trust within a group; such a history may increase social identity and reinforce an individual's predisposition toward trust. By providing social history in a double-blind, one-shot setting, we focus on the internalization of social norms, as opposed to other potential mechanisms for reciprocity such as reputation building.

In the social history treatment 28 additional pairs of subjects were run over three days. Each subject was given a report summarizing the decisions of the previous 32 pairs of subjects in our no history treatment. This report appears at the end of the instructions in Appendix A. For each level, \$0–10, the report details the number of times that amount was sent, the average

[5] Coleman notes that demand for norms increases with the existence of externalities between subjects. In the investment game such an externality exists since money triples only if it is sent, while return on investment depends on payback decisions. But why do we only observe positive average returns on \$5 and \$10. Elster notes that norms often have an all-or-nothing feature. In the investment game room B subjects are more likely to reciprocate when room A subjects send "all" of their money. Note that all may be interpreted as \$10, but it could also be interpreted as \$5 due to our experimental design. Subjects had all previously participated in individual choice experiments where they were guaranteed a minimum of \$5 (for showing up) which could not be used in the experiment. From past experience some subjects may have split their \$10 into the \$5 guarantee and \$5 for potential investment decisions.

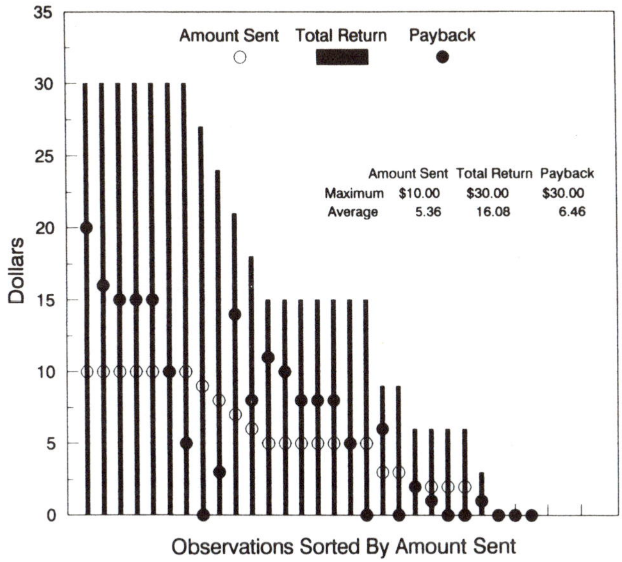

FIG. 3. Trust experiment results showing amount sent (○), total return (■), and payback (●). A social history was provided to the subjects.

payback (average amount returned), and the average net return (average amount returned minus average amount sent). In order to minimize any additional presentation effects in the instructions we referred to the report only in the following paragraph;

> "Each of you has received a report summarizing the decisions of the previous 32 pairs of subjects who have participated in this experiment in July. Please check the last page of the instructions to be sure you have this sheet."

If, in the no history treatment, subjects in room A failed to appreciate the dominant strategy property of the room B decisions, then providing a social history to room A makes subjects more aware of the existence of subjects in room B who do not reciprocate. This could result in a loss of trust, resulting in lower amounts sent. Such behavior should increase support for hypothesis N_0. Alternatively, room A subjects may focus on the positive net returns for the \$5 and \$10 levels. This focus could result in an increase in trust, resulting in more decisions to send either \$5 or \$10, providing increased support for hypothesis A_0. For room B subjects, social history may make keeping the money more acceptable, providing greater support for hypothesis N_1. Alternatively, social history may stimulate reciprocity when \$5 and \$10 are sent, providing support for hypotheses A_1–A_3.

Figure 3 graphs the results from these sessions. Data are sorted using

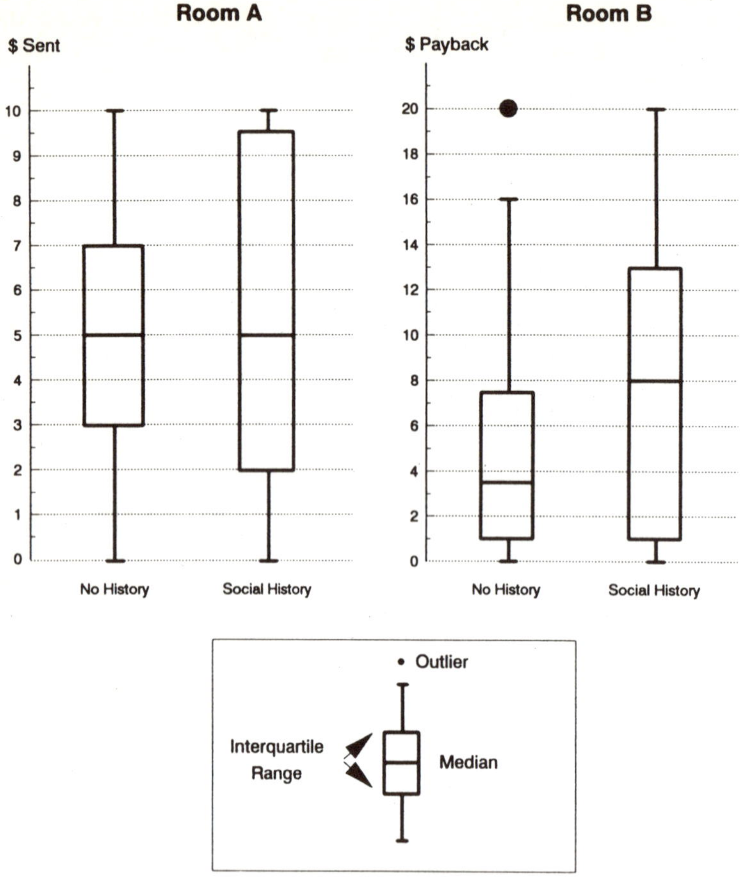

FIG. 4. Subjects' decision by room and treatment.

the same keys, amount sent and payback, as were used in Fig. 2. On the average room A subjects sent $5.36, resulting in an average payback of $6.46. Comparing paybacks under no history to paybacks under social history, a one-sided Wilcoxon rank–sum test ($r = 776$) is significant at the $p = 0.1$ level.

In Fig. 4 we summarize the data with box plots. These plots show a measure of location (the median) as a solid line, a measure of dispersion (the interquartile range) as a box and outliers (points) which are further than 1.5 times the interquartile range from the upper and lower quartiles. This range is shown as a vertical line which is drawn to the most extreme data point within 1.5 times the interquartile range from the upper and lower quartile boundaries. An immediate feature of the data is an increase in dispersion of the data, i.e., the interquartile range, in the social history treatment. This increase explains the reduced significance of statistical tests comparing no history with social history.

A. *Room A Decisions*

We make the following observations about room A decisions: (1) Only 3 of 28 subjects sent zero. This observation provides very little support for hypothesis N_0. (2) $5 and $10 are now sent 50% of the time. However, this increase in frequency of $5 and $10 amounts is not statistically significant. In the table included in Appendix B we compare average net return by amount sent. Using the same randomization test, explained in Section 3, we now reject (at $p = .06$) the null hypothesis that our sample of room A decisions was drawn from a uniform distribution over the amounts {0, 1, 2, . . . , 10}.

B. *Room B Decisions*

We make the following observations about room B decisions. (1) Of the 24 room B subjects who were sent $M_a >$ $1, 6 returned $0 or $1 to their counterparts; (2) 13 of the same 24 subjects returned more than their counterpart, sent resulting in positive net returns; (3) investments of $5 had an average payback of $7.14, while investments of $10.00 had an average payback of $13.17.

To examine Hypothesis *A*3 we calculate Spearman's rank correlation coefficient, r_s, between the paired room A and room B decisions. An $r_s =$ .34 suggests an increase in correlation between amounts sent and payback decisions when social history is provided. To test if the change in correlation between no history and social history is significant we use resampling. We generate 5000 sample points of the following form. First, we randomly assign our 60 paired observations between the two treatments with 32 pairs and 28 pairs; we then compute the difference in correlation statistics for our sample. From this empirical distribution we compute the probability, $p = .06$, that our resampled differences in correlation statistics are greater than or equal to our actual difference. We conclude that the change was significant.

5. PAYBACK DECISIONS AND EARNINGS

In Fig. 5 we graph the joint earnings of the 60 (room A, room B) pairs. The large outer triangle with points {(0,40), (10,10), and (30,10)} indicates the set of feasible earnings pairs. The shaded triangle {(10,30), (10,10), (30,10)} indicates the earnings pairs with non-negative net returns to room

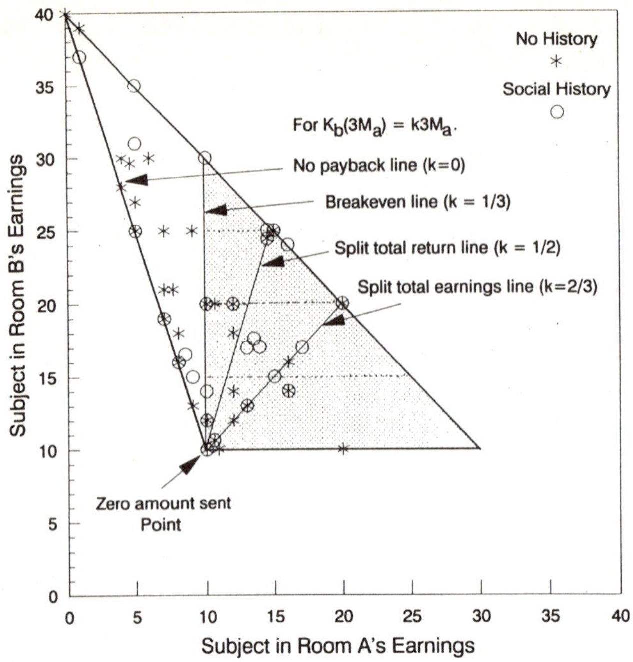

FIG. 5. Distribution of joint dollar earnings.

A, while the unshaded triangle {(0,40), (10,10), (10,30)} indicates the non-positive net returns to room A. If we write the amount returned as a fraction of the total return, i.e., $k_b(3M_a) = k3M_a$, then we can parameterize the following line segments: (1) When $k = 0$, subject b keeps all the money, i.e., the line segment with endpoints (0,40) and (10,10); (2) when $k = 1/3$, subject b returns the original amount sent, allowing subject a to break even, i.e., the line segment (10,10) with endpoints (10,10) and (10,30); (3) when $k = 1/2$, subject b splits the total return, $3M_a/2$, with subject a, i.e., the line segment with endpoints (10,10) and (15,25); (4) when $k = 2/3$, subject b splits the net return with subject a, i.e., the line segment with end points (10,10) and (20,20) which splits total earnings inclusive of show-up fees.

We have plotted the 32 no history pairs as asterisks and the 28 social history pairs as open circles. When points coincide we have offset them slightly. Using k as a measure of room B types and allowing the joint earnings pair to be wtihin a dollar of the type k prediction, then the four types $k = 0$, $k = 1/3$, $k = 1/2$, and $k = 2/3$ explain over 90% of the data. While the data suggest that social history increases the $k = 1/3$ and greater types, the increase is not statistically significant.

6. Conclusions

We have identified an experimental design where trust can be used for mutual gain. The double-blind and one-shot controls used in this design strengthen our conclusion that self interest alone cannot explain our results. In particular, these controls rule out reputations or contractual precommitments as explanations of subjects' behavior. In our initial no history treatment 30 of 32 room A subjects sent money, while 11 of these 30 decisions resulted in a payback greater than the amount sent. One explanation of the data is that room A subjects were willing to place a trust, by risking some amount of money, in the belief that there would be reciprocity; the room B subjects who reciprocated kept this trust. The remaining two-thirds may have been acted out of self interest, or alternatively they may not have interpreted the room A decisions as placing a trust and thus reciprocation was not an issue.

The social history treatment explores the interpretation that some subjects reciprocated because they were trusted. Given that two-thirds of the room B subjects did not reciprocate in the no history treatment, it seemed plausible that providing this information would cause room A subjects to send less and justify room B decisions to reciprocate less. This was not the case. Moving from no history to social history resulted in three observable effects. First, there is a shift in average return from a negative \$0.50 (no history) to a positive \$1.10 (social history). Since the average amount sent only increased by 20 cents, most of this change is accounted for by an increase in the average payback of \$1.80. Second, room A decisions become more systematic with respect to our randomization test. Our randomization results led us to the following direct comparison of behavior. Third, we observe an increased correlation between amounts sent and payback decisions.

Taken together our two treatments provide a strong rejection of the subgame perfect prediction that room A subjects will send no money. They did so 55 out of 60 times. Furthermore, we see reciprocation, but we also see room B types who did not reciprocate. Here the evidence is mixed. Some of the room B subjects who did not reciprocate may not have interpreted room A behavior as initiating a trust. The evidence on \$5 and \$10 amounts sent suggests that it may have been easier to interpret this as trust and thus served as focal points for trust. Further evidence comes from the social history treatment which was designed to increase subjects' propensity to believe in and use trust.

Trust can be used to explain a number of other experiments. In HMSS, 77 subjects in the double blind dictator games (DB1 and DB2), who received \$10 from the experimenter, sent an average of 11 cents for every dollar received; in contrast, the 55 room B subjects, who were sent money in both treatments of the investment game, sent back an average of 35 cents for every dollar received. This suggests that forward signaling, i.e., sending money in the investment game, may be essential for reciprocity. When subjects are simply endowed as a benevolent dictator by the experimenter (as in HMSS) there is no call for reciprocation. Reciprocity carries over into markets as well. Fehr *et al.* (1993) look at the effect of paying higher wages on subjects productivity where moral hazard exists. They find that subjects who are paid more are more likely to reciprocate by shirking less. McKelvey and Palfrey (1992) find that subjects in centipede games are more likely to pass, thus allowing the game to continue even though the subgame perfect prediction is to end the game. They explain their results in terms of a reputation model with altruistic types, i.e., those who pass no matter what. An alternative interpretation of their data is the existence of types who will keep a trust where the round-one decision to pass places a trust which can be kept in round two. The trust can be placed again in round three, and so on. However, consistent with the finding of payoff variability in the investment game, once sufficient reciprocity is achieved to make both players better off either player is likely to end the game. Given the existence of subjects who keep a trust, as much as one-third of the subjects in our no history experiment, the other subjects in the centipede game have an incentive to act as one of these types.

The ability to include trust and reciprocity as part of the rational choice paradigm would seem to allow better explanations of economic institutions. For example, there is strong evidence that (1) "framing" joint decision problems in terms of property rights and (2) implementing procedures for assigning such rights changes subject behavior; see for example HMSS or Hoffman and Spitzer (1982, 1985). But how do these changes in language and procedures affect behavior? Based on our study, one interpretation is that the language and institution of property rights is built on the behavioral primitives trust and reciprocity. Thus, by inventing property rights and allowing social history, society stimulates norms of behavior which further strengthen reciprocity. In earlier experiments property rights protect first movers from punishment, a negative form of reciprocity, when first movers make decisions which are more in their own self interest. By contrast, in the investment game, their is a property right when subject a sends part (or all) of subject a's show-up fee to room B, thus entrusting private property to another subject.

In conclusion, experiments on ultimatum game, repeated prisoners' dilemma games, and other extensive form games provide strong evidence that people do punish inappropriate behavior even though this is personally costly. Furthermore, subjects take this into account when they make their decisions. The investment game provides evidence that people are also willing to reward appropriate behavior and that this too is taken into account. Taken together, these results suggest that both positive and negative forms of reciprocity exist and must be taken into account in order to explain the development of institutional forms which reinforce the propensity to reciprocate. Our results provide strong support for current research efforts which attempt to measure trust, see Cummings *et al.* (1994), and efforts to integrate reciprocity into standard game theory, see Geanakopolos *et al.* (1989) and Rabin (1993).

Appendix A: Instructions for Trust Experiment

Instructions for Room A

You have been asked to participate in an economics experiment. The instructions you are about to read are self explanatory. We will not answer any questions during this experiment. If you have any questions, you should read back through these instructions. Now that the experiment has begun, we ask that you do not talk, at all, during this experiment.

In this experiment each of you will be paired with a different person who is in another room. You will not be told who these people are either during or after the experiment. This is room A, other participants are in room B. You will notice that there are other people in the same room with you who are also participating in this experiment. You will not be paired with any of these people. A person in room A, called monitor A, and a person in room B, called monitor B, will be chosen for today's experiment. The monitors will be in charge of the envelopes as explained below. In addition the monitors will verify that the instructions have been followed as they appear here.

Each person in room A and each person in room B has been given $10 as a show up fee for this experiment. Persons in room A will have the opportunity to send in an envelope, some, all, or none of their show up fee to a person in room B. Each dollar sent to room B will be tripled. For example, if you send an envelope which contains $2, the envelope will contain $6 when it reaches room B. If you send an envelope which contains $9, the envelope will contain $27 when it reaches room B. The person in room B will then decide how much money to send back to the person in room A and how much money to keep.

(For the social history treatment we added the following paragraph)
Each of you has received a report summarizing the decisions of the previous 32 pairs of subjects who have participated in this experiment during July. Please check the last page of the instructions to be sure you have this sheet.

The remainder of these instructions will explain exactly how this experiment is run. This experiment is structured so that no one, including the experimenters and monitors, will know the personal decision of people in either room A or room B. Since your decision is private we ask that you do not tell anyone your decision either during, or after, the experiment.

The experiment is conducted as follows: Twelve large unmarked envelopes have been placed in a box in room A. Each of these envelopes contains 10 one dollar bills (the show up fee for a person in room A), a smaller inner envelope, and a key in a sealed envelope marked KEY. The inner envelope and key are marked with the same letter of the alphabet. The monitor, in room A, will point to one person at a time, and hand that person an unmarked envelope from the box. The person who was pointed to will then go to one of the seats, with a large box on top and privately open the unmarked envelope inside the box. Only the person who opened the envelope will know which letter of the alphabet was in the envelope. Do not open the envelope marked KEY until you are told to do so. The monitor will then point to the next person, and continue in this fashion until everyone has made their decisions.

Each person in room A must decide how many dollar bills to put in the inner envelope. The person then pockets the remaining dollar bills and the envelope marked KEY. Examples: (1) Put $2 in the inner envelope, and pocket $8 as well as the envelope marked KEY. (2) Put $9 in the inner envelope, and pocket $1 as well as the envelope marked KEY. These are examples only, the actual decision is up to each person.

Once a person in room A has made a decision they should put the inner envelope back inside the large unmarked envelope, and return the unmarked envelope to the box marked return envelopes. Persons in room A should make sure that they have kept the envelope marked KEY as they will use this later in the experiment. Notice that each envelope returned will look exactly the same.

After all the envelopes have been put in the return box monitor A will transport the box to a recorder who is in the hallway. With monitor A observing, the recorder will then, one at a time, take the inner envelope out of the unmarked envelope and record on a blank sheet of paper, the letter on the envelope, and the amount of money in the envelope. While monitor A is observing, the recorder will then triple the amount of money in the inner envelope, and place the inner envelope back into the unmarked outer envelope. At this point, the recorder will signal the monitor from room B to come to the recorders desk. Once monitor B has arrived monitor A will be asked to return to room A.

Monitor B will then carry the box of envelopes to room B. Monitor B will then point to one person at a time, and hand that person an unmarked envelope from the box. The person who was called will then go to a seat with a large box on top and then privately open the outer envelope inside the box. The monitor will then point to the next person. Each person in room B must decide how many dollar bills to leave in the inner envelope. The person then pockets the remaining dollar bills. The inner envelope should then be placed in the unmarked outer envelope and the outer envelope should then be placed in the box marked return envelopes. The person in room B will then be asked to leave since the experiment is over for that person. When you leave we ask that you leave the building. After all the envelopes in room B are returned, monitor B will transport the box to the recorder in the hallway. The recorder will then, one at a time, open the inner envelope and record on a blank sheet of paper, the letter on the envelope, and the amount of money in the inner envelope. The recorder will then signal monitor A to come to the recorders desk. Once monitor A has arrived monitor B will return to room B.

When monitor A arrives the monitor and recorder will carry the box of envelopes to room C directly opposite room A. Room C contains mailboxes with identifying letters. The letters correspond to the letters on the inner envelopes. While the recorder observes, monitor A will place each inner envelope in the box with the corresponding letter. All the mailboxes will then be locked. The recorder will then go back to room B and monitor A will go to room A.

Monitor A will then point to one person at a time from room A. That person will then enter room C alone and open the envelope marked KEY. Inside this envelope is a lettered key which will open the mailbox with the corresponding letter. The inner envelope in the mailbox is the same one the person in room A started with. We have underlined the letters H and I on the key tags to make it clear which letter you have. The person from room A will then go to the appropriate mailbox, open it, take out the envelope, and remove the money. The person will then return the envelope to the mailbox and lock the mailbox. The person will then return the key to the envelope marked KEY and drop the envelope in the box just outside the door in the hallway. When you are called to go to room C you should take all your belongings since you will be asked to leave the building when you are done.

When everyone in room A has left, the experiment is over, and the monitors will be paid for their participation.

(Report included in Social History Treatment)
Summary of Previous Choices Aggregated by Amount Sent

Amount sent	0.00	1.00	2.00	3.00	4.00	5.00	6.00	7.00	8.00	9.00	10.00
Number of persons Choosing this amount	2	2	2	4	2	6	5	3	1	0	5
Average amount returned	0.00	.50	2.00	3.00	1.00	7.17	4.80	2.67	4.00		10.20
Amount sent	0.00	1.00	2.00	3.00	4.00	5.00	6.00	7.00	8.00		10.00
Average profit		−.50	0.00	0.00	−3.00	2.17	−1.20	−4.33	−4.00		0.20

Appendix B: Data from Experiments in Ordered Pairs

(Investment, Payback)

	No history			Social history		
	7/13/92	7/19/92	7/23/92	7/27/92	7/31/92	8/03/92
1	(7,1)	(5,7)	(6,12)	(5,11)	(3,0)	(1,1)
2	(3,0)	(10,0)	(10,15)	(10,15)	(2,0)	(10,20)
3	(7,6)	(5,0)	(3,6)	(2,2)	(10,5)	(7,14)
4	(5,11)	(8,4)	(6,8)	(5,8)	(2,0)	(10,15)
5	(3,1)	(5,15)	(6,1)	(0,0)	(5,0)	(3,6)
6	(2,4)	(0,0)	(10,15)	(2,1)	(5,10)	(10,10)
7	(6,0)	(7,1)	(10,1)	(10,16)	(8,3)	(6,8)
8	(4,1)	(1,0)	(6,3)	(10,15)	(5,8)	(5,8)
9	(10,20)	(3,5)	(4,1)	(5,5)	(0,0)	(0,0)
10	(5,5)	(2,0)	(0,0)	(9,0)		
11			(5,5)			
12			(1,1)			

References

Arrow, K. (1974). *The Limits Of Organization*. New York: Norton, York.

Camerer, C., Johnson, E., Rymon, T., and Sen, S. (1993). "Cognition and Framing in Sequential Bargaining for Gains and Losses," in *Frontiers of Game Theory*, (K. Binmore, A. Kirman, and P. Tuni, (Eds.), Cambridge, MA: MIT Press.

Cosmides, L., and Tooby, J. (1992). "Cognitive Adaptations for Social Exchange," in *The Adapted Mind*, (J. Barkow, L. Cosmides, and J. Tooby, Eds.). New York: Oxford Univ. Press.

Coleman, J. (1990). *Foundations of Social Choice Theory*. Cambridge, MA: Harvard Univ. Press.

Cummings, L., and Bromiley, P. (1995). "The Organizational Trust Inventory (OTI): Development and Validation," in *Trust in Organizations* (R. Kramer and T. Tyler, Eds.), Twin Oaks, CA: Sage.

Fehr, E., Kirchsteiger, G., and Riedl, A. (1993). "Does Fairness Prevent Market Clearing? An Experimental Investigation," *Quart. J. Econ.* **108,** 437–459.

Forsythe, R., Horowitz, J., Savin, N., and Sefton, M. (1994). "Replicability, Fairness and Pay in Experiments with Simple Bargaining Games," *Games Econ. Behav.* **6,** 347–369.

Geanakoplos, J., Pearce, D., and Stachetti, E. (1989). "Psychological Games and Sequential Rationality," *Games Econ. Behav.* **1,** 60–79.

Guth, W., and Kliment, H. (1993). "Competition or Cooperation: On the Evolutionary Economics Of Trust, Exploitation and Moral Attitudes," mimeo, University of Frankfurt.

Guth, W., Ockenfels, P., and Wendel (1993). "Efficiency by Trust in Fairness? Multiperiod Ultimatum Bargaining Experiments with an Increasing Cake," *Int. J. Game Theory* **22,** 51–73.

Harrison, G., and McCabe, K. (1993). "The Role of Experience for Testing Bargaining Theory in Experiments," *Res. Exp. Econ.* **5,** 137–169.

Hirshleifer, J. (1977). "Economics from a Biological Viewpoint," *J. Law Econ.* **20,** 1–52.

Hoffman, E., McCabe, K., Shachat, K., and Smith, V. (1994). "Preferences, Property Rights, and Anonymity in Bargaining Games," *Games Econ. Behav.* **7,** 346–380.

Hoffman, E., and Spitzer, M. (1982). "The Coase Theorem: Some Experimental Tests," *J. Law Econ.* **25,** 73–98.

Hoffman, E., and Spitzer, M. (1985). "Entitlements, Rights, and Fairness: An Experimental Examination of Subjects' Concepts of Distributive Justice," *J. Legal Studies* **15,** 254–297.

Kreps, D. M. (1990). "Corporate Culture and Economic Theory," in *Perspectives on Positive Political Economy* (J. Alt and K. Shepsle, Eds.). Cambridge: Cambridge Univ. Press.

McCabe, K., Rassenti, S., and Smith, V. (1994). "Forward and Backward Rationality in the Achievement of Cooperation," mimeo, Economic Science Laboratory, University of Arizona.

McKelvey, R., and Palfrey, T. (1992). "An Experimental Study of the Centipede Game," *Econometrica* **60,** 803–836.

Neelin, Sonnenschein, and Spiegel (1988). "A further test of noncooperative bargaining theory: Comment," *Amer. Econ. Rev.* **78**, 824–836.

Rabin, M. (1993). "Incorporating Fairness into Game Theory and Economics," *Amer. Econ. Rev.* **83,** 1281–1302.

Rosenthal, R. (1982). "Games of Perfect Information, Predatory Pricing, and the Chain-Store Paradox," *J. Econ. Theory* **25,** 92–100.

Schelling, T. (1980). *The Strategy Of Conflict.* Cambridge, MA: Harvard Univ. Press.

Selten, R. (1989). "Evolution, Learning, and Economic Behavior," the 1989 Nancy L. Schwartz Memorial Lecture, Northwest University, 1989.

Van Huyck, J., Battalio, R., and Walters, M. (1993). "Commitment versus Discretion in the Peasant–Dictator Game: Aggregate Analysis," mimeo, Texas A&M Economics.

Williamson, O. (1993). "Calculativeness, Trust, and Economic Organization," *J. Law Econ.* **36,** 453–486.

[21]

Experimental Economics, 3:81–100 (2000)

Trust, Reciprocity, and Social History: A Re-examination

ANDREAS ORTMANN*
Center for Adaptive Behavior and Cognition, Max Planck Institute for Human Development, Lentzeallee 94, 14195 Berlin, Germany
email: ortmann@mpib-berlin.mpg.de; andreas.ortmann@cerge.coni.cz

JOHN FITZGERALD AND CARL BOEING
Department of Economics, Bowdoin College, Brunswick, ME 04011, USA

Received February 11, 1998; Revised November 15, 1999

Abstract

Berg et al. (Games and Economic Behavior, 10, pp. 122–142, 1995) study trust and reciprocity in an investment setting. They find significant amounts of trust and reciprocity and conclude that trust is a guiding behavioral instinct (a "primitive" in their terminology). We modify the way information is presented to participants and, through a questionnaire, prompt strategic reasoning. To our surprise, none of our various treatments led to a reduction in the amount invested. Previously reported experimental results to the contrary did not survive replication. Our results suggest that those by Berg, Dickhaut, and McCabe are rather robust to changes in information presentation and strategic reasoning prompts. We discuss the implications of these findings.

Keywords: experimental economics, trust, reciprocity, information presentation, prompting strategic reasoning, experimental design, experimental implementation

JEL Classification: C72; C91

1. Introduction

Trust and reciprocity, if they could be shown to exist in two-person exchanges that are not repeated and are understood to be one-shot situations, would pose a serious challenge to many economists' strongly held belief that individuals act in their own self-interest. A phenomenon closely related to trust is kindness. Game theorists and experimental economists have wrestled with experimental results of public good experiments that seemed to suggest that kindness exists. These results have led to models that could explain kindness, and modifications of experimental design that might have induced it (Smith, 1991; Davis and Holt, 1993; Andreoni, 1995a, 1995b). Experimental economists in particular have become more sensitive to such design aspects as the impact of inter-subject and subject-experimenter interaction (Hoffman et al., 1994, 1996a; see also Ong and Weiss (forthcoming)).

*Please send all correspondence to 9 Jordan Avenue, Brunswick, ME 04011, USA (if writing from the USA) or the Berlin address (if writing from elsewhere).

In a carefully designed "double-blind" experiment incorporating subject-subject and subject-experimenter anonymity, Berg, Dickhaut, and McCabe studied trust and reciprocity in the following investment setting: Room A participants had to decide how much of their \$10 show-up fee to send to an anonymous counterpart in room B. Room A subjects had been told that the amount they sent would be tripled before it reached room B. Room B subjects then had to decide how much to keep for themselves and how much to return to the investor in room A. The unique subgame perfect equilibrium for this simple sequential game requires room A participants to send zero. Note that this equilibrium is a corner solution. Since errors can only occur in one direction, confusion or curiosity of subjects would inevitably show up as trust and/or reciprocity in the same way that confusion shows up as kindness in public good experiments featuring a corner solution (Andreoni, 1995a).

Berg and her colleagues employed two treatments for their experiment. The first was a No History treatment; the second was a Social History treatment in which the experimenters furnished subjects with the results of the first treatment from previous participants. Berg et al. found that subjects deviated from the subgame perfect equilibrium of (\$0, \$0), as room A subjects invested an average of \$5.16 and received an average payback of \$4.66 in the No History treatment.[1] In the Social History treatment, room A subjects invested an average of \$5.36 and received an even higher average payback of \$6.46. These results lead the authors to conclude that trust is a primitive which Berg et al. (1995) define as a guiding behavioral instinct applied to unfamiliar situations.

However, there are at least three other possible explanations for these results: confusion and/or lack of understanding of the nature of the experimental situation on the part of subjects, lack of saliency, and framing of the information provided in the Social History treatment (Andreoni, 1995a, 1995b; Smith, 1982; Smith and Walker, 1993; Tversky and Kahneman, 1986).

Framing issues may have arisen in the History treatment because Berg et al. furnished participants in room A with a table comparing the amount room A participants sent and the amount that room B participants returned. This representation focused on absolute dollar returns instead of proportions of available funds returned, which may have mislead subjects to believe that subjects in the earlier experiments returned money "fairly" when in fact, room B participants decided on uneven allocations. That such perceptions matter has been amply demonstrated in the relevant literature (Roth, 1995). Confusion and/or lack of understanding of the nature of the experimental situation may have arisen from the relatively long instructions and a fairly complicated experimental design. We modified two aspects of the design employed by Berg et al. to better understand these two issues. To facilitate comparison, we used their instructions and payoffs, ignoring the problem of saliency.

2. Experimental design

The subjects in rooms A and B were each given 10 one-dollar bills as a show-up fee. Subjects in room B then pocketed their show-up fee and subjects in room A had to decide how much of their \$10 to send to their counterparts in room B. The amount sent (M_a) was then tripled, resulting in a total amount of $3M_a$ to be received by room B subjects. Next, the room B subjects received the tripled money and had to decide how much to keep and how much to return to their counterparts in room A. This amount is denoted by $k_b(3M_a)$.

Thus the possible strategies faced by room A subjects are

$$M_a = \{0, 1, 2, \ldots, 10\}$$

and the possible strategies faced by room B subjects are

$$k_b(3M_a)\colon \{0, 3, 6, \ldots, 30\} \rightarrow \{0, 1, 2, \ldots, 30\}$$

We employed five treatments. The first was a baseline No History treatment which replicated the BDM baseline treatment. Our second treatment replicated the BDM Social History treatment by presenting the results from our baseline treatment as Berg and her colleagues did, i.e., by simply presenting the values of previous investments and returns in a table. Henceforth, we call this the BDM presentation.[2] The third treatment also replicated the BDM Social History treatment—with our first key modification. Specifically, instead of simply presenting the values of previous investments and returns in a table (as in the BDM presentation), we furnished *in addition* to this table the graph shown in figure 1. Note that we compare $k_b(3M_a)$ to $3M_a$ in this graph rather than $k_b(3M_a)$ to M_a. This frames the results in terms of the portion that room B participants returned to A, and it clearly shows room A participants that the returns were not equitable. Henceforth, we call this the OFB presentation.

The fourth treatment was a baseline No History treatment—with our second key modification. Specifically, we included a questionnaire for the room A participants which they were to complete prior to making a decision. We designed this questionnaire for two specific purposes. First, it was to ensure that room A subjects understood the design and considered their decisions carefully before making them. Second, it was to help subjects determine how much to invest by having them ponder the consequences of their decisions before they made them, thus reducing the potential for confusion. Specifically, we asked subjects to answer the following four questions.

1. How much money do you think you will send?
2. How much money will your room B counterpart receive if you send this much?
3. How much money do you think will be returned to you?
4. How much money would you return if you were in room B?

We hypothesized that the modifications in Treatment Three (which changed the way information was presented) and Treatment Four (which prompted strategic reasoning) would lead to significant drops in both the amount sent to room B from A, and consequently the amount sent back to room A from B. As we shall see, the modifications of Treatment Three and Four had no effect.

Treatment Five and Five R employed the modifications of Treatments Three and Four simultaneously. Treatment Five R is simply a replication of Treatment Five, for reason explained below. Table 1 summarizes the design and the date of the different treatments.[3]

Table 1. Experimental design and dates of implementation.

Treatments	*N* (pairs)	Date
1. Baseline (OFB-Base)	16	4/96
2. History (BDM presentation, no ques (OFB-Hist (BDM))	16	2/98
3. History (OFB presentation), no ques (OFB-Hist (OFB))	24	2/98
4. Baseline and questionnaire (OFB-ques)	12	10/96
5. History and questionnaire (OFB-H(OFB)Q)	18	5/96
5R. Replication of OFB-H(OFB)Q	16	9/99

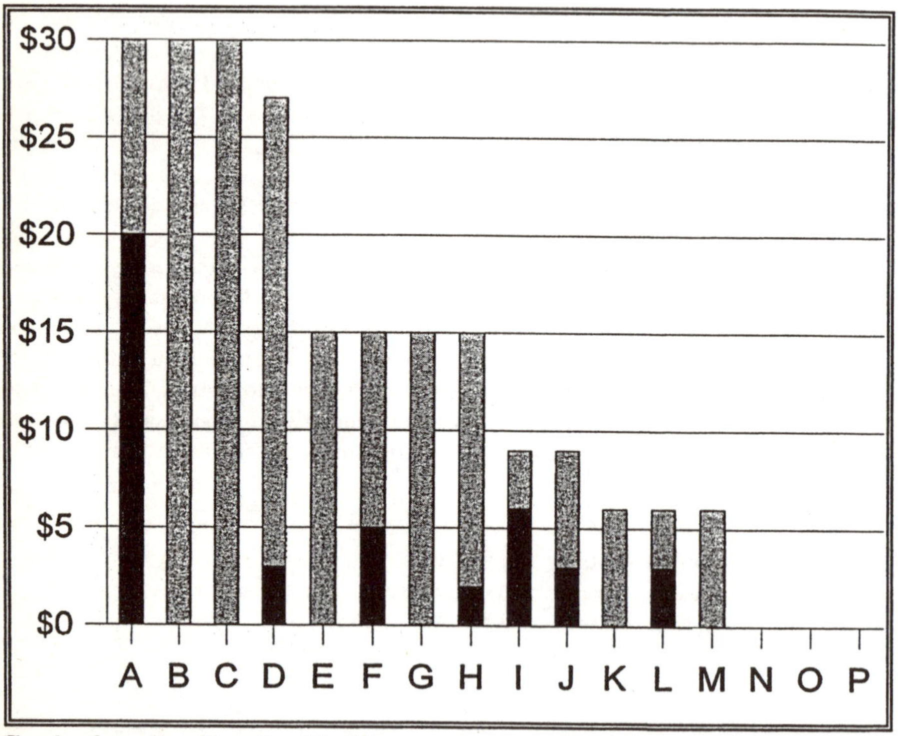

Graph of results of baseline No History treatment. This graph was used in our second treatment with the following text inserted into a box in the upper right corner: "Entire bar represents amount received by B. Shaded region represents amount returned to A. Please note: Subjects N, O and P sent $0 so the corresponding bars are not visible."

Figure 1. Baseline results.

3. Experimental implementation

The experiment was conducted in three separate rooms, A, B, and C, which were connected by a hallway. Rooms A and B contained participants, and room C contained the locked strong-boxes from which room A subjects retrieved their experimental earnings upon completion of the experiment. We began the experiment by randomly selecting a monitor in each room and then reading the instructions to the participants in room A and B. While the instructions were read to the participants, the monitors were instructed by one of the two experimenters in the hallway. After the instructions were read and the informed consent forms had been signed, the second experimenter retreated to the hallway and let the monitors take over.

The monitor ensured that the instructions were followed and silence was maintained. Once all subjects in room A had privately made their decisions regarding how much of their initial endowment to keep and how much to send, the monitor carried all the envelopes containing the investments to the experimenter in the hallway who, while the monitor watched, removed the money from the envelopes, tripled it, and recorded the amount sent. Monitor B was then summoned and was directed to distribute the envelopes randomly among room B subjects. Once all room B subjects had decided how much of the money in the envelopes to keep and how much to return, Monitor B carried the envelopes to the experimenter in the hallway. The experimenter again recorded the amount inside of the envelope, and proceeded to insert the envelopes into locked strong-boxes marked by distinct identification letters that corresponded to letters marking keys retained by room A subjects. Room A subjects then retrieved anonymously their payoffs from the appropriate strong-boxes and left the building. Once all subjects had left, the monitors were paid $10 and excused. (For details of the design, see Berg et al.) Exact instructions for all treatments are available directly from the corresponding author.

Table 1 details the number of subject pairs for each of the treatments.[4] Each subject pair had 2 participants, for a total of 204 participants. All subjects were recruited at Bowdoin College, a selective liberal arts college in Maine with a more homogeneous population (age, race) than is typical of many colleges and universities in the U.S.[5]

4. Results

Table 2 shows the mean and median contributions for all treatments. Table 3 shows tests for differences in treatment effects.

In our baseline, median investment was $4 with more than 80 percent of subjects investing (sending money to room B). As shown in Table 2, Berg et al. had a median investment of $5 with more than 90 percent of participants investing. We use a Mann-Whitney-Wilcoxon rank sum test (referred to as a Wilcoxon test in the sequel) to test for a shift in the distributions. Table 3 shows that we cannot reject that the distributions of investments are the same at the 5 percent level ($p = .31$).[6] Thus there is no significant difference in baseline results for the two studies. Figure 1 details the contributions and return amount from our study.

When Berg et al. used their social history treatment, contributions did not change much. The median remained at $5 and only 3 out of 28 subjects sent zero. They concluded that participants trust. As evidenced by Tables 2 and 3, none of our treatments led to

Table 2. Comparison of amounts sent.

	N (pairs)	Mean	Δ*	Median	Δ*
I. Berg, Dickhaut, McCabe (BDM)					
Baseline (BDM-Base)	32	5.2		5.0	
History (BDM-Hist)	28	5.4		5.0	
II. Our Results (OFB)					
1. Baseline (OFB-Base)	16	4.4		4.0	
2. History (BDM presentation), no Ques (OFB-Hist (BDM))	16	4.7	0.3	3.5	−0.5
3. History (OFB presentation), no Ques (OFB-Hist (OFB))	24	4.7	0.3	4.5	0.5
4. Baseline and Questionnaire (OFB-Ques)	12	5.8	1.4	5.5	1.5
5. History and Questionnaire (OFB-HQ)	18	2.2	−2.2	0.5	−3.5
5R. Replication of OFB-HQ	16	5.5	1.1	4.5	0.5
5 & 5R	34	3.7	−0.7	3.0	−1.0

Δ* = Magnitude and change of direction from our baseline treatment (OFB-Base).

significantly different results. This means that neither the way information is presented (BDM presentation, OFB presentation) nor strategic reasoning prompts (the questionnaire) matter statistically to our subject pool. In fact, as the results for treatment Five and its replication show, nor do these two modifications to the original design matter jointly if we pool the data.

Based on treatment Five alone, we previously reported results to the contrary. However, these results did not survive a replication whose results are reported as 5R in Tables 2 and 3. Interestingly, our treatment Five and its replication differ from each other in a statistically significant manner. Tables A5 and A5R present the data and summary statistics.

Since the History-and-Questionnaire treatment involved the use of the questionnaire, we can understand what kind of expectations about returns drove these decisions and whether expectations differed between the original treatment Five and its replication. Tables A5E and A5RE present questionnaire data and summary statistics.

The data in Tables A5E and A5RE allow one to tell a sensible story: On average, senders in both the original treatment Five and its replication expected to benefit from their investment. In fact, only 2 (out of 18 participants) in the original treatment and 3 (out of 16 participants) in the replication expected to come out worse. The 3 participants in the replication suggested they would have returned more than they expected to send.

The difference in results between the original treatment Five and its replication are clearly driven by the significantly different expectations about what would be returned. In the original treatment Five, 11 percent of participants expected back more than they sent. In the replication, 50 percent expected back more than they sent. These percentages differ significantly ($p = .016$) according to a t-test. Alternatively, participants in the original treatment Five expected that $2.56 would be returned on average; participants in the replication

Table 3. Summary of treatment results.

	BDM Baseline	BDM History	1 OFB Baseline	2 OFB Hist(BDM)	3 OFB Hist(OFB)	4 OFB BQ	5 OFB H(OFB)Q[4]	5R OFB H(OFB)Q	5 & 5R
BDM Baseline									
BDM History	same[a]								
1. OFB Baseline	same $p = .31$								
2. OFB Hist(BDM)[b]		differ $p = .54$	differ $p = .82$						
3. OFB Hist(OFB)[c]		same $p = .52$	same $p = .70$						
4. OFB BQ[d]			same $p = .44$						
5. OFB H(OFB)Q[e]		differ $p = .002$	differ $p = .04$						
5R OFB H(OFB)Q[e]		same $p = .97$	same $p = .50$				differ $p = .02$		
5 & 5R pooled		differ weakly $p = .06$	same $p = .41$		same $p = .23$	same $p = .16$			

[a] "Same" means amount sent are not significantly different for the two treatments using a Mann-Whitney Wilcoxon test for shift in distribution. "Differ" means significantly different at a 5% significance level. Differ weakly at a 10% significance level.
[b] Hist (BDM) = History (BDM presentation), no Ques.
[c] Hist (OFB) = History (OFB presentation), no Ques.
[d] OFB BQ = Baseline and Questionnaire.
[e] OFB H(OFB)Q = History (OFB presentation) and Questionnaire.

expected that \$6.875 would be returned on average. A Mann-Whitney test shows these expectations to be different at the 5% level ($p = .02$); a t-test of means shows them to be different at the 10% level ($p = .07$).

As Tables A5, A5R, A5E and A5RE demonstrate, on average expectations about amounts sent were remarkably on target (\$1.94 versus \$2.16 actually sent in the original treatment; \$5.625 versus \$5.50 actually sent in the replication). Participants' average expectations about returns, in contrast, were off target (only 35% of the average expected amount was returned in the original treatment; only 72% of the average expected amount was returned in the replication).

The question is: What accounts for the difference in expectations that we find in the original treatment Five and its replication? Given that location, set-up, instructions, and the experimenter who read them were the same, our prime suspect is the timing of the different treatments. As Table 1 shows, not only were different cohorts involved in original treatment and replication, the former had also been conducted at the end of the semester while the latter was conducted about two weeks after school started. That the majority of students participating in the replication were first-year students fresh off an orientation stressing community, honor code, etc. may have played a role. If indeed that were so, it would be disconcerting news, as experimental economists tend to work under the assumption that subject pool effects of this kind do not matter much (Ball and Cech, 1996). An informal questionnaire that we sent out to all participants in the replication after the session, and which had a response rate of 80%, indicated that the monitors had performed their assignment properly, that communication among participants did not take place, and that no other factors intervened in a systematic manner.

5. Discussion

Our re-examination of the well-known BDM results suggests that they are quite robust. Even a presentation mode whose focus is on relative rather than absolute returns together with strategic reasoning prompts do not, counter to our expectation, manage to derail them.

Do these results imply that trust is a primitive that participants use as guiding behavioral instinct in unfamiliar situations? On its face, yes. Other interpretations are possible though. First, we kept the stakes the same, i.e., we ignored the problem of saliency in our re-examination. That the level of payoffs can matter, has been amply demonstrated in the literature (e.g., Smith and Walker, 1993; Hertwig and Ortmann (forthcoming)).

Second, a significant number of participants may have unconsciously imported into the laboratory "the repeated game expectations that characterize their daily life" (Hoffman et al., 1996b, p. 300), especially in a microcosm like Bowdoin that very explicitly tries to instill a sense of community, ostracizes cheating, etc.

Third, it is questionable whether all participants understood the key characteristics of the experimental situation they were put in (e.g., Friedman, 1998; Binmore, 1999). The questionnaire data of treatments Five and its replication document that all senders expected positive albeit small returns on their investments. This expectation contradicts the results of previous experimental sessions which we presented to senders in both tabular and graphical form and which suggested that previous senders received, on average, only about 50% of their investment, and in any case, a small fraction of the tripled amount. While the questionnaire responses show that all senders understood the tripling mechanism, that suggest that a significant number may not have processed the data they were given. (More precisely, the participants in the original treatment Five apparently did, many participants in the replication did not.)

6. Conclusion

We replicated results reported in Berg et al. (1995) and investigated for this particular setting what it takes to get people to think strategically about it. Our results suggest that those by Berg and her colleagues are quite robust to changes in information presentation or/and strategic reasoning prompts, at least for the given payoffs. Our results also suggest that a significant number of participants had expectations that contradicted the available evidence. The source of those expectations is unclear.

Acknowledgments

We would like to thank two anonymous referees and John Dickhaut for their constructive comments.

Appendix

Table A1. Baseline (OFB-Base) (in dollars).

ID	Amount invested	Amount after triple	Amount returned
A	10	30	20
B	10	30	0
C	10	30	0
D	9	27	2
E	5	15	0
F	5	15	5
G	5	15	0
H	5	15	1
I	3	9	6
J	3	9	1
K	2	6	0
L	2	6	1
M	2	6	0
N	0	0	0
O	0	0	0
P	0	0	0
Totals	71.00	213.00	36.00
Mean	4.44	13.31	2.25

Table A2. History (BDM presentation), no Questionnaire (in dollars).

ID	Amount invested	Amount after triple	Amount returned
A	10	30	20
B	10	30	15
C	10	30	15
D	8	24	0
E	7	21	9
F	5	15	10
G	5	15	5
H	4	12	3
I	3	9	3
J	3	9	0
K	3	9	0
L	2	6	2
M	2	6	0
N	2	6	0
O	1	9	3
P	0	0	0
Totals	75	225	82
Mean	4.69	14.06	5.13

Table A3. History (OFB presentation), no Questionnaire (in dollars).

ID	Amount invested	Amount after triple	Amount returned
A	10	30	15
B	10	30	4
C	10	30	1
D	10	30	0
E	8	24	0
F	7	21	5
G	6	18	11
H	6	18	3
I	5	15	8
J	5	15	8
K	5	15	5
L	5	15	5
M	4	12	10

(*Continued on next page.*)

Table A3. (*Continued*).

ID	Amount invested	Amount after triple	Amount returned
N	4	12	1
O	3	9	5
P	3	9	4
Q	3	9	4
R	3	9	3
S	2	6	0
T	2	6	0
U	1	3	3
V	0	0	0
W	0	0	1
X	0	0	0
Totals	112	336	95
Mean	4.67	14.00	3.96

Table A4. Baseline and Questionnaire (in dollars).

ID	Amount invested	Amount after triple	Amount returned
A	10	30	20
B	10	30	20
C	10	30	18
D	10	30	14
E	9	27	1
F	7	21	8
G	4	12	4
H	4	12	3
I	3	9	2
J	2	6	0
K	0	0	0
L	0	0	0
Totals	69	207	90
Mean	5.75	17.25	7.20

Table A5. History and Questionnaire (OFB-H(OFB)Q) (in dollars).

ID	Amount invested	Amount after triple	Amount returned
A	10	30	5
B	10	30	0
C	5	15	0
D	3	9	7
E	3	9	0
F	3	9	0
G	2	6	2
H	2	6	1
I	1	3	1
J	0	0	0
K	0	0	0
L	0	0	0
M	0	0	0
N	0	0	0
O	0	0	0
P	0	0	0
Q	0	0	0
R	0	0	0
Totals	39.00	117.00	16.00
Mean	2.17	6.50	0.89

Table A5R. History and Questionnaire (OFB-H(OFB)Q)—replication.

ID	Amount invested	Amount after triple	Amount returned
A	10	30	20
B	10	30	15
C	10	30	10
D	10	30	10
E	10	30	0
F	10	30	0
G	8	24	16
H	5	15	1
I	4	12	6
J	4	12	0
K	3	9	2
L	3	9	0
M	1	3	0
N	0	0	0
O	0	0	0
P	0	0	0
Totals	88	264	80
Mean	5.50	16.50	5.00

Table A5E. Questionnaire data.

Send[a]		Returned[b]	Would[c]
10	<	20	20
10	<	15	15
5	=	5	5
3	=	3	4
3	>	1	3
2	>	0	0
1	=	1	1
1	=	1	1
0	=	0	0
0	=	0	0
0	=	0	0
0	=	0	0
0	=	0	0
0	=	0	0
0	=	0	0
0	=	0	0
0	=	0	0
0	=	0	0
1.94	<	2.56	<2.72

Note: Last line shows the mean for that column.
[a]"Send" = How much money do you think you will send?
[b]"Returned" = How much money do you think will be returned to you?
[c]"Would" = How much money would you return if you were in room B?

The following text consolidates the instructions for all 5 treatments reported in Ortmann, Fitzgerald, & Boeing, "Trust, Reciprocity, and Social History: A Reexamination" (for details please see Table 1: Experimental Design and Dates of Implementation.) The text below was used for all treatments; variations in the instructions for each treatment are shown in brackets {...} and denoted

- **"B" for Baseline treatment 1**
- **"H-BDM" for History (BDM presentation), no questionnaire treatment 2**
- **"H-OFB" for History (OFB presentation), no questionnaire treatment 3**
- **"Q" for Baseline and Questionnaire treatment 4**
- **"HQ" for History and Questionnaire treatments 5 and 5R**

Boldfaced text is commentary.

Table A5RE. Questionnaire data.

Send[a]		Returned[b]	Would[c]
10	<	20	30
10	<	20	20
10	<	15	15
10	<	15	15
10	<	15	15
10	>	0	15
8	>	4	10
5	>	0	10
4	<	6	2
3	<	4	4
3	<	4	0
3	=	3	4
3	=	3	3
1	=	1	0
0	=	0	0
0	=	0	0
5.625	<	6.875	<8.9375

Note: Last line shows the mean for that column.
[a]"Send" = How much money do you think you will send?
[b]"Returned" = How much money do you think will be returned to you?
[c]"Would" = How much money would you return if you were in room B?

Notes

1. It might have been more relevant to participants to report the average payback for those who invested. We followed the precedent set by Berg et al.
2. We used the results of *our* No History treatment to construct Social History. Arguably, one could consider this a different treatment. However, using one's own subjects was part of the original design. Furthermore, the results of our and BDM baseline treatments are not statistically different.
3. Note that the order in which the different sessions were conducted differs from the order in which they are presented in this paper.
4. Treatments were conducted in sessions of about 8 subject pairs each. Originally, we conducted two sessions for each of these treatments. However, the results of the two treatment Three sessions were divergent enough to warrant another session.
5. All communication during the recruitment process was through email. This recruitment process differs from the standard one (flyers, recruiting in selected classes.) Interestingly enough, the recruitment mode seems to affect the subject pool. In our experience, the traditional mode of recruitment led with some regularity to subject pools that had more male than female students. The recruitment process we have started to use in

this and other experiments seems to overcome that problem. For the experimental sessions reported here our participant pool was exactly 50% male.

6. We also examined the percentage of the initial investment that was returned although our change in instructions was not expected to affect returns. As explained in Berg et al., we use percent returned because it does not depend directly on the amount of dollars sent. The mean percent returned for those who received a positive amount in Berg et al. is 30% in the No History experiment, whereas we obtain 16%. The difference in distributions is moderate, although not significant at conventional levels based on a Wilcoxon test ($p = .12$).

References

Andreoni, J. (1995a). "Cooperation in Public Goods Experiments: Kindness or Confusion?" *American Economic Review*. 85(4), 891–904.

Andreoni, J. (1995b). "Warm-Glow Versus Cold-Prickle: The Effects of Positive and Negative Framing on Cooperation in Experiments." *Quarterly Journal of Economics*. 90(1), 1–21.

Ball, S.B. and Cech, P.A. (1996). "Subject Pool Choice and Treatment Effects in Economic Laboratory Research." *Research in Experimental Economics*. 6, 239–292.

Berg, J., Dickhaut, J., and McCabe, K. (1995). "Trust, Reciprocity, and Social History." *Games and Economic Behavior*. 10, 122–142.

Binmore, K. (1999). "Why Experiment in Economics?" *Economic Journal*. 109, 16–24.

Davis, D.D. and Holt, C.A. (1993). *Experimental Economics*. Princeton, NJ: Princeton University Press.

Friedman, D. (1998). "Monty Hall's Three Doors: Construction and Deconstruction of a Choice Anomaly." *American Economic Review*. 88(4), 933–946.

Hertwig, R. and Ortmann, A. (forthcoming). "Experimental Practices in Economics: A Challenge for Psychologists?" *Behavioral and Brain Sciences*.

Hoffman, E., McCabe, K., Shachat, K., and Smith, V. (1994). "Preferences, Property Rights, and Anonymity in Bargaining Games." *Games and Economic Behavior*. 7, 346–380.

Hoffman, E., McCabe, K., and Smith, V. (1996a). "Social Distance and Other-Regarding Behavior in Dictator Games." *American Economic Review*. 86(3), 653–660.

Hoffman, E., McCabe, K., and Smith, V. (1996b). "On Expectations and the Monetary Stakes in Ultimatum Games." *International Journal of Game Theory*. 25, 289–301.

Ong, A.D. and Weiss, D.J. (forthcoming). "The Impact of Anonymity on Responses to "Sensitive" Questions." *Journal of Applied Psychology*.

Roth, A.E. (1995). "Bargaining Experiments." In J.H. Kagel and A.E. Roth (eds.), *Handbook of Experimental Economics*, Princeton: Princeton University Press, pp. 253–348.

Smith, V. (1982). "Microeconomic Systems as an Experimental Science." *American Economic Review*. 72(5), 923–955.

Smith, V. (1991). "Rational Choice: The Contrast Between Economics and Psychology." *Journal of Political Economy*. 99(4), 977–997.

Smith, V. and Walker, J. (1993). "Monetary Rewards and Decision Cost in Experimental Economics." *Economic Inquiry*. 31(2), 245–261.

Tversky, A. and Kahneman, D. (1986). "Rational Choice and the Framing of Decisions." *Journal of Business*. 59, S251–S278.

Instructions (for room A)

You have been asked to participate in an economics experiment. The instructions you are about to read are self-explanatory. We will not answer any questions during this experiment. If you have any questions, you should read back through these instructions. Now that the experiment has begun, we ask that you do not talk, at all, during this experiment.

In this experiment each of you will be randomly paired with a different person who is in another room. You will not be told who these people are either during or after the experiment. This is room A, other participants are in room B. You will notice that there are other people in the same room with you who are also participating in this experiment. You will not be paired with any of these people. A person in room A, called monitor A, and a person in room B, called monitor B, will be chosen for today's experiment. The monitors will be in charge of the envelopes as explained below. In addition the monitors will verify that the instructions have been followed as they appear here. {**For Q add:** Participants in room A have also been supplied with a questionnaire and a pen. Please check now that you have these items. If you are missing anything, please let the experimenter know now. When you make your decision, we also ask that you complete the questionnaire.}

Each person in room A and each person in room B will been given $10 as a show-up fee for this experiment. Persons in room A will have the opportunity to send in an envelope, some, all, or none of their show-up fee to a person in room B. Each dollar sent to room B will be tripled before it reaches room B. For example, if you send an envelope which contains $2, the envelope will contain $6 when it reaches room B. If you send an envelope which contains $9, the envelope will contain $27 when it reaches room B. The person in room B will then decide how much money to send back to the person in room A and how much money to keep. (Recall that you are in room A.)

{**For H-OFB add:** Participants in room A (you) have also been supplied with a chart. (The chart is attached to these instructions.) Please check that you have these items now. If you are missing anything, please let the experimenter know now. The chart summarizes the results of previous experiments at Bowdoin. Please take a minute now to review the chart.}

{**For H-BDM add:** Participants in room A (you) have also been supplied with a chart and a bar-graph. (Chart and bar-graph are attached to these instructions.) Please check that you have these items now. If you are missing anything, please let the experimenter know now. The chart summarizes the results of previous experiments at Bowdoin, and the bar-graph below it illustrates these results. The entire bars (dark and white regions) on the bar-graph represent the amounts received by participants (A, B, . . . , P) in room B. The dark areas represent the portions of those amounts that participants in room B returned to their counterparts in room A. Please take a minute now to review bar-graph and chart.}

{**For HQ add:** Participants in room A (you) have also been supplied with a chart, a bar-graph, a questionnaire, and a pen. Please check that you have all four items. If you are missing anything, please let the experimenter know now. The chart summarizes the results of previous experiments at Bowdoin, and the bar-graph below it illustrates these results. The entire bars (dark and white regions) on the bar-graph represent the amounts received by participants (A, B, . . . , P) in room B. The dark areas represent the portions of those amounts that participants in room B returned to their counterparts in room A. Please take a minute now to review bar-graph and chart.}

{**For H-OFB, H-BDM, and HQ add:** You will have a chance to review this information after the instructions have been read, and again while you make your decision as to how much of your show-up fee to send.}

{**For HQ add:** When you make your decision, we also ask that you complete the questionnaire.}

[Please note: The bar-graph mentioned in the preceding paragraphs corresponded to figure 1; the chart presented the same information in the format documented in Berg et al. (1995)]

The remainder of these instructions will explain exactly how this experiment is run. This experiment is structured so that no one, including the experimenters and monitors, will know the personal decision of people in either room A or room B. Since your decision is private we ask that you do not tell anyone your decision either during, or after, the experiment.

The experiment is conducted as follows: Eight large unmarked envelopes have been placed in a box in a room A. Each of these envelopes contains 10 one-dollar bills (the show-up fee for a person in room A), a smaller inner envelope, and a key in a sealed envelope marked KEY. The inner envelope and key are marked with the same letter of the alphabet. The monitor, in room A, will point to one person at a time, and hand that person a large and unmarked envelope from the box. The person who was pointed to will then go to a seat with a box on top of the writing surface, and privately open the unmarked envelope inside the box. Only the person who opened the envelope will know which letter of the alphabet was in the envelope. Do not open the envelope marked KEY until you are told to do so. The monitor will then point to the next person, and continue in this fashion until everyone has made their decisions.

{**B:** Each person in room A must decide how many dollar bills to put in the inner envelope.} {**H-BDM:** Each person in room A should review the chart provided with these instructions. Then each person in room A must decide how many dollar bills to put in the inner envelope.} {**H-OFB:** Each person in room A should review the chart and the bar-graph provided with these instructions. Then each person in room A must decide how many dollar bills to put in the inner envelope.} {**Q:** Each person in room A must fill out the questionnaire at that point and decide how many dollars bills to put in the inner envelope together with the completed questionnaire.} {**HQ:** Each person in room A should review the chart and the bar-graph provided with these instructions. Persons in room A should then complete the questionnaire with their pen and fold it when done. Then each person in room A must decide how many dollar bills to put in the inner envelope.} The person then pockets the remaining dollar bills and the envelope marked KEY. Examples: (1) Put $9 in the inner envelope, and pocket $1 as well as the envelope marked KEY. (2) Put $2 in the inner envelope, and pocket $8 as well as the envelope marked KEY. These are examples only, the actual decision is up to each person.

Once a person in room A has made a decision they should put the inner envelope back inside the large unmarked envelope, and return the unmarked envelope to the box marked "return envelopes". Persons in room A should make sure that they have kept the envelope marked KEY as they will use this later in the experiment. Notice that each envelope returned will look exactly the same.

After all the envelopes have been put in the return box, monitor A will transport the box to a recorder who is in the hallway. With monitor A observing, the recorder will then, one at a time, take the inner envelope out of the unmarked envelope and record on a blank sheet of paper, the letter on the envelope, and the amount of money in the envelope. {**For Q and HQ add:** The recorder will retain the questionnaire.} While monitor A is observing, the recorder will then triple the amount of money in the inner envelope, and place the inner envelope back into the unmarked outer envelope. At this point, the recorder will signal the monitor from room B to come to the recorder's desk. Once monitor B has arrived, monitor A will be asked to return to room A.

Monitor B will then carry the box of envelopes to room B. Monitor B will then point to one person at a time, and hand that person an unmarked envelope from the box. The person who was called will then go to a seat with a box on top of the writing surface and then privately open the outer envelope inside the box. The monitor will then point to the next person. Each person in room B must decide how many dollar bills to leave in the inner envelope and how much to keep. The person then pockets the remaining dollar bills. The inner envelope should then be placed in the unmarked outer envelope and the outer envelope should then be placed in the box marked "return envelopes". The person in room B will then be asked to leave since the experiment is over for that person. After all the envelopes in room B are returned, monitor B will transport the box to the recorder in the hallway. The recorder will then, one at a time, open the inner envelope and record on a blank sheet of paper, the letter on the envelope, and the amount of money in the inner envelope. The recorder will then signal monitor A to come to the recorder's desk. Once monitor A has arrived monitor B will return to room B.

When monitor A arrives the monitor and recorder will carry the box of envelopes to room C adjacent to room A. Room C contains strong-boxes with identifying letters. The letters correspond to the letters on the inner envelopes. While the recorder observes, monitor A will place each inner envelope in the box with the corresponding letter. All the strong-boxes will then be locked. The recorder will then go back to his desk in the hallway and monitor A will go to room A.

Monitor A will then point to one person at a time from room A. That person will then enter room C alone and open the envelope marked KEY. Inside this envelope is a lettered key which will open the strong-box with the corresponding letter. The inner envelope in the strong-box is the same one the person in room A started with. The person from room A will then go to the appropriate strong-box, open it, take out the envelope, and remove the money. The person will then return the envelope to the strong-box and lock the strong-box. The person will then return the key to the envelope marked KEY and drop the envelope in the box marked "keydrop" just outside the door in the hallway. When you are called to go to room C you should take all your belongings since you will be asked to leave the building when you are done. {**For H-OFB add:** Please leave this copy of the instructions and the chart in room A.} {**For H-OFB add:** Please leave this copy of the instructions, the chart and the bar-graph in room A.} {**For HQ add:** Please leave this copy of the instructions, the chart, the bar-graph, and the pen in room A.}

When everyone in room A has left, the experiment is over, and the monitors will be paid for their participation.

Any questions?

[Collect informed consent form]

Instructions (for room B)

You have been asked to participate in an economics experiment. The instructions you are about to read are self-explanatory. We will not answer any questions during this experiment. If you have any questions, you should read back through these instructions. Now that the experiment has begun, we ask that you do not talk, at all, during this experiment.

In this experiment each of you will be randomly paired with a different person who is in another room. You will not be told who these people are either during or after the experiment. This is room B, other participants are in room A. You will notice that there are other people in the same room with you who are also participating in this experiment. You will not be paired with any of these people. A person in room A, called monitor A, and a person in room B, called monitor B, will be chosen for today's experiment. The monitors will be in charge of the envelopes as explained below. In addition the monitors will verify that the instructions have been followed as they appear here.

Each person in room A and each person in room B has been given $10 as a show-up fee for this experiment. Persons in room A will have the opportunity to send in an envelope, some, all, or none of their show-up fee to a person in room B. Each dollar sent to room B will be tripled before it reaches room B. For example, if you send an envelope which contains $2, the envelope will contain $6 when it reaches room B. If you send an envelope which contains $9, the envelope will contain $27 when it reaches room B. The person in room B will then decide how much money to send back to the person in room A and how much money to keep. (Recall that you are in room B.)

The remainder of these instructions will explain exactly how this experiment is run. This experiment is structured so that no one, including the experimenters and monitors, will know the personal decision of people in either room A or room B. Since your decision is private we ask that you do not tell anyone your decision either during, or after, the experiment.

The experiment is conducted as follows: Eight large unmarked envelopes have been placed in a box in a room A. Each of these envelopes contains 10 one-dollar bills (the show-up fee for a person in room A), a smaller inner envelope, and a key in a sealed envelope marked KEY. The inner envelope and key are marked with the same letter of the alphabet. The monitor, in room A, will point to one person at a time, and hand that person a large and unmarked envelope from the box. The person who was pointed to will then go to a seat with a box on top of the writing surface, and privately open the unmarked envelope inside the box. Only the person who opened the envelope will know which letter of the alphabet was in the envelope. The monitor will then point to the next person, and continue in this fashion until everyone has made their decisions.

Each person in room A must decide how many dollar bills to put in the inner envelope. The person then pockets the remaining dollar bills and the envelope marked KEY. Examples:

(1) Put $9 in the inner envelope, and pocket $1 as well as the envelope marked KEY.
(2) Put $2 in the inner envelope, and pocket $8 as well as the envelope marked KEY. These are examples only, the actual decision is up to each person.

Once a person in room A has made a decision they will put the inner envelope back inside the large unmarked envelope, and return the unmarked envelope to the box marked "return envelopes". Each envelope returned will look exactly the same.

After all the envelopes have been put in the return, box monitor A will transport the box to a recorder who is in the hallway. With monitor A observing, the recorder will then, one at a time, take the inner envelope out of the unmarked envelope and record on a blank sheet of paper, the letter on the envelope, and the amount of money in the envelope. While monitor A is observing, the recorder will then triple the amount of money in the inner envelope, and place the inner envelope back into the unmarked outer envelope. At this point, the recorder will signal the monitor from room B to come to the recorder's desk. Once monitor B has arrived, monitor A will be asked to return to room A.

Monitor B will then carry the box of envelopes to room B. Monitor B will then point to one person at a time, and hand that person an unmarked envelope from the box. The person who was called will then go to a seat with a box on top of the writing surface and then privately open the outer envelope inside the box. The monitor will then point to the next person. Each person in room B must decide how many dollar bills to leave in the inner envelope and how much to keep. The inner envelope should then be placed in the unmarked outer envelope and the outer envelope should then be placed in the box marked "return envelopes". The person in room B will then be asked to leave since the experiment is over for that person. When you leave we ask that you leave the building directly. After all the envelopes in room B are returned, monitor B will transport the box to the recorder in the hallway. The recorder will then, one at a time, open the inner envelope and record on a blank sheet of paper, the letter on the envelope, and the amount of money in the inner envelope. The recorder will then signal monitor A to come to the recorder's desk. Once monitor A has arrived, monitor B will return to room B.

When monitor A arrives the monitor and recorder will carry the box of envelopes to room C adjacent to room A. Room C contains strong-boxes with identifying letters. The letters correspond to the letters on the inner envelopes. While the recorder observes, monitor A will place each inner envelope in the box with the corresponding letter. All the strong-boxes will then be locked. The recorder will then go back to his desk in the hallway and monitor A will go to room A.

Monitor A will then point to one person at a time from room A. That person will then enter room C alone and open the envelope marked KEY. Inside this envelope is a lettered key which will open the strong-box with the corresponding letter. The inner envelope in the strong-box is the same one the person in room A started with. The person from room A will then go to the appropriate strong-box, open it, take out the envelope, and remove the money. The person will then return the envelope to the strong-box and lock the strong-box. The person will then return the key to the envelope marked KEY and drop the envelope in the box just outside the door in the hallway.

When everyone in room A has left, the experiment is over, and the monitors will be paid for their participation.

Any questions?

[Collect informed consent form]

[22]

Fairness as a Constraint on Profit Seeking: Entitlements in the Market

By DANIEL KAHNEMAN, JACK L. KNETSCH, AND RICHARD THALER*

Community standards of fairness for the setting of prices and wages were elicited by telephone surveys. In customer or labor markets, it is acceptable for a firm to raise prices (or cut wages) when profits are threatened and to maintain prices when costs diminish. It is unfair to exploit shifts in demand by raising prices or cutting wages. Several market anomalies are explained by assuming that these standards of fairness influence the behavior of firms.

Just as it is often useful to neglect friction in elementary mechanics, there may be good reasons to assume that firms seek their maximal profit as if they were subject only to legal and budgetary constraints. However, the patterns of sluggish or incomplete adjustment often observed in markets suggest that some additional constraints are operative. Several authors have used a notion of fairness to explain why many employers do not cut wages during periods of high unemployment (George Akerlof, 1979; Robert Solow, 1980). Arthur Okun (1981) went further in arguing that fairness also alters the outcomes in what he called customer markets—characterized by suppliers who are perceived as making their own pricing decisions, have some monopoly power (if only because search is costly), and often have repeat business with their clientele. Like labor markets, customer markets also sometimes fail to clear:

> ...firms in the sports and entertainment industries offer their customers tickets at standard prices for events that clearly generate excess demand. Popular new models of automobiles may have waiting lists that extend for months. Similarly, manufacturers in a number of industries operate with backlogs in booms and allocate shipments when they obviously could raise prices and reduce the queue. [p. 170]

Okun explained these observations by the hostile reaction of customers to price increases that are not justified by increased costs and are therefore viewed as unfair. He also noted that customers appear willing to accept "fair" price increases even when demand is slack, and commented that "...in practice, observed pricing behavior is a vast distance from do it yourself auctioneering" (p. 170).

The argument used by these authors to account for apparent deviations from the simple model of a profit-maximizing firm is that fair behavior is instrumental to the maximization of long-run profits. In Okun's model, customers who suspect that a supplier treats them unfairly are likely to start searching for alternatives; Akerlof (1980, 1982) suggested that firms invest in their reputation to produce goodwill among their customers and high morale among their employees; and Arrow argued that trusted suppliers may be able to operate in markets that are otherwise devastated by the lemons problem (Akerlof, 1970; Kenneth Arrow, 1973). In these approaches, the rules of fairness define the terms of an enforceable im-

*Kahneman: Department of Psychology, University of California, Berkeley, CA 94720; Knetsch, Department of Economics, Simon Fraser University; Thaler: Johnson School of Management, Cornell University. The research was carried out when Kahneman was at the University of British Columbia. It was supported by the Department of Fisheries and Oceans Canada. Kahneman and Thaler were also supported by the U.S. Office of Naval Research and the Alfred P. Sloan Foundation, respectively. Conversations with J. Brander, R. Frank and A. Tversky were very helpful.

plicit contract: Firms that behave unfairly are punished in the long run. A more radical assumption is that some firms apply fair policies even in situations that preclude enforcement—this is the view of the lay public, as shown in a later section of this paper.

If considerations of fairness do restrict the actions of profit-seeking firms, economic models might be enriched by a more detailed analysis of this constraint. Specifically, the rules that govern public perceptions of fairness should identify situations in which some firms will fail to exploit apparent opportunities to increase their profits. Near-rationality theory (Akerlof and Janet Yellen, 1985) suggests that such failures to maximize by a significant number of firms in a market can have large aggregate effects even in the presence of other firms that seek to take advantage of all available opportunities. Rules of fairness can also have significant economic effects through the medium of regulation. Indeed, Edward Zajac (forthcoming) has inferred general rules of fairness from public reactions to the behavior of regulated utilities.

The present research uses household surveys of public opinions to infer rules of fairness for conduct in the market from evaluations of particular actions by hypothetical firms.[1] The study has two main objectives: (*i*) to identify community standards of fairness that apply to price, rent, and wage setting by firms in varied circumstances; and (*ii*) to consider the possible implications of the rules of fairness for market outcomes.

The study was concerned with scenarios in which a *firm* (merchant, landlord, or employer) makes a pricing or wage-setting decision that affects the outcomes of one or more *transactors* (customers, tenants, or employees). The scenario was read to the participants, who evaluated the fairness of the action as in the following example:

Question 1. A hardware store has been selling snow shovels for $15. The morning after a large snowstorm, the store raises the price to $20. Please rate this action as:

Completely Fair Acceptable
Unfair Very Unfair

The two favorable and the two unfavorable categories are grouped in this report to indicate the proportions of respondents who judged the action acceptable or unfair. In this example, 82 percent of respondents ($N = 107$) considered it unfair for the hardware store to take advantage of the short-run increase in demand associated with a blizzard.

The approach of the present study is purely descriptive. Normative status is not claimed for the generalizations that are described as "rules of fairness," and the phrase "it is fair" is simply an abbreviation for "a substantial majority of the population studied thinks it fair." The paper considers in turn three determinants of fairness judgments: the reference transaction, the outcomes to the firm and to the transactors, and the occasion for the action of the firm. The final sections are concerned with the enforcement of fairness and with economic phenomena that the rules of fairness may help explain.

I. Reference Transactions

A central concept in analyzing the fairness of actions in which a firm sets the terms of future exchanges is the *reference transaction*, a relevant precedent that is characterized by a reference price or wage, and by a positive reference profit to the firm. The treatment is restricted to cases in which the fairness of the reference transaction is not itself in question.

The main findings of this research can be summarized by a principle of *dual entitlement*, which governs community standards of fairness: Transactors have an entitlement to the terms of the reference transaction and firms are entitled to their reference profit. A firm is not allowed to increase its profits by

[1] Data were collected between May 1984 and July 1985 in telephone surveys of randomly selected residents of two Canadian metropolitan areas: Toronto and Vancouver. Equal numbers of adult female and male respondents were interviewed for about ten minutes in calls made during evening hours. No more than five questions concerned with fairness were included in any interview, and contrasting questions that were to be compared were never put to the same respondents.

arbitrarily violating the entitlement of its transactors to the reference price, rent or wage (Max Bazerman, 1985; Zajac, forthcoming). When the reference profit of a firm is threatened, however, it may set new terms that protect its profit at transactors' expense.

Market prices, posted prices, and the history of previous transactions between a firm and a transactor can serve as reference transactions. When there is a history of similar transactions between firm and transactor, the most recent price, wage, or rent will be adopted for reference unless the terms of the previous transaction were explicitly temporary. For new transactions, prevailing competitive prices or wages provide the natural reference. The role of prior history in wage transactions is illustrated by the following pair of questions:

Question 2A. A small photocopying shop has one employee who has worked in the shop for six months and earns \$9 per hour. Business continues to be satisfactory, but a factory in the area has closed and unemployment has increased. Other small shops have now hired reliable workers at \$7 an hour to perform jobs similar to those done by the photocopy shop employee. The owner of the photocopying shop reduces the employee's wage to \$7.

($N = 98$) Acceptable 17% Unfair 83%

Question 2B. A small photocopying shop has one employee...[as in Question 2A]...The current employee leaves, and the owner decides to pay a replacement \$7 an hour.

($N = 125$) Acceptable 73% Unfair 27%

The current wage of an employee serves as reference for evaluating the fairness of future adjustments of that employee's wage—but not necessarily for evaluating the fairness of the wage paid to a replacement. The new worker does not have an entitlement to the former worker's wage rate. As the following question shows, the entitlement of an employee to a reference wage does not carry over to a new labor transaction, even with the same employer:

Question 3. A house painter employs two assistants and pays them \$9 per hour. The painter decides to quit house painting and go into the business of providing landscape services, where the going wage is lower. He reduces the workers' wages to \$7 per hour for the landscaping work.

($N = 94$) Acceptable 63% Unfair 37%

Note that the same reduction in wages that is judged acceptable by most respondents in Question 3 was judged unfair by 83 percent of the respondents to Question 2A.

Parallel results were obtained in questions concerning residential tenancy. As in the case of wages, many respondents apply different rules to a new tenant and to a tenant renewing a lease. A rent increase that is judged fair for a new lease may be unfair for a renewal. However, the circumstances under which the rules of fairness require landlords to bear such opportunity costs are narrowly defined. Few respondents consider it unfair for the landlord to sell the accommodation to another landlord who intends to raise the rents of sitting tenants, and even fewer believe that a landlord should make price concessions in selling an accommodation to its occupant.

The relevant reference transaction is not always unique. Disagreements about fairness are most likely to arise when alternative reference transactions can be invoked, each leading to a different assessment of the participants' outcomes. Agreement on general principles of fairness therefore does not preclude disputes about specific cases (see also Zajac, forthcoming). When competitors change their price or wage, for example, the current terms set by the firm and the new terms set by competitors define alternative reference transactions. Some people will consider it unfair for a firm not to raise its wages when competitors are increasing theirs. On the other hand, price increases that are not justified by increasing costs are judged less objectionable when competitors have led the way.

It should perhaps be emphasized that the reference transaction provides a basis for fairness judgments because it is normal, not necessarily because it is just. Psychological studies of adaptation suggest that any stable state of affairs tends to become accepted eventually, at least in the sense that alternatives to it no longer readily come to mind. Terms of exchange that are initially seen as unfair may in time acquire the status of a reference transaction. Thus, the gap between the behavior that people consider fair and the behavior that they expect in the marketplace tends to be rather small. This was confirmed in several scenarios, where different samples of respondents answered the two questions: "What does fairness require?" and "What do you think the firm would do?" The similarity of the answers suggests that people expect a substantial level of conformity to community standards—and also that they adapt their views of fairness to the norms of actual behavior.

II. The Coding of Outcomes

It is a commonplace that the fairness of an action depends in large part on the signs of its outcomes for the agent and for the individuals affected by it. The cardinal rule of fair behavior is surely that one person should not achieve a gain by simply imposing an equivalent loss on another.

In the present framework, the outcomes to the firm and to its transactors are defined as gains and losses in relation to the reference transaction. The transactor's outcome is simply the difference between the new terms set by the firm and the reference price, rent, or wage. The outcome to the firm is evaluated with respect to the reference profit, and incorporates the effect of exogenous shocks (for example, changes in wholesale prices) which alter the profit of the firm on a transaction at the reference terms. According to these definitions, the outcomes in the snow shovel example of Question 1 were a $5 gain to the firm and a $5 loss to the representative customer. However, had the same price increase been induced by a $5 increase in the wholesale price of snow shovels, the outcome to the firm would have been nil.

The issue of how to define relevant outcomes takes a similar form in studies of individuals' preferences and of judgments of fairness. In both domains, a descriptive analysis of people's judgments and choices involves rules of *naive accounting* that diverge in major ways from the standards of rationality assumed in economic analysis. People commonly evaluate outcomes as gains or losses relative to a neutral reference point rather than as endstates (Kahneman and Amos Tversky, 1979). In violation of normative standards, they are more sensitive to out-of-pocket costs than to opportunity costs and more sensitive to losses than to foregone gains (Kahneman and Tversky, 1984; Thaler, 1980). These characteristics of evaluation make preferences vulnerable to framing effects, in which inconsequential variations in the presentation of a choice problem affect the decision (Tversky and Kahneman, 1986).

The entitlements of firms and transactors induce similar asymmetries between gains and losses in fairness judgments. An action by a firm is more likely to be judged unfair if it causes a loss to its transactor than if it cancels or reduces a possible gain. Similarly, an action by a firm is more likely to be judged unfair if it achieves a gain to the firm than if it averts a loss. Different standards are applied to actions that are elicited by the threat of losses or by an opportunity to improve on a positive reference profit —a psychologically important distinction which is usually not represented in economic analysis.

Judgments of fairness are also susceptible to framing effects, in which form appears to overwhelm substance. One of these framing effects will be recognized as the money illusion, illustrated in the following questions:

Question 4A. A company is making a small profit. It is located in a community experiencing a recession with substantial unemployment but no inflation. There are many workers anxious to work at the company. The company decides to decrease wages and salaries 7% this year.

($N = 125$) Acceptable 38% Unfair 62%

Question 4B. ...with substantial unemployment and inflation of 12%...The company decides to increase salaries only 5% this year.

($N = 129$) Acceptable 78% Unfair 22%

Although the real income change is approximately the same in the two problems, the judgments of fairness are strikingly different. A wage cut is coded as a loss and consequently judged unfair. A nominal raise which does not compensate for inflation is more acceptable because it is coded as a gain to the employee, relative to the reference wage.

Analyses of individual choice suggest that the disutility associated with an outcome that is coded as a loss may be greater than the disutility of the same objective outcome when coded as the elimination of a gain. Thus, there may be less resistance to the cancellation of a discount or bonus than to an equivalent price increase or wage cut. As illustrated by the following questions, the same rule applies as well to fairness judgments.

Question 5A. A shortage has developed for a popular model of automobile, and customers must now wait two months for delivery. A dealer has been selling these cars at list price. Now the dealer prices this model at $200 above list price.

($N=130$) Acceptable 29% Unfair 71%

Question 5B. ...A dealer has been selling these cars at a discount of $200 below list price. Now the dealer sells this model only at list price.

($N=123$) Acceptable 58% Unfair 42%

The significant difference between the responses to Questions 5A and 5B (*chi-squared* = 20.91) indicates that the $200 price increase is not treated identically in the two problems. In Question 5A the increase is clearly coded as a loss relative to the unambiguous reference provided by the list price. In Question 5B the reference price is ambiguous, and the change can be coded either as a loss (if the reference price is the discounted price), or as the elimination of a gain (if the reference price is the list price). The relative leniency of judgments in Question 5B suggests that at least some respondents adopted the latter frame. The following questions illustrate the same effect in the case of wages:

Question 6A. A small company employs several people. The workers' incomes have been about average for the community. In recent months, business for the company has not increased as it had before. The owners reduce the workers' wages by 10 percent for the next year.

($N=100$) Acceptable 39% Unfair 61%

Question 6B. A small company employs several people. The workers have been receiving a 10 percent annual bonus each year and their total incomes have been about average for the community. In recent months, business for the company has not increased as it had before. The owners eliminate the workers' bonus for the year.

($N=98$) Acceptable 80% Unfair 20%

III. Occasions for Pricing Decisions

This section examines the rules of fairness that apply to three classes of occasions in which a firm may reconsider the terms that it sets for exchanges. (*i*) *Profit reductions*, for example, by rising costs or decreased demand for the product of the firm. (*ii*) *Profit increases*, for example, by efficiency gains or reduced costs. (*iii*) *Increases in market power*, for example, by temporary excess demand for goods, accommodations or jobs.

A. *Protecting Profit*

A random sample of adults contains many more customers, tenants, and employees than merchants, landlords, or employers. Nevertheless, most participants in the surveys clearly consider the firm to be entitled to its reference profit: They would allow a firm threatened by a reduction of its profit below a positive reference level to pass on the entire loss to its transactors, without compromising or sharing the pain. By large majorities, respondents endorsed the fairness of passing on increases in wholesale costs, in operating costs, and in the costs associated with a rental accommodation. The following two questions illustrate the range of situations to which this rule was found to apply.

Question 7. Suppose that, due to a transportation mixup, there is a local shortage of lettuce and the wholesale price has increased. A local grocer has bought the usual quantity of lettuce at a price that is 30 cents per head higher than normal. The grocer raises the price of lettuce to customers by 30 cents per head.

($N=101$) Acceptable 79% Unfair 21%

Question 8. A landlord owns and rents out a single small house to a tenant who is living on a fixed income. A higher rent would mean the tenant would have to move. Other small rental houses are available. The landlord's costs have increased substantially over the past year and the landlord raises the rent to cover the cost increases when the tenant's lease is due for renewal.

($N=151$) Acceptable 75% Unfair 25%

The answers to the last question, in particular, indicate that it is acceptable for firms to protect themselves from losses even when their transactors suffer substantial inconvenience as a result. The rules of fairness that yield such judgments do not correspond to norms of charity and do not reflect distributional concerns.

The attitude that permits the firm to protect a positive reference profit at the transactors' expense applies to employers as well as to merchants and landlords. When the profit of the employer in the labor transaction falls below the reference level, reductions of even nominal wages become acceptable. The next questions illustrate the strong effect of this variable.

Question 9A. A small company employs several workers and has been paying them average wages. There is severe unemployment in the area and the company could easily replace its current employees with good workers at a lower wage. The company has been making money. The owners reduce the current workers' wages by 5 percent.

($N=195$) Acceptable 23% Unfair 77%

Question 9B. ...The company has been losing money. The owners reduce the current workers' wages by 5 percent.

($N=195$) Acceptable 68% Unfair 32%

The effect of firm profitability was studied in greater detail in the context of a scenario in which Mr. Green, a gardener who employs two workers at $7 an hour, learns that other equally competent workers are willing to do the same work for $6 an hour. Some respondents were told that Mr. Green's business was doing well, others were told that it was doing poorly. The questions, presented in open format, required respondents to state "what is fair for Mr. Green to do in this situation," or "what is your best guess about what Mr. Green would do... ." The information about the current state of the business had a large effect. Replacing the employees or bargaining with them to achieve a lower wage was mentioned as fair by 67 percent of respondents when business was said to be poor, but only by 25 percent of respondents when business was good. The proportion guessing that Mr. Green would try to reduce his labor costs was 75 percent when he was said to be doing poorly, and 49 percent when he was said to be doing well. The differences were statistically reliable in both cases.

A firm is only allowed to protect itself at the transactor's expense against losses that pertain directly to the transaction at hand. Thus, it is unfair for a landlord to raise the rent on an accommodation to make up for the loss of another source of income. On the other hand, 62 percent of the respondents considered it acceptable for a landlord to charge a higher rent for apartments in one of two otherwise identical buildings, because a more costly foundation had been required in the construction of that building.

The assignment of costs to specific goods explains why it is generally unfair to raise the price of old stock when the price of new stock increases:

Question 10. A grocery store has several months supply of peanut butter in stock which it has on the shelves and in the storeroom. The owner hears that the wholesale price of peanut butter has increased and immediately raises the price on the current stock of peanut butter.

($N=147$) Acceptable 21% Unfair 79%

The principles of naive accounting apparently include a FIFO method of inventory cost allocation.

B. *The Allocation of Gains*

The data of the preceding section could be interpreted as evidence for a cost-plus rule of fair pricing, in which the supplier is expected to act as a broker in passing on marked-up costs (Okun). A critical test of this possible rule arises when the supplier's costs diminish: A strict cost-plus rule would require prices to come down accordingly. In contrast, a dual-entitlement view suggests that the firm is only prohibited from increasing its profit by causing a loss to its transactors. Increasing profits by retaining cost reductions does not violate the transactors' entitlement and may therefore be acceptable.

The results of our previous study (1986) indicated that community standards of fairness do not in fact restrict firms to the reference profit when their costs diminish, as a cost-plus rule would require. The questions used in these surveys presented a scenario of a monopolist supplier of a particular kind of table, who faces a $20 reduction of costs on tables that have been selling for $150. The respondents were asked to indicate whether "fairness requires" the supplier to lower the price, and if so, by how much. About one-half of the survey respondents felt that it was acceptable for the supplier to retain the entire benefit, and less than one-third would require the supplier to reduce the price by $20, as a cost-plus rule dictates. Further, and somewhat surprisingly, judgments of fairness did not reliably discriminate between primary producers and middlemen, or between savings due to lower input prices and to improved efficiency.

The conclusion that the rules of fairness permit the seller to keep part or all of any cost reduction was confirmed with the simpler method employed in the present study.

Question 11A. A small factory produces tables and sells all that it can make at $200 each. Because of changes in the price of materials, the cost of making each table has recently decreased by $40. The factory reduces its price for the tables by $20.

($N = 102$) Acceptable 79% Unfair 21%

Question 11B. ... the cost of making each table has recently decreased by $20. The factory does not change its price for the tables.

($N = 100$) Acceptable 53% Unfair 47%

The even division of opinions on Question 11B confirms the observations of the previous study. In conjunction with the results of the previous section, the findings support a dual-entitlement view: the rules of fairness permit a firm not to share in the losses that it imposes on its transactors, without imposing on it an unequivocal duty to share its gains with them.

C. *Exploitation of Increased Market Power*

The market power of a firm reflects the advantage to the transactor of the exchange which the firm offers, compared to the transactor's second-best alternative. For example, a blizzard increases the surplus associated with the purchase of a snow shovel at the regular price, compared to the alternatives of buying elsewhere or doing without a shovel. The respondents consider it unfair for the hardware store to capture any part of the increased surplus, because such an action would violate the customer's entitlement to the reference price. Similarly, it is unfair for a firm to exploit an excess in the supply of labor to cut wages (Question 2A), because this would violate the entitlement of employees to their reference wage.

As shown by the following routine example, the opposition to exploitation of shortages is not restricted to such extreme circumstances:

Question 12. A severe shortage of Red Delicious apples has developed in a community and none of the grocery stores or produce markets have any of this type of apple on their shelves. Other varieties of apples are plentiful in all of the stores. One grocer receives a single shipment of Red Delicious apples at the regular wholesale cost and raises the retail price of these Red Delicious apples by 25% over the regular price.

($N = 102$) Acceptable 37% Unfair 63%

Raising prices in response to a shortage is unfair even when close substitutes are readily available. A similar aversion to price rationing held as well for luxury items. For example, a majority of respondents thought it unfair for a popular restaurant to impose a $5 surcharge for Saturday night reservations.

Conventional economic analyses assume as a matter of course that excess demand for a good creates an opportunity for suppliers to raise prices, and that such increases will indeed occur. The profit-seeking adjustments that clear the market are in this view as natural as water finding its level—and as ethically neutral. The lay public does not share this indifference. Community standards of fairness effectively require the firm to absorb an opportunity cost in the presence of excess demand, by charging less than the clearing price or paying more than the clearing wage.

As might be expected from this analysis, it is unfair for a firm to take advantage of an increase in its monopoly power. Respondents were nearly unanimous in condemning a store that raises prices when its sole competitor in a community is temporarily forced to close. As shown in the next question, even a rather mild exploitation of monopoly power is considered unfair.

Question 13. A grocery chain has stores in many communities. Most of them face competition from other groceries. In one community the chain has no competition. Although its costs and volume of sales are the same there as elsewhere, the chain sets prices that average 5 percent higher than in other communities.

($N=101$) Acceptable 24% Unfair 76%

Responses to this and two additional versions of this question specifying average price increases of 10 and 15 percent did not differ significantly. The respondents clearly viewed such pricing practices as unfair, but were insensitive to the extent of the unwarranted increase.

A monopolist might attempt to increase profits by charging different customers as much as they are willing to pay. In conventional theory, the constraints that prevent a monopolist from using perfect price discrimination to capture all the consumers' surplus are asymmetric information and difficulties in preventing resale. The survey results suggest the addition of a further restraint: some forms of price discrimination are outrageous.

Question 14. A landlord rents out a small house. When the lease is due for renewal, the landlord learns that the tenant has taken a job very close to the house and is therefore unlikely to move. The landlord raises the rent $40 per month more than he was planning to do.

($N=157$) Acceptable 9% Unfair 91%

The near unanimity of responses to this and similar questions indicates that an action that deliberately exploits the special dependence of a particular individual is exceptionally offensive.

The introduction of an explicit auction to allocate scarce goods or jobs would also enable the firm to gain at the expense of its transactors, and is consequently judged unfair.

Question 15. A store has been sold out of the popular Cabbage Patch dolls for a month. A week before Christmas a single doll is discovered in a storeroom. The managers know that many customers would like to buy the doll. They announce over the store's public address system that the doll will be sold by auction to the customer who offers to pay the most.

($N=101$) Acceptable 26% Unfair 74%

Question 16. A business in a community with high unemployment needs to hire a new computer operator. Four candidates are judged to be completely qualified for the job. The manager asks the candidates to state the lowest salary they would be willing to accept, and then hires the one who demands the lowest salary.

($N=154$) Acceptable 36% Unfair 64%

The auction is opposed in both cases, presumably because the competition among potential buyers or employees benefits the firm. The opposition can in some cases be mitigated by eliminating this benefit. For example, a sentence added to Question 15, indicating that "the proceeds will go to

UNICEF" reduced the negative judgments of the doll auction from 74 to 21 percent.

The strong aversion to price rationing in these examples clearly does not extend to all uses of auctions. The individual who sells securities at twice the price paid for them a month ago is an object of admiration and envy—and is certainly not thought to be gouging. Why is it fair to sell a painting or a house at the market-clearing price, but not an apple, dinner reservation, job, or football game ticket? The rule of acceptability appears to be this: Goods for which an active resale market exists, and especially goods that serve as a store of value, can be sold freely by auction or other mechanisms allowing the seller to capture the maximum price. When resale is a realistic possibility, which is not the case for most consumer goods, the potential resale price reflects the higher value of the asset and the purchaser is therefore not perceived as sustaining a loss.

IV. Enforcement

Several considerations may deter a firm from violating community standards of fairness. First, a history or reputation of unfair dealing may induce potential transactors to take their business elsewhere, because of the element of trust that is present in many transactions. Second, transactors may avoid exchanges with offending firms at some cost to themselves, even when trust is not an issue. Finally, the individuals who make decisions on behalf of firms may have a preference for acting fairly. The role of reputation effects is widely recognized. This section presents some indications that a willingness to resist and to punish unfairness and an intrinsic motivation to be fair could also contribute to fair behavior in the marketplace.

A willingness to pay to resist and to punish unfairness has been demonstrated in incentive compatible laboratory experiments. In the ultimatum game devised by Werner Guth, Rolf Schmittberger, and Bernd Schwarze (1982), the participants are designated as allocators or recipients. Each allocator anonymously proposes a division of a fixed amount of money between himself (herself) and a recipient. The recipient either accepts the offer or rejects it, in which case both players get nothing. The standard game theoretic solution is for the allocator to make a token offer and for the recipient to accept it, but Guth et al. observed that many allocators offer an equal division and that recipients sometimes turn down positive offers. In our more detailed study of resistance to unfairness (1986), recipients were asked to indicate in advance how they wished to respond to a range of possible allocations: A majority of participants were willing to forsake $2 rather than accept an unfair allocation of $10.

Willingness to punish unfair actors was observed in another experiment, in which subjects were given the opportunity to share a sum of money evenly with one of two anonymous strangers, identified only by the allocation they had proposed to someone else in a previous round. About three-quarters of the undergraduate participants in this experiment elected to share $10 evenly with a stranger who had been fair to someone else, when the alternative was to share $12 evenly with an unfair allocator (see our other paper).

A willingness to punish unfairness was also expressed in the telephone surveys. For example, 68 percent of respondents said they would switch their patronage to a drugstore five minutes further away if the one closer to them raised its prices when a competitor was temporarily forced to close; and, in a separate sample, 69 percent indicated they would switch if the more convenient store discriminated against its older workers.

The costs of enforcing fairness are small in these examples—but effective enforcement in the marketplace can often be achieved at little cost to transactors. Retailers will have a substantial incentive to behave fairly if a large number of customers are prepared to drive an extra five minutes to avoid doing business with an unfair firm. The threat of future punishment when competitors enter may also deter a temporary monopolist from fully exploiting short-term profit opportunities.

In traditional economic theory, compliance with contracts depends on enforcement. It is a mild embarrassment to the standard model that experimental studies often produce fair behavior even in the absence of enforcement (Elizabeth Hoffman and Matthew Spitzer, 1982, 1985; our paper, 1986; Arvin Roth, Michael Malouf, and J. Keith Murninghan, 1981; Reinhard Selten, 1978). These observations, however, merely confirm common sense views of human behavior. Survey results indicate a belief that unenforced compliance to the rules of fairness is common. This belief was examined in two contexts: tipping in restaurants and sharp practice in automobile repairs.

Question 17A. If the service is satisfactory, how much of a tip do you think most people leave after ordering a meal costing $10 in a restaurant that they visit frequently?

($N = 122$) Mean response = $1.28

Question 17B. ...in a restaurant on a trip to another city that they do not expect to visit again?

($N = 124$) Mean response = $1.27

The respondents evidently do not treat the possibility of enforcement as a significant factor in the control of tipping. Their opinion is consistent with the widely observed adherence to a 15 percent tipping rule even by one-time customers who pay and tip by credit card, and have little reason to fear embarrassing retaliation by an irate server.

The common belief that tipping is controlled by intrinsic motivation can be accommodated with a standard microeconomic model by extending the utility function of individuals to include guilt and self-esteem. A more difficult question is whether firms, which the theory assumes to maximize profits, also fail to exploit some economic opportunities because of unenforced compliance with rules of fairness. The following questions elicited expectations about the behavior of a garage mechanic dealing with a regular customer or with a tourist.

Question 18A. [A man leaves his car with the mechanic at his regular / A tourist leaves his car at a] service station with instructions to replace an expensive part. After the [customer/tourist] leaves, the mechanic examines the car and discovers that it is not necessary to replace the part; it can be repaired cheaply. The mechanic would make much more money by replacing the part than by repairing it. Assuming the [customer/tourist] cannot be reached, what do you think the mechanic would do in this situation?

Make more money by replacing the part
customer: 60% tourist: 63%

Save the customer money by repairing the part
customer: 40% tourist: 37%

Question 18B. Of ten mechanics dealing with a [regular customer/tourist], how many would you expect to save the customer money by repairing the part?

Mean response
customer: 3.62 tourist: 3.72

The respondents do not approach garages with wide-eyed naive faith. It is therefore all the more noteworthy that they expect a tourist and a regular customer to be treated alike, in spite of the obvious difference between the two cases in the potential for any kind of enforcement, including reputation effects.[2]

Here again, there is no evidence that the public considers enforcement a significant factor. The respondents believe that most mechanics (usually excluding their own) would be less than saintly in this situation. However, they also appear to believe that the substantial minority of mechanics who would treat their customers fairly are not motivated in each case by the anticipation of sanctions.

V. Economic Consequences

The findings of this study suggest that many actions that are both profitable in the short run and not obviously dishonest are likely to be perceived as unfair exploitations of market power.[3] Such perceptions can have

[2] Other respondents were asked to assess the probable behavior of their own garage under similar circumstances: 88 percent expressed a belief that their garage would act fairly toward a regular customer, and 86 percent stated that their garage would treat a tourist and a regular customer similarly.

[3] This conclusion probably holds in social and cultural groups other than the Canadian urban samples

significant consequences if they find expression in legislation or regulation (Zajac, 1978; forthcoming). Further, even in the absence of government intervention, the actions of firms that wish to avoid a reputation for unfairness will depart in significant ways from the standard model of economic behavior. The survey results suggest four propositions about the effects of fairness considerations on the behavior of firms in customer markets, and a parallel set of hypotheses about labor markets.

A. *Fairness in Customer Markets*

PROPOSITION 1: *When excess demand in a customer market is unaccompanied by increases in suppliers' costs, the market will fail to clear in the short run.*

Evidence supporting this proposition was described by Phillip Cagan (1979), who concluded from a review of the behavior of prices that, "Empirical studies have long found that short-run shifts in demand have small and often insignificant effects [on prices]" (p. 18). Other consistent evidence comes from studies of disasters, where prices are often maintained at their reference levels although supplies are short (Douglas Dacy and Howard Kunreuther, 1969).

A particularly well-documented illustration of the behavior predicted in proposition 1 is provided by Alan Olmstead and Paul Rhode (1985). During the spring and summer of 1920 there was a severe gasoline shortage in the U.S. West Coast where Standard Oil of California (SOCal) was the dominant supplier. There were no government-imposed price controls, nor was there any threat of such controls, yet SOCal reacted by imposing allocation and rationing schemes while maintaining prices. Prices were actually higher in the East in the absence of any shortage. Significantly, Olmstead and Rhode note that the eastern firms had to purchase crude at higher prices while SOCal, being vertically integrated, had no such excuse for raising price. They conclude from confidential SOCal documents that SOCal officers "...were clearly concerned with their public image and tried to maintain the appearance of being 'fair'" (p. 1053).

PROPOSITION 2: *When a single supplier provides a family of goods for which there is differential demand without corresponding variation of input costs, shortages of the most valued items will occur.*

There is considerable support for this proposition in the pricing of sport and entertainment events, which are characterized by marked variation of demand for goods or services for which costs are about the same (Thaler, 1985). The survey responses suggest that charging the market-clearing price for the most popular goods would be judged unfair.

Proposition 2 applies to cases such as those of resort hotels that have in-season and out-of-season rates which correspond to predictable variations of demand. To the extent that constraints of fairness are operating, the price adjustments should be insufficient, with excess demand at the peak. Because naive accounting does not properly distinguish between marginal and average costs, customers and other observers are likely to adopt off-peak prices as a reference in evaluating the fairness of the price charged to peak customers. A revenue-maximizing (low) price in the off-season may suggest that the profits achievable at the peak are unfairly high. In spite of a substantial degree of within-season price variation in resort and ski hotels, it appears to be the rule that most of these establishments face excess demand during the peak weeks. One industry explanation is: "If you gouge them at Christmas, they won't be back in March."

PROPOSITION 3: *Price changes will be more responsive to variations of costs than to variations of demand, and more responsive to cost increases than to cost decreases.*

The high sensitivity of prices to short-run variations of costs is well documented

studied here, although the detailed rules of fairness for economic transactions may vary.

(Cagan). The idea of asymmetric price rigidity has a history of controversy (Timur Kuran, 1983; Solow; George Stigler and James Kindahl, 1970) and the issue is still unsettled. Changes of currency values offer a potential test of the hypothesis that cost increases tend to be passed on quickly and completely, whereas cost decreases can be retained at least in part. When the rate of exchange between two currencies changes after a prolonged period of stability, the prediction from Proposition 3 is that upward adjustments of import prices in one country will occur faster than the downward adjustments expected in the other.

PROPOSITION 4: *Price decreases will often take the form of discounts rather than reductions in the list or posted price.*

This proposition is strongly supported by the data of Stigler and Kindahl. Casual observation confirms that temporary discounts are much more common than temporary surcharges. Discounts have the important advantage that their subsequent cancellation will elicit less resistance than an increase in posted price. A temporary surcharge is especially aversive because it does not have the prospect of becoming a reference price, and can only be coded as a loss.

B. *Fairness in Labor Markets*

A consistent finding of this study is the similarity of the rules of fairness that apply to prices, rents, and wages. The correspondence extends to the economic predictions that may be derived for the behavior of wages in labor markets and of prices in customer markets. The first proposition about prices asserted that resistance to the exploitation of short-term fluctuations of demand could prevent markets from clearing. The corresponding prediction for labor markets is that wages will be relatively insensitive to excess supply.

The existence of wage stickiness is not in doubt, and numerous explanations have been offered for it. An entitlement model of this effect invokes an implicit contract between the worker and the firm. Like other implicit contract theories, such a model predicts that wage changes in a firm will be more sensitive to recent firm profits than to local labor market conditions. However, unlike the implicit contract theories that emphasize risk shifting (Costas Azariadis, 1975; Martin Baily, 1974; Donald Gordon, 1974), explanations in terms of fairness (Akerlof, 1979, 1982; Okun; Solow) lead to predictions of wage stickiness even in occupations that offer no prospects for long-term employment and therefore provide little protection from risk. Okun noted that "Casual empiricism about the casual labor market suggests that the Keynesian wage floor nonetheless operates; the pay of car washers or stock clerks is seldom cut in a recession, even when it is well above any statutory minimum wage" (1981, p. 82), and he concluded that the employment relation is governed by an "invisible handshake," rather than by the invisible hand (p. 89).

The dual-entitlement model differs from a Keynesian model of sticky wages, in which nominal wage changes are always nonnegative. The survey findings suggest that nominal wage cuts by a firm that is losing money or threatened with bankruptcy do not violate community standards of fairness. This modification of the sticky nominal wage dictum is related to Proposition 3 for customer markets. Just as they may raise prices to do so, firms may also cut wages to protect a positive reference profit.

Proposition 2 for customer markets asserted that the dispersion of prices for similar goods that cost the same to produce but differ in demand will be insufficient to clear the market. An analogous case in the labor market involves positions that are similar in nominal duties but are occupied by individuals who have different values in the employment market. The prediction is that differences in income will be insufficient to eliminate the excess demand for the individuals considered most valuable, and the excess supply of those considered most dispensable. This prediction applies both within and among occupations.

Robert Frank (1985) found that the individuals in a university who already are the most highly paid in each department are also the most likely targets for raiding. Frank explains the observed behavior in terms of envy and status. An analysis of this phenomenon in terms of fairness is the same as for the seasonal pricing of resort rooms: Just as prices that clear the market at peak demand will be perceived as gouging if the resort can also afford to operate at off-peak rates, a firm that can afford to pay its most valuable employees their market value may appear to grossly underpay their less-valued colleagues. A related prediction is that variations among departments will also be insufficient to clear the market. Although salaries are higher in academic departments that compete with the private sector than in others, the ratio of job openings to applicants is still lower in classics than in accounting.

The present analysis also suggests that firms that frame a portion of their compensation package as bonuses or profit sharing will encounter relatively little resistance to reductions of compensation during slack periods. This is the equivalent of Proposition 4. The relevant psychological principle is that losses are more aversive than objectively equivalent foregone gains. The same mechanism, combined with the money illusion, supports another prediction: Adjustments of real wages will be substantially greater in inflationary periods than in periods of stable prices, because the adjustments can then be achieved without making nominal cuts—which are always perceived as losses and are therefore strongly resisted. An unequal distribution of gains is more likely to appear fair than a reallocation in which there are losers.

This discussion has illustrated several ways in which the informal entitlements of customers or employees to the terms of reference transactions could enter an economic analysis. In cases such as the pricing of resort facilities, the concern of customers for fair pricing may permanently prevent the market from clearing. In other situations, the reluctance of firms to impose terms that can be perceived as unfair acts as a friction-like factor. The process of reaching equilibrium can be slowed down if no firm wants to be seen as a leader in moving to exploit changing market conditions. In some instances an initially unfair practice (for example, charging above list price for a popular car model) may spread slowly until it evolves into a new norm—and is no longer unfair. In all these cases, perceptions of transactors' entitlements affect the substantive outcomes of exchanges, altering or preventing the equilibria predicted by an analysis that omits fairness as a factor. In addition, considerations of fairness can affect the form rather than the substance of price or wage setting. Judgments of fairness are susceptible to substantial framing effects, and the present study gives reason to believe that firms have an incentive to frame the terms of exchanges so as to make them appear "fair."

REFERENCES

Akerlof, George A., "The Market for 'Lemons': Quality Uncertainty and the Market Mechanism," *Quarterly Journal of Economics*, August 1970, *84*, 488–500.

______, "The Case against Conservative Macroeconomics: An Inaugural Lecture," *Economica*, August 1979, *46*, 219–37.

______, "A Theory of Social Custom, of Which Unemployment May Be One Consequence," *Quarterly Journal of Economics*, June 1980, *94*, 749–75.

______, "Labor Contracts as Partial Gift Exchange," *Quarterly Journal of Economics*, November 1982, *97*, 543–69.

______ **and Yellen, Janet L.**, "Can Small Deviations from Rationality Make Significant Differences to Economic Equilibrium?," *American Economic Review*, September 1985, *75*, 708–20.

Arrow, Kenneth, "Social Responsibility and Economic Efficiency," *Public Policy*, Summer 1973, *21*, 303–17.

Azariadis, Costas, "Implicit Contracts and Unemployment Equilibria," *Journal of Political Economy*, December 1975, *83*, 1183–202.

Baily, Martin N., "Wages and Employment Under Uncertain Demand," *Review of Economic Studies*, January 1974, *41*, 37–50.

Bazerman, Max H., "Norms of Distributive Justice in Interest Arbitration," *Industrial* *and Labor Relations Review*, July 1985, *38*, 558–70.

Cagan, Phillip, *Persistent Inflation: Historical and Policy Essays*, New York: Columbia University Press, 1979.

Dacy, Douglas C. and Kunreuther, Howard, *The Economics of Natural Disasters*, New York: Free Press, 1969.

Frank, Robert H., *Choosing the Right Pond; Human Behavior and the Quest for Status*, New York: Oxford University Press, 1985.

Gordon, Donald F., "A Neo-Classical Theory of Keynesian Unemployment," *Economic Inquiry*, December 1974, *12*, 431–59.

Guth, Werner, Schmittberger, Rolf and Schwarze, Bernd, "An Experimental Analysis of Ultimatum Bargaining," *Journal of Economic Behavior and Organization*, 1982, *3*, 367–88.

Hoffman, Elizabeth and Spitzer, Matthew L., "The Coase Theorem: Some Experimental Tests," *Journal of Law and Economics*, April 1982, *25*, 73–98.

______ **and** ______ "Entitlements, Rights, and Fairness: An Experimental Examination of Subjects' Concepts of Distributive Justice," *Journal of Legal Studies*, June 1985, *14*, 259–97.

Kahneman, Daniel, Knetsch, Jack L. and Thaler, Richard, "Fairness and the Assumptions of Economics," *Journal of Business*, forthcoming, 1986.

______ **and Tversky, Amos,** "Prospect Theory: An Analysis of Decision Under Risk," *Econometrica*, March 1979, *47*, 263–91.

______ **and** ______, "Choices, Values, and Frames," *American Psychologist*, April 1984, *39*, 341–50.

Kuran, Timur, "Asymmetric Price Rigidity and Inflationary Bias," *American Economic Review*, June 1983, *73*, 373–82.

Okun, Arthur, *Prices and Quantities: A Macroeconomic Analysis*, Washington: The Brookings Institution, 1981.

Olmstead, Alan L. and Rhode, Paul, "Rationing Without Government: The West Coast Gas Famine of 1920," *American Economic Review*, December 1985, *75*, 1044–55.

Roth, Alvin, Malouf, Michael and Murnighan, J. Keith, "Sociological Versus Strategic Factors in Bargaining," *Journal of Economic Behavior and Organization*, June 1981, *2*, 153–77.

Selten, Reinhard, "The Equity Principle in Economic Behavior," in Hans W. Gottinger and Werner Leinfellner, eds., *Decision Theory and Social Ethics: Issues in Social Choice*, Dordrecht: D. Reidel, 1978, 289–301.

Solow, Robert M., "On Theories of Unemployment," *American Economic Review*, March 1980, *70*, 1–11.

Stigler, George J. and Kindahl, James K., *The Behavior of Industrial Prices*, NBER, New York: Columbia University Press, 1970.

Thaler, Richard, "Toward a Positive Theory of Consumer Choice," *Journal of Economic Behavior and Organization*, March 1980, *1*, 39–60.

______, "Mental Accounting and Consumer Choice," *Marketing Science*, Summer 1985, *4*, 199–214.

Tversky, Amos and Kahneman, Daniel, "Rational Choice and the Framing of Decisions," *Journal of Business*, forthcoming, 1986.

Zajac, Edward E., *Fairness or Efficiency: An Introduction to Public Utility Pricing*, Cambridge: Ballinger, 1978.

______, "Perceived Economic Justice: The example of Public Utility Regulation," in H. Peyton Young, ed., *Cost Allocation: Methods, Principles and Applications*, Amsterdam: North-Holland, forthcoming.

THE
QUARTERLY JOURNAL
OF ECONOMICS

Vol. XCVII November 1982 No. 4

LABOR CONTRACTS AS PARTIAL GIFT EXCHANGE*

GEORGE A. AKERLOF

This paper explains involuntary unemployment in terms of the response of firms to workers' group behavior. Workers' effort depends upon the norms determining a fair day's work. In order to affect those norms, firms may pay more than the market-clearing wage. Industries that pay consistently more than the market-clearing wage are primary, and those that pay only the market-clearing wage are secondary. Thus, this paper also gives a theory for division of labor markets between primary and secondary.

I. INTRODUCTION

In a study of social relations among workers at a utility company in the eastern United States, George Homans [1953, 1954] observed that a small group of young women (doing a job called "cash posting") exceeded the minimum work standards of the firm by a significant margin (i.e., on average by 15 percent). Most of these women neither desired nor expected promotion in the firm in return for their troubles. Why did they do it?

Section II shows that the standard neoclassical model cannot simultaneously explain both the behavior of the firm and the behavior of the cash posters. But, as shown in Section III, application of a standard sociological model does explain the behavior of both the young women and their employer. According to this model, in their interaction workers acquire sentiment for each other and also for the firm. As a consequence of sentiment for the firm, the workers acquire

* The author would like to thank William Dickens, Brian Main, Hajime Miyazaki, Janet L. Yellen, and two referees for invaluable help. He would also like to thank the National Science Foundation for generous financial support under Research Grant SOC 79-05562, administered by the Institute of Business and Economic Research of the University of California, Berkeley.

The Quarterly Journal of Economics, November 1982 CCC 0033-5533/82/040543-27$03.70

utility for an exchange of "gifts" with the firm—the amount of utility depending upon the so-called "norms" of gift exchange. On the worker's side, the "gift" given is work in excess of the minimum work standard; and on the firm's side the "gift" given is wages in excess of what these women could receive if they left their current jobs. As a consequence of worker sentiment for one another, the firm cannot deal with each worker individually, but rather must at least to some extent treat the group of workers with the same norms, collectively.

Norm–gift-exchange models have been used in many sociological studies to explain the behavior of workers. And these explanations are simple; properly understood, they are in tune with everyone's personal experiences of human behavior, so that they can be taken to have considerable generality. For that reason I feel confident in extrapolating such behavior beyond the narrow and particular instance of the "cash posters" to concern wage bargains and work conditions in some generality. Sections IV and V verbally explore the consequences of such behavior for wage determination; Sections VI and VII build formal mathematical models; and Section VIII gives conclusions.

This model of the microeconomics of the labor market is used to explain two phenomena that have not been successfully analyzed by more conventional economic theory. First, in most other analyses of unemployment, such as that of search theory [Phelps *et al.*, 1970], all unemployment is voluntary. In my analysis there are primary labor markets in which unemployed workers are unable to obtain jobs at the prevailing market wages. Second, the theory of dual labor markets [Doeringer and Piore, 1971] brings up the question as to which markets will be primary and which markets secondary. In the formal models developed in this paper, it is endogenously determined whether a market will be primary or secondary. Primary markets are those in which the gift component of labor input and wages is sizeable, and therefore wages are not market-clearing. Secondary labor markets are those in which wages are market-clearing.

The major feature of the usual model of implicit contracts due to Azariadis [1975] and Baily [1974] is risk-sharing agreements by the contracting agents over a span of time. These models have been taken as a vehicle for Okun's [1981, p. 133] description of labor and customer markets. This paper offers an alternative microfoundation for implicit contracts. Its emphasis is sociological. It focuses on the gift-exchange nature of employment arrangements, where the exchange is based partially on norms of behavior that are endogenously determined. This dependence of implicit contracts on *norms* of behavior (rather than on risk sharing) captures important aspects of Okun's description [1975, 1981] that have not been analyzed in the Azariadis-Baily framework.

According to this paper, norms of work effort are a major determinant of output. In emphasizing effort, it carries further the work of Leibenstein [1976] on X-efficiency. The focus on effort could also be expressed in Marxian terminology via the distinction between *labor power* and *labor* as in Edwards' recent book [1979] on the inevitable conflict between labor and management over the use of labor power.[1] In Edwards' terms this paper gives equilibrium models of the resolution of this conflict. Finally, it should be mentioned, Hirschman's concepts of *Exit*, *Voice*, and *Loyalty* [1970] can be expressed in terms of norms and gift exchange.

II. The Nonneoclassical Behavior of the Cash Posters or of the Eastern Utilities Co.

Economists usually assume that labor is hired as a factor of production and is put to work like capital. There is, however, one fundamental difference between labor and capital that is ignored by this assumption. Once a capitalist has hired capital, he is, over a fairly wide latitude, free to use it (or abuse it) as he wishes. However, having hired a laborer, management faces considerable restriction on how it can use its labor. Not only are there legal restrictions (such as OSHA regulations, child labor laws, etc.), but the willing cooperation of labor itself must usually be obtained for the firm to make the best use of the labor services.

Of course, standard economic theory does describe the nature of contracts when there are many possible standards of performance. According to standard theory, when a firm hires a laborer, there is an understanding by both parties that certain minimum standards of performance must be met. Furthermore, the contract may be *implicit* in the sense that workers need not be currently rewarded for their current performance but may earn chances for promotion with higher pay in the future in return for good performance in their current jobs. If this is the case, the firm need not have tight rules regarding work and compensation that very carefully specify the *quid pro quo* of pay for work, since injustices in the present can be compensated later. So standard theory can serve as a good approximation to reality even

1. For a review of the Marxian literature on this distinction, also see Edwards [1979].

TABLE I

WORK PERFORMANCE OF INDIVIDUAL CASH POSTERS

	Age in years	Time on job in years-months	Mean cards per hour	Mean errors per hour
Asnault	22	3–5	363	0.57
Burke	26	2–5	306	0.66
Coughlin	20	2–0	342	0.40
Donovan	20	1–9	308	0.79
Granara	21	1–3	438	0.65
Lo Presti	25	–11	317	0.03
Murphy	19	–7	439	0.62
Rourke	17	–4	323	0.82
Shaugnessy	23	–2	333	0.44
Urquhart	18	–2	361	0.49
Average	21.1	1–4	353	0.55

where very specific contracts relating effort or output to compensation would be quite expensive.

Against this background let us consider the study by Homans of "The Cash Posters." In this study a group of ten young women working as cash posters for a utility company in a New England city were interviewed and closely observed over a period of six months. The duty of a cash poster at Eastern Utilities was to record customers' payments on ledger cards at the time of receipt. The company's standard for such cash posting was 300 per hour, and careful records were made of the speed at which individual cash posters variously worked. Anyone who worked below the rate of 300 per hour received a mild rebuke from the supervisor. Table I adapted from Homan's article, "The Cash Posters," shows both the number of cash postings per hour of different workers and their rate of error.

Note from Table I that the average number of cash postings per hour (353) was 17.7 percent greater than the standard set by the company. The simple neoclassical theory of contracts cannot simultaneously explain why the faster persons did not reduce their speed to the standard; or, alternatively, why the firm did not increase the speed expected of its faster workers. The possibility that the faster workers worked harder than the standard for either increased pay or promotion was belied by the uniformity of wage for all cash posters and by the refusal of promotion by two cash posters. When promotion did occur, it was normally to a job considered more responsible than cash posting, but nevertheless paying the same wage. In addition, voluntary quits among the cash posters were quite frequent (with most of the young women leaving to be married), so that in most cases promotion was not a relevant consideration. Since pay was not dependent on effort and promotion was rarely a consideration, the standard economic model of contract would predict that workers set their work habits to meet the company's minimum standards of performance as long as they have marginal disutility for work at that level. On the other hand, if workers do have positive utility for work at this level, the lack of incentives for effort given by the firm should lead them to choose to work to the point where the marginal disutility of additional effort is just zero. But in that case the firm could increase its profits by increasing work standards for the faster workers. Unless their utility function is discontinuous, they would still prefer their current jobs to what they could obtain elsewhere at somewhat faster speeds of work.

Since output is easily observable, it is at least a bit surprising from the point of view of the neoclassical theory of contracts that workers are not paid wages proportional to their outputs. This constitutes another puzzlement regarding the system of industrial relations among the cash posters at Eastern Utilities, although a potential answer has been suggested by Etzioni [1971]. According to Etzioni, workers find pecuniary incentives, such as piece rates, "alienating."

The mysterious behavior of the cash posters and of Eastern Utilities in terms of neoclassical theory can be posed a bit more formally. Suppose for whatever reason (perhaps Etzioni's) that the firm has decided to pay the same wage $w = \overline{w}$ to all cash posters. Further, suppose that workers have a utility function $u(w,e)$, where w is the wage rate and e is effort. Workers, mindful of the firm's work rules, should choose their effort e to maximize

$$u(w,e), \tag{1}$$

subject to the constraints,

$$w = \overline{w} \tag{2}$$

$$e \geqq e_{\min}, \tag{3}$$

where $\overline{w}$ = \$1.05 per hour, the wage fixed for all cash posters, and $e_{\min}$ is the minimum effort necessary to accomplish the required 300 cash postings per hour.

Solution of this trivial maximization problem yields

$$e = e_{\min} \tag{4}$$

as long as $u_e < 0$ for $e \geqq e_{\min}$. On the assumption that utility is convex, there are two potential types of solutions. Each poses an empirical problem. If $u_e(\overline{w},e_{\min}) < 0$, the question arises—why did the workers not reduce their effort to 300 per hour? On the other hand, if $u_e(\overline{w},e_{\min}) > 0$, so that workers choose $u_e = 0$, why did the firm not raise the minimum standards for different workers above the point where $u_e = 0$? In either case the observation obtained is inconsistent with the neoclassical model.[2]

Of course, each cash poster may have a different utility function, and for some reason the firm may find it optimal to set the same minimum standard for all workers. For example, the rate perhaps cannot be set higher than 300 per hour in deference to the two workers who find the standard a bit onerous (as shown by Burke's and Donovan's performance in Table I, only 2 percent above the 300 minimum). But the question of why the same standard should be set for all workers can be answered only in terms of the interactions of workers among themselves and also with the firm. It is precisely in such terms that the next section poses the solution to the cash poster mystery.

Other potential objections such as the nonobservability of output and risk aversion by workers can be all but ruled out. Workers kept records of their outputs so output was easily observable; and workers did not work faster than the minimum out of fear of being sacked for falling below the minimum; as already mentioned, falling below the minimum occasioned no more than mild rebuke.

An explanation for either the firm's behavior or the workers' behavior must depend either on maximization of something other than profits by the firm or on interaction of the workers with each other and with the firm that alters their utility functions. It is to such a theory that we now turn.

III. Sociological Explanation of Cash Posters'–Eastern Utilities' Behavior

The previous section showed behavior by the cash posters inconsistent with a simple neoclassical theory of worker utility maximization and firm profit maximization. I do not doubt that there is some neoclassical model involving turnover costs or difficulty of ob-

2. The argument is just a bit subtle. If a worker with convex utility and positive marginal product for effort has a positive utility for wage income and zero disutility for added effort, the firm can increase his compensation and force him to work harder, to the advantage of both. If the worker was satisfied with his job before this additional trade, he will be even more satisfied afterwards, and therefore less willing to quit.

servation[3] which can explain the behavior of the firm and the cash posters, but given the failure of the simple model, the adequate model must of necessity be complicated. In contrast, this section presents a simple sociological explanation of the joint behavior of the cash posters and the Eastern Utilities Company.

According to a prominent school of sociological thought, the determinant of workers' effort is the norm of the work group. According to Elton Mayo [1949, p. 70], referring to the famous studies at the Hawthorne plant in the Bank Wiring Observation Room, "the working group as a whole actually determined the output of individual workers by reference to a standard, predetermined but clearly stated, that represented the group's conception of a fair day's work. The standard was rarely, if ever, in accord with the standards of the efficiency engineers."

According to an alternative, but equivalent, view of the cash posters' performance, they give a *gift* to the firm of work in excess of the minimum work required of 300 per hour. Offhand, it may seem absurd to view the worker as giving the firm a gift of any part of his work. Of course, the worker does not strictly give his labor as a gift to the firm; he expects a wage in return and, if not paid, will almost certainly sue in court. Likewise, the firm does not give the wage strictly as a gift. If the worker consistently fails to meet certain minimum standards, he will almost surely be dismissed. But above these minimum standards the worker's performance is freely determined. The norm (or "standard" as Mayo termed it) for the proper work effort is quite like the norm that determines the standards for gift giving at Christmas. Such gift giving is a trading relationship—in the sense that if one side of the exchange does not live up to expectations, the other side is also likely to curtail its activities.

The classic anthropological literature on the gift, particularly the essay by Marcel Mauss [1954], emphasizes this reciprocal nature of gift giving.[4] Mauss points out that, in the two major branches of Western European languages, the root for *poison* is the same as the root for *gift*, since in ancient German the word *gift* means both gift and poison, and the Greek word *δόσια* for poison, which is the root of the English *dose*, has the same root as the Greek word to *give*. The reason for the close association of the words for *gift* and *poison* in these ancient languages comes from the obligatory nature of reci-

3. For an interesting explanation of unemployment due to imperfect information, see Stoft [1980]. Solow [1980] supports the view that involuntary unemployment must be explained by sociological models of behavior.

4. A good, although not recent, review of the anthropology and sociology of gift exchange is Belshaw [1965]. See also Titmuss [1971].

procity of a gift, or, equivalently, the threat of harm that was believed to befall a recipient who failed to reciprocate. Although the magic has gone out of the sanctions behind repayment of most gifts, there are probably few in modern times who have never received a gift they did not want or who have not given a gift they considered to be inadequately appreciated.[5]

Why should there be any portion of labor that is given as a gift by the firm or of treatment of the worker by the firm that can be considered a gift? The answer to this question is at once trivial and profound. Persons who work for an institution (a firm in this case) tend to develop sentiment for their co-workers and for that institution; to a great extent they anthropomorphize these institutions (e.g., "the friendly bank"). For the same reasons that persons (brothers, for example) share gifts as showing sentiment for each other, it is natural that persons have utility for making gifts to institutions for which they have sentiment. Furthermore, if workers have an interest in the welfare of their coworkers, they gain utility if the firm relaxes pressure on the workers who are hard pressed; in return for reducing such pressure, better workers are often willing to work harder.

The giving of gifts is almost always determined by norms of behavior. In most cases the gift given is approximately in the range of what the recipient expects, and he reciprocates in kind. The norms of gift giving are determined by the relationship between the parties; thus, for example, it is expected that an increase in workers' productivity will be rewarded by increased wages to the workers. Much of union wage negotiations concerns the question of what constitutes a *fair* wage. To an economist who believes that wages are market-clearing or only determined by the relative bargaining power of the contractual parties, long discussions about the "fair wage" should have no bearing on the final settlement. But this notion neglects the fact that the average worker works harder than necessary according to the firm's work rules, and in return for this donation of goodwill and effort, he expects a fair wage from the firm.

This view of wages-effort as mutually reciprocal *gifts* leaves several unanswered questions. The firm decides not only work rules but also wages for each and every worker. Why should not Eastern Utilities set high standards of minimum effort and terminate all workers who are not capable of meeting or who are not willing to meet

5. It has been suggested to me by one referee that the analysis of labor contracts as partial gift exchange relates to the Freeman-Medoff argument [1979] on trade unions as collective voice. Reciprocal gift giving induces union formation because discontented workers find it more difficult to quit and find another job with gift giving than without. As in Mauss's analysis it is suggested that reciprocal gift giving i.e., mutual benevolence and dependence, go together with mutual hostility and militancy.

that standard (for example, Burke and Donovan in Table I)? Again there is a simple answer. In working together, workers acquire sentiment for each other. An increase in minimum standards that would put pressure on Burke and Donovan might easily be considered by the group as a whole as failure by the firm to reciprocate the group's collective donation of productivity 17.7 percent in excess of the minimum requirements. Indeed, although the details are unclear in Homans' account, there is indication that such a situation had arisen with respect to the cash posters. As Homans reports, "a couple of years before, when relations between the posters and a former division head were strained, there may have been some restriction on output."

In a different context, that of a soldier in basic training in World War II, it is revealed most clearly why better workers come to the aid of their fellows:

> If one is so favored by nature or training that he gets much more done, or done better, than his neighbor, he shows up that neighbor. The neighbor then gets rebukes or extra work. One cannot do this to any decent fellow who is trying his best, especially when you have to live side by side with him and watch his difficulties and sufferings. Therefore, the superior person—if he has any heart at all and if he is sensitive to the attitudes of his barracks mates—will help his less able neighbor to get along [Stouffer *et al.*, 1949, Vol. 2, p. 414].

Of course the cash posters were working under less extreme conditions. Nevertheless, they undoubtedly could have expressed their own reasons for helping each other in similar terms.

I have indicated the nature of the trade between firms and workers that is exemplified in the case study of the cash posters and that gives a consistent and plausible explanation for the behavior of both the firm and the workers; this explanation tells why workers exceed the minimum standards of work on the one hand, and why the firm does not raise these minimum standards on the other hand. But work standards are only one dimension of the treatment of workers. Another dimension is wages. For reasons similar to why minimum work standards are not necessarily set at the limit that workers will bear before leaving the firm, the optimal contract may not set wages at the minimum acceptable: if part of worker effort is a *gift*, likewise, part of wages paid should be a *gift*.

IV. Reference Groups

With the cash posters (or any other work group whose effort is determined not by the work rules but by the group's norms) the question arises: What does the group receive in return for working more than prescribed by the work rules? In the first place the worker may receive leniency in the work rules. Even if the worker habitually works at a speed in excess of work rules, he still benefits from leniency in two ways. First, he derives positive utility from the *gift* by the firm of potential leniency should he slacken his pace; second, as already mentioned, if he has sympathy for other members of the work group, he derives utility from the firm's generous treatment of other members of the group for whom the work rules are a binding constraint. Additionally, the firm may give remuneration in excess of that needed to obtain another worker of similar skills. Thus, excess remuneration and leniency of work rules constitute the major gifts by the firm to its workers.

Presumably, the gift of the worker to the firm, effort in excess of the work rules is linked to the gift of the firm to the worker. Following Mauss and others, reciprocity is a major feature of gift exchange (as also of market exchange).

The *quid pro quo* in gift exchange is, however, established at least slightly differently from market exchange. The norms for effort are established according to the conception of a fair day's work. (Note that Mayo described the work standard in precisely those terms.) In return the workers expect to be treated "fairly" by the firm. The conception of fair treatment has been the subject of considerable work by social psychologists and sociologists. For the most part it is not based on absolute standards, but, rather, on comparison of one's own situation with that of other persons.

According to Festinger [1954], persons have an innate psychological need to compare their actions and treatment with those of others. Persons use comparison with others as a guide to how they ought to behave or how they ought to be treated. The point should be clear to any parent with a young child. Consider the young child who has fallen but not hurt himself/herself. Such situations usually produce that momentary pause before the child decides whether s/he should cry. If the surrounding adults act as if the situation calls for crying, the child is likely to behave accordingly; however, if adults act as if s/he should not cry, the child is likely not to do so. In the context of this paper I wish to note that the child's behavior is not determined by the real phenomenon of being hurt, but rather by the social definition of the situation given by the norms of the surrounding adults. In this way the child calibrates his/her actions by the social standards set by others.[6]

6. For this point of view of social interaction, see Coser [1971] on Park, Mead, and Cooley. The idea of the "definition of the situation" is due to William I. Thomas.

How do people decide that they are fairly treated? There is no natural measure (just as there is no natural language). Merton [1957] has constructed a theory of how people determine the fairness of their treatment by reference to the treatment of reference individuals and treatment of reference groups.

In World War II the Research Branch of the Information and Education Division of the U.S. Department of War conducted a large number of surveys of soldiers' attitudes. Some of these attitudes appear paradoxical from a purely individualistic, utilitarian point of view. For example, in the Army Air Force, in which promotion rates were much higher than in the rest of the army, soldiers were much less satisfied with their chances of promotion than elsewhere. Or, as a second example, although all soldiers abroad showed strong desire to return to the United States, noncombat soldiers abroad showed little more dissatisfaction with army life than soldiers stationed in the United States. Merton [1957] explains these seemingly paradoxical findings (as well as many others) with the concept of the reference group. The soldier in the Air Force felt unsatisfied with his chances of promotion precisely because the promotion rate was high in the Air Force, thereby enabling him to compare himself with other personnel who had been promoted (and causing him to feel relatively deprived). Noncombat soldiers abroad felt relatively satisfied given their objective conditions because they compared their lot to that of combat soldiers abroad, whereas the soldiers in the United States felt relatively unsatisfied (relative to their objective conditions) because they compared their lot to that of civilians at home. In each of these cases the seemingly paradoxical behavior is quite natural when the soldiers' attitudes are explained in terms of their deprivation relative to that of the appropriate reference group.

At the same time that *The American Soldier* [1949, Volumes 1 and 2] shows how attitudes toward fairness are formed (e.g., through reference to the relative deprivation of the appropriate reference group), it also contains evidence consistent with our hypothesis that *group norms* determine performance (as we have suggested is the case with respect to the cash posters and had been found earlier in the studies by Mayo [1949] and Roethlisberger and Dickson [1947]). In this regard three specific findings are worthy of particular note.

First, the Research Branch chose to measure performance of combat units by the percentage of *nonbattle casualties.* This statistic is equivalent to the percentage of combat men who became ineffective for reasons other than wounds or other battle injuries. This statistic was chosen as the best proxy for the quality of the unit, since it is almost independent of the group's battle environment. It is, as well, unambiguously related to the quality of discipline in the unit: presumably, better organized units would lose smaller fractions of persons outside of battle. An excellent correlation was obtained [Stouffer, 1949, Vol. 2, p. 11] on a company-by-company basis between relatively favorable attitudes toward army life in interviews taken before the Normandy landing and the rate of nonbattle casualties following the Normandy landing in the three tested army divisions. This correlation of performance and attitude is a useful indicator that satisfaction in the job leads to improved job performance, justifying one aspect of our view that the firm will be willing to give a *gift* to the worker to increase his job satisfaction, so as, in turn, to increase his job performance.

There is one other noteworthy statistic from the same study. For one regiment (the Thirty-seventh Regiment of the Ninth Division) a graph was made plotting the percentage of nonbattle casualties of soldiers with and without previous combat experience in the same company. The graph shows a clear relation: in those companies in which the combat veterans had high rates of nonbattle casualties, the new recruits also had high rates (and vice versa). The correlation between the two statistics (taken across companies) was 80 percent [Stouffer, 1949, Vol. 2, p. 27]. This statistic is consistent with the hypothesis that members of a work group tend to take on the *group* norms, the companies with group norms more favorable to army life having fewer casualties among both new recruits and veterans. However, this conclusion follows of necessity only if the Research Branch was correct in its judgment that nonbattle casualties were independent of the environment; otherwise, such a correlation could be obtained because veterans and new recruits respond alike in their nonbattle casualties to changes in the environment.

Finally, there is the study by the Research Branch on the attitudes of soldiers in the Caribbean. It was hypothesized that there would be correlation between dissatisfaction and comfort. Perhaps surprisingly, at least to a very utilitarian view of motivations, the evidence showed at most only weak relation between dissatisfaction and the quality of soldiers' living conditions. This finding is useful in supporting our view that the morale of the working group (and indirectly its norms of work behavior) will depend largely on deprivation relative to that of reference individuals and reference groups, rather than depending on objective conditions alone.

This behavior of the American soldier is exactly consistent with our hypotheses concerning the behavior of the cash posters. We hypothesized (1) that the cash posters worked harder than required because of favorable work attitudes; (2) these attitudes, following Mayo *et al.*, were not just individual but also attitudes of the work group; (3) these attitudes depended in part upon workers' sense of fair treatment, where fairness was measured by comparison with persons similarly situated. In exact parallel *The American Soldier* shows (1) favorable attitudes were correlated with lower percentages of nonbattle casualties, both on a group-by-group basis and also on an individual basis. (2) The company-by-company correlation between performances of recruits and combat veterans demonstrates that performances were not randomly distributed over individuals but in fact varied systematically over groups. (There is considerable research in social psychology that shows how such patterns occur.) (3) Finally, attitudes of groups of soldiers toward the army can be systematically explained under the hypothesis that soldiers form their attitudes by comparing their situations to that of reference individuals or reference groups. I take the fact that the same model seems to apply to both the cash posters and the American soldier to be an indication of its universality.

V. The Fair Wage

The gift of the firm to the worker (in return for the worker's gift of hard work for the firm) consists in part of a wage that is fair in terms of the norms of this gift giving. Using reference-individual–reference-group theory, the fairness of this wage depends on how other persons in the worker's reference set are similarly treated. Although, persons do sometimes have reference groups, or reference individuals who are dissimilar [Hyman, 1942], in matters of fairness it is probably safe to suppose that most persons compare themselves to persons who are *similar*. In that case one argument of the perceived fairness of the wage will be the wages received by other similar workers. Such workers, of course, include workers who are employed; but, in addition, it includes workers in the reference set who are unemployed. While empirically unemployment at any moment is a fairly small fraction of the labor force, flows in and out of unemployment are large, and most workers have many friends and close relatives. The probability that a whole reference set be free of unemployment for a significant period (say a year) is not large for most persons.

There is one other argument to the reference wage. To the psychologist or sociologist, to say that persons compare their own behavior or treatment with that in the past is probably neither useful nor profound. But persons certainly do that, and some economic theory (for example, the Modigliani-Duesenberry peak income hypothesis) does depend on such behavior. Thus, one additional argument to the reference wage, in addition to the remuneration of similar employed and unemployed persons and their respective weights in the reference set, is past wages.

Consistent with this observation is the role of past wages in all labor negotiations. Labor disputes often concern the level of past wages, which are the benchmark for current negotiations. To cite a case in point, consider the General Motors strike of 1970. In the 1967–1970 contract wages were indexed, but an eight-cent-per-hour limit was placed on raises due to increases in the cost of living. The cost of living increased relative to wages by considerably more than eight cents per hour with a resultant level of wages twenty-six cents below the fully indexed level [Pearlstine, 1970]. The union claimed that the corporation had already received a windfall gain for the three years of the contract during which period wages were not fully indexed, and the negotiations should concern growth of the real wage from the fully indexed level; the company claimed negotiations should concern growth from the actual 1970 level. This matter was the most contentious issue in the settlement of a long strike.

Summing up all our discussion of the fair wage, the fair wage received by the worker depends on the effort he expends in excess of the work rules, the work rules themselves, the wages of other workers, the benefits of unemployed workers, as well as the number of such workers, and the worker's wages received in previous periods. Our theory of reference-group behavior thus yields a fair wage that looks very much like the wage paid in a Phillips curve:

$$w^f_{i,t+1} = f(w_{i,t}, w_0, b_u, u, e_i, e_0) \tag{5}$$

where

- $w^f_{i,t+1}$ is the perceived fair wage of individual i at $t + 1$
- $w_{i,t}$ is the actual wage of individual i in previous period(s)
- w_0 is the wage paid of others in the individual's reference set in current and previous periods
- b_u is unemployment benefits of individuals in the reference set in current and previous periods
- u is the number of unemployed in the reference set in current and previous periods
- e_i is the individual's work rules in current and previous periods

e_0 is the work rules of persons in the individual's reference set in current and previous periods.

Equation (5) is, of course, the basis for a Phillips curve of the traditional sort. It is important to note, however, that contrary to the Phillips relations obtained from search theory [Phelps *et al.*, 1970], (5) is not derived from market-clearing considerations. In general, there can be workers willing to enter gift relations with a firm, but no firms willing to enter gift relations with the workers. The next two sections model this occurrence. Our models are based upon the preceding discussion of reference groups and of the cash posters.

VI. A Model

This section and the next develop formal models that capture to some degree of accuracy most of the gift-giving idea in wage contracts. The ingredients of this model are spelled out in this section as follows.

1. *Norms* of effort on the part of workers in the work group. These norms depend on the work rules of the firm, the average wage paid by the firm, the incentive system of the firm (in terms of the different wages paid for different levels of output or effort), and the utility of co-workers in the firm who are part of the work group and for whom each worker has sympathy. All of these variables are endogenous to the firm. Exogenous to the firm, the norms depend on the returns to other persons in the workers' reference sets. In terms of our model these variables can be summarized by wages received by workers at other firms, the unemployment rate, and unemployment benefits. The model is considerably simplified by assuming only one time period. I do not see that this assumption takes anything away from the argument; it can be easily modified.

We thus summarize norms by the equation,

$$e_n = e_n(\{w(e,\epsilon)\},e_{\min},u_1,\ldots,u_J;w_0,u,b_u), \tag{6}$$

where

$\{w(e,\epsilon)\}$ is the function that relates wages of a worker of type ϵ to his effort; this is the remuneration system of the firm
$e_{\min}$ is the work rules
u_j is the utility of the jth worker in the firm
w_0 is the wage paid by other firms (perhaps a vector)
u is the unemployment rate
b_u is the unemployment benefit.

2. *Workers*. Each worker has a utility function. A worker who has been offered employment must decide on his level of effort and whether or not to accept employment at the terms offered. The utility of each worker depends on the norms for effort, the effort itself, and the wage rate if employed; it depends on the unemployment benefit if unemployed. A worker makes two choices. If offered employment (i.e., if the firm offers to "exchange gifts"), he must decide whether or not to accept the offer, and, if accepted, he must decide the size of the reciprocal gift. Thus, a worker of trait ϵ has a utility of working for the firm of

$$u(e_n,e,w,\epsilon), \tag{7}$$

and if not working for the firm, of

$$u(b_u,\epsilon).$$

If working for the firm, the worker chooses the level of effort e, which maximizes utility u, subject to the condition necessary to maintain his employment, that effort should exceed the firm's minimum requirement, $e \geqq e_{\min}$. Accordingly, the worker chooses a job, if offered, in preference to unemployment accordingly as

$$\max_{e \geqq e_{\min}} u(e_n,e,w,\epsilon) \tag{8}$$

is greater than or less than

$$u(b_u,\epsilon). \tag{9}$$

If a worker has more than one offer from different firms, he chooses the offer that maximizes his utility.

Across workers there is a distribution of tastes ϵ; we call this distribution function $f(\epsilon)$.

3. *Firms*. We are, finally, left with firm behavior. Firms have an output that depends on the work effort of the workers. This output q is

$$q = f(e_1,e_2,\ldots,e_J), \tag{10}$$

where J is the number of workers hired. e_j is the effort of worker j.

Firms pay wages in general according to type of worker ϵ and effort, so that $w = w(e,\epsilon)$.

Thus, wage cost is, accordingly,

$$\sum_{j=1}^{J} w(e_j,\epsilon_j),$$

where e_j is the effort of worker j and ϵ_j is the tastes of worker j.

The firm chooses the wage function $w(e,\epsilon)$, work rules, $e_{\min}$, and the number of workers it wishes to hire to maximize profits, which are

$$pf(e_1, \ldots, e_J) - \sum_{j=1}^{J} w(e_j, \epsilon_j), \tag{11}$$

where p is the price of output. The firm's behavior is subject to the constraint that a worker chooses whether or not to join the firm according to whether or not the firm is making the worker his best offer (including unemployment as an alternative); the firm also views e_n as endogenously determined.

Models may differ regarding the firm's knowledge of workers' tastes ϵ; in the models of the next section, where this is relevant, we assume that the probability that it chooses a worker of given tastes ϵ from the unemployment pool is random. That assumption, while convenient, could be modified.

The general model just described of norms-workers-firms is enough taken across all workers and firms to describe aggregate supply for a whole economy. Two such examples are explored in some detail in the next section. These examples describe major features of models with such norm-determined firm-worker interaction.

VII. Two Examples

According to the standard neoclassical model of the labor market, the firm purchases labor services in an optimal amount, *given the market wage.* This statement does not completely describe the firm's choice set, although in the *neoclassical* model the inaccuracy is of no importance. The neoclassical firm can purchase all the labor services it wishes if it pays a wage *at least as great as* the market wage. The firm chooses the wage and its purchases of labor services subject to this constraint. If the firm chooses a wage below the market-clearing level, it receives no labor. As far as its choice is concerned, it would be making the same decision if it demanded no labor and paid the market wage; and there is no advantage to choosing a wage in excess of the market rate. The firm's choice of wage therefore is always at the boundary: it will choose the optimal quantity of labor at the market-clearing wage.

However, once labor contracts are viewed in the context of gift exchange, it is not necessarily true that the firm will always choose wages on the boundary. In gift exchange the usual norm is that gifts should be more than the minimum required to keep the other party in the exchange relationship. In terms of the labor market this means that the worker who does no more than necessary to keep his job is the subject of at least some slight loss of reputation; reciprocally, the firm that pays its workers no more than the minimum necessary to retain them will also lose some reputation. In the neoclassical model the firm *never* chooses to pay more than the market-clearing wage because there is no advantage to doing so. In the gift-exchange model, however, the interior solution, in which the firm finds it advantageous to pay a wage in excess of the one at which it can acquire labor, may occur because there are some benefits (as well as costs) from paying a higher wage. Doubtless, this interior solution need not occur. Where it does occur, the labor market is primary. A worker entering the labor market will not automatically find work at the wage received by equally qualified employed persons. If the boundary solution occurs, in contrast, the labor market clears; the market is secondary, and a person in that market can readily obtain work at the wage received by current employees of similar qualifications.

The purpose of this section is to demonstrate by two specific examples the characteristics of the labor market in which gift exchange occurs in the sense that the workers' norm for effort depends upon their treatment by the firm. One example assumes that the firm's work rules are fixed, and with this assumption the equilibrium wage and unemployment are derived. The second example assumes that the real wage is fixed and demonstrates that work rules do not equilibrate supply and demand for labor in the sociological model (with norms) as they do in the neoclassical model. This model is specifically constructed with the behavior of the cash posters in mind.

Example I. Wages

Rather than present a model and show that there will be equilibrium unemployment, we work in reverse. All the parameters and functions of the model are chosen with the exception of the size of the labor force. It is then shown that appropriate particular choice of the size of the labor force will yield an equilibrium with unemployment rate u_0.

Let $\bar{l}$ workers per firm be the supply of labor. $\bar{l}$ will later be chosen to have a particular value to conform to the unemployment rate u_0, but that choice is at the end, not at the beginning of the story.

Let output q be a function of effort e and labor n according to the production function,

$$q = (en)^{\alpha}. \tag{12}$$

Let effort e of all workers be at the norm e_n. And let all workers be the same so that

$$e = e_n. \tag{13}$$

Let the effort norm be a function of the wage of the firm relative to the reference wage as

$$e_n = -a + b(w/w_r)^{\gamma}, \qquad \gamma < 1. \tag{14}$$

(Two considerations explain the particular choice of $e_n - w$ function (14). First, the firm chooses w to maximize the number of labor efficiency units per dollar spent. Solow [1979] has shown that such an internal maximum occurs where the elasticity of w with respect to e is equal to unity. And to insure that this choice of w yields the maximum effort per dollar of expenditure, the $e_n - w$ elasticity must be declining. The function (14) has been chosen accordingly with a declining $e_n - w$ elasticity. A second consideration is responsible for the negative intercept of $-a$. If positive effort is obtained at a 0 wage, a 0 wage [with infinite effort per dollar] is optimal.)

Let the reference wage w_r be the geometric mean,

$$w_r = w_0^{1-u}\, b_u^{u}, \tag{15}$$

where

u is the unemployment rate,
w_0 is the wage paid by other firms, and
b_u is the level of unemployment benefits.

Since the firm in question is the typical firm, it also follows that the employment by the firm n is the average number of employed persons per firm, or

$$n = (1 - u)\bar{l}. \tag{16}$$

Furthermore, again because the firm in question is the typical firm, its wage is the same as the wage of other firms, or

$$w = w_0. \tag{17}$$

Suppose that u is u_0. It will be shown that with appropriate choice of the parameter $\bar{l} = l_0$, the profit-maximizing firm will choose to hire an amount of labor $n = (1 - u_0)\bar{l}$ if its wage w is the same as the wage of other firms w_0. Consequently, u_0 is an equilibrium rate of unemployment with labor supply l_0.

The firm behaves in the following fashion. With unemployment at $u_0 > 0$, it can obtain all the workers it wants at any wage. Consequently, it chooses n and w to maximize profits, or

$$\Pi = (en)^{\alpha} - wn \tag{18}$$

subject to the constraints

$$e = e_n \tag{19}$$

$$e_n = -a + b(w/w_r)^{\gamma} \tag{20}$$

$$w_r = w_0^{1-u}\, b_u^{u}. \tag{21}$$

This maximization problem together with the condition $w = w_0$ yields the demand for labor n^d as a function of the unemployment rate u_0:

$$n^d = \left(\alpha^{-1} b_u \left(\frac{a\gamma}{1-\gamma}\right)^{-\alpha} \left(\frac{a}{b(1-\gamma)}\right)^{1/\gamma u_0}\right)^{1/(\alpha-1)}. \tag{22}$$

If n^d is consistent with the unemployment rate, then the supply of labor, which is as yet an unchosen parameter of our model, must be

$$\bar{l} = l_0 = \frac{n^d}{1-u_0} = (1-u_0)^{-1}\left(\alpha^{-1} b_u \left(\frac{a\gamma}{1-\gamma}\right)^{-\alpha} \times \left(\frac{a}{b(1-\gamma)}\right)^{1/\gamma u_0}\right)^{1/(\alpha-1)}. \tag{23}$$

With $\bar{l}$ chosen in this fashion according to the right-hand side of (23), our model has an equilibrium at the rate of unemployment u_0, where $0 < u_0 < 1$. Note that the unemployed would be willing to work at the wage paid employed workers, but firms will be unwilling to hire them at that wage, or one which is lower.

Moreover, it is also easy to construct an example in which the firm's choice of w is not interior. After all, if the coefficient $b = 0$ and $a < 0$, the example exactly corresponds to the neoclassical model verbally analyzed at the beginning of this section in which all markets cleared. In our analysis the property, whether or not markets clear, or, alternatively stated, whether labor markets are secondary or primary is endogenous.[7]

Example 2. Work Standards

The first example illustrated the possibility (and the accompanying discussion partially characterized that possibility) that the

7. Just because some markets clear does not mean that there is no unemployment. Unemployed workers may be waiting for an opportunity to take a primary sector job. See Hall [1975].

relation between work norms and wages will cause an economy-wide (or labor-market-wide) equilibrium with nonmarket-clearing prices because firms themselves find it advantageous to set wages above the minimum at which they can freely obtain labor.

Our discussion of the cash posters, however, was not concerned with wages but rather with work rules. According to the standard neoclassical model, even if for some reason wages are not fixed at market-clearing levels, still firms should adjust work rules to the point where supply and demand for labor are equal (*even at a nonequilibrial wage*). This section gives an example, in which the work rules will not equilibrate labor supply and demand. It is not the simplest example—partly because of our desire to make the model a faithful representation of the cash posters, and partially also because the reaction of workers to norms inherently involves a great deal of behavior that cannot easily be represented by simple linear functions.

Because in the standard neoclassical model work standards would equate demand and supply for labor even at a fixed nonequilibrating wage rate, we start with the assumption that the wage rate $\overline{w}$ is fixed. Although artificial, we could assume that the government has controlled wages. Certainly this occasionally happens when the government imposes certain forms of incomes policy.

Recall that among the cash posters some workers worked much above the work standard set by the firm (45 percent for Granara and Murphy) while some workers were quite close to the margin (only 2 percent above for Burke and Donovan).

To represent a model in which some workers are above the margin while other workers are at the margin, it is necessary to have at least two types of workers. For that reason our model has two groups of workers with different tastes. Poor workers form a fraction p of the work force. Good workers form a fraction $1 - p$.

In the story behind our model the firm is capable of identifying the tastes of workers only after they have joined the firm, but not before. In terms of the cash posters, who could have predicted that the almost equally outgoing and gregarious Murphy and Burke would have work records which were polar opposites? Homans hints that this difference may have occurred in part because Burke socialized primarily with a group of "ledger posters," while the rest of the cash posters socialized mainly among themselves. Certainly no personnel officer could have predicted such an occurrence.

Although the firm can measure performance easily once workers are hired, it is assumed that it cannot fire them without a reduction in the work norms. As a result, in the model constructed labor effort is observable ex post but not predictable ex ante.

Worker Behavior

Among the two types of workers, good workers who work for the firm have utility, denoted U^+, where

$$U^+ = A - B(e - (e_n + \epsilon))^2. \tag{24}$$

The parameter A depends on wages, but since they are assumed fixed, we have suppressed that dependency. Poor workers who work for the firm have utility, denoted U^-, where

$$U^- = A - B(e - (e_n - \epsilon))^2. \tag{25}$$

The parameters A and B are both positive, e_n is the norm of work effort, e is actual effort by the individual worker, and ϵ is a parameter reflecting the type of worker. U^+ and U^- are the utilities of good workers and bad workers, respectively, when working for the firm. Workers have the option of working for the firm with effort e and also the option of quitting and being unemployed. In that case their utility is assumed to be 0.

A worker who works for a firm maximizes his utility subject to abiding by the work rules of the firm. Thus, a good worker with utility function U^+ chooses e to maximize

$$A - B(e - (e_n + \epsilon))^2, \tag{26}$$

subject to the constraint

$$e \geqq e^+_{\min}, \tag{27}$$

where $e^+_{\min}$ is the minimum work standard set by the firm for good workers. Accordingly, for such a worker if U^+ working for the firm is positive, the worker chooses to work with effort e^+:

$$e^+ = \max(e^+_{\min}, e_n + \epsilon). \tag{28}$$

Similarly, if U^- working for the firm is positive, a poor worker chooses to work with effort e^-:

$$e^- = \max(e^-_{\min}, e_n - \epsilon). \tag{29}$$

Norms

The norms of behavior depend upon the work rules,

$$e_n = e_n(e^-_{\min}, e^+_{\min}). \tag{30}$$

Later it will be assumed that $e^-_{\min}$ and $e^+_{\min}$ have an effect on norms only insofar as they are a binding constraint on workers' effort.

Firm Behavior

On its side, the firm takes into account the reaction of the workers' effort to the norms and the reaction of the norms to work rules. In the case of excess supply of labor, where labor is freely available as long as U^+ and U^- are positive, the firm chooses $e^+_{\min}, e^-_{\min}$, and n to maximize profits, or

$$(\bar{e}(e^-_{\min}, e^+_{\min})n)^\alpha - \bar{w}n, \tag{31}$$

where $\bar{e}(\,)$ is the function combining (28), (29), and (30) with the appropriate weights to account for the dependence of average effort on work rules.

Accordingly, at an interior maximum the firm that can obtain all the labor it wishes will choose $e^-_{\min}$ and $e^+_{\min}$ to maximize $\bar{e}(e^-_{\min}, e^+_{\min})$, and its demand for labor according to the marginal product condition,

$$\alpha\bar{e}(e^{-*}_{\min}, e^{+*}_{\min})^\alpha n^{\alpha-1} = \bar{w}. \tag{32}$$

As long as n so chosen by the typical firm is less than $\bar{l}$, the demand for labor is less than the supply, and the assumption that the firm can obtain all the labor it wishes is justified.

Problems with obtaining an interior maximum. The question, however, arises, how there can be an interior maximum for $e^+_{\min}$ or $e^-_{\min}$. After all, why should the firm not increase $e^+_{\min}$ just up to the point where all good workers are on the verge of quitting? (In so doing, it also may have the added dividend of screening out the poorer workers.) In the real world workers usually apply sanctions against such behavior by the firm. For example, in the case of the cash posters, remember that Homans recorded a work slowdown in a previous dispute with a supervisor. In our model this is represented by the fact that as the work rules force workers to work sufficiently in excess of the norms, they quit.

Let the fraction p of poor workers be ½. Let the tastes parameter ϵ be 1. And let the parameters A and B in (24) and (25) be 2 and ½, respectively, so that

$$U^+ = 2 - \tfrac{1}{2}(e - (e_n + \epsilon))^2 \tag{33}$$

$$U^- = 2 - \tfrac{1}{2}(e - (e_n - \epsilon))^2. \tag{34}$$

Good workers, who maximize U^+, will choose

$$e = e_n + \epsilon \tag{35}$$

as long as they are unconstrained by the work rules. Similarly, if unconstrained, poor workers, who maximize U^-, will choose

$$e = e_n - \epsilon. \tag{36}$$

We assume that the work rules have an effect on the effort norm if and only if they are binding. Accordingly, the norm depends on $\max(e^+_{\min} - (e_n + \epsilon),0)$ and $\max(e^-_{\min} - (e_n - \epsilon),0)$. Furthermore, it is assumed that the norms are egalitarian in that a difference between the work rules for the two types of workers will have a negative effect on the norms.

Accordingly, the norm in this example follows the formula,

$$e_n = 6 - 0.8 \max(e^+_{\min} - (e_n + \epsilon), e^-_{\min} - (e_n - \epsilon), 0) - 20|e^+_{\min} - e^-_{\min}|. \tag{37}$$

The second term of (37) reflects the decline in the norm of effort as the work rules become increasingly binding on the workers' choice of effort. The third term reflects the effect on the norm of an inequality in the treatment of the two types of workers.

It is easy to check that the firm which wishes to maximize $\bar{e}$ will choose

$$e^+_{\min} = e^-_{\min} \leqq 5, \tag{38}$$

and at this maximum $\bar{e} = 6$.

I will sketch the proof. First, inequality in $e^+_{\min}$ and $e^-_{\min}$ causes such a large reduction in e_n (the coefficient of the last term of (37) being 20) that the firm always finds it advantageous to set $e^+_{\min} = e^-_{\min}$. In that case the formula for e_n (37) can be simplified to

$$e_n = 6 - 0.8 \max(e_{\min} - (e_n - \epsilon), 0). \tag{39}$$

A bit of algebra shows that with $\epsilon = 1$ (39) can be rewritten as

$$e_n = 6 \qquad e_{\min} \leqq 5 \tag{40A}$$

$$e_n = 30 - 4e_{\min} - 4 \qquad e_{\min} \geqq 5. \tag{40B}$$

It is easy to check using (34), (40A), (40B) and the value of $\epsilon = 1$ that U^- is positive if $e_{\min} < 5.4$ and negative if $e_{\min} > 5.4$. Similarly, U^+ is positive if $e_{\min} < 5.8$ and is negative for $e_{\min} > 5.8$.

Thus, in the range $0 \leqq e_{\min} < 5.4$ both good and bad workers are working. For $0 \leqq e_{\min} \leqq 5$ work rules are binding on neither good nor bad workers, and therefore

$$\bar{e} = \tfrac{1}{2}(e_n + \epsilon) + \tfrac{1}{2}(e_n - \epsilon) = e_n = 6, \qquad 0 \leqq e_{\min} \leqq 5. \tag{41}$$

For $5 < e_{\min} < 5.4$ work rules are binding on poor workers but not on good workers. U^- and U^+ are both positive so both good and bad workers are at work. Hence

$$\bar{e} = \tfrac{1}{2}(e_n + \epsilon) + \tfrac{1}{2}e_{\min} \qquad 5 < e_{\min} < 5.4 \tag{42}$$

$$= 13.5 - 1.5e_{\min} < 6 \qquad 5 < e_{\min} < 5.4. \tag{43}$$

By design of the example, for $e_{\min} > 5.4$ U^- is negative; also by (40B) for $e_{\min} > 5.4$, $e_n + \epsilon < e_{\min}$, so work rules are binding on good workers. U^+ is positive for $e_{\min} < 5.8$. Consequently, in the range $5.4 < e_{\min} < 5.8$ only good workers are at work, and since their effort is constrained by work rules,

$$\bar{e} = e_{\min} \qquad 5.4 < e_{\min} < 5.8. \tag{44}$$

For $e_{\min} > 5.8$ $\bar{e}$ is indeterminate, since U^+ and U^- are both negative. The number of workers willing to work is, however, 0. Hence $\bar{e}$ is maximized according to (41), (43), and (44) at $\bar{e} = 6$ with $e^+_{\min} = e^-_{\min} \leqq 5$.

To obtain an example with unemployment rate u_0, it is only necessary to choose $\bar{l} = l_0$ consistent with u_0 and the marginal productivity condition for labor demand so that

$$\bar{l} = l_0 = (1 - u_0)^{-1}(\alpha^{-1}6^{-\alpha}\overline{w})^{1/(\alpha-1)}. \tag{45}$$

Remark. This example corresponds exactly to cash poster behavior. The firm paid the same wage to all workers. One group of workers (a minority) worked at the work standard, or very close to it. Other workers worked above that standard. For reasons unspecified by Homans, but which are consistent with our model, the firm did not raise standards on either good workers or poor workers. At the equilibrium unemployment is involuntary.

VIII. Conclusion

This paper has explored the idea that labor contracts are partial gift exchanges. According to this idea, at least in part, wages are determined by, and in turn also influence, the norms of workers' effort; similarly, workers' effort is determined, at least in part, by these norms. A relation between the terms of exchange and norms is in our view what differentiates gift exchange from pure market exchange.

Indeed, while the norms may be greatly influenced by the same things as market prices, there is still a major difference between pure market exchange and gift exchange. In pure market exchange the maximum price at which a buyer is willing to purchase a commodity or factor service is the minimum at which the respective commodity or factor service is obtainable. Obversely, the minimum price at which a seller is willing to sell a commodity or factor service is the maximum at which the respective commodity or factor service can be sold. In gift exchange buyers may be willing to pay more than the minimum at which they can purchase a commodity or factor service because of the effect of the terms of exchange on the norms. Similarly, sellers may be willing to accept less than the maximum at which they can sell a commodity or factor service because of the effects of the terms of exchange on the norms. It has been shown that due to this behavior with gift exchange markets need not clear. Thus, the gift-exchange economy and the neoclassical economy differ in at least one fundamental respect. Future papers will explore further differences between the two models of exchange.

UNIVERSITY OF CALIFORNIA, BERKELEY

REFERENCES

Azariadis, C., "Implicit Contracts and Unemployment Equilibria," *Journal of Political Economy*, LXXXIII (Dec. 1975), 1183–1202.
Baily, M. N., "Wages and Employment Under Uncertain Demand," *Review of Economic Studies*, XLI (Jan. 1974), 37–50.
Belshaw, C. S., *Traditional Exchange and Modern Markets* (Englewood Cliffs, NJ: Prentice-Hall, 1965).
Coser, L. A., *Masters of Sociological Thought: Ideas in Historical and Social Context* (New York: Harcourt Brace Jovanovich, 1971).
Doeringer, P. B., and M. J. Piore, *Internal Labor Markets and Manpower Analysis* (Lexington, MA: D. C. Heath & Co., 1971).
Edwards, R., *Contested Terrain: The Transformation of the Workplace in the Twentieth Century* (New York: Basic Books, 1979).
Etzioni, A. W., *Modern Organizations* (Englewood Cliffs, NJ: Prentice-Hall, 1971).
Festinger, L., "A Theory of Social Comparison Processes," *Human Relations*, VII (1954), 117–40; reprinted in *Readings in Reference Group Therapy*, Herbert H. Hyman and Eleanor Singer, eds. (New York: The Free Press, 1968).
Freeman, R. L., and J. L. Medoff, "The Two Faces of Unionism," *The Public Interest*, No. 57 (Fall 1979), 69–93.
Hall, R. E., "The Rigidity of Wages and the Persistence of Unemployment." *Brookings Papers on Economic Activity*, III (1975), 301–49.
Hirschman, A. O., *Exit, Voice and Loyalty* (Cambridge: Harvard University Press, 1970).
Homans, G. C., "Status Among Clerical Workers," *Human Organization*, XII (Spring 1953), 5–10; reprinted in G. C. Homans, *Sentiments and Activities* (New York: Free Press of Glencoe, 1962).
——, "The Cash Posters," *American Sociological Review*, XIX (Dec. 1954), 724–33; reprinted in G. C. Homans, *Sentiments and Activities* (New York: Free Press of Glencoe, 1962).
Hyman, H. H., "The Psychology of Status," *Archives of Psychology*, No. 269 (1942); reprinted in part in *Readings in Reference Group Theory*, Herbert H. Hyman and Eleanor Singer, eds. (New York: The Free Press, 1968).
Leibenstein, H., *Beyond Economic Man: A New Foundation for Microeconomics* (Cambridge, MA: Harvard University Press, 1976).

Mauss, M., *The Gift: Forms and Functions of Exchange in Archaic Societies*, translated by Ian Cunnison (London: Cohen and West, 1954).
Mayo, E., *The Social Problems of an Industrial Civilization* (London: Routledge and Kegan Paul, 1949).
Merton, R. K., *Social Theory and Social Structure*, revised and enlarged edition (Glencoe, IL: The Free Press, 1957).
Okun, A., "Inflation: Its Mechanics and Welfare Costs," *Brookings Papers on Economic Activity*, II (1975), 366–73.
——, *Prices and Quantities: A Macroeconomic Analysis* (Washington, D.C.: The Brookings Institution, 1981).
Pearlstine, N., "Auto Pact Tension Eases; Strike Chances Viewed as Tied to Chrysler, GM Parleys," *Wall Street Journal*, CLXXVI, No. 48 (Sept. 4, 1970), 5, column 2.
Phelps, E. S. *et al.*, *The Microeconomic Foundations of Employment and Inflation Theory* (New York: Norton, 1970).
Roethlisberger, F. J., and W. J. Dickson, *Management and the Worker: An Account of a Research Program Conducted by the Western Electric Company, Hawthorne Works, Chicago* (Cambridge, MA: Harvard University Press, 1947).
Solow, R. H., "Another Possible Source of Wage Stickiness," *Journal of Macroeconomics*, I (Winter 1979), 79–82.
——, "On Theories of Unemployment," *American Economic Review*, LXX (March 1980), 1–10.
Stoft, S., "Cheat-Threat Theory," University of California Thesis Prospectus, August 1980.
Stouffer, S. A., E. A. Suchman, L. C. de Vinney, S. A. Star, and R. M. Williams, Jr., *The American Soldier: Adjustment During Army Life*, Vol. 1 (Princeton, NJ: Princeton University Press, 1949).
Stouffer, S. A., A. A. Lumsdaine, M. H. Lumsdaine, R. M. Williams, Jr., M. B. Smith, I. L. Jarvis, S. A. Star, and L. S. Cottrell, Jr., *The American Soldier: Combat and its Aftermath*, Vol. 2 (Princeton NJ: Princeton University Press, 1949).
Titmuss, R. M., *The Gift Relationship: From Human Blood to Social Policy* (New York: Random House, 1971).

[24]

Incorporating Fairness into Game Theory and Economics

By MATTHEW RABIN*

People like to help those who are helping them, and to hurt those who are hurting them. Outcomes reflecting such motivations are called fairness equilibria. Outcomes are mutual-max when each person maximizes the other's material payoffs, and mutual-min when each person minimizes the other's payoffs. It is shown that every mutual-max or mutual-min Nash equilibrium is a fairness equilibrium. If payoffs are small, fairness equilibria are roughly the set of mutual-max and mutual-min outcomes; if payoffs are large, fairness equilibria are roughly the set of Nash equilibria. Several economic examples are considered, and possible welfare implications of fairness are explored. (*JEL* A12, A13, D63, C70)

Most current economic models assume that people pursue only their own material self-interest and do not care about "social" goals. One exception to self-interest which has received some attention by economists is simple altruism: people may care not only about their own well-being, but also about the well-being of others. Yet psychological evidence indicates that most altruistic behavior is more complex: people do not seek uniformly to help other people; rather, they do so according to how generous these other people are being. Indeed, *the same people who are altrustic to other altruistic people are also motivated to hurt those who hurt them*. If somebody is being nice to you, fairness dictates that you be nice to him. If somebody is being mean to you, fairness allows—and vindictiveness dictates—that you be mean to him.

Clearly, these emotions have economic implications. If an employee has been exceptionally loyal, then a manger may feel some obligation to treat that employee well, even when it is not in his self-interest to do so. Other examples of economic behavior induced by social goals are voluntary reductions of water-use during droughts, conservation of energy to help solve the energy crisis (as documented, for instance, in Kenneth E. Train et al. [1987]), donations to public television stations, and many forms of voluntary labor. (Burton A. Weisbrod [1988] estimates that, in the United States, the total value of voluntary labor is $74 billion annually.)

On the negative side, a consumer may not buy a product sold by a monopolist at an "unfair" price, even if the material value to the consumer is greater than the price. By not buying, the consumer lowers his own material well-being so as to punish the monopolist. An employee who feels she has been mistreated by a firm may engage in acts of sabotage. Members of a striking labor union may strike longer than is in their material interests because they want to punish a firm for being unfair.

*Department of Economics, 787 Evans Hall, University of California, Berkeley, CA 94720. I thank Nikki Blasberg, Jeff Ely, April Franco, and especially Gadi Barlevy for research assistance; George Akerlof, Colin Camerer, Joe Farrell, Jonathan Feinstein, Ruth Given, Danny Kahneman, Annette Montgomery, Richard Thaler, and especially Bill Dickens for useful conversations; and Gadi Barlevy, Roland Benabou, Nikki Blasberg, Gary Bolton, Jeff Ely, April Franco, Drew Fudenberg, Rachel Kranton, Michael Lii, James Montgomery, Jim Ratliff, Halsey Rogers, Lones Smith, Jeff Zweibel, two anonymous referees, and especially Eddie Dekel-Tabak, Jim Fearon, Berkeley's David Levine, and Vai-Lam Mui for helpful comments on earlier drafts of this paper. I also thank the Institute of Business and Economic Research at the University of California-Berkeley for their funding of research assistance and the National Science Foundation (Grant SES92-10323) for financial support.

By modeling such emotions formally, one can begin to understand their economic and welfare implications more rigorously and more generally. In this paper, I develop a game-theoretic framework for incorporating such emotions into a broad range of economic models.[1] My framework incorporates the following three stylized facts:

(A) People are willing to sacrifice their own material well-being to help those who are being kind.
(B) People are willing to sacrifice their own material well-being to punish those who are being unkind.
(C) Both motivations (A) and (B) have a greater effect on behavior as the material cost of sacrificing becomes smaller.

In the next section, I briefly present some of the evidence from the psychological literature regarding these stylized facts. In Section II, I develop a game-theoretic solution concept "fairness equilibrium" that incorporates these stylized facts. Fairness equilibria do not in general constitute either a subset or a superset of Nash equilibria; that is, incorporating fairness considerations can both add new predictions to economic models and eliminate conventional predictions. In Section III, I present some general results about which outcomes in economic situations are likely to be fairness equilibria. The results demonstrate the special role of "mutual-max" outcomes (in which, given the other person's behavior, each person maximizes the other's material payoffs) and "mutual-min" outcomes (in which, given the other person's behavior, each person minimizes the other's material payoffs). The following results hold:

(i) Any Nash equilibrium that is either a mutual-max outcome or mutual-min outcome is also a fairness equilibrium.
(ii) If material payoffs are small, then, roughly, an outcome is a fairness equilibrium if and only if it is a mutual-max or a mutual-min outcome.
(iii) If material payoffs are large, then, roughly, an outcome is a fairness equilibrium if and only if it is a Nash equilibrium.

I hope this framework will eventually be used to study the implications of fairness in different economic situations. While I do not develop extended applications in this paper, Section IV contains examples illustrating the economic implications of my model of fairness. I develop a simple model of monopoly pricing and show that fairness implies that goods can only be sold at below the classical monopoly price. I then explore the implications of fairness in an extended labor example.

I consider some welfare implications of my model in Section V. Many researchers in welfare economics have long considered issues of fairness to be important in evaluating the desirability of different economic outcomes. Yet while such policy analysis incorporates economists' judgments of fairness and equity, it often ignores the concerns for fairness and equity of the economic actors being studied. By considering how people's attitudes toward fairness influence their behavior and well-being, my framework can help incorporate such concerns more directly into policy analysis and welfare economics.

While my model suggests that the behavioral implications of fairness are greatest when the material consequences of an economic interaction are not too large, there

[1]While many recognize the importance of social motivations in economic phenomena, these emotions have not been investigated widely within the formal apparatus of mainstream economics. Other researchers who have done so include George Akerlof (1982), Peter H. Huang and Ho-Mou Wu (1992), Vai-Lam Mui (1992), and Julio J. Rotemberg (1992); but these and other economic models have tended to be context-specific. While the current version of my model only applies to two-person complete-information games, it applies to *all* such games. If it is extended naturally, it will therefore have specific consequences in any economic or social situation that can be modeled by noncooperative game theory. (By its generality, my model may also contribute to psychological research. While some psychology researchers have tried to formulate general principles of behavior, I believe that noncooperative game theory provides a useful language for doing so more carefully. My model, for instance, helps demonstrate that some seemingly different behaviors in different contexts are explicable by common underlying principles.)

are several reasons why this does not imply that the economic implications of fairness are minor. First, while it is true that fairness influences behavior most when material stakes are small, it is not clear that it makes little difference when material stakes are large. Little empirical research on the economic implications of fairness has been conducted, and much anecdotal evidence suggests that people sacrifice substantial amounts of money to reward or punish kind or unkind behavior. Second, many major economic institutions, most notably decentralized markets, are best described as accumulations of minor economic interactions, so that the aggregate implications of departures from standard theory in these cases may be substantial. Third, the fairness component of a person's overall well-being can be influenced substantially by even small material changes.

Finally, even if material incentives in a situation are so large as to dominate behavior, fairness still matters. Welfare economics should be concerned not only with the efficient allocation of material goods, but also with designing institutions such that people are happy about the way they interact with others. For instance, if a person leaves an exchange in which he was treated unkindly, then his unhappiness at being so treated should be a consideration in evaluating the efficiency of that exchange. Armed with well-founded psychological assumptions, economists can start to address the nonmaterial benefits and costs of the free market and other institutions.[2]

I conclude the paper in Section VI with a discussion of some of the shortfalls of my model and an outline of possible extensions.

I. Fairness in Games: Some Evidence

In this section, I discuss some psychological research that demonstrates the stylized facts outlined in the Introduction. Consider fact A: "People are willing to sacrifice their own material well-being to help those who are being kind." The attempt to provide public goods without coercion is an archetypical example in which departures from pure self-interest can be beneficial to society, and it has been studied by psychologists as a means of testing for the existence of altruism and cooperation. Laboratory experiments of public goods have been conducted by, among others, John M. Orbell (1978), Gerald Marwell and Ruth Ames (1981), Werner Güth (1982), Alphons J. C. van de Kragt et al. (1983), R. Mark Isaac et al. (1984, 1985), Oliver Kim and Mark Walker (1984), James Andreoni (1988a, b), and Isaac James Walker (1988a, b). These experiments typically involve subjects choosing how much to contribute toward a public good, where the self-interested contribution is small or zero. The evidence from these experiments is that people cooperate to a degree greater than would be implied by pure self-interest. Many of these experiments are surveyed in Robyn M. Dawes and Richard H. Thaler (1988), who conclude that, for most experiments of one-shot public-good decisions in which the individually optimal contribution is close to 0 percent, the contribution rate ranges between 40 percent and 60 percent of the socially optimal level.[3]

These experiments indicate that contributions toward public goods are not, however, the result of "pure altruism," where people seek unconditionally to help others. Rather, the willingness to help seems highly contingent on the behavior of others. If people do not think that others are doing their fair share, then their enthusiasm for sacrificing for others is greatly diminished.

[2]Indeed, I show in Section V that there exist situations in which the unique fairness equilibrium leaves both players feeling that they have been treated unkindly. This means that negative emotions may be endogenously generated by particular economic structures. I also state and prove an unhappy theorem: *every* game contains at least one such "unkind equilibrium." That is, there does not exist any situation in which players necessarily depart with positive feelings.

[3]Further examples of stylized fact A can be found in Richard E. Goranson and Leonard Berkowitz (1966), Martin Greenberg and David Frisch (1972), Elizabeth Hoffman and Matthew Spitzer (1982), and Daniel Kahneman et al. (1986a, b).

Indeed, stylized fact B says that people will in some situations not only refuse to help others, but will sacrifice to hurt others who are being unfair. This idea has been most widely explored in the "ultimatum game," discussed at length in Thaler (1988). The ultimatum game consists of two people splitting some fixed amount of money X according to the following rules: a "proposer" offers some division of X to a "decider." If the decider says yes, they split the money according to the proposal. If the decider says no, they both get no money. The result of pure self-interest is clear: proposers will never offer more than a penny, and deciders should accept any offer of at least a penny. Yet experiments clearly reject such behavior. Data show that, even in one-shot settings, deciders are willing to punish unfair offers by rejecting them, and proposers tend to make fair offers.[4] Some papers illustrating stylized fact B are Goranson and Berkowitz (1966), Jerald Greenberg (1978), Güth et al. (1982), Kahneman et al. (1986a,b), and Alvin E. Roth et al. (1991).

Stylized fact C says that people will not be as willing to sacrifice a great amount of money to maintain fairness as they would be with small amounts of money. It is tested and partially confirmed in Gerald Leventhal and David Anderson (1970), but its validity is intuitive to most people. If the ultimatum game were conducted with $1, then most deciders would reject a proposed split of ($0.90, $0.10). If the ultimatum game were conducted with $10 million, the vast majority of deciders would accept a proposed split of ($9 million, $1 million).[5] Consider also the following example from Dawes and Thaler (1988 p. 145):

> In the rural areas around Ithaca it is common for farmers to put some fresh produce on a table by the road. There is a cash box on the table, and customers are expected to put money in the box in return for the vegetables they take. The box has just a small slit, so money can only be put in, not taken out. Also, the box is attached to the table, so no one can (easily) make off with the money. We think that the farmers who use this system have just about the right model of human nature. They feel that enough people will volunteer to pay for the fresh corn to make it worthwhile to put it out there. The farmers also know that if it were easy enough to take the money, someone would do so.

This example is in the spirit of stylized fact C: people succumb to the temptation to pursue their interests at the expense of others in proportion to the profitability of doing so.

From an economist's point of view, it matters not only whether stylized facts A–C are true, but whether they have important economic implications. Kahneman et al. (1986a,b) present strong arguments that these general issues are indeed important. For anyone unconvinced of the importance of social goals empirically or intuitively, one purpose of this paper is to help test the proposition theoretically: will adding fairness to economic models substantially alter conclusions? If so, in what situations will conclusions be altered, and in what way?

II. A Model

To formalize fairness, I adopt the framework developed by John Geanakoplos, David Pearce, and Ennio Stacchetti (1989) (hereafter, GPS). They modify conventional game theory by allowing payoffs to depend on players' *beliefs* as well as on their actions (see also Itzhak Gilboa and David Schmeidler, 1988).[6] While explicitly incorporating

[4]The decision by proposers to make fair offers can come from at least two motivations: self-interested proposers might be fair because they know unfair offers may be rejected, and proposers themselves have a preference for being fair.

[5]Clearly, however, a higher percentage of deciders would turn down an offer of ($9,999,999.90, $0.10) than turn down ($0.90, $0.10). In his footnote 6, Thaler (1988) concurs with these intuitions, while pointing out the obvious difficulty in financing experiments of the scale needed to test them fully.

[6]Outside the context of noncooperative game theory, Akerlof and William T. Dickens (1982) presented an earlier model incorporating beliefs directly into people's utility functions.

		Player 2: Opera	Player 2: Boxing
Player 1	Opera	2X, X	0, 0
	Boxing	0, 0	X, 2X

FIGURE 1. EXAMPLE 1: BATTLE OF THE SEXES

beliefs substantially complicates analysis, I argue that the approach is necessary to capture aspects of fairness. Fortunately, GPS show that many standard techniques and results have useful analogues in these "psychological games."

In developing my model of fairness, I extend the GPS approach with an additional step which I believe will prove essential for incorporating psychology into economic research: I derive psychological games from basic "material games." Whereas GPS provide a technique for analyzing games that already incorporate emotions, I use assumptions about fairness to derive psychological games from the more traditional material description of a situation. Doing so, I develop a model that can be applied generally and can be compared directly to standard economic analysis.

To motivate both the general framework and my specific model, consider Example 1 (see Fig. 1), where X is a positive number. (Throughout the paper, I shall represent games with the positive "scale variable" X. This allows me to consider the effects of increasing or decreasing a game's stakes without changing its fundamental strategic structure.) This is a standard battle-of-the-sexes game: two people prefer to go to the same event together, but each prefers a different event. Formally, both players prefer to play either (opera, opera) or (boxing, boxing) rather than not coordinating; but player 1 prefers (opera, opera), and player 2 prefers (boxing, boxing).

The payoffs are a function only of the moves made by the players. Suppose, however, that player 1 (say) cares not only about his own payoff, but depending on player 2's motives, he cares also about player 2's payoff. In particular, if player 2 seems to be intentionally helping player 1, then player 1 will be motivated to help player 2; if player 2 seems to be intentionally hurting player 1, then player 1 will wish to hurt player 2.

Suppose player 1 believes (a) that player 2 is playing boxing, and (b) that player 2 believes player 1 is playing boxing. Then player 1 concludes that player 2 is choosing an action that helps both players (playing opera would hurt both players). Because player 2 is not being either generous or mean, neither stylized fact A nor B applies. Thus, player 1 will be neutral about his effect on player 2 and will pursue his material self-interest by playing boxing. If this argument is repeated for player 2, one can show that, in the natural sense, (boxing, boxing) is an equilibrium: if it is common knowledge that this will be the outcome, then each player is maximizing his utility by playing his strategy.

Of course, (boxing, boxing) is a conventional Nash equilibrium in this game. To see the importance of fairness, suppose player 1 believes (a) that player 2 will play boxing, and (b) that player 2 believes that player 1 is playing opera. Now player 1 concludes that player 2 is lowering her own payoff in order to hurt him. Player 1 will therefore feel hostility toward player 2 and will wish to harm her. If this hostility is strong enough, player 1 may be willing to sacrifice his own material well-being, and play opera rather than boxing. Indeed, if both players have a strong enough emotional reaction to each other's behavior, then (opera, boxing) is an equilibrium. If it is common knowledge that they are playing this outcome, then, in the induced atmosphere of hostility, both players will wish to stick with it.

Notice the central role of expectations: player 1's payoffs do not depend simply on the actions taken, but also on his beliefs about player 2's motives. Could these emotions be directly modeled by transforming the payoffs, so that one could analyze this transformed game in the conventional way? This turns out to be impossible. In the natural sense, both of the equilibria discussed above are strict: each player strictly prefers to play his strategy given the equilibrium. In the equilibrium (boxing, boxing), player 1 strictly prefers playing boxing to opera. In the equilibrium (opera, boxing) player 1 strictly prefers opera to boxing. No matter what payoffs are chosen, these statements would be contradictory if payoffs depended solely on the actions taken. To formalize these preferences, therefore, it is necessary to develop a model that explicitly incorporates beliefs.[7] I now construct such a model, applicable to all two-person, finite-strategy games.

Consider a two-player, normal form game with (mixed) strategy sets S_1 and S_2 for players 1 and 2, derived from finite pure-strategy sets A_1 and A_2. Let $\pi_i : S_1 \times S_2 \rightarrow \mathbb{R}$ be player i's *material payoffs*.[8]

From this "material game," I now construct a "psychological game" as defined in GPS. I assume that each player's subjective expected utility when he chooses his strategy will depend on three factors: (i) his strategy, (ii) his beliefs about the other player's strategy choice, and (iii) his beliefs about the other player's beliefs about his strategy. Throughout, I shall use the following notation: $a_1 \in S_1$ and $a_2 \in S_2$ represent the strategies chosen by the two players; $b_1 \in S_1$ and $b_2 \in S_2$ represent, respectively, player 2's beliefs about what strategy player 1 is choosing, and player 1's beliefs about what strategy player 2 is choosing; $c_1 \in S_1$ and $c_2 \in S_2$ represent player 1's beliefs about what player 2 believes player 1's strategy is, and player 2's beliefs about what player 1 believes player 2's strategy is.

[7]My point here is that the results I get could not be gotten simply by respecifying the payoffs over the physical actions in the game. Van Kolpin (1993) argues that one can apply conventional game theory to these games by including the choice of beliefs as additional parts of players' strategies.

[8]I shall emphasize pure strategies in this paper, though formal definitions allow for mixed strategies, and all stated results apply to them. One reason I de-emphasize mixed strategies is that the characterization of preferences over mixed strategies is not straightforward. In psychological games, there can be a difference between interpreting mixed strategies literally as purposeful mixing by a player versus interpreting them as uncertainty by other players. Such issues of interpretation are less important in conventional game theory, and consequently incorporating mixed strategies is more straightforward.

The first step to incorporating fairness into the analysis is to define a "kindness function," $f_i(a_i, b_j)$, which measures how kind player i is being to player j. (I assume in this paper that players have a shared notion of kindness and fairness and that they apply these standards symmetrically. In Rabin (1992), I show that most of the results of this paper hold if multiple kindness functions are allowed.)

If player i believes that player j is choosing strategy b_j, how kind is player i being by choosing a_i? Player i is choosing the payoff pair $(\pi_i(a_i, b_j), \pi_j(b_j, a_i))$ from among the set of all payoffs feasible if player j is choosing strategy b_j [i.e., from among the set $\Pi(b_j) \equiv \{(\pi_i(a, b_j), \pi_j(b_j, a)) | a \in S_i\}$]. The players might have a variety of notions of how kind player i is being by choosing any given point in $\Pi(b_j)$. While I shall now proceed with a specific (and purposely simplistic) measure of kindness, I show in the Appendix that the results of this paper are valid for any kindness function that specifies the equitable payoffs as some rule for sharing along the Pareto frontier.

Let $\pi_j^{\mathrm{h}}(b_j)$ be player j's highest payoff in $\Pi(b_j)$, and let $\pi_j^{\ell}(b_j)$ be player j's lowest payoff *among points that are Pareto-efficient* in $\Pi(b_j)$. Let the "equitable payoff" be $\pi_j^{\mathrm{e}}(b_j) = [\pi_j^{\mathrm{h}}(b_j) + \pi_j^{\ell}(b_j)]/2$. When the Pareto frontier is linear, this payoff literally corresponds to the payoff player j would get if player i "splits the difference" with her among Pareto-efficient points. More generally, it provides a crude reference point against which to measure how generous player i is being to player j. Finally, let $\pi_j^{\min}(b_j)$ be the worst possible payoff for player j in the set $\Pi(b_j)$.

From these payoffs, I define the kindness function. This function captures how much more than or less than player j's equitable payoff player i believes he is giving to player j.

Definition 1: Player i's kindness to player j is given by

$$f_i(a_i, b_j) \equiv \frac{\pi_j(b_j, a_i) - \pi_j^{\mathrm{e}}(b_j)}{\pi_j^{\mathrm{h}}(b_j) - \pi_j^{\min}(b_j)}.$$

If $\pi_j^{\mathrm{h}}(b_j) - \pi_j^{\min}(b_j) = 0$, then $f_i(a_i, b_j) = 0$.

Note that $f_i = 0$ if and only if player i is trying to give player j her equitable payoff.[9] If $f_i < 0$, player i is giving player j less than her equitable payoff. Recalling the definition of the equitable payoff, there are two general ways for f_i to be negative: either player i is grabbing more than his share on the Pareto frontier of $\Pi(b_j)$ or he is choosing an inefficient point in $\Pi(b_j)$. Finally, $f_i > 0$ if player i is giving player j more than her equitable payoff. Recall that this can happen only if the Pareto frontier of $\Pi(b_j)$ is a nonsingleton; otherwise $\pi_j^{\mathrm{e}} = \pi_j^{\mathrm{h}}$.

I shall let the function $\tilde{f}_j(b_j, c_i)$ represent player i's beliefs about how kindly player j is treating him. While I shall keep the two notationally distinct, this function is formally equivalent to the function $f_j(a_j, b_i)$.

Definition 2: Player i's belief about how kind player j is being to him is given by

$$\tilde{f}_j(b_j, c_i) \equiv \frac{\pi_i(c_i, b_j) - \pi_i^{\mathrm{e}}(c_j)}{\pi_i^{\mathrm{h}}(c_i) - \pi_i^{\min}(c_i)}.$$

If $\pi_i^{\mathrm{h}}(c_i) - \pi_i^{\min}(c_i) = 0$, then $\tilde{f}_j(b_j, c_j) = 0$.

Because the kindness functions are normalized, the values of $f_i(\cdot)$ and $\tilde{f}_j(\cdot)$ must lie in the interval $[-1, \frac{1}{2}]$. Further, the kindness functions are insensitive to positive affine transformations of the material payoffs (overall utility, as defined shortly, will be sensitive to such transformations).

These kindness functions can now be used to specify fully the players' preferences. Each player i chooses a_i to maximize his expected utility $U_i(a_i, b_j, c_i)$, which incorporates both his material utility and the players' shared notion of fairness:

$$U_i(a_i, b_j, c_i)$$

$$\equiv \pi_i(a_i, b_j) + \tilde{f}_j(b_j, c_i) \cdot \left[1 + f_i(a_i, b_j)\right].$$

The central behavioral feature of these preferences reflects the original discussion. If player i believes that player j is treating him badly—$\tilde{f}_j(\cdot) < 0$—then player i wishes to treat player j badly, by choosing an action a_i such that $f_i(\cdot)$ is low or negative. If player j is treating player i kindly, then $\tilde{f}_j(\cdot)$ will be positive, and player i will wish to treat player j kindly. Of course, the specified utility function is such that players will trade off their preference for fairness against their material well-being, and material pursuits may override concerns for fairness.

Because the kindness functions are bounded above and below, this utility function reflects stylized fact C: the bigger the material payoffs, the less the players' behavior reflects their concern for fairness. Thus, the behavior in these games is sensitive to the scale of material payoffs. Obviously, I have not precisely determined the relative power of fairness versus material interest or even given units for the material payoffs; my results in specific examples are, therefore, only qualitative.

Notice that the preferences $V_i(a_i, b_j, c_i) \equiv \pi_i(a_i, b_j) + \tilde{f}_j(b_j, c_i) \cdot f_i(a_i, b_j)$ would yield precisely the same behavior as the utility function $U_i(a_i, b_j, c_i)$. I have made the preferences slightly more complicated so as to capture one bit of realism: whenever player j is treating player i unkindly, player i's overall utility will be lower than his material payoffs. That is, $\tilde{f}_j(\cdot) < 0$ implies $U_i(\cdot) \leq \pi_i(\cdot)$. If a person is treated badly, he leaves the situation bitter, and his ability to take revenge only partly makes up for the loss in welfare.[10]

Because these preferences form a psychological game, I can use the concept of *psychological Nash equilibrium* defined by GPS; this is simply the analog of Nash equilibrium for psychological games, imposing the additional condition that all higher-order

[9] When $\pi^{\mathrm{h}} = \pi^{\min}$, all of player i's responses to b_j yield player j the same payoff. Therefore, there is no issue of kindness, and $f_i = 0$.

[10] As Lones Smith has pointed out to me, however, this specification has one unrealistic implication: if player 1 is being "mean" to player 2 ($f_1 < 0$), then the nicer player 2 is to player 1, the happier is player 1, even if one ignores the implication for material payoffs. While this is perhaps correct if people enjoy making suckers of others, it is more likely that a player will feel guilty if he is mean to somebody who is nice to him.

beliefs match actual behavior. I shall call the solution concept thus defined "fairness equilibrium."[11]

Definition 3: The pair of strategies $(a_1, a_2) \in (S_1, S_2)$ is a *fairness equilibrium* if, for $i = 1,2,\ j \neq i$,

$$(1) \qquad a_i \in \arg\max_{a \in S_i} U_i(a, b_j, c_i)$$

$$(2) \qquad c_i = b_i = a_i.$$

Is this solution concept consistent with the earlier discussion of Example 1? In particular, is the "hostile" outcome (opera, boxing) a fairness equilibrium? If $c_1 = b_1 = a_1 =$ opera and $c_2 = b_2 = a_2 =$ boxing, then player 2 feels hostility, and $f_2 = -1$. Thus, player 1's utility from playing U is 0 (with $f_1 = -1$) and from playing boxing it is $X - 1$ (with $f_1 = 0$). Thus, if $X < 1$, player 1 prefers opera to boxing given these beliefs. Player 2 prefers boxing to opera. For $X < 1$, therefore, (opera, boxing) is an equilibrium. In this equilibrium, both players are hostile toward each other and unwilling to coordinate with the other if it means conceding to the other player.[12]

Because the players will feel no hostility if they coordinate, both (opera, opera) and (boxing, boxing) are also equilibria for all values of X. Again, these are conventional outcomes; the interesting implication of fairness in Example 1 is that the players' hostility may lead each to undertake costly punishment of the other. The game Prisoner's Dilemma shows, by contrast, that fairness may also lead each player to sacrifice to help the other player (see Fig. 2).

		Player 2: Cooperate	Player 2: Defect
Player 1	Cooperate	4X, 4X	0, 6X
	Defect	6X, 0	X, X

FIGURE 2. EXAMPLE 2: PRISONER'S DILEMMA

Consider the cooperative outcome, (cooperate, cooperate). If it is common knowledge to the players that they are playing (cooperate, cooperate), then each player knows that the other is sacrificing his own material well-being in order to help him. Each will thus want to help the other by playing cooperate, so long as the material gains from defecting are not too large. Thus, if X is small enough (less than $\frac{1}{4}$), (cooperate, cooperate) is a fairness equilibrium.

For any value of X, however, the Nash equilibrium (defect, defect) is also a fairness equilibrium. This is because if it is common knowledge that they are playing (defect, defect), then each player knows that the other is not willing to sacrifice X in order to give the other $6X$. Thus, both players will be hostile; in the outcome (defect, defect), each player is satisfying both his desire to hurt the other and his material self-interest.

The prisoner's dilemma illustrates two issues I discussed earlier. First, one cannot fully capture realistic behavior by invoking "pure altruism." In Example 2, both (cooperate, cooperate) and (defect, defect) are fairness equilibria, and I believe this prediction of the model is in line with reality. People sometimes cooperate, but if each expects the other player to defect, then they both will. Yet, having both of these as equilibria is inconsistent with pure altruism. Suppose that player 1's concern for player 2 were independent of player 2's behavior.

[11] GPS prove the existence of an equilibrium in all psychological games meeting certain continuity and convexity conditions. The kindness function used in the text does not yield utility functions that are everywhere continuous, so that GPS's theorem does not apply (although I have found no counterexamples to existence). As I discuss in Appendix A, continuous kindness functions that are very similar to the one used in the text, and for which all general results hold, can readily be constructed. Such kindness functions would guarantee existence using the GPS theorem.

[12] For $X < \frac{1}{2}$, (boxing, opera) is also an equilibrium. In this equilibrium, both players are with common knowledge "conceding," and both players feel hostile toward each other because both are giving up their best possible payoff in order to hurt the other player. The fact that, for $\frac{1}{2} < X \leq 1$, (opera, boxing) is an equilibrium, but (boxing, opera) is not, might suggest that (opera, boxing) is "more likely."

Then if he thought that player 2 was playing cooperate, he would play cooperate if and only if he were willing to give up $2X$ in order to help player 2 by $4X$; if player 1 thought that player 2 was playing defect, then he would play cooperate if and only if he were willing to give up X in order to help player 2 by $5X$. Clearly, then, if player 1 plays cooperate in response to cooperate, he would play cooperate in response to defect. In order to get the two equilibria, player 1 must care differentially about helping (or hurting) player 2 as a function of player 2's behavior.[13]

The second issue that the prisoner's dilemma illustrates is the role of intentionality in attitudes about fairness. Psychological evidence indicates that people determine the fairness of others according to their motives, not solely according to actions taken.[14] In game-theoretic terms, "motives" can be inferred from a player's choice of strategy from among those choices he has, so what strategy a player *could* have chosen (but did not) can be as important as what strategy he actually chooses. For example, people differentiate between those who take a generous action by choice and those who are forced to do so. Consider Example 3, depicted in Figure 3.

This is the "prisoner's dilemma" in which player 2 is forced to cooperate. It corresponds, for instance, to a case in which someone is forced to contribute to a public good. In this degenerate game, player 1 will always defect, so the unique fairness equilibrium is (defect, cooperate). This contrasts to the possibility of the (cooperate, cooperate) equilibrium in the prisoner's dilemma. The difference is that now player 1 will feel no positive regard for player 2's "decision" to cooperate, because player 2 is not voluntarily doing player 1 any favors; you are not grateful to somebody who is simply doing what he must.[15]

		Player 2
		C
Player 1	C	4X, 4X
	D	6X, 0

FIGURE 3. EXAMPLE 3: PRISONER'S NON-DILEMMA

		Player 2	
		Dare	Chicken
Player 1	Dare	-2X, -2X	2X, 0
	Chicken	0, 2X	X, X

FIGURE 4. EXAMPLE 4: CHICKEN

In both Examples 1 and 2, adding fairness creates new equilibria but does not get rid of any (strict) Nash equilibria. Example 4, the game "Chicken"[16] illustrates that fairness *can* rule out strict Nash equilibria (see Fig. 4).

This game is widely studied by political scientists, because it captures well situations in which nations challenge each other. Each country hopes to "dare" while the other country backs down [outcomes (dare, chicken) and (chicken, dare)]; but both dread most of all the outcome (dare, dare), in which neither nation backs down.

[13] Of course, I am ruling out "income effects" and the like as explanations; but that is clearly not what causes the multiplicity of equilibria in public-goods experiments.

[14] Greenberg and Frisch (1972) and Goranson and Berkowitz (1966) find evidence for this proposition, though not in as extreme a form as implied by my model.

[15] Player 1's complete indifference to player 2's plight here is because I have excluded any degree of pure altruism from my model. Indeed, many of the strong results throughout the paper are because I am ruling out pure altruism.

[16] While I will stick to the conventional name for this game, I note that it is extremely speciesist—there is little evidence that chickens are less brave than humans and other animals.

Consider the Nash equilibrium (dare, chicken), where player 1 "dares" and player 2 "chickens out." Is it a fairness equilibrium? In this outcome, it is common knowledge that player 1 is hurting player 2 to help himself. If X is small enough, player 2 would therefore deviate by playing dare, thus hurting both player 1 and himself. Thus, for small X, (dare, chicken) is not a fairness equilibrium; nor, obviously, is (chicken, dare). Both Nash equilibria are, for small enough X, inconsistent with fairness.

Whereas fairness does not rule out Nash equilibrium in Examples 1 and 2, it does so in Example 4. The next section presents several propositions about fairness equilibrium, including one pertaining to why fairness rules out Nash equilibria in Chicken, but not in Prisoner's Dilemma or Battle of the Sexes.

III. Some General Propositions

In the pure-strategy Nash equilibria of Battle of the Sexes, each taking the other player's strategy as given, each player is maximizing the other player's payoff by maximizing his own payoffs. Thus, each player can satisfy his own material interests without violating his sense of fairness. In the Nash equilibrium of Prisoner's Dilemma, each player is minimizing the other player's payoff by maximizing his own. Thus, bad will is generated, and "fairness" means that each player will try to hurt the other. Once again, players simultaneously satisfy their own material interests and their notions of fairness.

These two types of outcomes—where players mutually maximize each other's material payoffs, and where they mutually minimize each other's material payoffs—will play an important role in many of the results of this paper, so I define them formally:

Definition 4: A strategy pair $(a_1, a_2) \in (S_1, S_2)$ is a *mutual-max outcome* if, for $i = 1,2$, $j \neq i$, $a_i \in \arg\max_{a \in S_i} \pi_j(a, a_j)$.

Definition 5: A strategy pair $(a_1, a_2) \in (S_1, S_2)$ is a *mutual-min outcome* if, for $i = 1,2$, $j \neq i$, $a_i \in \arg\min_{a \in S_i} \pi_j(a, a_j)$.

The following definitions will also prove useful. Each of these definitions characterizes an outcome of a game in terms of the value of "kindness" f_i induced by each of the players.

Definition 6: (a) An outcome is *strictly positive* if, for $i = 1,2$, $f_i > 0$. (b) An outcome is *weakly positive* if, for $i = 1,2$, $f_i \geq 0$. (c) An outcome is *strictly negative* if, for $i = 1,2$, $f_i < 0$. (d) An outcome is *weakly negative* if, for $i = 1,2$, $f_i \leq 0$. (e) An outcome is *neutral* if, for $i = 1,2$, $f_i = 0$. (f) An outcome is *mixed* if, for $i = 1,2$, $j \neq i$, $f_i f_j < 0$.

Using these definitions, I state a proposition about two types of Nash equilibria that will necessarily also be fairness equilibria (all proofs are in Appendix B).

PROPOSITION 1: *Suppose that* (a_1, a_2) *is a Nash equilibrium, and either a mutual-max outcome or a mutual-min outcome. Then* (a_1, a_2) *is a fairness equilibrium.*

Note that the pure-strategy Nash equilibria in Chicken do not satisfy either premise of Proposition 1. In each, one player is maximizing the other's payoff, while the other is minimizing the first's payoff. If X is small enough, so that emotions dominate material payoffs, then the player who is being hurt will choose to hurt the other player, even when this action is self-destructive, and will play dare rather than chicken.

While Proposition 1 characterizes Nash equilibria that are necessarily fairness equilibria, Proposition 2 characterizes which outcomes—Nash or non-Nash—can possibly be fairness equilibria.

PROPOSITION 2: *Every fairness equilibrium outcome is either strictly positive or weakly negative.*

Proposition 2 shows that there will always be a certain symmetry of attitude in any fairness equilibrium. It will never be the case that, in equilibrium, one person is kind while the other is unkind.

While Propositions 1 and 2 pertain to all games, irrespective of the scale of material payoffs, I present in the remainder of this section several results that hold when material payoffs are either arbitrarily large or arbitrarily small. To do so, I will consider classes of games that differ only in the scale of the material payoffs. Given the set of strategies $S_1 \times S_2$ and the payoff functions $(\pi_1(a_1,a_2), \pi_2(a_1,a_2))$, let $\mathcal{G}$ be the set of games with strategies $S_1 \times S_2$ and, for all $X > 0$, material payoffs

$$(X \cdot \pi_1(a_1,a_2), X \cdot \pi_2(a_1,a_2)).$$

Let $G(X) \in \mathcal{G}$ be the game corresponding to a given value of X.

Consider Chicken again. It can be verified that, if X is small enough, then both (dare, dare) and (chicken, chicken) are fairness equilibria. Note that, while these two outcomes are (respectively) mutual-min and mutual-max outcomes, they are not Nash equilibria. Yet, when X is small, the fact that they are not equilibria in the "material" game is unimportant, because fairness considerations will start to dominate. Proposition 3 shows that the class of "strict" mutual-max and mutual-min outcomes are fairness equilibria for X small enough.

PROPOSITION 3: *For any outcome (a_1,a_2) that is either a strictly positive mutual-max outcome or a strictly negative mutual-min outcome, there exists an $\bar{X}$ such that, for all $X \in (0, \bar{X})$, (a_1,a_2) is a fairness equilibrium in $G(X)$.*

While Proposition 3 gives sufficient conditions for outcomes to be fairness equilibria when material payoffs are small, Proposition 4 gives conditions for which outcomes will not be fairness equilibria when material payoffs are small.

PROPOSITION 4: *Suppose that $(a_1,a_2) \in (S_1,S_2)$ is not a mutual-max income, nor a mutual-min outcome, nor a Nash equilibrium in which either player is unable to lower the payoffs of the other player. Then there exists an $\bar{X}$ such that, for all $X \in (0, \bar{X})$, (a_1,a_2) is not a fairness equilibrium in $G(X)$.*

Together, Propositions 3 and 4 state that, for games with very small material payoffs, finding the fairness equilibria consists approximately of finding the Nash equilibria in each of the following two hypothetical games: (i) the game in which each player tries to maximize the other player's material payoffs and (ii) the game in which each player tries to minimize the other player's material payoffs.

There are two caveats to this being a general characterization of the set of fairness equilibria in low-payoff games. First, Proposition 3 does not necessarily hold for mutual-max or mutual-min outcomes in which players are giving each other the equitable payoffs (i.e., when the outcomes are neutral). Thus, "non-strict" mutual-max and mutual-min outcomes need to be double-checked. Second, it is also necessary to check whether certain types of Nash equilibria in the original game are also fairness equilibria, even though they are neither mutual-max nor mutual-min outcomes. The potentially problematic Nash equilibria are those in which one of the players has no options that will lower the other's material payoffs.

I now turn to the case in which material payoffs are very large. Proposition 5 states essentially that as material payoffs become large, the players' behavior is dominated by material self-interest. In particular, players will play only Nash equilibria if the scale of payoffs is large enough.

PROPOSITION 5: *If (a_1,a_2) is a strict Nash equilibrium for games in $\mathcal{G}$, then there exists an $\bar{X}$ such that, for all $X > \bar{X}$, (a_1,a_2) is a fairness equilibrium in $G(X)$.*[17] *If (a_1,a_2) is not a Nash equilibrium for games in $\mathcal{G}$, then there exists an $\bar{X}$ such that, for all $X > \bar{X}$, (a_1,a_2) is not a fairness equilibrium in $G(X)$.*

The only caveat to the set of Nash equilibria being equivalent to the set of fairness equilibria when payoffs are large is that

[17] A Nash equilibrium is *strict* if each player is choosing his unique optimal strategy. Mixed-strategy Nash equilibria are, for instance, never strict, because they involve the players being indifferent among two or more actions.

some non-strict Nash equilibria are not fairness equilibria.

IV. Two Applications

One context in which fairness has been studied is monopoly pricing (see e.g., Thaler, 1985; Kahneman et al., 1986a,b). Might consumers see conventional monopoly prices as unfair and refuse to buy at such prices even when worth it in material terms? If this is the case, then even a profit-maximizing monopolist would price below the level predicted by standard economic theory. I now present a game-theoretic model of a monopoly and show that this intuition is an implication of fairness equilibrium.

I assume that a monopolist has costs c per unit of production, and a consumer values the product at v. These are common knowledge. The monopolist picks a price $p \in [c, v]$ as the consumer simultaneously picks a "reservation" price $r \in [c, v]$, above which he is not willing to pay. If $p \leq r$, then the good is sold at price p, and the payoffs are $p - c$ for the monopolist and $v - p$ for the consumer. If $p > r$, then there is no sale, and the payoffs are 0 for each player.

Though this is formally an infinite-strategy game, it can be analyzed using my model of fairness.[18] Applying Nash equilibrium allows any outcome. We might, however, further narrow our prediction, because the strategy $r = v$ for the consumer weakly dominates all other strategies (this would also be the result of subgame perfection if this were a sequential game, with the monopolist setting the price first). Thus, if players cared only about material payoffs, a reasonable outcome in this game is the equilibrium where $p = r = v$, so that the monopolist extracts all the surplus from trade.

What is the highest price consistent with a fairness equilibrium at which this product could be sold? First, what is the function $f_C(r, p)$, how fair the consumer is being to the monopolist? Given that the monopolist sets p, the only question is whether the monopolist gets profits $p - c$ or profits 0. If $r \geq p$, then the consumer is maximizing both the monopolist's and his own payoffs, so $f_C(r, p) = 0$. If $r < p$, then the consumer is minimizing the monopolist's payoffs, so $f_C(r, p) = -1$. One implication of this is that the monopolist will always exploit its position, because it will never feel positively toward the consumer; thus, $r > p$ cannot be a fairness equilibrium.

Because $r < p$ leads to no trade, this means that the only possibility for an equilibrium with trade is when $p = r$. How fair is the monopolist being to the consumer when $p = r = z$? Calculations show that $f_M(z, z) = [c - z]/2[v - c]$. Because I am considering only values of z between c and v, this number is negative. Any time the monopolist is not setting a price equal to its costs, the consumer thinks that the monopolist is being unfair. This is because the monopolist is choosing the price that extracts as much surplus as possible from the consumer, given the consumer's refusal to buy at a price higher than z.

To see whether $p = r = z$ is a fairness equilibrium for a given z, one must see whether the consumer would wish to deviate by setting $r < z$, thus eliminating the monopolist's profits. The consumer's total utility from $r < z$ is

$$U_C = 0 + f_M(z, z) \cdot [1 + -1] = 0.$$

The consumer's total utility from sticking with strategy $r = z$ is

$$U_C = v - z + f_M(z, z) \cdot [1 + 0]$$
$$= v - z + [c - z]/2[v - c].$$

Calculations show that the highest price consistent with fairness equilibrium is given

[18]Note, however, that I have artificially limited the strategy spaces of the players, requiring them to make only mutually beneficial offers; there are problems with the definitions of this paper if the payoff space of a game is unbounded. Moreover, though I believe that all results would be qualitatively similar with more realistic models, the exact answers provided here are sensitive to the specification of the strategy space.

by

$$z^* = [2v^2 - 2cv + c]/[1 + 2v - 2c].$$

This number is strictly less than v when $v > c$. Thus, the highest equilibrium price possible is lower than the conventional monopoly price when fairness is added to the equation. This reflects the arguments of Kahneman et al. (1986a,b): a monopolist interested in maximizing profits ought not to set price at "the monopoly price," because it should take consumers' attitudes toward fairness as a given.

I can further consider some limit results as the stakes become large in this game. Let the monopolist's costs and the consumer's value be $C \equiv cX$ and $V \equiv vX$, respectively. I represent the percentage of surplus that the monopolist is able to extract by $(z^* - C)/(V - C)$. Algebra shows that this equals $[2(V - C)]/[1 + 2(V - C)]$, and the limit of this as X becomes arbitrarily large is 1. That is, the monopolist is able to extract "practically all" of the surplus, because rejecting an offer for the sake of fairness is more costly for the consumer.

Another interesting implication of the model is that $dz^*/dc > 0$ for all parameter values. This means that the higher are the monopolist's costs, the higher the price the consumer will be willing to pay (assuming that the consumer knows the firm's costs). This is one interpretation of the results presented in Thaler (1985): consumers are willing to pay more for the same product from a high-cost firm than from a low-cost firm.

An area of economics where fairness has been widely discussed (more so than in monopoly pricing) is labor economics.[19] I now present an extended example that resembles the "gift-exchange" view of the employment relationship discussed in Akerlof (1982). Consider the situation in which a worker chooses an effort level and the firm simultaneously chooses a benefit level for the worker.[20] Formally, the worker chooses either a high or low effort level: $e \in \{H, L\}$. If $e = H$, the firm receives revenue $R > 0$, and the worker receives disutility γ. If $e = L$, the firm receives no revenue, and the worker experiences no disutility. Simultaneously, the firm chooses a benefit level $b \in [0, R]$. Material payoffs are as follows:

$$\pi_W = \begin{cases} b^{1/2} - \gamma & \text{if } e = H \\ b^{1/2} & \text{if } e = L \end{cases}$$

$$\pi_F = \begin{cases} (R - b)^{1/2} & \text{if } e = H \text{ and } b \leq R \\ 0 & \text{if } e = L \text{ or } b > R \end{cases}$$

where π_W is the worker's material payoffs, and π_F is the firm's material payoffs.[21]

This situation is essentially a continuous-strategy prisoner's dilemma, because each player has a dominant strategy: the worker maximizes his material payoffs by choosing $e = L$, and the firm maximizes its material payoffs by choosing $b = 0$. Thus, the unique Nash equilibrium is the nasty one in which $e = L$ and $b = 0$. Because this outcome is also a mutual-min outcome, this will be a fairness equilibrium in which the players feel negatively toward each other.

I now consider the possibility of a positive fairness equilibrium. First observe that the kindness of the worker to the firm is $f_W = \frac{1}{2}$ if the worker puts in high effort, and $f_W = -\frac{1}{2}$ if the worker puts in low effort. This is because $e = H$ involves the worker fully yielding along the Pareto frontier to the firm, and $e = L$ means that the worker is choosing the best Pareto-efficient point for himself, given the firm's choice of b.

Given the worker's choice of effort, the kindest the firm can be to the worker is to choose $b = R$; the least kind is clearly to choose $b = 0$. Therefore the equitable material payoff to the worker is $R^{1/2}/2 - \gamma$ if $e = H$, and $R^{1/2}/2$ if $e = L$. Using this, one

[19] For some examples discussing the role in labor economics of fairness and related issues, see Akerlof (1982), John Bishop (1987), James N. Baron (1988), David I. Levine (1991, 1993), and Rotemberg (1992). In Rabin (1992), I applied this model of fairness to several more examples from labor economics.

[20] This model is a version of one suggested to me by James Montgomery (pers. comm.).

[21] The assumptions that the parties are risk-averse and that the firm's payoff is 0 (rather than negative) if $e = L$ are made for convenience and are not essential.

can calculate that the kindness of the firm to the worker is given by $f_F = (b/R)^{1/2} - \frac{1}{2}$.

Using this, consider the possibility of a positive fairness equilibrium. What is the firm's utility if it is commonly known that the worker is setting $e = \text{H}$? It is given by

$$U_F = (R-b)^{1/2} + \tfrac{1}{2}\left[\tfrac{1}{2} + (b/R)^{1/2}\right].$$

Thus, the firm will maximize its utility by setting $\partial U_F/\partial b = 0$, and one gets the result that $b^* = R/(1+4R)$. With this level of b, the firm's kindness to the worker is $f_F^* = [1/(1+4R)]^{1/2} - \frac{1}{2}$.

Finally, in order for this to constitute a fairness equilibrium, it must be that the worker would wish to set $e = \text{H}$ rather than $e = \text{L}$. The two possible utility levels are:

$$U_W(e = \text{H}) = b^{1/2} - \gamma + \left\{[1/(1+4R)]^{1/2} - \tfrac{1}{2}\right\}\left(\tfrac{1}{2}\right)$$

$$U_W(e = \text{L}) = b^{1/2} + \left\{[1/(1+4R)]^{1/2} - \tfrac{1}{2}\right\}\left(-\tfrac{1}{2}\right).$$

Algebra yields the conclusion that the worker would not strictly prefer to choose $e = \text{L}$ if and only if

$$R \leq 0.25\left[1/(0.5+\gamma)^{1/2} - 1\right].$$

For all such combinations of R and γ, therefore, there exists a "gift-giving" equilibrium in which the worker sets $e = \text{H}$, and the firm gives the worker a bonus of $b^* = R/(1+4R)$. Note that the larger is γ, the smaller R must be for there to exist a gift-giving equilibrium. The reason for this is roughly as follows. If γ is large, the worker is very tempted to "cheat" the firm by not working hard. The only way he will not cheat is if the firm is being very kind. But the firm's material costs to yielding a given percentage of profits to the worker increases as R increases; thus, only if R is very small will the firm give the worker a generous enough share of profits to induce the worker to be kind.

		Player 2: Grab	Player 2: Share
Player 1	Grab	X, X	2X, 0
	Share	0, 2X	X, X

FIGURE 5. EXAMPLE 5: THE GRABBING GAME

In fact, if $\gamma \geq \frac{1}{2}$, then there is no gift-giving equilibrium, no matter how small is R. This is because the firm's material incentives are such that it will choose to be unkind to the worker, so that the worker will choose to be unkind to the firm. Thus, overall the model says that workers and firms will cooperate if neither is too tempted by material concerns to cheat.

V. Fairness and Welfare

I consider now some welfare implications of fairness.[22] My perspective here is that the full utility functions (combining material payoffs and "fairness payoffs") are the utility functions with which to determine social welfare. As such, I believe one should care not solely about how concerns for fairness support or interfere with material efficiency, but also about how these concerns affect people's overall welfare.

Consider Example 5 (see Fig. 5). In this game, two people are shopping, and there are two cans of soup left. Each person can either try to grab both cans, or not try to grab. If both grab or both do not grab, they each get one can; if one grabs, and the

[22]Robert H. Frank (1988, 1990) and others have explored how the existence of various emotions are understandable as adaptive evolutionary features of humans. While this view of emotions as "adaptive" may be broadly correct, Frank himself emphasizes that emotions can also be destructive in many situations. People's propensity for revenge can be harmful as well as helpful. My model of people's preferences for fairness will help economists do exactly what is done with "material" preferences—study how these preferences play out in different economic settings.

other does not, then the grabber gets both cans. This is a constant-sum version of the prisoner's dilemma: each player has a dominant strategy, and the unique Nash equilibrium is (grab, grab). As in the prisoner's dilemma, the noncooperative (grab, grab) outcome is a fairness equilibrium, no matter the value of X. For small X, however, the positive, mutual-max outcome (share, share) is also a fairness equilibrium. Moreover, because these two fairness equilibria yield the same material payoffs, (share, share) always Pareto-dominates (grab, grab).

Shopping for minor items is a situation in which people definitely care about material payoffs, and this concern drives the nature of the interaction; but they probably do not care a great deal about individual items. If two people fight over a couple of cans of goods, the social grief and bad tempers are likely to be of greater importance to the people than whether they get the cans. Indeed, while both (grab, grab) and (share, share) are fairness equilibria when material payoffs are arbitrarily small, the overall utility in each equilibrium is bounded away from zero.[23] *As the material payoffs involved become arbitrarily small, equilibrium utility levels do not necessarily become arbitrarily small.* This is realistic: no matter how minor the material implications, people's well-being is affected by the friendly or unfriendly behavior of others.

In Example 5, as with many examples in this paper, there is both a strictly positive and a strictly negative fairness equilibrium. Are there games that contain only positive or only negative fairness equilibria? If there are, this could be interpreted as saying that there are some economic situations that endogenously determine the friendliness or hostility of the people involved. More generally, one could consider the question of which types of economic structures are likely to generate which types of emotions.

The prisoner's dilemma illustrates that there do exist situations that endogenously generate hostility. Applying Proposition 5, the only fairness equilibrium of the prisoner's dilemma with very large material payoffs is the Nash equilibrium, where both players defect. This fairness equilibrium is strictly negative. Interpreting a negative fairness equilibrium as a situation in which parties become hostile to each other, this implies that if mutual cooperation is beneficial, but each person has an irresistible incentive to cheat when others are cooperating, then people will leave the situation feeling hostile.

Are there opposite, happier situations, in which the strategic logic of a situation dictates that people will depart on *good* terms? In other words, are there games for which all fairness equilibria yield strictly positive outcomes? Proposition 6 shows that the answer is no.[24]

PROPOSITION 6: *In every game, there exists a weakly negative fairness equilibrium.*

Proposition 6 states that it is never guaranteed that people will part with positive feelings. It implies a strong asymmetry in my model of fairness: there is a bias toward negative feelings. What causes this asymmetry? Recall that if a player is maximizing his own material payoffs, then he is being either mean or neutral to the other player, because being "nice" inherently involves sacrificing material well-being. Thus, while there are situations in which material self-interest tempts a player to be mean even if other players are being kind, material self-interest will never tempt a player to be kind when other players are being mean, because the

[23] In particular, the utility from (share, share) is positive for each player, and the utility from (grab, grab) is negative for each player: (share, share) Pareto-dominates (grab, grab). This again highlights the fact that social concerns take over when material payoffs are small.

[24] The proof of Proposition 6 invokes the existence theorem of GPS, which applies only if the kindness functions are continuous, so that technically I have established this result only when applying variants of the kindness functions that are continuous. See Appendix A for a discussion of the continuity assumption.

only way to be kind is to go against one's material self-interest.

VI. Discussion and Conclusion

The notion of fairness in this paper captures several important regularities of behavior but leaves out other issues. Evidence indicates, for instance, that people's notions of fairness are heavily influenced by the status quo and other reference points. For instance, Kahneman et al. (1986a,b) illustrate that the consumer's view of the fairness of prices charged by a firm can be heavily influenced by what that firm has charged in the past.

Extending the model to more general situations will create issues that do not arise in the simple two-person, normal-form, complete-information games discussed in this paper. The central distinction between two-person games and multiperson games is likely to be how a person behaves when he is hostile to some players but friendly toward others. The implications are clear if he is able to choose whom to help and whom to hurt; it is more problematic if he must choose either to help everybody or to hurt everybody, such as when choosing the contribution level to a public good. Does one contribute to reward those who have contributed or not contribute to punish those who have not contributed.

Extending the model to incomplete-information games is essential for applied research, but doing so will lead to important new issues. Because the theory depends so heavily on the motives of other players, and because interpreting other players' motives depends on beliefs about their payoffs and information, incomplete information is likely to have a dramatic effect on decision-making. Extending the model to sequential games is also essential for applied research. In conventional game theory, observing past behavior can provide information; in psychological games, it can conceivably change the motivations of the players. An important issue arises: can players "force" emotions; that is, can a first-mover do something that will compel a second player to regard him positively? One might imagine, for instance, that an analogue to Proposition 6 might no longer be true, and sequential games could perhaps be used as mechanisms that guarantee positive emotions.

		Player 2: Share	Player 2: Grab
Player 1	Trust	6X, 6X	0, 12X
	Dissolve	5X, 5X	5X, 5X

FIGURE 6. EXAMPLE 6: LEAVING A PARTNERSHIP

Finally, future research can also focus on modeling additional emotions. In Example 6, for instance, my model predicts no cooperation, whereas it seems plausible that cooperation would take place (see Fig. 6).[25]

This game represents the following situation. Players 1 and 2 are partners on a project that has thus far yielded total profits of $10X$. Player 1 must now withdraw from the project. If player 1 dissolves the partnership, the contract dictates that the players split the profits fifty-fifty. But total profits would be higher if player 1 leaves his resources in the project. To do so, however, he must forgo his contractual rights and trust player 2 to share the profits after the project is completed. So, player 1 must decide whether to "dissolve" or to "trust"; if he trusts player 2, then player 2 can either "grab" or "share."

What will happen? According to the notion of fairness in this paper, the only (pure-strategy) equilibrium is for player 1 to split the profits now, yielding an inefficient solution. The desirable outcome (trust, share) is not possible because player 2 will deviate. The reason is that he attributes no positive motive to player 1—while it is true that player 1 trusted player 2, he did so simply to increase his own expected material payoff. No kindness was involved.

One might think that (trust, share) is a reasonable outcome. This would be the outcome, for instance, if it is assumed that

[25]A related example was first suggested to me by Jim Fearon (pers. comm.).

players wish to be kind to those who trust them. If player 1 plays "trust" rather than "split," he is showing he trusts player 2. If player 2 feels kindly toward player 1 as a result of this trust, then he might not grab all the profits. If it is concluded that the idea that people are motivated to reward trust is psychologically sound, then it could be incorporated into formal models.

Appendix A: The Kindness Function Can Be Generalized

There is a broad class of kindness functions for which all of the results of this paper hold. Indeed, the proofs of all results contained in the body of the paper are general enough that they establish the results for the kindness functions that I now define.

Definition A1 requires that (i) fairness cannot lead to infinitely positive or infinitely negative utility, and (ii) how kind player i is being to player j is an increasing function of how high a material payoff player i is giving player j.

Definition A1: A kindness function is *bounded and increasing* if:

(i) there exists a number N such that $f_i(a_i, b_j) \in [-N, N]$ for all $a \in S_i$ and $b_j \in S_j$; and
(ii) $f_i(a_i, b_j) > f_i(a'_i, b_j)$ if and only if $\pi_j(b_j, a_i) > \pi_j(b_j, a'_i)$.

Definition A2 requires that the payoff that player j "deserves" is strictly between player j's worst and best Pareto-efficient payoffs, so long as the Pareto frontier is not a singleton.

Definition A2: Consider $\Pi(b_j)$, $\pi_j^{h}(b_j)$, and $\pi_j^{\ell}(b_j)$ as defined in the paper. A kindness function $f_i(a_i, b_j)$ is a *Pareto split* if there exists some $\pi_j^{e}(b_j)$ such that:

(i) $\pi_j(b_j, a_i) > \pi_j^{e}(b_j)$ implies that $f_i(a_i, b_j) > 0$; $\pi_j(b_j, a_i) = \pi_j^{e}(b_j)$ implies that $f_i(a_i, b_j) = 0$; and $\pi_j(b_j, a_i) < \pi_j^{e}(b_j)$ implies that $f_i(a_i, b_j) < 0$;
(ii) $\pi_j^{h}(b_j) \geq \pi_j^{e}(b_j) \geq \pi_j^{\ell}(b_j)$; and
(iii) if $\pi_j^{h}(b_j) > \pi_j^{\ell}(b_j)$, then $\pi_j^{h}(b_j) > \pi_j^{e}(b_j) > \pi_j^{\ell}(b_j)$.

Propositions 1, 2, and 6 are all true for any kindness function meeting Definitions A1 and A2. Propositions 3, 4, and 5, however, pertain to when material payoffs are made arbitrarily large or arbitrarily small. In order for these results to hold, one must guarantee that notions of the fairness of particular outcomes do not dramatically change when all payoffs are doubled (say). Definition A3 is a natural way to do so.

Definition A3: A kindness function $f_i(a_i, b_j)$ is *affine* if changing all payoffs for both players by the same affine transformation does not change the value of $f_i(a_i, b_j)$.

All the propositions in this paper hold for any kindness function meeting Definitions A1, A2, and A3. One substantial generalization allowed for here is that the kindness function can be sensitive to affine transformations of one player's payoffs. If all of player 2's payoffs are doubled, then it may be that fairness dictates that he get more—or less—than before. The definition and all of the limit results simply characterize what happens if *both* players' payoffs are comparably changed.

Knowing that the general results of this paper hold for a large class of kindness functions is also important should existence be problematic. While fairness equilibria exist in all of the examples of this paper, I have proved no general existence result and cannot invoke the existence theorem of GPS, because of possible discontinuities.

The kindness function in the text can be discontinuous in b_j at points where $\pi_j^{h}(b_j) = \pi_j^{min}(b_j)$; at such points, $\Pi(b_j)$ is a single point, and $f_i(a_i, b_j)$ is set equal to zero independent of a_i. The discontinuity comes from the fact that, by normalizing the kindness function by $[\pi_j^{h}(b_j) - \pi_j^{min}(b_j)]$, the kindness function can be bounded away from zero even when $\Pi(b_j)$ is arbitrarily small. While I chose this kindness function so as to emphasize that kindness or meanness can be large issues even when the stakes are small, this property could be made less extreme. For instance, one could choose the kindness function as

$$g_i(a_i, b_j)$$

$$\equiv \frac{\pi_j(b_j, a_i) - \pi_j^{\mathrm{e}}(b_j)}{(1-\gamma)[\pi_j^{\mathrm{h}}(b_j) - \pi_j^{\min}(b_j) + \gamma(\pi_j^{\max} - \pi_j^{\min})]}$$

where $\pi_j^{\max}$ and $\pi_j^{\min}$ are player j's maximum and minimum payoffs in the entire game. This kindness function is well-defined for all $\gamma \in (0,1]$, so long as $\pi_j^{\max} \neq \pi_j^{\min}$ (which is true unless one has a game in which no decisions by either player could possibly affect player j's payoff). A second type of discontinuity in the kindness functions is that $\pi_2^{\mathrm{e}}(b_2)$ can be discontinuous in b_2. This discontinuity can be smoothed out with the following definition: for $D > 0$, let

$$\pi_2^{\mathrm{e}}(b_2, D)$$

$$= \max_{b^* \in B_2}\{\pi_2^{\mathrm{e}}(b^*) + D\|b_2 - b^*\|\}.$$

It can be shown that $\pi_2^{\mathrm{e}}(b_2, D)$ is a well-defined function and is continuous in b_2. To construct a continuous kindness function (and thus allow the application of the GPS existence proof), one need merely replace π_2^{e} by $\pi_2^{\mathrm{e}}(b_2, D)$ in the above definition. It can be shown (proof available from the author upon request) that there exists a $D > 0$ defined for each game such that the resulting kindness function satisfies Definitions A1, A2, and A3 for all γ. Moreover, by choosing γ arbitrarily close to 0 and D arbitrarily large, one essentially defines kindness functions that are "smoothed" versions of that used in the paper.

While the precise kindness function used is not important to the qualitative results of this paper, the way I specify the overall utility function is perhaps more restrictive. One aspect that clearly determines some of the results in this paper is the fact that I completely exclude "pure altruism"; that is, I assume that unless player 2 is being kind to player 1, player 1 will have no desire to be kind to player 2. Psychological evidence suggests that, while people are substantially motivated by the type of "contingent altruism" I have incorporated into the model, pure altruism can also sometimes be important.

One natural way to expand the utility function to incorporate pure altruism would be as follows:

$$\tilde{U}_i(a_i, b_j, c_i)$$

$$\equiv \pi_i(a_i, b_j)$$

$$+ \left[\alpha + (1-\alpha)\tilde{f}_j(b_j, c_i)\right][1 + f_i(a_i, b_j)]$$

where $\alpha \in [0,1]$.

In this utility function, if $\alpha > 0$, then the player i will wish to be kind to player j even if player j is being "neutral" to player i. The relative importance of pure versus contingent altruism is captured by the parameter α; if α is small, then outcomes will be much as in the model of this paper; if α is close to 1, then pure altruism will dominate behavior.

As discussed above with regard to the kindness function, my model assumes that the fairness utility is completely independent of the scale of the material payoffs. Consider a situation in which a proposer's offer to split \$1 evenly is rejected by a decider. My model says that the proposer will leave the situation unhappy not only because he has no money, but because he was badly treated. Yet my model implies that the proposer will be as unhappy, *but no more so*, when leaving a situation in which the decider rejected an offer to split \$1 million evenly.

This seems unrealistic—the bitterness he feels should be larger the greater the harm done. The assumption could, however, be relaxed while maintaining all the general results of the paper. I could specify the utility function as:

$$U_i(a_i, b_j, c_i)$$

$$\equiv \pi_i(a_i, b_j) + G(X) \cdot \tilde{f}_j(b_j, c_i) \cdot [1 + f_i(a_i, b_j)]$$

where $G(X)$ is positive and increasing in X.[26]

[26]This specification and one of the conditions mentioned to maintain the limit results were suggested by Roland Benabou (pers. comm.).

This might create problems for the limit results of the paper. However, the conditions that $G(X)/X \to 0$ as $X \to \infty$ and that $G(X)$ is bounded away from 0 as $X \to 0$ would suffice for all propositions to hold. In this case, I am assuming that a person's fairness utility is less sensitive to the scale of payoffs than is his material utility, not that it is totally insensitive.

Appendix B: Proofs

PROOF OF PROPOSITION 1:

Since (a_1, a_2) is a Nash equilibrium, both players must be maximizing their material payoffs. First, suppose that (a_1, a_2) is a mutual-max outcome. Then both f_1 and f_2 must be nonnegative. Thus, both players have positive regard for the other. Since each player is choosing a strategy that maximizes both his own material well-being and the material well-being of the other player, this must maximize his overall utility.

Next, suppose that (a_1, a_2) is a mutual-min outcome. Then f_1 and f_2 will both be nonpositive, so that each player will be motivated to decrease the material well-being of the other. Since he is doing so while simultaneously maximizing his own material well-being, this must maximize his utility.

PROOF OF PROPOSITION 2:

Suppose that an outcome has one player being positive ($f_i > 0$), while the other player is not being positive ($f_j \leq 0$). If $f_i > 0$, then it must be that player i could increase his payoff in such a way that player j would be harmed, simply by changing his strategy to maximize his own material interest. If $f_j \leq 0$, it is inconsistent with utility maximization for player i not to do so; therefore, this outcome cannot be a fairness equilibrium. The only outcomes consistent with fairness equilibrium, therefore, are those for which both f_i and f_j are strictly positive, or neither is. This establishes the proposition.

PROOF OF PROPOSITION 3:

As $X \to 0$, the gain in material payoffs from changing a strategy approaches zero, and eventually it is dominated by the fairness payoffs. If (a_1, a_2) is a strictly positive mutual-max outcome, each player would strictly prefer to play a_i, since this uniquely maximizes the fairness product. Thus, this is a fairness equilibrium. If (a_1, a_2) is a strictly negative mutual-min outcome, each player would strictly prefer to play a_i, since this uniquely maximizes the fairness product. Thus, this too would be a fairness equilibrium.

PROOF OF PROPOSITION 4:

Suppose that (a_1, a_2) is not a Nash equilibrium. Then (without loss of generality) player 1 is not maximizing his material payoffs.

Suppose that player 1 is not minimizing player 2's payoffs. Then he is not minimizing f_1. Given that player 1 is also not maximizing his own material payoffs, this can be maximizing behavior only if $f_2 > 0$. Player 2 will choose $f_2 > 0$ only if $f_1 > 0$. Thus, both f_1 and f_2 are greater than 0; but if the material payoffs are small, this means that the players must choose to maximize f_1 and f_2, so that this must be a mutual-max outcome.

Suppose that player 1 is not maximizing player 2's payoffs. Then he is not maximizing f_1. If the payoffs are small, and given that player 1 is not maximizing his own payoffs, this implies that $f_2 < 0$. This means, as payoffs are small, that player 1 will minimize player 2's payoffs, so that $f_1 < 0$. If he does so, player 2 will in turn minimize player 1's payoffs. Thus, this outcome is a min-min outcome. This establishes that if (a_1, a_2) is not a mutual-max, mutual-min, or Nash equilibrium, then it will not be a fairness equilibrium for small enough X.

Now suppose that (a_1, a_2) *is* a Nash equilibrium, but one in which each player could lower the other player's material payoffs by changing his strategy. Suppose that (a_1, a_2) is not a mutual-max outcome. Then (without loss of generality) player 1 could increase player 2's material payoffs. Since player 1 is maximizing his own material payoffs in a way that hurts player 2, it is known that $f_1 < 0$. This can be optimal for small X only if $f_2 \leq 0$. If $f_2 < 0$, then earlier arguments imply that this must be a mutual-min outcome. Suppose $f_2 = 0$. Then this can be optimal for player 2 only if she has no choice of lowering player 1's payoffs; otherwise, the fact that $f_1 < 0$ would compel her to change strategies. This condition on player 2's choices directly contradicts the assumption that she *could* lower player 1's payoffs. This establishes the proposition.

PROOF OF PROPOSITION 5:

If (a_1, a_2) is a strict Nash equilibrium, then the difference in material payoffs from playing the equilibrium strategy versus a nonequilibrium strategy becomes arbitrarily large as X becomes arbitrarily large. Because the fairness gains and losses are independent of X, a_i eventually becomes a strict best reply to a_j as X becomes large.

If (a_1, a_2) is not a Nash equilibrium, then, for at least one player, the benefit in material payoffs from deviating from (a_1, a_2) becomes arbitrarily large as X becomes arbitrarily large. Because the fairness gains and losses are independent of X, a_i is eventually dominated by some other strategy with respect to a_j as X becomes large.

PROOF OF PROPOSITION 6:

From the material game, consider the psychological game from the preferences $V_i \equiv \pi_i(a_i, b_j) + \min[f_j(c_i, b_j), 0] \cdot \min[f_i(a_i, b_j), 0]$. When the kindness functions are continuous, GPS's general existence result means that this game has at least one equilibrium, (a_1^*, a_2^*). I will now argue that any such equilibrium is also a fairness equilibrium.

First, I show that, for $i = 1,2$, $f_i(a_i^*, a_j^*) \leq 0$. Suppose $f_i(a_i^*, a_j^*) > 0$. Let a_i' be such that $a_i' \in \arg\max_{a \in S_i} \pi_i(a, a_j^*)$. Then

$$V_i(a_i', a_j^*, a_i^*) > V_i(a_i^*, a_j^*, a_i^*)$$

which contradicts the premise. This is because the material payoff to i is higher with a_i' than with a_i^*, and because $f_i(a_i', a_j^*) \leq 0$, so that the fairness payoff cannot be any lower than from a_i^*.

Thus, for $i = 1,2$, $f_i(a_i^*, a_2^*) \leq 0$; but this implies that, for each player, maximizing $V_i(a_i, a_j^*, a_i^*)$ is the same as maximizing $U_i(a_i, a_j^*, a_i^*)$. Thus, (a_i^*, a_j^*) is a fairness equilibrium.

REFERENCES

Akerlof, George, "Labor Contracts as a Partial Gift Exchange," *Quarterly Journal of Economics*, November 1982, *97*, 543–69.

Akerlof, George and Dickens, William T., "The Economic Consequences of Cognitive Dissonance," *American Economic Review*, June 1982, *72*, 307–19.

Andreoni, James, (1988a) "Privately Provided Public Goods in a Large Economy: The Limits of Altruism," *Journal of Public Economics*, February 1988, *35*, 57–73.

______, (1988b) "Why Free Ride? Strategies and Learning in Public Goods Experiments," *Journal of Public Economics*, December 1988, *37*, 291–304.

Baron, James N., "The Employment Relation as a Social Relation," *Journal of the Japanese and International Economies*, December 1988, *2*, 492–525.

Bishop, John, "The Recognition and Reward of Employee Performance," *Journal of Labor Economics*, October 1987, *5*, S36–56.

Dawes, Robyn M. and Thaler, Richard H., "Anomalies: Cooperation," *Journal of Economic Perspectives*, Summer 1988, *2*, 187–98.

Frank, Robert H., *Passions Within Reason: The Strategic Role of the Emotions*, New York: Norton, 1988.

______, "A Theory of Moral Sentiments," in Jane J. Mansbridge, ed., *Beyond Self-Interest*, Chicago: University of Chicago Press, 1990, pp. 71–96.

Geanakoplos, John, Pearce, David and Stacchetti, Ennio, "Psychological Games and Sequential Rationality," *Games and Economic Behavior*, March 1989, *1*, 60–79.

Gilboa, Itzhak and Schmeidler, David, "Information Dependent Games: Can Common Sense Be Common Knowledge?" *Economics Letters*, 1988, *27* (3), 215–21.

Goranson, Richard E. and Berkowitz, Leonard, "Reciprocity and Responsibility Reactions to Prior Help," *Journal of Personality and Social Psychology*, February 1966, *3*, 227–32.

Greenberg, Jerald, "Effects of Reward Value and Retaliative Power on Allocation Decisions: Justice, Generosity or Greed?" *Journal of Personality and Social Psychology*, April 1978, *36*, 367–79.

Greenberg, Martin S. and Frisch, David, "Effect of Intentionality on Willingness to Reciporocate a Favor," *Journal of Experimental Social Psychology*, March 1972, *8*, 99–111.

Güth, Werner, Schmittberger, Rolf and Schwarze, Bernd, "An Experimental Analysis of Ultimatum Bargaining," *Journal of Economic Behavior and Organization*, December 1982, *3*, 367–88.

Hoffman, Elizabeth and Spitzer, Matthew, "The Coase Theorem: Some Experimental Tests," *Journal of Law and Economics*, April 1982, *75*, 73–98.

Huang, Peter H. and Wu, Ho-Mou, "Emotional Responses in Litigation," *International Review of Law and Economics*, March 1992, *12*, 31–44.

Isaac, R. Mark, McCue, Kenneth F. and Plott, Charles, "Public Goods Provision in an Experimental Environment," *Journal of Public Economics*, February 1985, *26*, 51–74.

______ **and Walker, James,** (1988a) "Group Size Effects in Public Goods Provision: The Voluntary Contribution Mechanism," *Quarterly Journal of Economics*, February 1988, *103*, 179–99.

______ **and** ______, (1988b) "Communication and Free-Riding Behavior: The Voluntary Contribution Mechanism," *Economic Inquiry*, October 1988, *26*, 585–608.

______, ______ **and Thomas, Susan H.,** "Divergent Evidence on Free Riding: An Experimental Examination of Possible Explanations," *Public Choice*, 1984, *43* (2), 113–49.

Kahneman, Daniel, Knetsch, Jack L. and Thaler, Richard H., (1986a) "Fairness as a Constraint on Profit Seeking: Entitlements in the Market," *American Economic Review*, September 1986, *76*, 728–41.

______, ______ **and** ______, (1986b) "Fairness and the Assumptions of Economics," *Journal of Business*, October 1986, *59*, S285–S300.

Kim, Oliver and Walker, Mark, "The Free Rider Problem: Experimental Evidence," *Public Choice*, 1984, *43* (1), 3–24.

Kolpin, Van, "Equilibrium Refinements in Psychological Games," *Games and Economic Behavior*, 1993 (forthcoming).

Leventhal, Gerald and Anderson, David, "Self-Interest and the Maintenance of Equity," *Journal of Personality and Social Psychology*, May 1970, *15*, 57–62.

Levine, David I., "Cohesiveness, Productivity, and Wage Dispersion," *Journal of Economic Behavior and Organization*, March 1991, *15*, 237–55.

______, "Fairness, Markets, and Ability To Pay: Evidence from Compensation Executives," *American Economic Review*, December 1993, *83* (5), 1241–59.

Marwell, Gerald and Ames, Ruth, "Economists Free Ride, Does Anyone Else?: Experiments on the Provision of Public Goods, IV," *Journal of Public Economics*, June 1981, *15*, 295–310.

Mui, Vai-Lam, "Two Essays in the Economics of Institutions: I. Envy," Ph.D. dissertation, Department of Economics, University of California-Berkeley, 1992.

Orbell, John M., Dawes, Robyn M. and van de Kragt, Alphons J. C., "Explaining Discussion Induced Cooperation," *Journal of Personality and Social Psychology*, May 1978, *54*, 811–19.

Rabin, Matthew, "Incorporating Fairness Into Game Theory and Economics," Department of Economics Working Paper No. 92-199, University of California-Berkeley, July 1992.

Rotemberg, Julio J., "Human Relations in the Workplace," mimeo, Massachusetts Institute of Technology, January 1992.

Roth, Alvin E., Prasnikar, Vesna, Okuno-Fujiwara, Masahiro and Zamir, Shmuel, "Bargaining and Market Behavior in Jerusalem, Ljubljana, Pittsburgh, and Tokyo: An Experimental Study," *American Economic Review*, December 1991, *81*, 1068–95.

Thaler, Richard H., "Mental Accounting and

Consumer Choice," *Marketing Science*, Summer 1985, *4*, 199–214.

______, "Anomalies: The Ultimatum Game," *Journal of Economic Perspectives*, Fall 1988, *2*, 195–207.

Train, Kenneth E., McFadden, Daniel L. and Goett, Andrew A., "Consumer Attitudes and Voluntary Rate Schedules for Public Utilities," *Review of Economics and Statistics*, August 1987, *64*, 383–91.

van de Kragt, Alphons J. C., Orbell, John M. and Dawes, Robyn M., "The Minimal Contributing Set as a Solution to Public Goods Problems," *American Political Science Review*, March 1983, *77*, 112–22.

Weisbrod, Burton A., *The Nonprofit Economy*, Cambridge, MA: Harvard University Press, 1988.

[25]

REVIEW OF ECONOMIC DYNAMICS **1**, 593–622 (1998)
ARTICLE NO. RD980023

Modeling Altruism and Spitefulness in Experiments*

David K. Levine

Department of Economics, University of California, Los Angeles, California 90024

Received June 23, 1997; revised October 21, 1997

We examine a simple theory of altruism in which players' payoffs are linear in their own monetary income and their opponents. The weight on the opponent's income is private information and varies in the population, depending, moreover, on what the opponent's coefficient is believed to be. Using results of ultimatum experiments and the final round of a centipede experiment, we are able to pin down relatively accurately what the distribution of altruism (and spite) in the population is. This distribution is then used with a reasonable degree of success to explain the results of the earlier rounds of centipede and the results of some public goods contribution games. In addition, we show that in a market game where the theory of selfish players does quite well, the theory of altruism makes exactly the same predictions as the theory of selfish players. *Journal of Economic Literature* Classification Numbers: C70, C72, D90, D92.

1. INTRODUCTION

Standard theory applied to the study of experiments generally examines a refinement of Nash equilibrium such as subgame perfection, and assumes that participants are selfish in the sense that they care only about their own monetary income.[1] Some (but not all) experiments cannot be explained by this theory. Two robust sets of experiments of this sort are those on ultimatum bargaining and public goods contribution games.

* This work was supported in part by the UCLA Academic Senate and by National Science Foundation grant SBR-93-20695. Discussions with Drew Fudenberg, Tom Palfrey, Robert Rosenthal, and John Van Huyck and comments by participants at the University of Chicago Theory Workshop, the UCLA Theory Workshop, The Harvard/MIT joint theory workshop, and the Hong Kong University of Science and Technology Theory Workshop are also gratefully acknowledged. I also thank Ramon Marimon and two anonymous referees for their guidance.

[1] There is much informal discussion of fairness, but little in the way of formal modeling applied to experiments.

1094-2025/98 $25.00

In ultimatum bargaining, the first player proposes a division of a fixed amount of money that may be accepted or rejected by the second player. According to the theory, any demand that leaves the second player with anything should be accepted, and consequently the proposer should either demand the entire amount or at least the greatest amount less than the entire amount. In fact, proposers do not demand nearly this amount, generally demanding between 50% and 60% of the total, and ungenerous demands that are significantly less than the entire amount are frequently rejected.

In public goods contribution games, players may make a costly donation to a common pool that provides a social benefit greater than the contribution. Because of the free rider problem, it is typically a dominant strategy not to contribute anything. Nevertheless, with as many as 10 or more players, some players contribute to the common pool.

One explanation of these phenomena is that the equilibrium concept is wrong, and this has been explored by a variety of authors, such as Binmore and Samuelson [2]. However, such explanations are difficult to accept, since in public goods games dominant strategies are involved, while in ultimatum bargaining it is puzzling that many demands leaving the second player with 30% or more of the total amount are rejected. The rejection of such an offer is not a failure of equilibrium theory, but a failure of the assumption of selfish players.

An alternative line of explanation is that players are not really selfish. One such explanation that is frequently discussed, particularly by the experimenters themselves, is that some notion of fairness plays a role in individual decision making. Rabin [17] has proposed a formal model of what this might mean. The model presented here is similar in spirit to Rabin's model, but does not depart from the ordinary assumptions of game theory. Moreover, Rabin examined only qualitative predictions of his model. The goal of this paper is to examine the quantitative implications of the theory: to what extent can a simple model of players who are not selfish explain the data from a variety of experiments, including both ultimatum and public goods games? A similar effort can be found in Andreoni and Miller [1]. That effort differs from this one in focusing only on public goods contribution games, and on altruism, but not spitefulness. In addition, they allow players to have nonlinear preferences over contributions.[2] They find, as do we, a remarkable degree of consistency in the attitude of players toward one another in different games.

[2] They assume that utility is defined over contributions in the particular game at hand, and not over total wealth. This, combined with nonlinearity, can lead to some of the same paradoxes that occur when non-Von Neumann--Morgenstern preferences are considered in decision theory. For example, it is possible to construct a series of problems involving contributions in such a way that the optimal solutions to the individual problems are suboptimal in the joint problem of solving the problems simultaneously.

The basic theory is that players care not only about their own monetary payoffs, but also about their opponent's monetary payoffs. The simplest such model is of the type described by many authors (see Ledyard [11], for example), in which utility is a linear function of both the player's own monetary payoff and his opponent's. It is convenient to normalize the coefficient on the own monetary payoff to 1. The question is, then, what is the coefficient on the other player's payoffs? Public goods contributions games suggest that this coefficient should be positive; ultimatum bargaining suggests that it should be negative (so that offers will be rejected). We adopt the point of view that the coefficient differs between different individuals in the population, with some individuals having positive coefficients and some negative coefficients, and with each individual's coefficient being private information. The theory gains strength from the hypothesis that this distribution is fixed across games of different types, so that the same distribution of coefficients should be used to explain, for example, both ultimatum bargaining and public goods contribution games.

In fact, this simple model is inadequate to explain even the results of ultimatum bargaining. From the rejection rates in the experiment, we can calculate how many players moving second must be spiteful and how spiteful they must be. However, the players moving first must be drawn from the same population, so we can use the distribution of spitefulness calculated from the rejection rates to compute what demands should be made by the players moving first. In fact, the demands that should be made, according to the theory, are substantially larger than those observed in the data.

As a result of this, we are led to a more complicated model of altruism. Introspection suggests that players care not only about other players' utility, but also that their attitudes toward other players depend on how they feel they are being treated. One way to model this is to use the psychological game approach of Rabin [17] and Geanakoplos et al. [7]. However, these models are complicated, and depart quite radically from ordinary choice theory. We will discuss the Rabin model in greater detail below. As an alternative, we propose a simpler model with the same flavor: players' weights on opponents' monetary payoffs depend both on their own coefficient of altruism (or spite), and on what they believe their opponents' coefficients to be. In particular, a more positive weight is placed on the money received by an opponent who is believed to be more altruistic, and a more negative weight on one that is believed to be more spiteful. Notice that the game played is now a signaling game, since players' actions will potentially reveal how altruistic they are, and their opponents care about this.

It is useful to think about the consequence this has in ultimatum bargaining. First, larger demands are a signal of greater spite. Hence the degree of altruism needed to explain the rejections is less than it would be in the absence of the signaling effect: even a relatively altruistic player may behave meanly to a player believed to be spiteful. In addition to demands being lower because players are less spiteful, demands are lower because an altruistic player will realize that acceptance of a large demand is a signal of an altruistic opponent, and consequently will be less desirous of making such a demand.

Using this model, we examine ultimatum bargaining experimental results due to Roth et al. [18]. We are able to fit the data quite well using the model, and pin down most of the distribution of altruism, except that the data contains little information about how altruistic the altruistic players are.

The departure of preferences from selfish preferences is substantial, so we next examine whether the model is consistent with other experiments in which the selfish theory together with subgame perfection has worked well. One example of such an experiment is the market experiment also reported in Roth et al. Here the selfish theory predicts the competitive equilibrium, and this is in fact what is observed. However, the structure of the game is such that there is little opportunity to transfer utility to or from other players. As a result, we show that regardless of how altruism is distributed in the population, there exist equilibria in which the coefficient of altruism does not matter, and that consequently these equilibria are the same as the equilibria of the selfish model.

We then turn to another well-known experiment inconsistent with selfishness and subgame perfection, the variation on grab-a-dollar studied by McKelvey and Palfrey [12]. In this experiment, a player may either grab or pass. If he passes, the money is doubled and his opponent gets the move, except in the final round. The grabber gets 80% of the money, his opponent 20%. This is structured so that with selfish players the unique Nash equilibrium is to grab immediately. In fact, only 8% of the population does so. However, as in ultimatum bargaining, there is also a simple failure of decision theory. A substantial fraction of players choose to give money away in the final round. So many do so that it is optimal for a selfish player to stay in as long as possible in hopes of getting lucky and meeting an altruistic opponent in the final round. The distribution of altruism from ultimatum is applied to study this game. The play in the final round pins down the extent to which the altruistic part of the population is altruistic, a parameter that could not be identified from the ultimatum experiment. This gives a complete distribution of altruism, and we find that play in the earlier rounds is generally consistent with this distribution. This is a genuine test of the theory in the sense that there are no free parameters available to explain play in the early rounds.

Finally, we turn to a public goods experiment by Isaac and Walker [8]. Here the model we use imperfectly represents the way in which the experiment was conducted, and the results of the experiments are not perfectly consistent with the distribution of altruism calculated in the other experiments. Nevertheless, the amount of altruism found in the public goods experiments is reasonably consistent with the amount and degree of altruism calculated from the other experiments.

In our concluding section we discuss in more detail the extent to which the simple theory succeeds in explaining experiments, and speculate on how it might apply in other experiments. One important issue we do not address is the issue of why players should be altruistic or spiteful. It is natural to speculate about evolutionary explanations for preferences of this type, and perhaps future research will identify evolutionary forces that lead to the types of preferences modeled here.

2. ALTRUISTIC PREFERENCES

We will be considering n person games with players $i = 1, \dots, n$. At terminal nodes of the extensive form, player i receives a *direct utility* of u_i. Player i also has a coefficient of altruism $-1 < a_i < 1$ and receives an *adjusted utility* of

$$v_i = u_i + \sum_{j \neq i} \frac{a_i + \lambda a_j}{1 + \lambda} u_j,$$

where $0 \leq \lambda \leq 1$. The objective of players is to maximize their adjusted utility. The adjusted utility reflects the player's own utility, and his regard for their opponents. If $a_i > 0$, we refer to the player as altruistic, as such a player has a positive regard for his opponents. If $a_i = 0$, we refer to the player as selfish, the usual case. If $a_i < 0$, we refer to the player as spiteful. The assumption that $-1 < a_i < 1$ means that no player has a higher regard for his opponents (positive or negative) than for himself.

The coefficient λ reflects the fact that players may have a higher regard for altruistic opponents than spiteful ones. When $\lambda = 0$, the model is one of pure altruism of the type discussed by Ledyard [11] as an explanation of the results of public goods contribution games. When $\lambda > 0$, the model can be regarded as incorporating an element of fairness, not in the sense that players have a particular target they consider "fair," but in the sense that they are willing to be more altruistic to an opponent who is more altruistic toward them. One of our major conclusions is that $\lambda = 0$ is not consistent with data from the ultimatum game.

Obviously the coefficient a_i is not independent of the units in which utility is measured, and utility must be measured in the "same" interpersonally comparable units for all players. The linearity of payoffs in opponents' utility may be taken as a convenient approximation. It has the important implication that players respect each other's preferences over outcomes and gambles. In general, players' regard for one another may depend on who the opponent is, but in the types of experiments we will be considering, players interact with each other anonymously, so regarding all opponents in a symmetric manner seems not only sensible, but necessary.

Prior to the start of play, players are drawn independently from a population with a distribution of altruism coefficients represented by a common cumulative distribution function $F(a_i)$. Each player i's altruism coefficient a_i is privately known, while the distribution F is common knowledge. Consequently, we model a particular game as a Bayesian game, augmented by the private information about types. It is of some importance in our analysis that players may reveal information about their altruism coefficient through their play. This can act as a signal of how they are likely to play in the future, and may change opponents' attitudes toward them (when $\lambda > 0$).

In studying experiments, we will identify the participants' utility with their monetary income from the experiment. Since the sums of money involved are trivial, it is hard to believe that curvature in the utility function can play much of a role in explaining behavior in the experiments. It is important to note, however, that the money that is not received by the participants reverts to the experimenter, and there is no reason for the subjects to feel differently about the experimenter than the other subjects. However, it does not seem sensible to identify the utility of the experimenter with the amount of money that reverts to him. Instead, we will assume that the marginal utility of the experimenter for money that is not disbursed to the subjects is zero, so that in effect, from the subject's point of view, the money is thrown away, and the altruism coefficient a_i does not matter. Notice that it is possible to design experiments to control more carefully for the effect of money that is not received by the subjects. Rather than having the money revert to the experimenter, one subject can be chosen to be the residual claimant, with all money not disbursed to the subjects being given to the residual claimant, who does not otherwise participate in the experiment. In this case, the utility of money not going to the participants other than the residual claimant can also be identified with money income, and the residual claimant should be viewed by the other subjects as having the population mean value of a_i. According to the theory, this should have an effect on the outcome of the experiment.

Our basic notion of equilibrium is that of sequential equilibrium: each player optimizes given preferences and beliefs that are derived from a limit of strictly mixed perturbations from equilibrium play and Bayes' law. As a technical aside, note that all of the games considered here are relatively simple, and sequentiality in these games coincides with the simpler notion of a perfect Bayes Nash equilibrium. As all of the distributions over types F we will consider have finite support, for any given monetary payoffs in a game, our theory of preferences induces an ordinary Bayesian game. This game can be analyzed by the ordinary tools of game theory: there are no new theorems or results about games of this type. The general theorems about sequential equilibria from Kreps and Wilson [9] apply directly. In particular, introducing altruistic preferences need not eliminate the multiplicity of equilibria. However, we should emphasize that the number of Nash equilibria is reduced by means of sensible refinements. The use of refinements has fallen into disrepute in the study of experiments, because these refinements (including sequentiality and subgame perfection) do quite poorly in describing actual play. However, that is not the case in this theory: once preferences for altruism and spite are taken into account, refinements do relatively well. Indeed, all of the equilibria we explicitly discuss are not only sequential, but satisfy the obvious monotonicity requirement on beliefs in a signaling game: beliefs are that the type most likely to deviate is the type for whom it is least disadvantageous.

We will explore the theory by means of quantitative examples drawn from the experimental literature. It is well known that there is considerable learning taking place in the early rounds of experiments. Since our model is a theory of equilibrium, we focus on experiments in which players get several opportunities to play, and focus on the outcome in the final rounds after the players have had time learn an equilibrium. Our goal is to explain why, even after the system appears to have stabilized, play does not resemble an equilibrium with traditional preferences. Our ideal experimental design is one in which players are matched with different opponents every period, so that we may legitimately ignore repeated game and reputational effects between rounds. With the exception of the public goods experiments of Isaac and Walker [8], all of the experiments reported here follow that design. The results of Isaac and Walker [8] are included because, despite the possibility that repeated effects might have mattered, the experimental design was well suited in other respects for examining the theory described here.

3. OTHER MODELS OF ALTRUISM AND FAIRNESS

Before studying specific experimental data using the model of altruism outlined in the previous section, it is useful to put the model in a broader perspective. The model described can be viewed as a particular parameterization of a class of models in which preferences depend on payoffs to an individual player and to his rivals, as well as depending on his own type and the type of his rivals. As we indicated, because of the stakes involved in the experimental setting, we have chosen a parameterization that is linear in monetary payoffs. This specification would obviously be unsuitable in a setting where the stakes were large.

Within the linear framework, we can consider a broader class of models in which adjusted utility is given by

$$v_i = u_i + \sum_{j \neq i} \beta_{ij} u_j,$$

and the coefficients β_{ij} are determined from players' types or other details about the game. For example, Ledyard [11] proposes a specification in which $\beta_{ij} = \gamma_i(u_j^f - u_j)$, where u_j^f is a "fair amount" which he does not define. A more detailed specification can be found in Rabin [17], who assumes that a player is interested in what is fair for himself, rather than what is fair for the other player. His specification is $\beta_{ij} = \gamma_i(u_i - u_i^f)$, where the "fair amount" is a fixed weighted average of the maximum and minimum Pareto efficient payoff, given player i's own choice of strategy, and the coefficient γ_i itself is endogenous in a somewhat complicated way. Both of these theories suppose that players care about whether their opponents play "fairly" and run into the problem that there is no obvious notion of fairness that applies to all games. The strategy of the specification we have chosen is to suppose that players do not care about whether their opponents play "fairly," but rather whether their opponents are nice people. This has the advantage that there is no need to answer the question of what is "fair."

4. ULTIMATUM

We begin with the study by Roth et al. [18] on ultimatum bargaining in four countries. The extensive form of this game is shown in Fig. 1.

Player 1 demands an amount x between 0 and \$10.[3] Player 2 may either accept or reject. If he accepts, player 1 gets the demanded amount, and player 2 gets the remainder of \$10. If he rejects, neither player receives anything.

In the usual selfish case where the altruism coefficient is $a_i = 0$ for all players, player 2 should accept any demand less than \$10. Subgame

[3] This is the base case. In countries other than the United States, payoffs were calibrated to match \$10 U.S. in local currency. In one treatment in the United States the payoff was \$30 rather than \$10. Since the magnitude of the payoffs does not matter for the theory here, we normalized all of the payoffs to \$10.

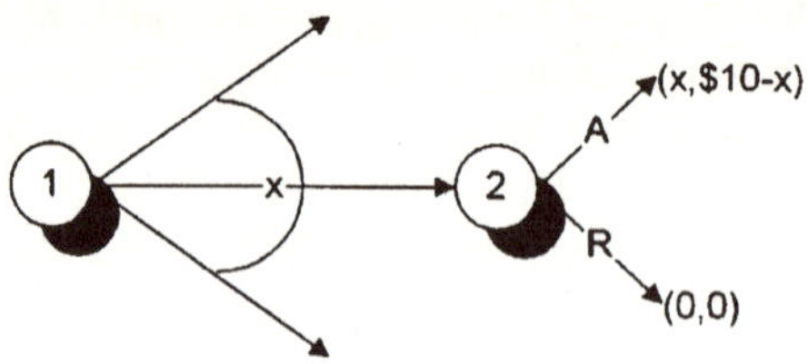

FIGURE 1

perfection then requires that player 1 demand at least $9.95.[4] The actual results of the experiments were quite different. Table I pools results[5] of the final (of 10) periods of play in the five experiments reported in Roth et al. [18], with payoffs normalized to $10. It should be emphasized that to eliminate as much as possible the effect of learning, only data are from the last of 10 rounds are used. The majority of players demanded no more than $6, and many demands of less than $10 are rejected.

The altruistic model has implications for this game, independent of the distribution F.

[4] Players were constrained to demands stated in units equivalent to $0.05.

[5] All four countries are pooled. There are differences between the results of the different treatments, but even with the pooled data, the evidence on altruism is very limited, as we shall see. While the differences are statistically significant, they are not large in absolute terms (in the United States demands were generally $5, in Israel generally $6). Since the theory says the treatments should not make a difference, we elected to pool the data.

TABLE I
Raw Ultimatum Data

Demand	Observations	Acceptance
$9.00	1	100%
$8.25	1	100%
$8.00	4	50%
$7.50	5	80%
$7.00	10	80%
$6.75	5	20%
$6.50	6	83%
$6.25	5	80%
$6.00	30	83%
$5.75	9	100%
$5.50	17	71%
$5.25	5	100%
$5.00	31	100%
$4.75	1	100%

PROPOSITION 1. *Regardless of F, in no sequential equilibrium will any demand be made for less than* \$5.00, *and any demand of* \$5.00 *or less will be accepted.*

Proof. First observe that $10 - x + \beta x > 0$ if $-1 < \beta$ and $x \leq 5$, so indeed, any demand of \$5.00 or less will be accepted. But $x + \beta(10 - x)$ is increasing in x for $\beta > -1$. Since a demand of less than \$5.00 can be increased without reducing the probability it will be accepted, it cannot be optimal to make such a demand. ∎

In fact, in the data only one demand of less than \$5.00 was ever made, and it was for \$4.75 and was accepted, so the data are consistent with Proposition 1.

To simplify the remainder of the analysis, it will be convenient to pool the results. The demands are grouped into three categories: demands in the range \$4.75–\$5.25 are treated as \$5.00 demands; demands in the range \$5.50 to \$6.50 are treated as \$6.00 demands; and demands of \$6.75 and higher are treated as \$7.00 demands. For simplicity, we will only allow players to make demands in even dollars. The pooled data are summarized in Table II; the column labeled Adjusted Acceptance is explained below.

We will assume that the distribution F of altruism coefficients places weight on three points $\bar{a} > a_0 > \underline{a}$. We refer to these as the altruistic, normal, and spiteful types of players. Since there are three demands made in equilibrium, and more altruistic types will prefer to make lower demands, we will look for an equilibrium in which the altruistic type demands \$5.00, the normal type \$6.00, and the spiteful type \$7.00. Consequently, the probabilities of the three types must be 0.28, 0.52, and 0.20, respectively, as this is the frequency of demands in the sample. The \$5.00 demand is clearly accepted by all three types. The \$6.00 demand is accepted by 82% of the population. However, because of sampling error, it is impossible to reject the hypothesis that the actual acceptance rate is 0.80 at less than a 28% level of confidence. Since 80% of the population corresponds to the spiteful types rejecting the demand, we will assume that this is in fact the actual acceptance rate (the column Adjusted Acceptance in Table II). In other words, we assume that the \$6.00 demand is rejected by the spiteful

TABLE II
Pooled Ultimatum Data

Demand	Observations	Frequency of observations	Accepted demands	Probability of acceptance	Adjusted acceptance
\$5.00	37	28%	37	1.00	1.00
\$6.00	67	52%	55	0.82	0.80
\$7.00	26	20%	17	0.65	0.65

types and accepted by the normal and altruistic types. The \$7.00 demand is accepted by 65% of the population, corresponding to all of the altruistic types (28%) and a fraction 71% ($0.71 \times 0.52 \approx 0.37$) of the normal types. This implies that the normal types must be indifferent between accepting and rejecting the \$7.00 demand.

Based on these considerations, we can characterize the parameters consistent with equilibrium by means of six incentive constraints given in Lemma A in the Appendix. Our next set of results examines more closely which parameter values are consistent with the data.

PROPOSITION 3. *There is no sequential equilibrium with* $\lambda = 0$.

Proof. Since the normal type must be indifferent to accepting or rejecting the \$7.00 demand, we have

$$3 + \frac{a_0 + \lambda \underline{a}}{1 + \lambda} 7 = 0$$

(also Eq. (6) in Lemma A). Setting $\lambda = 0$, we see that $a_0 = -3/7$; that is, the normal type must be relatively spiteful. But we may calculate in this case that the utility the normal type gets from making the \$6.00 demand is \$3.43, while the utility from making the \$7.00 demand is \$3.71. This contradicts the fact that the normal type must prefer the \$6.00 demand. ∎

This is actually a corollary of the next proposition, but we give a separate proof, because of the importance of the result. What this proposition says is that a model of pure altruism is not consistent with the data from the ultimatum experiments. The problem is that the acceptance of demands is such that players must be relatively spiteful. But spiteful players would not make the modest demands observed in ultimatum. We have experimented with several other specifications of the distribution of the coefficient of altruism in the model of pure altruism, and none can explain this feature of the data.

PROPOSITION 4. *In sequential equilibrium,* $-.301 \leq a_0 \leq -.095$, $-1 < \underline{a} < -0.73$, $0.584 \geq \lambda \geq 0.222$.

Proof. From manipulating the incentive constraints characterizing an equilibrium; see the Appendix for details. ∎

There are a variety of parameter values for which there are sequential equilibria consistent with the data. Each column of Table III gives a set of parameter values for which there exists an equilibrium of the type described that is consistent with the data.

As can be seen, a wide range of values of $\bar{a}$ is consistent with the data. Experimentation indicates somewhat less flexibility in the remaining pa-

TABLE III
Parameters Consistent with Equilibrium in Ultimatum

$\bar{a}$	0.10	0.30	0.40	0.90	0.90	0.90	0.90
a_0	−0.22	−0.22	−0.22	−0.22	−0.27	−0.26	−0.20
$\underline{a}$	−0.90	−0.90	−0.90	−0.90	−0.87	−0.90	−0.90
λ	0.45	0.45	0.45	0.45	0.36	0.35	0.49

rameters than is indicated in Proposition 3. In particular, it appears to be difficult to get $\underline{a}$ larger than -0.87 (versus the known upper bound of -0.73). Values of λ lower than 0.35 are difficult to find (against the known lower bound of 0.22). Values of λ higher than 0.49 are difficult to get, as against the known upper bound of 0.58. We were also unable to discover equilibria with values of a_0 below -0.2, although the known upper bound is only -0.301. The parameters $\lambda = 0.45$, $\underline{a} = -0.9$, and $a_0 = -0.22$ lie in the midrange of parameter values consistent with Proposition 3, and within the range of parameters experimentation shows is feasible. Moreover, from Table III, these parameters are consistent with a wide variety of different values of $\bar{a}$. In the remainder of the paper, in evaluating other experiments, we will somewhat arbitrarily choose to work with these parameter values.

While we have found a set of parameter values that is consistent with both sequential equilibrium and with the data, one question we have not yet answered is how much predictive power the theory has. In particular, for our favored parameter values, are there sequential equilibria other than the one found in the data? In particular, can there be a pooling equilibrium in which all players play the same way? The answer is affirmative:

PROPOSITION 5. *If* $\lambda = 0.45$, $a = -0.9$, $a_0 = -0.22$, $\bar{a} = 0.29$,[6] *and the corresponding probabilities of the spiteful, normal, and altruistic groups are* 0.20, 0.52, 0.28, *then there are two pooling equilibrium outcomes that are sequential: one in which all demands are* \$7.00, *and one in which all demands are* \$8.00. *In both cases, the sequential equilibrium offers are accepted by normal and altruistic types, and rejected by the spiteful types.*

Proof. By computation; see the Appendix. ∎

[6] The value of $\bar{a}$ is the estimate from the Centipede experiment discussed below, and is in the range consistent with the separating equilibrium observed in ultimatum.

The predictive power of the theory is about what we would expect from a signaling model. As usual, it is difficult to rule out pooling at different levels, and likely there are several separating equilibria as well as the one observed. On the other hand, it is by no means true that anything is an equilibrium, and indeed, we are able to rule out pooling equilibria at \$5.00, \$6.00, \$9.00 and \$10.00, which was not *a priori* obvious. Notice also that while these pooling equilibria are inconsistent with the data, they are considerably closer to the data than the equilibrium without altruism, in which only very large demands are made, and all are accepted.

5. COMPETITIVE AUCTION

For any value of λ, if the distribution F of altruism coefficient a is degenerate, placing all weight on $a = 0$, the model is the traditional model of all selfish players. Thus the extent to which the distribution F distributes weight away from the origin measures the extent to which the model is different from the selfish player model. To explain the ultimatum experiments, the departure from the selfish player model is quite large. For example, at least 20% of the population as a group has a mean coefficient of -0.73 or worse; even the middle group of 52% of the population seems to have a substantial degree of spite. In other words, we are proposing a substantial departure from the model of selfish agents. This, however, poses a potential problem: in many experiments, especially in market games, double oral auctions, and so forth, the model of selfish agents explains the data well. If the model proposed here is useful, then it must continue to explain the results of games already explained by the selfish player model.

From an intuitive perspective, the experiments in which the selfish player model has worked well are experiments with a high degree of competitiveness. In a relatively competitive environment, players can have a significant effect on their own utility, but it is difficult for them to transfer utility to or from other players. Consequently, we might expect that spite or altruism would play a very small role in such environments. To explore this issue, we turn now to another experiment conducted by Roth et al. under conditions very similar to those at the ultimatum experiment reported above. We argue that regardless of the distribution of altruism and spite in the population, we would expect to see the competitive equilibrium occur in this experiment (as was indeed observed).

In the market game experiment, nine identical buyers submit an offer to a single seller to buy an indivisible object worth nothing to the seller and \$10.00 to the buyer. If the seller accepts, he earns the highest price offered, and a buyer selected from the winning bids by lottery earns the difference between the object's value and the bid. Each player participates in 10 different market rounds with a changing population of buyers. This game has two subgame perfect equilibrium outcomes: either the price is \$10.00, or everyone bids \$9.95. In fact, by round 7 the price rose to \$9.95 or \$10.00 in every experiment, and typically this occurred much earlier.

Altruistic equilibria may be partially characterized by the following:

PROPOSITION 6. *In any sequential equilibrium, all offers of* \$5.00 *or better are accepted. There exist sequential equilibria in which buyer offers are independent of how altruistic they are and the seller always sells. If other buyer offers are independent of how altruistic they are and the seller always sells, then buyer preferences are independent of how altruistic the buyer is. Consequently, the set of sequential equilibria in which buyer offers are independent of how altruistic they are is independent of the distribution of altruism in the population.*

Proof. Let β be the coefficient of altruism adjusted for the opponent's altruism. If the seller accepts an offer of x, he gets $x + \beta(10 - x)$; if he rejects, he gets 0. Hence he accepts if $x + \beta(10 - x) \geq 0$. Since $\beta > -1$, this is true, provided that $x \geq \$5.00$, so all offers of \$5.00 or better are accepted, just as in the case of bargaining.

Turning to the buyers, if there are multiple offers at \$10.00, then no buyer can have any effect on his own utility, since the seller always gets \$10.00 and the buyer \$0.00, regardless of how any individual buyer deviates. More generally, suppose that buyer offers are independent of how altruistic the buyers are, and the seller always buys. The key observation is that by bidding low, a buyer does not prevent the transaction from taking place; he merely fails to get a valuable item for himself. In particular, if the buyer fails to buy, but the transaction takes place anyway, this yields a net benefit to the rest of the population of 10. In other words, an offer x accepted with probability p gives utility

$$p((10 - x) + \beta x) + (1 - p)\beta 10 = 10\beta + (1 - \beta)p(10 - x),$$

which, regardless of β, are the same preferences as $p(10 - x)$. Since preferences are independent of altruism, players are willing to use strategies that are independent of how altruistic they are, so every equilibrium without altruism is an equilibrium with altruism. ∎

6. CENTIPEDE

So far we have merely fit parameters to observations. When the model with $\lambda = 0$ did not fit the data, we simply introduced a new parameter to explain the results. To test the theory, we must hold fixed the parameters we found from ultimatum, and use them to explain the results of a different experiment. One famous experiment that is not explained well by selfish players is grab-a-dollar, and we will next examine such an experiment.

The specific experiment is a variation on grab-a-dollar that McKelvey and Palfrey [12] call the centipede game. The extensive form, together with the actual conditional probabilities of moves computed from the 29 experiments over the last 5 of 10 rounds of play, is reported in Fig. 2. In each round, players played against an opponent they had not previously played against, so repeated game effects should not be an issue here.

Without altruism, these results do not make much sense: Eighteen percent of player 2's that reach the final move choose to throw away money, for example. Moreover, with normal preferences, the unique Nash equilibrium is for all player 1's to drop out immediately. Note, however, that altruistic players may wish to give money away at the end, since the gain to the other player is much greater than the loss, and that this will give other players a reason to stay in the game. Notice also that there is a kind of reputation effect of the type discussed by Fudenberg and Levine [4], in the sense that by staying in, a player signals he is an altruistic type, and as a result is more likely to receive kind treatment from his opponent.

We will model this game using the same model of three types we used to analyze ultimatum. We will assume $\lambda = 0.45$, $\underline{a} = -0.9$, and $a_0 = -0.22$, which are parameters that have been narrowed down by the data on ultimatum. The probabilities of the spiteful, normal, and altruistic groups are 0.20, 0.52, 0.28, respectively. Notice that virtually no player 1's drop out in the first move, so that the distribution of types for the second time player 1 moves should be essentially the prior distribution. Moreover, in this second move by player 1, 25% of the players choose to continue, which, within the margin of sampling error, is quite close to the 28% of player 1's that are altruistic. So we will assume that in player 1's final move, all of the altruistic types pass, and all of the other types take, and we will analyze the modified data in Fig. 3.

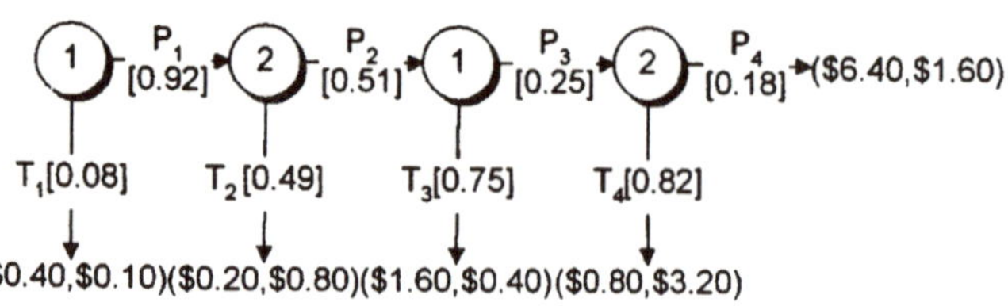

FIGURE 2

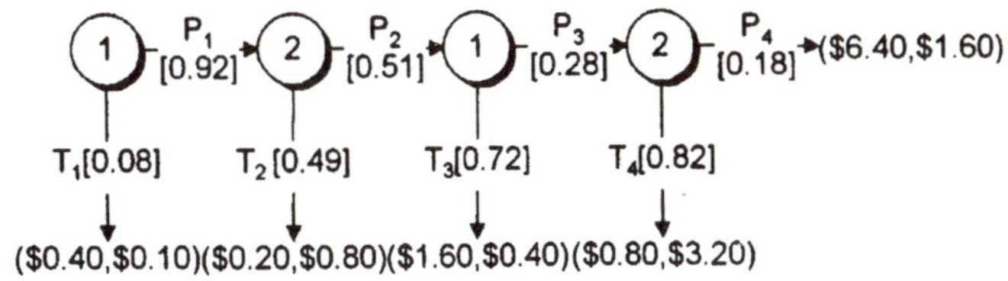

FIGURE 3

We examine the play of player 2's at the final node first. Since spiteful and normal types will drop out before altruists, and fewer players pass than the 28% of the population that are altruists, we conclude that the altruistic types must be indifferent between passing and taking. Since all player 1's are known to player 2 to be altruists at this point, this means that

$$3.20 + \frac{\bar{a} + \lambda\bar{a}}{1 + \lambda}0.80 = 1.60 + \frac{\bar{a} + \lambda\bar{a}}{1 + \lambda}6.40.$$

From this we may calculate $\bar{a} = 2/7 \approx 0.29$. This is one of the wide range of values consistent with the ultimatum data. Notice that this does not yet represent a test of the theory; we are merely calibrating the final parameter that was not pinned down by the ultimatum experiment. However, now that the entire distribution of altruism is pinned down, we can test the theory by asking whether the decisions of players in earlier rounds are consistent with the theory.

We consider player 1's final decision to pass or take. Since 51% of the player 2's of previously passed, including all of the altruistic player 2's, this means that $0.28/0.51 = 0.55$ of the player 2's are altruists and the remaining 0.45 are normal types. If player 1 takes, he then places a weight on his opponent's utility of

$$a_T \equiv \frac{a_0 + \lambda(0.55 \times \bar{a} + 0.45 \times a_0)}{1 + \lambda} = -0.13.$$

His utility if he takes is $1.60 + a_T 0.40 = 1.55$. On the other hand, if he passes, he has a 0.18 chance of an altruistic opponent and getting \$6.40 for himself and \$1.60 for the opponent, resulting in a utility of \$6.31. He also faces a 0.82 chance of an opponent who is $0.45/0.82 = 0.55$ likely to be normal and 0.45 likely to be altruistic. This yields a utility of \$0.33. Averaging over his opponent passing and taking in the final round yields the expected utility to passing of \$1.40, less than the utility of taking. In other words, the normal type should take. This implies that the spiteful

TABLE IV
Optimal Decisions in Centipede

Node	Type	Take utility	Pass utility	Difference
1's last move	a_0	\$1.55	\$1.40	\$0.14
2's first move	a_0	\$0.76	\$0.85	– \$0.09
1's first move	$\underline{a}$	\$0.33	\$0.49	– \$0.16

type should take, and it is apparent from the fact that the normal type is nearly indifferent that the altruistic type should pass. This is as the data suggest.

Continuing on in this way, we can, at each node, compute the utility from taking and passing as shown in Table IV. From the table we see that the spiteful type 1 player is willing nevertheless to pass in the first period. The only inconsistency is that the normal type of player 2 in his first move should be indifferent between passing and taking, and in fact prefers to pass. Notice, however, that we have made no effort to calibrate any of the parameters to the exact indifference of this type, and despite this, the preference for passing is very slight: a mere \$0.09 advantage. In fact, the data seem strikingly consistent with the model and the estimates of altruism and spitefulness from the ultimatum game and the final period of this game.

One way to understand how well this model explains the data is to compare it to the standard nonaltruistic model. In Fudenberg and Levine [5] we argue that an appropriate metric for measuring departures from the theory is the expected loss of players. We just calculated these losses for the altruism model. The results are summarized in Table V. Here the column marked Loss replicates the final column of Table IV. The column marked Population is the fraction of players (of both types) who suffer the loss. The second two columns report the same data for selfish players. The basis of the calculation is that it is optimal for a selfish player to pass in every round but the final one. In the penultimate round, player 1 can get an expected money gain of \$1.80 by passing; in his first move, player 2 gets

TABLE V
Comparing Losses in Centipede

Node	Altruism model		Standard model	
	Loss	Population	Loss	Population
1's last move	\$0.00		\$0.20	0.17
2's first move	\$0.09	0.17	\$0.38	0.23
1's first move	\$0.16	0.04	\$0.62	0.04

an expected money gain of \$1.18 by passing, while in the first move, it is worth \$1.02 for player 1 to pass. We do not include the losses of selfish player 1's that give money away in the final round, since in the altruism model we used these data to fit a free parameter. We can summarize the results of this table by computing an overall expectation: the deviation from the theory in the altruism model is an expected loss per player per game of about 1.5¢. By way of contrast, the deviation of the data from the standard model of selfish players is an expected loss per player per game of about 14.5¢, nearly an order of magnitude higher.

7. PUBLIC GOODS CONTRIBUTION GAME

It is well known that there is a great deal of altruism in public goods contribution games. Our examination of ultimatum bargaining and centipede suggests a relatively spiteful population with few (28%) altruists. Can this be reconciled with the large amount of altruism found in public goods contribution games? To answer this question, we examine a public goods contribution game studied by Isaac and Walker [8].

The game is a simultaneous move n person game, in which each individual must decide whether to contribute a number of tokens to a common pool, or consume them privately. If m_i is the number of tokens contributed (we may normalize so that the total number of available tokens per player is 1), the direct utility is given by

$$u_i = -m_i + \gamma \sum_{j=1}^{n} m_j.$$

There were four different treatments (pairs of values of γ, n), and each treatment was repeated six times.

As in the case of ultimatum and centipede, we assume $\lambda = 0.45$, $\underline{a} = -0.9$, $a_0 = -0.22$, and $\bar{a} = 0.29$. The corresponding probabilities of the spiteful, normal and altruistic groups are 0.20, 0.52, 0.28, respectively. We may calculate the mean population altruism equal to $\hat{a} = -0.21$. An individual contemplates a contribution to the public goods game, assuming his opponents are drawn randomly from a population with the mean degree of altruism,

$$\begin{aligned} v_i = & -m_i + \gamma(m_i + (n-1)\hat{m}_{-i}) \\ & + \frac{a_i + \lambda \hat{a}}{1+\lambda}(n-1)(-\hat{m}_{-i} + \gamma(m_i + (n-1)\hat{m}_{-i})), \end{aligned}$$

where $\hat{m}_{-1}$ is the mean contribution by players other than player i. Differentiating this with respect to his own contribution m_i, we see that the player will wish to contribute if and only if

$$-1 + \gamma + \frac{a_i + \lambda\hat{a}}{1 + \lambda}(n - 1)\gamma \geq 0.$$

From this we may compute the unique cut-off value a^* such that a player with a higher a degree of altruism contributes, and a player with a lower degree of altruism does not contribute. This is given by

$$a^* = \frac{(1 - \gamma)(1 + \lambda)}{(n - 1)\gamma} - \lambda\hat{a}.$$

Using $\lambda = 0.45$ and $\hat{a} = -0.21$, we can compute the different cut-off values corresponding to the different treatments.

In the actual experiment, four treatments were used, with different numbers of players and different values for the marginal per capital return γ. Following Isaac and Walker [8], we will consider the final round of play only; each treatment was repeated three times. The different treatments, the data from the experiments, and the cutoff values a are all reproduced in Table VI. The column labeled $\overline{m}$ reports the fraction of the population that would have had to contribute if all contributions were either zero or the maximum allowable.

We should begin by noting that the experimental design was not ideal, in the sense that it does not reflect the simple one-shot model we use to explain it. In fact, players played repeatedly against the same opponents, and we cannot be sure what information was revealed about their types prior to the final round reported above.

We should begin by observing that most players that contributed tokens contributed less than the maximum allowable. This is inconsistent with our theory. Because payoffs are linear in own and opponents' monetary payoff, except in the zero probability event of exact indifference, the contribution

TABLE VI
Contributions in a Public Goods Game

γ	n	$\overline{m}$	a^*
0.3	4	0.00	1.13
0.3	10	0.07	0.38
0.75	4	0.29	0.17
0.75	10	0.24	0.06

should either be the minimum or maximum allowable.[7] Although not part of the theory as exposited here, this failure is mitigated by the fact that, both theoretically (see Fudenberg and Levine [5]) and empirically (see McKelvey and Palfrey [13]), there is reason to believe that players near indifference randomize; the partial contribution can be the result of such randomization Because the theory cannot explain individual contributions, we take our objective to explain the aggregate contributions made by the population. This is measured by $\overline{m}$, the fraction of the population contributing all of their tokens required to match the aggregate contribution level.

In the first treatment, the theory predicts (since $a_i \leq 1$ for all players) that there should be no contributions, and indeed there are none. In the second treatment, our theory has 28% of the population altruistic with an average coefficient of 0.28; here we see 7% of the population with a coefficient of at least 0.38, consistent with the degree of altruism from the previous experiments.

The third treatment yields 29% of the population with a coefficient of at least 0.17, also generally consistent with 28% of the population having an average altruism coefficient of 0.28.

The final treatment is also generally consistent with the theory: 24% of the population has an altruism coefficient of at least 0.06. Notice, however, that there were fewer contributions in the fourth treatment than in the third treatment, despite the fact that the theory predicts the opposite. This is consistent, however, with the possibility that the anomalous results of the third treatment are due to sampling error: since each experiment was repeated three times, there are only 12 observations.

If we assume that the large fraction of contributions in the third treatment is due to sampling error, then we should conclude that the actual fraction of the population that would contribute should be 0.24—the fraction of altruists 0.28, less the 0.04 of the population who are altruists with coefficients below 0.17. If we assume three types of altruists with coefficients $0.06 + x$, $0.17 + x$, and $0.38 + x$ and frequencies 0.04, 0.17, and 0.07, having, according to our previous conclusions, a mean of $\bar{a} = 0.29$, then $x = 0.073$, and the three altruistic groups have coefficients of 0.133, 0.243, and 0.453.

[7] It is natural to speculate that this problem could be remedied by the type of nonlinear preferences considered by Andreoni and Miller [1]. However, while they are equally successful in predicting the aggregate outcome of these experiments, they also have little success in predicting the number of individuals who contribute nothing.

8. CONCLUSIONS

The theory fares relatively well in the experiments examined here, particularly in comparison to the selfish theory, which makes wildly wrong predictions, except in the market game. We can summarize in Fig. 4 the distribution of altruism coefficients that works relatively well.

The one really surprising feature of this distribution is the large mass of individuals with relatively negative coefficients—that is, the group of 20% of the population with mean coefficient -0.9.

We should point out the significance of this theory for games in which mixed strategy equilibria are observed. With selfish players, at the Nash equilibrium, a player can transfer money to or from his opponent at no cost (since he is indifferent). The deviation from Nash equilibrium depends on whether at the Nash equilibrium the marginal (indifferent) player is spiteful or altruistic. In the case in which the spiteful player is marginal, he will wish to transfer money away from his opponent. To prevent him from doing so, the opponent's strategy will have to be adjusted to keep him indifferent. In a symmetric game, this means that (with the usual perverse comparative statics of mixed strategies) equilibrium payoffs will be higher than would be the case with purely selfish players. It is known that non-zero-sum mixed equilibria differ systematically from Nash equilibria (see, for example, McKelvey and Palfrey [13]): it remains to be seen whether this can be explained by the population distribution of altruism reported here.

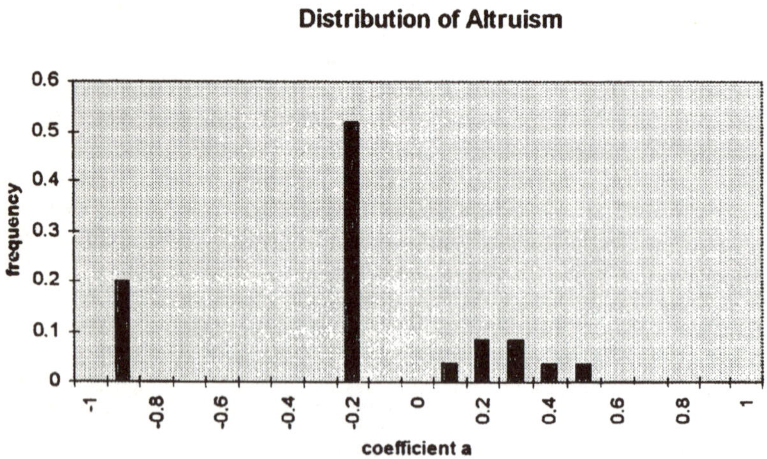

FIGURE 4

There are several experiments that cannot be explained by this theory: one such is the dictator experiment, in which one player decides whether or not to contribute money to an opponent. In these experiments contributions are positive, although with linear utility and $a_i < 1$, the theory predicts no contributions will ever be made.[8] It is possible to dismiss this result along the lines of the partial contributions in the public goods experiment: players who are very altruistic are nearly indifferent and are randomizing. In addition, we are unaware of any dictator experiments conducted in the same way as the experiments here, where players played repeatedly and had a chance to gain experience with the game.

A less radical departure from the predictions of the theory, but an important one, can be found in recent work by Van Huyck et al. [19]. This is a public goods experiment similar to Isaac and Walker's, except that players had the opportunity to be spiteful as well as altruistic. In fact, despite the fact that the estimates here are that many players are quite spiteful, very little spitefulness is observed in Van Huyck et al. [19]. There also appears to be less altruism than in Isaac and Walker's experiment, which suggests that the experimental conditions may have been different in an important way, but hardly begins to explain the lack of spitefulness. There are two significant ways in which the experiment of Van Huyck et al. differs from the experiments reported here, in which spitefulness appeared to play an important role (ultimatum and centipede). The game is a one-shot game, so players could not react to "spiteful" play by opponents, and the game is a four-player game rather than a two-player game.

The fact that there was less spitefulness with four players raises an issue about the theory: we have assumed that the altruism/spite coefficient is independent of how many opponents there are. This is sensible in the case of altruism, but one explanation of spite is that it is really "competitiveness," that is, the desire to outdo opponents. In this case, it is not the total utility of opponents that matters, but some measure of their average or maximum utility. However, while there is obviously much scope for the systematic study of how spite might vary with the number of opponents, even the simple adjustment of deflating our estimated spite coefficients by the number of opponents does not reduce predicted spiteful play to the low level observed by Van Huyck et al. This is evidence in favor of the hypothesis that the extensive form of the game matters: that is, that retaliation for past poor performance is not due only to signaling of types.

In discussing multiplayer public goods experiments, we should mention also the work of Palfrey and Prisbrey [15] on altruism and the warm glow

[8] The results of dictator are evidence in favor of the type of nonlineanty favored by Andreoni and Miller [1], and indeed, their experiments focus on dictator.

effect. They argue that the value of contributions to other players is not so important as the cost of the donation, that there is a "warm glow" effect in which players wish to incur a particular cost of contribution, regardless of the benefit. If the cost is lower, there will more contributions, but if the benefit is higher, there will be no increase in contribution. They study a four-person public goods contribution game in which players must decide whether to contribute a single token.[9] Each period each player would randomly draw a value ξ_i for his token, uniformly distributed on 1 to 20. If the token were kept, the value of the token would be paid; if the token were contributed, a fixed amount γ would be paid to each player. The monetary payoffs are given by

$$u_i = \xi_i - \xi_i m_i + \gamma \sum_{j=1}^{n} m_j.$$

Each player played 20 rounds with a fixed value of γ. They did this four times with different values of γ. Players were shuffled each round so as to minimize repeated game effects.[10] We consider only results from the second 10 rounds with each value of γ, so that players are relatively "experienced," and we can observe equilibrium behavior rather than learning behavior. Data from their experiment are reported in Table VII.[11] Because there are relatively few observations in each cell, the data are pooled as indicated in Table VII.

The most significant feature of these data is that it does not bear out the Palfrey and Prisbrey conclusion of a "warm glow" effect. For a given net cost of contributing $\xi_i - \gamma$, far more contributions are made when $\gamma = 15$ than when $\gamma = 3$; indeed, this is true whenever the cost of contribution is positive. This raises a methodological issue: their conclusion is based on a

[9] There was also a treatment in which players could contribute up to 9 tokens.
[10] A repeated game treatment was also considered with little consequence to the results.
[11] I am grateful to Tom Palfrey for providing me with the raw data.

TABLE VII
Pooled Palfrey/Prisbrey Results

	$\gamma = 3$		$\gamma = 15$	
$\xi_i - \gamma$	Gain ratio	$\overline{m}$	Gain ratio	$\overline{m}$
5	1.8	0.00	9.0	0.60
3–4	2.7	0.18	13.1	0.67
1–2	6.8	0.27	33.7	0.79
0	∞	0.88	∞	0.86

hypothesis test using maximum likelihood estimation in a fully specified model. To account for heterogeneity, they allow the warm glow effect to differ from player to player, but not the degree to which they are altruistic. As a result, the coefficient representing how altruistic players are (the weight on other players' utility) is effectively averaged over the population. Since, as the table above shows, for many players the slope was zero, this specification error leads them to substantially underestimate the extent to which a portion of the population was altruistic.

While the maximum likelihood approach deals well with the problem of sampling error, it deals poorly with specification error. The approach we have taken here is to use method of moments estimation, and, recognizing that the model is misspecified, to give easily interpretable measures of the departures from the theory. This, for example, is the approach we take in analyzing the centipede game, where we use the Fudenberg and Levine [5] approach of reporting players' losses. Similarly, while the model is clearly misspecified in the public goods experiment, failing as it does to explain the fact that individual players do not contribute all or nothing, we can ask whether it does a good job of predicting aggregate outcomes. This idea that the model may work well to explain features of the data we are interested in, while poorly describing some of the details we are less interested in, is extremely difficult to capture in a maximum likelihood approach.

Finally, we turn to other implications of the theory that could be tested in future experiments. For example, there is a set of implications of the theory for one-player games that has not been examined experimentally: The theory predicts that spiteful play should take place, even in a one-player setting. In other words, if a single player is given the option to deprive an opponent of money at a sufficiently modest cost to himself, then we should observe 20% or more of players availing themselves of this option. Moreover, in two-move games such as the best-shot game discussed by Prasnikar and Roth [16], in which all first players are observed to play the same way, the second mover should exhibit the same degree of altruism (or spite) when posed with the simple second-period decision problem with no first-player move.[12] In a similar vein, it is possible to confront players with the same choices faced by the second player in ultimatum bargaining, but also as a simple decision problem and with no first-period move. The theory predicts that this change will effect the play of the second players because of the absence of signaling by the first player, but it makes very

[12] In the full information best-shot reported in Prasnilcar and Roth [16], there is slightly less altruism and slightly less spite exhibited by the second player than in the experiments reported here. However, only eight second players were involved in the experiment, so sampling error is a major problem.

specific and easy-to-calculate predictions about the frequency of acceptance and rejections. Since this is a two-player experiment, it provides a more direct test than that of Van Huyck et al. that spite involves explicit retaliation and not merely signaling. Finally, a referee made the interesting suggestion that it would be possible to have players engage in dictator experiments, with their behavior in the experiment announced to their opponent in a subsequent ultimatum game. According to the theory, relatively ungenerous players in dictator should get poor offers in ultimatum.

APPENDIX

LEMMA A. *A sequential equilibrium matching the data will be given by parameters* $1 > \bar{a} > a_0 > \underline{a} > -1$, $0 \leq \lambda \leq 1$ *such that*

$$\left(6 + \frac{a_0 + \lambda(0.35\bar{a} + 0.65a_0)}{1+\lambda}4\right)0.8 - \left(5 + \frac{a_0 + \lambda(0.28\bar{a} + 0.52a_0 + 0.20\underline{a})}{1+\lambda}5\right) \geq 0 \tag{1}$$

$$\left(6 + \frac{\bar{a} + \lambda(0.35\bar{a} + 0.65a_0)}{1+\lambda}4\right)0.8 - \left(5 + \frac{\bar{a} + \lambda(0.28\bar{a} + 0.52a_0 + 0.20\underline{a})}{1+\lambda}5\right) \leq 0 \tag{2}$$

$$4 + \frac{\underline{a} + \lambda a_0}{1+\lambda}6 \leq 0 \tag{3}$$

$$\left(7 + \frac{\underline{a} + \lambda(0.43\bar{a} + 0.57a_0)}{1+\lambda}3\right)0.65 - \left(6 + \frac{\underline{a} + \lambda(0.35\bar{a} + 0.65a_0)}{1+\lambda}4\right)0.8 \geq 0 \tag{4}$$

$$\left(7 + \frac{a_0 + \lambda(0.43\bar{a} + 0.57a_0)}{1+\lambda}3\right)0.65 - \left(6 + \frac{a_0 + \lambda(0.35\bar{a} + 0.65a_0)}{1+\lambda}4\right)0.8 \leq 0 \tag{5}$$

$$3 + \frac{a_0 + \lambda \underline{a}}{1 + \lambda} 7 = 0 \tag{6}$$

$$\left(7 + \frac{\underline{a} + \lambda(0.43\bar{a} + 0.57a_0)}{1 + \lambda} 3\right) 0.65 \geq 2.80. \tag{7}$$

Proof. We first consider the \$5.00 demand. Since all types will accept this demand, the adjusted utility received by a player demanding this amount is

$$\left(5 + \frac{a + \lambda(0.28\bar{a} + 0.52a_0 + 0.20\underline{a})}{1 + \lambda} 5\right).$$

In addition, if the spiteful type accepts, all types will accept the demand. Since the demand is known to be made by the altruistic type, for the spiteful type to accept, we must have

$$5 + \frac{\underline{a} + \lambda \bar{a}}{1 + \lambda} 5 \geq 0.$$

However, this inequality is always satisfied for $\underline{a}, \bar{a} > -1$.

We turn next to the \$6.00 demand. Since only the altruistic and normal types accept this demand, the adjusted utility received by a player demanding this amount is

$$\left(6 + \frac{a + \lambda(0.35\bar{a} + 0.65a_0)}{1 + \lambda} 4\right) 0.8.$$

For the normal type, this must yield more utility than the \$5.00 demand (and therefore it does also for the spiteful type)

$$\left(6 + \frac{a_0 + \lambda(0.35\bar{a} + 0.65a_0)}{1 + \lambda} 4\right) 0.8 - \left(5 + \frac{a_0 + \lambda(0.28\bar{a} + 0.52a_0 + 0.20\underline{a})}{1 + \lambda} 5\right) \geq 0, \tag{1}$$

while for the altruistic type it must yield less utility,

$$\left(6 + \frac{\bar{a} + \lambda(0.35\bar{a} + 0.65a_0)}{1 + \lambda} 4\right) 0.8 - \left(5 + \frac{\bar{a} + \lambda(0.28\bar{a} + 0.52a_0 + 0.20\underline{a})}{1 + \lambda} 5\right) \leq 0. \tag{2}$$

Moreover, the spiteful type must reject, and the normal type accept (in which case the altruistic type will also accept) the \$6.00 demand. Since the demand is known to be made by the normal type for the spiteful type to reject, we must have

$$4 + \frac{\underline{a} + \lambda a_0}{1 + \lambda} 6 \leq 0, \tag{3}$$

while for the normal type to accept, we must have

$$4 + \frac{a_0 + \lambda a_0}{1 + \lambda} 6 = 4 + 6a_0 \geq 0.$$

Next we have the \$7.00 demand. Since the altruistic and 71% of the normal types accept this demand, the adjusted utility received by a player demanding this amount is

$$\left(7 + \frac{a + \lambda(0.43\bar{a} + 0.57a_0)}{1 + \lambda} 3\right) 0.65.$$

The spiteful type must prefer this to the \$6.00 demand, so that

$$\left(7 + \frac{\underline{a} + \lambda(0.43\bar{a} + 0.57a_0)}{1 + \lambda} 3\right) 0.65 - \left(6 + \frac{\underline{a} + \lambda(0.35\bar{a} + 0.65a_0)}{1 + \lambda} 4\right) 0.8 \geq 0, \tag{4}$$

while the normal type must prefer the \$6.00 demand yielding (5) (implying that the altruistic type does as well).

The normal type must be indifferent between accepting or rejecting the \$7.00 demand (in which case the spiteful player rejects, and the altruistic player accepts). Since the demand is known to be made by the spiteful player, this forces

$$3 + \frac{a_0 + \lambda \underline{a}}{1 + \lambda} 7 = 0. \tag{6}$$

Notice that this implies that a weighted average of a_0, $\underline{a}$ is equal to $-3/7$; since $a_0 > \underline{a}$, this implies that $a_0 > -3/7 > -2/3$, which implies the inequality above, that the normal player accepts the \$6.00 demand.

From Proposition 1, we may ignore demands of less than \$5.00. However, we need to consider demands of more than \$8.00.[13] Since in our proposed equilibrium, only spiteful types will demand as much as \$7.00, we consider the most favorable case for equilibrium, that in which beliefs are that any demand greater than \$7.00 is made by a spiteful type. Because the spiteful type has the most reason to make large demands, these beliefs are consistent with quite strong refinements, such as the intuitive criterion (Cho and Kreps [3]). Given these beliefs, it is clear that since normal types are indifferent between accepting and rejecting the \$7.00 demand, only the altruistic type will accept larger demands. Since it is most favorable for making large demands, let us suppose that the altruistic type is sufficiently altruistic as to accept all demands. In this case, if any type is to make a demand above \$7.00, the spiteful type will wish to do so, and will wish to demand a full \$10.00. The demand is accepted with probability 28%, corresponding to the fraction of altruistic types, so the expected utility is \$2.80. On the other hand, a demand of \$7.00 is accepted with probability 65%, and gives a spiteful type a utility of

$$\left(7 + \frac{a + \lambda(0.43\bar{a} + 0.57a_0)}{1 + \lambda} 3\right) 0.65 \geq 2.80. \tag{7}$$

PROPOSITION 4. *In sequential equilibrium* $-0.301 \leq a_0 \leq -0.095$, $-1 < \underline{a} < -0.73$, $0.584 \geq \lambda \geq 0.222$.

Proof. We begin by showing that the bounds $-0.301 \leq a_0 \leq -0.095$, $-1 < \underline{a} < -2/3$, $0.584 \geq \lambda \geq 0.222$ hold, then strengthen the bound on $\underline{a}$ as indicated below.

Note that the lower bound on λ follows from the bounds on a_0 and a, and Eq. (6), which may be solved for λ as a function of the other two variables. The upper bound on λ follows from substituting (6) into (3) and observing that $\underline{a} \geq -1$.

Note that Eq. (6) says that a convex combination of $\underline{a}$, a_0 is equal to $-3/7$. This implies immediately that $\underline{a} \leq -3/7 \leq a_0$. Solving (6) for λ and substituting into the condition (3) that the spiteful type reject the \$6 demand, we find

$$4 + \frac{6\underline{a}(\underline{a} + 3/7) - 6a_0(a_0 + 3/7)}{\underline{a} - a_0} \leq 0.$$

[13] There were actually 4.6% of the offers for \$8.00 or more (almost all for \$8 00), but we have elected to treat this as approximately zero.

Through straightforward algebraic manipulation, it can be shown that it is possible to satisfy this equation together with $\underline{a} \leq -3/7 \leq a_0$, only if $\underline{a} < -2/3$. Observing that if this condition can be satisfied at all, it can be satisfied when $\underline{a} = -1$, then yields the upper bound $a_0 \leq -0.095$.

Finally, substitute the solution of (6) for λ into (5), the condition that the normal type prefers to demand \$6.00 rather than \$7.00. Inspection of the resulting condition shows that if it can be satisfied at all, it can be satisfied when $\bar{a} = 1$. Making use of the condition that $\underline{a} < -2/3$ yields the lower bound $-0.301 \leq a_0$.

Finally, we can strengthen the bound on $\underline{a}$ by substituting (6) into (3) to find

$$a \leq -\frac{2 - (9/7)\lambda}{3(1 - \lambda)}.$$

Since the right-hand side is decreasing in λ, the largest value of $\underline{a}$ is obtained when λ takes on its smallest value of 0.22, yielding $a \leq -0.73$. ∎

PROPOSITION 5. *If* $\lambda = 0.45$, $\underline{a} = -0.9$, $a_0 = -0.22$, $\underline{a} = 0.29$[14] *and the corresponding probabilities of the spiteful, normal, and altruistic groups are* 0.20, 052, 0.28, *then there are two pooling equilibrium outcomes that are sequential: one in which all demands are* \$7.00, *and one in which all demands are* \$8.00. *In both cases, the sequential equilibrium offers are accepted by normal and altruistic types, and rejected by the spiteful types.*

Proof. Observe from our previous calculations that normal and altruistic players will accept a \$7.00 demand or less, even from a spiteful type; both will strictly prefer to accept a \$6.00 demand. Moreover, a spiteful type, regardless of beliefs about his opponent, faced with the acceptance of both normal and altruistic types, will always prefer to demand \$6.00 rather than getting \$5.00 for sure. This means that any pooling equilibrium must involve all players demanding at least \$6.00. Next, the population average altruism coefficient is $\hat{a} = -0.21$, so that both the normal and spiteful types will reject pooled demands of \$9.00 and \$10.00, and the spiteful type will reject all demands of more than \$5.00. This enables us to rule out a pooling equilibrium at \$6.00, since the altruistic type will prefer \$5.00 for certain to \$6.00 with 80% chance. We can similarly rule out pooling equilibria of \$9.00 and \$10.00, since the altruistic type will prefer \$5.00 for certain to even \$10.00 received with only a 28% probability. So this further narrows the range of pooling equilibria to \$7.00 and \$8.00 demands, which are accepted by the normal and altruistic type, and rejected by the spiteful

[14] The value of $\bar{a}$ is the estimate from the centipede experiment and is in the range consistent with the separating equilibrium observed in ultimatum.

type. These are equilibrium with off-equilibrium path play in which all types (including the altruistic type) reject $10.00 offers on the grounds that only spiteful types make them. In this case, even the spiteful type prefers to have a $7.00 offer accepted 80% of the time by an altruistic or normal type, to having a $9.00 offer accepted 28% of the time by the altruistic type. Similarly, the altruistic type prefers $7.00 80% of the time against $5.00 for certain. Consequently, both of these are equilibria. Notice that like the separating equilibrium, these pooling equilibria satisfy plausible refinements based on monotonicity: higher demands are thought to be made by less altruistic types. ∎

REFERENCES

1. J. Andreoni and J. H. Miller, "Giving According to GARP: An Experimental Study of Rationality and Altruism," University of Wisconsin, Madison, WI, 1996.
2. K. Binmore and L. Samuelson, "Evolutionary Drift and Equilibrium Selection," University College London, 1995.
3. I. Cho and D. Kreps, Signaling games and stable equilibria, *Quart. J. Econom.* **102** (1997), 179–221.
4. D. Fudenberg and D. K. Levine, Reputation and equilibrium selection in games with a patient player, *Econometrica* **57** (1989), 759–778.
5. D. Fudenberg and D. K. Levine, Consistency and cautious fictitious play, *J. Econom. Dynamics Control* **19** (1995), 1065–1090.
6. D. Fudenberg and D. K. Levine, Measuning subject's losses in experimental games, *Quart. J. Econom.* **112** (1997), 508–536.
7. J. Geanakoplos, D. Pearce, and E. Stacchetti, Psychological games and sequential rationality, *Games Econom. Behav.* **1** (1989), 60–79.
8. R. M. Isaac and J. M. Walker, Group size effects in public goods provision: the voluntary contribution mechanism, *Quart. J. Econom.* **103** (1988), 179–200.
9. D. Kreps and B. Wilson, Sequential equilibrium, *Economertica* **50** (1982), 863–894.
10. D. Kreps and R. Wilson, Reputation and imperfect information, *J. Econom. Theory* **50** (1982), 253–279.
11. J. Ledyard, Public goods: a survey of experimental research, *in* "Handbook of Experimental Economics" (J. Kagel and A. Roth, Eds.), Princeton Univ. Press, Princeton, NJ, 1995.
12. R. McKelvey and T. Palfrey, An experimental study of the centipede game, *Econometrica*, **60** (1992), 803–836.
13. R. McKelvey and T. Palfrey, Quantal response equilibria for normal form games, *Games Econom. Behav.* **10** (1995), 6–38.
14. P. Milgrom and J. Roberts, Predation, reputation and entry deterrence, *Econometrica* (1982), **50**, 443–460.
15. T. R. Palfrey and J. Prisbrey, Anomalous behavior in public goods experiments: how much and why? *Amer. Econom. Rev.* **87** (1987), 829–846.
16 V. Prasnikar and A. Roth, Considerations of fairness and strategy: experimental data from sequential games, *Quart. J. Econom.* **107** (1992), 865–888.
17. M. Rabin, Endogenous preferences in games, *Amer. Econom. Rev.* **83** (1993), 1281–1302.
18. A. E. Roth, V. Prasnikar, M. Okuno-Fujiwara, and S. Zamir, Bargaining and market behavior in Jerusalem, Liubljana, Pittsburgh, and Tokyo: an experimental study, *Amer. Econom. Rev.* **81** (1991), 1068–1095.
19. J. Van Huyck, R. Battalio, and F. Rankin, "On the Evolution of Convention: Evidence from Coordination Games," Texas A & M.

[26]

Economics and Philosophy, 2, 1986, 159–183. Printed in the United States of America.

THE CASE FOR A MULTIPLE-UTILITY CONCEPTION

AMITAI ETZIONI
George Washington University, Washington, D.C.

In recent decades, neoclassical economists have made heroic efforts to accommodate within the confines of the concept of rational utility maximization the fact that individual behavior is significantly affected by moral considerations. This article argues the merits of using an alternative approach: recognizing that individuals pursue at least two irreducible sources of value or "utility", pleasure and morality. The possibility that some additional utilities may have to be recognized is explored. This raises the concern that conceptual anarchy will break out, which in turn will force a search for a common denominator, and thus a return to one overarching utility. Arguments are presented to show that this concern is unfounded. The main focus of the article is a criticism of the monoutility conception and a brief for separating the sense of discharging one's moral obligations from all other satisfactions. The article first deals with general conceptual points, and then cites both everyday observations and empirical evidence in support of this position.

I. MONOUTILITY: TOO PARSIMONIOUS

A critic of the concept of utility used by economists is faced with the problem of shooting down a revolving target: no sooner has one idea been shot down, then a rather similar one appears, and before long, a

This article is a product of the Socio-Economic Project supported by George Washington University and the Center for Policy Research. I am grateful for comments on previous drafts to Michael S. McPherson, James Childress, Charles Dyke, and Daniel M. Hausman.

third jumps into sight, and soon thereafter, the first one reappears. Economists use three main variations of the concept of utility. First is the original concept, that of the pleasure of the self, coined by utilitarian philosophers and loaded with their psychological assumptions. The second, a much expanded version, increasingly (although not widely) used, encompasses the satisfactions an actor gains both from his own consumption as well as that of others; i.e., it includes satisfactions derived from benevolent acts and a certain understanding of community-minded duty. This concept is sometimes referred to as the interdependent utility (Boulding, 1978, p. 191; Lipsey and Steiner, 1975, p. 143). Finally, still other economists use the term utility as a formal attribute, a common denominator, according to which all specific quests for satisfaction can be ranked, which is needed to allow for mathematization (and to shore up the assumption of a monoutility world) but with no substantive attributes—a grand X. In the following discussion, to keep the targets apart, these concepts are referred to respectively as P-utility (pleasure), I-utility (interdependent), and X-utility (formal). They are all wanting, but for different reasons. The following discussion seeks to establish logical grounds (concerning proper conceptualization), as well as substantive ones, for keeping the concept of *satisfaction*, derived from doing what one likes, enjoys, and finds pleasurable, distinct from the sense of *affirmation* that accompanies living up to one's moral commitments, commitments that are often in themselves taxing rather than pleasurable. That is, for recognizing a moral "utility" above and beyond a P-, I-, or X-utility.

1. The Pleasure Utility

The original use of the term "utility" in modern economics was narrowly self-oriented and straightforwardly hedonistic: the gain of pleasure, the avoidance of pain. Bentham (1948, pp. 1–2) wrote, early in the nineteenth century: "Nature has placed mankind under the governance of two sovereign masters, *pain* and *pleasure*. . . . They govern us in all we do, in all we say, in all we think. . . . The *principle of utility* recognizes this subjection. . . ." Samuelson (1980, p. 48) explains, "As a customer you will buy a good because you feel it gives you satisfaction or 'utility.' "

To understand the source of this concept of utility it must be recalled that its origin and base are in utilitarian philosophy. It assumes that all means find their justification in the ends they serve; the ends give "utility" to the means. While it is possible to have a nonhedonistic utilitarian philosophy, in which the end that bestows value is not the self's pleasure, it is the hedonistic version of utilitarianism that lies at the root of modern economics. Happiness, satisfaction, and pleasure are used as synonyms (Walsh, 1970, pp. 21–26).

Pleasure is invested with moral approval; it is good while pain is evil. Bentham stressed that pain and pleasure are not only empirically our masters but also our normative guides: "It is for them *alone* to point out what we *ought* to do, as well as to determine what we shall do" (Bentham, 1948, p. 1, italics added). They, he added, set the standards of what is right and wrong. "The utilitarians suggested that actions by the self or by others whose consequences to the self are harmful (painful) are naturally deemed bad and arouse anger or punitive tendencies, and actions whose consequences are beneficial (pleasure) are naturally deemed good. . . ." (Kohlberg, 1968, p. 486). Once this gross value judgment about the moral goodness of pleasure is removed, and one takes into account that numerous acts are either pleasurable or moral but often not both (see below), the monoutility world is undermined. The door is then opened to the recognition that there are at least two major, distinct, irreducible sources of value widely recognized in nonutilitarian philosophies, in culture and in language, and "revealed" in behavior.

2. The Interdependent Utility

When the concept of P-utility is challenged as amoral, asocial, and as counter to basic facts about human behavior, including numerous community-minded, altruistic, cooperative, and loving acts, economists tend to point to a concept of utility that is, in effect, radically different but goes under the same name; one that contains service to others and commitment to values beyond the pleasure of self. A simple conceptual device is used: making consumption by *others* a source of the actor's pleasure (hence the term "interdependent" utility). When one person acts altruistically, it is said, the other person's pleasure has become a source of the ego's pleasure, part of the ego's utility.

This I-utility notion of gaining satisfaction from others' pleasure crosses over by degrees into the more abstract X-utility notion as the range of objects that may be a source of the ego's pleasure widens. Thus, besides caring about the extent of another's satisfactions, I may care about what particular goods he consumes, or about the well-being of plants and animals, or what have you. Here, the discussion concentrates on versions of the argument that retain the notion of the ego's psychological state of satisfaction as the ultimate source of motivation; purely formal versions of utility maximization are considered under "The Great X" below.

Note that the I-utility concept remains true to the hedonistic version of utilitarianism: altruistic acts must be explained by the *ego's* pleasure; true altruistic acts, acts of self-denial or sacrifice, are incompatible with the concept. What would motivate them? is the implied question. Of course, if one assumes that only the quest for pleasure (and avoidance of pain) *can* motivate people, one must conclude that saints enjoy their sacrifices, are masochistic. However, once one breaks out of the straitjacket of one utility, and allows for other factors to drive behavior, one sees that normal people do some things because they are right, whether or not they enjoy them. Indeed, over the centuries numerous theologians and philosophers have defined the uniqueness of human beings as compared to animals as the ability to pass judgment over one's urges instead of automatically yielding to them. True, not all such judgments must be ethical; they may, for instance, be aesthetic. However, moral factors are clearly central in defining such judgments.

Moreover, the all-inclusive expansion of the concept of utility violates the rules of sound conceptualization. Once a concept is defined so that it encompasses *all* the incidents that are members of a given category (in the case at hand, the motives for all human activities), it ceases to enhance one's ability to explain. The result is akin to that of multiplying all variables in an equation by one. As long as the ego's and the alter ego's pleasures are treated as equal in their status for the ego's utility, the concept ceases to differentiate. Thus, if someone gives me X new resources, I advance my utility when I use them to enhance my consumption, but I enhance it just as much when I give them to charity, or share them with those I love, or burn them the way the Kwakiutl do (Benedict, 1934, p. 143). Presuming I enjoy the fire, what does the concept add? It simply sprinkles whatever a person is after with the term "utility." Sadism, a quest for a fair or an unfair return, or for mutual affection all have the same status. To the degree that this "theory" aims to shed light on motivation, it constitutes a conceptual failure, because the purpose of introducing concepts is to call attention to meaningful distinctions. The same problem arose in the psychology of instincts, when people who were hungry were said to respond to their instinct, and those who were after sex, to their instinct, and so on. (Before that, the ancient Greeks populated the world with endless gods, "explaining" each event with the working of a god assigned to produce it.)

Leading economists have recognized the unproductive and tautological nature of this approach which states that whatever one does is said to "reveal" one's pleasure. As Stigler pointed out, "a reason, we would be saying, can always be found for whatever we observe man to do" which "turn[s] utility into a tautology" (1966, p. 57). "In the classical view, each consumer is a satisfaction maximizer, i.e., he is a rational egoist. . . . This assumption is so obviously contrary to fact that economists have turned it into a tautology. Any consumer behavior is by definition an attempt to maximize satisfaction" (Bowie and Simon, 1977, pp. 194–95). The authors go on to point out that as a result, "we no longer have an empirical theory about consumer behavior" and the theory becomes "utterly trivial" (ibid.). If one commits suicide, life "must have been" worse than death. In other situations in which some of the pleasures can be measured but still do not explain the act (such as a tax deduction that does not explain a gift because the deductions as a rule are lower in value), it is assumed that some other, unmeasured factor—say reputation in this case—"must" make up the difference. From a sociologist's viewpoint it is at least as plausible to hypothesize that the difference is due to a moral commitment.

Beyond undermining its explanatory power, the all-inclusive expansion of the concept of rational utility maximization undercuts a central thesis concerning the source of order in the economic system, a thesis that economists have advanced for centuries. As Adam Smith emphasized, the market system relies on each actor's pursuing his *self*-interest.

> It is not from the benevolence of the butcher, the brewer or the baker that we expect our dinner, but from their regard to their own interest. We address ourselves not to their humanity but to their self-love, and never talk to them of our own necessities but of their advantages (Smith, 1937 [1776], p. 14).

If there is no fundamental difference between "self-love" and love for others[1] Smith's whole thesis vanishes. Indeed, if people can derive pleasure directly from serving others and the community, there is no need for an invisible hand to tie their individualistic pursuits to the common good. Moreover, problems that might arise in coordinating nonselfish actions effectively would not necessarily be handled effectively by the invisible hand. It thus seems, on grounds of sound conceptualization, that the quest for self-satisfaction and seeking to serve others (the public included) out of a sense of moral obligation, are best kept apart.

1. A reviewer pointed out here that if one's altruism encompasses one's children, there is still a need for the invisible hand to order the relations among the households. This is quite true. However, to the extent that altruism encompasses those with whom one transacts, it supplements or replaces self-interest as the ordering mechanism. For evidence, see below.

3. The Great X

Another major attempt to shore up the monoutility paradigm is to suggest that the concept of utility, whatever its philosophical origins or the psychological "bedtime stories" it used to entail, should be treated as an abstract entity, without any content, neither pleasure nor consumption. It is merely the great common denominator, an X, into which all other values can be converted or by which all rank-ordering can be systematized. Hirshleifer put it succinctly: "What modern economists call 'utility' reflects *nothing* more than the rank ordering of preference" (1976, p. 85, italics added). "It [utility] need not refer to anything" (Little, 1957, p. 20).

This concept of X-utility, in its pure form, if it is taken as devoid of any content, and merely a formal factor according to which the various preferences can be ranked, must be given substantive content in order to be useful for scientific purposes. A means must be specified for determining what the preference rankings of the subjects of study actually are. A basic difficulty here is that the subjects' ranking or valuation of a set of objects will depend on the dimensions along which they are assessed. And because all empirical objects have multiple aspects such as calories, vitamins, minerals, and moral standings, their *value,* or *utility,* will depend on how they are viewed. Unlike mathematical symbols, objects do not have one clear value (Little, 1957, pp. 19ff.).

One way out of this dilemma would be to provide people with one or more criteria for ranking items (or "choices"); the selection of these criteria both introduces substance into the X-utility and raises the question of what it will be—merely pleasure, also morality, or some other utility—which is precisely the question the concept of X-utility seeks to avoid.

Modern economists circumvent this issue by an empiricist device; they draw on the subjects of study and observation, the consumers, the choice makers, to rank their preferences by whatever criteria are in the front or back of their minds, without asking them or otherwise seeking to establish what these criteria are. One way this is done is to ask people what they "prefer" (or which of two products or baskets of products they would rather "have" or "take"). Such questions reintroduce the pleasure utility because they evoke notions of consumption (or ownership, i.e., wealth or potential consumption). People will rank the same items quite differently if they are asked different ranking questions—say, what they value more—because this would bring to mind moral judgments. This is evident in a survey conducted by Juster. Americans were asked what they "benefit" from most. They responded in line with what they expected to be the morally approved answers, which is evident in the way their behavior diverges from their verbal rankings. Americans ranked highest, "talking with children" and seventeenth, "watching television," while it seems clear that in practice most Americans spend much more time watching TV than they ever do talking to their children (Juster, 1985).

To the extent that people are not asked but their choice-behavior is observed, or their ranking is said to be "revealed" in what they buy under various "constraints," especially of income, one runs into severe empirical difficulties. The problem is that it is not sufficient to show that at a given income level a rise in the price of coffee will lead people to buy more tea; one must deal with all the simultaneous changes in all other prices and "compensate" for the loss in across-the-board buying power. Even when this is attempted, under extremely simplified and controlled conditions of experiments with rats, the findings are extremely difficult to interpret (Kagel et al., 1975). Their applications to humans are dubious. Field experiments, such as the income maintenance and health coinsurance ones, run into very considerable, possibly unsurmounted, methodological difficulties. Several economists the author queried about this matter responded, at first, by stating that one need not know what motives "lurk" behind the preferences for the theory to be "very useful," "enormously illuminating," and for it to "allow to predict quite well people's behavior." When reminded of the difficulties listed above, they agreed that actually the predictive record "is quite weak." Indeed, they added, at best the theory predicts the direction of the change of behavior that results from changes in prices, not the magnitude.

Last but not least, the theory does not even seek to explain either the dynamics of preferences or what causes them, or how the consumers allocate their income among alternative goods to begin with. Such explanation is necessary because people change their preferences as the constraints under which they "implement" them change. Without a conception and measurement of preference dynamics, in which values play a pivotal role, a satisfactory theory of economic behavior is hard to imagine. The economist's assumption that people's preferences are "stable," ignores the most elementary observations of daily experience. The argument that absurd assumptions do not matter because the resulting theory is predicting successfully is highly questionable and, it is widely agreed, inadequate.

The suggestion that values and other factors that shape preferences are not the economists' turf, is but one more major reason for a paradigm change, to combine economics with psychology and sociology, to develop a socioeconomics, which in turn may provide for a richer but not overdetermining conception.

All this is not to deny that there may be economic applications within which one or another of these simplified utility theories—P or I or X—is serviceable; the point instead is that there *are* important ranges of human behavior—including some with significant economic aspects—where a more complex theory of motivation and choice is called for.

4. Antecedents

The suggestion that more than one utility is at work, and that one of them is moral, has been often raised before. However, most of those who embark on this road stop before completing the journey. They typically point to many reasons and considerable evidence that one should assume two utilities but then add, sometimes quite arbitrarily, that "after all," the two utilities can, somehow, be accommodated within one overarching one. Buchanan, for example, after a strong argument in favor of distinguishing between two motivational modes, one that he calls "economic self-interest" and the other that he terms "community," adds, in passing, that what "I label moral-ethical, can be analysed in a utility-maximization model" (1978, p. 366). Others whose work lies along this line include Harsanyi (1955), Thaler and Shefrin (1981), Margolis (1982), and Lindenberg (1983). A smaller number of authors called for recognizing two utilities (albeit not in exactly those words), but have not elaborated their reasons, provided amassed evidence, or spelled out an alternative conception. These include Sen (1977) and Hirschman (1984). We turn next to pick up where they left off. What is the nature of the moral "utility"? And once one recognizes two basic dimensions of valuations or utilities, must one open the flood gates to many more?

II. THE MORAL "UTILITY"

What constitutes a moral act? A visit with the relevant philosophical literature leads to the not surprising conclusion that philosophers, after being at it for many hundreds of years, have not yet produced a definitive definition of what is moral. Without attempting here to review the immense literature on the subject, the different approaches, or the difficulties each encounters, for the purposes at hand it suffices to consider moral acts those that meet four criteria, each necessary by itself but sufficient only in conjunction: moral acts reflect an imperative, a generalization, a symmetry when applied to others, and motivate intrinsically.

The *imperative* quality of moral acts is reflected in that persons who act morally feel they "must" behave that way, are obligated, duty bound. We are all familiar from personal experience or introspection with the sense that one ought to do something because it is right as distinguishable from doing it because it is enjoyable.

The notion of an imperative is close to the widely recognized fact that people set aside certain realms or spheres as important, compelling, "sacred" ones. Goodin (1980) sees people as treating moral principles as important and as doing so by setting them aside as a *differentiated,* distinct, set of considerations. Others, especially Durkheim and recently Walzer (1983), point out that people treat certain acts and considerations as "sacred" (which, of course, need not be religious).

One characteristic of such considerations, Goodin suggests, is to repudiate the instrumental rationality of considerations of costs and benefits. A person feels obligated to save a life, make a donation, and so on, without such calculations. Mothers dash into fires to save their children without stopping to calculate. Family members asked to donate a kidney to a child or sibling tend to respond with a quick positive commitment (Simmons et al., 1977). Indeed, the "instantaneousness" of the decision at hand is used by several researchers as one indication that a nondeliberative commitment is made (Fellner and Marshall, 1968).

Only after these moral principles are violated, do people enter into a second realm of decisions, in which moral considerations are weighed against others and calculations enter. This, by the way, explains why people *sometimes* calculate how much to give, and seek to establish what giving X dollars will do for their reputation, or what they will get in exchange, that is, exhibit what Goodin calls prudential morality; this should not be used to argue that they do not have *other* "sacred," nonnegotiable, moral commitments. Morality affects their choices in two different ways: by providing a sense of an absolute command, and as a source of preferences and a commitment to choose certain means, the moral ones, over others, but not at all costs.

People first sense an absolute command to act morally, but that does not mean that they will always heed it. That they are less likely to heed it if the costs are high does not indicate that there is no imperative; indeed, all other things being equal, it is what drives up the costs. On the other hand, if the moral commitment is not reflected in behavior but only in verbal expressions or "attitudes," then there is no imperative.

The need for additional criteria arises because there can be nonmoral imperatives; for example, obsessions with a forlorn love or even with an object, such as controlled substances or a fetish. The addition of the second and third criteria helps to segregate moral imperatives from others (Childress, 1977).

Individuals who act morally are able to *generalize* in the sense of justifying their acts to others and to themselves by general rules. Statements such as "because I want it" or "need it badly," do not meet this criterion because no generalization is entailed. Statements that one believes one ought to act in a certain manner because "these are *all* God's children" or "all men are born equal" are examples of generalizations. (For additional discussion of "general obligations," see Fishkin, 1982.)

Symmetry is required in that there must be a willingness to accord other, comparable people under comparable circumstances, the same standing or right. Racist ideologies, which otherwise have the appearance of moral systems in that they are compelling (to their believers) and generalizable, fail to qualify by this test.

Finally, moral acts *affirm or express a commitment,* rather than involve the consumption of a good or a service. Hence, they are *intrinsically* motivated and not subject to means-end analysis. Does the fact that moral acts are affected by costs not belie this characterization? Pure moral acts ignore costs, like the mother who dashes into the fire to save *her* child, the child she feels morally responsible for. Heath (1976, pp. 1–2) points out that the notions of the pursuit of a utility, of rational choice, and exchange behavior have been much extended to apply not only to market relations but also to friendship and even love. However, he observes, "excluded from this conception of exchange is behavior which is not motivated by the return but by a sense of duty or by some other internalized value. The action of the man who believes in the rightness of his cause and is not affected by the praise or blame of others cannot be included in the category of exchange." (See also Elster, 1979, ch. 4.) As to the argument that moral acts themselves are not impulsive acts but reflect deliberations and judgments (especially evident when one must sort out what course to follow when one is subject to conflicting moral claims), these deliberations are not of the same kind as means-end considerations; they require judgments among ends. Two major studies provide ample evidence that even consumption is often an act of communication and expression rather than of a choice behavior (Douglas, 1979; Thompson, 1979). (These are nonmoral acts that are intrinsically motivating, but that does not invalidate this criterion. It only shows that the universe of such acts is larger than that of moral acts and hence, as was already indicated, this criterion is necessary but not sufficient.)

The significance of the preceding observations should be explicated: Economists frequently argue that moral factors may affect preferences, together with many other factors, but they need not be examined separately because they are reflected in the preferences, and hence ultimately in the price, so one need not study what lurks behind the preferences. Several objections to this approach have already been listed to which it may be added that moral factors affect not only the preferences but also the "constraints." Well, respond the economists, then they will affect the costs. However, to the extent that moral factors sanctify one line of action or set of means over all others, or heavily favor one, they must be included in the analysis because, like oligopolistic or oligopsonistic factors, they rule out options that are preferable from a P-utility maximization viewpoint. A case in point is longshoremen who refuse to load ships that carry cargoes to Poland in protest against the regime's suppression of Solidarity, even if it means they lose some pay. This might be said to be an esoteric exception which, even if not explicable by some hidden pleasure or expediency, does not matter much. However, studies of labor relations are replete with evidence of loyalty of employees to the job, to management, and to the place of employment—and of commitments by higher ranking personnel to lower ranking ones. Economists have often recognized that as a result labor "markets" do not "clear," do not behave as they are expected (Thurow, 1983, ch. 7; Solow, 1980).

Furthermore, when one contemplates the substance of the term "moral behavior," the kinds of acts the term encompasses, one finds another reason to maintain its distinctiveness: moral acts are a source of value and of motivation other than pleasure. What one feels when one lives up to one's moral obligations, discharges one's duties, does "what is right," is distinct from the sense one has when one indulges one of the senses, satisfies a need, does things because they are "fun." *Indeed, many are explicitly based on the denial of pleasure in the name of the principle(s) evoked.* Doing penance, abstention from premarital sex, and Ramadan fasting are not what most people consider sources of pleasure. True, acting in line with one's moral precepts produces a kind of satisfaction, a sense of moral worth, but it's more the kind one gets when a hard day's work is done than the pleasure of getting off work early with full pay.

While pleasure and living up to one's moral commitments are not always or necessarily in conflict, they very often are in terms of their call on resources (the time, energy, and assets dedicated to one are often required by the other as well, a major factor, say, in the life of parents who work outside the home). Quite frequently pleasure-seeking acts and moral commitments are also incompatible in terms of the behavior expected and rewarded (e.g., when managers are under great pressure to increase profits but also not violate the rules of the game; using kickbacks or bribes to get more business are cases in point).

Moral commitments, here and throughout, unless otherwise indicated, refer to moral obligations that have been internalized, that individuals feel as their own, not to those they treat as external conditions to which they merely adapt. Internalization has been defined as part of the socialization process in which a person learns to "conform to rules in situations that arouse impulses to transgress and that lack surveillance and sanctions" (Kohlberg, 1968, p. 483). Social scientists may trace the genesis of one's moral commitments to one's parents, culture, peer or reference groups; but whatever their source, once internalized they become an integral part of the self. Thus, those who feel they ought to serve their country, God, or a cause, feel strongly—sometimes despite strong protestations from spouses, friends, and peers—that such actions are in line with *their* values, are *their* duty.

Does all this mean that the pursuit of pleasure or self-interest is immoral? Obviously not. There are significant areas within which their pursuit is judged to be legitimate, especially in economic activities. This discussion focuses on areas in which the two are in conflict only because it is in these areas that the distinct quality of acts that are judged to be moral stands out most clearly.

III. MORE THAN TWO?

Once the monoutility model is abandoned, why limit the category of utilities to two? Envy, anger, achieving social dominance, conformism, and xenophobia have been nominated as additions (Scitovsky, 1978, would add "novelty"). Psychologists have made long lists of motives or needs. The methodological significance of this challenge should not be overlooked. It is advanced by economists who argue that the existence of myriad "utilities" shows the need for *one* utility to order them all; that to abandon the reigning order leads to anarchy.

In response, one should note first that utilities (or dimensions of valuation) are not to be equated with specific needs, motives, goals, aspirations, preferences, or predispositions; they are analytical categories that encompass numerous concrete manifestations. Just as the concept of a P-utility encompasses numerous specific pleasures, there is no separate utility for sports-car-pleasure and lawn-pleasure, so the moral "utility" encompasses numerous expressions. Moreover, myriad specific needs, motives, goals, aspirations, preferences, and predispositions can be analyzed as an expression of two utilities.

There is, however, no reason to argue that it is logically necessary, or productive, to assume that there are only two utilities (or main sources of valuation), and no others may be considered. One candidate for a third utility that has often been cited is that of affection. It is part of Adam Smith's theory of moral sentiments, in which he sees people as balancing their own conscience with the demands of positive bonds to others.

The main question, though, is not whether one can discern a third (or fourth or fifth) utility, but whether one can keep the *number small,* to preserve parsimony. And one must ask for *the criteria* for introducing into one's paradigm new utilities versus subsuming an observed motive, drive, or preference in one that is already a member of one's paradigm or theory.

The answer is, in part, *pragmatic.* Utilities are not found in nature or on location in the brain; they are concepts we introduce to organize our thinking and the evidence we generate. The question is hence, in part, a matter of what "works," what is productive. For example, if we try to explain voting behavior in traditional utilitarian terms (as neoclassical economists have repeatedly done), voting makes no sense because it entails efforts and yields no specific return. (A voter cannot reasonably expect to affect the outcome of the elections.) Neoclassical economists deal with this "anomaly" by introducing ad hoc assumptions, suggesting that voters do "expect" to affect the elections after all, for various reasons. For example, they will turn out in larger numbers in close elections. (Actually, the correlation between turnout and closeness is weak and hence the concept of "expected" closeness is added, which is difficult to measure. And still the correlations remain weak [Hirshleifer, 1985, p. 55].) If, instead, one introduces another utility, *expressing* one's patriotic duty, one finds that there is a considerable correlation between the level of such a commitment and voting (Barry, 1978, p. 17; Godwin and Mitchell, 1982). One thus achieves higher predictive power, *without* any loss, indeed a gain, in parsimony, and the additional concept, which we shall see often "works" elsewhere, adds to our explanatory power by bringing to mind factors that the monoutility concept does not. For example, one criterion to be used in deciding whether or not a utility is to be added is whether or not it *significantly* enriches our predictive and explanatory powers without overdetermination.

Another criterion is *reducibility,* i.e., the ability to account for a phenomenon by categories already in the theory. For example, to the extent that one can show that affection is part pleasure (enjoy your friends) and part obligation (the dictum to treat others like one's self and not as a medium of exchange), the case for introducing a new category is weakened. However, if a factor, say some emotion like hatred, can be shown not to be accountable by our knowledge of people's moral predispositions and quests for pleasure, say if people's hatred drives them to do things that are both immoral and self-hurting (i.e., not pleasurable), a third category might be called for (Hirschman, 1977, pp. 38–66 traced the long history of opposition between "interests" and "passions.").

How can one foretell if these criteria will lead to conceptual anarchy, the result of the introduction of ever more utilities? Observing people's choices strongly suggests that while they are often subject to numerous forces, they experience them as the sum of a limited number of factors. Typically a person may feel that X is "fun" to do but for reason Y he feels he *ought* not to do it. True, in many situations a person may feel that X would be pleasurable for two, three, or more reasons (a winter vacation in the South may be relaxing and comfortably warm) while moral considerations may include conflicting obligations to spouse, children, and, say, the community. Nevertheless, people's thinking and behavior reveals that *they* reduce these numerous forces to a small number before the final choice. Most people usually feel torn in two or three ways, not umpteen ways; those that do are considered mentally ill. These summary feelings can guide us in developing the theory of utilities.

In the scope of this essay, the exercise cannot be completed by attempting to determine which exact number of summary concepts will prove to be the "right" one. This would involve exploring the cognitive and emotive organization of people's psyches, and the many complex issues raised by the notion of a multiple self. The question of how many facets there are is not merely a question of the convenience of "doing" science but also of the structure of what is found. Nor does it matter for the issues at hand whether the final number turns out to be three, four, or five. What have been indicated are the criteria that may be used in adding utilities or dimensions of value and why the result is expected to be a small number.

IV. CHALLENGING FINDINGS AND OBSERVATIONS

To this point, the essay has (a) argued that there are no principled reasons for insistence on adhering to the monoutility model, (b) indicated how the moral dimension of valuation can be characterized, and (c) defused the concern that the search for multiple "utilities" must eventuate in conceptual anarchy through identifying an excessive number of dimensions of valuation. The discussion has presumed that distinguishing between "moral" and "pleasurable" sources of valuation will prove fruitful through calling attention to and accounting for phenomena that strain the monoutility framework. The final verdict on this claim can only be the product of the kind of sustained research program this essay calls for. This section provides scattered evidence that suggests this program is promising. First, some evidence is cited that authentic altruistic behavior occurs and that such behavior is expressive rather than calculative. Second, the role of moral factors in *economic* behavior is illustrated. True, each of these items of behavior may be explained by some hidden rational considerations (economists have been quite ingenious in coming up with such explanations). The relative merit of these interpretations as compared to those given here is a matter of research called for but not carried out in this essay.

The second line of neoclassical defense is tackled next. Economists say in effect, "well, there may be moral imperatives but these can be explained by *economic* factors." Some evidence is presented to argue that moral acts are not reducible, that they have distinct attributes.

Moreover, the existence of irreducible moral factors, as suggested below, casts doubt about a core assumption of the choice theories that lies at the base of neoclassical economics: that people have clear preferences and can "trade off" relevant items.

1. Authentic Altruism and Expressive Behavior

A considerable body of experimental data supports the existence of significant amounts of authentic altruistic behavior, i.e., behavior in which there is no pleasure for the ego, directly or indirectly, or the costs (or, opportunities sacrificed) clearly outweigh the gains. Several experiments show that many people mail back "lost" wallets to strangers, cash intact (Hornstein et al., 1968). In another study, 64 percent of the subjects who had an opportunity to return a lost contribution to an "Institute for Research in Medicine" did so (Hornstein et al., 1971, p. 110; Hornstein, 1976, pp. 95–96). The cost involved is the cash and the postage and the trouble. The reward? Chiefly, the inner sense of having done what is right.

In some situations, many individuals who see others in distress rush to help them without calculating the consequences for themselves when they feel responsible, as mothers do for their children in houses on fire (Janis and Mann, 1977, p. 27). People who donate a kidney report doing so following an almost instantaneous decision, without deliberation of merits or costs (Fellner and Marshall, 1968). In a set of experiments designed to study "costly self-sacrificing" behavior, people were asked whether they would contribute bone marrow for strangers, not relatives (Schwartz, 1970, p. 283). Of those asked, 59 percent said they would donate; an additional 24 percent indicated at least a 50/50 chance that they would if called upon; 12 percent indicated a less than even chance that they would make such a contribution; only 5 percent said they would refuse outright (ibid., p. 289). Attitudes are not a firm predictor of behavior; the proportion of actual donors is likely to be significantly smaller but not trivial.

Latane and Darley (1970) sent researchers into, of all places, the streets of New York City, requesting help. High proportions of New

Yorkers did assist people they thought were in distress in a variety of situations. For example, an investigator who repeatedly fell down as drunk gained help from passersby in 70 percent of the staged episodes (Piliavin, Rodin, and Piliavin, 1969). For additional evidence and review of several of the studies cited see Rushton (1980) and Derlega and Grzelak (1982).

In many situations gifts are *not* given to elicit reciprocal gifts nor adjusted "in terms of marginal utilities to the recipients" (Wells, 1970, p. 47) but to *express* a family commitment or bond (Cheal, 1984, p. 1; Cheal, 1985), which illustrates that moral affirmations often entail no means-end analysis or choice, but, on the contrary, the one means deemed appropriate is fused to the goal. That is, the means and the goal are intrinsically linked in such a way that they cannot be separated and hence the question of the relative merit of the means at issue compared to some others simply does not apply. This is often the case in rituals. For instance, a *proper* bow is the only way to pay respect in certain South Korean relations. No other bow or mode of paying homage will do; indeed, they are perceived to show disrespect, because the proper means was not used. In the case of gifts, a variety of objects may be used but cash—even if more "efficient"—may be considered rather improper. That is, a whole different scheme of the process of action is involved than that implied in the notion of rational utility maximization.

2. A Factor in Economic Behavior

Commitments to moral values also affect economic activities. Consider saving behavior. Economists explain the level of saving mainly by the size of one's income (the higher one's income the more one saves), by the desire to provide for consumption in retirement, and by the level of interest rates. Together these factors explain part of the variance in the amount saved. However, there are at least three moral norms that also affect the amount saved: the extent to which one believes that it is immoral to be in debt; that one ought to save for its own sake (because "it is the right thing to do" and in order not to be dependent on the government or one's children); and that one ought to help one's children "start off in life". These moral commitments are affected in turn by the content and level of morality in society, by the norms of one's subculture (for example, these prosaving norms seem stronger in small towns than in the big cities), and by other noneconomic factors.

Economists have established that people save much more than can be explained by the desire to ensure their consumption after retirement. "At no age above sixty-five are Americans on an average dissaving" (Thurow, 1983, p. 221). Attempts have been made to explain this "excessive" saving by the need to hedge the "risk" that one will live longer than expected, but still there is a sizable unaccounted "surplus." This, in turn, is explained by older people's enjoyment of the consumption of their offspring "extending through several generations," according to one economist (Shorrocks, 1979, p. 416), and the "consumption of their [household's] descendants in all future generations," according to another (Laitner, 1979, p. 403). This seems an excessive attempt to stretch the consumption function; it is somewhat difficult to visualize how one can enjoy the consumption of one's yet-to-be-conceived offspring of offspring. Assuming a moral commitment to help one's own children seems at least as plausible.

Moral commitments reduce what economists have come to call "moral hazards." Specifically, *the stronger the moral underwriting of implicit contracts, the lower the administrative costs resulting in less of a need to buy hedge protection* (in case resources are not delivered, workers quit, and so on) *and to spend resources on legal action* (drafting explicit contracts, litigation). While reference here is to specific situations—for example, differences between those industries where one can ("usually") rely on one's word versus those where such reliance is less assured—the same point has been made about whole societies. It is common to note that because it is not possible to provide enough police, accountants, and inspectors to verify but a small segment of all the transactions that take place, economies and societies require that most of the transactions be based on voluntary compliance. This, in turn, is significantly affected by the relative *level* of morality within a given society (or subsociety), within a given historical period. To put it differently, to the extent that moral commitments enhance the resources that can be dedicated to the economic activity rather than to supervision and verification, a higher level of morality might increase productivity and even GNP. (On the role of employee thefts and other crimes in reducing productivity, see Denison, 1979.)

While economists tend to go to great lengths to explain behavior without resort to moral explanations (as just illustrated), when the role of moral factors is demonstrated they often suggest that these can be incorporated into neoclassical analysis by assuming that they are contained in the preferences or affect the "constraints." In effect, such a "concession" is greater than it may at first seem because moral factors are changing. This, in turn, leads one to realize that when economic behavior changes it may be due to changes in preferences, and not merely to those in constraints. For example, there is currently a neo-temperance movement in the United States that reduces the "preference" for alcohol. Nor is this the only instance. Without any change in taxes the temperance campaign of Father Matthew around 1850 in Ireland reduced that country's consumption of spirits from twelve million to five million gallons per annum (Hirshleifer, 1980, p. 11), indicative of a major window through which moral explanations may systematically enter the study of economic behavior.

3. The Irreducibility of Moral Behavior

Not only are there moral acts but their explanation cannot be "reduced" to other explanations because people who seek to live up to their moral commitments exhibit systematically and significantly different behavior from people who act to enhance their pleasures. These qualitative differences were noted by one of the major utilitarian philosophers, John Stuart Mill. He wrote, "certain social utilities . . . are vastly more important and therefore more absolute and imperative than any others are as a class . . ." and these utilities are "guarded by a sentiment not different in degree but in kind" (cited by Nisbett, 1981, p. 42). The essay turns next to spell out the distinctive qualities of behavior significantly affected by moral factors. The characterization is based on both everyday observations and social-science findings.

To the extent individuals act under the influence of moral commitments they are more likely to persevere when circumstances change, as compared to when they calculate costs and benefits. Conversely, the more individuals act in the calculative mode, the more likely they are to modify their behavior as circumstances change. For instance, moral behavior is more tenacious than economic behavior. Translated into economic terms, this suggests that *moral commitments "stretch out" the learning curve and are expected to increase transaction costs* when changes favored by economic rationality are inconsistent with moral conduct.

The learning curve reflects the time lapse and costs involved in improving performance. It demonstrates that people provided with information do not absorb it and act on it instantaneously, as was assumed by earlier—and even some present-day—economists. How long it takes and how many resources are required to achieve full absorption are also reflected. The more sharply it slopes, the lower the learning costs; the more stretched out, the higher. The shape of the curve is affected by nonmoral factors (for example, the complexity of the information to be absorbed). Assuming all these other factors are equal, learning is slower and more costly the higher the moral objections to what is being taught.

The concept of "transaction costs" has been introduced by economists to help explain "stickiness"—the observation that people will not modify their behavior even when such modifications are advantageous if the costs involved exceed the expected gain. Moral commitments are among the factors that affect the level of transaction costs. For instance, the stronger the moral commitment, the higher the return needed before the individuals involved will violate their implicit contracts in the face of changed economic circumstances that favor such a violation, and they will absorb more of an economic loss in order to live up to their obligation. For example, it is considered "improper" for professors to accept an offer in May from a competing university to start teaching in September in the same academic year (because it makes it difficult to replace such faculty so late in the year). The norm is said to be stronger in some universities (Ivy League?) than in others (Red Brick?). Hence, in May, it would take a larger salary differential to move a professor from the first kind of university than from the second. In short, moral behavior is "stickier" than amoral behavior.

Intrapsychic conflict between the pleasure and moral valuation of an item, whether the specific psychic mechanism that is activated is guilt, denial, or some other, *results in intrapsychic stress,* which in turn exacts costs that are not typical information or transaction costs: *they diminish the capacity of the actor.* A large body of research shows that under stress, people's decision making becomes less rational—if by acting rationally one means using available information, drawing proper conclusions, and so on. (For a masterful review of the findings, see Janis and Mann, 1979.) A major source of stress is "selling out" virtues one believes in, "prostituting" one's self.

4. "Dirty" Preferences and Encumbered Trades

Due to moral factors *choices do not reflect simple,* one-dimensional, preferences *but are multifaceted.* Economists tend to assume that all units of a specific item (at any one point in time) have one price; all offers and bids are made simultaneously, all bargains are struck, prices are set, and the market clears in a flash, for the whole process to start over again ("comparative statics"). However, everyday observations and experiments show that many purchases are accompanied or followed by feelings of guilt, shame, regrets, and other such feelings that, we shall see, are not merely ephemeral states of mind but have significant behavioral consequences. That is, preferences and behavior are often ambivalent, *and* moral factors which conflict with urges or drives or quests for pleasure are a major source of the ambivalence.

A simple example illustrates the point. It involves dieting, the activity in worship of the body on which millions of members of industrialized societies, especially those better off, focus their moral-like efforts: They feel guilty when they indulge (i.e., experience pleasure) and virtuous when they abstain (pain). One may observe a person who usually does not have desserts order them on three occasions in a row (say, during a holiday season) and then skip lunch on a fourth. An economist may suggest that the price of desserts first fell, and subsequently their cost sky-rocketed (assuming no change in income and other prices). It seems more explanatory to realize the connection between the events, the accumulation of, at first, not visible guilt being worked off (and "revealed in behavior" on the fourth occasion). It also will be more predictive. Guilt is, of course, not the only "accompanying" feeling of choice that has subsequent observable effects. The example is given but to highlight that a one-dimensional ranking overlooks much of what there is in a choice, including the role of moral factors that may not be revealed in every single choice, if viewed as unidimensional and complete unto itself.

Evidence of the existence of ambivalence, whether its source is moral conflict with pleasure or competing pleasures or otherwise, poses a difficulty for neoclassical economics. It is supposed to arise, in the "standard" model, only when consumers are indifferent among combinations of commodities. A lead article in an issue of the *American Economic Review,* the official scholarly publication of the American Economic Association, is dedicated to the puzzle of people whose behavior is said to reflect at one and the same time *two incompatible preferences* (Schelling, 1984). For instance, a man, who goes to a cocktail party, tells the host that when he gets drunk, the host should refuse his request for his car keys. What *is* the guest's preference? To drive drunk—then why ask to be refused the keys? Not to drive drunk—then why ask for the keys? Many more examples are given and considerable deliberation has been devoted to the dilemma. It exists, of course, only because the theory assumes that people will have one clear preference, reflecting one utility.

Because moral and pleasure "preferences" are qualitatively different, items or means of satisfying them cannot be simply "traded off" or substituted for one another, the way various consumer goods can be, which is an essential assumption for the basic concept of the market. If my marginal utility tells me to buy more oranges and fewer apples, there is no aftertaste (or residue) of guilt, shame, or sense of betrayal. But *when people choose to violate their moral precepts to enhance their pleasures, such post-hoc feelings are expected to accompany their actions* and these feelings in turn *have behavioral consequences.* As Hirschman puts it, in situations where individuals act in line with their preferences but in violation of their "meta preferences," often their moral values, the result is "regret and guilt over having preferred it" (1984, p. 13).

In experiments, people who were induced to tell a lie were twice as likely to volunteer to carry out a chore than those who did not lie. Fifty-five percent of shoppers who believed they broke a camera in a shop offered to help another shopper in a staged incident versus fifteen percent of a control group. (These and other studies are reviewed by Rushton, 1980, pp. 43–44.) The relationship is often more complex: a single transgression may lead to some guilt but only the cumulative effect of several will lead to one act of remorse. If an economic analogue can be given to such behavior it would be akin to charging consumers, retroactively but irregularly, for a random subset of past purchases, an additional mark up on items they already consumed, or charging them "extra" in the said manner, more for an item *other* than the one they bought. Guilt about one act spills over and attaches itself to other, seemingly unrelated, items.

The behavioral consequences are expected to include behavior sequences or cycles in which one or more acts are followed by bouts of morally approved behavior, and/or *an increased search for or commitment to offsetting (or "compensatory"), morally approved behavior;* for example, contributing to charity. Several experiments have shown positive correlations between responding to requests for help and *prior* "transgressions," correlations interpreted as the result of "guilt arousal" (Carlsmith and Gross, 1969, pp. 232–39; Sadalla and Wallace, 1966, pp. 187–94).

Conflicts between economic motives and moral beliefs, like other situations described by psychologists as governed by *dissonance,*[2] are expected to lead to inaction (one is caught between conflicting forces) and to *denial* (one acts one way but pretends, or firmly believes, that one acts differently). A simple example of the effects of dissonance is found in changed attitudes toward debt.

The success of credit cards and bank-check credit is attributable to the fact that they allow people to be in debt without having to deal with the dissonance between their feeling "debt is wrong" and their desire to use credit (Maital, 1982, pp. 142–43). People do not perceive these as loans or debt. (On effects of dissonance in the purchase of stocks, see Klausner, 1984, pp. 71–75.)

The discussion so far suggests that moral commitments cannot be exchanged for pleasurable acts without inner and behavioral consequences. It should be noted that many psychologists, from Sigmund Freud to Herbert Marcuse, have argued that the reverse also holds true: Basic urges or pleasures cannot be sublimated into socially approved behavior with full success, without residue. This, of course, lends further support to the thesis that the two concepts refer to behaviors that are substantively different, and are not reducible.

The inner structure of many moral decisions is systematically different from that of typical economic decisions. Unlike many economic

2. On the term, see Festinger, 1957; for an application by economists, see Akerlof and Dickens, 1982.

decisions, *many moral decisions are difficult to reverse (i.e., are asymmetrical), are very "lumpy" (or highly discontinuous), and reveal a high "notch effect" (a fear of passing a threshold that makes behavior sticky before passage but reluctance much diminished or lost once passage is completed).* Take, for example, the decisions concerning premarital sex many women used to face. There were basically three morally recognized positions: virginity, being sexually active, and being promiscuous. Each contained a very large range of behavior considered of the same basic merit; i.e., the decision was very lumpy. Also, once a woman "lost her virtue," or was known to be promiscuous, she found it almost impossible to reverse her moral status. Moreover, acts that had great value before passing the threshold (an incident of intercourse), have a much lower significance, lower value, once the transgression has occurred. That is, there is no standardization of the item at issue.

The same basic observations can be made about joining welfare. Before one joins, a welfare dollar may be worth only 80 cents, but once one joins, and one is stigmatized, the very next dollar will be worth the full (or nearly) 100 cents. And, even if one gets off welfare and no longer receives stigmatized income, the stigma is likely to linger. Taking out the first loan, for people who feel being in debt is a moral evil, is different from extending it or taking out a second one. (Denial here takes the form similar to that of using credit cards, which people do not consider in the same way [Maital, 1982, pp. 143ff.].) Selling one's home, especially if it is the first move, moving to a different city, especially if it is the first relocation, and first voluntary change of job may all reveal such a structure due to moral (and emotional) factors, all in sharp contrast to what economic transactions are assumed to be.

CONCLUSION

The article presents conceptual reasons and empirical indications for advancing a multiple-utility conception for the study of economic behavior, one that recognizes at least two sources of value: pleasure and morality. Attempts to accommodate moral behavior within the mono-utility model strain it. These efforts have pushed economists first to dilute the substance of the concept of utility to the point it ceased to differentiate. The concept of utility came to include both love for self and for others. In the process, Adam Smith's thesis, which assumes economic behavior is based on self-interest, is, in effect, abandoned. Later attempts to view the concept of utility as a completely contentless, formal concept render it a-empirical as all logical and mathematical concepts are, unless related to some other symbol.

The qualities of moral acts have been indicated and the often, but not necessarily, conflicting relationship between morality and pleasure was explicated. Evidence of authentic altruistic behavior has been cited. The role of moral factors in a variety of economic behaviors was indicated. Moral considerations, such as the arousal of guilt, were found to encumber preferences and choices. The level of morality was shown to be inversely related to the level of transaction costs. Limits that moral factors imposed on market relations were also discussed. In short, the distinction between pleasures and morals seems to be not only conceptually sound but also productive in accounting for the factors that drive economic behavior.

REFERENCES

Akerlof, George, and William T. Dickens. 1982. "The Economic Consequences of Cognitive Dissonance." *The American Economic Review* 72:307–19.

Barry, Brian. 1978. *Sociologists, Economists and Democracy*. Chicago: University of Chicago.

Benedict, Ruth. 1934. *Patterns of Culture*. Boston: Houghton Mifflin.

Bentham, Jeremy. 1948. *An Introduction to the Principles of Morals and Legislation*. New York: Hafner.

Boulding, Kenneth E. 1978. *Ecodynamics: A New Theory of Societal Evolution*. Beverly Hills: Sage.

Bowie, Norman E., and Robert L. Simon. 1977. *The Individual and the Political Order*. Englewood Cliffs, NJ: Prentice-Hall.

Buchanan, James M. 1978. "Markets, States, and the Extent of Morals." *American Economic Review* 2:364–68.

Carlsmith, J. M., and A. E. Gross. 1969. "Some Effects of Guilt on Compliance." *Journal of Personality and Social Psychology* 11:232–39.

Cheal, David J. 1984. "Wedding Gifts and the Making of Money." Paper Presented at the 79th Annual Meeting of the American Sociological Association, San Antonio, August 27–31.

———. 1985. "Moral Economy: Gift Giving in an Urban Society." *Winnipeg Area Study Report no. 5*. (January) Winnipeg: University of Winnipeg.

Childress, James F. 1977. "The Identification of Ethical Principles." *Journal of Religious Ethics* 5:39–68.

Curtin, Richard T., and Thomas S. Neubig. 1979. "Outstanding Debt Among American Households." In *Survey of Consumer Attitudes* (April). Ann Arbor: University of Michigan, pp. 1–2.

Denison, Edward F. 1979. *Accounting for Slower Economic Growth*. Washington, DC: Brookings.

Derlega, Valerian J., and Janusz Grzelak (Eds.). 1982. *Cooperation and Helping Behavior: Theories and Research*. New York: Academic Press.

Douglas, Mary, and Baron Isherwood. 1979. *The World of Goods*. New York: Basic Books.

Dyke, C. 1981. *Philosophy of Economics*. Englewood Cliffs, NJ: Prentice-Hall.

Elster, Jon. 1979. *Ulysses and the Sirens: Studies in Rationality*. New York: Cambridge University Press.

Etzioni, Amitai. 1984. *Capital Corruption*. New York: Harcourt, Brace, Jovanovich.

Fellner, C. H., and J. R. Marshall. 1968. "Twelve Kidney Donors." *Journal of the American Medical Association* 206:2703–7.

Festinger, Leon. 1957. *A Theory of Cognitive Dissonance*. Stanford, CA: Stanford University Press.

Fishkin, James S. 1982. *The Limits of Obligation*. New Haven, CT: Yale University Press.

Godwin, Kenneth, and Robert Cameron Mitchell. 1982. "Rational Models, Collective Goods and Nonelectoral Political Behavior." *Western Political Journal* 35:161–92.

Goodin, Robert E. 1980. "Making Moral Incentives Pay." *Policy Sciences* 12:131–45.

Harsanyi, John C. 1955. "Cardinal Welfare, Individualistic Ethics, and International Comparisons of Utility." *Journal of Political Economy* 63:309–21.

Heath, Anthony. 1976. *Rational Choice and Social Exchange.* New York: Cambridge University Press.

Hirschman, Albert O. 1984. "Against Parsimony: Three Easy Ways of Complicating Some Categories of Economic Discourse." *Bulletin: The American Academy of Arts and Sciences* 37(8):11–28.

Hirshleifer, Jack. 1976. *Price Theory and Application.* Englewood Cliffs, NJ: Prentice-Hall.

———. 1985. "The Expanding Domain of Economics." *The American Economic Review* 75(6):53–68.

Hornstein, H. A., E. Fisch, and M. Holmes. 1968. "Influence of a Model's Feelings about His Behavior and His Relevance as a Comparison of Other Observers' Helping Behavior." *Journal of Personal and Social Psychology* 10:222–26.

Hornstein, Harvey. 1976. *Cruelty and Kindness.* Englewood Cliffs, NJ: Prentice-Hall.

Hornstein, Harvey A., Hugo N. Masor, and Kenneth Sole. 1971. "Effects of Sentiment and Completion of a Helping Act on Observer Helping: A Case for Socially Mediated Zeigarnik Effects." *Journal of Personality and Social Psychology* 17:107–12.

Janis, Irving, and Leon Mann. 1977. *Decision Making: A Psychological Analysis of Conflict, Choice and Commitment.* New York: Free Press.

Juster, F. T. 1985. *Preferences for Work and Leisure.* Ann Arbor: University of Michigan, Institute for Social Research.

Kagel, John H., H. Rachlin, L. Green, R. Battalio, R. Basmann, and W. R. Klemm. 1975. "Experimental Studies of Consumer Demand Behavior Using Laboratory Animals." *Economic Inquiry* 13 (March):22–38.

Klausner, Michael. 1984. "Sociological Theory and the Behavior of Financial Markets." In Patricia A. Adler and Peter Adler (Eds.), *The Social Dynamics of Financial Markets.* Greenwich, Conn.: JAI Press.

Kohlberg, Lawrence. 1968. "Moral Development." In David L. Sills (Ed.), *International Encyclopedia of the Social Sciences,* vol. 10, pp. 483–93. New York: MacMillan and Free Press.

Laitner, John P. 1979. "Bequests, Golden-Age Capital Accumulation and Government Debt." *Economics* 46:403–14.

Latane, B., and J. M. Darley. 1970. *The Unresponsive Bystander: Why Doesn't He Help?* New York: Appleton-Century-Crofts.

Lindenberg, Siegwart. 1983. "Utility and Morality." *Kyklos* 36:450–68.

Lipsey, Richard, and Peter Steiner. 1975. *Economics.* New York: Harper and Row.

Little, I. M. D. 1957. *A Critique of Welfare Economics.* Oxford: Clarendon Press.

Maital, Shlomo. 1982. *Minds, Markets, and Money.* New York: Basic Books.

Margolis, Howard. 1982. *Selfishness, Altruism and Rationality: A Theory of Social Choice.* Cambridge: Cambridge University Press.

Moffit, R. 1983. "An Economic Model of Welfare Stigma." *American Economic Review* 73:1023–35.

Nisbett, Robert A. 1981. "Replies to Steven Kelman." *Regulation.* March/April: 42–43.

Piliavin, I. M., J. Rodin, and J. A. Piliavin. 1969. "Good Samaritanism: An Underground Phenomenon?" *Journal of Personality and Social Psychology* 13:289–99.

Rushton, J. Philippe. 1980. *Altruism, Socialization, and Society.* Englewood Cliffs, NJ: Prentice-Hall.

Sadalla, E., and J. Wallace. 1966. "Behavioral Consequences of Transgression." *Journal of Experimental Research in Personality* 1:187–94.

Samuelson, Paul A. 1980. *Economics.* 11th ed. New York: McGraw-Hill.

Schelling, Thomas. 1984. "Self-Command in Practice, in Policy, and in a Theory of Rational Choice." *American Economic Review* 74(2):1–11.

Schwartz, Shalom H. 1970. "Elicitation of Moral Obligation and Self-Sacrificing Behavior: An Experimental Study of Volunteering to be a Bone Marrow Donor." *Journal of Personality and Social Psychology* 15(4):283–93.

Scitovsky, Tibor. 1976. *The Joyless Economy.* New York: Oxford University Press.

Sen, Amartya K. 1977. "Rational Fools." *Philosophy and Public Affairs* 6(4):317–44.

Shorrocks, Anthony F. 1979. "On the Structure of Inter-generational Transfers Between Families." *Economica* 46:415–25.

Simmons, Roberta G., Susan D. Klein, and Robert L. Simmons. 1977. *Gift of Life: The Social and Psychological Impact of Organ Transplantation.* New York: Wiley.

Smith, Adam. 1937 (1776). *Wealth of Nations.* New York: Random House (Modern Library Edition).

Solow, Robert M. 1980. "On Theories of Unemployment." *American Economic Review* 70(1):1–11.

Stigler, George J. 1966. *The Theory of Price.* 3rd ed. New York: MacMillan.

Thaler, Richard, and H. M. Shefrin. 1981. "An Economic Theory of Self-Control." *Journal of Political Economy* 89:392–406.

Thompson, Michael. 1979. *Rubbish Theory: The Creation and Destruction of Value.* New York: Oxford University Press.

Thurow, Lester C. 1983. *Dangerous Currents.* New York: Random House.

Walsh, Vivian Charles. 1970. *Introduction to Contemporary Microeconomics.* New York: McGraw-Hill.

Walzer, Michael. 1983. *Spheres of Justice.* New York: Basic Books.

Wells, A. 1970. *Social Institutions.* London: Heinemann.

[27]

AMARTYA K. SEN

Rational Fools: A Critique of the Behavioral Foundations of Economic Theory

I

In his *Mathematical Psychics*, published in 1881, Edgeworth asserted that "the first principle of Economics is that every agent is actuated only by self-interest."[1] This view of man has been a persistent one in economic models, and the nature of economic theory seems to have been much influenced by this basic premise. In this essay I would like to examine some of the problems that have arisen from this conception of human beings.

I should mention that Edgeworth himself was quite aware that this so-called first principle of Economics was not a particularly realistic one. Indeed, he felt that "the concrete nineteenth century man is for the most part an impure egoist, a mixed utilitarian."[2] This raises the interesting question as to why Edgeworth spent so much of his time and talent in developing a line of inquiry the first principle of which he believed to be false. The issue is not why abstractions should be em-

This Herbert Spencer Lecture, delivered at Oxford University in October 1976, will appear in *Scientific Models and Man*, ed. H. Harris (forthcoming 1978) and is printed here by kind permission of Oxford University Press. For helpful comments on an earlier version, I am grateful to the Editors of this journal, and to Åke Andersson, Isaiah Berlin, Frank Hahn, Martin Hollis, Janos Kornai, Derek Parfit, Christopher Peacocke, and Tibor Scitovsky.

1. F.Y. Edgeworth, *Mathematical Psychics: An Essay on the Application of Mathematics to the Moral Sciences* (London, 1881), p. 16.

2. Edgeworth (1881), p. 104. In fact, he went on to make some interesting remarks on the results of "impure" egoism, admitting an element of sympathy for each other. The remarks have been investigated and analyzed by David Collard, "Edgeworth's Propositions on Altruism," *Economic Journal* 85 (1975).

ployed in pursuing general economic questions–the nature of the inquiry makes this inevitable–but why would one choose an assumption which he himself believed to be not merely inaccurate in detail but fundamentally mistaken? As we shall see, this question is of continuing interest to modern economics as well.

Part of the answer, as far as Edgeworth was concerned, undoubtedly lay in the fact that he did not think the assumption to be fundamentally mistaken in the *particular* types of activities to which he applied what he called "economical calculus": (i) war and (ii) contract. "Admitting that there exists in the higher parts of human nature a tendency towards and feeling after utilitarian institutions," he asked the rhetorical question: "could we seriously suppose that these moral considerations were relevant to war and trade; could eradicate the controlless core of human selfishness, or exercise an appreciable force in comparison with the impulse of self-interest."[3] He interpreted Sidgwick to have dispelled the "illusion" that "the interest of all is the interest of each," noting that Sidgwick found the "two supreme principles–Egoism and Utilitarianism" to be "irreconcilable, unless indeed by religion." "It is far from the spirit of the philosophy of pleasure to deprecate the importance of religion," wrote Edgeworth, "but in the present inquiry, and dealing with the lower elements of human nature, we should have to seek a more obvious transition, a more earthy passage, from the principle of self-interest to the principle, or at least the practice, of utilitarianism."[4]

Notice that the context of the debate is important to this argument. Edgeworth felt that he had established the acceptability of "egoism" as the fundamental behavioral assumption for his particular inquiry by demolishing the acceptability of "utilitarianism" as a description of actual behavior. Utilitarianism is, of course, far from being the only non-egoistic approach. Furthermore, between the claims of oneself and the claims of all lie the claims of a variety of groups–for example, families, friends, local communities, peer groups, and economic and social classes. The concepts of family responsibility, business ethics, class consciousness, and so on, relate to these intermediate areas of concern, and the dismissal of utilitarianism as a descriptive theory

3. Edgeworth, p. 52.
4. Ibid., pp. 52–53.

of behavior does not leave us with egoism as the only alternative. The relevance of some of these considerations to the economics of negotiations and contracts would be difficult to deny.

It must be noted that Edgeworth's query about the outcome of economic contact between purely self-seeking individuals had the merit of being immediately relevant to an abstract enquiry that had gone on for more than a hundred years already, and which was much discussed in debates involving Herbert Spencer, Henry Sidgwick, and other leading thinkers of the period. Two years before Edgeworth's *Mathematical Psychics* appeared, Herbert Spencer had published his elaborate analysis of the relation between egoism and altruism in *The Data of Ethics*. He had arrived at the comforting–if somewhat unclear –conclusion that "general happiness is to be achieved mainly through the adequate pursuit of their own happinesses by individuals; while, reciprocally, the happiness of individuals are to be achieved in part by their pursuit of the general happiness."[5] In the context of this relatively abstract enquiry, Edgeworth's tight economic analysis, based on a well-defined model of contracts between two self-seeking individuals, or between two types of (identical) self-seeking individuals, gave a clear answer to an old hypothetical question.

It appeared that in Edgeworth's model, based on egoistic behavior, there was a remarkable correspondence between exchange equilibria in competitive markets and what in modern economic terms is called "the core" of the economy. An outcome is said to be in "the core" of the economy if and only if it fulfills a set of conditions of unimprovability. These conditions, roughly speaking, are that not only is it the case that no one could be made better off without making somebody else worse off (the situation is what is called a "Pareto optimum"), but also that no one is worse off than he would be without trade, and that no coalition of individuals, by altering the trade among themselves, could on their own improve their own lot. Edgeworth showed that given certain general assumptions, any equilibrium that can emerge in a competitive market must satisfy these conditions and be in "the core." Thus, in Edgeworth's model the competitive market equilibria are, in this sense, undominated by any feasible alternative

5. H. Spencer, *The Data of Ethics* (London, 1879; extended edition, 1887), p. 238.

arrangement, given the initial distribution of endowments. More surprising in some ways was the converse result that if the number of individuals of each type were increased without limit, the core (representing such undominated outcomes) would shrink towards the set of competitive equilibria; that is, the core would not be much more extensive than the set of competitive equilibria. This pair of results has been much elaborated and extended in the recent literature on general equilibrium with similar models and with essentially the same behavioral assumptions.[6]

Being in the core, however, is not as such a momentous achievement from the point of view of social welfare. A person who starts off ill-endowed may stay poor and deprived even after the transactions, and if being in the core is all that competition offers, the propertyless person may be forgiven for not regarding this achievement as a "big deal." Edgeworth took some note of this by considering the problem of choice between different competitive equilibria. He observed that for the utilitarian good society, "competition requires to be supplemented by arbitration, and the basis of arbitration between self-interested contractors is the greatest possible sum-total utility."[7] Into the institutional aspects of such arbitration and the far-reaching implications of it for the distribution of property ownership, Edgeworth did not really enter, despite superficial appearance to the contrary. On the basis of the achievement of competition, however limited, Edgeworth felt entitled to be "biassed to a more conservative caution in reform." In calculating "the utility of pre-utilitarian institutions," Edgeworth felt impressed "with a view of Nature, not, as in the picture left by Mill, all bad, but a first approximation to the best."[8]

I am not concerned in this essay with examining whether the approximation is a rather remote one. (This I do believe to be the case even within the structure of assumptions used by Edgeworth, but it is not central to the subject of this paper.) I am concerned here with the view of man which forms part of Edgeworth's analysis and

6. See, especially, K.J. Arrow and F.H. Hahn, *General Competitive Analysis* (San Francisco, 1971).

7. Edgeworth, p. 56.

8. Ibid., p. 82.

survives more or less intact in much of modern economic theory. The view is, of course, a stylized one and geared specifically to tackling a relatively abstract dispute with which Spencer, Sidgwick, and several other leading contemporary thinkers were much concerned–namely, in what sense and to what extent would egoistic behavior achieve general good? Whether or not egoistic behavior is an accurate assumption in reality does not, of course, have any bearing on the accuracy of Edgeworth's answer to the question posed. Within the structure of a limited economic model it provided a clear-cut response to the abstract query about egoism and general good.

This particular debate has gone on for a long time and continues to provide motivation for many recent exercises in economic theory today. The limited nature of the query has had a decisive influence on the choice of economic models and the conception of human beings in them. In their distinguished text on general equilibrium theory, Arrow and Hahn state (pp. vi–vii):

> There is by now a long and fairly imposing line of economists from Adam Smith to the present who have sought to show that a decentralized economy motivated by self-interest and guided by price signals would be compatible with a coherent disposition of economic resources that could be regarded, in a well-defined sense, as superior to a large class of possible alternative dispositions. Moreover, the price signals would operate in a way to establish this degree of coherence. It is important to understand how surprising this claim must be to anyone not exposed to the tradition. The immediate "common sense" answer to the question "What will an economy motivated by individual greed and controlled by a very large number of different agents look like?" is probably: There will be chaos. That quite a different answer has long been claimed true and has indeed permeated the economic thinking of a large number of people who are in no way economists is itself sufficient ground for investigating it seriously. The proposition having been put forward and very seriously entertained, it is important to know not only whether it *is* true, but whether it *could* be true. A good deal of what follows is concerned with this last question, which seems to us to have considerable claims on the attention of economists.

The primary concern here is not with the relation of postulated models to the real economic world, but with the accuracy of answers to well-defined questions posed with preselected assumptions which severely constrain the nature of the models that can be admitted into the analysis. A specific concept of man is ingrained in the question itself, and there is no freedom to depart from this conception so long as one is engaged in answering this question. The nature of man in these current economic models continues, then, to reflect the particular formulation of certain general philosophical questions posed in the past. The realism of the chosen conception of man is simply not a part of this inquiry.

II

There is another nonempirical—and possibly simpler—reason why the conception of man in economic models tends to be that of a self-seeking egoist. It is possible to define a person's interests in such a way that no matter what he does he can be seen to be furthering his own interests in every isolated act of choice.[9] While formalized relatively recently in the context of the theory of revealed preference, this approach is of respectable antiquity, and Joseph Butler was already arguing against it in the Rolls Chapel two and a half centuries ago.[10] The reduction of man to a self-seeking animal depends in this approach on careful definition. If you are observed to choose x rejecting y, you are declared to have "revealed" a preference for x over y. Your personal utility is then defined as simply a numerical representation of this "preference," assigning a higher utility to a "preferred" alternative. With this set of definitions you can hardly escape maximizing your own utility, except through inconsistency. Of course, if you choose x and reject y on one occasion and then promptly proceed to do the exact opposite, you can prevent the revealed preference theorist

9. If a person's actions today affect his well-being in the future, then under this approach his future interests must be defined in terms of the way they are *assessed today*. In general, there is no reason to presume that the future interests as assessed today will coincide with those interests as assessed in the future. This adds an additional dimension to the problem, and I am grateful to Derek Parfit for convincing me of the conceptual importance of this question.

10. J. Butler, *Fifteen Sermons Preached at the Rolls Chapel* (London, 1726); see also T. Nagel, *The Possibility of Altruism* (Oxford, 1970), p. 81.

from assigning a preference ordering to you, thereby restraining him from stamping a utility function on you which you must be seen to be maximizing. He will then have to conclude that either you are inconsistent or your preferences are changing. You can frustrate the revealed-preference theorist through more sophisticated inconsistencies as well.[11] But if you are consistent, then no matter whether you are a single-minded egoist or a raving altruist or a class conscious militant, you will appear to be maximizing your own utility in this enchanted world of definitions. Borrowing from the terminology used in connection with taxation, if the Arrow-Hahn justification of the assumption of egoism amounts to an *avoidance* of the issue, the revealed preference approach looks more like a robust piece of *evasion*.

This approach of definitional egoism sometimes goes under the name of rational choice, and it involves nothing other than internal consistency. A person's choices are considered "rational" in this approach if and only if these choices can *all* be explained in terms of some preference relation consistent with the revealed preference definition, that is, if all his choices can be explained as the choosing of "most preferred" alternatives with respect to a postulated preference relation.[12] The rationale of this approach seems to be based on the idea that the only way of understanding a person's real preference is to examine his actual choices, and there is no choice-independent way of understanding someone's attitude towards alternatives. (This view, by the way, is not confined to economists only. When, many years ago, I had to take my qualifying examination in English Literature at Calcutta University, one of the questions we had to answer concerning *A Midsummer Night's Dream* was: Compare the characters of Hermia and Helena. Whom would you choose?)

I have tried to demonstrate elsewhere that once we eschew the curious definitions of preference and welfare, this approach presumes both too little and too much: too little because there are non-choice sources of information on preference and welfare as these terms are

11. See H.S. Houthakker, "Revealed Preference and the Utility Function," *Economica* 17 (1950); P.A. Samuelson, "The Problem of Integrability in Utility Theory," *Economica* 17 (1950).

12. For the main analytical results, see M.K. Richter, "Rational Choice," *Preference, Utility and Demand Theory*, ed. J.S. Chipman et al. (New York, 1971).

usually understood, and too much because choice may reflect a compromise among a variety of considerations of which personal welfare may be just one.[13]

The complex psychological issues underlying choice have recently been forcefully brought out by a number of penetrating studies dealing with consumer decisions[14] and production activities.[15] It is very much an open question as to whether these behavioral characteristics can be at all captured within the formal limits of consistent choice on which the welfare-maximization approach depends.[16]

III

Paul Samuelson has noted that many economists would "separate economics from sociology upon the basis of rational or irrational behavior, where these terms are defined in the penumbra of utility

13. A.K. Sen, "Behaviour and the Concept of Preference," *Economica* 40 (1973). See also S. Körner's important recent study, *Experience and Conduct* (Cambridge, 1971). Also T. Schwartz, "Von Wright's Theory of Human Welfare: A Critique," forthcoming in P.A. Schlipp, ed., *The Philosophy of Georg Henrik von Wright*; T. Majumdar, "The Concept of Man in Political Economy and Economics," mimeographed (Jawaharlal Nehru University, New Delhi, 1976); and F. Schick, "Rationality and Sociality," mimeographed (Rutgers University, Philosophy of Science Association, 1976).

14. See T. Scitovsky, *The Joyless Economy: An Inquiry into Human Satisfaction and Consumer Dissatisfaction* (London and New York, 1976). See also the general critique of the assumption of "rational" consumer behavior by J. Kornai, *Anti-Equilibrium* (Amsterdam and London, 1971), chap. 11; and the literature on "psychological choice models," in particular, D. McFadden, "Economic Applications of Psychological Choice Models" (presented at the Third World Econometric Congress, August 1975).

15. See H. Liebenstein, "Allocative Efficiency vs. x-Efficiency," *American Economic Review* 56 (1966). Also critiques of the traditional assumption of profit maximization in *business* behavior, particularly W.J. Baumol, *Business Behavior, Value and Growth* (New York, 1959); R. Marris, *The Economic Theory of Managerial Capitalism* (London, 1964); O. Williamson, *The Economics of Discretionary Behavior* (Chicago, 1967); and A. Silberston, "Price Behaviour of Firms," *Economic Journal* 80 (1970), reprinted in Royal Economic Society, *Surveys of Applied Economics*, vol. 1 (London, 1973).

16. On the required conditions of consistency for viewing choice in terms of a binary relation, see my "Choice Functions and Revealed Preference," *Review of Economic Studies* 38 (1971); H.G. Herzberger, "Ordinal Preference and Rational Choice," *Econometrica* 41 (1973); K. Suzumura, "Rational Choice and Revealed Preference," *Review of Economic Studies* 43 (1976); S. Kanger, "Choice Based on Preference," mimeographed (Uppsala University, 1976).

theory."[17] This view might well be resented, for good reasons, by sociologists, but the cross that economists have to bear in this view of the dichotomy can be seen if we note that the approach of "rational behavior," as it is typically interpreted, leads to a remarkably mute theory. Behavior, it appears, is to be "explained in terms of preferences, which are in turn defined only by behavior." Not surprisingly, excursions into circularities have been frequent. Nevertheless, Samuelson is undoubtedly right in asserting that the theory "is not in a technical sense *meaningless*."[18] The reason is quite simple. As we have already discussed, the approach does impose the requirement of internal consistency of observed choice, and this might well be refuted by actual observations, making the theory "meaningful" in the sense in which Samuelson's statement is intended.

The requirement of consistency does have surprising cutting power. Various general characteristics of demand relations can be derived from it. But in the present context, the main issue is the possibility of using the consistency requirement for actual *testing*. Samuelson specifies the need for "ideal observational conditions" for the implications of the approach to be "refuted or verified." This is not, however, easy to satisfy since, on the one hand, our love of variety makes it illegitimate to consider individual acts of choice as the proper units (rather than *sequences* of choices) while, on the other hand, lapse of time makes it difficult to distinguish between inconsistencies and changing tastes. There have, in fact, been very few systematic attempts at testing the consistency of people's day-to-day behavior, even though there have been interesting and useful contrived experiments on people's reactions to uncertainty under laboratory conditions. What counts as admissible evidence remains unsettled. If today you were to poll economists of different schools, you would almost certainly find the coexistence of beliefs (i) that the rational behavior theory is unfalsifiable, (ii) that it is falsifiable and so far unfalsified, and (iii) that it is falsifiable and indeed patently false.[19]

17. P.A. Samuelson, *The Foundation of Economics* (Cambridge, Mass., 1955), p. 90.

18. Ibid., p. 91.

19. The recent philosophical critiques of rational behavior theory include, among others, M. Hollis and E.J. Nell, *Rational Economic Man* (Cambridge, 1975); S. Wong, "On the Consistency and Completeness of Paul Samuelson's

However, for my purposes here this is not the central issue. Even if the required consistency were seen to obtain, it would still leave the question of egoism unresolved except in the purely definitional sense, as I have already noted. A consistent chooser can have any degree of egoism that we care to specify. It is, of course, true that in the special case of pure consumer choice over private goods, the revealed preference theorist tries to relate the person's "preference" or "utility" to his *own* bundle of commodities. This restriction arises, however, not from any guarantee that he is concerned only with his own interests, but from the fact that his own consumption bundle—or that of his family—is the only bundle over which he has direct *control* in his acts of choice. The question of egoism remains completely open.

I believe the question also requires a clearer formulation than it tends to receive, and to this question I shall now turn.

IV

As we consider departures from "unsympathetic isolation abstractly assumed in Economics," to use Edgeworth's words, we must distinguish between two separate concepts: (i) sympathy and (ii) commitment. The former corresponds to the case in which the concern for others directly affects one's own welfare. If the knowledge of torture of others makes you sick, it is a case of sympathy; if it does not make you feel personally worse off, but you think it is wrong and you are ready to do something to stop it, it is a case of commitment. I do not wish to claim that the words chosen have any very great merit, but the distinction is, I think, important. It can be argued that behavior based on sympathy is in an important sense egoistic, for one is oneself pleased at others' pleasure and pained at others' pain, and the pursuit of one's own utility may thus be helped by sympathetic action. It is action based on commitment rather than sympathy which would be non-egoistic in this sense. (Note, however, that the *existence* of sympathy does not imply that the action helpful to others must be *based on* sympathy in the sense that the action would not take place had one

Programme in the Theory of Consumer Behaviour" (Ph.D. thesis, Cambridge University, 1975, forthcoming). See also the pragmatic criticisms of Kornai, *Anti-Equilibrium*, chap. 11.

got less or no comfort from others' welfare. This question of *causation* is to be taken up presently.)

Sympathy is, in some ways, an easier concept to analyze than commitment. When a person's sense of well-being is psychologically dependent on someone else's welfare, it is a case of sympathy; other things given, the awareness of the increase in the welfare of the other person then makes this person directly better off. (Of course, when the influence is negative, the relation is better named "antipathy," but we can economize on terminology and stick to the term "sympathy," just noting that the relation can be positive or negative.) While sympathy relates similar things to each other—namely, welfares of different persons—commitment relates choice to anticipated levels of welfare. One way of defining commitment is in terms of a person choosing an act that he believes will yield a lower level of personal welfare to him than an alternative that is also available to him. Notice that the comparison is between *anticipated* welfare levels, and therefore this definition of commitment excludes acts that go against self-interest resulting purely from a failure to foresee consequences.

A more difficult question arises when a person's choice happens to coincide with the maximization of his anticipated personal welfare, but that is not the *reason* for his choice. If we wish to make room for this, we can expand the definition of commitment to include cases in which the person's choice, while maximizing anticipated personal welfare, would be unaffected under at least one counterfactual condition in which the act chosen would cease to maximize personal welfare. Commitment in this more inclusive sense may be difficult to ascertain not only in the context of others' choices but also in that of one's own, since it is not always clear what one would have done had the circumstances been different. This broader sense may have particular relevance when one acts on the basis of a concern for duty which, if violated, could cause remorse, but the action is really chosen out of the sense of duty rather than just to avoid the illfare resulting from the remorse that would occur if one were to act otherwise. (Of course, even the narrower sense of commitment will cover the case in which the illfare resulting from the remorse, if any, is *outweighed* by the gain in welfare.)

I have not yet referred to uncertainty concerning anticipated welfare. When this is introduced, the concept of sympathy is unaffected, but commitment will require reformulation. The necessary modifications will depend on the person's reaction to uncertainty. The simplest case is probably the one in which the person's idea of what a "lottery" offers to him in terms of personal gain is captured by the "expected utility" of personal welfare (that is, adding personal welfares from different outcomes weighted by the probability of occurrence of each outcome). In this case, the entire discussion is reformulated simply replacing personal welfare by *expected* personal welfare; commitment then involves choosing an action that yields a lower expected welfare than an alternative available action. (The broader sense can also be correspondingly modified.)

In the terminology of modern economic theory, sympathy is a case of "externality." Many models rule out externalities, for example, the standard model to establish that each competitive equilibrium is a Pareto optimum and belongs to the core of the economy. If the existence of sympathy were to be permitted in these models, some of these standard results would be upset, though by no means all of them.[20] But this would not require a serious revision of the basic structure of these models. On the other hand, commitment does involve, in a very real sense, counterpreferential choice, destroying the crucial assumption that a chosen alternative must be better than (or at least as good as) the others for the person choosing it, and this would certainly require that models be formulated in an essentially different way.

The contrast between sympathy and commitment may be illustrated with the story of two boys who find two apples, one large, one small. Boy *A* tells boy *B*, "You choose." *B* immediately picks the larger apple. *A* is upset and permits himself the remark that this was grossly unfair. "Why?" asks *B*. "Which one would *you* have chosen, if you were to choose rather than me?" "The smaller one, of course," *A* replies. *B* is now triumphant: "Then what are you complaining about? That's the one you've got!" *B* certainly wins this round of the argument, but in

20. See A.K. Sen, "Labour Allocation in a Co-operative Enterprise," *Review of Economic Studies* 33 (1966); S.G. Winter, Jr., "A Simple Remark on the Second Optimality Theorem of Welfare Economics," *Journal of Economic Theory* 1 (1969); Collard, "Edgeworth's Propositions"; G.C. Archibald and D. Donaldson, "Non-paternalism and Basic Theorems of Welfare Economics," *Canadian Journal of Economics* 9 (1976).

fact *A* would have lost nothing from *B*'s choice had his own hypothetical choice of the smaller apple been based on sympathy as opposed to commitment. *A*'s anger indicates that this was probably not the case.

Commitment is, of course, closely connected with one's morals. But moral this question is in a very broad sense, covering a variety of influences from religious to political, from the ill-understood to the well-argued. When, in Bernard Shaw's *The Devil's Disciple*, Judith Anderson interprets Richard Dudgeon's willingness to be hanged in place of her husband as arising from sympathy for him or love for her, Richard is adamant in his denial: "What I did last night, I did in cold blood, caring not half so much for your husband, or for you as I do for myself. I had no motive and no interest: all I can tell you is that when it came to the point whether I would take my neck out of the noose and put another man's into it, I could not do it."[21]

The characteristic of commitment with which I am most concerned here is the fact that it drives a wedge between personal choice and personal welfare, and much of traditional economic theory relies on the identity of the two. This identity is sometimes obscured by the ambiguity of the term "preference," since the normal use of the word permits the identification of preference with the concept of being better off, and at the same time it is not quite unnatural to define "preferred" as "chosen." I have no strong views on the "correct" use of the word "preference," and I would be satisfied as long as both uses are not *simultaneously* made, attempting an empirical assertion by virtue of two definitions.[22] The basic link between choice behavior and welfare achievements in the traditional models is severed as soon as commitment is admitted as an ingredient of choice.

V

"Fine," you might say, "but how relevant is all this to the kind of choices with which economists are concerned? Economics does not have much to do with Richard Dudgeon's march to the gallows." I

21. G.B. Shaw, *Three Plays for Puritans* (Harmondsworth, 1966), p. 94.

22. See my "Behaviour and the Concept of Preference," *Economica* 40 (1973); and Shick, "Rationality and Sociality."

think one should immediately agree that for many types of behavior, commitment is unlikely to be an important ingredient. In the private purchase of many consumer goods, the scope for the exercise of commitment may indeed be limited and may show up rather rarely in such exotic acts as the boycotting of South African avocados or the eschewing of Spanish holidays. Therefore, for many studies of consumer behavior and interpretations thereof, commitment may pose no great problem. Even sympathy may not be extremely important, the sources of interpersonal interdependence lying elsewhere, for example, in the desire to keep up with the Joneses or in being influenced by other people's habits.[23]

But economics is not concerned only with consumer behavior; nor is consumption confined to "private goods." One area in which the question of commitment is most important is that of the so-called public goods. These have to be contrasted with "private goods" which have the characteristic that they cannot be used by more than one person: if you ate a piece of apple pie, I wouldn't consider devouring it too. Not so with "public goods," for example, a road or a public park, which you and I may both be able to use. In many economic models private goods are the only ones around, and this is typically the case when the "invisible hand" is given the task of doing visible good. But, in fact, public goods are important in most economies and cover a wide range of services from roads and street lighting to defense. There is much evidence that the share of public goods in national consumption has grown rather dramatically in most countries in the world.

The problem of optimal allocation of public goods has also been much discussed, especially in the recent economic literature.[24] A lot

23. See J.S. Duesenberry, *Income, Saving and the Theory of Consumer Behavior* (Cambridge, Mass., 1949); S.J. Prais and H.S. Houthakker, *The Analysis of Family Budgets* (Cambridge, 1955); W. Gaertner, "A Dynamic Model of Interdependent Consumer Behaviour," mimeographed (Bielefeld University, 1973); R.A. Pollak, "Interdependent Preferences," *American Economic Review* 66 (1976).

24. See E. Lindahl, *Die Gerechtigkeit der Besteuerung* (Lund, 1919), translated in R.A. Musgrave and A. Peacock, *Classics in the Theory of Public Finance* (London, 1967); P.A. Samuelson, "The Pure Theory of Public Expenditure," *Review of Economic Studies* 21 (1954); R. Musgrave, *The Theory of Public Finance* (New York, 1959); L. Johansen, *Public Economics* (Amsterdam, 1966); D.K. Foley, "Lindahl's Solution and the Core of an Economy with Public Goods,"

of attention, in particular, has been devoted to the problem of correct revelation of preferences. This arises most obviously in the case of subscription schemes where a person is charged according to benefits received. The main problem centers on the fact that it is in everybody's interest to understate the benefit he expects, but this understatement may lead to the rejection of a public project which would have been justified if true benefits were known. Analysis of this difficulty, sometimes referred to as the "free rider" problem, has recently led to some extremely ingenious proposals for circumventing this inefficiency within the framework of egoistic action.[25] The reward mechanism is set up with such ungodly cunning that people have an incentive to reveal exactly their true willingness to pay for the public good in question. One difficulty in this solution arises from an assumed limitation of strategic possibilities open to the individual, the removal of which leads to an impossibility result.[26] Another difficulty concerns the fact that in giving people the incentive to reveal the truth, money is handed out and the income distribution shifts in a way unguided by distributional considerations. This effect can, of course, be undone by a redistribution of initial endowments and profit shares,[27] but that action obviously raises difficulties of its own.

Central to this problem is the assumption that when asked a ques-

Econometrica, 38 (1970); E. Malinvaud, "Prices for Individual Consumption, Quantity Indicators for Collective Consumption," *Review of Economic Studies* 39 (1972).

25. T. Groves and J. Ledyard, "Optimal Allocation of Public Goods: A Solution to the 'Free Rider Problem,'" Discussion Paper No. 144 (Center for Mathematical Studies in Economics and Management Science, Northwestern University, 1975); J. Green and J.J. Laffont, "On the Revelation of Preference for Public Goods," Technical Report No. 140 (Institute for Mathematical Studies in the Social Sciences, Stanford University, 1974). See also J. Dreze and D. de la Vallee Poussin, "A Tatonnement Process for Public Goods," *Review of Economic Studies* 38 (1971); E. Malinvaud, "A Planning Approach to the Public Goods Problem," *Swedish Journal of Economics* 73 (1971); V.L. Smith, "Incentive Compatible Experimental Processes for the Provision of Public Goods," mimeographed (Econometric Society Summer Meeting, Madison, 1976).

26. See J. Ledyard and D.J. Roberts, "On the Incentive Problem for Public Goods," Discussion Paper No. 116 (CMSEMS, Northwestern University, 1974). See also L. Hurwicz, "On Informationally Decentralized Systems," in R. Radner and B. McGuire, *Decisions and Organizations* (Amsterdam, 1972).

27. See Theorem 4.2 in Groves and Ledyard, "Optimal Allocation of Public Goods."

tion, the individual gives that answer which will maximize his personal gain. How good is this assumption? I doubt that in general it is very good. ("Where is the railway station?" he asks me. "There," I say, pointing at the post office, "and would you please post this letter for me on the way?" "Yes," he says, determined to open the envelope and check whether it contains something valuable.) Even in the particular context of revelation of preferences for public goods the gains-maximizing behavior may not be the best assumption. Leif Johansen, one of the major contributors to public economics, is, I think, right to question the assumption in this context:

> Economic theory in this, as well as in some other fields, tends to suggest that people are honest only to the extent that they have economic incentives for being so. This is a homo oeconomicus assumption which is far from being obviously true, and which needs confrontation with observed realities. In fact, a simple line of thought suggests that the assumption can hardly be true in its most extreme form. No society would be viable without some norms and rules of conduct. Such norms and rules are necessary for viability exactly in fields where strictly economic incentives are absent and cannot be created.[28]

What is at issue is not whether people invariably give an honest answer to every question, but whether they always give a gains-maximizing answer, or at any rate, whether they give gains-maximizing answers often enough to make that the appropriate general assumption for economic theory. The presence of non-gains-maximizing answers, including truthful ones, immediately brings in commitment as a part of behavior.

The question is relevant also to the recent literature on strategic voting. A number of beautiful analytical results have recently been established showing the impossibility of any voting procedure satisfying certain elementary requirements and making honest voting the

28. L. Johansen, "The Theory of Public Goods: Misplaced Emphasis" (Institute of Economics, University of Oslo, 1976). See also J.J. Laffont, "Macroeconomic Constraints, Economic Efficiency and Ethics," mimeographed (Harvard University, 1974); P. Bohm, "Estimating Demand for Public Goods: An Experiment," *European Economic Review* 3 (1972).

gains-maximizing strategy for everyone.[29] The correctness of these results is not in dispute, but is it appropriate to assume that people always do try to maximize personal gains in their voting behavior? Indeed, in large elections, it is difficult to show that any voter has any real prospect of affecting the outcome by his vote, and if voting involves some cost, the expected net gain from voting may typically be negative. Nevertheless, the proportion of turnout in large elections may still be quite high, and I have tried to argue elsewhere that in such elections people may often be "guided not so much by maximization of expected utility, but something much simpler, viz, just a desire to record one's true preference."[30] If this desire reflects a sense of commitment, then the behavior in question would be at variance with the view of man in traditional economic theory.

VI

The question of commitment is important in a number of other economic contexts.[31] It is central to the problem of work motivation, the importance of which for production performance can hardly be ignored.

It is certainly costly and may be impossible to devise a system of

29. A. Gibbard, "Manipulation of Voting Schemes: A General Result," *Econometrica* 41 (1973); M.A. Satterthwaite, "Strategy-proofness and Arrow's Conditions," *Journal of Economic Theory* 10 (1975); D. Schmeidler and H. Sonnenschein, "The Possibility of Non-manipulable Social Choice Functions" (CMSEMS, Northwestern University, 1974); B. Dutta and P.K. Pattanaik, "On Nicely Consistent Voting Systems" (Delhi School of Economics, 1975); P.K. Pattanaik, "Strategic Voting without Collusion under Binary and Democratic Group Decision Rules," *Review of Economic Studies* 42 (1975); B. Peleg, "Consistent Voting Systems" (Institute of Mathematics, Hebrew University, Jerusalem, 1976); A. Gibbard, "Social Decision, Strategic Behavior, and Best Outcomes: An Impossibility Result," Discussion Paper No. 224 (CMSEMS, Northwestern University, 1976).

30. See A.K. Sen, *Collective Choice and Social Welfare* (Edinburgh and San Francisco, 1970), p. 195.

31. See Ragnar Frisch's discussion of the need for "a realistic theoretical foundation for social policy" in his "Samarbeid mellom Politikere og Økonometrikere om Formuleringen av Politiske Preferenenser" (Socialøkonomen, 1971). (I am grateful to Leif Johansen for translating the relevant portions of the paper for me.) See also J.A. Mirrlees, "The Economics of Charitable Contributions," Econometric Society European meeting (Oslo, 1973).

supervision with rewards and punishment such that everyone has the incentive to exert himself. Every economic system has, therefore, tended to rely on the existence of attitudes toward work which supersedes the calculation of net gain from each unit of exertion. Social conditioning plays an extremely important part here.[32] I am persuaded that Britain's present economic difficulties have a great deal to do with work-motivation problems that lie outside the economics of rewards and punishments, and one reason why economists seem to have so little to contribute in this area is the neglect in traditional economic theory of this whole issue of commitment and the social relations surrounding it.[33]

These questions are connected, of course, with ethics, since moral reasoning influences one's actions, but in a broader sense these are matters of culture, of which morality is one part. Indeed, to take an extreme case, in the Chinese "cultural revolution" one of the primary aims was the increase of the sense of commitment with an eye on economic results: "the aim of the Great Proletarian Cultural Revolution is to revolutionize people's ideology and as a consequence to achieve greater, faster, better and more economical results in all fields of work."[34] Of course, China was experimenting with reducing dramatically the role of material incentives in production, which would

32. See A. Fox, *Beyond Contract: Work, Power and Trust Relations* (London, 1974); H.G. Nutzinger, "The Firm as a Social Institution: The Failure of a Contractarian Viewpoint," Working Paper No. 52 (Alfred Weber Institute, University of Heidelberg, 1976).

33. Cf. "Nor . . . should we forget the extent to which conventional theory ignores how and why work is organized within the firm and establishment in the way it is, what may be called the 'social relations' of the production process," R.A. Gordon, "Rigor and Relevance in a Changing Institutional Setting," Presidential Address, *American Economic Review* 66 (1976). See also R. Dahrendorf, *Class and Class Conflict in Industrial Society* (Stanford, 1959); O.E. Williamson, "The Evolution of Hierarchy: An Essay on the Organization of Work," Fels Discussion Paper No. 91 (University of Pennsylvania, 1976); and S.A. Marglin, "What Do Bosses Do? The Origins and Functions of Hierarchy in Capitalist Production," *Review of Radical Political Economics* 6 (1974).

34. "The Decision of the Central Committee of the Chinese Communist Party Concerning the Great Proletarian Cultural Revolution," adopted on 8 August 1966, reproduced in Joan Robinson, *The Cultural Revolution in China* (Harmondsworth, 1969). See also A.K. Sen, *On Economic Inequality* (Oxford, 1973); and C. Riskin, "Maoism and Motivation: A Discussion of Work Motivation in China," *Bulletin of Concerned Asian Scholars*, 1973.

certainly have increased the part that commitment was meant to play, but even within the traditional systems of payments, much reliance is usually placed on rules of conduct and modes of behavior that go beyond strictly economic incentives.[35] To run an organization *entirely* on incentives to personal gain is pretty much a hopeless task.

I will have a bit more to say presently on what might lie behind the sense of commitment, but I would like to emphasize at this stage that the morality or culture underlying it may well be of a limited kind—far removed from the grandeur of approaches such as utilitarianism. The "implicit collusions" that have been observed in business behavior in oligopolies seem to work on the basis of a system of mutual trust and sense of responsibility which has well-defined limits, and attempts at "universalization" of the same kind of behavior in other spheres of action may not go with it at all. There it is strictly a question of business ethics which is taken to apply within a fairly limited domain.

Similarly, in wage negotiations and in collective bargaining the sense of solidarity on either side may have well-defined limits, and may not fit in at all with an approach such as that of general utilitarianism. Edgeworth's implicit assumption, on which I commented earlier, that egoism and utilitarianism exhaust the possible alternative motivations, will be especially unhelpful in this context. While the field of commitment may be large, that of commitment based on utilitarianism and other universalized moral systems may well form a relatively small part of it.

VII

The economic theory of utility, which relates to the theory of rational behavior, is sometimes criticized for having too much structure; human beings are alleged to be "simpler" in reality. If our argument so far has been correct, precisely the opposite seems to be the case: traditional theory has *too little* structure. A person is given *one* preference ordering, and as and when the need arises this is supposed to reflect his interests, represent his welfare, summarize his idea of what should be done, and describe his actual choices and behavior. Can one prefer-

35. See Williamson, "The Evolution of Hierarchy," for a critical analysis of the recent literature in this area.

ence ordering do all these things? A person thus described may be "rational" in the limited sense of revealing no inconsistencies in his choice behavior, but if he has no use for these distinctions between quite different concepts, he must be a bit of a fool. The *purely* economic man is indeed close to being a social moron. Economic theory has been much preoccupied with this rational fool decked in the glory of his *one* all-purpose preference ordering. To make room for the different concepts related to his behavior we need a more elaborate structure.

What kind of a structure do we need? A bit more room up top is provided by John Harsanyi's important distinction between a person's "ethical" preferences and his "subjective" preferences: "the former must express what this individual prefers (or, rather would prefer), on the basis of impersonal social considerations alone, and the latter must express what he actually prefers, whether on the basis of his personal interests or on any other basis."[36] This dual structure permits us to distinguish between what a person thinks is good from the social point of view and what he regards as good from his own personal point of view. Presumably sympathy enters directly into the so-called subjective preference, but the role of commitment is left somewhat unclear. Insofar as a person's "subjective" preferences are taken to "define his utility function," the intention seems to be to exclude commitment from it, but an ambiguity arises from the fact that these are defined to "express his preferences in the full sense of the word as they actually are." Is this in the sense of choice, or in the sense of his conception of his own welfare? Perhaps Harsanyi intended the latter, since "ethical" preferences are by contrast given the role of expressing "what he prefers only in those possibly rare moments when he forces a special impartial and impersonal attitude on himself."[37] But what if he departs from his personal welfare maximization (including any sympathy), not through an impartial concern for all,[38] but through a sense of commitment to

36. J. Harsanyi, "Cardinal Welfare, Individualistic Ethics, and Interpersonal Comparisons of Utility," *Journal of Political Economy* 63 (1955): 315.

37. Ibid., pp. 315-316.

38. Note that for Harsanyi "an individual's preferences satisfy this requirement of impersonality if they indicate what social situation he would choose if he did not know what his general position would be in the new situation chosen

some particular group, say to the neighborhood or to the social class to which he belongs? The fact is we are still short of structure.

Even in expressing moral judgments from an impersonal point of view, a *dual* structure is deficient. Surely a preference ordering can be *more* ethical than another but *less* so than a third. We need more structure in this respect also. I have proposed elsewhere–at the 1972 Bristol conference on "practical reason"–that we need to consider *rankings of preference rankings* to express our moral judgments.[39] I would like to discuss this structure a bit more. A particular morality can be viewed, not just in terms of the "most moral" ranking of the set of alternative actions, but as a moral ranking of the rankings of actions (going well beyond the identification merely of the "most moral" ranking of actions). Let X be the set of alternative and mutually exclusive combinations of actions under consideration, and let Y be the set of rankings of the elements of X. A ranking of the set Y (consisting of action-rankings) will be called a meta-ranking of action-set X. It is my claim that a particular ranking of the action-set X is not articulate enough to express much about a given morality, and a more robust format is provided by choosing a meta-ranking of actions (that is, a ranking of Y rather than of X). Of course, such a meta-ranking may include *inter alia* the specification of a particular action-ranking as the "most moral," but insofar as actual behavior may be based on a compromise between claims of morality and the pursuit of various other objectives (including self-interest), one has to look also at the relative moral standings of those action-rankings that are *not* "most moral."

To illustrate, consider a set X of alternative action combinations and the following three rankings of this action-set X: ranking *A* represent-

(and in any of its alternatives) but rather had an equal chance of obtaining any of the social positions existing in this situation, from the highest down to the lowest" (p. 316).

39. A.K. Sen, "Choice, Orderings and Morality," in S. Körner, ed., *Practical Reason* (Oxford, 1974). See also J. Watkins' rejoinder and my reply in the same volume, and R.C. Jeffrey, "Preferences among Preferences," *Journal of Philosophy* 71 (1974); K. Binmore, "An Example in Group Preference," *Journal of Economic Theory* 10 (1975); and B.A. Weisbrod, "Toward a State-Preference Model of Utility Function Preferences: A Conceptual Note," mimeographed (University of Wisconsin, 1976).

ing my personal welfare ordering (thus, in some sense, representing my personal interests), ranking *B* reflecting my "isolated" personal interests ignoring sympathy (when such a separation is possible, which is not always so),[40] and ranking *C* in terms of which actual choices are made by me (when such choices are representable by a ranking, which again is not always so).[41] The "most moral" ranking *M* can, conceivably, be any of these rankings *A*, *B*, or *C*. Or else it can be some other ranking quite distinct from all three. (This will be the case if the actual choices of actions are not the "most moral" in terms of the moral system in question, and if, furthermore, the moral system requires sacrifice of some self-interest and also of "isolated" self-interest.) But even when some ranking *M* distinct from *A*, *B*, and *C* is identified as being at the top of the moral table, that still leaves open the question as to how *A*, *B*, and *C* may be ordered vis-à-vis each other. If, to take a particular example, it so happens that the pursuit of self-interest, including pleasure and pain from sympathy, is put morally above the pursuit of "isolated" self-interest (thereby leading to a partial coincidence of self-interest with morality), and the actual choices reflect a morally superior position to the pursuit of self-interest (perhaps due to a compromise in the moral direction), then the morality in question precipitates the meta-ranking *M*, *C*, *A*, *B*, in descending order. This, of course, goes well beyond specifying that *M* is "morally best."

The technique of meta-ranking permits a varying extent of moral articulation. It is not being claimed that a moral meta-ranking must be a *complete* ordering of the set Y, that is, must completely order all rankings of X. It can be a *partial* ordering, and I expect it often will be incomplete, but I should think that in most cases there will be no problem in going well beyond the limited expression permitted by the twofold specification of "ethical" and "subjective" preferences.

The rankings of action can, of course, be ordered also on grounds other than a particular system of morality: meta-ranking is a general

40. This presupposes some "independence" among the different elements influencing the level of overall welfare, implying some "separability." See W.M. Gorman, "Tricks with Utility Functions," in M. Artis and A.R. Nobay, eds., *Essays in Economic Analysis* (Cambridge, 1975).

41. See fn. 16 above.

technique usable under alternative interpretations of the meta-ranking relation. It can be used to describe a particular ideology or a set of political priorities or a system of class interests. In quite a different context, it can provide the format for expressing what preferences one would have preferred to have ("I wish I liked vegetarian foods more," or "I wish I didn't enjoy smoking so much"). Or it can be used to analyze the conflicts involved in addiction ("Given my current tastes, I am better off with heroin, but having heroin leads me to addiction, and I would have preferred not to have these tastes"). The tool of meta-rankings can be used in many different ways in distinct contexts.

This is clearly not the occasion to go into a detailed analysis of how this broader structure permits a better understanding of preference and behavior. A structure is not, of course, a theory, and alternative theories can be formulated using this structure. I should mention, however, that the structure demands much more information than is yielded by the observation of people's actual choices, which would at most reveal only the ranking *C*. It gives a role to introspection and to communication. To illustrate one use of the apparatus, I may refer to some technical results. Suppose I am trying to investigate your conception of your own welfare. You first specify the ranking *A* which represents your welfare ordering. But I want to go further and get an idea of your *cardinal* utility function, that is, roughly speaking, not only which ranking gives you more welfare but also by how much. I now ask you to order the different rankings in terms of their "closeness" to your actual welfare ranking *A*, much as a policeman uses the technique of photofit: is this more like him, or is that? If your answers reflect the fact that reversing a stronger preference makes the result more distant than reversing a weaker intensity of preference, your replies will satisfy certain consistency properties, and the order of rankings will permit us to compare your welfare *differences* between pairs. In fact, by considering higher and higher order rankings, we can determine your cardinal welfare function as closely as you care to specify.[42] I am not saying that this type of dialogue is the best way of discovering your welfare function, but it does illustrate that once we give

42. This result and some related ones emerged in discussions with Ken Binmore in 1975, but a projected joint paper reporting them is still, alas, unwritten. More work on this is currently being done also by R. Nader-Ispahani.

up the assumption that observing choices is the only source of data on welfare, a whole new world opens up, liberating us from the informational shackles of the traditional approach.

This broader structure has many other uses, for example, permitting a clearer analysis of *akrasia*—the weakness of will—and clarifying some conflicting considerations in the theory of liberty, which I have tried to discuss elsewhere.[43] It also helps in analyzing the development of behavior involving commitment in situations characterized by games such as the Prisoners' Dilemma.[44] This game is often treated, with some justice, as the classic case of failure of individualistic rationality. There are two players and each has two strategies, which we may call selfish and unselfish to make it easy to remember without my having to go into too much detail. Each player is better off personally by playing the selfish strategy *no* matter what the other does, but both are better off if both choose the unselfish rather than the selfish strategy. It is individually optimal to do the selfish thing: one can only affect one's own action and not that of the other, and given the other's strategy—no matter what—each player is better off being selfish. But this combination of selfish strategies, which results from self-seeking by both, produces an outcome that is worse for both than the result of both choosing the unselfish strategy. It can be shown that this conflict can exist even if the game is repeated many times.

Some people find it puzzling that individual self-seeking by each should produce an inferior outcome for all, but this, of course, is a well-known conflict, and has been discussed in general terms for a very long time. Indeed, it was the basis of Rousseau's famous distinc-

43. See Sen, "Choice, Orderings and Morality"; and also Sen, "Liberty, Unanimity and Rights," *Economica* 43 (1976). Note also the relevance of this structure in analyzing the incompleteness of the conception of liberty in terms of the ability to do what one *actually wishes*. Cf. "If I find that I am able to do little or nothing of what I wish, I need only contract or extinguish my wishes, and I am made free. If the tyrant (or 'hidden persuader') manages to condition his subjects (or customers) into losing their original wishes and embrace ('internalize') the form of life he has invented for them, he will, on this definition, have succeeded in liberating them." I. Berlin, "Two Concepts of Liberty," in *Four Essays on Liberty* (Oxford, 1969), pp. 139–140).

44. See R.D. Luce and H. Raiffa, *Games and Decisions* (New York, 1958); A. Rapoport and A.M. Chammah, *Prisoner's Dilemma: A Study in Conflict and Cooperation* (Ann Arbor, 1965); W.G. Runciman and A.K. Sen, "Games, Justice and the General Will," *Mind*, 74 (1965); N. Howard, *Paradoxes of Rationality* (Cambridge, Mass., 1971).

tion between the "general will" and the "will of all."[45] But the puzzle from the point of view of rational behavior lies in the fact that in actual situations people often do not follow the selfish strategy. Real life examples of this type of behavior in complex circumstances are well known, but even in controlled experiments in laboratory conditions people playing the Prisoners' Dilemma frequently do the unselfish thing.[46]

In interpreting these experimental results, the game theorist is tempted to put it down to the lack of intelligence of the players: "Evidently the run-of-the-mill players are not strategically sophisticated enough to have figured out that strategy DD [the selfish strategy] is the only rationally defensible strategy, and this intellectual short-coming saves them from losing."[47] A more fruitful approach may lie in permitting the possibility that the person is *more* sophisticated than the theory allows and that he has asked himself what type of preference he would like the other player to have, and on somewhat Kantian grounds has considered the case for himself having those preferences, or behaving *as if* he had them. This line of reasoning requires him to consider the modifications of the game that would be brought about by acting through commitment (in terms of "revealed preferences," this would look *as if* he had different preferences from the ones he actually had), and he has to assess alternative behavior norms in that light. I have discussed these issues elsewhere;[48] thus I shall simply note here that the apparatus of *ranking of rankings* assists the reasoning which involves considering the merits of having different types of preferences (or of acting as if one had them).

VIII

Admitting behavior based on commitment would, of course have far-reaching consequences on the nature of many economic models. I

45. See Runciman and Sen.

46. See, for example, L.B. Lave, "An Empirical Approach to the Prisoner's Dilemma Game," *Quarterly Journal of Economics* 76 (1962), and Rapoport and Chammah, *Prisoner's Dilemma.*

47. Rapoport and Chammah, p. 29.

48. Sen, "Choice, Orderings and Morality." See also K. Baier, "Rationality and Morality," and A.K. Sen, "Rationality and Morality: A Reply," both forthcoming in *Erkenntnis*; K. Baier, *The Moral Point of View* (Ithaca, 1958); and Fred Schick's analysis, "Rationality and Sociality."

have tried to show why this change is necessary and why the consequences may well be serious. Many issues remain unresolved, including the empirical importance of commitment as a part of behavior, which would vary, as I have argued, from field to field. I have also indicated why the empirical evidence for this cannot be sought in the mere observation of actual choices, and must involve other sources of information, including introspection and discussion.

There remains, however, the issue as to whether this view of man amounts to seeing him as an irrational creature. Much depends on the concept of rationality used, and many alternative characterizations exist. In the sense of *consistency* of choice, there is no reason to think that admitting commitment must imply any departure from rationality. This is, however, a weak sense of rationality.

The other concept of rationality prevalent in economics identifies it with the possibility of justifying each act in terms of self-interest: when act x is chosen by person i and act y rejected, this implies that i's personal interests are expected by i to be better served by x than by y. There are, it seems to me, three distinct elements in this approach. First, it is a consequentialist view: judging acts by conseqences only.[49] Second, it is an approach of *act* evaluation rather than *rule* evaluation. And third, the only consequences considered in evaluating acts are those on one's own interests, everything else being at best an intermediate product. It is clearly possible to dispute the claims of each of these elements to being a necessary part of the conception of rationality in the dictionary sense of "the power of being able to exercise one's reason." Moreover, arguments for rejecting the straightjacket of each of these three principles are not hard to find. The case for actions based on commitment can arise from the violation of any of these three principles. Commitment sometimes relates to a sense of obligation going beyond the consequences. Sometimes the lack of personal gain in particular *acts* is accepted by considering the value of *rules* of behavior. But even within a consequentialist act-evaluation framework, the exclusion of any consideration other than self-interest seems to impose a wholly arbitrary limitation on the notion of rationality.

49. On the nature of "consequentialism" and problems engendered by it, see B. Williams, "A Critique of Utilitarianism," in J.J.C. Smart and B. Williams, *Utilitarianism: For and Against* (Cambridge, 1973).

Henry Sidgwick noted the arbitrary nature of the assumption of egoism:

If the Utilitarian has to answer the question, "Why should I sacrifice my own happiness for the greater happiness of another?" it must surely be admissible to ask the Egoist, "Why should I sacrifice a present pleasure for one in the future? Why should I concern myself about my own future feelings any more than about the feelings of other persons?" It undoubtedly seems to Common Sense paradoxical to ask for a reason why one should seek one's own happiness on the whole; but I do not see how the demand can be repudiated as absurd by those who adopt views of the extreme empirical school of psychologists, although those views are commonly supposed to have a close affinity with Egoistic Hedonism. Grant that the Ego is merely a system of coherent phenomena, that the permanent identical "I" is not a fact but a fiction, as Hume and his followers maintain; why, then, should one part of the series of feelings into which the Ego is resolved be concerned with another part of the same series, any more than with any other series?[50]

The view of rationality that identifies it with consequentialist act-evaluation using self-interest can be questioned from any of these three angles. Admitting commitment as a part of behavior implies no denial of reasoned assessment as a basis for action.

There is not much merit in spending a lot of effort in debating the "proper" definition of rationality. The term is used in many different senses, and none of the criticisms of the behavioral foundations of economic theory presented here stands or falls on the definition chosen. The main issue is the acceptability of the assumption of the invariable pursuit of self-interest in each act. Calling that type of behavior rational, or departures from it irrational, does not change the relevance of these criticisms, though it does produce an arbitrarily narrow definition of rationality. This paper has not been concerned with

50. H. Sidgwick, *The Method of Ethics* (London, 1874; 7th ed., 1907), pp. 418-419. See also Nagel's forceful exposition of the thesis that "altruism itself depends on a recogniton of the reality of other persons, and on the equivalent capacity to regard oneself as merely one individual among many." *The Possibility of Altruism*, p. 1.

the question as to whether human behavior is better described as rational or irrational. The main thesis has been the need to accommodate commitment as a part of behavior. Commitment does not presuppose reasoning, but it does not exclude it; in fact, insofar as consequences on others have to be more clearly understood and assessed in terms of one's values and instincts, the scope for reasoning may well expand. I have tried to analyze the structural extensions in the conception of preference made necessary by behavior based on reasoned assessment of commitment. Preferences as rankings have to be replaced by a richer structure involving meta-rankings and related concepts.

I have also argued against viewing behavior in terms of the traditional dichotomy between egoism and universalized moral systems (such as utilitarianism). Groups intermediate between oneself and all, such as class and community, provide the focus of many actions involving commitment. The rejection of egoism as description of motivation does not, therefore, imply the acceptance of some universalized morality as the basis of actual behavior. Nor does it make human beings excessively noble.

Nor, of course, does the use of reasoning imply remarkable wisdom.

> It is as true as Caesar's name was Kaiser,
> That no economist was ever wiser,

said Robert Frost in playful praise of the contemporary economist. Perhaps a similarly dubious tribute can be paid to the economic man in our modified conception. If he shines at all, he shines in comparison –in contrast–with the dominant image of the rational fool.

ELSEVIER

Journal of Economic Behavior & Organization
Vol. 40 (1999) 373–386

JOURNAL OF
Economic Behavior
& Organization

www.elsevier.com/locate/econbase

Sentimental fools: a critique of Amartya Sen's notion of commitment

Elias L. Khalil *

1338 E. Hyde Park Blvd., #3, Chicago, IL 60615, USA

Received 25 October 1997; received in revised form 8 February 1999; accepted 11 March 1999

Abstract

Commitment is problematic because one sometimes pursues it against one's interest. To solve it, the paper proposes a distinction between 'non-binding' and 'binding' commitments. Non-binding commitment is about ambition, such as becoming a great chef, which bolsters welfare in the pecuniary sense as well as self-respect. In contrast, 'binding commitment' is about honesty. While it diminishes welfare, it augments self-integrity. The neoclassical view reduces both commitments to interest, while the multiple-self approach separates both commitments from interest. The separation permits the confusion of sentimental fools, who enter commitments without regard to interest, with rational sentimentalists, who take interest into consideration.

JEL classification: D0

Keywords: Substantive interest; Non-binding commitment; Binding commitment; Sentimental fools; Rational fools; Rational sentimentalists; Guilt; Disgrace (shame); Embarrassment; Substantive preference; Symbolic preference (self-respect and self-integrity); Lethargic will; Crooked will

1. Introduction

Given that commitment appears to negate interest, some theorists, such as Amartya Sen, propose that agents have conflicting selves. Defenders of the standard approach, on the other hand, deny the existence of the problem; they simply regard commitment as an ordinary preference stemming from a unitary self. While this paper recognizes the phenomenon of commitment as a problem, it tries to solve it without appealing to the multiple-self view.

* Tel.: +1-773-548-7638; fax: +1-773-702-8490
E-mail address: elkhalil@midway.uchicago.edu (E.L. Khalil)

0167-2681/99/$ – see front matter
PII: S0167-2681(99)00060-8

	Incentive -responsiveness	Examples	Reward	Negation of preference
Substantive interest	Very responsive	Demand for food, clothes, entertainment	Substantive preference (welfare)	irrational
Non-binding commitment	Responsive (after trying hard enough)	Career or idealistic pursuits	Symbolic preference (self-respect)	Weak will (lethargic will)
Binding commitment	Not responsive	Honesty, no shirking, fairness	Symbolic preference (self-integrity)	Weak will (crooked will)

Fig. 1. The three preferences.

It does so by distinguishing two kinds of commitment and how each relates differently to interest–a necessary distinction to discern admirable acts from sentimental foolishness.

Let us start with three kinds of preferences, which may overlap, facing the self (*S*):

Situation 1: S decides to enter a training program in the culinary art of French cuisine because the going wage rate for chefs, given the cost of training and the responsibility of the job, is more attractive than other options.

Situation 2: In addition to Situation 1, *S* has been impressed by the creative art involved in French cooking. He takes on a commitment to try to become the best chef in the city.

Situation 3: In addition to Situation 2, *S* takes on the commitment to be truthful. In specific, he prepares, in light of his advertisement, dishes made only from fresh ingredients, even when the pecuniary benefit from a cheating strategy is unambiguously greater than expected pecuniary cost resulting possibly from a tarnished market reputation.

Situation 1 involves what I call '*substantive interest*', pecuniary calculation. Situation 2 consists of '*non-binding commitment*' because the promise cannot be obligatory given that the agent is uncertain whether he can fulfill it. Situation 3 entails '*binding commitment*' because the agent is certain that he can meet his obligation. The agent fulfills his binding commitment to enjoy self-integrity. If he fulfills it exclusively out of substantive calculation concerning penalty, it would fail to generate the sense of self-integrity.

While Situation 2 advances substantive preference, Situation 3 by definition reduces it. Nonetheless, both kinds of commitment satisfy a sense of selfhood, dubbed here 'symbolic preference' as opposed to 'substantive preference'. As summed up in Fig. 1, while the negation of one's substantive interest would be irrational, the negation of either kind of commitment is usually described as the result of weak will. There are two kinds of weak will ('lethargic' and 'crooked'), and two kinds of symbolic preference ('self-respect' and 'self-integrity'), following the two kinds of commitment.

The paper commences with some motivation (Section 1). It distinguishes binding from non-binding commitments (Section 2) and preference from choice (Section 3). Many authors confuse non-binding with binding commitment, which lead them to separate commitment per se from substantive interest (Section 4). Such a separation entails that the agent is constituted of multiple selves (Section 5). Such a view, in turn, makes it impossible to distinguish sentimental fools from rational sentimentalists (Section 6).

2. Motivation

While the three situations are about self-concern, one can equally illustrate them by other-concerns such as altruism, public spiritedness, or patriotism. The conjectured distinction among the three preferences has two payoffs, practical and theoretical. Regarding the practical payoff, the debate about income redistribution can be clarified on the ground of whether it is prompted by altruism, which pertains to substantive interest, or is instigated by fairness, which involves binding commitment. If a redistribution policy is prompted by altruism, one has to weigh the efficiency advantage versus side-effect disadvantages such as the weakening of incentives. But if the policy is prompted by fairness, on the basis of some social contract entered under the veil of ignorance (Rawls, 1971), one would conceive differently the so-called weakening of incentives: It would be in one's right, as specified by the social contract, not to work below a guaranteed social wage.

If there is no difference between commitment and interest, the judicial system's main goal would be the deterrence of crime rather than the vindication of justice. Therefore, it would be cheaper to punish rich criminals with high fines rather than with jail sentences–as long as both methods are equivalent in deterring crime. However, people usually abhor the idea of fining rich criminals rather than putting them in jail. The abhorrence is inexplicable if one views commitment as a substantive preference. Moreover, the distinction between the two kinds of commitment will make it clear, as shown below, why the negation of non-binding commitment is only a cause for embarrassment, while the negation of binding commitment is usually seen as shameful. In fact, the distinction would provide a ground for why laws commanding charity, as distinct from upholding justice, can be counterproductive.

In addition, if one views internal organs, such as kidneys, to be 'gifts of life', one would regard the legalization of their trade as repugnant, no different from prostitution (Radin, 1996; cf. Arrow, 1997). One would see the legalization of the market for organs as a violation of binding commitments which the agent, although implicitly, makes with one's sense of identity. Some experts argue that legalization of the organs market would actually decrease the total organs available similarly to how the legalization of blood donation in the US has hindered the supply of blood (Stewart, 1992). While substantive preference rises as a result of the legalization, it may not rise enough to offset the weakening of symbolic preference which acts as a motive in institutions where the marketing of organs is prohibited.

Regarding the theoretical payoff, the focus here, *the proposed three-way distinction promises to supersede the shortcomings of both the unitary-self and multiple-self approaches.* [1] The standard, unitary-self view does not recognize the interest/commitment distinction. When commitments are not the outcome of strategic repetitive games, the standard approach treats them as preferences reducible to substantive preference function which

[1] I use the term 'multiple-self' to express inconsistent preferences, where the agent is assumed to contain a 'moral self' as opposed to 'material self.' In this sense, my usage differs from Richard Posner's (Posner, 1995, ch. 4). Posner takes the term to denote conflicting needs, where agents are seen as trying to accommodate pressing needs arising from work, family, church, and so on (also see Kuran, 1995, pp. 43–44]. In the sense of inconsistent preferences, the multiple-self view is advanced by Amartya Sen (1982), John Harsanyi (1955), Thomas Schelling (1984), Amitai Etzioni (1986), Gregory Kavka (1991), and Jon Elster (Elster, 1986; cf. Hausman and McPherson, 1993). It is beyond the scope here to contrast fully the multiple- and unitary-self approaches (Khalil, 1995, 1996, 1997b, 1998).

is the object of optimization. On the other hand, the multiple-self approach recognizes the interest/commitment difference. But it treats non-binding commitment as not different from binding commitment. The treatment entails that commitment stems from a self separate from the one which expresses substantive interest. Such a view, as detailed below with respect to Sen's, makes it impossible to distinguish sentimental fools from rational sentimentalists.

The paper evaluates the advantages of the proposed three-way distinction vis-à-vis Sen's work. In his 1977 celebrated paper, Sen [(Sen, 1977) (reprinted 1982, ch. 4] argues that the reduction of commitment to interest implies that agents are 'rational fools' because they are ready, in response to change of relative price or income, to cheat without the feeling of shame (disgrace) and to quit projects at the first appearance of difficulty without the feeling of embarrassment. It is true that casual observations of normal agents who occasionally cheat and, as soon as the project becomes harder, quit indicate that they experience shame and embarrassment--an experience alien to the rational fools inhabiting the unitary-self world.

However, Sen's separation of commitment from interest invites from the rear window another kind of fools, what is coined here 'sentimental fools'. Sentimental fools are ready to incur costs unjustified by expected benefits, such as jumping off a ship in the middle of the ocean to retrieve a toy for a crying child. Sen is correct that the collapsing of commitment with interest engenders a world of rational fools, but his radical separation of interest and commitment engenders a world of sentimental fools. *To avoid rational fools à la unitary-self view and sentimental fools à la multiple-self view, we should neither collapse interest and commitment nor separate them radically*. It is possible to achieve this task with the help of the proposed distinction between non-binding and binding commitments.

3. The commitment dichotomy

The difference between the two kinds of commitment is not that binding commitment is coerced, while the other is optional. Both are voluntary. No one coerces *S* in Situation 3 to advertize his fresh ingredients. Moreover, the difference between the two is not that binding commitment is a promise to a second party, while the other is a personal promise. Binding commitment can be made with the self, as when one refuses to accept payment for blood donation or sexual pleasure. Also, the issue is not that binding commitment is a non-binding one made in the past. All non-binding commitments move into the past once they are made.

Rather, the main difference lies with regard to ability. In Situation 1, *S* is maximizing substantive preference which is assumed to be within one's ability. In Situation 2, *S* is also pursuing substantive preference, but not in the strict optimization sense. The goal is rather expressive of *S*'s self-image, an image to which *S* makes a non-binding commitment. The commitment is non-binding because *S* is uncertain whether *S* has the ability to sustain the necessary effort to carry it through. *S* may eventually have to give up the commitment if it impairs sufficiently his substantive interest. However, insofar as *S* acts to attain such a goal, it affords *S* symbolic preference which goes beyond substantive preference. In contrast, in Situation 3, *S* is obliged by a binding commitment–pursued even in single-shot games–not to cheat or disown one's identity, which can be extended to be loyal to one's family, country,

E.L. Khalil / J. of Economic Behavior & Org. 40 (1999) 373–386 377

tribe, and religion. The commitment is binding because S is certain that S has the ability to sustain the necessary effort to carry it through.

In other words, *while the agent's ability is not in question in binding commitment, it is so in non-binding commitment* (Khalil, 1997a). In binding commitment, the agent promises to be honest, not to sell or buy sexual pleasure (prostitution), not to accept money for donated blood, not to accept bribes, or to sell his country's secrets to the enemy when it is clear that such a promise is within his ability. Given that ability is not in doubt, the reason behind the commitment, therefore, is to counter the opportunistic gain which would arise from cheating. In contrast, in non-binding commitment, the agent promises to pursue a career or advance a public cause despite anticipated arduous hurdles. The promise is needed in order to sustain one's effort given that the ability of the actor with regard to the challenge is uncertain. This situation is similar to the commitment to climb a mountain, whose height and terrain are quite known to the actor, but would be an uncertain challenge for him because he has not tried it before. If the actor quits after trying hard enough, the actor would not be labeled (by himself or others) a 'quitter', i.e., someone who lacks fortitude. In contrast, the actor would be labeled 'corrupt' if he, as long as he is not in a state of destitute, accepts a bribe irrespective of its size. While the commitment to climb the mountain is contingent on an uncertain ability and hence is non-binding, the commitment to rebuff bribes is not contingent on ability and hence is binding.

Further, each kind of commitment relates differently to substantive interest. While Situation 1 and Situation 2 augment substantive preference, Situation 2 additionally attains symbolic preference, in specific 'self-respect', for exhibiting tenacity. In contrast, Situation 3 originates symbolic preference, in specific 'self-integrity', for acting honestly, but only at the expense of lowering substantive preference as clearly in the case of single-shot games. [2] One may appeal to unreflected habit (Mueller, 1986) in explaining why one would act honestly in single-shot games. However, such an appeal is an option of last resort because it invokes ad hoc reasoning. A better explanation is that the agent in Situation 3 is optimizing a function which includes, besides the familiar substantive preference, self-integrity. While self-integrity arises from honesty which may lower substantive interest, self-respect stems from pursuing an ambition which enhances substantive interest.

Another way to distinguish between the two commitments is to discern two kinds of weak will or temptations. When one gives up the pursuit of a non-binding commitment at the first sign of difficulty, as in Situation 2, his will can be characterized as 'lethargic'. This differs from violating binding commitment, as cheating customers in Situation 3, where the will can be depicted as 'crooked'. While lethargic will engenders the feeling of 'embarrassment', crooked will gives rise to the feeling of 'shame' for the simple reason that lethargic will invites complacency while crooked will is about duplicity. One can, with respect to binding commitment, be characterized by a crooked will while,

[2] The proposed term 'symbolic preference' resembles Timur Kuran's (Kuran, 1995) 'expressive utility' (see Khalil, 1999). There is one difference, however. The term 'symbolic' is merely an umbrella category, while Kuran's 'expressive' is a concept which supposedly denotes a single preference function. To wit, Kuran, similar to many other writers on the subject, does not distinguish between the two radically different kinds of commitment and the consequently different kinds of symbolic preference. Aside from lexicon, symbolic preference is a category rather than a concept which denotes a phenomenon.

with regard to non-binding commitment, be characterized by a non-lethargic, tenacious will.[3]

Anxiety-driven actions which may indicate neurosis (see Lewis, 1971) are motivated by guilt. Such actions may fail to highlight the proposed difference between the two kinds of weak will. The term 'guilt', as used below, exposes situations where action is motivated by anxiety rather than by preference. The term denotes suboptimal preference which one may choose out of lack of self-assertion, boldness, or self-confidence. As Charles Taylor (1995, pp. 142) argues, turning away from the crushing burden of medieval Catholic notion of 'sin' or, in contemporary vernacular, 'guilt', amounts to liberation: "To break with a good to which one cannot really subscribe is a liberation in anyone's language." There are other ways to establish the commitment dichotomy. At least concerning the three ways mentioned so far, they do not provide a clear-cut blueprint on how to classify unambiguously actual preferences. Many acts, such as volunteering resources to a homeless shelter, can be composite ones, blending the motives of altruism (i.e. substantive interest) with ambition (i.e. non-binding commitment to take pride in one's neighborhood) and justice (i.e. binding commitment to the unlucky ones in society). At least theoretically, however, it is possible to discern the three preferences and two kinds of commitment they entail.

4. The divergence of preference and choice

Among others, Becker (1996), Kuran (1995), and Sunstein (1997) propose other reasons, beside guilt-driven anxiety, behind the preference/choice divergence. To note, the set of concepts offered by each author is geared to solve a particular problem, rather than to solve the preference/choice divergence per se.

For example, Becker, with other co-authors, tries to account for addiction, where agents choose bundles which are contrary to their preferences. He reasons that the preference/choice divergence is only apparent: Addiction, similar to habits, is the outcome of rational choice when consumption is intertemporally nonseparable. His account implies that observed preference/choice divergence is really the divergence of choice from, what I dub here, 'fanciful preference'. In the case of addiction, the addict may wish to quit, but his preference might be fanciful when, given the hardship of quitting, it is beyond his budget constraint. The preference for a drug-free life style might be as fanciful as the dream of a school teacher with limited income to own a mansion in the French Riviera. Becker's theory should not be misunderstood as stating that it is impossible to quit addiction or to live in a mansion with servants. Rather, to attain such objectives, the addict or the school teacher must expend enormous cost to cultivate appropriate new habits, such as socializing with non-addicts or augmenting additional human capital. Otherwise, to close the gap between choice and fanciful preference, the agent must adjust the fanciful preference as he learns from information. Further, Becker's theory should not be misunderstood as failing to recognize the possibility of pathology, the persistence of the gap between choice and fanciful preference. But such persistence is the result of the misfunctioning of information processing. So, the

[3] The analyses of Davidson (1980) and Jon Elster (1983) mostly focus on crooked will.

persistence of the gap is reasoned to be the outcome of special characteristic of information, not expressive of a gap between choice and feasible preference.

Becker's reasoning shows that if one wants to assert the preference/choice divergence thesis, one must first treat preference as *feasible*. This seems to be the case with Frankfurt's (Frankfurt, 1971) notion of 'free will' with regard to 'second order preference' or what came to be called 'metapreference' (also see Jeffrey, 1974; McPherson, 1980; Hahn, 1982). One may prefer choosing drugs over education, while one simultaneously prefers the preference for education over drugs at the meta level. For such a metapreference to be non-trivial, George (1993) explicitly distinguishes metapreference from 'regret' which is associated with particular choices. In such choices, regret express situations where alternative options are fanciful, i.e., beyond one's budget constraint.

On the other hand, Kuran studies the preference/choice divergence with a focus on the dynamics between private preferences and hostile public opinion. He argues that agents may not act on their private preferences if they do not jibe with public preferences. Kuran's main objective is not to solve the preference/choice divergence in general. Rather, he tries to account for abrupt changes in public preferences. To Kuran, agents may 'live a lie' in public, falsify their private preferences to secure the approval of others. Such 'preference falsification' is justified i.e., not judged as indicative of insincerity or dishonesty only when the disapproval of the public involves severe persecution. For Kuran's purpose, the preference/choice divergence is relevant only insofar as it sheds light on the divergence of private preference from public choice. Thus, this particular divergence stems from historical accidents of coercive social-political environments. In the absence of such an environment, and especially when public opinion values maverick and eccentric private preferences, there is no need for public choice to diverge from private preference. Nonetheless, Kuran's thesis is useful here. It clarifies one issue. If one wants to assert the preference/choice divergence thesis, one must be clear that the issue is about *truthful* choice where the approval of others is irrelevant.

Further, Sunstein investigates the preference/choice divergence with a focus on how societal corrupting norms may push choice away from true preference. He maintains that preferences are fuzzy and, hence, susceptible to the manipulation of unenlightened societal norms such as the pursuit of vanity. This entails that there is a need for state intervention in order to align choices with true preferences. Sunstein's thesis about the deviation of choice from true preference does not fully coincide with the preference/choice deviation discussed here. For one thing, there would be no divergence if the public is fully enlightened even to the satisfaction of the benevolent state. Nonetheless, Sunstein's discussion clarifies one issue. If one wants to assert the preference/choice divergence thesis, one must be clear that the issue is about the divergence of choice from *enlightened* preference.

5. Lumping non-binding with binding commitments

Sen (1982, p. 1; 1985, 1993, 1995) proposes the preference/choice divergence from a different angle. He argues, contrary to the axioms of the theory of revealed preference, one should not assume a priori that behavior is internally consistent. Empirical study should rather determine whether, in a particular case, choice matches preference. While the paper does not quibble with this thesis, Sen extends the thesis to imply that the agent has multiple selves. This implication is unwarranted. To show this, we need to unpack Sen's confusing categories. The confusion arises from a terminological twist which equates the preference/choice divergence with the interest/commitment distinction. He reaches such an identification by equating the terms 'preference' with 'interest', on one hand, and 'choice' with 'commitment', on the other.

While the issue is not about lexicon, this paper employs 'preference' to denote both interest and commitment, and utilizes 'choice' to indicate action which may deviate from preference. When Sen equates preference with interest and choice with commitment, he can claim with such a terminological twist that the interest/commitment distinction is necessarily implied by the accepted preference/choice divergence. With this lexicon, Sen overlooks the commitment dichotomy when he lumps both kinds of commitment in one concept and, in turn, opposes it to interest as if each kind of commitment relates in the same way to interest. For instance, he explicitly opposes 'commitment' and 'sympathy'. He illustrates it by distinguishing two separate motives behind the opposition to torture: one is out of principle and the other is out of sympathy in the sense of caring about the substantive interest of the other (Sen, 1982, pp. 91–92). He further illustrates the difference:

> The contrast between sympathy and commitment may be illustrated with the story of two boys who find two apples, one large, one small. Boy *A* tells boy *B*, 'You choose'. *B* immediately picks the larger apple. *A* is upset and permits himself the remark that this was grossly unfair. 'Why?' asks *B*. 'Which one would *you* have chosen, if you were to choose rather than me?' 'The smaller one, of course', *A* replies. *B* is now triumphant: 'Then what are you complaining about? That's the one you've got!' *B* certainly wins this round of argument, but in fact *A* would have lost nothing from *B*'s choice had his own hypothetical choice of the smaller apple been based on sympathy as opposed to commitment. *A*'s anger indicates that this was probably not the case (Sen, 1982, p. 93) also see (Sen, 1993, p. 501).[4]

It is clear that Sen places 'sympathy' in the substantive interest (welfare) function, while he treats 'commitment' as a category which *reduces* that function.

Sen's interest/commitment opposition makes sense if the word 'commitment' strictly denotes binding commitment. However, Sen uses the term to also denote non-binding commitment such as the commitment 'to exert' oneself, which rather augments rather than reduces substantive interest (Sen, 1982, pp. 97–98).

Sen uses the same term to discuss the binding rule of justice to abstain from the use of torture and to express striving towards challenging goals, as working harder for a better future. Sen must have treated non-binding commitment as binding when he argues in many places that commitment *per se* always lowers substantive interest (welfare) (e.g. Sen, 1982, p. 93). For Sen, 'commitment does involve, in a very real sense, counterpreferential choice' [Ibid.]. Such an interest/commitment opposition overlooks that non-binding commitment

[4] Sen (1997, p. 747) repeats the same observation with regard to the tendency of an agent not to grab immediately his favorite chair in a party or snatch his favorite fruit from the host's tray. Sen dismisses the view that such etiquettes are ways which allow an actor to sympathize with the intensity of preferences of others [Ibid., p. 747n]. He maintains that it arises either from the concern over reputation, social commitment to a moral imperative, or conventional rule following.

Fig. 2. Sen's meta-ranking.

buttresses interest. As discussed next, the opposition leads to a particular view of ranking of preferences, the multiple-self view. As shown later, such a view cannot afford the conceptual tools needed to distinguish sentimental fools from rational sentimentalists.

6. Meta-ranking of preferences and the multiple-self view

Sen welcomes John Harsanyi's (Harsanyi, 1955, 1986, 1988) distinction between 'ethical' and 'subjective' preferences. While the former expresses what the person prefers 'on the basis of impersonal social considerations alone,' the latter denotes what the person actually prefers 'on the basis of his personal interests or on any other basis' [Ibid., p. 315]. This sociological approach generally defines the 'good' from the social rather than the individual standpoint. For Sen (1982, p. 100), however, Harsanyi's '*dual* structure is deficient.' First, 'actual' behavior may express ethical consideration and, second, 'a preference ordering can be *more* ethical than another but *less* so than a third.' Sen proposes 'more structure' involving the rankings of preference rankings, which follows Frankfurt (1971). Sen's meta-ranking entails two sets, X and Y (Sen, 1982, p. 100). As reconstructed in Fig. 2, set X includes bundles B_j, where B_1 can be five apples for the self and three apples for the group. Set Y includes elements A through Z where each specifies a ranking of B_j. The A ranking may specify B_1 preferable to B_2 and the B ranking may stipulate the opposite. The set Y is nothing other than a multitude of preference functions which are exclusive. Each actor ($a_i = a_1, a_2, \ldots, a_n$) has a meta-ranking ($Y_i^m$) which expresses 'a particular system of morality' (Ibid., p. 101). For a_n, e.g., the appropriate system is Y_n^m where, e.g., $B > K > \ldots > H$.

Insofar as an agent is able to rank the different rankings means that the multitude of preference functions are consistent and commensurable. So, as Jon Elster (Elster, 1986, pp. 11–13) assesses, meta-ranking is the articulation of one general category capable of ordering more particular sets of preferences. David George (1998) contrasts the idea of metapreference to the multiple-self approach. To one interpretation at least, when the preferences subject to ranking involve varied substantive interests, meta-ranking of preference is merely a more sophisticated formulation of the unitary preference function. In this light, Howard Margolis's (Margolis, 1982) theory is in the tradition of metapreference: He postulates that behavior expresses a compromise between two functions, 'self-interest' and 'social motivation.' This entails a meta-function to which the two different selves (selfish and altruist) reconcile.

In contrast, Sen uses meta-ranking to advance a multiple-self conception of preference where commitment is not even a preference which can be reconciled with welfare. Nonetheless, Sen's employment of the meta-ranking lexicon cannot deliver the blow that Sen wants to inflict on conventional theory. Sen somewhat recognizes the shortcoming when he calls

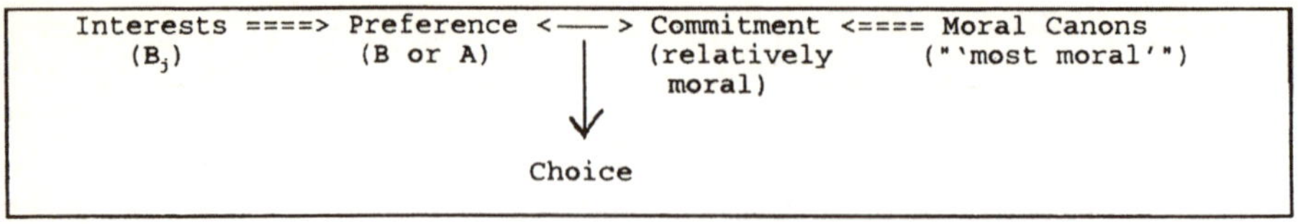

Fig. 3. Reconstruction of Sen's multiple-self view.

meta-ranking a 'general technique' (Sen, 1982, p. 101). That is, meta-ranking is not a specific technique to model commitment. To wit, a_n can apply any particular moral system to rank the ranking elements (Sen, 1982, p. 100–101).[5] To take a step further, D includes the commitment to some particular group, say to the neighborhood or to the social class to which he belongs. To Sen, the 'most moral' ranking M, where he uses 'M' in the sense of a particular meta-ranking (Y_n^m), can be any of the ranking of A, B, D, and so one. That is, a_1 (whose $M_1 = Y_1^m$) may rank B (isolated interests) preferable to D (commitment to group), while agent a_2 (whose $M_1 = Y_2^m$) ranks them in reverse. There is nothing in the idea of meta-ranking which entails anything about a conflict between commitment and interest (or 'preference' in Sen's lexicon). The agent can simply change his meta-ranking as he pleases. Thus, the idea of meta-ranking fits like hand in glove with the traditional notion of commensurable preference functions.

Sen extricates himself from this traditional implication to assert the thesis that commitment is counter-preferential by making a subtle confusion. He suddenly states, following his definition of M as a meta-ranking (Y_i^m), that M can also be defined as an element of the set Y as if the two uses are logically equivalent (Sen, 1982, p. 101). Obviously, the class cannot be a member of itself: M cannot be Y_i^m and simultaneously an element in the Y set. Y_i^m, or what Sen calls the 'most moral' ranking M,' is how to arrange the ranking elements A through Z and, hence, Y_i^m cannot logically be 'some other ranking quite distinct' from the others. Once one considers Y_i^m (the 'most moral') an element in the set Y, the set Y stops being about meta-ranking preference function. It becomes a single-ranking preference function where B_j are arranged according to one criterion: from the less moral B and A elements to the most moral element M. Sen justifies what amounts to the abandonment of meta-ranking and adoption of single-ranking by asserting that 'moral system requires sacrifice of some self-interest.' This amounts to admitting that the meta-ranking lexicon cannot capture Sen's thesis, viz., the moral system requires sacrifice (Sen, 1982, p. 101). In this single-ranking, Sen views choice as a compromise between less desirable preference functions and the ideal 'most moral' ranking (Sen, 1982, p. 100).This entails a multiple-self view, as Fig. 3 shows. Sen's agenda is not about the meta-ranking of preference functions which would approximate the unitary-self approach. It is rather about the inherent opposition between the 'most moral' commitments and substantive interests (welfare). So, Sen's view does not depart from Harsanyi's 'dual structure.' Sen merely adds intermediate selves, ones infused with sympathy (A) and actual choices (C), between the two opposite poles. Thus, Sen's multiple-self approach is ultimately based on the opposition between interest and moral commitments. Such an opposition stems from the fact that Sen (1987, p. 55n)

[5] It is inconsistent to regard C as an element of the set Y (i.e. a separate preference function) as well as a general category representing any other element which is actually acted upon.

ultimately aims at providing the '*foundation*' of the relevance of basic needs fulfillment. As John Rawls (1988) argues, this amounts to providing a 'comprehensive doctrine' or some unique view of the good which is contrary to Rawls's view of the 'political conception' of justice. Notwithstanding Sen's (Sen, 1990) defense, Sen's comprehensive doctrine stems from his wanting to ground non-binding commitment, upon which interpersonal preference is conducted, on the solid foundation of binding commitment, i.e., justice. (Sen, 1990, p. 112). The search for such a solid foundation entails the conception of moral canons as stemming from a source separate from substantive preference (Sen, 1980). Such a separation may explain why the multiple-self view cannot ultimately delineate sentimental fools from rational sentimentalists.

7. Origin of sentimental fools

Given his multiple-self view, Sen fails to differentiate sentimental fools from rational sentimentalists. For instance, he misread Bernard Shaw's *The Devil's Disciple*. While Shaw exposes the motive of Richard Dudgeon, the protagonist of the play, as an exemplar of sentimental foolishness which characterizes moral dogmatists, Sen celebrates it:

> Commitment is, of course, closely connected with one's morals. But moral this question [sic] is in a very broad sense, covering a variety of influences from religious to political, from the ill-understood to the well argued. When, in Bernard Shaw's *The Devil's Disciple*, Judith Anderson interprets Richard Dudgeon's willingness to be hanged in place of her husband as arising from sympathy for him or love for her, Richard is adamant in his denial: 'What I did last night, I did in cold blood, caring not half so much for your husband, or for you as I do for myself. I had no motive and no interest: all I can tell you is that when it came to the point whether I would take my neck out of the noose and put another man's into it, I could not do it' [Sen, 1982, pp. 93–94].

To substantiate, the play takes place in New England in 1777 as the British troops try to quell the American rebellion. They went to Judith Anderson's house to arrest her husband, Reverend Anderson, on charges of treason. They mistook Richard as the Reverend. Richard chose not to reveal his identity not because he cares about the Reverend but rather because of a binding commitment. As confirmed by Shaw (1931, p. xxvi) in a section in the preface notably titled 'On Diabolinian Ethics,' Richard tells Judith 'the obvious truth that he would have done as much for any stranger that the law of his own nature, and no interest nor lust whatsoever, forbad him to cry out that the hangman's noose should be taken off his neck only to be put on another man's.'

Richard acquired the 'devil's disciple' title for making mockery of pious, but hypocritical Puritans. Richard revelled the persona of the iconoclast who does not lead a mendacious life. He desired to show that he is more moral than the false Puritans who surround him.[6] This desire blinded him as he came to realize later. To complete the sentence from which Sen takes his quote, Richard did not know why he did not reveal his identity, which would not endanger the Reverend's life. He confessed: 'I see myself as a fool for my pains' (Shaw, 1931, p. 52). Richard viewed his life as a failure: He failed to achieve some kind of moral

[6] For a general background on Shaw and psychoanalysis, see Arthur Nethercot (1969) and Sidney Albert (1971).

purity and saw the chance of dying in place of the Reverend as an opportunity to redeem himself. The opportunity blinded him from realizing that the declared purpose viz., saving the Reverend's life, can be achieved without endangering his own. Richard recognized his sentimental foolishness later when Reverend Anderson was able to save Richard's life without endangering his own. At the end, Richard stated that he 'behaved like a fool' [Ibid. p. 74]. Judith answered that he acted "like a hero." Richard replied: "much the same thing, perhaps." With some bitterness towards himself, however, Richard retracts his statement: "But no: if I had been any good, I should have done for you [Reverend Anderson] what you did for me, instead of making a vain sacrifice." So, Richard's sacrifice did not arise from rational sentimentality, where benefit is evaluated in light of its cost. At least for Shaw, Richard is a sentimental fool, a Puritan who treated non-binding commitment (care about the welfare of others) as binding, i.e., as oblivious to cost. It is not surprising that Sen, who failed to distinguish the two commitments in relation to cost, also failed to detect Richard's sentimental or anxiety-driven foolishness.

8. Conclusions

The paper is organized around four interrelated points. First, non-binding differs from binding commitment in many ways, especially how each relates to substantive interest. Second, the lumping of non-binding with binding commitments entails that non-binding commitment, similar to binding one, is contrary to interest. Third, such lumping leads, à la Sen, to a multiple-self view which radically separates commitment *per se* from interest. Fourth, such a view makes it impossible to distinguish sentimental fools from rational sentimentalists. To distinguish the two, we need to distinguish the two kinds of commitment and how each relates to interest, which need not necessarily invoke the unitary-self view.

While the paper employs Sen's preference/choice divergence thesis, it criticizes Sen's conception of commitment as radically separate from substantive interest. The paper argues that commitment should be considered as a special kind of preference. *While commitment is not reducible to interest à la unitary-self view, commitment is contingent on interest contrary to the multiple-self view.* The paper proposes two variants of this contingency. First, commitment is non-binding when the agent pursues forward-looking interest which would test his ability. Second, commitment is binding when the agent fulfills a past promise which does not concern the testing of ability. Thus, non-binding commitment, such as the pursuit of a career, and binding commitment, such as honesty, relate differently to substantive interest.

The paper shows how moral dogmatism or Puritanism arises when one treats non-binding principles as binding ones. While observance of the rules of justice is absolute, principles like urging higher self-fulfilling goals, kindness, loyalty, group solidarity, the aversion of divorce and abortion, and altruism are subject to deliberation in light of other competing demands. In his useful argument that law is not simply a system of absolute rules, Ronald Dworkin (1977) maintains that principles are wide-ranging and cannot be followed in an absolute manner. In fact, most principles involve conflicts between two goods or two claims, which demands one to compare and apply the cost-benefit calculations. This is not the case with rights. The payment of what one owes the grocer does not involve deciding among countervailing interests. It rather arises from a binding commitment which counters, at least in single-shot games, substantive interest.

The paper portrays a picture of the archeology of the self which is less simplistic than the standard one. However, the picture is a coherent one because it represents commitments as preferences and, in turn, relates them to substantive interest. While such a parsimonious representation conserves the aesthetic quality which typifies the unitary-self approach, it avoids a number of anomalies which faces the approach such as the origins of embarrassment and shame, the quest after justice even beyond what is justified by deterrence, the inexplicable decline of supply of internal organs once their market is legalized, and so on. Such anomalies would make standard economic theory vulnerable to attacks from other branches of social science armed with non-parsimonious, multiple-self conceptions.

Acknowledgements

The paper was supported by research fellowships from the Alexandre von Humboldt Foundation (Germany) and the Earhart Foundation and benefitted from the readings of Amartya Sen, Howard Margolis, Cass Sunstein, anonymous refrees, and especially Steven Joyce. The technical help of Carole Brown is acknowledged. The usual caveat applies.

References

Albert, Sidney P., 1971. Reflections on Shaw and psychoanalysis. Modern Drama 14 (2), 169–194.

Arrow, Kenneth J., 1997. Invaluable goods. Journal of Economic Literature 35 (2), 757–765.

Becker, Gary S., 1996. Accounting for Tastes. Harvard University Press, Cambridge, MA.

Davidson, D., 1980. How is Weakness of Will Possible? In: Davidson, D., Essays on Actions and Events, ch. 2. Oxford University Press, Oxford.

Dworkin, Ronald M., 1977. Is law a System of Rules? In: Dworkin R.M, (Ed.), The Philosophy of Law. Oxford University Press, Oxford.

Elster, Jon, 1983. Sour Grapes: Studies in the Subversion of Rationality. Cambridge University Press, Cambridge.

Elster, Jon (Ed.), 1986. The Multiple Self. Cambridge University Press, Cambridge.

Etzioni, Amitai, 1986. The case for a multiple-preference conception. Economics and Philosophy 2 (2), 159–183.

Frankfurt, Harry M., 1971. Freedom of the will and the concept of a person. Philosophical Review 68 (1), 5–20.

George, David, 1993. Does the market create preferred preferences?. Review of Social Economy 51 (3), 323–346.

George, David, 1998. Coping rationally with unpreferred preferences. Eastern Economic Journaling 24 (2), 181–194.

Hahn, Frank, 1982. One Some Difficulties of the Utilitarian Economist. In: Sen, Amatya, Williams, Bernard (Eds.), Utilitarianism and Beyond. Cambridge University Press, Cambridge, pp. 187–198.

Harsanyi, John C., 1955. Cardinal welfare, individualistic ethics, and international comparisons of preference. Journal of Political Economy 63, 309–321.

Harsanyi, John C., 1986. Individual Utilities and Utilitarian Ethics. In: Diekmann, Andreas, Mitter, Peter (Eds.), Paradoxical Effects of Social Behavior: Essays in Honor of Anatol Rapoport. Physica-Verlag, Heidelberg, pp. 1–12.

Harsanyi, John C., 1986. Rational Behavior and Bargaining Equilibrium in Games and Social Situations. Cambridge University Press, Cambridge.

Hausman, Daniel M., McPherson, Michael S., 1993. Taking ethics seriously: Economics and contemporary moral philosophy. Journal of Economic Literature 31 (2), 671–731.

Jeffrey, R.C., 1974. Preferences Among Preferences, The Journal of Philosophy 377–391.

Kavka, Gregory S., 1991. Is individual choice less problematic than collective choice?. Economics and Philosophy 7 (2), 143–165.
Khalil, Elias L., 1995. On the scope of economics: What is the question?. Finnish Economic Papers 8 (1), 38–53.
Khalil, Elias L., 1996. What is economic action? From Marshall and Robbins to Polanyi and Becker. Journal of the History of Economic Thought 18 (1), 13–36.
Khalil, Elias L., 1997a. Buridan's ass, risk, uncertainty, and self-competition: A theory of entrepreneurship. Kyklos 50 (2), 147–163.
Khalil, Elias L., 1997b. Etzioni versus Becker: Do moral sentiments differ from ordinary tastes?. De Economist 145 (4), 491–520.
Khalil, Elias L., 1999. Symbolic Products: Prestige, Pride and Identity Goods. Theory and Decision, in press.
Kuran, Timur, 1995. Private Truths, Public Lies: The Social Consequences of Preference Falsification. Harvard University Press, Cambrdige, MA.
Lewis, Helen Block, 1971. Shame and Guilt in Neurosis. International Universities Press, New York.
Margolis, Howard, 1982. Selfishness, Altruism and Rationality: A Theory of Social Choice, Cambridge University Press, Cambridge.
McPherson, Michael S., 1980. Liberty and the higher pleasures. In defense of mill. Economic Inquiry 8 (2), 314–320.
Mueller, D., 1986. Rational egoism vs. adaptive egoism. Public Choice 51, 3–23.
Nethercot, Arthur H., 1969. Bernard Shaw and psychoanalysis. Modern Drama 11 (4), 356–375.
Posner, Richard A., 1995. Aging and Old Age. University of Chicago Press, Chicago.
Radin, Margaret Jane, 1996. Contested Commodities. Harvard University Press, Cambridge, MA.
Rawls, John;, 1971. A Theory of Justice. Harvard University Press, Cambridge, MA.
Rawls, John, 1988. The Priority of right and ideas of the good. Philosophy and Public Affairs 17 (4), 251–276.
Schelling, Thomas C., 1984b. Choice and Consequence. Harvard University Press, Cambridge, MA.
Sen, Amartya K., 1977. Rational fools: A critique of the behavioral foundations of economic theory (Reprinted in Sen, 1982, ch. 4). Philosophy & Public Affairs) 6 (4), 317–344.
Sen, Amartya K., 1980-1981. Plural Preference. Proceedings of the Aristotelian Society, pp. 193–215.
Sen, Amartya K., 1982. Choice, Welfare and Measurement. Basil Blackwell, Oxford.
Sen, Amartya K., 1985. Goals, commitment, and identity. Journal of Law, Economics and Organization 1 (2), 341–355.
Sen, Amartya K., 1987. On Ethics and Economics. Basil Blackwell, Oxford.
Sen, Amartya K., 1990. Justice: Means versus freedoms. Philosophy and Public Affairs 19 (2), 111–121.
Sen, Amartya K., 1993. Internal consistency of choice. Econometrica 61 (3), 495–521.
Sen, Amartya K., 1995. Is the Idea of Purely Internal Consistency of Choice Bizarre? In: Altham, J.E.J., Harrison, Ross (Eds.), World, Mind and Ethics: Essays on the Ethical Philosophy of Bernard Williams. Cambridge University Press, Cambridge, pp. 19–31.
Sen, Amartya K., 1997. Maximization and the act of choice. Econometrica 65 (4), 745–779.
Shaw, Bernard,1931. Three Plays for Puritans: The Devil's Disciple, Caesar and Cleopatra, and Captain Brassbound's Conversion. Constable and Company, London, 1900.
Stewart, Hamish, 1992. Rationality and the market for human blood. Journal of Economic Behavior and Organization 19 (2), 125–143.
Sunstein, Cass R., 1997. Free Markets and Social Justice. Oxford University Press, Oxford.
Taylor, Charles, 1995. A most peculiar institution. In: Altham, J.E.J., Harrison, Ross (Eds.), World, Mind and Ethics: Essays on the Ethical Philosophy of Bernard Williams. Cambridge University Press, Cambridge, pp. 132–155.

Part III
Trust as Trait

[29]

KYKLOS, Vol. 39 – 1986 – Fasc. 2, 245–266

Evolution and Stability of Cooperation without Enforceable Contracts

ULRICH WITT*

I. INTRODUCTION

Many economic interactions are not based on codified entitlement rights or on exhaustive judicial arrangements, nevertheless, mutual expectations are met. Similarly, in many cases where a formal judicial basis does exist, but enforcement costs are prohibitive, an expected need to enforce the unwritten contract would discourage interaction from the outset. Such interactions, however, do often occur, in fact, they constitute a large fraction of the exchange activities run in the economic system. What then are the conditions that allow this to happen? Apparently, the *w*illingness of an individual to *a*dhere to a *n*on-codified *c*ommitment (somebody else's claim) – henceforth abbreviated *WANC* – plays a decisive role. As the problem is put here, *WANC* cannot be entirely explained by the availability of more or less cheap and effective legal remedies. So, what induces an economic agent to comply with obligations which he could safely default?

In the economic theory of property rights, *WANC* is often made an exogenous factor which varies parametrically with the institutional setting. Its impact is only indirectly considered when specifying a transaction cost vector. In the context of a static model such a view may be appropriate. By contrast, in a dynamic perspective a more detailed

* Universität Mannheim, BRD. – Earlier versions of this paper have been presented to the European Association of Law and Economics Workshop Berlin, June 1985, and to the Public Choice Society Annual Meeting Baltimore, USA 1986. I wish to thank J. IRVING-LESSMANN, M. KRAFT, R. SCHMACHTENBERG, and P. WEISE for helpful comments.

understanding is required. This is so because changes in *WANC* may be more rapid, but no less effective for the actually observed structure of interactions, than a change in the legal position through either judicial interpretation or new legislation.

The theoretical discussion in this paper starts in *Section II* from the prisoner's dilemma (pd) problem which seems appropriate for dealing with some of the features sketched above. The significance of this problem has been stressed in recent years in a growing body of literature concerned with the explanation of cooperative phenomena, norms, and 'institutions' in social and economic interaction [Rapoport and Chammah 1965, Taylor 1976, Ullmann-Margalit 1977, Schotter 1981, Axelrod 1984]. As is known from game-theoretic considerations, there are at least two possible explanations for *WANC*, i.e. cooperative instead of non-cooperative behavior, in the context of pd-models. First, *WANC* can be deduced from individual optimizing behavior if the respective interaction is to be repeated infinitely [Taylor 1976, Kurz 1977] or if the number of replications is finite but uncertain (and some additional conditions are met, see Kreps, Milgrom, Roberts, and Wilson [1982]). Second, *WANC* may be a rational attitude if non-cooperative behavior ('cheating') brings with it the threat of proscription or retaliatory activity. Anyway, the pay-off structure is actually transformed in such a way that the original pd disappears. In the first case, a super-game with different pay-offs results; in the second case, the original pd-game is extended into a threat game [see, e.g. Rapoport, Guyer, and Gordon 1976].

Contrary to the usual procedure, the present paper emphasizes the second approach (*Section III*) since it seems more akin to the quasi-contractual situation as well as to the evolutionary perspective adopted here. According to the latter, economic agents are alert, trying both to improve their lot actively and ingeniously and to avoid being harmed. In doing so, the agents are not entirely bound to simple, rather passive reactions whether derived from an optimization or not[1]. Man disposes of

1. The 'policing'-strategy [Schotter 1981] or some variant of the 'tit-for-tat'-rule [see Rapoport and Chammah 1965, 207–208] might be mentioned here. In biological evolution genetically programmed cooperative behavior following the 'tit-for-tat'-rule seems to have had a reproductional advantage. It can be observed therefore, even among most primitive organism [Axelrod 1984, ch. 5]. It seems highly plausible that man also has it in some form or other among his inherited, elementary behavior. But these parts of behavior beyond conscious control are not the whole story.

a large creative potential which may be utilized to influence other peoples' behavior. Preaching, indoctrination, threat – the various forms of human communication [see BOULDING 1977] – are at an agent's disposal if he tries to make others behave in a desired way. In order to understand the impact of these mechanisms a more detailed behavioral theory must be available, of course. The threat game-approach suggested here seems able to integrate relevant behavioral hypotheses on social learning, norm-internalization, cognitive consistency, etc. as sketched in *Section IV.*

Drawing on the behavioral foundations, *Section V* outlines a basic pattern in the evolution of economic cooperation which is built on non-codified claims. It is shown that there is a potential instability or, in a more dramatic diction, a 'critical mass' problem involved in these kinds of interaction. Some factors, established through correlated individual attitudes, exert a controlling influence. As long as they prevail, *WANC* is quite strictly maintained between interacting agents. Once the controlling factors are sufficiently weakened however, *WANC* is quickly lost and the corresponding interactions break down, everybody being worse off. The potential advantages of retaining or returning to *WANC* can lead to a spontaneous emergence of new subpopulations, internally restoring interactions based on non-codified claims. It seems, however, that, together with a reduced domain in which transactions occur, more formalized, enforceable, contractual behavior and costly resort to lawyers and the judicial system can as well evolve, since this is often more compatible with the individual behavioral patterns which led to the break-down of *WANC.* Some concluding remarks follow in *Section VI.*

II. WILLINGNESS TO ADHERE TO NON-CODIFIED CLAIMS AND THE PRISONER'S DILEMMA

Consider a presentation of the problem we are concerned with here as a prisoner's dilemma in the most elementary form of a 2×2 game in *Figure 1.* Two individuals agree upon, in unwritten assurances, to provide a mutual service, say. Each individual has to decide whether he will comply with his assurance before he knows what the other has decided. If both comply, both can gain compared to the situation where both violate the unwritten stipulations. If, however, one individual honors his obligations while the other does not, the defaulting individual appears to get something free and is thus even better off, while the other suffers a real loss. In order to illustrate the point, a perfectly symmetric situation is presupposed in *Figure 1* and, for convenience, numerical values are assigned to each individual's outcome given his own decision and that of the other individual[2].

Figure 1

Individual outcomes with respect to compliance with unwritten stipulations (upper right corner in the cells – individual 1; lower left corner – individual 2)

		Individual 1	
		comply (c)	don't comply (d)
Individual 2	comply (c)	N = 1 N = 1	B = 2 F = − 1
	don't comply (d)	F = -1 B = 2	T = 0 T = 0

It is easy to see that, according to this presentation, whatever individual 1 chooses to do, individual 2 gets a better outcome if he decides not to comply (d is a dominant strategy). Since the situation is symmetric, it is rational for both to choose d. This means, that non-cooperation is the only equilibrium point in this game. The quasi-contractual arrangement would not become effective although both individuals would find it desirable – hence the dilemma. The situation is in principle unchanged, if the two individuals make their decisions one after the other. Rational behavior does not here lead to *WANC*, the basis for cooperation. However, this result conflicts with evidence from specific experimental as well as from general empirical observations[3].

Apparently, real decision makers perceive or imagine institutional and environmental factors that are absent from the simple presentation

2. The only restriction which has to be satisfied in the arbitrary choice of these values is that they must not contradict the preference order on the outcomes as indicated by the capital letters B, N, T, F for best, next best, third, fourth respectively.

3. For instance, RAPOPORT [1980, p. 287] reports that in experiments in which test persons picked up 'from the street' were required to do the game in *Figure 1* in its one-shot version still 40% of them chose action c. Moreover, in their extensive experimentation with repeated pd-games RAPOPORT and CHAMMAH [1965] found mutually cooperative behaviour in the majority of cases under various conditions. For an empirical study on non-contractual arrangements prevailing in US-American business relations see MACAULAY [1963].

of the situation as a pd in *Figure 1*. These factors have a significant effect on the behavior making it differ from that predicted above. Any contract, written or unwritten, is embedded in a relational context [MACNEIL 1973/74]. First, information and workable decision heuristics are available from past experience. Second, and with respect to the following even more important, the future is a source of further options, a basic fact taken into account by the agents even if the future events are only imperfectly or wishfully anticipated.

One possible theoretical extension which tries to capture some features of the relational context is a dynamic version. The fact that many interactions of the above kind are actually ongoing ones has been expressed by several writers by the assumption that the game in *Figure 1* is repeated over again. In this case a super-game results in which, for any finite sequence of playings, the dominant strategy unfortunately remains choosing d all the time[4]. Only in some special cases, mentioned in the introduction, does a cooperative result obtain.

For the present problem of (quasi-)contractual agreements a dynamic version comes up against an additional problem. If a sequence of playings with simultaneously chosen actions d cannot be excluded, as in the case of a finite number of repetitions, a paradoxical situation ensues. Two agents continually attempt to reach contractual agreements though both patently violate them. This paradox can be avoided when the supergame is modified so as to recognize explicitly a prior choice stage. At this prior stage a decision is taken either to enter or not to enter a contractual arrangement with some particular person. The modified super-game, however, does not either allow cooperation to be deduced for a finite sequence of playings[5].

4. The proof is by backward induction. Let n be the number of replications. Then in the n-th playing it is rational to choose action d by analogy to the simple pd-model. Since this is known in the n-1-th playing, d is decided there too. The proposition follows by working back this way to the first playing.

5. Let the individual outcomes in one playing of the modified supergame be those in the extended matrix below where actions c and d are now conditional on the decision 'contracting accepted' (ca). To be specific, let us assume further that the decision 'contracting refused' (cr) is chosen if and only if the opponent has decided on d sometime previously. Then, an agent who is repeatedly involved in contractual arrangements and thus in the position of effectively choosing between c and d must have previously withstood the temptation to choose d. It follows that the modified supergame has a peculiar property.

Thus, the kind of dynamic extension of the elementary pd-game just discussed does not seem to lead to very satisfactory results if compared to the high frequency of empirically observed cooperative behavior even in interactions which are repeated a strongly limited number of times[6]. The relevance of the behavioral model underlying this approach seems questionable. Indeed, it will be argued below that a more satisfactory different model is one which takes into account several insights from

		Individual 1		
		c/ca	d/ca	cr
	c/ca	1 1	2 -1	0 0
Individual 2	d/ca	-1 2	0 0	0 0
	cr	0 0	0 0	0 0

The sequence of playings with the two agents involved establishes a process starting from the submatrix which consists of the four upper left cells. It remains there as long as both agents choose c, i.e. the upper left cell. Once d occurs, however, the process shifts in the next playing to the bottom line and the right column which represent absorbing states of the process. (Contracting is terminated between the two individuals.) In other words, as long as the process is in the upper left submatrix any single playing is a potential transition game which can basically be represented by a game like that in *Figure 1.* The supergame perspective only requires the rational agent to see the temporary extra gain from defaulting against the discounted future losses from his spoiled contractual capacity. As a consequence, in a single transition game the expected streams of outcomes from deciding c or d now can lead to pay-offs which are quite different from those of the one-shot game. Nevertheless, with single playing pay-offs as those in the extend matrix and a non-negative discount rate a t-th playing always exists in n playings, $t < n < \infty$, in which it is rational for both agents to choose d and the transition is induced. Since this is anticipated in a playing before the t-th one, it is rational to induce the transition then. Again working backwards to the first playing we end up with the non-cooperative result – d is chosen simultaneously and no further (quasi-)contracting occurs among the two agents.

6. *WANC* most certainly prevails if the interactions are based on kinship, friendship, or business ties, i.e. are continually, though, of course, not infinitely, pursued on the basis of almost perfect communication among all individuals involved. In this special case, the fear of losing reputation and trustworthiness due to own non-cooperative ('cheating') behavior being reported to everybody else is usually a disciplining factor, see TULLOCK [1985].

psychological research on learning and personality factors. Another theoretical extension of the elementary pd-game can provide a key which allows the argument to be developed further. To this we turn in the next section.

III. DOES THREAT BRING ABOUT COMPLIANCE?

In this section we will show that the elementary pd-game in *Figure 1* can be changed if an additional move is available which allows agents to respond to the opponent's choice post festum. This is a dynamic extension in a very rudimentary form. But it suffices to capture an important feature of reality: that in most cases people have the option of making trouble for someone who has upset them. This option, the basis of threat, can be utilized to affect the opponent's decision strategically ex ante. Hence, in this perspective, a transformation of the elementary pd-game to a threat-game is straightforward. As will become evident, however, in the present context the theoretical extension once initiated by that transformation must be carried even further and must call attention to the general behavioral foundation of the model.

In order to bring out the essential point let us assume a non-repetitive interaction. Two agents meet, e.g., and engage in a single transaction which requires them to deliver independently something of, say, a certain quality which can only be assessed some time after delivery. They do not explicitly set out the mutual obligations in a written contract but tacitly expect that the transaction will be correctly completed. Obviously, *WANC* is required on both sides if this expectation is to be met but, according to the elementary pd-game in the previous section, it will not result if the choices are rational. Now consider the situation where individual 1 decides on c in *Figure 1* – for whatever reason – whereas individual 2 chooses d. Agent 1 then gets the sucker's pay-off while agent 2 does well. The former is presumably upset by this and may well decide spontaneously to look out for retaliatory action. Since people are quite inventive, when motivated, in finding ways to get back at others, agent 1 will usually have the power to spoil things for agent 2. The problem is that agent 1 can achieve this effect only by himself suffering additional losses in time, energy, resources, etc.

The extended game in *Figure 2* reproduces these characteristics. Two actions are available in addition to action d. The agents can either take

Figure 2

Individual outcomes if retaliatory action is possible (threat game)

		Individual 1 r/c	n/c	d
	r/c	N=1 / N=1	N=1 / N=1	Q=-1 / L=-2
Individual 2	n/c	N=1 / N=1	N=1 / N=1	B=2 / F=-1
	d	L=-2 / Q=-1	F=-1 / B=2	T=0 / T=0

retaliatory measures when they have decided c and are fooled (r/c) or can refrain from doing so (n/c). Note that when one agent choses d and the other r/c the pay-off Q of the non-cooperative agents is made negative (–1) at the cost of increasing the retaliator's loss (to –2, the worst result at all i.e. $|L| > |F|$). On the other hand, the pay-off structure resulting from combinations of the actions d and n/c is the same as the one in *Figure 1.* (The elementary pd-game appears again in the lower right submatrix in *Figure 2.*)

An inspection of the actions available to the individuals in the extended game shows that there is no longer a clear-cut solution such as the equilibrium in pure strategies in the elementary pd-game. But action n/c weakly dominates action r/c. So, if it turns out that agent 1 decided c while agent 2 chose d, the decision to retaliate would clearly contradict the rationality principle. It is a puzzling fact, at least to the economist, that despite this irrationality verdict it can quite commonly be observed that people are motivated to take revenge on cheats[7].

7. One could speculate that this kind of sponaneous, yet 'irrational', response is a part of our genetically programmed, inherited reaction patterns. TRIVERS [1971], for instance, argues that what he calls 'reciprocal altruism' (identical to cooperative action in the pd) is enforced by 'moral aggression', a mainly genetically determined response behaviour. Since cooperation certainly has increased the survival fitness in those early stages of the human phylogenesis in which a strong selection pressure prevailed, any such aggressive behavior favouring actual cooperation could have had a selectional advantage and could thus have been genetically fixed. In order to explain the process of propagation this reasoning is not sufficient, however. The aggressive,

The extended game can also, of course, be given an ex ante interpretation. This does not resolve the puzzle but might permit discussion about it to be postponed. In fact, there are two ex ante interpretations of the game in *Figure 2.* According to one the dominated action r/c might be omitted altogether. Then we are back in the original pd with the non-cooperative outcome. Alternatively action r/c can be included and a special form of a threat game postulated (for a general definition see RAPOPORT, GUYER, and GORDON [1976, 21]). Imagine agent 1 announces that he is definitely committing himself to action r/c regardless of what agent 2 decides. If agent 2 believes this announcement and inspects the outcomes available to him within the first column, he cannot do better than choosing c (in which case whether either agent 1 or 2 would actually decide r/c or n/c will not be revealed). The threat of retaliation will have succeeded. Moreover, in this interpretation the mutually cooperative behavior, i.e. *WANC*, so often observed, can be deduced.

Unfortunately, the threat game-interpretation has two serious defects. The first is general and is connected with the credibility of the self - commitment to r/c. Why should agent 2 be convinced of the threat in view of the excessive cost this would impose on his opponent if 2 were to choose d? The second defect is specific to the context of unwritten, quasi-contractual cooperation based on the tacit expectation that no sanctions will be necessary. How can these conditions be brought into line with the idea of threat? If threat had been deemed necessary, enforceable written contracts with clearly defined remedies would have been available.

Now, realize that both defects would be eliminated if the seemingly puzzling, spontaneous impulse to retaliate, mentioned above, is indeed so common that a sufficiently high probability of its occurrence is tacitly presupposed by the interacting individuals. In that case, however, the model based on the threat-game interpretation of *Figure 2* would appear somewhat inconsistent. In the context of the otherwise game-theoretic reasoning based on the rationality concept one essential argument would have to be stated by recourse on an irrational act, the decision to retaliate. If the rationality assumption were generally applied the threat

retaliatory response consumes resources which might otherwise be used for reproductive activities. Hence it entails a genetic disadvantage to the single individual. For a more detailed discussion of this complex see WITT [1985].

of action r/c, adopted with a high frequency, would be beneficial to all but would not occur because of the individually incurred costs of retaliation – something like a public good problem. Thus, an explanation of *WANC* and, in turn, of the widespread practice of unwritten contractual arrangements, which draws on a structure of pay-offs like that in *Figure 2*, has to be given a more elaborated behavioral foundation. The next step to be taken now is therefore a short digression into those hypotheses on empirical regularities in human behavior which seem to be relevant to the present problem.

IV. LEARNING, INTERNALIZED STANDARDS OF CONDUCT, AND THE FREQUENCY ASPECT

According to social learning theory [BANDURA 1973], development and modification of human – economic as well as other – behavior is subject mainly to two principles[8]. On the one hand, the frequency and strength of reinforcement of a chosen action influences the probability of the particular action being chosen again in a similar situation. Positively or negatively reinforcing events can be success and failure, rewarding and punishing reactions from other persons (the social environment), and, in certain cases, also self-corroboration. This kind of learning, i.e. alteration of behavior, follows essentially the subconscious conditioning known from simple stimulus-response patterns. On the other hand, there is cognitive learning, which can intervene into the basic process just mentioned and override its results. This kind of learning is led by insight but also by observation and imitation of 'social models', that is, the behavior of other individuals.

With respect to some elementary pattern of conduct like *WANC* (i.e. reliability) this theory implies that such a pattern can systematically be

8. In terms of the behavioral model used in micro-economics based on the concepts of an individual preference order on imaginable actions, a constrained set of feasible actions and the maximum choice rule (optimization hypothesis) the following hypotheses can be interpreted as an empirically confirmed, psychological, theory of preference formation and change, for a detailed discussion see WITT [1986, ch. III].

elicited by positive reinforcement as well as by repeated presentation and recommendation of credible 'social models' (e.g. by preaching, indoctrination, advertising, etc.). The social learning process in which an individual adopts the respective standards from his/her environment starts in his/her childhood, but it is not restricted to it. Rather it constitutes an ongoing though decelerating process. Notice that the result of the individual learning process in a certain time span is strongly dependent on the state of the individual's environment in that time span, i.e. on the standards of conduct held by the other individuals. This follows from the fact that reinforcement is determined by the environmental reaction according to the respective standards as well as from the fact that the models of standards of conduct currently practiced are what is offered for adoption by the environment.

The process of adoption sketched this way can also be described as one of habitualization. The individual usually 'internalizes' successful patterns of conduct by using them continually over time. That is, he/she starts to reproduce the underlying standards as normative statements addressed to him-/herself as well as to others (see Opp [1982] for an instructive description). The striving for cognitive consistency then requires him/her to avoid opportunistic behavior, i.e. choices contradicting the adopted standard[9]. Thus, if an individual has, under educational pressure, adopted a cooperative, reliable, pattern of conduct, *WANC* will most probably be displayed by him/her in the situations we are concerned with here. Typically, such an individual will also react aggressively if others, who are expected or claim to conform to the same standard, violate it.

To summarize, the roughly sketched behavioral hypotheses predict that types of behavior will emerge and gradually change in complex, interactive learning processes in a population. These types can be distinguished by their standards of conduct. Due to the natural variance in personality factors and to differences in the personal life history there will usually be several types. This result will certainly carry over to our problem. Thus, beyond the narrow concept of rationality, different, but

9. For a short discussion of what happens if a conflict cannot be avoided see Schlicht [1984].

still predictable, ways of reacting to the situation represented in *Figure 2* should empirically be expected[10].

For the purpose of demonstration the most simple case with only two types will be considered in what follows. Assume that according to current moral standards most individuals in the relevant population at a given point in time have been educated to behave cooperatively, reliably, i.e. in a non-opportunistic way. Let us denote these people as being 'social' type S, who choose action r/c in *Figure 2* as an attitude. Because of the natural variance in character, temper, and other inherited personal dispositions and because of different lessons drawn from the observation of different 'social models', there are also individuals who adopt a deviant pattern of conduct, being out for their own advantage. We denote these people as being 'opportunistic' type P, who decide rationally in the original sense on the actions available in the threat game.

In the newly gained perspective, the previous orientation towards two isolated individuals in a single game is no longer exhaustive. Attention must also be paid to the population of individuals and the frequencies with which the identified behavioral types are present there. Lacking further information, we can assume, as a first approximation, that in an arbitrarily selected, single interaction (game) any two individuals from the population will be equally likely to meet. Whether in this interaction *WANC* will prevail and, hence, the agreement be mutually complied with depends, under these conditions, on the frequencies of the behavioral types in the population. So too, does the frequency with which *WANC* occurs in a set of independent interactions (i.e. interactions not repeatedly done, the same individuals being involved).

Moreover, the frequency aspect becomes decisive with respect to the dynamics of *WANC* and the evolution of the contractual behavior.

10. For a different argument with the same result see Heiner [1983]. Indeed, the identification and characterization of different empirical types of players is one of the major achievements of the systematic experimental investigation of 2×2 games [Rapoport 1980, 288]. The apparent conflict with the rationality assumption (in the sense of choosing the most preferred feasible action in *Figure 2*) could be 'resolved' by an adequate specification of what the pay-offs in *Figures 1* and *2* express: No doubt, it is possible to rationalize any of the different empirically observed types of behavior as optimizing behavior, if appropriate arguments are added to the utility function to represent a preference for cooperativeness, retaliation etc. However, such an operation would not create any new insights.

According to the suggested social learning process model, the frequencies of the behavioral types can systematically change with their relative success and their recommendation as main causes, both of which are frequency – dependent. This will affect *WANC*. For instance, an S-type individual entering a population of P-individuals will suffer heavy losses without really being able to change conditions. Thus he/she will hardly qualify as a successful 'social mode'. Rather he/she will learn to abandon his/her pattern of conduct (or leave the population) so that *WANC* cannot gain foothold. On the other side, a limited number of P-individuals in a population of S-individuals will not have much reason to call the tacitly expected threat in question. If he/she nevertheless is going to 'test' the credibility of his/her expectation there is a high probability that he/she will be punished. Hence there is a disincentive for him/her to deviate from displaying *WANC*. If he/she is mostly inclined to choose action n/c, the impression that there are mostly cooperative individuals in the population will be reinforced. An unstable situation might, however, turn up in between these polar cases. Thus, a new evolutionary dimension comes in here in this approach to explaining compliance to informal obligations. A simple mathematical model can help to clarify some implications.

V. STABILITY AND CHANGE IN (QUASI-)CONTRACTUAL BEHAVIOR – AN EVOLUTIONARY PERSPECTIVE

Consider a large population of individuals potentially interacting with each other in a given period of time t. Interactions effectively taking place are assumed to challenge *WANC* as described earlier. At most, one interaction is carried out per individual in t and two individuals are always involved. For convenience, it is assumed that any two in the population have the same chance of meeting. Once confronted with each other, the agents face the problem described by the game in *Figure 2*. In order to simplify the exposition let the pay-offs in each game be the same and given in monetary units like those denoted in *Figure 2*. Now suppose there are two types of behavior in the population, a P-type and an S-type (see the previous section). The respective relative frequencies are p_t, $0 \leq p_t \leq 1$, and $s_t = 1 - p_t$. Under these assumptions, the average share of effective interactions in t in which individuals of type P (of type S) meet can be determined as p_t^2 (as s_t^2). The average share of mixed interactions is $1 - p_t^2 - s_t^2$. It will be assumed that the agents do not know ex ante which type the individual they are involved with is nor what the mean shares p_t and s_t are.

Individuals of type P maximize their utility which is supposed to be a linear function of their pay-offs. We assume that they decide action n/c with a frequency reflecting how credible they believe the tacit threat of retaliation is. If they feel sure of meeting a S-type individual, they cannot do better than choose n/c; if not, the best choice depends on what they believe their opponent's assessment of them might be. This is a somewhat undetermined situation. In order to proceed further, it is assumed here that P-type individuals (i) suspect each other of being non-cooperative, and (ii) with an aggregate share p_t happen to have guessed that they are involved with a P-type opponent. Hence, without being aware of this fact[11], they have decided d with a relative frequency p_t and n/c with the tail frequency. Since, by definition, S-type individuals always choose action r/c, the assumptions introduced up to now allow us to deduce the relative frequency w of *WANC* being displayed (i.e. actions r/c *and* n/c) as

$$w_t = s_t^2 + 2p_t s_t^2 + p_t^2 s_t^2 = 1 - 2p_t^2 + p_t^4 \qquad (1)$$

Following the theory sketched in the previous section, the individuals behave according to the standard of conduct they have adopted. But, in the course of time, it is possible for the adopted standard to change. In the simple framework of only two behavioral types, any such alterations can, of course, only be expressed as a transition from the P-type to the S-type and vica versa. Correspondingly, we have to cast here the social learning process theory in terms of adequate transition hypotheses, which determine how p_t and s_t change from period to period if interactions are carried out according to the above assumptions. Since the relative shares of the two types add up to one, only one transition function will completely describe the dynamics of the population change.

11. This follows from the assumption that the true values of p_t and s_t are not known. Note that if they were known the optimal decision would be strictly bimodal: d if $r > 2/3$, n/c otherwise (given the pay-offs in *Figure 2*).

COOPERATION WITHOUT ENFORCEABLE CONTRACTS

In the social learning process model two forces can bring about behavioral changes. On the one hand there is the observation of a 'social model', a common pattern of conduct supported by preaching, recommendation, etc., that can induce people to adopt (perhaps in a long, gradual process) that pattern. On the other hand, success and failure achieved by acting according to the adopted standard play a role. The latter force works essentially as described by conditioning models: success reinforces, failure weakens the tendency to maintain the currently adopted standard. Let us turn to the first effect. In a simple way it can be described by the transition function.

$$p_t = p_{t-1} + (1 - w_{t-1})(1 - p_{t-1}) - w_{t-1}p_{t-1} \tag{2}$$

The last term on the right hand side of (2) represents the 'outflux', i.e. individuals switching from P-type to S-type behavior. In accordance with the theory, this term depends on the relative frequency with which *WANC*, the 'social model' authoritative for S-type behavior, has been corroborated in the current interactions. Note that 'disguised' P-type individuals (having chosen n/c) contribute to the corroboration effect. Furthermore, the size of the pool which individuals can leave is decisive here. The second term on the right hand side of (2) represent the 'influx' from S-type to P-type behavior occurring at the same time, i.e. the share of individuals who have abandonded their 'social' standard of conduct under the influence of the alternative 'model'. Inserting (1) into (2) we get

$$p_t = 2p_{t-1}^2 - p_{t-1}^4 \tag{3}$$

The second effect can most simply be modeled by drawing on the average pay-offs realized by the two types of behavior. Clearly, they are frequency dependent. If we denote the various pay-offs by capital letters as in *Figure 2*, then the average pay-off of the S-types is

$$\pi_t^s = N - Np_t - (N - L)p_t^2 + (N - L)p_t^3 \tag{4}$$

The average pay-off of the P-types is respectively

$$\pi_t^P = Np_t - (N - Q)p_t^2 + (B + F - N - Q)p_t^3 - (B + F - N - T)p_t^4 \tag{5}$$

Furthermore, let us introduce as a measure for the relative success of the P-types

$$u_t \begin{cases} = \dfrac{\pi_t^P}{\pi_t^s + \pi_t^P} & \text{for } \pi_t^P \geq 0, \pi_t^s \geq 0 \\ = 1 & \text{for } \pi_t^P \geq 0, \pi_t^s < 0 \\ = 0 & \text{for } \pi_t^P < 0, \pi_t^s \geq 0 \\ = \dfrac{\pi_t^s}{\pi_t^s + \pi_t^P} & \text{for } \pi_t^P < 0, \pi_t^s < 0. \end{cases} \quad (6)$$

Analogously to (2), the influx into the P-type population can then be made dependent on the product of the relative success of the P-types and the relative size of the S-type group (indicating how many people would be able to switch at all if dissatisfied). By similar reasoning we get the outflux form the P-type population into the S-type group by the product of the tails. Thus,

$$p_t = p_{t-1} + u_{t-1}(1 - p_{t-1}) - (1 - u_{t-1})\, p_{t-1} \quad (7)$$

is the corresponding transition function for the second effect. After some transformations using (4), (5) and (6) the function yields for the numerical specification given in *Figure 2*

$$p_t \begin{cases} = \dfrac{p_{t-1} - 2p_{t-1}^2 + p_{t-1}^3}{1 - 5p_{t-1}^2 + 4p_{t-1}^3} & \text{for } p_{t-1} \leq \dfrac{1}{\sqrt{3}} \\ = 1 & \text{otherwise.} \end{cases} \quad (8)$$

The graphs of functions (3) and (8) are plotted in *Figure 3*. With respect to the impact of 'social model'-learning, (3) displays an unstable equilibrium in $p^* = (\sqrt{5}-1)/2 \simeq 0.618$ in *Figure 3*. This means that once p exeeds p* the S-type will, according to this hypothesis, be driven out of the population. Below p* the P-type cannot gain foothold as indicated exemplarily by the one stepped time-path drawn in *Figure 3*. Thus, in p* the P-type subpopulation has reached a 'critical mass'. Concerning reinforcement learning (8) shows a similar phenomenon. However, the unstable equilibrium $p^{**} = 0.5 < p^*$. (The higher p* value is due to the fact that, because of their expectations, some 'disguised' P-type individuals are induced to behave socially thus corroborating the 'social model'.) Moreover, once p** is exceeded, the P-type will propagate very quickly (one possible time path has been drawn). This is due to the quickly increasing retaliation costs making action r/c a rather selfdefeating strategy.

The combined effect of the two learning hypotheses depends on how sensitive the population is on average to custom, preaching, indoctrina-

Figure 3

Graphs of the transition functions (3) and (8)

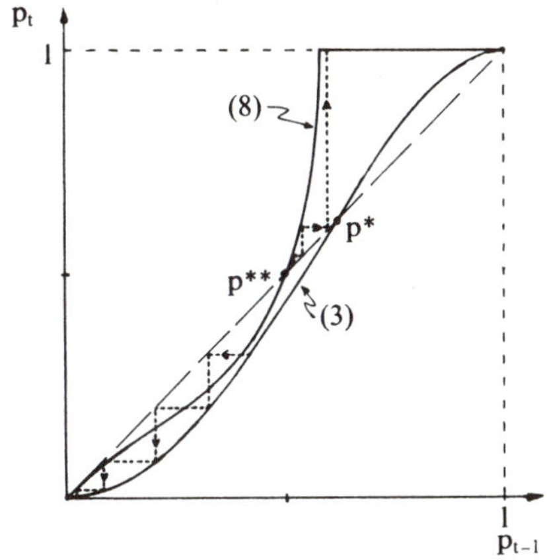

tion, etc. If this can be expressed by a sociality parameter α, varying from o (no orientation at all towards prevailing custom) to 1 (exclusive orientation on what is recommended by common practice) (2) and (7) yield the combined transition hypothesis

$$p_t = p_{t-1} + \alpha[(1 - w_{t-1})(1 - p_{t-1}) - w_{t-1}p_{t-1}] \\ + (1 - \alpha)[u_{t-1}(1 - p_{t-1}) - (1 - u_{t-1})p_{t-1}]. \tag{9}$$

Using the numerical specification given in *Figure 2* the graph of (9) is situated between those of (3) and (8) in *Figure 3*, the two limiting cases.

Now we are able to discuss the evolution of the patterns of conduct in the population, i.e. towards *WANC*, as implied by the social learning process model. Assume as an initial condition an average frequency $p_t = 0$[12]. Since the actual values may be subject to random disturbances and effects from historical events it can happen, however, that the realization $P_0 > 0$, e.g., because of an occasional variation in the size of the potentially interacting population. Assume $\alpha = 1$ so that (3) is valid. Then a large range exists within which the S-type remains predominant. As long as $P_0 \leq p^*$ *WANC* will not be endangered. If $\alpha = 0$, on the other

12. In an alternative scenario we can start from an unstable equilibrium being reached in the composition of P- and S-types in the population. Then, very small random fluctuations in the composition can induce drastically differing evolutions driving either the S- or the P-type out of the population.

side (i.e. if it is the pecuniary success which matters for the average adoption of behavioral patterns), then the range of tolerance is smaller. This is even more so, if either L increases or Q decreases absolutely or both happen, since, in that case, the graph of (8) becomes steeper, and p** shifts to the left[13].

Hence, the stronger the 'materialistic' orientation of the population (the smaller α) and the lower the comparative efficiency of one monetary unit sacrificed for retaliatory actions, the more to the left the critical mass point and the higher the probability of a fluctuation exceeding the compensating power of the S-type population so that the process capsizes. If this happens *WANC* dies out in the population. The informal, (quasi-) contractual interactions break down. This process, once get started, is irreversible, except that systematic forces are activated which shift p_t back beyond the critical mass point[14]. Since (9) is formulated in average frequencies, one such systematic force may be one leading to a strong reduction of the population combined with an effective discrimination against P-type individuals, that means, the emergence of relatively homogenous S-type subpopulations.

VI. CONCLUSIONS

In the introduction the question was how *WANC* and hence (quasi-) contractual cooperation can come about as a widespread mode of

13. From equations (4) to (7) it follows that the equilibrium condition in general terms is

$$p = \frac{Np - (N-Q)p^2 + (B+F-N-Q)p^3 - (B+F-N-T)p^4}{N - (2N-L-Q)p^2 + (B+F-L-Q)p^3 - (B+F-N-T)p^4}$$

provided

$$\pi_t^P \geq 0, \pi_t^s \geq 0$$

Inserting all parameter values given in *Figure 2* except those for L and Q a quadratic equation results for which a root p**, $0 < p^{**} < 1$, can be determined as

$$p^{**} = \frac{2-2Q}{2-2Q-2L}$$

Since $Q < 0$, $L < 0$ this yields $dp^{**}/dQ < 0$ and $dp^{**}/dL > 0$ as asserted.

14. Of course, a situation $p_t = 1$, once established, could also be overcome by fluctuations in the reverse direction since an analogous reasoning, starting from $s_t = 0$ as an inital condition, is possible.

interaction in view of the fact that tacit obligations can easily be defaulted if it is advantageous to do so. To answer the question we proceeded in three steps. First, we gave the conflict a more instructive representation in game-theoretic terms and discussed several game variants. Second, we departed from the narrow, static, behavioral background of the rationality concept in game theory. A model of a social learning process, drawing on empirically confirmed hypotheses from neighboring disciplines was suggested. To demonstrate some of its implications, the most simple case of two different attitudes towards *WANC*, which could result from such a process, was discussed. Third, the inherent dynamics of such an approach were made explicit in a model of a frequency dependent evolution of *WANC* and the corresponding behavior.

A general answer can now be given on this basis as follows. Provided moral standards and corresponding 'social models', e.g. in education, which make people adopt a cooperative, reliable, standard of conduct with a high frequency prevail and provided further, that 'moral aggression' is displayed against those who violate this standard, then *WANC* and the corresponding contractual practices can gain widespread use in a population of interacting agents and these will be self-reinforcing. However, such a situation is sensitive to systematic shifts in the acceptance of moral standards as well as to non-systematic (random) shifts in the composition of the population. Once the frequency of individuals who have adopted a cooperative attitude falls below a critical level, the increasingly destructive losses they have to bear in the interactions with defaulting individuals will induce them to reorient themselves. Moreover, this will detract from the cooperative attitude as a worth-while 'social model'. This, in turn, will decrease the frequency still further until *WANC* is driven out of the population.

Once the turn-over gets started contractual practices have to change. Written contracts (incurring higher transaction costs) which include the specification of legal remedies etc. have to be substituted for the former quasi-contractual arrangements. Because of the higher transaction costs there is an incentive for cooperative individuals who are still present in the population to separate out and form a homogenous subpopulation. For this to succeed it must be possible, of course, to discriminate against 'cheaters' who have an even greater incentive to insinuate themselves into the subpopulation. This is difficult to achieve. High entrance fees

ULRICH WITT

(requiring repeated interactions), pledges, or intensive moral suasion on the basis of group-specific religious or ideological practices may be devices used to overcome the problem. It is possible, however, that the social learning process induces an abandonment of *WANC* much more quickly than such a subpopulation can be established. In that case an incentive structure emerges which makes the dilemma of costly contractual practices unavoidable.

As it stands, the answer sketched here builds on a critical component: the prevalence of certain moral standards and 'social models'. How these come about is not explained, yet it is not outside the scope of the present theory. One possible way of reasoning with respect to this problem is outlined in HAYEK [1967], another in OPP [1982]. But even without further extensions in this direction, the approach presented in this paper is more generally applicable. In particular, it could be applied to the quite common problem in many domains of economics of determining the aggregate effect of a changing composition in the prevailing types of behavior. A phenomenon which, because of its very similar structure [see, e.g. BUCHANAN 1975, 64–68], might be a good candidate for a direct transfer is the consent to and the change of constitutional orders.

REFERENCES

Axelrod, R.: *The Evolution of Cooperation,* New York: Basic Books, 1984.

BANDURA, A.: *Social Learning Theory,* Englewood Cliffs: Prentice-Hall, 1973.

BOULDING, K. E.: 'Prices and Other Institutions', *Journal of Economic Issues,* Vol. 11 (1977), 809–821.

BUCHANAN, J.: *The Limits of Liberty: Between Anarchy and Leviathan,* Chicago, University of Chicago Press, 1975.

HAYEK, F. A.: 'Notes on the Evolution of Systems of Rules of Conduct', in: F. A. HAYEK, *Studies in Philosophy, Politics and Economics,* London: Kegan Paul, 1967, 66–81.

HEINER, R. A.: 'The Origin of Predictable Behavior', *American Economic Review,* Vol. 73 (1983), 560–595.

KREPS, D. M.; MILGROM, P.; ROBERTS, J. and WILSON, R.: 'Rational Cooperation in the Finitely Repeated Prisoners' Dilemma', *Journal of Economic Theory,* Vol. 27 (1982), 245–252.

KURZ, M.: 'Altruistic Equilibrium', in: B. BALASSA and R. NELSON (eds.): *Economic Progress, Private Values, and Public Policy: Essays in Honor of William Fellner,* Amsterdam: North-Holland, 1977, 177–20.

COOPERATION WITHOUT ENFORCEABLE CONTRACTS

MACAULAY, S.: 'Non-Contractual Relations in Business: A Preliminary Study', *American Sociological Review*, Vol. 28 (1963), 55–67.

MACNEIL, I. R.: 'The Many Futures of Contracts', *Southern California Law Review*, Vol. 47 (1973/74), 691–816.

OPP, K. D.: 'The Evolutionary Emergence of Norms', *British Journal of Social Psychology*, Vol. 21 (1982), 139–149.

RAPOPORT, A.: *Mathematische Methoden in den Sozialwissenschaften* (Mathematical Methods in Social Sciences), Würzburg: Physica-Verlag 1980.

RAPOPORT, A. and CHAMMAH, A. M.: *Prisoner's Dilemma*, Ann Arbor: University of Michigan Press, 1965.

RAPOPORT, A.; GUYER, M. J. and GORDON, O. G.: *The 2×2 Game*, Ann Arbor: University of Michigan Press, 1976.

SCHLICHT, E.: 'Cognitive Dissonance in Economics', in: H. TODT (ed.): *Normengeleitetes Verhalten in den Sozialwissenschaften*, Berlin: Duncker & Humblot 1984, 61–81.

SCHOTTER, A.: *The Economic Theory of Social Institutions*, Cambridge: Cambridge University Press, 1981.

TAYLOR, M.: *Anarchy and Cooperation*, London: J. Wiley & Sons, 1976.

TIVERS, R. L.: 'The Evolution of Reciprocal Altruism', *Quarterly Review of Biology*, Vol. 46 (1971), 35–57.

TULLOCK, G.: 'Adam Smith and the Prisoners' Dilemma', *Quarterly Journal of Economics*, Vol. 100 (1985).

ULLMANN-MARGALIT, E.: *The Emergence of Norms*, New York: Oxford University Press, 1978.

WITT, U.: 'Economic Behavior and Biological Evolution – Some Remarks on the Sociobiology Debate', *Zeitschrift für die gesamte Staatswissenschaft*, (Journal of Institutional and Theoretical Economics), Vol. 141 (1985), 365–389.

WITT, U.: *Individualistische Grundlagen der Evolutorischen Ökonomik* (Individualistic Foundations of Evolutionary Economics), Tübingen: Mohr, 1986.

ZUSAMMENFASSUNG

Ökonomische Transaktionen können oft nicht auf der Basis erschöpfender rechtlicher Regelungen und vereinbarter Zwangsmittel abgewickelt werden. Es ist dann nicht auszuschliessen, dass eine Seite ihre Verpflichtungen unzulänglich erfüllt, während die andere sie in vollem Umfang leistet. Eine ähnliche Situation kann auftreten, wenn formelle rechtliche Ansprüche zwar bestehen, sich aber wegen prohibitiver Durchsetzungskosten nicht realisieren lassen. Der Logik des Gefangenen-Dilemmas folgend sind in solchen Situationen regelmässig Anreize zu einem nicht oder nicht vollständigen Erfüllen von Vereinbarungen zu erwarten. Dennoch finden Transaktionen häufig auf einer scheinbar so wenig gesicherten Basis statt, ohne dass es zu einer Verletzung der wechselseitigen Verpflichtungen kommt. Zur Erklärung dieses empirischen Phänomens wird eine Theorie des häufigkeitsabhängigen Lernverhaltens vorgeschlagen, das in verschiedenen Gruppen der interagierenden Individuen auftritt. Der Ansatz lässt sich verallgemeinern, um die Bedingungen zu klären, unter denen in einem evolutorischen Prozess eine Vielzahl gesellschaftlicher Gefangenen-Dilemma-Situationen vermieden wird.

SUMMARY

Strict legal arrangements and sanctions against default are frequently absent in economic transactions. Even where such arrangements exist, enforcement costs are often prohibitive. Prisoner's dilemma logic shows that in these situations the incentive to default is strong. Nevertheless, although such transactions are common, default is rather rare. To explain this a theory of frequency dependent learning behaviour within groups of interacting agents is suggested. The approach can be generalized to indicate conditions under which many societal prisoner's dilemma situations can be prevented in the course of an evolutionary process.

RÉSUMÉ

Les dispositions et les sanctions légales contre le manquement aux engagements sont fréquemment absentes dans les transactions économiques. Même lorsque ces dispositions existent, les coûts de leur mise en application sont souvent prohibitifs. La logique du dilemme du prisonnier montre que, dans ces situations, il existe une forte incitation au non-respect des engagements. Cependant, bien que ces transactions soient fréquentes, le manquement aux engagements est plutôt rare. Pour expliquer ceci, l'auteur suggère de recourir à la théorie du comportement de la fréquence d'apprentissage du défenseur à l'intérieur de groupes d'agents réagissant réciproquement. Cette approche peut se généraliser pour déterminer les conditions dans lesquelles on peut empêcher le développement de bien des situations sociales du dilemme du prisonnier.

[30]

German Economic Review 1(1): 83–110

Co-evolution of Preferences and Information in Simple Games of Trust

Werner Güth
Humboldt University, Berlin

Hartmut Kliemt
Gerhard-Mercator University, GH, Duisburg

Bezalel Peleg
Hebrew University of Jerusalem and Copenhagen Business School

Abstract. *In standard rational choice modelling decisions are made according to given information and preferences. In the model presented here the 'information technology' of individual decision-makers as well as their preferences evolve in a dynamic process. In this process decisions are made rationally by players who differ in their informational as well as in their preference type. Relative success of alternative decisions feeds back on the type composition of the population which in turn influences rational decision-making. An indirect evolutionary analysis of an elementary yet important basic game of trust shows that under certain parameter constellations the population dynamics of the evolutionary process specify a unique completely mixed rest point. However, as opposed to previous studies of preference formation in the game of trust there is no convergence to but only circumventing the rest point if the informational status of individuals evolves rather than being chosen strategically.*

1. INTRODUCTION

In standard rational choice modelling, decision-makers decide completely opportunistically in view of the anticipated causal consequences of each of their decisions taken separately. In standard models of evolutionary game theory, choices are treated as if being determined by a program or a disposition specifying how to choose in each of a whole class of decision situations. Though models that focus on either of the two extremes have provided valuable insights, in the real world human decision-making is located somewhere between the extremes on which standard models focus. It is influenced by the expected future and by the experienced past. Therefore, in our efforts to model and understand social behavior we should not confine ourselves to isolating one of these factors by abstracting away the other one but rather try to reach the middle ground between the traditional extreme modelling assumptions. We feel that an indirect evolutionary approach is particularly well suited for this task.

Our subsequent discussion of the co-evolution of preferences and information in a simple game of trust will integrate 'expectational pull' and 'adaptive push' in a single model. In previous indirect evolutionary analyses of trust problems (see Güth and Kliemt, 1995) we focused on the evolution of preferences while assuming that players could strategically decide about the acquisition of costly information. As opposed to that we shall now treat the emergence of information conditions in basic trust situations as endogenous to the evolutionary process. More specifically, in Section 2 we lay out our basic trust game and the background idea of the indirect evolutionary approach. In Section 3 we consider two extreme information conditions and solve the basic games for both. In one of the two polar extremes players who must decide on whether to trust or not to trust are completely uninformed about their co-player's type. In the other polar case they are completely informed in that regard. In the next section, 4, it is described how players' preferences to behave trustworthily and their ability to detect that disposition in others may evolve in a co-evolutionary process. Players are either completely informed I-types whose detection technology truthfully reveals their co-player's type with complete reliability at cost C or they are totally uninformed U-types whose detection technology is costless but so unreliable that they are left completely in the dark about their co-player's type. Section 5 considers whether under the extreme information conditions associated with different player types there are any population compositions which are dynamically stable along both the preference and the information dimension. Section 6 generalizes the argument to the intermediate case in which a 'C, μ' information technology providing merely a stochastic signal about the co-player's type is available at cost $C > 0$. Section 7 puts our results into perspective and relates them to other approaches as pursued either by ourselves or others.

2. THE TRUST PREDICAMENT

Owing to the fact that human decision-makers are endowed with the distinctly human faculty to make opportunistically rational choices social interaction is soaked with problems of trust. Mutually advantageous forms of cooperation may be closed off since they require that one partner move first without a guarantee that the other(s) will reciprocate. Thus the 'trust predicament' emerges.

The essentials of interaction situations that can give rise to problems of trust are represented in Figure 1. The tree of Figure 1 should not be misinterpreted as

Preference and Information in Simple Games of Trust

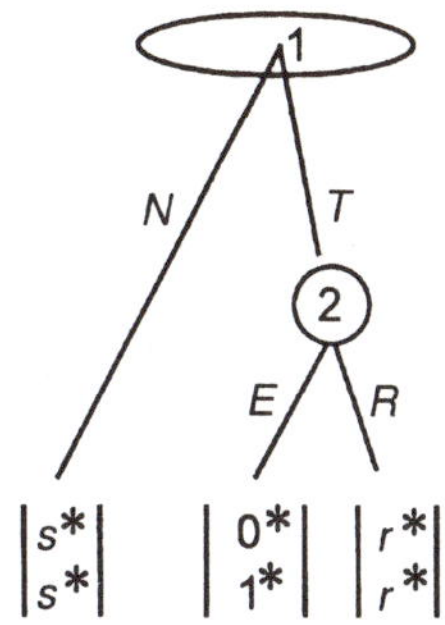

$1^* > r^* > s^* > 0^*$

Figure 1

a game in the proper sense of that term. The starred entries at the ends of the branches of the tree are not payoffs representing subjective preferences. They rather represent objective or material rewards as measured for instance in monetary or other units including such possibilities as increases in the number of offspring.

For individuals whose preferences can be represented by a payoff function which in fact coincides with the material payoffs – whose preferences are 'linear in money' – the objective situation of Figure 1 is transformed into a game of trust by simply dropping the 'stars'. In that game, under the conventional background assumption of common knowledge of the tree, rational choice dictates that the first mover choose *N* since he foresees that the second mover rationally chooses *E*. Both players end up with *s* in terms of their subjective evaluations and with s^* in objective terms while they could have realized $r > s$ or $r^* > s^*$ respectively. The Pareto superior result is closed off.

There are several conceivable 'solutions' for problems of trust (see, for fine overviews over social situations involving problems of trust, Fukuyama, 1995; Landa, 1994; Seligman, 1997). The institutions of promise and contract form a case in point. These institutions confer commitment power on individuals (see, on the fundamental role of power conferring rules, the seminal analysis in Hart, 1961). Being endowed with commitment power individuals can choose to modify their expected future payoffs in a preceding strategic move. To put it otherwise, by their preceding (contractual) promise individuals can render themselves 'trustworthy' or – more formally speaking – choose to play a modified subgame.

Institutional solutions to trust problems are what rational-choice theorists would focus on naturally. Other social theorists have traditionally drawn attention to the 'internalization of norms'. Such an internalization gives rise to a modification of preferences as well, however, without a preceding strategic choice of the affected individual. We feel that rational-choice theorists, rather

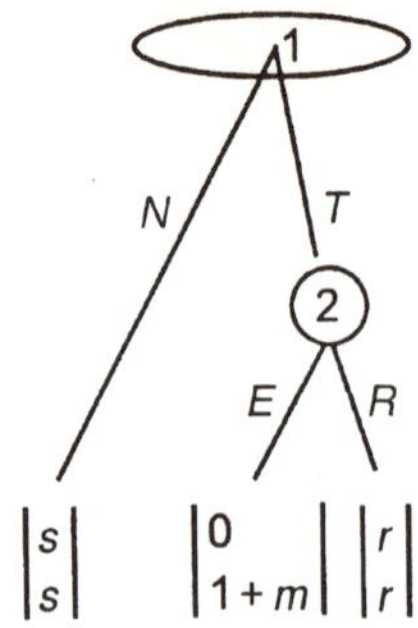

$1 > r > s > 0$

Figure 2

than rejecting the 'internalization of norms' out of hand as obscure or ad hoc, should better seek ways to integrate it in their models. Besides extrinsic motivation which rests on the subjective perceptions of the objective reward structure of an action situation, intrinsic motivation which derives from other sources like norm internalization can be a central element of decision-making (see, in an economic vein on intrinsic motivation, Frey, 1997).

In Figure 2 a purely subjective motivational component not based directly on objective rewards shows up as the payoff component, *m*. Wheeling in such a motivational factor like *m* would be purely ad hoc if we let it rest with that. But we shall treat *m* as an endogenous parameter of our model. In doing so we distinguish two player types, the trustworthy $\underline{m}$-type for whom in the role of the second mover due to $\underline{m}+1 < r(\underline{m} < r-1 < 0)$ the choice of *R* is rational and the untrustworthy $\overline{m}$-type for whom, because of $\overline{m}+1 > r(\overline{m} > r-1)$, the choice of *E* is rational. Since all values of *m* that fulfill the same preceding inequalities are behaviorally equivalent it suffices to focus on two types. Accordingly in our discussion of the evolution of the population's type composition each of the two types represents a whole interval of behaviorally equivalent values of *m*.

In previous work we considered how type-dependent differences between the trustworthy and untrustworthy types' decision-making would bring about differential evolutionary success – as measured along the objective dimension of material reward. We studied the evolution of the composition of a population of trustworthy and untrustworthy types under various parameter constellations and modelling assumptions. But we focused exclusively on the evolution of preferences. With respect to information we relied on the assumption that players could choose strategically whether or not to acquire information of reliability μ at some cost *C*. Now we assume that informed I-type players who are endowed with a 'C, μ' technology emerge in the evolutionary process and survive if they are more successful than the uninformed U-type players who do not incur the cost but remain totally uninformed about their co-player's type. Unlike other evolutionary approaches (see for instance the discussion of the evolutionary dynamics of crime in Cressman *et al.*, 1998) ours is still indirect in other regards. Even though the informed players simply emerge, rational strategic choices in the stage games are still explicitly modelled rather than eliminated altogether.

3. BASIC GAMES OF TRUST AND THEIR SOLUTION

3.1. Basic games of trust as played by the uninformed and the informed

Imagine a game of trust as described in Figure 2. Assume further that the game is played by U-type players who do not know their co-player's preference parameter m or, as we shall also say, they are ignorant of their co-player's 'moral' type. Assignment of moral types can be modelled in the conventional way as the outcome of a fictitious random move in which 'nature' or 'player 0' chooses the types of the players. Since only the trustworthiness of the second mover affects the outcome of the game we can neglect the 'moral' type of the player who ends up in the first-mover role. We need to model only the type assignment for the second-mover role.

In our model, 'nature' or 'player 0' starts by assigning first- and second-mover roles to players 1 and 2, respectively, in a random move with an equal likelihood of 1/2 for either of the two roles. With probability q, corresponding to the share q of trustworthy $\underline{m}$-types in the population, player 0 'chooses' in the previously mentioned fictitious random move that the second mover be a trustworthy $\underline{m}$-type. Afterwards the game of trust of Figure 2 is played according to type and role assignment as fixed in the preceding random moves. The tree shown in Figure 3 emerges.

As indicated above, this tree models the game among U-type players. When assigned the first-mover role their detection technology does not reveal any information on the type of the second mover. However, if there exist I-type individuals then these types in the role of the first mover – due to their perfect detection technology – have complete information on the second mover's type. With an I-type as player 1 and a U-type as player 2 the game is characterized by the graph shown in Figure 4. As for the other assignments of information types: if only player 2 is an informed type her information sets become singletons, while player 1 cannot discriminate. If both players are informed then all information sets are singletons.

3.2 Solutions of trust games played by different informational and moral types

Assume that the population share of I-types is $p \in [0, 1]$ while that of U-types is $1 - p$. Assume further that the population share q of trustworthy $\underline{m}$-types

W. Güth, H. Kliemt and B. Peleg

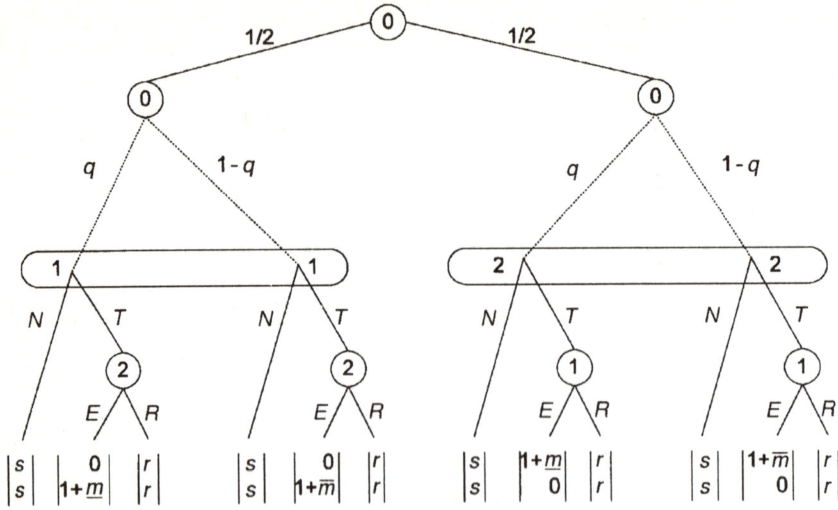

$m_i = \underline{m}$ or $m_i = \overline{m}$ for $i = 1, 2$ and $\underline{m} < r - 1 < \overline{m}$, $1 > r > s > 0$

Figure 3 U-type player 1 and U-type player 2

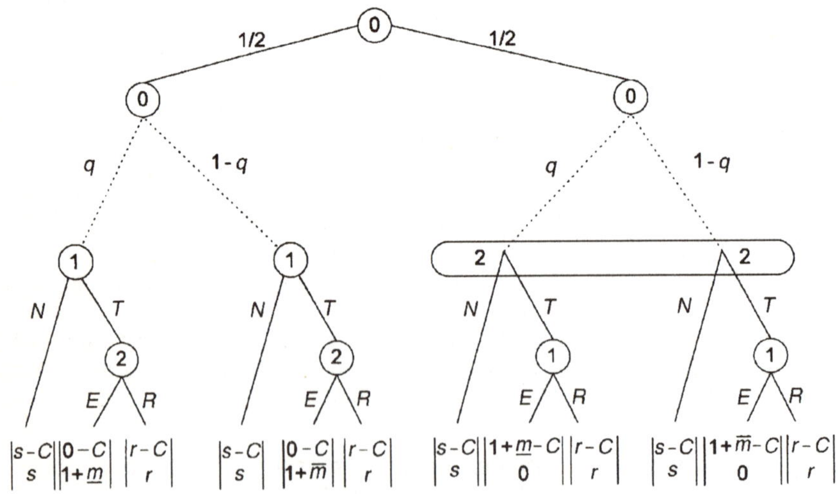

$m_i = \underline{m}$ or $m_i = \overline{m}$ for $i = 1, 2$ and $\underline{m} < r - 1 < \overline{m}$, $1 > r > s > 0, C \geq 0$

Figure 4 I-type player 1 and U-type player 2

and the complementary share $1-q$ of untrustworthy $\overline{m}$-types is common knowledge among the players. Looking at the game recursively let us start with the behavior in the role of the second mover. Obviously, for behavior in second-mover roles the informational type does not matter. Only the 'moral' type of being trustworthy or untrustworthy is then relevant: in second-mover roles trustworthy $\underline{m}$-types will choose R while untrustworthy $\overline{m}$-types choose E.

On the other hand, in the first-mover role the moral type of the decision-maker is behaviorally irrelevant. But choosers of different informational types tend to choose differently in first-mover roles. The uninformed U-type, who does not have access to specific type information and therefore must rely on the prior probability q of meeting a trustworthy second mover will choose to trust if $qr+(1-q)0>s$ (i.e. $q>s/r$) and not to trust if $qr+(1-q)0<s$ (i.e. $q<s/r$) (as shall subsequently become obvious: the degenerate case $q=s/r$ can be neglected for the purposes at hand). The decisions of the fully informed I-type will, however, be determined completely by his knowledge of the second mover's type: if the second mover is a trustworthy $\underline{m}$-type, an I-type first mover, expecting r rather than s, chooses T; if the second mover is an untrustworthy $\overline{m}$-type, the I-type first mover, expecting s rather than 0, decides on N.

In principle we have to consider four combinations of informational and moral aspects and thus four player types: $\underline{m}$-I-types, $\underline{m}$-U-types, $\overline{m}$-I-types and $\overline{m}$-U-types. However, since in first-mover roles players independent of their own moral type choose according to their informational type whereas in second-mover roles moral type is all that matters is the moral and informational dimensions of the problem are 'separable'. It suffices in the subsequent discussion of the evolutionary dynamics of the population composition to consider the relative survival prospects of U- vs I-types independently of their own moral type while the relative success of the $\underline{m}$- vs $\overline{m}$-types does not depend on their informational type.

4. EVOLUTIONARY DYNAMICS

Let us now investigate how p and q evolve if the preceding games are played among randomly paired players chosen from an infinite population of individuals of the four 'moral-cum-informational' types. Our basic assumption is that q increases (decreases) when the $\underline{m}$-types are more (less) successful than $\overline{m}$-types in basic games. Similarly, p is assumed to increase (decrease) whenever I-types are more (less) successful than U-types.

Since we assume that players are randomly drawn from a population containing infinitely many individuals of all types the average expected success of different types will have 0 variance, i.e. each type's average success is not stochastic while that of the individuals belonging to the different types may well be. In view of this we can directly relate the decrease and increase in population shares p and q to expected payoffs and these in turn to their objective ('starred') counterparts – the 'currency' in which relative success in evolutionary competition is ultimately determined.

Now, starting with relative success of informational types, consider the expectations of an I-type as opposed to those of a U-type. For the sake of specificity assume, initially, that the situation sketched in Figure 4 obtains. Player 1 is an I-type and player 2 a U-type. Player 1 has incurred a sunk cost of C. Whether or not this makes him better off than a U-type player 1 depends on the value of the information to which he gains access. So let us look at the value of the information.

With a probability of $\frac{1}{2}$ player 1 expects to play as a first and with equal likelihood as a second mover. Before matching and before role assignment player 1's expectations for the contingency of becoming the first mover depend solely on the population composition parameter q. This parameter describes how likely it is that he be paired with a trustworthy co-player whom he then would recognize since, as an I-type first-mover, player 1 can perfectly discriminate between trustworthy and untrustworthy second movers. Thus before matching and role assignment I-type player 1 expects $\frac{1}{2}[qr + (1 - q)s]$ from the first-mover role. As compared to that a U-type player 1 would expect $\frac{1}{2}[qr + (1 - q)0]$, for $q > s/r$, and $\frac{1}{2}s$, for $q < s/r$.

When assigned the second-mover role I-type player 1's information about first-mover player 2's type is strategically irrelevant. The I-type, like the U-type second mover, plays solely according to his own moral type. In the case described in Figure 4 both types of player 1 are dealing with an uninformed player 2 in the first-mover role. Behavior of such a U-type player depends solely on the relation between q and s/r. Thus, under the information conditions depicted in Figure 4, I-type and U-type players of identical moral type have identical expectations in second-mover roles.

It is obvious that the preceding line of argument applies to all combinations of types assigned to players 1 and 2: I-type and U-type players of identical moral type have identical expectations in second-mover roles as determined by their co-player's informational type (and, of course, independently of the first-mover co-player's moral type).

If the identical expectations of I-types and U-types in second-mover roles are W then before role assignment and matching the expectation of both informationally different but morally identical types of player 1 are $\frac{1}{2}W$. The same term $\frac{1}{2}W$ forms part of the expectation $R_I(q)$ of the informed I-type and of the expectation $R_U(q)$ of the uninformed U-type. Therefore the payoff in second-mover roles cannot differentiate between morally identical types that differ only along the informational dimension. Payoff in second-mover roles can therefore be neglected in the determination of relative evolutionary success of morally identical alternative informational types.

Taking into account this observation we can focus solely on differential success of alternative informational types in first-mover roles. Moreover, since we are dealing with an infinite population in which expectations directly translate into relative success of different types we get – after multiplying by 2 – the following simplified success functions for I-types and U-types:

$$R_{\mathrm{I}}(q) = qr + (1 - q)s - 2C \tag{4.1}$$

$$R_{\mathrm{U}}(q) = \begin{cases} s & \text{for } q < s/r \\ qr & \text{for } q > s/r \end{cases} \tag{4.2}$$

For $R_{\mathrm{I}}(q) > R_{\mathrm{U}}(q)$ to be fulfilled it is necessary that

$$2C < \frac{s}{r}(r - s) \tag{4.3}$$

and

$$\frac{2C}{r - s} < q < \frac{s - 2C}{s} \tag{4.4}$$

apply. The left-hand side of (4.4) emerges for $s/r > q$ and the right-hand side for $s/r < q$. If the interval for q characterized by (4.4) is non-empty, this in turn implies that (4.3) obtains as well. Moreover, if (4.4) holds good and thus the necessary condition, (4.3), for a non-empty interval applies as well, then $q = s/r$ will always be an element of that non-empty interval.

The negation of (4.3) is $2C \geq (s/r)(r - s)$. If $2C$ is strictly greater than the right-hand side of the inequality there are no populations of trustworthy and untrustworthy types such that the informed would do better than the uninformed type. Due to the high 'fixed cost' of being an informed type, I-types are eventually driven out of the population. In the degenerate case in which (4.3) becomes an equality with an empty interval (4.4), the population share p of informed individuals will almost always decline too.

Up to now we relied on the sign of $R_{\mathrm{I}}(q) - R_{\mathrm{U}}(q)$ as indicating the direction of change. We have for all $t \geq 0$:

$$R_{\mathrm{I}}(q_t) - R_{\mathrm{U}}(q_t) = \begin{cases} (r - s)q_t - 2C & \text{for } q_t < s/r \\ s - 2C - sq_t & \text{for } q_t > s/r \end{cases} \tag{4.5}$$

Clearly, under any plausible specification of the dynamic process, as long as $R_{\mathrm{I}}(q_t) - R_{\mathrm{U}}(q_t) > 0, p_t$ should increase through time.

To say anything about the dynamic process itself we need to specify it. So let us postulate here without further justification that the dynamic process can be described by a linear relationship:

$$\dot{p}_t = k[R_{\mathrm{I}}(q_t) - R_{\mathrm{U}}(q_t)] \tag{4.6}$$

where k is a positive constant. (In a somewhat different but related context p_t may be interpreted as a mixed strategy whose dynamics is justified in a learning context as for instance in Arthur, 1993, and Posch, 1997, who refer to a Polya-

W. Güth, H. Kliemt and B. Peleg

type urn model while other stochastic dynamics like those discussed in Hofbauer and Schlag, 1998, would be inconsistent with the rational-choice assumptions introduced in Section 3.2 above.)

Turning to the dynamics of q let us assume initially that (4.3) obtains and that there is a permanent influx (mutation) of I-types such that there are always some informed individuals around. Thus, even if $p_t \to 0$ for $t \to \infty$, the population share p_t of informed I-types is always positive.

In second-mover roles differential success of moral types depends on the population share p of informed types in first-mover roles. For an $\underline{m}$-type second mover we therefore get:

$$R_{\underline{m}}(p) = \begin{cases} pr + (1-p)s & \text{for } q < s/r \\ r & \text{for } q > s/r \end{cases} \tag{4.7}$$

and for an $\overline{m}$-type

$$R_{\overline{m}} = \begin{cases} s & \text{for } q < s/r \\ ps + (1-p)1 & \text{for } q > s/r \end{cases} \tag{4.8}$$

$R_{\underline{m}}(p) - R_{\overline{m}}(p) > 0$ is fulfilled for $q < s/r$ since, by assumption, $p > 0$ and $r > s$. Therefore, for $q < s/r$ and $p > 0$ the share q of $\underline{m}$-types increases while for $q > s/r$:

$$p > \frac{1-r}{1-s} \tag{4.9}$$

is required for that to be the case. Thus an increase of q is to be expected unless $q > s/r$ and (4.9) is reversed. In the latter case, $R_{\underline{m}}(p) - R_{\overline{m}}(p) < 0$ and q will decrease.

Again, in view of the difference

$$R_{\underline{m}}(p) - R_{\overline{m}}(p) = \begin{cases} (r-s)p_t & \text{for } q < s/r \\ (1-s)p_t - (1-r) & \text{for } q > s/r \end{cases} \tag{4.10}$$

we specify the dynamic process by postulating the linear relationship

$$\dot{q}_t = h[R_{\underline{m}}(p_t) - R_{\overline{m}}(p_t)] \tag{4.11}$$

where h is a positive constant.

If the reverse of relation (4.3) applies we know from the preceding argument about the dynamics of p that the informed I-types will tend to be driven out of the population entirely. However, if one assumes – as we did above and shall do after the following brief digression – that there is a permanent influx of I-types such that $p_t > 0$ then $p_t = 0$ is merely a limit result. Still, it may be noted that $p_t = 0$ corresponds to a generic case, if the type-revealing signal that is received in first-mover roles becomes stochastic. Therefore it seems appropriate to look at the limiting constellation somewhat more carefully rather than to dismiss it out of hand.

Preference and Information in Simple Games of Trust

Suspending the assumption $p_t > 0$ let us for the time being and for the sake of simplicity suppose that I-types have been driven out completely and therefore all players are uninformed U-types. Though all are U-types some may be trustworthy and others untrustworthy. However, since all are uninformed the game of Figure 3 is played throughout. Now, it is obvious that in the game as displayed in Figure 3, untrustworthy second movers – regardless of their informational characteristics in first-mover roles and the costs they would incur then – have an advantage over trustworthy ones if they find a trusting first mover. In first-mover roles uninformed first movers, regardless of their own moral type, will rationally choose to trust as long as $q > s/r$. Thus, in that realm in a population of uninformed U-types the population share q of the trustworthy will decline. On the other hand, since in case $q < s/r$ first movers should rationally choose N throughout, nothing could differentiate between types leaving the population composition unaltered. Therefore all (p, q) with $p = 0$ and $q < s/r$ would be rest points, though with degenerate attraction sets.

Assuming that decision-makers, even though they are rational, are prone to commit occasional mistakes uninformed first movers would occasionally mistakenly choose to trust even if $q < s/r$. Then the untrustworthy could have an advantage over the trustworthy types beyond the threshold of $q = s/r$ and the population share q of trustworthy individuals would tend to decline over the whole interval (0, 1], though the decline would be slowed down for $q < s/r$. Figures 5 and 6 sum up the preceding discussion of the dynamics of p and q.

5. STABILITY OF *p*, *q* CONSTELLATIONS

A rest point (p^*, q^*) of the p, q dynamics is characterized by vanishing rates of change $\dot{p}_t$ and $\dot{q}_t$:

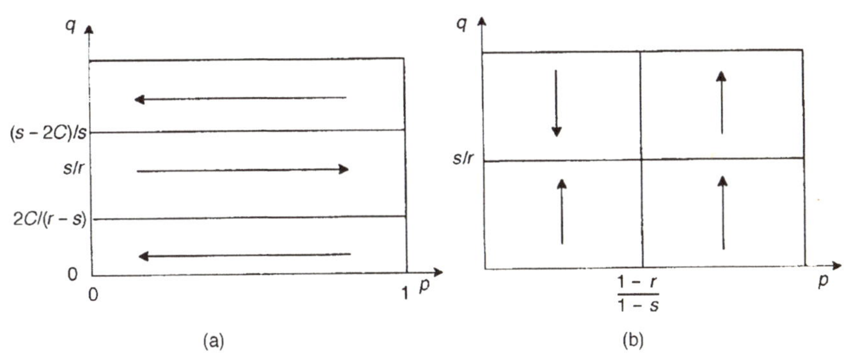

Figure 5a, b The direction in which p and q change for $2C < (s/r)(r - s)$

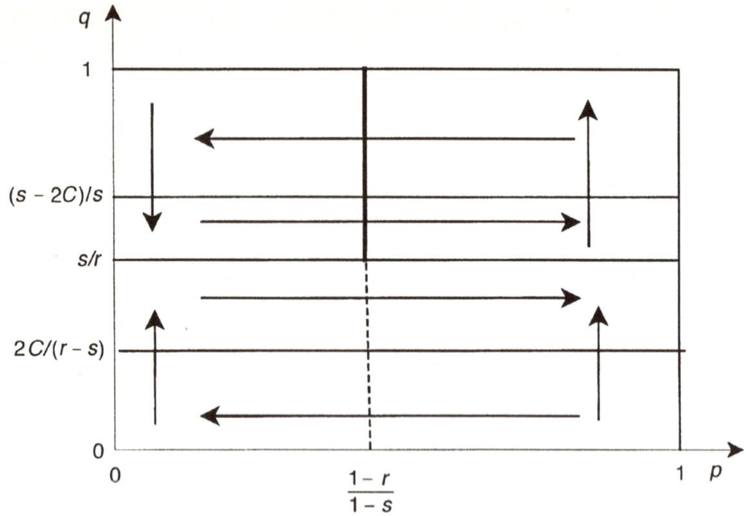

Figure 6 The p, q dynamics for $2C < (s/r)(r - s)$

$$(\dot{p}_t, \dot{q}_t) = (k[R_I(q^*) - R_U(q^*)], h[R_{\underline{m}}(p^*) - R_{\overline{m}}(p^*)]) = (0, 0) \tag{5.1}$$

Since $p_t > 0$ and $q_t < s/r$ imply $\dot{q}_t > 0$ there are no rest points

$$(p, q) \in [0, 1]^2 \quad \text{with } q < s/r \text{ and } p > 0 \tag{5.2}$$

Therefore in the range $q < s/r$ only the points from the line segment $[p = 0, q \le s/r)$ or – in case of trembles (on how 'general trembles' may affect results, see Gale *et al.*, 1995) – possibly the point $(p, q) = (0, 0)$ can be rest points (with degenerate attraction sets). In the degenerate case $q = s/r$ the first moving player is indifferent between *N* and *T*. There is no unique solution play for the first moving player. Since changes in the population composition depend on play and since the first-mover's play cannot be predicted, $(\dot{p}_t, \dot{q}_t)$ is not determined. Hardly anything can be said about this case.

Other p, q constellations can be at rest only if they are an element of

$$E := \{(p, q) \in [0, 1]^2 | q > s/r\} \tag{5.3}$$

Moreover, if $(p, q) \in E$ and thus $q > s/r$, then $p > (1 - r)/(1 - s)$ implies $R_{\underline{m}}(p) - R_{\overline{m}}(p) > 0$ and $p < (1 - r)/(1 - s)$ implies $R_{\underline{m}}(p) - R_{\overline{m}}(p) < 0$ (see Figures 5 and 6). From this consideration it is already obvious that rest points in *E* must fulfill $p = (1 - r)/(1 - s)$. Analogous arguments show that it is necessary for a rest point that $q = (s - 2C)/s$ be fulfilled, too. Thus there can only be one point that fulfills both necessary conditions. Since together the two conditions imply vanishing rates of change along both dimensions the unique rest point in *E* is

Preference and Information in Simple Games of Trust

$$(p^*, q^*) = \left(\frac{1-r}{1-s}, \frac{s-2C}{s}\right) \tag{5.4}$$

In the rest point (p^*, q^*) the rates of change $\dot{p}_t, \dot{q}_t$ vanish. Intuitively speaking there is no 'push away' from (p^*, q^*) since for sufficiently small perturbations the dynamic process will remain arbitrarily close to that state. More formally, (p^*, q^*) is stable in the sense that for every $\epsilon > 0$ and the corresponding neighborhood under the Euclidean norm $d(\cdots)$ there is a $\delta > 0$ and a corresponding neighborhood of (p^*, q^*) such that for a 'starting point' (p_0, q_0) with $d((p^*, q^*), (p_0, q_0)) < \delta$ we have $d((p^*, q^*), (p_t, q_t)) < \epsilon$ for all $t \geq 0$.

Though stable, the point (p^*, q^*) is, however, not (locally) asymptotically stable. To be (locally) asymptotically stable there must not only be no 'push away' from (p^*, q^*) but rather some 'pull towards' it. More formally, (p^*, q^*) is *not* (locally) asymptotically stable, since there exists no $\epsilon > 0$ such that for all starting points (p_0, q_0) with $d((p^*, q^*), (p_0, q_0)) < \epsilon$ we have $\lim_{t\to\infty}(p_t, q_t) = (p^*, q^*)$. These claims are demonstrated in the subsequent discussion of the time path of (p_t, q_t), $t \geq 0$, for all initial $(p_0, q_0) \in E$.

For $(p_t, q_t) \in E$ we have $q_t > s/r$. Inserting (4.5) into (4.6) and (4.10) into (4.11) yields

$$\dot{p}_t = k[s - 2C - sq_t] \quad k > 0 \tag{5.5}$$

$$\dot{q}_t = h[(1-s)p_t - (1-r)] \quad h > 0 \tag{5.6}$$

Solving (5.5) for q_t and taking the derivative with respect to time yields

$$\dot{q}_t = -\frac{1}{ks}\ddot{p}_t \tag{5.7}$$

and, using (5.7) on (5.6):

$$\ddot{p}_t + khs(1-s)p_t = khs(1-r) \tag{5.8}$$

A constant solution to the inhomogeneous differential equation (5.8) is

$$p_t = c \quad \text{where } c = \frac{1-r}{1-s} \tag{5.9}$$

For the homogeneous equation

$$\ddot{p}_t b^2 p_t = 0 \quad \text{with } b^2 = khs(1-s) \tag{5.10}$$

two independent solutions are given by

$$p_t = \sin(tb) \quad \text{and} \quad p_t = \cos(tb) \tag{5.11}$$

All solutions can be expressed as

W. Güth, H. Kliemt and B. Peleg

$$p_t = c + \lambda_1 \sin(tb) + \lambda_2 \cos(tb) \quad \text{for some } \lambda_1, \lambda_2 \in R \tag{5.12}$$

Taking the derivative

$$\dot{p}_t = \lambda_1 b \cos(tb) - \lambda_2 b \sin(tb) \tag{5.13}$$

using it on (5.5) and solving for q_t we have

$$q_t = \frac{s - 2C}{s} + \frac{b}{ks}[\lambda_2 \sin(tb) - \lambda_1 \cos(tb)] \tag{5.14}$$

From (5.12) and (5.14) it is obvious that the p_t, q_t dynamics are periodic since sin and cos are periodic. Regardless of the two positive factors k and h, any initial p_t, q_t constellation will be revisited indefinitely. Moreover, from any initial $(p_t, q_t) \neq (p^*, q^*)$ with $q_t > s/r$ the dynamic process will not be attracted to the unique rest point $(p^*, q^*) = [(1 - r)/(1 - s), (s - 2C)/s]$ in E. The attraction set of (p^*, q^*) is $\{(p^*, q^*)\}$.

In view of general mathematical insights into the structure of (time) continuous processes in R^2 this result is hardly surprising. A process starting at some $(p, q) \in E$ must either converge to some (p^*, q^*) or be periodic. In our case periodicity ensues because linearity and, for that matter, 'separability' prevent convergence. (For related illustrations of the same basic facts in a direct social evolutionary setting see Friedman, 1991; Cressman *et al.*, 1998; and Posch, 1997.)

The preceding considerations rule out any stronger statements about attractors of the dynamic process. We can, however, characterize the periodic process somewhat further. In doing so let us first define two other auxiliary constants

$$d := \frac{ks}{b} \quad \text{and} \quad e := k\frac{s - 2C}{b}$$

Using these constants we can rewrite (5.12) and (5.14) as

$$p_t - c = \lambda_1 \sin(tb) + \lambda_2 \cos(tb) \tag{5.12'}$$

$$dq_t - e = \lambda_2 \sin(tb) - \lambda_1 \cos(tb) \tag{5.14'}$$

After multiplying the first equation by λ_2, the second by λ_1 and subtracting the results we get

$$\cos(bt) = \frac{\lambda_2(p_t - c) - \lambda_1(dq_t - e)}{\lambda_1^2 + \lambda_2^2} \tag{5.15}$$

whereas multiplying the first equation by λ_1, the second by λ_2 and adding the results yields

Preference and Information in Simple Games of Trust

$$\sin(bt) = \frac{\lambda_1(p_t - c) + \lambda_2(dq_t - e)}{\lambda_1^2 + \lambda_2^2} \tag{5.16}$$

Using $\cos^2(bt) + \sin^2(bt) = 1$ we get

$$[\lambda_2(p_t - c) - \lambda_1(dq_t - e)]^2 + [\lambda_1(p_t - c) + \lambda_2(dq_t - e)]^2 = [\lambda_1^2 + \lambda_2^2]^2$$

and from this

$$(p_t - c)^2 + (dq_t - e)^2 = \lambda_1^2 + \lambda_2^2 \tag{5.17}$$

The p_t, q_t process cycles on an ellipse around the unique rest point in E, namely $(p^*, q^*) = [(1 - r)/(1 - s), (s - 2C)/s] = (c, e/d)$. The time span for a complete cycle, Δt, can be calculated by considering $p_t = p_{t+\Delta t}$ in equation (5.12′); that is

$$\lambda_1 \sin(tb) + \lambda_2 \cos(tb) = \lambda_1 \sin([t + \Delta t]b) + \lambda_2 \cos([t + \Delta t]b) \tag{5.18}$$

Owing to the periodicity 2π of sin as well as of cos we can conclude that $2\pi = \Delta tb$ and thus

$$\Delta t = 2\pi/b = \frac{2\pi}{\sqrt{khs(1 - s)}} \tag{5.19}$$

The two parameters k and h allow for different volatilities of the adaptive processes along the informational or p-dimension and the moral or q-dimension of the population composition. The length of the 'cycle' of the dynamic process in which the population composition changes through time is determined as a function of the product $khs(1 - s)$: the larger the factor kh the shorter the cycle. Analogously, the larger the factor $s(1 - s)$, i.e. the closer s is to $\frac{1}{2}$, the shorter the cycle.

Finally, for all k, h and any starting point $(p_0, q_0) \in E$ the coefficients are uniquely determined by equations (5.12′) and (5.14′) as

$$p_0 - c = \lambda_2 \tag{5.20}$$

$$dq_0 - e = -\lambda_1 \tag{5.21}$$

where c is a function of the exogenous parameters r, s, while b and d are functions of k, h and again the exogenous parameter s. For all k, h and all $(p_0, q_0) \in E$ the time trajectories of the p_t, q_t process can be determined. As (5.17) shows, this process stays on the same graph while its cycle length depends on kh and $s(1 - s)$. For all $t > 0$ we have:

$$p_t - c = (e - dq_0) \sin(bt) + (p_0 - c) \cos(bt) \tag{5.12″}$$

$$dq_t - e = (p_0 - c) \sin(bt) + (dq_0 - e) \cos(bt) \tag{5.14″}$$

The results reached thus far are quite robust. As is shown in the mathematical appendix the linear adjustment process specified in equations (4.6) and (4.11) can be generalized and it can also be secured that an adjustment process starting in the interior of E will remain there.

6. IMPERFECT TYPE DETECTION

The preceding discussion focused on polar extremes. Either U-types were assigned first-mover roles and a game with purely private information on the second mover's moral type was played, or I-types playing in the first-mover role could perfectly discriminate between the trustworthy and untrustworthy second movers. Obviously the middle ground between these extremes is of great interest. In situations involving problems of trust the information status of real-world decision-makers more often than not seems neither to correspond to that of fully informed I-types nor to that of completely ignorant U-types. It seems quite realistic that real-world decision-makers command what we shall call a 'C, μ' technology. This information 'technology' – using the term 'technology' in its widest sense including long acquaintance, detective services, other individuals' looks etc. – provides some information of the second mover's type. More specifically, partially informed I′-type individuals have access to a stochastic signal which reveals the co-player's type with probability $\mu > \frac{1}{2}$. Gaining access they incur, however, some sunk cost $C > 0$.

If the second mover is a trustworthy $\underline{m}$-type then an imperfectly informed first mover receives with probabilty $\underline{\mu}$ the signal '$\underline{m}$'. With probability $(1 - \underline{\mu})$ the signal received at cost $C > 0$ from an $\underline{m}$-type is '$\overline{m}$'. If the second mover is an $\overline{m}$-type then with probability $\bar{\mu}$ the true type is revealed by the signal '$\overline{m}$' while with complementary probability $1 - \bar{\mu}$ the signal '$\underline{m}$' misleadingly indicates a trustworthy type even though it is received from an untrustworthy $\overline{m}$-type.

We require

$$\tfrac{1}{2} < \underline{\mu}, \bar{\mu} \leq 1 \tag{6.1}$$

Knowing the population share q of trustworthy $\underline{m}$-types in the population, all players should rationally endorse the prior probability q of encountering a trustworthy second mover. Beyond this, U-type players do not command information about their second-moving co-player's moral type. But (incompletely) informed I′-type players in first-mover roles receive a type signal indicating with probability $\mu = \underline{\mu}, \bar{\mu}$ their second-moving co-player's true type. Obviously the probability of receiving the signal '$\underline{m}$' is $q\underline{\mu} + (1 - q)(1 - \bar{\mu})$ so that the posterior probability for a trustworthy $\underline{m}$-type individual in the second-mover role after receiving the signal '$\underline{m}$' is $q\underline{\mu}/[q\underline{\mu} + (1 - q)(1 - \bar{\mu})]$. Analogously, the probability of receiving the signal '$\overline{m}$' is $q(1 - \underline{\mu}) + (1 - q)\bar{\mu}$. After receiving the signal '$\overline{m}$' the posterior probability for an untrustworthy $\overline{m}$-type in the second-mover role is $(1-q)\bar{\mu}/[q(1-\underline{\mu})+(1-q)\bar{\mu}]$ while after that signal the posterior probability for a trustworthy $\underline{m}$-type is $q(1-\underline{\mu})/[q(1-\underline{\mu})+(1-q)\bar{\mu}]$.

After receiving signal '$\underline{m}$' an imperfectly informed $\bar{\text{I}}'$-type should rationally prefer to trust, T, over showing no trust, N, in the role of the first mover if

$$\frac{q\underline{\mu}}{q\underline{\mu}+(1-q)(1-\bar{\mu})}r > s \tag{6.2}$$

while after receiving the signal '$\overline{m}$' he should rationally prefer N over T if

$$\frac{q(1-\underline{\mu})}{q(1-\underline{\mu})+(1-q)\bar{\mu}}r < s \tag{6.3}$$

For convenience set

$$R := \frac{q\underline{\mu}}{q\underline{\mu}+(1-q)(1-\bar{\mu})} \qquad L := \frac{q(1-\underline{\mu})}{q(1-\underline{\mu})+(1-q)\bar{\mu}} \tag{6.4}$$

Observe that $1 > q > 0$ and $\frac{1}{2} < \underline{\mu}, \bar{\mu} < 1$ imply

$$1 > R > L > 0 \tag{6.5}$$

I′-type players will follow the signal '$\underline{m}$' by choosing T only if $R > s/r$, and they will follow the signal '$\overline{m}$' by choosing N only if $L < s/r$. Thus I′-type players will follow both signals only if

$$\frac{s}{r} \in (L, R) \tag{6.6}$$

Now, note that the relation $R > s/r$ is equivalent to

$$q > \frac{s(1-\bar{\mu})}{\underline{\mu}(r-s)+(1-\bar{\mu})s} \tag{6.2′}$$

while relation $L < s/r$ is equivalent to

$$q < \frac{s\bar{\mu}}{(1-\underline{\mu})(r-s)+\bar{\mu}s} \tag{6.3′}$$

Set

$$J := \frac{s(1-\bar{\mu})}{\underline{\mu}(r-s)+(1-\bar{\mu})s} \quad \text{and} \quad H := \frac{s\bar{\mu}}{(1-\underline{\mu})(r-s)+\bar{\mu}s} \tag{6.7}$$

The assumption $\frac{1}{2} < \underline{\mu}, \bar{\mu}$, implies

$$0 < J < H < 1 \tag{6.5′}$$

W. Güth, H. Kliemt and B. Peleg

Observe also that $s/r < R \Leftrightarrow q > J$ and $L < s/r \Leftrightarrow q < H$ and thus

$$\frac{s}{r} \in (L, R) \Leftrightarrow q \in (J, H) \tag{6.8}$$

Only for (6.8) can type differentiation take place. For, I′-type players should be expected to behave exactly like U-type players whenever $s/r \notin (L, R)$ – i.e., $s/r \geq R$ or $s/r \leq L$ – and thus also $q \notin (J, H)$ – i.e., $q \leq J$ or $H \leq q$. To see this, assume first that the I′-type players ignore the signal '$\underline{m}$' because of $R \leq s/r$. Note, $(R > s/r \Leftrightarrow q > J) \Leftrightarrow (q \leq J \Leftrightarrow R \leq s/r)$. Moreover $\frac{1}{2} < \underline{\mu}, \bar{\mu}$, implies $(r - s)(1 - \bar{\mu}) < \underline{\mu}(r - s)$ and $(r - s)(1 - \bar{\mu}) < \underline{\mu}(r - s) \Leftrightarrow J < s/r$. Therefore for $R \leq s/r$ we get $s/r > J \geq q$. Because of $s/r > q$ all U-type players should rationally choose not to trust in the first-mover role while the I′-types should not let the signal '$\underline{m}$' induce them to deviate from the strategy suggested by $q < s/r$. Moreover, since $R > L$ the I′-types should follow the signal '$\overline{m}$' and thus in that contingency should certainly behave like the U-types, too. In sum, nothing can differentiate between I′-types and U-types if $s/r \geq R$.

Turning to the other conceivable violation of (6.8), assume second, $s/r \leq L$. Note $s/r \leq L \Leftrightarrow H \leq q$. Moreover, $\frac{1}{2} < \underline{\mu}, \bar{\mu}$ implies

$$q \geq H \Leftrightarrow q \geq \frac{s}{\frac{(1 - \underline{\mu})}{\bar{\mu}}(r - s) + s}$$

The latter implies $q > [s/(r - s + s)] = s/r$. Therefore all U-type players should choose T, if $s/r \leq L$. Note that $s/r \leq L$ is the negation of (6.3). It is therefore not the case that the I′-type should choose N over T after receiving an '$\overline{m}$' signal. He should rather ignore that signal and decide on T. Should the I′-type receive an '$\underline{m}$' signal he should certainly choose to trust if $s/r \leq L < R$. In sum, if $s/r \leq L$ nothing can differentiate between U-types and I′-types.

The upshot of the preceding discussion is that for $q \notin (J, H)$ – or, for that matter, $s/r \notin (L, R)$ – nothing can differentiate between uninformed U-types and (incompletely) informed I′-types. If (6.8) is not fulfilled, all types behave like U-types. Therefore the case $s/r \notin (L, R)[q \notin (J, H)]$ corresponds to that of $p = 0$ for which we have shown elsewhere that – at least in the presence of occasional mistakes – there is a single universal attractor for q, namely $q = 0$ (see Güth and Kliemt, 1994). For $q_t > H$, of course, the dynamic process will eventually yield $q_t \in (J, H)$ whereas for $q_t < J$ the range will never be reached. Since $q_t < J$ implies $R_U(q) > R_{I'}(q)$ and thus a decrease of p, now the line segment $[p = 0, J)$ or – in case of occasional mistakes – the rest point $(p, q) = (0, 0)$ have a generic attraction set, namely all (p, q), with $q < J$. The points $(p, q) = (0, q)$ with $0 < q < s/r$ remain rest points with degenerate attraction sets. In our remaining discussion of the case of incompletely informed I′-type players we focus on $q_t \in (J, H)$.

Studying the dynamics of p and q we must again consider the relative reproductive success of I′-types as compared to U-types and of $\underline{m}$-types as compared to $\overline{m}$-types. The condition $R_{I'}(q) - R_U(q) > 0$ now reads:

Preference and Information in Simple Games of Trust

$$\{q[\underline{\mu}r + (1 - \underline{\mu})s] + (1 - q)[\bar{\mu}s + (1 - \bar{\mu})0] - 2C\} - s > 0 \quad \text{if } q < s/r \tag{6.9}$$

$$q > \frac{s(1 - \bar{\mu}) + 2C}{\underline{\mu}(r - s) + (1 - \bar{\mu})s} \tag{6.9'}$$

Similarly,

$$\{q[\underline{\mu}r + (1 - \underline{\mu})s] + (1 - q)[\bar{\mu}s + (1 - \bar{\mu})0] - 2C\} - qr > 0 \quad \text{if } q > s/r \tag{6.10}$$

$$q > \frac{s\bar{\mu} - 2C}{(1 - \underline{\mu})(r - s) + \bar{\mu}s} \tag{6.10'}$$

Again for notational convenience

$$U := \frac{s(1 - \bar{\mu}) + 2C}{\underline{\mu}(r - s) + (1 - \bar{\mu})s} \quad \text{and} \quad O := \frac{s\bar{\mu} - 2C}{(1 - \underline{\mu})(r - s) + \bar{\mu}s} \tag{6.11}$$

For $q \in (U, O)$ the population share p of I′-types should be expected to increase whereas a decrease must be expected for $q \notin [U, O]$. Owing to $C > 0$ we get

$$H > O > \frac{s}{r} > U > J \tag{6.12}$$

as long as

$$2C < \frac{s}{r}(r - s)(\underline{\mu} + \bar{\mu} - 1) \tag{6.13}$$

This being said about the informational dimension let us now turn to the moral dimension. As before, we rely on $p > 0$ when studying the case $q < s/r$.

Recall that moral type matters only in second-mover roles. At the same time differential success of moral types depends on the population share p of informed types in first-mover roles. Thus we get for an $\underline{m}$-type second mover

$$R_{\underline{m}}(p) = \begin{cases} p(\underline{\mu}r + (1 - \underline{\mu})s) + (1 - p)s & \text{for } q < s/r \\ p(\underline{\mu}r + (1 - \underline{\mu})s) + (1 - p)r & \text{for } q > s/r \end{cases} \tag{6.14}$$

and for an $\overline{m}$-type

$$R_{\overline{m}}(p) = \begin{cases} p(\bar{\mu}s + (1 - \bar{\mu})1) + (1 - p)s & \text{for } q < s/r \\ p(\bar{\mu}s + (1 - \bar{\mu})1) + (1 - p)1 & \text{for } q > s/r \end{cases} \tag{6.15}$$

$R_{\underline{m}}(p) - R_{\overline{m}}(p) > 0$ holds good for $q > s/r$ if

W. Güth, H. Kliemt and B. Peleg

$$p > \frac{1-r}{\bar{\mu}(1-s)+(r-s)(\underline{\mu}-1)} \tag{6.16}$$

$R_{\underline{m}}(p) - R_{\overline{m}}(p) > 0$ holds good for $q < s/r$ if

$$\frac{\underline{\mu}}{1-\bar{\mu}} > \frac{1-s}{r-s} \tag{6.17}$$

Note that (6.16) emerges only for $\bar{\mu}(1-s) > (r-s)(1-\underline{\mu})$ or $(1-s)/(r-s) > (1-\underline{\mu})/\bar{\mu}$ otherwise the relation would be reversed with a negative right-hand side requiring a negative p. The relations (6.16) and (6.17) can be fulfilled both for parameter constellations with

$$\frac{1-s}{r-s} \in \left(\frac{1-\underline{\mu}}{\bar{\mu}}, \frac{\underline{\mu}}{1-\bar{\mu}}\right)$$

Only then can the presence of informed I′-types drive a population share $q_t < s/r$ beyond the threshold beyond which the uninformed U-types have good reason to always trust. $R_{\underline{m}}(p) - R_{\overline{m}}(p) < 0$ applies if, in case of $q > s/r$, (6.16) is reversed. In particular this will always be the case for $(1-s)/(r-s) < (1-\underline{\mu})/\bar{\mu}$. For this parameter constellation growth of the population share q of trustworthy individuals is possible only over the range $[0, s/r)$. Of course, $R_{\underline{m}}(p) - R_{\overline{m}}(p) < 0$ also holds good if in case $q < s/r$ relation (6.17) is reversed to $\underline{\mu}/(1-\bar{\mu}) < (1-s)/(r-s)$.

Again, after defining for convenience

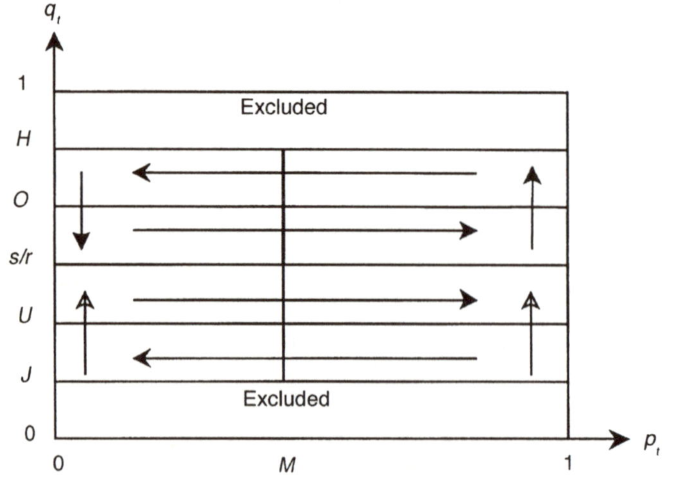

Figure 7 Equation (6.17)

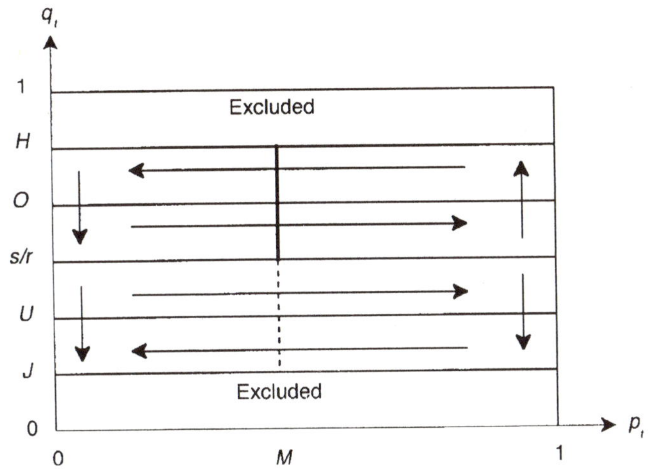

Figure 8 Equation (6.17) reversed

$$M := \frac{1-r}{\bar{\mu}(1-s)+(r-s)(\underline{\mu}-1)} \tag{6.18}$$

our considerations can be summed up graphically by Figures 7 and 8. Note that we restricted attention to parameter constellations satisfying $2C < (s/r)(r-s)(\underline{\mu}+\bar{\mu}-1)$. As a final step let us now turn to the dynamics in $E = \{(p,q) \in [0,1]^2 | q > s/r\}$ if this set contains a unique rest point. We assume that $p > 0$ and $(1-s)/(r-s) > (1-\underline{\mu})/\bar{\mu}$ obtain. Owing to $q > s/r$ we can, as before in the case of differential equations (5.5) and (5.6), restrict attention to two generalized differential equations:

$$\dot{p}_t = k[R_{\mathrm{I'}}(q) - R_{\mathrm{U}}(q)] = k[\{\underline{\mu}(r-s)+(1-\bar{\mu})s-r\}q_t+\bar{\mu}s-2C] \tag{6.19}$$

$$\dot{q}_t = h[R_{\underline{m}}(p) - R_{\overline{m}}(p)] = 1[\{\bar{\mu}(1-s)+(r-s)(\underline{\mu}-1)\}p_t-1+r] \tag{6.20}$$

Making the same basic assumptions about the characteristics of the dynamic process $\dot{p}_t$ again emerges as an (affin) linear function of q_t and $\dot{q}_t$ as an (affin) linear function of p_t. As in the extreme parameter constellation $\bar{\mu} = \underline{\mu} = 1$, the unique rest point

$$(p^*,q^*) = (M,O) = \left(\frac{s\bar{\mu}-2C}{(1-\underline{\mu})(r-s)+\bar{\mu}s}, \frac{1-r}{\bar{\mu}(1-s)+(r-s)(\underline{\mu}-1)}\right) \tag{6.21}$$

of E has merely the degenerate attraction set $\{(p^*,q^*)\}$. All other starting points $(p,q) \in E$ lead to indefinite cycling around the unique rest point (p^*,q^*).

Comparing the results of Sections 4 and 5, in which perfect type detection was assumed, with those of Section 6 shows that the central qualitative results carry over from the deterministic case characterized by $\bar{\mu} = \underline{\mu} = 1$ to stochastic cases characterized by imperfect type detection. We can thus answer the obvious query whether the assumption of perfect type detection might be so extreme as to render irrelevant all results reached under this premise. There is a clear continuity between the extreme idealization of perfect type detection and the more realistic case of imperfect type detection such that the extreme can be approximated by the less extreme case. On the other hand, basic insights gained by studying the somewhat more transparent extreme case carry over to less idealized situations. However, certain differences remain and it is instructive to look briefly at some of them in a 'comparative statics' kind of way.

It has already been pointed out that in the case of perfect type detection the 'length of the cycle' around the rest point

$$(p^*, q^*) = \left(\frac{1-r}{1-s}, \frac{s-2C}{s}\right)$$

depends only on s: the closer s approaches $\frac{1}{2}$, the shorter the cycle. The first coordinate $(1-r)/(1-s)$ of the rest point will decrease towards 0 if r increases towards 1 and increases towards 1 if r decreases towards s. The second coordinate $[s-2C]/s$ depends on s and C and will increase towards 1 if C decreases towards 0 while approaching s/r if C increases towards $(s/2r)(r-s)$. Moreover, in (5.5) and (5.6) only the parameter s influences the coefficients of p_t and q_t.

In (6.19) and (6.20) the parameters r, s and $\bar{\mu}, \underline{\mu}$ all enter the determination of the coefficients of p_t and q_t. Likewise the rest point depends on r, s and $\bar{\mu}, \underline{\mu}$, as well as on C. The influence of $\underline{\mu}$ on outcomes decreases if $r-s$ decreases while the influence of $\bar{\mu}$ is strongly linked with s. This illustrates how the analysis of the imperfect type detection case can differentiate between the error of trusting somebody who does not deserve it – which happens with probability $(1-p)(1-\bar{\mu})$ – and the error of failing to trust a trustworthy partner – which occurs with probability $p(1-\underline{\mu})$.

7. CONCLUDING REMARKS

The preceding exercise offers, on the one hand, some interesting insights into methodological problems of rational choice modelling (in a wide sense of that term) and, on the other hand, substantial results about trust relationships. To start with the latter, it is intuitively plausible that the prospects of trustworthy individuals as opposed to untrustworthy ones crucially depend on the existence of individuals who can to some extent discriminate between trustworthy and untrustworthy partners. In our model – provided that the conditions for following the signal are fulfilled – the (costly) information on individuals' trustworthiness leads to a discrimination between types. If the signal indicates a trustworthy second mover this leads to a choice of T in first-mover roles even if $q < s/r$. If the signal received indicates an untrustworthy type, N is chosen even if $q > s/r$. This corroborates the somewhat elementary yet extremely important insight that the stability of cooperation in view of the trust predicament depends at least as much on the presence of the faculty and inclination to discriminate in the role of the trustor as on the disposition to act fairly as a trustee.

In our model discrimination expresses itself – in the realm in which following the signal is rational – by signal-dependent choices of N and T. In social reality it may express itself in somewhat different, though related, forms. In particular, players may be able to choose their interaction partners and thus to discriminate against the untrustworthy by refusing to interact with them in the first place. Moreover, the free choice of partners could include both the option of repeating interactions with the same partner and of ending them. If that is the case, 'the shadow of the future' (Axelrod, 1984) or 'the discipline of continuous dealings' (Smith, 1776/1976) might be operative as well. The presence of this shadow would tend to diminish the value of type discrimination by inducing trustworthy behavior by all types. (For simulation studies of the discipline of continuous dealings in the presence of an exit option see, for example, Schüßler, 1990; Vanberg and Congleton, 1992; and on inducing the untrustworthy to behave as if trustworthy, of course, Kreps *et al.*, 1982.)

This being said and explicitly acknowledging that other factors may discriminate between trustworthy and untrustworthy individuals as well we feel that it is of great importance to go beyond the intuitively plausible and to gain a somewhat better understanding of the impact of alternative information conditions on the relative survival prospects of trustworthy, non-opportunistic and untrustworthy, opportunistic individuals. That such a closer look may yield quite surprising insights is borne out by comparing the results of the present with our former applications of the indirect evolutionary approach to trust problems.

Formerly we have studied the influence of 'C, μ' technologies of different reliability on the population composition under the premise that the players could choose strategically whether or not they would acquire specific type information of reliability μ at cost C. Under this condition, depending on the parameter constellation, either only $p = 0$, or $p = 0$ and $p = p^* > s/r$, would be evolutionarily stable population compositions with attraction sets whose union would comprise the whole interval [0, 1]. In the present model all the basic assumptions are the same with the only exception that the information technology now is not chosen but rather some players are endowed or, for that matter, stuck with this costly technology without that being their own choice. Under both assumptions, that of the strategic choice of the information technology and that of its evolution, bimorphic rest points or evolutionarily stable population compositions that contain opportunistic as well as non-opportunistic types may emerge. However, interestingly enough, at least under very natural and simple assumptions about the dynamics of the evolutionary process, the effects on the population composition are qualitatively very different from the case in which the costs of being informed are subject to a strategic choice: in the model in which information evolves along with preferences there need not be a generic attractor corresponding to the stable bimorphism in the model in which information conditions are strategically chosen.

Relating this to our social experience it seems to suggest that the presence of some 'zealots' who are for some reason or other averse to being exploited or are preoccupied with knowing their partners' true character can have a fundamental impact on the character of social interaction (for a somewhat parallel argument see Coleman, 1983). To put it very bluntly, 'nosiness' may not be such a bad thing altogether. We might even represent it by an intrinsic motivational factor expressing a zealous preference for defending oneself against exploitation even at high extrinsic or objective costs C. Such inclinations may lead to building up the population share of trustworthy individuals in situations where nobody would rationally invest in costly information technologies. For informed individuals will seek out the trustworthy in situations in which the population share of the trustworthy is too low for rendering the choice of T rational. Owing to this, the trustworthy will have a slight differential advantage over the untrustworthy unless this effect is overcompensated by mistaken choices of T that are made without a signal or due to a misleading one.

In fact, even in our former model in which players made a strategic decision about acquiring the information technology the same kind of argument may apply. As long as individuals once in a while invest in a 'C, μ' technology even though it is not rational to do so this – without any zealotry – may be sufficient to secure to the trustworthy an advantage over the untrustworthy. In the presence of such mistaken investments in information $p_t > 0$ will be fulfilled throughout. Again, once in a while trustworthy second movers will be singled out and will be trusted in an environment in which there are too few trustworthy to show trust generally. As in the presence of zealots this will bring about a differential advantage for the trustworthy if it is not overcompensated by mistaken choices of T among those who do not command a specific type of information. The latter may seem a big if, though, if one takes into account how mistakes of different kinds may compensate each other.

Avoiding a formal analysis of mistake-driven evolutionary processes here let us only remark that in those cases in which $p_t > 0$ is sufficiently large to provide a differential advantage for the trustworthy over the untrustworthy a self-supporting process of the following kind may be operative: initially there are too few trustworthy around to make seeking them out worthwhile. But after a while that may change and the informed may have an advantage over the uninformed and thus their population share might increase as well.

Of course, as our model shows, after going beyond a certain threshold the decrease of trustworthy individuals – and for that matter also of informed individuals – will eventually be unavoidable. Still, there might be some institutional means or other to stabilize population shares p of trustworthy individuals once they have grown beyond a certain threshold. This seems to be quite interesting from a policy point of view, too. Admittedly it is speculative, though not completely so since within the framework of our indirect evolutionary approach to the trust predicament it can be shown that the proper workings of a court system depend on the presence of sufficiently many non-opportunistic individuals if adjudicators cannot be selected according to their trustworthiness and thus 'judges are no better than the rest of us' (see Brennan *et al.*, 1997).

Letting our discussion of substantial issues rest with this we may finally turn to some methodological problems. Since we have touched on these issues already in our preceding discussion of the substantial trust problem we can be quite brief. We feel that our models suggest that we explore more carefully what may be regarded as varying 'degrees of indirectness' in the evolutionary approach. Evolutionary models might reach from the extreme of a completely indirect evolutionary approach in which even the faculty to make opportunistically rational choices itself is viewed as endogenous to or emergent from an evolutionary process (see Güth and Kliemt, 1998), over the still extreme more standard direct evolutionary approach in which all behavior evolves without opportunistically rational choices playing a role, to models in which some decisions are modelled as opportunistically rational in the standard sense while the information conditions evolve along with some aspects of preferences, to models in which some information conditions as well as the substantial decisions are subject to opportunistically rational choice while certain aspects of the preferences are emergent, to extreme models in which even the utility function for some game can be chosen strategically (though one may have some second thoughts about that claim as, for instance, made in Frank, 1987). Observing that there is almost a continuum of models of varying degrees of indirectness it seems clear that further research should look at the pros and cons of alternative degrees of indirectness. Doing this we may hope to gain not only additional methodological but also some new insights into such eternal problems like that of 'nature and nurture'.

ACKNOWLEDGMENTS

The authors gratefully acknowledge improvements suggested by Karl Schlag and Urs Schweizer.

MATHEMATICAL APPENDIX TO SECTION 5

Denote the interior of E by

W. Güth, H. Kliemt and B. Peleg

$$E^0 := \{(p,q)|0 < p < 1 \text{ and } s/r < q < 1\} \tag{A.1}$$

A function f, f:[0, 1]→[0, 1], is a smoothing function if:

$$f(0) = 0 \tag{A.2}$$

$$\exists \epsilon, 0 < \epsilon < \frac{1}{2}\left(1 - \frac{s}{r}\right) : x \geq \epsilon \Rightarrow f(x) = 1 \tag{A.3}$$

$$x \in (0, \epsilon) \Rightarrow 1 > f(x) > 0 \tag{A.4}$$

$$f \text{ is continuous and non-decreasing} \tag{A.5}$$

$$\int_0^\epsilon \frac{dx}{f(x)} = \infty \tag{A.6}$$

We can substitute h, k in equations (5.5) and (5.6) by smoothing functions f_i and $g_i, i = 1, 2$, to get

$$\dot{p}_t = [s - 2C - sq_t]f_1(p_t)g_1(1 - p_t) \tag{A.7}$$

$$\dot{q}_t = [(1 - s)p_t - (1 - r)]f_2\left(q_t - \frac{s}{r}\right)g_2(1 - q_t) \tag{A.8}$$

Proposition

For all solutions $(p_t, q_t)_{t \geq 0}$ of equations (A.7) and (A.8) we have:

$$(p_0, q_0) \in E^0 \Rightarrow \forall t : (p_t, q_t) \in E^0$$

To prove the proposition we utilize equations (A.7) and (A.8) to derive

$$\frac{dp_t}{dq_t} = \frac{\dot{p}_t}{\dot{q}_t} = \frac{[s - 2C - sq_t]f_1(p_t)g_1(1 - p_t)}{[(1 - s)p_t - (1 - r)]f_2(q_t - [s/r])g_2(1 - q_t)} \tag{A.9}$$

and then separate variables by transforming it into

$$\frac{[(1 - s)p_t - (1 - r)]}{f_1(p_t)g_1(1 - p_t)}dp_t + \frac{sq_t + 2C - s}{f_2(q_t - [s/r])g_2(1 - q_t)}dq_t = 0 \tag{A.10}$$

For any $(p, q) \in E^0$

$$U(p,q) := \int_{p^*}^{p} \frac{[(1 - s)\bar{p} - (1 - r)]}{f_1(\bar{p})g_1(1 - \bar{p})}d\bar{p} + \int_{q^*}^{q} \frac{s\bar{q} + 2C - s}{f_2(\bar{q} - [s/r])g_2(1 - \bar{q})}d\bar{q} \tag{A.11}$$

Preference and Information in Simple Games of Trust

is a potential function for (A.10). Owing to the next two observations, (i) and (ii), the function $-U(\cdot,\cdot)$ is single peaked on E^0 with a unique maximum at the point $(p^*, q^*) = ((1-r)/(1-s), (s-2C)/s)$:

(i) The derivative dU/dt of $U(\cdot,\cdot)$ along the line segment

$$\{(p^*, q^*) + t[(p, q) - (p^*, q^*)] | t \in [0, 1]\}$$

with $(p, q) \neq (p^*, q^*)$is

$$\frac{dU(p(t), q(t))}{dt} = \frac{\partial U}{\partial \bar{p}}\frac{d\bar{p}}{dt} + \frac{\partial U}{\partial \bar{q}}\frac{d\bar{q}}{dt}$$

$$= \frac{(1-s)(\bar{p}-p^*)(p-p^*)}{f_1(\bar{p})g_1(1-\bar{p})} + \frac{s(\bar{q}-q^*)(q-q^*)}{f_2(\bar{q}-[s/r])g_2(1-\bar{q})}, (\bar{p}, \bar{q}) \neq (p^*, q^*)$$

Since $(\bar{p}-p^*)(p-p^*) \geq 0$ and $(\bar{q}-q^*)(q-q^*) \geq 0$ the function U strictly increases with t. $U(p, q)$ increases along all rays emanating from (p^*, q^*) and the level lines of $U(\cdot,\cdot)$ are bounded in length.

(ii) Because of (A.6) and (A.11) a level line of $U(\cdot,\cdot)$ cannot intersect the boundary of E^0. Moreover, the trajectory of a solution is a level line of $U(\cdot,\cdot)$ since $U(p, q)$ is given as the integral of (A.9) and (A.10) respectively. Thus for any initial point $(p_0, q_0) \in E^0$ the solution will remain in E^0.

As already argued the iso-level curves of $U(p, q)$, i.e. the sets,

$$I(p, q) = \{(\bar{p}, \bar{q}) \in E^0 | U(\bar{p}, \bar{q}) = U(p, q)\} \quad \text{(A.12)}$$

for $(p, q) \in E^0$ are the trajectories $(p_t, q_t)_{t \geq 0}$ of the dynamic system (A.7) and (A.8) for some $(p_0, q_0) \in E^0$. As in the special case of equations (5.5) and (5.6) the system (A.7) and (A.8) with $(p_0, q_0) \in E^0$ is dynamically though not asymptotically stable. Cycling around (p^*, q^*) is in this sense a robust result.

Solution trajectories starting in E^0 remain in E^0 under quite general transformations: Let ϕ and φ be continuous and strictly increasing on $[-1, 1]$ such that $\phi(0) = 0 = \varphi(0)$. Instead of equalities (A.7) and (A.8) we now consider

$$\dot{p}_t = \phi([s - 2C - sq_t])f_1(p_t)g_1(1-p_t) \quad \text{(A.13)}$$

$$\dot{q}_t = \varphi([(1-s)p_t - (1-r)])f_2\left(q_t - \frac{s}{r}\right)g_2(1-q_t) \quad \text{(A.14)}$$

The results stated in (i) and (ii) as derived in our previous discussion of the special case (A.7) and (A.8) carry over to (A.13) and (A.14). Cycling around (p^*, q^*) is thus not brought about by the linearity assumption made in specifying (4.6) and (4.11) respectively, but emerges quite generally when preferences and information co-evolve as described here.

REFERENCES

Arthur, W. B. (1993), 'On Designing Economic Agents that Behave like Human Agents', *Journal of Evolutionary Economics* 3, 1–22.

Axelrod, R. (1984), *The Evolution of Cooperation*, Basic Books, New York.

Brennan, H. G., W. Güth and H. Kliemt (1997), 'Trust in the Shadow of the Courts', Discussion Paper No. 9789, Center for Economic Research, Tilburg.

Coleman, J. S. (1983), 'Free Riders and Zealots', in: W. Sodeur *et al.* (eds), *Ökonomische Erklärungen sozialen Verhaltens*, Verlag der Kooperative, Duisburg, pp. 135–152.

Cressman, Ross, William G. Morrison and Jean-Francois Wen (1998), 'On the Evolutionary Dynamics of Crime', *Canadian Economics Association* 31(5), 1101–1117.

Frank, R. (1987), 'If Homo Economicus Could Choose His Own Utility Function, Would He Want One with a Conscience?', *American Economic Review* 77(4), 593–604.

Frey, B. S. (1997), *Not Just for the Money. An Economic Theory of Personal Motivation*, Edward Elgar, Cheltenham.

Friedman, Daniel (1991), 'Evolutionary Games in Economics', *Econometrica* 59(3), 637–666.

Fukuyama, F. (1995), *Trust. The Social Virtues and the Creation of Prosperity*, Free Press, New York.

Gale, John, Kenneth G. Binmore and Larry Samuelson (1995), 'Learning to be Imperfect: The Ultimatum Game', *Games and Economic Behavior* 8, 56–90.

Güth, W. and H. Kliemt (1994), 'Competition or Co-operation: On the Evolutionary Economics of Trust, Exploitation and Moral Attitudes', *Metroeconomica* 45(2), 155–187.

Güth, W. and H. Kliemt (1995), 'Evolutionarily Stable Co-operative Commitments', *Humboldt University Discussion Paper, Economics Series* 53.

Güth, W. and H. Kliemt (1998), 'The Indirect Evolutionary Approach', *Rationality and Society* 10(3), 377–399.

Hart, H. L. A. (1961), *The Concept of Law*, Clarendon Press, Oxford.

Hofbauer, Josef and Karl H. Schlag (1998), 'Sophisticated Imitation in Cyclic Games', Rheinische Friedrich-Wilhelms-Universität, Bonn. Sonderforschungsbereich 303, Discussion Paper No. B-427.

Kreps, D., P. Milgrom, J. Roberts and R. Wilson (1982), 'Rational Cooperation in the Finitely-Repeated Prisoners' Dilemma', *Journal of Economic Theory* 27, 245–252.

Landa, J. (1994), *Trust, Ethnicity, and Identity*, University of Michigan Press, Ann Arbor, MI.

Posch, Martin (1997), 'Cycling in a Stochastic Learning Algorithm for Normal Form Games', *Journal of Evolutionary Economics* 7, 193–207.

Schüßler, R. (1990), *Kooperation unter Egoisten*, Oldenbourg, München.

Seligman, A. (1997), *The Problem of Trust*, Princeton University Press, Princeton, NJ.

Smith, A. (1776/1976), *An Inquiry into the Nature and Causes of the Wealth of Nations*, Liberty Press, Indianapolis.

Vanberg, V. J. and R. D. Congleton (1992), 'Rationality, Morality and Exit', *American Political Science Review* 86, 418–427.

[31]

Explaining Reciprocal Behavior in Simple Strategic Games: An Evolutionary Approach

Werner Güth and Menahem E. Yaari

Reciprocal behavior is a tendency on the part of individuals who perceive the behavior of others as being beneficial or harmful to themselves to respond in kind. To simplify matters, our analysis concentrates on situations where it is harm that is being reciprocated. Here, individual A is said to harm another individual B if it is common knowledge that the negative consequences of A's act are serious for B and that A is causing them.

The basic problem of reciprocal behavior is to explain why people engage in costly retribution when the damage to themselves is unpreventable. Our main approach to this problem is the concept of evolutionary stability: we shall try to show that mutants endowed with an incentive to reciprocate have a higher reproductive success. More specifically, it is assumed that, while individual behavior is guided both by the desire to reproduce and the incentive to reciprocate, reproductive success is purely a function of the resources earned via strategic interaction.

Our model is a simple, two-person game where initially both players must choose independently between a fair and an unfair proposal. The game ends immediately if both players pick the same proposal, and this common proposal is then implemented. Payoffs to both players are higher in the case of mutual fairness. In the case of diverging proposals, the player who has chosen fairly can prevent his or her greedy partner from enjoying the fruits of his or her greed, that is, he or she can reciprocate even though the reproductive resources of the fair proposal are no longer available to him or her.

The game to be discussed is simple, but a similar analysis can be performed for more complex game models with more than two players and more than two sequential decision stages. A more important shortcoming of our analysis is that we assume individual rationality for given preferences, al-

The authors gratefully acknowledge helpful comments by Reinhard Selten, Eric van Damme, Franz Weissing, Ulrich Witt, and an anonymous referee as well as the financial support of the German Science Foundation DFG and the Israel Foundations Trustees.

though one might also want to derive individual rationality as an evolutionarily stable strategy (ESS; see, e.g., Maynard Smith and Price 1973; Maynard Smith 1982; Selten 1983; Van Damme 1987). One could, for instance, assume two time dimensions so that evolution of behavior for given preferences can develop much faster than the evolution of preferences themselves. Here we do not engage in this more ambitious endeavor but only indicate its likely results.

Another restrictive assumption is complete information, in the sense of both players being aware of each other's preferences, including the desire to reciprocate. A similar analysis is possible for a game model where players are not sure whether their opponents will want to reciprocate. This can be done simply by allowing the opponent to be one of several possible types, with different tendencies for reciprocal behavior. In a further study we shall explore a model that includes the situations of complete and mutually incomplete information as well as the situations of asymmetric incomplete information as special cases.

Our approach can be regarded as a new way of viewing individual preferences. Instead of assuming that individual preferences are exogenously given, we think of an evolutionary process where preferences are determined as evolutionarily stable strategies. An objection to this approach might be that human evolution is much too slow to explain the rather rapid changes in human preferences often observed. We would accept this criticism if our approach were used to explain changes in preferences for consumer products. But for preferences relating to basic human attitudes, such as the desire for reciprocity, this argument does not apply. The desire for reciprocity is not a recent fancy but a typical trait of humans in general, going back to early primates. This point has been discussed by Trivers (1971). (Indeed, reciprocity has been observed also in monkeys, our old ancestors. See, e.g., Maynard Smith 1978.)

In the next section we shall describe our simple game model. This game is analysed in the third section for any pattern of preference for reciprocal behavior. With the help of these results we show, in the fourth section, that the desire for reciprocity can be an evolutionarily stable strategy. We conclude the chapter by summarizing and briefly indicating our further plans for the study of reciprocal behavior.

The Game Model

Two interacting individuals, called player 1 and player 2, are engaged in the game shown in figure 1 in extensive form.

The game starts with the first move of player 1. The moves of player 1 are indicated by capital letters, the ones of player 2 by lowercase letters. The

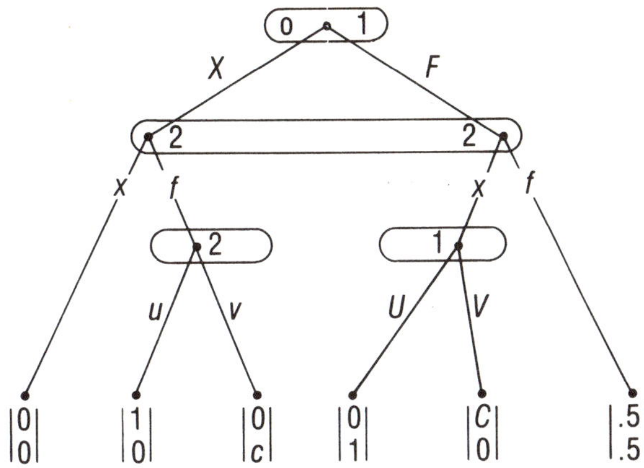

Fig. 1. The game in extensive form with players 1 and 2

letters X and x stand for exploiting the other player, whereas F and f represent the fair treatment move. The label at each decision node indicates the player whose turn it is to move. Note that the two decision nodes following 1's initial move belong to the same information set for player 2, that is, player 2 has to decide between x and f without knowing 1's previous decision. Thus, both players have to decide independently between their exploitative and their fair treatment move.

We imagine that both individuals have to decide how to split a resource whose consumption is positively related to reproductive success. Without loss of generality, the size of this resource can be normalized at 1. In the case of (X,x), where both sides choose to exploit each other, we envisage a very inefficient conflict settlement, for example, risky fights with serious injuries, so that neither party can gain any reproductive success. In the case of (F,f), where both sides choose to treat each other fairly, the result is an equal distribution of the available resource. The payoff vectors (0,0) for (X,x) and (0.5,0.5) for (F,f) should be interpreted either as the amount of resource available for consumption by the two agents or as the reproductive success resulting from consuming it. Since any ordinal transformation of individual payoffs will not affect our results and since reproductive success is assumed to be strictly increasing in resource intake, either interpretation can be used to derive our results.

In the case where the two agents choose opposite moves, that is, (X,f) and (F,x), the player who has made the fair proposal is allowed to decide whether to yield (U, respectively u) or whether to reciprocate (V, respectively v), that is, to prevent the other from enjoying what he or she greedily has taken away. If he yields, then all the resource and all the reproductive success goes to the other (selfish) player. This explains the payoff vectors (1,0) for the play (X,f,u) and (0,1) for the play (F,x,U). If this player chooses to reciprocate, then neither player can enjoy the resource, that is, both players have no resource intake and therefore the same reproductive success, as in the case of (X,x). Ordinarily, this would mean that the payoff vectors for the plays (X,f,v) and (F,x,V) are both (0,0). It is at this point that our analysis departs from customary tradition: We assume that, as far as reproductive success is concerned, vector (0,0) is, indeed, the outcome for both (X,f,v) and (F,x,V). However, as far as agents' preferences are concerned, we assume the outcomes to be $(0,c)$ and $(C,0)$, respectively, and we think of parameters c and C as being determined in an evolutionary process.

The case of $C > 0$ and $c > 0$ is one where both players get satisfaction from reciprocating, in the case of $C < 0$ and $c < 0$ the costs of reciprocation outweigh its pleasures. What we shall attempt to do is show that the situation with $C > 0$ and $c > 0$ is more likely to evolve if the preference patterns expressed by parameters C and c are determined through genetic mutation and evolution.

As long as the game in figure 1 is analyzed solely in terms of pure strategies, there is no loss of generality in assuming that parameters c and C can take on just two value, one positive and the other negative. Consequently, let us assume:

$$C \in \{C_+, C_-\} \quad \text{and} \quad c \in \{c_+, c_-\}, \tag{1}$$

with

$$C_+ > 0 > C_- \quad \text{and} \quad c_+ > 0 > c_-. \tag{2}$$

Note that in the evolutionary game, where parameters c and C themselves are chosen, mixed strategies *are* possible, and they are achieved through distributions of types in the population.

The four possible specifications (C,c) of genetically determined payoff parameters give rise to four different games (in fig. 1) that can be identified by their parameter configurations.

$$(C,c) = \begin{cases} (C_+, c_+) \\ (C_+, c_-) \\ (C_-, c_+) \\ (C_-, c_-) \end{cases} \tag{3}$$

This implicitly assumes that a player knows whether his or her opponent is a reciprocating or a yielding type, that is, that the game is one of complete information. If a player has only probabilistic beliefs concerning the type of his or her opponent, the analysis of the game would have to involve all types of players that are expected with positive probability. What we essentially exclude is the possibility that a yielding type might choose (strategically) to mimic a reciprocating type. A further study will explore a model where such a behavior is possible.

In the next section we will solve the four games shown in figure 1 corresponding to the four possible parameter configurations (C,c) in equation 3. With the help of these results, we then can determine the evolutionarily stable configuration (C,c) of genetically determined preferences guiding reciprocal behavior.

Solution of Games

Let s_i and $\hat{s}_i$ be two possible strategies of player i. We say that s_i dominates $\hat{s}_i$ if, for all possible strategy combinations of player i's opponents, s_i is never a worse reply than $\hat{s}_i$ and if s_i is a better reply than $\hat{s}_i$ to at least one such strategy combination. The strategies that survive repeated elimination of dominated strategies are simply called undominated strategies. For the solution of the four games (C,c), described by figure 1 and equation 3, we will require the choice of undominated strategies by all players. For the case at hand, repeated elimination of dominated strategies yields a unique strategy for both players in all four games (C,c). Therefore, we can determine the solutions of all four games by relying merely on this rather weak rationality condition.

It should be noted that rationality in the sense that players choose undominated strategies can be derived as evolutionarily stable behavior. Imagine a situation where a player i has only two strategies, s_i and $\hat{s}_i$, and where s_i dominates $\hat{s}_i$ with payoffs being positively related to reproductive success. If behavior is genetically determined, all possible strategy combinations of i's coplayers might show up as a result of mutation. Thus, permanent invasion of the population by mutants will completely drive out all $\hat{s}_i$ gene types, since they yield a lower reproductive success than s_i in every completely mixed population where no possible gene constellation is excluded. Unfortunately, this argument cannot be simply extended so that it also applies to repeated elimination of dominated strategies. Another approach would be to model genetically determined learning behavior and to explore whether this will lead to the use of undominated strategies. This indicates that there might be ways to derive rationality in the sense of undominated strategies instead of simply assuming it by an evolutionary analysis whose time unit is infinitesimal in comparison with the time unit that is applicable for changes in the genetically determined incentives for reciprocal behavior.

The Game $(C,c) = (C_+,c_+)$

In case of $C = C_+$ and $c = c_+$, the strategies prescribing moves U and u, respectively, are obviously dominated, that is, both players will reciprocate whenever they have the choice to do so. Thus, after eliminating all strategies prescribing moves U and u, both players have just two possible strategies left, namely XV and FV for player 1 and xv and fv for player 2. The payoff structure for this restricted game is shown in table 1.

In table 1, it can easily be seen that FV is always better than XV regardless which of the two possible strategies player 2 is going to use. Similarly, fv dominates xv in the restricted game. Thus, repeated elimination of dominated strategies yields the unique solution $s = (s_1,s_2) = (FV,fv)$, that is, both players choose fair play, since their opponent is firmly committed to reciprocate. To summarize:

Observation 1. In the case of $(C,c) = (C_+,c_+)$, the solution of the game is the strategy vector (FV,fv).

The Game $(C,c) = (C_-,c_-)$

For $C = C_-$ and $c = c_-$ the strategies prescribing moves V and v, respectively, are dominated. Eliminating these dominated strategies yields the restricted game shown in table 2.

If the opponent is selfish (chooses X or x, as appropriate), then the player's own choice does not matter. But if the opponent is fair (chooses F or f, as appropriate), then the choice of selfish behavior is clearly better. Thus, repeated elimination of dominated strategies yields the solution (XU,xu). Since no one is going to reciprocate, both players make selfish proposals and thereby lose all the available resources.

Observation 2. In the case of $(C,c) = (C_-,c_-)$, the solution of the game is the strategy vector (XU,xu).

TABLE 1. Bimatrix Game Resulting after Elimination of the Dominated Moves *U* and *u* for $(C,c) = (C_+,c_+)$

	Player 2	
Player 1	xv	fv
XV	(0,0)	$(0,c_+)$
FV	$(C_+,0)$	(0.5,0.5)

TABLE 2. Bimatrix Game Resulting after Elimination of the Dominated Moves V and v for $(C,c) = (C_-,c_-)$

	Player 2	
Player 1	*xu*	*fu*
XU	(0,0)	(1,0)
FU	(0,1)	(0.5,0.5)

The Games $(C,c) = (C_+,c_-)$ and $(C,c) = (C_-,c_+)$

Due to the symmetry of the game, it suffices to consider one of the two possible situations with different incentives for both players to reciprocate. In the case of $(C,c) = (C_+,c_-)$, all strategies s_1 prescribing move U and all strategies s_2 prescribing v are dominated. The restricted game after eliminating all these strategies is shown in table 3.

Obviously, *fu* dominates *xu*. Eliminating *xu* now makes *FV* a dominated strategy of player 1. Thus, the solution for $(C,c) = (C_+,c_-)$ is (XV,fu), that is, the player who is willing to reciprocate can exploit the other player. For $(C,c) = (C_-,c_+)$, the analogous result is (FU,xv).

Observation 3. The solution of the game is the strategy vector (XV,fu) for $(C,c) = (C_+c_-)$ and (FU,xv) for $(C,c) = (C_-,c_+)$.

Evolutionary Analysis of Incentives for Reciprocal Behavior

With the help of the preceding results, we will now determine the evolutionarily stable parameter configuration (C,c). Let $G = [S_1,S_2; H = (H_1,H_2)]$ be a symmetric game in normal form, that is,

TABLE 3. Bimatrix Game Resulting after Elimination of the Dominated Moves U and v for $(C,c) = (C_+,c_-)$

	Player 2	
Player 1	*xu*	*fu*
XV	(0,0)	(1,0)
FV	$(C_+,0)$	(0.5,0.5)

$$S_1 = S_2$$

$$H_1(s_1,s_2) = H_2(s_2,s_1)$$

for all

$$(s_1,s_2) \in S_1 \times S_2,$$

where S_1 and S_2 are the sets of pure strategies s_1 and s_2, respectively, and where $H_i(s_1,s_2)$ measures i's reproductive success for the strategy vector (s_1,s_2), $i = 1, 2$. All pure strategies s_i in S_i and mixed strategies $q_i(\cdot)$ with

$$q_i(s_i) \geq 0,\ s_i \in S_i, \quad \text{and} \quad \sum_{s_i \in S_i} q_i(s_i) = 1$$

are considered as possible mutants. We identify the pure strategy s_i with the mixed strategy $q_i(\cdot)$ satisfying $q_i(s_i) = 1$ and denote the set of mixed strategies $q_i(\cdot)$ by Q_i. The payoff functions $H_i(\cdot)$ can be extended from $S_1 \times S_2$ to $Q_1 \times Q_2$ in the canonical way:

$$H_i(q_1,q_2) = \sum_{(s_1,s_2) \in S_1 \times S_2} q_1(s_1)q_2(s_2)H_i(s_1,s_2)\,. \tag{4}$$

A strategy $q_i(\cdot) \in Q_i$ is evolutionarily stable (see Maynard Smith and Price 1973; Maynard Smith 1982; Selten 1983; Van Damme 1987) if the following two conditions hold:

$$H_i(q_i,q_i) \geq H_i(\hat{q}_i,q_i) \quad \text{for all} \quad \hat{q}_i \in Q_i, \tag{5}$$

and

$$H_i(q_i,\hat{q}_i) > H_i(\hat{q}_i,\hat{q}_i) \quad \text{for all} \quad \hat{q}_i \in Q_i$$

$$\text{with} \quad H_i(\hat{q}_i,q_i) = H_i(q_i,q_i). \tag{6}$$

Condition 5 says that the evolutionarily stable strategy $q_i(\cdot)$ must be optimal given that the population consists of $q_i(\cdot)$ strategies only. If there is no unique best reply against a population consisting of $q_i(\cdot)$ types only, then, according to condition 6, the evolutionarily stable strategy $q_i(\cdot)$ must be better than any other optimal reply $\hat{q}_i(\cdot)$ against $\hat{q}_i(\cdot)$ in a population consisting of $\hat{q}_i(\cdot)$ types only.

The concept of evolutionary stability as defined here tries to capture, in a static way, the essential aspects of an equilibrium state of a dynamic evolutionary process. Condition 5 implies that, in a population containing the same evolutionarily stable strategy only, there exists no mutant which is better adjusted to this environment. If there would be an equally optimal reply to such an environment, then condition 6 rules out that this mutant can spread out in the population since, in any mixed population with the evolutionarily stable strategy and this mutant, the evolutionarily stable strategy earns a higher reproductive success.

For the evolutionary analysis, we consider both possible parameter values of C and c, respectively, as well as all probability mixtures of both values as possible mutants, that is,

$$S_1 = \{C_+, C_-\} \quad \text{and} \quad S_2 = \{c_+, c_-\}.$$

The reproductive success for all four strategy combinations (C,c) is determined by the solution payoffs for the (C,c) games where one, of course, has to keep in mind that the payoff parameters C and c are completely unrelated to reproductive success. According to observations 1, 2, and 3, the reproductive success for the four possible strategy combinations (C,c) is shown in table 4.

For each of the four possible constellations (C,c) of gene types, the first (second) matrix component measures the reproductive success of player 1(2). With the help of table 4, one can easily see that there exists a unique, evolutionary stable strategy, namely

$$C = C_+ \quad \text{and} \quad c = c_+, \tag{7}$$

since this gene type is always the only optimal best reply regardless of how the population is divided between the two possible gene types.

Proposition. For the game of figure 1 and the space of mutants as described by table 4 there exists a unique evolutionarily stable strategy

TABLE 4. Bimatrix with the Reproductive Success for Both Players and All Four Possible Constellations (*C,c*) of Gene Types

	Player 2	
Player 1	c_+	c_-
C_+	(0.5,0.5)	(1,0)
C_-	(0,1)	(0,0)

$C = C_+$ and $c = c_+$, respectively, according to which both players are genetically programmed to exercise reciprocal behavior.

The proposition implies that, after possible adjustments due to short-lived new mutants, the population will settle down to a state where all individuals possess a desire to reciprocate. It thus provides a possible explanation for why humans and their early ancestors developed such a desire to respond harmfully to harm and kindly to kindness. The main reason for our result is that people who allow others to exploit them will finally be exploited and that one will not be exploited if one is genetically determined to reciprocate. Thus, genetic implementation of reciprocity helps to avoid inefficient outcomes due to mutual attempts to exploit others.

If the reciprocal acts *V* and *v*, respectively, were not available, the game of figure 1 would simplify to the degenerate Prisoner's Dilemma game shown in table 5. This game has the unique solution

$$s = (s_1, s_2) = (XU, xu)$$

in undominated strategies. According to the proposition, this inefficient result will be avoided if retaliatory acts are possible and players can genetically develop a preference for reciprocity. It is, of course, well known that retaliatory precommitment will resolve the Prisoner's Dilemma (see, e.g., Witt 1986). Here our purpose is to suggest an evolutionary setting and to show that such retaliatory precommitment would, in fact, be evolutionarily stable.

We have restricted ourselves to a very simple model where there is no effort or time cost of punishing that psychic satisfaction from retaliation would have to overcome. Of course, nothing would change if such costs are always smaller than the absolute value of the desire for revenge. But there may be circumstances where this is not true and where cooperation may fail, since retaliation is not self-enforcing. Another restriction of our analysis is that it considers only genetic evolution and not cultural evolution (see, e.g., Boyd and Richerson 1985). One reason is that we feel less confident modeling cultural evolution and speculating about its stability conditions. Since cultural

TABLE 5. Bimatrix Representation of Figure 1 When Moves *V* and *v*, Respectively, Are Not Available

	Player 2	
Player 1	*xu*	*fu*
XU	(0,0)	(1,0)
FU	(0,1)	(0.5,0.5)

changes are often inspired by other coexisting cultures and not only by rare mutants, the stability properties of evolutionarily stable strategies, for instance, may not be appropriate for cultural evolution.

In the meanwhile, our model has been generalized in two ways (see Güth 1991). First, we have given up the assumption of perfect behavioral control, that is, an unintended action will now also be used due to small mistake probabilities. The more general and complex model allows the investigation of the incentives for developing a better behavioral control. More important, we were also able to generalize our results to situations where there is incomplete information about reciprocal incentives, that is, one knows their own reciprocal incentive but not that of the other individual. In such situations, 'desire for revenge' is also the only evolutionarily stable strategy, as is the case when reciprocal incentives are common knowledge.

Peter Ockenfels (1989) has applied our basic approach to Prisoner's Dilemma games that can be played either simultaneously or sequentially as games of perfect information. Players are assumed to have genetically determined preferences either for using their cooperative strategy or only for mutual cooperation, which strategies are totally unrelated to reproductive success. Unfortunately, such games can have multiple equilibria so that Ockenfels has to rely on equilibrium selection. To justify preferences for cooperation as an evolutionarily stable strategy when one is only incompletely informed about the opponent's preference type, Ockenfels assumes that a defective type will be recognized with positive probability. A similar situation has been analysed by Frank (1987), who assumes that player in Prisoner's Dilemma games can be either honest (reliable cooperators) or dishonest (defecting from cooperation) and that honesty can be signaled perfectly or imperfectly. By comparing the expected payoffs of honest players (who cannot defect) and dishonest players for all possible compositions of the population, Frank derives the evolutionary dynamics and the evolutionarily stable composition of the population.

Final Remarks

The desire for reciprocity is a well-known fact (see, e.g., Gouldner 1960; Young 1986) and can be easily explored experimentally. We do not assume this desire to be exogenously given, but rather we try to derive it by applying the concept of evolutionary stability. Of course, our approach cannot be used to explain momentary human preferences, since biological evolution is very slow in comparison with changes in preferences for consumer products. Only incentives for basic behavioral attitudes such as reciprocity (see Trivers 1971) can be approached through a model of genetic evolution.

Our model shows that reciprocal behavior may help avoid inefficiencies resulting from individual selfishness. One would, therefore, like to explore ways of ensuring efficient results through mechanisms guaranteeing reciprocity. A game in which reciprocity is self-enforcing can be called a reciprocal mechanism. Our own example of a reciprocal mechanism rests on the idea of going back to the "biological game" and demonstrating the evolutionary stability of preferences for reciprocity.

REFERENCES

Boyd, R., and Richerson, P. 1985. *Culture and the Evolutionary Process*. Chicago: University of Chicago Press.

Frank, R. H. 1987. "If Homo Economicus Could Choose His Own Utility Function, Would He Want One with a Conscience?" *American Economic Review* 7:593–604.

Gouldner, A. W. 1960. "The Norm of Reciprocity: A Preliminary Statement." *American Sociological Review* 25:161–78.

Güth, W. 1991. "Incomplete Information about Reciprocal Incentives—An Evolutionary Approach to Explaining Cooperative Behavior." Working Paper. University of Frankfurt. Photocopy.

Maynard Smith, J. 1978. "The Evolution of Behavior." *Scientific American*, September, 136–45.

Maynard Smith, J. 1982. *Evolution and the Theory of Games*. Cambridge: Cambridge University Press.

Maynard Smith, J., and Price, G. R. 1973. "The Logic of Animal Conflict." *Nature* 246:15–18.

Ockenfels, P. 1989. "Cooperation in Prisoner's Dilemma Games—An Evolutionary Approach." Working Paper. University of Frankfurt. Photocopy.

Selten, R. 1983. "Evolutionary Stability in Extensive Two-Person Games." *Mathematical Social Sciences* 5:269–363.

Trivers, R. L. 1971. "The Evolution of Reciprocal Altruism." *Quarterly Review of Biology* 46:35–57.

Van Damme, E. 1987. *Stability and Perfection of Nash Equilibria*. Berlin: Springer-Verlag.

Witt, U. 1986. "Evolution and Stability of Cooperation without Enforceable Contracts." *Kyklos* 39:245–66.

Young, G. A., Jr. 1986. "Patterns of Threat and Punishment Reciprocity in a Conflict Setting." *Journal for Personality of Social Psychology* 51:541–46.

[32]

J. theor. Biol. (2000) **206,** 169–179
doi:10.1006/jtbi.2000.2111, available online at http://www.idealibrary.com on IDEAL®

Strong Reciprocity and Human Sociality

HERBERT GINTIS*

Department of Economics, University of Massachusetts, Amherst, U.S.A.

(*Received on* 15 *June* 1999, *Accepted in revised form on* 22 *May* 2000)

Human groups maintain a high level of sociality despite a low level of relatedness among group members. This paper reviews the evidence for an empirically identifiable form of prosocial behavior in humans, which we call "strong reciprocity", that may in part explain human sociality. A strong reciprocator is predisposed to cooperate with others and punish non-cooperators, even when this behavior cannot be justified in terms of extended kinship or reciprocal altruism. We present a simple model, stylized but plausible, of the evolutionary emergence of strong reciprocity.

1. Introduction

Human groups maintain a high level of sociality despite a low level of relatedness among group members. Three approaches have been offered to explain this phenomenon: reciprocal altruism (Trivers, 1971; Axelrod & Hamilton, 1981), cultural group selection (Cavalli-Sforza *et al.*, 1981; Boyd & Richerson, 1985) and genetically based altruism (Lumsden & Wilson, 1981; Simon, 1993; Wilson & Dugatkin, 1997; Sober & Wilson, 1998). These approaches are complementary and doubtless all contribute to the explanation of human sociality. The analysis of altruism, however, has tended to argue the plausibility of altruism in general, rather than isolating particular human traits that might have emerged from a group selection process.

This paper reviews the evidence for one such trait—an empirically identifiable form of prosocial behavior in humans that probably has a significant genetic component. We call this "strong reciprocity". A strong reciprocator is predisposed to cooperate with others and punish non-cooperators, even when this behavior cannot be justified in terms of self-interest, extended kinship, or reciprocal altruism. We present a simple yet plausible model of the evolutionary emergence of strong reciprocity.

2. The Conditions for Sustaining Cooperation

A group of n individuals faces in each time period a "public goods game" in which each member, by sacrificing an amount $c > 0$, contributes an amount $b > c$ shared equally by the other members of the group (all costs and benefits are in fitness units).*

*E-mail: hgintis@mediaone.net, web: http://www-unix.oit.umass.edu/~gintis

* For a review of the evidence concerning cooperation in non-humans and humans, see Dugatkin (1997) and Dugatkin (1998), respectively. Following Axelrod & Hamilton (1981), most models deal with repeated two-person interactions, although Boyd & Richerson (1988, 1992) and a few others deal with larger groups. Sethi & Somanathan (1996) is close to this paper in modeling endogenous punishment in a public goods game, but their model predicts the absence of punishers in equilibrium, a result at variance with observed behavior in human society.

0022-5193/00/180169 + 11 $35.00/0

If all members cooperate, each receives a net payoff of $b - c > 0$. However, the only Nash equilibrium in this game is universal defection, in which no member contributes, and all members have baseline fitness zero (an arbitrary constant can be added to all fitnesses to account for the growth rate of the overall population). We also assume an individual not in a cooperating group has baseline fitness zero.

While cooperation is not an equilibrium outcome in a single play of this public goods game, it can be sustained under appropriate conditions if the game is repeated. Specifically, suppose a member's contribution is publicly observable, and in any period a player who fails to contribute c is ostracized from the group. Suppose also that group disbands spontaneously at the end of a given period (due to war, pestilence, climate change, and the like) with probability $1 - \delta$. Let π be a member's total expected fitness when contributing, assuming all other members contribute. Then π can be determined by noting that the current period net fitness gain is $b - c$, plus with probability δ the game is continued and again has value π in the next period. Therefore, we have $\pi = b - c + \delta\pi$, which gives†

$$\pi = \frac{b - c}{1 - \delta}. \quad (1)$$

A player will contribute, then, as long as $(b - c)/(1 - \delta) > b$, since by not contributing, the member earns b during the current period, but is ostracized at the end of the period. Rearranging terms in this inequality, we get

Theorem 1. *Suppose c is the fitness cost to a group member of cooperating, b is the fitness gain to others in the group when a member cooperates, and δ is a discount factor representing the probability that the group will remain constituted for at least one more period.‡ Then cooperation can be sustained in the repeated public goods game if and only if*

$$\frac{c}{b} \leq \delta.$$

Theorem 1 is of course a completely standard result. With $n = 2$ is analogous to Hamilton's (1964) inclusive fitness criterion (where δ represents the degree of relatedness), Triver's (1971) reciprocal altruism mechanism (where $\delta = 1$), and Axelrod's (1984) condition for cooperation in the repeated prisoner's dilemma. However, the explicit presence of the discount factor δ in Theorem 1 makes it clear that, *however, great the net benefits of cooperation, if groups disband with high probability, then cooperation among self-interested agents cannot be sustained.*§ Moreover, periodic social crises are not implausible, since population contractions were likely common in the evolutionary history of *Homo sapiens* (Boone & Kessler, 1999). The very low rate of growth of the human population over the whole pre-historic period, plus the high rate of human population growth in even poor contemporary foraging societies in good times (Keckler, 1997), suggests periodic crises occurred in the past. Moreover, flattened mortality profiles of pre-historic skeletal populations indicate population crashes ranging from 10 to 54% at a mean rate of once in 30 years (Keckler, 1997). Finally, optimal foraging models of hunter–gatherer societies often predict stable limit cycles (Belovsky, 1988).

In contrast to the self-interested agents assumed in Theorem 1, a strong reciprocator cooperates and punishes non-cooperators without considering the value of δ, i.e. even when the probability of future interactions is low. As we shall see, when δ is low, the presence of strong reciprocators can allow the group to secure the benefits of cooperation. However, strong reciprocators are altruists, since they bear surveillance and punishment costs not borne by

† Equation (1) can also be derived by noting that $(b - c)\delta^n$ is the expected return in period n, so we have $\pi = (b - c)(1 + \delta + \delta^2 + \cdots) = (b - c)/(1 - \delta)$.

‡ In general, the discount factor δ is the ratio of the contribution to fitness of a unit payoff in the next period to a unit payoff in the current period. In addition to the probability of group dissolution, this ratio generally depends, among other things, on an individual's age and health. We abstract from these factors in this paper.

§ To my knowledge, endogenous variation in the discount factor δ, central to explaining a high frequency of strong reciprocators in this paper, has not previously been modeled. Nor has the relationship between group longevity and the prevalence of reciprocal altruism in non-human species been subjected to systematic empirical investigation. See, however, Dugatkin & Alfieri (1992).

self-interested group members, so they can persist in equilibrium only if certain conditions, which we develop below, are satisfied.

3. Experimental Evidence for Strong Reciprocity

An extensive body of evidence suggests that a considerable fraction of the population, in many different societies, and under many different social conditions, including complete anonymity, behave like the strong reciprocator. We here review laboratory evidence concerning the *public goods game* as modeled in the previous section. For additional evidence, including the results of dictator, ultimatum, common pool resource and trust games, see Güth & Tietz (1990), Roth (1995), and Camerer & Thaler (1995), and for analytical models, see Gintis (2000).

The public goods game is a direct test of strong reciprocity, and is designed to illuminate such behaviors as contributing to team and community goals, as well as punishing non-contributors. Public goods experiments were first undertaken by the sociologist G. Marwell, the psychologist R. Dawes, the political scientist J. Orbell, and the economists R. Isaac and J. Walker in the late 1970s and early 1980s [see Ledyard (1995) for a summary of this research and an extensive bibliography]. The following is a typical public good game, using a protocol studied by Fehr & Gächter (2000).

Each round of the game consists of each subject being grouped with three other subjects under conditions of strict anonymity. Each subject is then given 20 "points", redeemable at the end of the experimental session for real money. Each subject then places some number of the 20 points in a "common account", and the remainder in the subject's "private account". The experimenter then tells the subjects how many points were contributed to the common account, and adds to the private account of each subject 40% of the total amount in the common account. It follows that if a subject contributes his whole 20 points to the common account, each player will receive eight points at the end of the round. In effect, by cooperating a player loses 12 points but his teammates gain 24 points. In terms of our model of the previous section, $c = 12$ and $b = 24$. The experiment continues for exactly ten rounds, and the subjects are informed of this fact at the start of the experiment.

Clearly, full free riding is a dominant strategy in the public goods game. Public goods experiments, however, show that only a fraction of subjects conform to the self-interested model, contributing nothing to the common account. Rather, subjects begin by contributing on average about half of their endowment to the public account. The level of contributions decays over the course of the ten rounds, until in the final rounds most players are behaving in a self-interested manner (Dawes & Thaler, 1988; Ledyard, 1995). In a meta-study of 12 public goods experiments Fehr & Schmidt (1999) found that in the early rounds, average and median contribution levels ranged from 40 to 60% of the endowment, but in the final period 73% of all individuals ($N = 1042$) contributed nothing, and many of the remaining players contributed close to zero. These results are not compatible with the self-interested actor model, which predicts zero contribution on all rounds, though they might be predicted by a reciprocal altruism model, since the chance to reciprocate declines as end of the experiment approaches. However, we shall see that this is not in fact the explanation of moderate but deteriorating levels of cooperation in the public goods game.

The explanation of the decay of cooperation offered by subjects when debriefed after the experiment is that cooperative subjects became angry at others who contributed less than themselves, and retaliated against free-riding low contributors in the only way available to them—by lowering their own contributions (Andreoni, 1995). Experimental evidence supports this interpretation. When subjects are allowed to punish non-contributors, they do so at a cost to themselves (Dawes *et al.*, 1986; Sato, 1987; Yamagishi, 1988a, b, 1992).

For instance, in Ostrom *et al.* (1992) subjects interacted for 25 periods in a public goods game, and by paying a "fee", subjects could impose costs on other subjects by "fining" them. Since fining costs the individual who uses it, but the benefits of increased compliance accrue to the group as a whole, the only Nash equilibrium in this game that does not depend on incredible threats is for no player to pay the fee, so no player is ever punished for defecting, and all players defect by contributing nothing to the common pool. However, the authors found a significant level of punishing behavior.

The design of the Ostrom–Walker–Gardner study allowed individuals to engage in strategic behavior, since costly punishment of defectors could increase cooperation in future periods, yielding a positive net return for the retaliator. Fehr & Gächter (2000) set up an experimental situation in which the possibility of strategic punishment was removed. They used a ten-round public goods game with costly punishment, employing three different methods of assigning members to groups.|| There were sufficient subjects to run between 10 and 18 groups simultaneously. Under the *Personal* treatment, the four subjects remained in the same group for all ten periods. Under the *Stranger* treatment, the subjects were randomly reassigned after each round. Finally, under the *Perfect Stranger* treatment the subjects were randomly reassigned and assured that they would never meet another subject more than once (in this case, the number of rounds had to be reduced from ten to six to accommodate the size of the subject pool). Subjects earned an average of about $35 for an experimental session.

Fehr & Gächter (2000) performed their experiment for ten rounds with punishment and ten rounds without. Their results are illustrated in Fig. 1. We see that when costly punishment is permitted, cooperation does not deteriorate, and in the partner game, despite strict anonymity, cooperation increases almost to full cooperation, even on the final round. When punishment is not permitted, however, the same subjects experience the deterioration of cooperation found in previous public goods games.

The contrast between the partner effect and the two stranger effects is worth noting. In the latter

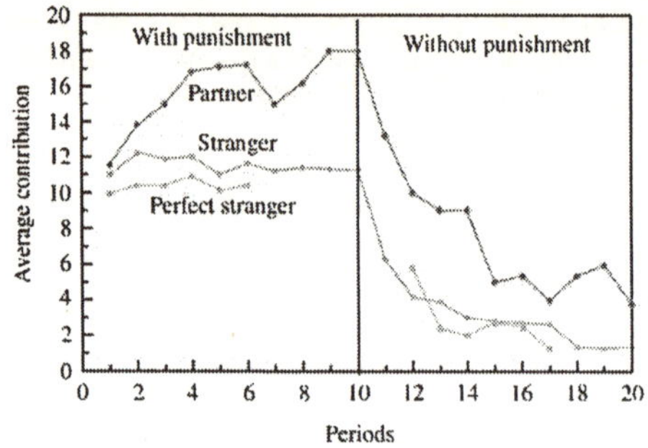

FIG. 1. Average contributions over time in the partner, stranger, and perfect stranger treatments when the punishment conditions is played first (adapted from Fehr & Gächter, 2000).

case, punishment prevented the deterioration of cooperation, whereas in the former case punishment led to an increase in participation over time, until near full cooperation was achieved. This result suggest that subjects are motivated by the personal desire to punish free riders (the stranger treatment), but are even more strongly motivated when there is an identifiable group, to which they belong, whose cooperative effort is impaired by free riding (the partner treatment). The prosociality of strong reciprocity is thus more strongly manifested, the more coherent and permanent the group in question.

4. The Evolution of Strong Reciprocity

A critical weakness of reciprocal altruism is that when a social group is threatened with extinction or dispersal, say through war, pestilence, or famine, cooperation is most needed for survival. But the discount factor δ, which is the probability of group survival for one period, decreases sharply when the group is threatened, since the probability that the group will dissolve increases. Thus, *precisely when a group is most in need of prosocial behavior, cooperation based on reciprocal altruism will collapse*, since the discount factor then falls to a level rendering defection an optimal behavior for self-interested agents.

But strong reciprocity can sustain cooperation in the face of such a threat to the group, and

||Imposing a punishment was quite costly in this experiment. Low levels of punishment (one or two points) was equally costly to punisher and punishee, with higher levels of punishment being relatively more costly to the punisher. Imposing a ten-point punishment—the highest level permitted—cost the punisher 30 points. As we argue below, in human societies we expect the costs of punishing to be quite low compared to the costs of being punished. Thus, this experiment is strongly biased against finding strong reciprocity.

hence, might have an evolutionary advantage in situations where groups are frequently threatened. Strong reciprocators, however, are altruists in that they increase the fitness of unrelated individuals at a cost to themselves. For, unlike self-interested agents, who cooperate and punish only if this maximizes their within-group fitness payoff, strong reciprocators cooperate even when this involves a fitness penalty. If strong reciprocity is an evolutionary adaptation, it must be a considerable benefit to a group to have strong reciprocators, and the group benefits must outweight the individuals costs.¶

These benefits and costs are conveniently represented in terms of Price's equation (1970), which we express as follows (Frank, 1998). Suppose there are groups $i = 1, \ldots, m$, and let q_i be the fraction of the population in group i. Let π_i be the mean fitness of group i, so $\bar{\pi} = \sum_i q_i \pi_i$ is the mean fitness of the whole population. Groups grow from one period to the next in proportion to their relative fitness, so if q_i' is the fraction of the population in group i in the next period, then

$$q_i' = q_i \frac{\pi_i}{\bar{\pi}}.$$

Suppose there is a trait with frequency f_i in group i, so the frequency of the trait in the whole population is $\bar{f} = \sum_i q_i f_i$. If π_i' and f_i' are the mean fitness of group i and the frequency of the trait in group i in the next period, respectively, then $\bar{f}' = \sum_i q_i' f_i'$, and writing $\Delta f_i = f_i' - f_i$, we have

$$\begin{aligned}\bar{f}' - \bar{f} &= \sum q_i' f_i' - \sum q_i f_i \\ &= \sum q_i \frac{\pi_i}{\bar{\pi}}(f_i + \Delta f_i) - \sum q_i f_i \\ &= \sum q_i \left(\frac{\pi_i}{\bar{\pi}} - 1\right) f_i + \sum q_i \frac{\pi_i}{\bar{\pi}} \Delta f_i.\end{aligned}$$

Now, writing $\Delta \bar{f} = \bar{f}' - \bar{f}$, this becomes

$$\bar{\pi} \Delta \bar{f} = \sum q_i (\pi_i - \bar{\pi}) f_i + \sum q_i \pi_i \Delta f_i. \quad (2)$$

¶ This model is an instance of analysing *trait groups* in *structured demes*, to use the terminology of Wilson (1977), to which the reader can refer for a general treatment with numerous applications of behavioral ecology. See also Soltis *et al.* (1995) and references therein.

The second term in eqn (2) is just $\mathbf{E}[\pi \Delta f]$, the expected value of $\pi \Delta f$, over all groups, weighted by the relative size of the groups. If the trait in question renders individuals bearing it less fit than other group members, this term will be negative, since $\Delta f_i < 0$ within each group. To interpret the first term, note that the covariance between the variables π and f is given by

$$\mathrm{cov}(\pi, f) = \sum_i q_i (\pi_i - \bar{\pi})(f_i - \bar{f}).$$

and since $\sum_i q_i (\pi_i - \bar{\pi}) \bar{f} = 0$, we can write eqn (2) as

$$\bar{\pi} \Delta \bar{f} = \mathrm{cov}(\pi, f) + \mathbf{E}[\pi \Delta f]. \quad (3)$$

Strong reciprocity can thus persist in equilibrium if and only if $\mathrm{cov}(\pi, f) > -\mathbf{E}[\pi \Delta f]$ where f is the frequency of the strong reciprocity trait and π is group fitness.

Suppose now that in each "good" period the group will persist into the next period with probability δ^*, while in a "bad" period, which occurs with probability p, the group persists with probability $\delta_* < \delta^*$ provided members cooperate, but dissolves with probability one if members do not cooperate.

At the beginning of each period, prior to members deciding whether or not to cooperate, the state of the group for that period is revealed. Let π^* be the total fitness of a member if all members cooperate, and the state of the group is "good", and let π_* be the total fitness if members cooperate and the state is "bad". Then, the expected fitness before the state is revealed is $\pi = p\pi_* + (1 - p)\pi^*$, and using the same argument as in the derivation of eqn (1), we have the following recursion equations:

$$\pi^* = b - c + \delta^* \pi,$$

$$\pi_* = b - c + \delta_* \pi,$$

which entail

$$\pi^* = \frac{1 + p(\delta^* - \delta_*)}{1 - \delta^* + p(\delta^* - \delta_*)}(b - c), \quad (4)$$

$$\pi_* = \frac{1 - (1 - p)(\delta^* - \delta_*)}{1 - \delta^* + p(\delta^* - \delta_*)}(b - c), \quad (5)$$

$$\pi = \frac{1}{1 - \delta^* + p(\delta^* - \delta_*)}(b - c). \qquad (6)$$

When can cooperation be sustained? Clearly, if it is worthwhile for an agent to cooperate in a bad period, it is worthwhile to cooperate in a good period, so we need only check the bad period case. The current benefit of defecting is c, so the condition for cooperation is $c < \delta_* \pi$. There is a Nash equilibrium in which members thus cooperate in the good state but not in the bad when the following inequalities hold:

$$\delta^* \pi > c > \delta_* \pi. \qquad (7)$$

We assume these inequalities hold.

Suppose group i has a fraction f_i of strong reciprocators, who cooperate and punish independent of whether the state of the group is good or bad. Suppose each strong reciprocator inflicts a total amount of harm $h > 0$ on non-cooperators, at a personal cost of retaliation $c_r > 0$. Because of eqn (7), in a bad state self-interested agents always defect unless punished by strong reciprocators. If there are n_i group members, in a bad state $n_i(1 - f_i)$ defect, and the total harm inflicted on those caught is $n_i f_i h$, so the harm per defector imposed by strong reciprocators is $f_i h/(1 - f_i)$. The gain from defecting in eqn (7) now becomes $c - f_i h/(1 - f_i)$. Thus, if the fraction f_i of strong reciprocators is at least

$$f_* = \frac{c - \pi\delta_*}{c - \pi\delta_* + h}, \qquad (8)$$

complete cooperation will hold. Note that f_* lies strictly between zero and one. Equation (8), where π is given by eqn (6), leads to the following.

Theorem 2. *The minimum fraction f_* of strong reciprocators needed to induce cooperation is lowered by a decrease in the probability p of the bad state, an increase in the probability of survival δ_* in the bad state, and/or an increase in the amount of harm h per strong reciprocator inflicted upon non-cooperators.*

These properties of the model have a straightforward interpretation. A decrease in p raises the fitness value π of being in a cooperative group, thus lowering the fitness gain $c - \delta_* \pi$ from defecting in the bad state, which reduces the amount of punishment needed to induce self-interested members to cooperate. An increase in δ_* also raises π, and hence lowers $c - \delta_* \pi$, with the same result.

The fact that an increase in h allows for cooperation with a smaller fraction of strong reciprocators is completely obvious from eqn (8), but is perhaps the most interesting of these properties since, as a result of the superior tool-making and hunting ability of *Homo sapiens*, the ability to inflict costly punishment (high h) at a low cost to the punisher (low c_r), probably distinguishes humans from other species that live in groups and recognizing individuals, hence for which reciprocal altruism might occur. While size, strength, and vigor generally determine the outcome of animal disputes, victory often involving great cost even to the winner, in human societies even a small number of attackers can defeat the most formidable single enemy at very low fitness cost to the attackers through the use of coordination, stealth and deadly weapons.

Bingham (1999) has stressed the importance of the superior abilities of humans in clubbing and throwing projectiles as compared with other primates, citing Goodall (1964) and Plooij (1978) on the relative advantage of humans, and Darlington (1975), Fifer (1987), and Isaac (1987) on the importance of these traits in human evolution. Calvin (1983) argues that humans are unique in possessing the same neural machinery for rapid manual–brachial movements that allow for precision stone-throwing. Theorem 2 suggests one reason why these factors favor the evolution of strong reciprocity.

If $f_i < f_*$ there will be no cooperation in a bad period (we continue to assume the parameters of the model are such that there is always cooperation in the good period). In this situation, the group disbands. Using the same argument as that leading to eqn (1), we see that the fitness π_s of members of such non-cooperative groups satisfies the recursion equation $\pi_s = (1 - p)(b - c + \delta^* \pi_s)$, so

$$\pi_s = \frac{1 - p}{1 - (1 - p)\delta^*}(b - c). \qquad (9)$$

Our assumption that there is always cooperation in the good state requires that $\delta^* \pi_s > b$, which becomes

$$\frac{\delta^*(1-p)}{1-(1-p)\delta^*}(b-c) > b.$$

Note that the relative fitness benefit from being in a cooperative group is

$$\Delta\pi = \pi - \pi_s = p\pi \frac{1-(1-p)(\delta^* - \delta_*)}{1-(1-p)\delta^*} > 0. \quad (10)$$

For example, suppose $p = 0.95$, so the expected duration of a group exposed only to "good" states is 20 years, suppose $p = 0.10$, so a "bad" period occurs in one year out of ten, and suppose $\delta_* = 0.25$, so a cooperating group survives with 25% probability in a "bad" period. Then, $\Delta\pi/\pi = 0.255$, i.e., the cooperating group enjoys a 25.5% fitness advantage over the non-cooperating group.

We suppose that the fraction of strong reciprocators in a group is common knowledge, and strong reciprocators punish defectors only in groups where $f_i \geqslant f_*$, and in doing so they each incur the fixed fitness cost of retaliation c_r.** We shall interpret c_r as a surveillance cost, and since punishment is unnecessary except in "bad" periods, strong reciprocators will incur this cost only with probability p, so the expected fitness cost of being a strong reciprocator is pc_r.††

** This common knowledge assumption is strong, but it could be dropped by assuming that the single-stage public goods game is played several times in each time period. The level of punishment in the first stage would then correctly signal the frequency of strong reciprocity in the group, so that the common knowledge assumption would hold for the remaining stages. This alternative has the added benefit of being a more plausible representation of human cooperation, and it provided a natural interpretation of c_r as the cost of punishing in the first stage. On the other hand, in this case, stronger assumptions would be needed to conclude that a small fraction of strong reciprocators could invade a population of self-interested types, since strong reciprocators are now less fit that self-interested types in uncooperative groups. We shall forego this more sophisticated model as it would unnecessarily complicate our exposition.

†† An alternative, perhaps more plausible, pair of assumptions is that c_r is expended only when non-cooperation is actually detected, and either the public goods game is multi-stage, as in the previous footnote, or there is some source of stochasticity (for instance imperfect signaling or variable agent behavior) that leads to a positive level of punishment even in cooperative groups. The treatment of c_r as a surveillance cost is simpler and leads to the identical result that strong reciprocators incur positive costs even in a cooperative equilibrium.

We will use Price's equation to chart the dynamics of strong reciprocity, which in this case says the change $\Delta\bar{f}$ in the fraction of strong reciprocators in the population is given by

$$\Delta\bar{f} = \frac{1}{\bar{\pi}}\mathrm{cov}(\pi, f) + \frac{1}{\bar{\pi}}\mathbf{E}[\pi\Delta f], \quad (11)$$

where $\bar{\pi}$ is the mean fitness of the population. Let q_f be the fraction of the population in cooperative groups, so

$$q_f = \sum_{f_i \geqslant f_*} q_i, \quad (12)$$

The fitness of each member of a group with $f_i \geqslant f_*$ (resp. $f_i < f_*$) is π (resp. π_s), so the average fitness is $\bar{\pi} = q_f\pi + (1-q_f)\pi_s$. We then have

$$\frac{1}{\bar{\pi}}\mathbf{E}[\pi\Delta f] = \sum_{f_i \geqslant f^*} q_i f_i \frac{\pi}{\bar{\pi}}(-pc_r). \quad (13)$$

Algebraic manipulation gives

$$\frac{\pi}{\bar{\pi}} = \frac{1-\delta^*(1-p)}{1-\delta^*(1-p)-p(1-q_f)(1-(\delta^*-\delta_*)(1-p))},$$

so if we let $f_c = \sum_{f_i \geqslant f^*} q_i f_i / q_f$, which is the mean fraction of strong reciprocators in cooperative groups, then eqn (13) becomes

$$\frac{1}{\bar{\pi}}\mathbf{E}[\pi\Delta x] = -\frac{c_r f_c p q_f (1-\delta^*(1-p))}{1-\delta^*(1-p)-p(1-q_f)(1-(\delta^*-\delta_*)(1-p))}. \quad (14)$$

To evaluate the covariance term, we define $f_s = \sum_{f_i < f^*} q_i f_i/(1-q_f)$, which is the mean frequency of strong reciprocators in non-cooperative groups. Then we have

$$\frac{1}{\bar{\pi}}\mathrm{cov}(\pi_i, f_i) = \frac{(f_c - f_s)pq_f(1-q_f)(1-(\delta^*-\delta_*)(1-p))}{1-\delta^*(1-p)-p(1-q_f)(1-(\delta^*-\delta_*)(1-p))}. \quad (15)$$

The condition for the increase in strong reciprocity is that the sum of eqns (14) and (15) be positive, which for $q_f > 0$ reduces to

$$\left(1 + \frac{\delta_*(1-p)}{1-\delta^*(1-p)}\right)\frac{f_c - f_s}{f_c}(1 - q_f) > c_r. \quad (16)$$

Note that $0 < q_f < 1$ implies $0 \leqslant f_s < f_c$, so we have the following.

Theorem 3. *Suppose the discount factor is δ^* in a good period and $\delta_*(<\delta^*)$ in a bad period, and bad periods occur with probability $p > 0$. Suppose eqn (7) holds, so there is cooperation in the good but not the bad periods in groups in which the fraction of strong reciprocators is less than f_*, given by eqn (8). Then if the fraction of strong reciprocators in cooperative groups is strictly positive ($q_f > 0$), eqn (16) is the condition for an increase in the fraction of strong reciprocators in the population.*

Let $\bar{f} = f_s(1 - q_f) + f_c q_f$, which is the frequency of strong reciprocity in the whole population. To close the model and thus determine the equilibrium value of $\bar{f}$, we must develop a plausible mechanism for the assignment of individuals to groups, thereby determining f_c and f_s as functions of $\bar{f}$. We shall adopt the conservative assumption that new groups form by the assignment of self-interested individuals and strong reciprocators in proportion to their frequency in the population, so that there is no assortative interaction in the formation of new groups.‡‡

For simplicity, we assume a *fixed size founder process*, in which newly formed groups are of a fixed size k, and the number of such groups is effectively infinite, so that the frequency of strong reciprocators in a group is given by the binomial distribution, i.e. we assume sampling with replacement in the assignment of individuals to groups.§§ The probability p_k that a newly formed group satisfies $f \geqslant f_*$ is then given by

$$p_k = \sum_{r \geqslant f_* k}^{k} \binom{k}{r} \bar{f}^r (1 - \bar{f})^{k-r}, \quad (17)$$

the frequency of strong reciprocators in such groups is given by

$$f_c = \frac{1}{kp_k} \sum_{r \geqslant f_* k}^{k} r \binom{k}{r} \bar{f}^r (1 - \bar{f})^{k-r}, \quad (18)$$

and the frequency of strong reciprocators in groups with $f < f_*$ is given by

$$f_s = (\bar{f} - f_c q_f)/(1 - q_f), \quad (19)$$

where q_f is given by eqn (12). It follows that eqn (16) cannot be satisfied when $\bar{f} = 1$, since in this case $q_f = 1$. On the other hand, $\bar{f} \geqslant q_f f_c \geqslant q_f f_*$, so when $\bar{f}$ is small, so is q_f. Then eqn (19) shows that when $\bar{f}$ is small, so is f_s. But $f_c \geqslant f_*$, so both the second and third terms eqn (16) approach unity for small $\bar{f}$. This proves the theorem.

Theorem 4. *Under the conditions of Theorem 3, and assuming a fixed size founder process, in newly forming groups self-interested agents can always invade a population of strong reciprocators, and when the cost c_r of punishing non-cooperators is sufficiently low, a small fraction $\bar{f}$ of strong reciprocators can always invade a population of self-interested agents.*

Theorems 2 and 4 suggest the central importance of the amount of harm h an agent can inflict on non-cooperators and the cost c_r the agent incurs doing so. As long as there is a positive fraction of strong reciprocators in the population, eqn (8) shows that sufficiently large h implies $q_f > 0$, where Theorem 2 applies. Theorem 2 then asserts that for sufficiently low cost of retaliation c_r, strong reciprocators can invade a

‡‡ It is generally understood, of course, that the maintenance of altruistic behavior depends on assortative interactions. William Hamilton (1975) first noted that kin selection is based on assortative interactions. Others who have contributed to the theory of assortative interactions include Wilson (1977), Boyd (1982), Michod (1982), Wade (1985), and Boyd & Richerson (1993). Assortative interactions in our model take the form of groups with a high frequency of strong reciprocators lasting longer than other groups.

§§ For a more general analysis of this case, see Cohen & Eshel (1976). Note that the assumption of sampling with replacement assumes that population size is effectively infinite, so there are an infinite number of strong reciprocators as long as $\bar{f} > 0$.

population of self-interested agents.|||| Under no condition, however, can strong reciprocators drive self-interested agents to extinction, since eqn (16) is necessarily violated when q_f is near unity.

Simulating this model (I used Mathematica 3.0) allows us to assess the plausibility of the parameters involved and the nature of the equilibrium fraction $\bar{f}^*$ of strong reciprocators in the population. In equilibrium, eqn (16) must hold as an equality, since the fraction of strong reciprocators in newly formed groups must be equal to that of the population as a whole.

Equations (17) and (18) allow us to estimate the left-hand side (l.h.s.) of eqn (16). The first term on the l.h.s. is a number greater than unity that, for plausible values of the parameters, lies between 1.0 and 4.0. For instance, if $\delta^* = 0.95$, $\delta_* \leqslant 0.25$, and $p \geqslant 0.10$, this factor has a minimum of 1.00 and a maximum of 2.47. The lower curve in Fig. 2 shows the equilibrium fraction $\bar{f}^*$ of strong reciprocators for values of c_r from 0.05 to 1, when $\delta^* = 0.95$, $\delta_* = 0.10$, $p = 0.10$, there are 40 members per group, and $f_* = 3/8$ must be strong reciprocators to induce cooperation in the bad state. The upper curve shows the same relationship when there are eight members per group. The latter curve would be relevant if groups are composed of a small number of "families", and the strong reciprocity characteristic is highly heritable within families. It is clear from Fig. 2 that the incidence of strong reciprocity can be much higher, especially when the cost of retaliation c_r is high, when family assortative interaction occurs.¶¶

||||Our model thus strongly supports Bingham's (1999) stress on physical factors in explaining cooperation among humans. Bingham makes the stronger claim that human cooperation is based on "coalitional enforcement" by self-interested agents. This claim is doubtful because coalitional enforcement is a form of reciprocal altruism, which we have shown fails when there is a high probability of group dissolution. Moreover, as we have seen, human revenge and retaliation does not follow the logic of self-interested behavior.

¶¶Models of assortative interaction taking families as a behavioral unit include Wilson (1977), Boyd (1982), Michod (1982), Wade (1985), and Boyd & Richerson (1993). The argument that hunter–gatherer groups in both recent and Pleistocene periods have consisted of a small coalition of families made by Kaplan & Hill (1985), Blurton-Jones (1987), Knauft (1991), Boehm (1993), and Hawkes (1993).

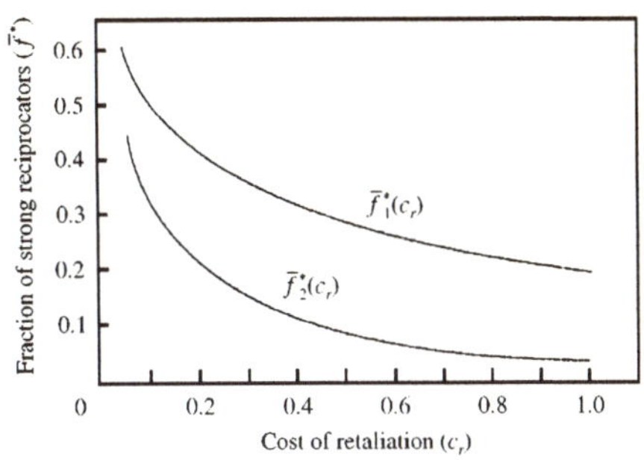

FIG. 2. The equilibrium fraction of strong reciprocating families: a computer simulation.

5. Conclusion

Reciprocal altruism leads to a high level of cooperation in human societies, and many behavioral scientists believe that reciprocal altruism is sufficient to explain human sociality. Economists are particularly favorable to this belief, since reciprocal altruism is a behavior supported by the so-called *rational actor model*, in which much of the economic analysis is presumed.

However, laboratory experiments, conducted in many different social settings by different research groups, consistently show that people tend to behave prosocially and punish antisocial behavior, at a cost to themselves, even when the probability of future interactions is extremely low, or zero. We call this *strong reciprocity*, in contrast with the *weak reciprocity* associated with reciprocal altruism, because the former behavior is robust in the face of changes in the probability of future interaction.

I have stressed the laboratory experiments in this paper because the controlled environment of the laboratory is conducive to isolating the strong reciprocity motive from other bases for cooperation and punishment. It would be remiss, however, not to mention the prevalence of strong reciprocity in the everyday operation of human society. Two categories of behavior immediately come to mind. First, in many circumstances people retaliate against others, at considerable personal cost, when the possibility of gains through future interaction is remote or zero. Victims of crime, for instance, spend time and energy ensuring that the perpetrators are apprehended and receive harsh sentences, and jilted or betrayed lovers retaliate at great personal cost—often reducing their biological fitness to zero.

A second manifestation of strong reciprocity is evident in the propensity of humans to engage in episodic collective action towards transforming social norms and political regimes. Movements for civil rights, civil liberties, and political democracy in authoritarian states are responsible for creating modern liberal democracies, yet participation in such movements cannot usually be explained in terms of self-interest or reciprocal altruism (Bowles & Gintis, 1986). Non-participators in collective action, such as "scab workers" during a trade union strike, or "traitors" in a civil war, are spontaneously ostracized and punished, while guerrillas and underground freedom fighters are widely supported, often at great cost to the supporters. Without strong reciprocity, then, human society would likely be quite differently organized than it is, and we likely would be considerably less successful as a species.

Strong reciprocity is a form of altruism, in that it benefits group members at a cost to the strong reciprocators themselves. This paper shows that there is a plausible evolutionary model supporting the emergence of strong reciprocity. This model based on the notion that societies periodically experience extinction-threatening events, and reciprocal altruism will fail to motivate self-interested individuals in such periods, thus exacerbating the threat and increasing the likelihood of group extinction. If the fraction of strong reciprocators is sufficiently high, even self-interested agents can be induced to cooperate in such situations, thus lowering the probability of group extinction.

I would like to thank Lee Alan Dugatkin, Ernst Fehr, David Sloan Wilson, and the referees of this journal for helpful comments, Samuel Bowles and Robert Boyd for many extended discussions of these issues, and the MacArthur Foundation for financial support.

REFERENCES

Andreoni, J. (1995). Cooperation in public goods experiments: kindness or confusion. *Am. Econ. Rev.* **85**, 891–904.

Axelrod, R. (1984). *The Evolution of Cooperation*. New York: Basic Books.

Axelrod, R. & Hamilton, W. D. (1981). The evolution of cooperation. *Science* **211**, 1390–1396.

Belovsky, G. (1988). An optimal foraging-based model of hunter-gatherer population dynamics. *J. Anthropol. Archaeol.* 329–372.

Bingham, P. M. (1999). Human uniqueness: a general theory. *Quart. Rev. Biol.* **74**, 133–169.

Blurton-Jones, N. G. (1987). Tolerated theft: suggestions about the ecology and evolution of sharing, hoarding, and scrounging. *Soc. Sci. Inf.* **26**, 31–54.

Boehm, C. (1993). Egalitarian behavior and reverse dominance hierarchy. *Curr. Anthropol.* **34**, 227–254.

Boone, J. L. & Karen, L. K. (1999). More status or more children? Social status, fertility reduction, and long-term fitness. *Evol. Human Behav.* **20**, 257–277.

Bowles, S. & Gintis, H. (1986). *Democracy and Capitalism: Property, Community, and the Contradictions of Modern Social Thought*. New York: Basic Books.

Boyd, R. (1982). Density dependent mortality and the evolution of social behavior. *Animal Behav.* **30**, 972–982.

Boyd, R. & Richerson, P. J. (1985). *Culture and the Evolutionary Process*. Chicago: University of Chicago Press.

Boyd, R. & Richerson, P. J. (1988). The evolution of reciprocity in sizable groups. *J. theor. Biol.* **132**, 337–356.

Boyd, R. & Richerson, P. J. (1992). Punishment allows the evolution of cooperation (or anything else) in sizeable groups. *Ethol. Sociobiol.* **113**, 171–195.

Boyd, R. & Richerson, P. J. (1993). Effect of phenotypic variation of kin selection. *Proc. Nat. Acad. Sci. U.S.A.* **77**, 7506–7509.

Calvin, W. H. (1983). A stone's throw and its launch window: timing precision and its implications for language and hominid brains. *J. theor. Biol.* **104**, 121–135.

Camerer, C. & Thaler, R. (1995). Ultimatums, dictators, and manners. *J. Econ. Perspect.* **9**, 209–219.

Cavalli-Sforza, Luigi, L. & Feldman, M. W. (1981). *Cultural Transmission and Evolution*. Princeton, NJ: Princeton University Press.

Cohen, D. & Eshel, I. (1976). On the founder effect and the evolution of altruistic traits. *Theor. Popul. Biol.* **10**, 276–302.

Darlington, P. J. (1975). Group selection, altruism, reinforcement and throwing in human evolution. *Proc. Nat. Acad. Sci. U.S.A.* **72**, 3748–3752.

Dawes, R. M., Orbell, J. M. & Van de Kragt, J. C. (1986). Organizing groups for collective action. *Am. Pol. Sci. Rev.* **80**, 1171–1185.

Dugatkin, L. A. (1997). *Cooperation among Animals*. New York: Oxford University Press.

Dugatkin, L. A. (1998). Game theory and cooperation. In: *Game Theory and Animal Behavior* (Dugatkin, L. A. & Reeve, H. K., eds), pp. 38–63. Oxford: Oxford University Press.

Dugatkin, L. A. & Alfieri, M. (1992). Interpopulational difference in the cooperative strategy used during predator inspection in the guppy. *Evol. Ecol.* **6**, 519–526.

Fehr, E. & Schmidt, K. M. (1999). A theory of fairness, competition, and cooperation. *Quart. J. Econom.* **114**, 817–868.

Fehr, E. & Gächter, S. (2000). Cooperation and punishment. *Am. Econom. Rev.* (in press).

Fifer, F. C. (1987). The adoption of bipedalism by the hominids: a new hypothesis. *Human Evol.* **2**, 135–147.

FRANK, S. A. (1998). *Foundations of Social Evolution*. Princeton: Princeton University Press.

GINTIS, H. (2000). *Game Theory Evolving*. Princeton, NJ: Princeton University Press.

GOODALL, J. (1964). Tool-using and aimed throwing in a community of free-living chimpanzees. *Nature* **201,** 1264-1266.

GÜTH, W. & TIETZ, R. (1990). Ultimatum bargaining behavior: a survey and comparison of experimental results. *J. Econom. Psychol.* **11,** 417-449.

HAMILTON, W. D. (1964). The genetical evolution of social behavior. *J. theor. Biol.* **37,** 1-16, 17-52.

HAMILTON, W. D. (1975). Innate social aptitudes of man: an approach from evolutionary genetics. In: *Biosocial Anthropology* (Fox, R., ed.), pp. 115-132. New York: John Wiley & Sons.

HAWKES, K. (1993). Why hunter-gatherers work: an ancient version of the problem of public goods. *Curr. Anthropol.* **34,** 341-361.

ISAAC, B. (1987). Throwing and human evolution. *African Archeol. Rev.* **5,** 3-17.

KAPLAN, H. & HILL, K. (1985). Hunting ability and reproductive success among male ache foragers: preliminary results. *Curr. Anthropol.* **26,** 131-133.

KECKLER, C. N. W. (1997). Catastrophic mortality in simulations of forager age-of-death: where did all the humans go? In: *Integrating Archaeological Demography: Multidisciplinary Approaches to Prehistoric Populations. Center for Archaeological Investigations, Occasional Papers, No.* 24. (Paine, R., ed.), pp. 205-228. Carbondale, IL: Southern Illinois University Press.

KNAUFT, B. (1991). Violence and sociality in human evolution. *Curr. Anthropol.* **32,** 391-428.

LEDYARD, J. O. (1995). Public goods: a survey of experimental research. In: *The Handbook of Experimental Economics*. pp. 111-194. (Kagel, J. H. & Roth, A. E. eds), Princeton, NJ: Princeton University Press.

LUMSDEN, C. J. & WILSON, E. O. (1981). *Genes, Mind, and Culture: The Coevolutionary Process*. Cambridge, MA: Harvard University Press.

ROBYN DAWES, M. & THALER, R. (1988). Cooperation. *J. Econom. Perspect.* **2,** 187-197.

MICHOD, R. (1982). The theory of kin selection. *Ann. Rev. Ecol. Systems* **13,** 23-55.

OSTROM, E., WALKER, J. & GARDNER, R. (1992). Covenants with and without a sword: self-governance is possible. *Am. Pol. Sci. Rev.* **86,** 404-417.

PLOOIJ, F. X. (1978). Tool-using during chimpanzees bushpig hunt. *Carnivore* **1,** 103-106.

PRICE, G. R. (1970). Selection and covariance. *Nature* **227,** 520-521.

ROTH, A. (1995). Bargaining experiments. In: *The Handbook of Experimental Economics* (Kagel, J. & Roth, A., eds). Princeton, NJ: Princeton University Press.

SATO, K. (1987). Distribution and the cost of maintaining common property resources. *J. Expl. Soc. Psychol.* **23,** 19-31.

SETHI, R. & SOMANATHAN, E. (1996). The evolution of social norms in common property resource use. *Am. Econom. Rev.* **86,** 766-788.

SIMON, H. A. (1993). Altruism and economics. *Am. Econom. Rev.* **83,** 156-161.

SOBER, E. & WILSON, D. S. (1998). *Unto Others: The Evolution and Psychology of Unselfish Behavior*. Cambridge, MA: Harvard University Press.

SOLTIS, J., BOYD, R. & RICHERSON, P. (1995). Can group-functional behaviors evolve by cultural group selection: an empirical test. *Curr. Anthropol.* **36,** 473-483.

TRIVERS, R. L. (1971). The evolution of reciprocal altruism. *Quart. Rev. Biol.* **46,** 35-57.

WADE, M. J. (1985). Soft selection, hard selection, kin selection and group selection. *Am. Nat.* **125,** 61-73.

WILSON, D. S. (1977). Structure demes and the evolution of group-advantageous traits. *Am. Nat.* **111,** 157-185.

WILSON, D. S. & DUGATKIN, L. A. (1997). Group selection and assortative interactions. *Am. Nat.* **149,** 336-351.

YAMAGISHI, T. (1988a). The provision of a sanctioning system in the United States and Japan. *Soc. Psychol. Quart.* **51,** 265-271.

YAMAGISHI, T. (1988b). Seriousness of social dilemmas and the provision of a sanctioning system. *Soc. Psychol. Quart.* **51,** 32-42.

YAMAGISHI, T. (1992). Group size and the provision of a sanctioning system in a social dilemma. In: *Social Dilemmas: Theoretical Issues and Research Findings* (Liebrand, W. B. G., Messick, D. M. & Wilke, H. A. M., eds), pp. 267-287. Oxford: Pergamon Press.

[33]

If *Homo Economicus* Could Choose His Own Utility Function, Would He Want One with a Conscience?

By ROBERT H. FRANK*

A blush may reveal a lie and cause great embarrassment at the moment. But in situations that require trust, there can be great advantage in being known to be a blusher. This paper develops a model in which tastes are determined endogenously for their capacity to help solve the so-called precommitment problem. The tastes that emerge are very different from those assumed in conventional models of rational choice.

The rational choice model takes tastes as given,[1] and assumes that people pursue self-interest. The model performs well much of the time, yet apparent contradictions abound. Travelers on interstate highways leave tips for waitresses they will never see again. Participants in bloody family feuds seek revenge even at ruinous cost to themselves. People walk away from profitable transactions whose terms they believe to be "unfair." The British spend vast sums to defend the desolate Falklands, even though they have little empire left against which to deter future aggression. In these and countless other ways, people do not seem to be maximizing utility functions of the usual sort.

In this paper, I investigate the familiar theme that seemingly irrational behavior can sometimes be explained without departing from the utility-maximization framework. Efforts along these lines have generally focused on a more careful assessment of the constraints people face. The alternative I explore here is to suggest that tastes differ in systematic ways from those portrayed in standard economic models. Instead of treating tastes as a datum, I retreat a step and ask, "What kind of tastes would maximize the attainment of selfish objectives?" This is essentially the behavioral biologist's approach (W. D. Hamilton, 1964; E. O. Wilson, 1975, 1978; Richard Dawkins, 1976; Robert Trivers, 1985). It treats tastes not as ends in themselves, but as means for attaining important material objectives.[2]

My focus is a specific example in which people have opportunities to cheat without possibility of reprisal. This example illustrates that it will sometimes be in a selfish person's interest to have a utility function that predisposes him not to cheat, even when he is *certain* he would not be caught. The example also suggests other specific elements of the utility function that might help people resolve important market failures and bargaining problems. The common feature of

*Professor of Economics, Department of Economics, Cornell University, Ithaca, NY 14853. I thank Robert Trivers, Jack Hirshleifer, Thomas Schelling, Robert Axelrod, Henry Hansmann, Thomas Eisner, Simon Levin, Stephen Emlen, Elizabeth Adkins Regan, and an anonymous referee for encouragement and helpful comments on an earlier draft. This research was supported by National Science Foundation Grant No. SES-8605829.

[1]Gary Becker and George Stigler (1977) provide the clearest statement of the modern economists' hands-off approach to tastes. For three recent exceptions that are closely related to the theme of this paper, see Thomas Schelling (1978), George Akerlof (1983), and Jack Hirshleifer (1984). See also Hirshleifer (1977; 1978a, b), Philip Coelho (1985), Paul Rubin and Chris Paul (1979), Rubin (1982), and myself (1985a, b; 1986, 1988).

[2]In the biologist's view, tastes are no different from other characteristics. All are selected for their capacity to promote survival and reproduction. A wolf who "likes" to stand up to intruders runs the risk of serious injury. But because the animal is known to have that preference, it may do much better, on the average, than one who is known to prefer passive retreat. If so, the success conferred by this taste will lead to an increase in its frequency in the gene pool.

these problems is that their solution requires people to make *ex ante* commitments to behave in ways that will not be self-serving *ex post*.

I. The Commitment Problem

Thomas Schelling (1960) provides a vivid illustration of this class of problems. He describes a kidnapper who suddenly gets cold feet. He wants to set his victim free, but is afraid he will go to the police. In return for his freedom, the victim gladly promises not to do so. The problem, of course, is that both realize that it will no longer be in his interest to keep this promise once he is free. And so the kidnapper reluctantly concludes he must kill his victim.

Schelling suggests the following way out of the dilemma: "If the victim has commited an offense whose disclosure would lead to blackmail, he may confess it; if not, he might commit one in the presence of his captor, to create a bond that will ensure his silence" (1960, pp. 43–44). The blackmailable act serves here as a "commitment device," something that provides the victim with an incentive to keep his promise. The need for such devices arises frequently in the course of economic interaction.

II. The Costs of Monitoring and the Breakdown of Cooperation

Consider, for example, the case of a joint venture. Numerous opportunities exist in which it is possible to increase output through cooperation. Unfortunately, however, performance in many such ventures is either impossible or prohibitively costly to monitor.

It follows that a tendency to cheat when there is no possibility of punishment will often eliminate opportunities for mutual gain. Consider a joint venture in which *A* and *B* may either behave honestly or dishonestly. Suppose the payoffs to the four possible combinations of strategies are as given in Table 1, where *H* denotes honest, *D* denotes dishonest, and where $x_4 > x_3 > x_2 > x_1$. Suppose also that the parties interact only once, so that cheating cannot be penalized. These payoffs create a prisoner's dilemma. *D* is the dominant strategy, even though the resultant payoff, x_2, is lower than if each had chosen *H*.[3] Parties *A* and *B* need a commitment device of the sort described by Schelling.

TABLE 1—THE PAYOFFS TO *A* FROM INTERACTION WITH *B*

		B	
		H	*D*
A	*H*	x_3	x_1
	D	x_4	x_2

III. The Conscience as a Commitment Device

Schelling's device worked by altering the relevant material incentives, an approach that will not always be practical. Fortunately, commitment devices can also work in other ways. Consider, for example, a person with the capacity to experience strong feelings of guilt upon breaking a promise—that is, a person with a conscience. This person will often honor his promises even when material incentives favor breaking them. It is precisely this capacity of emotional forces to override rational calculations that makes them candidates for commitment devices.

Of course, merely *having* a conscience does not solve the commitment problem; one's potential trading partners must also know about it. But how can they? Surely it is insufficient for a person merely to *declare* how he or she feels. ("I have a conscience. Trust me.") A strategically important emotion can be communicated credibly only if it is accompanied by a signal that is at least partially insulated from direct control.

[3]Robert Axelrod (1984), Trivers (1971), and others have demonstrated the tendency for cooperation to emerge in repeated prisoner's dilemmas. My focus here is on whether cooperation can be self-serving when the game is played only once, or, if played more than once, when cheating cannot be detected. For an excellent survey of biological models of cooperation and altruism, see Hirshleifer (1977).

Many observable physical symptoms of emotional arousal satisfy this requirement. Posture, the rate of respiration, the pitch and timbre of the voice, perspiration, facial muscle tone and expression, movement of the eyes, and a host of other readily observable physical symptoms vary systematically with a person's affective condition (Melvin Konner, 1982; Paul Ekman, 1985). In most people, at least some of these symptoms are almost completely insulated from voluntary control (Ekman; Charles Darwin, 1872). If natural selection caused (Darwin), or even permitted, these symptoms to convey such feelings as fear, joy, and grief, there is no reason why it could not have allowed these same symptoms to be related in a characteristic way to feelings of guilt as well.[4]

If there are gains from appearing to be trustworthy, opportunists will inevitably attempt to mimic the symptoms of trustworthiness. Needless to say, character traits would be useless as commitment devices if people who lacked them could *perfectly* mimic their symptoms. But mimicry usually entails costs of its own, and is thus seldom perfect.[5] Granted, lie detection, even the highly technical sort practiced by experienced professionals, is subject to error (David Lykken, 1981). Even so, clues to deceit are reliable in a probabilistic sense and, as will become clear, this is all that is needed for the conscience to serve as a commitment device.

For the sake of discussion, suppose that a mutant did in fact appear with a conscience accompanied by a statistically reliable signal. How might such a mutant have fared? In models of natural selection, a gene for a given trait will increase in frequency relative to its alleles (alternative genes on the same locus) if the trait leads, on average, to a higher material payoff. We must thus compare the mutant's expected payoff to that of persons who lack a conscience. The next section develops a formal model for this purpose.[6]

IV. An Illustrative Model

Consider a population each of whose members bears one of two traits, H or D. Those bearing H are honest, those bearing D are not.[7] To be honest here means to refrain from cheating one's partner in a cooperative venture, even when cheating cannot be punished. To be dishonest means always to cheat under the same circumstances.

Suppose people face one of two options:

1) They may pair with someone in a joint venture whose payoffs are as given above in Table 1. This venture will occur only once and dishonest behavior cannot be punished; or

[4] Trivers argues that guilt could have evolved within the framework of his reciprocal altruism model as a means of protecting people against the possibility of being caught cheating: "...it is possible that the common psychological assumption that one feels guilt even when one behaves badly in private is based on the fact that many transgressions are *likely* to become public knowledge" (1971, p. 50).

[5] There are abundant cases in nature where mimics coexist with the genuine bearers of a trait for extended periods. For example, there are butterflies, such as the monarch, whose strategy for defending themselves is to have developed a foul taste. This taste itself would be useless unless predators had some way of telling which butterflies to avoid. And so the monarch has developed a conspicuous pattern of wing markings that its predators have learned to interpret for this purpose. The safety afforded by these wing markings has created a profitable opportunity for mutant butterflies who bear similar markings but lack the bad taste that normally accompanies them. Merely by looking like the unpalatable monarchs, viceroy butterflies have escaped predation without having had to expend the bodily resources required to produce the objectionable taste itself. Coexistence of the two types implies that mimicry is either incomplete or else imposes important costs on the viceroy. For an illuminating discussion of the phenomenon of deceptive signaling in animals, see John Krebs and Dawkins (1984).

[6] For a more reader-friendly version of this model, see my forthcoming book (1988, ch. 3).

[7] More precisely, imagine a population with two alleles, a_1 and a_2, at a given genetic locus. Individuals homozygous in a_1 are "honest," those homozygous in a_2 are not. Regardless of what effect honest behavior may have on fitness, each allele in heterozygous individuals will be affected equally by the interactions of these individuals with others. We may thus disregard these individuals when analyzing the competition between a_1 and a_2. In the text, H refers to individuals homozygous in a_1, D to those homozygous in a_2.

2) They may pair with someone in an alternative venture in which behavior can be perfectly monitored. Call this the "work-alone" option, because it does not involve activities that require trust. It too will occur only once, and its payoff is x_2 for each person, irrespective of the combinations of types who interact. Thus, the work-alone option offers the same payoff as when two dishonest persons interact in venture 1.

Many readers will find it more plausible to assume that persons who cheat one another in venture 1 do *worse* than those who participate in ventures that do not require trust (i.e., to assume a payoff larger than x_2 for the work-alone option). But since the goal of this exercise is to see whether honest persons can prosper in the material world, I retain the more conservative assumption that the work-alone option pays only x_2. If honest persons can survive with that payoff, they will certainly do so with an even higher one.

Since working alone pays only x_2, it will never appeal to a dishonest person, who can always do at least as well in venture 1. Its obvious attraction for an honest person is that there is no chance of being cheated; the downside, however, is that its payoff is less than x_3, the gain from successful cooperation in venture 1. (More below on how honest persons choose between the two options.)

In addition to their behavioral differences, let the H's and D's differ with respect to the genes that influence some observable characteristic S, which is also influenced by random environmental forces. More specifically, suppose that the observable characteristic for person i takes the value,

$$S_i = \mu_i + \varepsilon_i,$$

where $\mu_i = \mu_H$ if i is honest, $= \mu_D$ if i is dishonest, $\mu_H > \mu_D$, and ε_i is an independently, identically distributed random variable with zero mean. The μ_i component of S_i is heritable, the ε_i component is not.

Case 1: *A Perfectly Reliable Signal*. If the variance of ε_i were zero, everyone could tell with certainty whether any given person was an H or a D. In that case, H's would pair only with other H's in venture 1, and would receive a payoff of x_3. The D's would be left to pair with one another, for which they would receive only x_2. Thus, if the signal that accompanied each trait were *perfectly* reliable, the H's would soon drive the D's to extinction.

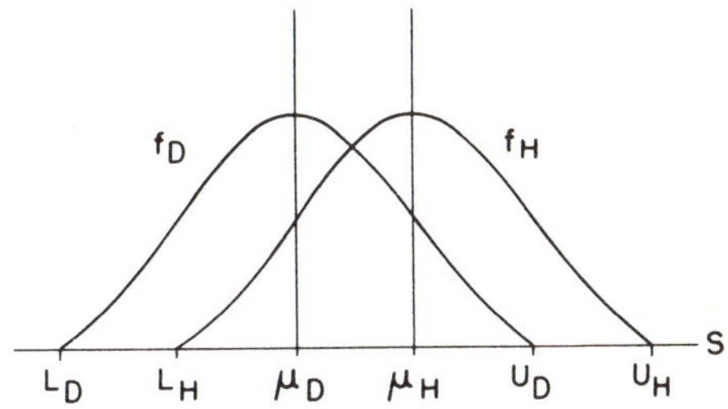

FIGURE 1. PROBABILITY DENSITIES FOR AN OBSERVABLE SIGNAL OF TRUSTWORTHINESS

Case 2: *Imperfect Signals*. By contrast, when ε_i has sufficiently large variance, S_i provides merely a measure of the probability that i is trustworthy. As an illustration of this more interesting case, suppose people draw their S values independently from the probability densities f_D and f_H shown in Figure 1.[8]

In terms of the earlier discussion, the relative position of the two densities reflects imperfect mimicry by the D's of the trait used by the H's to identify themselves as trustworthy. For the densities shown, whose ranges do not overlap completely, we are sure that individuals with $S > U_D$ are honest, and that those with $S < L_H$ are dishonest. Individuals whose S values lie in the region

[8]Each density shown in Figure 1 is derived from the standard normal density, $f(S)$, in the following manner: First the tails are truncated at two standard deviations from the mean by subtracting $f(2)$ from every point. Let I denote the area under the resulting functions. The functions are then normalized by dividing each by I. Letting 2 and 3 be the respective means, we thus have

$$f_H = (1/\sqrt{2\pi})(1/I)\left[\exp(-(x-3)^2/2) - \exp(-2)\right],$$

and

$$f_D = (1/\sqrt{2\pi})(1/I)\left[\exp(-(x-2)^2/2) - \exp(-2)\right].$$

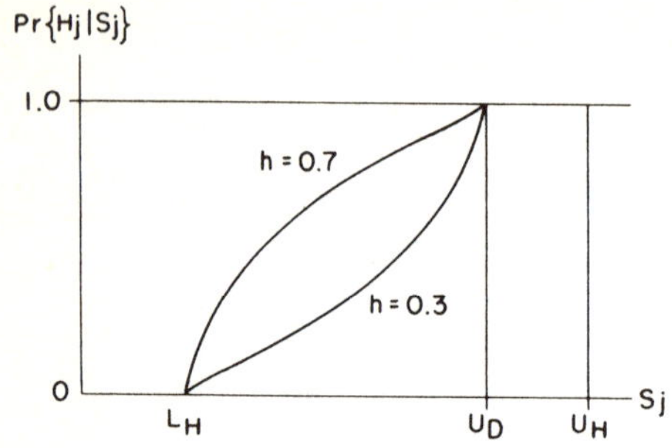

FIGURE 2. THE PROBABILITY OF BEING HONEST, CONDITIONAL ON S

where the two densities overlap may be either H or D. If h denotes the proportion of the population bearing H, the probability that an individual j with $S = S_j$ is honest is then given by

$$(1) \quad \Pr\{H_j|S_j\} = \frac{hf_H(S_j)}{hf_H(S_j)+(1-h)f_D(S_j)}.$$

For the two densities shown in Figure 1, $\Pr\{H_j|S_j\}$ is plotted in Figure 2 for two different values of h.

A. *The Threshold Signal Value*

Given the payoffs in Table 1, both H's and D's will clearly do best by interacting (if they choose venture 1) with other individuals whom they believe to be H's. Consider the problem confronting individual i, who is H and must decide whether to interact with individual j, who has $S = S_j$. Let $E(X_{ij}|S_j)$ denote the expected payoff to i from pairing with this individual. If the alternative is the work-alone option (which has payoff x_2), the condition that makes it worth i's while to work with j is given by

$$(2) \quad E(X_{ij}|S_j) = x_3\Pr\{H_j|S_j\} + x_1\left[1-\Pr\{H_j|S_j\}\right] \geq x_2.$$

Call S^* the value of S_j that satisfies $E(X_{ij}|S_j) = x_2$. The value S^* is the smallest value of S_j for which it would be as attractive for i to work with j as to work alone. Using the densities from Figure 1, this threshold signal value is shown in Figure 3 for the particular case of $h = 1/2$ and $x_2 = (x_1 + x_3)/2$.

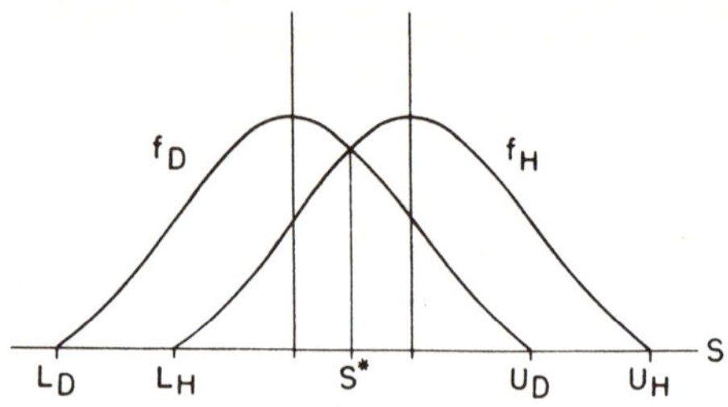

FIGURE 3. THE THRESHOLD SIGNAL VALUE WHEN $h = 1/2$ AND $x_2 = (x_1 + x_3)/2$

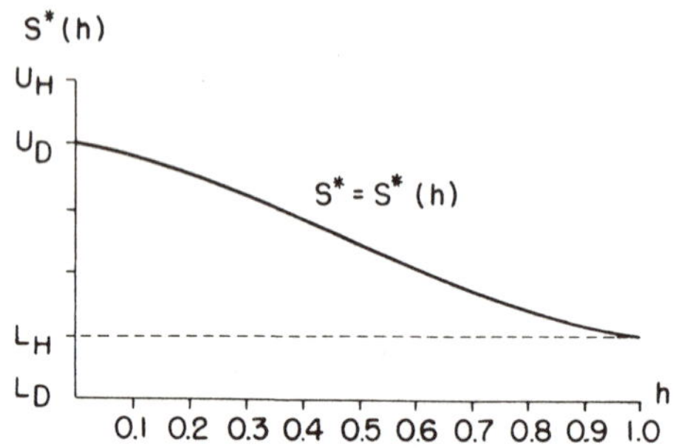

FIGURE 4. THE THRESHOLD SIGNAL VALUE AS A FUNCTION OF h

Using equations (1) and (2), it can easily be shown that S^* is a decreasing function of h: As the proportion of the population that is honest grows, it becomes ever more probable that an individual whose S lies between L_H and U_D is honest, and ever more likely, therefore, that the expected payoff from interacting with that individual will exceed x_2. It is also easy to show that S^* decreases with increases in $(x_3 - x_2)$ and increases with increases in $(x_2 - x_1)$. The greater the payoff to successful cooperation, and the smaller the penalty for being cheated, the lower will be the threshold signal for cooperation. For the particular case of $(x_4 - x_3) = (x_3 - x_2)$

$=(x_2-x_1)=x_1$, the schedule $S^*(h)$ that corresponds to the densities from Figure 1 is plotted in Figure 4.

B. *The Sorting Process Whereby Interacting Pairs Form*

It is not strictly correct to say that an individual who is honest faces only the alternatives of working alone or working with someone with $S=S_j$. There are other members of the population besides j; and, of those with $S>S^*$, i will want to choose a partner with the highest possible S value. The problem is that *everyone* prefers to interact with such a partner, and there are only so many of them to go around.

The bearer of a high S value, whether he is honest or not, owns a valuable asset. The natural way to exploit it will be to use it to attract a partner whose own S value is also high. Without going into technical details, it can be seen that the outcome will be for the two with the highest S values to pair up, then the next two, and so on, until all those with $S \geq S^*$ are paired. Needless to say, the expected total payoff to any pair increases with the S values of its members. If the population is sufficiently dense, as assumed here, the S values within each pair will be virtually the same.[9]

C. *The Expected Payoff Functions*

With the foregoing discussion in mind, let us now investigate what happens if a mutation provides a small toehold for the H's in a population that initially consisted entirely of D's. Will the H's make headway or be driven to extinction? To answer this question, we must compare the average payoffs for H's and D's, denoted $E(X|H)$ and $E(X|D)$, respectively, when h is near zero. To calculate $E(X|H)$, note from equations (1) and (2) that $S^*(h)$ approaches U_D as h approaches zero (see Figure 4). As the share of the population that is honest approaches zero, the rational strategy for an honest person, in the limit, is to interact only with people whose S values lie to the right of U_D —that is, with people who are certain to be honest. As h approaches zero, the expected payoff to the H's thus approaches the limiting value

$$(3)\quad \lim_{h\to 0} E(X|H) = x_3\int_{U_D}^{U_H} f_H(S)\,dS + x_2\int_{L_H}^{U_D} f_H(S)\,dS.$$

The second term on the right-hand side of equation (3) reflects the fact that an H with $S<U_D$ does best by not interacting—that is, by choosing the work-alone option. (He would be delighted to interact with an H with $S>U_D$, but that person would not agree to interact with *him*.)

The corresponding limiting expected payoff for the D's is simply x_2. So when the proportion of the population that is honest is very small, we have $E(X|H)>E(X|D)$, which means h will grow.

What if we had started at the opposite extreme—in a population in which the proportion of D's was near zero? In the limit, the decision rule for the H's would be "interact with anyone whose S value exceeds L_H." As h approaches one, the expected payoff for the D's would thus approach

$$(4)\quad \lim_{h\to 1} E(X|D) = x_2\int_{L_D}^{L_H} f_D(S)\,dS + x_4\int_{L_H}^{U_D} f_D(S)\,dS.$$

The corresponding expected payoff for H will approach x_3 as h approaches one. Comparing the right-hand side of equation (4) with x_3, we see that the former will be larger for sufficiently large values of x_2 or x_4, or

[9] In less dense populations, S values could differ within pairs, suggesting that the member in any pair with the lower S value might have to pay his partner in order to induce him to participate. Any such transfer payments will obviously not affect the average payoff to members of a cooperating pair. Even if the assumption of dense populations did not hold, therefore, complications of this sort would create no difficulties: We are concerned only with average payoffs to the two genotypes here.

for sufficiently extensive overlap of the ranges of f_H and f_D. Assuming that $E(X|D)$ does exceed x_3 for values of h close to one, h will then begin to fall.

To investigate the behavior of this population as it evolves away from either of the two pure states, we need general expressions for $E(X|H)$ and $E(X|D)$.

The first step in finding $E(X|H)$ is to use equations (1) and (2) to find S^* as a function of h (as was done to generate Figure 4). Given $S^*(h)$, we then calculate P_H and P_D, the respective shares of the honest and dishonest populations with $S > S^*$:

$$(5) \qquad P_H = \int_{S^*}^{U_H} f_H(S)\,dS;$$

$$(6) \qquad P_D = \int_{S^*}^{U_D} f_D(S)\,dS.$$

Given equations (5) and (6), $E(X|H)$ can be computed as a weighted sum of the payoffs from (1) working alone, (2) interacting with someone who is honest, and (3) interacting with someone who is dishonest. Noting that $(1-P_H)$ is the probability that an honest individual works alone, and using $\lambda = hP_H/(hP_H+(1-h)P_D)$ to denote the share of the population with $S > S^*$ that is honest, we have

$$(7) \qquad E(X|H) = (1-P_H)x_2 + P_H[\lambda x_3 + (1-\lambda)x_1].$$

In like fashion, $E(X|D)$ can be calculated as a weighted sum of the payoffs to working alone, interacting with someone who is honest, and interacting with someone who is dishonest:

$$(8) \qquad E(X|D) = (1-P_D)x_2 + P_D[\lambda x_4 + (1-\lambda)x_2].$$

For my illustrative densities from Figure 1, $E(X|H)$ and $E(X|D)$ are plotted as functions of h in Figure 5. Both $E(X|H)$ and $E(X|D)$ will in general be increasing functions of h. For the particular densities from Figure 1, the two curves cross exactly once.

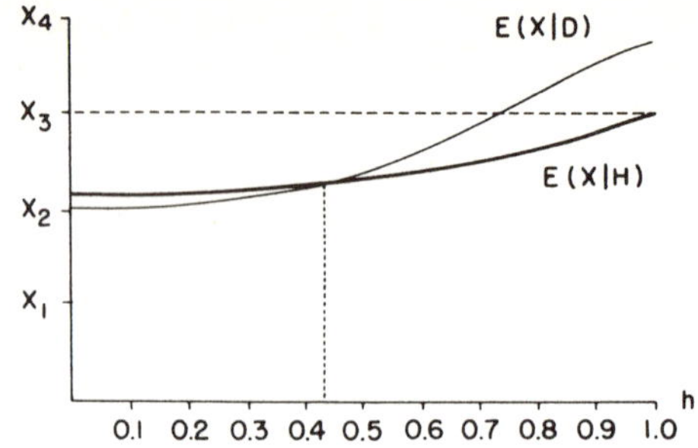

FIGURE 5. EXPECTED PAYOFFS FOR H AND D

The equilibrium value of h is the one for which $E(X|D)$ and $E(X|H)$ intersect. For an equilibrium to be stable, $E(X|H)$ must cross $E(X|D)$ from above. Since $E(X|H)$ will always be greater than $E(X|D)$ at $h = 0$, the intersection of the two curves (assuming they intersect at all) will thus correspond to a stable equilibrium value of h, like the one depicted in Figure 5.

Case 3: *Costs of Scrutiny*. The model can be made more complete, and the existence of an equilibrium assured, if we add the assumption that resources must be expended in order to inspect the S values of others. Let us assume specifically that these values can be observed only by people who have borne the cost C of becoming sensitized.

First consider the limiting case of a population in which h approaches zero. A necessary condition for any interaction to occur at all is that $x_3 - C > x_2$. Assuming that condition is met, only those honest persons whose own S values exceed U_D will find it worthwhile to spend C to become sensitized. H's with $S < U_D$ will work alone (because there is no prospect of their finding an H with whom to interact). Thus the latter H's will receive payoff x_2, the same as $E(X|D)$ when h is zero. No D's will pay to become sensitized because they too have no chance of finding an unclaimed H, so the expected payoff for D's here is x_2. For very small values of h, then, some H's will fare the same as the D's, others better. Thus, as before, h will grow when it starts near zero.

For values of h near one, no one will find it worthwhile to pay C to become sensitized. With everyone's S thus effectively out of sight, even D's with $S < L_H$ will find honest partners with whom to interact. $E(X|D)$ will thus approach x_4 as h approaches one. So, unlike the case where S could be observed for free, it is no longer possible for the H's to take over the entire population, regardless of how close x_3 may be to x_4.

A key step in understanding the nature of the equilibrium that results when h starts near zero is to recognize that it will always be most strongly in the interests of those with the highest S values to bear the expense of becoming sensitized. To see this, recall from the earlier discussion that the bearer of a high S value owns a valuable asset he can use to attract a partner whose own S value is also high. It is in the interests of bearers of high S values to interact with others who are H. And, having become sensitized, they are then able to identify others with high S values (the people who are most likely to be H) and interact with them. Persons with relatively low S values, who can only hope to claim a partner whose own S value is also low, therefore face a lower expected payoff to the investment of becoming sensitized.

Knowing this enables one to conclude that the equilibrium h must be sufficiently low that it pays at least *some* of the population to become sensitized. This can be shown by noting that, if the contrary is assumed, we get a contradiction. That is, suppose it is assumed that, in equilibrium, the expected payoff to the person with the highest S value is higher if he does *not* become sensitized. Recall that his expected payoff if he had become sensitized, call it $E(X,C)$, would be

$$E(X,C) = x_3 - C, \tag{9}$$

which is already assumed to be greater than x_2. We know that if it does not pay the H with the highest S value to become sensitized, it does not pay any other H to do so either. And when nobody pays C, the odds of H's with low S values pairing successfully are the same as for those with high S values. *All* of the H's must thus expect a payoff higher than x_2. This means it pays all of the H's to interact, and all will expect the same payoff, call it $E(X,0)$:

$$E(X,0) = hx_3 + (1-h)x_1. \tag{10}$$

But the expected payoff for each D when everyone interacts is $hx_4 + (1-h)x_2$, which is clearly larger than $E(X,0)$.

Thus, if it is assumed that the equilibrium h is so large that it does not pay even those with the highest S values to become sensitized, we are forced to conclude that the expected payoff to D exceeds the expected payoff to H at that value of h. This means that it could not have been an equilibrium value after all. The equilibrium h must therefore be small enough that it is in the interests of at least those with the highest S values to become sensitized.

To gain further insight into the nature of the equilibrium here, let us again consider a population in which h started near zero and has grown to some positive value, say, h_0. At h_0, who will interact with whom, and in whose interests will it be to become sensitized? We can show it will pay those persons with S greater than some threshold value, $S^*(h_0) < U_D$, to become sensitized and interact with others with like S values. And we can also show that it may or may not pay H's with $S < S^*(h_0)$—that is, those who do not find it profitable to become sensitized—to interact at random with other members of the truncated population (people with $S < S^*(h_0)$).

The threshold value $S^*(h_0)$ is determined as follows. Again making use of the notation defined in equations (5) and (6), note that

$$1 - P_H = \int_{L_H}^{S^*(h_0)} f_H(S)\, dS; \tag{11}$$

$$1 - P_D = \int_{L_D}^{S^*(h_0)} f_D(S)\, dS, \tag{12}$$

are the respective shares of the honest and dishonest populations for which $S < S^*(h_0)$. Let $\delta = (1 - P_H)h_0/[(1 - P_H)h_0 + (1 -$

$P_D)(1-h_0)]$ denote the share of this truncated population that is honest. $S^*(h_0)$ is the value of S that solves the following equation:

$$(13)\quad \Pr\{H|S^*(h_0)\}x_3 + (1-\Pr\{H|S^*(h_0)\})x_1 - C = \max\{x_2, \delta x_3 + (1-\delta)x_1\}.$$

The left-hand side of equation (13) is the expected payoff to an H with $S = S^*(h_0)$ who pays C to become sensitized and then interacts with someone with the same S value (see equation (1)). The second expression within the brackets on the right-hand side of equation (13) is the expected payoff to that same H (or, for that matter, to any other H) if he does not become sensitized and interacts with a randomly chosen person from the truncated population (again, those D's and H's with $S < S^*(h_0)$). If x_2 is larger than that figure, as it is likely to be for small values of h_0, all H's with $S < S^*(h_0)$ will work alone. Otherwise all H's will interact —those with $S > S^*(h_0)$ interacting with others with $S > S^*(h_0)$, those with $S < S^*(h_0)$ interacting with randomly chosen members of the remaining population. Depending on the particular densities used for f_H and f_D, either outcome is possible.

Once $S^*(h_0)$ is determined, it is straightforward, albeit tedious, to calculate $E(X|H)$ and $E(X|D)$. Using the rule that h grows when $E(X|H) > E(X|D)$, the equilibrium value of h is the one for which the two expected payoff curves cross. If we again employ the densities from Figure 1, and use $C = x_1/4$, the expected payoff curves and the equilibrium h are as depicted in Figure 6.

Two features of Figure 6 merit discussion. Note first the discontinuities in the two payoff curves. To see why these occur, recall that it would not be in the interests of anyone to pay the costs of scrutiny if the population initially consisted almost entirely of H's. All of the H's, even those with the highest S values, expect a higher payoff interacting at random with people from the population at large. For values of h close to one, the expected payoff to the D's exceeds that to the H's, which, as noted earlier, causes h to fall. Once h reaches the value for which

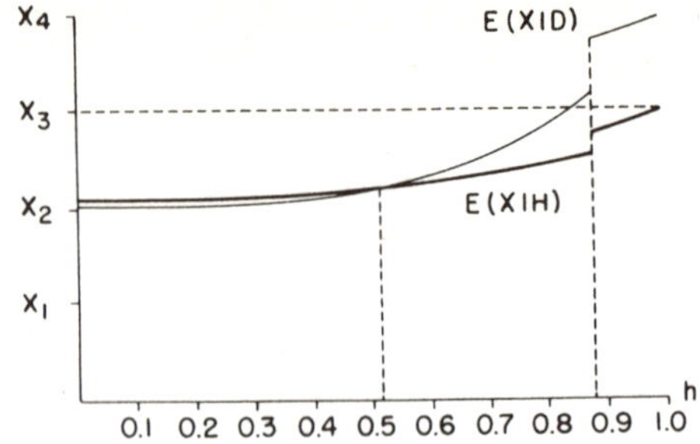

FIGURE 6. EQUILIBRIUM WHEN THERE ARE COSTS OF SCRUTINY

$$(14)\quad E(X,0) = hx_3 + (1-h)x_1 = x_3 - C,$$

however, it abruptly becomes in the interests of those H's with $S > U_D$ to become sensitized, thereby to interact selectively with one another, rather than with individuals chosen at random. At the value of h that solves equation (14), the H's who incur the costs of becoming sensitized are exactly compensated for those costs by the higher gains from selective interaction. But their sudden unavailability for interaction with the remainder of the population produces an abrupt decline in everyone else's expected payoff. This decline is reflected in the discontinuities in the expected payoff curves in Figure 6.

Note also that the equilibrium value of h in Figure 6 is larger than the corresponding value in Figure 5. Although the costs of scrutiny reduce the expected payoffs to both groups in absolute terms, the reduction is more pronounced for the D's. This happens because the costs of scrutiny cause the schedule $S^*(h)$ to shift to the right. And given that f_D lies to the left of f_H, any such shift in $S^*(h)$ will cause a proportionally greater reduction to the D's payoff than to the H's. It is perhaps fitting that, in their struggle with the D's, the H's are abetted by the fact that it requires some effort to observe the symptoms of trustworthiness.

This model treats people as if they were either honest or dishonest. In reality, however, honesty is not a binary trait. A more fully articulated theory would likely predict the coexistence of honest and dishonest impulses within each individual. The resulting environment would be one in which people search hopefully for others they can trust, while remaining ever vigilant against the possibility of being cheated—in short, an environment very much like the one that confronts us.

This outcome is at once in harmony with the economists' view that people pursue self-interest and with their critics' view that people often transcend selfish tendencies. The clear irony is that the gains from cooperation cannot be fully exploited here unless one adopts at the outset what everyone would call a genuinely unselfish point of view.[10]

The model thus suggests that people will often refrain from cheating not because they fear being caught, but because cheating simply makes them feel bad. This view is consistent with an extensive body of empirical evidence assembled by Jerome Kagan; as he summarizes his interpretation of that evidence:

> Construction of a persuasive rational basis for behaving morally has been the problem on which most moral philosophers have stubbed their toes. I believe they will continue to do so until they recognize what Chinese philosophers have known for a long time: namely, feeling, not logic, sustains the superego. [1984, p. *xiv*]

Feelings may indeed sustain the superego. But in the model discussed here, it is logic that ultimately sustains those feelings.

V. Other Aspects of the Utility Function

A. *Concerns About Fairness*

Like feelings of guilt, concerns about fairness may also play a useful role in the utility function.[11] People often walk away from profitable opportunities when they perceive the terms of a transaction to be "unfair." To make sense of such behavior in the framework of conventional economic models, we must imagine that they are investing in the development of reputations for being tough bargainers. That may sometimes be so. But much of the time people walk away just because they would feel even worse if they did not. And even the strategy of developing a tough reputation would be much easier to execute if people actually *disliked* participating in profitable, but one-sided, transactions. People who felt that way would not be lying when they threatened to abandon negotiations. Their preference structure would serve, in effect, as a commitment device, one that makes it in their interests to reject an unfair bargain.

B. *Anger and Vengeance*

Anger, too, often motivates behavior that does not appear self-serving. Customers who are wronged by a supplier may give up several days of their time and suffer much inconvenience in the process of tracking down a $50 refund. People often behave this way even when they are visiting distant locations, where there is no reasonable prospect that their behavior will help them develop reputations for toughness. The proximate cause is that behaving any other way would leave them feeling angry and frustrated.

Viewing tastes as commitment devices suggests a clear rationale for such behavior. If a capacity for anger is observable in a person, suppliers will know he is commited to seek redress, even if it does not "pay" him to do so. This, in turn, makes it rational for the buyer to trust the supplier, even

[10] This is not to say, of course, that we never encounter the more narrowly selfish utility function generally assumed by economists. People of the sort who inhabit economic models surely do exist; but most of us (economists included!) make every effort to steer clear of them.

[11] See my book (1985b, chs. 2,5,6).

when some dimensions of product quality cannot be observed before purchase. The buyer's capacity for anger thus benefits both himself *and* the supplier. For, as George Akerlof's lemons model demonstrates (1970), the alternative here would be for no transaction to take place at all.

VI. Concluding Remarks

Tastes are important. Seemingly minor alterations in the utility function can produce large changes in the conclusions that emerge from economic models. As I have emphasized elsewhere (1984a, b; 1985a, b), the presence of concerns about relative position will affect the wages people earn and also how they spend them. Similarly, the presence of a capacity for anger makes it easier to understand a variety of behaviors that are difficult to rationalize by reference to utility functions of the usual sort.[12] Finally, conscience and other moral sentiments also play a powerful role in the choices people make.

Modern economists regard behaviors arising from these emotions as lying outside the scope of our standard model. But it is neither necessary nor productive to view them this way. Our utility-maximization framework has proven its usefulness for understanding and predicing human behavior. With more careful attention to the specification of the utility function, the territory to which this model applies can be greatly expanded.

[12] Hirshleifer (1978b) makes a similar point.

REFERENCES

Akerlof, George, "The Market for 'Lemons'," *Quarterly Journal of Economics*, August 1970, *84*, 488–500.

______, "Loyalty Filters," *American Economic Review*, March 1983, *73*, 54–63.

Axelrod, Robert, *The Evolution of Cooperation*, New York: Basic Books, 1984.

Becker, Gary and Stigler, George, "De Gustibus Non Est Disputandum," *American Economic Review*, March 1977, *67*, 76–90.

Coelho, Philip, "An Examination into the Causes of Economic Growth: Status as an Economic Good," *Research in Law and Economics*, 1985, 7, 89–116.

Darwin, Charles, *The Expression of Emotions in Man and Animals* (1872), Chicago: University of Chicago Press, 1965.

Dawkins, Richard, *The Selfish Gene*, New York: Oxford University Press, 1976.

Ekman, Paul, *Telling Lies*, New York: W. W. Norton, 1985.

Frank, Robert H., (1984a) "Interdependent Preferences and the Competitive Wage Structure," *Rand Journal of Economics*, Winter 1984, *15*, 510–20.

______, (1984b) "Are Workers Paid Their Marginal Products?," *American Economic Review*, September 1984, *74*, 549–71.

______, (1985a) "The Demand for Unobservable and Other Nonpositional Goods," *American Economic Review*, March 1985, *75*, 101–16.

______, (1985b) *Choosing the Right Pond*, New York: Oxford University Press, 1985.

______, "The Nature of the Utility Function," in A. MacFadyen and H. MacFadyen, eds., *Economic Psychology*, Amsterdam: North-Holland, 1986.

______, *Beyond Self-Interest: Prisoner's Dilemmas and the Strategic Role of the Emotions*, New York: W. W. Norton, 1988.

Hamilton, W. D., "The Genetical Theory of Social Behavior," *Journal of Theoretical Biology*, 1964, *7*, 1–32.

Hirshleifer, Jack, "Economics from a Biological Viewpoint," *Journal of Law and Economics*, April 1977, 20:1–52.

______, (1978a) "Competition, Cooperation, and Conflict in Economics and Biology," *American Economic Review Proceedings*, May 1978, *68*, 238–43.

______, (1978b) "Natural Economy Versus Political Economy," *Journal of Social and Biological Structures*, October 1978, *1*, 319–37.

______, "The Emotions as Guarantors of Threats and Promises," Department of Economics Working Paper No. 337, UCLA, August 1984.

Kagan, Jerome, *The Nature of the Child*, New York: Basic Books, 1984.

Konner, Melvin, *The Tangled Wing*, New York: Holt, Rinehart, and Winston, 1982.

Krebs, John R. and Dawkins, Richard, "Animal Signals: Mind Reading and Manipulation," in J. R. Krebs and N. B. Davies, eds., *Behavioral Ecology: An Evolutionary Approach*, 2nd ed., Sunderland: Sinauer Associates, 1984.

Lykken, David T., *A Tremor in the Blood*, New York: McGraw-Hill, 1981.

Rubin, Paul, "Evolved Ethics and Efficient Ethics," *Journal of Economic Behavior and Organization*, June/Sept. 1982, *3*, 161–74.

______, **and Paul, Chris,** "An Evolutionary Model of Taste for Risk," *Economic Inquiry*, October 1979, *17*, 585–96.

Schelling, Thomas C., *The Strategy of Conflict*, New York: Oxford University Press, 1960.

______, "Altruism, Meanness, and Other Potentially Strategic Behaviors," *American Economic Review Proceedings*, May 1978, *68*, 229–30.

Trivers, Robert L., "The Evolution of Reciprocal Altruism," *Quarterly Review of Biology*, March 1971, *46*, 35–57.

______, *Social Evolution*, Menlo Park: Benjamin/Cummings, 1985.

Wilson, Edward O., *Sociobiology*, Cambridge: Belknap Press, Harvard University Press, 1975.

______, *On Human Nature*, Cambridge: Harvard University Press, 1978.

[34]

On the Emotions as Guarantors of Threats and Promises

Jack Hirshleifer

The role of the passions or emotions in supporting civil society has been discussed by social theorists and moral philosophers since earliest times. Adam Smith, in particular, whose name is more usually associated with the claim that an economic system may function effectively even when men act only in accordance with calculated self-interest, was actually very concerned with aspects of human nature that set limits upon the pursuit of self-interest: "Nature, when she formed man for society, endowed him with an original desire to please, and an original aversion to offend his brethren. She taught him to feel pleasure in their favourable, and pain in their unfavourable regard. She rendered their approbation most flattering and most agreeable to him for its own sake; and their disapprobation most mortifying and most offensive." [1] More intriguing than his appreciation of the force of "positive" emotions like benevolence and sympathy are Smith's insights into how even the more dubious passions—pride, vanity, and ambition—may promote the interests of society.[2] This point had of course already been made by Mandeville in *The Fable of the Bees* (1714). But Smith comes closer to my theme here in his argument that these "negative" sentiments can be most socially useful precisely when they drive people to undertake activities *beyond the bounds of pragmatic self-interest*. Thus, of a "poor man's son ... visited with ambition" Adam Smith says,

> For this purpose he makes his court to all mankind; he serves those whom he hates, and is obsequious to those whom he despises. Through the whole of his life he pursues the idea of a certain artificial and elegant repose which he may never arrive at, for which he sacrifices a real tranquillity that is at all times in his power, and which, if in the extremity of old age he should at last attain to it, he will find to be in no respect preferable to that humble security and contentment which he had abandoned for it.[3]
>
> And it is well that nature imposes upon us in this manner. It is this deception which arouses and keeps in continual motion the industry of mankind. It is this which first prompted them to cultivate the ground, to build houses, to found cities and common-wealths, and to

invent and improve all the sciences and arts, which ennoble and embellish human life.[4,5]

The point I shall be making is somewhat different, however. The emotions, positive or negative, can indeed be socially useful in driving a person to act beyond the bounds of pragmatic self-interest. But paradoxically the consequence is not necessarily adverse for himself. A person can sometimes best further his self-interest by *not* intending to pursue it. Methodologically speaking also, I shall be advancing somewhat beyond the classical discussions referred to above, in providing a systematic *analysis* of the precise ways in which different emotional sets may promote or subvert socially advantageous arrangements. My discussion follows a lead by Becker (1976), who demonstrated how "altruism" can, in effect, force cooperation upon a completely selfish partner (the "Rotten-Kid Theorem"). I shall try to show more generally here how, and up to what limits, positive or negative emotions can serve a constructive role as guarantors of *threats* or *promises* in social interactions.

If a mutually desired objective is to be achieved, it is often necessary that one or more of the parties forgo the opportunity to reap a self-interested gain. Intelligence permits reasoning beings to "look around the corner," to visualize the advantages of *not* pursuing immediate self-interest. But the problem of securing the necessary coordination of actions remains. A meeting of the minds—a contract, to use that term in its broadest sense—does not generally suffice; some method of *enforcing* (or otherwise guaranteeing) performance is generally required.[6]

The most obvious method of enforcement is through the legal-judicial system. But it has long been appreciated that in some cases contracts may be self-enforcing (Macaulay, 1963), the key point being that fear of losing profitable future business with a trading partner may suffice to deter defection here and now. This topic has recently been studied by Telser (1980), using the analytical model of the repeated-play Prisoners' Dilemma ("supergame" theory, in the standard jargon). The difficulty is the well-known incentive to defect at the last round of play. This obstacle can be overcome, so that the contract becomes self-enforcing, when the number of rounds is infinite or at least if there is a sufficiently high probability of play always continuing for another round (see also Luce and Raiffa, 1957, p. 102).

In contrast with this line of discussion, I shall be dealing solely with single-round games. But my analysis will not be limited to Prisoners' Dilemma, which is only one of a number of distinct payoff environments combining a mutual gain from cooperation with a self-interested motive to defect. In the situations to be considered the possibility of enforcement stems from an assumed asymmetric game protocol, such that one of the players "has the last word" (Hirshleifer, 1977) and thus is potentially in a position to confer reward or punishment. Since offers of reward or punishment are contingent strategies, we are in the realm of "metagames" in the jargon of the trade (Howard, 1971; Thompson and Faith, 1981).

In what follows I shall first briefly discuss the nature of threats versus promises in different payoff environments. Then I shall provide an explicit analysis for several different categories of emotions. Finally, I shall speculate upon the possible reasons why emotions, and other limitations upon "rationality," have survived as part of the human constitution.

1

An individual who makes a threat or promise is pledging to respond in a contingent way to another's actions, with the goal of influencing the other party's choice. The intended effect would presumably always be to the threatener's advantage, though not necessarily to the other's disadvantage. The only other point worthy of special note is that a promise or threat must be *to do something that the individual would not otherwise be motivated to do*. That is what distinguishes these pledges from mere forecasts, however informative, of one's likely responses to another's actions (see also Schelling, 1960, chapter 2).

Matrix 1 illustrates a Prisoners' Dilemma payoff environment, where 4 represents the highest and 1 the lowest of the ordinally ranked returns to each of the players (see figure 14.1). Here and throughout, unless indicated to the contrary, the Column player moves first so that it is the Row player who "has the last word." It is then possible to define *contingent* strategies

Matrix 1

Prisoners' Dilemma

	LOYAL	DEFECT
LOYAL	3,3 #	1,4
DEFECT	4,1	2,2*

Matrix 1A

Expanded Prisoners' Dilemma

	LOYAL	DEFECT
LOYAL	3,3	1,4
DEFECT	4,1	2,2
TIT FOR TAT	3,3	2,2
REVERSAL	4,1	1,4

Matrix 2

Chicken

	DOVE	HAWK
DOVE	3,3 #	2,4*
HAWK	4,2**	1,1

Figure 14.1

for Row. Let the two elementary strategies available to each player be LOYAL and DEFECT. Row's additional contingent strategies can be termed TIT FOR TAT (play LOYAL in response to LOYAL, and DEFECT in response to DEFECT) and REVERSAL (play DEFECT in response to LOYAL, and LOYAL in response to DEFECT). It is standard to represent these contingent strategies by additional rows in the game's normal form, as in the "expanded" Matrix 1A. However, for my purposes it suffices to deal directly with the underlying Matrix 1, where it is easy enough to visualize the effects of threats or promises on the part of the Row player.

With Column having the first move, suppose that Row—even though he may contemplate or even intend a contingent strategy like TIT FOR TAT—cannot *guarantee* to Column that he will be following it. Then, returning to Matrix 1, Column will surely choose DEFECT. (For, his choice of LOYAL would be responded to by Row's DEFECT, leaving Column with his worst payoff of 1.) Row will of course answer Column's DEFECT with his own DEFECT. Thus the parties end up at the cell of Matrix 1 marked with a star; the payoffs are 2 each—their next-to-worst outcomes in each case.[7] This is of course the traditional "trap" equilibrium of Prisoners' Dilemma,[8] a seemingly paradoxical result since, by cooperation, the parties could have reaped their next-to-best payoff of 3 each.

This Pareto-superior 3,3 outcome (marked with a # in Matrix 1) would indeed be achieved if Row could guarantee abiding by a *promise* to play LOYAL in response to LOYAL on Column's part. Column, if he could rely upon that promise, then would play LOYAL on the first move. What makes Row's utterance a promise (rather than a forecast) is that he offers *not to do* what he is in fact motivated to do when his turn comes up. In promising LOYAL, Row engages himself to confer a benefit upon Column, at a cost to himself, should the latter first choose LOYAL himself. But that Row will play DEFECT in response to DEFECT is only a forecast and not a threat, since Row would be doing that anyway.

To illustrate an actual *threat*, consider the almost equally famous payoff environment known as the game of Chicken (Matrix 2). Holding to the ornithological metaphor, the two strategies can be called HAWK and DOVE. If Row cannot guarantee performance of a contingent strategy, then Column, having the first move, must inspect Row's response to each of his choices. Evidently, Column's best first move is the "less cooperative" HAWK strategy, leading to an asymmetrical 2,4 outcome in his favor (starred in the matrix). In order to influence Column to change his strategy, Row would have to guarantee execution of a *threat* to play HAWK in response to HAWK. Once again, that is an engagement to do something at a cost to himself, but now the action imposes a *loss* on Column. If Column bows to the threat and plays DOVE instead, Row now plays HAWK leading to the reversed payoff outcome 4,2 in Row's favor (double-starred in the matrix).

On the other hand, Row might sweeten the deal by issuing a *threat-and-promise*. That is, in addition to the aforesaid threat to play HAWK in response to HAWK, he could promise to forgo part of his gain and respond to DOVE with DOVE. Then, the parties could achieve the symmetrical 3,3 outcome (marked # in Matrix 2). It might seem puzzling that, if Row's threat is solid enough to work, he would ever choose to reduce his gain by combining a threat and a promise. But throughout this paper we are contemplating the possibility that parties might, owing to emotional limits upon self-interested rationality, *not* necessarily do what it is in their material advantage to do. In such circumstances, threat-and-promise might conceivably trigger a less hostile response than threat alone.

2

In this section I shall examine the consequences of two different scaled classes of emotion: (1) the malevolence/benevolence spectrum and (2) the anger/gratitude spectrum. The first category is *action-independent*, the second is *action-dependent*. I shall continue to employ the assumption throughout that one player always has the first move; in fact, let us call him First. The other player, Second, is therefore the one who may be in a position to confer reward or punishment.

Benevolence/Malevolence

Figures 14.2a and 14.2b illustrate benevolence and malevolence *on the part of the last mover*, Second. Thus it is Second's indifference curves that are being pictured, on axes representing the two parties' material incomes Y_S and Y_F. In figure 14.2a Y_S and Y_F are both *goods* for a benevolent Second, so his indifference curves have the familiar negative slope. In figure 14.2b his own income Y_S remains of course a good for Second, but now Y_F is a *bad* from his point of view. Hence the abnormal indifference curve map in figure 14.2b.

I shall also be assuming that Second always has the power to transfer income to First, or else to deprive him of income, if he chooses—in each case, at a cost to himself. Specifically, in the transfer mode Second can increase First's income Y_F by giving up his own income Y_S on a 1 : 1 basis. (Note the dashed 135° "transfer lines" *TT* in figure 14.2a, where the arrows attached indicate the direction of movement.) In the deprivation mode, Second can reduce First's income but again only by incurring an assumed equal cost himself—indicated by the dashed 45° "deprivation lines" *DD* in figure 14.2b. (Once again, the arrows indicate the possible direction of movement.)

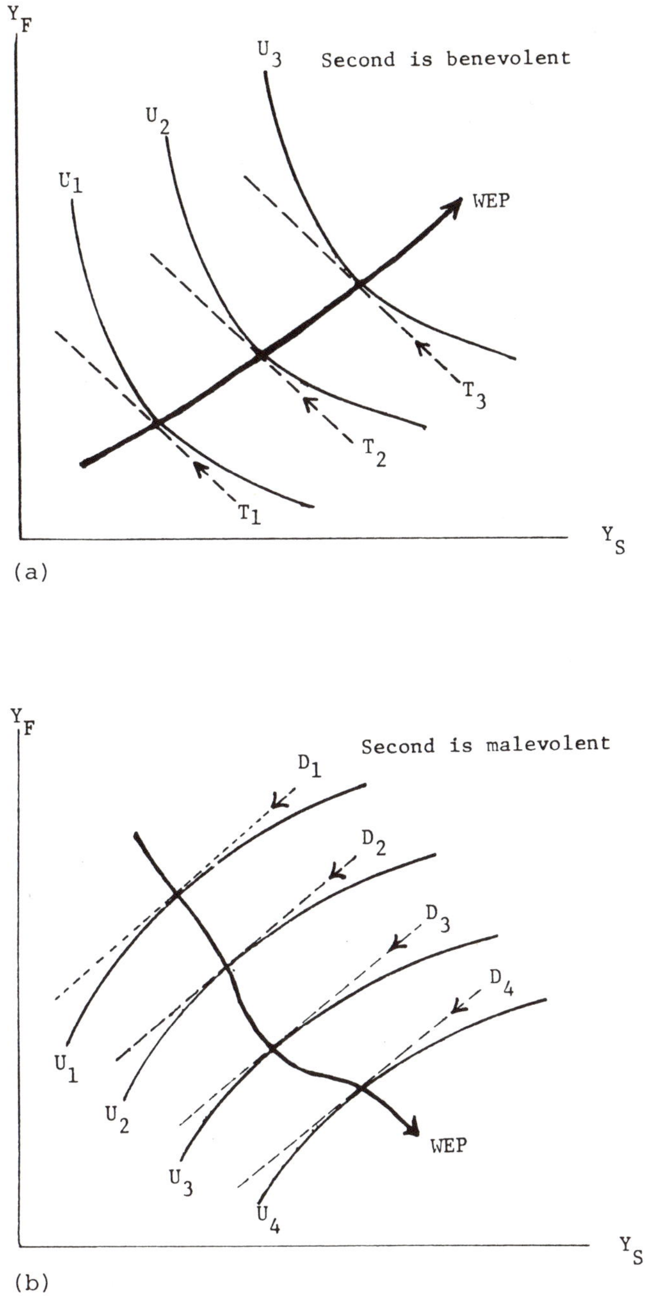

Figure 14.2
Benevolence versus malevolence.

In figure 14.2a the *WEP* curve (a "Wealth Expansion Path") connects all the tangencies of Second's benevolent indifference curves with the 135° transfer lines. It follows immediately that, provided the starting position is to the *southeast* of the *WEP* curve (that is, provided he is relatively well off and First relatively poorly off to begin with), Second will always transfer exactly that amount of income leading him to a final solution along *WEP*. Similarly, in figure 14.2b the *WEP* curve connects all the tangencies of Second's malevolent indifference curves with the 45° deprivation lines. Here Second will always impose enough deprivation to end up along *WEP*, provided the starting position is to the *northeast*. (That is, provided both parties are relatively well endowed with income to begin with. Second must be reasonably wealthy in order to afford the cost of inflicting the deprivation, while First must be well off to begin with else the initial situation would not be intolerable to a malevolent Second.)

Another property of the *WEP* curves will be important in what follows. In figure 14.2a *WEP* has positive slope throughout. This indicates that, as a benevolent Second grows wealthier, he will want to choose positions involving greater Y_S and greater Y_F *both*. That is, as he becomes richer, he wants to end up with more income for himself and more income for the object of his benevolence. This represents a special, though reasonable, assumption, that Y_S and Y_F are both "superior" goods from Second's point of view.[9] By a corresponding argument, in figure 14.2b the curve *WEP* has negative slope. As Second becomes richer, he prefers to so arrange matters as to have more income himself while leaving the target of his malevolence worse off.

Now we turn to the decisions available to the first mover. It will be assumed that a joint productive opportunity boundary like *QQ'* in figure 14.3 always exists, and that First has the sole choice of the productive arrangements to be made—i.e., he determines the point to be chosen along *QQ'*. Furthermore, for simplicity First is assumed throughout to be merely self-interested, neither benevolent nor malevolent.[10] It then follows that, in the absence of any anticipated reaction from Second, First would always simply prefer the most northerly position along *QQ'*—point *M* in the diagram. As it happens, the joint productive arrangements represented by point *M* do generate some income for Second as well, but this is a merely incidental fact from First's selfish point of view.

But now note the position of Second's (solid) Wealth Expansion Path *WEP* in figure 14.3. This indicates that, beyond point *X*, where *WEP* cuts *QQ'*, Second regards himself as wealthy enough to display some benevolence toward First. Thus, First, should he choose his short-sightedly selfish optimum, M, would end up doing better than this—since Second would benevolently transfer enough income to him along the transfer line T_1T_1 to end up at point *N* that lies to the north of *M*. But that is still not the best

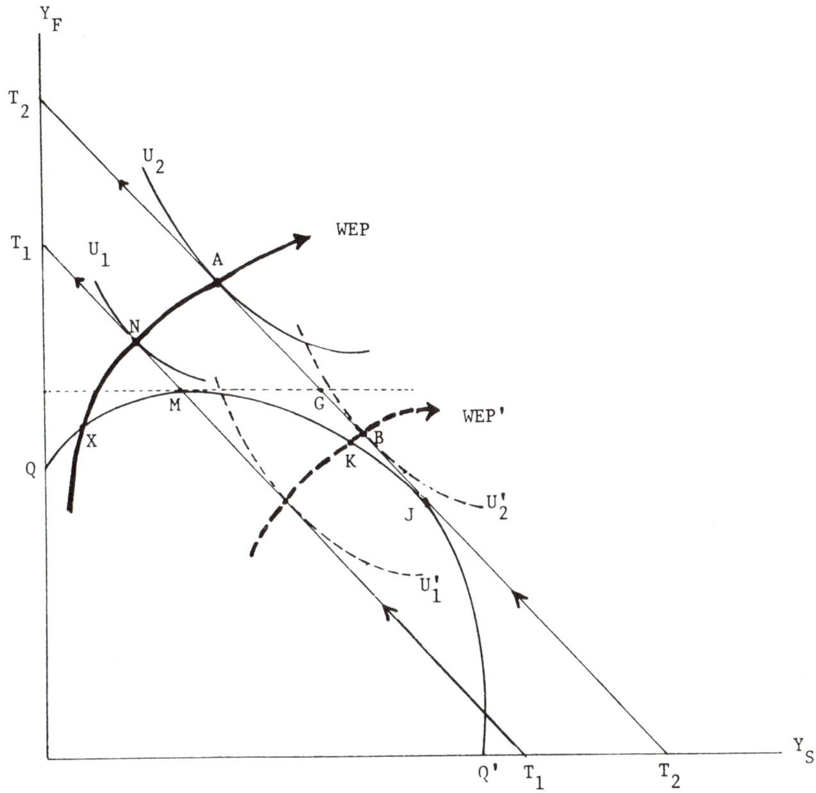

Figure 14.3
The Rotten-Kid Theorem—benevolence as guarantor of a promise.

that a *far-sightedly* selfish First could achieve. In fact, it will be evident from the diagram that First should choose point *J*, where *QQ'* is tangent to the highest attainable 135° transfer line T_2T_2. True, in the short run, First will have sacrificed income on behalf of Second. But the latter will then benevolently transfer enough of his enlarged income to First so as to achieve a final indifference-curve tangency at point *A*. From the selfish First player's point of view, *A* is better than (north of) *N*. In fact, *A* represents the largest income attainable by First under the conditions assumed.

That, however, is not the surprising part of this result. The real point is, not only does "enlightened self-interest" lead the selfish first mover to a better outcome thanks to a predictable benefit from Second's benevolence, but the latter gains as well! And the gain to Second is not merely in terms of his psychic satisfaction from seeing First better off. Even in the crassly material sense, the benevolent second mover himself has gained from his generosity. His own material income Y_S is greater at point *A* than it would have been otherwise, i.e., had the selfish First player chosen point *M* along *QQ'*.

What has happened here is that Second's benevolence guaranteed an implicit "promise" to reward First, a necessary condition for securing co-operation from a merely self-interested individual. The second mover's "hard-core altruism" has served to elicit the first mover's pragmatic or "soft-core altruism."[11]

Another aspect of the constructive role played by benevolence is brought out if we look at the alternative (dashed) Wealth Expansion Path *WEP'* in figure 14.3. This curve is associated with a different possible set of preferences for Second, suggest by the dashed indifference curves *U'*. These alternative preferences are *qualitatively* similar in that they also represent benevolent tastes, but now to a *quantitatively* lesser degree. In these altered circumstances, if First were to choose the jointly cooperative position *J* along *QQ'* as before, Second would then transfer a smaller amount to him—so that the parties would end up at position *B* along *WEP'* rather than at A along *WEP*. But, for the selfish First player, position *B* is inferior to his short-sightedly selfish optimum, *M*. The conclusion: far-sighted or enlightened self-interest may not suffice to achieve mutual improvement, in the absence of a *sufficiently strong degree* of benevolence on the part of the player having the last move.

Of course, in the latter situation Second could still *promise* to provide First with a sufficient reward to induce cooperation—say, by pledging to choose position *A* if First selects *J* along *QQ'*. But by assumption there is nothing to guarantee Second's promise—save his own benevolence, which is here inadequate. In fact, there is a critical threshold degree of benevolence on the part of Second needed to elicit cooperation from First. To wit, to provide enough inducement for a far-sightedly selfish First to choose point *J*, Second's benevolent Wealth Expansion Path must cut the transfer line T_2T_2 north of its intersection with the dotted line through *M*. Thus, lots of love may do the trick where a little love achieves nothing at all!

If benevolence can serve as guarantor of a *promise* by the party having the last word, can malevolence serve as a guarantor of a *threat*? It surely can, but the overall effect is not to elicit cooperation, if we hold to the assumption that the *WEP* curve in figure 14.4 (compare figure 14.2b) has negative slope throughout. (That is, the richer Second gets, the more he can afford to and want to spend on depriving First.) In figure 14.4 then, should the first mover short-sightedly choose the most northerly position *M* along *QQ'*, he will have empowered a malevolent Second to impoverish him to the degree represented by the final position *L*. If First were instead to choose the efficient productive point *J*, he would end up still worse off at

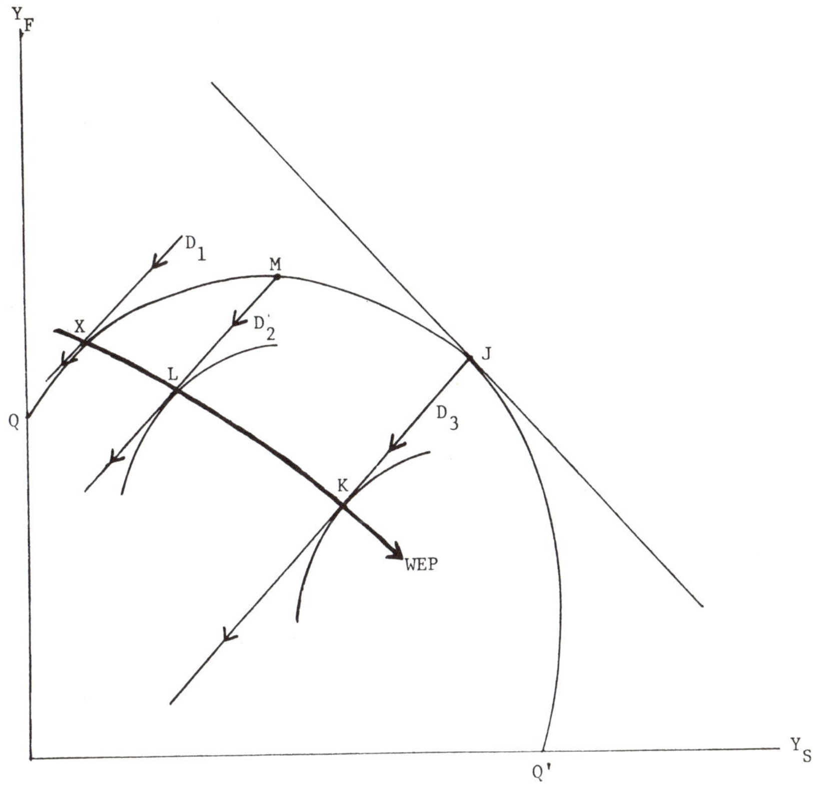

Figure 14.4
Malevolence and threat.

K. Evidently a selfish First does best to choose point *X*, where he is initially poorer but where Second is also so poor that he cannot afford (or at least does not care) to incur costs to impose any further deprivation upon him. Thus malevolence guarantees execution of a threat, but the consequence is that *both* parties are worse off—in terms of psychic satisfaction and in terms of material income as well.

Gratitude/Anger

I now turn to the *action-dependent* emotional scale ranging from gratitude at the positive end to anger at the negative end of the spectrum. The question as before will be whether these emotions can guarantee execution of threats or promises and thereby promote achievement of mutually beneficial solutions.

Allowing for the possibility that malevolence and benevolence represented a departure from the economist's standard assumption of self-interested behavior, but did not otherwise do violence to the picture of economic man as a rational utilitarian calculator. An individual who values other people's income (positively or negatively) as well as his own can nevertheless coolly go about his business of calculating a preferred final outcome in the light of his given preferences and opportunities.[12] But I am now introducing a much more serious departure from the standard assumptions of the economist—to wit, the idea that an individual can be *passionate*, in the sense of "losing control" and doing what he does not really want to do (on this see Schelling, 1980). Or an alternative (and my preferred) interpretation would be that what he wants to do need not depend only upon the final outcome in the utilitarian sense—i.e., strictly upon the ultimate distribution of incomes between the two parties—but rather may be *action-dependent*. An income distribution that could be tolerable as an accidental or random event, for example, might lead to violent revolt if seen to be the result of conscious choice on the part of another economic agent. Common observation tells us that, whatever the textbooks assume, such behavior is in fact very important in the makeup of normal human beings. I shall be showing that, at least in certain circumstances, such nonutilitarian behavior[13] makes ultimate utilitarian sense!

Since preferences are now assumed action-dependent, we can no longer postulate a fixed preference map defined simply over the parties' incomes Y_F and Y_S. Nevertheless, it is possible to place plausible restrictions upon how a second mover influenced by anger/gratitude motivations would respond to choices by a first mover. (By analogy with the foregoing, I assume here that only Second is subject to anger/gratitude emotions, First remaining throughout a coolly calculating and self-interested economic man.) In figure 14.5, Second's responses to First's choice along QQ' are summarized diagrammatically by his Anger/Gratitude Response (AGR) curve. This curve might take on a number of possible shapes, subject to the restrictions that (1) increasing wealth empowers Second to spend more either on transferring income to or else withdrawing income from First, but (2) the more "cooperative" is First's behavior (i.e., the more his choice along QQ' approaches point J), the less is Second's anger and/or the greater is Second's gratitude—with the obvious implication for his willingness to confer benefit or injury upon the other.[14]

In figure 14.5 the "effective anger" region of Second's AGR curve extends from point X to point M along the opportunity boundary QQ'. (If First were to choose any point to the west of X along QQ', Second might be even angrier still, but too impoverished to do anything about it.) As First's choice hypothetically shifts to the east of X so as to provide Second with more income, the latter can *increasingly afford to* react in an angry way but becomes *decreasingly inclined* to do so. Beyond the crossover at M,

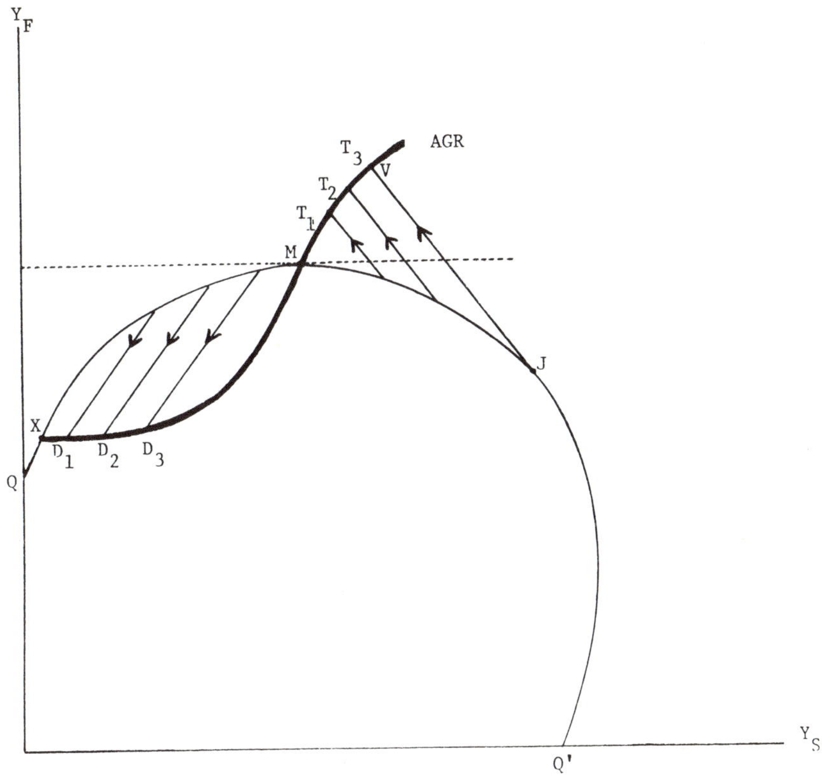

Figure 14.5
The Anger/Gratitude Response (AGR) curve—threat and promise.

Second enters his "effective gratitude" region. Here as his income grows thanks to First's making a more cooperative productive decision, Second is increasingly more able to react (now in a positive grateful way) and is also increasingly inclined to do so. Thus in the effective anger region, between *X* and *M*, the gap between *QQ'* and *AGR* first widens and then narrows. But in the effective gratitude region beyond the crossover at *M* the gap increasingly widens as Second's income increases. This type of situation, it may be noted, corresponds to the *threat-and-promise* contingent behavior mentioned in section 1.[15]

The outcome of the pattern pictured in figure 14.5 is at point *V*. The efficient productive solution is achieved (at *J* on *QQ'*) plus a redistribution thereafter in such a way that both parties are better off in comparison with First's simple selfish solution at point *M*. But this is only one of quite a number of possible consequences of an anger-gratitude scaled reaction pattern.

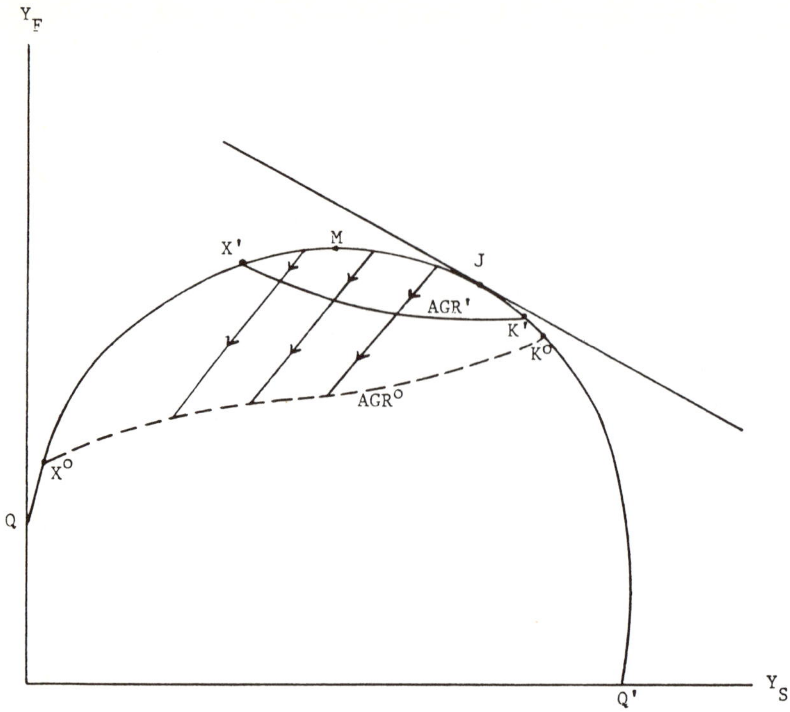

Figure 14.6
Effective and ineffective *AGR* curves.

Two other possibilities are pictured in figure 14.6. Here, in contrast to figure 14.5, anger is the dominant emotion influencing Second's behavior. However, this can have very different implications, as illustrated by the alternative *AGR* curves pictured—the (dashed) AGR° versus the (solid) AGR'. In each case, by assumption here the crossover point along QQ' lies to the east of the efficient productive solution *J*; Second does not give up his wrath until he is very well treated indeed. If Second's emotional set corresponds to AGR°, the best choice for First along $X^\circ K^\circ$ is at point K°. Second's threat has worked so effectively as to force First to make a big sacrifice—going not merely beyond First's simple selfish optimum, *M*, but even beyond the jointly efficient outcome. If Second's AGR' curve is applicable, on the other hand, First will prefer point X'. Second's threat does not work at all. Or rather it works *to the disadvantage* of both parties, in view of the steps First will take to escape the threat. X' is inferior for both, not merely in comparison with what could have been achieved by Second's making a transfer after First chooses the jointly efficient outcome *J*, but even in comparison with First's simple selfish outcome *M*.

What is the difference between the two cases? AGR' represents a relatively "small" threat in comparison with AGR°—it does not take hold at all until point X' rather than X°, and it inflicts smaller punishment throughout the relevant range. This feature is not the essential, however. The important feature is the overall *slope* of the AGR curve. That is, no matter whether the magnitude of the threat is large or small, its effectiveness depends upon the "appeasing" effect of each increment of compliance. A sufficient appeasing effect would be reflected by a positively sloped *AGR* curve, like AGR° in figure 14.6. Here a coolly calculating First can always do better by complying, up to the limit of feasibility at point K°. But if Second's anger is never sufficiently appeased, as reflected by the negatively sloped AGR' in the diagram, First can minimize the loss to himself by non-compliance—to the disadvantage of Second as well.

While many other pictures can be drawn illustrating interesting possibilities, the following points summarize the key considerations:

1. The rationally selfish first mover will want and (assuming that he has the relevant information) be able to achieve the most northerly point along the *AGR* curve that represents Second's scaled emotional response to his behavior.
2. Second's *AGR* curve will typically take off at some interior point *X along QQ'*, where he begins to have income enough to be able to indulge his anger. The *AGR* curve may have positive or negative slope, but will eventually cross *QQ'* again at a point where First's move has become generous enough to appease Second's anger.
3. If *anger* is Second's dominating emotion, reflected by an *AGR* curve that does not cut *QQ'* until some point *K* to the east of the efficient point *J*, then the solution for First—the most northerly point along *AGR* (unless *M* is higher still)—will tend to be toward one extreme or the other, depending upon whether the slope of the *AGR* curve is predominantly positive or negative. If the slope is predominantly positive, there are typically positive *marginal* payoffs to First of appeasement, of bowing to the threat. It does not matter how heavy a punishment Second might impose in aggregate, but only how he reacts, on the margin, to First's concessions. A positively sloped *AGR* function thus tends toward an excellent outcome for Second, with First appeasing him heavily. If, on the other hand, the slope of the *AGR* curve is predominantly negative, First typically suffers negative marginal payoffs from making concessions. Here the typical outcome is toward the other extreme, at point *X* where Second is left too poor to inflict punishment. Of course, here First will end up poor as well.
4. But if *gratitude* is Second's dominating emotion, reflected by an *AGR* crossing *QQ'* to the west of point *J*, the efficient solution tends

to be achieved—provided again that the *AGR* curve has positive slope. Both parties then end up better off than at First's simple selfish optimum.

3

Biologists and anthropologists have been long concerned with explaining the great gap between human intellectual capacities and those of the nonhuman primates, an advance that appears to go beyond the adaptive environmental requirements of primitive man (Washburn, 1960; Rose, 1980; Staddon, 1981). But equally mysterious, perhaps, is the survival of those *limitations* upon self-interested rationality we term the passions or emotions. In *The Expression of the Emotions*, Charles Darwin emphasized the universality of these emotions over the human species, and also their continuity with behaviors visible among animals. Of course, there would be no special need to explain survival of the passions if they are only "imperfections." Since the development of any trait involves some energetic cost, or at least some opportunity cost in terms of other capacities that have to be sacrificed, we do not need to explain why all living beings are not unlimitedly fecund, powerful beyond measure, or as speedy as light. But we ought not prejudge the question as to whether the observed limitations upon the human ability to pursue self-interested rationality are really no more than imperfections—might not these seeming disabilities actually be functional?

The thrust of the argument here has been that certain patterns of environmental payoffs to interpersonal cooperative opportunities can make retention of a capacity for emotion materially profitable. In this paper I distinguished between the *action-independent* versus the *action-dependent* passions. The first category was illustrated by non-self-interested motivations (the malevolence/benevolence spectrum), the second by impairment of the ability to calculate owing to reactive "loss of control" (the anger/gratitude spectrum). Given that one party in a social interaction is a selfish and perfectly rational calculator, it turns out that there are circumstances in which it is indeed profitable for the other to diverge from self-interested rationality—in accordance with one or both of these emotional scales.

As a related point, evolutionary biologists have also been concerned to explain the survival of "altruism" on the one hand and "spite" on the other. Despite the psychological connotations of these terms, the interpretation in the standard literature has been entirely operational rather than motivational: "altruism" is taken to mean acting so as to help another organism, at a cost to oneself, while "spite" refers to incurring a cost so as to injure another. Since evolutionary success is a selfish criterion,[16] the biological literature has attempted to explore the different patterns by which proximate sacrifice, the cost incurred to benefit or to injure another organism, can ultimately pay off through some indirect route [for example, in the case of "altruism," if one's beneficiaries are kin (Hamilton, 1964) or if an other-benefiting act leads to adequate reciprocation (Trivers, 1971)]. This paper, in contrast, directly attacks the problem of motivation. (Hence it is not applicable to lower organisms lacking the capacity for emotions.) What it examines are possible mechanisms whereby individuals may be led to supply the reward or punishment (the positive or negative reciprocation) that make certain forms of social cooperation possible. The vague terms "altruism" and "spite" are inadequate to describe the subtly different forms that these reciprocations may take.

In summary, the models analyzed here represent a special but illuminating case. It was assumed that, in a given payoff environment, a merely self-interested and accurately calculating party has the first move, after which a possibly emotion-influenced agent makes his choice in response. When it comes to the action-independent emotions—the malevolence/benevolence spectrum—*benevolence* can serve to guarantee a promise, but *malevolence* is not generally effective in guaranteeing execution of a threat. (A curious yet important point is that just a little benevolence may not work either—a generosity threshold must be overcome.) As for the action-dependent reactions, the anger/gratitude scale, *gratitude* has effects rather parallel with benevolence, but *anger* tends to be more effective than malevolence in securing cooperation. The key reason for the difference is that malevolence becomes a more powerful force as the responding party's wealth increases, a factor that strongly inhibits any desire on the part of the first mover to enrich the other by cooperation. But anger tends to erode as the first mover's choice shifts toward cooperation, hence may provide the needed inducement for achieving a mutually beneficial arrangement. The most general and interesting conclusions are that (i) absence of self-interest can pay off *even measured in terms of material selfish gain*, and, a parallel but quite distinct point, (ii) the loss of control that makes calculated behavior impossible can be more profitable than calculated optimization. (It follows that a coolly calculating individual might more or less successfully *pretend* to be driven by passion-dominated responses. Furthermore, in this pretense he need not be seeking a merely selfish goal!)

Analytically, this paper demonstrates the not-so-paradoxical fact that it is possible to analyze, in terms of effects upon rationally calculated self-interest, the consequences of non-self-interested motivations and of limitations upon the ability to calculate. The economist must go beyond the assumption of "economic man" precisely because of the economic advantage of *not* behaving like economic man—an advantage that presumably explains why the world is not populated solely by economic men.

I would like also to indicate some of the limitations of the analysis, which suggest directions for generalization:

1. The analysis here does not pretend to explain *all* the behaviors and attitudes we think of as emotions, but only certain of these, which are alleged to help guarantee the execution of contracts. Other types of emotions also serve important functions—for example, fear, which makes us flee danger, or romantic love, which helps us win mates—but are not relevant to the purpose at hand. Coming closer to the topic here, there are still other sentiments that bear upon the kinds of interpersonal transactions a group of individuals can arrive at, but which I have not studied—envy, pride, and shame are among them.
2. I have dealt only with one-time interactions. There is already a considerable body of literature dealing with repeated interactions, in which refusal to continue a business relationship with a defecting trading partner may alone suffice to enforce a contract. Nevertheless, I suspect the anger/gratitude response pattern is an important additional factor, providing a degree of extra support where mere refusal of future business cannot carry all the weight of maintaining a social relationship.
3. The postulated division of responsibility, whereby the first mover has free choice of productive arrangements while the second mover can only react by a reward or deprivation response, is of course a special assumption. But I do not believe it is unduly restrictive. We could equally well imagine the first mover as making some preliminary choice that narrows down the productive or other options available, after which the second mover makes a "finalizing" decision, possibly including productive aspects as well. The assumed special shapes of the functions could also be easily generalized. If the productive opportunity locus were to become less concave-downward (i.e., if QQ' in the diagrams were to approach a linear or even a convex-downward shape), the potential mutual gain via productive coordination would be reduced. Cooperation will then, other things being equal, become less likely.[17] And similarly, one could allow for different "exchange rates" in the second mover's ability to transfer or to deprive the other party, with predictable consequences for the efficacy of the second mover's ability to exert influence upon the other.
4. I considered only interactions between a self-interested coolly calculating party on the one hand, and an emotion-driven individual on the other, where the latter has the last move. If the time sequence were reversed, what I have called "threat" and "promise" would evidently not be successful.
5. Finally, the analysis here hints at a more daring suggestion. *Leader-*

ship involves to a significant extent the function of conferring reward or punishment upon other members of the society, i.e., serving as second mover in many social interactions. While the role of leader is often simply seized by the strongest and/or cleverest, there also is commonly some degree of popular consent involved. Might it not be the case that the "inspirational" or "charismatic" quality that we look for in leaders is an extraordinary capacity to transcend self-interested motivations, to be passionately driven by action-dependent, non-utilitarian goals? There are of course merely self-interested, calculating princes who would follow Machiavelli's advice: "Therefore, a prudent ruler ought not to keep faith when by so doing it would be against his interest, and when the reasons which made him bind himself no longer exist" (*The Prince*, XVIII). But such a ruler would likely find it difficult to elicit from citizens that extra measure of devoted cooperation upon which the survival of his regime may depend. So, even the most Machiavellian of princes is likely at least to *simulate* the possession of genuine action-independent or action-dependent passions—what Boulding (1969) has called the heroic ethic.

Notes

1. Smith, *Moral Sentiments*, p. 212.
2. On this, see especially Coase (1976), pp. 536, 542–543.
3. *Moral Sentiments*, p. 300.
4. Ibid., p. 303.
5. Compare also the Talmudic argument that even the evil impulse instilled by God in man is "very good": "Were it not for that impulse, a man would not build a house, marry a wife, beget children or conduct business affairs" (Cohen, 1949).
6. Sometimes a meeting of the minds can suffice, as in adoption of a convention that no one has any incentive to violate. Agreeing to drive on the right (left), or to meet under the clock at Grand Central Station, are possible examples (on this see Schelling, 1978a, chapter 3). I have shown that such coordination tends automatically to emerge under particular types of social environments (Hirshleifer, 1982, p. 14).
7. It might be thought that this analysis is over-elaborate in that DEFECT is by inspection a "dominant" strategy for each player given the payoffs of Matrix 1. But dominance arguments must be used with great care in sequential-play protocols. It is easy to demonstrate underlying payoff matrices where the *first* mover would want to emply a "dominated" strategy, since he can thereby influence the other player's responding choice. Schelling (1978b) provides a number of illustrations: for example, to keep you from kidnapping my children I may give away all my wealth.
8. The starred cell is also the unique "Nash equilibrium" of the usual (simultaneous move) Prisoners' Dilemma. However, we are dealing here with a sequential-move rather than a simultaneous-move game. It would be possible, using the appropriate expanded matrix in each case, to expand the Nash equilibrium idea to cover sequential-move games, but I shall not in fact be using that solution concept.
9. While superior goods are the normal pattern, standard economic models allow for the possibility of "inferior" goods—i.e., goods of which less is chosen as the consumer

becomes richer. This possibility can, however, be excluded here. Note that if Y_F were an inferior good for Second, then First would be motivated to impoverish his benefactor! Even if this were infeasible, First would also be motivated to impoverish himself. If First throws away $10, Second would then rationally compensate him by more than the $10 lost. If Y_F were inferior over any range, this process would continue until Y_F entered a range where it was no longer inferior, unless Second became bankrupt before this point was reached (see Becker, 1981, Chapter 8).

10. The proposition of this section can easily be extended to cover a benevolent or malevolent First. In particular, there can be instances where Second's benevolence can induce cooperation even from a malevolent First, to their mutual gain.
11. The terminology is due to E. O. Wilson (1978). However, the point made here diverges from Wilson's. He was concerned to contrast the weakness of "hard-core altruism" (benevolence) *compared* to "soft-core altruism" (enlightened self-interest) as organizers of cooperation in large social units. The analysis here indicates that the two factors may sometimes *complement* one another in a socially useful way.
12. Such models of interpersonal consumption preferences have been employed by a number of economists, including Boulding (1962, chapter 2), and Becker (1971).
13. It would be possible, by a somewhat forced twist of terminology, to interpret passionate behavior as rational choice—for example, by having the individual's preferences (as to benevolence or malevolence) be responsive to the other's actions. But passionate behavior, the essential character of which involves loss of control and heedlessness of consequences, cannot be fitted smoothly into the utilitarian mold.
14. While there is some diagrammatic similarity between the *AGR* and the previous *WEP* curves, they stand logically on quite a different footing. An *AGR* curve *could* also be interpreted as a locus of tangencies of transfer lines (or deprivation lines) with the second mover's indifference curves. But, the crucial point is, owing to the emotional action-dependent effects, Second's entire indifference curve map changes in response to First's choice along *QQ'*.
15. Of course a person capable *only* of anger can only guarantee execution of threats; a person capable only of gratitude is similarly restricted to promises. Having such a narrow repertoire of behaviors may be less costly, but restricts the contingent strategies available.
16. "Natural selection will never produce in a being any structure more injurious than beneficial to that being, for natural selection acts solely by and for the good of each" (Darwin, *Origin of Species*, chapter 6).
17. See Friedman (1980).

References

Becker, Gary S. (1971). A Theory of Social Interactions. *J. Polit. Econ.* 82:1063–1093.

Becker, Gary S. (1976). Altruism, Egoism, and Genetic Fitness: Economics and Sociobiology. *J. Econ. Lit.* 14:817–828.

Becker, Gary S. (1981). *A Treatise on the Family*. Cambridge, MA: Harvard University Press.

Boulding, Kenneth E. (1962). *Conflict and Defense*. New York: Harper & Row.

Boulding, Kenneth E. (1969). Economics as a Moral Science. *Am. Econ. Rev.* 59.

Coase, R. H. (1976). Adam Smith's View of Man. *J. Law & Econ.* 19.

Cohen, A, (1949). *Everyman's Talmud*, New American ed. New York: E. P. Dutton.

Darwin, Charles (1872/1859). *The Origin of Species by Means of Natural Selection*, 6th ed. (1st ed., 1859).

Darwin, Charles (1872). *The Expression of the Emotions in Man and Animals.*

Friedman, David (1980). Many, Few, One: Social Harmony and the Shrunken Choice Set. *Am Econ. Rev.* 70.
Hamilton, W. D. (1964). The Genetical Evolution of Social Behavior, I. *J. Theor. Biol.* 7:1–17.
Hirshleifer, J. (1977). Shakespeare vs. Becker on Altruism: the Importance of Having the Last Word. *J. Econ. Lit.* 15:500–502.
Hirshleifer, J. (1982). Evolutionary Models in Economics and Law: Cooperation versus Conflict strategies. *Res. In Law & Econ.* 4:1–60.
Howard, Nigel (1971). *Paradoxes of Rationality.* Cambridge, MA: MIT Press.
Luce, R. Duncan, and Howard Raiffa (1957). *Games and Decisions.* New York: Wiley.
Macaulay, Stewart (1963). Non-Contractual Relations in Business. *Am. Sociol. Rev.* 28:55–67.
Rose, Michael (1980). The Mental Arms Race Amplifier. *Human Ecology* 8:285–293.
Schelling, Thomas C. (1960). *The Strategy of Conflict.* London: Oxford University Press.
Schelling, Thomas C. (1978a). *Micromotives and Macrobehavior.* New York: Norton.
Schelling, Thomas C. (1978b). Altruism, Meanness, and Other Potentially Strategic Behaviors. *American Economic Review* 68:229–230.
Schelling, Thomas C. (1980). The Intimate Contest for Self-Command. *The Public Interest* 60.
Smith, Adam (1969). *The Theory of Moral Sentiments,* ed. E. G. West. Indianapolis: Liberty Classics.
Staddon, J. E. R. (1981). On a Possible Relation between Cultural Transmission and Genetical evolution. In P. P. G. Bateson and P. H. Klopfer (eds.), *Advantages of Diversity,* vol. 4, New York: Plenum, pp. 135–145.
Telser, L. G. (1980). A Theory of Self-Enforcing Agreements. *J. of Bus.* 53:27–45.
Thompson, Earl A., and Roger L. Faith (1981). A Pure Theory of Strategic Behavior and Social Institutions. *Am. Econ. Rev.* 71:366–380.
Trivers, Robert L. (1971). The Evolution of Reciprocal Altruism. *Quart. Rev. Biol.* 46:35–58.
Washburn (1960). Tools and Human Evolution. *Sc. Am.* 203:63–75.
Wilson, Edward O. (1978). Altruism. *Harvard Mag.* 81.

ELSEVIER

Journal of Economic Psychology 22 (2001) 617–640

JOURNAL OF Economic Psychology

www.elsevier.com/locate/joep

The value of a smile: Game theory with a human face

Jörn P.W. Scharlemann [a,1], Catherine C. Eckel [b,*], Alex Kacelnik [a], Rick K. Wilson [c,2]

[a] *Department of Zoology, University of Oxford, South Parks Road, Oxford OX1 3PS, UK*

[b] *Department of Economics (0316), Virginia Polytechnic Institute and State University, Blacksburg, VA 24061, USA*

[c] *Department of Political Science, Rice University, Houston, TX 77251-1892, USA*

Received 1 October 1999; accepted 22 February 2001

Abstract

Many economists and biologists view cooperation as anomalous: animals (including humans) that pursue their own self-interest have superior survival odds to their altruistic or cooperative neighbors. However, in many situations there are substantial gains to the group that can achieve cooperation among its members, and to individuals who are members of those groups. For an individual, the key to successful cooperation is the ability to identify cooperative partners. The ability to signal and detect the intention to cooperate would be a very valuable skill for humans to posses.

Smiling is frequently observed in social interactions between humans, and may be used as a signal of the intention to cooperate. However, given that humans have the ability to smile falsely, the ability to detect intentions may go far beyond the ability to recognize a smile. In the present study, we examine the value of a smile in a simple bargaining context. 120 subjects participate in a laboratory experiment consisting of a simple two-person, one-shot "trust" game with monetary payoffs. Each subject is shown a photograph of his partner prior to the

* Corresponding author. Tel.: +1-540-231-7707; fax: +1-540-231-5097.

E-mail addresses: jpws2@cam.ac.uk (J.P.W. Scharlemann), eckelc@vt.edu (C.C. Eckel), rkw@rice.edu (R.K. Wilson).

[1] Present address: Conservation Biology Group, Department of Zoology, University of Cambridge, Downing Street, Cambridge CB2 3EJ, UK. Tel: +44-1223-331698.

[2] Tel.: +1-713-527-8101.

PII: S0167-4870(01)00059-9

game; the photograph is taken from a collection that includes one smiling and one non-smiling image for each of 60 individuals. These photographs are also rated by a separate set of subjects who complete a semantic differential survey on affective and behavioral interpretations of the images.

Results lend some support to the prediction that smiles can elicit cooperation among strangers in a one-shot interaction. Other characteristics of faces also appear to elicit cooperation. Factor analysis of the survey data reveals an important factor, termed "cooperation", which is strongly related to trusting behavior in the game. This factor is correlated with smiling, but is somewhat more strongly predictive of behavior than a smile alone. In addition, males are found to be more cooperative, especially towards female images, whereas females are least cooperative towards female images.

PsycINFO classification: 3040; 2360

JEL classification: C7; C91

Keywords: Trust; Behavioral game theory; Facial expressions; Sex differences

1. Introduction

Imagine two persons facing one another for the first time in a social exchange, where there are potential gains to both parties. They know nothing about one another, but each has to make a decision and those decisions will jointly affect their payoffs. How does each anticipate the other's actions? How does one judge whether a partner is trustworthy or predict if trust will be reciprocated?

Strategic behavior involves actors choosing strategies contingent on the anticipated actions of others. Actors forecast the choices of others based on a vector of characteristics, which can be either inherent or intentional. Clearly actors embody inherent characteristics, such as gender, ethnicity, or age, that signal a type. Individuals display additional signals through attire, language, and facial expressions. Both inherent and intentional signals provide information and influence strategic choice.

Humans perform many actions, purposively taken with full knowledge of their consequences, which appear to be "irrational"; i.e., if they did not perform these actions, they would be better off, at least in the short term. In particular people often put themselves in a position where they must rely on another person to reciprocate a potentially costly trusting move. Examples include ordering software over the internet, leaving an automobile with a valet service, or buying a bottle of fine wine at a new wine shop. In each case we turn over something of value (a credit card number, a car or money) expecting to receive something in return, but at the same time risk exposing ourselves to possible exploitation by "cheaters". The Internet firm may credit our account and never send the software. The valet may abscond with the car. The wine may be ruined, having been improperly stored. But people routinely trust others and successfully avoid cheaters. How?

This paper focuses on a cue that may affect the beliefs held by actors playing a simple game, and affect their willingness to risk an initial trusting move. We argue that the facial expression of a counterpart contains information that is used by an actor in formulating beliefs and subsequent actions. This research presents findings from experiments designed to test the effect of facial expressions on trusting behavior. We examine the effect of a smile on strategy choice in a simple bargaining game, while controlling for sex-pairings. Two questions are addressed: (1) Does smiling elicit trust among strangers? (2) Is there a difference between the sexes in assessing trust?

This is the first of a planned series of studies examining the social signaling of cooperation through facial expressions. Our purpose in this initial study is to discover any existing regularity in the relationship between the decision to trust and the facial characteristics of a partner. We isolate the effect of the facial expression of a partner on the decision to trust in a two-person, sequential game; facial expressions are predetermined, and constitute the controlled stimulus in our experiments. We do not examine actual attempts to signal cooperation – whether genuine or deceptive – on the part of partners to a potential exchange, and so do not test for subjects' ability to accurately signal or detect intentions. Plans for future research that will examine these issues are discussed in the final section.

2. Motivation

The tension between self-interest and the common good is most frequently studied in the context of prisoners' dilemma and public goods games. In these games, if individuals choose an individually rational strategy, collectively inefficient outcomes result. On the other hand, there are cooperative strategies that, if taken by both players, yield outcomes that make everyone better off. Choosing the cooperative strategy is risky, because cheaters can always take advantage of the cooperator. In a prisoner's dilemma game, defecting leaves the cheater better off and makes the cooperator worse off. In an exchange relationship the same is true. An actor who takes an initial move that trusts another to deliver on an exchange will be left worse off if that trust is not reciprocated. The key to a successful exchange is choosing a trustworthy partner. If cooperators could easily identify cheaters, cooperation could flourish without the risk of a betrayal of trust.

Any mechanism designed to identify cooperators is likely to run into trouble because cheaters have a strong incentive to mimic cooperators. Consider a population of cooperators and defectors where cooperators are easily identified (assume they have a C on their foreheads), and cooperators can interact selectively with one another. Defectors on the other hand will be left to interact with one another, resulting in a lower payoff. Under such conditions it would pay defectors to mimic the co-operators' signal by marking a C on their foreheads. If defectors are perfect mimics, the feature looses all its power to signal a distinction, resulting in random pairings of cooperators and defectors.

This problem has been extensively discussed in the literature on evolution of animal signals, where optimal interacting strategies are seen as resulting from natural selection on both receivers and signalers. In general, theoretical biologists assume that for signals to be "evolutionarily stable" (i.e. for selection on signalers and on receivers to preserve both signaling and responding), signals must make the receiver act so as to favor the signaler. But this response must confer an advantage to the receiver as well. However, since signalers benefit from the signaling regardless of the reliability of the information that is signaled, there must be some selective check on signaling, and this is normally assumed to be a differential cost of signaling true and false information; i.e. signaling false information should be more costly than signaling veridically (Grafen, 1990; Zahavi, 1977; Hamilton & Zuk, 1982). This is cost is referred to as a *handicap*.

If we view smiling as a biological signal, a biologist would ask, what could act as a handicap in this case? At least two forms of handicap may be relevant to smiling. On one hand, it may be that producing a smile has a differential cost depending on the signaler's state, so that the balance of costs and benefits to the signaler inhibits indiscriminate smiling, and this in turn preserves the benefit of responding to the smile. Alternatively, smiles may act as "revealing handicaps", that is signals that are not costly to produce, but that have the effect of exposing the quality of the signaler to the receiver. For example, a receiver may be judging the quality of the signaler's teeth, and smiling exposes the teeth. Receivers may take a non-smiling individual as one who refuses to reveal her quality and hence discriminate against her.[3]

[3] The paradigmatic biological example of a revealing handicap is a feather arrangement or bare skin patch that allows the observer a better judgement of the potential damage due to parasites: individuals with high parasite resistance would develop particularly revealing feather arrangements or skin patches, forcing the rest to follow suit.

Thus, from a biological point of view, honest signals, such as true or Duchenne smiles (D-smiles) (Ekman, Friesen, & Davidson, 1990), will be maintained in a population either because smiling is differentially costly according some characteristic of the signaler, or because it reveals this characteristic to the receiver. In the context of this study, the relevant characteristic is "trustworthiness" or "cooperativeness" or a related trait that increases the benefit expected from trusting the counterpart.

There is at least circumstantial evidence that smiling is difficult to fake. Duchenne de Boulogne (1862) stated that "it will be simple for me to show that there are some emotions that man cannot stimulate or portray artificially on the face; the attentive observer is always able to recognize a false smile...", and Duchenne's views resonate with everyday subjective experience. Faking a D-smile is not possible for the majority of humans,[4] and this is consistent with the idea that it represents an honest signal; but the nature of its cost or the reason why it would be an uncheatable revealing indicator remain unknown.

Two experimental studies provide evidence that people can identify cooperators with some success. Frank, Ekman, and Friesen (1993) show that people are reasonably good at predicting the actions of their partners in a prisoner's dilemma game if subjects have observed one another for 30 minutes prior to making their decisions. Brown, Palameta, and Moore (1999) use video-clips of self-reported altruists and non-altruists and find that subjects do well in distinguishing between the two. They conclude that the two types send quite different non-verbal signals that other subjects are able to read. In short, there appear to be reliable signals that lead people to draw inferences about others.

What is the source of the signals used by individuals to facilitate prediction? An extensive literature on facial expressions contends that the human face is a rich source of social signals (Darwin, 1872; Ekman, 1982; Fridlund, 1994). While researchers debate whether the face leaks emotions or whether the face is purposively used to display social content, there is general agreement that humans are attuned to the messages emanating from the face.

A smile is a particularly common and effective signal and its function has been extensively studied (e.g. Ekman, Friesen, & Ellsworth, 1982, 1990). For example the ability to smile and to recognize a smile is developed very early in

[4] According to Frank (1988) only about 10% of the population are born with or later acquire voluntary control of all facial muscles, with actor Woody Allen a prominent example. Only those people are able to deliberately fake a D smile, others would require lengthy practice to gain voluntary control of these muscles.

life (Bruce & Young, 1998). Humans are able to recognize smiles at twice the distance of other facial expressions (Walk & Walters, 1988). Smiles can induce pleasure in the observer, or even in the smiler (Surakka & Hietanen, 1998).

Smiles are not just for show; they also have an impact on the behavior of others. For example, there is some evidence that newscasters' smiles can influence candidate choice (Mullen et al., 1986). Additional evidence shows that waitresses receive significantly larger tips when smiling (Tidd & Lochard, 1978). Finally, LaFrance and Hecht (1995) show that smiling generates leniency, with people who smile receiving lesser sentences for a given criminal conviction.

Observable characteristics other than smiles may also signal conventions for behavior. A characteristic such as sex or age may be correlated with the tendency to cooperate, and so may be treated as a signal of "type". For example, both sex and age are identifiable from still photographs (Zebrowitz, 1997), and so constitute readily perceived signals. Elderly persons are sometimes thought of as more cooperative (or vulnerable to cheaters). While women are considered the "cooperative sex", surveys of sex differences in bargaining games find women are sometimes more and sometimes less cooperative, contingent on the decision environment (Sell, 1997; Walters & Stuchlmacher, 1998; Eckel & Grossman, in press).

We report results of two studies designed to test whether people routinely use facial characteristics to forecast the actions of others. The first study, a questionnaire, elicits perceptions of a set of facial images. Both male and female subjects and facial images are used, and the images display either a smiling or neutral facial expression. In the second study, a decision-making experiment, we control the facial characteristics of a counterpart presented to a subject in a game with financial stakes. Subjects first observe a facial image of their "counterpart", taken from the same set of images. Subjects then play a simple bargaining game with in which they are asked to choose whether to trust the person depicted in the photograph.

3. Methods and results

3.1. Study 1: Questionnaire

3.1.1. Design

A questionnaire was designed to elicit perceptions of the facial features of pictures used in the decision-making experiment below. A subject observed one black-and-white photograph and was then presented with 25 word pairs of opposite meaning as a paper and pencil task. All words were taken from Anderson (1968), and the pairs were matched using extreme ratings on his listing. (The word pairs were pre-tested in a group of 12 under a different task.) For each word pair subjects were asked to rate the photograph based on a three-point scale by choosing the word on the left, the word on the right, or "cannot tell". For example, consider the sad/happy wording pairing: if "sad" was chosen, it was coded as a rating of −1; if the subject selected "happy" the rating was 1; if the subject could not decide which word pair best fit, then a neutral rating of 0 was assigned. Table 1 lists the items included in the questionnaire and the percentage choosing the category.

Sixty photographic models were used, with two poses for each model: a smile and a neutral expression. Of the models, 47 were male and 13 were

Table 1
Word-pair items for questionnaire (percent choosing each alternative)

Word 1	Percentage	Cannot tell %	Percentage	Word 2
Good	25.8	58.3	15.8	Bad
Strong	42.5	40.8	16.7	Weak
Calm	45.8	32.5	21.7	Excitable
Kind	26.7	56.7	16.7	Cruel
Attractive	28.3	34.2	37.5	Unattractive
Trusting	21.7	39.2	39.2	Suspicious
Pleasant	42.5	40.0	17.5	Unpleasant
Tough	43.3	44.2	12.5	Fragile
Active	46.7	25.8	27.5	Passive
Friendly	48.3	34.2	17.5	Unfriendly
Cooperative	21.7	44.2	34.2	Competitive
Forgiving	18.3	59.2	22.5	Vengeful
Honest	25.0	53.3	21.7	Dishonest
Generous	18.3	58.3	23.3	Selfish
Trustworthy	29.2	46.7	24.2	Untrustworthy
Considerate	23.3	53.3	23.3	Inconsiderate
Sincere	23.3	60.8	15.8	Deceitful
Benevolent	23.3	60.8	15.8	Malevolent
Domineering	35.8	48.3	15.8	Submissive
Happy	40.8	40.0	19.2	Sad
Male	80.8	0.0	19.2	Female
Forthright	34.2	50.8	15.0	Scheming
Content	44.2	38.3	17.5	Frustrated
Secure	34.2	46.7	19.2	Insecure
Amiable	41.7	38.3	20.0	Hostile

Note: Because of rounding, not all rows sum to 100%.

female. The photographs were taken from the Psychological Image Collection at Stirling (PICS), Psychology Department, University of Stirling.[5] The 120 photographs were coded as either smiling or not smiling *for a given model*, and there is quite a bit of variation across models in the degree to which the facial expressions differ. While the faces we use are listed on the site as reflecting different facial expressions, no details are given about what the models were told when the photographs were taken.[6] One hundred and twenty graduate students and staff from a major British university participated in the questionnaire study (57 males and 63 females). The photographic images were assigned randomly to subjects, while the order of the word pairs was the same for all subjects. If all items on the questionnaire were answered with "cannot tell", the particular questionnaire was discarded, and the face assigned to a new subject.[7]

3.1.2. Results

Table 1 contains questionnaire items and aggregate ratings. We tested for and found no response bias in the questionnaire. For the analysis, word pair items were reordered in a consistent direction, and factor analysis, with a varimax rotation, was used to create scales across the word pair items. The three distinct factors with an eigenvalue above 1.0 were recovered. Five items are strongly correlated with the first factor, which we term *cooperative*: friendly/unfriendly, cooperative/non-cooperative, forgiving/unforgiving, happy/sad, and amiable/hostile. The second factor, which we term *trustworthy*, is strongly correlated with the items: honest/dishonest, trustworthy/untrustworthy, and sincere/insincere. The final factor, which we term *tough*, includes the items: strong/weak, tough/fragile, domineering/submissive, and secure/insecure. The factors identified in the analysis are intuitively appealing, and their importance is consistent with standard negotiation tactics (for example, see Foster, 1992).

The three factor loadings produce continuous measures that can be used in the analysis of behavior that follows. To give a sense of the structure of

[5] The URL for this site is: http://brl.rice.edu/JEP2001/index.html. The PICS database is a collection of images that has been used in psychological research. Previous research using these photographs was concerned with visual perception, memory and processing.

[6] We can be fairly certain that the subjects were not told to act as if they are signalling willingness to cooperate in a social exchange, however. The absence of the intention to signal may bias our results in the direction of a finding of no effect.

[7] Nine males and nine females (15% of all questionnaires) answered all questions with "cannot tell". Those questionnaires were discarded and 18 new subjects were used.

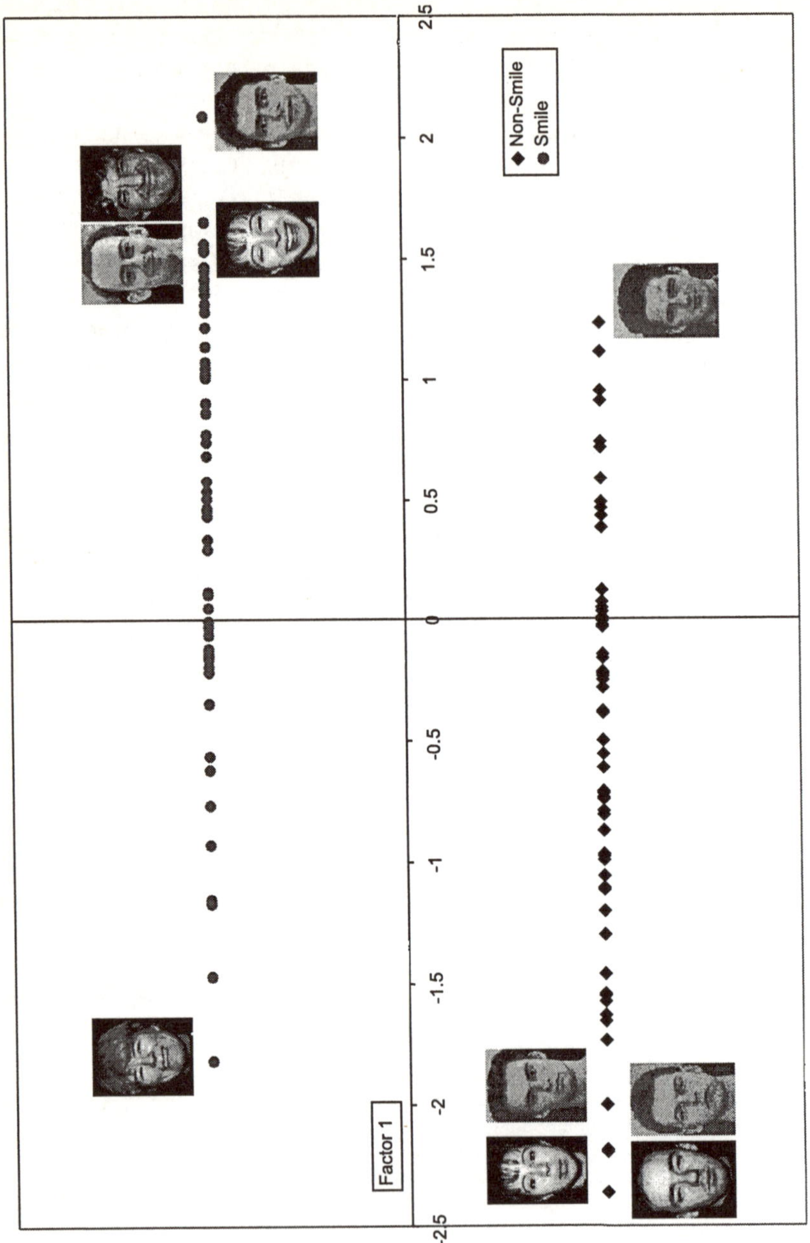

Fig. 1. Plot of factor 1 (cooperative) loadings by smiling and non-smiling images.

Factor 1, for example, we construct Fig. 1. The factor loading for *cooperation* is measured on the horizontal axis. Pictures coded as smiling are plotted above the axis, those that are coded non-smiling are below the axis. A *t*-test comparing the average factor loading for smiling versus non-smiling faces indicates a significant difference, with smiling photographs receiving higher scores ($t = 6.16$, $p < 0.001$). It is clear from the figure that Factor 1 is correlated with smiling ($\rho = 0.49$), but also incorporates other characteristics of the faces. While the ratings are not significantly related to the sex of the image or the rater, subjects apparently are able to perceive additional information in the faces apart from their smile.[8]

Several representative photographs are placed approximately at their positions on the Factor 1 distribution. Smiling and non-smiling faces that are rated highest and lowest on Factor 1 are shown. The photographs at the bottom left that are rated as non-smiling all exhibit dour expressions. Those at the top extreme right, and rated as smiling, exhibit inviting expressions. From these photographs it appears the factor loading does a fine job of discriminating between smiles and non-smiles. This is evident when comparing photographs of the same person; for example the non-smiling female at the bottom left is rated much lower than her smiling photograph at the upper right of the figure.

There is more to this factor than smiling and non-smiling images, however. Two photographs are included which are at the opposite ends of their distributions. The female model at the extreme left, but coded as smiling, is older and has a grimacing expression. The male model at the lower right is coded as non-smiling, but he carries a slight grin. While the images are coded correctly relative to their pair, it is clear that respondents perceive other attributes of these faces when viewed independently of each other.

These independent ratings indicate that there are at least three characteristics linked with the photographs. The first factor, which we have termed *cooperative*, is related to the presence or absence of a smile. The second and third factors are unrelated to a smile; instead they tap dimensions of *trust-*

[8] At the suggestion of a referee we estimated linear regression models for *cooperation* and *trustworthy* (as dependent variables) with the sex of the photograph, the age of the photograph (1 = under 21, 2 = 21–30, 3 = over 30), and the sex of the rater as independent variables. We find that neither the sex of the photo nor of the rater is significantly related to either scale. Age is also not significant in the *cooperation* equation, but is positively and significantly related to the *trustworthiness* index. However, the value is small: a one-point increase in the age scale is associated with an increase in the trustworthiness index of 0.015. Each model explained about 1% of the variance in the respective index. Details of the estimates are available on request.

worthiness and *toughness*. All three factors are viewed as capturing important attributes for actors in bargaining settings. We use this information in our second study.

3.2. Study 2: "Trust" game

3.2.1. Experimental design and justification

The second study is designed to investigate the extent to which subjects trust a smiling or non-smiling counterpart in a game with financial stakes. Survey information allows us to measure the subjective response of our subjects to the faces, but the impact on behavior of these perceptions is a separate issue. Economists predict that the incentive structure of the game should dominate any perceptions about a counterpart, while most psychologists would predict the faces should matter for behavior.

The experiment is a three-factor design ($2 \times 2 \times 2$) with factors consisting of the sex of the subject, the sex of the photograph, and whether the image is smiling. Each subject is randomly assigned one of the photographic images described above as a "counterpart" for a simple bargaining game. The subjects are led to believe that they are playing the pictured subject, but in fact play against a pre-programmed strategy, as explained below.[9]

While we prefer experiments where subjects are not deceived in any way, this design required that we present paired images for our stimulus. Experimental control over the content of the images necessitated some degree of deception. In our experiment we have fixed the signals being sent by the counterpart in order to maintain maximum control of the stimulus. Moreover, our design requires that we present these same faces for rating by different subjects. In both experiments, having one smiling and one unsmiling version of the same person adds experimental control.

As a rule, we agree that deception should be avoided in laboratory experiments. However, there are times when deception is both necessary and justified, as Bonetti (1998a,b), points out. We were careful in these experiments to meet the APA guidelines for deception and do not believe our results can be called into question based on its use. While the focus of our paper is not deception, but rather the effect of controlled stimuli on subjects' decisions, we detour briefly here to addressing common reactions among

[9] A version of the game can be found at http://brl.rice.edu/joep2001 or is available from the first author on request.

experimental economists to the issue of deceiving subjects. Three issues appear to be at stake.

First, there is the argument that deception will undermine the credibility of all experiments and so the validity of all experimental results. This view seems to have little empirical support. Bonnetti's survey suggests that even a strong expectation of deception rarely affects behavior relative to a control group, implying that even if subjects anticipate deception, their behavior will be unaffected. Many members of subject pools at most universities have participated in psychology experiments as a course requirement, so the subject pools used by experimental economists may already be contaminated to some extent by the expectation of deception. We attempted to minimize potential impact by conducting the experiment using a subject pool that is unlikely ever to participate in any other experiment, so their experience is unlikely to contaminate anyone else's subject pool.[10]

Second, deception can be used in a way that undermines the motivational basis for subjects (and this is the important point that Hey (1998) makes in his response to Bonnetti). It is crucial that subjects be motivated by the monetary incentives in experiments. If deception affects a subject's payoffs, preventing the subject from earning a maximal amount or otherwise breaking the linkage between actions and outcomes, then deception undermines the research results. This is where we draw the line in our own research.[11]

Third, the suspicion of deception may bias the results of the experiment itself. While, as mentioned above, there is little evidence to support this claim, neither we nor any other experimentalist can rule it out, as we have no way of removing the expectation of deception from our subjects' minds. We did our best to convince subjects that our claims were true, using the procedure described below. If subjects suspected deception, our best guess of the effect on their behavior is that it would make them less likely to trust, regardless of the stimulus, and, if anything, is likely to diminish the magnitude of any differences in response to stimuli. If there is a bias, it is in the direction of finding a null result.

Minor deception is sometimes necessary (or cost-effective) for achieving the desired level of experimental control over stimuli or feedback. In our experiment, control requires that subjects be presented with paired sets of

[10] If the reader believes that undergraduates read academic papers, some may come to know of the deception, and be affected by it.

[11] In our experiment deception does not harm subject's earnings. The deception component of this experiment did not break the linkage between the subject's action and the resulting outcome. Subjects were not misled about their own performance on the task, nor were decisions made that would deprive subjects of earnings.

faces. A single face is presented in two versions: one smiling, and one unsmiling. Without this control we cannot be certain whether our result is due to a smile, or due to some other difference between any two different faces. This led us to control the facial expressions by setting them ahead of time. Other experimental designs can be used to test related notions: we discuss some possibilities in a concluding section.

3.2.2. Procedure

The subjects are seated at a computer terminal for the duration of the experiment. Subjects participate in a variation on the Trust game (Berg, Dickhaut, & McCabe, 1995) shown in Fig. 2. The game is structured as follows. At the first node of the decision tree, the subject chooses between two alternatives. A move to the right ends the experiment: the subject earns £1.00, and her counterpart £0.50. A downward move passes the choice to the second player, who then faces a similar choice to end the experiment (giving the second player £1.25 and the first player £0.80) or to pass the move back to player 1. The first player then has a choice between £1.00 and £1.20 for each of the players. The unique subgame-perfect Nash equilibrium for this game has the first mover terminating the game at the first node.[12] However, there are gains to both players if there is trust and reciprocity. An initial "trusting" move is problematic because the second player has an incentive to quit at the second node, leaving the first player worse off; but if that trusting move is reciprocated, then both players are better off than at the Nash equilibrium.[13]

We take care to convince subjects of the credibility of the situation. At the outset, subjects are photographed using a small camera placed on top of the monitor, and this picture is shown to them before they view the counterpart's photograph. This is done to heighten the sense that subjects are playing against a counterpart at another computer in a separate room. Subjects are given detailed on-screen instructions including two examples with games without the trust-game incentive structure. Subjects then are shown a black-and-white photograph (stimulus face) of their apparent counterpart. Pho-

[12] The game is similar in structure to a centipede game (McKelvey & Palfrey, 1992).

[13] We acknowledge that higher incentives would have been preferable. A recent survey by Camerer and Hogarth (1999) indicates that beyond a minimal level, higher incentives rarely matter. While the level of incentives may affect variance (in our context, lessening the likelihood that any significant effects would be found), it rarely affects levels of behavior and is even less likely to affect comparative statics of treatments. In addition we note that Burham et al. (2000) find very similar overall levels of trust in a game with a similar structure and much higher incentive levels.

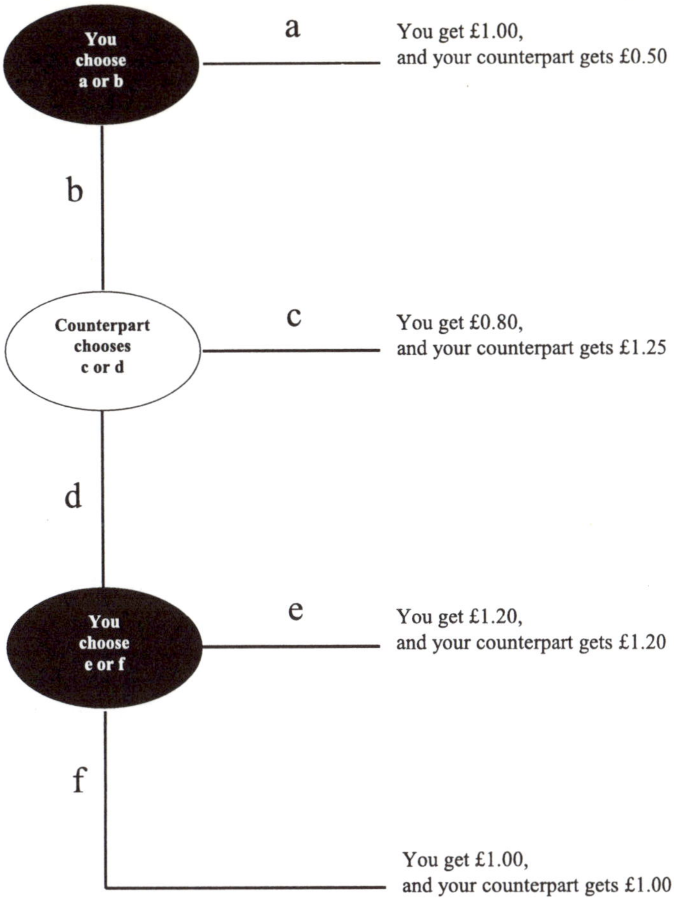

Fig. 2. Game used in the experiment.

tographs are visible as a smaller side picture while the game is played. After finishing the game subjects are asked to respond to an on-screen questionnaire. At the end of the questionnaire subjects are paid in cash the amount of money they earn (£1.20 or £1.00, depending on their choice).

In this game, subjects always are assigned to move first. The first move is the most interesting, as it indicates whether a subject declines to trust her counterpart by choosing the Nash equilibrium strategy, or trusts by passing to the counterpart. When subjects choose to pass, they are told to wait for their counterpart to make a decision. The computer is pre-programmed so that the counterpart always chooses to reciprocate, then gives subjects the final choice.[14]

Subjects consisted of 120 graduate students and staff from a variety of Oxford University departments and colleges, solicited by email and by posters distributed to departments and colleges within the vicinity of the Department of Zoology. Subjects were required to book a specific slot to participate in the experiment and a reminder was sent a day before their experimental session. A total of 120 sessions (one subject per session) were conducted for this study. Of these subjects, a total of 58 were male (48.3%).

3.2.3. *Results*

Our principal conjecture is that smiling facial expressions act like a signal intended to induce a cooperative move.[15] In the analysis that follows, we analyze the value of a smile, then incorporate the factor analysis above into further analysis of the game.

Summary results are shown in Table 2.[16] Subjects trust smiling counterparts in 68.3% of decisions, and non-smiling counterparts in 55.0% of decisions. Using a one-tailed proportions test for paired samples, we can reject the hypothesis that the smiling and non-smiling counterparts are trusted equally ($t = 1.66$, $p = 0.051$).[17]

As shown in the bottom row of the table, male subjects chose to trust in 69% of decisions, while females trusted in 54.8% of decisions. The sex difference, while substantial, is not significant at traditional levels ($\chi^2(1) = 2.530$, $p = 0.112$). Male subjects show greater discrimination between smiling and non-smiling faces: males trust smilers in 79.3% and non-smilers in 58.6%

[14] The last choice, between terminal branches *e* and *f*, tests if subjects make rational choices, i.e. are able to differentiate between £1.20 (branch *e*) and £1.00 (branch *f*). Any subjects making the irrational choice of branch *f* were excluded from the analysis.

[15] See Eckel and Wilson (1997, 1998) for studies that make the same point in a somewhat different design.

[16] Of the 131 subjects participating in the study, three were excluded because of incomplete pairing (i.e. only one face of the pair was shown), four because of technical problems (computer or camera crashed) and another four because they made the irrational choice (branch *f*) (3% of subjects reacted irrationally). Of the remaining 120 subjects used for analysis, seven (6.2%) reported that the instructions were unclear. The average duration of experiment, including instructions and on-screen questionnaire, was about 8 min. Of 50 subjects who commented on the game only four (or 8%) stated that they believed their counterpart was not a real person.

[17] While paired samples tests are rare, such a test is entirely appropriate in this setting. Each model presented two different images, one smiling and one not smiling. Consequently we can pair the responses to the two images. This finding shows that smiles affect "trust" in this experiment. A standard *t*-test gives a similar result. See Kimmel (1957) on the use of one-tailed tests.

Table 2
Proportion of subjects choosing to trust by type of decision maker and characteristics of faces

Facial image	Decision maker		
	Male	Female	All
Male-neutral	0.565	0.583	0.574
Male-smiling	0.739	0.625	0.681
All male	0.652	0.604	0.628
Female-neutral	0.667	0.286	0.462
Female-smiling	1.000	0.429	0.692
All female	0.833	0.357	0.577
All neutral	0.586	0.516	0.550
All smiling	0.793	0.581	0.683
All faces	**0.690**	**0.548**	**0.617**

of decisions, while females trust smilers in 58.1% and non-smilers in 51.6% of decisions. The statistical reliability of this result is greater for males than for females ($\chi^2(1) = 2.90$, $p = 0.089$), and ($\chi^2(1) = 0.261$, $p = 0.61$, respectively).

The experimental design provides four subject/counterpart sex dyads. We can reject the hypothesis that all four sex pairings lead to equal degrees of trust ($\chi^2(3) = 6.649, p = 0.085$). Male subjects are more likely to trust female counterparts and females are more likely to trust male counterparts. However, the difference between same-sex dyads (male/male and female/female) and opposite-sex dyads (male/female, female/male) is not significant ($\chi^2(1) = 0.564, p = 0.453$). Finally, the sex of the counterpart has no significant main effect on trust overall ($\chi^2(1) = 0.222, p = 0.638$).

We conducted a multivariate probit regression analysis of the decisions by the subjects, incorporating all of the elements of the experimental design. Table 3 presents the results. The dependent variable in the regressions is bivariate and equal to one if the subject chose to trust the counterpart. The estimates predict the probability that a subject will make a decision to trust. Model 1 tests the effect of a smile on the decision to trust in a simple model that includes only an intercept and the variable Smile, which is equal to 1 if the face is coded as smiling, and 0 otherwise. The coefficient on Smile has the predicted sign, and is statistically significant using a one-tailed test at the 0.10 level. Model 2 permits the effect of a smile to vary according to the sex of the decision maker by interacting the variable "Smile" with sex. While the effect is positive in both cases, only for male subjects is it statistically significant. This indicates that men are more influenced by the smile of a counterpart.

Table 3
Probit regression results: dependent variable = trust

Variable	Model 1	Model 2	Model 3	Model 4
Intercept	0.126	0.126		
	(0.162)	(0.162)		
	(0.439)	(0.439)		
Smile	**0.351**			
	(0.233)			
	(0.066)[a]			
Smile X		**0.692**	**0.631**	
Male subject		(0.309)	(0.360)	
		(0.013)[a]	(0.040)[a]	
Smile X		0.077	0.169	
Female subject		(0.279)	(0.323)	
		(0.390)[a]	(0.301)[a]	
Factor 1X				**0.467**
Male subject				(0.217)
				(0.016)[a]
Factor 1X				0.135
Female subject				(0.162)
				(0.202)[a]
Male subject with Male face			0.092	**0.424**
			(0.254)	(0.197)
			(0.714)	(0.031)
Male subject with female face			0.731	**1.346**
			(0.466)	(0.512)
			(0.116)	(0.008)
Female subject with male face			0.077	0.257
			(0.243)	(0.184)
			(0.720)	(0.161)
Female subject with female face			−0.453	−0.407
			(0.383)	(0.350)
			(0.236)	(0.245)
Log likelihood	−78.75	−77.15	−74.75	−73.51

Standard errors for coefficients shown in parentheses; *p*-values are in italics; bold indicates significant at $p \leqslant 0.10$.
[a] Indicates a one-tailed test.

Models 1 and 2 implicitly assume that all subject-pairings are the same. Model 3 includes the sex-pairings as dummy variables, to allow for heterogeneity across pairings. (Note that this specification requires that the intercept be dropped.) The coefficients and significance levels on the Smile variables are stable across the two models. Male subjects are more trusting with female faces, but female subjects trust female faces less than male faces. Using likelihood ratio tests, the hypothesis that men treat male and female faces the same cannot be rejected (i.e. a model that allows the two coefficients to be different does not account for significantly more of the variation in the dependent variable than a model that constrains the coefficients to be the same, $\chi^2(1) = 1.82$, $p = 0.177$), but women are significantly less trusting of female faces ($\chi^2(1) = 2.70$, $p = 0.100$).

Perhaps it is not merely the counterpart's smile and sex that are interpreted as a signal of the intention to cooperate, but some other aspect of their faces. We conducted additional regressions, replacing the Smile with Factors 1–3. To our surprise, the inclusion of Factors 2 and 3 in the regression had no effect on its explanatory power (results not reported here). The coefficients were never close to statistical significance, and their inclusion did not affect the coefficients on the other variables. In Model 4 we replace Smile with Factor 1 derived in the previous section. [18] Consistent with the previous model, males are more responsive to the counterpart's smile than females. Once more, men are more likely to trust female faces, and women to trust male faces. In this specification of the model, we are able to reject the hypothesis of equal treatment of male and female faces for both men and women. (For male subjects, $\chi^2(1) = 3.34$, $p = 0.068$); for female subjects, ($\chi^2(1) = 2.92$, $p = 0.087$).

To provide additional intuition for these results, we calculate the probabilities of taking a trusting move based on the parameters from Model 4 for both male and female subjects. As the loading on the cooperative factor increases, the probability that males will select a trust move rises from 0.22 to 0.97. By contrast, the probability that females will take a trusting move slowly rises from 0.22 to 0.48. [19] The males appear to be more responsive to inviting faces, as measured by Factor 1, than females.

4. Discussion

The main results of this study are that: (1) smiling, at the margin, positively affects trust among strangers, (2) facial features can affect cooperation,

[18] We also ran regressions similar to Models 1 and 2 substituting Factor 1 for Smile, with similar results. Using a log-likelihood test we can reject that the four sex-pairings exhibit the same levels of trust, making Model 4 the appropriate specification. In addition, we tested for the effect of Factors 2 and 3 in these models; the coefficients on Factors 2 and 3 are never significant, and their exclusion does not affect the magnitude or significance of the other variables. For models 3 and 4, we also test for an interaction effect between the four sex pairings and Smile, and find no significant effect.

[19] These calculations use the Factor 1 interaction with the male or female subject and fix the additional parameter from Model 4 to be a same sex pairing. For example, when estimating the male probability, the parameters for the male by Factor 1 parameter was used as well as the male/male sex pairing parameter. Using opposite-sex pairings would result in more extreme differences between the sexes.

regardless of smiling, and (3) both males and females are more trusting toward members of the opposite sex. To our knowledge, ours is the first test of the effect of facial expressions on behavior in a controlled laboratory environment with financial stakes.

Smiling increases trust among strangers. Subjects were more likely to trust photographs of smiling persons than non-smiling photographs of the same persons. The result is significant in a one-tailed, matched-pairs proportions test, as well as in regression analysis. We interpret this to mean that subjects were able to detect a difference in facial expression, and that facial expression affected the subjects' beliefs about the trustworthiness of the counterpart represented by the facial image. Thus smiling appears to serve as an informative stimulus to elicit trusting behavior.

Our results are somewhat more convincing when we consider that several factors might bias our results toward a null finding. First, the photographs of counterparts were taken under artificial conditions unrelated to the experimental environment. As far as we know, the photographic models were simply instructed to display a particular expression "smile!", and were not told what their expressions would be used for. Most social signals are tied to a social context, but these photographic models were given no such context. It may well be that if the models knew their expressions would be a signal in a bargaining game, they would have offered facial expressions that could be interpreted more readily.

Second, there is considerable variability across smiles. Other than our questionnaire ratings, we made no attempt to directly rate the physical attributes of the smiles, or to categorize them as true or false smiles. This could be achieved by using the Facial Action Coding System (FACS) developed by Ekman and Friesen (1982). If smiles are effective signals, then true smiles should have a much stronger effect than false smiles.

Third, the use of still photographs biases the perception of the facial expressions. With still photographs, judgements are derived from permanent physiognomic features rather than transient muscle movements (e.g., facial wrinkles cannot be distinguished from wrinkles caused by muscle action), and the natural flow of behavior may be mutilated into meaningless units (Ekman et al., 1982). Social communication is 'a structure not of objects but of events'; therefore dynamic footage of facial expression may be a more appropriate means of eliciting naturalistic viewing patterns to expression-dependent facial features (Nahm, Perret, Amaral, & Albright, 1997).

Fourth, we have not considered the attractiveness of faces. Some images might be perceived as more attractive than others, regardless of whether they are smiling. Lau (1982) found that smiling and sex had significant effects on attractiveness. Moreover, physical attractiveness has a powerful effect on perceptions of intelligence and predictions of success (Zebrowitz, 1997, Chapters 6 and 7), and is rewarded in the marketplace across a wide sample of professions (Biddle & Hamermesh, 1998; Hamermesh & Biddle, 1994). We plan an investigation of the effect of attractiveness on trust and other aspects of bargaining.

Finally, the questionnaire responses (study 1) make it clear that facial features other than smiling may be important in communicating intentions. Our first factor, which was most strongly correlated with trusting behavior, does more than differentiate between smiling and non-smiling images. It also captures something about the "niceness" of the photographic image. As we have labeled the factor, it appears to be an invitation to cooperate.

Another potential shortcoming of our study is its reliance on fictional counterparts. In future work we plan to implement an alternative design in which counterparts can freely send their own signal – a smile or frown. Since each subject controls the facial expression that is sent, we will no longer have the degree of control (two expressions for each face) that the current study provides. The experiment presented here controls one side of the signaling problem. Now that we have established the effect of a smile in a controlled setting we can move on to the more complicated design.[20]

Relating our results to others, we see that the overall level of trust is somewhat lower than that found in most other studies, though our restricted trust game is sufficiently different from other studies to make that comparison difficult. Our game gives subjects the option to trust their counterpart with 20% of their payoff, with the possibility of doubling the amount if the trust is reciprocated; i.e., subjects give up £0.20 for a potential gain of an additional £0.20. In other studies, subjects choose the amount they wish to entrust their counterpart. In a study where the trusted amount triples in value, Berg et al. (1995) find that 87.5% of subjects trust their counterparts with at least 20% of their endowment; in a face-to-face design, Glaeser, Laibson, Scheinkman, and Soutter (2000) double the trusted amount, and find a somewhat higher level of trust among Harvard University undergraduates. Both of these studies have average payoffs about five times the level of our study.

[20] Both referees suggested design variations similar to those we had planned.

While Berg et al., does not examine individual differences in amounts entrusted, the Glaeser et al., study tests for sex differences (among other things) and finds no significant differences in behavior of women and men or across sex pairings. Croson and Buchan (1999) finds that while women and men are equally likely to trust an anonymous partner, women are more likely to reciprocate trust. One similar study (Burnham, McCabe, & Smith, 2000) finds very similar overall levels of trust in a somewhat more complex restricted trust game. They find that when subtle difference in instructions (describing subjects as "partners" rather than "opponents") are used to cue cooperative intentions, subjects are more likely to trust and reciprocate trust. Since our counterparts are simulated players, the relationship between facial characteristics and reciprocity cannot be examined: that is a topic for further study. None of the previous studies examines facial expressions, nor compares face-to-face with anonymous pairings in a common design.

There is considerable evidence that face-to-face interaction leads to different results from anonymous interaction in bargaining games. For example, Frohlich and Oppenheimer (1998) show that face-to-face communication in comparison to e-mail contact improved the joint prisoner's dilemma outcome of subjects. Roth (1995, 295–304) notes that face-to-face interaction is more likely to lead to efficient outcomes and equal distributions. In a time when more and more interactions take place via telephones and electronic mail, it is important to understand the role of nonverbal communication in face-to-face interactions. Video-conferencing and video-telephones might allow sufficient facial communication resulting in similar cooperative outcomes as face-to-face interactions. Further research is required in this direction as well.

In addition to the role of facial expressions, our results indicate that both male and female subjects are more trusting of members of the opposite sex. Our analysis provides some evidence that both women and men respond differently to male than to female facial expressions. Consistent with numerous findings from social psychology, these findings might be explained by subjects having a sexual interest in their counterparts. For example, Tidd and Lochard (1978) show that men gave larger tips than women to a smiling waitress, whereas there was no difference in tips when the waitress was not smiling. The simplest explanation might be that men earn more than women, but Tidd and Lochard also suggest that men might be motivated to give larger tips as a way of signaling interest to a women who is issuing a friendly (smiling) expression.

We also find that male subjects discriminate more between smiling and non-smiling counterparts whereas female subjects cooperate at similar levels regardless of facial expression. An explanation of this result might be an effect of dominance. Individuals in subordinate roles smile more than individuals in power positions, regardless of their gender, as shown by Deutsch (1990) in simulated interview situations. Since men are more commonly in dominant positions, they might be more receptive to smiles than females. Therefore men might discriminate more between smiling and non-smiling faces. It may also be that women, who are known to smile more than men (Hinsz & Tomhave, 1991), do not regard smiling as an important, or honest, signal, because it has been overused.

Our research suggests that actors draw meaning from facial expressions. They use that meaning to condition their own behavior. The change in their own behavior may be due to the effect of facial expressions on beliefs about the counterpart, which are then used to formulate behavioral strategies. Inviting facial expressions may lead subjects to be more likely to forego a safe, best response (Nash equilibrium) strategy in favor of a risky, cooperative (trusting) behavioral strategy.

Thus, smiling is used by humans who are interacting in a one-shot game with strangers. This scenario is self-consistent, and would be evolutionarily stable if the signal were more costly to produce in the absence of the appropriate emotion. But as we discussed above, this assertion leaves the reason for the emotional reliability of smiling obscure. One likely explanation relates to the conditions in which human social behavior evolved. Humans are universally social and tended to live in small groups, and hence one-shot interactions may have been a rarity in their evolutionary history. Group living subjects interact repetitively, and reputations count because a fake smiler will be eventually recognized through her record, and hence discriminated against. When reputation for truthful expression of emotion is important, one might expect the evolution of psychological mechanisms that enforce it. If this interpretation is true, the evolved mechanisms will still be present in modern social conditions, when we sometimes interact with waiters once or play a one-shot trust game in the computer with a perfect stranger. Smiling to strangers may be a relic of our tribal past.

Acknowledgements

The experiments were conducted as part of a M.Sc. Thesis completed by the first author, Department of Zoology, Oxford University. He gratefully acknowledges the support of a BBSRC studentship. Eckel and Wilson acknowledge the support of the US National Science Foundation.

References

Anderson, N. H. (1968). Likableness ratings of 555 personality-trait words. *Journal of Personality and Social Psychology*, *9* (3), 272–279.

Berg, J., Dickhaut, J., & McCabe, K. (1995). Trust, reciprocity and social history. *Games and Economic Behavior*, *10*, 122–142.

Biddle, J., & Hamermesh, D. S. (1998). Beauty, productivity, and discrimination: Lawyers' looks and lucre. *Journal of Labor Economics*, *16* (1), 172–201.

Bonetti, S. (1998a). Experimental economics and deception. *Journal of Economic Psychology*, *19* (3), 377–395.

Bonetti, S. (1998b). Experimental economics and deception: response. *Journal of Economic Psychology*, *19* (3), 411–414.

Brown, W. M., Palameta, B., & Moore, C. (1999). *The evolution of altruist-detection: can humans decode nonverbal signals of cooperative demeanor*? Paper presented at the annual Meeting of the Human Behavior and Evolution Society, Salt Lake City, UT, June 2–6, 1999.

Bruce, V., & Young, A. (1998). *In the eye of the beholder*. Oxford: Oxford University Press.

Burnham, T., McCabe, K., & Smith, V. L. (2000). Friend-or-foe intentionality priming in an extensive form trust game. *Journal of Economic Behavior and Organization*, *43* (1), 57–73.

Camerer, C., & Hogarth, R. (1999). The effects of financial incentives in experiments: A review and capital–labor–production framework. *Journal of Risk and Uncertainty*, *19* (1–3), 7–42.

Croson, R., & Buchan, N. (1999). Gender and culture: International experimental evidence from trust games. *American Economic Review*, *89* (2), 386–391.

Darwin, C. (1872). *The expression of the emotions in man and animals*. London: John Murray.

Deutsch, F. M. (1990). Status, sex, and smiling: The effect of role on smiling in men and women. *Personality and Social Psychology Bulletin*, *16*, 531–540.

Duchenne de Boulogne, G.-B. d. B. (1862). *The mechanism of human facial expression or an electro-physiological analysis of the expression of the emotions*. Edited & translated by R. A. Cuthbertson (1990). *Studies in emotion and social interaction*. Cambridge: Cambridge University Press.

Eckel, C. C., & Grossman, P. (in press). Differences in the economic decisions of men and women: Experimental evidence. In C. Plott & V. Smith (Eds.), *Handbook of experimental results*. New York: Elsevier, forthcoming.

Eckel, C. C., & Wilson, R. K. (1997). *The human face of game theory*. Paper presented at the annual meeting of the Economic Science Association, Tucson, AZ, September 19–20, 1997.

Eckel, C. C., & Wilson, R. K. (1998). *Reputation formation in simple bargaining games*. Paper presented at the Midwest Political Science Association Meeting, Chicago, IL, 23–25 April, 1998.

Ekman, P. (Ed.). (1982). *Emotion in the human face. Studies in emotion and social interaction*. Cambridge: Cambridge University Press.

Ekman, P., & Friesen, W. V. (1982). Measuring facial movement with the Facial Action Coding System. In P. Ekman (Ed.), *Emotion in the human face* (pp. 178–211). Cambridge: Cambridge University Press.

Ekman, P., Friesen, W. V., & Davidson, R. J. (1990). The duchenne smile – emotional expression and brain physiology II. *Journal of Personality and Social Psychology*, *58*, 342–353.

Ekman, P., Friesen, W. V., Ellsworth, P. (1982). Methodological decisions. In P. Ekman (Ed.), *Emotion in the human face* (pp. 22–38). Cambridge: Cambridge University Press.

Foster, D. A. (1992). *Bargaining across borders: How to negotiate business successfully anywhere in the world*. New York: McGraw-Hill.

Frank, R. H. (1988). *Passions within reasons: The strategic role of the emotions.* New York: W.W. Norton.
Frank, M. G., Ekman, P., & Friesen, W. V. (1993). Behavioral markers and recognizability of the smile of enjoyment. *Journal of Personality and Social Psychology*, *64*, 83–93.
Fridlund, A. J. (1994). *Human facial expression: An evolutionary view.* San Diego: Academic Press.
Frohlich, N., & Oppenheimer, J. (1998). Some consequences of e-mail vs. face-to-face communication in experiment. *Journal of Economic Behavior and Organization*, *35*, 389–403.
Glaeser, E., Laibson, D. I, Scheinkman, J. A., & Soutter, C. L. (2000). Measuring trust. *Quarterly Journal of Economics*, *115* (3), 811–846.
Grafen, A. (1990). Biological signals as handicaps. *Journal of Theoretical Biology*, *144*, 517–546.
Hamermesh, D. S., & Biddle, J. E. (1994). Beauty and the labor market. *American Economic Review*, *84* (5), 1174–1194.
Hamilton, W. D., & Zuk, M. (1982). Heritable true fitness and bright birds: a role for parasites? *Science*, *218*, 384–387.
Hey, J. (1998). Experimental economics and deception: A comment. *Journal of Economic Psychology*, *19* (3), 397–401.
Hinsz, V. B., & Tomhave, J. A. (1991). Smile and (half) the world smiles with you, frown and you frown alone. *Personality and Social Psychology Bulletin*, *17*, 586–592.
Kimmel, H. D. (1957). Three criteria for the use of one-tailed tests. *Psychology Bulletin*, *54*, 351–353.
LaFrance, M., & Hecht, M. A. (1995). Why smiles generate leniency. *Personality and Social Psychology Bulletin*, *21*, 207–214.
Lau, S. (1982). The effect on smiling on person perception. *Journal of Social Psychology*, *117*, 63–67.
McKelvey, R. D., & Palfrey, T. R. (1992). An experimental study of the centipede game. *Econometrica*, *60*, 803.
Mullen, B., Futrell, D., Stairs, D., Tice, D. M., Dawson, K. E., Riordan, C. A., Kennedy, J. G., Baumeister, R. F., Radloff, C. E., Goethals, G. R., & Rosenfeld, P. (1986). Newscasters facial expressions and voting-behavior of viewers – can a smile elect a president? *Journal of Personality and Social Psychology*, *51*, 291–295.
Nahm, F. K. D., Perret, A., Amaral, D. G., & Albright, T. D. (1997). How do monkeys look at faces? *Journal of Cognitive Neuroscience*, *9*, 611–623.
Roth, A. (1995). Bargaining Experiments. In J. H. Kagel & A. E. Roth (Eds.), *The handbook of experimental economics.* Princeton, NJ: Princeton University Press.
Sell, J. (1997). Gender, strategies, and contributions to public goods. *Social Psychology Quarterly*, *60* (3), 252–265.
Surakka, V., & Hietanen, J. K. (1998). Facial and emotional reactions to duchenne and non-duchenne smiles. *International Journal of Psychophysiology*, *29*, 23–33.
Tidd, K. L., & Lochard, J. S. (1978). Monetary significance of the affiliative smile: A case for reciprocal altruism. *Bulletin of the Psychonomic Society*, *11*, 344–346.
Walk, R. D., & Walters, K. L. (1988). Perception of the smile and other emotions of the body and face at different distances. *Bulletin of the Psychonomic Society*, *26*, 510–510.
Walters, A., Stuchlmacher, A., & Meyer, L. (1998). Gender and negotiator competitiveness: A meta-analysis. *Organizational Behavior and Human Decision Processes*, *76* (1), 1–29.
Zahavi, A. (1977). The cost of honesty (further remarks on the handicap principle). *Journal of Theoretical Biology*, *67*, 146–151.
Zebrowitz, L. A. (1997). *Reading faces: Window to the soul?* Boulder, CO: Westview Press.

[36]

Games and Economic Behavior **33,** 90–116 (2000)
doi:10.1006/game.1999.0762, available online at http://www.idealibrary.com on IDEAL®

An Experiment on the Hypothesis of Involuntary Truth-Signalling in Bargaining[1]

Axel Ockenfels

Faculty of Economics and Management, University of Magdeburg, Germany

and

Reinhard Selten

University of Bonn, Germany

Received February 1, 1999

We examine face-to-face interaction in a two-person bargaining game with incomplete information in which each bargainer can either have costs to be subtracted from his/her bargaining agreement payoff or not. The bargaining events are observed by onlookers who guess the cost situations of the participants. The work of D. Gauthier (1978, *Morals by Agreement*. Oxford: Clarendon) and R. H. Frank (1988, *Passions Within Reason: The Strategic Role of Emotions*. New York: Norton) suggests that the onlookers' detection accuracy exceeds chance accuracy because of involuntary signals inherent in the behavior of the bargainers. It is shown that cost guesses are somewhat more accurate than chance. This effect, however, is entirely explainable by the onlookers' information about objective features of the bargaining process. *Journal of Economic Literature* Classification Numbers: C70, C91, D70, D82. © 2000 Academic Press

Key Words: bargaining experiment; face-to-face interaction; truth-signalling.

1. INTRODUCTION

It is often suggested in the literature that bargainers cannot convincingly lie because they cannot avoid involuntary signals like facial movements or voice inflection which provide hints about the emotional state of

[1] The authors thank the team of the Magdeburg Laboratory for Experimental Economics "MAXLAB" for the aid in collecting the data. Financial support by the Deutsche Forschungsgesellschaft is gratefully acknowledged. Corresponding author: Axel Ockenfels, Faculty of Economics and Management, University of Magdeburg, P.O. Box 4120, D-39016 Magdeburg, Germany. E-mail: axel.ockenfels@ww.uni-magdeburg.de.

0899-8256/00 $35.00

the speaker. The philosopher David Gauthier, for instance, built his theory of "morals by agreement" on the premise that people are "translucent" in the sense that they are able "to detect others' sincerity or insincerity" (1978, p. 181). Also, many papers in evolutionary game theory are based on this assertion which we shall refer to as the *hypothesis of involuntary truth-signalling* in the following. Frank's (1987, 1988) approach to the evolution of cooperation in prisoner's dilemmas as well as Robson's (1990) biological "secret handshake" model may be the most prominent models that make use of the hypothesis of involuntary truth-signalling in an evolutionary context. Varieties of the hypothesis of involuntary truth-signalling have been proposed by Hirshleifer (1987) and Schelling (1978) in papers which have found less attention, and probably also by others. As far as we know, however, nobody has ever supplied convincing empirical evidence for the hypothesis in a bargaining context. Gauthier and Frank explicitly put the hypothesis of involuntary truth-signalling into such a context. It is therefore of interest to examine the hypothesis in experimental bargaining games.

In an experiment by Frank *et al.* (1993) subjects, before playing a prisoner's dilemma, had the opportunity to talk to their opponents about the problem and were then asked to predict whether they would cooperate or not. It turned out that they succeeded much more than randomly expected in correctly predicting non-cooperative behavior but to a much (although not significantly) smaller extent cooperative behavior. The paper does not report the content of the conversations. It is possible that some subjects openly or implicitly declared that they did not want to cooperate and therefore were expected not to do so.[2] Therefore the experiment does not clarify what was deducible from verbal statements and what was due to the recognition of involuntary signals. Moreover, the payoff scheme was such that most of the variance was due to a random payoff component added in order to make it impossible for the subject to find out afterward whether an opponent has cooperated or not. Therefore the behavior in the games was relatively unimportant for the final payoff. There was no payment for the correctness of the prediction.

In the psychological literature the question of whether deception can be detected has been addressed in quite a number of investigations. An overview is given by Zuckerman *et al.* (1981). In these studies subjects are usually told by the experimenter whether they should lie or tell the truth and no monetary incentives are supplied. A typical task was that a subject

[2]There is, however, a very brief sketch of the content of "many" of the subjects' conversations in Frank (1988, Chap. 7) which suggests that subjects did not explicitly announce that they were going to defect. Yet, in a similar prisoner's dilemma experiment by Brosig (1998) a non-negligible share of subjects explicitly and some implicitly stated that they would not cooperate.

should talk badly about somebody else whom he or she liked and appreciated or he or she should praise somebody whom he or she did not think to be worthy of praise at all. In the paper by Zuckerman *et al.* (1981, p. 26) we find the following summarizing statement:

> In fact, the examination of actual percentage accuracy indicates that most of the results fall in the 0.45–0.60 range with a chance level of 0.5 (see Kraut, 1980; Knapp and Comadena, 1979; Miller and Burgoon, 1981).[3]

The paper also investigates the basis of this detection capability. Treatment conditions varied according to whether the face or the body could be seen or not and whether speech could be heard or not. Surprisingly, the highest detection capability was observed when speech could be heard and the body could be observed but not the face. This suggests that facial clues are misleading rather than informative. Moreover, most of what is transmitted by speech seems to be discovered also by those who only saw transcripts. Zuckerman *et al.* (1981, p. 27) summarize the results as follows:

> The surprising finding, of course, is the power (i.e., the accuracy) of the word, either written or spoken. The assumption that non-verbal channels are more important in the communication of deception than the verbal clues is simply not true (see DePaulo, Rosenthal, Green, and Rosenkrantz, 1981).

The psychological studies suggest that the hypothesis of involuntary truth-signalling may have some merit even if the effects are weak. However, this may be due to the nature of the task because subjects told to tell lies may feel quite different about this than a bargainer who misrepresents his or her situation. Therefore it is of interest to investigate the hypothesis of involuntary truth-signalling in the context of bargaining experiments. Unlike the subjects in most psychological experiments, the subjects in the environment of our bargaining experiment are motivated by non-negligible monetary incentives and are free to choose whether they want to tell the truth or not.[4]

The bargaining situation with incomplete information underlying our experiment is very simple. Two bargainers have to divide a fixed sum of money but they may or may not have costs to be deducted from the bargaining results in case of an agreement. There is two-sided incomplete information about the cost situation of the other player. Selten (1975) applied the noncooperative model by Harsanyi and Selten (1972) to this bargaining situation. Experiments on the basis of the same noncooperative bargaining

[3] Similar summarizing statements can be found in articles by Gilovich *et al.* (1998), Anderson *et al.* (1999), and others.

[4] The design of our experiments is similar to unpublished pilot experiments by Selten and Stoecker (1978) performed at the University of Bielefeld under less controlled conditions. Bargainers and onlookers were non-academics visiting the university at an "open day." The results with respect to the capability of detection were similar to those of the study reported here. However, bargaining was not video-taped and the number of bargaining events was rather small. Many questions raised here cannot be examined with the help of this material.

model were performed by Hogatt *et al.* (1978). Kuon (1994) theoretically and experimentally applied the Rubinstein model (1985a,b) of alternating bid bargaining to a similar situation. The experiments presented here are not based on a complex noncooperative bargaining model but on face-to-face interaction followed by just one round of simultaneous agreement proposals.

2. THE EXPERIMENT

The experiment consisted of two sessions. In each session 24 subjects participated as bargainers. In addition to this a number of other subjects, 42 in session 1 and 46 in session 2, had the role of onlookers. The bargainers were students of the University of Magdeburg studying a variety of fields, mostly economics, in different semesters. We tried to avoid bargaining between people who were acquainted with each other. Bargainers were only matched into a bargaining pair if they declared that they did not know each other. All onlookers were students of economics.

2.1. *Procedure*

A session was a sequence of 12 bargaining events. In each bargaining event two subjects bargained about the division of DM 30. The bargaining was face-to-face, observed by the onlookers, and video-taped. The bargainers separately arrived about 20 minutes before their bargaining events, read the instructions, and gave up all rights with respect to the video recordings to the experimenter (see Appendix A for all instructions). Then the bargainers had to throw a dice in order to determine whether they would have costs of DM 12 or not. In the case of a throw of 1, 2, 3 subjects had costs and in the case of a throw of 4, 5, 6 there were no costs. The cost situation of a bargainer was private information. The costs were subtracted from the subject's agreement payoff if agreement was reached.

At the start of the bargaining event, two bargainers were brought to a lecture hall, where they talked for maximally 10 minutes. The bargainers could stop their conversation earlier if they wanted to do so. Afterward each bargainer separately and secretly filled in forms in which each of both wrote down the agreement reached according to his or her understanding. Moreover, each of them had to fill in a guess about whether the other one had costs or not. Afterward both bargainers, one after another, were led to a separate room where the payments were made, unobserved by the other bargainer and the onlookers. If both forms agreed with respect to the division of the DM 30, payments according to the agreement were made with costs deducted if there were any. If the forms were in disagreement the bargainers received zero payoffs from the game. In addition to the payoff from the game, each bargainer received a show up fee of DM 10. Overall, average bargainer earnings were DM 19.88 with a minimum of DM 10 and a maximum of DM 29. The average time needed for the whole experiment was about half an hour.

Onlookers were fully informed about the bargaining rules. They were seated in the lecture hall such that they had a good view of the bargainers but could not communicate with their neighbors. The task of the onlookers was to guess who among the bargainers had costs and who had no costs. The guessed cost situation for each bargainer was marked with a cross in a decision form. The onlookers were paid according to the following scheme in each session: DM 300 were divided among those who had the highest number of correct guesses achieved, DM 100 were divided among those who had the second highest number of correct guesses, and DM 50 were divided among those who had the third highest number of correct guesses. The maximum earnings in sessions 1 and 2 were DM 100 and DM 300, respectively. Session 1 lasted about 80 minutes and session 2 about 70 minutes.

2.2. *Remarks*

Theoretically it is possible that an agreement is reached in which one bargainer with costs receives less than DM 12. In the instructions the bargainers were told that in the case of costs they had to insist on at least DM 12 if they did not want to face a loss. Losses would be deducted from the show up fee. In fact, losses did not occur.

The instructions explicitly told the subjects to try to maximize their payoffs. This was done in order to direct attention as much as possible to the money payoff.

The experimental setup did not permit a bargainer to prove to the other one that he or she had costs. Also, after the bargaining, it was kept secret whether a bargainer had costs or not. The onlookers did not get any information about which of their guesses were correct.

Bargainers were not permitted to communicate with each other before the bargaining and were separated after the bargaining event in order to provide no easy opportunities for retrospective communication. They were also not able to see any bargaining events other than their own. Communication among onlookers was prohibited and successfully prevented.

3. EXPERIMENTAL DATA

Table I shows the results of all bargaining events. In the following we explain the entries in the table together with some summary remarks:

TABLE I
Bargaining Data

1 Bargainer Identification number	2 Bargaining costs	3 Outcome (DM)	4 Correctly guessed by opponent	5 Onlooker hit rate (%)	6 Cost assertion	7 First aggressive demand	8 First fair demand	9 Bargaining time (min)	10 Male/ female	11 Economics student
1A	0	15.0	1	78.6*	0	0	1	0.5	m	ec
1B	0	15.0	1	71.4*	0	0	0		m	n-ec
2A	0	15.0	0	83.3*	0	0	0	0.3	m	ec
2B	1	15.0	0	28.6*	0	0	1		m	n-ec
3A	1	15.0	0	66.7*	1	0	0	1.0	m	ec
3B	0	15.0	0	54.8	1 (f)	0	1		m	n-ec
4A	1	0.0	0	38.1	1	0	1	8.0	m	n-ec
4B	1	0.0	0	71.4*	1 (f)	1	0		m	ec
5A	1	15.0	1	57.1	0	0	0	0.7	f	n-ec
5B	1	15.0	0	81.0*	0	1	1		f	ec
6A	1	15.0	0	54.8	1 (f)	1	1	3.0	m	ec
6B	1	15.0	1	38.1	1	0	0		m	n-ec
7A	0	15.0	0	42.9	0	1	0	10.0	m	ec
7B	1	15.0	0	19.0*	1	0	1		m	ec
8A	1	15.0	0	7.1*	1 (f)	0	1	3.0	m	ec
8B	1	15.0	1	54.8	1	1	0		m	n-ec
9A	0	15.0	1	50.0	1 (f)	1	1	1.5	m	ec
9B	0	15.0	1	69.0*	1	0	0		m	ec
10A	0	15.0	1	76.2*	0	0	0	0.2	m	ec
10B	0	15.0	1	92.9*	0	0	1		f	ec
11A	0	13.0	1	100.0	0	0	1	1.0	m	ec
11B	0	17.0	0	14.3*	1	1	0		m	ec
12A	1	16.0	1	47.6	1	1	0	5.0	m	ec
12B	0	14.0	1	90.5*	1 (f)	0	1		m	ec
13A	0	17.5	0	32.6*	1	1	0	2.3	m	n-ec
13B	0	12.5	1	87.0*	0	0	0		m	n-ec
14A	1	15.0	0	60.9	1 (f)	1	1	3.3	f	ec
14B	0	15.0	1	41.3	1	0	0		m	ec

ctd. overleaf

TABLE I
(Continued)

1 Bargainer Identification number	2 Bargaining costs	3 Outcome (DM)	4 Correctly guessed by opponent	5 Onlooker hit rate (%)	6 Cost assertion	7 First aggressive demand	8 First fair demand	9 Bargaining time (min)	10 Male/ female	11 Economics student
15A	1	15.0	0	34.8	0	0	0	0.7	f	ec
15B	1	15.0	1	32.6*	0	0	1		m	ec
16A	0	15.0	1	56.5	0	0	0	0.8	m	n-ec
16B	1	15.0	0	52.2	0	1	1		f	ec
17A	0	18.0	1	19.6*	1	1	0	3.6	m	ec
17B	0	12.0	1	95.7*	0	0	1		m	ec
18A	0	19.0	0	6.5*	0	1	0	1.2	m	ec
18B	0	11.0	0	93.5*	0	0	1		m	ec
19A	1	15.0	1	26.1*	1	0	1	4.0	m	ec
19B	1	15.0	1	76.1*	1 (f)	1	0		f	n-ec
20A	0	15.0	0	54.3	1	0	0	1.2	m	ec
20B	1	15.0	0	21.7*	0	0	1		m	n-ec
21A	0	15.0	1	91.3*	0	0	0	0.2	m	n-ec
21B	0	15.0	1	93.5*	0	0	1		m	n-ec
22A	0	15.0	1	50.0	1 (f)	1	0	0.3	f	ec
22B	0	15.0	1	45.7	1	0	1		m	ec
23A	0	15.0	0	21.7*	1	1	0	2.4	m	ec
23B	0	15.0	1	54.3	0	0	1		f	n-ec
24A	0	15.0	0	73.9*	0	1	0	0.9	m	ec
24B	1	15.0	0	39.1	0	0	1		m	n-ec
Average session 1	50.0%	13.75	50.0%	57.8%	58.3%	33.3%	50.0%	2.85	87.5% males	70.8% ec
Average session 2	33.3%	15.00	54.2%	52.5%	41.7%	37.5%	45.8%	1.74	75.0% males	62.5% ec
Average both sessions	41.7%	14.38	52.1%	55.2%	50.0%	35.4%	47.9%	2.30	81.3% males	66.7% ec

Column 1 (bargainer identification number): Each bargainer has an identification number consisting of the bargaining event number and a letter A or B. The first 12 bargaining event numbers refer to session 1 and the second 12 to session 2.

Column 2 (bargaining costs): The entry is 1 if the bargainer had costs and 0 if he or she had none. In session 1, 12 out of the 24 bargainers had costs whereas in session 2 only 8 out of the 24 bargainers had costs.

Column 3 (outcome): The entry shows the game payoff in German marks before the deduction of costs. Eighteen of the 24 bargaining pairs agreed on DM 15 for each of both. Conflict was reached only in one case. In five cases an agreement was reached in which one bargainer received more than the other.

Column 4 (correctly guessed by opponent): In the case of an entry of 1 the opponent correctly guessed whether the bargainer had costs or not. In the case of an entry of 0 the opponent's guess was wrong. The percentage of correct guesses by bargainers in both sessions is 52.1%.

Column 5 (onlooker hit rate): The entry is the percentage of correct guesses over all onlookers of the session. The star indicates significance according to the two-sided binomial test at the significance level of 5%. The test is based on the null hypothesis that both guesses are equally probable. The average percentage of correct guesses by onlookers in both sessions is 55.2%.

Column 6 (cost assertion): An entry of 1 indicates that the bargainer explicitly asserted in the bargaining event that he or she had costs. In the case of an entry of 0 he or she did not make such an assertion. In those bargaining events in which both bargainers asserted costs, an "(f)" indicates that the bargainer was the first of both who asserted to have costs.

Twelve of the 20 bargainers who had costs correctly asserted that they had costs. Twelve of the 28 bargainers without costs falsely asserted that they had costs. Nobody ever said explicitly that they had no costs.

Column 7 (first aggressive demand): We use the term "aggressive" for demands of more than DM 15 and an entry of 1 indicates that the bargainer was the first one to make an aggressive demand. Otherwise the entry is 0. If one of both bargainers has an entry of 1, obviously the other one must have an entry of 0. In seven cases, none of both bargainers asked for more than DM 15 for themselves so that both entries are 0.

Column 8 (first fair demand): We refer to a demand of exactly DM 15 as "fair." An entry of 1 indicates that the bargainer was the first one to make a fair demand. Otherwise the entry is 0. In bargaining event 13 neither of the bargainers had an entry of 1 because an aggressive demand was accepted before a fair demand was made. In all other cases there was a player who first faced a fair demand.

Column 9 (bargaining time): The entry shows the time until the end of the bargaining conversations in minutes. The maximum of 10 minutes was reached only once in bargaining event 7. The average bargaining time was 2.30 minutes.

Column 10 (male/female): "m" stands for male and "f" for female. Nine out of the 48 bargainers were female.

Column 11 (economics student): "ec" stands for economics student and "n-ec" for other students. Thirty-two of the 48 bargainers studied economics.

4. OVERALL DETECTION CAPABILITY

In this section, we look at whether the data show a significant overall detection capability or, in other words, whether the percentage of correct guesses is significantly higher than the randomly expected 50%. However, we do not want to make the assumption that the probabilities of correct guesses are the same for different onlookers and different bargainers judged by the same onlookers. If there is no overall detection capability one would expect a mean value of 12 correct guesses of an onlooker.

Figure 1 shows the distribution of the 88 numbers of correct guesses of an onlooker.[5] The mode and the median of the distribution is 14 and the mean is 13.22. We test the null hypothesis that the data summarized by Fig. 1 are a sample from a distribution with mean value 12. This hypothesis is rejected by the Wilcoxon signed rank test on a very high level of significance ($p =$ 0.000, two-sided). As we shall see later, this result needs to be interpreted with care. In some cases it is easy to make a correct guess on the basis of very simple criteria which have nothing to do with involuntary signalling of truth.

We now turn our attention to the guesses of the bargainers about their opponent's cost situation. These guesses are correct in only 52.1% of all cases. In comparison to the onlookers who correctly guessed in 55.2% of all cases (cf. Table I), the bargainers were less accurate. The difference between the two numbers is very small and seems to be compatible with the idea that the probability of a correct guess is not different for bargainers and onlookers. It is difficult, however, to support this impression by an

[5]The individual guesses of all onlookers are shown in Table IV in Appendix B.

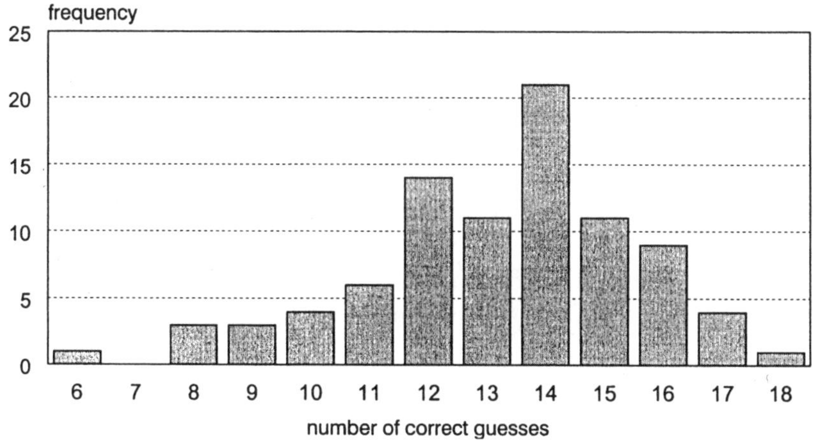

FIG. 1. Distribution of correct guesses of an onlooker.

adequate statistical test, since probabilities must be suspected to be different for different onlookers and for different bargainers judged by the same onlookers.

The bargainers' judgements on the cost situations of their opponents correlate with the onlooker hit rates (columns 4 and 5 in Table I). The biserial rank correlation coefficient is 0.337 which is not very high but the associated Mann–Whitney U-test is significant at the level $p = 0.021$ (two-sided).

Figure 2 shows the distribution of onlooker hit rates over bargainers listed in column 5 of Table I. The figure also exhibits the theoretical distri-

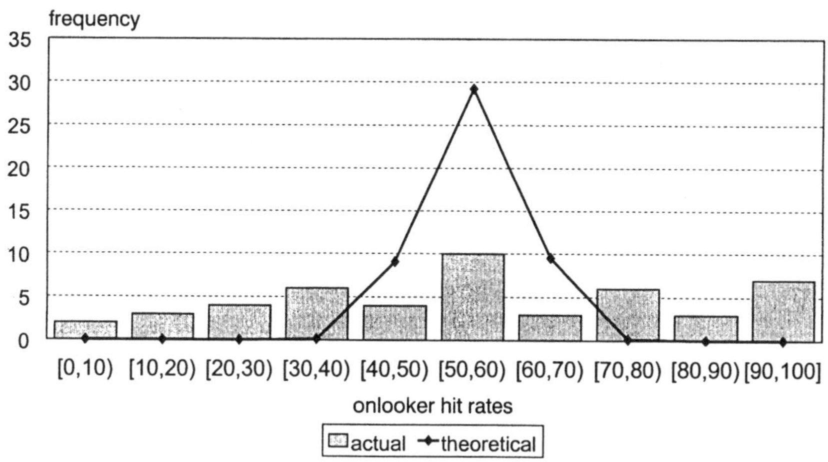

FIG. 2. Distribution of hit rates over bargainers.

bution which would be obtained if the probability of a correct guess were the same for every bargainer, namely, the observed overall relative frequency 55.2% of correct guesses, and also independent of each other.

Obviously, the theoretical distribution does not agree with the data. According to the theoretical distribution, at least one hit rate either greater than 80% or smaller than 30% has a probability of less than 5%. Nevertheless such hit rates are observed in 19 of 48 cases.

Our findings suggest that the probabilities of a correct guess by an onlooker are different for different bargainers. It appears that the cost situation of the bargainer is easy to assess in some cases and very difficult to be correctly guessed in some other cases.

As we have explained above, the stars in column 5 indicate that the corresponding onlooker hit rate is different from 50% at the two-sided significance level of 5%. This is the case for 29 of the 48 hit rates. In 18 of these 29 cases the hit rates are above 50%, but in 11 cases they are below. For these 11 bargainers the guesses of the onlookers are significantly worse than random. As far as there is a capability of detecting the true cost situations, it fails miserably in these cases.

5. THE INFLUENCE OF OBJECTIVE FEATURES OF THE BARGAINING PROCESS ON THE CORRECTNESS OF GUESSES

Why is it that onlookers have a very good capability to judge the cost situations of some bargainers and a very bad capability for others? In order to find the reasons, we analyze the objective features of the bargaining process in this section. By objective features we mean characteristics of the bargaining process which can either be clearly seen in the transcripts or which are in other ways apparent from the bargaining process without any information coming from visual channels like facial expression and body postures or auditory channels like voice intonation. Such features are the final bargaining result and the bargaining time. The features clearly indicated by the transcripts are the cost assertions and the first aggressive and first fair demand. In this respect the transcripts are unambiguous.[6]

In connection with the objective features of the bargaining process, three different questions suggest themselves: Which objective features are good indicators of the cost situations of the bargainers? To what extent are these objective features responsible for the fact that onlookers judge the true cost situations somewhat more accurately than randomly expected? Which other features influence the guesses of the onlookers?

[6]The transcripts (in German) are available from the authors upon request.

In the following, we shall first look at those features which are good indicators of the actual cost situation; these are the final bargaining result and the bargaining time. It will then be shown that these features are responsible for the better than randomly guessing success of the onlookers. Finally, we shall present a probit analysis of the onlookers' guessing behavior that takes into account other objective features.

5.1. *Actual Costs, Cost Guesses, and Final Bargaining Results*

In five bargaining events the final bargaining result was asymmetric in the sense that an agreement was reached in which one bargainer received a higher share of the gross payoff of DM 30 than the other one. In such situations the onlookers tend to judge that the bargainer with the higher gross payoff has costs and the bargainer with the lower payoff has no costs. In fact, on average over all five bargaining events, the onlookers guess in 75% that the bargainer with the higher gross payoff has costs and in 93.6% of all cases that the bargainer with the lower gross payoff has no costs. The second tendency is fully justified in each of the five cases. The bargainers with the lower gross payoffs have no costs. The first tendency, however, is mistaken. Among all five bargainers with a higher gross payoff, only one has costs.[7]

The data just discussed show that a lower gross payoff in an asymmetric final result is a good indicator of no costs. Contrary to this, however, a higher gross payoff is not a good indicator of costs. For instance, the bargainer with the highest gross profit (DM 19) had no costs, but 93.5% of the onlookers guessed that he had costs.

The guessing tendencies of the onlookers in face of asymmetric bargaining results are also reflected by a highly significant negative rank correlation coefficient of -0.540 ($p = 0.001$, two-sided) between a bargainer's gross payoff and the onlooker hit rates (columns 3 and 5 in Table I). The onlookers make strong use of the fact that a lower gross payoff is a good indicator for no costs and thereby improve their hit rates.

Conflict with zero payoffs for both bargainers was reached in only one bargaining event. In this event, both bargainers had costs. For one of the bargainers, 62% of the onlookers guessed that he had costs but for the other one only 29%. One might think that a conflict indicates a high probability

[7] In three of the five cases the lower gross payoff was higher than DM 12, in one it was DM 12, and in another one it was DM 11. At least in the last case it is almost obvious that the bargainer with the lower gross payoff had no costs, even if it was not excluded by the rules that participants with costs accepted less than their costs of DM 12.

for both bargainers having costs. However, in the one case observed in our data, the onlookers do not seem to be guided by such considerations.

5.2. *Actual Costs, Cost Guesses, and Bargaining Time*

Five bargaining events ended after extremely short times of at most half a minute. In all these cases an agreement of equal gross payoffs of DM 15 was reached. Within half a minute, the bargainers cannot do much more than to express their willingness to accept a fair division. This led us to the decision to draw the line between extremely short and other bargaining events at half a minute.

Only 1 of the 10 bargainers involved in the five extremely short bargaining events had costs; 9 had no costs. The onlookers had the tendency to make a guess of no costs if the bargaining time was extremely short. On average a bargainer involved in the five bargaining events was judged by 75% of the onlookers to have no costs. Also, the 1 bargainer who had costs was judged by 70% of the onlookers not to have costs. The average hit rate for the short bargaining events is 71.1%.

In the bargaining events lasting for more than half a minute, 50% of the bargainers had costs and the onlookers on average judged 55% of them to have no costs. The average hit rate in these cases is only 51%.

Within the bargaining events lasting more than half a minute, there seems to be no difference between longer and shorter bargaining times with respect to the actual cost situations. Median tests used to examine these questions do not yield significant results. However, there is a sharp difference between the extremely short and the longer bargaining events. A four field table χ^2-test yields a significance of $p = 0.022$ (two-sided) for the difference of actual costs.

As we have seen, a short bargaining time is a good indicator of both bargainers having no costs. The onlookers make use of this indicator and thereby increase their hit rates considerably above random level in these cases.[8]

5.3. *Hit Rates Unaided by Bargaining Time and Result Asymmetry*

In this section, we want to examine whether the objective criteria based on short bargaining time and lower gross payoff in asymmetric results ex-

[8]It is remarkable that in bargaining experiments with anonymous interaction there is a concentration of agreements reached in the very last seconds before the deadline. Roth *et al.* (1988, p. 806), for instance, state that the deadline effect is "one of the clearest phenomena observed in bargaining experiments to date". In our face-to-face experiments, however, only 2 out of 24 bargaining events were still going on in the last two minutes.

plain the fact that onlookers succeed in achieving hit rates which on the average are significantly better than random. For this purpose, we define an *adjusted hit rate*. In order to do this, we look at the *reduced set* of bargainers without the 10 participants involved in extremely short bargaining events and the 5 participants who received lower gross payoffs than their opponents. The adjusted hit rate of an onlooker is his or her hit rate for the remaining bargainers in this reduced set.

The mean adjusted hit rate of the 88 onlookers is 44.5%. Based on a normal approximation we can compute a 99%-confidence interval for the mean of the distribution of adjusted hit rates. The lower bound of this confidence interval is 41.07% and the upper bound is 47.99%.

It is safe to conclude that without the criteria of extremely short bargaining time and lower gross payoff in an asymmetric bargaining result, the capability of the onlookers to make correct judgements about the true cost situations is worse than random. The upper limit of the 99% confidence interval is clearly below 50%.

Obviously, these results speak against the involuntary truth-signalling hypothesis. Unaided by the objective criteria of short bargaining time and lower gross payoff, the onlookers do not perceive involuntary signals which help them to form correct guesses. On the contrary, to some extent, onlookers seemed to be systematically misled as the 99%-confidence interval suggests.

5.4. *Correlations among Objective Features and Their Relation to Actual Costs*

It is the purpose of this section to describe the interrelationship between the objective features of the bargaining process and their connection with actual costs. In addition to the criteria of lower gross payoff and short bargaining time, we also look at the presence of cost assertion, first aggressive demand, and first fair demand (columns 6, 7, and 8 in Table I). All these features are 0–1 variables. The value of the lower gross payoff criterion is defined as 1 if the gross payoff is lower than DM 15 and 0 otherwise. Similarly, the value of the short bargaining time criterion is defined as 1 if the bargaining time does not exceed half a minute and 0 otherwise.

The correlations among the objective features are shown in Table II. The table also shows correlations with the presence of actual costs (according to column 2 in Table II). The significance of correlations of the lower gross payoff and short bargaining time criteria with actual costs confirm what has been pointed out earlier in this respect. The other three correlations of actual costs with the remaining three objective features are not significant.

There are only two significant correlations among the objective features: one between the short bargaining time criterion and cost assertion and one

TABLE II
Correlations among Objective Features and Their Relation to Actual Costs

Objective features	Short bargaining time	Cost assertion	First aggressive demand	First fair demand	Actual bargaining costs
Lower gross payoff	−0.175	−0.205	−0.253	0.219	−0.288[a]
Short bargaining time		−0.308[a]	−0.273	0.021	−0.330[a]
Cost assertion			0.305[a]	−0.125	0.169
First aggressive demand				−0.274	0.081
First fair demand					0.204

[a] Significant on the 5% level (two-sided).

between cost assertion and first aggressive demand. The first one is due to the fact that cost assertions are not typical for short bargaining times. The second one may be due to a tendency to buttress first aggressive demands by cost assertions.

The positive correlation between first fair demand and actual bargaining costs is in an unexpected direction. It suggests that somebody with costs is more likely to make a first fair demand than somebody without costs. However, this effect is not significant. All other correlations are in the expected directions.

A correlation which is not expressed by Table II is that between the presence of cost assertions of both bargainers in the same bargaining event. The data convey the impression that a cost assertion on one side is responded by a cost assertion by the other side. In order to examine this impression statistically, we construct a null hypothesis based on a simple theory proceeding from the assumption that bargainers with and without costs have probabilities of making a cost assertion which do not depend on the situation and the behavior on the other side. We estimate the probabilities by the relative frequencies observed in the data and then compute expected values for the numbers of bargaining events with two, one, or no cost assertions. With this simple theory as null hypothesis, we performed a χ^2-test which yields a significance of $p = 0.055$ (two-sided). The test confirms the impression that a cost assertion on one side provokes a defense by a cost assertion on the other side. Not only the number of cases in which both bargainers made a cost assertion but also the number of those in which none of them made a cost assertion is greater than randomly expected under the null hypothesis.

TABLE III
Probit Model

Variables	Coefficient values	t-values
Constant	−1.770	−11.236
Lower gross payoff	−1.093	−7.826
Short bargaining time	−0.427	−5.315
Cost assertion	0.140	2.215
First aggressive demand	0.610	9.215
First fair demand	−0.242	−3.968

5.5. *A Probit Analysis*

In the following we want to look at which objective features have a significant influence on the guessing behavior of the onlookers. We shall try to answer this question with the help of a probit model. Table III shows the results. The independent variables are the five objective features discussed above (cf. Table II) and the dependent variable is the guess of an onlooker about the cost situation of a bargainer (cf. Table IV in Appendix B). There are 88 onlookers, each of whom had to make 24 guesses.

Admittedly, the probit analysis makes strong independence assumptions which are unlikely to be satisfied. The same behavior is attributed to each onlooker and all guessing events are assumed to be independent of each other. Nevertheless, the probit analysis has some descriptive relevance even if the underlying model cannot really be taken seriously.[9]

The statistical analysis indicates that all five objective features have significant influence on the cost guesses. In particular, the probit analysis reveals a strong influence of the variable first aggressive demand on the cost guess. This influence is smaller than that of the lower gross payoff criterion but greater than that of the short bargaining time criterion. The strong influence of the variable first aggressive demand in the probit analysis is in contrast to the small correlation of the variable with actual costs. This suggests that trying to make the first aggressive demand is to some extent effective in conveying the impression of costs. To a lesser degree something similar

[9]We also performed Mann–Whitney U-tests which for every one of the five variables compared the 88 independent hit rates for the criterion value zero with the hit rates for the value one. All these tests are significant on the 1%-level (two-sided). For the variables first aggressive demand, first fair demand, and cost assertion, the same tests were performed for the adjusted hit rates. These tests are significant at the 1%-level (two-sided) for first fair and first aggressive demand and yield $p = 0.073$ (two-sided) for cost assertion. All effects point into the same direction as in the probit analysis.

can be said about cost assertions. The first fair demand, however, seems to suggest an absence of costs to the onlookers, even if the correlation with actual costs is slightly positive.

The influence of the cost assertions on the guesses of the onlookers does not seem to depend on whether they are correct or not. Twelve bargainers correctly assert that they have costs and twelve others make false cost assertions. In the case of true cost assertions, 47% of the onlookers on average guess the presence of costs. The corresponding percentage for false cost assertions is 55%. The reduced set of bargainers underlying the adjusted hit rates shows a similar picture. Here, the percentages are 47% for 11 true cost assertions and 51% for 6 false cost assertions. The differences between the percentages are in the opposite direction of what one would expect according to the involuntary truth-signalling hypothesis.

6. CONCLUSIONS

The results of our experiments clearly speak against the involuntary truth-signalling hypothesis. As we have seen, the capability of onlookers to make cost guesses which are somewhat more frequently correct than randomly expected can entirely be explained by the objective criteria of lower gross payoff and short bargaining time. These readily available features of the bargaining process (and not involuntary signals) enable the onlookers to guess somewhat more accurately than chance.

The adjusted hit rates which eliminate the influences of the two objective criteria reveal a guessing accuracy worse than chance. The 99%-confidence interval for the mean of the adjusted hit rates has a lower bound of 0.41 and an upper bound of 0.48. One can conclude that at least on average the onlookers not only fail to profit from involuntary signals but are even somewhat misled by what they observe if they cannot rely on the criteria of lower gross payoff and short bargaining time.

We have also seen in Section 5.5 that on average the onlookers cannot distinguish true from false cost assertions. Of course, these findings do not exclude the possibility that among the onlookers there are some whose truth detection capabilities are much better than the average and others for whom these capabilities are much lower than the average.[10] However, as far as we can see, the data show no evidence in this direction. In any

[10]Ekman and his co-authors conducted extensive subject pool studies in these contexts and provide evidence that some "professional lie catchers" can achieve high accuracy rates (see Ekman, 1985, and Ekman *et al.*, 1999 and the references cited therein).

case, the assumption of a widely spread culturally acquired truth detection capability does not find support by our experimental study.

In the literature, we often find comparisons between face-to-face and anonymous game interaction (Dawes *et al.*, 1977; Orbell *et al.*, 1988; Isaac and Walker, 1988; Frey and Bohnet, 1995; Sally, 1995; Valley *et al.*, 1998; Frohlich and Oppenheimer, 1998; Brosig *et al.*, 1999). The general conclusion is that face-to-face interaction leads to more cooperation and more egalitarian outcomes. In this connection, one sometimes finds explanations based on the involuntary truth-signalling hypothesis referring to the theoretical work of Robert Frank. Although our study does not examine the difference between formal anonymous interaction and face-to-face bargaining, our results suggest that any differences which may be there are not due to involuntary truth-signalling. Yet alternative explanations are not difficult to find. Face-to-face interaction may per se create more cooperation, more trust, and more consideration of the interests of the other participants (cf. Roth, 1995, for a related point of view).

The involuntary truth-signalling hypothesis may have some merit in other contexts as they occur in the psychological experiments discussed in Section 1. Involuntary truth-signalling, however, does not seem to take place in the context of bargaining situations.

APPENDIX A: WRITTEN DIRECTIONS (TRANSLATION FROM GERMAN)

Rules for Bargainers

Everybody knows that it is difficult in negotiations to assess how far the bargaining partner can give in, e.g., when buying a used car. In our experiment you will be placed in the following bargaining position, in which bargaining skills are required.

1. You bargain with a randomly chosen bargaining partner about the division of DM 30.

2. Before the bargaining event, you throw a dice in order to determine whether you have costs of DM 12 or not. In the case of a throw of 1, 2, 3 you have costs and in the case of a throw of 4, 5, 6 you do not have costs. In the case of costs, DM 12 are subtracted from your bargaining outcome. Your cost situation will be marked at the bottom of this page. Nobody except you and the experimenter knows your cost situation. You do not know whether your bargaining partner has costs. Nor will the information about the cost situation of any bargainer be revealed to anyone after the experiment has been completed.

3. The bargaining event lasts maximally 10 minutes but could stop earlier if you want it to. After the bargaining event, each of the bargainers writes down the agreement reached according to his or her understanding in the *bargainer form* on the next page. If the bargainer forms match in the division of the DM 30 you receive a corresponding payoff deducted by

the costs if you have costs. Note that a bargainer with costs has to demand at least DM 12 if he or she does not want to suffer a loss. (Losses are deducted from the DM 10 that each bargainer receives for the participation in the experiment.) If the bargainers cannot agree upon a division, if the bargainer forms do not match, or if the outcomes sum up to more than DM 30, neither bargainer receives a payoff from the bargaining.

4. The bargaining is video-taped and observed by students.
5. Try to realize the highest possible payoff.

From now on until the end of the experiment you are not permitted to communicate with other participants outside the bargaining event. If you have any questions, please raise your hand.

○ costs ○ no costs

Statement

1. I agree that I am video- and audio-taped during my participation in the experiment. I waive all claims that may arise in connection with the taping.
2. I agree that the tapes are preserved by the university for an indefinite time and are used for scientific analyses.

Date : Signature :

Bargainer Form

Bargainer identification number: ☐

<u>Please fill in:</u>

Field of Study: ☐

Sex: ○ m ○ f

<u>Division of DM 30:</u>

for me: ☐ **DM**

for my bargaining partner: ☐ **DM**

I guess that my bargaining partner...

○ **had costs.** ○ **had no costs.**

Rules for Onlookers

In a moment you will be witness of 12 bargaining events in which your assessment skills are demanded. Earlier, the bargainers obtained the following bargaining instructions:

1. You bargain with a randomly chosen bargaining partner about the division of DM 30.

2. Before the bargaining event, you throw a dice in order to determine whether you have costs of DM 12 or not. In the case of a throw of 1, 2, 3 you have costs and in the case of a throw of 4, 5, 6 you do not have costs. In the case of costs, DM 12 are subtracted from your bargaining outcome. Your cost situation will be marked at the bottom of this page. Nobody except you and the experimenter knows your cost situation. You do not know whether your bargaining partner has costs. Nor will the information about the cost situation of any bargainer be revealed to anyone after the experiment has been completed.

3. The bargaining event lasts maximally 10 minutes but could stop earlier if you want it to. After the bargaining event, each of the bargainers writes down the agreement reached according to his or her understanding in the *bargainer form* on the next page. If the bargainer forms match in the division of the DM 30 you receive a corresponding payoff deducted by the costs if you have costs. Note that a bargainer with costs has to demand at least DM 12 if he or she does not want to suffer a loss. (Losses are deducted from the DM 10 that each bargainer receives for the participation in the experiment.) If the bargainers cannot agree upon a division, if the bargainer forms do not match, or if the outcomes sum up to more than DM 30, neither bargainer receives a payoff from the bargaining.

4. The bargaining is video-taped and observed by students.

5. Try to realize the highest possible payoff.

Your task is to guess from the bargaining process who among the 24 bargainers has costs and who has no costs. In a bargaining event, one, both, or neither bargainer may have costs. DM 300 are divided among those onlookers who achieve the highest number of correct guesses, DM 100 are divided among those who achieve the second highest number, and DM 50 among those who have the third highest number.

From now on until the end of the experiment you are not permitted to communicate in any form during the whole experiment. If you have any questions, please raise your hand now.

Onlooker Form

Onlooker identification number: [ ]

Field of study: [ ]

Sex: ○ m ○ f

Please mark the bargainers who you think have costs with a cross:

Bargaining event	Bargainer *A*	Bargainer *B*
1		
2		
3		
4		
5		
6		
7		
8		
9		
10		
11		
12		

APPENDIX B: ONLOOKER DATA

The following table shows the individual guesses of all onlookers as well as their gender. The onlookers in each session are sorted according to their numbers of correct guesses. All onlookers are undergraduate students of economics.

TABLE IV
Onlooker Data

Session 1 Onlooker	1A	1B	2A	2B	3A	3B	4A	4B	5A	5B	6A	6B	7A	7B	8A	8B	9A	9B	10A	10B	11A	11B	12A	12B	Male/ female
1	0	0	0	0	1	0	0	1	1	1	1	1	0	0	0	1	1	0	0	0	0	1	0	0	f
2	0	0	0	0	1	1	1	1	1	1	0	1	0	1	0	0	0	1	0	0	0	1	1	0	f
3	0	0	0	0	1	0	0	1	1	1	1	1	0	0	0	0	0	0	0	0	0	1	0	0	m
4	0	0	0	1	1	1	0	1	1	1	0	0	1	0	0	1	0	0	0	0	0	1	1	0	f
5	1	1	0	1	0	0	1	0	1	1	0	1	1	0	1	1	0	0	0	0	0	1	1	0	f
6	0	1	0	0	1	0	1	1	0	1	1	1	1	1	0	0	1	0	0	0	0	1	1	0	f
7	0	0	0	0	1	0	0	1	1	1	1	0	1	0	0	1	0	0	1	0	0	1	1	0	m
8	0	0	0	0	1	0	0	1	0	1	0	1	0	0	0	1	1	0	0	0	0	1	1	0	m
9	0	0	0	1	1	0	0	1	1	1	1	0	1	0	0	1	0	1	0	0	0	1	0	0	m
10	0	0	0	0	1	1	1	1	0	1	0	0	0	0	0	0	0	0	0	0	0	0	1	0	m
11	0	1	0	0	1	1	1	1	0	0	0	1	0	1	0	1	0	0	0	0	0	1	1	0	m
12	1	1	0	1	0	0	0	1	1	1	1	0	1	0	0	1	0	0	0	0	0	1	1	0	f
13	0	0	0	0	0	1	1	1	1	1	0	0	0	0	0	1	0	0	0	0	0	1	0	0	f
14	1	0	0	1	0	0	1	1	1	1	1	0	0	0	1	0	0	1	1	1	0	1	1	0	f
15	0	1	1	1	0	1	1	1	1	1	1	0	1	1	0	1	0	0	0	0	0	1	0	0	f
16	0	0	0	1	1	0	1	1	0	0	1	0	0	0	0	0	1	0	1	0	0	1	1	0	f
17	0	0	1	1	0	1	1	0	1	1	1	0	0	1	0	1	0	1	0	0	0	1	0	0	m
18	0	1	0	1	0	0	0	0	1	1	0	0	0	1	0	0	1	0	0	0	0	0	1	0	m
19	1	0	0	1	1	1	0	0	1	1	1	0	1	0	0	1	1	0	0	0	0	1	1	0	f
20	1	0	0	1	1	1	0	0	0	1	1	0	1	0	1	1	1	0	1	0	0	0	1	0	f
21	0	1	0	0	1	1	1	1	0	1	0	0	1	0	0	1	0	0	0	0	0	1	1	0	f
22	0	0	0	0	1	1	0	1	1	1	1	1	1	1	0	0	1	1	0	0	0	1	0	0	f
23	1	0	0	0	1	0	0	1	0	0	0	1	1	0	0	1	0	0	0	0	0	1	1	0	m
24	1	0	0	0	1	1	1	1	0	1	1	0	0	0	0	1	1	0	0	0	0	1	1	1	m
25	0	1	0	0	1	1	1	1	0	1	1	1	0	0	0	0	1	0	0	0	0	1	0	0	m
26	0	1	0	0	1	0	0	0	1	1	1	0	1	0	0	1	0	0	1	0	0	1	1	0	m
27	0	0	0	0	1	1	0	1	0	1	1	0	0	0	0	0	0	0	0	0	0	1	0	0	m
28	0	0	0	0	1	1	0	1	1	1	1	1	1	0	0	1	1	0	0	0	0	1	0	1	m
29	0	0	0	0	1	1	0	1	0	1	1	1	1	0	0	1	1	0	0	0	0	1	0	0	m

ctd. overleaf

TABLE IV
(Continued)

Session 1 Onlooker	1A	1B	2A	2B	3A	3B	4A	4B	5A	5B	6A	6B	7A	7B	8A	8B	9A	9B	10A	10B	11A	11B	12A	12B	Male/ female
30	0	0	0	0	1	0	0	0	0	1	1	1	1	0	0	0	0	1	0	0	0	1	1	0	m
31	0	0	0	0	0	1	1	1	0	1	0	0	0	1	0	1	1	0	0	0	0	1	1	1	m
32	1	0	0	0	0	0	1	1	0	1	0	0	0	0	0	1	1	0	0	0	0	1	0	0	f
33	0	0	1	1	1	0	1	1	1	0	0	0	0	0	0	0	1	1	0	0	0	1	0	0	m
34	0	0	0	0	1	1	0	1	0	1	1	0	1	0	0	0	1	0	0	0	0	1	0	0	f
35	0	0	0	0	1	1	0	1	1	1	1	0	1	0	0	0	1	1	0	0	0	1	0	0	f
36	0	1	0	0	1	0	0	0	1	1	0	1	1	0	0	1	1	1	0	0	0	1	0	0	m
37	0	0	1	0	0	0	0	0	1	0	0	1	1	0	0	0	0	0	1	0	0	0	0	0	m
38	0	0	0	0	1	0	0	1	0	1	0	1	1	0	0	1	1	1	1	0	0	1	0	1	m
39	0	1	0	0	0	0	0	1	0	0	1	0	1	0	0	0	1	1	0	0	0	0	0	0	m
40	0	1	1	0	0	0	0	0	1	0	0	0	0	0	0	0	0	1	1	0	0	0	0	0	m
41	0	0	1	0	0	0	0	0	1	0	0	0	1	0	0	0	0	0	1	1	0	1	0	0	m
42	1	0	1	0	0	0	0	0	1	1	0	0	1	0	0	0	1	1	1	1	0	1	0	0	m
Average Session 1 (%)	21.4	28.6	16.7	28.6	66.7	45.2	38.1	71.4	57.1	81.0	54.8	38.1	57.1	19.0	7.1	54.8	50.0	31.0	23.8	7.1	0.0	85.7	47.6	9.5	59.5 males

Session 2 Onlooker	13A	13B	14A	14B	15A	15B	16A	16B	17A	17B	18A	18B	19A	19B	20A	20B	21A	21B	22A	22B	23A	23B	24A	24B	Male/ female
43	1	0	1	0	1	1	0	1	1	0	1	0	1	1	0	1	0	0	0	0	1	1	0	0	f
44	0	1	1	0	1	0	0	1	1	0	1	0	1	1	0	1	0	0	1	1	1	0	0	1	f
45	1	0	1	0	1	1	1	1	1	0	1	0	1	1	0	1	0	0	1	1	1	0	1	1	f
46	0	0	1	1	1	1	0	0	1	0	1	0	0	1	0	1	0	0	1	0	0	1	1	0	m
47	1	0	0	0	1	0	0	0	0	0	1	0	0	1	0	0	0	0	0	0	0	0	1	0	f
48	0	0	1	0	0	0	0	1	1	0	1	0	0	1	0	1	0	0	1	1	1	1	0	1	m
49	0	0	1	0	0	0	1	1	1	0	1	0	0	1	0	0	0	0	0	0	1	0	1	1	f

TABLE IV
(Continued)

Session 2 Onlooker	13A	13B	14A	14B	15A	15B	16A	16B	17A	17B	18A	18B	19A	19B	20A	20B	21A	21B	22A	22B	23A	23B	24A	24B	Male/ female
50	0	0	0	1	0	1	1	1	0	0	1	0	0	1	0	0	0	0	0	1	1	0	0	0	m
51	1	0	1	0	0	0	1	1	1	0	1	0	0	1	0	0	0	0	0	0	1	0	0	0	m
52	1	0	1	0	0	0	1	1	1	0	1	0	0	1	0	0	0	0	0	0	1	0	0	0	m
53	0	0	1	1	0	0	0	0	1	0	1	0	0	1	1	0	0	0	1	0	0	0	0	1	m
54	0	0	1	0	1	1	0	0	1	0	1	0	0	1	1	0	0	0	1	1	1	1	0	1	m
55	1	1	1	1	1	0	1	1	1	0	1	0	0	1	0	0	0	0	0	0	0	0	0	0	m
56	1	1	1	1	1	1	0	0	0	0	0	0	0	1	0	0	0	0	1	1	1	0	0	0	f
57	1	0	1	1	0	1	0	1	0	0	1	0	0	1	0	0	0	0	0	1	1	1	0	0	m
58	0	0	0	1	0	0	0	1	1	0	1	0	0	0	0	0	0	0	1	0	0	0	0	0	f
59	1	0	0	1	1	1	0	1	1	0	1	0	0	1	0	0	0	0	1	0	1	1	0	0	f
60	1	0	1	0	0	0	0	0	1	0	1	0	0	1	0	0	0	0	0	1	1	0	0	0	m
61	1	0	0	1	0	0	1	1	1	0	1	0	0	1	0	0	0	0	0	0	1	0	0	1	m
62	1	0	1	0	0	0	0	0	1	0	1	0	1	1	1	0	0	0	0	0	1	0	1	0	m
63	1	0	0	1	1	0	1	1	0	0	1	0	0	0	1	1	0	0	1	0	0	1	0	1	m
64	1	0	1	1	0	0	1	1	1	0	1	0	0	1	1	1	0	0	0	1	1	0	0	1	m
65	0	1	0	1	1	1	0	0	0	0	1	0	1	0	1	0	1	1	0	0	1	0	0	1	f
66	1	0	1	0	0	0	0	0	1	0	1	0	1	1	0	0	0	0	1	1	1	1	0	1	m
67	0	0	1	0	0	0	1	1	1	0	1	0	0	1	1	0	0	0	1	1	1	0	0	0	m
68	1	0	1	1	0	1	0	0	1	0	1	0	0	1	1	1	0	0	0	1	1	1	0	0	m
69	0	0	0	1	0	0	0	1	1	0	1	0	0	1	1	0	0	0	0	1	1	0	0	0	m
70	1	0	1	0	0	1	1	1	1	0	1	0	1	1	1	0	1	1	0	1	0	1	0	0	f
71	1	0	0	0	1	0	0	0	1	0	1	0	0	1	1	0	0	0	0	1	1	1	0	1	f
72	0	0	1	0	0	1	0	0	1	0	1	0	0	0	1	0	1	0	0	1	1	1	0	1	f
73	0	0	0	1	1	0	0	0	1	0	1	0	0	1	1	0	0	0	1	0	1	1	0	1	f
74	1	1	0	1	0	0	0	1	0	1	0	1	1	0	0	0	0	0	0	0	1	1	0	1	f
75	1	0	1	1	1	1	1	0	1	0	1	0	0	1	1	0	0	0	1	0	1	0	0	0	m
76	1	0	1	1	0	0	1	1	0	0	1	0	0	1	1	0	0	0	1	1	0	0	0	0	f
77	1	0	1	1	0	0	1	0	1	0	1	0	0	1	0	0	0	0	1	0	1	0	0	1	f

ctd. overleaf

TABLE IV
(Continued)

Session 2 Onlooker	13A	13B	14A	14B	15A	15B	16A	16B	17A	17B	18A	18B	19A	19B	20A	20B	21A	21B	22A	22B	23A	23B	24A	24B	Male/ female
78	1	0	0	1	0	0	0	0	1	0	1	0	0	1	0	0	0	0	0	1	1	0	0	0	m
79	1	0	1	1	0	0	0	0	0	1	0	1	1	0	0	0	0	0	0	1	1	1	0	0	m
80	0	0	0	1	1	0	1	1	1	0	1	0	1	0	0	0	0	0	1	1	1	0	1	0	m
81	0	1	0	1	0	0	1	1	1	0	1	0	1	0	0	1	0	0	1	1	1	1	0	1	m
82	1	0	0	0	1	0	1	1	1	0	1	0	0	1	1	1	0	0	1	1	1	1	1	0	m
83	1	0	1	0	0	0	1	1	1	0	1	0	1	1	1	0	0	0	1	1	1	1	1	0	f
84	1	0	0	1	0	1	0	0	1	0	1	0	0	0	1	0	1	1	0	0	0	1	0	1	m
85	1	0	1	1	0	0	0	0	1	0	1	0	0	1	0	0	0	0	1	1	1	1	1	0	f
86	1	0	0	0	0	0	0	0	1	0	1	1	0	0	1	0	0	0	0	0	0	1	1	0	m
87	1	0	1	1	0	0	1	0	1	0	1	0	0	1	1	0	0	0	1	1	1	0	1	0	f
88	1	0	0	1	0	1	1	0	1	0	1	0	0	0	1	0	0	0	1	0	1	0	1	0	f
Average session 2 (%)	67.4	13.0	60.9	58.7	34.8	32.6	43.5	52.2	80.4	4.3	93.5	6.5	26.1	76.1	45.7	21.7	8.7	6.5	50.0	54.3	78.3	45.7	26.1	39.1	56.5 males

REFERENCES

Anderson, D. E., Ansfield, M. E., and DePaulo, B. M. (1999). "Love's Best Habit: Deception in the Context of Relationships," in *The Social Context of Nonverbal Behavior* (P. Philippot, R. S. Feldman, and E. J. Coats, Eds.), pp. 372–409. Cambridge, UK: Cambridge Univ. Press.

Brosig, J. (1998). "Communication and Individual Cooperation—An Experiment," Discussion Paper, University of Magdeburg.

Brosig, J., Ockenfels, A., and Weimann, J. (1999). "Does Communication Enhance Cooperation?" Discussion Paper, University of Magdeburg.

Dawes, R. M., McTavish, J., and Shaklee, H. (1977). "Behavior, Communication, and Assumptions about Other People's Behavior in a Commons Dilemma Situation," *J. Personality Soc. Psychol.* **35**, 1–11.

DePaulo, B. M., Rosenthal, R., Green, C. R., and Rosenkrantz, J. (1981). "Verbal and Nonverbal Revealingness in Deceptive and Nondeceptive Communications," Discussion Paper, University of Virginia.

Ekman, P. (1985). *Telling Lies—Clues to Deceit in the Marketplace, Politics, and Marriage.* New York/London: Norton.

Ekman, P., O'Sullivan, M., and Frank. M. G. (1999). "A Few can Catch a Liar," *Psych. Sci.* **10**, 263–266.

Frank, R. H. (1987). "If Homo Economicus Could Choose His Own Utility Function, Would He Want One with a Conscience?," *Amer. Econ. Rev.* **77**, 593–604.

Frank, R. H. (1988). *Passions Within Reason: The Strategic Role of Emotions*. New York: Norton.

Frank, R. H., Gilovich, T., and Regan, D. T. (1993). "The Evolution of One-Shot Cooperation: An Experiment," *Ethol. Sociobiol.* **14**, 247–256.

Frey, B. S., and Bohnet, I. (1995). "Institutions Affect Fairness: Experimental Investigations," *J. Institutional Theoretical Econ.* **151**, 286–303.

Frohlich, N., and Oppenheimer, J. (1998). "Some Consequences of E-mail vs. Face-to-Face Communication in Experiment," *J. Econ. Behav. Organ.* **35**, 389–403.

Gauthier, D. (1978). *Morals by Agreement*. Oxford: Clarendon Press.

Gilovich, T., Medvec, V. H., and Savitsky, K. (1998). "The Illusion of Transparency: Biased Assessments of Other's Ability to Read One's Emotional States," *J. Personality Social Psychol.* **75**, 332–346.

Harsanyi, J. C., and Selten, R. (1972). "A Generalized Nash Solution for Two-Person Bargaining Games with Incomplete Information," *Management Sci.* **18**, P80–P106.

Hirshleifer, J. (1987). "On the Emotions as Guarantors of Threats and Promises," in *The Latest on the Best: Essays in Evolution and Optimality* (J. Dupre, Ed.), pp. 307–326. Cambridge, MA: MIT Press.

Hoggatt, A. C., Selten, R., Crockett, D., Gill, S., and Moore, J. (1978). "Bargaining Experiments with Incomplete Information," in *Bargaining Behavior, Contributions to Experimental Economics*, Vol. 7 (H. Sauermann, Ed.), pp. 127–178. Tübingen: Mohr.

Isaac, R. M., and Walker, J. M. (1988). "Communication and Free Riding Behavior: The Voluntary Contribution Mechanism," *Econ. Inquiry* **26**, 585–608.

Knapp, M. L., and Comadena, M. E. (1979). "Telling It Like It Isn't: A Review of Theory and Research on Deceptive Communications," *Human Comm. Res.* **5**, 270–285.

Kraut, R. E. (1980). "Humans as Lie Detectors: Some Second Thoughts," *J. Comm.* **30**, 209–216.

Kuon, B. (1994). *Two-Person Bargaining Experiments with Incomplete Information*. Berlin: Springer-Verlag.

Miller, G. R., and Burgoon, J. K. (1981). "Factors Affecting Assessments of Witness Credibility," in *The Psychology of the Courtroom* (R. Bray and N. Kerr, Eds.). New York: Academic Press.

Orbell, J. M., van de Kragt, A. J. C., and Dawes, R. (1988). "Explaining Discussion-Induced Cooperation," *J. Personality Social Psychol.* **54**, 811–819.

Robson, A. (1990). "Efficiency in Evolutionary Games: Darwin, Nash and the Secret Handshake," *J. Theoretical Biol.* **144**, 379–396.

Roth, A. E. (1995). "Bargaining Experiments," in *Handbook of Experimental Economics* (J. Kagel and A. E. Roth, Eds.), pp. 253–348. Princeton, NJ: Princeton Univ. Press.

Roth, A. E., Murnighan, J. K., and Schoumaker, F. (1988). "The Deadline Effect in Bargaining: Some Experimental Evidence," *Amer. Econ. Rev.* **78**, 806–823.

Rubinstein, A. (1985a). "A Bargaining Model with Incomplete Information about Time Preferences," *Econometrica* **53**, 1151–1172.

Rubinstein, A. (1985b). "Choice of Conjectures in a Bargaining Game with Incomplete Information," in *Game Theoretic Models of Bargaining* (A. E. Roth, Ed.), pp. 99–114. Cambridge, UK: Cambridge Univ. Press.

Sally, D. F. (1995). "Conversation and Cooperation in Social Dilemmas: Experimental Evidence from 1958 to 1992," *Rationality Soc.* **7**, 58–92.

Schelling, T. (1978). "Altruism, Meanness, and other Potentially Strategic Behaviors," *Amer. Econ. Rev.* **68**, 229–230.

Selten, R. (1975). "Bargaining under Incomplete Information—A Numerical Example," in *Dynamische Wirtschaftsanalyse* (O. Becker and R. Richter, Eds.), pp. 136–168. Tübingen: Mohr.

Valley, K. L., Moag, J., and Bazerman, M. H. (1998). "'A Matter of Trust': Effects of Communication on the Efficiency and Distribution of Outcomes," *J. Econ. Behav. Organ.* **34**, 211–238.

Zuckerman, M., DePaulo, B. M., and Rosenthal, R. (1981). "Verbal and Nonverbal Communication of Deception," *Adv. Exp. Social Psychol.* **14**, 1–59.

Name Index